Handbook of Globalization, Governance, and Public Administration

PUBLIC ADMINISTRATION AND PUBLIC POLICY

A Comprehensive Publication Program

Executive Editor

JACK RABIN
Professor of Public Administration and Public Policy
School of Public Affairs
The Capital College
The Pennsylvania State University—Harrisburg
Middletown, Pennsylvania

Assistant to the Executive Editor
T. Aaron Wachhaus, Jr.

1. *Public Administration as a Developing Discipline,* Robert T. Golembiewski
2. *Comparative National Policies on Health Care,* Milton I. Roemer, M.D.
3. *Exclusionary Injustice: The Problem of Illegally Obtained Evidence,* Steven R. Schlesinger
5. *Organization Development in Public Administration,* edited by Robert T. Golembiewski and William B. Eddy
7. *Approaches to Planned Change,* Robert T. Golembiewski
8. *Program Evaluation at HEW,* edited by James G. Abert
9. *The States and the Metropolis,* Patricia S. Florestano and Vincent L. Marando
11. *Changing Bureaucracies: Understanding the Organization before Selecting the Approach,* William A. Medina
12. *Handbook on Public Budgeting and Financial Management,* edited by Jack Rabin and Thomas D. Lynch
15. *Handbook on Public Personnel Administration and Labor Relations,* edited by Jack Rabin, Thomas Vocino, W. Bartley Hildreth, and Gerald J. Miller
19. *Handbook of Organization Management,* edited by William B. Eddy
22. *Politics and Administration: Woodrow Wilson and American Public Administration,* edited by Jack Rabin and James S. Bowman
23. *Making and Managing Policy: Formulation, Analysis, Evaluation,* edited by G. Ronald Gilbert
25. *Decision Making in the Public Sector,* edited by Lloyd G. Nigro
26. *Managing Administration,* edited by Jack Rabin, Samuel Humes, and Brian S. Morgan
27. *Public Personnel Update,* edited by Michael Cohen and Robert T. Golembiewski
28. *State and Local Government Administration,* edited by Jack Rabin and Don Dodd
29. *Public Administration: A Bibliographic Guide to the Literature,* Howard E. McCurdy

31. *Handbook of Information Resource Management,* edited by Jack Rabin and Edward M. Jackowski
32. *Public Administration in Developed Democracies: A Comparative Study,* edited by Donald C. Rowat
33. *The Politics of Terrorism: Third Edition,* edited by Michael Stohl
34. *Handbook on Human Services Administration,* edited by Jack Rabin and Marcia B. Steinhauer
36. *Ethics for Bureaucrats: An Essay on Law and Values, Second Edition,* John A. Rohr
37. *The Guide to the Foundations of Public Administration,* Daniel W. Martin
39. *Terrorism and Emergency Management: Policy and Administration,* William L. Waugh, Jr.
40. *Organizational Behavior and Public Management: Second Edition,* Michael L. Vasu, Debra W. Stewart, and G. David Garson
43. *Government Financial Management Theory,* Gerald J. Miller
46. *Handbook of Public Budgeting,* edited by Jack Rabin
49. *Handbook of Court Administration and Management,* edited by Steven W. Hays and Cole Blease Graham, Jr.
50. *Handbook of Comparative Public Budgeting and Financial Management,* edited by Thomas D. Lynch and Lawrence L. Martin
53. *Encyclopedia of Policy Studies: Second Edition,* edited by Stuart S. Nagel
54. *Handbook of Regulation and Administrative Law,* edited by David H. Rosenbloom and Richard D. Schwartz
55. *Handbook of Bureaucracy,* edited by Ali Farazmand
56. *Handbook of Public Sector Labor Relations,* edited by Jack Rabin, Thomas Vocino, W. Bartley Hildreth, and Gerald J. Miller
57. *Practical Public Management,* Robert T. Golembiewski
58. *Handbook of Public Personnel Administration,* edited by Jack Rabin, Thomas Vocino, W. Bartley Hildreth, and Gerald J. Miller
60. *Handbook of Debt Management,* edited by Gerald J. Miller
61. *Public Administration and Law: Second Edition,* David H. Rosenbloom and Rosemary O'Leary
62. *Handbook of Local Government Administration,* edited by John J. Gargan
63. *Handbook of Administrative Communication,* edited by James L. Garnett and Alexander Kouzmin
64. *Public Budgeting and Finance: Fourth Edition,* edited by Robert T. Golembiewski and Jack Rabin
65. *Handbook of Public Administration: Second Edition,* edited by Jack Rabin, W. Bartley Hildreth, and Gerald J. Miller
67. *Handbook of Public Finance,* edited by Fred Thompson and Mark T. Green
68. *Organizational Behavior and Public Management: Third Edition,* Michael L. Vasu, Debra W. Stewart, and G. David Garson
69. *Handbook of Economic Development,* edited by Kuotsai Tom Liou
70. *Handbook of Health Administration and Policy,* edited by Anne Osborne Kilpatrick and James A. Johnson
71. *Handbook of Research Methods in Public Administration,* edited by Gerald J. Miller and Marcia L. Whicker

72. *Handbook on Taxation*, edited by W. Bartley Hildreth and James A. Richardson
73. *Handbook of Comparative Public Administration in the Asia-Pacific Basin*, edited by Hoi-kwok Wong and Hon S. Chan
74. *Handbook of Global Environmental Policy and Administration,* edited by Dennis L. Soden and Brent S. Steel
75. *Handbook of State Government Administration,* edited by John J. Gargan
76. *Handbook of Global Legal Policy,* edited by Stuart S. Nagel
78. *Handbook of Global Economic Policy,* edited by Stuart S. Nagel
79. *Handbook of Strategic Management: Second Edition,* edited by Jack Rabin, Gerald J. Miller, and W. Bartley Hildreth
80. *Handbook of Global International Policy,* edited by Stuart S. Nagel
81. *Handbook of Organizational Consultation: Second Edition,* edited by Robert T. Golembiewski
82. *Handbook of Global Political Policy,* edited by Stuart S. Nagel
83. *Handbook of Global Technology Policy,* edited by Stuart S. Nagel
84. *Handbook of Criminal Justice Administration*, edited by M. A. DuPont-Morales, Michael K. Hooper, and Judy H. Schmidt
85. *Labor Relations in the Public Sector: Third Edition*, edited by Richard C. Kearney
86. *Handbook of Administrative Ethics: Second Edition,* edited by Terry L. Cooper
87. *Handbook of Organizational Behavior: Second Edition*, edited by Robert T. Golembiewski
88. *Handbook of Global Social Policy,* edited by Stuart S. Nagel and Amy Robb
89. *Public Administration: A Comparative Perspective, Sixth Edition,* Ferrel Heady
90. *Handbook of Public Quality Management*, edited by Ronald J. Stupak and Peter M. Leitner
91. *Handbook of Public Management Practice and Reform*, edited by Kuotsai Tom Liou
92. *Personnel Management in Government: Politics and Process, Fifth Edition,* Jay M. Shafritz, Norma M. Riccucci, David H. Rosenbloom, Katherine C. Naff, and Albert C. Hyde
93. *Handbook of Crisis and Emergency Management*, edited by Ali Farazmand
94. *Handbook of Comparative and Development Public Administration: Second Edition,* edited by Ali Farazmand
95. *Financial Planning and Management in Public Organizations,* Alan Walter Steiss and Emeka O. Cyprian Nwagwu
96. *Handbook of International Health Care Systems,* edited by Khi V. Thai, Edward T. Wimberley, and Sharon M. McManus
97. *Handbook of Monetary Policy,* edited by Jack Rabin and Glenn L. Stevens
98. *Handbook of Fiscal Policy,* edited by Jack Rabin and Glenn L. Stevens
99. *Public Administration: An Interdisciplinary Critical Analysis,* edited by Eran Vigoda
100. *Ironies in Organizational Development: Second Edition, Revised and Expanded,* edited by Robert T. Golembiewski

101. *Science and Technology of Terrorism and Counterterrorism*, edited by Tushar K. Ghosh, Mark A. Prelas, Dabir S. Viswanath, and Sudarshan K. Loyalka
102. *Strategic Management for Public and Nonprofit Organizations*, Alan Walter Steiss
103. *Case Studies in Public Budgeting and Financial Management: Second Edition*, edited by Aman Khan and W. Bartley Hildreth
104. *Handbook of Conflict Management*, edited by William J. Pammer, Jr. and Jerri Killian
105. *Chaos Organization and Disaster Management*, Alan Kirschenbaum
106. *Handbook of Gay, Lesbian, Bisexual, and Transgender Administration and Policy*, edited by Wallace Swan
107. *Public Productivity Handbook: Second Edition*, edited by Marc Holzer
108. *Handbook of Developmental Policy Studies*, edited by Gedeon M. Mudacumura, Desta Mebratu and M. Shamsul Haque
109. *Bioterrorism in Medical and Healthcare Administration*, Laure Paquette
110. *International Public Policy and Management: Policy Learning Beyond Regional, Cultural, and Political Boundaries*, edited by David Levi-Faur and Eran Vigoda-Gadot
111. *Handbook of Public Information Systems, Second Edition*, edited by G. David Garson
112. *Handbook of Public Sector Economics*, edited by Donijo Robbins
113. *Handbook of Public Administration and Policy in the European Union*, edited by M. Peter van der Hoek
114. *Nonproliferation Issues for Weapons of Mass Destruction*, Mark A. Prelas and Michael S. Peck
115. *Common Ground, Common Future: Moral Agency in Public Administration, Professions, and Citizenship*, Charles Garofalo and Dean Geuras
116. *Handbook of Organization Theory and Management: The Philosophical Approach, Second Edition*, edited by Thomas D. Lynch and Peter L. Cruise
117. *International Development Governance*, edited by Ahmed Shafiqul Huque and Habib Zafarullah
118. *Sustainable Development Policy and Administration*, edited by Gedeon M. Mudacumura, Desta Mebratu, and M. Shamsul Haque
119. *Public Financial Management*, edited by Howard A. Frank
120. *Handbook of Juvenile Justice: Theory and Practice*, edited by Barbara Sims and Pamela Preston
121. *Emerging Infectious Diseases and the Threat to Occupational Health in the U.S. and Canada*, edited by William Charney
122. *Handbook of Technology Management in Public Administration*, edited by David Greisler and Ronald J. Stupak
123. *Handbook of Decision Making*, edited by Goktug Morcol
124. *Handbook of Public Administration, Third Edition*, edited by Jack Rabin
125. *Handbook of Public Policy Analysis*, edited by Frank Fischer, Gerald J. Miller, and Mara S. Sidney
126. *Elements of Effective Governance: Measurement, Accountability and Participation*, edited by Kathe Callahan
127. *Handbook of Transportation Policy and Administration*, edited by Jeremy Plant

128. *Art and Practice of Court Administration,* Alexander B. Aikman
129. *Handbook of Globalization, Governance, and Public Administration,* Ali Farazmand and Jack Pinkowski

Available Electronically

Principles and Practices of Public Administration, edited by Jack Rabin, Robert F. Munzenrider, and Sherrie M. Bartell

PublicADMINISTRATION*netBASE*

Handbook of Globalization, Governance, and Public Administration

Ali Farazmand
Florida Atlantic University
Fort Lauderdale, Florida, U.S.A.

Jack Pinkowski
Nova Southeastern University
Fort Lauderdale, Florida, U.S.A.

CRC is an imprint of the Taylor & Francis Group,
an informa business

CRC Press
Taylor & Francis Group
6000 Broken Sound Parkway NW, Suite 300
Boca Raton, FL 33487-2742

Printed in the United States of America on acid-free paper
10 9 8 7 6 5 4 3 2 1

International Standard Book Number-10: 0-8493-3726-7 (Hardcover)
International Standard Book Number-13: 978-0-8493-3726-0 (Hardcover)

Library of Congress Cataloging-in-Publication Data

Handbook of globalization, governance, and public administration / [edited by]
Ali Farazmand, Jack Pinkowski.
p. cm. -- (Public administration and public policy ; 129)
Includes bibliographical references and index.
ISBN 0-8493-3726-7
1. Public administration--Handbooks, manuals, etc. 2. Globalization--Handbooks, manuals, etc. I. Farazmand, Ali. II. Pinkowski, Jack. III. Series.

JF1351.H269 2006
351--dc22 2006040716

Visit the Taylor & Francis Web site at
http://www.taylorandfrancis.com

and the CRC Press Web site at
http://www.crcpress.com

Preface

The purpose of this encyclopedic handbook on an increasingly important subject is to present original material on diverse issues and aspects of globalization, governance, and public administration to answer the need for a growing, worldwide, cross-disciplinary, multifaceted interest in globalization with various implications for public administration, public management, and governance. Up until now there has been no single resource to untangle the web of complex and multilevel issues connected with globalization to serve as a starting point for understanding the complicated relationships between globalization and the public sector. This handbook will serve a primer on the issues and a guide to inform a wide spectrum of interested parties including practitioners, academics, research scholars, public officials, corporate managers, researchers and students of political science, economics, finance, cross-cultural studies, human resource management, public policy, and business and public administration. There are a wide range of issues, perspectives, case studies, and analytical and theoretical aspects that are included in this volume.

The handbook is organized into nine parts of related topics. Section I, "Concepts, Meanings, and Theoretical Perspectives," sets the conceptual framework for our coverage of globalization in the public administration context. Essays in Section I present several definitions and a brief historical overview related to how globalization has developed and impacted governance and the practice of public management. The multidimensional process is presented as one that is perceived and received differently based on one's cultural perspective. Globalization transcends national borders and national cultures so that the cultural state of the world has now become more linked to the flow of information and knowledge. However, from a critical standpoint, the process whereby globalization develops from information and communications technologies is challenged as a process that is driven by design, resulting in directed change and challenges. The designing forces behind globalization are said to promote global hegemony and to serve self-interests of global corporations and dominant power players in world politics and economics. This has impacts on people and countries that are not equally distributed among all nations. Although nations and public administration continue to exist, the assertion is made that globalization presents new threats especially to national sovereignty and the environment and tends to increase poverty and inequality worldwide, both producing global insecurity.

Section II, "Consequences and Implications for Public Administration," and Section III, "Consequences and Implications for Governance," include 14 chapters on various consequences and implications for public administration and governance. The social dimensions of globalization, specifically demographic changes, present a predicament in transitional governments such as the former East Germany. One result of unification across boundaries is the blurring of client identity that has implications for public management and the lack of clear agreement on what is in the public interest. The public interest changes depending on the configuration of the community it serves. This also has to do with regulation of professions and regulated occupations. Yet another result of global integration has substantial implications for national security and international health interests across changing national borders where the residents on both sides have in common family and their shared cultural identity. Besides the political and economic factors, negative side effects of globalization extend to cultural disruption, especially where the government institutions are weak and world standards are imposed on previously isolated regimes and reinforced by rapid electronic communications.

Much of the worldwide dissemination of information concerning globalization is filtered through traditional print and electronic media reports. E-government is prescribed as a counterbalancing influence for the public administrator to communicate directly with the public. Information and communication technologies also create new venues for individuals and partisan groups to reach out across borders to sway public opinion that allows both for greater participation in democratic governance as well as the ability for one individual with a computer connected to the Internet to proffer propaganda and critical commentary intended to undermine established regimes. In general, globalization has resulted in a shift in worldwide power from elected representatives or nation's elites to nonelected corporate elites, international non-governmental bureaucrats, and individuals.

The national administrations must increasingly interact with international organizations and laws that govern them, resulting in increasing importance of alliances with other states spanning issues and borders. Political power results from social energy and successful governments find it essential to delegate authority without losing it. Non-state actors are more and more important in global governance. International organizations figure importantly in coordination, cooperation, and decisions concerning international norms, standards, trade, and human rights. Governance under globalization means understanding and integrating national goals with the collective goals of the international community. Consequently, government may have become secondary to the transformation of governance, i.e., how well institutions serve their clientele. However, globally powerful states of the North still tend to dominate through major avenues of global supranational organizations and economic institutions.

In three separate sections of the handbook, we include various accounts of transformations and administrative reforms. Section IV, "Globalization and Administrative Reform and Reorganization," includes the global view to restructuring governance and administration including "New Public Management" and pervasive privatization with associated diminution of accountability due to the increased autonomy given to private firms, agencies, and state-owned companies. Theoretical constructs are proposed for developing nations whereas others address the generally overlooked linkage between the drive for increased outputs and the limitations of human resources and its consequences tied to motivation and job satisfaction. Another chapter looks at the European Community as a case study of successful supranational governance, albeit with crises, failures, and occasional stagnation.

Section V is dedicated to country-specific case studies of administrative reforms and reorganizations in the Asia-Pacific region including the Philippines, Japan, China, and Hong Kong. In Hong Kong, the bureaucracy was the driving force and provided leadership to the reform movement. The administrative system there is credited with managing the social tensions triggered by major changes in society and the Hong Kong economy. These studies highlight the reform agenda including restructuring, privatization, decentralization, e-government, and efforts to increase transparency and accountability to make administration more responsive and responsible to the social equity and efficiency issues of the time. The difficulty of permanent reform is highlighted as the desire to abolish former regimes or consolidate government organizations that must face established vested interests both within the bureaucracy and from the private sector. Such resistance must be overcome for reforms to be successful. Some of the reforms in China are said to parallel those of New Public Management style reforms, i.e., downsizing, decentralization, market-orientation, contracting-out, and desire to increase transparency and improve public service.

Administrative reforms and reorganizations in Africa and India are the subject area of the chapters in Section VI. Obstacles to meaningful decentralization and measures for strengthening decentralization in the African continent are covered. The effectiveness of decentralization to local governments in Africa remains limited because of their dependence on the central government for financial resources and limited autonomy, inadequate grass roots participation, and the lack of committed bureaucratic leadership. Privatization efforts in Botswana are shown to have implications for a changing role of the state following public–private partnerships. The view of the private sector changed compared to colonial times when private enterprise was viewed as a means of exploitation and the creator of income disparities in the country. Now it is considered the engine of growth and new public–private partnerships continue to be developed, partly out of the realization that performance of public enterprises has been disappointing. This has resulted in a new role for the state as a protector of the public interest and monitor of the performance of the privatized undertakings.

A traditional village in India is highlighted as an example of the paradox of development wherein land has been taken for development but the promised developmental tasks have not been forthcoming; instead it has resulted in corruption and exploitation. The conclusion calls for sustainable development under globalization to be grounded in community bonding with local deliberations in community-based institutions whereas governments seek growth through market expansion across borders worldwide. The strategies for good governance in India and developing nations are addressed along with an examination of what constitutes bad governance. Information communication technology is put forward as a tool to demystify governance reforms by facilitating transparency and accountability.

In Section VII, "Globalization: Comparative, Development, and Global Public Administration," we present chapters dealing with development that is driven by transnational corporations, which may actually result in underdevelopment. Although large international corporations may drive economic development, they do so with their own interest first and may not consider human rights for the citizens in the growth of the economy. Another chapter looks at imperialism as the extension of the globally more powerful states' power over resources or resource flows within another state's sovereignty to the exclusive benefit of the globalizing imperial state. Under globalization we see the exercise of power by private corporations and alliances of states that are not specifically tied to the national state where the power is influenced. In the public service context, this means self-serving behavior for private or state elite's interests irrespective of the "public interest."

Sustainable development is the subject of another chapter that calls for a multidimensional environment including coordination of intersectoral relationships, policy domains, and microlevel feasibility with less hierarchical bureaucracy. International development management is treated in a separate chapter. We also include here, instead of in Section VI, a case study in an African country because it is focused on development logic and globalization as forces behind ideology-driven reforms. The conclusion is that in the case of Ghana, crosscultural borrowing from different cultures should allow the development of a globalized public administration system capable of responding to both global and local needs relying on the interdisciplinary nature of the field; global–local interplay is required.

Section VIII, "Globalization: Issues in Public Management," includes chapters on public sector management reforms intended to improve productivity with greater transparency. These include incentive systems, competition, privatization, and accountability standards. A case study in Russia compares the ability to autonomously generate revenues on the local level as well as local incentives to increase the tax base. Failing such incentives and rewards, regional and local governments are at the mercy of the central government, which results in increases in revenue-sharing formulas that offset any local gains.

A separate chapter focuses on ethics in the public sector to guide ethical decision making. The transformation of governance is the topic of a chapter that discusses increasingly international affairs by subnational governments. Energy policy is a global concern arising out of the mismatch between resource and production capacity and consumption demands. It pits consumers and business interests against the local public interest that may only be moderated by supranational, large utilities, and international organizations. Countries face the challenge of international trade and the need for foreign investment for competitive advantage versus domestic opportunities, resulting in diverting their resources to the foreign sector. Corporate interests and investors frequently control these outcomes. The key differences between "market driving" compared to "market-driven" business strategies, in the context of the global market environment, is the subject of another chapter.

Section IX, "Globalization and the Future of Governance and Public Administration," looks at the prospects for change in the coming century in the issues and implications from globalization. This includes an environmental ethic and the legacy that is being created for future generations borne out of consuming society's penchant for greater energy demands and natural resources degradation and corporate exploitation. One approach to altering the direction of change is change itself in the manner that we educate and train future public sector workers. This includes ethical training and consciousness to outcomes, unintended consequences, and negative externalities. Public health concerns and climatic change are covered in individual chapters. Both topics can cause drastic, rapid, and irreversible harm to our species. Regarding public administration, partisan, ideological conflict, and international forces have found their way into many aspects of public management including an area once thought immune to external influences such as the orderliness and predictability of local government budgeting.

The combined forces of globalization and its implications resulting in privatization, marketization, downsizing, corporatization, outsourcing, cross-border administration, and other topics included in this volume result in a challenge for public administration in this era. Revitalization of the field rests in part on the need to understand the multifaceted causes and implications covered in the broad spectrum of issues in this handbook.

The more than 60 contributors to the handbook include many established scholars and practitioners from around the world who share their individual expertise and unique perspectives on these phenomena. It is our collective hope that this handbook will serve as a library reference work and major textbook to fill the present need and stimulate future research on these topics.

We express our gratitude to all of the contributing authors who have been very patient throughout the extended process of bringing this project to fruition. We express our sincere appreciation to all the contributors for their prompt attention to requests for revisions, rewrites, and timely submission of their manuscripts during the extended time necessary to coordinate them all. Our original publisher, Marcel Dekker, Inc., was sold to the Taylor & Francis group during the time we were preparing and assembling manuscripts for this book. We are thankful that our new publisher, Rich O'Hanley, proved to be just as interested in our project and most cooperative during the transition. Our production editor, Claire Miller, was very understanding and helpful during the changeover period between publishers and the entire production staff at Taylor & Francis and CRC Press proved to be a joy to work with.

Finally, we would like to acknowledge the support of other individuals who made this project possible. Jack Rabin, the Public Administration and Public Policy series editor, has always been supportive and encouraged our efforts without reservation. We also thank Sami Ullah, Lynn Schweitzer, Mary Feeney, and Associate Dean J. Preston Jones at the H. Wayne Huizenga School of Business and Entrepreneurship at Nova Southeastern University who provided assistance in marketing our call for manuscripts, organizing the submissions, maintaining the database, communicating with the publishers and authors, and carrying out related tasks that enabled us to keep organized and complete the project.

Ali Farazmand
Jack Pinkowski

Editors

Ali Farazmand is professor of public administration at Florida Atlantic University, Fort Lauderdale, Florida. where he teaches graduate MPA and Ph.D. courses in organization theory and behavior, organizational change and public management, globalization, personnel and labor relations, bureaucratic politics and administrative theory, ethics, and intellectual development of public administration.

Professor Farazmand's research and publications include over 18 authored and edited books and handbooks, and over 80 journal articles and book chapters. An internationally renowned scholar, Farazmand is also an active member of several international professional associations that include the American Political Science Association (APSA), American Society for Public Administration (ASPA), International Association of Schools and Institutes of Administration (IASIA), Eastern Regional Organization of Public Administration (EROPA), and International Studies Association (ISA), to name a few. Farazmand is also the founding editor in chief of the new globally refereed journal, *Public Organization Review: a Global Journal*. He has served as academic consultant/advisor to the United Nations on governance, public administration, and globalization and administration, preparing and presenting discussion papers at UN sponsored international conferences worldwide.

Professor Farazmand received the B.A. degree in business administration from Tehran University; the M.S. degree in educational administration from Syracuse University; the Master of Public Administration (M.P.A.) and the Ph.D. degree in public administration from the Maxwell School of Syracuse University, New York.

Jack Pinkowski is the founding director of the Institute of Government and Public Policy (IGPP) of the H. Wayne Huizenga School of Business and Entrepreneurship at Nova Southeastern University, Fort Lauderdale, Florida. The IGPP serves the community by applying business management and cross-discipline expertise in collaboration across the university to solve problems and conduct research on public sector issues.

With more than twenty-five years as a successful business entrepreneur, Dr. Pinkowski combines real-world experience with academic credentials that enhance teaching in the classroom and applied research. His business entities have included the import-export trade with Southeast Asia, Central

America, and Europe. Pinkowski has served as a principal researcher or facilitator on many local government projects including: public/private economic development initiatives; strategic community visioning processes; transportation intermodal planning for urban redevelopment; and emergency management needs analysis, among others. He teaches the capstone course in the Master of Public Administration program as well as other masters and doctoral courses on government budgeting, public financial management, organization theory, ethics, economic systems, economic development, and comparative government and economic systems. His research interests include various issues in public finance, economic development, globalization, international economic and organizational impacts of the Internet, the evolution of e-commerce and its impacts on state and local government finance, and other issues of public policy.

Dr. Pinkowski earned the Ph.D. from Florida Atlantic University in Boca Raton, Florida, the M.P.A. from Georgia Southern University in Statesboro, Georgia, and the B.A. degree from Temple University in Philadelphia, Pennsylvania.

Contributors

Jonathan F. Anderson, Ph.D.
Department of Public Administration
University of Alaska Southeast
Juneau, Alaska

Anna A. Anickeeva, Ph.D.
Volgograd State University
Volgograd, Russia

Jane Beckett-Camarata, Ph.D.
Department of Political Science
Kent State University
Kent, Ohio

Richard Blake, Ph.D.
Department of Social Work
Seton Hall University
South Orange, New Jersey

Madlyn M. Bonimy, M.A.
Institute of Government
Tennessee State University
Antioch, Tennessee

Derick W. Brinkerhoff, Ed.D.
RTI International (Research Triangle Institute)
Washington, D.C.

Jennifer M. Brinkerhoff, Ph.D.
George Washington University
Washington, D.C.

Tom Christensen, Ph.D.
Department of Political Science
University of Oslo
Oslo, Norway

Peter L. Cruise, Ph.D.
Health and Community Services
California State University
Chico, California

Robert F. Durant, Ph.D.
American University
Washington, D.C.

O.P. Dwivedi, Ph.D.
Fellow of the Royal Society (Canada)
University of Guelph
Guelph, Ontario, Canada

Ali Farazmand, Ph.D.
School of Public Administration
Florida Atlantic University
Fort Lauderdale, Florida

Mary Farrell, Ph.D.
Centre d'Etudes et de Recherches Internationales
Sciences Po University
Paris, France

Lon S. Felker, Ph.D.
Department of Economics, Finance, and Urban Studies
East Tennessee State University
Johnson City, Tennessee

Patrick Fisher, Ph.D.
Seton Hall University
South Orange, New Jersey

Jean-Claude Garcia-Zamor, Ph.D.
School of Policy and Management
Florida International University
Miami, Florida

Heather Getha-Taylor
Campbell Public Affairs Institute
Maxwell School of Citizenship and Public Affairs
Syracuse University
Syracuse, New York

Robert P. Goss, J.D., Ph.D.
Graduate Public Policy Program
Brigham Young University
Provo, Utah

Peter Fuseini Haruna, Ph.D.
Department of Social Sciences
Texas A&M International University
Laredo, Texas

Catherine Horiuchi, D.P.A.
College of Professional Studies
University of San Francisco
San Francisco, California

Ahmed Shafiqul Huque, Ph.D.
Department of Political Science
McMaster University
Hamilton, Ontario, Canada

Kalu N. Kalu, Ph.D.
Department of Political Science and Public Administration
Auburn University at Montgomery
Montgomery, Alabama

Yuko Kaneko
Faculty of Literature and Social Sciences
University of Yamagata
Yamagata, Japan

Naim Kapucu, Ph.D.
Department of Public Administration
University of Central Florida
Orlando, Florida

Keith Kelly, M.A.
Henry W. Bloch School of Business and Public Administration
University of Missouri — Kansas City
Kansas City, Missouri

Renu Khator, Ph.D.
Office of Academic Affairs
University of South Florida
Tampa, Florida

Peter H. Koehn, Ph.D.
Department of Political Science
University of Montana — Missoula
Missoula, Montana

Per Lægreid, Ph.D.
University of Bergen
Bergen, Norway

Paulette Laubsch, D.P.A.
School of Administrative Science
Fairleigh Dickinson University
Teaneck, New Jersey

Mordecai Lee, Ph.D.
Department of Governmental Affairs
University of Wisconsin Milwaukee
Milwaukee, Wisconsin

Platon N. Rigos, Ph.D.
Department of Government and International Affairs
University of South Florida
Tampa, Florida

Susan Scott, M.B.A.
Calyptus Consulting Group
Lexington, Massachusetts

Keshav C. Sharma, Ph.D.
Department of Political and Administrative Studies
University of Botswana
Gaborone, Botswana

Helen K. Simon, D.B.A.
Florida International University
Miami, Florida

Amita Singh, Ph.D.
Centre for the Study of Law and Governance
Jawaharlal Nehru University
New Delhi, India

Itoko Suzuki, Ph.D.
Department of Public Administration
Ritsumeikan Asia Pacific University (APU)
Beppu City
Oita, Japan

Leslie Cauthen Tworoger, D.B.A.
H. Wayne Huizenga School of Business and Entrepreneurship
Nova Southeastern University
Fort Lauderdale, Florida

Christopher Van Vliet, M.P.A.
City of Lauderdale Lakes, Florida

Curtis Ventriss, Ph.D.
Rubenstein School of Environment and Natural Resources
University of Vermont
Burlington, Vermont

Herbert H. Werlin, Ph.D.
Independent Consultant
College Park, Maryland

Clay G. Wescott, Ph.D.
Asian Development Bank
Manila, Philippines

Pan G. Yatrakis, Ph.D.
Nova Southeastern University
Fort Lauderdale, Florida

Mengzhong Zhang, Ph.D.
US/China Public Administration Secretariat (ASPA) and
National Center for Public Productivity (NCPP)
Nanyang Technology University
Singapore

Contents

SECTION III: CONSEQUENCES AND IMPLICATIONS FOR GOVERNANCE

SECTION IV: GLOBALIZATION AND ADMINISTRATIVE REFORM AND REORGANIZATION

SECTION V: ADMINISTRATIVE REFORM AND REORGANIZATION IN THE ASIA–PACIFIC REGION

SECTION VI: ADMINISTRATIVE REFORM AND REORGANIZATION IN AFRICA–INDIA

SECTION VII: GLOBALIZATION: COMPARATIVE, DEVELOPMENT AND GLOBAL PUBLIC ADMINISTRATION

SECTION VIII: GLOBALIZATION: ISSUES IN PUBLIC MANAGEMENT

SECTION IX: GLOBALIZATION AND THE FUTURE OF GOVERNANCE AND PUBLIC ADMINISTRATION

I

CONCEPTS, MEANINGS, AND THEORETICAL PERSPECTIVES

Chapter 1

Globalization: A Theoretical Analysis with Implications for Governance and Public Administration

Ali Farazmand

CONTENTS

Introduction

The dramatic changes of the last 25 years have shaken up the entire world and produced profound changes and transformations in governments, political systems, governance, public administration, and civic society–state relations. Many old and traditional ways of thinking have been replaced by new ways of thinking, ideas, and perceptions regarding philosophy and management of governance, economy, and international relations. Similarly, many institutional changes have altered traditional structural forms and the substance of governance and administration. Indeed, it seems the whole world has turned upside down and the institutions have turned inside out or outside in.

If we look closely at the features of this new stage of world development, it would not be an exaggeration to claim that the dawn of a new civilization has begun with the rapid fall of the established, industrial civilization with which many parts of the world are still trying to catch up. While a few are making leaping advancements in individual and group life, the majority of the world population is still desperately struggling to survive. Concepts of *rupture* and *uncertainty* have replaced the term *rapid* to describe change or development. The result seems to be rupturing the transformation with temporary life and characteristics. This global phenomenon has many profound implications for societies, peoples, governments, and public administration systems.

Change is both inevitable and necessary, and it is often good for promoting dynamic systems, but chaotic change coupled with rupturing events can have potentially devastating consequences for many while presenting opportunities for some. Quantitative changes are important in shaping the structures and values of the societies, governments, and humanity, but it is the qualitative changes that alter the long-standing characteristics of human civilization. It is the massive qualitative changes that are now taking place and altering the planet Earth, and its societies and communities.

The high mark of these changes is "globalization," a concept that has become popular worldwide. It has appeared in scholarships, in political discussions, in various media, and in all circles of human inquiry all over the world. The term has captured many imaginary as well as practical ways of life and governance systems. Few terms in modern history have ever been used as frequently as the term "globalization." There is no single definition of the term, yet globalization has evoked various conceptual and intellectual, as well as political and economic reactions worldwide.

Indeed, numerous scholars and politicians and numerous ideological perspectives have expressed different ways to describe the changes associated with globalization. For example, Huntington (1996) speaks of the "clash of civilizations" in a divided world of East and West, Islamic and other Asian religious-based cultures, on the one hand, and Judaic–Christian culture with a self-declared higher moral ground to dominate and subsume all other cultures on the other. Fukuyama (1992) predicts, rather superficially and prematurely, "the end of history and of the last man" (due to the fall of the Soviet system in USSR), and advises all governments and states to abandon their existence and leave everything to market institutions to perform the functions from A to Z. Korbin (1996) indicates a "return to medievalism," with its feudal features of serfdom, bondage, and baron-ruled slavery system. Handy speaks of the "age of unreason," in which doing the unthinkable and thinking the unreasonable are expected in the process of governing political systems and managing modern organizations of public and private sectors.

These expressions reflect major points of view on the rupturing qualitative changes worldwide. They present interesting points that merit consideration and analysis, but they also tend to exaggerate and oversimplify the rapid changes of the present and underestimate or misunderstand the dynamic process of dialectical change and transformation of the future, a process that has characterized the history of world civilizations from the earliest time; they will continue to surprise thinkers of fixating ideas in the future.

The world is experiencing a high degree of globalism representing ideological, political, organizational, and economic phenomena at the turn of the 21st century, and of globalization, which is a process of worldwide integration and transcendence. What does globalization mean? What are the theoretical underpinnings of globalization? And what does it mean for the state, governance, and public administration?

This chapter addresses these fundamental questions and offers a theoretical analysis of globalization with some implications for governance and public administration. A political economy approach is used to explain the changes of globalization within the process of continuity in the historical development of political and administrative systems. The section "Big Changes and the Challenge of Globalization," discusses "big changes" producing globalization with expressed concerns for the fate of governance and public administration; "Meaning of Globalism and Globalization," the meanings of globalization and globalism; "Theoretical Perspective: A Bird's Eye View," a theoretical analysis of different perspectives on globalization; and "Conclusion," (Part V) some implications for governance and public administration.

Big Changes and the Challenge of Globalization

Change has always been a driving force for transformations throughout history. However, several "big changes" of the last 25 years or so seem to have taken the entire world by surprise, shaken up many traditional systems and ways of life, and produced new worldwide transformations in governments, governance, state–society relations, and public administration. In the realms of international relations and politics, arguments for a "world order" have emerged with attempts for global convergence and a new world order. Consequently, discussions have proliferated around the concepts of "convergence theory," "corporate hegemony theory," "late capitalism and global imperialism theory," and various globalization theories that represent different perspectives, viewpoints, ideological tendencies, and socioeconomic as well as ecological and technological orientations. For a detailed treatment of these and other theories, see my forthcoming book, *Globalization, Governance, and Administration* (Farazmand, forthcoming).

This spectrum of widespread perspectives covers a scope of scholarly discussions that range from left to right with many in between. It is beyond the scope of this chapter to delve into the details of this subject matter. However, for our purpose, an outline of these mega changes is presented to set the rest of the chapter materials in order.

Generally speaking, three broad, mega changes of worldwide significance have occurred that have caused revolutionary transformations in governments, governance, state–society relations, and public administration.

The first mega change is technological innovation in general, but most importantly of the computer, Internet, information, and satellite communications that have produced giant steps toward world integration and removal of many artificial barriers in learning about other nations and peoples around the world, with the ability to communicate instantaneously around the globe. This technological innovation is just the beginning of a long-term global change that will develop in the future. Acquiring knowledge and information today is made easy by striking a key on the computer board. The need to travel to libraries and information centers is disappearing fast, and access to worldwide information is instantaneous. No longer can governments and state or corporate institutions dictate to citizens or employees what they should or should not know or read.

However, this does not mean a total loss of boundaries of nationalism, or sense of national sovereignty and identity, though these concepts are being challenged already. Formation of supranational organizations such as the European Union (EU) is an example. Other organizations like EU may emerge or are emerging. At the same time, atomization, rise of nationalism, and small-scale identity formation — ethic, religious, etc. — are also developing, a contradictory development opposite of the supranational and collective identity concepts. This dual problem of collective and individual identity syndrome (or what I have called a dual identity syndrome — DIS) will continue to play an important role in national governance, international relations and politics, and public administration as well as culture.

Huntington's concept of "clash of civilizations" with a vision of Western civilization's hegemony over all others will meet its own antithesis, and indeed it has already met with such opposition in the world. This theory will produce nothing but a catastrophe for the world.

The second mega change of global significance is an extension of the first, that is the technological advancement in military and space areas. Although there is nothing new about this realm of technological innovations, as there have always been advancements of some sort throughout history, this time is different in that the ability of certain superpower nations, especially the United States, to master knowledge, skills, and tools to dominate the world via military threats through sky, land, and water has reached the level of global supremacy. Although deterrent forces of global scale still exist and may pose a serious challenge to the "supremacy," in the absence of the Soviet Union they do not possess an equal and countervailing balance of power. Besides, the global military supremacy of the United States as the only mega-superpower has already contributed to the establishment of an ideological doctrine of "global hegemony" within the top-ruling elite circles of the country, with the projection of subsuming the entire world as the new frontier realm of operation under the U.S. global leadership, a position that is denounced by many countries of the world (e.g., France, Russia, China, North Korea, Iran).

The assumption of such global hegemonic rule is explained by this new "hegemony doctrine" with sacred missions of serving American national interests worldwide with no limit to its fields of operation (read it as a global field), on the one hand, and the self-proclaimed ideological crusade of promoting Western ideas, culture, and Judaic Christianity along with the values and institutions of capitalism, on the other. This is done by both the peaceful means of diplomatic maneuvers, ideological slogans of freedom and democracy, financial tools, coercion, violence, and direct wars and the occupation of other nations that may pose resistance or challenge. This is the projection that the dominant elites have for the United States as the most dominant superpower of the world in the new century. The principles of "the Project for the New American Century," signed by some inner circle elites and political figures, including the current president George W. Bush, vice-president Dick Cheney, and defense secretary, Donald Rumsfeld, and others, clearly state the projection of American power in the world as a global empire in the 21st century.

This new global project, no doubt, raises many alarms to other nation-states trying to survive: the Europeans find the solution in the formation of the EU organization, the developing countries of different continents look for other alliances of similar fashion, and Islamic countries have their Organization of the Islamic Countries. However, these regional or associational organizations will not serve them an effective leverage against the new global super baron for a wide range of economic, political, cultural, and military reasons. Most developing countries are familiar with this new global power reconfiguration and are used to its tricks and objectives. Most of them have experienced direct colonialism first, and then indirect or neocolonialism in the age of imperialism before and during the Cold War era.

However, what is different at this time is the absence of the alternative global superpower, the former Soviet Union (the USSR) that tended to maintain a countervailing balance of power worldwide and offered alternative realms of existence free from the global hegemony of neocolonialism or imperialism of the late corporate capitalism. Today, the threat of "military intervention by remote control," along with economic and diplomatic weapons, is used to push the "doctrine of global hegemony" and operationalize the "Project for the American Century" across the globe. This will keep the "Iron Triangles" of all fields profitably busy, especially in the military-industrial complex (MIC), agriculture, and information technology, to name a few. No doubt, this global assumption of supremacy creates its own antithesis of counterbalancing forces, alliances, superpowers, and possible grand conflicts. In the meantime, smaller nations feeling threatened and squeezed will attempt every possible way to survive and maintain a degree of autonomy and independence by acquiring means of deterrent power such as nuclear weapons and long-range missiles that can reach desired targets.

The proponents of rapid globalization of corporate capitalism, as we will see later in this chapter, view this development of survival strategy and self-reliance by some developing nations both dangerous and useless. Dangerous, because it poses a challenge to the "global hegemony doctrine" and causes a security threat to the new monopolistic world order; these nations or governments, therefore, must be prevented from developing such power that can lead them to further independence, development, and autonomy in the global village. Examples include North Korea, postrevolutionary Iran, and Libya; the latter has already been convinced through negotiations and its nuclear project has been terminated. North Korea insists on its atomic power production unless its security is guaranteed by a nonaggression agreement signed by the United States. Iran insists on its legitimate right to possess and develop nuclear technology for peaceful purposes but rejects it for military atomic weapon purposes, just like the advanced nations of the West, or India and Pakistan or Israel that already possess such nuclear weapons.

The proponents of globalization of corporate capitalism also call these nations' attempts for self-reliance and autonomy useless because they see no need for it, as the whole world is converging into one through the economic power of market capitalism, in which corporations rule the world and Western supremacy of military and economic domination is unstoppable (see, for example, Fukuyama, (1992).

The third, and perhaps the most important, change of the late 20th century was the sudden and shocking collapse of the Soviet Union as the countervailing superpower of the world. The fall of the USSR ended the era of a bipolar global world order in which the two superpowers, the U.S. and the USSR, competed for world domination, control, and expansion of their spheres of influence. Developing countries of the world were divided more or less under these two global superpowers with two opposing ideological, political, social, and cultural orientations; for several decades, they had enjoyed some safety nets of protection zones created by the opposing superpowers. Yet, while Cold War characterized the two superpower relations, hot wars were always fought in developing and less developed nations that represented the extended arms of the superpowers in the battlefield.

With the sudden fall of the Soviet Union, this global bipolar world order was ended along with the Cold War drama, but immediately, a new global world order was proclaimed by the Western capitalist powers, especially the United States, which now claims to assume global leadership with projected plans of hegemony, domination, and control, all in the name of ideological and doctrinal slogans of market supremacy, corporate capitalism as the most advanced organization of economic system, liberal values of freedom and liberty, property, Western style of democracy, and Judaic–Christian religious values of the Western civilization (Huntington, 1996).

It is beyond the scope of this chapter to discuss the reasons why the USSR collapsed, but at least two broad multitudes of factors contributed to the phenomenon: one was internal and the other external. Internally, the system was new and was in experimentation for decades, therefore many trials and errors. Obviously, the system was surrounded from all fronts by hostile forces of capitalism that did everything they could to defeat the system. The country's overemphasis on military, defense, and space technological achievements, no doubt, gained the system tremendous recognition, respect, and ability as a superpower to check the abuses of the Western superpower and make a key difference in shaping and reshaping global politics and international relations. However, this superpower achievement was gained at a price domestically vis-à-vis its citizens, their consumer expectations, and the problems of managing a gigantic economy and society. Public management was a big project of the Soviet system, yet its dynamics failed to catch up with the latest in the world and with that of the Soviet achievements in the military and space areas.

While the fall of the Soviet Union was a sad tragedy for the poor, the working classes, and the less developed nations hoping to develop on a noncapitalist path of sustainable development free from mass inequality of the capitalist order, the capitalist world of the West in general and the United States in particular cheered the collapse and celebrated the biggest change of the world in the last quarter of the 20th century. What a change! It gave the proponents of capitalism a boost of morale, a new source of energy, and a new claim of legitimacy for capitalist system of economy and society over socialism and all other forms of economic organization; market supremacy has since been a global slogan of Western powers, corporate leaders, politicians, academic circles, consulting think-tank organizations, and even religious leaders.

These and other equally or less important changes of the last 25 years seem to have turned the world upside down and caused massive transformation in all aspects of life, society, politics, and administration. They have contributed to the new, contending theories of global world order and globalization. But, then, what does globalization mean?

Meaning of Globalism and Globalization

Diversity and confusion characterize the meaning of globalism and globalization. These terms mean different things to people with different worldviews, ideologies, and knowledge bases. Thus, no single definition can be used to explain globalism and globalization. Notwithstanding, the impacts of knowledge on governance and public administration have been inconclusive and confusing with the subject being studied. Because public administration constitutes the core of the state and its governance (Holden, 1997), any changes in the character of the state means corresponding changes in governance and administration, and changes in governance and public administration are reflected in the character of the state.

Globalization and the State

Some scholars have already claimed the "end of the state and administration" (Stever, 1988). Others point to the irrelevance of the state or "state indifferent" in the new logic of global capitalism. Others may see their earlier dream of global "cosmocorporations" come through, seeing states as irrelevant. These arguments are hardly new. As far as globalism and world systems are concerned, both have existed since the turn of the 20th century and both were accentuated by the rise of the USSR and its ideological claim of world socialism.

The demise of the state was predicted by certain liberal internationalists as well as by some Marxist-Leninists early in the 20th century. Lenin's seminal work, *Imperialism: The Highest Stage of Capitalism* (1965), focused on the growth and role of multinational corporations in modern capitalism, making the state redundant to serve the interests of transworld corporate elites. The recent argument of "transnationalism," which appeared in the 1970s, has also gained momentum. More recently, the works on globalization and new world order allude to the conclusion that the days of the state are numbered (Ohmae, 1995).

Similarly, scholars of governance and public administration have predicted the creation of a new world order beyond nation-states by global corporations and the emergence of a "global village" and a "world government" with "global management". However, with the exception of a few scholarly works (Farazmand, 1994, 1999, 2001a,b), little critical analysis of the terms *globalism*, *globalization*, and *new world order* have been offered in public administration. Others, however, have vocally refuted the idea of the end of the state. For example, Scholte (1997) has argued the persistence of the nation-states with all implications for public administration. Hirst and Thompson (1996), Zysman (1996), have argued that globalization has been exaggerated and that the states remain strong with crucial functions of governance. In fact, some political scientists like Skcopol (1985), who "brought the state back in" to their disciplines during the 1980s, have maintained their skepticism about the disappearance of the state from history. As a result, the process of globalization has produced opposing and controversial trains of thought, concerning the fate of the state in modern governance: one predicting the end of the state, another arguing on the persistence of the state and national governance, and still others with other perspectives in between, as we will see later in this chapter.

What is most important is the impact of globalism and globalization on governance and public administration. The fact is that these phenomena have changed the nature and character of the state and public administration worldwide. There have been "retreating shifts" in the quality and quantity of state power and authority (Strange, 1996; Graycar, 1983), away from the welfare state and transformed into a security-militarized and coercive "corporate state" (Farazmand, 1997a,b, 1999, 2001b). No matter what perspective is adopted, the end results have been increasing fiscal crisis of the state, accompanied by a serious crisis of governability, insecurity in the midst of increased militarization of the world, and further crises of human insecurity worldwide, a vicious cycle that only feeds into more crises in the age of globalization and increasing inequality.

Using a political economy approach, this chapter treats the concepts of globalism and globalization as phenomena produced by historical changes within the broader framework of continuity. Unlike assertions by some, as in the *End of History and the Man* (Fukuyama, 1992), this chapter considers globalization as an expected historical, dialectical development of late capitalism and argues that globalization is caused by the dynamic nature of rapid accumulation of surplus at the global level. The dynamic nature of capitalist political economy in its latest development has shifted in favor of financial capital as opposed to the earlier production nature of the capital. It has shifted from national to global capitalism. Change and continuity are dialectical characteristics of the development of socioeconomic systems. The qualitative and quantitative changes of the last few decades have altered the nature of capitalist economies and their respective structures and organizations of governance and administration. These changes started after World War II and have accelerated since the 1970s. But the state will persist, I have argued.

Elsewhere (1999, 2004), I have argued that globalization has been caused by several factors, including the economic factors of surplus accumulation of capital, the state, domestic constraints, innovations in information technology, international institutions, and ideology. In turn, globalization has caused significant consequences for the capitalist state, its governance, and its public administration. The core of the state and administration persists in the broader sense of continuity. But major changes have been occurring, as a consequence of globalization, that alter the nature and character of the state and public administration from the traditional welfare administrative state to that of the corporate welfare state. Thus, global capitalism is analyzed in the context of the world political economy. In this context, globalization is considered more broadly than capitalism alone.

Capitalism needs the state and the state is not independent from capital; the elites of both work together in the globalization process because it serves both. Unfortunately, little has been studied on the causal relationship among the aspects of globalization, the state, sound governance, and public administration. With the rise of globalization of financial capital and ideological globalism, the very identity of nation-states and their sovereignty has been challenged.

What Does Globalism Mean?

Globalism means an ideological system with global wings of operations, strategic points, and integration. Like the term capitalism, globalism recognizes no territorial limits or boundaries and claims the entire realm of the world. As a concept, globalism is a global system of capitalist order, as proclaimed by the ideology of globalizing corporations and the globalizing superpower "states" that guard and promote them. Thus, globalism is an ideological, organizational, political, and economic phenomenon of the late 20th century, but its origin may be traced to the 19th century and even earlier times.

Globalism denotes integration and convergence of world powers, cultures, economic systems, organizational arrangements, and administrative practices. It reflects concentration, centralization, and a melding of differences to produce universal symbols, modules, norms, values, and structures. Therefore, globalism is the institutionalization of global peoples, structures, values, norms, socioeconomic systems, and power relationships toward a unifying system of structures and values. As such, globalism is a worldly ideology to which conformity and compliance are required or at least expected.

Once operationally established and institutionalized, globalism will be extremely difficult to resist though not impossible. However, it will also generate its countervailing dialectical forces of resistance from all over the world, forces that oppose oppression, exploitation, domination, and threat to human and national identity. The great Russian philosopher Dostoevsky once observed that "man will engage in self-destruction to preserve his identity." This may be true, but will it matter to the "power holders" of globalization in the age of late capitalism? What can the powerless do in the face of powerful?

What Does Globalization Mean?

While globalism is an ideological system, globalization is a process and a means to achieve the goals of globalism and serves its interests. Globalization has meant many things to many people. The ideas are diverse, interchangeable, and broad, so much so that it is easy to fall into a definition trap. For example, economists consider globalization as an advance step toward a fully integrated world market. Political scientists view it as a march away from the conventionally defined concept of state with territorial sovereignty and the emergence of supranational and global governing bodies under a new world order (Falk, 1997). Business school scholars and consultants see globalization as unlimited opportunities in a "borderless world" (Ohmae, 1990). Others view globalization as a phenomenon driven only by private-sector corporations, not governments (Strange, 1996). These viewpoints reflect different lenses of seeing the world, and they promote the interests they are supposed to serve.

Meanings and theories of globalization are expanding with time, as globalization is not an entirely new concept or reality. Indeed, globalization has a long history. Perhaps the first time in history that globalization was conceptualized and even realized to a great extent in the ancient world was by Cyrus the Great, who by conquering virtually the entire known world founded the first world-state Achaemenid Persian Empire in 550 B.C. Unlike the Romans, who attempted centuries later to assimilate all subject peoples into one Roman culture, Cyrus envisioned a united and unified empire of Persia with a "synthesis of civilizations" many of whom were in place before the arrival of Aryans on the Iranian plateau; under this new global empire all civilizations were free to practice their cultures, traditions, and values under the novel system of "tolerant governance," in which slavery was abolished and freedom of religion, language, and cultures was assured by Cyrus the Great's Universal Charter of Human Rights, the first ever issued in human history (for more details, see Olmstead, 1948; Frye, 1975; Farazmand, 2001a).

Cyrus's globalization vision lasted for over 200 years, only to be followed by another globalization figure, Alexander the Great, whose vision was to establish a Hellenic world, a vision that did not last too long, for it soon was recaptured by the Parthian Empire of Persia in the East and the newcomer Roman Empire of the West. For the next 800 years, the world was ruled mainly by these two key superpowers, along with China in the Far East. The rise of the Islamic Empire in the 7th century was another attempt to form a global community of devout Muslims (Islamic Ummat) then facing the yet another contending globalizing force of Christianity. The subsequent rise and fall of other great empires of the West and the East in the last five centuries have shown how many times earlier attempts at the globalization game have been played out in human history.

Thus, early concepts and forms of globalization have been around for over 2500 years. Why then a surge of globalization discussion in the last 20 years? The answer to this question must be found in the "big changes" outlined earlier in this chapter.

Today, a cursory review of the monumental literature on globalization reveals diverse meanings and theoretical perspectives. Grouping together their common threads, we find several meanings and contending views as presented below. Aside from the viewpoints and meanings of globalization pointed out earlier in this section, it is important to note that all discussions of globalization deal with the question of borders, "the territorial demarcations of state jurisdictions, and associated issues of governance, economy, identity, and community" (Scholte, 1997, p. 430). Following this guidance, we discern six meanings of globalization:

1. *Globalization as internationalization* means an increase in cross-border relations among organizations, identities (including human and governmental) and communities beyond national jurisdictional boundaries. Originated centuries ago, internationalization grew with the rise of international trade and other aspects of economic and political relations among nations. Although governance and public administration have become more internationalized, such internationalization is not new either and

has been a common practice after World War II, and the Cold War era epitomized this 20th century phenomenon (Waldo, 1980; Riggs, 1994).

2. *Globalization as border openness* has similar limitations and is not new, as the borders of the capitalist nations, constrained by legal and political limitations, have never been closed to each other. The former East European and Soviet Union are exceptions, which are no part of the whole world of capitalism. Thus, border openness has some validity but is not a major departure from the earlier meanings of globalization, and is certainly not a strong defining one. Its validity rests in increased cross-border migrations, communications, financial transactions, and cultural relationships. Its purported idea of a borderless, integrated world would be characterized by a unified global economy, a global government, a homogenous global culture, and, by implication, a global system of governance and public administration (Scholte, 1997). This is a very commonly used notion of globalization about which much has been written and discussed in American political science and public administration literature in the 1990s. The Internet and other means of information technology have contributed to this meaning of globalization of governance and public administration with an idea of "thinking globally and acting locally," adjusting to global situations, and learning to adapt to global changes. The concepts of "new world," "global village," "global governance," and "global management" seem to characterize this notion of globalization and its implications for the state and public administration.

As noted above, this notion of globalization is also limited and redundant, and not new because it has been expressed for almost three centuries. The anti-cameralists raised it in favor of capitalist development, the liberal internationalists raised it against the doctrine of balance of power in the early 20th century, the transnationalists raised it against the "realist's" view of nationalist and state sovereignty proclamations in international relations (Scholte, 1997), and the socialist internationalists advanced it (led by the USSR) through the Communist International (Comintern) proclamation in the 1930s.

3. *Globalization as a process* has a useful meaning but when considered alone misses some points. Using a political economy view, this notion refers to globalization not as a phenomenon, but a process, a continuing process of capital accumulation in modern capitalism that has been going on for centuries. Only recently has it been intensifying as a result of the availability of modern technology. Therefore, it is nothing new. Accordingly, capitalism is "in its innermost essence an expanding system both internally and externally. Once rooted, it both grows and spreads" (Sweezy, 1997, p. 1). Beginning with the recession of 1974–1975, three trends have contributed to the accelerated rate of capital accumulation at the global level: the decreased growth rate, the "worldwide proliferation of monopolistic

(or oligopolistic) multinational corporation," and the "financialization of the capital accumulation process" (Sweezy, 1997, pp. 1–2). A quickening of globalization has taken place, but all three trends are traced to the changes in the internal process of capital accumulation.

4. *Globalization as ideology* has always been a major force driving ideas and systems, including capitalist systems. Ideology embodies values, norms, sanctions, and internalizing cultural bounding that tend to mold mind and soul among human beings towards specific, ideal forms of structure and processes with goals either manifest or implicitly pulling actions and behaviors. The ideological underpinnings of Western capitalist democracy act as a driving force to globalize American and Western European liberal democracy. The massive amount of information, including propaganda, which spreads throughout the world through the media, the press, through computers and satellite communication systems, offers an image of an ideal political system for other countries to emulate. The key words *freedom, individualism, free market enterprise*, and *plural democracy* have characterized this ideological force of globalization (Lindblom, 2001). Important and effective as this perspective may have been, this normative force of globalization also says little about the political economy of the state, governance, and public administration.

5. *Globalization as a phenomenon* means globalization as a cause-and-effect phenomenon in late capitalism, but it means a new phenomenon explained by nonlinear, noncausal, and chaotic events. The first is a political economy meaning used and preferred by this author, and the second is explained by chaos theory, which also has relevance to this subject, yet not powerful enough to solely define globalization. Sharing the view of the capital accumulation process, the first view treats globalization as a cause of world capitalism's endless effort to reach global markets for accelerated accumulation of capital during the stagnant era of the 1970s. Globalization has also produced significant consequences for the state and other institutions in the society, whose territorial borders have not only become somewhat borderless, but more importantly *transcended*. Here, the globe has become a single place, a village so to speak.

This view of globalization is useful for understanding global changes in the political economy of nations. The above meanings provide a set of explanations that help us understand globalization in the following manner:

6. *Globalization as both a transcending phenomenon and a continuing process of capital accumulation*. This meaning considers globalization as a process of surplus accumulation by global capitalism — a constant process of expansion into new frontiers and opportunities for increasing capital accumulation at the global level. It also views globalization as a phenomenon caused by the accelerated process of global capital

accumulation — a phenomenon that has manifested its negative and positive impacts almost everywhere. Not all nations are equally affected by this process. The countries of the North are the prime beneficiaries of this process, while the poor nations of the South are the dumping grounds of this global phenomenon of globalization. Unlike the Third World countries, which have been plagued by the devastating effects of globalization by multinational and transnational corporations for decades, the peoples, institutions, and communities of the advanced industrial countries of the North did not experience the impact of globalization until recently. Now the chicken has come home to roost for the latter countries and communities in the West too. New forces of globalization, namely China, are also entering the playing field, as inequality in power is a key factor.

It is this qualitative change spurred by the new globalization process that has caused concerns and "new consequences" for the nation-states in the dominant West. Therefore, this perspective of globalization is rather novel and complementary to the views noted above in that it adds an innovative idea to the conceptualization of the term. It considers the state as an active institutional player in the process of globalization and in dealing with its consequences. Other factors such as information technology also have played a key role.

Thus, we see a wide range of meanings that attempt to explain globalization. Adding to the list we may include the sectoral instruments, namely technological globalization, economic globalization, and a host of political, social, cultural, and academic globalization. Still, others may explain the recent development of globalization in several stages, beginning from the early 20th century divide of the world into socialism and capitalism, formation of the League of Nations, World War II, and the rise of the United Nations, rise of multinational and transnational corporations, and the fall of the Soviet Union in 1991. All these prints have useful explanatory power, but they all are parts of the above-mentioned political economy meaning of globalization, as the key to understanding globalization is the factors of power, economic accumulation, territorial boundaries, and control.

Theoretical Perspectives: A Bird's Eye View

The meanings and ideas detailed above lead us to a summary of theoretical perspectives outlined as follows. Broadly speaking three theoretical perspectives explain the heavy literature on globalization: the proponents, the opponents, and those in the middle.

1. The proponents of globalization see a new world of opportunities to economically and culturally integrate the world of nations and their peoples into "one place," a global village. Communication technologies of the

Internet, e-mails, information systems, and all other related means enable people worldwide to connect, obtain information, and purchase goods and services from anywhere in the world. This market theory of capitalist globalization sees the world population as costumers and the entire globe as marketplaces, many of which were not explored before.

The proponents see capitalism as the only legitimate system of economy and society that recognizes no national boundaries, state-imposed limitations, or constraints forced by geographical or climatic conditions, as the Internet and other technologies enable free flow of capital across the world, and instantaneous communication and financial transactions to take place anywhere in the world. These proponents (Fukuyama, 1992; Ohmae, 1995; Gates, 1995; Huntington, 1996, to name a few) view globalization as the stampede of a herd on the run, and nothing can stop it; any force or nation that stands in its way will be crushed and annihilated. Therefore, they advise all nation-states and governments to abandon their unique ideas, forms and systems of governance and administration as well as markets and join this "global herd" that can run all economies and market systems. In return, they will benefit from its largess of economy of scale, efficiency, and state-of-the-art technological advantages.

Any resistance to this global herd mentality will be futile and pointless, as its military machine (read this as the United States and NATO alliance) will crush all resistance with violence and war. Thus, globalization by violence of war is also the option available to the globalizing herd — the transworld corporations and their backing state military might. This view also dismisses any possibility of social revolutions by peoples across the world, as this new global empire (the runaway herd) will crush it with its military as well as economic and technological might; no hope for such revolutionary changes to counter globalization.

These proponents of globalization envision the entire globe politically and ideologically converging into the Western values of market capitalism run by corporations, political values of liberalism, individual freedom (as long as they do not oppose the globalization), and liberty to do private business and become agents of the global marketplace and its organization of transworld corporations, and hence "agencification" (Farazmand, 2002) of the world. Governments must also privatize and contract out all functions of public service, including military and security, and as the private business sector grows bigger, so does the globalization of market capitalism, and hence market supremacy over socialism and all other mixed forms of economy and society that characterized the world of capitalism for much of the 20th century. This was also known as "mixed economy and welfare state" with an administrative state to perform public service functions. This theory of globalization sees no legitimate alternative to market capitalism and Western supremacy, and therefore must be crushed to pave the way in the entire world for its operations.

While privatization and outsourcing expedite the globalization process, "new public management" and a host of other "new ideas" in culture, governance, and organization theory have been promoted worldwide to serve as intellectual engines of education, training, and cultural transformation of governments, public managers, and administrators, and peoples around the globe (see, for example, Lindblom, 2001; Donohue and Nye, 2002).

2. The opponents of globalization view it a serious threat to the world of peoples, nation-states, cultures, governments, national sovereignty, democracy and self-determination, communities, individual freedom, and public administration. The opponents warn against global convergence by global corporations, which are merging and re-merging together to monopolize economic, financial, and political powers, and are therefore able to dictate political, social, and other policies to governments, communities, and people, hence their threat to national sovereignty and democratic rights of peoples and communities worldwide.

The opponents also warn against monopolization of economic organization and power in the global marketplace as it constrains individual choices and freedom. Moreover, they warn against the convergence theory, as the "cultural uniqueness" of peoples and nations will be destroyed in favor of consumer culture, which only benefits the ruling capitalist elites, corporate barons, and governments that protect and promote them worldwide. They see the rise of a new global imperialism through Americanization of the world and led by the U.S. global empire. The consequences of this globalization, they argue, are too many to name, but include increasing exploitation of cheap labor, massive poverty, political repression against all forms of resistance to this global order, and rise of all kinds of human wage slavery, mercenary labor, and global bondage. Loss of local and national autonomy, sovereignty, and democratic self-determination under the new world order of global dictatorship is a dangerous development that all peoples and nation-states must oppose and prevent from happening (for example, see Cerny, 1995; Dugger, 1989; Gill and Law, 1988; Cox, 1993; Korten, 1995; Mander and Goldsmith, 1996; Farazmand, 1999).

The opponents are also critical of globalization of capitalism and corporate hegemony, for they see the potential end of public administration (Stever, 1988) and the growth of global "insecurity" rather than peace and security (Scholte, 1997). They warn against the false promise of the proponents, who claim that wars will be rare and peace will prevail worldwide, and point to increasing potentials for conflicts and wars, including direct wars of interventions and occupation of developing nations by the globalizing western powers. Recent wars and occupation of Afghanistan and Iraq by the United States are live testimonies to this warning.

In fact, the warnings continue, threat of direct military violence by the globalizing superpower, the United States, through "nuclear" weapons against resisting nation-states has increased rather than decreased. Such threats have been made by the current U.S. president, George W. Bush and other ruling elites against such countries as Iran and North Korea, both possessing capabilities to develop nuclear technologies, though mostly for peaceful purposes of energy production, a legitimate right that all nation-states have.

These global threats, coupled with increasing global inequality and poverty, promote global insecurity rather than the other way around. The opponents see the concept of "global village" not run democratically by village members, but unequally by the "strong" and more powerful ones, the barons with economic power and powerful military weapons (Harvey, 1995). This will take us back to medieval systems of feudalism and slavery (Korbin, 1996; Farazmand, 1999, 2004, forthcoming), and drive millions if not billions of hard working people in a "race to the bottom" (Brecher and Costello, 1994).

3. The third theoretical perspective, the work of this author included, on globalization reflects on realities, some unpleasant but also some positive ones, regarding the phenomenon and the process of globalization. This perspective is also complex as it represents several theoretical streams, some of which may appear to contradict each other. For example, one view argues that the world must reach the verge of destruction by the inequality-driven destructive forces of capitalism so that all peoples and weaker nations will rise in a global revolution to overthrow it in favor of the alternative systems. Another stream argues that the world of people and the oppressed do not have to suffer long by waiting for that destructive stage of capitalism to be ended by a revolution; globalization must be opposed and its negative consequences and impacts must be exposed through mass education for global awareness, collective actions, and more. In other words, resistance to globalization of corporate capitalism must be organized and intensified so the ruling barons of globalization are forced to retreat and modify their policies and accept the will of peoples worldwide.

Differences aside, this broad theoretical view sees globalization as an inevitable continuity in the process of global accumulation of corporate capitalism as the last stage of capitalist development, that is the global organization of world capitalism in search of new frontiers with no national or other barriers. It also sees globalization as an inevitable phenomenon of social and economic development in world history, a byproduct phenomenon of historical development in human history. The fact is globalization cannot be stopped, but it can be modified by opposition, collective action, and people power.

Thus, while resisting the adverse impacts of globalization, strategies and plans of action need to be developed to adjust and adapt to the new global conditions, to manage and cope with new realities, and to develop strategic choices to build local, regional, and national capacities for autonomy and democratic independence and to preserve local and national identities in culture, values, and economic bases. This is a huge challenge facing nation-states and governance systems, leaders, and public administration in theory and practice. Proponents of this third perspective are many, and are still growing (for example, see, Korten, 1995; Strange, 1996; Scholte, 1997; Farazmand, 1999, 2004, forthcoming; to name a few).

Such a social and historical development necessarily entails negative as well as some positive consequences; both come together. For example, the Internet and other information and communication technologies facilitate global access and connectedness, but they also serve the ruling elites, capitalist class of governance and administration, the village barons, the exploiters, the employers, and all other organizations of administration and governance a powerful tool of oppression and exploitation.

Proponents of this perspective, this author included, acknowledge some benefits of globalization, but warn against its severe consequences inflicted on developing nations, the poor, the powerless, and weak, and working class people worldwide.

Conclusion: Implications for Governance and Public Administration

What does the above analysis of globalization mean for governance and public administration? First, we need to make a distinction between "globalization as a self-directed process," a process that develops automatically as a result of technological and communications innovation and other international relations, on the one hand, and the process of globalization driven by design and by forces that make it happen, on the other. The first process is inevitable and is like many other phenomena that develop with time.

The second process is most important to understanding the forces behind globalization, underpinning ideologies, and the consequences that they produce for people, communities, environment, nation-states, governments, and public administration systems. In fact, as noted earlier, globalization has many consequences, both positive and negative, for societies and their governance systems. These impacts are not equally distributed to all nations, and by far the rich nations of the North are prime beneficiaries, while developing nations are the marginal receivers of any benefits, if any at all. Indeed, the latter countries are the prime receivers of the adverse or the negative impacts of globalization, a subject beyond the limits of this chapter.

Briefly noted, several implications may be drawn for governance and public administration:

First, globalization does not end the state, and by extension public administration. Thus, governance and public administration are in fact alive and will continue to persist. The bureaucracy will grow larger, rather than shrink, but its character will be security–military oriented, and its behavior will be coercive and repressive to maintain social control, order and stability, and its primary role will be to fight terrorism, the new global enemy created by the destructive behaviors of corporate capitalism and globalizing imperialism.

Second, however, the character and the role and behavior of the state and public administration change as result of globalization of corporate capitalism. In fact, there is a global transformation of the state and public administration from the traditional balancing mixed state to a new, market-driven and corporate-state ruled by transworld corporations and with the market ideology, that is the state is here to stay, but it is to serve the interests of the corporate capitalism. The new state is also coercive with a tendency to militarize the world for security purposes so the market can operate with peace. Public administration in this transformation process is also changed from a public interest oriented administrative system to a noncivilian, security-oriented police system of administration to achieve the mission of social control and capital accumulation. This is what public administration of corporate capitalism is all about: from public administration to administration of the public.

Third is the threat of globalization to state sovereignty, democracy and individual freedom, and to national independence in developing countries. Even the advanced countries of the West are not totally immune from this development, as globalization forces and supranational organizations such as the World Bank (WB), International Monetary Fund (IMF), the United Nations, and the World Trade Organization (WTO) as well as a host of other international agreements can force member-states to adopt globalization decisions that may go against national interests. Serving primarily the interests of the globalizing superpower nations — the United States, the Europeans, and the transworld corporations — such institutions as IMF and WB actually increase poverty and underdevelopment; they are the "lords of poverty" (Hankock, 1989).

Fourth, globalization also threatens the environment and ecological systems, as globalizing forces — corporations — always look for production environments with little or no regulations and labor legislation. They move to other global locations overnight once pressures for environmental regulations and against cheap labor exploitation mount in existing countries.

Fifth, globalization tends to increase poverty and inequality worldwide (Hankock, 1989), and it causes more unemployment through technological innovations, drains governing systems with tax subsidies and tax expenditures, and demands massive expenditures on security and military functions for policing and social control. The result is the increasing crisis in governance and public administration known as the "fiscal crisis" (O'Connor, 1973). This will lead to increased public disenchantment, frustration, unemployment-driven problems, and eventual social revolutions at home and worldwide (LeFeber, 1984).

Finally, globalization will produce more war, not less, as globalizing forces and institutions will use violence to promote the goals of corporate globalization. At the same time, pressures to resist these global mercenary-like capitalists will likely rise, a system that tends to drive almost every one except the ruling elites and riches of the North to a global race deep to the "bottom" (Korten, 1995). And the globalization of Western or American "cultural imperialism" in the guise of consumption, sex, drugs, pornography, and violence will eventually backfire with resentment and revolutionary attempts to revive local and indigenous cultural values (Said, 1993). This is a lesson that history has taught us over and over again, and the rise and fall of great empires attests to this historical truth (Kennedy, 1989).

What can and should be done? There are ways and means, strategies, and policies that can be adopted to counter the destructive force of this runaway global capitalism. This is a subject that requires a separate chapter presentation. See my forthcoming works, *Globalization, Governance, and Administration* and *Public Administration in the Age of Globalization.*

References

Brecher, J. and T. Costello (1994). *Global Village, Or Global Pillage: Economic Reconstruction from the Bottom Up.* Boston, MA: South End Press.

Cerny, P.G. (1995). "Globalization and the Changing Logic of Collective Action." *International Organization.* 49 (Autumn): 595–625.

Cox, R.W. (1993). "Structural Issues of Global Governance." In S. Gill, ed. *Gramci, Historical Materialism, and International Relations.* Cambridge: Cambridge University Press, pp. 259–289.

Donohue, J. and J. Nye, eds. (2002). *Market-Based Governance.* Washington, D.C.: Brookings Institution.

Falk, R. (1997). "States of Siege: Will Globalization Win Out?" *International Affairs.* 73 (January): 124–125.

Farazmand, A. (1994). "The New World Order and Global Public Administration: A Critical Essay." In J.-C. Garcia-Zamor and R. Khator, eds. *Public Administration in the Global Village.* Westport, CT: Praeger, pp. 62–81.

——(1997a). "From Civil to Non-Civil Administration: The Biggest Challenge to the State and Public Administration." Paper presented at the 1997 ASPA Conference, Philadelphia, July.

——(1997b). "Institutionalization of the New Administrative State/Role." Paper Presented at the 1997 Annual Conference of the American Political Science Association (APSA), Washington, D.C., August 28–31.

——(1999). "Globalization and Public Administration." *Public Administration Review.* Nov./Dec./ 59 (6): 509–522.

——(2001a). *Handbook of Comparative and Development Administration*, 2nd edition. Revised and expanded into 76 chapters/1200 pages. New York: Marcel Dekker.

——(2001b). *Privatization or Public Enterprise Reform?* Westport, CT: Praeger.

——(2002). "Privatization and Globalization: A Critical Analysis with Implications for Public Management Education and Training." *International Review of Administrative Sciences.* 68 (3): 355–371.

——(2004). *Sound Governance: Policy and Administrative Innovations.* Westport, CT: Praeger.

——(forthcoming-a). *Globalization, Governance, and Administration.*

——(forthcoming-b). *Public Administration in the Age of Globalization.*

Frye, R. (1975). *The Golden Age of Persia.* New York: Harper & Row.

Fukuyama, F. (1992). *The End of History: The Last Man.* New York: Avon Books.

Gates, B. (1995). *The Road Ahead.* London: Viking.

Gill, S. and D. Law (1988). *The Global Political Economy.* Baltimore, MD: Johns Hopkins University Press.

Graycar, A. (1983). *Retreat from the Welfare State.* Sydney: Allen & Unwin.

Handy, C. (1992). *The Age of Paradox.* Boston: Harvard Business School Press.

Hankock, G. (1989). *Lords of Poverty.* New York: Atlantic Monthly Press.

Harvey, R. (1995). *The Return of the Strong: The Drift to Global Disorder.* London: Macmillan.

Heady, F. (1998). "Comparative and International Public Administration: Building Intellectual Bridges." *Public Administration Review.* 58 (1): 32–39.

Hirst, P. and G. Thompson (1996). *Globalization in Question: The International Economy and the Possibilities of Governance.* Cambridge: Polity.

Holden M. (1997). "Political Power and the Centrality of Administration." In A. Farazmand, ed. *Modern Systems of Government: Exploring the Role of Bureaucrats and Politicians.* Thousand Oaks, CA: Sage, pp. 125–154.

Huntington, S. (1996). *The Clash of Civilizations and the Remaking of World Order.* New York: Simon & Schuster.

Kennedy, P. (1989). *The Rise and Fall of the Great Powers: Economic Change and Military Conflict.* New York: Vintage Books.

Korbin, S. (1996). "Back to the Future: Neomedievalism and the Postmodern Digital World Economy." *Journal of International Affairs.* 51 (2): 367–409.

Korten, D. (1995). *When Corporations Rule the World.* West Hartford, CT: Kumarian Press.

LeFeber, W. (1984). *Inevitable Revolutions: The United States in Central America.* New York: Norton.

Lenin, V. (1965). *Imperialism: The Highest Stage of Capitalism.* Peking, China: Foreign Languages Press.

Lindblom, C. (2001). *The Market System.* New Haven: Yale University Press.

Mander, J. and E. Goldsmith, eds. (1996). *The Case Against the Global Economy and for a Return toward Local.* San Francisco: Sierra Club Books.

Mann, M. (1980). *States, War and Capitalism.* Oxford, UK: Blackwell.

O'Connor, J. (1973). *The Fiscal Crisis of the State.* New York: Harper & Row.

Ohmae, K. (1990). *The Borderless World.* London: Collins.

——(1995). *The End of the Nation-State: The Rise of Regional Economies.* London: Harper-Collins.

Olmstead, A. (1948). *History of the Persian Empire: The Achaemenid Period.* Chicago: University of Chicago Press.

Riggs, F. (1994). "Global Forces and the Discipline of Public Administration." In J.-C. Garcia-Zamor and R. Khator, eds. *Public Administration in the Global Village.* Westport, CT: Praeger, pp. 17–44.

Said, E. (1993). *Culture and Imperialism.* New York: Alfred A. Knopf.

Scholte, J.A. (1997). "Global Capitalism and the State." *International Affairs.* 73 (3): 427–452.

Skocpol, T. (1985). "Bringing the State Back in: Strategies of Analysis in Current Research." In B.E. Peter, D. Rueschemeyer, and T. Skocpol, eds. *Bringing the State Back in.* Cambridge, UK: Cambridge University Press.

Stever, J. (1988). *The End of Public Administration.* New York: Transnational Publications.

Strange, S. (1996). *The Retreat of the State: Diffusion of Power in the World Economy.* Cambridge: Cambridge University Press.

Sweezy, P. (1997, September). "More (or less) on Globalization." *Monthly Review.* 49 (4): 1–2.

Waldo, D. (1980/1990). *The Enterprise of Public Administration.* Navota, CA: Chandler & Sharp.

Zysman, J. (1996)."The Myth of a 'Global' Economy: Enduring National Foundations and Emerging Regional Realities." *New Political Economy.* 1 (July): 157–184.

Chapter 2

Cultural Globalization

Nasser Momayezi

CONTENTS

Introduction

Globalization is not a one-dimensional phenomenon, but a multidimensional process involving domains of activity and interaction. Scholars defining globalization in terms of a multidimensional process (Axford, 1995; Waters, 1995; Friedman, 1999; Halliday, 1999) draw their analytical frameworks from the social sciences, namely sociology, economics, and political science. Some of these frameworks tend to view culture as the driver for global economic and political interdependence. The world has experienced successive waves of what we now call globalization. These periods have all shared certain characteristics: the expansion of trade, the diffusion of technology, extensive migration, and the cross-fertilization of diverse cultures — a mix that should give pause to those who perceive globalization narrowly, as a process nurtured strictly by economic forces. Indeed, any analytical account of globalization would be woefully inadequate without an examination of its cultural dimension. A number of prominent scholars have emphasized the centrality of culture to contemporary debates on globalization. As sociologist John Tomlinson puts it: "Globalization lies at the heart of modern culture; cultural practices lie at the heart of globalization" (Tomlinson, 1999, p. 1). Indeed, the understanding of globalization as involving several dimensions including cultural issues is now common (Hall, 1991; Axford, 1995; Robertson, 1992). Giddens (1990) sees cultural globalization as a fundamental aspect of globalization. In 1994 he stated that "Globalization is not only, or even primarily, an economic phenomenon; and it should not be equated with the emergence of a 'world system'" (pp. 4–5).

The globalization of culture has a long history. The formations of the world's great religions are profound examples of the capacity of ideas and beliefs to cross great distances with decisive social impacts. No less important are the great premodern empires such as the Roman Empire, which, in the absence of direct military and political control, held its domains together through a shred and extensive ruling class culture. However, from the 18th century, as European empires expanded and a series of technological innovations began to have far-reaching practical effects, new forms of cultural globalization crystallized. The most important ideas and arguments to emerge from the West during this era were science, liberalism, and socialism (Held et al., 1999, Archibagi et al. 1998).

However, in the period since the World War II and particularly since the end of the Cold War, the degree and intensity, the speed, and the sheer volume of cultural communication are unsurpassed at a global level. Thomas Friedman argues that the globalization system, which replaced the Cold War system, is a "dynamic ongoing process that involves the inexorable integration of markets, nation-states and technologies to a degree never witnessed before" (Friedman, 2001, p. 297). The global diffusion of radio, television, the Internet, satellite and digital technologies has made instantaneous communication possible, has rendered many border checks and control over information ineffective, and has exposed an enormous constituency to diverse cultural outputs and values (Silverstone, 2001). In contrast to earlier periods, in which states and theocracies were central to cultural globalization, the current era is one in which the corporations have replaced states and theocracies as the key producers and distributors of cultural products.

The world has become more interdependent. Even the most authoritarian governments are barely able to stem the influx of goods, services, investments, drugs, pop culture, disease, money, and secrets. Mass communications have put every government, even the most oppressive one, in media fishbowls, in which their gaffs and crimes are inevitably exposed to the world. National governments are less able to control the access of their population to new ideas, culture, and information that flows freely through multiple, transnational communication channels: phones, fax, the Internet, television, and films.

This chapter explores the impact of globalization of communication and cultural life on national culture, and the future impact of cultural flows on our sense of personal and national identities.

Cultural Globalization and Communication

Cultural globalization stems from the technological revolution and economic globalization, which together foster the flow of cultural goods such as symbols, morals, values, religion, philosophy, music, literature, and popular entertainment (Rapley, 2004). With advances in technology, communications, and transportation, the activities of states are being internationalized to a degree not previously experienced. Communication technology has indeed transformed the way individuals communicate and the way they learn from one another. The political and cultural barriers that separate us are mitigated by the technological channels connecting us. Faxes, modems, and cellular phones serve the global economy and transcend national politics and culture. In communications, for example, from 1970 to 1990 the cost of an international telephone call fell by more than 90 percent; in the 1980s telecommunications traffic increased by about 20 percent a year, and by the late 1990s over 50 million people were using the Internet. Indeed, the spread of ideas through media, television, videos, and the Internet seems to be contributing to the emergence of global culture (United Nations Development Program, Human development report 1997, p. 83).

The rapid diffusion of political and economic ideas around the globe has resulted in a clash of traditions within non-Western civilizations. This is a clash within the civilizations rather than between the civilizations as predicted by Samuel Huntington (1996). The new communication technologies have made control difficult for countries such as China and Iran, which have closed-door policies, to restrain access to the Internet. The new technologies have transformed the conduct of cultural, economic, and political life everywhere. As Rosa Gomez Dierks points out people in non-Western countries are challenging their own traditional culture, for example, Iranians pressuring their Islamic government to reverse itself, to open its economy, and to democratize and secularize national politics (2001). Likewise, the caste system in India is being challenged by members of lower castes who demand political equality and representation. Digital images of Indian villagers, Iranian and Chinese students communicating by cellular phone and fax to mobilize national reform movements are a clear reminder that the communications revolution indeed represents the "death of distance" (*The Economist*, October 1999, p. 7).

Japanese business strategist Kenichi Omhae argues that more profound cultural and generational cleavages are occurring in Japanese society, as Japanese teenagers of the 1990s have learned a different set of perceptions and social values from those of their parents and grandparents. This generation he argues is much less accepting of traditional Japanese notions of authority and conformity, is much more culturally open, questioning, and creative: "Everything, finally, is open to considered choice, initiative, creativity and daring" (1995, p. 36). This shift results, Ohmae claims, from the use of computers, computer games, and interactive multimedia: "watching how a kid from another culture whom you've never seen before reveals character and mind-set through programming style" (p. 37).

The Internet is the key organizing principle of globalization, because it is the vehicle by which individuals, governments, and private firms are interconnected around the globe. In the past half century, over 62 percent of the 192 sovereign states around the world have become democratic, representing over 58 percent of the world's population (Diamond and Platnner, 1999). One of the possible reasons for the increasing number of democratic regimes across the globe could well be the fast and vast diffusion of information. Competitive, fair, and free political elections in recent decades may be explained by the democratization of information across Eastern Europe, the Western hemisphere, Asia, and Africa. In these areas, democratic regimes are increasingly replacing the authoritarian and repressive regimes (Dierks, 2001, p. 29).

The driving forces behind cultural globalization are the companies rather than countries. Today, global corporations have much more impact on local, national culture than the publishing houses as in previous eras. The last few decades have witnessed the rapid development of new communication media, and the era was constantly characterized as the Information Age — one in which information could be a key to the power and affluence. To the developing countries it was increasingly clear that the flow of information was continuing along the one-way street from the West to the rest of the world. Critics of multinational capitalism frequently complain of its tendency toward cultural convergence and homogenization. Hamelink, in his book *Cultural Autonomy in Global Communications* (1983), acknowledges that cultural homogenization or synchronization is closely connected to the spread of global capitalism. Hamelink argues that certain processes of cultural convergence are under way, and that these are new processes. He also argues that cultural synchronization is to be deplored on the grounds that it is a threat to cultural autonomy.

Does globalization increase cultural homogeneity, or does it lead to greater diversity and heterogeneity? Or, to put the matter into less academic terms, does globalization make people more alike or more different?

Arguments for Cultural Homogeneity

Some believe that the prominent icons of popular culture, like Coca-Cola, blue jeans, rock music, and McDonald's Golden Arches will dissolve all cultural differences in a dull and colorless homogeneity throughout the world, and they also believe that the driving forces behind this homogenization are the mass media. American and European companies are spreading their powerful images, sound, and advertising on unprepared peoples, which are designed to increase profits of capitalist firms. This phenomenon is called neocolonialism. As the argument goes, because direct politico-military control could no longer be practiced, neocolonist powers turned to symbolic and psychological means of control, which was conveniently facilitated by the rapid integration of global communications system and, especially, by the proliferation of television. Pushing mainly the American culture, they argue, promotes ideologies of consumption, instant gratification, self-absorption, and the like, which is consistent with mass media's spread of global capitalism. Suddenly, people all over Africa and the rest of the non-Westernized regions of the world appear to be imbibing materialistic and individualistic values, which were previously associated with the Western culture.

Tomlinson (1999) emphasizes that global cultural flows are directed by powerful international media corporations that utilize new communication technologies to shape societies and identities. There is a clear oligopolistic tendency as a few globalized firms have come to control up to 85 percent of the dissemination of works, in both film and record industries. As images and ideas can more easily and rapidly be transmitted from one place to another, they profoundly impact the way people experience their everyday lives. Culture remains no longer tied to fixed localities such as town and nation, but acquires new meanings that reflect dominant themes emerging in a global context. This interconnectivity caused by cultural globalization challenges parochial values and identities, because they undermine the linkages that connect culture to fixity of location. Similarly, the Arab critics of globalization argue that the "imbalance flow of western economic views and lifestyle heading for one direction, from rich countries to the poorer and from giant industrial states to the developing nations, have made in effect these lesser countries under invasion by the global socioeconomic forces of industrialized west... In fact, this rapid economic, technological, social, and political intrusion of foreign culture into the Arab world may put their cultural magnitude in jeopardy and will force people to fear for the loss of their religious and social characteristics" (Moussalli, 2003, p. 2).

In the same vein, some scholars argue that these processes have facilitated the rise of increasingly homogenized global culture underwritten by the Anglo-American value system. Referring to the global diffusion of American values, consumer goods, and lifestyle as "Americanization," these authors analyze the ways in which such forms of cultural imperialism are overwhelming the more vulnerable cultures. American sociologist George Ritzer, for example, coined the term "McDonaldization" to describe the wide-ranging process by which the principles of the fast-food restaurant are coming to dominate more and more stores of American society as well as the rest of the world. In the long run, McDonaldization leads to the eclipse of cultural diversity and dehumanization of social relations (1993). Like other mammoth, multinational corporations, McDonald's sells a brand — that is, it sells homogeneity. It attracts customers with comforting promise that wherever they roam, wherever on the globe they find themselves, no matter what cultural challenges they face, a Big Mac and fries will always look and taste the same.

The prominent American political theorist Benjamin R. Barber also enters the normative realm when he warns his readers against cultural imperialism of what he calls "McWorld" — a soulless consumer market. For Barber, McWorld is a product of a superficial American popular culture assembled in the 1950s and 1960s and driven by expansionist commercial interest: "Its template is American, its for style . . . Music, video, theater, books, and theme parks . . . are all constructed as image exports creating a common taste around common logos, advertising, slogans, stars, songs, brand names, jingles, and trademarks" (Barber, 1996, p. 17). He claims that the colonizing tendencies of McWorld provoke cultural and political resistance in the form of "Jihad" — the parochial impulse to reject and repel Western homogenization forces wherever they can be found. Fueled by the furies of ethnonationalism or religious fundamentalism, Jihad represents the dark side of cultural particularism. Guided by opposing visions of homogeneity, Jihad and McWorld are dialectically interlocked in a bitter cultural struggle for popular allegiance. Barber insists that ultimately both these forces work against a participatory form of democracy, for they are equally prone to undermine civil liberties and thus thwart the possibility of global democratic future.

The proponents of the cultural homogenization thesis offer ample empirical evidence for their interpretation. They point to American Indians wearing Nike sneakers, people in sub-Sahara purchasing Texaco baseball caps, and Palestinian youth proudly displaying their Chicago Bulls sweatshirts in downtown Ramallah. Documenting the spread of Anglo-American culture, which is facilitated by the deregulation and convergence of global media and electronic communication systems, some commentators even go so far as to insist that there no longer exist any viable alternatives to the

"Americanization" of the world. For example, French political economist Serge Latouche argues that the media-driven, consumerist push toward "planetary uniformity" according to Anglo-American norms and values will inevitably result in a worldwide "standardization of lifestyle" (1996, p. 3).

In reaction to the cultural domination or cultural imperialism, less developed countries called for a "New World Information Order" (NWIO). These countries pleaded their case against the domination of Western media in UNESCO and other UN forums, arguing that restrictions should be placed on Western cultural propagation and that aid should flow to the former colonies to improve their nascent communication systems. However, global media, including the production of music and film, are monopolized by a few powerful Western corporations. It is estimated, for example, that in 1997, more than 280 million households around the world had access to MTV. Local TV stations in an increasing number of African countries, to maintain their audience, have resorted to organizing their broadcasts in Western fashion complete with Western shows, superficial news broadcasts, and Western style advertisements. Television broadcasts all over the world increasingly resemble each other as do the products in the fields of music, film, and publishing. The result of this cultural process of homogenization is that "a large section of the world's population dreams of living like Cosby & Co. or like the characters in any other stereotype American soap opera" (Akande, 2002, p. 3).

Cultural globalization destroys diversity and displaces the opportunity to sustain decent human life through an assortment of many different cultures. It is more a consequence of power concentration in the global media and manufacturing companies than the people's own wish to abandon their cultural identity and diversity. Circulation and distribution as well as production structures are now experiencing the phenomena of convergence, concentration, and massification and have thus become the main factors of cultural homogenization.

Argument against Cultural Homogenization

It is one thing to acknowledge the powerful cultural logic of global capitalism, but it is quite another to assert that the cultural diversity existing on our planet is destined to vanish (Appadurai, 1996). In fact, several influential academics offer contrary assessments that link globalization to new forms of cultural diversity. Roland Robertson (1992), for example, contends that global cultural flows often reinvigorate local cultural niches. Arguing that cultural globalization always takes place in local contexts, Robertson predicts a pluralization of the world as localities produce a variety of unique cultural responses to global forces. The result is not increasing cultural homogenization, but "glocalization" — a complex interaction of the global and local cultures, characterized by cultural borrowing. These interactions lead to a complex mixture of both homogenizing and heterogenizing impulses. Often referred to as "hybridization" or "creolization," the process of cultural mixing is reflected in music, film, fashion, language, and other forms of symbolic expression. Diversity not only exists between cultures, but also within cultures. All cultures are plural, creol, hybrid, and multicultural from within. There are no more authentic, pure, traditional, and isolated cultures in the world, even if they ever existed at all.

There is little evidence that all cultures are heading in the same direction. "The history of the world, rather than moving toward cultural homogenization, has demonstrated the opposite; a trend to cultural differentiation and cultural complexity" (King, 1991, p. 16). Philippe Legrain, a chief economist in Europe, argues that "globalization not only increase[s] individual freedom, but also revitalizes cultural artifacts through foreign influences, technologies, and markets. Thriving cultures are not set in stone. They are forever changing from within and without. Each generation challenges the previous one; science and technology alter the way we see ourselves and the world; fashions come and go; experience and events influence our belief; outsiders affect us for good and ill" (Legrain, 2003, p. B8). Though the vast majority of cultural products come from the United States, this does not amount to a simple case of cultural imperialism. You can choose to drink Coke and eat McDonald's without becoming American in any meaningful sense. Legrain continues to argue that "the really profound cultural changes have little to do with Coca-Cola. Western ideas about liberalism and science are taking root almost everywhere, while Europe and North America are becoming multicultural societies through immigration, mainly from developing countries. Foreigners are changing America as they adopt its ways. Half of the 50 million new inhabitants expected in America in the next 25 years will be immigrants or the children of immigrants. Technology is reshaping culture: just think of the Internet. Individual choice is fragmenting the imposed uniformity of national cultures. New hybrid cultures are emerging, and the regional ones re-emerging. National identity is not disappearing, but the bonds of nationality are loosening" (B9, B10). Stanley Hoffmann makes similar observations:

> Economic life takes place on a global scale, but human identity remains national — hence the strong resistance to cultural homogenization. Over the centuries, increasingly centralized states have expanded their functions and tried to forge a sense of common identity for their subjects. But no central power in the world can do the same thing today, even in the European Union. There, a single currency and advanced economic coordination have not yet produced a unified economy or strong central institutions endowed with legal autonomy, nor have they resulted in a sense of post-national

> citizenship. The march from national identity to one that would be both national and European has only just begun. A world very partially unified by technology still has no collective consciousness or collective solidarity. What states are unwilling to do the world market cannot do all by itself, especially in engendering a sense of world citizenship. (2004/2005, 5)

National cultures are much stronger than people seem to think. One of the surprising features of our global age is how robust national and local cultures have proved to be (Appadurai, 1990). National institutions remain central to public life whereas national audiences constantly reinterpret foreign products in novel ways. In fact, the available evidence suggests that national and local cultures remain robust; national institutions in many states continue to have a central impact on public life; national television and radio broadcasting continue to enjoy substantial audiences. The organization of the press and the news coverage retain strong national roots and imported foreign products are constantly read and interpreted in novel ways by national audiences, that is, they become rapidly indigenized (Miller, 1992; Liebes and Elihu, 1993; Thompson, 1995, 1998). Moreover, the evidence indicates that there is no simple, common global pool of memories; no common global way of thinking; and no universal history in and through which people can unite. There is only a manifold set of political meanings and systems through which any new global awareness, or multicultural politics, or human rights discourse must struggle for influence (Bozeman, 1984; Silverstone, 2001). Given the deep roots of national cultures and ethno-histories, and many ways in which they are often refashioned, this can hardly be a surprise. Despite the vast flows of information, imagery, and people around the world, there are only a few signs, at best, of a universal or global history in the making, and a few signs of a decline in importance of nationalism.

The globalist's emphasis that globalization is "globalizing Western culture and Western cultural icons" is overstated. In most countries loyalty and identity are stubbornly rooted in traditional ethic, regional, and national communities. However, Norris notes that, in the long term, public opinion is moving in a more international direction (2000). Generations brought up with Yahoo, MTV, and CNN affirm this trend and are more likely to have some sense of global identification, although it remains to be seen whether this tendency crystallizes into a majority position and whether it generates a clearly focused political orientation.

Conclusion

It is widely asserted that we live in an era in which the greater part of social life is determined by a global process, and in which national cultures, national economies, and national borders are dissolving. Globalization is understood as a multidimensional process that connects individuals, governments, and firms across national boundaries. It is a process that includes technological, economic, political, and cultural dimensions. Undoubtedly, telecommunication technology is the key organizing principle of globalization, because it is the vehicle by which individuals, governments, and private firms are interconnected around the globe.

The cultural state of the world can be interpreted as being intrinsically linked to the flow of information and knowledge. Today, it is the media, which are the primary channels for cultural globalization, that are at the heart of issues about cultural pluralism, given their economic power and their influence on our symbolic order. The fact that the internationalization of information has provided networks of communication and interaction between different cultures of the world is clear and certain. There are genuine causes for concern about the rate at which cultures (non-Western) are being undermined in a world that is bound together by ever-stronger economies. However, it is an exaggeration to speak of vanishing cultures, and it is equally naive to believe that cultures can be protected against foreign influences. There is no doubt that the magnification of global media networks and satellite communication technologies enable some dominant powers to have a truly global reach. The Americans thus have been successful in supporting firms that can profitably disseminate American images, ideas, and values throughout the world. They have understood that the best way to sell themselves is to create desires and dreams.

It is impossible to ignore the threat of Western cultural influences on non-Western cultures. However, we need to find ways to ensure balanced exchanges between societies and cultures that are equal in dignity and are able to reflect critically and honestly on their values, practices, and adaptation to the changing world conditions. It is as important for a society and culture as it is for a country to see its language, values, and views of the world shared and carried by others. Obviously, it would be an excessive form of cultural fundamentalism to suggest that non-Western countries should try and keep everything exactly as it is, rather than allowing culture to develop.

References

Akande, W. November 10, 2002. "The Drawbacks of Cultural Globalization," Yellow-Times.org. http: //yellowtimes.org/article.php?sid = 848&mode = ...

Appadurai, A. 1996. *Modernity at Large: Cultural Dimensions of Globalization*. Minneapolis: University of Minnesota Press.

Appadurai, A. 1990. "Disjuncture and Difference in the Global Culture," *Public Culture*. 2(2): 1–24.

Archibugi, D., Held, D. and Kohler, M. (eds) 1998. *Re-Imagining Political Community: Studies in Cosmopolitan Democracy*. Cambridge: Polity Press.

Axford, B. 1995. *The Global System: Economics, Politics and Culture*. Cambridge: Polity Press.

Barber, B.R. 1996. *Jihad vs. McWorld*. New York: Ballantine Books.

Bozeman, A.B. 1984. "The International Order in Multicultural World," in H. Bull and A. Watson (eds), *The Expansion of International Society*. Oxford: Oxford University press.

Dierks, R.G. 2001. *Introduction to Globalization: Political and Economic Perspectives for the New Country*. Chicago: Burnham Inc., Publishers.

Friedman, T.L. 1999. *The Lexus and the Olive Tree: Understanding Globalization*. New York: Farrar, Straus and Giroux.

Friedman, T.L. 2001. "The World is Ten Years Old: The New Era of Globalization," in C.W. Kegley, Jr. and E.R. Wittkopf (eds), *The Global Agenda*. 5th ed. Boston: McGraw Hill.

Giddens, A. 1990. *The Consequences of Modernity*. Cambridge: Cambridge University Press.

Hall, S. 1991. "The Local and the Global: Globalization and Ethnicities," in A.D. King (ed.), *Culture Globalization and the World-System*, pp. 19–30.

Halliday, F. 1999. "The Chimera of the International University," *International Affairs*. 75:99–120.

Hamelink, C.J. 1983. *Cultural Autonomy in Global Communications: Planning National Information Policy*. New York: Longman.

Hoffmann, S. 2004/2005. "Clash of Globalization," in H.E. Purkitt (ed.), *World Politics*. 25th ed. IA, Dubuque: McGraw-Hill/Dushkin.

Held, D., Anthony, G.M., David, G., and Jonathan, P. 1999. *Global Transformations: Politics, Economics and Culture*. Stanford, CA: Stanford University Press.

Huntington, S.P. 1996. *The Clash of Civilizations and the Remaking of World Order*. New York, NY: Simon & Schuster Inc.

King, A.D. (ed.) 1991. *Culture, Globalization and the World System: Contemporary Conditions for the Representation of Identity*. London: Macmillan.

Latouche, S. 1996. *The Westernization of the World*. Cambridge: Polity Press.

Legrain, P. 2003. "Cultural Globalization is not Americanization," *Chronicle of Higher Education*, May 9.

Liebes, T. and Elihu, K. 1993. *The Export of Meaning: Cross-Cultural Readings of Dallas*. Cambridge: Polity Press.

Miller, D. 1992. "The Young and Restless in Trinidad: A Case of the Local and the Global in Mass Consumption," in R. Silverstone and E. Hirsch (eds), *Consuming Technology*. London: Routledge.

Moussalli, M. 2003. "Impact of Globalization," *Daily Star*, August 25.

Norris, P. 2000. "Global Governance and Cosmopolitan Citizens," in J.S. Nye and J.D. Donahue (eds), *Governance in a Globalizing World*. Washington, DC: Brookings Institution Press.

Omhae, K. 1995. *The End of the Nation State: The Rise and Fall of Regional Economies*. London: Harper & Collins.

Rapley, J. 2004. *Globalization and Inequality: Neoliberalism's Downward Spiral.* Boulder, CO: Lynne Rienner Publishers.

Re-Imagining Political Community Studies in Cosmopolitan Democracy. Cambridge: Polity Press.

Ritzer, G. 1993. *The McDonaldization of Society: An Investigation into the Changing Character of Contemporary Social Life.* Thousand Oaks, CA: Pine Forge Press.

Robertson, R. 1992. *Globalization: Social Theory and Global Culture.* London: Sage.

Silverstone, R. 2001. "Finding a Voice: Minorities, Media and the Global Commons," *Emergences.* 11(1):13–27.

"The Conquest of Location," *The Economist.* October 9, 1999, p. 7.

Thompson, J. 1995. *The Media and Modernity: A Social Theory of the Media.* Cambridge: Polity Press.

Thompson, J. 1998. "Community Identity and World Citizenship," in Archibugi et al. 1998. *Re-Imagining Political Community Studies in Cosmopolitan Democracy.* Cambridge: Polity Press.

Tomlinson. J. 1999. *Globalization and Culture.* Chicago: The University of Chicago Press.

United Nations Development Program (UNDP). Human Development Report, 1997. New York; Oxford University Press.

Waters, M. 1995. *Globalization.* 2nd ed. London: Routledge.

Chapter 3

Planning for Change: Globalization and American Public Administration

Madlyn M. Bonimy

CONTENTS

Globalization: Some Definitions

Webster's *Third New International Dictionary* (1986, p. 965) defines globalization as "the act of globalizing or condition of being globalized." In this sense, globalization relates to and involves the interdependency of the entire world and a decreased emphasis on narrow or provincial actions and policies. Gary-Vaughn (2002, pp. 20–21) explains further how, with globalization "many barriers assumed to have separated governments, peoples, and cultures no longer exist." Another author, Luke (1998, p. 987), agrees and writes how globalization links "all the states of the modern world, to one degree or another economically, politically, and environmentally."

Thus economically, as Luke underscores: "where once the world economy was dominated by only a few nations, the globally interdependent economy is characterized by more widely shared economic power and influence among governmental and nongovernmental institutions. [And this] has eroded political sovereignty and diminished the power of the nation-state to control its economy directly" (1998, p. 987). Then, politically, Luke stresses how globalization has "diffused political power broadly among an expanding number of governmental and nongovernmental actors, dramatically increasing political pluralism in world politics. [Thus] the relative role of the nation-state in international affairs declines as global interdependence increases" (1998, p. 987). And finally, environmentally, globalization involves environmental spillovers. Again, Luke argues how "regional problems arise when neighboring countries share a common natural resource and one country's actions spill over borders and affect others, such as transboundary pollution and management of international rivers or regional seas" (1998, p. 987).

Therefore, the changes that the phenomenon of globalization will occasion — a world shrinking into a "global village," increasing economic integration, cross-border spillovers, increasing political pluralism, and the internationalization of domestic affairs, for example — will have a profound impact on the practice of American public administration. And, in particular, the occupational sector, enterprises, and activities that deal with the formulation and implementation of policy of governmental and other public programs and the management of such programs.

Globalization: A Historical Overview

It was after World War II that the concept of globalization emerged (Luke, 1998; Farazmand 1999; Kettl, 2000). Farazmand (1999) even goes further and credits Mikhail Gorbachev with this new way of global thinking and restructuring. Farazmand (1999, p. 510) argues how Gorbachev "called for global restructuring, openness, an end to the Cold War, peace for all, [and] superpower cooperation..." Similarly, Luke (1998), Farazmand (1999), and Kettl (2000) agree that since the 1970s the significant advances in global communication and information technology have bound the world's countries and communities, thus connecting them more closely together than ever before.

Consequently, communication technology such as fax as well as information and computer technology, in the form of the Internet and the World Wide Web in particular, exemplify contemporary globalization. These technologically enhanced tools have forever changed the globe, producing rapid communication. In fact, no other technological innovation has the same capability to transcend national boundaries (Scott & O'Sullivan, 2002, p. 233). And in transcending national boundaries, globalization has been facilitated by this connection and coordination among peoples, governments, and nongovernmental organizations. Along with information technology, transportation technology (Luke, 1998, p. 985) too has further reduced geographic space. The result is a borderless world characterized by a unified global economy and global government.

Besides technological innovation, globalization has developed, and again, since the 1970s, because of the surplus accumulation of corporate capital. Farazmand (1999, p. 512) discusses how the surplus accumulation of corporate capital has crossed territorial boundaries, reaching a high point after the 1970s and its zenith in the 1990s. This capital accumulation at the global level marks a significant shift from national to global capitalism. Farazmand (1999, p. 512) correctly points out that: "surplus (or profit) accumulation is the lifeblood of capitalism which needs constant expansion at any cost." And a high rate of surplus accumulation has contributed to a "transworld mobility of corporations" (Farazmand, 1999, p. 512). Accordingly, this transworld mobility of corporations has led to the concentration of corporate power at the global level and to the creation of a globalizing class of transnational corporations, also called multinationals. In fact, the number of global corporations increased from 3,500 in 1960 to 40,000 in 1995, representing 40 percent of the world's total commerce (Farazmand, 1999, p. 513). Another author, Reich (1991, p. 30), also contributes to this discussion about multinationals adding how this concentrated global corporate structure has created a world government beyond nation-states — and, in fact, a new world government of managerial elites who can influence public policy and administrative decisions. Farazmand (1999, pp. 516–518) provides a good example of this situation when he writes how a few transnational elites can prescribe and dictate public policy in local communities. One example is when global corporations close factories overnight and take their business overseas for more profitable locations without consulting local people. This new world government has implications for public administration as multinationals are expected to expand in this globalized age.

Our historical overview of how globalization developed ends with a look at a third major cause — the dominance of international institutions. Since the 1970s, the United Nations and its key affiliated organizations such as the World Bank, the International Monetary Fund (IMF), and the World Trade Organization (WTO) have been the powerful institutions in this process (Luke, 1998; Farazmand, 1999; Kettl, 2000; O'Toole & Hanf, 2002). We also point out here that the United States dominates the United Nations agencies, as it is a key donor of international aid. Yet, the United States, the current world's sole superpower, has found itself unable to act alone because, in the international debate, the federal government has become more marginalized as formal organizations like the United Nations and the WTO have become stronger (Kettl, 2000, p. 491). Then, too, as Farazmand (1999, p. 515) argues the decisions and the codes of conduct of these supraterritorial organizations are binding over the nation-state affecting their administrative systems. Consequently, in this globalized world, governments must devise new strategies for effective management of global processes. The new realities of the globalized world call for building an administrative capacity and apparatus for tackling transnational issues and institutions.

Globalization: What Will It Mean for the Practice of American Public Administration?

With globalization, public administration enters a new era of administration. This new administration era broadens the scope and the practice of public administration. Here, we discuss three critical changes for the practice of public administration.

Public Administration from Self-Governance to World/Transnational Governance

Stoker (1998, p. 17) and Huque (2001, p. 1291) define governance as "a new process of governing." Stoker adds how this new process of governing signifies a change in the meaning of government and a new method by which society is governed (1998, p. 17). Accordingly, today, because of globalization, society has a new method of governing and public administration has also adopted a new method. Public administration is now intertwined in the world's governance. Thus, with the increasing degree of interdependence in the world, public administration can no longer just content itself with domestic, internal, territorial, or parochial issues. The critical policy problems — for example, jobs, immigration, environmental quality, and public health — have become globally interdependent and this forces public administration to think, act, and manage in global terms as well.

For example, Luke (1998, p. 989) argues how pollution has no boundaries and thus is a global issue calling for cross-border solutions. Then, Huddelston (2000, p. 678) emphasizes how public health too must shift to deal with global matters such as infectious diseases, various viruses (Ebola, and the recent outbreak of the severe acute respiratory syndrome (SARS), which requires quarantining mass numbers of people, nationals as well as visiting foreigners, for instance), and emergency preparedness against terrorist attacks. Huddelston (2000, p. 672) also reports how public administrators are overwhelmed with problems of immigration, legal and illegal, induced by poverty, repression, and civil wars in distant lands. These examples confirm that public administrators are already heavily enmeshed with policy and programs that extend well beyond the borders. American public administration is maneuvering in the international system of world/transnational governance and as such administrative decision makers are confronted with new challenges to which no single actor can respond. The emerging governance pattern is one of multilateral agreements.

Public Administration to Transnational Administrative Structure

With increasing global interdependence, there has been a major change in the configuration of public administration as transnational developments are changing administration. Therefore, government, particularly at the national level, has had to reorganize itself structurally to deal with transnational issues.

"The basic structure of American government comes from the New Deal days" as Kettl explains (2000, p. 488). It is basically a vertical system of hierarchical bureaucracies and signifies a government driven by functional specialization and process control. Kettl (2000, p. 495) adds how this model is "the keystone of democratic accountability" — in this vertical relationship, elected policy makers delegate authority to administrators in exchange for accountability for results. However, today, as a result of globalization, public administration must now adapt to deal with horizontal networks. These horizontal networks exhibit a distinctive pattern of multilateral decision making involving governments, intergovernmental bodies, and a variety of international nongovernmental organizations (O'Toole & Hanf, 2002, p. 160).

O'Toole and Hanf (2002, pp. 160–162) further underscore how "the global expanse has become a highly complex mixed-actor system . . . with many networks and many functionally specific regimes coexisting." Hence, in terms of a transnational administrative structure, public administration is moving toward: "disaggregated, multilevel, institutionally, complex, interdependent arrays" (O'Toole & Hanf: 2002, p. 160). And no federal cabinet-level department is untouched, for they all have specialized units to deal with the international aspects of their mission (Kettl, 2000, p. 492). Nevertheless, a major problem of horizontal networks is that they undermine accountability. And Kettl (2000, p. 494) stresses how "the spread of horizontal relationships muddies accountability. They replace hierarchical authority with networks . . . where administrative responsibility is widely shared and where no one is truly in charge." In short, diffused accountability is prevalent in joint action.

Public Administration to Transnational Collaborative Management

A new era of administration is emerging as evidenced by both the increasing importance of global governance and its transnational-networked administrative structures. In future years, it would seem, that the United States, a dominant and significant player in the globalizing world, will have to work more closely and as a partner with other countries to achieve its global policy aims. And for the most part, it appears that transnational collaborative management will be used to organize and manage shared problems in this complex and polycentric setting. Several writers recognize this move to transnational collaborative management with its various managerial strategies.

For example, Farazmand (1999, p. 519) points out how "as guardians of global community interests, public administrators have a global responsibility to act in a coordinated manner." O'Toole and Hanf (2002, p. 160) argue how "participants in any case cannot achieve something on their own. [As a result] Government actors find themselves necessarily engaged in forms of collaborative management." O'Toole and Hanf (2002, pp. 163–164) further explain how both decision making and problem solving have been reconfigured to "transnational decision making" and "mutual problem solving." With this global dimension, it is now imperative to collaborate. Collaborative management, says O'Toole and Hanf (2002, pp. 163–164), is the means to deal with issues like terrorism, for instance, that "surpass the resources and problem-solving capacities of territorially defined units."

Finally, Luke (1998, p. 989) reports how "nations must engage in cooperative action and collaborative initiatives across traditional boundaries and jurisdictions." Partnerships, alliances, and various forms of interorganizational strategies are thus fundamental. Similarly, cooperative actions that are typified by bargaining and negotiation are essential. And we point out here that when it comes to bargaining and negotiation, administrators are not solely reactive to the international regime. As a matter of fact, O'Toole and Hanf (2002, p. 165) are quick to explain how, for example, "administrators are involved from the outset in conducting analyses, outlining options [and] framing negotiating positions. . . . "

So even though national decision makers will be expected to be the principal decision makers at an international level, engaging in various forms of transnational cooperation, their international commitments carry implications to subnational public administration — particularly, to state and local levels, where the implementation of international obligations by national authorities requires coordination and collaboration among agencies that share responsibilities. All things considered, transnational collaborative management is the emerging management strategy required for cross-border solutions and will enable public administrators to manage cooperatively in the networked arrangements of global disparate actors.

Globalization: How Can Public Administration/ Administrators Plan for the Changes?

With globalization, the focus of administrative work will be reshaped. Administrative work, as Mudacumura (2000, p. 2052) confirms, is reshaped on a global scale by the existence of complex interdependencies and interconnections that have crystallized the environmental context of public administration. This new environmental context of public administration demands new skills and tools in planning for change. The change literature (Kotter & Schlesinger, 1979; Senge, 1990), for example, argues how change will happen, for it is the only constant in life. Therefore, of utmost importance in planning for change is clearly leading the direction of change and possessing knowledge and skills in planning for it.

Thus, administrators must become aware of globalization and its interrelated processes, for their own effective and responsible functioning. In planning for change, public administrators must be proactive, rather than reactive; be inclusive with more points of view; make decisions with enough knowledge; work on the common good, rather than their own preferences; and finally, emphasize collective responsibility (Halet, 1997).

With regards to including more viewpoints, Farazmand (1999, p. 518) outlines how the space for citizen involvement has been shrinking with globalization. Nevertheless, the future legitimacy of public administration will be based on citizen involvement. Thus, in planning for change and globalization, public administrators must engage citizens in the administration of public affairs and encourage them to play a proactive role in managing societal resources. Public administrators must also build a sense of community and foster values of citizenship and community/public interest.

Similarly, when it comes to making decisions with enough knowledge, Farazmand (1999, p. 518) underscores how in planning for change and globalization, practitioners must broaden their personal and professional worldviews. Public administrators must examine public administration from a comparative, international, and global perspective, thus expanding their knowledge about different peoples and cultures. Consequently, with broadened personal and professional worldviews, public administrators can appreciate the cultural, institutional, and religious underpinnings of the administrative cultures of other nations. In addition, scholars like Haque (2002, p. 177) believe that in planning for change and globalization public managers must receive training in cross-cultural administrative systems.

With the complex interconnections that now seem to define public administration, administrators must learn how to maintain, on a global scale, adequate levels of cooperation. Luke (1998, p. 989) warns how with the increasing interdependence comes the increased potential for conflict and confrontation. Consequently, in planning for change and globalization, public administrators will need skills in conflict management, including brainstorming, building consensus, and problem solving. And conflict management strategies that nurture shared stakes in solving common global issues need to be designed (Luke, 1998, p. 989).

Additionally, in planning for change and globalization, Mudacumura (2002, p. 2070) points out how an administrator will increasingly become a team captain or even first among equals; thus, there is a growing need to stress participatory management skills in global change.

Finally, in planning for change and globalization, several authors, for example, Farazmand (1999), Luke (1998), and Kirkwood (2001) discuss a number of educational strategies to assist future public administrators. Farazmand (1999, p. 518) argues how public administrators need exposure to studies that will help them to generate generalizations across global spaces. Luke (1998, p. 989) mentions how global interdependence demands heightened understanding of cultures, markets, and languages of other countries. Luke (*ibid.*), again, goes on to explain how not only a broadened international perspective is required, but also increased skills in international communications and foreign languages that will enable public administrators to observe, think, and act in an interdependent world are required. Additionally of importance, stresses Farazmand (1999, p. 518), is for public administrators to "learn how to discuss exports, deal with foreign officials, and develop a greater understanding of capital markets." In the final analysis, as Kirkwood (2001, p. 10) points out, leaders of the 21st century need education that focus on the world with emphasis, for example, on cross-cultural awareness, multiple perspectives, comprehension and appreciation of cultures, and knowledge of global issues and the world as an interrelated system.

Altogether, it would seem that public administrators must adapt to the changing environmental context of global public administration. They must lead the direction of change and possess knowledge, skill, and education in planning for it.

Conclusion

This chapter has sketched in a variety of ways how globalization has changed the practice of public administration. The discussion has first touched on public administration heavily involved in world governance, then adding a new horizontal administrative structure, and finally moving to transnational collaborative management. The gist of the argument is that globalization is on the move: The globe has become smaller and physical boundaries have become irrelevant. Accordingly, this borderless world of globalization demands that nations engage in cooperative action to solve common international issues, and that administrators develop a broadened worldview managerial perspective.

This chapter has also presented several problems that globalization will induce vis-à-vis the practice of public administration: (1) Diffused accountability inherent in joint action as American administrators will be asked to enforce norms set in the global political community — the WTO and the IMF, for example; (2) Diminished governance as government is less able to govern in origin and scope. This means that cross-border problems, for instance, infectious diseases and terrorist attacks require cross-border solutions, administration, and coordination; and (3) Lessened legitimacy, because an administration that has diffused accountability and diminished governance has little legitimacy.

Nonetheless, globalization has set the agenda to which American public administration must respond. American public administration must thus plan for the changes of globalization by leading the direction of change and possessing knowledge and skills in planning for it. Finally, there must be educational strategies to assist future public administrators, including multicultural learning designed to learn more about other peoples, cultures, and languages.

Altogether, it would seem that in a world that is becoming highly globalized, both American public administration in the 21st century and its leaders have little choice but to actively embrace globalization. In so doing, however, American public administration enters a new era of administration and some degree of challenge lies ahead for it.

References

Farazmand, A. (1999). "Globalization and Public Administration," *Public Administration Review*, 59(6): 509–522.

Gary-Vaughn, G. (2002). "Global Interdependence," *Journal of Family and Consumer Sciences*, 94(3): 20–21.

Halet, M.J. (1997). *Organization Theory, Modern Symbolic and Postmodern Perspectives*. Cambridge, MA: Oxford University Press.

Haque, S.M. (2002). "Government Responses to Terrorism: Critical Views of their Impacts on People and Public Administration," *Public Administration Review*, 62(Special Issue): 170–180.

Huddelston, M.W. (2000). "Onto the Darkling Plain: Globalization and the American Public Service in the Twenty-First Century," *Journal of Public Administration Research and Theory*, 10(4): 665–684.

Huque, A.S. (2001). "Governance and Public Management: The South Asian Context," *International Journal of Public Administration*, 24(12): 1289–1300.

Kettl, D.F. (2000). "The Transformation of Governance: Globalization, Devolution, and the Role of Government," *Public Administration Review*, 60(6): 488–497.

Kirkwood, T.F. (2001). "Our Global Age Requires Global Education: Clarifying Definitional Ambiguities," *The Social Studies*, 92(1): 10–15.

Kotter, J.P. and L.A. Schlesinger (1979). "Choosing Strategies for Change," *Harvard Business Review*, 57(2): 106–114.

Luke, J.S. (1998). "Global Interdependence," in J.M. Shafritz, editor in chief, *International Encyclopedia of Public Policy and Administration*, vol. 3, Boulder, CO: Westview Press, pp. 984–989.

Mudacumura, G.M. (2000). "Participative Management in Global Transformational Change," *International Journal of Public Administration*, 23(12): 2051–2077.

O'Toole, L.J. Jr. and K.I. Hanf (2002). "American Public Administration and Impacts of International Governance," *Public Administration Review*, 62(Special Issue): 158–167.

Reich, R.B. (1991). *The Work of Nations: Preparing for 21st Century Capitalism*, New York: Simon & Schuster.

Scott, T.J. and M. O'Sullivan (2002). "Essential Web Sites to Research the Globalization Process." *The Social Studies, 93*(5): 232–236.

Senge, P. (1990). *The Fifth Discipline: The Art and Practice of the Learning Organization*, London: Century.

Stoker, G. (1998). "Governance as Theory: Five Propositions," *International Social Science Journal*, 53(170): 17–28.

Webster, M. (1986). *Third New International Dictionary*, Springfield, MA: Merriam Webster Inc. (Philippines copyright).

CONSEQUENCES AND IMPLICATIONS FOR PUBLIC ADMINISTRATION

Chapter 4

The Challenge of Globalization to Public Administration Identity

Jonathan F. Anderson

CONTENTS

> "The rapid progress of globalization has brought about a veritable disintegration of the world's borders. Before our eyes, the illusory nature of these former cultural and economic boundaries has been exposed during the last decade. The winds of changes have amended the context within which governments operate and with that, the purview and methods of their

public administrators. Policy makers now find themselves working in international environments. Consequently, they have to take into consideration the global implications of their domestic policies."

Walter Broadnax (2004)

"Government in the United States has, thus, become increasingly intertwined in the world's governance.... These changes...have culminated, however, into a fundamental transformation of governance — a transformation that poses substantial challenges for public institutions and how we manage them."

Donald Kettl (2000)

Introduction

As our world encounters increasingly rapid technological and social changes, it can be imagined as both shrinking and expanding, as both becoming one, and flying apart, shattering into individual pieces. Centrifugal and centripetal forces tear at our conception of the world. Whereas this perspective is not new (Toffler, 1970; Waldo, 1971; Huntington, 1971), increasingly rapid advances in technology have made continuous change the new norm. Whereas the fault lines, cleavages, and conceptual borders of society have changed, public administration's identity has remained traditionally, and almost exclusively, located in the geographically bound world of the state. Concepts of the "public interest" are similarly geographically aligned. Little attention is paid to the pressures exerted on the identity of "public manager" in this globalized, postmodern age. This chapter articulates the need for a conversation about the impact of globalization on the identity of public administration and particularly the public manager.

Centripetal Forces

It is a cliché to say that the world is becoming smaller, but the reality impacts our lives daily. Advances in transportation and communication make distances less relevant. We can reach any point on the Earth in less than a day (assuming we have the economic resources). People and governments of the past took days, weeks, or months to communicate with each other. Now such interaction is almost instantaneous. In the past, events happening on one side of the world might never be known outside that region. Now events in isolated locations are broadcast to the rest of the world almost immediately, sometimes even before governments are aware of them. Humans are more connected to each other than ever before. Radio, television, and the Internet connections encroach across every geographical boundary. The Internet facilitates conversations and instantaneous exchange of information. We are increasingly acquainted, if not intimate, with those who were previously strangers.

This explosion of communication has spawned a nascent monoculture that asserts itself even upon isolated communities (Anderson, 2001). The world distribution of movies, music, sports, fashions, and clothing promotes common ideas of appearance, behavior, music, and style. Barber's (1995) McWorld is a reality, with a McDonald's (and a KFC and a Burger King and a Pizza Hut) on every corner. Millions around the world sport the same logo-embossed clothing — or at least a pirated rip-off. Increasingly corporations have branches and distribution networks in a variety of countries. Small independent stores, unable to compete with the familiar big box stores, are forced out of business. Along with this homogenization comes the comfort and security of familiarity. We know what to expect from stores that are clones of those in our hometown. The world is coming together, and we are closer to one another because of these new technologies.

Centrifugal Forces

But the cliché, "familiarity breeds contempt" is also true, as the more we know of each other, the more we react to each other (Volkan, 1988; Barash, 1994). Positive and negative passions are heightened among those who are closest to each other and share commonalities. Families and neighbors know each other most intimately. They are brought together by similarities and driven apart by differences. With communication and transportation revolutions we have come to know those at a distance almost as intimately as those next door. The foreign countries of the past were exotic and distant, and did not impact our lives. You could close your eyes or turn your back. You knew they were there, somewhere, but they were not relevant to local realities. Today, a strike in India impacts service delivery in the United States. An incident in the Middle East immediately changes the price of gasoline at the corner pump. Jobs are lost not only because of a downturn in the economy, but also because someone is hired on the other side of the world (Lehoczky, 2004).

There are positive results from this intimacy. We form global connections and bonds. We share interests and memberships in transnational organizations. A natural disaster in any part of the world is reported immediately, and foreign aid arrives quickly. The explosion of technological and logistical changes results in drastic reductions of prices for consumer products, making yesterday's luxuries accessible to a much larger percentage of the world's population. However, not only consumer products are available worldwide, but also tools of destruction (Balser, 2000).

Increased intimacy and increased technological advances contribute to a rising number of wars fought by civilians or paramilitaries and to personal conflict and personal wars, wars of neighbor destroying neighbor, and atrocities committed against former friends (Bercovitch, 2003; Sollenberg & Wallensteen, 2001).

Ethnic, cultural, and religious alliances cross borders, fueling complex and overlapping conflict configurations. Those who formerly fought for their land, now fight for their identity, which is based on characteristics that may not stop at state boundaries. Even as we come to know each other better, a paradoxical breakdown of civic-society fuels ethnic conflict (e.g., Varshney, 2002).

This increase in contact, facilitated by technology, is exacerbated by massive increase in population (also facilitated by technology). Our burgeoning population in the past 100 years has grown from about 1.5 billion in 1900 to over 6 billion in 2000, with over 70 million people added to the Earth annually (U.S. Census Bureau, 2004), forcing us to live physically closer at the same time the communication and logistics revolutions move us psychically closer. The more personal our contact, the more personal is the conflict. Familiarity does, indeed, appear to breed contempt. Centripetal forces are catalysts for the centrifugal.

Globalization blurs traditional lines of identity. Homogenized values make it difficult to say just who we are. Sassen (1998) in *Globalization and its Discontents* notes an "unmooring of identities from what have been traditional sources of identity such as the nation or the village" (p. xxxii), and that "globalization is a process that generates contradictory spaces characterized by contestation, internal differentiation, continuous border crossings" (p. xxxiv).

The foregoing is not a new analysis. We see and hear such critiques daily. A complementary, if somewhat less familiar, analysis is the changing nature of the state.

The Decline of the State

The concept of a "sovereign" state assumes control of human interactions within geographical borders. The state has a number of traditional responsibilities. It provides political security and stability through armed forces and law enforcement. It provides economic stability through regulation of markets. The modern welfare state may also provide education and a variety of social services. Whereas private and nonprofit entities may also provide services, the state regulates, coordinates, and sometimes funds those organizations.

In recent years multinational organizations have begun to undertake roles previously performed exclusively by the nation-state. Immediately after World War II a system of collective defense organizations was created, central among which were NATO and the Warsaw Pact (Van Creveld, 1999). At the same time, multinational political organizations also arose. The most recent example is the European Union where laws and policies cross national borders, and sovereignty becomes nebulous (Cananea, 2003). This chipping away at the sovereign powers of the state raises questions of "governability" (Howe, 2002) or what Boggs (2001) calls "political atrophy."

The concept of legitimate military actor has also shifted toward multinational organizations (Long, 1994; Smolowe & Angelo, 1992). Where previously the state was the only legitimate user of force, now in the international arena, forces of the individual state are often seen as illegitimate. Legitimacy is achieved through agreements within and among multinational organizations. The Korean War was designated as United Nation's action. The U.S. action in Vietnam had international participation that was continually cited as evidence of legitimacy. Both Persian Gulf wars were composed of coalitions of nations. It is more or less accepted that, other than defense from invasion, legitimate international use of force now demands a multinational response.

Even more than military security, economic organization and regulation have been internationalized. The explosive growth in communication and logistical technologies enables corporations to be worldwide organizations. Transnational corporations have been around for years, but they are now responsible for increasing percentages of national economies. Foreign ownership in local companies has increased and lowered regulatory barriers (Kleinert, 2001). Increasing foreign investment in local economies is a normative goal for most developed countries. The International Monetary Fund (IMF) and the World Trade Organization (WTO) both advocate facilitating such investment (*The Age*, 2003).

As corporations expand across borders, individual states have less control over them, weakening state regulatory power. Omae (1990) asserts that national economies no longer exist in an age of globalization. To fill this governance gap international treaties create international regulations. The WTO, IMF, and World Bank share in the regulation of state economies, reducing individual state sovereignty and creating what Bennett (2004) calls a "Network Commonwealth" of states.

As corporate ownership is internationalized, there is an increasing need for more international agreements and regulations. And with the increase in the multilateral organizations, perforce, comes a decline in the power of the individual state. Although this conclusion is not new, there has been little discussion about the impact of globalization on the role and identity of public managers.

Issue Networks

Network theories have begun to address the changing governance landscape. Intergovernmental relations scholars focus on network management as key to local government effectiveness (Kickert et al. 1997; Klijn & Koppenjan, 2000; Agranoff & McGuire, 2003). Yet, there is a tendency to assume that public managers "manage" or "facilitate" the networks in which they participate. Agranoff and McGuire (2001, p. 679) note "our analysis of economic development puts municipalities at the hub of horizontal and vertical connections as they engage in contacts and transactions with multiple federal and state agencies and interlocal players." There is also a strong normative assumption that public managers represent an aggregate public interest. Klijn and Koppenjan (2000, p. 135) conclude that "government's special resources and its unique legitimacy as representative of the common interest make it the outstanding candidate for fulfilling the role of network manager."

The Role of Public Managers

Public managers are traditionally charged to serve the public interest (Herring, 1936; ASPA Code of Ethics, 2005), and in that service many dedicated public servants find their professional identity (Brewer et al. 2000; Perry & Wise, 1990). (The Constitution gives little guidance to U.S. public managers, and the federal oath of office [U.S. Code] simply calls for public managers to "support and defend the Constitution of the United States.") (U.S. Code, 2005) Yet, identifying the public interest is a difficult task. Lippmann's (1955, p. 42) classic definition of the public interest is "what men would choose if they saw clearly, thought rationally, acted disinterestedly and benevolently." Harmon (1969) identifies an array of roles for the public managers based on varieties of responsiveness and advocacy.

Guidance for public managers may come from four legitimizing sources: legal frameworks, elected officials, personal expertise, or directly from citizens. All four have conceptual difficulties. Guidance from legal structures and legislators can be vague, incomplete, and sometimes contradictory. Guidance from personal expertise may be subjective, parochial, and unrepresentative, whereas guidance from citizens may be emotionally manipulated or biased in favor of the educated, the vocal, and the accessible.

In the traditional (Harmon's "rationalist") understanding, articulated by Fox and Miller (1995) as the loop model of democracy (see Figure 4.1), citizens express their interests through election of public officials. Public policy promulgated by elected officials is, by definition, the public interest.

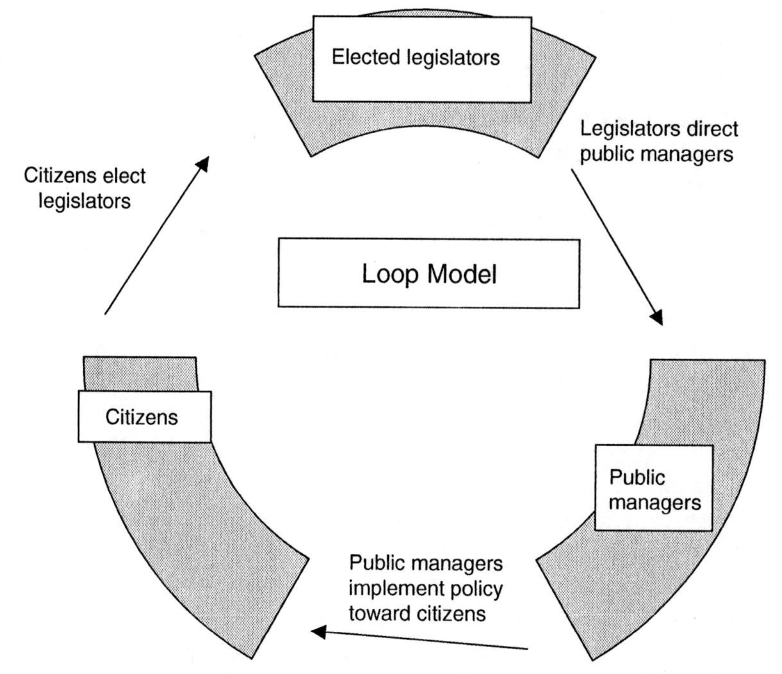

Figure 4.1 Loop model.

Elected officials tell public managers what to do, and public managers carry out that articulated public interest. The public interest is synonymous with legislation because of the assumption that, in a democracy, legislators' actions are the will of the people. The role of the public managers is to follow the directions of the elected representatives.

Whereas the public manager has always been called upon to serve the "public interest," most agree that the "loop model" is not a true reflection of reality. Citizens may choose candidates for reasons unrelated to policy preferences. Elected officials act for a variety of reasons, and the resulting legislation may or may not be the true preference of the electorate. Legislators have their own understanding of words and concepts. Compromise language takes advantage of those differences, resulting in legislation that is vague, and leaves policy details for public agencies and courts to sort out. This ambiguity and complexity make the rationalist loop model impractical to serve as anything more than a loose framework for public manager actions. This has led scholars across the ideological spectrum to propose alternative routes to the public interest.

Frederickson and others from the Minnowbrook conference (Marini, 1971) believe that the role of public managers is to ensure that our governmental system truly represents all citizens. They claim that many citizens are under-represented. In other words the current constitutional structure does not accurately reflect the public interest, because it marginalizes segments of the polity. The "New Public Administration" called on public managers to ensure social equity by identifying the needs of, and advocating for the disempowered and disenfranchised.

The participatory approach epitomized by King et al. in *Government is Us* (1998) critiques governance as not accomplishing its democratic purpose. The public policy process is closed to the majority of the population, and public managers are called to involve citizens directly in public administration planning, decision making, and action (Box, 1998; Denhardt & Denhardt, 2000, 2003). The call for citizen participation is so ingrained in public administration as to be conventional wisdom (ASPA Code of Ethic, 2005). It is the responsibility of public managers to interact directly with citizens to help ascertain the public interest. Figure 4.2 presents the model where public managers synthesize public policy from the input of legislators and citizens, plus the public managers' interaction with marginalized groups.

Legal approaches see executive branch agencies as partners in a constitutional framework where they balance other powers. Long (1949, p. 259) wrote that "the bureaucracy is recognized by all interested groups as a major channel of representation to such an extent that

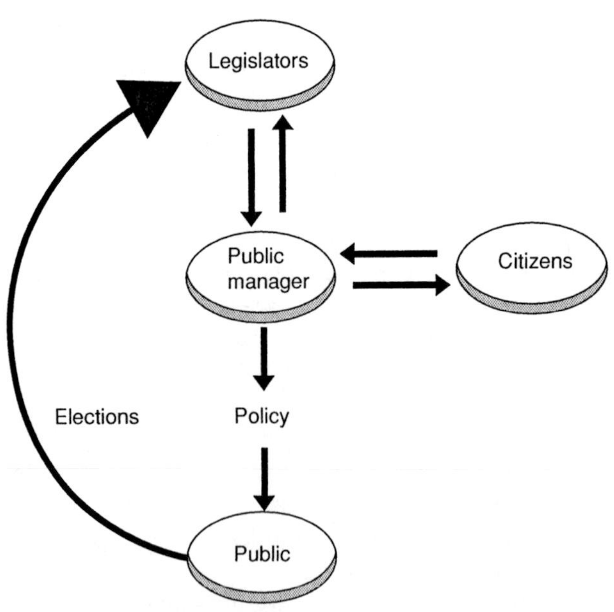

Figure 4.2 Public manager and citizens.

Congress rightly feels the competition of a rival." Rohr (1986) in *To Run a Constitution* argues that public administration is essentially a fourth branch of government. He conceives of public administration as a balancing force and a semi-independent actor in the democratic process, contributing to the checks and balances conceived of by the Constitutional framers. The conception of public managers as "balance" assumes that without such balance the democratic purposes of the Constitution will not be fulfilled.

Personal and technical expertise approaches are advanced by those who call for an increased separation of politics and administration. Lowi (1969) and others identify the problem of governance as too much pluralism, and call for a more independent public administration, free from the control of "interest group liberalism." This perspective believes public managers can best identify the public interest without the influence of political pressures. This concept is echoed by Zakaria (2003) who calls for a public administration more insulated from the ephemeral moods of the masses. The role of public managers is that of an unbiased expert, protected from the whims of democratic mood swings.

Behn (1995) is similarly concerned with undue influence on public managers, but this time from elected officials. Recalling the civil service reforms of the 19th century, and Wilson's division of politics and administration, Behn bemoans interference from legislators. He wants public managers to have more discretion and to be insulated from the "micromanagement" of elected officials. Implicitly, he declares that legislators do not accurately identify the public interest, and that public managers should be allowed more independence to carry out their tasks. The role of public managers is to be the rational expert. New Public Management and Public Choice models similarly advocate decentralization and increased managerial discretion (Osborne & Gaebler, 1992; Barzelay, 1992). The underlying assumption is that the public interest is best identified and carried out by semiautonomous, objective technocrats, insulated from the influences of both legislators and citizens, allowing them to make implementation decisions, unbiased by interest groups. Figure 4.3 illustrates this model.

The unifying assumption of these varied perspectives is that the existing governance structure fails to adequately articulate the public interest, and, therefore, public managers need to take independent action. All conceive of a public administration with direct links to the polity (rather than through legislators), either interactive or analytical. Whereas these analyses shift a portion of the identification of the public interest to public managers, they do not specify where that interest can be found or of what it comprises.

Although participation advocates focus on process, and identify multiple publics, they still assume those publics are located within the public manager's political jurisdiction. For instance, Denhardt and Denhardt (2000,

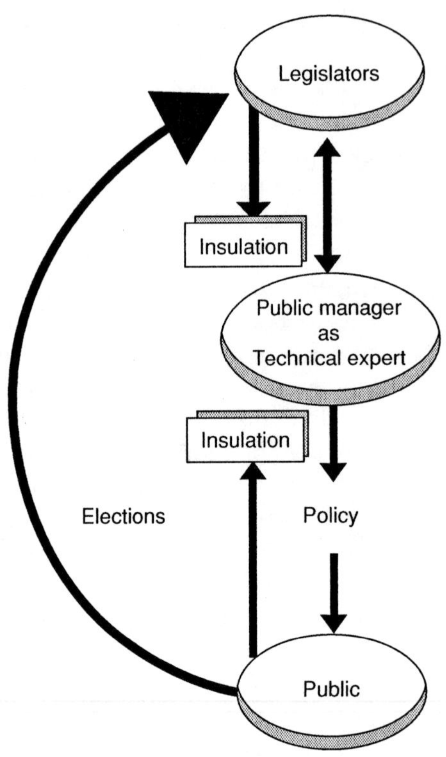

Figure 4.3 Expert public manager insulated from influence.

p. 553) note that government is "no longer in charge" and has become "another player," but still assume a public manager-centric model where managers control the agenda, bring the proper players to the table, and facilitate, negotiate, and broker solutions. In an outstanding exploration of these dynamics, Kettl (2000) asks how government can ensure accountability in an environment where vertical hierarchies are replaced by horizontal cross-governmental networks. Yet, he too locates his analysis within an American governmental environment. Whereas acknowledging the complexity of the world, this approach still places the public manager at the center of a circle, juggling, coordinating, and "managing" various geographically bounded publics to arrive at a consensual policy.

Network approaches speak of serving and interacting with "society," but the unspoken assumption is that "society" lies within national boundaries. Even postmodern approaches (Fox & Miller, 1995; McSwite, 2002; Habermas, 1984; Abel & Sementelli, 2004), whereas emphasizing discourse or critical theory, appear to take for granted a single public policy system centered around public managers. Figure 4.4 illustrates this model.

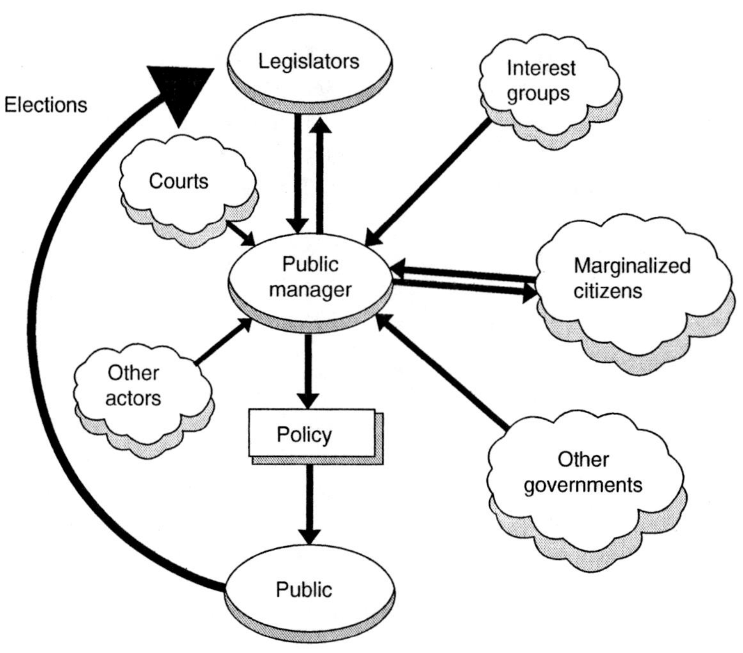

Figure 4.4 Public manager-centric model.

Globalization and the Public Interest: Who or What Public?

Once public managers leave the secure (but deceptive) simplicity of the loop model of democracy and seek to directly ascertain a "public" interest, they must confront the fact that there are many publics (O'Toole, 1997). Individuals and groups have conflicting interests. The interests of the city conflict with the interests of the state. States' interests conflict with the national interest. The interests of one trade group conflict with another trade group. The interests of developers conflict with the interests of environmentalists.

In the transnational system, citizen interests are no longer limited to the boundaries of the political unit. Their identities are linked not only to geographic location, but also to economic or interest-based communities that transcend borders. Sassen (1998, pp. 195–196) notes that information industries, finance, and advanced corporate services "tend to have a space economy that is transnational and is partly embedded in electronic spaces that override conventional jurisdictions and boundaries."

Public managers are challenged to confront both the divisions within their jurisdiction and the diversity of interests between jurisdictions. Public manager-centric models effectively address within-jurisdiction divisions by challenging mangers to facilitate consensus among competing interests. Interests may be diverse, but they are still found within the borders of the larger polity and it is possible to conceive of a larger, polity-wide public interest. The problem is one of facilitating consensus, and the public manager is the neutral (and normatively admirable) facilitator. Network analysis addresses cross-jurisdictional challenges, but still within a polity based on national boundaries.

The postmodern challenge begins with the fact that local jurisdictions are part of larger polities, that picket fence or marble cake federalism requires state, federal, and local cooperation, and that horizontal cooperation between jurisdictions may be required to achieve local goals. This challenge is met by the creation of intergovernmental task forces and working groups. Public managers are agents who advocate the interests of their principals, but their principals do not constitute the universe of those impacted by the policy, but only a subset of it. "Public" is relative, diverse, and geographically fragmented. Within the policy network, there are multiple publics of which the public manager represents only one. The "public interest" for a policy network that crosses boundaries is defined differently by each jurisdiction-bound public manager.

In a public manager-centric model, the public manager is not an advocate, but a facilitator, an unbiased third party, seeking to "bring us all together." This fits well with the normative self-image of a neutral, unbiased, objective public manager, seeking the collective public interest. If a subgroup within the polity argues for a "self-serving" policy, the public manager reminds the subgroup of the larger public interest. In the intergovernmental network the public manager assumes the role of the subgroup representative. Calls to see the broader interest above and beyond the represented polity will not honor their role as agents advocating the interests of their principals. Rather than the normatively positive image of objective neutral, the public manager becomes advocate for a special interest — in this case a geographic political jurisdiction. Kass (1989) examines this clash of identity between objective facilitator and interest-group advocate, but he frames his call for an ethical basis of agency theory specifically in "American public administration" bypassing the challenges of globalization.

The globalized world adds an additional layer to this identity challenge. In the globalized world, interest groups, or publics, crosscut national boundaries. Environmental and economic impacts of trade and pollution ignore cartographic borders. The growing emphasis on outsourcing and privatization driven by the New Public Management movement results in state activities carried out by transnational private and nonprofit organizations raising crucial questions of accountability (Choudhury & Ahmed, 2002) and the capacity for self-management (Kettl, 2000). Transnational regulatory regimes create new constituencies and shared interests that do not stop at national boundaries. "Political demands are no longer directed to one state-based interlocutor" (Radcliffe, 2001).

Broad public policy issues and interests may be controlled by nonstate institutions with varied interest boundaries. When issues cross national borders, transnational working groups of policy participants can be established, which may or may not function under the aegis of a state. The public interest for each public manager is constructed from the group each represents. There is no single universal public to which the public manager delivers policy, rather the policy implementation universe contains multiple policy systems within which the public manager may represent the entire or simply a fraction of the affected public. With the realization that there are many publics, the public manager is no longer at the center of the process. Figure 4.5 portrays the globalized, postmodern policy model where there are multiple publics and multiple policy makers. The public manager assumes the role of advocate for a particular geographically based interest group, rather than coordinator or facilitator of a centralized policy stream.

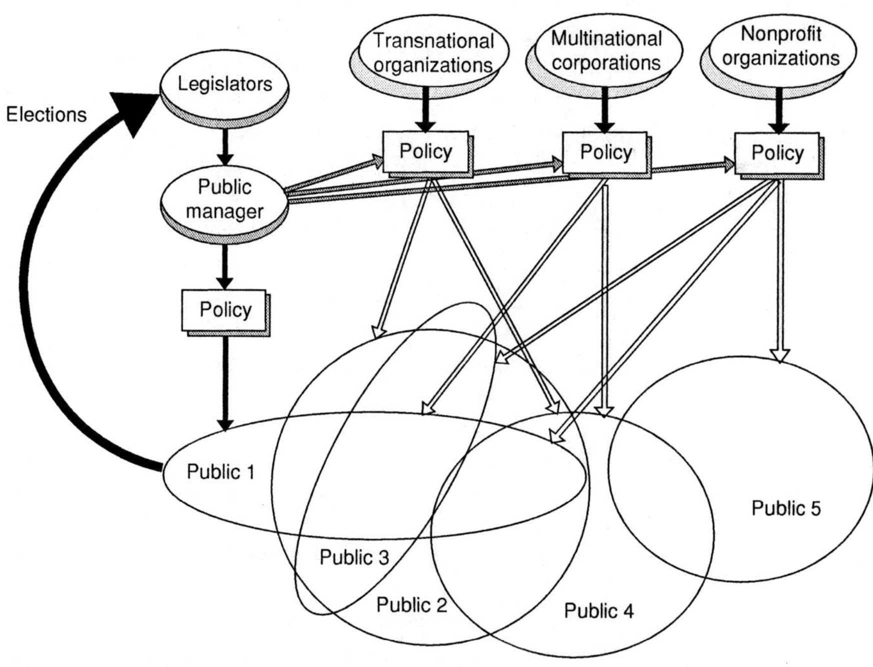

Figure 4.5 Globalized public policy process.

The Dilemma of the Public Manager: More Questions than Answers

The construction of a public interest is dependent upon a specification of constituent group. As extra-national political and interest groupings are created, the boundary of "public" may assume a variety of configurations. As noted earlier, public managers tend to normatively construct their identity as servant of the public interest, and public administration scholars often call on public managers to interface directly with that "public." As the concept of "publics" evolves, the individual public manager is challenged to reformulate his or her identity.

Who does the public manager serve, as the public interest changes depending on the configuration of people or entities considered? As issue networks crosscut geographical boundaries, so conceptualization of "publics" are re-formed. As the scope and power of the state diminishes, the power and centrality of the public manager likewise diminishes. As policies are implemented by structures and institutions that crosscut government boundaries, the public manager's role is to advocate a particular interest configuration, rather than be an objective, unbiased facilitator. Theories of public service motivation, public service ethics, and social psychology must be reconsidered as the public manager's role moves from center to periphery.

This article begins a conversation on the consequences of an increasingly global and networked world. Public managers are "faced with the continuous challenges of building trans-jurisdictional network capacities in order to implement policies that respect international agreements and national priorities" (Broadnax, 2004). Public administration must adapt "to deal effectively with the horizontal networks that have been layered on top of the traditional vertical system" (Kettl, 2000). "The new transnational administrative law needs a proper theoretical foundation which cannot be that of the state" (Cananea, 2003). The challenge for public administration is to reconceptualize the role of public managers in a globalized world where public interests crosscut and transcend the governments that public managers represent.

References

Abel, C. and A. Sementelli, 2004. *Evolutionary Critical Theory and Its Role in Public Affairs*. Armonk, NY: M.E. Sharpe.

Agranoff, R. and M. McGuire. 2001. American Federalism and the Search for Models of Management. *Public Administration Review* 61(6): 671–682.

Agranoff, R. and M. McGuire. 2003. *Collaborative Public Management: New Strategies for Local Governments*. Washington, DC: Georgetown University Press.

Anderson, J. 2001. Northern Communities and the State: Is Resistance 'Futile?' *Northern Review* 23: 9–16.

ASPA Code of Ethics. American Society for Public Administration. Accessed online March 9, 2005. http://www.aspanet.org/scriptcontent/index_codeofethics.cfm.

Balser, M. 2000. Armed to the Teeth. *UN Chronicle* 37(1): 24.

Barash, D. 1994. *Beloved Enemies: Our Need for Opponents.* Amherst, NY: Prometheus Books.

Barber, B. 1995. *Jihad vs. McWorld.* New York: Times Books.

Barzelay, M. 1992. *Breaking Through Bureaucracy: A New Vision for Managing in Government.* Berkeley, CA: University of California Press.

Behn, R. 1995. The Big Questions of Public Management. *Public Administration Review* 55(4): 313–324.

Bennett, J.C. 2004. Networking Nation States. *National Interest* 74: 17–30.

Bercovitch, J. 2003. Managing Internationalized Ethnic Conflict. *World Affairs* 166(1): 56–68.

Boggs, C. 2001. Economic Globalization and Political Atrophy. *Democracy and Nature* 7(2): 303–316.

Box, R. 1998. *Citizen Governance.* Thousand Oaks, CA: Sage.

Brewer, G., S. Selden, and R. Facer. 2000. Individual Conceptions of Public Service Motivation. *Public Administration Review* 60(3): 254–264.

Broadnax, W. 2004. We Have Truly Become a World without Borders. *PA Times.* January: 16.

Cananea, G. 2003. Beyond the State: The Europeanization and Globalization of Procedural Administrative Law. *European Public Law* 9(4): 563–578.

Choudhury, E. and S. Ahmed. 2002. The Shifting Meaning of Governance: Public Accountability of Third Sector Organizations in an Emergent Global Regime. *International Journal of Public Administration* 25(4): 561–588.

Denhardt, R. and J. Denhardt. 2000. The New Public Service: Serving Rather than Steering. *Public Administration Review* 60(6): 549–559.

Denhardt, J. and R. Denhardt. 2003. *The New Public Service: Serving not Steering.* Armonk, NY: M.E. Sharpe.

Fox, C. and H. Miller. 1995. *Postmodern Public Administration.* Thousand Oaks, CA: Sage.

Habermas, J. 1984. *The Theory of Communicative Action.* Boston: Beacon Press.

Harmon, M. 1969. Administrative Policy Formulation and the Public Interest. *Public Administration Review* 29(5): 483–491.

Herring, E.P 1936. *Public Administration and the Public Interest.* New York: McGraw-Hill.

Howe, L.E. 2002. Administrative Law and Governmentality: Politics and Discretion in a Changing State of Sovereignty. *Administrative Theory and Praxis* 24(1): 55–80.

Huntington, S. 1971. The Change to Change: Modernization, Development and Politics. *Comparative Politics* 3(3): 283–322.

Kass, H.D. 1989. Exploring Agency as a Basis for Ethical Theory in American Public Administration. *International Journal of Public Administration* 12(6): 949–969.

Kettl, D.F. 2000. The Transformation of Governance: Globalization, Devolution and the Role of Government. *Public Administration Review* 60(6): 488–497.

Kickert, W.J.M., E.-H. Klijn, and J.F.M. Koppenjan (eds.). 1997. *Managing Complex Networks: Strategies for the Public Sector.* Thousand Oaks, CA: Sage.

King, C., C. Stivers, and R. Box. 1998. *Government is Us: Public Administration in an Anti-Government Era.* Thousand Oaks, CA: Sage.

Kleinert, J. 2001. The Role of Multinational Organizations in Globalization: An Empirical Overview. Kiel Institute of World Economics Working Paper 1069. Accessed online June 26, 2004. http://www.uni-kiel.de/ifw/pub/kap/2001/kap1069.pdf.

Klijn, E.H. and J.F.M. Koppenjan. 2000. Public Management and Policy Networks: Foundations of a Network Approach to Governance. *Public Management(UK)* 2(2): 135–157.

Lehoczky, E. 2004. White-Collar Jobs May Be Next to Move Overseas. *Boston Globe* Online Edition, May 16, 2004. Accessed online June 26, 2004. http://bostonworks.boston.com/globe/articles/051604_outsource.html.

Lippmann, W. 1955. *The Public Philosophy.* Boston: Little, Brown & Company.

Long, N.E. 1949. Power and Administration. *Public Administration Review* 9(4): 257–264.

Long, E.L. Jr. 1994. Legitimate Force. *Christian Century* 111(1): 5–6.

Lowi, T. 1969. *The End of Liberalism: Ideology, Policy and the Crisis of Public Authority.* New York: Norton.

Marini, F. (ed). 1971. *Toward a New Public Administration: the Minnowbrook Perspective.* Scranton, PA: Chandler.

McSwite, O.C. 2002. *Invitation to Public Administration.* Armonk, NY: M.E. Sharpe.

Omae, K. 1990. *The Borderless World: Power and Strategy in the Interlinked Economy.* New York: Harper Business.

Osborne, D. and T. Gaebler. 1992. *Reinventing Government: How the Entrepreneurial Spirit is Transforming the Public Sector.* Reading, MA: Addison-Wesley.

O'Toole, L.J. Jr. 1997. The Implications for Democracy in a Networked Bureaucratic World. *Journal of Public Administration Research and Theory* 7(3): 443–459.

Perry, J. and L.R. Wise. 1990. The Motivational Bases of Public Service. *Public Administration Review* 50(3): 367–373.

Radcliffe, S.A. 2001. Development, the State and Transnational Political Connections: State and Subject Formations in Latin America. *Global Networks* 1(1): 19–36.

Rohr, J. 1986. *To Run a Constitution: the Legitimacy of the Administrative State.* Lawrence, KA: University Press of Kansas.

Sassen, S. 1998. *Globalization and its Discontents.* New York: New Press.

Smolowe, J. and B. Angelo. 1992. The U.N. Marches In. *Time* 139(12) March 23, 1992: 32–33.

Sollenberg M. and P. Wallensteen. 2001. Major Armed Conflicts. *Journal of Peace Research* 38: 629–644.

The Age. 2003. IMF, World Bank Push Free Trade. August 22, Melbourne Australia Accessed online June 26, 2004. http://www.theage.com.au/articles/2003/08/22/1061482264603.html.

Toffler, A. 1970. *Future Shock.* New York: Random House.

U.S. Census Bureau. 2004. Accessed online June 26, 2004, http://www.census.gov/ipc/www/world.html.

U.S. Code, Title V, Part III, Subpart B, Chapter 33, Subchapter II, Section 3331. Accessed online March 8, 2005, http://www.access.gpo.gov/uscode/title5/partiii_subpartb_chapter33_subchapterii_.html.

Van Creveld, M. 1999. *The Rise and Decline of the State*. New York: Cambridge University Press.

Varshney, A. 2002. *Ethnic Conflict and Civic Life: Hindus and Muslims in India*. New Haven: Yale University Press.

Volkan, V. 1988. *The Need to Have Enemies and Allies: From Clinical Practice to International Relationships*. Northvale, NJ: Jason Aronson Inc.

Waldo, D. 1971. *Public Administration in a Time of Turbulence*. Scranton, PA: Chandler.

Zakaria, F. 2003. *The Future of Freedom: Illiberal Democracy at Home and Abroad*. New York: W.W. Norton.

Chapter 5

Globalization and Its Impact on Strategic Security

Christopher Van Vliet

CONTENTS

Globalization is the international system that replaced the Cold War system. With it came the integration of capital, technology, and information across national borders in an attempt to create a single global market. We have all seen evidence of the tension and conflicts that exist between this interconnected system and the ancient forces of culture, geography, tradition, and community that feel brutalized by it and resist its intrusion. However, globalization is with us, whether we like it or not. While some might argue that the September 11, 2001 attacks resulted from its processes that had begun a generation earlier, it is these processes that will, in the long run, provide the United States and the rest of the world with the security that they desire and deserve. The challenge lies in ensuring everyone has a stake in globalization.

New Balances, New Threats

The Cold War system was built exclusively around nation-states, and it was balanced at the center by two superpowers: the United States and the Soviet Union. The globalization system, according to Thomas Friedman, is built around three balances: the traditional balance between nation-states; that between nation-states and global markets; and the most recent — the balance between individuals and nation-states. These super-empowered individuals, some of whom are quite dangerous, are now able to act directly on the world stage without the traditional mediation of governments, corporations, or any other public or private institutions (Friedman, 2000, pp. 12–13).

Since the end of the Cold War, weak or failing states have probably become the single most important problem for international order. Chester Crocker tells us that the problem is not the absence of nations but the absence of states with the legitimacy and authority to manage their affairs (Crocker, 2003, p. 37). Weak or failing states commit human rights abuses, provoke humanitarian disasters, drive massive waves of immigration, and attack their neighbors. Since September 11th, the vast majority of international crises have involved weak or failing states. The failed state of Afghanistan was so weak that it was hijacked by a non-state actor, the terrorist organization Al Qaeda, and served as a base for global terrorist operations. The attacks reinforced the ways in which violence had become democratized. Traditional forms of deterrence or containment are not effective against this type of non-state actor. For that reason, security concerns demand reaching inside of states and changing their regime to prevent future threats from arising. "The failed state problem that was seen previously as largely a humanitarian or human rights issue, has suddenly taken on a major security dimension" (Fukuyama, 2004, pp. 92–93). Moreover, it was a "general failure of the historical imagination," says Michael Ignatieff, "an inability of the post-Cold War West to grasp that the emerging crisis of state order in so many overlapping zones of the world — from Egypt to Afghanistan — would eventually become a security threat at home" (Ignatieff, 2003, p. 170).

Islamist fundamentalism, radical Islam, or what Walter Russell Mead more properly calls "Arabian fascism," has surfaced as the greatest security threat facing the United States and the international community. Arabian fascism is a totalitarian ideology inspired by a mythologized vision of the past. It attracts not only Arabs but all those for whom the early Islamic wars of religion and conquest represent a golden age. It aims to restore this past by force, not only in the world of Islam, but ultimately throughout the world. This fascism comes in two forms: secular and religious. The totalitarian ideologies now tormenting the Muslim world include the secular fascism of the Ba'ath Party of Iraq and the religious fascism of Osama bin Laden. Both movements believe in subordinating the rights of individuals and eliminating the independence of civil society in favor of a totalitarian politics. "Both movements," says Mead, "recognize no limits on the right of their leaders to command their followers to carry out lawless violence against innocent civilians and both are deadly enemies of freedom and peace" (Mead, 2004, p. 176).

Policies or Identity

A persistent question posed by president George W. Bush is, "Why do the terrorists hate us?" Are Islamic terrorists and increasingly much of the Muslim world incited by the United States' policies or do they simply hate our existence and what we represent? Professor Noam Chomsky believes that there are specific policies that have enflamed the potential "support base" for Islamic terrorism. Policies relating to the Israel–Palestine issue, sanctions in Iraq, and more fundamentally, U.S. support for corrupt and repressive regimes that undermine democracy and development. Anger in the Muslim world, he says, does not spring from resentment of our freedom and democracy, their own cultural failings tracing back many centuries, and their alleged inability to take part in globalization (Chomsky, 2003, pp. 213–214).

His sentiments echo those of Michael Scheuer, a senior U.S. intelligence official who, writing under the name, "Anonymous," explains that the United States is hated across the Islamic world because of specific government policies and actions. That hatred, he says, is concrete and martial not abstract and intellectual, and it will grow for the foreseeable future. Scheuer lists six U.S. policies that Osama bin Laden repeatedly refers to as anti-Muslim. They are: U.S. support for Israel that keeps Palestinians in the Israelis' thrall; U.S. and other Western troops on the Arabian Peninsula; U.S. occupation of Iraq and Afghanistan; U.S. support for Russia, India, and China against their Muslim militants; U.S. pressure on Arab energy producers to keep oil prices low; and U.S. support for apostate, corrupt, and tyrannical Muslim governments (Anonymous, 2004, pp. 240–241). Since bin Laden has no center of gravity in the traditional sense, that is, no economy, no cities, no homeland, no power grids, no regular military, etc., his center of gravity lies in the list of current U.S. policies toward the Muslim world. It is that *status quo*, according to Scheuer, that enrages Muslims around the globe, no matter their view of Al Qaeda's martial actions, and gives bin Laden's efforts to instigate a worldwide anti-U.S. defensive jihad with virtually unlimited room for growth. He warns that so long as this fact is unrecognized by Americans and their leaders, bin Laden will keep winning the strategic war, even while continuing to suffer tactical losses (Anonymous, 2004, p. 263).

Other scholars and strategic thinkers reject the argument that it is our policies and not our identity that have created this rabid hatred. Jean Bethke Elshtain contends that changes in our policies would not satisfy Islamists because they loathe us for who we are and what our society represents. Even as the radicals indict specific U.S. actions, both past and present, bin Laden labels us "pagans" and "infidels."

> To Islamists, infidels are those who believe in separation of church and state. Infidels profess the wrong religion, or the wrong version of a religion, or no religion at all. Infidels believe in civic and personal freedom. Infidels educate women and give them a public presence and role. Infidels intermarry across lines of religion. Infidels believe that all people have human rights. Whatever else the United States might do on the world scene to allay the concerns of its opponents, it cannot repeal its founding constitutional principles, which condemn it in the eyes of such fundamentalists
>
> Elshtain, 2003, pp. 3–4

Elshtain argues then that even if we were to alter our policies, we could not repeal our commitment to personal freedom. We could not negate the First Amendment to the U.S. Constitution, which guarantees the free exercise of any religion. Radical Islamists desire an official religion, and they would impose it everywhere they could, through terror if necessary. Our belief in freedom and our basic ideals are nonnegotiable. Thus, the terrorists despise us for what we are and what we represent. Francis Fukuyama reinforces this view by analyzing first-person accounts, reports, fatwas or legal opinions and the manuals of Islamist extremists. His article in *Newsweek*, "Their Target: The Modern World," explains that extremist groups celebrated September 11th because it humbled a society that they believed was at its core corrupt. This corruption originates in their view from secularism itself. "What they hate is that the state in Western societies should be dedicated to religious tolerance and pluralism, rather than trying to serve religious truth" (Fukuyama, as cited in Elshtain, 2003, pp. 22–23).

A Failure of Modernity

The Islamic world must overcome its consistent impulse to blame others for all of its failures. Poverty and bitterness can be attributed directly to the obscenely rich ruling families in places like Saudi Arabia and Jordan. Keeping the populace ignorant is a deliberate strategy of the jihadists who feed on poverty and ignorance whereas faulting secular rulers and the corrupt West. Muslim states and societies are decaying although their ancient competitors flourish. The Islamic world cannot progress without fundamental and pervasive changes in virtually every public and private sphere. According to strategic thinker Ralph Peters, "a billion people, as proud as they are ill-governed and ill-prepared for modern life, have found they cannot compete with other civilizations on a single front — not even in terror, for the West will, out of demonstrated need, learn to terrorize the terrorists" (Peters, 2004, p. 6). Islam, rather than shifting blame, must make a far more difficult choice of attempting to build tolerant, more equitable, open, and honest societies, reject a mythologized past, and embrace a challenging future. There is a hadith or a tradition that is attributed to the Prophet Muhammad that the condition of a people will not change unless they change it themselves. Islamic civilization cannot prosper under modern conditions as long as it is antimeritocratic, oppresses and torments women, mocks the rule of law, neglects education, and lacks a work ethic. The Islamic world, says Peters, will continue to do more harm to its own people than it has done or will ever be able to do to the West.

Islamist fundamentalism is an extreme repudiation of modernity or the processes of globalization, but even more tragically, most of the Muslim world is a textbook example of the "failure of modernity." It is afflicted by poverty, ignorance, and tyranny. Muslims fault American economic dominance and exploitation and America's support for many corrupt Muslim tyrants who serve its purposes. A potent combination of low productivity and a high birth rate in the Middle East has led to a caustic situation with a large and rapidly growing population of unemployed, uneducated, and frustrated young men. The United Nations and the World Bank inform us that the Arab world continues to lose more ground to the West, in areas such as job creation, education, technology, and productivity. Even more frustrating is that the rapidly rising economies of East Asia, in countries such as Korea, Taiwan and Singapore, are also leaving Arab nations behind. Eminent scholar Bernard Lewis presents a bleak and devastating picture of Arab underdevelopment. "The GDP (Gross Domestic Product) in all Arab countries combined stood at $531.2 billion in 1999 — less than that of a single European country, Spain ($595.5 billion)" (Lewis, 2003, p. 116). A listing of book sales among 27 countries begins with the United States and ends with Vietnam with not a single mention of a Muslim state.

Further evidence of underdevelopment can be gleaned from a report on Arab Human Development in 2002, which was prepared by a committee of Arab intellectuals and published under the auspices of the United Nations. It revealed that the entire Arab world, with 300 million people, translates about 330 books annually, one fifth of the number that Greece does with its 11 million people. According to the World Bank, in 2000 the average annual income in Muslim countries from Morocco to Bangladesh was only half the world average. In the 1990s, the combined gross national products of three of Israel's Arab neighbors, Jordan, Syria, and Lebanon, were significantly smaller than that of Israel alone. According to the United Nations statistics, on a per capita basis, the contrast was even grimmer. Israel's per capita GDP was 3.5 times that of Lebanon and Syria, 12 times that of Jordan, and 13.5 times that of Egypt (Lewis, 2003, p. 117). The people of the Middle East, thanks to modern media and communications, are painfully aware of the deep and expanding gulf between the opportunities of the free world outside their borders and the desperate and appalling conditions within them. Widespread and better modernization and an acceptance of globalization are the answers for some. Others, however, believe globalization itself is the problem.

Disconnectedness Portends Danger

Thomas Barnett, a former senior strategic researcher and professor at the U.S. Naval War College, calls globalization America's "gift to history" and explains why its wide dissemination is critical not only to our security, but the security of the entire world. The Pentagon is still in shock at the rapid dissolution of the Soviet Union and has spent the 1990s grasping for a long-term military strategy to replace containment. According to Barnett, our enemy is neither a religion (Islam) nor a place (the Middle East), but a condition — disconnectedness (Barnett, 2004, p. 49). Those parts of the world where terrorism and unrest are brewing are characterized by a disconnectedness from the globalizing world and disconnectedness portends danger.

In regions of the world where globalization is thick with network connectivity, financial transactions, liberal media flows, and collective security you find stable governments, rising standards of living and low murder rates. Barnett labels these parts of the world the Functioning Core, or Core. In areas where globalization is thinning or absent you discover politically repressive regimes, widespread poverty and disease, routine mass murder and most importantly, the breeding grounds that incubate the next generation of global terrorists. He refers to these parts of the world as the Non-Integrating Gap, or Gap. An analysis of U.S. military responses since the end of the Cold War reinforces this relationship between globalization and connectivity. There has been an overwhelming concentration of military activity in regions of the world that are excluded from globalization's growing Core, such as the Caribbean Rim, virtually all of Africa, the Balkans, the Caucasus, Central Asia, the Middle East, Southwest Asia, and much of Southeast Asia. This is roughly one third of the world's population. Demographically, most are young and are labeled low or low–middle income by the World Bank (less than $3000 annual per capita).

America's goal must be to promote "rule sets" that are shared by both the Core and the Gap. When we see countries moving toward acceptance of globalization's economic rule sets, we should also expect to see a similar acceptance of emerging political and security rule sets that define fair play among nations, firms, and even individuals, not just in trade but also in terms of war. America does not commit herself to war simply because she dislikes a certain religion or people, or even a bad ruler. She intervenes when the rule sets are being so blatantly violated that the offending parties need to be stopped and removed from power. Rule sets encourage and protect connectivity, and growing connectivity is ultimately stabilizing. The Pentagon needs to focus on roughly 5 percent of both the states and transnational actors that tend to bend or break the security rule sets. By dealing with that fraction firmly and consistently, "it sends the right signals to the rest of the community that playing by the rules pays off" (Barnett, 2004, p. 353).

Barnett's suggested strategy contains three basic goals. Increase the Core's immune system capabilities to respond to 9/11-like "system perturbations" or disturbances. Work the seam states or countries like Mexico, Brazil, South Africa, Morocco, Algeria, Greece, Turkey, Pakistan, Thailand, Malaysia, the Philippines and Indonesia to firewall the Core from the Gap's worst exports, such as terror, drugs, and pandemic diseases. Finally, he insists that we must progressively shrink the Gap by continuing to export security to its greatest trouble spots. He adds that the United States should expect to put in the largest share of the security effort to support globalization's advance since it enjoys its benefits disproportionately. This transaction should be pursued out of rational self-interest.

Failed States

Sovereign nation-states have seen their power erode over the last generation and much of this reduction has been for the good. All too powerful states, primarily dictatorships in the 20th century, tyrannized populations and committed acts of aggression against their neighbors. Others, due to excessive state scope, impeded economic growth and were characterized by a variety of dysfunctions and inefficiencies. The trend has been to cut back the size of state sectors and to transfer functions that have been improperly appropriated to the market or to civil society. The global economy has weakened the autonomy of sovereign nation-states by increasing the mobility of information, capital, and to a lesser extent, labor. Francis Fukuyama reminds us that the chief issue for global politics today is not how to cut back on stateness but how to build it up. He explains that for individual societies and for the global community, the withering away of the state is not a prelude to utopia but a recipe for disaster.

The crucial problem facing poor countries that obstructs their possibilities for economic development is their inadequate level of institutional development. These countries do not require extensive states, but do need strong and effective states to provide the necessary state functions. At the end of the Cold War, we witnessed the emergence of a group of failed and troubled states from Europe to South Asia. These weak states have posed threats to international order because they are the source of conflict and violations of human rights and because they have become potential breeding grounds for a new kind of terrorism they can reach into the developed world. Strengthening these states through various forms of nation-building is a task that has become vital to international security and the future of world order (Fukuyama, 2004, p. 120). In the absence of sovereign nation-states, Fukuyama warns, we are left with multinational corporations, non-governmental organizations, international organizations, crime syndicates, and terrorist groups, which seldom possess both power and legitimacy at the same time. Radical Islam would never have succeeded in winning followers if the Muslim countries that won independence from the European empires had been able to convert dreams of self-determination into the reality of competent, rule-abiding states. America has inherited this crisis of self-determination from the empires of the past, which now manifests itself in the "desire of Islamists to build theocratic tyrannies on the ruins of failed nationalist dreams" (Ignatieff, 2003, pp. 170–171).

Unilateralism, Preemption, and Hegemony

Assumptions about America's strategic security, scholar John Lewis Gaddis tells us, have been impacted by three surprise attacks in its history: the British attack of Washington and the burning of the White House and the Capitol in 1814; the Japanese attack of Pearl Harbor in 1941; and the Al Qaeda attacks of September 11, 2001. Following the burning of Washington in 1814, Secretary of State John Quincy Adams approved Andrew Jackson's invasion of Florida, which was then a possession of a very weak Spain. This controversial decision was supposedly designed to subdue marauding border gangs made up of Indians and former slaves, but the real objective was to attack British adventurers based in the territory and ultimately seize it for the United States. Jackson argued that the move would preempt any attack from Great Britain, the Spanish, or their continental allies. Adams' plan was to prevent balance-of-power politics from breaking out on the North American continent similar to what existed in Europe. Through a strategy of unilateralism and preemption, Adams sought to maintain strength beyond challenge. For the United States to survive and prosper, it had to be the preeminent power on the continent. Otherwise it would descend into competitions over "rocks" and "fish ponds" (Gaddis, 2004, p. 26).

America withdrew from this strategy following the attack on Pearl Harbor in 1941 and instead began to cooperate with its allies on an intercontinental scale to defeat authoritarianism. However, we are now witnessing the Bush Doctrine, a grand strategy whose foundations are based in the 19th century tradition of unilateralism, preemption, and hegemony, projected this time on a global scale. Gaddis suggests that Spanish Florida would today be described as a failed state. Adams, in a controversial diplomatic note at the time, told the Spanish that they must either garrison enough troops to secure the territory or "cede to the United States a province . . . which is in fact a derelict, open to the occupancy of every enemy, civilized or savage, of the United States, and serving no other earthly purpose than as a post of annoyance to them" (Gaddis, 2004, p. 17). Today, in a world where rogue regimes and terrorists seek to obtain and detonate nuclear weapons and where nation-crippling technologies are becoming more portable and deadly, the globe is now the frontier. The United States is no longer protected by its geography and a balance-of-power politics is no longer feasible.

The essence of the Bush Doctrine is that America must maintain a preponderance of power or as President Bush announced at West Point in June 2002: "America has, and intends to keep, military strengths beyond challenge" (Gaddis, 2004, p. 30). A strategy of preemption or, more properly preventive war will put the United States in a position of governing potentially hostile populations in countries that threaten it with terrorism, as we have seen in Afghanistan and Iraq. Gaddis warns, however, that an empire acting unilaterally and without alliances may end up creating more threats than that actually exist. President Bush's "National Security Strategy," published in September 2002, elaborated on the West Point speech and stated that the goal of American foreign policy is to "extend the benefits of freedom across the globe." It further declared that:

> We will actively work to bring the hope of democracy, development, free markets, and free trade to every corner of the world . . . America must stand firmly for the nonnegotiable demands of human dignity: the rule of law;

> limits on the absolute power of the state; free speech; freedom of worship; equal justice; respect for women; religious and ethnic tolerance; and respect for private property.
>
> Ferguson, 2004, p. 23

Is Democracy the Answer?

The administration believes, then, that democracy is the path to security in the Middle East. Thomas Friedman notes that while expanding globalization is critical, particularly for developing countries, it is equally important to democratize their political systems at the same time. The democratic process will give the public in these countries a sense of ownership over the painful process of economic policy reform. A politics of sustainable globalization requires a new social bargain between workers, financiers, and governments. A pure market vision alone, he says, is too brutal and not sustainable. Globalization and strategic security become stabilized by democratizing globalization, that is by making it work for more and more people all the time. That is why countries that are adjusting best to globalization today are not necessarily the richest ones, such as Saudi Arabia, Nigeria, or Iran, but rather the most democratic ones like Poland, Taiwan, Thailand, and Korea.

Distinguished professor Samuel Huntington, however, offers the antithesis to this argument and warns that terrorism and the Middle East's general anti-Americanism do not originate from the absence of democracy but from "civilizational" differences. He says that democratization and globalization have done little to erode these differences in the region. The security of the United States and other democratic societies depends not on trying to impose their own values on cultures where they cannot possibly take root, but rather on maintaining the "multicivilizational character of global politics" (Huntington, 1996, p. 21). The Bush National Security Strategy soundly challenges Huntington's theory and argues that 9/11 demonstrated that we could not coexist with our enemies. Furthermore, if Muslims themselves are so divided on the benefits of globalization, perhaps democratization might be the answer.

Historian Niall Ferguson believes that the world needs an effective liberal empire and that the United States is best suited for the job. He points to the success of economic globalization in the world's two most populous countries, China and India, where the per capita incomes have risen rapidly. However, even though international inequality is diminishing, Ferguson stresses the recurring theme that there are parts of the world (the Gap) where legal and political institutions are in a condition of such collapse or corruption that their populations are effectively cut off (disconnected) from any hope of prosperity. The existence of states, which through either weakness (failed) or malice, encourage terrorist organizations committed to wrecking a liberal world order, is a problem that must be confronted with. He, like Friedman, advises that economic globalization needs to be underwritten politically, as it was a century ago (Ferguson, 2004, p. 301).

Former National Security Advisor, Zbigniew Brzezinski, cautions that if America promotes and pursues democracy in the Muslim world with a fanatical zeal that ignores the historical and cultural traditions of Islam, the project could backfire. While it is true that America successfully imposed democracy upon Germany and Japan after World War II, there were social foundations on which we were able to construct democratic constitutions. Brzezinski suggests that the situation in the Middle East will be more challenging and that the push for democratization will require "historical patience" and "cultural sensitivity." Muslim countries such as Turkey, Morocco, and even Iran, despite its fundamentalist posture, seem to demonstrate that: "when democratization takes place through organic growth and not through dogmatic imposition by an alien force, Islamic societies also gradually absorb and assimilate a democratic political culture" (Brzezinski, 2004, p. 225).

Conductivity, Not Empire

Discussions of empire, freedom, liberty, or democracy are premature and irrelevant in the context of Thomas Barnett's proposed operating theory. Much like Brzezinski, he explains that America cannot command societies to bypass their histories and suddenly discharge the hatreds that have developed throughout the years. What America can offer, according to Barnett, is the choice of "connectivity" to escape isolation and safety within which freedom finds practical expression. He emphasizes that none of this can be imposed, but only offered. "Globalization," he says, "does not come with a ruler, but with rules" (Barnett, 2004, p. 356). Thus, the goal should be broadband economic and social conductivity, not mandating content, such as democratic transformation. Offering connectivity only involves enforcing minimal rule sets. Imposing our political system on other societies is a more complicated and dangerous matter. Our role in providing globalization's security should be that of shrinking the Gap on those actors who willfully disregard its emerging rule sets.

Those Americans who favor an isolationist policy in the wake of the 9/11 attacks ignore the fact that if we do not deal with these troubled regions now, we will have to deal with them in the future. These disconnected places must be invited to participate and have a stake in globalization. It is not a question of the United States seeking to extend its power or become a neo-imperialist global centurion, but instead a case of simply quelling the efforts of those who will kill to preserve a society's disconnectedness. Bringing order to the frontier zones is the primary task and it must be done without denying the local people their rights to some degree of self-determination. Michael Ignatieff reminds us that while Americans possess global power, they do not seek global domination. "They cannot rebuild each failed state or appease each anti-American hatred, and the more they try, the more they expose themselves to the overreach that eventually undermined the classical empires of old" (Ignatieff, 2003, p. 169).

The Role of Soft Power

President Bush's new security strategy or the Bush Doctrine is correct in assessing that the "privatization of war" by transnational groups like Al Qaeda is a major historical change in world politics that must be addressed. However, his strategic vision has never been clearly elucidated to the public and the world, and the Bush administration appears to be fumbling over how to implement this new strategy. Bush's strategy relies heavily on American military power or hard power and this is certainly indispensable in our fight against terrorism. America, though, is not properly utilizing another weapon at its disposal and that is its soft power.

Soft power is the attraction of our culture and ideals. Our ability to persuade and attract others is a necessary complement to our military might. We defeated the Taliban government in Afghanistan, but that victory accounted for less than a quarter of the Al Qaeda transnational network, which is believed to have cells in 60 countries. Success in places like Hamburg or Kuala Lumpur depends on close civilian cooperation, sharing of intelligence, coordinating police work across borders and tracing global financial flows. Whereas America's partners work with us partly out of self-interest, the inherent attractiveness of U.S. policies can and does influence their degree of cooperation. More importantly, the current struggle against Islamist terrorism is a contest whose outcome is closely tied to a civil war between moderates and extremists within Islamic civilization. According to Joseph Nye, Jr., former Assistant Secretary of Defense, the United States and other advanced democracies will only win if moderate Muslims win, and the ability to attract the moderates is critical to victory. We need to appeal to moderates and use "public diplomacy" more effectively to seek out common ground (Nye, 2004, p. 131).

Thomas Kean, former governor of New Jersey and chairman of the national commission that produced the *9/11 Report* agrees. He says the

West must offer an alternative to the media manipulation occurring in the Muslim world, primarily through the Al Jazeera news outlet. Kean questions how a man, supposedly living in a cave (Osama bin Laden), has been able to "outcommunicate" us. America must convey, for example, through public diplomacy and our media that we have protected Muslims in the past, in places like Bosnia, Kosovo, and Somalia. Institutions such as the International Monetary Fund, the World Trade Organization, and the United Nations play a role in enhancing a country's soft power, as well. Countries encounter less resistance to their wishes when they make their power legitimate, in the eyes of others. If a country's culture and values are attractive and persuasive and it uses institutions and follows rules that encourage other countries to conduct their affairs in ways it prefers, the benefits are obvious. The Bush Doctrine, then, which seeks to identify and eliminate terrorists wherever they are together with the regimes that harbor them, must expand its approach to include soft power as part of its overall strategic plan.

References

Anonymous. (2004). *Imperial Hubris: Why the West Is Losing the War on Terror.* Dulles, VA: Brassey's Inc.

Barnett, T.P.M. (2004). *The Pentagon's New Map: War and Peace in the Twenty-First Century.* New York, NY: G.P. Putnam's Sons.

Brzezinski, Z. (2004). *The Choice: Global Domination or Global Leadership.* New York, NY: Basic Books.

Chomsky, N. (2003). *Hegemony or Survival: America's Quest for Global Dominance.* New York, NY: Metropolitan Books.

Crocker, C.A. (2003, September/October). Engaging Failed States. *Foreign Affairs.* Volume 82 No 5.

Elshtain, J.B. (2003). *Just War against Terror: The Burden of American Power in a Violent World.* New York, NY: Basic Books.

Ferguson, N. (2004). *Colossus: The Price of America's Empire.* New York, NY: The Penguin Press.

Friedman, T.L. (2000). *The Lexus and the Olive Tree.* New York, NY: Farrar, Straus and Giroux.

Fukuyama, F. (2004). *State-Building: Governance and World Order in the 21st Century.* Ithaca, NY: Cornell University Press.

Gaddis, J.L. (2004). *Surprise, Security, and the American Experience.* Cambridge, MA: Harvard University Press.

Huntington, S.P. (1996). *The Clash of Civilizations and the Remaking of World Order.* New York, NY: Touchtone.

Ignatieff, M. January 5, 2003. The Burden. *New York Times Magazine.*

Lewis, B. (2003). *The Crisis of Islam: Holy War and Unholy Terror.* New York, NY: The Modern Library.

Mead, W.R. (2004). *Power, Terror, Peace and War: America's Grand Strategy in a World at Risk.* New York, NY: Alfred A. Knopf.

Nye, J. JR. (2004). *Soft Power: The Means to Success in World Politics.* New York, NY: Public Affairs.

Peters, R. (2004). *Beyond Terror: Strategy in a Changing World.* Mechanicsburg, PA: Stackpole Books.

Chapter 6

Nation-Building: An Appraisal

John D. Montgomery

CONTENTS

Any serious appraisal of nation-building should begin by recognizing the historical reality that no external force can build a nation. What it can do is make a state more viable or improve its responsiveness to its people, and even that end is not easily achieved being a nation. For, being a nation requires more than the sheer exercise of authority. It rests on a voluntary sense of public community, which is derived historically from a confluence of ethnic, economic, and political factors. What international or domestic statesmen can do, on the other hand, is to contribute to state-building, in the hope of achieving a quality of governance that extends throughout a nation. To call that process nation-building transcends reality, but for the sake of convenience most of us accept the misnomer.

Both the U.S. State Department and the Pentagon are reluctant about the process anyway, regarding it as a distraction from more "serious" enterprises like diplomacy and war. It is their sad fate, time after relentless time, to find themselves engaged in it.

The American public mind ignores both this linguistic indulgence and professional skepticism. Thus the World Wide Web offers an extensive bibliography (Questia.com lists 435,000 books and articles on nation-building, without running out of confirmatory historical experience). Even in jaded Europe, political voices were indulged in nation-building aspirations for Afghanistan before they balked at applying it in Iraq and perhaps still in other post-combat countries, in spite of the probability that "regime change" would serve the international order better than the *status quo*. Yet advocates of nation-building can describe successes in the troubled aftermath of the fall of the Soviet empire and the hundreds of development programs in Africa and Asia that have implied a nation-building impulse. Interest in the subject has even made it a commercially viable subject for publishers and writers, with the result that Buy.com is prepared to offer access to more than a million "products," for which it can claim 5 million customers. And dozens of governments, international bodies, and non-governmental organizations could cite decades of their own earnest experience if they wished to qualify themselves as experts in the field.

Upon reflection, however, their conclusions are not encouraging: almost all of these sources echo the same trenchant proposition that nation-building usually fails. The policy implication is to avoid excessive ambition for it — but the nation-building temptation returns nevertheless even among seasoned politicians, who are willing to ignore the unwelcome corollary that some countries may be unsuitable for it.

As a historical principle, the proposition is easily affirmed by observing most of the attempts to install an enduring democracy to replace an authoritarian system. The failures can be ascribed either to a hostile context (insecurity and instability of the "patient") or to an imperfect process (conceptual and operational inadequacies on the part of the "doctor"). "Contextual" failures appear in countries that lack the experience of accountable governance, a condition that is all the more distressing when the "doctor" intervenes, as a result of an impulsive or ideological gesture instead of an appraisal of the context of action. "Process" failures reveal how fragmentary is the contemporary understanding of the necessary ingredients of viability in modern states. To be sure, there have been advances in the theory and practice of governance that should restrain too much irrational exuberance, but no theory would encourage immediate hopes of bringing about a simple, spectacular regime change in a failed state. In fact, most of the nation-building histories that are regarded as successes have taken the form of modest disaggregated improvements that helped raise the "patient" out of a chronic state of morbidity. For, serious nation-building cannot occur during periods of chronic insecurity.

Yet there are cases of the more ambitious forms of nation-building. Some large-scale operations of the past have generated perhaps misleading expectations for the prospects of introducing stable, democratic, or accountable government. For example, one careful study of seven cases (Japan, Germany, Somalia, Haiti, Bosnia, Kosovo, and Afghanistan) has even identified principles that seem to explain these successful cases: all took place in the presence of adequate levels of security; all displayed a high degree of donor commitment as measured by the cost of the operation, the manpower employed, and the duration of the military presence. Those that were undertaken bilaterally proved to be less complex or time-consuming than international operations, but the latter, despite the additional effort, seem to have produced a more thoroughgoing transition to a new regime and have developed stronger regional relationships.[1]

The more modest and less comprehensive successes consisted of isolated improvements that were introduced piecemeal in the form of foreign aid or induced institution-building. Such relatively unpretentious programs have improved many countries' educational systems, health programs, agricultural services, economic planning units, and military organizations, as a result of efforts by both international assistance agencies and non-governmental organizations. Similar results were once celebrated as a consequence of 19th century imperial assistance, but even the most benign colonialism rarely succeeded in introducing a sustained Westminster system, however much it was desired. They did achieve some degree of political competition and a professionalized bureaucracy that occasionally continued under independence, however, after the departure of imperial captains and kings. These forms of nation-building were more likely to survive as the result of a series of pragmatic ameliorative measures than as an externally imposed form of permanent revolution.

Both aspects of nation-building — the partial, pragmatic and the holistic, ideological — have contributed to or induced some form of "regime change" that is sufficient to sustain the hope among international donors which well-intentioned future interventions can "install" or at least "encourage" democracy, by providing decisive support to hope for a "positive" political development. What seems to come to mind is that few of the large-scale efforts (Germany, Japan, South Korea, and Panama) persisted for more than a decade, in contrast to equally ambitious programs that produced a new regime which lasted barely three years (Cuba, Haiti, Nicaragua, Cambodia, and Vietnam) or even less (Grenada and Dominican Republic).[2]

Clearly, however, the less ambitious enterprises were the more successful ones. The first cases dated as far back as Truman's Point IV program, in which international assistance was able to contribute significantly to the infrastructures of good governance while leaving it to the indigenous populations to do the rest. Such interventions began with citizen-service activities, beginning with the expansion of educational opportunities, technical improvements in agriculture, and public health initiatives.

A second, more comprehensive tier of assistance began to emerge with improvements in economic planning, the mobilization of community participation in self-help programs, and the stimulation of active political movements. Taken together, these efforts merged into a comprehensive (though unacknowledged) "donors' model" of activities that were deemed to serve political and economic objectives of the post-war international order.

These traditional forms of technical assistance drew heavily on Western experiences, which were stripped of "political interference" where possible. Their successes included improvements in educational resources, agricultural productivity, and public health standards. These improvements were not without state-building significance. Relevant aid programs generally strengthened central authorities even when they were intended to benefit local organizations because they required the channeling of added resources to national ministries. Donors soon became aware of this issue; it has become increasingly common for aid projects to operate below the level of both national and provincial authorities. One strategy has been to place resources directly in the hands of traditional community leaders to encourage them to join in developing new elements in the civil society. Such efforts risk alienating the national leadership, however, especially when they support local "warlords" at the expense of stabilizing the internal security.

In time, political consequences began to influence foreign aid aspirations. Donor programs that had begun by rebuilding governance and administrative capacity, to develop the infrastructure to make good use of foreign aid, began to consider political development objectives as appropriate in themselves. Newly independent countries and post-conflict economies shared a general need for strengthened governmental macroeconomic management capability, as a result of which aid programs addressed questions of national budgeting, expenditure control, public sector investment management, central bank functions, and revenue collection. But there was an increasing recognition of the need for improved processes of governance through civil service reforms, decentralization schemes, and attention to citizen participation programs.[3] These interventions were still presented as politically immaculate where possible, however, to avoid invasive aspects of foreign aid.

But recognition was growing that institutional infrastructure was not merely technical. It as well included observance of the need for rule of law, as a result of which coherent legislation was introduced to enhance the legal framework for economic activity and to advance an effective and independent judiciary. Efforts to encourage the viability of the rule of law included offering legislative advice, suggestions for judicial reform, and recommended improvements in public access to courts. The international requirements of statecraft also received assistance in matters such as protecting foreign direct investment, promoting liberal trade, advancing the cause of free speech through assistance to the media, and even strengthening the prospects of a vital civil society, through support to advocacy groups and professional associations. The protection of human rights by publicly condemning violations became an important element in an emergent practice of nation-building.

These elements of a "donors' model" permitted international development agencies to advance their preferences for the internal affairs of ailing states, without overtly seeking to promote regime change. Yet, they could contribute constituent elements to the task of nation-building. It was clear that sectoral or microlevel successes were more likely to survive than large-scale institutional reforms that were intended as regime changes. All that donors could reasonably hope was that such "good things go together" and produce some benevolent spillover from each limited success.

The prospects for these modest aspirations exceeded the public expectations for foreign aid.[4] Although no one could claim that such assistance had produced new democracies, it is clear that some of its results extended beyond the sectoral or microlevel at which it functioned.[5]

Current doctrine continues to regard such efforts as promising. Programs aimed at promoting the rule of law, for example, are considered to have had significant impacts in Latin America and East Europe in situations where local institutions have received financial and technical assistance from abroad,[6] foreign aid has contributed to a productive economy when competitive organizations are encouraged.[7] Freedom of speech and media diversity have risen more frequently when there is a conspicuous foreign presence than without it, even in the face of setbacks when critics venture too far; human rights are at least as much protected by foreign intervention as by domestic politics.[8] Finally, for all their impreciseness, the techniques of good governance over the many years have contributed to productivity as a result of or advances in accountability, transparency, efficiency, reduced corruption, support to competitive markets, and emergent agricultural technology.[9]

These spillover effects are enhanced when programs serve purposes of equity and opportunity and when they reinforce institutions of self-governance and enrich a public sense of national identity and purpose.[10] To be sure, democracy is not guaranteed by such measures. Not all support to decentralization of power necessarily contributes to democratization unless it is accompanied by a formal devolution of authority; even elections, however popular, do not necessarily increase responsibility in government. The historical data is insufficient to prove that such characteristics have to be first developed or that there is any other dependable means to identify a necessary sequence in their rise. But some tentative principles emerge: it often develops that competitiveness among economic enterprises precedes such developments, including a cluster of conditions like freedom of speech, human rights, and the rule of law. These recurrent circumstances offer modest support to the priority that donors currently assign to the development of a competitive market economy.[11] There is wisdom nevertheless in treating each variable as an independent opportunity, addressing them one by one without expecting that any of them will bring improvement throughout the social system.

These experiences reinforce the wisdom of refraining from wholesale efforts to transplant democratic institutions and democratic politics.[12] It is a disconcerting fact that induced democratic processes have sometimes perpetuated conflictual divisions in a society that should have been moving toward cooperation and compromise. Even supposedly democratic forms of group action such as party and electoral systems have promoted ethnic schisms and polarized the political behavior of competing groups. The roots of such institutions need to be indigenous to avoid the kind of politics that release and stimulate group antagonisms and elevate repressed fears that sometimes emerge when authoritarian control is relinquished.

In short, it is possible to identify areas of success in supporting democratic institutions through foreign aid. The rule of law has advanced significantly in Latin America and East Europe where local institutions have received financial and technical assistance from abroad[13]; a productive economy has perhaps been the most conspicuous product of foreign aid, especially when enterprises have been competitive[14] and outward-based, even when they risk falling into a new form of colonization[15]; free speech and media diversity have accompanied a foreign presence, sometimes at the cost of sustaining excessively daring critics[16]; human rights have been protected more by foreign intervention than by domestic politics[17]; and for all its impreciseness, the congeries of technical qualities involved in good governance have included special elements immediately associated with productivity, such as emergent agricultural technology,[18] as well as advances in accountability,[19] transparency, efficiency, absence of corruption, and support to competitive markets, which are the hallmarks of government most preferred by the international banks. There is often a spillover effect in well-designed aid projects that serve purposes of equity and opportunity, while reinforcing institutional aims and enriching a public sense of national identity and purpose.[21]

There are even some historical principles that tentatively suggest sequences in the experience of foreign aid. Studies of the rise of democratic states have emphasized the importance of attaining institutional strength at the center first, before local autocrats or other rival groups can interrupt a transition to a responsible government. Programs to promote the rule of law, support media diversity, and train a corps of professional civil servants are usually introduced before competitive elections and partisan activism.[21] It is certain to be expected, however, that these relationships would apply as much to the Islamic world as to the modernizing polities anywhere: They are not merely an expression of Western donors' preferences. The path to development there, as elsewhere, will be shaped more by indigenous factors and events in the field rather than by donors' underlying values. Whatever may be the role of political culture,[22] most scholars agree that nothing in the Islamic world, resistant as it may appear to be in the aftermath of chronic wars in the Middle East, makes democratic aspirations impossible.[23]

Not all aid is directed at democratic outcomes. Donors' models range from the hope of constructing Islamic states, inspired by the Koran, to hopes of the former Soviet Union for East Germany, North Korea, China, and newly independent Eastern states. On the whole, however, current doctrine associated with nation-building derives from liberal democratic states.

The opportunity to participate directly in constitutional innovations occurs only rarely, however, notably in cases involving peacemaking or in restraining assertions of an aggressive sovereignty. The most likely of such interventions occur at moments when there is international action to end or prevent wars, following traditional Westphalian views of national integrity and sovereignty. In recent years, the UN, the World Bank, and several Western governments have provided advice and good offices about issues of statecraft following chaos and insecurity. In such cases, internal conditions sometimes appear as prerequisites to peaceful relations, thus apparently justifying the exertion of powerful pressures to reform as part of a peace settlement. Most recently, the international community enthusiastically offered modest technical assistance to Afghanistan in constitution drafting, including logistical and other support to the Loya Jirga, a national assembly that served as a prelude to the formation of a constitutional national government. Bosnia, too, was the occasion for an international agreement regarding the internal governance that was pressed upon several unwilling parties.

Out of respect for the national sovereignty of members, international agencies cannot maintain a standing capacity to engage in nation-building. Some observers, including the present author, have suggested the creation of a body of professionals to perform these functions for bilateral relationships.[24] But it is still desirable to reduce the reluctant resort to sheer nation amateurism in both bilateral and international efforts by developing professional traditions on the basis of a growing reservoir of experience. If necessary, a standing non-governmental organization could perform the same function.

Nation-building doctrines have emerged from history, from careful appraisals of diplomacy and statesmanship, and from general propositions developed in political science, economics, and other systematic reviews of experience. It is not necessary to act out of serendipity and political accident to gain access to the most promising areas of intervention on behalf of improved and sustained political development. Even there, nation-building is highly experimental and perhaps should be undertaken only if the donors are willing to contemplate failure and if they are willing to mobilize a significant professional capacity drawing upon the talents of foreign assistance agencies, from the scattered elements in the diplomatic corps, and from the scholarly and commercial communities with experience in political development.

To seek such professionalism will be a major task of international leadership in the coming decades.

References

1. Dobbins, J., J.G. McGinn, K.C. Seth, G. Jones, R. Lal, A. Rathmell, R. Swanger, and A. Timilsina, *America's Role in Nation-Building: From Germany to Iraq* (Santa Monica, CA: RAND, 2004).
2. Pei, M. and S. Kasper, "Lessons from the Past: The American Record on Nation Building," Policy Brief 24 (Washington, D.C.: Carnegie Endowment for International Peace, 2003)
3. Rondinelli, D.A., "International Goals and Strategies for Afghanistan's Development: Reconstruction and Beyond," in J.D. Montgomery and D.A. Rondinelli, eds., *Beyond Reconstruction in Afghanistan: Lessons from Development Experience* (New York: Palgrave MacMillan, 2004).
4. Morawetz, D., *Twenty-Five Years of Economic Development* (Baltimore, MD: Johns Hopkins University Press, 1977); Cassen, R. et al., "Does Aid Work?" Report to an Intergovernmental Task Force (Oxford: Oxford University Press, 1986); Krueger, A.O., C. Michalopoulos, and V.W. Ruttan, *Aid and Development* (Baltimore, MD: Johns Hopkins University Press, 1989), pp. 1–10.
5. Muscat, R.J., *Investing in Peace: How Development Aid Can Prevent or Promote Conflict* (Armonk, NY: M.E. Sharpe, 2002), p. 38.
6. Carothers, T., *Aiding Democracy Abroad: The Learning Curve* (Washington, D.C.: Carnegie Endowment for International Peace, 1999), pp. 163–177.
7. Cassen, R. and Associates, "Does Aid Work?" Report to an Intergovernmental Task Force (Oxford: Clarendon Press, 1987), pp. 321–333.
8. Montgomery, J.D., ed., *Human Rights: Positive Policies in Asia and the Pacific Rim* (Hollis, NH: Hollis Publishing Co., 1998).
9. Cassen, R. and Associates, "Does Aid Work?" Report to an Intergovernmental Task Force (Oxford: Clarendon Press, 1987), pp. 97–100.
10. Ruttan, V.W., "What Happened to Political Development?" *Economic Development and Cultural Change*, 39(2) (1991), pp. 265–292.

11. Fraser Institute, Annual Economic Freedom of the World Report, June 2003, at www.FreeTheWorld.com.
12. Carothers, T., *Aiding Democracy Abroad: The Learning Curve* (Washington, D.C.: Carnegie Endowment for International Peace, 1999).
13. Carothers, T., *Aiding Democracy Abroad: The Learning Curve* (Washington, D.C.: Carnegie Endowment for International Peace, 1999), pp. 163–177.
14. Cassen, R. and Associates, "Does Aid Work?" Report to an Intergovernmental Task Force (Oxford: Clarendon Press, 1987), pp. 321–333.
15. Krueger, A.O., C. Michalopoulos, and V.W. Ruttan, *Aid and Development* (Baltimore, MD: Johns Hopkins University Press, 1989), p. 306.
16. Carothers, T., *Aiding Democracy Abroad: The Learning Curve* (Washington, D.C.: Carnegie Endowment for International Peace, 1999), pp. 235–244.
17. Montgomery, J.D., ed., *Human Rights: Positive Policies in Asia and the Pacific Rim* (Hollis, NH: Hollis Publishing Co., 1998).
18. Carothers, T. *Aiding Democracy Abroad: The Learning Curve* (Washington, D.C: Carnegie Endowment for International Peace, 1999), pp. 60, 117–131.
19. Carothers, T. *Aiding Democracy Abroad: The Learning Curve* (Washington, D.C: Carnegie Endowment for International Peace, 1999), pp. 97–100.
20. Muscat, op. cit., pp. 74–99, Ruttan, "What Happened to Political Development?", op. cit., p. 276.
21. Mansfield, E.D. and J. Snyder, "Democratic Transitions, Institutional Strength, and War." *International Organization*, 56(2) (Spring 2002), pp. 297–337.
22. Harrison, L., E. Harrison, and S.P. Huntington, *Culture Matters: How Values Shape Human Progress* (New York: Basis Books, 2000).
23. Seligson, M.A., "The Renaissance of Political Culture or the Renaissance of the Ecological Fallacy," *Comparative Politics*, 34(3) (April 2002), pp. 273–292.
24. Tessler, M., "Islam and Democracy in the Middle East, The Impact of Religious Orientations and Attitudes toward Democracy in Four Arab Countries," *Comparative Politics*, 34(3) (April 2002), pp. 337–354.
25. Rondinelli, D.A. and J.D. Montgomery, "Does the United States Need a Nation-Building Agency?" *Foreign Service Journal*, 81(12) (2004), pp. 56–60.

Chapter 7

Globalization and the Regulation of Professions

Robert P. Goss

CONTENTS

Globalization is fetching substantial change in both governmental and voluntary self-regulation of professions and occupations. The stodgy, even creaking, system of fragmented professional regulation in nations around the world is undergoing metamorphosis. Occupational regulation in the

United States has been moving from one largely undertaken and overseen by 50 states to one more amenable to national interests, from one operated to satisfy domestic stakeholder to one more international in scope, and from one largely governmental to one more dependent upon non-governmental interests and organizations. These changes in professional regulation mirror the development of American public administration from one characterized as the Old Public Administration into one more like the New Public Service, yet applicable globally. The changes reflect the applicability of different political, economic, and administrative theories too. Corresponding adjustments regulating professions within other nations are also proceeding rapidly because of globalization.

Impact of Globalization on the Regulation of Professions and Occupations

The flow of technology, knowledge, people, values, and ideas across national borders has affected not only the world's economic order, but also the international and the intranational political order. Several hundred years of U.S. history have demonstrated movement from colonial dependence to independence, but more recently from independence to hemispheric and global interdependence. The 1787 Constitution met the need for a common market in goods and services among the collective 13 American states, subject to the police power of the states where trade was open with no state-imposed tariffs, but globalization has now broadened that concept through free-trade agreements to much of the world. However, such agreements now include diminution of non-tariff barriers as well, and have the effect within the United States of amending the 50 states common market. Specifically, the free movement and use of professional services across states, nations, and continents fosters recognition of *bona fide* professional and occupational credentials. Correspondingly, trade in services has diminished those who do not meet appropriate standards and fomented efforts within the United States and other nations for change. Economic, political, and free trade forces will continue into the immediate future.

What is the status of governmental regulation on professions and occupations? What about voluntary self-regulation? And where is such regulation headed in the future? In responding to such questions, this chapter does not cover only a single profession. Rather, it deals broadly with the changing nature of intranational, national, and transnational bases for occupational and professional credentialing and licensure because of globalization. It identifies past and current models now in use because of globalization, and offers ideas and suggestions about the future of globalized professional services regulation. Thousands of associations of professionals in the United States and around the world, billions of consumers, and thousands of governmental agencies and nonprofit regulatory organizations are and will be affected by these developments. Moreover, an understanding of them is fundamental for those engaged in policy analysis and the making of public policy, as well as administering policies dealing with occupations. Simply stated, globalization is changing both the rules and the means by which professions and occupations are regulated. Reassessing alternatives in light of new directions resulting from globalization may provide governmental policymakers and the leaders of nonprofit organizations and businesses, as well as billions of consumers, with potentially better ways of serving both the public and specific stakeholders through professional services regulation.

Traditional Regulation of Occupations

In many nations governments regulate occupations. The conventional distinction between professions on the one hand, and occupations on the other, involves the advanced nature of the required education, training, and preparation necessary to provide services to the public; historically, there was a mental rather than manual work distinction as well. The general public tends to accept as professions those occupations providing essential services that are prestigious, in part, due to their required extensive preparation and training. In federal governmental systems the regulation of occupations is often at the state or provincial level. So it has evolved in the United States, with governmental regulation in the United States having a long history. Among the first colonial or state regulation was Virginia's medical practice act in 1639, occurring well before the United States was formed. The Constitution's Tenth Amendment confirmed the concept that licensure was the responsibility of the states. In the 1800s state licensure for physicians, dentists, pharmacists, attorneys, and teachers began occurring in earnest, and in the 20th century dozens of additional groups became licensed — barbers, funeral directors, accountants, nurses, real estate brokers, chiropractors, etc.[1]

During the Progressive Era, the foundations of American public administration were laid and built upon. The Old Public Administration asserted a separation between policymaking on the one hand, and implementation of policy on the other. Yet the implementers of professional services regulation were increasingly called upon to make policy themselves. Policymaking included the advancement of social well-being through Keynesian economics from the New Deal through the post-World War II period. Arguments for a welfare economics approach to state licensing involved public benefits, including assurances to consumers of high-quality services by only competent individuals in lieu of unregulated individuals endangering the public's health, safety, or economic well-being. However, such a public interest rationale or theory and the corresponding "market failure" concept justifying governmental action for reasons such as "asymmetric information," where professionals know so much more than consumers as a basis for state action, has been challenged by critics.[2]

In other nations there has been a preference for professions to regulate themselves. The United Kingdom serves as an example of professional self-regulation, where associations have monitored education requirements, accredited educational programs and training requirements, awarded and renewed licenses, controlled aspects of practice, and disciplined recalcitrant members.[3] But in many countries, including the United States, there have been varying degrees of self-regulation for professions.[4] Of course, guilds have existed since the Middle Ages, with their activities directed at the protection of the interests of their members as well as contributions to the communities in which they worked. In the view of critics, however, an association of professionals does not generally have as its primary goal protection or benefit of the general public. Instead, a professional association seeks principally to advantage its own members. Critics of state licensure activities have indicated that licensure should not have as a consideration, the improvement of business conditions for the licensed profession; in particular, an association's influence in the operation and staffing of a state licensure board should be minimized.[5] The capture of regulatory agencies by special interests has produced restrictions on entry into the profession and higher costs for consumers. Both incrementalism and public choice theory suggest that government officials, including those serving on state licensing or comparable boards, as well as those charged with administering such professional regulation, may have, as motivation, something less than that of *homo politicus* — a public-spirited actor interested in the well-being of the public — and more like that of *homo economicus* — an individual seeking to maximize personal benefits. Capture theory, incrementalism, and particularly public choice theory have led to skepticism about whether "market failures" in private regulation identified by professional associations properly serve as a basis for governmental action in the form of state regulation. Critics have charged that state-sanctioned monopolies over the supply, provision, and regulation of services have more likely demonstrated "government failure" that should be mitigated through a market-like solution where credentials can and do compete. For emerging occupations it is often more difficult to secure state licensure because of "sunrise" provisions in many states, requiring the costs and benefits of proposed licensure to be demonstrated to the legislature, and so new occupations have sought private-sector credentialing instead. In the late 1970s and 1980s the Old Public

Administration and public interest theory were being reconsidered, and the New Public Management and public choice theory were ushered in.

"Credentialing" is a generic term for licensure, certification, and registration,[6] although it is often used to include educational diplomas as well.[7] "Licensing" is a process by which a government agency grants individuals permission to engage in a specified profession or occupation, upon finding that individual applicants have attained the minimal degree of competency required to ensure that the public's health, safety, or economic well-being will be reasonably well protected.[8] "Certification" is a process by which a governmental or non-governmental organization grants authority to use a specified title to an individual, who has met predetermined qualifications.[9] The primary purpose of licensure and certification is to protect the public,[10] if the programs are well-designed. Compared with licensing, which is the most restrictive form of occupational regulation, "registration" is the least restrictive form of regulation or credentialing, usually consisting of requiring individuals to file their names, addresses, and qualifications with a government agency before practicing an occupation or profession.[11]

State licensure and voluntary regulation have grown since 1980, when over 800 occupations and professions were regulated at the state government level in the United States compared with 1100 in 2004,[12] whereas professions unable to secure state licensure have often turned to voluntary self-regulation through nonprofit organizations. Requirements for initial licensing and certification have historically included one or more of the 4Es — education, experience, examination, and ethics — for initial licensure or certification. In addition, there have often been requirements to continue to maintain one's licensure or certification. For example, regulatory bodies have applied continuing education or continuing competency requirements, as well as required adherence to practice standards and codes of ethics; these have been enforced by the power of government agencies as well as nonprofit organizations that investigate complaints and take disciplinary action against licensees and certificants failing to comply.[13]

Admission to practice a given occupation by means of licensure is generally confined to one state or area of jurisdiction. Often states will engage in "reciprocity" arrangements — whereby one state may communicate to a second state that it will accept the other's licensees if that state will accept its licensees in return — on a bilateral or multilateral basis so that a licensee who moves to or practices in another state may be able to secure permission to practice in more than one state without going through a new qualifications process. Yet this is frequently difficult, and reciprocity is not the norm. "Endorsement" is also a process used by states to recognize the professional qualifications of those in a particular discipline that have been licensed in other states. Here the state makes a judgment whether a specific candidate has met comparable (but not necessarily equivalent) standards or other requirements. If affirmative, the applicant is admitted to practice in the second state by means of endorsement. If reciprocity or endorsement is not universally available within the states for occupations and professions, the challenge of applying such approaches to globalized professions is augmented. Writers have recommended that the broader public — beyond the regulated profession or occupation itself — be heard on regulatory matters. In particular, when a legislature is considering whether to enact a law to license an occupational group, when a regulated group is proposing rules and regulations that could determine entry-level standards, professional practices, or ethical obligations, or when a legislative body is considering whether to sunset or continue a regulatory board, the voice of the general public ought to be discerned.[14]

In the United States, competition policy has been expressed in the form of the Sherman Antitrust Act of 1890 with enforcement responsibilities assigned to the U.S. Department of Justice and to the Federal Trade Commission (FTC). Charged to protect consumer interests through investigations involving rules of conduct for various professional associations, the FTC has frowned upon agreements that might limit competition.[15] On the other hand, the U.S. Supreme Court in the case *Parker vs. Brown* (1943) has determined that the Congress did not intend to limit the states' sovereign regulatory power when it passed the antitrust laws, and thus, under a dual system of government in which the states are sovereign under the constitutional principle of federalism, actions of the state itself are shielded from federal antitrust scrutiny when state conduct is in furtherance of a clearly articulated state policy and actively supervised by the state. This "state action" doctrine generally does not cover a non-sovereign state licensing board simply asserting a public interest rationale for its actions because it has assumed delegated responsibility from the state legislature; rather, it must be an articulated state policy determined by a sovereign entity like the legislature or state supreme court. However, courts have found that state-level boards and similar entities with private participants can be exempted from the active supervision requirement where they perform a public function and are directly accountable to the state, such as state bars or state boards of accountancy.[16] Although the FTC cannot use its enforcement authority to challenge competitive restraints, it can and does seek to persuade policymakers of the benefits of competition. For example, it has worked with state legislatures and state licensing bodies to set aside or temper attempts to restrict advertising and prevent competition from those outside the profession.[17] These activities have represented applications of public choice theory replacing public interest theory.

The U.S. Supreme Court has also declared the use of professional credentials and designations from *bona fide* organizations as protected commercial free speech. In *Bates vs. State Bar of Arizona* 433 U.S. 350

(1977), the court found that the prohibition on the advertising of professional services violated the First and Fourteenth Amendments. In *Ibanez vs. Florida Department of Business and Professional Regulation*, 512 U.S. 136 (1994) the Court found that a state licensing board dealing with accountancy may not constitutionaly prohibit an attorney from including in her advertising truthful references that she is a Certified Public Accountant and Certified Financial Planner. Commercial advertising does merit First Amendment protection given the important functions it serves in society, such as providing consumers with valuable information. The proper use of both *bona fide* nonprofit and governmental occupational qualifications was upheld.

In addition to the licensing and certification elements of credentialing, there exists a third element called accreditation. Within the United States six regional nonprofit organizations accredit colleges and universities on a regional basis, and more than 50 accrediting organizations review school programs for individual professions.[18] The Council for Higher Education Accreditation (CHEA), recognized by the U.S. Department of Education, is currently the organization that carries out this recognition function in the private sector as a non-governmental entity. The National Commission for Certifying Agencies (NCCA) is similarly a nonprofit organization that accredits programs of certifying bodies which meet its rigorous standards.[19] Typically, accreditation deals with programs or an organization, whereas licensing and certification are applied to individuals.[20]

Neighboring nations of the United States — and those also parties to the North American Free Trade Agreement (NAFTA) — have differing credentialing processes. Under the Canadian constitution, the provincial governments have complete jurisdiction over education. Moreover, there is no federal department or ministry of education. Autonomous and professional self-regulation in Canada applies to universities and professionals. The Association of Accrediting Agencies of Canada (AAAC), formed in 1994 to monitor trends and support accreditors of professional education, has served as a Canadian network for professional accrediting bodies. Educational accreditation in Canada has been similarly voluntary, such that the quality of professional education is the responsibility of both the professions and the post-secondary educational institutions within which the professional schools are housed. Accordingly, the role of national, educational, and non-governmental professional associations has been powerful in the development of education standards and accreditation.[21]

In Mexico, the higher education and licensing procedures used are very different from those of Canada and the United States. Undergraduate study programs are specialized along subjects of study (*carreras*), leading to a professional degree. The programs are lengthy, with heavy course loads. Upon graduation the student is granted licensure to legally practice the profession in addition to receiving the university degree. Accordingly, University undergraduate studies in Mexico are called "*licenciatura*" studies. The National Autonomous University of Mexico (Universidad Nacional Autonoma de Mexico or UNAM) is the entity that performs accreditation of the study programs for post-secondary educational institutions.[22] In some other Latin American nations, such as Chile, the accreditation system is similar to that of Mexico.[23]

Tensions Involving Domestic Professional Regulation with Globalization

Globalization as a term represents the concept of increasing integration and interchange between people, businesses, organizations, nations, and governments. Alterations in means of communication and the modes of transportation have improved the speed and frequency with which people, products, services, and ideas move about the globe. Notwithstanding time and distance, communities and societies have become more connected. The global community is also fostered through immigration and emigration.

Although the term globalization is relatively new, international cooperation in standards-setting is not recent. The internationalization of standards began a century ago with the formation of the International Electrotechnical Commission (IEC) in 1906, followed by the International Standards Association in 1926. The current International Organization for Standardization (ISO) was formed in 1946 as the world's largest developer of standards — initially technical standards for products because exports and imports representing international commerce would be impossible without similar standards. More recently, ISO has worked on service standards, and its determinations are useful to governments and regulatory bodies, to conformity assessment professionals in both the public and private sectors, and to consumers or users of services. There are many stakeholders within the 148 national standards institutes that make up this non-governmental organization (NGO) developing market-driven, voluntary consensus standards. Founding bodies for the ISO were the national standards bodies of 26 countries, including in the United States the current American National Standards Institute (ANSI), itself a nonprofit organization founded by several professional societies and three federal agencies. Although the ISO does not regulate or legislate, its voluntary standards can become market requirements through adoption in countries as part of specific regulatory frameworks or by reference in legislation for which standards serve as a technical basis. ISO standards represent agreements among the participating standards institutes, are significant in scope and size, and are properly termed global standards. In 2003, ISO issued international standard

ISO/IEC 170024 providing guidelines or a global benchmark for organizations managing certification of personnel in any profession or trade.[24] And in 2004, the organization issued ISO/IEC 17011 covering similar requirements for accreditation bodies to insure that they operate in a consistent, comparable, and reliable manner worldwide.[25]

One year after the creation of ISO the General Agreement on Tariffs and Trade (GATT) was signed, providing an international forum that encouraged free trade between member countries through regulating and reducing tariffs on traded goods, and by providing a common mechanism for resolving trade disputes. Nonetheless, continued growth in the world's economic order depended upon the free movement of not just products, but also services.[26] Services are the largest productive sector in most national economies, with the share of services in the national products of most nations having risen steadily in the last several decades. In 2001 services reached 72 percent of GDP in developed nations and 52 percent in developing countries,[27] making the services sector the largest and fastest-growing sector of the world economy.[28] In the United States the service sector comprises 80 percent of U.S. employment and 64 percent of U.S. GDP. The size of the service sector means significant value results from reducing barriers to trade in services. For example, the Office of the U.S. Trade Representative (USTR) has cited a University of Michigan study estimating that a one third cut in global barriers to trade in services would increase U.S. annual income by $150 billion, or about $2100 per American family of four, and total elimination of barriers in services would raise U.S. annual income by $450 billion, or about $6380 per family of four.[29]

Increasing global trade necessitates producers and consumers moving from one nation to another, producers establishing a presence in another nation, or freer cross-border transportable services.[30] Professional mobility does not only mean that an individual be able to physically travel from one jurisdiction to another, but also encompasses virtual mobility where the outcomes of a professional's work are free to circulate without losing their validity.[31] Thus, professional services barriers can involve those where the provider never leaves her political jurisdiction, or the economic control of her service firm in the provider's country, but where the delivery of the service depends upon means like satellite delivery or fiber optic communications, telecommunications, film, videotape, audio recordings, as well as written materials.[32] Professionals follow product and services industries in moving overseas and around the globe, increase their use of the Internet and other communications systems, immigrate or emigrate with their practice skills, and otherwise broaden their international ties.

For individuals, businesses, organizations, and governments the globalization of professions creates challenges associated with having practitioners credentialed within one jurisdiction practicing in a different jurisdiction. The use of e-mail, the Internet, and satellite communications makes it possible for the practice of an occupation to cross jurisdictional boundaries even if the individual practitioner never leaves his or her geographical locale. Telepractice, for example, has come to mean professionals providing interactive, long-distance services to a consumer in another location.[33] A health practitioner located in an urban area may be able to monitor the heartbeat of a homebound patient in a rural area of another state with an electronic stethoscope. A surgeon in one country can direct a person in a second nation in repairing a patient's heart. Architects and engineers may send drawings using the Internet, whereas lawyers may send contracts.[34] Interstate, international, and interjurisdictional practice are becoming increasingly common for professions because of globalization. The effects of globalization include more than the invention and use of technological tools associated with it; they include the educational preparation of the individual, the credentialing of that person, the delivery of services by the credentialed person, and the person's continuing competency after first being credentialed.

The lack of international recognition of credentials — the inability to recognize professional credentials from one nation to another — is not the problem of a single profession or occupation. Rather, it is pervasive and crosses virtually all disciplines. Each day practitioners engage in informal conversations between and among themselves, irrespective of their native countries, regarding advancement of their knowledge in the field, the application of concepts and theories, and principles to the specific circumstances of clients, and freedoms and constraints regarding their work. Occasionally, international meetings and conferences are organized for formal discussion and resolution purposes. One such conference in 1995, sponsored by the Paris-based Organization for Economic Cooperation and Development (OECD) created in 1960, identified key obstacles to the internationalization of professional services: (1) lack of appropriate access to local practice; (2) restrictions concerning the establishment of firms; and (3) local presence and nationality requirements.[35] At this session the OECD chair of the Committee on Competition Law and Policy noted that increased international competition would help mitigate the identified three major abuses of professional regulation: (1) entry requirements, including limitations in establishing a practice; (2) fee-setting, including those wrongly justified by a presumed need to avoid price competition; and (3) ethics rules, such as those constraining the consumer's right to change suppliers and thus prevent fluidity of the market.[36] Also at this meeting consumer representatives voiced their view that the public would be best served by a competitive market with choices and the necessary information and means to exercise those choices. From a consumer perspective there were only two legitimate purposes of professional regulation: (1) protection of the public that uses professional services; and (2) protection of the integrity and quality of the profession.[37]

Not surprisingly, complaints regarding the insular and nontransportable nature of credentials have only partly come from professionals themselves, for many still have single geographic community perspectives. Consumer advocates, economists, and governmental officials charged with protecting the public interest within a nation have voiced concerns. In the United States the FTC is responsible to ensure that markets operate efficiently and benefit consumers through lower prices, innovation, and choice among products and services. Its consumer protection mission is also designed to help consumers make informed choices about their purchases, and thereby maximize benefits for consumers.[38] Yet grievances against and alternatives to the structure of singularly domestic professional services regulation have recently come with greater force from outside individual nations.[39] The globalization decade of the 1990s began a strong expansion in trade and economic integration that highlighted some problems. Following the Canada–U.S. Free Trade Agreement in 1988, the North American Free Trade Area (NAFTA) was negotiated in 1992 and became effective in 1994. The World Trade Organization (WTO) and its corresponding General Agreement on Services (GATS) were agreed to in 1994 and became effective in 1995, and there have been continued activities with the Asia–Pacific Economic Cooperation Forum (APEC) begun in 1989, the 1994 proposal for a Free Trade Area of the Americas (FTAA), as well as several bilateral trade agreements. Because of the importance of NAFTA and GATS, the design and impact of these two agreements are stressed in this chapter.

NAFTA's Chapter 12 did not automatically extend the right of professionals to practice in other countries. Rather, the agreement required that the professionals from NAFTA countries be given "national treatment" — nondiscriminatory access to certification and licensing procedures.[40] Under NAFTA's Article 1210, Canada, Mexico, and the United States were each obligated to ensure that their licensing and certification of nationals "does not constitute an unnecessary barrier to trade" and "is based on objective and transparent criteria, such as competence and the ability to provide a service," "is not more burdensome than necessary to ensure the quality of a service," and "does not constitute a restriction on the cross-border provision of a service." Within the first two years of the agreement each nation was to "eliminate any citizenship or permanent residency requirement for the licensing and certification of professional service providers." Although no national government is required to extend recognition of education, experience, or licenses and certifications obtained in other nations, it must afford interested parties "an adequate opportunity to demonstrate that education, experience, licenses or certifications obtained in another nation should also be recognized." Moreover, a comprehension of the significant functions undertaken by non-governmental bodies was explicitly recognized in Article 1213, where any reference to a federal, state, or provincial government was defined to include "any non-governmental body in the exercise of any regulatory, administrative or other governmental authority delegated to it by such government." In NAFTA's Annex 1210 dealing with professional services nations are obligated to "encourage the relevant bodies in their respective territories to develop mutually acceptable professional standards and criteria for licensing and certification of professional service providers to provide recommendations on mutual recognition" including education, examinations, work experience, conduct and ethics, professional development and re-certification, scope of practice, and "encourage their respective competent authorities, where appropriate, to adopt those recommendations within a mutually agreed period." These NAFTA commitments to change occupational regulation were critical, but they were succeeded by at least equally important commitments reached under GATS.

At the government-to-government meeting in Marrakech, Morocco, in 1994, ministers signed documents involving the creation of the General Agreement on Trade in Services (GATS) and the framework for establishing the intergovernmental organization called the World Trade Organization (WTO). In contrast with GATT that dealt with goods, GATS was an extension of the trading system into the services sector. Individual WTO member nations are responsible for monitoring their compliance with these agreements; the WTO does operate a dispute settlement system for member nations, however. Ambassador Charlene Barshefsky described the WTO in a speech to the Institute for International Economics on April 15, 1998:

> ...The role of the WTO is not to demand a system of uniform regulation nor to detract in any respect from the absolute right of governments to establish a particular set of regulatory norms, provided they are neither discriminatory, arbitrary, nor disguised barriers to trade. Rather, the role of the WTO is to ensure that national regulatory practices are fully transparent and not politically directed. This includes the principles of genuine national treatment and due process, commitments to publish and make widely available all regulations and to ensure that it is those public regulations and not others that are actually applied. Inherent in the need for clear, enforceable rules is also the need for impartial regulators.[41]

GATS has two general rules applicable to WTO member nations, including their subnational governments and non-governmental bodies, relevant to professional services — Article VI that deals with domestic regulation of the professions, and Article VII that covers the recognition of qualifications. Even future free-trade agreements entered into by WTO members must be in keeping with these provisions. Article VI, Domestic Regulation, calls upon WTO members to reasonably, objectively, and impartially administer specific commitments made, and to generally assure that qualification requirements and procedures, technical standards and licensing requirements do not constitute unnecessary barriers to trade in services. A Council for Trade in Services was authorized to develop particular guidelines for specific professions — and when done WTO members must adhere to those guidelines — based on objective and transparent criteria such as competence and the ability to supply the service, regulating in a manner not more burdensome than necessary to ensure the quality of service and, in the case of licensing procedures, not having them serve as a restriction on the supply of service. Article VI also acknowledges "international standards" of relevant international organizations, meaning entities whose membership is open to the appropriate bodies of at least all WTO members. Article VII, Recognition, calls upon WTO members to "work in cooperation with intergovernmental and non-governmental organizations toward the establishment and adoption of common international standards and criteria for recognition and common international standards for the practice of relevant services trades and professions." WTO members are expected to set their own "standards or criteria for the authorization, licensing or certification of service suppliers" and without discrimination "recognize the education or experience obtained, requirements met, or license or certifications granted" in other countries through harmonization, agreements with another country, or accord them recognition unilaterally. These procedures and verification of qualifications requirements affect both governmental and non-governmental entities within countries and thus respect and give assurance to these bodies about their functions.[42]

When federal governments enter into international trade agreements on a global level, they often become acutely conscious of barriers at the state or provincial level of government. This occurred in Canada, which recognized that it was easier to trade between the United States and Canada than it was to trade between Canadian provinces. In 1994, the provincial and territorial governments of Canada signed an Agreement on Internal Trade (AIT) with the objective "to reduce and eliminate to the extent possible, barriers to the free movement of persons, goods, services and investments within Canada and to establish an open, efficient and stable domestic market." Chapter 7 of AIT, applied to measures adopted or maintained by the provinces and territories that create barriers to mobility, such as occupational standards, licensing, certification, registration, or residency requirements for workers.[43] The Office of the U.S. Trade Representative (USTR) has encouraged state governments and non-governmental organizations to remove barriers to trade in services where they exist, but in GATS negotiations USTR has recognized that the "United States and sub-federal governments will continue to be able to establish, maintain, and fully enforce domestic laws protecting consumers, health, safety, and the environment."[44] Indeed, the federal government continues to be reluctant to become involved in state occupational licensing, although the commerce and supremacy clauses of the Constitution could be used as a basis for doing so.[45]

A more assertive posture has been taken by the European Union (EU). The European approach to barriers for trade in services has represented a response to both WTO and EU needs. Prior to the expansion of the EU to 25 countries in May 2004, it had sought to achieve the reality of a more truly common market for professional services — both through its Competition Directorate General (DG), which urges member states to abate restrictions, like advertising limitations and price-fixing arrangements, and through its Internal Market DG, which cuts administrative burdens and excessive conditions that inhibit EU businesses and professional service providers from offering services across borders or opening operations in other nations.[46] In February 2004, after the completion of a study, covering the six professions of lawyers, notaries, accountants, architects, engineers, and pharmacists, that was a part of the Competition DG, the Commission announced that it was calling on its member states to abolish restrictions unless they are "clearly justified by the public interest." The research study reaffirmed economic theory and capture theory that governmental regulatory bodies bend toward the will of those being regulated instead of the larger public interest, concluding that "economic benefits are being gained by highly regulated professions at the expense of consumer welfare," that there is a "negative correlation between the degree of regulation and the productivity," that "none of the markets for professional services has experienced the dire consequences of market breakdown predicted by theories based on the presence of conditions known as market failure," and so "the predictions of public interest theory seem wide of the mark, and that, on the contrary, regulation could be reduced."[47] Noted Commissioner Mario Monti at the October 2003 European Commission Conference on Professional Regulation:

> I put the emphasis upon the Lisbon goal . . . aiming at making Europe the most competitive and dynamic knowledge-based economy in the world. . . . In the U.S., the professions or authorities have indeed done away with some of the most serious restraints on competition and are considering some further relaxation of the existing rules. Nevertheless, even today members of a profession cannot necessarily practice in another State. To me this means that in some ways the EU could, if it so wished, be more progressive than the U.S. in this important sector of the economy. . . . In the U.S. the Federal Trade Commission has highlighted that citizens of one State are often forced to absorb the costs imposed by another States' anti-competitive regulations. . . . This also limits consumers' choice and may have adverse effects on employment.[48]

The Competition DG became effective on May 2004.

The EU Internal Market DG may come into effect by 2007; the matter is still under consideration. But unlike the Competition DG, its application is limited to EU nationals. Non-EU professionals, even those qualified and licensed in one of the EU countries, will still need a separate license to operate as licensed professionals in other EU states, and will not benefit from the Internal Market DG. Of course, GATS allows negotiation of mutual recognition agreements on a bilateral or a regional basis, as long as the parties to the agreement afford an adequate opportunity for other WTO members to enter into that agreement or a similar agreement.[49] For the Internal Market DG, the EU noted that the rights of EU citizens to establish themselves or to provide services in any of the EU countries are fundamental principles of the European Community law, and regulations that only recognize professional qualifications of the particular jurisdiction present obstacles to these fundamental freedoms. The proposed directive would have the effect of replacing 15 existing directives in dealing with the recognition of professional qualifications, described as constituting the first comprehensive modernization of the community system since it was conceived 40 years ago.

Concepts and Models of Global Professional Services Regulation

Globalization has fostered increasingly more frequent interchanges among government regulators, regulated professionals and businesses, and the respective national organizations representing their interests. Florini and Simmons indicate that the three fundamental international actors — states, the private sector, and civil society — vary greatly in their ability, with governments having coercive power, firms possessing economic power, and the third sector commanding moral authority.[50] But combinations of these three may offer both "hard" and "soft" power policy options, and perhaps global decision making requires all three plus intergovernmental organizations.[51] Both regional and global networks of government officials and professionals have arisen and meetings involving them have created NAFTA and GATS as well as organizations like the WTO, ISO, and OECD, permitting both official and unofficial governmental actors to address common problems on a regional or global scale. It is these intergovernmental organizations (IGOs) and non-governmental organizations (NGOs) — and additional networks and organizations composed of public or private individuals and organizations generated from them and others — that are a key feature of world order in the 21st century and represent good public policy according to Slaughter.[52] Their expansive regulatory reach allows government officials, nonprofit regulators, and business and professional interests to cooperate on a continuing basis, exchange information about their activities, develop databases and best practices, provide technical assistance, harmonize approaches to the regulation of professions, and improve compliance with international standards and norms, achieving results not through the application of coercive or hard but rather persuasive or soft power. Slaughter notes that such self-regulatory networks can be understood as a type of global governance. Yet with political authority still held by national governments, there appears an increasing disjunction between transnational challenges and the capacity of mostly national systems to solve them. These transnational systems that are emerging to resolve problems are not accountable directly to people affected by their policies, and no real constituency elects international entities composed of governments, businesses, and professional interests.[53]

Rather than thinking of these IGOs as entities representing the collective interests of unitary states or nations, Slaughter urges us to look upon them as performing legislative, adjudicatory, and administrative functions for nations. Accordingly, although nations exist in the world as crucial actors, they are "disaggregated" and relate to other nations through channels that represent some element or portion of their sovereignty, including the regulation of specific professions and occupations. Through the lens of disaggregated rather than unitary states, policymakers and others can view a changed international political system, and through these government official networks, parts of unitary and federal governments will make and enforce global rules.[54] Within the United States, counterpart government officials have long been connected horizontally across states through nonprofits that they have controlled to assist specific state regulatory agencies in performing their missions, but horizontal government networks now link counterpart national officials (and such state federations) across national borders. Correspondingly, there are vertical government networks linking national and state governmental officials with their supranational counterparts.[55] Horizontal and vertical IGOs and NGOs are truly features of the reformed international regulatory scheme, and they represent "governance" in professional regulation,[56] and the new description of the revised public sector.[57]

For individuals, governments, and nonprofit regulators of occupations, approaches to professional regulation include: (1) a unilateral approach — where a governmental or authoritative body recognizes credentials; (2) a bilateral approach — where two governmental or authoritative bodies recognize the credentials of the other; and (3) a multilateral approach — where several governmental or authoritative bodies mutually recognize credentials.[58] The unilateral approach has been rendered inappropriate or unworkable in many situations because of the explosion in the global economy, in favor of a reciprocal form of recognition.[59] The multilateral approach has received the most attention. For example, professional associations in Europe have used group registers to recognize qualifications like "European Biologist," "European Geologist," and "European Chemist."[60] The formation of the EU itself has fostered creation of federations of national professional associations within Europe, and those federation functions have included support for lobbying in Brussels as well as for country-specific national professional associations.[61] The establishment of NAFTA and GATS under WTO with oversight to foster professional regulatory changes, the expansion of ISO standards into occupational regulation, and the formation of singular international professional federations and NGOs all illustrate this multilateral approach. A description of six particular professions, which follows in this chapter, unfolds the applicability of each of these unilateral, bilateral, and multilateral approaches to regulation and governance. But before undertaking a U.S. domestic and vertical description of these six fields, however, it is helpful to understand the roles and functions of several U.S.-based organizations, whose memberships horizontally cut across many professions and occupations, but which have responded to global developments with vertical adjustments. They are presented in the order of their chronological creation.

The Council on Licensure, Enforcement and Regulation (CLEAR), an affiliate of the Council of State Governments, was organized more than 25 years ago with a membership consisting of not only government regulators responsible for licensure, certification, or registration processes of credentialing, but also members that included the professions and occupations regulated by government. Within its membership are those engaged in the regulation of occupations as diverse as accountancy, architecture, engineering, investment advising, law, and nursing. CLEAR's focus has been on the common interests in government regulation; it actually operates a certification program for government investigators and inspectors with a consumer protection thrust. Although originally an organization with a U.S. focus, its membership has come to embrace substantial numbers of Canadian organizations and other individuals. Global trends have encouraged CLEAR in recent years to describe itself as an international resource for professional regulation stakeholders. Recent annual meetings have increasingly featured participants and research drawn from nations on other continents. Moreover, CLEAR has a London office, and an expressed interest in closer ties with the regulatory communities in Europe and Australasia.

In contrast with CLEAR's focus on government credentialing and regulation, the National Organization for Competency Assurance (NOCA) has concentrated more on non-governmental credentialing, particularly certifying bodies. NOCA is an Internal Revenue Code 501(c)(3) membership body that formerly had a U.S. focus but has changed due to international expansion (NOCA, 2004), such that member assistance often involves credentialing efforts globally.[62] NCCA is an administratively independent entity that is the accrediting body for NOCA; in contrast with NOCA, it has no members. Originally, NCCA was the National Commission for Health Certifying Agencies (NCHCA) that in 1977 developed standards of excellence for voluntary certification cooperatively with the federal government.[63] A certifying program may be accredited if its standards meet or exceed the NCCA accreditation standards, and certification programs so accredited may display the NCCA seal in their literature. NCCA places strong reliance upon a "job analysis" delineating the tasks, criticality, and functions performed by professionals, who accurately demonstrate the skills and knowledge (core body of knowledge) necessary to perform in the particular discipline. A keen or robust emphasis during the NCCA review of a certification program is placed upon the reliability and validity of the testing elements, to be sure that they are consistent with widely accepted legal and psychometric requirements.[64]

The Center for Quality Assurance in International Education (CQAIE) is a collaborative endeavor of the higher education and the competency assurance communities. Physically located with other higher education organizations in Washington, D.C., it also promotes the globalization of professions, holding periodic conferences on issues dealing with the effects of NAFTA and other trade agreements on education and the professions.

The International Accreditation Forum, Inc. (IAF) was formed in 2001 as a world association of Conformity Assessment Accreditation Bodies. Unlike the other bodies above, its roots are international. The IAF's principal function is to develop a single worldwide program of conformity assessment that reduces the risks of businesses and customers by assuring them their certifications may be relied upon. It does this through accreditation, assuring the competency and impartiality of the body accredited, with consequential benefits to governments and consumers through regular surveillance that certification bodies are independent and competent.

The work of U.S.-based nonprofit organizations, such as CLEAR, NOCA, NCCA, CQAIE, and the internationally based IAF, often helps to transmit ideas through policy diffusion across occupations and professions. They are joined by some silo-like NGOs that characterize professions by spreading ideas and concepts vertically within their own fields. Individuals involved in these entities sometimes have used a lexicon including "global licensure," "global certification," and "global accreditation," perhaps inaccurately. In discussing the prospect of "global licensure" the director of the New Mexico Board of Examiners for Architects identified the possibilities of an international entity to determine policy issues and authenticate credentials, certification through professional associations, administration through a body like the United Nations, a compact or international governmental agreement, or having professionals in different states or nations create an umbrella global certification agency that might help keep costs and the supporting credentialing infrastructure at reasonable levels for participating local bodies.[65] In addition to IGO models represented by the WTO and the individual freestanding professional bodies covering individual professions spanning many nations, there are existing NGOs who are adapting themselves to the need for transnational regulation of occupations, including the ISO.

Globalization has represented a potentially expanding market for credentials offered both inside and outside the United States. For United States and other national professional certification programs desiring to extend their efforts beyond their own boundaries, there appear four possible models: (1) simply offering the certification outside the nation with the understanding that is a certification based in a specific nation; (2) modify the certification for use within another country; (3) creating an international credential; and (4) creating an international federation of related credentialing bodies. These are all examples for global certification, but it may be necessary to understand the trademark legal effects of these alternatives.[66]

Transformation in Several Specific Professions

Changes underway in six professional fields serve to illustrate the breadth and scope of the effect of globalization upon governmental and voluntary regulation schemes in the United States and elsewhere.

Accountancy

In the United States each of the 50 states has a state board of accountancy that establishes standards for professional competency and required educational quality to be licensed to practice accountancy in that state as a Certified Public Accountant (CPA). Although licensure requirements vary somewhat among states, most have education, examination, and experience requirements, and some have ethics requirements. Historically, licensure in one state has not permitted a CPA to practice in another state. The National Association of State Boards of Accountancy (NASBA), a nonprofit entity representing the 54 state and territorial boards, assists its members in performing their regulatory functions. For example, NASBA's National Registry of Continuing Professional Education Sponsors lists organizations that provide high-quality continuing education in accordance with nationally recognized standards, and its Quality Assurance Service recognizes organizations that provide self-study courses of the required caliber.

Educational accreditation for accountancy is performed by the Association to Advance Collegiate Schools of Business (AACSB International), a not-for-profit corporation of approximately 900 members representing colleges, universities, and business and professional organizations. Founded in 1916, AACSB began its accreditation function with the adoption of the first standards in 1919. Additional standards for programs in accountancy were adopted in 1980, and revised sets of standards that are relevant and applicable to all business programs globally and which support and encourage excellence in management education worldwide were adopted in 2003.

The Uniform Certified Public Accountant Examination is designed to assess the knowledge and skills that entry-level CPAs need to practice public accountancy. This licensure test has been developed by the American Institute of Certified Public Accountants (AICPA), a nonprofit membership association, and is administered only in the United States. NASBA offers the International Uniform CPA Qualification Examination (IQEX) to qualifying candidates, which exists to facilitate the U.S. CPA qualification process for accounting professionals from other countries whose professional bodies have entered into mutual recognition agreements (MRAs) with the AICPA and NASBA. Such agreements are in effect only with the Canadian Institute of Chartered Accountants (CICA), the Institute of Chartered Accountants in Australia (ICAA), CPA Australia, and the Instituto Mexicano De Contadores Publicos (IMCP), but additional MRAs with others are anticipated in future.

Accounting is one of the most globalized professions, representing the need for accuracy, materiality, and timeliness in financial and performance information and measures. There is keen interest in international standard-setting for accounting; developing nations, for instance, must have an accounting system capable of measuring enterprise performance, and credit agencies and banks require harmonized standards across borders.[67] Measured by revenues, the "Big Four" firms — PricewaterhouseCoopers, Deloitte Touche Tohmatsu, and Ernst & Young all headquartered in New York, and KPMG headquartered in Amsterdam — dominate this field. Each of them has thousands of partners, tens of thousands of employees, offices around the world, and annual revenues greater than $10 billion. Big four revenues alone are estimated to be one third of all global accounting services revenues; these firms audit the majority of publicly listed companies in developed nations (78 percent in the United States, 80 percent in Japan and Italy, 90 percent in the Netherlands, and 97 percent in the United Kingdom), and they have a national presence in all but 43 countries. The spread of accounting firms around the globe initially occurred as they followed their clients who moved outside their home countries, but their continuing expansion abroad is often based upon non-equity (i.e., licensing) forms of investment because of national regulatory constraints, such as the right of national practice only being granted to national firms that have majority ownership and management control. These barriers have often resulted in expansion of operations by adding members to a network of firms which are usually separate legally, and locally owned and managed as partnerships.[68]

To advance the profession of accountancy internationally, the International Federation of Accountants was formed in 1977, representing 128 member bodies in 91 countries and more than two million professional accountants. A federation of national professional bodies, it has produced a set of international standards on auditing, ethics, education, financial and management accounting, and the public sector. Even earlier in 1973 the International Accounting Standards Committee was formed to work for harmonization in financial reporting.[69]

Under NAFTA, the countries of Canada, Mexico, and the United States agreed to eliminate all residency requirements for certification to practice accountancy. National governments upon signing the treaty allowed a two-year period for provincial and state governments to file reservations, and Annex 1205.5 of the agreement encouraged the relevant regulatory bodies in countries to develop mutually acceptable standards and criteria for licensing and certification.[70] The Certified General Accountants (CGA) of Canada and the Canadian Institute of Chartered Accountants in Canada (CICA), and in the United States both the NASBA and the AICPA, proceeded to establish qualification appraisal boards to review the standards for accounting credentialing in other nations, thus facilitating reciprocity agreements with professional accounting bodies in other countries.[71] Such initiatives in Canada and the United States were undertaken because in both nations accountancy is regulated at the provincial or state level. In Canada there are three national accounting organizations — CGA, CICA, and the Management Accountants of Canada — and in Mexico the profession is similarly segmented; but the Mexican government created a Committee for the International Practice of Accountancy that is representative of all the accounting organizations in that country.[72]

Beyond North American developments, the Working Party on Professional Services (WPPS), a former committee of the WTO, had focused on MRAs and on legally binding rules and principles for regulation of the accountancy profession. The OECD conducted a study of four professions including accounting, reviewing licensing and regulatory measures in its member countries; its work product was shared with the WPPS.[73] WPPS developed guidelines for the negotiation of MRAs in accounting in 1997 and disciplines for regulation of the accounting profession in 1998, both of which have been adopted by the WTO.[74] The Working Party on Domestic Regulation (WPDR), successor of the WPPS, is considering whether to establish similar disciplines for additional professions.[75]

Following the approval of NAFTA and the establishment of the WTO and its WPPS, NASBA and AICPA jointly developed a Uniform Accountancy Act (UAA) in 1998 in large measure because of the globalization of business, demographic shifts in the profession, and legal challenges to the regulatory system in place at the time.[76] UAA represented model legislation that the groups sought to have enacted by each of the 50 states, and excellent progress in state adoption of this model legislation has occurred. UAA contains the concept of "substantial equivalency" to provide greater ease of mobility across state lines, both in-person and electronically. Thus, a CPA who has a license in good standing from one state that follows the UAA criteria would be qualified to practice in another state that subscribes to the UAA as well. If a CPA moves to another state and wishes to practice there or be employed there, he or she is required to obtain a reciprocal license. NASBA established a National Qualification Appraisal Service (NQAS) to help both state boards and individual CPAs to make determinations of "substantial equivalency." There is symmetry between NASBA's work through NQAS in determining whether a state's licensure requirements are substantially equivalent under the UAA and the concept of international reciprocity under the International Qualifications Appraisal Board (IQAB) established by NASBA and the AICPA.[77]

As a result of NAFTA and GATS agreements, and the broader forces of globalization affecting the interests of accountants, their national and international organizations, the interests of multinational corporations and large accounting firms, and the interests of state boards of accountancy, the status of state regulation of accountancy is more uniform and reciprocal, and mutual recognition of accounting credentials and those who hold them is occurring, both between U.S. states and among nations. The profession of accountancy has fostered support networks where domestic and international IGOs and NGOs are involved in regulating, coordinating, and managing activities associated with accountancy credentialing.

Architecture

All 50 states require individuals to be licensed (although the term used is "registered") before they may call themselves architects or contract to provide architectural services. Licensure requirements usually include a professional degree in architecture, a period of practical training or internship, and passage of the Architect Registration Examination. Typically, the state regulatory authority is vested in a state board of architecture comprised of architects and others. Without registration issued by the state board, one may not engage in the practice of architecture nor use the title "architect" within a state. State boards may discipline architects whose practice does not meet minimum standards of professional conduct, and they typically have continuing professional development requirements as well. The National Architectural Accrediting Board (NAAB) is the agency authorized to accredit professional degree programs in architecture, and most state registration boards in the United States require any applicant for licensure to have graduated from a NAAB-accredited program.[78]

As early as 1920, it became evident to state architectural boards that architects conducted their practice in several states and therefore needed to obtain registration from multiple states. The nonprofit National Council of Architectural Registration Boards (NCARB) was formed as a federation of all state boards that regulate the practice of architecture. The national certification developed by NCARB permits individual architects to more easily respond to opportunities for business in other states; it simplifies and facilitates the registration process because every state board has recognized the NCARB certifying process as adequately rigorous. The NCARB develops the Architect Registration Examination as the written test used by all states, offers "monograph quizzes" online as evidence of successful completion of continuing education requirements, and also develops "Legislative Guidelines and Model Law" to assist state legislatures and member state boards to promote a uniform regulatory framework within states.[79] Either as a part of a sunset review process or a general performance review process, boards that license or register architects have been proposed for abolition from time to time; a recent example came from the August 2004 California Performance Review titled "Government for the People for a Change" that recommended the architects board be eliminated while retaining regulatory functions in a proposed new Department of Commerce and Consumer Protection.

The International Union of Architects (UIA) was founded in 1948 as a federation of national organizations. In 1999 its assembly unanimously approved the UIA Accord on Recommended International Standards of Professionalism in Architectural Practice and nine other policy guidelines, as global standards; China and the United States served as the joint secretariat for the UIA Professional Practice Program.[80] These standards were greatly influenced by GATS and the WTO's Council for Trade in Services. The UIA sees itself as a relevant international organization whose standards should be taken into account by the Council in judging conformity to GATS, including facilitating the portability of professional credentials across borders. It has published specific procedures on reciprocity.[81]

Architecture has been characterized as a profession without boundaries for decades. The American Institute of Architects (AIA) is the U.S. professional membership organization, and has as members approximately half of all registered architects, many of whom are registered in multiple states. Through "reciprocity" available via the NCARB certification process, a registered architect in one state can apply for registration in another jurisdiction by having the NCARB process documentation or by presenting documentation that he or she meets that jurisdiction's registration requirements. Agreements like NAFTA and GATS have promoted this domestic reciprocity concept to an international level. By 1999, NCARB certificate holders could practice in Canada and Canadian architects could similarly practice in the United States through the establishment of an inter-recognition agreement. When the requirements of other nations have both some similar and dissimilar aspects, the NCARB has used bilateral accords where architects from other nations are granted the opportunity to practice in the United States by affiliation with a U.S. architect.[82] In 2002, the Architects Accreditation Council of Australia (AACA), an organization that represents eight state and territorial architects' registration boards, and NCARB announced a Protocol for Practice that allows architects in Australia and the United States holding a NCARB certificate to practice in one another's country in association with a licensed architect. Globalization has encouraged the AACA to develop cooperative agreements with other countries, and the NCARB to ratify similar protocols for practice with the Czech Republic and New Zealand, an MRA and Bilateral Accord with China, and a full MRA with Canada. AIA and NCARB together have signed a Memorandum of Intent and Understanding with the national registration authorities of Canada and Mexico.

Since 2002, several architectural organizations of the United States and European Union have been engaged in discussions to establish mutual recognition. NCARB, AIA, and the Architects' Council of Europe (ACE) are concluding negotiations for such an MRA. This arrangement is expected to be implemented by regulatory jurisdictions in Europe and the United States in 2005, and make it easier for both United States and European architects to provide services in each other's market. It should enable an architect, who is duly licensed in a U.S. jurisdiction, to be recognized as an architect in any EU member state, and any architect meeting the requirements of EU Directive 85/384/EEC in any member state of the European Union may similarly be recognized as an architect within the United States based on the approval actions of individual state boards of architecture.

The profession of architecture has undergone significant changes because of globalization. Professional regulation recognized the need for mobility among the states in United States early, but recent international developments have made possible greater recognition of credentialing among nations, including but not limited to licensure. The functions of NCARB in providing architect certification acceptable to all states has been central to progress fostered through both IGOs and NGOs.

Engineering

The engineering profession is less self-regulated and is more closely associated with corporations than are other professions.[83] Beginning engineering graduates usually work under the supervision of experienced engineers and may receive training. While acquiring knowledge and experience, engineers may be assigned increasingly difficult projects with greater independence and decision making. All states require licensure for engineers offering services directly to the public (professional engineering), but even engineers who will not prepare, sign, and submit engineering plans to a public authority for approval, or provide services to private clients requiring licensure, may still seek that enhanced status. Engineers so licensed, called Professional Engineers (PEs), include civil, electrical, mechanical, chemical, and other engineers. Generally licensing requires a degree from an accredited engineering program, four years of relevant work experience, and successful completion of a competency examination. Recent graduates can start the licensing process by taking the examination in two stages. The initial fundamentals examination can be taken upon graduation, and individuals who pass are called Engineers in Training (EIT) or Engineer Interns (EI). After acquiring suitable work experience, EITs can take the second examination. Many states also impose post-licensure continuing education requirements, and most states recognize licensure from sister states provided the manner in which the initial license was obtained meets or exceeds their own licensure requirements.

State licensing boards for PEs perform the regulatory functions of licensure and relicensure, and possess investigative and disciplinary powers. The National Council of Examiners for Engineering and Surveying (NCEES) is the nonprofit organization of state licensing boards that assists its members in performing these very activities. It encourages the elimination of state-specific engineering examinations, for example, in favor of a national one that will promote comity,[84] develops and scores the licensure examinations for engineering, offers a model Engineering Practice Act for state legislatures to consider, maintains a records program service for professionals that facilitates the process of licensure in multiple states, and coordinates with international organizations to promote licensure of all engineers. In the United States the title engineer can be used by individuals not licensed as PEs; less than 20 percent of engineering graduates become licensed and some educators, engineering firms, and policymakers are thought indifferent to the idea of licensure.[85] In 2003 NCEES created a separate entity to administer the engineering examinations called Engineering and Land Surveying Examination Services (ELSES); ELSES, LLC is a limited liability company managed by NCEES. Similar to the California recommendations regarding the board regulating architects, the California

Performance Review in August 2004 also recommended abolition of the California Board of Registration for Professional Engineers and Land Surveyors with those functions to be performed by a new Department of Commerce and Consumer Affairs.

The engineering profession has been profoundly impacted by globalization, resulting in calls for greater mobility.[86] Realization of the effect of globalization upon the practice of engineering resulted in a report by the American Society of Mechanical Engineers in 1999 explaining factors such as licensing requirements, treaties, trade agreements, as well as codes and standards that may exist to restrict or enhance the cross-border flow of engineering services.[87] Mechanical engineers are expected to adapt and support the efforts of their employers to achieve competitive advantage in a global market.[88] Globalization is causing a basic shift in the location of research, design, and development in the electrical engineering profession; essentially the field follows the market. Where once multinational companies may have looked to engineers from the United States or Europe to design-at-a-distance, they now look to native engineers in China, India, and other parts of Asia as they seek to increase their manufacturing and marketing presence there.[89] Engineering transnational corporations (TNCs) often provide training to their employees, and the profession of engineering is among the services identified as part of the shift toward services in the World Investment Report.[90] The World Federation of Engineering Organizations (WFEO) has noted that engineering has been an international profession for at least a century.[91] WFEO itself was formed in 1968, with the support of the United Nations Educational, Scientific and Cultural Organization (UNESCO), to advance the engineering profession worldwide, working with governments and business entities. This Paris-based NGO does concern itself with harmonizing global standards in engineering and facilitating global mobility for engineers. Its U.S. member is the American Association of Engineering Societies (AAES).

Accreditation of U.S. college and university programs in engineering is the responsibility of the Accreditation Board for Engineering and Technology (ABET), a federation of 30 U.S. professional and technical societies representing many fields that has provided higher education quality assurance for 70 years. Beyond accrediting more than 2500 programs at over 500 colleges and universities, it also seeks to promote mobility of technical professionals through activities such as the development of mutual recognition of systems of accreditation, the determination of substantial equivalency of programs, and the evaluation of educational credentials. In 1989 ABET and similar accreditation bodies in Australia, Canada, Ireland, Hong Kong, New Zealand, South Africa, and the United Kingdom signed the Washington Accord, establishing that graduates of engineering education programs accredited by any of them in their nations are prepared to practice engineering at the entry level. Although the licensing or registration of professional engineers is not directly covered by this Washington Accord, the signatory accrediting bodies agreed to work to assure that regulatory entities for engineers accept the substantial equivalency of academic programs they accredit. ABET, for example, offers a service of assessment of credentials, Engineering Credentials Evaluation International (ECEI), for those educated outside the United States that is useful to state licensing boards. Japan was added as a provisional member in 2001, and in 2003, provisional membership status was conferred by the signatory countries of the Washington Accord upon accreditation agencies in Germany, Malaysia, and Singapore. Additional national organizations are expected to be added in the future, and provisional membership of these bodies may eventually result in full signatory status.

In 1989, three U.S. organizations — ABET, NCEES, and the National Society of Professional Engineers (NSPE), a professional association of credentialed engineers — established the United States Council for International Engineering Practice (USCIEP) to negotiate on behalf of the three organizations to identify constraints to practice, recommend procedures to eliminate any artificial constraints, and promote cross-border practice. After the approval of NAFTA, which included negotiation with counterparts in Canada and Mexico to develop a Mutual Recognition Document (MRD) for engineering services, the relevant professional bodies of Canada, Mexico, and the United States signed an MRD on June 5, 1995. By 1998, it seemed ready to be implemented in all jurisdictions in Canada and Mexico, but only Texas among the states had announced its intention to implement the agreement.[92] However, just as in the case of NAFTA, there was much debate and controversy involved in the signing of the MRD; so the signing of this MRD did not close debate and controversy within USCIEP over the nationally normed examinations given by the state boards in the U.S. or over the details of the temporary licensure provisions within the MRD. As a result, USCIEP concluded to seek a negotiated resolution of these differences with its counterpart organizations in Canada and Mexico.[93] Subsequently, USCIEP expressed its concern with the document developed by Canada, Mexico, and the Texas Board of Professional Engineers in September 2002 to implement the NAFTA MRD procedures for temporary licensure of those wishing to practice in one another's jurisdictions because it seemed inconsistent with the model law supported by U.S. engineering licensing boards across the United States.[94] The sticking point is the licensure examination required by the states for PE; similar examinations are not required in Canada and Mexico for licensure. In recognition that a psychometrically sound competency examination for licensure is an important differentiator between engineers who are PE licensed and those who are not, state boards are not yet ready to accept through mutual recognition those not yet demonstrating that qualification needed to protect the health and safety of the public.

More recently USCIEP and two other international organizations — the Asia–Pacific Economic Cooperation (APEC) Engineer Coordinating Committee and the Engineers Mobility Forum (EMF) — have sought to improve professional mobility through international decentralized registries that foster opportunities for engineers to work on international projects. EMF was a former subcommittee of the Washington Accord signatories, but became an independent entity in 1997 with participating countries — Australia, Canada, Hong Kong, Ireland, Japan, Korea, Malaysia, New Zealand, South Africa, United Kingdom, and the United States. The APEC Engineer Register was launched in 2000 by professional bodies and regulatory authorities to help remove barriers to professional mobility in Australia, Canada, Hong Kong, Japan, Korea, Malaysia, and New Zealand; eligible individuals from Indonesia and the United States have since been added. The European Engineering Federation (FEANI) has similarly developed a register of "European Engineers."[95] And in South America there is continuing work toward common standards in engineering through MERCOSUR (the Market of the South) involving Argentina, Brazil, Paraguay, and Uruguay.[96]

Like the professions of accountancy and architecture, engineering has clearly been affected by globalization. Some elements of the process for U.S. state licensure have become simplified and easier, but the requirement of passing the licensure examination, an important distinction between being an engineer and a PE, has not been fundamentally modified. Accordingly, progress on mutual recognition or reciprocity under NAFTA and GATS has occurred more slowly for engineering because state licensure in the United States does require passage of a competency examination that other nations do not administer. On the other hand, mutual recognition dealing with the education of engineers and accreditation is progressing.

Financial Planning

Financial planning involves the process of determining whether and how an individual can meet life goals through proper management of financial resources. This holistic approach to personal finance developed from the limitations and inadequacies of U.S. segmented advisors in the fields of insurance (life, health, property, and casualty), investments (securities and real estate), taxation, employee benefits, and estate planning. From the late 1960s onward individual clients sought comprehensive advice from practitioners to deal with the financial implications of greater longevity, increased career mobility involving more than one employer, the expansion in employer use of defined-benefit — 401(k) and 403(b) plans — that shift the risk of investments to individuals in lieu of the employer bearing such risk under traditional defined-benefit or pension plans, the availability and use of new individual retirement accounts (IRAs), more complexity in federal and state tax laws, the increased likelihood of second marriages and stepchildren, and the challenging financial situations of individuals moving from state to state or nation to nation or holding property or other investments outside their domicile. Some practitioners in specific fields like investments and securities, insurance, employee benefits, taxation, and estate planning began to call themselves financial planners or advisors to denote the greater scope of their interest in serving clients, but there was not always a corresponding level competence in handling topics and client issues outside of their particular training. These and related concerns caused the Consumer Federation of America (CFA) and the American Association of Retired Persons (AARP) to raise questions, and in 1988 the U.S. House Committee on Energy and Commerce, Subcommittee on Telecommunications and Finance to hold hearings and receive a report from the staff of the U.S. Securities and Exchange Commission.[97] Some college graduates actually sought to begin their careers as broad-based financial planners, but during this period the several government regulatory schemes — both federal and state — involving investment advice, securities, insurance, accountancy, and law were bound by statutory limitations and the unwillingness of the regulated occupations to change those frameworks if doing so might advantage competitors.

Individuals interested in offering personal financial planning services were drawn to educational programs that provided them broader but necessary educational preparation for the field of financial planning, and a nonprofit regulatory framework developed in the United States to fill the void left by numerous silo-like government regulatory schemes for specific occupations. In the United States there are more than 300 educational programs offered through nearly 200 colleges and universities registered with the Certified Financial Planner Board of Standards, Inc. (CFP Board), an IRC 501(c)(3) nonprofit organization, as covering the more than 100 financial planning topics that several financial planner job analysis studies have indicated as necessary for practice. The CFP Board, created in 1985, does not accredit educational programs, but its functions are analogous to accrediting agencies. The certification program offered by the CFP Board, however, has been accredited by the NCCA. Successful completion of an approved educational program satisfies the educational requirement and allows an individual to take the two-day certification examination offered nationally and internationally several times a year. Passage of this competency test, demonstration of experience, and completion of an ethics declaration and agreement entitles the applicant to use the certification marks — Certified Financial Planner® and CFP®. Continuing certification requires adherence to the ethical code, practice standards, and continuing education. Oversight and administration of both pre- and post-certification processes, including an ethics and standards enforcement disciplinary process to protect the public, is performed by the professional regulatory organization for its 50,000 CFP certificants (the CFP Board does not have members) in the United States. Membership associations for financial planners in the United States include the Financial Planning Association, the National Association of Personal Financial Advisors, the Society of Financial Service Professionals, and the American Institute of Certified Public Accountants' Personal Financial Planning Membership Section.

In addition to the nonprofit regulatory framework provided by the CFP Board for those financial planners who are certified, financial planners are regulated by governments. Specific activities performed by financial planners — such as investment advice or the sale of securities or insurance — are overseen by state and federal agencies. These include state securities agencies regulating individuals as investment adviser representatives and securities salespersons, and state insurance departments regulating individuals as insurance agents, brokers, or consultants (for life, health, property, and casualty insurance purposes). Practitioners may also be regulated as attorneys or accountants if they are so licensed by states. The vast majority of financial planners, whether certified or not, fall under both state securities and state insurance regulatory schemes.[98] Individuals with the certification, and those holding similar *bona fide* credentials from other bodies such as the AICPA and the American College, have found some governmental licensure processes easier. For example, state insurance departments often exempt such individuals from some further pre-licensing examinations, and state securities agencies have exempted them from Uniform Investment Adviser Examinations 65 and 66.

The North American Securities Administrators Association (NASAA) was organized in 1919 and consists of government securities administrators of the 50 states, the District of Columbia, Puerto Rico, Canada, and Mexico. It has worked closely with the National Conference of Commissioners on Uniform State Laws (NCCUSL) to develop model laws, including the Uniform Securities Act, and to have that act adopted by state legislatures. Under the federal 1996 National Securities Markets Improvement Act (NSMIA) the U.S. Securities and Exchange Commission (SEC) registers investment adviser firms with $25 million or more in assets under management, and states register investment adviser companies or firms with under $25 million in assets under management. States also license individuals who provide investment advice regarding buying and selling securities for a fee separate from other services; they are called investment adviser representatives and include financial planners offering investment advice to clients. For many years state securities agencies did not have competency examinations for individuals providing investment advice to consumers[99]; but following passage of NSMIA, the states were the only registering authority for about two thirds of the firms as well as all investment adviser representatives, so in 1997 NASAA developed a memorandum of understanding that supported competency examination development.[100] The SEC and NASAA have jointly developed the Investment Adviser Registration Depository (IARD) program, built and operated by the National Association of Securities Dealers, Inc. (NASD). In 2002, NASAA indicated that IARD would enable financial planners and other investment advisers to become licensed with regulators online, saving both time and money. Two years earlier, NASAA's president had testified before the U.S. Senate Banking Committee that because of globalization, new electronic technologies and increasing numbers of consumer investors, regulators at all levels of government need to "take a fresh look at what they do, how they do it and its impact on industry and consumers."[101] He also noted that the National Governors' Association and the National Association of Insurance Commissioners (NAIC) had adopted similar statements because of the changing role of government in the global economy.

NAIC was formed in 1871 to coordinate regulation of multistate insurers. The oldest state officials' organization, the NAIC also serves as an accrediting body for its state agency members. The federal 1945 McCarran–Ferguson Act was enacted to allow states to continue to regulate the insurance business after the U.S. Supreme Court, in *U.S. South-Eastern Underwriters Association* (overturning an 1869 decision in *Paul vs. Virginia*) declared insurance to be interstate commerce within the authority of Congress to regulate; under McCarran–Ferguson insurance is exempt from some federal antitrust statutes to the extent that it is regulated by the states. In recognition of this act, yet being sensitive to the plight of consumers and insurers but particularly to insurance agents, brokers, and consultants who were having significant difficulty obtaining state licensure efficiently from multiple state insurance departments, Congress enacted and President Clinton signed the Financial Services Modernization Act of 1999, the Gramm–Leach–Bliley Act (GLBA). As the most sweeping federal legislation to affect the state-regulated insurance industry since the McCarran–Ferguson Act, GLBA required that unless states made their insurance licensure laws both substantially uniform and fully reciprocal within three years, a National Association of Registered Agents and Brokers (NARAB), a quasi-independent organization to be established by the federal government, would be created to govern the licensure of insurance agents, brokers, and consultants in all states. The National Conference of Insurance Legislators (NCOIL) and the National Conference of State Legislatures (NCSL) worked with NAIC and others to pass model legislation known as the Producer Licensing Model Act (PLMA) and forestall federal preemption. By August 2004, 49 states had passed the PLMA, 41 states had been certified by NAIC as meeting GLBA requirements for licensure reciprocity, 49 states were using the same application form for licensure (Uniform Non-Resident Application), and 30 states were processing non-resident applications electronically through the National Insurance Producer Registry (NIPR), a nonprofit affiliate of the NAIC incorporated in 1996 to make uniform the insurance producer licensing process for the benefit of regulators, insurers, producers, and consumers. NIPR is a comprehensive source of licensing, demographic appointment, and market conduct data for over 3.8 million producers. The federal threat to state regulation of insurance through NARAB had caused state legislators and others to respond to the need for efficiency, uniformity, and reciprocity to help maintain a U.S. competitive edge in the increasingly global economy.[102] In a corresponding effort to preserve states' authority to regulate the insurance market, NAIC, NCSL, NCOIL, and the insurance industry have created an Interstate Insurance Product Regulation Compact (IIPRC) to allow insurers to market their products nationally more quickly and efficiently to be responsive to the industry and beneficial to the consumers. This is a national multistate public authority to receive, review, and quickly make regulatory decisions on insurance product filings consistent with national uniform standards created by the Compact's member states.[103]

Global connections among federal and state security regulators and their counterparts in other nations largely occur within the International Organization of Securities Commissioners (IOSCO) created in 1984. Similar connections between state insurance regulators and their counterparts from other countries largely occur through the International Association of Insurance Supervisors (IAIS) created in the 1990s. Both of these IGOs have been termed transgovernmental networks by Slaughter, but there are also corresponding networks for financial planning NGOs as well.

Interest in personal financial planning within other nations was spawned by similar internal forces as described above for the United States. Moreover, the increasing propensity of clients to have personal investments, business dealings, and employment with persons and organizations in other nations, which include more travel and communications for both clients and financial planners, fostered increasingly frequent interchanges among practitioners in the financial planning field. An international assembly of financial planning regulatory bodies, the International CFP Council, was formed as an advisory and subsidiary body of the CFP Board by both the Australian financial planning organization and the CFP Board in 1990. Subsequently, members from Asia, Africa, Europe, and North and South America that qualified were added. In October 2004, the International CFP Council became the independent Financial Planning Standards Board; it handles accreditation of programs for all national financial planning organizations outside the United States. These include accrediting programs for certification of individuals in Australia, Austria, Brazil, Canada, Chinese Taipei, France, Germany, Hong Kong, India, Japan, Malaysia, New Zealand, Republic of Korea, Singapore, South Africa, Switzerland, and the United Kingdom, as well as the rules for the use of certification marks across borders covering nearly 50,000 certificants outside the United States based upon common standards.

In addition to the international network of individuals and national organizations represented within the Financial Planning Standards Board associated with certification marks — Certified Financial Planner® and CFP® — in different nations, this network of groups and individuals has also chosen to work through the ISO and national affiliate organizations associated with ISO, including the American National Standards Institute (ANSI) in the United States. ISO Technical Committee 222, Personal Financial Planning, has been charged with standardization in the field of personal financial planning, including the certification of practitioners and the processes they use in working with clients.[104] ANSI serves as secretariat for TC 222 and has designated the CFP Board to serve as its agent. Since 2000 its decision to establish this financial planning technical committee, the ISO has issued in 2003 an international standard dealing with conformity assessment (assurance that services measure up to the particular relevant standard), covering the general requirements for bodies operating programs for the certification of individuals (ISO/IEC 17024). This ISO standard has spawned affiliate activities in accreditation of certification programs based upon ISO/IEC 17024; ANSI was the first national body to do so in March 2003, announcing that its efforts would protect the integrity of individual certification programs, and promote consumer and public confidence.[105]

In the field of personal financial planning the federal–state government division of responsibilities has not always been clear and has been much less cooperative. In recent years more clarity and coordination have developed because of federal legislation for both insurance and the giving of investment advice. Still, the U.S. financial planning occupation has been adapted to preexisting government regulation of some subdisciplines with broader voluntary nonprofit regulation, partly because the existing regulatory systems had strong "iron triangle" reinforcement that was not receptive to much change. Moreover, global interest in the field of personal financial planning and the corresponding international nonprofit network of standards-setting and professional associations within many nations grew rapidly along side of the vertical but narrower government regulatory scheme for insurance and securities regulation represented by IAIS and IOSCO. These IGO and NGO combinations have spawned a global governance system that is more complicated than in other professions, and is still evolving. For personal financial planning such developments would have occurred even without specific NAFTA and GATS provisions, but globalization has fostered greater reliance upon nonprofit certification.

Law

Attorneys, counselors at law, or lawyers are individuals who have been authorized by the highest state court in a specific U.S. jurisdiction to use such titles and to practice law. Federal courts and federal agencies set their own standards for lawyers litigating or appearing in proceedings before them.[106] Prelicensing requirements for lawyers generally include education represented by a law degree, and the passing of a bar examination. Law schools are accredited by the American Bar Association's Council on Legal Education and Admission to the Bar; the American Bar Association (ABA) is a membership organization representing about half of all U.S. practicing attorneys. The bar examination for a state usually consists of a Multistate Bar Examination and the Multistate Professional Responsibility Examination, prepared by the National Conference of Bar Examiners (NCBE), a nonprofit 501(c)(3) corporation formed in 1931 to develop, maintain, and apply uniform standards of education and character and to test for eligibility to practice law. Most states also have an essay portion to supplement these bar examinations, and these singularly state-specific exams are prepared by the individual state bar examiners. Postlicensing requirements for lawyers include continuing education and adherence to ethical codes.

The International Bar Association (IBA) was founded in 1947 by representatives of 34 bar associations inspired by the vision of the United Nations. In 1970, individual lawyers were able to join IBA, and in that same year the Section on Business Law was formed. Membership has grown to nearly 200 bar associations and over 16,000 individual lawyers, who promote the exchange of information and the practice of law globally, seek to preserve the independence of the profession and the judiciary and support human rights of interest to lawyers worldwide.

There have been impediments to the licensing of foreign lawyers in the 50 states for decades, even beyond the challenges faced by attorneys licensed in one state not being able to practice in other states; it is not an easy process except where specific reciprocity treatment is available.[107] EU has less limitations for mobility among lawyers in specific EU countries than does the United States for mobility from state to state. Nonetheless, globalization of legal services continues. In 1999 legal services were the third largest export in the business services sector, and during the 1990s the growth of U.S. legal services was about 10 percent annually, during which time the U.S. exported more in legal services than it imported.[108] The U.S., U.K., and Australian law firms dominate international legal services as they were the only ones listed in the top 20 legal service TNCs in 2002.[109] Legal fields covered by such firms include antitrust and trade, banking and finance, intellectual property, real estate, environment, and tourism. Services provided to clients are dominated by large TNC clients with the lawyering provided heavily dependent upon host-country specific skills. This is because the legal code under which these firms operate is unique, with a country's values, culture, and beliefs superimposed. Legal services TNCs typically organize their activities in the form of partnerships with host-nation firms that are thoroughly familiar with norms and standards.[110]

Among the many reasons for globalization of legal services one has been the growth and complexity of the role of the multinational "General Counsel" in corporations. This also has been one factor propelling the need for a review of national or state admission requirements and limitations in the practice of law. The increase in number, prestige, and authority of in-house counsel, along with the globalization of business and capital markets, added to the expectation that in-house counsel were to be proactive in protecting their employers from possible suits, and forced the general counsel of global organizations to wrestle with unfamiliar, cultural, ethical, and legal challenges.[111]

Changes in the individual state requirements for law practice have been slower than for other professions. In less than half of the states, individuals licensed to practice law in a country outside the United States are eligible to be "foreign legal consultants" for the limited purpose of just giving legal advice to clients regarding the laws of jurisdictions other than that of the United States; this has made more difficult the likelihood of achieving reciprocity for U.S. lawyers in other nations, even though U.S. lawyers are being called upon to analyze and understand international law and the laws of other countries.[112] NAFTA promotes the use of foreign legal consultant arrangements within its three member nations, with benefits including the advancement of legitimate client interests.[113] Among the reasons for the slow pace of change is the inherently self-regulatory framework of attorney regulation, which occurs under the oversight of the judicial branch of state government (California is an exception, with the legislature setting basic standards), arguably more insulated from the interests of the general public than regulation of other professions under partisan elections for the executive and legislative branches.

After the turn of the 21st century the work of the WTO's Working Party on Domestic Regulation (WPDR) caused great discussion and ferment among the legal profession that is largely self-regulated. Following approval by the WTO Council on Services in Trade of the Disciplines for the Accountancy Sector in 1998 and establishment of the WPDR, it undertook to secure comments from the IBA about the applicability of such disciplines to legal services. For example, some within the WPDR have thought that the accountancy disciplines could be applied to other professionals on a horizontal basis. WTO member nations also sought to secure comments and suggestions from legal organizations within those nations. The September 19, 2002 Federal Register requested comments on the Doha Development Agenda negotiations concerning both goods and services. In general, legal services organizations in the United States have been slow to provide feedback, and there has been a relatively low level of awareness about GATS among U.S. groups.[114] This was not true for Canada, however, as the Canadian Bar Association (CBA) and others have been active in making their views available to the Canadian Department of Industry and the Department of Foreign Affairs and International Trade. The CBA opposed the horizontal application of the disciplines for accountancy to the legal profession, noting that "the legal profession should not be covered by a common generic set of professional disciplines," that "the legal profession must be self-regulating," and that the profession "through the law societies, must be able to determine the standards of admission into the profession, establish standards and rules which govern members of the profession, and discipline those who fail to meet these standards," partly because "with the exception of general principles underlying broad doctrines such as the 'common law' or 'civil law,' legal rules are jurisdiction-specific."[115] In the United States the profession of law is regulated by the state courts, and the separation of powers doctrine has been invoked to shield the law profession from a regulatory scheme that was crafted by federal executive branch officials under GATS. In 2003, ABA Center for Professional Responsibility launched a new Web page on the topic of GATS and legal services to stimulate communications.[116] The IBA replied to the WPDR invitation in 2003, suggesting changes to the disciplines so that they could properly apply to legal services. It is not clear the extent to which, if at all, the legal services sector will be covered horizontally by any WPDR-adopted disciplines, but comments from WTO officials have indicated that they believe that legal professionals will benefit from liberalizing legal services around the globe more than any other profession.[117]

Although globalization has greatly affected the practice of some aspects of the legal profession, others aspects of law have appeared more insulated from such pressures. The self-regulatory nature of legal practice in some nations has permitted many attorneys to pretty much continue to practice both civil and criminal law within their confined states and provinces. Moreover, the differences between common law systems of some nations (United Kingdom, United States, India, Malaysia, and former British Commonwealth countries), based upon non-statutory law developed by courts, and civil law-based legal systems in most of the world, have posed challenges to greater interest and pressures for uniformity and reciprocity. Yet the practice of law may over time have global WTO or other disciplines adopted.

Nursing

Nursing regulation within the United States involves governmental oversight provided for nursing practice in each state. It is regulated because it is one health profession that poses risk of harm to the public if practiced by someone who is unprepared and incompetent. Some believe that consumers may not have sufficient information and experience to identify an unqualified healthcare provider, and the public is therefore highly vulnerable to unsafe and incompetent practitioners. State boards of nursing permit only those individuals to practice nursing who have met their qualifications. The National Council of State Boards of Nursing, Inc. (NCSBN) is the non-profit entity composed of all 50 state boards of nursing; it assists its members with their regulatory functions and develops licensing examinations in nursing, including those for registered nurses and licensed practical nurses (LPNs) or vocational nurses (VNs). It also develops model laws for state legislatures and state boards to consider, such as the Nurse Practice Act, which typically defines nursing and the boundaries and scope of nursing practice, the types of licenses and titles to be used and the requirements for licensure, and identifies grounds for disciplinary action.[118] Registered nurses (RNs) constitute the largest healthcare occupation, with about 2.3 million in the United States; this title generally requires graduation from an approved nursing program and passing a national licensing examination.[119] Among state boards of nursing there are some variations in regulating advance practice nurses.

It is the National League for Nursing Accrediting Commission (NLNAC), a nonprofit organization and a subsidiary of the National League for Nursing, which serves as the national accrediting body for all types of nursing education programs. It is recognized by the U.S. Department of Education and other federal agencies, the National Council of State Boards of Nursing (NCSBN), and the Council for Higher Education Accreditation (CHEA). For some U.S. nurses, certification in a specialty is required; for others it is voluntary. Certification may be offered by several organizations, but the American Nurses Credentialing Center (ANCC), a subsidiary of the American Nurses Association, an organization of 150,000 nurses, is the largest. Many of its certification programs have been accredited by NCCA; some states seek certification programs to be accredited by an independent commission. In an effort to promote and validate nursing excellence around the world, ANCC established "Credentialing International" in 1999 that includes certification of specialists and advance practice nurses, accreditation of continuing education providers for nurses, and a "Magnet Recognition" of nursing services effort to deal with nursing shortages and deteriorating work environments for nurses.

Healthcare, specifically nursing, has been changed by globalization; unrelenting external forces are transforming the healthcare system and nursing practice. The advent of the Internet, telehealth, and global migration has been the driving force, breaking down barriers to the interstate practice of nursing.[120] Patients through the Internet have access to a primary care provider, a specialist, online professional help, online pharmacy, and online self-help; healthcare providers in addition to providing care are also facilitators of self-managed care.[121] The demand for foreign nurses remains high in the United States, as the nation struggles to replace nurses who have retired or changed professions. The Commission on Graduates of Foreign Nursing Schools (CGFNS), a nonprofit entity, was organized in the late 1970s to facilitate a review of credentials and certify nurses and other healthcare providers, and otherwise assists migrating nurses and others to determine if they are qualified to be able to practice in the United States and meet state licensure requirements. The continuing shortage of nurses in the United States has fostered a review of how healthcare providers can recruit Canadian or Mexican nurses who qualify for TN nonimmigrant status under NAFTA.[122]

Nurses began exploring the possibility of mutual recognition under NAFTA by 1998.[134] The challenge of NAFTA to develop mutually acceptable standards for licensure and certification, intended to permit greater mobility of professionals across the borders of Canada, Mexico, and the United States, was manifested early, and it led representatives of the nursing profession in 1993 to undertake what came to be termed the "Trilateral Initiative for North American Nursing." This cooperative endeavor, overseen by CGFNS, involved nursing professionals from the three nations in a broad-based assessment project with a short-range objective of gaining common understanding of nursing in these nations, and the long-term goal of having common education and practice standards in several phases.[123] Genuine differences involving licensure, registration, and certification were found, including ongoing competency requirements. Meanwhile, telepractice and other activities within the United States propelled many nurses to agree to an interstate compact, which upon implementation would enable nurses to move from state to state.[124] This internal U.S. mutual recognition model of nurse licensure allows a nurse to have one license (in his or her state of residency) and to practice in other states (both physical and electronic), subject to each state's practice law and regulation. Under mutual recognition, a nurse may practice across state lines unless otherwise restricted. Since 1998, the Nurse Licensure Compact has included RNs and LPNs or VNs. In 2002 the NCSBN approved model language for a licensure compact for advance practice registered nurses (APRNs), with only those states that have adopted the LPN/VN Nurse Licensure Compact able to implement a compact for APRNs. In 2004, states began entering this newer compact, the mechanism that the states are using to adopt the mutual recognition model. Even within some states, however, the concept of nursing regulation through compact has been controversial. The attorneys general of both Kansas and Nebraska, for example, had issued opinions that the Nurse Licensure Compact was unconstitutional because it violates the state's rights to regulate nursing practice.[125]

The International Council of Nurses (ICN), founded in 1899, is a federation of national nurses' associations in over 120 countries. Headquartered in Geneva, Switzerland, it is dedicated to advance nursing worldwide and influencing policy. For example, it has published standards for "telenursing" programs.[126] It also encourages and tracks the development of MRAs. Australia and New Zealand have been engaged in efforts to develop cross-border nurse practitioner standards, and signed the Trans-Tasman Mutual Recognition Agreement in 1997. Moreover, the ANC/NCNZ Memorandum of Cooperation in 2001 is moving both those nations toward harmonizing the standards of nurses across their jurisdictions.[127] ICN has reported that an MRA under NAFTA is still under negotiation, but the Caribbean Community and Common Market (CARICOM) MRA is underway permitting reciprocity, as is another one for the Eastern, Central, and Southern African College of Nursing (ECSACON) dealing with standards of practice and the core content of education.[128] Meanwhile, within the United States, the NCSBN announced in 2004 that it has selected the first three international locations — England, Hong Kong, and South Korea — where it will offer its National Council for Licensure Examination (NCLEX) (both registered nurse and practical nurse), beginning in 2005, for U.S. domestic nurse licensure purposes.

Healthcare is among the most sensitive fields for government professional services regulation. Medical practice was among the first to be regulated in the United States because of the obvious public health, welfare, and safety risks. Notwithstanding increasing interest regarding professional mobility, reciprocity, and uniformity broadly in medicine, and specifically in nursing, public interest theory concerns about the unqualified not practicing is still extant. Accordingly, the credentialing barriers and existing qualification requirements for the practice of nursing are undergoing change more slowly than other professions. However, U.S. internal reciprocity and uniformity is occurring with state compacts supported by the NCSBN and other nursing organizations, and there seems to be growing influence for the operation of these state compacts.

Conclusions and the Feasible Future

National governments — and state or provincial governments within federal systems — are losing some ability to both assert and implement occupational regulatory policy within their territorial borders. International and domestic expectations and pressures for substantial equivalency, reciprocity, harmonization, mutual recognition, and uniformity are succeeding — slowly in some fields and with greater alacrity in others. Political boundaries still exist, but globalization has reduced the meaning of borders (both virtual and actual), and they have become porous. Elites and experts in the nonprofit and business sectors are increasingly aiding and abetting government officials in the development and establishment of international norms and standards through transnational organizations. Writers Reinecke and Slaughter suggest that governance is replacing government, with governance representing a hodgepodge of private and public international entities through which public policy is created and administered.[129]

Clear notions of governmental sovereignty and distinctions between the public, nonprofit, and business sectors have been blurred. Whereas the Old Public Administration generally included only those who worked in government agencies, especially those receiving merit appointments in the civil service, the multisectored New Public Service now includes individuals working within the governmental and the public-serving nonprofit communities.[130] Graduating college seniors themselves think of the nonprofit sector when they hear the words "public service,"[131] and National Association of Schools of Public Affairs and Administration (NASPAA) schools have been increasingly channeling their graduates to public service employment in the nonprofit and business sectors. Public service thus includes all individuals providing goods and services for governments, including workers directly employed by governments but also some in nonprofit organizations and private businesses.[132] The scope and breadth of the New Public Service[133] is illustrated in Table 7.1 using the numerous government agencies, nonprofits, IGOs, and NGOs considered in this chapter.

Table 7.1 further shows the critical U.S. domestic role filled by nonprofit organizations and federations composed of state regulatory boards and agencies. As both nonprofits and IGOs, these entities in the professional fields of accountancy, architecture, engineering, insurance, investment advising, and nursing serve as national networks of state government officials and have become the principal means by which state regulatory agencies cooperate in the United States. States have delegated selected functions to such entities, or to special subsidiaries or creations of these federations. Thus, there has been an accretion of power and authority by them because their activities dealing with examinations, certification, record-keeping, model laws, etc. are central to domestic and international encouragement

Table 7.1 Classification of Organizations

	Name of Agency or Organization	OPA	NPS	Nonprofit	IGO	NGO
1.	Accreditation Board for Engineering and Technology (ABET)		a	x		x
2.	American Association of Engineering Societies (AAES)			x		x
3.	American Association of Retired Persons (AARP)			x		x
4.	American Bar Association (ABA)		c	x		x
5.	American Bar Association's Council on Legal Education and Admission to the Bar		a	x		x
6.	American Institute of Architects (AIA)			x		x
7.	American Institute of Certified Public Accountants (AICPA)		e	x		x
8.	American National Standards Institute (ANSI)		ac	x		x
9.	American Nurses Association (ANA)			x		x
10.	American Nurses Credentialing Center (ANCC)		c	x		x
11.	American Society of Mechanical Engineers (ASME)			x		x
12.	Architects Accreditation Council of Australia (AACA)		a	x		x
13.	Architects' Council of Europe (ACE)			x		x
14.	Association of Accrediting Agencies of Canada (AAAC)		a	x		x
15.	Association to Advance Collegiate Schools of Business (AACSB)		a	x		x
16.	California Board of Registration for Professional Engineers and Land Surveyors (CBRPELS)	x	x			
17.	Canadian Bar Association (CBA)			x		x
18.	Canadian Department of Industry	x	x			
19.	Canadian Department of Foreign Affairs and Trade	x	x			
20.	Canadian Institute of Chartered Accountants (CICA)			x		x
21.	Consumer Federation of America (CFA)			x		x
22.	Center for Quality Assurance in International Education (CQAIE)		x	x		x
23.	Certified Financial Planner Board of Standards, Inc. (CFP Board)		x	x		x

(continued)

Table 7.1 (continued) Classification of Organizations

	Name of Agency or Organization	OPA	NPS	Nonprofit	IGO	NGO
24.	Certified General Accountants – Canada (CGA)			x		x
25.	Commission on Graduates of Foreign Nursing Schools (CGFNS)		c	x		x
26.	Council for Higher Education Accreditation (CHEA)		x	x		x
27.	Council on Licensure, Enforcement and Regulation (CLEAR)		x	x	x	
28.	Engineering and Land Surveying Examination Services (ESLES)		x	x	x	
29.	European Engineering Federation (FEANI)			x		x
30.	Financial Planner Standards Board (FPSB)		x	x		x
31.	Financial Planning Association (FPA)			x		x
32.	Florida Department of Business and Professional Regulation	x	x			
33.	International Accreditation Forum (IAF)		a	x		x
34.	International Association of Insurance Supervisors (IAIS)		x	x	x	
35.	International Bar Association (IBA)			x		x
36.	International Council of Nurses (ICN)			x		x
37.	International Electrotechnical Commission (IEC)		x	x		x
38.	International Federation of Accountants (IFA)			x		x
39.	International Organization for Standardization (ISO)		x	x		x
40.	International Organization of Securities Commissioners (IOSCO)		x	x	x	
41.	International Qualifications Appraisal Board (IQAB)		c	x		x
42.	International Union of Architects (UIA)			x		x
43.	Interstate Insurance Product Regulation Compact (IIPRC)		x	x	x	

44.	Institute of Chartered Accountants in Australia (ICAA)			x		x
45.	Instituto Mexicano De Contadores Publicos (IMCP)			x		x
46.	National Architectural Accrediting Board (NAAB)		a	x		x
47.	National Association of Insurance Commissioners (NAIC)		x	x	x	
48.	National Association of Personal Financial Advisors (NAPFA)			x		x
49.	National Association of Securities Dealers, Inc. (NASD)		e	x		x
50.	National Association of State Boards of Accountancy (NASBA)		x	x	x	
51.	National Autonomous University of Mexico (UNAM)		x	x		
52.	National Commission for Certifying Agencies (NCCA)		a	c		c
53.	National Conference of Bar Examiners (NCBE)		e	x		x
54.	National Conference of Commissioners on Uniform State Laws (NCCUSL)		x	x		x
55.	National Conference of Insurance Legislators (NCOIL)		x	x	x	
56.	National Conference of State Legislatures (NCSL)	x	x	x	x	
57.	National Council of Architectural Registration Boards (NCARB)		x	x	x	
58.	National Council of Examiners for Engineering and Surveying (NCEES)		x	x	x	
59.	National Council of State Boards of Nursing (NCSBN)		x	x	x	
60.	National Governors' Association (NGA)		x	x	x	
61.	National Insurance Producer Registry (NIPR)		x	x		x
62.	National League for Nursing (NLN)			x		x
63.	National League for Nursing Accreditation (NLNAC)		a	x		x
64.	National Organization for Competency Assurance (NOCA)		c	x		x
65.	National Society of Professional Engineers (NSPE)			x		x
66.	North American Securities Administrators Association (NASAA)		x		x	

(continued)

Table 7.1 (continued) Classification of Organizations

	Name of Agency or Organization	OPA	NPS	Nonprofit	*I*GO	NGO
67.	Nurse Licensure Compact		x	x	x	
68.	Office of the U.S. Trade Representative (USTR)	x	x			
69.	Organization for Economic Cooperation and Development (OECD)		x	x		x
70.	Society of Financial Service Professionals (SFSP)			x		x
71.	Texas Board of Professional Engineers (TBPE)	x	x			
72.	United Nations Educational, Scientific and Cultural Organization (UNESCO)		x	x	x	
73.	United States Council for International Engineering Practice (USCIEP)		a	x		x
74.	U.S. Department of Education	x	x			
75.	U.S. Department of Justice	x	x			
76.	U.S. Federal Trade Commission	x	x			
77.	U.S. Securities and Exchange Commission	x	x			
78.	U.S. Supreme Court	x	x			
79.	Working Party on Domestic Regulation (WPDR) of the WTO		x	x	x	
80.	Working Party on Professional Services (WPPS) of the WTO		x	x	x	
81.	World Federation of Engineering Organizations (WFEO)			x		x
82.	World Trade Organization (WTO)		x	x	x	

Key: OPA = Workers are government employees in the Old Public Administration.
NPS = Workers in this organization are in the New Public Service.
a = Qualifies for accreditation purposes.
c = Qualifies for certification purposes.
e = Qualifies for examination purposes.
x = Qualifies an organization as a nonprofit, intergovernmental organization or non-governmental organization.

for state regulatory boards as well as state legislatures to move toward more uniformity. Economies of scale have also played a significant part. And the expertise and leadership assembled through the NCCUSL, CLEAR, NOCA, NCCA, and others have been important as well. Generally, there has been a willingness to assent to the collective wisdom and judgment exercised by these nonprofit entities and elites on behalf of regulatory boards and legislatures. Truly we have governance through networks in the professional services sphere within the United States.

Concurrently with state government coordination and cooperation through nonprofits to perform governmental licensure functions, there has been greater movement for individual certification and program accreditation through nonprofits. The public and private sectors have each come to increasingly rely upon voluntary certification and accreditation, beyond governmental licensure, as a means to provide competency assurance to the general public, consumers, businesses, and even government institutions. Because courts and agencies of government, employers, professions, and others often ask, "Who reviewed your certification program?" Providers of certification programs themselves seek an independent assessment of what they do. The adoption of sunrise and sunset provisions within states has had the effect of diminishing the numbers of occupations that have been granted government regulation from what might have otherwise occurred. Although relatively few have been entirely deregulated, more occupations have never become regulated by government because estimated costs were projected to outweigh the benefits of licensure. Privatization through voluntary certification programs has flourished. Moreover, licensure and certification are not mutually exclusive options. Indeed, many state bar organizations have recognized certification and specialization for attorneys, whether that specialization certification has been provided by the state bars in some capacity or by recognized national or regional certification agencies. Similarly, the medical field has long had certification of medical specialties for its practitioners that are licensed. As described for architecture, NCARB itself operates a certification program. States, business employers, and consumers have encouraged the establishment and use of *bona fide* credentials, even as new occupations have been defined or old ones redefined such as through the North American Industry Classification System.[134] The importance of credentialing individuals through licensure or certification has in turn driven the need for accreditation of both governmental and nonprofit agencies performing such activities. The result has been a strengthening of credentialing processes within the United States in the nonprofit realm. Perhaps this would have occurred to some extent without globalization, but certainly it has been augmented by it.

It is more difficult still to delegate functions formerly performed by state and national governments to international nonprofits, whether IGOs or NGOs. There are political and legal hurdles. And after all there are language and custom differences for many; however, the United States as a multiethnic nation from immigration may have an advantage with its relative heterogeneity. But in most cases there exists no entity that could take on responsibilities internationally in the same way as nonprofit organizations in the United States composed of state regulatory board members cooperate together through existing institutions. Nonetheless, the potential is there, and some early steps have been taken. With the establishment and expansion of operations of the WTO and ISO, regional and global agreements like NAFTA and GATS, the creation of IGOs such as IOSCO and IAIS, and the formation of NGO bodies like the IFA, the UIA, the WFEO, the Financial Planning Standards Board, the IBA, and the ICN for the identified professions above, as well as the advancement of public choice theory, a profound shift has taken place in the roles of the public, private, and nonprofit sectors. A new and more global nonprofit sector has emerged, composed of IGOs and of NGOs that have filled space unoccupied because of limitations on both government and business. Just as NGOs have assumed a significant role in international relief and development activities,[135] they are doing so for professional regulation administered through both government agencies and nonprofit entities.

Further liberalization of trade in services is likely, with concomitant effects on credentialing. For many nations, including the United States, additional regional and bilateral trade agreements are possible — examples include the Free Trade Area of the Americas and individual bilateral agreements. There will be more nations joining the WTO too. The concept of a global license to practice a profession is not immediately feasible through the varied and separate nation-state domestic regulatory schemes, but it may be substantially accomplished through networks of IGOs and NGOs involved with credentialing over time. Global certification of individuals based upon non-governmental standards may be more possible than global licensure, but it is still daunting for trademarks that are still subject to the laws of political jurisdictions even where marks licensing is used. Global accreditation may be more likely than the first two, yet still formidable. Movement toward global licensure or registration, certification or accreditation, may spawn the creation or expansion of single-profession entities that cover only one occupation, or may result in the adaptation of existing organizations or the creation of new bodies encompassing a multitude of occupations. As documented in this chapter, both approaches exemplify institutional theory that includes governance or network theory seeing organizations as bounded social constructs of rules, norms, and the expectations that constrain individual and social choice and behavior.

Institutionalism assumes that policy preferences are neither exogenous nor stable but are molded through collective experience, institutions, education, and particularly professions.[136]

International leadership in the regulation of professions varies. For some fields the United States appears to lead and for other fields the U.S. profession seems to respond to the lead of others. Leading and responding models may be occupation-specific. But through trade agreements, international membership organizations, and international IGOs and NGOs, professional interests, organizations, and businesses can and do influence the nature of U.S. occupational regulation and that of all other nations. Recent EU Directives and policies from other nations pose challenges to traditional public interest theory and the Old Public Administration system of national and subnational governmental regulation. Some applications suggest that public choice or economic theory continues to spread, with a corresponding emphasis on New Public Management in implementation. Globalization forces may be expected to promote centralization over decentralization actions, yet for nations with federal systems, legal instruments are likely to continue to be sensitive to subnational regulatory structures and processes. Even with slow movement greater uniformity within and among nations appears a trend.

In the United States the drafting and approval of national trade and other documents will continue to recognize the police power of state governments to engage in the traditional regulatory functions involving the licensure of professions and occupations. This inherent right of state governments, evidenced by the Tenth Amendment, to impose upon private rights reasonable restrictions related to promotion and maintenance of the health, safety, morals, and general welfare of the public, *North Dakota vs. Cromwell* 9 NW2d 914 (1943), has been accepted in many court cases. Whether in the form of federal legislation, federal court decisions, approved treaties, presidential orders, and federal agency regulations, there is a political desire not to run afoul of the principle of federalism. Thus, professionals that are parties to MRAs with their counterparts in other countries should not assume that the U.S. government will enforce the provisions of any such agreements concluded by those U.S. professional organizations, for it is the states that will need to implement these agreements.[137] On the other hand, there exists a widening consensus about removing barriers to professional services with resultant benefits, so even within the United States there may be a confluence of problems, politics, and policies[138] that might result in federal preemption of professional regulation in a specific field if the lack of reciprocity or uniformity adversely and sufficiently affects interstate and foreign commerce, such as was perceived by Congress dealing with insurance agents, brokers, and consultants. The fundamental nature of the U.S. domestic common market was initially one eliminating tariffs between the states. Now that non-tariff barrier diminishment has become more important, the forces of globalization (not limited to trade agreements) are placing stiffer constraints upon regulation by the both state governments and nonprofit entities. As long as there is perceptible movement toward a lessening of credentialing barriers, any wide or forceful federal response is unlikely.

Perhaps a more likely scenario to achieve uniformity and reciprocity, consistent with principle of state primacy in occupational regulation, involves interstate compacts in the United States, as formal agreements between two or more states, interstate compacts represent sovereign state cooperation without the involvement of the national government. Examples are the Nurse Licensure Compact and the IIPRC. Some may involve the *de facto* exercise of discretion moving to a compact administrative entity making decisions. Very few compacts, however, ultimately include all states or even a majority of them,[139] and this is a weakness. Nonetheless, in the Nurse Licensure Compact the states continue to have authority for determining licensure requirements and disciplinary actions.

It is not inconceivable that governmental regulation of the professions could occur on a regional or international basis. But if states within the United States have difficulty in delegating functions to a state compact entity, which they may oversee and from which they can remove themselves, how likely is a more global governmental body that is imbued with the authority to act for nations not sharing a common culture and norms? Conceptually a common governmental body could be set up or an existing one be used. Yet the critics of "governmental failure" on a national or subnational basis are not prone to find support for more governmental regulation on a global scale, and the transfer of any element of sovereignty is jealously guarded. More probable is voluntary action by interest groups working together to bestow authority upon a new or existing NGO to perform regulation of a profession outside of a governmental structure on an international basis. Such privatization of international regulation might not be entirely self-regulation of the profession, but rather a more balanced regulation with consumer and other groups working cooperatively with professional associations, and involve possibly oversight by governmental regulatory representatives.

Greater privatization of state regulation or deregulation, more reliance upon voluntary certification in lieu of governmental licensure, the increasing interests of professions and businesses and consumers to reduce barriers to trade in services between states and among nations, the accretion of capacity and authority to IGO nonprofits in the United States to act on behalf of the states collectively, some additional acceptance of uniform state laws, the relative likelihood of some additional use of interstate compacts, and many other factors are all likely to mean a reduction in some of the high-quality barriers loosely identified as constituting the past and current state of regulation for occupations and professions in the United States, and perhaps other nations. Centralizing tendencies toward uniformity and reciprocity seem more prevalent and stronger than decentralizing tendencies. Consequently, professional regulation from a U.S. perspective is likely to look less governmental, more voluntary, and more subject to market decision making by service users, consumers, businesses, and practitioners of the professions. The rising importance of non-state actors in the nonprofit and business sectors suggests the possible application of additional elitism and pluralism for professional regulation, both nationally and internationally. Singular existing professions may develop distinctive cultures and mores that span nations, but new professions and occupations may be based less and less on national customs and traditions and more on regional or international commonalties. Greater acceptance of economic and capture theory, greater consumerism, and a change of direction on the part of professions themselves, and particularly the elites within them, regarding the perceived value of state regulation for their professions compared with the benefits and costs of deregulation, are evident. Accordingly, national identities and regulatory frameworks will still matter, but may matter relatively less. The old reliance upon governmental authority and coercion is giving way to a New Public Service that explicitly recognizes the growing roles and functions of nonprofits and NGOs and the application of persuasion and "soft" power to achieve accepted norms and standards developed and accepted internationally. Globalization is reworking as well as redefining the professions.[140] Nation-state regulation of professions and occupations is still a descriptive hallmark, but the future of public policy and public administration within this domain will continue to undergo substantial change.

References

1. Shimberg, B., Roederer, D. (1994). *Questions a Legislator Should Ask.* 2nd ed. Lexington, KY: The Council on Licensure, Enforcement and Regulation, pp. 1–2.
2. Teske, P. (2004). *Regulation in the States.* Washington, D.C.: Brookings Institution Press, pp. 32–33; Shimberg, B. (2000). The role that licensure plays in society. In: Schoon, C.G., Smith I.L., eds. *The Licensure and Certification Mission.* New York: Professional Examination Service, pp. 150–151.
3. Evetts, J. (1999, July). Regulation of professions in global economies: dimensions of acquired regulation. Paper Presented at the Meeting of the Advancement of Socio-Economics, Madison, WI. Available at http://www.sase.org/conf1999/papers/julia_evetts.pdf (accessed December 15, 2004).
4. Jacobs, J.A. (1992). *Certification and Accreditation Law Handbook.* Washington, D.C.: American Society for Association Executives, p. 1.

5. Schoon, C.C. and Smith I.L. (2000). *The Licensure and Certification Mission: Legal, Social, and Political Foundations*. New York: Professional Examination Service, p. 11.
6. Shimberg, B. and Roederer, D. (1994). *Questions a Legislator Should Ask*. 2nd ed. Lexington, KY: The Council on Licensure, Enforcement and Regulation, p. 34.
7. Committee to Develop Standards for Educational and Psychological Testing (1999). *Standards for Educational and Psychological Testing*. Washington, D.C.: American Psychological Association, p. 174.
8. Committee to Develop Standards for Educational and Psychological Testing (1999). *Standards for Educational and Psychological Testing*. Washington, D.C.: American Psychological Association, p. 177; Shimberg, B. (1980). *Occupational Licensing: A Public Perspective*. Princeton, NJ: Educational Testing Service, p. 20.
9. Committee to Develop Standards for Educational and Psychological Testing (1999). *Standards for Educational and Psychological Testing*. Washington, D.C.: American Psychological Association, p. 172; Reaves, R.P. (1993). *The Law of Professional Licensing and Certification*. 2nd ed. Montgomery, AL: Publications for Professionals, p. 10; Shimberg, B. (1980). *Occupational Licensing: A Public Perspective*. Princeton, NJ: Educational Testing Service, p. 21.
10. Committee to Develop Standards for Educational and Psychological Testing (1985). *Standards for Educational and Psychological Testing*. Washington, D.C.: American Psychological Association, p. 63.
11. Shimberg, B. and Roederer, D. (1994). *Questions a Legislator Should Ask*. 2nd ed. Lexington, KY: The Council on Licensure, Enforcement and Regulation, p. 37.
12. Brinegar, P. (2004). Trends and Issues in State Professional Licensing. In: *The Book of the States 2004*. Lexington, KY: Council of State Governments, p. 447; Shimberg, B. (1980). *Occupational Licensing: A Public Perspective*. Princeton, NJ: Educational Testing Service, p. 4.
13. Bobby, C. (1997). Quality assurance and the professions: U.S. model of accreditation, certification, and licensure. In: Lenn, M.P., Campos, L., eds. *Globalization of the Professions and the Quality Imperative: Professional Accreditation, Certification, and Licensure*. Madison, WI: Magna Publications, p. 39; Shimberg, B. (1980). *Occupational Licensing: A Public Perspective*. Princeton, NJ: Educational Testing Service, pp. 31 and 215.
14. Shimberg, B. (1980). *Occupational Licensing: A Public Perspective*. Princeton, NJ: Educational Testing Service, p. 221.
15. Federal Trade Commission (2003). *A Positive Agenda for Consumers: The FTC Year in Review*. Washington, D.C.: FTC, p. 4.
16. Federal Trade Commission State Action Task Force (2003, September). *Report of the State Action Task Force. Washington, D.C.: FTC, pp. 1, 7 and 18; Earles vs. State Board of Certified Public Accountants of Louisiana, 139 F.3d 1033*, 1041; *Hass vs. Oregon State Bar, 883 F.2d* 1460.
17. Federal Trade Commission (2003). *A Positive Agenda for Consumers: The FTC Year In Review*. Washington, D.C.: FTC, p. 21.
18. Ascher, B. (1997). New trade agreements: implications for education and the professions. In: Lenn, M.P., Campos, L., eds. *Globalization of the Professions*

and the Quality Imperative: Professional Accreditation, Certification, and Licensure. Madison, WI: Magna Publications, p. 29.

19. Schoon, C.C. and Smith I.L. (2000). *The Licensure and Certification Mission: Legal, Social, and Political Foundations.* New York: Professional Examination Service, p. 18; Maronde, J.L. (1996). Introduction to the standards for accreditation of national certification organizations. In: Browning, A.H., Bugbee, A.C. Jr., Mullins, M.A., eds. *Certification: A NOCA Handbook.* Washington, D.C.: National Organization for Competency Assurance, pp. x–xi.
20. Bobby, C. (1997). Quality assurance and the professions: U.S. model of accreditation, certification, and licensure. In: Lenn, M.P., Campos, L., eds. *Globalization of the Professions and the Quality Imperative: Professional Accreditation, Certification, and Licensure.* Madison, WI: Magna Publications, p. 39; Fabrey, L. (1996). Basic psychometric principles. In: Browning, A.H., Bugbee, A.C. Jr., Mullins, M.A., eds. *Certification: A NOCA Handbook.* Washington, D.C.: National Organization for Competency Assurance, pp. 2–3.
21. McBride, W. (1997). International perspectives: the Canadian system of professional quality assurance. In: Lenn, M.P., Campos, L., eds. *Globalization of the Professions and the Quality Imperative: Professional Accreditation, Certification, and Licensure.* Madison, WI: Magna Publications, p. 42; Klaiman, D.G. (1997). Association of accrediting agencies in Canada. In: Lenn, M. P., Campos, L., eds. *Globalization of the Professions and the Quality Imperative: Professional Accreditation, Certification, and Licensure.* Madison, WI: Magna Publications, p. 45.
22. Malo, S. (1999). The road to accreditation in Mexico: the case of the UNAM. In: Lenn, M.P., Miller, B.D., eds. *The Foundations of Globalization of Higher Education and the Professions.* Washington, D.C.: The Center for Quality Assurance in International Education, p. 77.
23. Lemaitre, M.J. (1997). Accreditation in Chile. In: Lenn, M.P., Campos, L., eds. *Globalization of the Professions and the Quality Imperative: Professional Accreditation, Certification, and Licensure.* Madison, WI: Magna Publications, p. 50.
24. International Organization for Standardization (2002). Annual Report 2002. Geneva, Switzerland: ISO, p. 13.
25. International Organization for Standardization (2004, November 15). *ISO/IEC Standard for "One-Stop Accreditation" to Boost Cross-Border Trade.* Geneva, Switzerland: ISO, p. 1.
26. Fugate, D.L. and Zimmerman, A. (1996). International services marketing: a review of structural barriers, regulatory limitations, and marketing responses. *Journal of Professional Services Marketing*, 13(2): 37.
27. United Nations Conference on Trade and Development (2004). World Investment Report 2004: The Shift Toward Services. New York: UNCTAD, p. 97.
28. World Trade Organization (2001). *GATS — Fact and Fiction.* Geneva, Switzerland: WTO, pp. 3 and 4.
29. United States Trade Representative (2003, March 31). *U.S. Services Offers in WTO Trade Talks.* Washington, D.C.: USTR.

30. World Trade Organization (2001). *GATS — Fact and Fiction*. Geneva, Switzerland: WTO, p. 1; Mukherjee, N. (1992). Multinational negotiations and trade barriers and entry strategy alternatives: strategic marketing implications. *Journal of Small Business Management*, 29(6): 45.
31. Augusti, G. (1999). European engineering formation: the problem of transnational recognition. *European Journal of Engineering Education*, 24(1): 8.
32. Fugate, D.L. and Zimmerman, A. (1996). International services marketing: a review of structural barriers, regulatory limitations, and marketing responses. *Journal of Professional Services Marketing*, 13(2): 51.
33. Brinegar, P. and McGinley, M. (1998). *Telepractice and Professional Licensing: A Guide for Legislators*. Lexington, KY: The Council on Licensure, Enforcement and Regulation, p. 1.
34. Ascher, B. (1999). Education and the professions: international activities, products and by-products. In: Lenn, M.P., Miller, B.D., eds. *The Foundations of Globalization of Higher Education and the Professions*. Washington, D.C.: The Center for Quality Assurance in International Education, p. 15.
35. Knapp, U. (1997). International trade in professional services: assessing barriers and encouraging reform. In: Lenn, M.P., Campos, L., eds. *Globalization of the Professions and the Quality Imperative: Professional Accreditation, Certification, and Licensure*. Madison, WI: Magna Publications, p. 11.
36. Knapp, U. (1997). International trade in professional services: assessing barriers and encouraging reform. In: Lenn, M.P., Campos, L., eds. *Globalization of the Professions and the Quality Imperative: Professional Accreditation, Certification, and Licensure*. Madison, WI: Magna Publications, p. 13.
37. Knapp, U. (1997). International trade in professional services: assessing barriers and encouraging reform. In: Lenn, M.P., Campos, L., eds. *Globalization of the Professions and the Quality Imperative: Professional Accreditation, Certification, and Licensure*. Madison, WI: Magna Publications, pp. 13–14.
38. Federal Trade Commission (2003, June). *A Positive Agenda for Consumers: The FTC Year in Review*. Washington, D.C.: FTC, p. 1.
39. Evetts, J. (1999). The European professional federations: occupational regulation in European markets. *The International Scope Review*, 1 Winter(2): 15.
40. Lloyd-Jones, J. (1999). Global governance of accounting education and accreditation: dream or reality? In: Lenn, M.P., Miller, B.D., eds. *The Foundations of Globalization of Higher Education and the Professions*. Washington, D.C.: The Center for Quality Assurance in International Education, p. 97.
41. Ascher, B. (1999). Education and the professions: international activities, products and by-products. In: Lenn, M.P., Miller, B.D., eds. *The Foundations of Globalization of Higher Education and the Professions*. Washington, D.C.: The Center for Quality Assurance in International Education, p. 16.
42. Lloyd-Jones, J. (1999). Global governance of accounting education and accreditation: dream or reality?" In: Lenn, M.P., Miller, B.D., eds. *The Foundations of Globalization of Higher Education and the Professions*. Washington, D.C.: The Center for Quality Assurance in International Education, p. 96.
43. Rondeau, M. and Walsh, B. (1997). Canada's agreement on internal trade: the labor mobility. In: Lenn, M.P. and Campos, L., eds. *Globalization of the*

Professions and the Quality Imperative: Professional Accreditation, Certification, and Licensure. Madison, WI: Magna Publications, pp. 61–63; Ascher, B. (1999). Education and the professions: international activities, products and by-products. In: Lenn, M.P., Miller, B.D., eds. *The Foundations of Globalization of Higher Education and the Professions.* Washington, D.C.: The Center for Quality Assurance in International Education, p. 20.

44. United States Trade Representative (2003, March 31). *Facts on Services Offer: Opening Dynamic New Markets.* Washington, D.C.: USTR.
45. Brinegar, P. (2004). Trends and issues in state professional licensing. In: *The Book of the States 2004.* Lexington, KY: Council of State Governments, p. 447.
46. Ascher, B. (2004, April 26). *Toward a Borderless Market for Professional Services.* Washington, D.C.: American Antitrust Institute, p. 1. Available at http://www.antitrustinstitute.org/recent2/316.cfm (accessed December 15, 2004)
47. Paterson, I., Fink, M., Ogus, A. (2003). *Economic Impact of Regulation in the Field of Liberal Professions in Different Member States.* Brussels: Belgium European Commission, DG Competition, pp. 127–128.
48. Monti, M. (2003, October 28). Comments and concluding remarks of Commissioner Mario Monti at the Conference for Professional Regulation. Brussels: Belgium European Commission, pp. 1–4. Available at http://europa.eu.int/comm/competition/liberalization/conference/speeches/mario_monti.pdf (accessed November 8, 2004).
49. Ascher, B. (2004, April 26). Toward a Borderless Market for Professional Services. Washington, D.C.: American Antitrust Institute, p. 4. Available at http://www.antitrustinstitute.org/recent2/316.cfm (accessed December 15, 2004).
50. Florini, A., Simmons, P.J. (2000). What the world needs now? In: Florini, A., ed. *The Third Force: The Rise of Transnational Civil Society.* Washington, D.C.: Japan Center for International Exchange and Carnegie Endowment for International Peace, p. 10.
51. Florini, A. (2003). *The Coming Democracy: New Rules for Running a New World.* Washington, D.C.: Island Press, p. 207.
52. Slaughter, A. (2004). *A New World Order.* Princeton, NJ: Princeton University Press, pp. 1 and 261.
53. Florini, A. (2003). *The Coming Democracy: New Rules for Running a New World.* Washington, D.C.: Island Press, p. 10.
54. Slaughter, A. (2004). *A New World Order.* Princeton, NJ: Princeton University Press, pp. 2–7.
55. Slaughter, A. (2004). *A New World Order.* Princeton, NJ: Princeton University Press, p. 13.
56. Florini, A. (2003). *The Coming Democracy: New Rules for Running a New World.* Washington, D.C.: Island Press, p. 5.
57. Goldsmith, S. and Eggers, W.D. (2004). *Governing by Network: The New Shape of the Public Sector.* Washington, D.C.: Brookings Institution Press.
58. Jefferies, D. and Evetts, J. (2000). Approaches to the international recognition of qualifications in engineering and the sciences. *European Journal of Engineering Education,* 25(1): 100.

59. International Council of Nurses (2004). *Fact sheet on Mutual Recognition Agreements (MRAs)*. Geneva, Switzerland: ICN, p. 1.
60. Jefferies, D. and Evetts, J. (2000). Approaches to the international recognition of qualifications in engineering and the sciences. *European Journal of Engineering Education*, 25(1): 102.
61. Evetts, J. (1999). The European professional federations: occupational regulation in European markets. *The International Scope Review*, 1(2):1–20.
62. Delk, W. (2004). Promoting your credentials in faraway places: benefits and caveats of exporting your credentialing program abroad. *Association Management* (June):57–62.
63. Maronde, J.L. (1996). Introduction to the standards for accreditation of national certification organizations. In: Browning, A.H., Bugbee, A.C. Jr., Mullins, M.A., eds. *Certification: A NOCA Handbook*. Washington, D.C.: National Organization for Competency Assurance, p. x.
64. Committee to Develop Standards for Educational and Psychological Testing (1999). *Standards for Educational and Psychological Testing*. Washington, D.C.: American Psychological Association.
65. Knauer, D.J. (1999). The globaiization of professional practice. In: Lenn, M.P., Miller, B.D., eds. *The Foundations of Globalization of Higher Education and the Professions*. Washington, D.C.: The Center for Quality Assurance in International Education, p. 54.
66. Knapp, L.G. and Knapp, J.E. (2002). *The Business of Certification: A Comprehensive Guide to Developing a Successful Program*. Washington, D.C.: American Society of Association Executives, p. 123.
67. Lloyd-Jones, J. (1999). Global governance of accounting education and accreditation: dream or reality? In: Lenn, M.P., Miller, B.D., eds. *The Foundations of Globalization of Higher Education and the Professions*. Washington, D.C.: The Center for Quality Assurance in International Education, p. 96.
68. United Nations Conference on Trade and Development (2004). World Investment Report 2004: The Shift Toward Services. New York: UNCTAD, p. 110.
69. Lloyd-Jones, J. (1999). Global governance of accounting education and accreditation: dream or reality? In: Lenn, M.P., Miller, B.D., eds. *The Foundations of Globalization of Higher Education and the Professions*. Washington, D.C.: The Center for Quality Assurance in International Education, p. 96.
70. Lloyd-Jones, J. (1999). Global governance of accounting education and accreditation: dream or reality? In: Lenn, M.P., Miller, B.D., eds. *The Foundations of Globalization of Higher Education and the Professions*. Washington, D.C.: The Center for Quality Assurance in International Education, p. 97.
71. Holstrum, G.L. (1999). Competency and educational quality assurance in accounting: global issues from a U.S. perspective. In: Lenn, M.P., Miller, B.D., eds. *The Foundations of Globalization of Higher Education and the Professions*. Washington, D.C.: The Center for Quality Assurance in International Education, p. 93.
72. Lloyd-Jones, J. (1999). Global governance of accounting education and accreditation: dream or reality? In: Lenn, M.P., Miller, B.D., eds. *The Foundations*

of Globalization of Higher Education and the Professions. Washington, D.C.: The Center for Quality Assurance in International Education, p. 98.

73. Ascher, B. (1999). Education and the professions: international activities, products and by-products. In: Lenn, M.P., Miller, B.D., eds. *The Foundations of Globalization of Higher Education and the Professions.* Washington, D.C.: The Center for Quality Assurance in International Education, pp. 16–17.
74. World Trade Organization (1997, May 28). Guidelines for Mutual Recognition Agreements or Arrangements in the Accountancy Sector. Document 97–2295; World Trade Organization (1998, December 14). Disciplines on Domestic Regulation in the Accountancy Sector. Document 98–5140.
75. Ascher, B. (2004, April 26). Toward a Borderless Market for Professional Services. Washington, D.C.: American Antitrust Institute, p. 4. Available at http://www.antitrustinstitute.org/recent2/316.cfm (accessed December 15, 2004).
76. Holstrum, G.L. (1999). Competency and educational quality assurance in accounting: global issues from a U.S. perspective. In: Lenn, M.P. and Miller, B.D., eds. *The Foundations of Globalization of Higher Education and the Professions.* Washington, D.C.: The Center for Quality Assurance in International Education, p. 92.
77. Holstrum, G.L. (1999). Competency and educational quality assurance in accounting: global issues from a U.S. perspective. In: Lenn, M.P. and Miller, B.D., eds. *The Foundations of Globalization of Higher Education and the Professions.* Washington, D.C.: The Center for Quality Assurance in International Education, p. 97.
78. National Council of Architectural Registration Boards (1999). *The Regulation of Architecture in the United States.* Washington, D.C.: NCARB, p. 2.
79. National Council of Architectural Registration Boards (1999). *The Regulation of Architecture in the United States.* Washington, D.C.: NCARB, pp. 2–3.
80. International Union of Architects (1999). Recommended Guidelines for the UIA Accord on Recommended International Standards of Professionalism in Architectural Practice Policy on Registration/Licensing/Certification of the Practice of Architecture. Paris: UIA, p. 1. Available at http://www.uia-architects.org/image/PDF/Pro Pra/Intro.pdf.
81. International Union of Architects (1999). Recommended Guidelines for the UIA Accord on Recommended International Standards of Professionalism in Architectural Practice Policy on Registration/Licensing/Certification of the Practice of Architecture. Paris: UIA, p. 1. Available at http://www.uia-architects.org/image/PDF/Pro Pra/Appendix.pdf.
82. National Council of Architectural Registration Boards (1999). *The Regulation of Architecture in the United States.* Washington, D.C.: NCARB, p. 3.
83. Kennedy, M.D. and Weiner, E.S. (2003, January). The articulation of international expertise in the professions. Paper presented at a Revising Borders Meeting at Duke University, Durham NC, p. 20. Available at http://www.umich.edu/~iinet/iisite/pubs/01.2003.mkennedy.duke.final2.htm (accessed December 10, 2004).
84. National Council of Examiners for Engineering and Surveying (2003, December). *Licensure Exchange*, p. 13.

85. National Council of Examiners for Engineering and Surveying (2003, March). *Report of the Engineering Licensure Qualifications Task Force.* Clemson, SC: NCEES, pp. 30–31.
86. Ascher, B. (2001, February). Engineers get organized to face obstacles in international mobility. *Engineering Times*, 23(2): 2.
87. Falcioni, J. (1999, March). Engineering globally. *Mechanical Engineering*, 121(3): 4.
88. Roe, K.K. (1999). The global generation. *Mechanical Engineering.* Available at http://www.memagazine.org/supparch/mepower99/global/global.html (accessed December 8, 2004).
89. Conner, M. (2004). Jobs follow the market. *EDN* (November): 44.
90. United Nations Conference on Trade and Development (2004). World Investment Report 2004: The Shift toward Services. New York: UNCTAD, pp. 135 and 145.
91. World Federation of Engineering Organizations (2004). *Introduction.* Available at http://www.unesco.org/wfeo/introduction.html (accessed December 15, 2004).
92. Ascher, B. (1999). Education and the professions: international activities, products and by-products. In: Lenn, M.P., Miller, B.D., eds. *The Foundations of Globalization of Higher Education and the Professions.* Washington, D.C.: The Center for Quality Assurance in International Education, p. 17.
93. Lewis, G.L. Jr. (1999). Engineering mobility under the North American Free Trade Agreement (NAFTA). In: Lenn, M.P., Miller, B.D., eds. *The Foundations of Globalization of Higher Education and the Professions.* Washington, D.C.: The Center for Quality Assurance in International Education, p. 147.
94. National Council of Examiners for Engineering and Surveying (2003, August). *Licensure Exchange*, 7(4): 11–12.
95. Jefferies, D. and Evetts, J. (2000). Approaches to the international recognition of qualifications in engineering and the sciences. *European Journal of Engineering Education*, 25(1): 101; Evetts, J. (1999). The European professional federations: occupational regulation in European markets. *The International Scope Review*, 1(2): 9.
96. Lemaitre, M.J. (2004, June). Toward common professional standards in Engineering, Medicine, and Agronomy: the Case of MERCOSUR (the Market of the South). Paper Presented at the Conference Professional Accreditation and Certification: Gateways to Quality and Mobility in the Americas, Mexico City, Mexico.
97. Staff of the United States Securities and Exchange Commission (1988). Report on financial planners to the house committee on energy and commerce, subcommittee on telecommunications and finance. Washington, D.C.: SEC, February.
98. Macey, J.R. (2002). Regulation of Financial Planners: A White Paper Prepared for the Financial Planning Association. Atlanta, GA: Financial Planning Association.
99. Goss, R.P. (1995, October). Statement and testimony on the regulation of financial planners. Paper Presented to the NASAA Financial Planners/Investment Advisers Committee, Vancouver, Canada; Goss, R.P. (1995, December).

Statement and testimony and the regulation of financial planners. Paper Presented to the NASAA Task Force on the Future of Shared State and Federal Securities Regulation, St. Michaels, MD.

100. Chauncey Group International (1998). *Job Analysis Abstract for the North American Securities Administrators Association.* Princeton, NJ: The Chauncey Group International, p. 1.
101. North American Administrators Association (2000). *State Securities Regulators Unanimously Adopt Vision for Future.* Montreal, Canada: NASAA, September 19.
102. National Conference of Insurance Legislators (2000). Statement of Deputy Speaker Clare Farragher of New Jersey, NCOIL President, before the Subcommittee on Securities of the Committee on Banking, Housing and Urban Affairs, U.S. Senate, April 12, 2000. Available at http://www.ncoil.org/ (accessed December 15, 2004).
103. Calvo, C. (2003, March). Insurance regulation: a time for change. *State Legislatures.* Available at http://www.ncsl.org/programs/pubs/SLmag/2003/303insur.htm (accessed December 15, 2004).
104. International Organization for Standardization (2002). Annual Report 2002. Geneva, Switzerland: ISO, p. 12.
105. American National Standards Institute (2003, March 3). *ANSI Launches Accreditation Program for Personnel Certification Bodies.* Washington, D.C.: ANSI. Available at http://www.ansi.org/news_publications/latest_headlines.aspx?menuid = 7 (accessed December 15, 2004).
106. Goebel, R.J. (2000). Legal practice rights of domestic and foreign lawyers in the United States. *International and Comparative Law Quarterly*, 49: 416–417.
107. Needham, C. (1998). The licensing of foreign legal consultants in the United States. *Fordham International Law Journal*, 21(4): 1126–1151; Goebel, R.J. (2000). Legal practice rights of domestic and foreign lawyers in the United States. *International and Comparative Law Quarterly*, 49: 413–445.
108. Terry, L.S. (2001). GATS' applicability to transnational lawyering and its potential impact on U.S. state regulation of lawyers. *Vanderbilt Journal of Transnational Law*, 34: 994–996.
109. United Nations Conference on Trade and Development (2004). World Investment Report 2004: The Shift toward Services. New York: UNCTAD, p. 326.
110. United Nations Conference on Trade and Development (2004). World Investment Report 2004: The Shift toward Services. New York: UNCTAD, p. 112.
111. Daly, M.C. (1997). The cultural, ethical, and legal challenges in lawyering for a global organization: the role of the general counsel. *Emory Law Journal*, 46(3): 1057 and 1109.
112. Needham, C. (1998). The licensing of foreign legal consultants in the United States. *Fordham International Law Journal*, 21(4): 1126–1129.
113. Goebel, R.J. (2000). Legal practice rights of domestic and foreign lawyers in the United States. *International and Comparative Law Quarterly*, 49: 415.
114. Terry. L.S. (2002). Legal services sector and the Doha development agenda: response to 67 Federal Register 59086 (September 19, 2002). Letter to Ms. Gloria Blue, Executive Secretary of the U.S. Trade Policy Staff Committee

dated October 28, 2002, p. 4. Available at http://www.abanet.org/cpr/gats/terry_ustr.pdf (accessed December 15, 2004).

115. Canadian Bar Association (2000). Submission on the General Agreement on Trade in Services and the Legal Profession: The Accountancy Disciplines as a Model for the Legal Profession. Ottawa, Canada: CBA, pp. 3–4 and 14.
116. Terry, L.S. (2003). What will the WTO disciplines apply to? Distinguishing among market access, national treatment and Article VI: 4 measures when applying the GATS to legal services. *The Professional Lawyer* (2003 Symposium): 84.
117. Council on Licensure, Enforcement and Regulation (2004, Fall). *International News*, 21(4): 1.
118. NCSBN website. Available at http://www.ncsbn.org/regulation/index.asp (accessed December 15, 2004).
119. U.S. Department of Labor, Bureau of Labor Statistics (2004). *Occupational Outlook Handbook 2004–05*, p. 1. Available at http://www.bls.gov/oco/home.htm (accessed December 15, 2004).
120. Fernandez, R.D. and Herbert, G.J. (2004). Global licensure: new modalities of treatment and care require the development of new structures and systems to access care. *Nursing Administration Quarterly* (April–June): 131.
121. Ferguson, T. (2000). Introduction: the Internet revolution. *Pfizer Journal*, 4(2): 7.
122. Lebowitz, L.M. (2003). Immigration strategies for hiring staff. *Nursing Homes*, 52(5): 42.
123. Davis, C. (1999). An update on the Trilateral Initiative for North American nursing. In: Lenn, M.P., Miller, B.D., eds. *The Foundations of Globalization of Higher Education and the Professions*. Washington, D.C.: The Center for Quality Assurance in International Education, p. 109.
124. Ascher, B. (1999). Education and the professions: international activities, products and by-products. In: Lenn, M.P., Miller, B.D., eds. *The Foundations of Globalization of Higher Education and the Professions*. Washington, D.C.: The Center for Quality Assurance in International Education, p. 20.
125. Robinette, A. (2002). *Multi-state Licensure: What is it? What are the Concerns? How does it Affect Nursing Practice?* Jefferson City, MO: Missouri Nurses Association, p. 2.
126. International Council of Nurses (2001). *International Professional Standards for Telenursing Programmes*. Available at http://www.icn.ch/matters_telenursing.htm (accessed December 15, 2004).
127. Council on Licensure, Enforcement and Regulation (2004, Spring). *International News*, 21(1): 1.
128. International Council of Nurses (2004). *Mutual Recognition Agreements (MRAs)*. Available at http://www.icn.ch/matters_mra.htm (accessed December 15, 2004).
129. Reinicke, W.H. (1998). *Global Public Policy: Governing without Government?* Washington, D.C.: The Brookings Institution; Slaughter, A. (2004). *A New World Order*. Princeton, NJ: Princeton University Press, p. 262.
130. Frederickson, H.G. (1999). The repositioning of American public administration. *PS: Political Science and Politics*, XXXII(4): 703.

131. Light, P.C. (2003). *In Search of Public Service.* Washington, D.C.: Brookings Institution. Available at http://www.brook.edu/gs/cps/light20030603.htm (accessed December 15, 2004).
132. Light, P.C. (1999) *The New Public Service.* Washington, D.C.: Brookings Institution Press, p. 1.
133. Denhardt, J.V., Denhardt, R.B. (2003). *The New Public Service: Serving, Not Steering.* Armonk, NY: M.E. Sharpe; Denhardt, R.B, Denhardt, J.V. (2000). The New Public Service: serving rather than steering. *Public Administration Review,* 60(6): 549–559; Light, P.C. (1999) *The New Public Service.* Washington, D.C.: Brookings Institution Press.
134. Ascher, B. (1999). Education and the professions: international activities, products and by-products. In: Lenn, M.P. and Miller, B.D., eds. *The Foundations of Globalization of Higher Education and the Professions.* Washington, D.C.: The Center for Quality Assurance in International Education, p. 19.
135. Lindenberg, M., Bryant. C. (2001). *Going Global.* Bloomfield, CT: Kumarian Press, Inc., p. 1.
136. Frederickson, H.G, Smith, K.B. (2003). *The Public Administration Theory Primer.* Bolder, CO: Westview Press, pp. 67–71.
137. Ascher, B. (2004, April 26). *Toward a Borderless Market for Professional Services.* Washington, D.C.: American Antitrust Institute, p. 4. Available at http://www.antitrustinstitute.org/recent2/316.cfm (accessed December 15, 2004).
138. Kingdon, J.W. (1995). *Agendas, Alternatives, and Public Policies.* 2nd ed. New York: Addison-Wesley Educational Publishers, p. 201.
139. Bowman, A. (2004). Trends and issues in interstate cooperation. In: *The Book of the States 2004.* Lexington, KY: The Council of State Governments, p. 36.
140. Evetts, J. (1999). The European professional federations: occupational regulation in European markets. *The International Scope Review,* 1(2):15.

Chapter 8

Globalization and Media Coverage of Public Administration

Mordecai Lee

CONTENTS

Introduction

Comparative and international administration has generally paid little attention to media issues. For example, administrative–media relations are not addressed in the overviews and handbooks from Heady (2001), Hyden (1997), Garcia-Zamor and Khator (1994), Baker (1994), Dwivedi and

Henderson (1990), and Rowat (1988). Whereas the first edition of Farazmand's handbook did not include any entries for media relations, the second edition had one (Farazmand, 1991, 2001). That entry, by Kalantari, focused on the role of the media in the United States, its impact on the political system, and a short discussion of the implications of these trends on public administration (Kalantari, 2001). Although a helpful contribution, it did not address the broader scope of agency–media relations from international and comparative perspectives. A contributing factor to the minor attention paid to media relations is partly related to the limited ability to draw generalizations between the wide variety of the governmental and media systems of contemporary nation-states (Lenn, 1996, p. 441; Grunig, 1997, pp. 270–271).

An attempt to find such literature in other related fields provided equally meager results. In public administration writings, according to Martin, the study of agency relations with the press "is one of the more dramatic examples of a subject from which Public Administration has borrowed only a scattering of the available literature" (Martin, 1989, p. 148). According to Garnett, all aspects of communication, whether internal or external, have "been underemphasized in public administration practice and scholarship relative to its importance to the enterprise of public administration" (Garnett, 1997, p. 6).

Similar results are found in political science. It has dedicated substantial attention to the reporter–politician relationship in democracies, both regarding coverage of candidates, campaigns, and elections, as well as coverage of elected officials once in office (Jacobs & Shapiro, 1996; Lipset, 1996, pp. 285–287; Patterson, 1996a,b; Nimmo & Newsome, 1997; Nye, 1997; Alger, 1998; Gans, 1998). However, the field generally focuses less on the relationship between the administrative side of government and the news media. Nearly 40 years ago, Hiebert noted that there were very few studies of the public information function in the U.S. federal government or research that would be relevant to public information practitioners (Hiebert, 1968, p. 6). Since then, little has changed. McKerns noted that the focus of the government–media literature "has been largely myopic, i.e., the primary focus has been on the relationship at the federal level and between the president and the news media in particular" (McKerns, 1985, p. 20). Nimmo and Swanson summed up research in political communications by noting that "even more rare are analyses of bureaucratic communication" (Nimmo & Swanson, 1990, p. 28).

Finally, the literature of media studies regarding the government generally focuses on elected officials, politics, and public policy making. Little separate attention is paid to the nonelected side of government, the bureaucracy. For example, Asante's comprehensive review of the literature did not identify a subfield regarding media coverage of public administration in the section on the government–press connection (Asante, 1997, pp. 11–49).

The following two sections provide a brief summary of the limited available knowledge about how the media covers public administration from a comparative and international perspective.

Media Coverage of Public Administration: First World Nations

An assessment of the trends in media coverage of American public administration concluded that it has been diminishing quantitatively. Further, the reduced coverage has been assuming a greater negative tone; with reporters often framing their stories with archetypal story lines, such as "wasteful bureaucrats," "citizen victimized by bureaucracy," and "agency ignoring real needs" (Lee, 1999, pp. 454–455). The overall impact is that "the bureaucracy and other institutions of government, with little influence and access to the media, get victimized and condemned without proper investigation" by reporters who are driven by a different agenda (Kalantari, 2001, p. 881).

These patterns are spreading to other countries also. Negrine and Papathanassopoulos reported on the Americanization of political communications throughout the world: "Indeed, as television becomes the main source of information for most people, the fact that its own development has been greatly influenced by the U.S. experience increases the connections between practices in the United States and elsewhere" (Negrine & Papathanassopoulos, 1996, p. 53; Patterson, 1998 makes a comparable point). Similarly, the growing importance of talk radio in the United States has spread to other countries, such as Hong Kong, as well (Lee, 2002a).

Several reports by the Organisation for Economic Co-operation and Development (OECD) suggest that the trends regarding U.S. media coverage of public administration are also occurring in other First World countries. OECD consists of 30 of the most economically advanced nations, which have a free-market economic system and a democratic political system. At its "Ministerial Symposium on the Future of Public Service" representatives expressed concern over pressures from the media for rapid responses to problems. In particular, they felt that "the part played by the media, clearly vital to the functioning of democracy and oversight of administrative action, can be disruptive if decision-makers are subjected to permanent inquisition" (OECD, 1996, Session Two, p. 4). As a result of this, a year later OECD issued a public management paper noting general trends in media coverage similar to ones occurring in the United States, including a basic "spin" that is increasingly cynical, superficial, and sensational. This negative trend was compounded in OECD nations by a media focus on scandal, real or fabricated crises and policy failure. Another trend in media coverage is a sense of urgency and expectation of immediate response that has the effect of skewing policy agendas and decision-making. However, "what is urgent is not always what is most important" (Washington, 1997, p. 30).

Although Japan is a democratic and an economically advanced nation like the United States, media coverage of the bureaucracy has been significantly different. Notwithstanding its modern media institutions that are on par with those of the United States, Japan's media gives much greater coverage to the administrative state than U.S. media. According to Krauss, Japanese television had had an "exceptionally large percentage of stories related to the bureaucracy and its advisory councils in Japan (together occupying 36 percent in the Japanese sample versus only 2 percent for mentions of bureaucracy in the American sample)" (Krauss, 1996, p. 99). Whereas U.S. media is executive-centered and input oriented, Japanese media is bureaucracy-centered and output oriented. Krauss concludes that "the portrayal of politics and government, particularly the administrative state, is one of the most important and seemingly distinctive aspects of the content of NHK television news compared to American network news" (Krauss, 1996, p. 102).

This significant difference can be partly attributed to the general cultural factors, but Freeman (2000) attributes it largely to the prevalence of press clubs in Japan. These press-based information cartels limit competition between reporters from different media outlets who are assigned to the same beat. Furthermore, most assignments are institution-based, normally corresponding to major administrative departments. Press clubs have the effect of giving bureaucrats the ability to assert control and define their own agendas.

One similarity between U.S. and Japanese media trends is that "saturation television news coverage in Japan of bizarre events easily rivals its American counterparts" (Pharr, 1997, p. 136) that can have the effect of slowly crowding out the current extensive coverage of bureaucracy. This, again, confirms the trend of the globalization of American-style media coverage of public administration.

Media Coverage of Public Administration: Eastern Europe

According to Édes, one of the ongoing problems for government information officers in the transitional countries of Eastern Europe is what he calls "immature media." Somewhat comparable to some Western media trends, he noted that "some newspapers make little effort to report in a balanced, objective manner, and resort to sensationalism to attract readers" (Édes, 2000, p. 463).

Earlier, O'Neill had noted the Americanization of television coverage of government news in Eastern Europe, describing it as aggressive, critical, reckless, and sensational (O'Neill, 1993, p. 155). He concluded that "however much these trends may vary from country to country, they are traveling in the same general direction: toward various degrees of mediacracy, in which TV politics replaces old patterns of governance, . . . and instant public emotions override reflection and deliberation in the making of policy" (O'Neill, 1993, p. 156).

A newspaper reporter from Germany who was assigned to cover southeastern Europe noted "because of a journalist's constraints always to cover 'headline-news', important background stories on subjects like public administration reform never or seldom are written" (Rub, 1996, p. 47). Kimble suggested that in the successor states to the Soviet Union, which had been dominated by the administrative apparatus, the emergence of market economies, personal freedom, and democracy meant, "government is becoming irrelevant" (Kimble, 1998). Diminished media coverage of the bureaucracy, she argued, reflected evolving citizen perceptions of those institutions that are now important in their lives and those that no longer are.

What to Do? Practitioner Responses to the Globalization of Media Treatment of Public Administration

The preceding sections have demonstrated that the academic research and reports from practitioners indicate early signs of the trends of globalization regarding press coverage of public administration in the United States, including reduction in quantity and an increasingly negative tone in quality. These patterns are gradually manifesting themselves in other countries as well. This trend is currently most noticeable in the First World nations, which are economically, socially, and politically at levels comparable to that of the United States. However, as a broad generalization, the 21st century era of globalization suggests that these trends will eventually encompass all nations, not just the First World countries. If so, what is the modern-era public administrator to do?

Training

Public administration education has gradually reduced its focus on the importance of external communications, public relations, and media skills

(Lee, 1998). However, with the emergence of the digital era as one of the most important driving factors of globalization, training in the use of information outside the bureaucracy is as important as it is in-house. If "knowledge is power," then certainly in the Information Age effective government administrators need techniques for communicating with the public. In fact, information has become such an important commodity in the globalized world that some theorists are now suggesting that in the next phase of the digital era, the citizenry will assert that it must be given formal legal and constitutional rights to information from government (Bovens, 2002). In this context, government managers-in-training need to include external relations in their curriculum and that current practitioners would benefit by seeking continuing education and professional development in this area.

In a separate piece, this author has suggested a specific and detailed curriculum outline for public information, including the purposes, audiences, and techniques that government managers can use to accomplish their responsibilities (Lee, 2000). The key is to avoid the temptation of focusing on learning techniques in a sterile context. Rather, the appropriate techniques emerge from the purpose and audience in each specific circumstance. Therefore, selection of communication techniques should be the last step of the process for the practitioner, rather than the first. Certainly, media relations is a narrower subject within the larger rubric of external relations, but public administrators can use public information and external communications strategies very effectively for many other related and important missions, not just media relations (Weiss, 2002; Freeman & Nelson, 2003).

Given the global trend of the Americanization of media coverage of public administration, practitioners particularly need to hone their skills for dealing with an increasingly unfair, distracted, trivia-obsessed, and crisis-driven press corps. Some specific recommendations include (Lee, 1999, pp. 455–458):

- Becoming a policy entrepreneur, especially focusing on the importance of the "problem definition" stage of public issues and concerns.
- Learning to speak in short and pithy sound-bites and being able to express a position in ten words or less.
- Making it as easy as possible for reporters to cover the agency.
- Communicating through multiple mass media, not just the "traditional" ones.
- Seeking allies in the press corps, especially individual reporters who are concerned about a problem and would be willing to publicize it.
- Involving the agency's public affairs staff in decision-making at the highest level of the organization.

- Putting a human face on the issue the agency is involved in, by bringing forward a client or customer who would be likely to appear sympathetic to the reporters and the audience.

Some practical and useful handbooks on conducting media relations have been published for U.S. practitioners including Brown (2002), Cohen and Eimicke (2002, Chap. 11), Krey (2000), Bjornlund (1996), and Wade (1993). Assuming that the globalization of media relations in public administration is indeed a gradual Americanization of it, some elements of these training guides can be useful for international practitioners where similar trends are occurring.

E-Government and Direct Reporting to the Citizenry

The emerging global concept of e-government has the potential of revolutionizing many elements of public administration, governance, and democracy (Kakabadse et al., 2003; Margetts, 2003). In particular, direct government-to-citizen (G2C) e-gov and the emerging phenomenon of e-democracy offer the practitioner an efficient, inexpensive, and mass-reaching way to communicate *directly* with the citizenry. For the first time, by using e-gov technology the public administrator can bypass the press corps and exchange information with the public-at-large. In this respect, e-gov provides an alternative to the traditional reliance of government on the mass media to provide information to the public. Until now, public administrators could only communicate this information to the citizenry *indirectly* through the press. That, of course, has meant that reporters had the power to define the agenda and control what information would reach the individudal members of the public. However, in traditional public administration theory, government managers were also assigned the normative obligation of direct public reporting to keep the citizenry informed of their activities and record (Beyle, 1928; Lee, 2002b). One of the fullest flowerings of institutionalizing public reporting in the United States was the establishment of the Office of Government Reports by President Franklin Roosevelt within the Executive Office of the President. The mission of that agency, which existed from 1939 to 1942 and then from 1946 to 1948, was to keep the public informed of the programs and activities of the Executive Branch and to report back to the president on public opinion (Lee, 2005b).

When it is considered from the perspective of purpose, the obligation of the public administrator to engage in media relations is to account to the citizenry, albeit indirectly through the media. If the rationale for media relations is to engage in public reporting, then the emergence of the digital era permits the practice of public reporting to continue, simply doing it in a slightly different way, directly to the citizenry rather than indirectly through media relations.

The technological capability, provided by e-gov, for government managers to be able to report directly to the citizens without dependence on the media has been called *e-reporting*. Increasingly, public sector organizations are using the Internet to provide information to the citizenry. This helps contribute to the basic need for an informed public in those forms of governance that call for, whether directly or indirectly, the consent of the governed. Certainly, notwithstanding the many variations on democratic government, the *sine qua non* of popular sovereignty is an informed public. Regardless of the details, the expectation is that in a republic, public opinion is of utmost importance.

Until now, the role of the free press has been to serve as an instrument of democracy, by being the only channel that governments can use to inform the citizenry of their activities and then be held accountable by public opinion. Now, G2C e-gov technology permits public managers to engage in e-reporting by keeping the citizenry informed through the Internet, websites, e-mail, and other digital technology applications (Lee, 2005a). In a sense, the technology contributing to globalization of public administration includes the expansion of the definition of traditional media relations to include direct e-reporting to the citizenry. Some best practices in e-reporting include:

- Report consistently, for example at least annually.
- Make it easy to find it on a government's homepage.
- Make it easy for a lay citizen to read and understand.
- Include photographs, charts, and other visual aids to communicate the record of the agency in nonverbal forms also.
- Keep it short, since lay citizens are not interested in too much detail.
- Present performance management information.
- Use performance management results that closely correlate to the interests of the citizens, rather than those that would interest managers and policy decision makers.
- Create a feedback loop for citizens to give their opinions, ask questions, and get involved.

More generally, OECD has strongly encouraged public managers to enhance their direct interactions with citizens as a way of promoting citizen engagement. Efforts such as providing information to the public, engaging in consultation with the citizenry, and increasing public participation in policy making contribute not only to better public administration, but also help to balance out the traditional dependence of the government manager on press relations to reach the public (Caddy & Vergez 2001, 2003; Gramberger, 2001). In fact, improved standing with the public can strengthen the political standing of a government agency and helps it in withstanding future pressures and unwanted interference.

In conclusion, the globalization of media relations in public administration presents both problems and responses to the government manager. The Americanization of press coverage of government is contributing to a style of coverage that is increasingly negative, episodic, scandal-driven, and uninformative. However, to counterbalance that spreading phenomenon, the global trend towards e-government is providing the public administrator with new capabilities of communicating directly with the public. This has the potential of discounting the potential harmful effects of the international trends in the media coverage. In this regard, the 20th century focus on press relations in public administration is being superseded, thanks to technological advances, into a managerial activity that could be called public relations — in the best sense of that term. The key, as always, for public administrators is to be adaptable and fleet-footed in implementing their role of keeping the citizenry informed of their activities, stewardship, and record.

Acknowledgment

An earlier and shorter version of the literature review portion of this chapter was presented in "Journalists and administrators: International and comparative trends in relations between the media and public administration," in the February 2000 issue of *Global Network*, the e-newsletter of the section on Comparative and International Administration of the American Society for Public Administration. Retrieved September 23, 2004: http://www.uncc.edu/stwalker/sica/GN1.html.

References

Alger, D. (1998). Megamedia, the State of Journalism, and Democracy. *Harvard International Journal of Press/Politics, 3*, 126–133.

Asante, C.E. (Compiler) (1997). *Press Freedom and Development: A Research Guide and Selected Bibliography*. Westport, CT: Greenwood.

Baker, R. (ed.) (1994). *Comparative Public Management: Putting U.S. Public Policy and Implementation in Context*. Westport, CT: Praeger.

Beyle, H.C. (1928). *Governmental Reporting in Chicago*. Chicago: University of Chicago Press.

Bjornlund, L. (1996). *Media Relations for Local Governments: Communicating for Results*. Washington, D.C.: International City/County Management Association.

Bovens, M. (2002). Information Rights: Citizenship in the Information Society. *Journal of Political Philosophy, 10*, 317–341.

Brown, L. (2002). *Your Public Best: The Complete Guide To Making Successful Public Appearances in the Meeting Room, on the Platform, and on TV* (2nd ed.). New York: Newmarket Press.

Caddy, J. and Vergez, C. (2001). *Citizens as Partners: Information, Consultation, and Public Participation in Policy-Making*. Paris: Organisation for Economic Co-operation and Development.

Caddy, J. and Vergez, C. (eds.) (2003). *Promise and Problems of E-Democracy: Challenges of Online Citizen Engagement*. Paris: Organisation for Economic Co-operation and Development.

Cohen, S. and Eimicke, W. (2002). *The Effective Public Manager: Achieving Success in a Changing Government* (3rd ed.). San Francisco: Jossey-Bass.

Dwivedi, O.P. and Henderson, K.M. (eds.) (1990). *Public Administration in World Perspective*. Ames, IA: University of Iowa Press.

Édes, B.W. (2000). The Role of Government Information Officers. *Journal of Government Information, 23*, 455–469.

Farazmand, A. (ed.) (1991). *Handbook of Comparative and Development Public Administration*. New York: Marcel Dekker.

Farazmand, A. (ed.) (2001). *Handbook of Comparative and Development Public Administration* (2nd ed.). New York: Marcel Dekker.

Freeman, L.A. (2000). *Closing the Shop: Information Cartels and Japan's Mass Media*. Princeton, NJ: Princeton University Press.

Freeman, M. and Nelson, S. (2003). Communications in Local Government: A Business Planning Model. *IQ Reports* (monograph series of the International City/County Management Association), *35* (4).

Gans, H.J. (1998). What Can Journalists Actually Do for American Democracy? *Harvard International Journal of Press/Politics, 3*, 6–12.

Garcia-Zamor, J.-C. and Khator, R. (eds) (1994). *Public Administration in the Global Village*. Westport, CT: Praeger.

Garnett, J.L. (1997). Administrative Communication: Domain, Threats, and Legitimacy. In J.L. Garnett and A. Kouzmin (eds), *Handbook of Administrative Communication*. New York: Marcel Dekker (pp. 1–20).

Gramberger, M.R. (2001). *Citizens as Partners: OECD Handbook on Information, Consultation, and Public Participation in Policy-Making*. Paris: Organisation for Economic Co-operation and Development.

Grunig, J.E. (1997). Public Relations Management in Government and Business. In J.L. Garnett and A. Kouzmin (eds), *Handbook of Administrative Communication*. New York: Marcel Dekker (pp. 241–283).

Heady, F. (2001). *Public Administration: A Comparative Perspective* (6th ed.). New York: Marcel Dekker.

Hiebert, R.E. (1968). Introduction. In R.E. Hiebert and C.E. Spitzer (eds), *The Voice of Government*. New York: John Wiley & Sons (pp. 3–7).

Hyden, G. (1997). Democratization and Administration. In A. Hadenius (ed.), *Democracy's Victory and Crisis: Nobel Symposium No. 93*. Cambridge, UK: Cambridge University Press (pp. 242–259).

Jacobs, L.R. and Shapiro, R.Y. (1996). Toward the Integrated Study of Political Communications, Public Opinion, and the Policy-Making Process. *PS: Political Science and Politics, 29*, 10–13.

Kakabadse, A., Kakabadse, N.K. and Kouzmin, A. (2003). Reinventing the Democratic Governance Project Through Information Technology? A Growing Agenda for Debate. *Public Administration Review, 63*, 44–60.

Kalantari, B. (2001). Media and the Bureaucracy in the United States. In A. Farazmand (ed.), *Handbook of Comparative and Development Public Administration* (2nd ed.). New York: Marcel Dekker (pp. 877–883).

Kimble, D. (1998). *Postcards from the Edge: Reflections on International and Comparative Administration at Mid-Life* (Panel session). 59th annual national meeting of the American Society for Public Administration (ASPA), May 9–13, 1998 in Seattle, WA, USA.

Krauss, E.S. (1996). Portraying the State: NHK Television News and Politics. In S.J. Pharr and E.S. Krauss (eds), *Media and Politics in Japan*. Honolulu, HI: University of Hawaii Press (pp. 89–129).

Krey, D. (2000). *Delivering the Message: A Resource Guide for Public Information Officials* (2nd ed.). Sacramento, CA: California Association of Public Information Officials.

Lee, M. (1998). Public Relations in Public Administration: A Disappearing Act in Public Administration Education. *Public Relations Review, 24*, 509–520.

Lee, M. (1999). Reporters and Bureaucrats: Public Relations Counter-Strategies by Public Administrators in an Era of Media Disinterest in Government. *Public Relations Review, 25*, 451–463.

Lee, M. (2000). Public Information in Government Organizations: A Review and Curriculum Outline of External Relations in Public Administration. *Public Administration and Management: An Interactive Journal, 5*, 183–214. Retrieved September 23, 2004, from http://www.pamij.com/5_4/5_4_4_pubinfo.pdf.

Lee, F.L.F. (2002a). Radio Phone-in Talk Shows as Politically Significant Infotainment in Hong Kong. *Harvard International Journal of Press/Politics, 7*, 57–79.

Lee, M. (2002b). Intersectoral Differences in Public Affairs: The Duty of Public Reporting in Public Administration. *Journal of Public Affairs, 2*, 33–43.

Lee, M. (2005a). E-Reporting: Using Managing for Results Data to Strengthen Democratic Accountability. In J.M. Kamensky and A. Morales (eds), *Managing for Results 2005*. Lanham, MD: Rowman & Littlefield (pp. 141–195). Also available online as a monograph, retrieved September 23, 2004 from http://www.businessofgovernment.org/pdfs/Lee_Report.pdf.

Lee, M. (2005b). *The First Presidential Communications Agency: FDR's Office of Government Reports*. Albany, NY: State University of New York Press.

Lenn, D.J. (1996). International Public Affairs: Managing Within the Global Village. In L.B. Dennis (ed.), *Practical Public Affairs in an Era of Change: A Communications Guide For Business, Government, and College*. Lanham, MD: Public Relations Society of American and University Press of America (pp. 435–456).

Lipset, S.M. (1996). *American Exceptionalism: A Double-Edged Sword*. New York: W.W. Norton.

Margetts, H. (2003). Electronic Government: A Revolution in Public Administration? In B.G. Peters and J. Pierre (eds), *Handbook of Public Administration*. London: Sage Publications (pp. 366–376).

Martin, D.W. (1989). *The Guide to the Foundations of Public Administration*. New York: Marcel Dekker.

McKerns, J.P. (1985). *News Media and Public Policy: An Annotated Bibliography*. New York: Garland.

Negrine, R. and Papathanassopoulos, S. (1996). The "Americanization" of Political Communication: A Critique. *Harvard International Journal of Press/Politics, 1*, 45–62.

Nimmo, D. and Newsome, C. (1997). *Political Commentators in the United States in the 20th Century: A Bio-Critical Sourcebook*. Westport, CT: Greenwood.

Nimmo, D. and Swanson, D.L. (1990). The Field of Political Communication: Beyond the Voter Persuasion Paradigm. In D.L. Swanson and D. Nimmo (eds), *New Directions in Political Communication: A Resource Book*. Newberry Park, CA: Sage (pp. 7–47).

Nye, J.S., Jr. (1997). The Media and Declining Confidence in Government. *Harvard International Journal of Press/Politics, 2*, 4–9.

O'Neill, M.J. (1993). *The Roar of the Crowd: How Television and People Power Are Changing the World*. New York: Random House.

Organisation for Economic Co-operation and Development (1996). Ministerial Symposium on the Future of Public Services. Paris: Organisation for Economic Co-operation and Development. Retrieved September 23, 2004, from http://www1.oecd.org/puma/gvrnance/minister/session2.htm.

Patterson, T.E. (1996a). Bad News, Bad Governance. *Annals of the American Academy of Political and Social Science, 546*, 97–108.

Patterson, T.E. (1996b). Bad News, Period. *PS: Political Science & Politics, 29*, 17–20.

Patterson, T.E. (1998). Time and News: The Media's Limitations as an Instrument of Democracy. *International Political Science Review, 19*, 55–67.

Pharr, S.J. (1997). Japanese Videocracy. *Harvard International Journal of Press/Politics*, 2(1), 130–138.

Rowat, D.C. (ed.) (1988). *Public Administration in Developed Democracies: A Comparative Study*. New York: Marcel Dekker.

Rub, M. (1996). Press Relations with Governments in Emerging Democracies. In *Effective Communications Between the Public Service and the Media*. SIGMA Papers No. 9 Paris: Organisation for Economic Co-operation and Development (pp. 44–47). Retrieved September 23, 2004, from http://www.sigmaweb.org/PDF/SIGMA_SP09_96E.PDF.

Wade, J. (1993). *Dealing Effectively with the Media: What Local Government Officials Need to Know about Print, Radio and Television Interviews*. Washington, D.C.: National League of Cities.

Washington, S. (1997). Consultation and Communications: Integrating Multiple Interests into Policy; Managing Media Relations. Public Management Occasional Papers No. 17. Paris: Organisation for Economic Co-operation and Development.

Weiss, J.A. (2002). Public Information. In L.M. Salamon (ed.), *The Tools of Government: A Guide to the New Governance*. New York: Oxford University Press (pp. 217–254).

Chapter 9

The Etiology of Transnational Health Security in the Age of Globalization

Elizabeth Sharpe Overman

CONTENTS

Introduction

The accelerated convergence of people associated with intensified globalization is transforming the health situation worldwide. Understanding what makes health a transnational security issue hinges on an awareness of evolution and ecological interdependence. Medical professionals are finding that the etiology of contemporary health security lies not in health events of the last 150 years but rather stretches back 100,000 years to our human beginnings. The assumption was that scientific enterprise coupled with technological development would continue to successfully generate breathtaking advances in health care. This paradigm was premised on the belief that the 30-year increase in the human life span and the dramatic decline in the deadly diseases of smallpox, leprosy, and polio meant that the dangers of infections were a thing of the past. The U.S. Surgeon General announced in 1969 that the health battles of the future were to be waged, exclusively, against chronic and degenerative diseases, and problems of aging. Scientific technology that rapidly distinguished between different kinds of germs lent itself to diagnosis so rapid that the long-term damaging effects of many diseases were marginalized. The reigning epidemiological theory ushering in these advances was based on the fruition of a 19th century model, which witnessed a 150-year decline of infectious disease in North America and Europe and suggested that the diseases would simply disappear, especially as a country developed or modernized. The health situation appeared to be stabilized and even static in wealthy countries.

The new millennium, however, has been accompanied by a reemergence of the "classic diseases" in more toxic, biotic resistant forms accompanied by the appearance of new infectious diseases such as AIDS, Legionnaire's disease, Ebola virus, toxic shock syndrome, multiple drug-resistant tuberculosis, severe acute respiratory syndrome (SARS), and a host of others. This chapter points out that these changes occurred because public health predictors took too narrow a view geographically and temporally. They looked only at a century or two instead of the entire sweep of human history. They failed to recognize that diseases come and go when there are major changes in social relations, among populations, the kinds of food we eat, and the way we use the land. When we change our relations with nature, we also change epidemiology and the opportunities for infection. With or without bioterrorist attacks, the health situation is in constant flux and as we are learning, it always has been. This makes health a transnational security issue in this era of hyperglobalization.

The Sweep of Human History

The emergent globalized public health paradigm begins about 100,000 years ago. A series of migrations out of Africa, first to the geographically contiguous Middle East and then to most of the habitable world scattered humankind in discrete communities across the face of the globe. This ended about 15,000 years ago when the tendency to slowly reintegrate began to merge previously scattered human populations into ever larger units as the barriers among them gradually disappeared. Human interaction combined with technological, social, and cultural exchange across the continents set the world's people on the path of increasing interdependence that it has been following ever since.

Each step in this reintegration of human populations has had significant ecological, political, and socioeconomic consequences, not the least of which has been the insecurity associated with the emergence and the spread of disease. Viruses, bacteria, and various animals and plants have never respected human boundaries. Microbes sailing in the winds or the waters have accompanied travelers, be they explorers, migrants, merchants, missionaries, or mercenaries, mostly with no effect. There have been times, however, when the introduction of microbes has reshaped the entire societies and their accompanying ecosystems, altering the course of human history.

The bones of our paleoithic ancestors reveal that as hunters and gatherers we consumed a wide range of food, which prevented the onset of any of the deficiency diseases related to malnutrition. Pestilence, plagues, and epidemics became permanent problems for humans when paleolithic hunters and gatherers settled down in one place and domesticated animals and various grains in order to produce a narrow range of food crops. The adoption of agriculture and the transition to settled societies exposed humans to diseases they had never encountered before with a resultant deterioration in health. For the first time, not only were a large number of humans living side by side, but many people were sharing living space with animals. Thus began the transfer of diseases and infections between humans and their animals. Cowpox evolved into smallpox; rinderpest and canine distemper became measles; tuberculosis and diphtheria evolved from cattle; influenza from hogs; and the common cold from horses. Leprosy came from the water buffalo and SARS from chickens. As the diseases established themselves in human organisms, they began to spread to new areas with the acceleration of human contact.

The sheer concentration of large human populations offered potential disease organisms a rich and accessible food supply. A steady supply of food led to a vast and rapid increase in the number of people, and soon sustained the merger of clans and tribes into cities and kingdoms. Slowly microorganisms grew and multiplied in human villages as they gave way to cities and robust civilizations. Human proximity, a new experience, became the social norm even though it continues to challenge human health. The emergence of larger administrative units, such as empires, brought previously isolated peoples and microorganisms together. Human populations have to reach specific sizes to sustain infectious disease and they did so with the emergence of the Roman Empire in the West and the Han Empire in the East. Infections became powerful agents of human tragedy as each empire was wracked by strange diseases killing from a quarter to a third of the population at a time. The rise of the Mongol Empire united almost all of China and Korea as well as central Asia, Russia, Iran, and Iraq at a time when caravan traffic across Asia and down into central Africa brought diverse people into contact with one another and lead to the appearance of new diseases. At the same time populations in Europe were expanding, setting the stage for the successive waves of pneumonic and bubonic plague. Sometimes as many as 40 percent of the residents in urban areas perished in a single outbreak. The age of European exploration and colonization brought even more people into contact with one another. The microorganisms that accompanied conquerors, particularly those causing smallpox, measles, typhus, malaria, and yellow fever, killed nearly two thirds of the indigenous populations in the Americas. World War I triggered the annual global influenza epidemics we struggle with today. The HIV/AIDS pandemic that is ravaging Africa, the Caribbean, and parts of East Asia is another example.

From this perspective, one can see that the struggle for existence between different forms of life on Earth is an endless chain of parasitism that we call infection. The typhus louse, the plague flea, and the yellow-fever mosquito have had far more power over the fates of nations than all the warfare combined. Huge societies have collapsed in the face of malaria. Armies have crumbled into rabbles under the onslaught of cholera, spirilla, dysentery, typhoid bacilli, or syphilis. The tsetse fly has devastated huge expanse of humanity.

Microbes evolve to feed on the nutrients within the human body. In response, the human body has evolved three primary ways to fend off dangerous microbes. The best response mechanism available to humans is natural selection. In an epidemic people with genes for resistance to that particular microbe are more likely to survive than people lacking such genes. With repeated exposure, existing human populations will consist of a higher proportion of individuals with the genes for resistance, those without the genes having perished. But the development of these genes can come at an evolutionary price. Sickle-cell, for example, evolved as a protection against malaria and sleeping sickness. Today it can cause anemia or a deoxygenated blood system. Tay-Sachs evolved initially as a protection against tuberculosis and today it causes cancer. Cystic fibrosis, which evolved as a protection from bacterial diarrhea, now causes the lung tissue to solidify to the point of suffocation. The second method, which fends off an invasion of lethal microbes, is the human body's ability to develop a fever and kill germs through the application of heat. The development of vaccinations is the third method of stimulating antibodies or white cell production to the extent that the human body is no longer susceptible to the disease-causing microbes. The evolutionary paradox is that as humans develop more and better agents to confound the infectious microorganisms, the stronger, more varied, and complex they become in response.

We know that microbes jump from animals to humans and back. The major killers of humanity throughout our recent history — smallpox, flu, tuberculosis, malaria, plague, measles, and cholera — are infectious diseases that evolved from diseases of animals, even though most of the microbes responsible for our own epidemic illnesses are now almost confined to humans. Bubonic plague originated in Mesopotamia about the middle of the 11th century, and spread by rats serving as hosts to fleas, with the disease killing an estimated 25,000,000 people. The greatest single epidemic in 20th century human history was that of influenza, derived from a mix of chickens, geese, and hogs, which killed 21 million people at the end of World War I. Until World War II, more victims of war died of war-borne microbes than of battle wounds. It was smallpox, not the military might of the Spanish in 1520, which gave Europeans a decisive advantage in Mexico. Mexico's initial population of about 20 million plummeted to about 1.6 million. For the New World as a whole, the Indian population decline in a century or two following Columbus's arrival is estimated to have been as large as 95 percent. The main killers were Old World germs to which Indians had never been exposed, and against which they therefore had neither an immune nor a genetic resistance.

The original inhabitants of the Americas had not been exposed to diseases such as smallpox, measles, influenza, plague, tuberculosis, typhus, cholera, and malaria. These were the contaminants to which Eurasians, for the most part, were either genetic resistant or immune by the 1400s. This paradox can be attributed to the availability of useful livestock. Those microbes responsible for the infectious diseases of crowded human societies evolved from very similar ancestral microbes causing infectious diseases of the domestic animals with which food producers came into daily contact around 10,000 years ago. Eurasia harbored many domestic animal species and hence developed many such microbes, whereas the Americas harbored few domesticable animal species and therefore many fewer microbes. The question of animal origins of human disease underlies the broadest pattern of human history and is one of the most important contemporary issues today. AIDS, for example, is an explosively spreading human disease that appears to have evolved from a virus resident in wild African monkeys. Another example is the emergence of bovine spongiform encephalopathy (BSE), also called mad cow disease, in the Great Britain. BSE spread to humans as a new variant of Creutzfeld-Jakob disease.

In the 20th century the development of a single-type vaccine against all forms of clinical smallpox, combined with the absence of any reservoir of smallpox virus in nature, made possible the attempt by the World Health Organization to eradicate smallpox from the world. This immense project involved following all contact of every case of smallpox with timely vaccinations to prevent the spread of infection. Smallpox is estimated to have caused 2,000,000 deaths in 1967. No cases were reported from 1977 to 1980, with the exception of two cases in England in 1978 whose source was a laboratory virus. Routine smallpox vaccination has been discontinued, and the virus was stored in four laboratories throughout the world, ready to be made into vaccine if it was ever necessary. Some of the smallpox vials have disappeared from their resident laboratories, raising the possibility that the disease could be used in weapons production programs. AIDS will soon surpass the Bubonic plague as the world's worst pandemic if a vaccine is not found and the 40 million plus people living with HIV/AIDS do not receive the necessary anti-retroviral drugs that could prolong their life. Since the beginning of the epidemic in the late 1970s, 21.8 million people have died. In the next 10–15 years as many as 65 million people could succumb to the disease.

Epidemic diseases move rapidly through human populations spreading microbes until everyone is either dead, recovered, or immune. At that point the disease dies out until a new crop of virgin hosts appears. Infectious diseases that visit us as epidemics share five common characteristics. First, they spread quickly and efficiently from an infected person to a nearby healthy person. Second, the illness is acute. That is people either die shortly or recover completely. Third, those who recover develop antibodies. Fourth, these diseases tend to be restricted to humans. And, fifth, the diseases need a human population that is sufficiently numerous and densely packed, or a new population of susceptible children available for infection by the time the disease would otherwise wane.

Epidemic diseases are also known as crowd diseases. Diseases become successful as epidemics only when the population becomes more vulnerable because the social infrastructure that would have controlled the disease vectors has crumbled. A population of a few hundred thousand sustains measles. We know there are diseases that require a quarter million people to be self-sustaining. As life conditions change, so do opportunities for disease. In the 21st century we may find out which diseases will emerge in crowded populations of 10 or 20 million.

Transnational Security

Over the time human populations have coevolved with millions of other animal and plant species and even larger numbers of potentially pathogenic microorganisms. Those germs that spread the best leave the most offspring and are favored by natural selection. Science regards death of the host as the accidental by-product of infectious disease. The ideal host for any microbe is the one that continues to broadcast the offspring into more and more hosts. The bacteria from cholera diarrheal fluid making its way into the municipal water supply is an example of this. In the current period of increasing dependence and globalized urbanization, many of the once banished microbes are returning, having successfully developed evolved mechanisms to counter the weapons that once banished them. At the root of the resurgence of old infectious diseases is an evolutionary paradox. The more vigorously we have assailed the world of microorganisms, the more varied the repertoire of bacterial and viral strains have been thrown up against us. People, plants, and animals are all coming into contact with new environments through expanded trade and more rapid transportation. Globalization opens societies through economic integration, which could lead to the disappearance of national borders, which inhibit the free flow of people and goods among regions. Patterns of human settlement and behavior are in flux, fostering a resurgence of pathogenic microorganisms combined with the worldwide spread of various kinds of other potentially destructive disease species. This makes health a transnational security issue.

Historically, national security issues are focused exclusively on the nation-state. In a hyperglobalizing environment, health is an arena of shared mutual concern. Public health failures can result in failed regions with devastated economic and social structures. There is a connection between economic growth, vitality, and health. The AIDS/HIV pandemic is a dramatic example of how precipitous population declines cause businesses to lose competitiveness through lower productivity. In countries ravaged by the pandemic, tourism and foreign direct investment falter, skilled workers emigrate, the tax base shrinks, government resources are redirected to health care, and education declines. International action may be necessary to avoid a descent into chaos and preserve health, education, police, and other public services. Global disease surveillance and response systems are not enough. Medical goods and services must be disbursed to prevent the spread of infectious disease. Those countries in the developed world that lead the world in the development of medical technology and medical research and development, possess a global public good, which may be called upon to foster transnational health security by sharing their knowledge and resources with less competitive countries and regions. The need for effective global health security systems comes at a time when governments, the principal authorities for health care implementation strategies, are decentralizing. As political, economic, and developmental activities become transnationalized at all levels and among all types of organizations in complex decentralized networks, centralized structures that traditionally controlled the processes of international activities and decision making will lose influence. This will also impact global public health.

Conclusion

Microbes move seamlessly, crossing national borders with ease. Whereas diseases are transnational, health care delivery systems are national, stopping at borders. The globalized nature of the threat facing the world's population implies that global integration will be sustainable only if systems for regulating and policing it keep improving as well. If the free flow of people, goods, capital, and ideas is important, common prevention and protective measures that facilitate legitimate cross-border movements must be enacted. This calls for enhanced national governments that work co-operatively with other enhanced national governments.

What we are learning is that life on Earth depends on the maintenance of a number of delicate balances between a whole array of complex processes. The most important task in all human history has been to find a way of extracting enough resources for maintaining life — food, clothing, shelter, energy, and other material goods — from differing and dynamic natural ecosystems. The problem for human societies has been to balance various demands against the ability of the ecosystems to withstand the resulting pressures. This is the global health challenge that confronts the whole of humanity.

Further Reading

Billings, J. and J.C. Cantor (2002). "Access," *Health Care Delivery in the United States*, A.R. Kovner and S. Jonas, editors, New York: Springer, pp. 395–426.

Brainard, L.S. (2003). "Role for Health in the Fight against International Poverty," *Biological Security and Public Health*, K.M. Campbell and P. Zelikow, editors, Washington, D.C.: The Aspen Institute, pp. 73–84.

Bulliet, R.W., P.K. Crossley, D.R. Headrick, S.W. Hirsch, L.L. Johnson, and D. Northrup (2001). *The Earth and Its People: A Global History*, New York: Houghton Mifflin Company.

Chyba, C.F. (2004). "Toward Biological Security," *Terrorism and Counterrorism*, R.D. Howard and R.L. Sawyer, editors, Guilford, CT: McGraw-Hill/Duskin, pp. 198–207.

Clinton, W.J. (1993, September 22). *Address of the President to the Joint Session of Congress*, Office of the Press Secretary, Washington, D.C.: The White House.

Collaborative Trilateral Conference: Bringing Health and Health Science into the Foreign Policy Mainstream (April 2003). "Beyond Ditchley: Bringing Health and Health Science into the Foreign Policy Mainstream," *Rand Center for Domestic and International Security*, Santa Monica, CA: Rand, pp. 1–17. (Unattributed.)

Davis, L.E. (2003). "Globalization's Security Implications," Rand Issue Paper, Santa Monica, CA: Rand, pp. 1–8.

Diamond, J. (1997). *Guns, Germs, and Steel*, New York: W.W. Norton.

Fascell, D.B. (2003, October 26). "The Caribbean's Worst Plague: HIV/AIDS," *Revista Inter-Forum*, Vol. 4, 1–4.

Flynn, S.F. (2004). "American the Vulnerable," *Homeland Security*, First Edition, J.B. Thomas, editor, Guilford, CT: McGraw-Hill/Dushkin, pp. 2–8.

Garrison, F.H. (1929). *History of Medicine*, London: W.B. Saunders.

Gilpin, R. (2000). *The Challenge of Global Capitalism*, Princeton, NJ: Princeton University Press.

Gottschalk, M. (1999). "The Missing Millions: Organized Labor, Business, and the Defeat of Clinton's Health Security Act," *Journal of Health Politics, Policy and Law*, 24(3), 489–523.

Griffoli, T.M. (2002). *On the Questions of Globalization: Guidance from History, Inspiration for Tomorrow*, Geneva: Graduate Institute of International Studies.

Held, D., A. McGrew, D. Goldblatt, and J. Perraton (1999). *Global Transformation Politics, Economics and Culture*, Stanford, CA: Stanford University.

Heymann, D.L. (2003). "Emerging and Epidemic-Prone Diseases: Threats to Public Health Security," *Biological Security & Public Health*, K.M. Campbell and P. Zelikow, editors, Washington, D.C.: Aspen Strategy Group, pp. 49–56.

Inside Washington Publishers (IWP) (1996, January 15). "Environmental Security Could Become Part of Military's Worldwide Missions," *Defense Environment Alert*, Vol. 1, p. 1.

Jun, J.S. and D.S. Wright (1996). *Globalization and Decentralization: Institutional Contexts, Policy Issues, and Intergovernmental Relations in Japan and the United States*, Washington, D.C.: Georgetown University Press, p. 1.

Kaplan, R.D. (2002). "Fort Leavenworth and the Eclipse of Nationhood," *The Atlantic Monthly*, 278(3), 74–90.

Keohane, R.O. and J.S. Nye, Jr (2000). "Introduction," in J.S. Nye and J.D. Donahue, editors, *Governance in a Globalizing World*, Washington, D.C.: Brookings Institution Press.

Lappe, M. (1994). *Evolutionary Medicine: Rethinking the Origins of Disease*, San Francisco: Sierra Club Books,

Lechner, F.J. and J. Boli (2000). *The Globalization Reader*, Oxford, England: Blackwell Publishers.

Levins, R. (September, 2002). "A Report on the Crisis in U.S. Public Health," *Monthly Review*, 52(4), 8–33.

Love, M.C. (2003). *Beyond Sovereignty*, Belmont, CA: Wadsworth-Thomson.

McNeill, W.H. (1976). *Plagues and Peoples*, New York: Doubleday.

Mongan, J.J. (1995). "Anatomy and Physiology of Health Reform's Failure," *Health Affairs*, 14(1), 99–101, as quoted in Shi, L. and D.A. Singh, editors (2001). *Delivering Health Care in America*, Gaithersburg, MD: An Aspen Publication, p. 96.

National Intelligence Council (January, 2000). *The Global Infectious Disease: Threat and Its Implications for the United States*, as quoted in Kassalow, J.S. (2001). *Why Health is Important to U.S. Foreign Policy*, Washington, D.C.: Council on Foreign Relations, Milbank Memorial Fund.

O'Brien, K. and J. Nusbaum (October 12, 2000). "Intelligence Gathering Asymmetric Threats," *Jane's Intelligence Review*, October 12, 1.

Pilch, R.F. (2004). "The Bioterrorist Threat in the United States," *Terrorism and Counterrorism*, R.D. Howard and R.L. Sawyer, editors, Guilford, CT: McGraw-Hill/Duskin, pp. 208–242.

Pirages, D. (1995). "Microsecurity: Disease Organisms and Human Well Being," *Washington Quarterly,* Autumn.

Pirages, D. and P. Runci (2003). "Ecological Interdependence and the Spread of Infectious Disease," *Beyond Sovereignty*, M.C. Love, editor, Belmont, CA: Thomas Wadsworth, pp. 245–266.

Russell, D.H. and R.L. Sawyer, editors (2004). *Terrorism and Counterrorism*, Guilford, CT: McGraw-Hill/Duskin.

Shi, L. and D.A. Singh (2001). *Delivering Health Care in America: A Systems Approach*, Gaithersburg, MD: Aspen.

Sloan, S. (September, 2002). "Organizing for National Security: The Challenge of Bureaucratic Innovation in the War against Terrorism," *Public Administration Review*, 62(Special Issue), 124–137.

Smithson, A.E. (2003). "The Role of International Institutions in Detection, Deterrence, and Prevention," *Biological Security and Public Health*, K.M. Campbell and P. Zelikow, editors, Washington, D.C.: The Aspen Institute.

Weisskopf, M.G., H.A. Anderson, S. Foldy, L.P. Hanrahan, K. Blair, T.J. Torok, P.D. Rumm (2002). "Heat Wave Morbidity and Mortality, Milwaukee, Wis, 1999 vs 1995: An Improved Response?," *American Journal of Public Health,* 92(5), 830–833.

Zinsser, H. (1963). *Rats, Lice and History*, Boston: Little, Brown and Company.

Chapter 10

Globalization and Public Administration Education: A Process of Mutual Transformation in the Former Soviet Union and Central and Eastern Europe

G. Arno Loessner

CONTENTS

Overview

Two great forces are converging in the 21st century: globalization and civil society. The former benefits from a well-coordinated effort by multinational corporations intent upon competition on a "level playing field." Globalization standardizes the conduct of business and flows of capital across national borders (Beck, 2000, as cited in Beynon & Dunkerley, 2000, p. 4).[1] Firms should compete on the basis of price and product quality. Predictably, those with economic power try to define the rules of the game for those who want to play. Some rules guide transfer and tenure of property ownership. Others enhance competition and transparency. The intent is to reduce the risk of doing business by creating a business atmosphere of stability and predictability.

Side effects of globalization may include economic, political, and cultural disruption. Rules that standardize practices can disconnect people from their cultures. In countries with weak institutions, these side effects may be worse than the ills they are intended to address (Friedman, 2000; Held, 1999, as quoted in Beynon & Dunkerley, 2000, p. 8).

Globalization in the former Soviet Union and Central and Eastern Europe (FSU/CEE) following the "revolution" of 1989–90 has demonstrated negative side effects. World standards reinforced by rapid electronic communications have been imposed on weak institutions after more than four decades of isolation. Reducing the impact of these side effects and restoring social and economic stability will require a stronger civil society, a product of higher education reform in the fields of public administration and public policy.

Globalization and the Former Soviet Union and Central and Eastern Europe

The rapid and severe decline of economic well-being in the FSU/CEE region is unique, resulting in a rate of increase in poverty since 1989 greater than in any other region of the world (World Bank, 2000). Unlike China, which has

[1]Beck makes a distinction between globality, globalism, and globalization. "Globality" refers to the fact that we are increasingly living in a world society in the sense that the notion of closed spaces has become illusory... from now on nothing which happens on our planet is only a limited local event. "Globalism" is the view that the world market is now powerful enough to supplant (local and national) political action. "Globalization" describes the processes through which sovereign national states are criss-crossed and undermined by transnational factors with varying prospects of power, orientations, identities, and networks. The term globalization in this paper incorporates each of these concepts.

achieved notable economic success by pragmatically maintaining its planned economy while introducing market economy principles in parallel to it, the FSU/CEE region suffers from a hasty adoption of Western economic models that have caused social and political turmoil (Lau et al., 2000; McIntyre, 2001; Sachs, 2001). Whereas there have been high yet fairly stable levels of inequality in Latin America over some time, the deterioration of the income distribution in the FSU/CEE region occurred in only a decade, "... a change of unprecedented magnitude and speed" (World Bank, 2000, p. 139). There is little question that globalization is a primary factor in explaining the economic hardships and increasing disparities in income and wealth that threaten the fabric of these (FSU/CEE) societies.

Rather than an attack by young intellectuals intent upon demonizing capitalism, as vocal dissent against globalization may be characterized (Bhagwati, 2002), the complaint is that traditional patterns of life were uprooted in response to pressure for change before workable substitutes were in place. In contrast to the majority of poor people in developing countries, citizens of this region are educated, accustomed to employment, and expecting pensions after retirement (World Bank, 2000, p. 32). The shock to the psyche of the region has been particularly severe.

Countries in the FSU/CEE region are very much in need of becoming players in the global marketplace. They enjoy a comparative advantage of low cost, highly skilled workers in economies that are in search of international credit and trade opportunities to exploit the business advantages that these factors provide. Several CEE countries are either newly admitted or trying to meet the criteria required to join the European Union (EU). It is not surprising, therefore, that 9 of the 45 most globalized countries in the world are found in this region[2] (Foreign Policy Magazine Globalization Index, 2003, pp. 60–72).

Some say that advisers and politicians in the region have been hiding behind the rhetoric of globalization to avoid accepting responsibility for fiscal and economic failure (McIntyre, 2001; Smadja, 1997). Others conclude that the problems arise from a combination of long-term institutional insufficiency exacerbated by effects of globalization (Sachs; World Bank). Although exact causes are debated, the fact is that governments have tried to meet global expectations by reducing resources for traditional social programs (social dumping) and weakening environmental regulations (regulatory arbitrage).

Predictably, these attempts to make foreign direct investment more attractive have actually discouraged investment, undermined citizen confidence in governments, and helped encourage organized crime and

---

[2]The 9 EU countries and their ranks in the list of top 45 globalized countries in the world are: Czech Republic (15), Croatia (22), Hungary (23), Slovenia (25), Slovakia (27), Poland (32), Romania (40), Ukraine (42), and Russia (45). Romania expects to join the EU in 2007.

corruption — a situation that makes the process of organizing and delivering public administration education all the more complicated and all the more necessary (McIntyre, 2001; World Bank, 2000 and 2003). Moreover, the CEO of the International Labor Organization, complaining about the negative impact of globalization on employment, concludes that the outcomes are good for corporations and bad for employees. "We see a situation where high productivity, high-quality, high technology are no longer linked to the notion of higher wages. We see a new world where instead of creating new jobs, high productivity is destroying jobs." This is, of course a transition. But nobody knows how long the transition will last. We see a situation where there is a complete delinkage between the fate of the corporation and the fate of its employees. "If I want to put it in extreme form, you might say that the better the corporation is today, the shakier is the fate of the employee" (Smadja, p. 2).

Globalization and Higher Education

If other cultures are to function effectively in the international marketplace, it will be necessary that they have an informed electorate and responsive public officials. This means an educational effort consistent with international educational standards that concurrently steers university teaching, research, and public service activities to meet the needs of civil society. Teaching and research in the field of public administration and public affairs education must be at the heart of this educational reform.

Accomplishing such reform will require several changes in the way higher education is conducted, ranging from institutional governance and management practices to rethinking traditional faculty roles and pedagogical practices. Should educators place a priority on reform? The World Bank thinks so:

> Under state socialism, many countries attained high rates of participation in education, producing large numbers of skilled graduates, and cutting edge research. Achievements in tertiary education were particularly noteworthy in mathematics, natural sciences and engineering. However, the introduction of a market economy resulted in a sharp decline in public funding for colleges, universities and scientific academies...the quickening pace of both social and technological change increased the rate at which skills became obsolete and undermined the effectiveness of the hyper-specialization that had characterized tertiary education under socialism. Demand for broad skills such as critical analysis, problem solving and teamwork greatly increased. Colleges, universities and scientific academies in Russia and other transition economies are struggling to adjust to these new realities.
>
> World Bank (2003, p. 2)

American Land Grant institutions have extended higher education into the community. Perhaps this successful approach of integrating public service in research and teaching might be adapted in FSU/CEE, keeping in mind lessons learned from the mistakes of rapid adjustments during the 1990s. It is interesting to consider how these reforms may be facilitated by globalization, in what might be termed a process of mutual transformation.

Enrollments in post-secondary education are increasing rapidly in FSU/CEE, partly in response to the opportunities of the global marketplace (UNESCO, 1995) (Table 10.1). Students, no longer captives of the state higher education system, are in a stronger position as consumers. They want relevance in university education and academic credentials that permit advanced study and career opportunities abroad. The word "relevant" might mean qualified teachers imbedding examples from applied research in their teaching, as suggested by this review of programs in the Czech Republic:

> There are some problems common to all public administration programs in the Czech Republic, even within faculties with many of the prerequisites for the field. Of primary importance is the lack of coordination of teaching and research activities in faculties of public administration, as well as the fact that research tends to lag behind teaching efforts. At present, this condition is, to a certain extent, justified by the short history of public administration as an academic field and the fact that initial efforts were focused on building curricula. In the future, however, the lack of coordination between these essential areas will become problematic and may lead to a substantial decrease in the competitiveness of the field with classic economic, legal, sociological and geographic disciplines. In addition, the issue of improving the quality of teaching must be addressed, particularly by introducing young qualified faculty. This is especially true in many regional academic institutions.
>
> NISPAcee (2000)

Should their universities fail them, they may be expected to take advantage of enhanced opportunities for student mobility. As countries gain membership in the EU, their citizens enjoy the same tuition at European universities as other EU nationals. In Britain, the difference is a maximum tuition charge of £1125 instead of £16,000, the amount charged for residents of non-EU countries. Most pay nothing, because their family's earned income is below the £21,475 threshold that applies in England. This has resulted in a 30 percent increase in demand in the United Kingdom for university placements from nonresident applicants (Halpin, 2005).

Unfortunately, improvements in mobility are not yet significant enough in many FSU/CEE countries to influence the higher education market. The loss of the traditional social safety net experienced since 1990 has meant that many students are still needed at home to help provide for family; so

Table 10.1 Post-Secondary Education in CEE, Selected Data, 1998–01

Country	*Population 2000 (000)*	*Enrollment 1998–99*	*Enrollment 1999–00*	*Enrollment 2000–01*	*Enrollment 2000–01 as percent of population*	*percent GDP spent on tertiary ed.*[a]
Belarus	1,582	353,108	377,167	437,995	27.7	6.0 percent
Bulgaria[b]	1,161	270,007	261,321	247,006	21.3	NA
Czech. Rep.[c]	10,293	231,224	253,695	260,044	NA	4.5
Estonia	206	48,684	53,613	57,778	28.0	7.6
Georgia[c]	5,335	130,164	137,046	140,629	NA	NA
Hungary	1,468	279,397	307,071	330,549	22.5	5.2
Kazakhstan	2,956	323,949	370,321	445,651	15.1	NA
Latvia	346	82,042	91,237	102,783	29.7	5.9
Lithuania	533	107,419	121,904	135,923	25.5	NA
Poland	6,559	1,399,090	1,579,571	1,774,985	27.1	5.3
Romania	3,612	407,720	452,621	533,152	14.8	3.6
Russian Fed.	22,753	NA	NA	7,224,014	31.7	3.1
Slovakia[c]	5,380	122,886	135,914	143,909	NA	4.2
Slovenia	291	79,126	83,816	91,494	31.4	NA

Source: UNESCO.
[a]Most recent year during the period 1998–01.
[b]Reductions in enrollments in Bulgaria may be attributed to reported 5.4 percent reduction in population between 1995 and 2000.
[c]Population for various years from www.gazetteer.de/home.htm
NA: Not available

although the potential for increased mobility is improved, most students and their families currently lack the financial resources to take advantage of it. Student mobility is likely in the future to become an important globalization-inspired factor contributing to education change in this region, but it is not likely to be influential in the near term. Reform that may be experienced will probably have to come from within.

Are the conditions present to help nurture such reform? An important factor that is stimulating reform from within is the demand from new groups of higher education consumers. An emerging practice of training of civil servants creates a new higher education clientele not known to FSU/CEE universities prior to 1990. These students and other "nontraditional" students from the private sector and their employers expect high-quality educational product and student services. This trend is changing the nature of the civil service[3] requiring universities to look at new ways of doing business to achieve both pedagogical reforms and budget savings (Johnstone, 2002).

Some of these changes have the potential to impact the way students learn. For example, FSU/CEE students and faculty may spend 30–35 hours a week in classroom lectures. University public administration departments in the region are seeking new approaches to allow more time to be spent in problem-based and service learning and the development of relevant case studies. These pedagogical changes present potential opportunities for American faculty to make an important contribution in the region if a process of adaptation of American norms in curriculum and practice can be developed in working relationships with Western universities.

FSU/CEE faculty teach public policy and public management using U.S., Western European, and Australian cases and examples. The use of applied research and service learning as teaching tools is needed to give greater meaning and relevance to public administration education in the region and to link learning to practice. Gaining this dimension in public administration education is also likely to help students and faculty tailor public administration education to local areas' needs — the essence of the mutual transformation process that may help reform local institutions and educational processes.

Service learning and applied research can be controversial and new techniques usually require new skills on the part of faculty, new sources

---

[3]"The excessive presence of political ideology in the civil service interfered with objective decision-making and led to political criteria guiding civil service appointments over professional qualifications. This clearly had a negative effect on the education of civil servants to the detriment of individuals with the necessary skills for such positions. Other factors, in particular the constant economic downgrading of the 'non-productive' sphere and the civil service, also affected the quality of public administration. In addition, arts and humanities education, and, particularly in the 1950s, legal education were undervalued and preference was given to technical subjects, which were more distant by their nature from public administration." http://www.nispa.sk/reports/Czech/Part1.htm

of funding, and new relationships for universities in the community.[4] In the West, faculty may experience some local controversy after the production of a public policy study report. This has not been the experience in FSU/CEE. Implementing these reforms will require an established university presence in the community by stronger university rectors (presidents), who will need to work with advisory and governing boards, of which there is little to no experience in the region. Rectors will need to find independent sources of funding to help faculty establish community linkages (Marga, 2002).

As strong relations with civil society become a more important part of public affairs education, the activity will help university managers rely less upon top-down direction from the central education ministries. But these changes will take time, in part, because rectors currently lack sufficient authority to make them. The practice of university public service activity has often not been clear to university officials or to the public officials they might serve. Under the previous system, the university did not train those responsible for public functions or conduct surveys or applied research or policy forums. The development of capacity in these practices provides an opportunity for American faculty in this region.

Another significant constraint is the process by which rectors are selected (Frenyo, 2002). Currently, faculty and students in the university senate elect rectors for terms of four or five years' duration, usually with a two-term limit. Largely symbolic, prior to 1989, senates have become more influential. External boards and donors may be expected to want to play by different rules if a more "Western" corporate management style is adopted. For example, prior to 1989, it was often common practice that deans and department heads would go around the rector to make budget deals directly with the Ministry of Education (Prof. Dr. Joze Mencinger, Rector of the University of Ljubljana, Slovenia, personal communication. April 2, 1999). These practices would have to change as rectors become CEOs working for governing boards in a new approach to governance and financial support.

Principles of academic freedom, institutional autonomy, and accountability are not well rooted in FSU/CEE. Universities lack experience in institutional advancement and advocacy, and have little incentive for entrepreneurship in university management (Petrin et al., 2002).[5] In addition, government officials are inexperienced with academic–industry relations, often resulting in universities in the region encouraged to develop links

---

[4]A recent example is the election of a member of the PA faculty at Babes–Bolyai University as Mayor of Cluj–Napoca, the city in which the University is located. The University had very little contact with the previous Mayor, but is now involved in applied research, student internships, and other service-learning applications that involve the city.

[5]One university described the process used in buying computers. University officials decided on the machine they wanted and ordered as many units as their budget permitted. There was no

with overseas corporations, rather than relying on local experience (Etzkowitz et al., 1998, p. 153). Pressures from the global educational marketplace will likely be a necessary catalyst for change in traditional university practices, because the role of universities in the region has been that of guardian and interpreter of culture, oriented more to preservation than to change. Higher education leaders, who are more likely to emphasize the place of their institutions in history than their potential as societal change agents, often describe their universities as one of the oldest universities in their country.

Public administration faculty may also be expected to resist change. Some resistance has come from inexperience with Western concepts and teaching methods, whereas some is based in a reluctance to change direct advisory relationships (paid consultancies) with local clients that have helped supplement meager university salaries. Faculty salaries will have to be increased if they are to devote the time necessary to achieve a Western-style-service learning approach to public affairs education. Unfortunately, most universities in the region currently lack the resources to raise faculty salaries sufficiently to accomplish this.

The Network of Institutes of Public Affairs/Administration in Central and Eastern Europe (NISPAcee), with 109 institutional members in 21 countries, was organized with the assistance of the U.S. National Association of Schools of Public Affairs and Public Administration (NASPAA) to facilitate intra-regional and international exchanges on matters of public affairs education and practice. This is a means of "globalizing" public administration education, in which FSU/CEE universities seek best practice adaptation. European-wide convergence of higher education standards, a major thrust of the Bologna Declaration of 1999, is another influence of globalization that may help bring about reforms in the practice of public affairs education. The Declaration recognizes a role for higher education in a competitive global environment: "We must in particular look at the objective of increasing the international competitiveness of the European system of higher education. The vitality and efficiency of any civilization can be measured by the appeal that its culture has for other countries. We need to ensure that the European higher education system acquires a world-wide degree of attraction equal to our extraordinary cultural and scientific traditions" (Bologna Declaration, 1999).

Preparing students for the new environment influenced by globalization requires new subjects and approaches to learning. Just as it is important to

---

consideration of having firms compete for the order; no effort to buy some from each of several vendors, with the understanding that the vendors that provided the best price and service would be preferred in future orders; and no request that potential vendors consider contributing a certain number of units as a way to promote future sales to graduates and help a resource-poor university meet its needs. It will take time to change these practices.

understand the role of profit to the economic engine of a society, it is also important to appreciate the distribution of responsibilities of the public and nonprofit sectors in a three-sector economy (Weisbrod, 1975). There is a need for new courses in ethics in public administration, environmental policies, social welfare policies, public–private partnerships, efficiency and effectiveness in the public sector and the development of new types of public administration, and for discussions of balance between theory and practice, policy and management, qualitative and quantitative, specialization and core knowledge skills (Barth, 2002; Denhardt, 2001).

Universities seek to accommodate local stakeholders in an effort to be accepted in their societies, while also asserting their autonomy in research, teaching, admissions, and university management practices (Marga, 2003). In addition, universities must attend to external factors to meet international expectations. All this can be quite confusing and frustrating, particularly in the social sciences, where unlike engineering and the "hard sciences," there is not likely to have been close working communications and connections with the West during the previous system.

Faculty and students who were asked to rationalize the previous social and economic system may now be called upon to critique it and prepare it for change. Faculty and administrators are pressing for modernization and "westernization" of public affairs education programs (NISPAcee, 2002). Public administration faculty need partnerships with governments and the private and nonprofit sectors to further develop emerging public service activities. An increasing number of institutions are offering degrees in public policy and public administration, despite a paucity of relevant experience.[6]

Transition in public administration education has not come easily. Central government ministries have been reluctant to share resources and power with universities. They have resisted experimentation necessary to develop public administration degrees that meet local needs. Some universities, lacking adequate guidance, have launched programs without adequate resources and without pretesting the market. Misdirection and confusion have, in some cases, been accompanied by lack of probity in admissions, grading, and the awarding of degrees (Frenyo, 2002).

[6]An example of this point is found in a statement from an NISPAcee report of evaluation of public administration programs generally in Romania: "Comparative courses in public administration programs, especially courses that concern the EU, are slowly being introduced. These include courses in comparative administration systems, European integration, etc. Although this tendency is now fairly well developed in comparison to 1991, it is still not of major significance or importance. Nevertheless, the trend is to develop this part of the curriculum, especially because of the larger movement of the Romanian higher education system towards Western models and the need to modernize the Romanian public administration system." http://www.nispa.sk/reports/Romania/Part5.htm

Despite false starts and frustration, the sense of urgency to accomplish educational change is palpable. After decades of isolation, university leaders and stakeholders are considering new models of university reform and modernization to achieve a status of international competitiveness. Hasty adoption of Western models has caused great hardship, leading to the conclusion that practices elsewhere may not necessarily be "best practice" for this region; or even if they are best practice, they should be adapted to local needs, not adopted hastily. Using this approach, the adaptation of American experience by FSU/CEE universities may indeed insure a process of mutual transformation.

The author gratefully acknowledges assistance for this chapter from the Salzburg Seminar in American Studies and the Morris Library at the University of Delaware.

References

Barth, T.J. (2002). Reflections on building an MPA program: Faculty discussions worth having [electronic version]. *Journal of Public Affairs Education, 8*(4): 253–261.

Beynon, J., and Dunkerley, D. (eds.) (2000). *Globalization: The Reader.* New York: Routledge.

Bhagwati, J. (2002). Coping with antiglobalization. *Foreign Affairs, 8*(1): 2–8.

Bologna Declaration of 1999 (1999, June). Retrieved April 29, 2005 from http://www.unige.ch/cre/activities/Bologna%20Forum/Bologne1999/bologna%20-declaration.htm

Denhardt, R. (2001). The big questions in public administration education. *Public Administration Review, 6*(5): 526–534.

Etzkowitz, H., Webster, A., and Healey, P. (eds.) (1998). *Capitalizing Knowledge: New Intersections of Industry and Academia.* Albany, New York: SUNY Press.

Foreign Policy Magazine Globalization Index (2003). Measuring globalization: who's up, who's down? *Foreign Policy, 134*: 60–72.

Frenyo, L. (2002). Democratic inefficiency in higher education governance and management in transition societies of the former East Bloc. In *Universities Project Final Report, 1997–2002.* Salzburg, Austria: Salzburg Seminar. Retrieved April 25, 2005 from http://www.salzburgseminar.org/UP

Halpin, T. (2005, January 27). Universities pay the price of European expansion. *TimesOnline.* Retrieved April 30, 2005 from http://timesonline.co.uk/article/0,3561–1458287,00html

Johnstone, D. (2002). Free higher education: who can afford the myth? *In Universities Project Final Report, 1997–2002.* Salzburg, Austria: Salzburg Seminar. Retrieved April 25, 2005 from http://www.salzburgseminar.org/UP

Lau, L., Qian, Y., and Roland, G. (2000). Reform without losers: an interpretation of China's dual track approach to transition. *Journal of Political Economy, 108*(1): 120–133.

Marga, A. (2002). Choices for a high performance university. In Universities Project Final Report, 1997–2002. Salzburg, Austria: Salzburg Seminar. Retrieved April 25, 2005 from http://www.salzburgseminar.org/UP

Marga, A. (2003). *University Reform Today*, 2nd ed. Cluj–Napoca, Romania: Cluj University Press.

McIntyre, R. (2001). Globalization and the role of the state: lessons from central and Eastern Europe. *The Ecumenical Review*, *53*(4): 447–479.

NISPAcee (2000). Comparative analysis of the contents of public administration programmes. Retrieved April 25, 2005 from http://www.nispa.sk/reports/Czech/Part4.htm

NISPAcee (2002). Evaluation of academic programs in the field of public administration. Retrieved April 25, 2005 from http://www.nispa.sk/reports/Romania/part5.htm.

Petrin, T., Vitez, R. and Mesl, M. (2002). Sustainable Regional Development: Experiences from Slovenia. In Jean Pyle and Robert Forant (eds.) *Globalization, Universities and Issues of Sustainable Human Development*. Edward Elgar. Northampton.

Sachs, J. (2001). The strategic significance of global inequality. *The Washington Quarterly*, *24*(3): 187–198.

Smadja, C. (1997). Globalization and enterprises: playing the winner takes all game. ILO Enterprise Forum 96. Geneva: International Labor Organization. Retrieved April 25, 2005 from www.ilo.org/public/english/employment/ent/entforum/forum96

UNESCO (1995). Policy paper for change and development in higher education. Retrieved April 30, 2005 from http://unesco.unesco.org/images/0009/000989/098992e.pdf

Weisbrod, B.A. (1975). Toward a theory of the voluntary nonprofit sector in a three-sector economy. In E.S. Phelps (ed.), *Altruism, Morality, and Economic Theory*. New York: Russell Sage Foundation, pp. 171–195.

World Bank (2000). Making transition work for everyone: poverty and inequality in Europe and Central Asia. Washington, D.C.

World Bank (2003, March 25). Modern tertiary education key to harnessing global knowledge economy: Bank says Russia's science and technology tradition is valuable asset in modernizing high-tech knowledge industries. Press release. Moscow.

CONSEQUENCES AND IMPLICATIONS FOR GOVERNANCE

Chapter 11

Globalization and Information and Communications Technology Influences on Democratic Governance

Jack Pinkowski

CONTENTS

Introduction

In his book *1984*, Orwell (1961) envisioned a future that would be surmounted by electronic communication wherein citizens would be constantly monitored and controlled by "Big Brother." According to Orwell's scenario, information technology would evolve as an instrument of oppression, resulting in citizens viewing their government with suspicion because all their behaviors, attitudes, opinions, actions, political views, and religious beliefs would be recorded in databases by the surveillance instruments of the authoritative state. The end result would be substantial enhancement of state political power at the expense of personal freedoms, human rights, individuality, and democracy.

Technology would ultimately pose a threat to liberty without respect for human rights in the name of the omnipresent nation-state. The states of the world would be diminished in number as an outcome of the behemoths getting more powerful through their control of knowledge and recorded history. In *1984*'s world, only three countries would remain with most of the Western world part of Oceania. And the three state powers would be continuously at war with each other. Individuality would be inhibited and squelched. The totalitarian state would maintain power through censors and Thought Police who monitor everybody's behavior, thoughts, and ideas. Democracy would become an underground movement, and conformity would be the only sane path to survival.

The world has changed substantially, especially regarding technology, since Orwell penned *1984* at mid-century, but the future did not turn out the way he envisioned. The number of countries has not been reduced to just three but has grown progressively over the last 40 years, so that there are now 170 or more nation-states in the world (Dicken, 1998). Orwell was right though, in that technological change would be a hallmark of the era and knowledge would be a source of power. But its consequences for the human condition, governance, and democracy are quite different. In fact, assessment of these outcomes at the beginning of the 21st century is far from certain. This chapter presents an overview of globalization and democracy with a focus on information and communications technology and how it can contribute to individual freedom and free expression. At the same time that technology allows for individual expression and facilitates participative governance, it has the potential to be a tool of propaganda and special interests, not all that far from Orwell's dark model.

Globalization and Technology

Globalization in some form has been with us for as long as men have ventured out to trade around the world. One consequence of world trade has always been the intermingling of ideas and cultures. Mercantilism, colonialism, and the worldwide factory are arguably contemporary manifestations of exploitation in the name of utilitarianism as described by Bentham (1843/1962) and Mill (1863/1987). In this view, for the sake of the greatest good for the greatness number, it would be alright to oppress a small minority if it benefits the great majority.

The Internet and the World Wide Web[1] have intertwined the technologically advanced segments of the world's population with the consequence that power has been shifted downward to the individual at the expense of the nation-state. This may actually reinforce democracy in that the voice of the individual has been provided with more political freedom. People and individuals have a voice that can be heard. Globalization has been attributed to the spread of democratic governments and increased legitimacy for newly created ones in recent years (Grindle, 2000). But as the Internet and worldwide computing and telephonic communication continue to expand and influence the daily lives of people around the world, public confidence in government has declined in many democratic countries (Nye, 1997). This is a paradox. Suffice is to say that democracy has been transformed.

As a marketplace for ideas, the Internet functions as if it were a town hall meeting reaching out to disparate audiences in cyberspace. Computer-aided communications have indeed been employed in town meetings to facilitate communication between citizens and their elected representatives (Guthrie & Dutton, 1992; Hacker, 1996). Breakthroughs in information technology enable the world's population to access information about distant regimes in addition to keeping abreast of their hometown governments. New social forms do not necessarily emerge as a consequence of technology. But over the last several decades of the 20th century, the interaction between technology and globalization has resulted in changes in world geopolitics. It has resulted in new ways of producing goods and services and has more freely spread ideas as a byproduct of interaction in global business exchanges.

The production chain for goods is worldwide following cheap labor, abundant natural resources, relaxed environmental regulation, and the flow of capital, all of which are augmented by technology and communications. Negative externalities are disregarded in the name of corporate profitability. In the most egregious terms, this includes pollution of the environment,

[1]Although often used synonymously, these two terms are different. The Internet is the architecture of a "network of networks" that links computers globally. It allows any computer to communicate with any other computer in the world as long as they are connected to the Internet. The World Wide Web, or Web, is a popular way of accessing information and is expressly designed for information sharing. It often utilizes browsers to share documents containing graphics, sounds, video, and text.

depletion of natural resources, diminishing quality of life, substandard healthcare, unsafe working conditions, and nonexistent social safety nets. New information technologies allow capital to be shifted throughout the globe between economies literally overnight (Castells, 2000). Financial consequences that span borders equally hastily can have disastrous effects on local currency and markets.

The new means of communications and managing firms means that component parts can be sourced from anywhere in the worldwide production chain. Cairncross (1997) has described this as the "death of distance" where the reduction in the cost of communications is probably the single most important force shaping society in the new century. When we call a telephone number or key a Web site for information and services, we could be communicating with a representative working halfway around the world. The physical location is totally transparent to the inquirer. The interaction of the different cultures has the potential to influence each of their thinking even to the extent of attitude, work habits, schedules, and spoken accents. This cultural globalization contributes to a social and cultural admixture for all participants (Rosendorf, 2000). In one sense this is considered economic development, yet it may be at the expense of exported jobs in another region of the world, such as concerning U.S. steel mills, garments, and textiles manufacturing.

Although technological change has the power to revolutionize the way people live, it also has the potential for a profound effect on how they are governed with implications for the sovereignty of international borders, international trade, and democracy. Dictatorial regimes want more than ever to control their media including what appears on television, in print, and now what is permitted over the Internet. Although social conditions do not directly determine the types of technology in use within a specific community, governments can affect general financial conditions that suffocate or accelerate the process of technological modernization. This has been true throughout history. Neither technology nor business alone could have developed the global economy. The decisive agents in this evolution were governments, especially in the wealthiest countries. The policy changes that shaped the foundation for globalization were deregulation of domestic economic activity in terms of financial markets, the privatization of publicly controlled enterprises, and liberalization of international trade and investment (Castells, 2000).

The information technology revolution has been instrumental in restructuring capitalist systems in the last several decades in comparison to the consummate collapse of statism, at least in the Soviet model. In contrast, the Chinese model, which seems to embrace capitalism and integration in global economic networks, is leading to structural changes and likely will lead to internal political conflicts and institutional change in the coming years (Castells, 2000). Globalization, along with changes in communications technologies, works together and complements social and economic progress. The networked society depends on "interconnectedness" that supports the knowledge economy. The benefits of globalization however have not as yet been distributed equally among countries, populations, or families, and the poorest within any community have been least positioned to benefit (Grindle, 2000).

Significant changes in local control over public services and resources, private investment, and privatization have consequences for governments too. In some cases, they are leading to global governance and reduced control by local governments over opportunities for development (Strange, 1996). Globalization has negatively affected transparency and accountability thereby shifting power from elected officials as direct representatives of the people to nonelected corporate officers, trade officials, and international, non-governmental organization bureaucrats.

The Information Technology Revolution: A Power Shift

The power shift from the central authority nation-state to the individual is augmented by the growth of multinational business firms, relatively cheap and quick worldwide air travel, and satellite communications that effectively make transnational corporations more powerful than many states. It also makes them able to disregard many cross-border restrictions with impunity (Korten, 2001). The biggest problem with the power that international corporations have amassed is that it has not been accompanied by corresponding obligations to workers and consumers. Consideration has been given to neither the preservation of natural resources nor the impacts on neighbors through unintended consequences and negative externalities. Nevertheless, the appeal, convenience, and affordability of worldwide commerce contribute to the pursuit of methodological individualism on the microfirm level, as well as for Fortune 500 firms. Today's worldwide entrepreneurs also include "mom-and-pop" businesses who market on the Internet and ship via FedEx or UPS Worldwide, with instantaneous, secure, online credit card payments. These changes are described as the "third industrial revolution," or the technological revolution, due to the impact of computers and communications technology (Drucker, 1999).

Toffler (1981) parsed human civilization into three "waves." The First Wave was an agrarian-based culture, lasting over thousands of years. The decisive change associated with the transformation brought about by this revolution was that people stopped hunting and gathering. Instead of following their food, they developed food sources on the land they occupied for extended time periods. Socially speaking, this led to extended families and the development of farms. Communication and history during this era was through oral narratives (Toffler & Toffler, 1995).

The Second Wave of human development was the industrial age that lasted a few hundred years. Coming after the Middle Ages, feudal power gave way to commercial organizations because they had the greater ability to mass produce with uniformity and lower prices. As the guilds of craftsmen lost influence, nation-states grew to protect business interests. Cities developed as efficient places to coordinate people and material movements for the manufacture of goods and the provision of specialized personal services. Governmental services developed and with them developed the associated decision making to manage cooperating as well as competing human activities. Adam Smith (1776) prescribed the need for governments and a system of laws as essential to protecting capital. Governments came to be the repository for coin of the realm as work became specialized and workers received pay in currency instead of barter in exchange for their labor. Work moved from the home to the factory. When money became more important than land, governments started taxing money, both income and profits, for support to enable them to provide public services. The invention of moveable type meant that information and communication could be shared among greater numbers of people over greater distances. The American Civil War was essentially a clash of the Second Wave, the industrial North, with the First Wave, the agrarian South.

In the Third Wave, material things have become secondary to the transfer of information. This wave has only been apparent since the 1950s. It grew out of the need to track money resulting from the success of the industrial wave where business investment and capital management started to become more complex. In the information age, factory work is less important than knowledge work because factory work is no longer completed from start to finish in one place. Knowledge work can be done anywhere and transferred around the world. Careers and senior employees who know the traditions of the firm are less valuable because information systems themselves keep the information as the repository of knowledge. Oral accounts are no longer passed on as in earlier ages as people spend less time interacting with people. Cell phones are ubiquitous. People communicate electronically and spend less time communicating face-to-face. Everyone is online everywhere as thirst for information is insatiable, instantaneous communication is unavoidable, and the amount of new information keeps expanding. Location and distance are no longer relevant, except in the use of real estate. Mass customization has led to mass sameness. The big losers in this evolution are the middlemen, the brokers, and the traders as now direct-to-consumer is the business model. This disintermediation also extends to politics and governance.

The industrial revolution at the turn of the 19th century demanded energy to power machinery. The governmental regulations over industrial power supplies were based upon the need for intergovernmental cooperation in the production and delivery of large scale power supplies, such as with hydroelectric dams and power transmissions lines. As an outcome, the size and influence of government grew.

With the immigrant workforce and expansion of the industrial base at the turn of the 20th century, police forces and public fire companies were necessary to maintain order amongst disparate workers in dense urban areas. Public schools were necessary for parents who began to work away from home in factories. Capital for infrastructure needed to be accumulated for massive infrastructure projects like railroads, canals, and highways, which led to further regulation and taxation. This also led to growth in government.

Globalization has enhanced the technological revolution so that firms now readily operate in multiple jurisdictions simultaneously with vertical supply chains that are coordinated with high technology and electronic communications. Now, big business marshals its own resources, capital flows, and supply chains around the world where it is their own best interest. This frequently is at the expense of taxing systems of the nation-states and may result in negative consequences for workers' rights.

The shift in commercial activity to avoid taxation will result in smaller government that is more focused on the ways it provides services and regulates business. The new role in the diminished state may be one of informing, monitoring, and measuring services instead of providing them directly (Cairncross, 1997). Geographical boundaries will continue to diminish as the prime determinant of government authority. Today, governments are frequently considered as just one source of authority among many that influence the market (Strange, 1996).

Since the emergence of the state in mid-17th century, growing commerce and globalization have been accompanied by growth in nation-states as the dominant form of governance to facilitate international economic relationships. Governance of national economies was synonymous with government by nation-states with legitimate control over sovereign territory. However, governance is a function that can be performed by a variety of actors including states, non-state actors, private, national, and international institutions as well (Hirst & Thompson, 1996). As an expression of weakened power of individual nation-states under globalization, we see more supraregional associations such as trading blocs, free-trade areas, customs unions, common markets, and economic unions.

With the Internet, individuals can take on causes that even large organizations avoid because of their overhead and interlocking boards of directors (Anderson & Anthony, 1986; Dooley, 1969). Power is shifting and diffusing to include more individual power, small businesses, and small non-governmental organizations. But like tabloid newspapers and celebrity magazines, the Internet is a medium where extreme statements attract attention and unfounded allegations including totally fabricated accounts and intentional misstatements gain authority.

Weblogs (a.k.a. Blogs): The Fifth Estate or Challenge to Democratic Governance?

With the power of the Internet, individuals, as well as representatives of formal or informal groups, have new power in advancing partisan causes without regard to authority or geopolitical boundaries (Davis, 1999; Kamarck & Nye, 2002; Wilhelm, 2000). The latest challenge to democratic governance, trust in government, and respect for traditional authoritative institutions around the world is the persuasive political power of weblogs.

The weblog, or blog, is a hybrid of a personal diary and a public discussion board that welcomes continual commentary on some subject of interest. The word "blog" is new to the English language and started entering dictionaries in the early 21st century, but it is quickly gaining usage around the world. Reportedly, blogs started around 1998 as only 23 blogs were known to exist at the beginning of 1999 (Franke-Ruta, 2005). According to a blog tracking Web site (http://www.Technorati.com), a new blog is created nowadays every 7.4 seconds. The site is currently tracking more than 10 million weblogs.

"Blog" was named as 2004's word of the year by Merriam-Webster Online in recognition of its popularity and increased use in the technology lexicon. The dictionary now defines a blog as "a Web site that contains an online personal journal with reflections, comments, and often hyperlinks provided by the writer" (http://www.m-w.com/info/04words.htm).

Weblogs represent an Internet community of special interest where communications are spread by e-mail among technology-savvy, proactive participants. The Internet community is significant because it has joined other human associations adding to personal affiliation options such as family, church, professional association, workplace, and civil society (Dyson, 1998). There are thousands of weblogs that are formed to express and advance the personal thoughts and beliefs of their writers, often among strangers and antiestablishment. It fits with the postindustrial shift in human values that emphasizes the individual at the expense of, and with diminished respect for, authority and institutions (Inglehart, 1997).

Whether blogs should be classified as "freedom of speech" or a tool of anarchists may rely on the interpretation of the reader. When it transcends political boundaries or even when the message recipients are entirely within one political state, a blog represents the exertion of political influence outside the scope of checks and balances, media scrutiny, or ethical accountability that traditionally protects society against the abuse of a few zealots. Nevertheless, recent successes in marshalling public opinion that have resulted in embarrassment for the establishment would support blogs as yet another element in the decline of the primacy of the nation-state as the center of power.

News and Views

One might argue that lobbyists, for many causes, are essentially no different in their attempts to influence policy. Indeed, the Internet has been described as electronic lobbying (Davis, 1999). Unlike lobbyists, who represent others, bloggers frequently include individualists who have no financial or institutional backing, just access to a computer and an opinion. They can expedite their message to a mass audience with no need for editorial review or fact-checking. Because blogging requires no credentials, careless reporting and baseless charges are possible. Editors in traditional journalism and peer review in academic publication help to mitigate this problem, but it is given wide abandon in blogging journalism (Albritton, 2003). These new political advocates have another substantial advantage over other players in advancing their cause: speed. We have seen terrorist and extremist groups claim responsibility on their Web sites for bombings, plane explosions, and murders even while the flames are raging. Sometimes these are with the express intention of influencing democratic elections. Unlike most Web sites, weblogs invite the viewer to contribute to their argument. By merely accumulating individual opinions and claims, support for an idea or a position grows in commonality among a disparate assembly of Internet users.

The only credibility the bloggers offer is that they usually link to their source (McKinney, 2005). However, those hyperlinked URLs can quickly become dead links and are generally beyond authoritative accountability. As evidence of their emergence as a new source for up-to-the-minute contemporary news and views, some have suggested that libraries include blogs along with other print media in their periodicals collections (Gordon, 2005). The bloggers even have the power to influence the conventional media.

An Internet blog using the moniker Power Line is credited with bringing about veteran journalist Dan Rather's early retirement (McKinney, 2005). Power Line was named the "Blog of the Year" by *Time* magazine for it (Time, 2004). In a dramatic account of the power of Internet communications, the Power Line site was one of the first to compile evidence regarding the flaws in the story that President George W. Bush's service record as reported on the weekly television news magazine, *60 Minutes*, might be bogus. It eventually led to retraction by CBS News of their story on the president's military service record in the Texas Air National Guard and Rather's retirement, one year earlier than planned (Pein, 2005).

The simplicity and alacrity of the blog is well illustrated by this case: One of the bloggers at Power Line received an e-mail from a reader after the original story was telecast. The e-mail was posted with two paragraphs and a link to a threaded discussion on another Internet site, questioning the news story; within an hour an additional 50 e-mail messages were added by other readers with additional information suggesting the documents were fraudulent (McKinney, 2005). The media establishment had effectively been trumped by the antiestablishment, "an army of citizen journalists" (Kurtz, 2004).

Weblogs have the power to make mainstream journalists more accountable, but they also have the power to manipulate information for personal interests. The White House issued the first of its kind press pass to a blogger, Garret Graff, in 2005 to allow him admittance to press briefings, thereby joining the ranks of the White House press corps (Greeley, 2005). Although there are an estimated 1 million professional journalists in the United States, there are an estimated 8 million bloggers, and there could be as many as 280 million (Welch, 2005). The phenomenon is spreading around the world.

The power of their large numbers was evidenced in the global sharing of news in the aftermath of the Indian Ocean tsunami in December 2004. The capacity of the traditional media in remote locations was eclipsed by online dissemination of personal accounts from citizen journalists. Their accounts and various online postings made their way to publication in print and broadcast media to complement conventional media and perhaps did a better job (Waldman, 2005). With the power to compete with the "fourth estate," comes the power to influence democratic elections.

Journalists have had the power to speak and make others pay attention to causes and concerns of their editorial choosing, which has acted as a check on abuses by the government aristocracy, the clergy, and other elites. In doing so, they uphold democratic values and advance the public interest. Now, individual bloggers can attend to similar objectives as traditional journalists, and their digital age journalism may constitute the "fifth estate."

Political Persuasion

The influence of the Internet community and bloggers was dramatically showcased in the presidential election bid of former Vermont governor, Howard Dean, in the 2004 U.S. presidential election (Cone, 2003; Whitney,

2004; www.bloggingofthepresident.com). The blog in Dean's campaign was used to build his community of supporters and inspired thousands of citizens to get involved. The Dean blog helped to frame the campaign ideologically and provide an effective means to fund his campaign activities. Dean's early campaign success may also have been due to the weakened power of the traditional broadcast media to build grassroots support for candidates (Lessig, 2003).

In an online fund-raiser, Dean was able to raise more money than Dick Cheney on the same weekend at a $2000-a-plate luncheon for the campaign (Palser, 2003). Dean was not the only politician to demonstrate the power of bloggers and partisan Internet journalism in elections (Walker, 2004). Senate Democratic leader, Tom Daschle, was defeated by John Thune in South Dakota by bloggers in Thune's campaign (Crowley, 2005). This approach builds on prior Internet-mediated campaigns that proved successful. John McCain raised millions of dollars in 2000 and signed up tens of thousands of supporters through his Web site (Lizza, 2003). Jesse Ventura, the former professional wrestler, who won election as governor of Minnesota, used a Web site in 1998 to raise contributions for his campaign (Holmes, 2001).

The first Internet sites for presidential candidates appeared in 1996, but these were limited to one-way communication including biographical information, platform positions, organization addresses, and press releases (Davis, 1999). The clear, demonstrated impact by bloggers on the U.S. political campaigns is persuasive and will no doubt be used by political activists around the world and across all geopolitical boundaries. What should be clear from the American experience is that bloggers are not journalists. They function more like partisan operatives, whose ideological agenda should be scrutinized and weighed when relying upon them for useful information. Bloggers in any case clearly now have the power to support democratic agendas and to undermine democracy.

International Ideology

The open dialog, typically welcome by blogs, may pose a threat to the establishment. Such communication is illegal in some Muslim countries and may be a vital source for spreading democracy. As a factor in globalization, it represents the uncensored spreading of ideas. It has the power to put the individual, ordinary voter on the soapbox of public opinion, on par with society's powerful elites. Blogs rely on personal views of democracy.

The first Iranian weblog was launched in 2001 (Corrick, 2005). The Internet has been described as "effectively the only unrestricted interactive medium accessible to Iranians" (http://www.stop.censoring.us/). The use of weblogs goes both ways: It can advocate for causes or censor political candidates whose views are not tolerated by the ruling party (ITIran, March 27, 2005). Consequently, the Iranian government has taken to filtering the blogs on the part of the Internet Service Providers (ISPs). Especially in fundamentalist countries, authorities believe that free expression, such as that of the webloggers, should be filtered because their views present a risk to youth in terms of immoral and sacrilegious messages. When President George W. Bush labeled Iran as part of the Axis of Evil in his State of the Union Message, a weblog was quickly created dedicated to Iranian people who are against military attacks on Iran. "Iranians for Peace" welcome the opinions of Iranian people around the globe who are in opposition to war, and they believe that their support base extends around the world, not just within the Iranian borders (http://nowarforiran.blogspot.com).

Since the Iranian Revolution in the 1970s, there has been a thriving cultural underground that has kept young Iranians exposed to and interested in other points of view (Wright, 2000). Most Iranian blogs are in English, which reflects this outreach to other cultures around the world. Farsi is now tied with French as the second most common language used in blogs. There are an estimated 100,000 active Iranian blogs (Siamdoust, 2005). Blogs are especially important in giving women a voice in the Muslim world (Corrick, 2005). The door to some countries has been closed for ideological and political reasons. But bloggers are stepping in to function as alternative media to exchange information, opinion, and analysis. Sometimes, as with North Korea, these have been labeled a "jungle of lies." Yet these eyes of the world in-country may provide the only means for relating events in distant countries to the outside world, including its collaborative and supranational monitoring institutions such as the United Nations (MacKinnon, 2004).

Governance and the Individual

Although the number of nations has not been reduced as Orwell's *1984* assumed (Orwell, 1961), the nations are shrinking in terms of their functions. Land is less important than an educated populace, currency and precious metals' stockpiles are less important than capital flows, and parochial interests are less important than international economy as a whole (Rosecrance, 1999). In previous eras, leaders of states were obsessed with accumulating more territory. The underlying assumption had been that land is the key to production, resources, and power. The ability for such nation-states to achieve their goals was thought to rest upon their economic power, military power, and political power.

Today's new conception of state power has to do with modern technology and knowledge research. New value is placed on income that comes not only from manufacturing, but also from product design, marketing, financing, and human creativity as applied to commerce (Florida, 2002). When real economic power is decoupled from land, production and people can move to wherever the creative class of workers prefers to live and work in the world. Corporate downsizing has contributed to the new class of worker who functions very well in virtual space. These individuals do not think in terms of the state protecting their capital or government regulations as necessary for their well-being. In earlier "waves" of technological revolution, the growth of the nation-state was accepted as necessary outcome contributing to the public good. Knowledge workers have become more individualistic.

Corporate marketing is now increasingly aimed at Internet users rather than mainstream media because of the proven power of persuasion. This trend portends diminished role if not the elimination of the public relations middlemen (Shenk, 1997). Governments face new challenges to enforce jurisdictional issues as the lines of "legitimate" authority are more blurred (Dyson, 1998). This challenges fundamental conceptions of jurisdiction based on physical place and consent of the governed. E-commerce and direct-to-consumer sales have direct consequences for government revenues and budgets, and ultimately their ability to provide traditional services.

At the same time, governments are using e-government initiatives to bring services directly to their constituents via the Internet, thereby "marketing" themselves to enhance the value and utility of their services. This includes citizen involvement and feedback, in addition to routine services like applying for building permits and paying taxes online. The digital revolution is remaking two intertwined relationships between people and their government: the one between government and the citizen consumer or customer; the other between government and the citizen-owner or shareholder (Tapscott & Agnew, 1999).

The virtual economies lead to more open government because the flow of ideas, capital, and production is aided by open borders. The feat of conquering other states to gain access to resources and markets is less important when commerce, trade, and capital flows are virtual. Still, as Adam Smith (1776) cautioned, successful business depends on a system of laws and courts to enforce them to protect the businessman's capital. The new role of the state includes protecting international factors of production. After all, foreign capital must have legal safeguards if direct foreign investment is to continue to be important to growth of domestic production. We still need governments for this purpose and for many other noneconomic reasons. Protecting human rights, implementing social policy on the local level, social inequity and redistributing income, providing public goods, assuring safety nets for the poor, and regulating financial and energy markets are still very important government roles. But there is growing power of the individual to function outside of the state. The new paradigm breaks down hierarchies and creates new power structures that empower individuals and elites.

The dissemination of so much information opens the door to spurious information and perhaps too many choices. Internet-based groups effectively lobby the policy-making process for the sake of their own agenda. They represent new political groups that can reach a mass audience and their constituency instantaneously. Traditional groups may become organizational dinosaurs in the cyberspace age (Davis, 1999). The political power will shift to smaller, less well-financed groups based on the passionate, technology-savvy constituents who capitalize on the low overhead, and low-cost communication possible via the Internet. But Internet lobbying is not party neutral; it favors libertarians, free markets, advocates for deregulated, decentralized government and otherwise conservative issues (Shenk, 1997).

Conclusion

Free communication across borders results in greater sharing of ideas and balance of power between citizens and their government. The Internet connects people and organizations across borders, across the world, allowing them to share the same interests, curiosities, complaints, and aspirations. The global village has a presence in every village with an Internet connection. When citizens are better informed, public choice theory suggests they will make better decisions as to which jurisdiction to live within, based on the package of services available from their government (Buchanan & Tullock, 1962).

The Internet can be used to collect information that is not usually available to the public, and therefore makes possible a new era of openness and transparency (Davis, 1999). When Newt Gingrich was elected Speaker of the U.S. House of Representatives in 1995, one of his first acts was to make all U.S. Congressional documents available online in order to "change the balance of power" in favor of the citizen and away from the traditional power brokers and lobbyists (Shenk, 1997, p. 173). In theory, citizens can make their views known to others and vote on policy decisions in direct democracy (Fountain, 2002; Toffler & Toffler, 1995). This is now also possible on the individual level through weblogs and other content-rich Web sites outside the hierarchy and bureaucracy of traditional political parties.

Information technology and communications advancements create new venues for citizens to engage in political activity, including, for example, joining interest groups, voting in elections, and participating in online political forums (Wilhelm, 2000). World Wide Web sites can be pro-West, spreading American culture, as well as anti-American, supporting stinging attacks on American foreign policy (Barber & Schulz, 1996). As always, in the court of public opinion, leaders have to understand that democracy is about sharing one's opinions in general and cannot be regulated in truly open societies. For example, a Web site in China was established in 1999 by *People's Daily* as a vehicle for the Communist Party to involve citizens in anti-American rhetoric following the U.S. bombing of the Chinese embassy in Belgrade. "Emboldened by their freedom to discuss China–U.S. relations, users have now moved on to domestic issues, offering stinging attacks on corruption, bad government and social inequality" (Gilley, 2001, p. 64).

The Internet and the information and communications technology revolution of the late 20th century provide new means for people to participate in democratic governance. It has given new powers to individuals that equals or are greater to powers once held strictly by society's elites. Worldwide commerce and human interchanges that are aided by globalization have meant sharing of ideas and opinions on a global scale. If these are not repressed by nation-states or ideological governmental interests, unfettered freedom of expression will result in profound change in who governs, how we govern, and how satisfied we are with our representatives. It also provides new power to anonymity where all participants online are truly equal because they are shed of their physical and social baggage. It seems that this contributes quite well toward a model of enhanced democracy and democratic governance, or not, depending on one's own ideology.

References

Albritton, C. (2003). "Blogging from Iraq." *Nieman Reports*, 57(3). Cambridge, MA: Harvard University Press, pp. 82–85.

Anderson, C.A., and R.N. Anthony (1986). *The New Corporate Directors*. New York: John Wiley & Sons.

Barber, B.R., and A. Schulz (eds.) (1996). *Jihad vs. McWorld: How the Planet is Both Falling Apart and Coming Together— And What This Means for Democracy.* New York: Times Books.

Bentham, J. (1843/1962). In *The Works of Jeremy Bentham*. Bowring, J. (ed.) New York: Russell & Russell.

Buchanan, J.M., and G. Tullock (1962). *The Calculus of Consent.* Ann Arbor, MI: University of Michigan Press.

Cairncross, F. (1997) *The Death of Distance: How the Communications Revolution Will Change Our Lives.* Boston, MA: Harvard Business School Press.

Castells, M. (2000). *The Rise of the Network Society*, 2nd ed. Oxford, UK: Blackwell Publishers.

Cone, E. (2003). "The marketing of the President 2004." *Baseline*, 1(25). New York: Ziff Davis Media, p. 32.

Corrick, K. (2005). "Bloggers strike first," *New Statesman*, 18; Feb 14, 846. London, p. 19.

Crowley, M. (2005). "Local Yokels: Bloggers and partisan Internet journalists helped elect J. Thune to the Senate." *The New Republic*, 232(9): 11–12.

Davis, R. (1999). *The Web of Politics: The Internet's Impact on the American Political System*. Oxford: Oxford University Press.

Dicken, P. (1998). *Global Shift: Transforming the World Economy*. New York: The Guilford Press.

Dooley, P.C. (1969). "The interlocking directorate." *American Economic Review*, 59(3): 314–323.

Drucker, P. (1999). Beyond the information revolution. *Atlantic Monthly, 284*(4): pp. 47–57.

Dyson, E. (1998). *Release 2.1: A Design for Living in the Digital Age*. New York: Broadway Books.

Florida, R. (2002). *The Rise of the Creative Class: And How It's Transforming Work, Leisure, Community and Everyday Life*. New York: Basic Books.

Fountain, J.E. (2002). "Toward a theory of federal bureaucracy for the twenty-first century." In Kamarck, E.C., and J.S. Nye, Jr. (eds.) *Governance.Com: Democracy in the Information Age*. Washington, D.C.: Brookings, pp. 117–140.

Franke-Ruta, G. (2005). "Blog rolled." *American Prospect*, 16(4): 39–42.

Gilley, B. (2001). "Trojan Horse: A chat site run by the Communist Party is delivering stinging criticism — of the party." *Far Eastern Economic Review*, 21: 64.

Gordon, R.S. (2005). "Revenge of the Nexgen people." *Library Journal*, 130(9): 78.

Greeley, A.H. (2005). "Blogger admitted to White House." *The Harvard Crimson*, March 10, 2005.

Grindle, M.S. (2000). "Ready or not: The developing world and globalization." In Nye, J.S., Jr., and J.D. Donahue (eds.) *Governance in a Globalizing World*. Washington, D.C.: Brookings, pp. 178–207.

Guthrie, K.K., and W.H. Dutton (1992). "The politics of citizen access technology: The development of public information utilities in four cities." *Policy Studies Journal*, 20(4): 574–597.

Hacker, K.L. (1996). "Missing links in the evolution of electronic democratization." *Media, Culture & Society*, 18: 213–232.

Hirst, P., and G. Thompson (1996). *Globalization in Question*. Cambridge, MA: Polity Press.

Holmes, D. (2001). *eGov: eBusiness Strategies for Government*. London: Nicholas Brealey Publishing.

Inglehart, R. (1997). "Postmaterialist values and the erosion of institutional authority." In Nye, J.S., Jr., P.D. Zeilkow, and D.C. King (eds.) *Why People Don't Trust Government*. Cambridge, MA: Harvard University Press, pp. 217–236.

Kamarck, E.C. and Nye, J.S. Jr. (eds.) (2002). *Governance. Com: Democracy in the Information Age*. Washington, DC: Brookings Press.

Korten, D.C. (2001). *When Corporations Rule the World*, 2nd ed. Bloomfield, CT: Kumarian Press.

Kurtz, H. (2004). "After blogs got hits, CBS got a black eye." *The Washington Post*, September 20, p. C01.

Lessig, L. (2003). "The new road to the White House." *Wired*, 11(11): 136.

Lizza, R. (2003) "Dean.com." *The New Republic*, 228(21), June 2, p. 10.

MacKinnon, R. (2004). "Blogging North Korea." *Nieman Reports*, 58(3). Cambridge, MA: Harvard University Press, pp. 103–107.

McKinney, M. (2005). "Bloggers exult in Rather departure," *Minneapolis-St. Paul Star Tribune*, March 10, p. A8.

Mill, J.S. (1863/1987). *Utilitarianism*. Buffalo, NY: Prometheus Books.

Nye, J.S., Jr. (1997). "The decline in confidence in government." In Nye, J.S., Jr. P.D. Zeilkow, and D.C. King (eds.) *Why People Don't Trust Government*. Cambridge, MA: Harvard University Press, pp. 1–2.

Orwell, G. (1961). *1984*. New York: New American Library.

Palser, B. (2003). "Virtual campaigning." *American Journalism Review*, 25(7), p. 62, Oct/Nov.

Pein, C. (2005). "Blog-Gate." *Columbia Journalism Review*, 43(5), Jan/Feb. New York: Columbia University, pp. 30–35.

Rosecrance, R. (1999). *The Rise of the Virtual State: Wealth and Power in the Coming Century*. New York: Basic Books.

Rosendorf, N.M. (2000) "Social and cultural globalization: concepts, history, and America's role." In Nye, J.S., Jr. and J.D. Donahue (eds.) *Governance in a Globalizing World*. Washington, D.C.: Brookings, pp. 109–134.

Shenk, D. (1997). *Data Smog: Surviving the Information Glut*. San Francisco, CA: Harper Collins.

Siamdoust, N. (2005). "Blogwatch." *Time*, May 9, 2005.

Smith, Adam (1776/1904). *An Inquiry into the Nature and Causes of the Wealth of Nations*. First published in 1776. Fifth ed. London: Methuen & Co.

Strange, S. (1996). *The Retreat of the State: The Diffusion of World Power in the New Economy*. Cambridge, MA: Cambridge University Press.

Tapscott, D., and D. Agnew (1999). "Governance in the digital economy." *Finance & Development*, 36(4): 34–37.

Time (2004). "Time names President George W. Bush 2004 person of the year." *Time*, December 19.

Toffler, A. (1981). *The Third Wave*. New York: Bantam Books.

Toffler, A., and H. Toffler (1995). *Creating a New Civilization: The Politics of the Third Wave*. Atlanta, GA: Turner Publishing.

Waldman, S. (2005). "Arriving at the digital news age." *Nieman Reports*, 59(1). Cambridge, MA: Harvard University Press, pp. 78–79.

Walker, L. (2004). "Bloggers gain attention in 2004 election." *The Washington Post*, Nov. 4, p. E01.

Welch, M. (2005). "Who gets to play journalist?." *Reason*, 37(2). Research Library, p. 18.

Whitney, W.H. (2004). "Digital politics." *Columbia Journalism Review*, 42(6). New York: Columbia University, p. 9.

Wilhelm, A.G. (2000). *Democracy in the Digital Age: Challenges to Political Life in Cyberspace*. New York: Routledge.

Wright, R. (2000). *The Last Great Revolution: Turmoil and Transformation in Iran*. New York: Alfred A. Knopf.

Chapter 12

Regional Integration, Regionalism and Public Administration: Bridging the Global–National Divide in Decision Making and Policy Implementation

Mary Farrell

CONTENTS

Broadly speaking, public administration is the implementation of policy within a state framework. More concretely, it is fair to describe the core of what public administration is about, in terms of taking care of the state's and international organizations' business by civil servants within the executive branch of government. Two things stand out in this description of public administration. The first is the arena of action in which public administration is performed, namely the state with its territorial, juridical, and political boundaries clearly defined. The second feature that is highlighted in the above definition refers to the scope of activities within the remit of contemporary public administration. The national public administration is concerned with issues and policies emanating from the government of the particular nation-state and increasingly must engage with the policies and laws of international organizations.

The modern state interacts with the international system to a significant extent, and this is true for both rich and poor countries. The pattern of interaction and cooperation is evolving in new ways, and although war is still a causal factor in a more negative form of interaction, today international cooperation between states is largely of a more peaceful nature. The conquest of territory is much less a motivating factor behind a state's decision to engage in cross-border activity, though the conquest of international markets has become a dominant objective in the foreign policies of advanced and developing countries alike. In all parts of the world, states have become enmeshed in an ever-growing number of alliances with other states, for purposes that are both diverse and complex, and covering issue areas spanning the economic, social, cultural, environmental, and security, to name a few.

This dense pattern of cooperation is shaped by both formal and informal arrangements, by legal and quasilegal agreements, sometimes conducted within the framework of international organizations, and other times through the loose coordination that takes place under an intergovernmental umbrella. Whatever the legal and institutional arrangements that are decided upon, each and every case of nation-state involvement in international cooperation imposes a new set of responsibilities upon the national administration, with consequences for public management and the resources available for the efficient operation of its role, and indeed for the nature of the governance system. Instead of pursuing the designated role of the national bureaucracy in the Westphalian nation-state, implementing the policy of the national government while subject to the scrutiny of the national parliament and acting within the framework of the national legal system, contemporary public administration faces a much more complex set of tasks. Public administration is faced with implementation of policies that have not been agreed through the customary national political process.

In effect, the diverse nature of new responsibilities, which are imposed upon the public administration by the state's set of preferences for international cooperation, is reflected in the resulting agreements signed and the membership of various international organizations, all of which call into question the traditional relationship between the state and national public administration. The essential stability among the judiciary, the legislature, and the executive branch of government is threatened, as laws and policies decided outside the territory of the state must now be implemented within the political jurisdiction of the state by the public administration arm of the national political authorities (Majone, 1996).

This chapter sets out to examine one case of such deterritorialization, in the form of the regional agreements between sovereign states. Regionalism is not a recent phenomenon, but it is increasingly becoming a preferred solution to common problems and shared interests for many countries in the advanced and developing parts of the world. There is a distinction to be made here between international agreements or treaties (formal or nonbinding) among sovereign states, the international organizations comprising membership of sovereign states established for a specific function or purpose, and the diverse forms of regional cooperation arrangements in different parts of the world, reflected in such regional integration arrangements as the European Union (EU), the Association of South-East Asian Nations (ASEAN), the Economic Community of West African States (ECOWAS), the North American Free Trade Area (NAFTA), or the Common Market of the South (Mercosur). It is the latter forms of cooperation that this chapter is concerned with.

The chapter is structured along the following lines. In the section "Regional Integration: from Concept to Practice," an examination of the different conceptual approaches to regional integration and varying definitions in the literature suggest a diversity of perceptions by academic commentators, an explicit result of the different disciplinary attempts to understand this real-world form of cooperation. Having worked our way through the disciplinary and conceptual definitions, the next section "Regional Integration and Globalization" moves on to examine the nature of the relationship between regionalism and globalism. There have been two broad schools of thought on this question, an early school which saw regionalism (especially regional economic integration) as a stepping stone to globalization (that is, to a global open trading system), and a contrasting position held by those who saw regionalism as a response and defensive reaction to the threats and challenges emanating from the unstoppable forces of globalization (Breslin et al., 2002). Here, an attempt will be made to tease out the complexities of this relationship beyond the fixed views of these polar positions.

The key concern of the chapter is to explore the impact of regionalism on public administration and to assess the changing nature of national governance in the context of the development of regionalism. No matter what form regional cooperation may take in any given region (i.e., whether more or less intergovernmental), the cooperating states make certain commitments and arrive at decisions and agreements on courses of action to be implemented subsequently in each country. At the implementation stage, the responsibility falls to the public bureaucracy in each state to activate the agreements and commitments made by the respective governments. At this point, fulfilling the responsibilities, entered into through international commitments, is more than just extra work for already over-worked public officials. As a minimum, regionalism requires a division of responsibilities, functions, and decision making between the national and regional (i.e. supranational) levels. In many cases, this division will extend to the subnational level, thereby creating a multilevel governance system (Hooghe & Marks, 2001).

In the section "Modes of Governance," the discussion is focused upon an exposition of modes of governance in the framework of regionalism, and the section "Implications for Public Administration" considers the implications for public administration. The concluding section takes stock of the likely future challenges facing public administration in the face of continued interest in regional cooperation among countries around the world. Despite this shared interest in regional cooperation, however, it is clear that regions are taking an independent approach toward developing the type of regional model that best reflects the particular socioeconomic, political, and historical circumstances of each region. This variety in the forms of regional cooperation makes the task of identifying implications for public administration more difficult, and also more challenging as an intellectual exercise. Ultimately, students and public policy practitioners must take into account the political and practical consequences for public administration, arising from the fact of having to implement policies and programmes originating outside the national political and legislative framework.

Regional Integration: From Concept to Practice

One of the immediate reactions to the perusal of the academic literature on regionalism is the diversity of concepts and terminology (Fawcett & Hurrell, 1995; Laursen, 2003). Indeed, it is evident that there is little agreement on the substantive definitions and this then presents problems for our intention to explain the significance for public administration of such arrangements. For one thing, the use of such different terms as regionalism, regionalization, and regional integration requires us to consider whether and to what extent different terms are used to explain different phenomena, or whether in practice the phenomena are the same, but the use of terminology reflects different schools of thought or disciplinary background, or even priorities shaped by the academic study of particular regions (loosely described in current academic parlance as area studies).

Given the complexity of the phenomenon under study, many authors have attempted to elucidate the issues by a preliminary conceptualization of the notion of region (Rosamond, 2000; Fawcett, 2004). Fawcett begins her discussion of regionalism by providing a definition of what is a region. The region can be defined in terms of geographic space, thereby embracing a number of countries, not all of which need to share borders. Or, the region can be conceived of as a zone, embracing groups of states with some identifiable patterns of behavior (Fawcett, 2004, p. 432). A region can be understood as an "imagined community," where the states are bound together by a sense of shared history, culture, identity, and common experience and customs, thus placing the region in a comparable situation to that of a nation.

Generally, a region will comprise a group of states that are linked together (loosely or otherwise) by a shared bond of mutual interdependence, and some geographical relationship. Fawcett adds a qualifying statement that regions need not conform to state boundaries, a qualification that opens up the possibility of regions with subnational and supranational political entities. Taking into account the existence of state, substate, and supranational entities in the region should alert us to the fact that non-state actors can also be important in shaping and defining the activities and programmes of the region — including business and labor interests, environmental groups, non-governmental organizations, and other elements of civil society.

If we turn from the definition of a region to the concepts associated with regional processes, it is not always clear that simply defining what we mean by region will allow clarity in explaining regionalism, regionalization, and regional integration. Regionalism is commonly understood as a state-led project, where states and non-state actors cooperate and coordinate policies and strategies in the region. Cooperation is driven by the shared interests of the participants, and the common purpose to pursue and promote common goals in certain issue areas — economic, trade, money, security, resource management, conflict resolution, and peace building. This is certainly not an exhaustive list of action areas, and in any given regionalist project the precise set of activities will reflect the political preferences and resources of the participating states, as well as the political commitment of each state. Each regional project has its own set of priorities, and there is no real necessity to start with one issue area and proceed logically to cooperate in the next issue area by following some functional logic.

Clearly, some regions already have their priorities for action, determined by the particular set of sociopolitical, historical, or other circumstances in the region. In West Africa, for instance, ECOWAS began with the aim of fostering economic integration among the member states, but is now increasingly embroiled in attempts to restore stability to the conflict-ridden countries of the region. Hence, what was originally envisaged as an economic community is by default having to take on security activities and develop a regional role as peacemaker. Similarly, the ASEAN began as a security community, a goal that was explicit in its mandate and actions over three decades (Öjendal, 2004; MacFarlane, 2004). By 1990s, the member states were beginning to consider new policies and projects in the economic arena with proposals under consideration to establish a form of monetary cooperation, and an Asian Economic Community. From its inception, the EU had the intention to create an economic community, but there was no doubt that the underlying rationale was based upon concerns with security, prevention of war, and creating unity in Europe to withstand the encroaching communism and Soviet expansion. But the political goal of European unity was to be achieved through economic means (Haas, 1958).

Regionalism can take different forms and is illustrated along a continuum between "soft regionalism," with a sense of regional identity, of awareness, or community, to "hard regionalism," where regional actors, groups, and networks interact on a supranational basis often through formal institutional arrangements and organizations (van Ham, 2001). Regionalism is thus a state-led project, involving also other non-state actors (Hettne et al., 1999). Moreover, a regionalist project has both vertical and horizontal dimensions, bringing in subnational and supranational actors and linking them together within the framework of a system of multilevel governance (Marks et al., 1996).

Continuing with the task of clarifying the terminology, we can introduce another term: regionalization. Often regionalization and regionalism are used interchangeably, however those analysts who distinguish between these two terms are concerned to draw out a differentiation based upon processes and actors. Regionalization is therefore understood as a process of integration arising out of the activities of firms, markets, capital flows, and generally the strategies of companies. In simple terms the distinction comes down to differentiating between top-down, state-led projects and bottom-up processes pushing for greater regional economic (trade) integration. Similar bottom-up processes of regionalization can be identified in non-trade activities, particularly in the arena of security. For example, the spillover effects arising out of conflict in one country can produce regional responses to contain the conflict — essentially in the form of an unplanned set of actions by the regional actors, producing the effect of creating a sense of regional community and identity (Allison, 2004).

Although regionalism and regionalization processes constitute distinct and separate phenomena, it would be wrong to overstate the differences between them or to suggest that the two are not interlinked. Regionalization processes can be spontaneous, producing a concentration of activity at the regional level (activities that range across the economic, social, security, legal, and illegal) and helping to create a sense of regional identity or to foster regional organizations. But in a world where states continue to hold territorial and political sovereignty as core elements of the Westphalian nation-state, the kind of activities and processes associated with regionalization will depend very much upon the political will of these states in the region, and the collective and individual decisions and policies of the respective states. The regionalization of trade, for instance, has been facilitated to a large extent because of the decisions to remove national tariff and nontariff barriers, as well as other trade-promoting policies in the participating states.

Clearly, there arises the question as to which comes first — the state-led regionalism project or the regionalization processes that prompt a political response and collective action on the part of the states within the region. If we look at the many examples across the world, the evidence suggests that in some cases regionalisms may prompt further processes of regionalization, although elsewhere the emergence of regionalization activities opens up a governance space to which states have then to respond to address a political deficit, or a perceived threat to sovereignty. One way around this confusion over regionalism and regionalization is to be found within the literature in regional integration. The study of regional integration goes back to 1950s, and can be found in both political science and economics contributions. Ernst Haas, one of the most influential contributors to the field of regional integration, explained how and why nation-states decide to cooperate in a sustained and reiterative process, seeking common interests (Haas, 1958). Regional integration involves processes of cooperation, rather than movement toward a defined outcome. The primary actors are to be found at several levels — subnational, national, and supranational. At the national level, actors include interest groups, political parties, national bureaucrats, although at the supranational level, regional organizations (i.e., supranational institutions) also play a role in managing cooperation, diffusing tensions among sovereign states with competing interests, mediating between different interest groups, and proposing policy initiatives.

For Haas, the initial impetus for regional integration came from the economic sector, which he described as the most dynamic and with a high degree of interdependence. Consequently, integration in one economic sector gave rise to the need for integration in a related sector, either to protect the gains from integration already in place, or to address the negative externalities of existing integration. One illustration of this type of "spillover" is the case of market (economic) integration, which may require an additional integrative step to make the market integration work more successfully by establishing a single currency — the one market, one money principle which the European Commission advocated in its strategy to persuade the European states to give up their currency in favor of a single currency, the euro.

In the economics literature, the classic model of economic integration was expounded by Balassa at the beginning of 1960s (Balassa, 1962). In the Balassa model of economic integration, formal cooperation takes place between states to create a free-trade area, where tariffs and other nontariff barriers are removed on internal trade between the participating countries Although each country retains its own tariff on trade with third countries (nonmembers of the free-trade area). Balassa suggested a progressive movement of liberalization and integration in stages, moving from the free-trade area to a customs union, a common market, a monetary union, and ultimately an economic and political union. Each stage implies deeper integration, greater coordination of national economic policies, and widening of the issue areas and policies that would be subject to coordination.

Issues in this economic approach to regional integration were the likely impact upon welfare arising out of trade liberalization, the impact upon trade patterns, and the effect of increased competition upon national firms and industries. These considerations remain of paramount importance in the contemporary world, and have taken on a political salience that was not at all evident in the original Balassa model. Since the original formulation, the number and scope of regional integration arrangements in all parts of the world has been extended. Much of these agreements take the form of free-trade agreements, although some aspire to move toward deeper integration at a later stage, possibly through the establishment of a customs union or a common market (Estevadeordal et al., 2004). In practice, a significant number of these free-trade agreements never move beyond this stage, and some never reach the stage of being a comprehensive free-trade area.

Yet the reasons for initiating regional integration arrangements remain valid over time. States and economic actors may have their separate interests in seeing regional integration emerge, but they also share common interests in the project, and, in the processes inherent to regional integration. Economic actors gain from the economics of scale associated with a larger market, and a reduction of transaction costs associated with market exchange, as well as cost advantages associated with the ability to locate production in a lower-cost partner country. As integration processes develop, participating countries may opt for further coordination or harmonization of policies and common rules on trade, industrial standards, taxation, and labor market regulation.

Deeper integration may follow with decisions on cooperation and macroeconomic policy coordination, common fiscal and monetary policies, and common social policies — ultimately, perhaps a regional transfer or redistributive mechanism to ensure balanced integration, to compensate the losers, and to help individual countries and subnational regions to bear the burden of adjustment to the demands of deepening integration. Even when the goal is economic integration, it remains essential to compensate the losers and to support efforts at adjustment to the pressures arising from increased levels of competition, so as to ensure the political viability of economic integration. These pressures can have economic, social, or environmental consequences, not all of which may have been anticipated with the initial decision to cooperate.

The foregoing discussion of regional integration presents two very important conclusions with implications for how we interpret the phenomena, and also the causal connections with national (and international) public administration. Firstly, regional integration involves a process rather than an outcome. It is not a teleological process, whereby the participating states are moving toward some inexorable destination predetermined by the architects of regional integration. Contrary to earlier studies and critiques, regional integration represents ongoing processes of interaction between myriad actors at different levels (firms, governments, bureaucrats, non-governmental organizations, interest groups, and supranational institutions), without any destination firmly established. As interests change, and the external circumstances alter, the pressures emanating from the internal and external environment will give rise to new patterns of cooperation.

Secondly, regional integration encompasses both a political and an economic dimension, with the two interacting in a complex and mutually reinforcing manner. The answer to the question, "Is integration an economic or a political phenomenon?", has to recognize the interaction between political forces and economic actors played out at regional, national, and subnational level.

Regional Integration and Globalization

The renewed interest in regional integration since 1980s has coincided with the spread of globalization (Gilpin, 2000). The topic of globalization has itself attracted much attention across the academic community and among the wider general public, generating intense, if often confused, debate over the causes and the likely impact. Not surprisingly, the debate over globalization has intensified in recent years with the emergence of an anti-globalization movement and counter-tendencies that have spread from the advanced countries to the developing ones. Of particular concern in the debate over globalization has been the question of the uneven distribution of the benefits, and the unequal impact of the negative consequences associated with such aspects as financial instability, uneven growth and underdevelopment, income inequalities, and poverty. Despite these reservations, globalization processes proceed unabated and largely uncontested in the international arenas of power.

Described as an intensification of economic flows (trade, capital, investment) at the international level, and an increase in the level of international or global interdependence, globalization has resulted in a deterritorialization of economic activities and a weakening of state autonomy. It also has a cultural dimension, manifested in the spread of ideas, values and, for many, producing a cultural hegemony with the dominance of Western values and the promotion of a consumerist society (Held et al., 1999).

Where does regional integration fit into these broader processes of globalization? Is regional integration a stepping stone toward globalization? Or, an alternative way of organizing economic and political relations at the regional level, thereby strengthening the economic and sociopolitical ties between the participating countries, their citizens, economies, and political leaders? In fact, regional integration is both a stepping stone toward globalization and an alternative way of regionalizing relations between political and economic actors (Mansfield & Milner, 2001). Much of the current regional integration arrangements involve preferential trade liberalization agreements among the participating countries, and are exempted (under GATT article 24) from the World Trade Organization (WTO) rules that preferential agreements should be extended to all trading partners.

Because the regional trading blocs are permitted under the WTO rules regarding the maintenance of a "global" open trading system, regional trade agreements may therefore be considered as stepping stones toward globalization. In a similar vein, many regional integration arrangements around the world have adopted neoliberal policies and values, embracing the ideology of the market on a collective scale, reflecting a convergence of the dominant ideas system to be found within the WTO and other international institutions.

Despite this seeming convergence of ideas and values among the prominent actors in regional integration, there is also reason to suggest that regional actors have fashioned the form of regional integration to address precise regional problems and meet specific goals and objectives, to conform with the particular set of circumstances and national preferences. For example, in the wake of the Asian financial crisis of 1997 the countries of the ASEAN grouping began to give serious consideration to deepening monetary cooperation and, later on, to direct their attention to deeper trade integration. The EU enlargement to 25 states was first mooted at the beginning of 1990s in the aftermath of the collapse of the Soviet Union and the subsequent instability in the counties on the EU's eastern borders — thereby making the widening of integration a security issue. Sometime later, it became clear that a larger EU also meant a larger market, and therefore an attractive option for the firms and industries of Western Europe facing a largely saturated and certainly low-growth market in the EU-15.

In 1990s, regional integration exhibited a renewed vigor in Europe, Asia, the Americas, and Africa (Farrell and Hettne, 2005). The success of the European integration model prompted reaction, albeit with different motivations. The North American Free Trade Area (NAFTA) was an attempt to construct regional integration so as to act as a counterweight to the European bloc and a possible 'Fortress Europe' that might erect protectionist barriers against imports from the United States. In Africa, regional integration was revived at the continental level in the decision to establish the African Union, a proposal for a very formal and highly institutionalized form of regional integration, modeled on the EU system. In Latin America, Mercosur was established at the beginning of 1990s, and also initially modeled on the EU. However, regional integration in Latin America failed to secure real progress in policy areas, in part due to the rivalry between the two largest countries Brazil and Argentina.

Despite the references to the "EU model," there is no serious intent on the part of the regional actors around the world to adopt the "European model" (Wiener & Diez, 2004). Although it may be possible or even desirable to take lessons from the European experience, in practice each regional community appears to be developing a model of regional integration appropriate to the particular political, socioeconomic, and cultural, as well as historical conditions, prevailing in the region. Just as there are real obstacles to the application elsewhere of a particular development model which produced good results in an individual country, so also with regional integration models. What works in Europe, for instance, may not work in Asia due to differences in social and political relations, distinct value systems, domestic political preferences, and other conditions that have been historically determined in each region.

Modes of Governance

One of the striking aspects in a study of regional integration is the disparity between different arrangements and the diverse record of successful cooperation. Although some regional groupings are successful, others begin well and subsequently run out of steam, and they eventually disappear or remain moribund until a change of circumstances or a crisis encourages regional actors to revive cooperation to provide shared solutions to common problems. The issue of why some integration schemes are successful and others fail was explained by Mattli (1999) in terms of the degree of commitment on the part of political leaders toward making regional integration work and, for economic actors, the potential gains should be significant. Simply signing a regional integration agreement (whether it relates to a free-trade area or a more substantial form of integration that includes economic and political dimensions) does not make it a substantive reality. Indeed, for many of the regional trade agreements that were signed in recent years, the lack of foresight over the implications and follow-up has deterred real progress toward the kind of liberalization suggested in the founding text of the trade agreement. Moreover, the process of integration takes time and the requisite political commitment by the heads of state (signatories to the agreement) to actually make the necessary administrative, legal, and political changes at national level. This is where public administration becomes most directly involved — somewhere down the road from the actual signing of the agreement.

However, in individual states public administration is, or should be, involved at an earlier stage before the commitment to enter into a regional integration arrangement. In the normal course of events, the national public administration officials are engaged in formulating strategies relating to the implementation of government policy, and often this requires working with different branches of government to identify national interests and priorities. Domestic politics involves the reconciliation of diverse national interests, and in international relations the national government must also adopt positions and negotiating strategies that take account of different national interests. Public administration is closely bound up with the process of devising policies for government, and doing so in a manner that incorporates and reflects the diversity of national interests.

Once an agreement is reached by a group of countries to establish a regional integration arrangement, the agreement must be implemented. Implementation is largely the responsibility of the national public administration in each of the signatory states. Even an agreement by national governments to integrate their economies will involve a multistage process of establishing common rules, regulations, and policies, some of which will be written into the agreement, although other policies result from the interpretation of the spirit of the treaty or the general principles and objectives of the regional integration agreement (or treaty). Regional integration is therefore a process that evolves over time. In the course of implementing the arrangement, governments must take a decision regarding the overall nature of the integrative arrangements. Should integration adopt formal or informal structures to coordinate the activities and policies decided upon by the participating countries? Formal structures tend to take the form of a supranational organization dedicated to the task of coordinating the policies and initiatives adopted by the member governments. In practice, the mandate of the supranational organizations can vary widely, depending upon the preferences of the participating states and usually these responsibilities are set out in the founding treaty or agreement establishing the regional integration arrangement (Archer, 2001).

Informal structures of regional integration tend toward looser coordination mechanisms and limited institutionalization. This has been the model adopted by the ASEAN, and typically there is a stronger emphasis on maintaining national sovereignty. The categorization of regional integration arrangements into formal and informal structures is intended to give a general representation of what are really two ideal types. However, regional integration arrangements can incorporate elements of both formal and informal structures — in other words, combining both supranationality and intergovernmentalism in policy making and implementation, and mechanisms for reconciling different interests or resolving conflicts. Regional integration arrangements can therefore be represented as a continuum linking intergovernmentalism and supranationalism (Sandholtz & Stone Sweet, 1998).

At the intergovernmental end of the spectrum, the national governments are the key actors in intergovernmental politics, and the decisions they make are the product of bargaining and negotiation. Integral to the whole process is the relative power of the individual states and the preferences of each state as determined by the reconciliation of domestic interests and politics. At the other end of the continuum, supranational governance is reflected in centralized governmental structures that possess jurisdiction over specific policy domains within the territory of the member states (Andersen & Eliassen, 2001). As a result, the supranational organization can shape the behavior of states and other actors, including both public and private sectors. Within this continuum it is possible to situate any given policy domain under regional integration, or to characterize the development of regional integration as a whole. We can, for instance, use this continuum to situate existing regional integration arrangements, such as Mercosur, NAFTA, ASEAN, or ECOWAS. It is a useful organizing framework, but should be considered together with the detailed analysis of actual political and policy developments in each case.

As regional integration develops, the arrangements become more complex and the horizontal and vertical linkages between social, economic, and political actors evolve and are strengthened. Vertical linkages are established and develop over time between actors organized at the supranational level and actors organized at the national and subnational levels (Marks et al., 1996). These vertical linkages become stable over time, as repeated interactions solidify relations of trust and engender habits of cooperation. Horizontal linkages in the form of interactions between groups of actors in one member state with actors organized in another can also evolve with regional integration. Such horizontal linkages, or "patterned interaction," can occur between governments, national public administrations, local authorities, interest groups, or other actors seeking to influence the regional integration process in some way or another. Integration involves this process of evolving horizontal and vertical linkages — and a gradually evolving multilevel governance framework, linking supranational, national, and subnational levels of policy making.

Implications for Public Administration

Regional integration changes the context in which the national public administration operates, and the very nature of what public administration does. Instead of implementing policies and delivering services at the behest of the national government, and as decided and approved in the national parliament, the national public administration must implement policies that are the outcome and product of decisions arrived at through the regional cooperation framework. Although the national government is still very much involved in formulating the policies that the public administration is then expected to implement, these policies are the result of a complex process of interstate bargaining and negotiation to arrive at common interests.

In a more supranational form of regional integration where the national public administration must respond more directly to the policies established by the supranational organization, national officials have to be well informed regarding the international context in which they operate, and continually update their knowledge of regional developments. National public administration officials are increasingly required to coordinate the national level policy with that of the regional level, and to align national and regional mechanisms for coordination. New national policies may have to be placed in a regional context, and national officials will be required to engage in more regional dialogue, and to involve their counterparts from other member states.

Regional integration may impact upon how policies are implemented and services delivered. Some policy domains will move to a supranational level with greater harmonization and the development of common policies. In other policy domains, there may be an agreement to implement policy at national level, or to subdivide implementation between national and subnational levels. In the case of European integration, there has been a gradual realignment of subnational, national, and supranational levels of authority, with local authorities engaging more directly with the European level and in some cases using the opportunity to bypass the national government (especially evident in the domain of regional policy).

As markets and economies become more integrated, there is greater competition and the increased opportunity for cross-border trade and provision of services. The market is no longer national, and the service customer (or service provider) may neither originate from within the territory nor be subject to the jurisdiction of the national public administration. This deterritorialization arising out of the processes of regional integration has implications for the regulatory and other policies of the national administration. Public services can be delivered by nonnational providers, or consumed beyond the national boundaries. Public services, such as education, healthcare, public utilities, are potentially subject to the impact of these deterritorialization processes. Consequently, regional integration can have a radical impact in terms of changing the relationship between the public sector provider and the consumer. The coordination function of national public administration will in such instances become more important, as different national government departments become involved in policy implementation.

In addition to the impact on how policies are made and implemented, regional integration can also have significant implications for resources within public administration, not least human and financial resources. This is not simply an issue of numbers, whether of personnel or the budgetary resources required to implement an increasingly complex range of activities in an expanding policy domain. There is the broader consideration of state capacity, especially in the context of regional integration involving developing countries. The pursuit and effective implementation of a regional integration strategy is dependent not just on the political commitment of the participating governments. Equally important is the capacity of the state, and its public administration, to implement policies agreed at regional level. Therefore, developing countries need to have the capacity to coordinate national and regional level initiatives, to be able to initiate regional level dialogue where appropriate, and to represent and defend national interests in regional negotiations. Capacity for integration will vary from region to region, in part dependent upon the nature and form of regional integration in each case and what is therefore required from the participant states in terms of policy adaptation, judicial reform, institutional innovation, and political change.

Capacity for regional integration is defined by the adaptive capability of the national public administration in each country. But two other factors play an important role: the quality of personnel in the public administration and the readiness and ability of the public administration to "think regional." This latter requirement emanates from the fact that regional integration involves the gradual emergence of new sites of decision making, and new centers of power on the one hand, and also from the explicit desire of the states themselves to create a form of regional integration. Turning the regional integration intention into reality will require a shift in the attitudes and frames of reference of national actors, including public actors and national administrations. Recent theoretical work within the constructivist school in international relations, when applied to the study of regional integration, emphasizes the importance of the social interactions among actors in terms of shaping identities and interests (Rosamond, 2000). Interests are not predetermined and fixed but emerge out of the processes of social interaction. This interaction can allow for the gradual emergence of a regional identity and facilitate the ability to "think regional."

National administrations are naturally embedded in national social structures, and accustomed to think in terms of the national context. However, neither the national governments and the public administration nor the emerging regional entity is a static concept. Globalization and regional integration constitute challenges to the traditional nation-state from "above." But the state is also being challenged from "below," through pressures for decentralization, delegation, and even privatization. So, what are the future challenges for the national public administration in the context of the evolving processes associated with regional integration?

Conclusion

Regional integration has attracted the attention of academic scholars and the policy community with the increasing popularity of integration over the past couple of decades. Even with the diverse record of success across regional integration schemes, the general view is that regional integration will continue to feature prominently in the politics between states (Breslin et al., 2002). Although the level of research into the topic is considerable, especially in the disciplines of political science, economics, and international relations, there has been comparatively little work done on the impact of the integration process on national administrations and public services, with the possible exception of the European integration experience. Consequently, the question is still to be answered. In part, the dynamic nature of integration makes it difficult to assess its impact upon public administration. Also, each integration model has its own particular configuration of policy domains, and a distribution of authority between the national and supranational level that varies from one policy area to another, making it difficult to assess the nature and extent of integration on the national competence.

In the literature on public management reform, recent work suggests an international convergence in public management systems (Peters & Pierre, 1998). However, there is no firm consensus on the degree of convergence, and some suggestion that even among the most similar countries, the extent of convergence has been overstated. How to explain this discrepancy? It is one thing to acknowledge that a shared discourse may be taking place in different countries, and that common decisions are adopted by countries within a regional integration framework (or through participation in international treaties), but it is quite another thing to claim that public administration systems are converging in terms of how the work is done or the results that are achieved. As the preceding discussion suggests, there are good reasons to consider the issue of how national public administration is affected by regional integration, and how the national level can make an impact at the regional level.

The current interest in regional integration suggests that both the demand and supply conditions identified by Mattli (1999) continue to operate. Yet, there are problems that remain. First, there is the issue of the legitimacy of policy decisions made beyond the level of the state but have to be implemented by national public administration. The so-called jurisdictional gap presents a problem for the national administration that must be resolved in order not to undermine the credibility of the national administration. There are possible lines of action to address the legitimacy problem. One is to extend the supervisory and review activities of the national parliaments, and to enhance the monitoring of regional integration processes by parliamentary committees that can then report back to the national parliament. Similarly, national governments regularly inform national parliaments about the commitments entered into as part of membership of the regional integration scheme.

Second, there is the issue of who is "in" and who is excluded from the policy-making arena associated with regional integration. This is the "participation gap" identified with both global and regional governance systems. Because the regional level is closer to the national level, and also increasingly the level where more decisions and policies are made that are likely to impact on national administration, it is imperative to address this particular deficit by ensuring that all relevant interests are included, and particularly important to enhance the participation of civil society. Regional integration has tended to involve political elites and economic interests (especially large corporations), yet it is becoming more evident that popular support is essential to ensure the continued relevance of regional integration for the broadest societal interests (Tsakatika, 2005). The challenge is to make regional governance work, and the responsibility is on respective national authorities to ensure that the national populace can identify with a political project that is democratic and inclusive of the wider interests.

Third, regional governance and policy making is often characterized by the "incentive gap," the problem of how to make implementation work. Even in long-established regional integration schemes like the EU, implementation of decisions made at the supranational level is uneven and patchy in certain policy domains. Elsewhere, the implementation gap is more acute, and especially in regional integration involving developing countries. Addressing this particular problem means the simultaneous attack on the other challenges already identified — the jurisdictional and participation gaps — although national governments must continue to back up the rhetoric of regional cooperation and integration with substantive political commitment and action. Ultimately regional integration will work to the extent that it is promoted by national governments, and the policies jointly decided upon are implemented by national public administration. No state can function without a public administration, and the public service is essential to both national and regional (i.e., supranational) level policy making. Without an effective national public administration, regional integration attempts will be doomed to failure — not least, regional integration among developing countries.

References

Allison, R. (2004) Regionalism, regional structures and security management in Central Asia. *International Affairs* 80(3): 463–483.

Andersen, S.S., Eliassen, K.A. (2001) *Making Policy in Europe*, 2nd ed. London: Sage.

Archer, C. (2001) *International Organizations*, 3rd ed. London: Routledge.

Balassa, B. (1962) *The Theory of Economic Integration*. London: Allen and Unwin.

Breslin, S., Hughes, C.W., Phillips, N., Rosamond, B. (2002) *New Regionalisms in the Global Political Economy. Theories and Cases*. London: Routledge.

Estevadeordal, A., Rodrik, D., Taylor, A.M., Velasco, A. (2004) *Integrating the Americas: FTAA and Beyond*. Harvard: Harvard University Press.

Farrell, M., Hettne, B., eds. (2005) *Global Politics of Regionalism. Theory and Practice*. London: Pluto.

Fawcett, L. (2004) Exploring regional domains: A comparative history of regionalism. *International Affairs* 80(3): 429–446.

Fawcett, L., Hurrell, A. (1995) *Regionalism in World Politics*. Oxford: Oxford University Press.

Gilpin, R. (2000) *The Challenge of Global Capitalism. The World Economy in the 21st Century*. Princeton: Princeton University Press.

Haas, E. (1958) *The Uniting of Europe*. Stanford: Stanford University Press.

Held, D., McGrew, A., Goldblatt, D., Perraton, J. (1999) *Global Transformations: Politics, Economics and Culture*. Cambridge: Polity Press.

Hettne, B., Inotai, A., Sunkel, O., eds. (1999) *Globalism and the New Regionalism*. Basingstoke: Macmillan, UNU/WIDER.

Hooghe, L., Marks, G. (2001) *Multi-Level Governance and European Integration*. Lanham, MD: Rownan and Littlefield.

Laursen, F. (2003) *Comparative Regional Integration: Theoretical Perspectives*. Aldershot: Ashgate.

MacFarlane, S.N. (2004) The United States and regionalism in Central Asia. *International Affairs* 80(3): 447–461.

Majone, G. (1996) *Regulating Europe*. London: Routledge.

Mansfield, E.D., Milner, H. (2001) The new wave of regionalism. In: Diehl, P.F. ed. *The Politics of Global Governance*. Boulder, CO: Lynne Rienner.

Marks, G., Scharpf, F.W., Schmitter, P.C., Streeck, W. (1996) *Governance in the European Union*. London: Sage.

Mattli, W. (1999) *The Logic of Regional Integration: Europe and Beyond*. Cambridge: Cambridge University Press.

Öjendal, J. (2004) Back to the future? Regionalism in South-East Asia under unilateral pressure. *International Affairs* 80(3): 519–533.

Peters, B.G., Pierre, J. (1998) Governance without government? Rethinking public administration. *Journal of Public Administration Research and Theory* 8(2): 223–243.

Rosamond, B. (2000) *Theories of European Integration*. Basingstoke: Palgrave.

Sandholtz, W., Stone Sweet, A. (1998) *European Integration and Supranational Governance*. Oxford: Oxford University Press.

Tsakatika, M. (2005) Claims to legitimacy: The European Commission between continuity and change. *Journal of Common Market Studies* 43(1): 193–220.

van Ham, P. (2001) *European Integration and the Postmodern Condition: Governance, Democracy, Identity*. London: Routledge.

Wiener, A., Diez, T. (2004) *European Integration Theory*. Oxford: Oxford University Press.

Chapter 13

Globalization and Governance: Explaining Success and Failure

Herbert H. Werlin

CONTENTS

Introduction

If we are to believe Thomas L. Friedman's 1999 bestseller, *The Lexus and the Olive Tree*, countries that attempt to avoid globalization are doomed to poverty. This is because, "the more you let market forces rule and the more you open your economy to free trade and competition, the more efficient and flourishing your economy will be" (Friedman, 1999, pp. 8–9). Using World Bank statistics, Friedman goes on to point out that between 1975 and 1997, the number of countries with liberal economic regimes had expanded from 8 percent of countries (amounting to $23 billion of direct foreign investment) to 28 percent of countries ($644 billion of direct foreign investment). According to Friedman, what has made globalization, "inexorable," has been a combination of international developments (the end of the Cold War and, with it, the triumph of capitalism, urbanization, international finance, and American culture) and technological developments (computerization, miniaturization, fiber optics, the Internet, cable and satellite television, automation, much faster and cheaper forms of transportation, and the handling of goods and services).

However, even if we agree with Friedman that there is no way to avoid globalization, we can still ask ourselves, "is it a good thing?" After all, the angry protests and the riotous behavior of thousands of demonstrators at recent meetings of the international finance organizations, the World Trade Organization, and the finance ministers of wealthy states cannot be completely ignored, however much we may be offended by it. This is why it is useful to come to grips with a thoughtful presentation of the antiglobalization case by the former Peruvian diplomat, Oswaldo de Rivero in his 2001 book, *The Myth of Development: Non-Viable Economies of the 21st Century*.

Perhaps without doing too much injustice to this book, de Rivero's arguments can be boiled down to the following: (1) Only a small number of countries (the city states of Hong Kong and Singapore, together with Taiwan and South Korea) have been able to take full advantage of globalization. (2) Despite globalization, 30 percent of the world's working age population remain unemployed and 40 percent of the population of Latin America, Asia, and Africa live below the poverty line, on less than one dollar a day. (3) Globalization has intensified problems of overpopulation, urbanization, waste or mismanagement of resources, poverty, unemployment, pollution, crime, inequality, oppression, and erosion of national sovereignty. (4) Because 75 percent of the world's population live in impoverished countries, they lack the financial, scientific, and technological resources to be competitive in a world dominated by a small number of transnational corporations, with decreasing need for unskilled labor and raw materials. (5) The economic policies supporting globalization pushed by the World Bank, the International Monetary Fund (IMF), and the leaders of wealthy countries, including comparative advantage, structural adjustment, free trade, liberalization, deregulation, and privatization, have proved to be mistaken, counterproductive, and harmful to the poor. (6) Even when countries attempt globalization, they face high tariffs and subsidies to protect the products most exported by developing countries, such as food, clothes, and textiles.

Two more recent books (Stiglitz, 2003; Bhagwati, 2004) bring the debate into focus, not so much over the "benefits of globalization," but, rather, on the "the consequences of globalization" and how to protect countries from these consequences. Although both the books point to some of the same problems regarding globalization (e.g., dangers of intensifying unemployment, monopolization, corruption, inequality, environmental neglect, excessive production, labor exploitation, foreign capital flight, and financial failure or instability), Stiglitz sees them more inevitable and intractable than Bhagwati does. In this regard, Stiglitz's assertion (p. 5) that "to many in the developing world, globalization has not brought the promised economic benefits" can be compared to Bhagwati's enthusiastic position (p. 240): "The debate, then should be not about whether we should be content with the pace at which economic prosperity, aided by globalization, proceeds to reduce, say, child labor, but about what additional policy instruments can we deploy to accelerate that pace."

Whereas both these distinguished economists recognize the importance of governmental policies and their implementation in maximizing the advantages of globalization and minimizing its disadvantages, they do not seem to fully appreciate or understand the importance of public administration in this regard. Consequently, I suggest that Stiglitz may be overemphasizing the deleterious impact of the so-called "Washington Consensus Policies" (privatization, deregulation, financial market liberalization, free trade, and balanced budgets), whereas Bhagwati may be underemphasizing it. According to Stiglitz, Poland, which ignored the IMF's economic policy prescriptions, has done better than the Czech Republic, one of the "IMF's star pupils." (p. 156) Yet, as of 2003, economic conditions were better in the Czech Republic than in Poland (*The Economist*, 2004, p. 83).

In regard to structural adjustment requirements imposed by the World Bank, Stiglitz is far more critical than Bhagwati. But as we look at a particular country (Uganda, as presented by Stiglitz, p. 76), it is not the school fees insisted upon by the World Bank or IMF that reduce educational opportunity but, rather, poor public administration, combined with inappropriate policies. In Uganda, more than three times is spent on the education of the wealthiest fifth of the country than on the education of the poorest, and much of the money intended for schools is either stolen or diverted (World Bank Development Committee, 2004, ch. 7, pp. 8–9). One can add that the teacher absentee rate in Uganda has been estimated at about 25 percent. While I would agree with Bhagwati (p. 162) that free trade cannot be blamed for Jamaica's failure to attract international investment, I would place far more emphasis (as I do in this chapter) on the government's corruption and mismanagement for this failure.

Stiglitz (p. 6) notes the hypocrisy of wealthy countries — pushing free trade on poor countries, while maintaining many forms of protectionism. In this regard, he might have quoted a recent World Bank publication: "OECD protection rates for sugar are frequently above 200 percent, and its support to sugar producers of $6.4 billion per year roughly equals developing country exports" (World Bank Development Committee, 2004, Chapter 1, p. 10). However, without justifying the protectionism of developed countries, Bhagwati (p. 232) uses World Bank research to point out that tariff rates for agriculture, textiles and clothing, and industrial products are actually higher in the developing countries than in the developed countries. Yet, regardless of existing impediments to trade, it is amazing what poor countries can do to promote their exports when determined to do so. Vietnam, for example (*The Economist,* May 8, 2004, p. 39), not only has developed diversified exports, but also has found new markets for products encountering higher tariffs (such as catfish).

Political Power as Social Energy

On the American Political Science Association's Web site, it is recognized that there is more than one definition of politics. Yet, the only one mentioned, presumably derived from Harold Lasswell's 1936 book, is "who get what, when, and how." This is explained as follows: "Almost always the political process involves competition for scarce resources." To me this seems to be a unidimensional definition of politics, emphasizing partisanship (rather than statesmanship or governance) and, as such, is misleading and counterproductive. And above all, as explained in this chapter, it prevents us from understanding political power. Consequently, it distorts our understanding of political words such as democracy, corruption, and decentralization and thus prevents us from linking political science to public administration.

Ask a political scientist what he or she means by "politics." The reaction is likely to be a mixture of irritation and confusion. Introductory political science textbooks frequently use the meaning of politics as "the authoritative allocation of values" and "the pursuit of power" without indicating the relationship between these concepts (Norquest, 1991, pp. 504–505). Yet, values cannot simply be imposed (behavior, yes; values, no) and power cannot be pursued within an empty framework. The process of inculcating values requires a strong relationship between leaders and followers. Such a relationship cannot develop unless the struggle for power is carried out within an acceptable framework.

Imagine watching the Olympics and seeing it only as the competitive struggle for victory. How many gold, silver, and bronze medals an individual or nation wins then becomes most important. However, if there is no consensus on every aspect of the competitive process (rules, officiating, equipment, facilities, etc.), the competition is meaningless. How to build consensus to maximize the competitive process is, of course, the responsibility of leadership. This is where we need my suggested overall definition of politics: the relationship of leadership to followership for the purpose of governance, presented in the next section, introducing political elasticity (PE) theory.

I believe that behaviorally oriented political scientists prefer seeing politics simply as "a struggle for competitive advantage" because political power is then seen as similar to money and, as such, is easier to measure that way. Consequently, they often end up distorting or trivializing political situations and phenomena. Above all, they fail to solve the so-called "mysteries of development" that have been presented in my various publications (e.g., Werlin, 1998, 2000, 2003): (1) Why is it that autocratic governments are sometimes more effective (though usually not) in promoting development than their more democratic counterparts? (2) Why is it that more developed countries (MDCs) tend to be both more centralized and more decentralized than less developed countries (LDCs)? (3) Why is corruption more devastating for poor countries than rich countries? (4) What explains the capacity of certain countries (such as Singapore) to do "cultural engineering?" (5) Why is it that economic globalization has had a more positive impact on some countries than on others? For this reason, we have to introduce an "elastic" concept of political power, recognizing that we cannot altogether escape the "tautological trap" (seeing what we want to see) in doing so. In this regard, PE theory is no different from other theories in political science which "may be likened to a net that is cast out to capture political phenomena, which are then drawn in and sorted in a way that seems meaningful and relevant to the particular thinker." (Wolin, 1960, p. 21).

An elastic concept of political power enables us to conceptualize it as a form of social energy, rather than merely a resource to be fought over in a competitive way. This analogy to physical energy also suggests that, while energy is essential to life, it can also be highly destructive, inert, or counterproductive. In illustrating political power as a form of social energy, I am going to introduce a personal note, using a recent trip to Berlin (June, 2003), seeing how it has changed in the 75 years (1928) since my father had visited it on his way to Moscow to study the origins of the Soviet system for a University of Chicago history Ph.D. dissertation. Although visits to other

German cities are useful, one can find "within the borders of Greater Berlin" a "microcosm" of German problems (Heneghan, 2002, p. 236). Concentrating on political power, one can observe the following manifestations:

Dynamic

In his 1928 unpublished diary, my father found Berlin to be remarkably clean and neat: "By contrast to American cities of anything like its size, its preeminence in these characteristics is only the more unchallengeable. There is none of those begrimed and besmoked buildings as in Chicago, for example. I have yet to see a cluttered-up backyard or alley, yet to see empty lots with the grass uncut and piled high with rusty iron, old lumber, and other junk." In regard to art, science, industry, and technology, Berlin was clearly one of the great centers of civilization.

Devastating

Under Hitler's Third Reich (1933–1945), political power within Berlin and the rest of Germany became totalitarian, as described by Friedrich and Brzezinski (1956) with the following characteristics: an official ideology, a single mass party, terroristic police control, near-complete domination of mass communication, and central direction of the economy. The devastation wrought was overwhelming as to be generally considered "unprecedented": a brutal war of conquest, genocide, the deaths of 40 million people, extensive slave labor, and, within Germany, enormous economic, intellectual, and cultural loss (Turner, 1987, pp. 3–7).

Miraculous

Despite the Soviet efforts to divide, isolate, and undermine Berlin during the Cold War, West Berliners enjoyed the "economic miracle" and welfare-state capitalism associated with the Christian Democratic leadership of Konrad Adenauer and Ludwig Erhard during the 1950s and 1960s. By the end of the 1950s, the Federal Republic was "ranked second only to the United States in world trade," with low levels of inflation and unemployment and "one of the world's largest currency reserves" (Turner, 1987, p. 61). For the first time, prosperity became associated with political stability, labor union participation, burden-sharing, democracy, and a highly elaborate welfare state. It was not only a time of cultural and educational renaissance but also reconstruction as well, with an estimated quarter of the country's housing having to be rebuilt.

Lethargic

How to characterize political power under the German Democratic Republic (1945–1989) remains unclear: semi-totalitarian, post-Stalinist, Sovietized, tutelary, and so forth, "linked, however indirectly, to the normative aims of those speaking and writing?" (Kocka, 1997, pp. 17–18). However described, the regime was authoritarian and repressive, undermining spontaneity, innovation, and adaptability. Although not obviously inelastic in comparison to LDCs in much of the world, East German factories, in comparison to their West German counterparts, "suffered from outdated technology, environmental problems, delays in resolving property ownership issues, and low productivity" (Smith, 1999, p. 117). According to some observers, the character of East Germans had become so deformed by years of socialization under communism that it would take generations to overcome their "pathological disabilities" (e.g., Baylis, 1999, p. 26).

Revitalized

Whereas scholars and journalists recently visiting East Berlin and East Germany recognize the difficulties that remain to be overcome, most seem impressed by what has so far been accomplished. Heneghan's finding in 2002 (Heneghan, 2002, p. 61) probably remains valid, that the unemployment rate is still twice as high as that in the West and the average household purchasing power is about 70 percent as much. Yet, despite the view often expressed by economists that "full integration will take 30 or 40 years" and that "in the meantime continuing financial transfers from West to East will be necessary," East German firms may be able to adapt better than their West German competitors to the Euro (Smith, 1999, p. 232). Consequently, "Thomas Mann would have been pleased to see how European his Germany had turned out to be by the end of the tumultuous century" (Heneghan, 2002, p. 238).

We can end this section by noting that the Marshall Plan was clearly a great success in West Germany in facilitating the transformation that has occurred. But this would have been impossible without the country's underlying political software (as explained in the next section). Where political software is inadequate, foreign aid (as administered by the World Bank) has been largely unsuccessful. Although how to encourage LDCs to take more advantage of globalization opportunities will be left to the last section of this chapter, the political software requisites noted in the next section suggest possibilities. In any case, I hope that what I have written here will call attention to the need to rethink the meaning of political power and what has to happen for it to be effective. In so doing, we may be able to dissipate the "intellectual chaos" associated with political power (Baldwin, 1989, p. 2).

Political Elasticity Theory

Because PE theory is essential to our effort to better understand the capacity of countries to use political power for their globalization efforts, its five propositions are presented here:

1. The more governments or those in authority can integrate and alternate soft forms of political power (linking incentives to persuasion) with hard forms (including disincentives and coercion), the more effective they will be.
2. As leaders integrate and alternate soft and hard forms of power, their political power takes on "rubber band" and "balloon" characteristics, allowing them to (a) decentralize or delegate power by various methods without losing control and (b) expand their influence in ways that predictably affect the behavior of wider circles of citizens, participants, and subordinates.
3. Political elasticity depends partly on the selection of appropriate political hardware (including "objective" forms of organization, regulation, procedure, and technology) but mostly on the enhancement of political software (i.e., policies and practices that foster respectful relations between leaders and followers).
4. The effectiveness of political software is directly proportional to the government's success in establishing acceptable goals, hiring qualified personnel, encouraging training, delegating responsibility, stimulating motivation and competition, paying attention to morale, expanding two-way flows of communication, promoting legitimacy, maintaining supervision, cultivating contractors, protecting independent spheres of authority, and developing conflict resolution procedures. Inasmuch as a government fails to do any of these commonsensical requirements (with appropriate variations), its efforts to reform both micro- and macro-administration are going to be problematic. Yet, progress can be measured on the basis of steps taken to improve any aspect of these requirements.
5. Enhancing political software requires a balancing of two forms of struggle — for competitive advantage and for consensus — suggested by the various meanings of politics found in Wolin's 1960 study of political thought (Wolin, 1960, pp. 10, 42, 66, 363). Within the framework of his overarching definition of politics (the relationship of leadership to followership for the purpose of governance), measures taken to increase advantage may be considered "primary politics" (i.e., partisanship) and measures taken to build consensus may be considered "secondary politics" (i.e., statesmanship).

Three Success Stories

In the literature on economic development, we find various explanations given as to why some countries benefit far more than others from globalization: geographic, cultural, sociological (ethnic, religious, racial, and other divisions), political (particularly, the existence of democracy), and the choice of economic policies. Although all of these explanations are relevant, I find them inadequate in explaining why globalization helps some countries more than others.

In thinking about the relationship of globalization to development, we might link it to an earlier body of literature having to do with "growth without development," underscoring the fact that development is more than the production of goods and services or per capita gross national product (GNP) (Lindenberg, 1993, p. 15). A 1966 Northwestern University study of Liberia (Clower et al., 1966) showed clearly how unsatisfactory GNP per capita figures are. While Liberia's per capita GNP in 1965 (US $642) put it then within the category of a "mid-level" country by the World Bank standard, 75 percent of the population remained illiterate and 75 percent of the national income went to foreign households, business firms, and the political elite. Thus, this study concluded that much of the growth that occurred during the post-World War II years had not led to meaningful development. A similar conclusion has been reached by students of Soviet development, noting that the "low quality of goods and services produced obscured statistics showing above median world growth prior to 1990" (Easterly & Fisher, 2000, p. 481).

In regard to the potential benefits of globalization, PE theory points to the importance of an "enabling environment," which can be fostered but not dictated by government. This is why an effective public administration is essential. In emphasizing governance, I find myself somewhat alone, inasmuch as social scientists (particularly economists and political scientists) tend to ignore it (Werlin, 2000). Economists (especially at the World Bank and the IMF) who promote structural adjustment often minimize the role of government in favor of liberalization, deregulation, privatization, and reliance of the market place. Political scientists seem more concerned with who governs and the selection of policies (so-called "rational choice") than the quality of governance and and the implementation of policies.Only a small percentage of articles in journals dealing with comparative politics, political development, and economic development are primarily concerned with public administration.

The three "success stories" that will be presented in this section illustrate the "message" of PE theory, that, as countries prosper, political power takes on "rubber band" and "balloon" characteristics. If we see political power as nothing more than the product of physical and legal resources, it is likely to manifest itself as coercion or corruption, thereby appearing to be "real political power" as defined (Baldwin, 1989, p. 201) by Robert Dahl ("the ability of A to get B to do something he would not otherwise have done") but, as such, essentially inelastic. In other words, whereas A can force B to surrender his resources, he cannot force B to productively invest them. PE theory allows us (as noted earlier) to see political power as a "form of social energy" and, as such, that is essential for globalization purposes, much as physical energy is essential for biological life. In each of the following cases, governmental effectiveness can be seen as dependent upon the quality of relations between leaders and followers, rather than merely the monopoly of coercive authority.

The Netherlands

The Netherlands is a remarkable country in many ways. It is one of the most densely populated countries of the world, with 27 percent of it below sea level, protected by its famous dikes. Yet, it was judged by the 1996 UN Human Development Report to have the best living conditions, including the lowest unemployment rates, within the European Union (Hunt, 2000).

For purposes of this chapter, I will concentrate on the fact that the Netherlands ranks third worldwide (after the United States and France) in agricultural export value — an achievement that clearly would be impossible without a high quality of governance, including merging of centralization and decentralization. On the one hand, the Netherlands appears to be highly centralized inasmuch as the central government appoints mayors, provides more than two thirds of municipal revenues for specific purposes, and determines the policies and guidelines for provincial and local administration (Andeweg & Irwin, 1993). On the other hand, the Netherlands is also a decentralized state in which local governments have considerable autonomy (Jones, 1995; Toonen, 1996). Within the limits set by central and provincial officials, each municipality prepares its own plans and regulations, following extensive discussions, negotiations, and opportunities for objection. According to Wintle (2000, p. 149), under the Dutch model, "the state is highly centralized, big-spending and all-powerful, but that does not and need not threaten in any way the integrity of the component units."

"Elastic decentralization" (to use my terminology) is evident in the complex private sector–public sector (sometimes characterized as "corporatist") linkages that are responsible for agricultural, as well as industrial, development in the Netherlands. These linkages have been promoted since the 1930s by provincial institutes for economic development (van Zanden, 1998). Associated with them is a tight infrastructure of agricultural research, education, rural banks, cooperatives, commercial firms, advisory councils, parastatal organizations, and extension services to encourage and facilitate new products, production techniques, and marketing opportunities. While 80 percent of farmers are organized, they are divided among "pillarized" groups (Catholic, Protestant, Socialist, Liberal, etc.). What makes this fragmented system politically elastic is the respect for independent experts, for the judiciary (including various bodies of administrative justice and appeal), and for the existing system of formal and informal consultations. Above all, there is a devotion to the politics of accommodation, pragmatism, and consensus.

One can point to the example of political inelasticity in the Netherlands (Hendriks & Toonen, 2001). How to prevent excessive water use and pollution, for example, has been particularly difficult. Nevertheless, politicians are able to turn to "incrementalism" — "a process of shared perception, negotiation, and trade-off" (Bekkers & Lips, 2001).

South Korea

Because economists seldom understand the power of politics, their analysis of economic problems and opportunities can be quite misleading. When political leaders are as firmly committed to economic development, as they were (and still are) in Korea, they can cause the most rational recommendations stemming from comparative advantage, cost–benefit, and other forms of analyses to appear mistaken and even ridiculous. In other words, they can make economic progress by disregarding the prevailing economic advice. This "school of dissent" has been led by Amsden (1994, p. 96), who points out that, in the Korean case, "getting prices wrong" has been essential in accounting for its amazing industrialization success.

Amsden (1994, p. 113) suggests that state-guided capitalism has become controversial in South Korea, particularly because of the criticism of Korean economists influenced by the "conservative, anti-government Chicago school." The truth is, she concludes, there is no scientific evidence to back up the contention that either Japan or Korea could have grown faster with less government intervention. Johnson (1994, p. 470) notes in this regard that neoclassical economic theorists who prevail at the World Bank and other international organizations remain very defensive about the achievements of state-guided capitalism, "which they did not anticipate and still cannot fully explain using their purely economic concepts."

Comparing Korea's industrialization with that of India, Lee (1991, p. 470) suggests that Korean leaders were able to free themselves from orthodox or classical economic thinking only because they respected it. In other words, Korean leaders often distorted market incentives and disincentives to compete in the world market; but they were "pragmatic and bold enough to reform the entire incentive and economic management regime when circumstances dictated it."

South Korea's industrialization efforts would have certainly failed if its administration had not been politically elastic, recognizing that it was an authoritarian regime until the 1990s. The history of its industrialization effort presented here should illustrate that fact.

Whereas in 1960, the Korean civil service was viewed "as a corrupt and inept institution," and by the 1970s, it had "become one of the most reputable in the developing world" (World Bank, 1993, p. 176). South Korea has followed the Japanese "best product" policy in public employment practices, selecting top graduates of Seoul National University for the majority of the senior positions in politically and economically important agencies. Although President Park during the 1960s and the 1970s and President Chun during the 1980s surrounded themselves with "palace guards" (particularly classmates from the Korean Military Academy) and patron–client networks to satisfy partisan needs in ministries like construction, both balanced them with highly qualified civilians with advanced degrees in key economic ministries (Kim, 1991, p. 321).

South Korea had to face problems of corruption associated with the *chaebol* (financially linked companies). The practices of the *chaebol* include: use of corporate money for personal purposes, cross-payment guarantees among subsidiaries, dubious book-keeping practices (for example, inflating sales or assets and deflating debts), false names for bank deposits, and misuse of the banks (or financial institutions) for careless investments. As pointed out by Cheng et al. (1999, p. 105), "it was generally accepted for businesses to provide gifts, services and even cash for bureaucrats as a way of keeping relations with various ministries on a solid footing." This capitalistic corruption is considered responsible for the financial crisis that struck South Korea in November 1997, requiring the IMF's most expensive rescue operation (amounting to $55 billion). Within one year, the percentage of Koreans living in poverty nearly tripled from 8.5 to 22.9 percent (Dahlman & Andersson, 2000, p. 47).

Since 1997, there has been an improvement in the quality of the Korean civil service. Although public sector employment has been reduced from 7 percent to 5 percent of the total employment, civil servant wages have been increased at par with comparable private sector employees. The result has been a much greater administrative capacity to deal with capitalistic corruption, according to Jung-in (2002), facilitated by the fact that "the institutional landscape of the Korean economy has changed dramatically over the past four years." This conclusion is underscored by the Organization for Economic Co-operation and Development (OECD, 2000, p. 15), pointing out that in Korea there has been "a rapid and profound reorientation in administrative, legal and economic policies," bringing the country "closer to the mainstream of good regulatory practices in OECD countries." What also seems to be making a difference, according to the OECD (2000, pp. 15–16) "has been a surge in the number of non-governmental organizations in recent years, to over 8000," willing and able to fight for the interests of consumers, labor, and good government.

In 1969, the South Korean government borrowed from the World Bank to create a network of vocational training institutions near the industries, so that instructors could analyze the needs of these industries and also the experts from the industries could serve as part-time tutors (Werlin, 1998, pp. 278–284). A Curriculum Research and Development Department within the Ministry of Education was created to facilitate the introduction of computer technology, new textbooks and equipment, a national testing service, and "models of excellence" approach. By tying their vocational education system to five-year economic development plans and to manpower the projections, the schools were able to find employment for 81 percent of their graduates and to keep the dropout rates low.

The development of industrial parks in South Korea has been facilitated by the domination of a small number of conglomerates (the *chaebols*) along German and Japanese lines, together with a close partnership among government agencies, universities, and corporations. President Park developed a "reverse brain drain," attracting Koreans, who were studying and working abroad, to fill the top ranks of industries and research institutes (Clifford, 1994, p. 110). "Over a thousand scientists were repatriated with financial support from the government between 1968 and 1989" (Lall, 1997, p. 23).

According to Gibney (1992, pp. 128–129), the Korean government has been particularly concerned with the expansion of electronics, in which Korea (as of 1990) ranked fourth in the world. Pae (1992, p. 484) points out that the Daeduck Science and Research Center expanded from 1970 to 1990 to accommodate about 40 research institutes and three universities. By the end of 1990s, about 5 percent of Korea's GNP went for Research and Development (R&D), which was considered "an unprecedented rate of investment in technological activity. . . . " (Lall, 1997, p. 26). This investment supported the efforts of nearly 3000 research establishments, including more than 1000 R&D units in universities and colleges, and 200 public research establishments. Moreover, the government has been contributing about $25 million annually in recent years to give small businesses access to the same kind of planning, management, and accounting tools that big businesses use, particularly with the goal of making electronic about one third (up from 12 percent currently) of business transactions by 2005 (Ihlwan, 2003, p. 26).

In analyzing the implications of South Korea's industrial development, Lall (1997, pp. 31–32) suggests that "the design of structural adjustment programs has to be very different from the essentially neo-liberal approach recommended by institutions like the World Bank today." In looking at the Korean experience, economists must pay attention to such political factors as the determination of leaders to create skilled and independent bureaucracies and to overcome entrenched vested interests. In doing so, they can go on to generalize that the economic potential of countries rests upon these factors, thereby incorporating them in their theories.

Whereas the Dahlman and Andersson report (Dahlman & Anderson, 2000, pp. 31–32) is somewhat critical of Korea's "misallocation of investments" and "impediments to high-value-added services," it points out that, as of 1997, there were 48 researchers per 10,000 labor force in Korea, as against only 6 in Mexico. Because of the existence of a well-educated population combined with "aggressive capital investment on a large-scale, modern facilities, risk taking, and vigorous domestic rivalry," Korea has been able to recover from its 1997 financial crisis with unemployment falling to 4.4 percent by the end of 1999 (Dahlman & Andersson, 2000, p. 96).

Although Korea had to face difficult competition from China, it has been able to maintain a comparative advantage in regard to the delivery time, reliability, and technological sophistication of its products. For example, although prior to 1974, South Korea did not even have a shipbuilding industry, it is currently vying with Japan for world leadership in this industry, specializing in double-hull tankers that are highly automated and computerized (Kirk, 2003, pp. W1, W7). Even when recognizing the alleged "unfair subsidies" to this industry received in the form of loans from government-owned banks, observers note that Korea's dominant share of world shipbuilding would not have been possible without its highly educated and motivated workforce.

Singapore

Singapore has been described as a "sub-fascist state," in which the "vulnerability" of the island republic is used as a pretext "to crack down on democratic critics" (Haas, 1999, p. 39). Despite periodic elections, the government has used a single-party system to suppress dissent, detain without trial, intimidate newspapers and radical trade unions, and enact antidemocratic laws and administrative regulations. Although the regime does employ overt repression, it prefers to use "the bankrupting libel suit" as a tool to discourage political dissent (Beng-Huat, 1994, pp. 655–657).

Lee Kwan Yew, Singapore's prime minister from 1959 until his resignation in 1990, has always been ambivalent about democracy. Whereas in a 1992 speech in the Philippines, he proclaimed that "what a country needs to develop is discipline more than democracy," he explained to a Chinese delegation to Singapore that year "that social control could not depend on discipline alone," adding "people had to have a decent life with reasonable housing and social amenities if they were to lead moral and upright lives. They had to accept the basic principles of our system of government..." (Lee Kwan Yew, 2000, pp. 304, 646).

At the beginning of 1997, the ruling People's Action Party (PAP) increased its seats (leaving only two in opposition) in Parliament and its share of the vote (reaching 65 percent) over 1991. It did so, however, by threatening to delay the upgrading of public housing estates and planned infrastructure projects in opposition-supporting constituencies. These tactics, together with those used to discourage opposition candidates in the November 3, 2001 elections, are seen as essential to prevent "rampant individualism, social instability, and decadence" (Neher, 1999, pp. 48–49). Yet, they were a crude manifestation of "hard politics": "what you get depends upon how you vote!" As explained by Mutalib (2000, p. 317), "an illiberal, (soft) authoritarian form of governance is certainly preferable to liberal democracy" because "economic growth demands much sacrifice from the people," which they might not be willing to support if given a choice.

Although liberal democracy is clearly undermined in Singapore, classical democracy is evident in various ways. Survey data indicates a high degree of public respect for the government in regard to property rights, the legal system, honesty, reliability, business environment, and lack of corruption (Huff, 1999). The Lee Kuan Yew government transformed its bureaucracy over a 25-year period from one that was somewhat inefficient and corrupt into probably the most respected in Asia, including personnel who are carefully selected, highly paid, and trained, with excellent equipment and working conditions, and properly motivated and controlled. Although the jury system has been eliminated, both the Swiss-based Institute for Management Development and the Hong Kong-based Political and Economic Risk Consultancy ranked Singapore's judicial system as the best in Asia during the 1990s (Lee Kwan Yew, 2000, pp. 219–220). Transparency International Web site lists Singapore as among the world's least corrupt countries. In a book that is quite critical of authoritarian rule in Singapore, one of the authors points out that "Singapore does enjoy substantive democracy," including due process of law, equality of opportunity, and "a modicum of civil liberties" (Neher, 1999, p. 51).

Lee Kwan Yew, in his recent (2000) autobiography, is proud of the cultural engineering that occurred under his rule from 1959 to 1990, transforming a population that was largely uneducated, illiterate in English, impoverished, and without professional or technical skills into a one comparable to what exists in the most advanced countries. By the end of the 1990s, 40 percent of eligible youth (as against 5 percent in 1970s) were enrolled in higher education, facilitating the annual export of $60 billion worth of high-tech products, which was about one third more than exported by China (*The Economist* November 10, 2001, p. 11). In the process, two disadvantaged sections of the population (women and Malays) have especially benefited. Between 1970 and 1990, the percentage of women aged 25 to 29 years with a secondary of college education doubled, those in wage-earning employed increased by 20 percent, and the fertility rate was reduced by 70 percent (Werlin, 1998, pp. 219–220). With the financial support and encouragement of the government, the independent Association of Muslim Professionals became very successful during the 1990s in quadrupling the percentage (from 7 to 28 percent) of Malay students undertaking higher education, so that a higher percentage of Malays in Singapore hold administrative or professional positions than in Malaysia, thereby also reducing their hostility toward the Chinese majority (Lee Kwan Yew, 2000, p. 209). Yet, animosity remains insofar as the government has not found a way to completely integrate the various racial and religious communities and, at the same time, respect their differences. Allowing veiled schoolgirls seems to be the most vexing problem made more difficult by "Singapore's knee-jerk rejection of all but the mildest dissent" (*The Economist*, February 9, 2002a, p. 37).

Lee Kwan Yew's cultural engineering would not have been successful without a high quality of political software. In my case study of Singapore's successful public housing program, I found government officials remarkably responsive to changing needs and demands (Werlin, 1998, pp. 231–234). University planning professors, in the interviews that I had with them in 1990, were impressed, not only by the willingness of officials to listen to their criticisms and suggestions, but also by their willingness to fund research on existing and emerging problems. In this regard, Mutalib (2000, p. 337) reports on the willingness of the government in 1998 to revise its economic policies (including cost-cutting measures, lowering of fees and taxes, and a reduction in employers' social security contributions), taking unusual steps to swing public opinion in favor of radical reform. During a recession in the mid-1980s, employees of even profitable firms agreed to a significant reduction in salaries as a result of a "tripartite" advisory council composed of government, employees, and labor. This was facilitated by "vocal and frank comment on all public policies" carried out in the press, parliament, public forums, and grass roots institutions" (Chee, 1986; Campus & Root, 1996, p. 81). Likewise, in response to the 1998 Asian financial crisis, the parliamentary designated committee on Singapore's competitiveness made a number of painful recommendations, including reducing total wage costs by up to 20 percent, which were acceptable only because of the existing high-quality political software (Leong, 2000).

Since 1990, under Prime Minister Goh Chok Tong, there have been more experiments to expand two-way flows of communication: community development councils, a speakers' corner, an award for the best public suggestions for improving the functioning of the courts, and a liberalization of registration requirements for groups or societies. Leong (2000, pp. 436–455), a political science lecturer at the National University of Singapore, has summarized what the current situation is, indicating that constructive criticism is to be encouraged, but not counterproductive statements or activities, particularly having to do with racial, ethnic, and religious differences. The permission granted to political satires is an indication of the recent flexibility and tolerance existing in Singapore. However, what Leong (2000, p. 442) refers to as, "this love–hate attitude among policy makers for citizen input" seems to be reflected in a remark of Prime Minister Goh that while those "who put forth their views in very well-meaning ways will receive a very gentle and very well-meaning reply," those who try to undermine the authority of the government through snide remarks and mockery "must expect a very, very hard blow from the government in return."

Although Singapore has slipped since 2000 in its place as the world's top trading nation in terms of trade as a proportion of gross domestic product (GDP), it "has consistently placed among the most competitive economies in the world for a long time," being more competitive than Switzerland, Japan, Sweden, Germany, and the United States, according to studies of the United Nations Industrial Development Organization (UNIDO) (Audretsch, 2003). Despite criticism that "the economy is excessively state managed," both domestic and foreign entrepreneurs continue to find opportunities here in "high-end electronics, process chemicals, pharmaceuticals and biomedical sciences" (Bhaskaran, 2003, p. 154).

An article by Kam (2001), a professor in Singapore National University's business school, underscores some of the reasons why Singapore is such an attractive place for multinational corporations (MNCs): (1) the government's Research and Development (R&D) expenditure (increasing sixfold between 1987 and 1998); (2) an impressive growth of research scientists and engineers; (3) the sponsorship of an increasing number of public R&D institutions; (4) the widening enrolment in technology courses at the local universities and polytechnic institutions; (5) the increase in spin-offs from universities and public R&D institutions; (6) the rapid growth of public research institutes and centers; (7) the increase in patents filed by Singapore-based organizations; (8) the encouragement of technology deployment efforts, particularly advanced manufacturing and internet technologies; (9) a very liberal immigration policy to attract foreign talent; (10) incentives for MNCs to send Singaporean engineers overseas to acquire new technical skills; (11) the offering of investment incentives to MNCs to upgrade operations; and (12) the promotion of science parks and incubators (places to help newly emerging companies). Without the linking of improved training, infrastructure, finance, research, labor relations, and marketing arrangements, Singapore's globalization efforts, particularly in electronics, would not have been possible.

Three Failure Stories

In seeing political power as a form of social energy, using PE theory, it should be appropriate to underscore the basic point made in this chapter that political power tends to take a more politically elastic form in MDCs than in LDCs. I emphasize the word, "tends," because there are examples of "political inelasticity" in MDCs and "political elasticity" in LDCs. In this regard, Costa Rica (which is clearly an LDC) may be doing a better job than the United States in protecting its "ecological treasures" (Newton & Dillingham, 1994).

Some scholars do not regard persuasion as a form of power because they equate "power with the capacity to compel obedience in the face of opposition" (Wrong, 1979, p. 22). In fact, coercion without persuasion is likely to be ineffective because it indicates a poor quality of political software. Although political software (as indicated in the propositions of PE theory) requires a series of commonsensical steps, it is by no means an easy or inexpensive process. In this regard, Peters (1991, p. 153) quotes V.O. Key to the effect that "the average voter is no fool; he or she generally understands what is being done with taxes and services." In 1998 Swedes were the most heavily taxed people in the world, with tax receipts amounting to 52 percent of GDP (about twice the European Community average); but their willingness to pay this amount stemmed from their belief that they were receiving "a fair return in services for their taxes" (Peters, 1991, p. 160). In Nigeria, on the other hand, people have successfully resisted paying local taxes because there has been so little progress toward administrative efficiency and effectiveness (Phillips, 1991). In Onitsha, for example, officials threatened to cut off water service to those failing to pay property taxes. However, because services were unreliable and mismanaged, taxpayers considered the threat meaningless (Dillinger, 1991, p. 28).

Goerner and Thompson (1996, p. 28) note that although political philosophers define political authority "as a monopoly of the means of coercive physical force," they have failed to deal with the paradox of "a coercive public order to guarantee individualistic liberty." Where there is a high quality of political software, there is no real problem in this regard. In LDCs, on the other hand, we constantly see evidence of "political inelasticity." This is clearest in Africa under "predatory rule" where authoritarianism coexists "with a definite lack of authority" (Fatton, 1992, p. 28).

Although African leaders have a great capacity for exercising coercion, they have only a limited capacity for governance. This may be because governance in Africa "is more a matter of seamanship and less one of navigation — that is staying afloat rather than going somewhere" (Jackson & Rosberg, 1982, p. 18).

The case studies below are intended to explain why is it that LDCs are less effective than MDCs in creating wealth, a high standard of living, and the implementation of policies. Insofar as political power in LDCs lacks rubber band and balloon characteristics, it will not be energetic enough for beneficial globalization. As such, these case studies are also relevant in dealing with the "mysteries of development" that were presented at the beginning of this chapter.

Ghana

While Ghana has about the same population size as the Netherlands (15–20 million), it is far more dependent on agriculture. Whereas in the Netherlands, manufacturing accounts for 70 percent of merchandise export, Ghana depends on agriculture for nearly half of GDP and export earnings and 70 percent of employment (Chibber and Leechor, 1993, p. 29). This would not be a problem if Ghana utilized its agricultural potential. Ghana's most lucrative agricultural product remains cocoa. However, its share of the world market has dropped from 30 percent in 1970 to about 10 percent, without much likelihood of recovery. According to a 1993 study of the OECD, Ghana has a clear competitive advantage in many crops (in addition to cocoa): coffee, rubber, maize, sorghum, cotton, tobacco, pineapples, and oil palm (Alpine & Pickett, 1993).

Agricultural output has risen in recent years at an average rate of only 2 percent per annum, as against a population growth rate of 3 percent. The growth of food crops, livestock, and fishing output has been particularly slow. Because only about half of Ghana's arable area is cultivated, agricultural export opportunities are being missed. For example, although Ghana could be exporting more and better pineapples than Costa Rica, in 1994 it managed only $5 million worth, as against $45 million worth for Costa Rica that year (Buckley, 1996, pp. A1, A12–A13). Likewise, offshore fish stocks could also be better utilized. Horticultural exports certainly could be expanded, considering that Kenya (which has a much longer flying time to Europe) successfully exports horticultural products (consisting now of 70 percent of its produce), thereby reducing its reliance on coffee and tea (Africa Region, 2003).

The inability of the government to significantly expand agricultural productivity clearly stems from underlying bottlenecks to rural development

(Chibber et al., 1993 Bahal et al., 1993;). Perhaps most serious of all is the lack of feeder roads, of which an estimated 60 percent are in poor condition. This means that rural Ghana remains a "footpath economy," with farmers (most of whom are women) having to spend much of their time head-loading commodities. The government has not even helped in providing fuel-efficient cooking stoves, small carts, wheelbarrows, and bicycles, which could also promote local artisanal and small-scale industry. There is also an inadequate availability of simple equipment for conditioning, processing, and preserving crops. And very few farmers have access to irrigation, credit, fertilizer, insecticides, animal husbandry services, and other inputs taken for granted in MDCs. Because of the traditional tenure system (without individual ownership of land), there is little incentive for land improvement and credit provision.

The research and extension systems remain uncoordinated and ineffective. Much of their staff is untrained or without funds and vehicles to get to the rural areas. Although recently there has been an effort to make better use of non-governmental organizations (NGOs) to assist farmers, they have so far "failed to incorporate farmers' issues into research activities..." (Puplampu, 2003, pp. 148–149). Thus, horticulture export, which could be profitably expanded, is discouraged. And more severe problems, such as soil fertility loss, soil erosion, and deforestation (estimated to cost 4 percent of GDP per year) cannot be addressed. Because of the poor transportation and storage systems, the cost of marketing food accounts for about 70 percent of the retail price of agricultural produce. Although Ghana has successfully expanded its export of tropical fruits and vegetables in recent years, crop losses remain high because of problems of storage, infrastructure, technology, and quality control (Memorandum of the President, 2004, pp. 7–8).

The Ghanaian government has failed to mobilize the self-help efforts of rural areas. Although in 1988 it embarked on an extensive program of decentralization to district assemblies (DAs), it remains an extremely centralized country. All but about two percent of DA revenue comes from the central government. DAs generally lack qualified staff to do financial planning, budgeting, revenue collection, expenditure control, and accounting. The staff sent by the central government tends to be inadequate in number, unqualified, poorly paid, and rotated every few years without regard for local needs and personal preferences. Moreover, the performance of staff is seldom audited or supervised. Consultations with DAs are rare, even on priorities and budgetary needs. The shortage of personnel at the local level is related, not only to the unattractive conditions of work, but also to the lack of authority and poor social infrastructure (Ayee, 2003, p. 77). While local governments have the authority to collect revenue, they seldom have the capacity and willingness to do so, leaving them unable "to reconcile shrinking revenue bases with increasing expenditure levels" (Ayee, 2003, p. 72). Since DAs are so dependent upon the central government for funds, projects often have to be suspended because of the irregular disbursements of proceeds.

Civil servants generally consider their postings in rural areas a hardship because of the lack of adequate housing, infrastructure, family services, and resources to carry out their assigned tasks. In rural areas, the infant mortality rate is 30 percent higher and child mortality rate is 20 percent higher than in urban areas. Lack of medical facilities in rural areas is only a part of the reason for this. Of far greater importance is the fact that only 20 percent of the rural population (as against about 70 percent of the urban population) has access to safe water sources (Bahal et al., 1993, p. 25). Especially unhappy are the secondary and university graduates who are required to spend a year in villages doing low-level jobs (Peil, 1996, p. 56). They are seldom paid enough to cover accommodation and food. Consequently, officials are unable to inspire or facilitate the sort of cooperation essential for community development.

Over the years, the Ghanaian government has attempted a variety of programs, usually with foreign aid, to help farmers. But none has worked very well. In 1975, for example, the government established the National Council on Women and Development (NCWD), particularly to help women in agriculture and agriculturally based enterprises inasmuch as women comprise much of the rural labor force. So far, however, according to a study by Chao (1999, p. 57), the NCWD has been ineffective for various administrative reasons: rapid turnover in leadership, unqualified staff, low pay, poor conditions of service, inadequate resources and mobility, etc. Moreover, women's limited access to education, land, appropriate technology, transportation, capital, and storage facilities makes it very difficult to help them (Kesson-Smith & Tettey, 2003).

Ghana's Technology Consultancy Center was set up in 1972 as an autonomous unit within the Kumasi University of Science and Technology. It received assistance from a number of sources, particularly the London-based Intermediate Technology Development Group. Much of its effort was directed at assisting a huge informal industrial area near Kumasi called Suame Magazine. Smillie (1986, pp. 10–12) described it as a dismal place where more than 40,000 workers struggled without reliable credit, water, sanitation, electricity, and roads, using rudimentary buildings, techniques, and equipment. Employees in the small establishments (typically consisting of a master with three or four assistants) were industrious and enterprising but seldom knew much about materials, safety, or engineering. According to Smillie (1986, p. 11), "none of the workers understood how an internal combustion engine worked, making simple diagnosis, testing and maintenance virtually impossible." Smillie (1986) gives several examples of Canadian and American foreign aid projects, during the 1970s and early

1980s, to expand or improve Ghanaian industrial parks that were frustrated or delayed by various factors, most important of which stemmed from governmental indifference. In 1982, Ghanaian officials never even bothered to meet a visiting Canadian team.

The same discouraging situation persists. The uncompetitive nature of Ghanaian firms is reflective of the fact that few employ quality control personnel, practice regular maintenance of their equipment, have research and development capabilities, use interchangeable parts, and "produce large quantities of goods of consistent quality to precise delivery schedules" (Berman, 2003, pp. 36–37). During the 1990s, the average rate of growth of the manufacturing subsector was about 2.5 percent. The share of manufacturing in Ghana's GDP then remained at around 10 percent. This slow growth is attributed to the governmental discouragement and to the fact that "opportunities were constrained by the presence of public enterprises with powerful political connections" (Chhibber and Leechor, 1994, p. 177). Summarizing the situation at the end of the 1990s, Berman (2003, p. 23) writes that, despite some renewed economic growth, the unemployed in the cities could not expect anything more than "self-employment in the informal sector." While the business climate has improved somewhat since 2000, the most recent economic surveys "suggest that small- and medium-size firms bear a relatively high share of the costs of the business environment in Ghana, preventing them from expanding and reaching a size sufficient for entering world markets" (Memorandum of the President, 2004, p. 11).

Under the rule of Jerry Rawlings, from the beginning of 1982 to the end of 2000, business associations were treated with disrespect (Kraus, 2002). Among their problems were high interest rates, lack of credit and access to foreign currency, ruinous inflation, suppression of communication media and any form of dissent, arbitrary governmental action, and denial of the rule of law. Reasons for this seem to include, not simply ethnic considerations and hostility to capitalism, but also a fear that "wealth acquired by successful business people will be used to support the opposition groups rather than the incumbent government" (Arthur, 2003, p. 170; Adjibolosoo, 2000). This accounts for "the low levels of trust that entrepreneurs have in institutional arrangements" characterized by a political system without transparency (Arthur, 2003, p. 175).

Without a well-functioning legal system that can ensure individual rights and provide a credible means of resolving conflicts, Herbst (1993, p. 162) points out that the Ghanaian investment climate remains unattractive. After the 1992 election, the President urged Ghanaians to avoid products made by companies supporting the opposition parties (Buckley, 1996, p. A13). Several of these companies were nationalized, including the nation's largest tobacco company, with some 1000 workers. The ability of owners to legally fight such actions were doubtful inasmuch as the bureaucracy and the courts did "not effectively enforce the most basic of the institutional and legal conditions of capitalism" (Berman, 2003, p. 38). When Ghanaian journalists attempted to expose the corruption of the Chief Justice of the Supreme Court, they were fined and imprisoned on the grounds "that truth was not an acceptable defence" (Tettey, 2003, pp. 94–95).

The untrustworthiness of the banking system may account for the fact that Ghana's "savings performance is notably poor in comparison to all low-income countries" (Armstrong, 1996, p. 37). Moreover, the sort of "export mentality" that exists in South Korea has not emerged, which is indicated by the lack of an export credit facility, an export bank, and a system for exempting duties on imports needed to promote exports (Armstrong, 1996, p. 97). This partly explains the low level of foreign investment — about 4 percent of Ghana's GDP, as against 18 percent in South Korea during the 1970s and between 12 and 18 percent in Southeast Asia (Campos & Root, 1996, p. 123). Yet, this is the result, not of cultural impediments, but of political ones since, when given a chance, Ghanaians can be very entrepreneurial. On the other hand, they cannot be expected to overcome a persistent "vicious circle" consisting of nepotism and patronage, discretionary abuse by politicians and officials, and "the lack of enforcement of clear rules of the game" (Berman, 2003, pp. 38–39).

As it is, the government has not provided employment opportunities and a stimulating learning environment for the nearly 25,000 students enrolled in its three universities, six polytechnics, and seven colleges. During the 1990s, only about 15 percent of the 250,000 young people annually coming out of the school system found jobs (Chibber et al., 1993, p. 25). They faced the fact that, in urban areas, unemployment often exceeded 25 percent. Even those with degrees in science and engineering are discouraged. Although business courses are popular, there are few jobs available and, for the reasons mentioned above, individual entrepreneurship remains extremely difficult. Even when entrepreneurs find funding for research and development, they are discouraged by constant power disruptions and greedy land owners. Yet, when given appropriate opportunities and incentives, they "can demonstrate their drive, initiative and capabilities against the odds . . . " (Arthur, 2003, pp. 172–173).

Jamaica

What makes classical democracy essential for economic development is that it is also necessary for a high quality of political software. Liberal democracy, on the other hand, can be quite counterproductive unless it is balanced by classical democracy. This point calls into question Lord Acton's famous assertion, "Power tends to corrupt and absolute power corrupts absolutely" (quoted, Caiden, 2001, p. 16). In other words, using Wolin's two sides of politics noted earlier, partisanship and statesmanship, we can also make a distinction between primary and secondary corruption. Under primary corruption, manifestations of greed (associated with corruption) are somewhat controlled by the political system; under secondary corruption, there is no such control. Primary corruption would be similar to a normal basketball game, in which competent referees call the fouls; secondary corruption would be a basketball game, in which the referees were corrupt, so that fouling became so prevalent as to be almost meaningless.

A social scientist comparing Singapore and Jamaica in the early 1960s (each with population then of about 1.6 million and a GDP per capita of $400), when independence from Great Britain was looming, might have predicted a much brighter future for Jamaica, despite problems stemming from colonial rule, racial tension, and the dangers of hurricanes and earthquakes (Norris, 1962). In 1960 Jamaica was the world's primary source of bauxite and alumina. Its Industrial Development Corporation was responsible for 30 factories and over 300 manufactured items. Although its agricultural exports consisted largely of plantation products such as sugar, bananas, citrus fruits, and coconuts, it was promoting various exotic fruits and spices, suitable for smallholder production. The country's beauty gave it tremendous potential as a tourist center, particularly after the Cuban revolution. Jamaica's potential for export-led growth was enhanced by its geographical proximity to North America and its English-speaking workforce. At the same time, Singapore had no natural resources and was suffering from severe racial, religious, and political turmoil, intensified by its traumatic 1965 separation from Malaysia.

The situation now obviously is very different, indicated by the great disparity in per capita income: compare Singapore, nearly $30,000 (with a 6.5 percent annual growth) with Jamaica, less than $4,000 (with negative growth for most of the last 25 years). Whereas Singapore's government has managed to eliminate persistent poverty, unemployment, and crime, Jamaica's government has been unable to break the linkage between high teenage pregnancy rates (40 percent), female-headed households (40 percent), school dropout and failure rates (one third of those from poor households), poverty (one third of the population), unemployment (16 percent), and extremely high rates of ordinary and violent crime (Human and Social Development Group, 1997). Whereas Singapore has been able to undertake some of the world's best programs in public housing, public transportation, urban planning, public health, and public education, Jamaica's efforts have largely failed. Between 1965 and 1995, the World Bank lent Jamaica $1.3 billion for 62 projects, of which 52 were evaluated as unsuccessful in regard to outcome, sustainability, and institutional improvement (Caribbean Country Management Unit, 2000, p. 19).

Jamaica, in contrast to Singapore, has maintained a vigorous two-party system since independence, with the People's National Party and the opposition Jamaica Labor Party alternating in power about every ten years. However, both political parties regularly employ criminal gangs (assisted to some extent by police and civil servants) to mobilize political support, distribute favors, and intimidate opponents. These parties have divided the country into "garrisons," within which illegal acts are allowed so long as they contribute toward electoral victory: "The sharing in the spoils provides a basis for community support for the justification of hatred, murder and mayhem against the opposition" (Figueroa & Sives, 2002, p. 98). The origin of the violence goes back to the 1970s, when community leaders (known as "dons") were armed by the parties, given control of patronage, and used as enforcers in the turf wars that divided the country.

The civil service, the judicial system, and the police have lost citizens' respect as their effectiveness has been undermined by inadequate pay, training, expertise, and even drug money (Hudson & Seyer, 2000). According to *The Economist* (November 1, 2003a, p. 36), extortion by gang leaders adds 40 percent to project costs, amounting to "an official tax of perhaps $100 million a year," further encouraging violent turf wars between rival gangs and contributing to debt, which "eats up 60 percent of Jamaica's tax revenues." Moreover, insofar as "those who make and enforce the laws of a country are perceived to be intimately involved in illegal activities," the "legitimacy of national institutions" is undermined (Figueroa & Sives, 2002, p. 100). Whereas various efforts have been made to improve the functioning of the Jamaican bureaucracy, it has not been able to escape "the problems of weak performance and poor quality in the delivery of service to the public" (Ferguson, 2002, p. 23). Not much can be expected when "the complex network of corruption and illegality" continues "to undermine the integrity of many of the country's institutions and has had a significant impact on the value systems to which people increasingly adhere" (Figueroa & Sives, 2002, p. 100).

The consequences of a democratic political system, in which partisanship is more apparent than statesmanship, were once again revealed in July 2001, when riots broke out in the Tivoli Gardens neighborhood of West Kingston, causing much destruction, personal injury, and loss of more than 25 lives (Gonzales, 2001, p. A3). The violence broke about when the police went into the community, led by Edward Seaga, the former prime minister and leader of the opposition Jamaica Labor Party, looking for illegal weapons. "Homes, shops, factories, schools, and other community buildings have been abandoned and lands that could be redeveloped close to the center of Kingston lie in ruins" (Gonzales, 2001, p. A3). In the case of Jamaica, political disorder clearly results from bad governance, rather than from such common causes of political instability as racial, religious, or ethnic differences. In other words, party bosses have used political gangsters and lower class partisans to bring "their zero-sum communal loyalties and their savage violence and predatory instincts into national politics" (Gray, 2003, p. 78).

Because primary or liberal democracy has taken a dysfunctional form in Jamaica, contrary to the conventional assumption, it has intensified corruption. At the same time, there is not enough secondary democracy here to prevent persistent mismanagement of the economy manifesting itself in slow growth, budgetary shortfalls, inflation, and unpayable debt. Parastatals (of which some 150 remain) have been used by the government to undermine the economy because they are "monitored only in exceptional circumstances" (Harrigan, 1998, p. 17). Moreover, banks, credit unions, and insurance companies continue to be undercapitalized, undersupervised, and underregulated, with the public usually kept in the dark about this mismanagement (Dean, 1998; Henke, 1999). Public expenditure is hidden, first of all, from the IMF, and, secondly, from the legislature and the public, indicating that these methods "are linked to the workings of clientelist politics" (Harrigan, 1998, p. 17).

How the resulting political inelasticity has undermined business development is indicated in a recent World Bank report showing a connection between, on the one hand, the "factionalized civil society" and the "parallel system of government in inner cities" and, on the other hand, the "low respect for law and order" and "low national pride" (Caribbean Country Management Unit, 2000, Section E). Businesses must not only pay kickbacks and bribes, but also "there is pressure to employ workers and contractors based on political affiliation rather than competence" (Figueroa & Sives, 2002, pp. 99–100). A combination of "politically inspired gangsters, heroic bandits, and left-wing gunmen" have "robbed banks, challenged the security forces with hit-and-run tactics, and mocked the rule of the two parties" (Gray, 2003, p. 90). Until there is more evidence of classical (secondary) democracy, Jamaica will certainly be unable to escape its poverty, violence, and misery, even though, culturally, it may remain more exciting than puritanical and authoritarian Singapore.

Mexico

Mexico's experience with export-oriented manufacturing (the so-called "maquiladora corporations" — generally, direct subsidiaries of transnational firms) goes back to 1965, when it was set up along the border areas in cooperation with the American government to discourage illegal migration, while protecting domestic manufacturers (Cooney, 2001). Under this arrangement, imports of raw materials and parts from the United States were allowed without duties or restrictions on the condition that the finished goods were sent back to the United States, with taxes paid only on the value added by the Mexican workers. Yet, by 1980 it was clear that there was more needed to be done, which was indicated by a number of factors then affecting Mexico: (1) extensive oil income amounting to more than 75 percent of export earnings; (2) the increase of foreign debt to nearly $80 billion (making it the most indebted nation in the world by 1982); (3) an inflation rate reaching nearly 30 percent (going up to almost 100 percent by 1982); and (4) an overvalued exchange rate (Damian, 2000).

Mexico was required under structural adjustment policies, which were imposed by the IMF and the World Bank from the 1980s onward, to adopt an "export-at-all costs" strategy. Under it, Mexico eliminated most import licenses and import prices, cut subsidies for industrial and agricultural inputs, privatized a high percentage of state enterprises, drastically reduced tariffs and rigid controls on foreign investment, joined the General Agreement on Tariffs and Trade (GATT), entered into the North American Free Trade Agreement (NAFTA), and signed trade agreements with many Latin American countries. Consequently, as of 2000, Mexico was earning more from maquiladora exports (which expanded by about 200 percent from 1994 to 2000) than from oil exports. Whereas in 1985, oil accounted for more than 55 percent of total exports and manufacturing, 30 percent, this ratio was reversed by 1995, with the oil share falling to under 11 percent and manufacturing, 85 percent of export composition. During the 1990s, Mexico had the highest rate of export growth in the world (making it the world's eighth largest exporter and the United States' second biggest trading partner after Canada) and accounted for nearly one fourth of the total GDP of Latin America and the Caribbean (Levy & Bruhn, 2001, p. 11). In 1998–1999, it sold about $35 billion worth of high-tech products, nearly as much as China, which has more than ten times Mexico's population. In 2000, Mexico had a $20 billion trade surplus with the United States. Consequently, Mexico came to be viewed "as a model of economic reform worthy of emulation by other nations" (Kelly, 2001, p. 84).

Despite Mexico's achievements, there has been an increase in the level of poverty, indicating that per capita growth has been about one third that achieved under import-substitution from 1940 – 1980. Real wages dropped 40 percent during the 1980s and fell even further during the 1990s. During the 1990s, per capita growth was less than 3 percent annually, as against 6 percent annually from 1950 to 1980 (Damien, 2000, p. 29). In 1996, 42 percent of the Mexican population was reported to be living below the poverty line (an increase of nearly 75 percent from 1989), which was partly a result of the terrible financial crisis of 1994–1995.

Severe poverty affects especially rural Mexico, containing (as of 1998) 25 percent of the population but accounting for nearly 60 percent of those in extreme poverty (Tulchin & Selee, 2003 Peters, 2000;). Because nearly three fourths of all Mexican households in 1996 were considered at least somewhat impoverished, the expectation that NAFTA membership would reduce illegal migration to the United States (where wages are ten times higher) proved illusory. An estimated 60 percent of the economically active population continue to work within the informal sector and, as such, lack the protection of social security, unemployment insurance, and other social safety provisions found in most industrialized countries (Latin America and the Caribbean Region, 2001, p. 5).

On the Human Development Index (combining per capita income, health, and adult literacy statistics), Mexico scores 78.6, as against 80.1 in Costa Rica, despite Mexico's higher per capita purchasing power (25.5 percent of that of the United States, as against 19.9 percent in Costa Rica). However, one can point to other indications of the failure of the Mexican government to use its economic success for a higher standard of living. Mexico's illiteracy rate remains at about 13 percent, as against about 6 percent in such an impoverished country as Cuba (Peters, 2000, p. 163). Although Mexican education has improved in recent years, with the average child receiving 7.7 years of schooling, the poorest 10 percent of children, particularly in rural areas, receive only a few years of education under extremely inadequate conditions (Levy & Bruhn, 2001, p. 11; *The Economist*, 2001, pp. 25–26).

Whereas Mexico and Poland had about the same per capita purchasing power in 2000, the percentage of the adult population in Mexico with upper secondary education was 21.2 percent, as against 54.3 percent in Poland; and Mexico was then spending 50 percent less than Poland on each primary school student ($935 as against $1435). Mexico spends only 2.8 percent of its GDP on health as against 4.2 percent in Poland, partly resulting in an infant mortality rate (per 1000 live births) three times higher (30 compared to 10) than that of Poland. Perhaps more significant is that, whereas almost all Poles now have access to adequate water sources and sanitation, the comparative percentages for Mexico are 83 and 66 (OECD, 2001, 2002).

Globalization may have increased income inequality in Mexico, with the top 20 percent of households expanding their share of total income from 49.5 percent in 1984 to 58.2 percent in 2000, leaving Mexico with one of the most unequal income distributions in the world. The top decile of the population now accounts for more than 40 percent of the nation's income, as against only about one third in 1984 (Cypher, 2003, pp. 29–30). Globalization seems also to have intensified "territorial polarization" in Mexico, with the states south of Mexico City largely excluded from export activities. Summarizing the impact of the "neoliberal model of development" for Mexico, Cooney (2001, p. 80) concludes that, while it may be useful for the elite, "the benefits for the majority of Mexicans appear minimal if not nonexistent."

Inequality in Mexico, as in the United States, is certainly associated with racial and cultural divisions. While one quarter to one third of Mexico's poor are indigenous, indigenous people make up about 60 percent of the extreme poor. This is particularly true in rural areas where the typical pattern remains of indigenous landless peasants working for white large landholders (the *latifundios)*, who are protected by private militias, soldiers, and police. This has resulted in the Zapatista rebellion in the state of Chiapas. However, no more than 10 percent of Mexicans speak primarily an Indian language, and, despite Mexico's diversity, "the degree of homogenity is increasing" (Levy & Bruhn, 2001, p. 25).

Because of the lack of attention to governance in much of the social science literature on Mexico, we have to use a variety of specialized sources. Transparency International's 2001 Corruption Perception Index (available on its Web site) puts Mexico at 3.7 (slightly higher than Egypt). OECD reports are also useful. A 1999 report (OECD, 1999, pp. 251–252) having to do with regulatory reform in Mexico notes that "the enforcement of regulations is problematic in Mexico," adding "complex and unclear regulation, and difficulties at the judicial level with interpretation and enforcement, have meant that Mexican regulation has long been the source of considerable uncertainty and confusion to the citizen." In Mexico civil society "remains thin and uneven compared with advanced industrial democracies" (Levy & Bruhn, 2001, p. 75). Consequently, Mexico's own anti-corruption czar estimates that corruption costs the country about 10 percent of its GDP — twice the education budget (Rosenberg, 2003).

The recent murder of Digna Ochoa, one of Mexico's most prominent human rights attorneys raised concerns about the ability of President Vincente Fox's government to transform the political culture. In much of Mexico, law enforcement agents cannot be distinguished from the criminals they are supposed to arrest. The payment of bribes is so common that is difficult to determine if this practice results more from "extortion" or voluntary "gift-giving." Indeed, according to a recent study by Mexican sociologists, the police are taught by their colleagues and superiors how to extort money from businesses and citizens, which partly accounts for the fact that only about 8 percent of crimes are solved and suspects who pay bribes are usually let go (Botello & Rivera, 2000). In 1994, even the violent Brazilian cities of Rio de Janeiro and Sao Paulo reported more than 16 percent of crimes resolved, as against only 2.6 percent in Mexico City that year (Elizondo, 2003, p. 44). On the other hand, more than half of the 22,000 prisoners in Mexico City's jails are there for offenses so slight that human rights advocates (and, increasingly, city officials) "say that they never should have been jailed in the first place" (Sullivan & Jordan, 2002, pp. A1, A10). The arbitrary nature of Mexico's legal system is underscored by the fact that there are no jury trials and that in many cases, the judge never even sees the defendant.

The failure of the legal system has been most apparent in Ciudad Juárez where nearly 400 women "all of them poor and with virtually no political influence" have been tortured, raped, and killed since 1990 with justice being undermined by bungled autopsies, falsified evidence, and use of torture to obtain confessions, according to an Amnesty International report (Forero, 2003, p. A6). "Intolerable killings" occur here, as this report goes on to emphasize, because of a combination of "indifference, lack of will, negligence, or inability."

Toward the end of the 1990s, the attorney general admitted that 80 percent of the federal police engaged in corruption; and, despite President Vincente Fox's campaign against corruption, the most recent report of Transparency Mexico (the local arm of Transparency International) suggests that residents of Mexico City have to pay bribes for almost a quarter of the government services they receive, with businesses particularly targeted (Levy & Bruhn, 2001, p. 17). So lucrative is this situation for policemen that many bribe their way into police positions, disregarding the fact that their official pay is very low. Corrupt police officers may be responsible for the fact that Mexico ranks second in the world (next to Colombia) in kidnapping, with more than 3000 cases in 2003 (*The Economist*, June 19, 2004, p. 37).

In Mexico, freedom of the press is undermined by the fact that journalists, editors, and publishers are often paid (or given financial inducements) by the government or criminal elements to exercise "self-censorship," therefore preferring "to follow the corruption-paved avenue to mobility offered by members of the state rather than attack the system" (Morris, 1991, p. 52). Those who resist (as happened to more than 30 reporters during the late 1980s) may well be murdered. In the last 16 years, three journalists have been assassinated in Tijuana for reporting about government corruption and drug trafficking (Sullivan and Jordan, 2004, A18).

The lack of trust in the police and the courts accounts for the increasing tendency of citizens to resort to mob justice, "including lynchings and beatings of suspects caught in the act" (Levy & Bruhn, 2001, p. 17). Because torture has been "standard operating procedure" in the Mexican legal system, there is a profound lack of trust in the judiciary (Weiner, 2001, p. A10). To reform it is going to require a complete overhaul of the justice system, including changing the nature of criminal investigations and judicial standards. Many criminals escape simply because cases are delayed, thrown out on technicalities, or undermined by the lack of a national police database. During the 1990s, there were major efforts to reform the judicial system; but, according to a study by Domingo (2000, p. 742). the "alarming persistence of human rights violations, high levels of inefficiency in the administration of justice, overburdened courts, and the continuing crises of corruption scandals and political violence undermine the notion that the rule of law is advancing in Mexico." In 2001, a United Nations special rapporteur on human rights in Mexico claimed that seven out of ten federal judges were corrupt (*The Economist*, June 29, 2002b, p. 36).

The fact that an estimated 2.5 percent of Mexico's GNP and 8 percent of its export earnings are derived from the illegal drug trade greatly increases the difficulty of reforming the system (Levy & Bruhn, 2001, p. 222). The increasing use of soldiers to prevent peasants from growing the raw material for this trade has become controversial in this regard. For example, while soldiers are frequently accused of human rights violations, they are tried in military courts where, despite President Fox's promises of reform, "there has not been a single conviction" since he came to power (*The Economist*, June 29, 2002b, p. 36). Recent studies have generally concluded that "human rights violations are the worst in rural, and especially indigenous regions of the country" (Levy & Bruhn, 2001, p. 107).

While Mexico may have improved the quality of administration in recent years, it still remains very weak. In 1998, the OECD (1998, p. 113) (which tends to be very diplomatic) reported that "Mexico does not have a true civil service as this term is understood in other OECD countries, with the exception of a few Ministries" and that management and training are very inadequate. Observers of Mexican administration point to a variety of weaknesses. According to an article in *The Economist* (May 12, 2001, p. 42), "there are few evaluations, either inside or outside government, of how well it performs," thereby facilitating the corrupt handling or mismanagement of contracts as well as the inefficient performance of work. The practices of ministries are often opaque; and insofar as there are no instruments to force them to comply with regulations, there is also no effective oversight. Because about a third of officials are affected by the sexenio system (the change in government every six years), those who gain power often consider it their right "to partake of the system's spoils." Consequently, meritocratic considerations are less important than loyalty, deference, and services that clients can provide to patrons; and corruption here "is less a sickly deviation from Weberian health, than the cartilage and collagen which holds a sprawling body politics together" (Knight, 1996, p. 231).

Mexico's poor quality of governance undermines business development in all sorts of ways. Whereas Korea spends 13.3 percent of GDP on education, Mexico spends less than 5 percent. In regard to researchers per 10,000 labor force and scientific publications per 100,000 population, Mexico is far behind South Korea and other comparable countries. Moreover, unlike other industrial nations, where on average the private sector undertakes in excess of 40 percent of national outlays for R&D, in Mexico, it accounts for only about 17 percent of the total.

What has kept Mexico from spending more on education and social expenditure is the failure of the government to increase tax revenue much about 10 percent of GDP, as against 23.6 percent in Korea. Social expenditure in Mexico as a percent of GDP (14.7) is the lowest for any OECD member, which means that it is about 50 percent lower than that of Korea. Moreover, according to Elizondo (2003, p. 46), "because the quality of expenditure is usually poor, the result is a very low provision of public goods when compared to the taxes collected." A vicious circle therefore exists, with the bureaucracy inefficient, poorly paid, and corrupt and thus unable to cope with the needs of society, and, at the same time, the unwillingness of taxpayers to pay more because "they do not perceive the benefits of their taxes" (Elizondo, 2003, p. 46).

Perhaps even more serious is the failure of the banking system to facilitate business development. Bank credit to the private sector in Mexico stands at less than 10 percent of GDP, as against 30 percent in Brazil and 52 percent in the United States (Malkin, 2004, pp. W1, W7). The average cost of a banking transaction, including the use of checking accounts and debit and credit cards in Mexico is $1.62, compared with 52 cents in the United States. Only about 70 percent of Mexicans (including 40 percent of those in formal employment) use commercial banks or have contact with financial services (*The Economist*, August 9, 2003b, p. 61).

While officials are anxious for more Mexicans to have access to banking and credit, they have failed to supervise existing financial institutions and enforce regulation, thereby discouraging expansion of the banking system. It is not so much lack of capital that prevents Mexican banks from lending more, but rather, a "reluctance to lend to risky borrowers under a soft legal system" (Herrmann, 2002, p. 43), Moreover, without a more efficient and trustworthy bureaucracy, it is difficult to enforce repayment of loans and appropriate accounting rules, which further undermines the system.

Conclusion: Helping Countries to Globalize

In the case of Asia, it is clear that globalization has caused a significant decrease in those living below $1 a day (Ravallion, 2004, p. 65). With the good performances of India and China, the percentage of the world's population below $1 a day has declined from 33 percent in 1981 to about 18 percent in 2001. However, while the percentage of miserably poor has fallen in Asia since the early 1980s, it has roughly doubled in Africa. Whereas one in ten of the world's poorest then lived in Africa, it is now about one in three.

Considering Africa's economic retrogression, Professor Jeffrey Sachs (2004, pp. 19–21), a special advisor to the UN secretary general on the Millennium Development Goals, advocates about a tripling of foreign aid (from $8 billion to $25 billion a year), with about half of this amount going to Africa, to be administered by the International Development Association

(IDA) of the World Bank. While I entirely agree that Africa needs such financial assistance, I remain skeptical because of the history of World Bank's antipoverty efforts over the years.

While the world's wealthy countries have provided an estimated $1 trillion to developing countries since World War II, the primary responsibility of helping these countries has been given to the World Bank, including several hundred billion dollars of loans for projects and economic reform. With its staff of over 10,000, including the International Bank for Reconstruction and Development (IBRD) and the International Development Association (IDA), the Bank made loans totaling $19.5 billion and worked in 100 countries in 2002. For the poorest countries, assistance is largely channeled through the IDA, almost without interest charges. Nearly half of new loans are for IDA projects, and lending for economic policy reform has reached more than 50 percent of Bank lending. Moreover, using a research budget of about $25 million, the Bank remains the primary source of data and social science research. As such, it determines the direction these countries should be moving in and establishes the benchmarks of how well they are doing.

Despite success over the years in facilitating global improvements in infant survival, life expectancy, agricultural output, and adult literacy, World Bank loans appear to cause countries to become increasingly indebted and, therefore, more impoverished. On the whole, only a minority of World Bank projects have been judged by the Bank itself to be "sustainable" and, for the poorest, often most indebted countries, less than one in four (Rich, 2002). While policy reform projects (the so-called "structural adjustment lending") has been at times unfairly criticized (disregarding the need for adequate tax collecting or cost recovery), a 1997 evaluation found only 19 percent of the projects performing satisfactorily (Rich, 2002, p. 27).

The World Bank's own evaluation reports have emphasized its failure to carry out "its self-proclaimed goals of poverty alleviation and environmentally sustainable development" (Pincus & Winters, 2002, p. 22). At the end of the 20th century, the Bank economists determined that the "average income in the richest 20 countries is 37 times the average in the poorest 20 — a gap that has doubled in the past 40 years" (World Bank, 2000, p. 3). This indicates that, despite economic growth in some countries, the dismantling of socialist economies, extensive globalization, large amounts of foreign aid, and many donor assisted projects, at least 75 percent of the world's population live in countries with a per capita income of less than $1000, with about half of the world (2.7 billion) living on $2 a day (Ravallion, 2004, p. 65).

My own research (Werlin, 1998) suggests various reasons why the World Bank has not been more successful; and this analysis has been underscored by a more recent book edited by Pincus and Winters (2002). Perhaps the biggest factor remains the political software inadequacies within borrowing countries. However, the Bank staff have to work under conditions established by its main shareholders, particularly the United States, accounting for the three most persistent explanations for failure:

1. *The culture of loan approval.* A major study of the World Bank (the 1992 Wapenhans Report) drew attention to the pressures on Bank staff to "favor the formulation and approval of new projects over the monitoring and supervision of ongoing projects." After all, staff need to keep busy; governments need the loans; good relationships with borrowers are essential; and pressure from contractors or businesses in donor countries cannot be easily resisted. When all is said and done, the Bank's board and management still focus on "staff/dollars lent." This means that staff are rewarded "for moving projects through the approval process at a faster pace, and having a client (borrower) orientation — not for policy compliance" (Rich, 2002, p. 29).
2. *The World Bank's political constraints.* The World Bank is "forbidden from engaging in political activity by its own rules." While the Bank is increasingly willing to deal with such political issues as governance, decentralization, and civil society, it "must remain on guard against accusations of meddling in domestic political affairs, not only because its *Articles of Agreement* require it to do so, but also because its authority as a development bank — and hence its attractiveness to donor countries — depends largely on its claim to "technical, objective expertise" (Pincus, 2002, p. 84). However, efforts to keep a project "apolitical" has political consequences that cannot be avoided. For example, to really help farmers, the Bank has "to confront the political realities behind its rhetorical edifice of participation, partnership, and support for civil society" (Sender, 2002, p. 199). The truth is, all reform efforts have political implications. For example, programs to help African rural women may be impossible without "an accessible court that is independent of local male notables" (Sender, 2002, p. 198).
3. *The unwillingness to confront underlying problems.* For the reasons already mentioned, the solutions generally promoted by the World Bank (privatization, reducing government expenditure, trade and financial liberalization, deregulation, and the other reforms associated with the so-called "Washington Consensus") tend to be naive as well as unrealistic. Even the Bank's approach to the problem of corruption is often technocratic requiring borrowers to expand expertise, including "workshops for everyone from elementary school principals to judges to bureaucrats," rather than dealing with underlying problems (Winters, 2002, p. 112). While the authors of an important World Bank 1997 document on corruption recognize that it may stem from "the

way power is exercised and retained," they then consider it to be an "untouchable realm" (Winters, 2002, p. 113). Although noneconomists (particularly, anthropologists and sociologists) are increasingly used by the World Bank, they do not really "challenge the economics and economists of the World Bank and can have the effect of strengthening their position and scope" (Werlin, 1998, p. 319).

An Alternative Approach

Using PE theory, it can be argued that countries are poor because political power cannot be easily delegated or decentralized and, as such, cannot predictably control or affect the behavior or their populations. What is essential is the development of political software (consensus building), which requires various commonsensical steps that have been presented. Progress can be measured on the basis of steps to improve any aspect of them.

If this analysis is correct, the World Bank must act more like an ordinary bank — requiring justification for loans, rather than being simply a source for loans, and starting with small loans, gradually increasing their size and scope based on the progress made. While the Bank must avoid partisan or "primary politics" (particularly, getting involved in elections), it cannot avoid "secondary politics" (the consensus building essential for political software development). In the process of introducing technocratic considerations, the underlying factors needed for development must always be emphasized.

There is a saying that the more impoverished a country (or individual) is, the more tightly closed is the door to reform, with the lock having to be opened from inside. While I believe that a heavy-handed approach would be counterproductive, I suggest that the following approaches might be experimented with: (1) requiring prior reform — making sure, for example, that a country has the capacity and the willingness to repair old roads before new roads are financed; (2) intensifying pressure in various ways — terminating ineffective projects following the dissemination of explanatory reports and holding of public hearings, which the press would be encouraged to cover; and (3) promoting competition — getting countries at similar levels of per capita income to compete for project support, based upon the quality of governance.

I also have in mind making structural adjustment and debt-relief contingent a competitive process after the amounts potentially available to each eligible country are suggested. Each of these countries would be expected to determine its quantifiable goals, strategies for achieving them, and timetables for doing so. Taking into account the governmental improvements of this country in comparison to those of other highly indebted or impoverished countries, evaluators (led perhaps by Transparency International, the world's leading anticorruption organization) would periodically announce how much countries would receive, together with justifications, encouraging countries to keep trying for additional funds. The objective would be to make structural adjustment and debt relief "prizes to be worked for," rather than "gifts to be waited for." Otherwise, they are likely to be wasted.

What is suggested here is that the path to reform is much the same, regardless of cultural or other differences between the countries, indicated by success stories in Malawi and Peru, showing that progress can be made even under authoritarian and corrupt leaders based on the implementation of political software requisites (Werlin, 1998). Under President Banda in Malawi, road repair was made a national priority. A management system was installed, using microcomputers to provide the needed information at various levels of organization. Workshops were also established to set objectives for the implementation of all repair activities. In addition, there was a comparison of work performance between districts, creating a spirit of competition and an incentive for supervisors to perform to the limits of their potential. Consequently, as of 1990, only 6 percent of Malawi's paved roads and 16 percent of its unpaved roads were in bad shape, compared to an estimated one quarter of paved roads and 40 percent of unpaved roads being in a similar dismal shape in Sub-Saharan Africa as a whole. In Peru, the percentage of the GDP collected in taxes nearly tripled during the early 1990s (from less than 5 percent to nearly 15 percent) when the tax collecting agency (*Sunat*) was professionalized.

This underscores the importance of inducing the country itself to create an appropriate project unit: identifying needed positions; requiring staff to take examinations to compete for these positions, and giving salaries comparable to those in the private sector. Only when the World Bank is satisfied with the quality of this unit would the project begin. Another possibility is simply a "grant-in-aid" system, in which community efforts are matched by the government (supported by the Bank). This worked quite well in Egypt during the 1980s under a "village improvement program."

However, such projects are difficult without a national commitment to improve the quality of governance. To foster this commitment, the World Bank needs to support programs for which there is the greatest enthusiasm. Such enthusiasm can easily be undermined by evidence of corruption. This is what happened in Kenya in the 1980s when powerful people ceased to pay property taxes and service charges, thereby causing residents of World Bank-supported housing projects to riot when they were also required to pay these taxes and charges (Stren, 1989, p. 33).

As a professor, I used to tell my students that "it is as difficult to help poor countries as it is the beggars on urban streets." In other words, when beggars suffer from alcoholism, drugs, or various forms of mental illness, you can give them charity but never make them independent of it. Likewise, unless the World Bank is willing to go deep into the underlying causes of poverty, even at the risk of alienating shareholders and executive directors, it will never be really successful. While the Bank's *Articles of Agreement* certainly disallow interference in domestic political affairs, they also "vest the Bank with unambiguous rights and responsibilities to safeguard the integrity of its loan funds" (Winters, 2002, p. 106). Indeed, the Bank and its directors could eventually be sued in the World Court by indebted countries "for willfully and illegally contributing to their criminal debt burden" (Winters, 2002, p. 106).

A Final Note: The Case of Liberia

As an example of "what not to do" is a report released at the end of January 2004 by the United Nations and the World Bank suggesting that Liberia needed about $500 million in stabilization aid during the next two years. According to an article in *The New York Times* there was a donors conference in February 2004, attended by Secretary of State Colin Powell and French Foreign Minister Dominique de Villepin to discuss this report, with the United States promising about $200 million for this effort (Sengupta, 2004, p. A6).

Without denying the desperate situation in Liberia, it can be argued that the World Bank should start out with only a small loan, requiring Liberia to show significant progress in improving its public administration along the lines earlier suggested, before any additional funds were released. As it is, Liberia is one of the most corrupt and mismanaged countries in the world. Under these circumstances, a small grant-in-aid would be much more appropriate, with additional financial support given only when the Liberian government demonstrated real progress in effectively dealing with its most serious problems. Otherwise, however carefully supervised by foreign officials, the money is likely to be wasted unless Liberian leaders are induced to come to grips with their fundamental weaknesses. This might also give supporters of reform within Liberia itself the encouragement they need to successfully carry on their struggle.

My own analysis of the situation is based on my experience reviewing in the late 1980s a World Bank urban project in Monrovia, Liberia that was undertaken at the end of the 1970s (Werlin, 1990). Although this project was considered a failure insofar as the institutional reform efforts were never implemented, including a reform of accounting systems, building codes, revenue collection, and fiscal discipline, there were possibilities that were missed, such as the following:

1. *Mobilizing potential reformers.* There were experienced and capable Liberians both within the country and outside it anxious for reform who could have been used. Moreover, the Bank could have turned for additional assistance to churches, ethnic associations, and mutual-help groups which were active in Monrovia.
2. *Sponsoring public workshops.* It was discovered during a "Project Launch Workshop," held after the project had begun that many of the city's leaders and much of the population were unaware of the project's origins or purposes. This suggests the importance of periodically sponsoring such workshops to provide a time for serious dialogue about Liberia's political policies and practices.
3. *Using incremental rather than blueprint procedures.* If a step-by-step approach had been used for the Monrovia project, step one could have included the institutional reforms essential for step two, which could have concentrated upon infrastructural investments and capital works, to be followed by additional steps essential for overall urban development. The entire project, accordingly, could have been presented as a multisectoral urban loan package, with funds released, based upon progress in institutional development.

For any reform to work, leaders must be convinced that it is in their own self-interest. This is apparently what caused the Kenyan government under President Daniel arap Moi, despite his corrupt and authoritarian ways, to privatize Kenya Airways in 1996, under a partnership with KLM (Africa Region, 2003, p. 101). His motivation was apparently a desire to please a growing African business elite anxious for the success of tourism and horticultural exports to Europe. Consequently, Kenya (despite continuing problems with crime, corruption, and mismanagement) remains the dominant airline hub in the region, sustaining the tourist industry and facilitating the development of a first class horticultural industry. Although in the case of Liberia there is no guarantee that leaders will be motivated to allow any type of reform, they might be influenced by the linkage of extensive foreign aid to reform efforts, assuming that these efforts also have the support of an enlightened public opinion which might be reached by the World Bank officials who recognize the importance of doing so.

References

Adjibolosoo, S. (2003). Ethnicity and the Development of National Consciousness: A Human Factor Analysis. In W.J. Tettey, K.P. Puplampu, and B.J. Berman (Eds.), *Critical Perspectives in Politics and Socio-Economic Development in Ghana* (pp. 107–134). Leiden: Brill.

Africa Region (2003). *Kenya: A Policy Agenda to Restore Growth*. Washington, D.C.: World Bank.

Alpine, R.W.L. and J. Pickett (1993). *Agricultural Liberalization and Economic Growth in Ghana and Côte Ivoire*. Paris: OECD.

Amsden, A.H. (1994). The Spectre of Anglo-Saxonization is Haunting South Korea. In D.H. Kim and T.Y. Kong (Eds.), *Economic Development in the Republic of Korea* (pp. 84–120). Boulder, CO: Westview.

Andeweg, R. and G.A. Irwin (1993). *Dutch Government and Politics*. New York: St. Martin's.

Armstrong, R.P. (1996). *Ghana: Country Assistance Review: A Study in Development Effectiveness*. Washington, D.C.: World Bank OED.

Arthur, P. (2003). The Implications of State Policy for Micro-Enterprise Development. In W.J. Tettey, K.P. Puplampu, and B.J. Berman (Eds.), *Critical Perspectives in Politics and Socio-Economic Development in Ghana* (pp. 158–175). Leiden: Brill.

Audretsch, D.B. (2003). Entrepreneurship, Innovation and Globalization: Does Singapore Need a New Approach. In R.S. Rajan (Ed.), *Sustaining Competitiveness in the New Global Economy: The Experience of Singapore* (pp. 206–233). Singapore: Institute of Policy Studies.

Ayee, J.R.A. (2003). Local Government, Decentralization, and State Capacity in Ghana. In W.J. Tettey, K.P. Puplampu, and B.J. Berman (Eds.), *Critical Perspectives in Politics and Socio-Economic Development in Ghana* (pp. 47–73). Leiden: Brill.

Bahal, J. (1993). *Strengthening Local Initiative & Building Local Capacity in Ghana*. Washington, D.C.: World Bank.

Baldwin, D.A. (1989). *Paradoxes of Power*. New York and Oxford: Blackwell.

Baylis, T.A. (1999). Institutional Destruction and Reconstruction. In P.J. Smith (Ed.), *After the Wall: Eastern Germany since 1989* (pp. 26–43). Boulder, CO: Westview.

Bekkers, V.J.J.M. and A.M.B. Lips (2001). Water Management in the Netherlands. In F. Hendriks and T.A.J. Toonen. (Eds.), *Polder Politics: The Re-invention of Consensus* (pp. 135–152) Burlington, VT: Ashgate.

Beng-Huat, C. (1994). Arrested Development: Democratization in Singapore. *Third World Quarterly* 15(2): 655–677.

Berman, B. (2003). Capitalism Incomplete. In W.J. Tettey, K.P. Puplampu, and B.J. Berman (Eds.), *Critical Perspectives in Politics and Socio-Economic Development in Ghana* (pp. 22–43). Leiden: Brill.

Bhagwati, J. (2004). *In Defense of Globalization*. New York: Oxford.

Bhaskaran, M. (2003). Structural Challenges Facing the Singapore Economy. In R.S. Rajan (Ed.), *Sustaining Competitiveness in the New Global Economy: The Experience of Singapore* (pp. 154–171), Cheltenham, UK: Elgar.

Botello, C. and Lopez Rivera, A. (2000). Inside the Mexican Police. *World Policy Journal* 12(September): 61–70.

Buckley, S. Waves of Trade Leaves Africa Parched. *The Washington Post* (December 31, 1996), pp. A1, A11–A12.

Caiden, G.E. (2001). Corruption and Governance. In G.E. Caiden, O.P. Dwivedi, and J. Jabbra (Eds.), *Where Corruption Lives* (pp. 15–38). Bloomfield, CN: Kumarian.

Campos, J.E. and H.L. Root (1996). *The Key to the Asian Miracle.* Washington, D.C.: Brookings.

Caribbean Country Management Unit (2000). *Country Assistance Strategy.* Washington, D.C.: World Bank Report No. 21187-JM.

Chao, S. (1999). *Ghana: Gender Analysis and Policymaking for Development.* Washington, D.C.: World Bank.

Chee, C.C. (1986). Singapore in 1986. *Asian Survey* 26(2): 159–163.

Cheng, T-J., S. Haggard, and D. Kang (1999). Institutions and Growth in Korea and Taiwan: The Bureaucracy. In Y. Akyuz (Ed.), *East Asian Development: New Perspectives* (pp. 97–119). London: Cass.

Chhibber, A. and C. Leechor (1993). *Ghana 2000 and Beyond.* Washington, D.C.: World Bank Africa Regional Office.

Clifford, M.I. (1994). *Troubled Tiger: Businessmen, Bureaucrats, and Generals in South Korea.* Armonk, NY: Sharpe.

Clower, R.W., D. George, M. Harwitch, and A.A. Walters (1966). *Growth Without Development: An Economic Analysis.* Evanston, IL: Northwestern University Press.

Cooney, P. (2001). The Mexican Crisis and the Maquiladora Boom. *Latin American Perspectives* 28(September): 55–83.

Cypher, J.M. (2003). Developing Disarticulation Within the Mexican Economy. *Latin American Perspectives* 28(September): 29–54.

Dahlman, C. and T. Andersson (2000). *Korea and the Knowledge-based Economy.* Washington, D.C.: World Bank Institute.

Damian, A. (2000). *Adjustment, Poverty and Employment in Mexico.* Hampshire, UK: Ashgate.

de Rivero, O. (2001). *The Myth of Development: Non-Viable Economies of the 21st Century.* New York: Zed Books.

Dean, J.W. (1998). Can Financial Liberalization Come too Soon? Jamaica in the 1990s. *Social and Economic Studies* 47(4): 7–33.

Dillinger, W. (1991). *Urban Property Tax Reform.* Washington, D.C.: World Bank.

Domingo, P. (2000). Judicial Independence: The Politics of the Supreme Court in Mexico. *Journal of Latin American Studies* 32(Autumn): 720–743.

Easterly, E. and S. Fischer (2000). What Can We Learn from the Soviet Collapse? *Finance and Development* (December), 2–5.

The Economist (2001). *Pocket Book in Figures.* London: The Economist.

The Economist (2002a). The Sun Rises, February 9:37 London: The Economist.

The Economist (2002b). Corrupt Judges, June 29:36.

The Economist (2003a). Extortion in Jamaica, November 1:36 London: The Economist.

The Economist (2003b). Competing with China, August 9:61.

The Economist (2004). *The World in 2003.* London: The Economist.

Elizondo, C. (2003). After the Second of July: Challenges and Opportunities. In J.S. Tulchin and A.D. Selee (Eds.), *Mexico's Politics and Society in Transition* (pp. 29–54). Boulder, CO: Rienner.

Fatton, R. Jr. (1992). *Predatory Rule: State and Civil Society in Africa.* Boulder, CO: Rienner.

Figueroa, M. and A. Sives (2002). Homogenous Voting, Electoral Manipulation and The "Garrison" Process in Post-Independence Jamaica. *Commonwealth and Comparative Studies* 40(1): 81–108.

Forero, J. Rights Group Faults Police in Deaths of Women in Mexico. *The New York Times* (August 12, 2003). p. A6.

Friedman, T.L. (1999). *The Lotus and the Olive Tree.* New York: Anchor.

Friedrich, C.J. and Z.K. Brzezinski (1956). *Totalitarian Dictatorship and Autocracy.* New York: Praeger.

Gibney, F. (1992). *Korea's Quiet Revolution: From Garrison State to Democracy.* New York: Walker.

Goerner, E.A. and W.J. Thompson (1996). Politics and Coercion. *Political Theory* 24(4): 620–652.

Gonzalez, D. Riots Point out Jamaican Fault Line. *New York Times* (July 15, 2001). p. A3.

Gray, O. (2003). Predatory Politics and the Political Impasse in Jamaica. *Small Axe* 13(March): 72–94.

Haas, M. (1999). Arrested Development in Singapore. In M. Haas (Ed.), *The Singapore Puzzle* (pp. 2–42). London: Praeger.

Harrigan, J. (1998). Effects of the IMF and the World Bank on Public Expenditure Accountability in Jamaica. *Public Administration and Development* 18(1): 5–23.

Hendriks, F. and T.A.J. Toonen (2001). *Polder Politics: The Re-invention of Consensus Democracy in the Netherlands.* Burlington, VT: Ashgate.

Heneghan, T. (2002). *Unchained Eagle: Germany After the Wall.* London: Reuters.

Henke, H. (1999). Jamaica's Decision to Pursue a Neoliberal Development Strategy. *Latin American Perspectives* 26(1): 7–33.

Herbst, J. (1993). *The Politics of Reform in Ghana, 1982–1991.* Berkeley and LA: University of California press.

Herrmann, P. (2002). Corporate Strategy in Mexico: The Long Road to Internationalization." In A.M. Bissessar (Ed.), *Public Transfer, New Public Management and Globalization* (pp. 35–55). Lanham, MD: University Press of America.

Hudson, R.A. and D.J. Seyer (2002). Jamaica. In S.A. Meditz and D.M. Hanratty (Eds.), *Commonwealth Caribbean: A Regional Study* (pp. 120–147). Washington, D.C.: Department of the Army.

Huff, W.G. (1999). Turning the Corner in Singapore's Development State? *Asian Survey* 33(2): 214–242.

Human and Social Development Group (1997). *Violence and Urban Poverty in Jamaica: Breaking the Cycle.* Washington, D.C.: World Bank.

Hunt, J. (2000). *Culture Shock: Netherlands.* Portland, OR: Graphic Arts.

Ihlwan, M. Small Business Gets Wired in a Big Way. *Business Week* (September 1, 2003). p. 26.

Jackson, R.H. and C.G. Rosberg (1982). *Personal Rule in Black Africa: Prince, Autocrat, Prophet, Tyrant.* Berkeley and LA University of California Press.

Johnson, C. (1994). What is the Best System of National Economic Management for Korea? In L.-J. Cho and Y.H. Kim (Eds.), *Korea's Political Economy: An Institutional Perspective* (pp. 70–94). Boulder, CO: Westview.

Jones, T. (1995). *Policing and Democracy in the Netherlands.* London: Policy Studies Institute.

Jung-in, J. (2002). Laws, Rules, and Old Habits in a New World: A Summary of Post Crisis Institutional Changes. *Korea Journal* 41(January): 74–75.

Kam, W.P. (2001). From Leveraging Multinational Corporations to Fostering Entrepreneurship. In L. Low and D.M. Johnston (Eds.), *Singapore Inc.: Public Policy Options in the Third Millennium* (pp. 35–84). Singapore: Asia Pacific.

Kelly, T.J. (2001). Neoliberal Reforms and Rural Poverty. Latin American Perspectives 28 (September): 84–103.

Kesson-Smith, C. and W.J. Tettey (2003). Citizenship, Customary Law, and Gendered Jurisdiction: A Socio-Legal Perspective. In W.J. Tettey, K.P. Puplampu, and B.J. Berman (Eds.), *Critical Perspectives in Politics and Socio-Economic Development in Ghana* (pp. 305–332). London: Brill.

Kim, D.H. (1991). Alternative Social Development Strategies for Korea in the 1990s. In G.E. Caiden and B.W. Kim (Eds.), *A Dragon's Progress: Development Administration in Korea* (pp. 9–18). West Hartford, CN: Kumarian.

Kirk, D. Shipbuilders Steer Past South Korea's Economic Downturn. *The New York Times* (September 24, 2003). pp. W1, W7.

Knight, A. (1996). Corruption in Twentieth Century Mexico. In W. Little and E. Posado-Carbo (Eds.), *Political Corruption in Europe and Latin America* (pp. 220–245). London and New York: Macmillan Press and St. Martin's Press.

Kocka, J. (1997). The GDR: A Special Kind of Modern Dictatorship. In K.H. Jarausch (Ed.), *Dictatorship as Experience: Towards a Socio-Cultural History of the GDR* (pp. 12–27). New York and Oxford: Berghahn.

Kraus, J. (2002). Capital, Power and Business Associations in the African Political Economy: A Tale of Two Countries, Ghana and Nigeria. *Journal of Modern African Studies* 40(3): 395–436.

Lall, S. (1997). Industrial Development and Technology. In D.H. Kim and T.Y. Kongs (Eds.), *The Korean Peninsula in Transition* (pp. 12–40). New York and London: Macmillan and St. Martin's Press.

Lasswell, H.D. (1936). *Politics: Who Gets What, When, How.* New York: McGraw-Hill.

Latin America and the Caribbean Region (2001). *Mexico's Land Policy: A Decade After the Ejido Reform.* Washington, D.C.: World Bank Report No. 22187-ME.

Lee Kwan Yew (2000). *From Third World to First: The Singapore Story.* Westport, CN: Praeger.

Lee, S.C. (1991). Industrial Development and Technology. In D.H. Kim and T.Y. Kong (Eds.), *Economic Development in the Republic of Korea: A Policy Perspective* (pp. 455–475). Honolulu: East-West Center.

Leechor, C. (1994). Ghana: Frontrunner in Development. In I. Husain and R. Faruqee (Eds.), *Adjustment in Africa: Lessons from Country Case Studies* (pp. 153–180). Washington, D.C.: World Bank.

Leong, H.K. (2000). Citizen Participation and Policy Making in Singapore. *Asia Survey* 40(1): 436–455.

Levy, D.C. and K. Bruhn (2001). *Mexico: The Struggle for Democratic Development.* Berkeley and LA: University of California.

Lindenberg, M.M. (1993). *The Human Development Race: Improving the Quality of Life in Developing Countries*. San Francisco, CA: ICS Press.

Malkin, E. Pressure Builds on Mexican Banks to Ease Credit. *The New York Times* (April 7, 2004). pp. W1, W7.

Memorandum of the President (2004). *Country Assistance Strategy of the World Bank Group for the Republic of Ghana*. Washington, D.C.: World Bank Report 27838-GH.

Morris, S.D. (1991). *Corruption and Politics in Contemporary Mexico*. Tuscaloosa, AB: University of Alabama.

Mutalib, H. (2000). Illiberal Democracy and the Future of Opposition in Singapore. *Third World Quarterly* 21(1): 313–338.

Neher, C.D. (1999). The Case for Singapore. In M. Haas (Ed.), *The Singapore Puzzle* (pp. 39–54). Westport, CN: Praeger.

Newton, L.H. and C.K. Dillingham (1994). *Watersheds: Classic Cases in Environmental Ethics*. Belmont, CA: Wadsworth.

Norquest, D.A. (1991). A Unifying Conception of Politics. *PS: Political Science & Politics* 24(3): 504–505.

Norris, K. (1962). *Jamaica: The Search for an Identity*. London: Oxford University.

Organization for Economic Co-operation and Development (OECD) (1998). *Decentralization and Local Infrastructure in* Mexico. Paris: OECD.

Organization for Economic Co-operation and Development (OECD) (1999). *Regulatory Reform in Mexico*. Paris: OECD.

Organization for Economic Co-operation and Development (OECD) (2000). *Regulatory Reform in Korea*. Paris: OECD.

Organization for Economic Co-operation and Development (OECD) (2001, 2002). *OECD in Figures*. Paris: OECD.

Pae, S.M. (1992). *Korea Leading Developing Nations: Economy, Democracy, and Welfare*. Lanham, MD: University Press of America.

Peil, M. (1996). Ghana's Universities and Their Government: An Ambiguous Relationship. *Issues* 24(1): 52–56.

Peters, B.G. (1991). *The Politics of Taxation: A Comparative Perspective*. Cambridge, MA: Blackwell.

Peters, E.D. (2000). *Polarizing Mexico: The Impact of Liberalization Strategy*. Boulder, CO: Lynne Rienner.

Phillips, A.O. (1991). Four Decades of Federalism in Nigeria. *Publius*, 21(4): 103–112.

Pincus, J.R. (2002). State Simplification and Institution Building in a World Bank-Financed Development Project. In J.R. Pincus and J.A. Winters (Eds.), *Reinventing the World Bank*, (pp. 76–100). Ithaca, NY: Cornell.

Pincus, J.R. and J.A. Winters (2002). Reinventing the World Bank. In J.R. Pincus and J.A. Winters (Eds.), *Reinventing the World Bank* (pp. 1–25). Ithaca, NY: Cornell.

Puplampu, K.P. (2003). State-NGO Relations and Agricultural Sector Development. In W.J. Tettey, K.P. Puplampu, and B.J. Berman (Eds.), *Critical Perspectives on Politics and Socio-Economic Development in Ghana* (pp. 129–157). Leiden and Boston: Brill.

Ravallion, M. *The Economist* (April 10, 2004). p. 65.

Rich, B. (2002). The World Bank Under James Wolfensohn. In J.R. Pincus and J.A. Winters (Eds.), *Reinventing the World Bank* (pp. 26–53). Ithaca, NY: Cornell.

Rosenberg, T. The Taint of the Greased Palm. *The New York Times Magazine* (August 10, 2003). pp. 28–33.

Sachs, J. Developing Africa's Economy. *The Economist* (May 22, 2004). pp. 19–21.

Sender, J. (2002). Reassessing the Role of the World Bank in Sub-Saharan Africa. In J.R. Pincus and J.A. Winters (Eds.), *Reinventing the World Bank* (pp. 185–202). Ithaca, NY: Cornell.

Sengupta, S. Liberia Needs $500 million, Report Says. *The New York Times* (February 2, 2004). p. A6.

Smillie, I. (1986). *No Condition Permanent: Pump Priming Ghana's Industrial Revolution.* London: Intermediate Technology.

Smith, P.J. (1999). The Illusory Economic Miracle. In P.J. Smith (Ed.), *After the Wall: Eastern Germany since 1989* (pp. 110–133). Boulder, CO: Westview.

Stiglitz, J.E. (2003). *Globalization and its Discontents.* New York: Norton.

Stren, R.E. (1989). Urban Government in Africa. In R.E. Stren and R.R. White (Eds.), *African Cities in Crisis* (pp. 20–42). Boulder, CO: Westview.

Sullivan, K. and M. Jordan, Disparate Justice Imprisons Mexico's Poor. *The Washington Post* (July 6, 2002). pp. A1, A10.

Sullivan, K. and M. Jordan, Gunmen Kill Editor of Tijuana Newspaper. *The Washington Post* (June 23, 2004). p. A18.

Tettey, W.J. (2003). The Mass Media, Political Expression, and Democratic Transition. In W.J. Tettey, K.P. Puplampu, and B.J. Berman (Eds.), *Critical Perspectives in Politics and Socio-Economic Development in Ghana* (pp. 90–107). Leiden: Brill.

Toonen, T.A.J. (1996). On the Administrative Condition of Politics: Administrative Transformation in the Netherlands. *West European Politics* 19(3): 609–632.

Tulchin, J.S. and A.S. Selee (2003). Introduction. In J.S. Tulchin and A.S. Selee (Eds.), *Mexico's Politics and Society in Transition* (pp. 5–25). Boulder, CO: Lynne Rienner.

Turner, H.A. Jr. (1987). *The Two Germanies since 1945.* New Haven: Yale.

van Zanden, J. (1998). *The Economic History of the Netherlands.* London: Routledge.

Wapenhans, W.W. (1992). *The Wapenhans Report.* Washington, D.C.: World Bank.

Weiner, J. Mexico's New Leader Vows to End Longstanding Impunity for Torture in Justice System. *The New York Times* (March 18, 2001). A18.

Werlin, H.H. (1990). Decentralization and Culture: The Case of Monrovia, Liberia. *Public Administration and Development* 10(3) 251–262.

Werlin, H.H. (1998). *The Mysteries of Development: Studies Using Political Elasticity Theory.* Lanham, MD: University Press of America.

Werlin, H.H. (2000). Linking Public Administration to Comparative Politics. *PS: Political Science and Politics*, 33(3): 581–588.

Werlin, H.H. (2003). Poor Nations, Rich Nations: A Theory of Governance. *Public Administration Review* 63(3): 329–342.

Winters, J.A. (2002). Criminal Debt. In J.R. Pincus and J.A. Winters (Eds.), *Reinventing the World Bank* (pp. 101–130). Ithaca, NY: Cornell.

Wintle, M. (2000). Pillarisation, Consociation and Vertical Pluralism in the Netherlands: A European View. *West European Politics* 23(3): 139–152.

Wolin, S.S. (1960). *Politics and Vision: Continuity and Innovation in Western Political Thought.* Boston: Little, Brown.

World Bank (1993). *The East Asian Miracle: Economic Growth and Public Policy.* Washington, D.C.: World Bank.

World Bank (2000). *World Development Report.* Washington, D.C.: World Bank.

World Bank Development Committee (2004). *Global Monitoring Report.* Washington, D.C.: World Bank.

Wrong, D.H. (1979). *Power: Its Forms, Bases and Uses.* New York: Harper and Row.

Chapter 14

Global Governance, the UN Secretariat, and International Public Administration

Itoko Suzuki

CONTENTS

Introduction

Purpose

After nearly 60 years of existence of the United Nations, it was gratifying for the present and former UN staff (the author was a staff member of the UN during 1969–1999) to hear the news that our Secretary-General Kofi Annan received 2002 Nobel Peace Prize together with the United Nations. The United Nations was created in 1945 with the objectives of maintaining peace and security and to achieve international cooperation in solving international problems. The founding period environment has tremendously changed since. Especially now, we see strong impact of globalization, and yet we still see the states having the final authority in deciding the fates of our global community. Nevertheless, non-state actors including the inter-governmental organizations (IGOs) (as well as non-government organizations (NGOs) and private sector firms) have increasingly become important in global governance in which the United Nations is playing a crucial role. The United Nations is the most comprehensive (issue-wise) IGO in the present world, as the United Nations is currently managing many more international regimes. The United Nations is the most universal international institution with a membership of 191 states. Any state, member, or nonmember of the United Nations can bring into the United Nations (General Assembly) any issue for its solution. The United Nations is often considered to have legitimacy (of course depending on issues) even to bind nonmembers. When the present world community does not possess the world government, the United Nations is taking a crucial role in global governance.

It is well known by now that the Secretary-General is not only the chief administrative officer of the United Nations Secretariat, but also has been recognized as a creator, in his capacity officially as an advisor to the international community, of the partnerships beyond the member states, of all actors representing and seeking the preservations of global human interests, which can sometimes override national interests. The Nobel Prize awarded to the Secretary-General symbolizes, of course, his excellent personal capacity, but also the importance of the leadership of the Secretary-General of the United Nations in the current international community, which is assisted by the staff of the UN Secretariat.

The UN Secretariat is, according to the Article 7 of the UN Charter, one of the major entities of the United Nations together with the General Assembly and the Councils (we do not argue in the context of this chapter about the International Court of Justice, which is also a major UN entity). In the governance framework, whether it is at the level of national, local, or international, actors are not only governments, but also non-state actors. In the global governance, the UN Secretariat, not an IGO by itself, but as a global actor of governance, is increasingly emphasizing the relationships and networks harmonizing among the state and non-state actors including IGOs, private firms, and NGOs.[1] The UN Secretariat, represented by the Secretary-General, is a focal point to link all "the peoples" of the world in managing global or international regimes, as it provides forum of dialogue, discussions, negotiations, coordination, and decisions and advices for the world community of many actors and networks. For managing these regimes, and all the other activities of the United Nations, the UN Secretariat mobilizes and allocates major administrative resources including normative, financial, human, and informational from and to member states as well as many other actors in the international community. The UN Secretariat is obviously situated in the main street of the international public administration. It is not possible to clarify the system of global governance. But it can organize some facts that the international public administration is making global governance a practical reality.

This chapter tries to review, from the experience of a former UN official engaged in the international public administration, some salient functions and resources of the UN Secretariat, as they evolve the international public administration, and attempts to identify major roles of the UN Secretariat for the global governance. In doing so, this chapter sketches some peculiar phenomenon of the international public administration, which intersects with the UN Secretariat.

This chapter does not argue, define, or prescribe any theory or theoretical foundations of international public administration or global governance. Even with the limited and nonacademic scope, this review will hopefully serve to be a step toward many future investigations of issues in the international public administration as it evolves in and through the UN Secretariat.

---

[1]See the detailed concept of networking described in Takeo Uchida (2002). Introduction: Roles and Challenges of the UN Secretariat in Global Governance. In: The Japan Association for United Nations Studies, ed. *The United Nations Secretariat as a Global Actor.* Tokyo: Kokusai Shoin. Prof. J. Ruggie described how the UN Global Compact was designed in his article (Ruggie, J.G. (2001). The Global Compact as Learning Network. *Global Governance* 7(4) (Oct.–Dec.), 371–378). Secretary-General Kofi Annan reiterated the importance of non-state actors in his Millennium Report, http://www.un.org/millennium/sg/report/ch1.pdf (accessed November 1, 2004).

International Public Administration Used in the Context of This Chapter

There are many definitions, approaches, and interests to be covered in international public administration. The terms such as "international," or "public administration" are defined invariably and their usages are numerous. Each definition involves each historical context, possesses different purpose, and levels, and each definition itself is still the object of further argument. This essay tries to avoid such arguments, and is looking only into the process of the international public administration which evolves, in and through the UN Secretariat. As stated earlier, the UN Secretariat is one of the three major entities of the United Nations together with the General Assembly, and Councils that are the IGOs. There may be many other international public administration phenomena intersecting these IGOs, which are beyond the purview of this chapter.

The UN Secretariat is a legal international public institution, which procures its resource, allocates, and distributes in the global governance, which aims at cooperation among various actors in managing world orders. Analogous to national public administration in which resources procurement and distribution are managed by the public system and organizations, international public administration is the public administration of international issue or issues pertaining to the allocation of public goods beyond and across the national border via coordination or cooperation. As international administration requires coordination or cooperation for issues between nations, diplomacy can be international public administration. If so, international public administration has been exercised much before interdependent relations among sovereign states have been clearly recognized to have emerged. This chapter does not deal with such arguments, nor does it deal with the UN administration *per se*. This chapter will argue only one aspect of international public administration as it evolves in and through the international organization called the UN Secretariat. While international public administration is evolving in various levels of governance and many public systems, this chapter will deal with the international public administration system as it is exploited in the UN Secretariat that has its own resources and functions.

The UN Secretariat is an international public organization. The organization for the objectives between and among the states is the organizing principle of the international public administration. According to Mitrany,[2] the cooperation among the states is possible, and that possibility is actually

[2]Mitrany, D. (1966). A Working Peace System. Chicago, quoted in Shiroyama, H. (1997). *The Structure and Process of International Administration*. Tokyo: University of Tokyo Press, p. 13. The author is much indebted to Prof. Shiroyama for his theories and thrusts presented in this book and another cited in footnote 6 that have inspired her.

enabling the international public administration. In other words, as Woolf[3] puts it, international public interests can be possibly shared by and among states. Taking into account these organizing principles of international public administration, and the resources cited above for the UN Secretariat, several functions exercised by the UN Secretariat will be reviewed in the following sections, as we try to understand the salient characteristics of the international public administration in and through the UN Secretariat.

International Public Administration in the Context of Global Governance

Positioning of the United Nations

The current world is not an anarchical society; the world is not always with uncontrollable disorders. Global governance theory or theories try to identify positively, what issues exist now in the global community, and how the states, international organizations and civil society can cooperate toward its solution. In this context, current international public administration is deploying the cooperative activity without a central world government. As neither global governance nor international public administration have yet developed their systems, the real substance of either global governance or international public administration cannot always assure effective results. However, in a world of uncertainty, particularly in the international community, global governance can provide a framework or at least the possibility of a framework in which many actors of international community can cooperate toward responding to globally threatening issues.

For one thing, the United Nations as an IGO created in the half of the 20th century has since been serving as an indispensable institution in the international community, despite its defective parts, and has served the global interests and by working for the solution of major international issues. If the international community shares the global governance, that means, according to Prof. Joseph Nye, "cooperative power"[4] is exploited in the international community in which each actor is implicitly required to act civil. Also the United Nations is required by its Charter that member states ("we the people") act in "tolerance."[5]

---

[3]Woolf, L. (1916). International Governance, quoted in Shiroyama, H. (1997). *The Structure and Process of International Administration*. Tokyo: University of Tokyo Press, p. 11.
[4]Keohane, R.O., and Nye, J.S. (2000). Introduction. In: Nye, J.S. and, Donahue, J.D. eds. *Governance in a Globalizing World*. Washington, D.C.: Brookings Institution Press, pp. 1–41.
[5]UN Charter, Preamble. http://www.un.org/aboutun/charter/index.html.

The United Nations and its system organizations including the World Bank, International Monetary Fund (IMF), United Nations Educational, Scientific, and Cultural Organization (UNESCO), International Labor Organization (ILO), World Health Organization (WHO), Food and Agriculture Organization (FAO), and other specialized agencies as well as United Nations Development Program (UNDP), United Nations Environment Program (UNEP), and other funds and programs plus UN regional commissions, altogether constitute "the UN system." Each entity has its own designated principles, norms, rules, procedures, and financial and human resources. It organizes dialogues, coordination, cooperation, and formulates agreements and policies. Current global governance is decentralized. Decentralized systems mean that there is no single world order applicable for all global or international issues, and each issue is identified, reviewed, and solved with the relevant regime or regimes. The current world community has organized so many international regimes and these are managed in a fragmented, not always coordinated manner. Thus, decentralized does not mean that the world is regionally, or territorially decentralized, but the solution to the global issues can create each regime to be solved. Many global and international regimes have been created and many are with each UN system organization as the focal point. These activities are possible when the above-cited co-opted soft power, compliance, or tolerance is available in the international community.

Global Governance and the UN Secretariat

Although it is known that the United Nations consists, organizationally of General Assembly, Councils, and the Secretariat, the UN Secretariat performs more than administrative functions of the United Nations, which is an IGO. Regime management and coordination, or the policy process with the initial norm and issue identification starts often with the UN Secretariat. As a permanent organization, UN Secretariat has budget, the international civil service system, and other resources. The UN Secretariat is an important actor of the global governance with the rest of the actors, state, and non-state and IGOs including UN General Assembly and UN Councils.

The UN Charter stipulates that the Secretary-General is the chief administrative officer of the organization in its Article 97. However, the role of the Secretariat is not specifically stated. Chapter XV of the Charter does not explicitly state that the UN Secretariat is an administrative organ, although, the staff member's neutrality as international civil servants who must be responsible only to the organization (United Nations) is stipulated. However, since its Article 99 stipulating that the Secretary-General, the head of the Secretariat, may bring to the attention of the Security Council (sometimes a primary decision-making institution in the United Nations above the General Assembly) any matter in his opinion may threaten the maintenance of international peace and security, can be interpreted that he can lead, and advise the international community. Then his staff, international officials employed in the Secretariat as international civil servants, need to function in this capacity (of course in support of the Secretary-General) as well. One of the recent advisory acts of the Secretary-General to the international community was his expression of the opinion dated February 1, 2005 over the Nepalese King's decision of national emergency and his dismantlement of the government. The Secretary-General expressed his strong concern and advised to restore the democratic procedure to the nation. The UN staff are not after all the staff of the national governments and solely work for the chief administrative officer of the United Nations. The following sections of this chapter discuss the functions, not all but some illustrative, performed by the UN Secretariat in the UN General Assembly and Councils, to clarify further the roles of the UN Secretariat.

The UN Secretariat in the "Legislative" Process

Governance functions can generally be divided into the three branches: legislative, executive, and judicial. In the UN governance, these functions are not categorically decentralized. As stated earlier, the United Nations, as an IGO, possesses three major organizations, General Assembly (as a quasilegislative body for all members), Councils, and the Secretariat. The UN Charter stipulates more clearly the roles of General Assembly and the Councils than the role of the UN Secretariat. Unlike the national governance, the three divisions, legislative, judicial, and executive (administrative), are not fully clarified for the United Nations either.

For instance, the UN General Assembly is usually considered as the legislative body, but it does not always possess the authorities accepted by all member states in their decisions including declarations, resolutions, or decisions. They sometimes could bind or restrain the member states, but not always. UN General Assembly is not strictly a legislative body like the congresses of states.

On the other hand, many norms and rules have been created by the (through) United Nations as international laws or "soft laws." The United Nations has formed many regimes in the international community. Most of the soft laws take the shape of recommendations even if they are part of the UN resolutions and decisions in the General Assembly (or UN-organized conferences). Some of the decisions take the form of legal documents like treaties that would bind the states signed and ratified with the United Nations (and then often nonmember states as well). Legal powers to bind or restrain states differ according to each decision. Often, resolutions remain just as resolutions. But in many cases, they are taken up by national congresses through the state governments, and if ratified, relevant national laws are to be formulated or revised. Then legal authorities arise in the national community, and if accumulated from many states subsequently in the international community. Even if UN resolutions are not to become part of domestic laws (due to opposition in the national parliament or for some other reasons), UN resolution often functions in the domestic congress and public administration (Prime Minister or Foreign Ministry, for example) as a norm to be respected or cannot be totally ignored by the government of a country. In this manner the UN General Assembly functions as a *de facto* legislative entity in the global governance.

The relevance of the above descriptions in the context of this article is the fact that the draft of these important resolutions or decisions (possibly prospective national rules or laws) are often prepared by a relevant staff of the Secretariat, after consultations and negotiations made with the governments of the member states. Before the draft decision or resolution is submitted to the General Assembly, in the formulation, the staff in charge in the UN Secretariat make a number of direct contacts with the counterpart staff of the permanent missions of the member governments in the committee or plenary meetings of the General Assembly. For one decision or resolution, that secretariat staff member may become the *de facto* focal point for representatives of many member states in the General Assembly. The UN staff have no authority to organize the decision on the subject, but make horizontal contacts with delegations of the member countries, to organize policy contents and coordinate many different interests of countries. In the international administration, nonhierarchical coordination is performed. Because the General Assembly does not possess its own secretariat, the members of the UN Secretariat perform the functions of the General Assembly Secretariat. The policy formulation process in the General Assembly involves intersects between the member states and the UN Secretariat, which shapes the international public administration phenomenon.

Similar situation arises in the UN Councils, which are the managing boards of the United Nations. For instance, in the Economic and Social Council (ECOSOC), the Department of Economic and Social Affairs (DESA) serves as the Secretariat of the Council and its staff in charge of the particular issue takes the similar position as in the General Assembly, and performs drafting policies, resolutions, or decisions for the submission to the Council sessions in coordination with the delegations of the member states as well as with other intergovernmental bodies, particularly within the UN system.

In the United Nations, General Assembly is a "congress," but the General Assembly is not represented by the national congressmen with the rights to represent the state governance. Bureaucrats of the government of the member states represent the government, negotiate with the Secretariat and representatives of other member states, and remain the mainstream of the delegation in the General Assembly. In this way, the elected officials of the state governance do not represent the General Assembly. As such, many diplomats consider General Assembly as the administrative body governed by international public administration.

The UN Secretariat in the Judicial Process

As another function of governance, judicial function is exercised in the United Nations by the International Court of Justice and the UN Security Council, when it decides the sanction, and by the World Trade Organization (WTO) that has judicial functions as well. But the exercise of the judicial function is not limited to these organizations only.

Judicial function of governance is mainly the function to apply and interpret the laws. In the United Nations, each regime is usually equipped with the review function to be undertaken if not annually, every few years. General Assembly and the Councils monitor the maintenance and the management of the respective rules and the regimes. Monitoring is a preliminary function of the judiciary, as well as the function of public administration to manage the regime. For instance, if some countries are found not to be complying with the regimes, secretariat (Secretary-General, and therefore UN professionals) can inform the Security Council (that action may lead to a sanction), and the staff members who assisted the legislation of the regime may in fact monitor the resolution pertaining the particular regime. In this way, in the UN administration, judicial function of governance is deeply embedded in the regime administration, which also shapes an international public administration phenomenon through the monitoring function. In fact, monitoring is in practice mandated in many UN organizations, programs, and projects.

Additionally, for instance, during the peacekeeping operations (PKO) in Cambodia that lacked at that time the judicial system of a national government, the United Nations used the PKO (UN Secretariat staff) itself to exercise the judicial function of the state. In that case, the United Nations administered the judicial function of the state as the temporary "World Government."[6]

---

[6]Shiroyama, H. (2001). International Administration: An Indispensable Element in Global Governance. In: Watanabe, A., and Tsuchiyama, J., eds. (2001). *Global Governance: In Search of Order without Government*. Tokyo: University of Tokyo Press, pp. 146–167. Also, Hoshino, T. (2001). International Organization: An Agent of Governance. In: Watanabe, A, and Tsuchiyama, J., eds. (2001). *Global Governance: In Search of Order without Government*. Tokyo: University of Tokyo Press, pp. 168–191.

Coordination in the Nonhierarchical International Administration

Coordination is one of the important functions of public administration. Coordination integrates and harmonizes all functions that are decentralized in a central government to maintain integrity of public administration. In the United Nations, secretariat staff is destined to be involved in coordinating the interests of member states in the General Assembly and Council secretariats for formulating draft policies in respective substantive area. Specific substantive area has been managed by each UN program or specialized institution that forms part of the UN system. For the management of each regime and each substantive area, and when common framework for the member states is explored, UN staff members try to coordinate the interests among the UN institutions as well as between the UN system and the member state governments. Coordination is an important function in international public administration as well.

Staff members of the United Nations make nonhierarchical coordination with the member states and among the intergovernmental bodies. Probably much more horizontal relations take forms under the nonhierarchical coordination through the UN Secretariat than the relations between the state bureaucrats with the state congressmen. Some characteristics and the nature of "coordination" in the UN Secretariat will be further analyzed below.

Due to the importance of the coordination, the UN Secretariat (Secretary-General) is constantly and even now under reform of the coordination mechanisms in the United Nations at several levels. For the UN system wide coordination, Chief Executives Board (CEB) for Coordination[7] — formerly the Administrative Committee on Coordination (ACC) — is the forum which brings the executive heads of all organizations to further coordination and cooperation on the whole range of substantive and management issues facing the UN system. Chaired by the Secretary-General of the United Nations, the Board meets twice annually. It is composed of the Executive Heads of the 28 member organizations including United Nations, ILO, FAO, UNESCO, the Bretton Woods institutions, other specialized agencies, funds and programs and the WTO.

For the UN resource coordination, Committee for Programme Coordination (CPC) coordinates all programs of the UN system before the annual budget coordination; 34 prominent representatives (ambassadors or ministers) of member states are selected in the General Assembly as members for the CPC. For budget coordination before the General Assembly adopts the

---

[7]On the coordination of the UN system and other level of coordination, see http://ceb.unsystem.org/ for details.

biennium budget of the United Nations, Fifth Committee and Advisory Committee for Administrative and Budgetary Questions (ACABQ) of the General Assembly performed coordination within the General Assembly's budgetary process after the CPC finishes program coordination. ACABQ as an advisory body consists of 16 government officials selected in the General Assembly on the basis of individual and professional capacity. CPC and ACABQ are found among some involved Secretariat staff to express strong authority to the Secretariat as they "check" programs and budgets prepared by the Secretariat staff. Security Council and ECOSOC coordinate in semi-annual meetings relevant policies; additionally each committee and program under each council does organize annual meeting to coordinate the interests of member states, NGOs, and scientific professional's opinions for policy integration. Representatives of relevant UN agencies are also invited to these meetings to express opinions.

Each specialized agency, UN fund, and program has its own coordination mechanism with relevant organizations and member states. For instance, World Bank Consultation Group meeting does coordinate their activities with those of the relevant UN agencies and representatives of member states, relevant NGOs. Similarly, UNDP Round Table organized for each country (UNDP has many permanent representative offices in member states) annually coordinates technical cooperation resources for a particular country from all UN agencies with participation of representatives of member states.

DESA of the United Nations is a secretariat of ECOSOC, and has the function of coordination of activities of all the substantive programs, agencies, and regional commissions under ECOSOC. Each year before the regular General Assembly session starts in September, it organizes coordination meeting twice a year in Geneva and in New York alternately, for the coordination of programs of budgets and resource procurements. All relevant UN agencies and heads of the programs participate in the respective coordination meetings together with the representatives of the member states of the ECOSOC.

Each substantive program of the DESA also holds meetings, as a committee or expert group with government representatives for resource and norm coordination; independent experts and NGOs provide comments for new technology use, norms, etc. rather than resource coordination.

In all the levels, coordination with the delegates of member states forms the shape of international public administration. Global governance exploits heavily the UN Secretariat, which often takes initiatives or a role of focal point for coordination of interests of diverse actors, government or non-government, of the international community.

Coordination practiced in the United Nations is a function of international public administration. It differs somehow from the coordination function of the domestic public administration. The difference may be firstly explained in the differences in coordination and cooperation.

Coordination and cooperation are two different functions in administration. Coordination and cooperation are usually differentiated with the following criteria: equity in the rule (order); commonality of objectives (limiting participants); threat to the autonomy. Coordination is undertaken to seek total integrity of the whole public administration system and often reveals commonality among the institutions and threatens the autonomy of each entity. In the international administration, each actor, whether it is the government of a member state (has a sovereignty), or a UN agency, or other international organization, has high degree of autonomy in the international community. Even for coordination among the UN entities, UN headquarters has difficulty in coordinating the interests of relevant UN agencies. Coordination threatens the autonomy. The process of coordination sometimes creates hostile relations, contrary to the function of the coordination. Coordination and co-opted activities are derived in the name of cooperation. For instance, interagency cooperation, a product after "coordination," is reached with a written agreement of cooperation to avoid misunderstanding to occur later based on ambiguity.

Under the system of nonhierarchy, which is the environment in the international public administration, coordination of common objectives is difficult. Even in domestic governance, interministry coordination is not easy as it functions in the nonhierarchical system.

Under the nonhierarchical system, cooperation and compliance are sought by way of negotiation. International community functions with the availability of common objectives and goals. For global governance to function (co-opted control of each other in a nonhierarchical system without central governing institution), negotiation is a key function, and negotiating to reach a cooperation activity is making some coordination possible in the international community.

In addition to these two reasons, i.e., high autonomy of each actor and nonhierarchical system, that are making coordination difficult in the international public administration, another reason may be the difficulty of creating trust in the multicultural community. For instance, in the recent UN management training programs, working in a multicultural environment and how to cooperate with different cultures are major topics. These training programs are sometimes offered as joint program for UN and member states' officials. This circumstance only would indicate the difficulty to work in the multicultural organization.

Because of the insufficient coordination, overlapping activities and programs emerge in the global governance. Difficulty or lack of coordination might make it easy to create overlapping institutions in the UN system, which led to the criticism of the UN system on account of redundant activities, although some critiques argue, redundancy is sometimes useful to supplement decentralized activities.

Advocacy as an International Public Administration Function

National public administration nowadays requires increasingly more activities to advocate, calling attention, providing adequate information for the security of the nationals. National government these days requests cooperation of citizens to comply with a new norm for environment, food and health, safety and security, etc. rather than issuing a restraining order or sanction. The United Nations as a focal point of norm and regime creation and management takes advocacy as an important function. In fact, advocacy is not only a role of the United Nations but is embedded in the functions of the UN Secretariat staff. As such it is an important function of the international public administration like coordination, cooperation, and negotiation as described above.

Most of the UN organizations provide advocacy programs to disseminate norms and related information to the world community. The UN Secretariat staff consume substantial energy and resources for exercising this advocacy function. The United Nations organizes world conferences not only to generate norms but also to advocate the norms and to solicit support for the new norms. In line with the planning, organizing, staffing, directing, coordinating, and budgeting (POSDCORB), once itemized major functions of the traditional public administration, advocating can be added, as an important function of the UN Secretariat (including its staff). Advocating can make negotiation for coordination with state authorities easier, as advocacy succeeds, soliciting cooperation for coordination of common interests with the states can be easier. Counterparts in negotiation will listen to the points of arguments when they find intellectual (normative) authority. Often coordination can be stagnated, as it is a difficult task for the UN staff members, advocating is a more promising (as well as more appealing and gratifying) function, rather uniquely heavy loaded in the international public administration for the UN staff to engage.

This heavy weight of the advocacy is due to the unique mission of the United Nations to provide global public goods or manage new norms and regimes. In the exercise of the function, the UN Secretariat interacts not only with the governments of the member states, but also with non-governmental organizations and the civil society.

Due to limited resources, the UN Secretariat cannot advocate systematically the new norms to the international community. For instance, the UN Public Administration Program used to provide assistance to national policy support for new norms, and training (each year average 30–50 countries with some 20 professional staff including interregional and technical advisors with the help of residential/field project professionals) mainly in the technical cooperation projects funded by UNDP, World Bank, or Official Development Assistance (ODAs). Many developing countries request technical assistance, but the United Nations has limited resources despite the Secretariat (meaning staff) efforts to tap additional resources from more generous member states' governments. Of course some developing countries do not wish the intervention of the United Nations. With these limitations, UN norms and regimes have been advocated to member states.

Advocating can be compared with such administrative function in the state public administration, as administrative guidance, that is exercised to bring the society to a desired circumstance or standard. Administrative guidance is enabled from the cognition that the public administration side is good and then to some extent that guidance engineer people and organizations to a better situation. In the case of the international public administration, most of the member states and their citizens acknowledge generally that the United Nations is a "good" (or "goodness") organization (United Nations is after all an intermediate global public good) that is protecting nationals, international community, and global interests.

Advocacy function is still underdeveloped and there is no established definition for this function neither in public administration nor in the international public administration. This function can be further reviewed and evaluated in connection with the validity and the legitimacy of the role of the UN Secretariat in the context of the international public administration.

Resource Allocations of the UN Secretariat

Public administration can be often most simply viewed as allocation of scarce public resources. Major resources of public administration are rules (laws, regimes, norms, treaties, decisions, etc., in the context of the United Nations), and financial, human, and information resources. In the context of the international public administration, coordination (when difficult, cooperation and negotiation for) resource allocations among member states, between the states and the United Nations, and among the UN agencies was discussed in earlier section as an important administrative function. The system in resource allocations is not well developed for the United Nations, as often criticized in the case of allocation of financial resources. This paper is not intended to describe the details of these functions or resources. This section will highlight some limited aspects of the allocation of resources of the United Nations, so that the roles of the UN Secretariat, which exploits the international public administration can be further clarified.

Financial Resources

The UN Secretariat experienced throughout its history many financial crises and tried to rectify the problems. The United Nations cannot levy the tax to member states and instead requires their assessed contribution. Each member state pays its dues based on the established principles of assessed contribution. The amount is in accordance to the commensurable national economic ability. Although the United Nations cannot actually enforce member states to comply, if a country fails to provide assessed contribution for more than two years, it is supposed to lose the status of membership, although such a rule is not always exercised.

The UN budget is biennial and each program of the United Nations needs to submit the annual budget and the execution report to the relevant Council and then to the General Assembly. PKO budget is separate, but is similarly assessed to each member state. The United States of America is a number one contributor for both, but the ceiling of the assessed amount to a single member is now provided.

In addition to assessed contribution, the United Nations receives voluntary contribution. Development-oriented entities of the United Nations such as UNDP, United Nations Children's Fund (UNICEF), and FAO as well as UN Secretariat receive voluntary contributions. Voluntary contribution includes both regular contribution, which resembles the regular budget contribution, and the *ad hoc* voluntary contribution based on the will of a particular government or on the requests of the UN Secretariat. In the context of this chapter, it is important to describe the latter case.

Large amount of voluntary contribution to developmental agencies like UNICEF, UNDP, United Nations High Commissioner for Refugees (UNHCR) naturally can be politically influenced. Contributing governments can specify the areas. Many programs and funds in economic and social areas in the UN system very much rely on the voluntary contribution to organize activities. Some countries are well known to be interested in the issue of women's rights, whereas others for instance, in environmental activities. Their national policies determine to which areas or the countries to contribute voluntarily. This means that the UN administration is much dependent on the will of the sovereign states. However, overall, financial resources are said to have been secured by the cooperation from many developed countries to the multilateral institution (United Nations) without distorting the rules of the United Nations or disrupting the UN norms.

A UN staff member can also take initiative to tap the voluntary contribution to his or her own work. The UN Secretariat can sometimes be politicized because of this possibility in which the staff can be linked to the financial resources of a country. However, UN staff, as an international civil servant, cannot receive any influence (any country cannot instruct UN staff) based on the principles of neutrality sanctioned by the UN staff rules based on the UN Charter. In addition to the aforementioned roundtable (of UNDP) or consultation group meeting of each UN office, coordination on the voluntary contribution is regularly organized among the aid-providing countries and UN agencies. Because the UN developmental agencies organize pledging conferences inviting all interested states, all states are well informed which country pledges or contributes to what areas and how much. By such consultation and coordination meeting, overlaps (too much) or too obvious tied provision are tried to be minimized.

Although the official UN members are the governments of member states, the financial resources can be tapped not only from the governments but also from the private sector and civil society organizations, as well as individual citizens. It is well known that UNICEF is selling its goods and receives contribution from the airline passengers. One Japanese diplomat once suggested the airline travel tax to be levied as a UN tax. Many ideas have been presented to secure financial resources. Followed by $1 trillion contribution by Ted Turner, large-scale contribution from Bill Gates and others have been tapped. Private contribution is usually welcomed by the financially "poor" UN Secretariat. These circumstances can be interpreted as the financial resources administration of the United Nations being always uncertain, compared to the financial administration of the national government.

Human Resources[8]

Again this chapter is not intended to analyze the UN human resources system. This chapter highlights the difficulty of the UN Secretariat to secure human resources to manage the international public administration. Permanent staff, who are employed as professionals in the UN Secretariat, are international civil servants recruited based on professional qualifications and equitable regional representation. Neutrality (to remain independent from governments) and geographical representation are important principles in a multicultural organization. It is both a merit and desirability to secure international professional officials service (international civil service) based on geographical representation, as most of the UN activities require

[8]For useful references, see (a) Kuyama, S. (2002). The International Civil Service: Origins, Principles and Composition. In: The Japan Association for United Nations Studies, ed. *The United Nations Secretariat as a Global Actor*. Tokyo: Kokusai Shoin; (b) Tashiro, K. (2002). Activities and Prospects of the International Civil Service. In: The Japan Association for United Nations Studies, ed. *The United Nations Secretariat as a Global Actor*. Tokyo: Kokusai Shoin; and (c) Mauritzen, H. (1990). *The International Civil Service: A Study of Bureaucracy: International Organizations*. Brookfield, VA: Dartmouth.

knowledge of the countries and the region in addition to the professional knowledge.

In recruitment, each member state is offered to contribute candidates for the professional posts. It is not always possible for a country to contribute the desired level of human resources based on the regional representation principle. For instance, Japan, as a number two financial contributor, cannot meet even one half of the desired level of human resource contribution to the UN Secretariat, whereas the countries such as the Philippines are often over-represented. These realities are not desirable in light of the principle of diversity.

In addition to the regular professional staff, professional staff members with limited length of appointment, such as advisors and experts work in the UN Secretariat and projects. These temporary staff who are employed for the work of staff or advisors and experts are also important UN human resources.

What matters most is the quality of these professionals working in and for the Secretariat. Recruitment method, promotion, human resource management is very much different from those of the national civil service. International Civil Service Commission and the UN human resource management offices have provided rules and methods for how to secure and maintain best quality and efficiency as well as regional representation in the UN human resources. With all the devices and constant reforms in the human resource management within the UN Secretariat, the Secretariat would still need improvement in human resource management, which can only be possible when the member states take more interest in the human resource management (and not intervention).

Major difficulties in the human resource management arise from the fact that the standard setting of human resources is extremely difficult in international administration, as the job of the international civil servant is not always attractive to some countries due to their economic and cultural differences. Additionally UN staff members, whether in security area or development assistance area, often engage in fieldwork that entails danger and risks. Negotiations with member state representatives for new standard setting or regime management are not an easy task. In a nonhierarchical system, administrative authority is not bestowed to the UN officials unlike the national public administration systems. There are many "predicaments" to becoming UN officials.

Internally, the UN staff members work under the regulation of international civil service and in a hierarchal bureaucratic system, like any national civil service. And the UN bureaucratic system requires staff members to be independent from any national government. However, staff members have their own cultural ties and bureaucratic cultural background of their country of origin. They may sometimes tend to psychologically rely upon the ties of their original country. UN human resource management is in peculiar difficulties as staff members have their own bureaucratic culture, which contributes to mosaic bureaucratic system that may in turn lead to highly unorganized management in the UN Secretariat. Working in international public administration, particularly in the UN Secretariat, means individual staff members are away for a long period of time from their homeland, and are compelled to live in a closed society of different cultural settings from their homeland. These peculiar circumstances are making human resource management extremely difficult.

A realistic and systematic survey on these aspects and as well as other human resource management predicaments can be undertaken to improve the human resource and resource management of the UN Secretariat. As it is the people who manage the regimes and norms of the United Nations, the future of the intergovernmental organization is indeed dependent on how well the UN Secretariat can secure the better quality of human resources and their management.

Information Resources

Information collection and dissemination are entrusted activities of any office or program in the United Nations. Staff of the UN Secretariat is assigned to collect, organize, and analyze the information received from the member states and other sources.

The UN Public Administration Progamme of DESA, for instance, collects and disseminates information on innovative experiences of countries in administrative reforms or governance capacity building. Expert committee meetings and field projects are good sources for information collection and they are organized in close cooperation with relevant UN offices and organizations such as the UNDP, World Bank, regional commissions as well as other specialized UN agencies, as stated earlier, to share relevant information.

The UN Secretariat staff members develop information networks for the respective program activities to facilitate information collection and dissemination functions of the UN Secretariat. Collected information is analyzed and used for drawing new international public policies, as disseminated in the resolutions, declarations or decisions in the Council and General Assembly eventually to be developed as rules or regimes or even UN treaties.

Member state governments are not the only sources in most of the UN offices and programs, which deal with issues of development or humanitarian affairs, NGOs are important sources for information collection and strategy building. Of course, information collection in the international public administration cannot be always systematic, or automatic. Some

NGOs are vocal and others are quieter. Despite these discrepancies, UN information has contributed to the policy and strategy building of many member states, particularly developing countries, where the information from other countries is scarce and information collection abilities are not always sufficient. To developing countries, certain assistance (to retrieve information) is provided through development cooperation projects or advisory services.

Summarizing the Roles of the UN Secretariat

From the foregoing discussions on some functions performed by the UN Secretariat of the United Nations, the distinctive roles of the Secretariat can be summarized in the following. These roles unfold the unique phenomenon of the international public administration intersecting the UN Secretariat as exhibited in the above sections.

Instrument for Global Public Policy Making

The UN Secretariat services the secretariat of the legislative bodies (decision making) of the United Nations including the General Assembly and Councils, and serves to a certain degree a judicial process particularly through its monitoring function. The UN Secretariat prepares forums for discussion, debates, and decision making. These decisions include international standards, rules, norms, and regimes in practically all areas, such as human rights, women's rights, transportation, trade, environment, labor, health, education, etc. In the "legislative" process, the UN Secretariat categorizes and clarifies the issues, directly negotiates and "coordinates" with member states and NGOs to synthesize common interests. "Coordination," cooperation, and negotiation are important international administrative functions performed in the UN Secretariat as discussed in the section "Coordination in the Nonhierarchical International Administration" of this chapter. This chapter also argued that the UN Secretariat, although not an IGO, but as an aide to the Secretary-General who performs as an advisor to the international community, directly coordinates and negotiates with member states and other actors in global governance.

Information Clearing Center for International Networking

To implement UN-mandated activities, the UN Secretariat collects information from the member states as well as other sources, and disseminates them to the world community. The UN Secretariat (in many programs and

UN organizations) has established many information networks for their program, regime, or rule management. The role of the UN Secretariat in information collection and networking is expected to serve the information clearing function for the international community. Information resource management in the UN Secretariat has been discussed in the section "Information Resources" as part of the international public administration.

Monitoring UN Decisions, Resolutions, International Laws, and Rules

As the UN Secretariat serves the secretariat of the decision-making bodies of the United Nations, whether it is the Security Council, or General Assembly, or of the ILO, or International Atomic Energy Agency (IAEA), as well as many international regimes, these decision and regime implementation are monitored in fact by the secretariat. Often the same staff who have served the decision-making secretariat do monitor the progress of the implementation of the decision or regime, including any violation through information collection.

Advocacy of Norms, Rules, Standards, and Regimes

As discussed earlier, the Secretariat staff does engage substantial time and resources for advocating the new and emerging rules and norms to be spread in the member states and international community. This chapter argued in the section "Advocacy as an International Public Administration Function" that advocating is uniquely a heavy function that forms a part of the international public administration.

Advisory and Technical Assistance

The Secretariat organizes advisory and technical assistance activities, with the resources provided by member states as well as non-governmental sources. The advisory function may be an auxiliary function of advocacy and the function may be performed based on the availability of resources, but mainly addressed to norm or standard setting in the member states, particularly in developing countries, mostly upon request.

Mobilizing and Allocating Resources

The international administration system is often discussed as a system of resource allocation of the UN Secretariat. The UN Secretariat as a permanent institution with budget has to manage administrative resources including financial, human, and informational. Material resources and infrastructure (building and others) are also procured and managed in the UN Secretariat. These resources are mobilized and allocated by the Secretariat from mainly member state governments but from other sources as well, as discussed in the section "Resource Allocations of the UN Secretariat." Resource procurement, allocations, coordination and negotiation with the member states and among the UN institutions (mostly IGOs) also evolve as the international public administration phenomenon as discussed in the foregoing sections.

Toward Reforms of the International Public Administration

In this chapter, some limited aspects of the international public administration which the UN Secretariat exploits for global governance were discussed. Global governance cannot be possible without the international public administration. In the United Nations, international administration evolves in all governance branches including legislative, judicial, and executive. This does not mean that global governance is practiced with legitimacy or responsible fully to the international community. Global governance system has not yet been clearly designed, but the international administration is responding to the global governance objectives and remains a major enabling part of the system. This chapter, however, neither verifies the effectiveness of the international administration nor does it assert that the administrative phenomenon exhibited by the activities of the UN Secretariat is all international public administration. In fact it is only one scope of international public administration. Even with such a limited scope in the future, it is desirable to evaluate the accountability (mainly to the member states) of the international public administration and effectiveness (degree of contribution to the international community) in the context of global governance.

Evaluation in public administration is relatively a new experiment and its indicators and methods are not adequately established yet even for the evaluation of national public administration. The standards applicable to the national public administration evaluation such as the accountability, legitimacy, equity, transparency, or legal framework may not be applicable to the international public administration as they are. The UN Secretariat has been the target of criticism on account of expanded bureaucratic system, inefficiency, difficulty of coordination among the organizations of the UN system, lack of financial resources, etc. The UN Secretariat has constantly been reformed internally by the initiatives of the Secretary-General[9] and the member states. The end of the 2004 report of the High Level Panel[10] recommended many reforms in order for the United Nations to become better and more responsible actor for global governance. To improve the international public administration that intersects with the UN Secretariat is only one aspect of the expected UN reforms, but even for that purpose, establishing the appropriate evaluation indicators is acutely needed.

Selected Bibliography

Articles

Ruggie, J.G. (1975). International Responses to Technology: Concepts and Trends. *International Organization* 29–3, 557–583.

Ruggie, J.G. (2001). The Global Compact as Learning Network. *Global Governance* 7(4) (Oct.–Dec.), 371–378.

Books

Axford, B. (1995). *The Global System: Economics, Politics and Culture.* New York: St. Martin's Press.

Center for UN Reform Education (2003). *A Reader on Second Assembly and Parliamentary Proposals.* New York: Center for UN Reform Education.

Center for UN Reform Education (2003). *2003–2004 Handbook of Proposals for UN Reform.* 2nd edition. Wayne, NJ: Center for UN Reform Education.

Coicaud, J-M., and Heiskanen, V., eds. (2001). *The Legitimacy of International Organizations.* Tokyo: The UN University Press.

De Cooker, C., ed. UNITAR (1990). International Administration: Law and Management Practices in International Organizations. London: Martinus Nijhoff Publishers.

Diel, P.F. (2001). *The Politics of Global Governance: International Organizations in an Interdependent World.* 2nd edition. London: Rienner.

Division of Public Administration and Development Management, UN/DESA (1998). Rethinking Public Administration: An Overview. New York: United Nations.

Fukuda, K. (2003). *New Aspects of International Administration: Issues and Perspectives.* Tokyo: Yuhikaku.

Imamura, T. (1997). *Basic Theories of Public Administration.* Tokyo: Sampou Shobou.

---

[9]UN reforms, web site of the United Nations in http://www.un.org/reform/chron. Also United Nations document "We the People; Millennium Report of the Secretary-General, March 2000, in www.un.org/millenium/sg/report.

[10]Report of the High Level Panel on Threats, Challenges and Change (2004). A More Secure World: Our Shared Responsibility: Executive Summary. New York: United Nations. Detailed full version also available in the www.un.org/secureworld/report2.pdf.

Kaul, I., Grunberg, I., and Stern, M.A., eds. (1999). *Global Public Goods: International Cooperation in the 21st Century*. New York, Oxford: Oxford University Press.

Mauritzen, H. (1990). *The International Civil Service: A Study of Bureaucracy: International Organizations*. Brookfield, VA: Dartmouth.

Mogami, T. (1996). *International Organizations*. Tokyo: University of Tokyo Press.

Muldoon, Jr., J.P. (2004). *The Architecture of Global Governance: An Introduction to the Study of International Organizations*. Oxford: Westview.

Nelson, J. Report Commissioned by the UN Global Compact Office (2002). *Building Partnerships*. New York: United Nations.

Report of the High Level Panel on Threats, Challenges, and Change (2004). A More Secure World: Our Shared Responsibility: Executive Summary. New York: United Nations.

Rittberger, V., ed. (2001). *Global Governance and the United Nations System*. Tokyo: UN University Press.

Roberts, A., and Kingsbury, B., eds. (1996). *United Nations, Divided World*. 2nd edition. Oxford: Clarendon Press.

Rosenau, J., and Czempiel, E.O., eds. (1991). *Governance without Government*. Cambridge: Cambridge University Press.

Shiroyama, H. (1997). *The Structure and Process of International Administration*. Tokyo: University of Tokyo Press.

The Japan Association for United Nations Studies (2002). *The United Nations Secretariat as a Global Actor*. Tokyo: Kokusai Shoin.

Tsuji, K. (1965). *Modern Public Administration Theories and Reality: Compilation of Special Articles in Celebration of Prof. Masamichi Royama's 70th Birthday*. Tokyo: Keiso Shobou.

UN Commission on Global Governance (1995). *Our Global Neighborhood*. New York: Oxford University Press.

UN Department of Economic and Social Affairs (1999). *Governance in Africa: Consolidating the Institutional Foundations*. New York: United Nations.

UN Department of Economic and Social Affairs. (2000). *Building Partnerships for Good Governance: The Spirit and the Reality of South–South Cooperation*. New York: United Nations.

UN Department of Economic and Social Affairs (2001). *World Public Sector Report: Globalization and the State 2001*. New York: United Nations.

UN Department of Economic and Social Affairs (2002). *Human Resources Development for Eco-Partnership Building in Local Governance*. New York: United Nations.

Vayrynen, R., ed. (1999). *Globalization and Global Governance*. Oxford: Rowman and Littlefield.

Walzer, M. (1997). *On Toleration*. New Haven: Yale University Press.

Watanabe, A., and Tsuchiyama, J., eds. (2001). *Global Governance: In Search of Order without Government*. Tokyo: University of Tokyo Press.

Yokota, Y., ed. (2001). *Theory and Practice of International Organizations*. Tokyo: Kokusai Shoin.

Young, O.R., ed. (2000). *Global Governance: Drawing Insights from the Environmental Experience*. 2nd printing. Cambridge, MA: The MIT Press.

Ziring, L., Riggs, R., and Plano, J. (2000). *The United Nations: International Organization and World Politics*. 3rd edition. New York: Wordsworth.

Book chapters

Hoshino, T. (2001). International Organization: An Agent of Governance. In: Watanabe, A., and Tsuchiyama, J., eds. (2001). *Global Governance: In Search of Order without Government*. Tokyo: University of Tokyo Press, pp. 168–191.

Keohane, R.O., and Nye, J.S. (2000). Introduction. In: Nye, J.S., and Donahue, J.D. eds. *Governance in a Globalizing World*. Washington, D.C.: Brookings Institution Press, pp. 1–41.

Kuyama, S. (2002). The International Civil Service: Origins, Principles, and Composition. In: The Japan Association for United Nations Studies, ed. *The United Nations Secretariat as a Global Actor*. Tokyo: Kokusai Shoin.

Nigro, F., and Nigro, L.G. (1973). International Administration. In: *Modern Public Administration*. 3rd edition. New York: Harper and Row, pp. 438–458.

Ruggie, J. (1983). International Regimes, Transactions, and Change: Embedded Liberalism in the Postwar Economic Order. In: Krasner, S., ed. *International Regimes*. Ithaca, NY: Cornell University Press.

Shiroyama, H. (2001). International Administration: An Indispensable Element in Global Governance. In: Watanabe, A., and Tsuchiyama, J., eds. (2001). *Global Governance: In Search of Order without Government*. Tokyo: University of Tokyo Press, pp. 146–167.

Simai, M. (1994). The Governance of International Intergovernmental Organizations. In: *The Future of Global Governance: Managing Risk and Change in the International System*. Washington, D.C.: United States Institute of Peace Press, pp. 315–335.

Tashiro, K. (2002). Activities and Prospects of the International Civil Service. In: The Japan Association for United Nations Studies, ed. *The United Nations Secretariat as a Global Actor*. Tokyo: Kokusai Shoin.

Uchida, T. (2002). Introduction: Roles and Challenges of the UN Secretariat. In: The Japan Association for United Nations Studies, ed. *The United Nations Secretariat as a Global Actor*. Tokyo: Kokusai Shoin.

Electronic Publications

http://www.un.org/millennium/sg/report/ch1 (accessed November 1, 2004)
http://www.un.org/reform/chron (accessed October 1, 2004)
http://ceb.unsystem.org/ (accessed February, 2005)
http://www.un.org/aboutun/charter/index (accessed February, 2005)

Chapter 15

Global Governance and National Governance: How Mutually Exclusive?

Kalu N. Kalu

CONTENTS

Global Governance: An Enduring Myth?

In the new lexicon of international cooperation, the words "globalization" and "global governance" have become ubiquitous household names. But these are abstract concepts without qualitative meaning. Although "globalization" is often preceded by the understanding that information technology and digital communications have brought peoples and cultures more closely, the concept of "global governance" while idealistic in its presentation, still lacks the institutional context for its realization. Nation-states continue to abide by their own rules and have remained quite reticent in the protection of their sovereignties.

In the new mantra of global governance, how to integrate disparate national goals with the collective goal of the international community is the foremost challenge for public administration in the 21st century. And there is also the crucial problem of decision making: who decides how we govern and under what conditions? Among some of the models that have been utilized in various attempts at collective governance, especially the European Union in its formative years was the principle of unanimity on important decisions as well as in imposing sanctions. In a world caught between the defense of state sovereignty and supremacy in the international system, the very application of the principle of unanimity becomes a *liberum veto* that paralyzes the whole governance system and the underlying regimes which it represents.

To say that the world is unipolar and that it is becoming one through globalization is all too suggestive (Waltz, 1999, p. 10). The point remains that global or world politics has not taken over from national politics; trade and technology do not determine a single best way to organize a polity and its economy, and national systems, naturally, display a great deal of resilience (Waltz, 1999, p. 6). Without the national state, deeply rooted in the past, evolved through ages of growth, expressing profound feeling of peoples trained in the habit of common obedience, these organs of global governance would be merely mechanisms without a driving, controlling, or directing force (Pollard, 1918, p. 30). The world ends up with an artificial unity, which will sooner or later break down under the strain of natural forces or the nostalgia of distant nationalism.

The point is that people are not coming together in the political or cultural sense of the term. It is true that communication and transportation have facilitated transcultural immigration but it is yet to facilitate transcultural integration. There is also an equal tendency to mistake the global spread of multinational corporations (including McDonald's) as an indication of the "homogenization of cultures" (see Kettl, 2000, p. 492); rather what we have is the "globalization of markets." The two are different. Second, Kettl (2000) also points out that such cultural integration has been facilitated by the fact that "the Internet has helped to cement English as the global language and has fueled rapid communication" (Kettl, 2000, p. 492). However, the use of the Internet has not eliminated other native languages besides English, and many Internet softwares are also written in languages other than English. It can therefore be said that the use of the Internet, although it may have increased the frequency of cross-cultural communication, has not necessarily brought about the homogenization of cultures.

The same dialectic applies to international immigration encouraged by increasing and cheaper modes of transportation, communications, and commerce. As can be observed in the United States, many immigrant populations have been quite successful in carving out for themselves their own territory from the larger American real estate pie. They surround themselves with traditional and cultural artifacts from their home countries as a symbol of identity as well as affinity. The Chinatowns, the barrios, and various ethnic enclaves in many urban centers are good examples of resilient subcultures within the larger American cultural domain.

Ironically, much of the discussions on globalization have focused on the interdependence of markets, but not on how the integration of markets, politics, and culture can facilitate the creation of a regime for global governance. Though it has been much overlooked in the literature, there is a stark difference between globalization and global governance. Whereas globalization involves a greater level of structural (market, technological, communication) interdependence among societies and nations, global governance involves the functional integration of critical systems (politics, culture, policy) of national sovereignty. But the problem here is that "sovereignty is strongly egalitarian with respect to state rights and motivates states to resist external interference in their affairs. Hence, given that the institution of sovereignty alone would induce subordinate state actors to resist external control, the problem in "informal empire" (a global governance system) is to create identities and interests that subordinates would not otherwise have (Wendt & Friedheim, 1995, pp. 700–701).

Bureaucratic Flux: Test Cases in Administrative Complexity

Unfolding events of the post–Cold War period coupled with the rude awakening of September 11, 2001 has generated increased ambiguity about the course of globalization and what it portends for public administration and governance in an increasingly restless world. As political leaders ruminate over the proper context for a seemingly complex system of "global governance," the question remains: who governs the world, and how?

In May 2003, a subtle event in U.S. Iraq policy that may have gone unnoticed by many occurred. Retired Lt. General Jay Garner, who had served barely two months as the interim U.S. civilian administrator for Iraq, was replaced by Ambassador L. Paul Bremer, a career diplomat from the State Department. It was a palace coup that saw the State Department take over postwar Iraq policy from the Department of Defense. The underground war between the Defense and State Departments has ended and it was a tempered victory of "diplomacy" over violence or use of "force." It was also a recognition of the fact that the military lacks the administrative preparation to run the infrastructure of a civilian government, nor is it able to weave through the cultural and political milestones characteristic of Middle East politics. As Donald Rumsfeld licked his wounds, he invited Lt. General Garner to stand beside him at a Defense Department press briefing. It was a ceremonial and face-saving attempt to soothe the now-wounded ego of the poor retired general. He was already out of service and the rest was nothing more than an unseemly diplomatic nicety.

The lieutenant general can be said to have set himself up for the kind of subtle embarrassment he may have received as a result of being removed from Iraq. First, at the formal end of the war, he opted to run Iraq from a safe distance in Kuwait, and later from the southern city of Basra. He was quite late in moving to Baghdad to restore order and to establish his presence. This created a vacuum that enabled Ahmed Chalabi, the erstwhile leader of the Iraqi National Congress to beat him to it and move to Baghdad. Chalabi's credibility and legitimacy was already established in the eyes of the ordinary Iraqis and Lt. General Garner never recovered from it. Second, instead of staying in Baghdad to deal with the daily crisis and anarchy, he found time to travel to Kurdistan in the northern part of the country where there was already relative peace, and where he was already a recognizable face there as a result of his military expedition there in the post-1991 Gulf war period. While Baghdad burned, the picture of Lt. General Garner decorated with showers of praises and collars of flower rings by men, women, and children of Kurdistan may have roiled deep thinkers within the Bush administration, hence his fate was sealed. A few days later, he was recalled to Washington.

Having now taken over the reins as the Interim Civilian Administrator for Iraq, L. Paul Bremer (State Department) has to report to Donald Rumsfeld (Defense), while General Sanchez (the Army field commander in Iraq) had to be subservient or at least take policy orders from Bremer. Despite the rather political nature of this relationship, chaos and anarchy continued to dwell in Iraq as many more coalition soldiers continue to be killed. To get a handle on the situation, the Bush administration in October 2003 created what is called an Iraqi Stabilization Group headed by Condoleeza Rice (National Security Adviser) to take over postwar Iraq policy. Select deputies from the State and Defense departments were chosen to work under her as the administration's response to the rising level of volatility in Iraq. Many saw this as a sidelining of the State and Defense departments, whereas others saw it as a mild vote of no confidence in the way postwar Iraq administration was conducted. Others also saw it as another unnecessary layer of authority that can only hamstrung the military to do what is necessary to stop the seething guerrilla insurgency in Iraq. In the end, it was a triumph of the unitary actor model over the organizational and bureaucratic politics of the State and Defense departments that prevailed. It was the decision of the President to eventually reassign and combine specific responsibilities pertinent to his Iraq policy and how it should be governed. There are many lessons to be learned from the above event.

Administrative Norms and the Challenge of Global Governance

But by its various pronouncements, there was little doubt that the collective thinking of the Bush administration was firmly rooted in an earlier tradition. In a Fox News interview by Brit Hume on September 22, 2003, President Bush made a statement to the effect that "a free Iraq will be a significant dynamic in changing attitudes in the Middle East. Free societies are peaceful societies." It was believed that the democratic gene, once firmly planted in Iraq, would have a multiplier effect throughout the rest of the region and beyond. As the famous Yale historian John Lewis Gaddis (2003) pointed out in a PBS-sponsored analysis of the Bush doctrine, "this grand strategy is actually looking toward the culmination of the Wilsonian project of a world safe for democracy, even in the Middle East. And the long-term dimension of it reflects a kind of thinking not only about what do we have to do tomorrow or next week, but where do we want to come out at the end of this process. While this brand of thinking is not new, at least in its fundamental principles, it harbors a strong historical precedent."

The inauguration of Woodrow Wilson on March 4, 1913 as the 28th President of the United States was perhaps, the first in the history of this country when presidential public policy transcended the philosophical ideals of a scholar-diplomat. Such ideals not only projected a kind of liberal activism in domestic politics, but also served as a mantra for the pontification of an American global leadership and supremacy, and a world made peaceful for democracy. The period from 1914 to 1920 were challenging years that tested the viability as well as the inherent truism in what has now become the Wilsonian doctrine: a peaceful world founded on democracy, with American leadership and tutelage as the anchor. World War I started in Europe in 1914, but the United States at Wilson's insistence, maintained neutrality until it was broken two-and-half years later in 1917 after a long trail of diplomatic vacillations.

Although Wilson had argued that "belligerency would end all chances of American mediation in the conflict," the United States reluctantly entered the war on the side of the Allies against Germany, "simply to end the war and bring the carnage to an end." There was also the hope that ending the war would allow for a reasonable peace settlement and the reconstruction of a new world order — a thinking that eventually crystallized in the fated Draft Covenant for a League of Nations. In 1919, the Treaty of Versailles ended World War I, and the belligerents signed an armistice. But to be seen as a war to end all wars, Wilson utilized his diplomatic acumen to introduce a Draft Covenant for the creation of a League of Nations as part of the final resolution of the Treaty of Versailles. His ideal was derailed after the U.S Senate (led by the fiery Henry Cabot Lodge of Massachusetts) failed to garner enough votes to ratify both the Treaty of Versailles and the Draft League Covenant.

As a leader in foreign affairs, who guided the American people from provincialism toward world leadership and responsibilities, Wilson's internationalist idealism evolved out of his personal scholarship, the circumstances of the moment, and his own personal moral upbringing. He began to evince keen interest in foreign affairs for the first time in the late 1890s and early 1900s. He was reacting in part to new shifts in international power, as well as changes in American thinking about the future role of the United States in world affairs as a consequence of the Venezuelan controversy with Great Britain, the war with Spain, the extension of American interests to the Far East, and the acquisition of an overseas empire (Link, 1979, p. 3).

Though it lasted for approximately four months, Wilson saw especially the war with Spain (1898) as the end of American isolation and the inevitable beginning of a new era in which the United States would have to play a widening role in world politics. As he wrote later on in the 15th reprinting of the "Congressional Government," "much of the most important change to be noticed is the result of the war with Spain upon the lodgment and exercise of power within our federal system: the greatly increased power and opportunity for constructive statesmanship given the President, by the plunge into international politics and into the administration of distant dependencies, which has been that war's most striking and momentous consequence" (Wilson, 1956, pp. 22–23). "The American people were now neighbors to the world, whether they like it or not, and could not escape the coming challenges by ignoring them" (Link, 1979, p. 3).

Benign Hegemony: Governance in a Transformative World

In defeat, Wilson's internationalism left less of a sad postscript as opposed to an enduring challenge facing modern democracies in light of the realist politics of the international system. There are three ideals that remain even more relevant today: enshrining democracy among countries of the world, creating conditions for peaceful coexistence and cooperation (democratic peace), and the U.S. moral leadership in matters of international affairs. Despite its failures and chequered existence, the United Nations as a multilateral concept has come to be generally regarded as "vindication" of Wilson's idealism. With limited or no enforcement mechanism, and founded on a liberal doctrine of international peace and cooperation, it has nonetheless proven to lack the "collective" capacity to enforce many of its crucial resolutions.

The United Nations has harbored a historic inclination to avoid the use of force unless prodded by a powerful interest behind the scene. Because rules governing international behavior are generally flaunted by member states when matters of state sovereignty and national interest collide with the collective will of the international community, the United Nations can be effective only to the extent that member states are willing to grant it. The abstract (psychological) notion of the United Nations as a conglomerate of nations-states serves more to temper the independent excesses of member states than any expectation of punishment after-the-fact. In the contemporary world that we live, there are ample reasons to come to this conclusion. The United Nations would probably not have sanctioned (due to disagreement within the membership) the Korean War without the singular commitment of the United States; the same applies to the civil war in the Congo in the 1960s, as well as the Persian Gulf War of 1991. Although the United Nations was unable to inject itself wholly into the Balkan conflict, the United States went in under the umbrella of North Atlantic Treaty Organization (NATO) forces. Before that, it was Somalia where the United States took on the leadership role whereas the United Nations played a secondary role.

As the Cold War came to an end, many regions of the world have suddenly unearthed deep-seated animosities between states, within states, and among ethnic groups, such that we now have more regional conflicts than we did in the period of the Cold War. In his *The Coming Anarchy*, Robert Kaplan (1994) was quite poignant in his prophetic assessment of the post–Cold War international regime. He points out that in a "moonscape" over which peoples have migrated and settled in patterns that obliterate borders, the end of the Cold War will bring on a cruel process of natural selection among existing states. No longer will these states be so firmly propped up by the West or the Soviet Union. Also in his article *Why We Will Soon Miss the Cold War*, John Mearsheimer (2002) bemoaned the fact that the rigid bipolar alliance structure which sustained the Cold War, and invariably the "long peace" for the past 45 years would now be replaced by a multipolar system of power asymmetries; and power asymmetries (in the absence of a hegemon) more often than not invite wars. In the ensuing flux and uncertainty of the international system, as nation-states come together, as national interests collide and break away, who governs and how becomes of utmost importance.

There is certainly a case to be made for a model founded on the concept of benign hegemony since in fundamental ways, some of this may have already become evident. The United States is the only country that can organize and lead a military coalition, as it did in Iraq and the Balkans. Some states have little choice but to participate, partly because of the pressure the strong can bring to bear on the weak and partly because of the needs of the latter (Waltz, 1999, p. 10). Where the United Nations has failed in the governance and enforcement of international resolutions and regimes, the United States seems to have succeeded through benign hegemony in "taming" state appetite for nuclear weaponry and proliferation (Libya, Iran, North Korea), or by outright use of force as leader of a coalition of countries (Iraq, Afghanistan, the Balkans). Ironically, she may have (at least by default) become the "quasi-hegemon" of the contemporary international system — a possibility that, among other things, so worried the U.S. Senate as it voted in 1919 to kill President Wilson's vision for the League of Nations. The international leadership that Wilson had idealized for the United States can in fundamental ways be amenable to the doctrine of benign hegemony. But to do that would require a modification of Wilson's concept of the administrative state in light of the exigencies of the moment, and the role of public administration in adapting to changes within and between nations in the international environment.

The Political Context: Upholding the Nation-State

Due to technological advances in communication, the decline in the number of centralized economies, a wave of liberal democracies and free-market economies emerging in Eastern Europe and South-East Asia, the rising economic punch of the European Union, the teething economic pains in Russia, and the rise of China and her "abbreviated" brand of capitalism, many have argued that the world is moving toward a politically borderless and highly interdependent global economy that will foster prosperity, international cooperation, and world peace through democracy. A corollary of this position is that the American economic and political system has become the model for the world (Mansbach & Rhodes, 2003, p. 288). But how would the emerging model be governed?

Although most "politicians have grasped the policy implication of the democratic peace theory, using it to justify actions, even military actions, which are intended to create or defend democracies" (Ziegler, 2000, p. 140), this premise fits right into the corner of the current Bush administration's policy toward authoritarian nondemocratic regimes like Saddam Hussein's Iraq and others similarly disposed. In a Russert NBC "Meet the Press" program held on February 8, 2004, Tim Russert posed a question to President Bush at the Oval Office: "Mr. President, why are we (U.S. Soldiers) now engaging in nation-building in Iraq?" President Bush responded: "Our troops are trained to fight and win wars, and therefore to make peace possible. But to make peace possible, it is permissible to engage in nation-building. In the end, a free Iraq will change the world; a free Iraq will make it possible for our kids to grow up in a safer world."

Accepting the fact that the new Bush doctrine mirrors elements of the Wilsonian democratic peace idealism, in the sense that the virtue of peaceful coexistence among nation-states is a desirable end, they both differ in how the democratic peace ought to be secured. Wilson's belief in the pacific resolution of international disputes, the use of war as a last resort, was severely criticized as both timid and unrealistic in light of the realist propensities in the behavior of states. While "his conviction that all error resided in governments and that people were always and everywhere virtuous led him into some of the gravest follies of the Paris Peace Conference; the point remains that in much of the 20th-century world, "democracies are (were), by and large, naturally pacific and mutually compatible in ways that dictatorships, personal or collective, are (were) not" (Nicholas, 1968, pp. 184–185). It was the same sense of realism that led to much of the early criticisms of the Wilsonian doctrine.

But unlike the Wilsonian doctrine, "the current U.S. National Security strategy does not envision that U.S. interests and general world stability can be safeguarded without the presence and sometimes active application of American political, economic, and military power worldwide. Thus, embodied in the strategy is a clear expansion of the demands placed on the military, in responding to terrorism abroad and ensuring the security of the American homeland, in maintaining American preeminence as a military power, and in preempting attacks against the United States by terrorists and rogue states, particularly attacks that might involve weapons of mass destruction" (Davis & Shapiro, 2003, p. 8). Although it departs from past doctrines in its succinct statement of the intention of the United States to act militarily, and if necessary, alone to preemptively protect the interests and security of the country, Davis and Shapiro (2003) also point out that the goal reflects the central notion that U.S. leadership presents an opportunity as well as a duty to use American power and influence to make the world safe for democracy.

As the only superpower in world politics, the United States has found itself in a quandary: How to reconcile issues of domestic politics in the context of playing a pragmatic role in an international system characterized by flux and violence? Traditional issues of foreign policy, security, and defense remain the province of nation-states, so too are macroeconomic and monetary policies (Ohmae, 1993, p. 80), as well as taxation and public investment needed to provide the necessary infrastructure and incentives for managing the welfare state. Some Americans believe that the United States benignly provides a necessary minimum of management of the international system and that because of its moderation, other states will continue to appreciate, or at least accept, its services (Waltz, 1999, p. 11). However, continued appreciation of United States' role in the international system very much depends on the mix of models it applies in doing so. Certainly, time has changed and the pacific approach to internationalism which Wilson employed in the early 1900s may not be as expedient for dealing with most of today's circumstances; especially in an era when foreign, economic, and defense policies play equal roles in shaping the contours and direction of national security policy.

The Economic Context: Global Market Regime

The idea of economic globalization is a concept that captures key developments in international trade, finance, and foreign direct investment by transnational corporations (TNCs). As Mansbach and Rhodes (2003, p. 284) point out, since the end of World War II, international trade has greatly expanded and has become a much more important factor in both domestic and international economic affairs. Whereas the volume of international trade had grown by only 0.5 percent annually between 1913 and 1948, it grew at an annual rate of 7 percent from 1948 to 1973. Nonetheless and over the course of the postwar era, trade has grown from 7 to 21 percent of total world income, as the value of world trade has increased from $57 billion in 1947 to $6 trillion in the 1990s. In the course of these developments, most trade barriers have declined, various multilateral trade regimes like the General Agreement on Trade and Tariffs (GATT), the Uruguay Round, World Trade Organization (WTO), and many others have been negotiated among nation-states. The European Union has emerged as an imperial economic market with no tariffs, open trade borders, and a uniform currency to facilitate trade and policy coordination between member states.

However, when we talk about globalization, it rarely suggests that national boundaries are shifting nor are state policies becoming merged. Rather most of what we see is an increasing level of communication or transactions between nation-states coordinated not necessarily by a uniformity of interests, but by a regime of rules anchored within the market system. We refer to this as the free market or free enterprise doctrine — characterized by various clichés like open borders, antiprotectionism, free trade, most favored nation status, and so. The governance mechanism that holds this relationship together is not based on institutional frameworks but on an almost universal acceptance that the market doctrine is supreme both in the creation and in the distribution of wealth. At the center of this relationship is the critical role of TNCs and their ability to demonstrate visible presence and independence in almost every part of the globe.

For the fact that the market regime that govern, the operation of TNCs operates (at least in theory) outside of the political domain of nation-states, it becomes difficult to develop a uniform rule to check potential excesses. "Although states have a variety of weapons they can use against TNCs, among them taxation, capital controls, regulation, and nationalization, they rarely do so because they need corporate investment. Hence when the interests of states and that of TNCs collide, both may be losers" (Mansbach, 2000, p. 199). Even when they have no political intent, corporate decisions may have important political consequences, over which governments have little control (Mansbach, 2000, p. 201). Although there is a general agreement on the increased role of the market and of globalization as integrating forces in an emerging global community, there is growing ambivalence regarding the ability of the market to maintain international peace and global order.

Many have argued that the only thing that has changed is that the proclivity of nation-states to compete with each other has only shifted, but this time, into the economic arena. Because most countries in the developing world are not able to compete on the same economic plane as the industrialized countries of the West, economic globalization therefore leads to increasing levels of poverty, unemployment, indebtedness, inequality among nation-states, environmental degradation, and international currency speculation to the detriment of poor countries. Even the postwar international rules and institutions created within the Bretton Woods system have also come under intense criticism as being heavy-handed and overly paternalistic when it comes to assisting poor countries to properly manage their economic policies.

Whereas critics point to the fact that the West's gain in the context of globalization has been at the expense of developing countries, the already meager share of the global income of the poorest people in the world has dropped from 2.3 to 1.4 percent in the last decade, and continues to decline. Hence, many poor countries have become, not participants, but spectators in the international surge of economic globalization. Even among industrialized countries and as the process of international economic integration takes place against the backdrop of retreating governments and diminished social obligations, the need for social insurance for the vast majority of the population continues to grow (Rodrik, 1997, p. 21). However, "it is one mistake for government to restrict and distort market activity, reducing competition and perpetuating privileges; it is another to assume that market forces will automatically create opportunities for those at the margin" (Birdsall, 1998, p. 80). "The bottom line is that international trade and open markets are less of a problem than worldwide changes in the technology of production that favor skilled workers everywhere" (Birdsall, 1998, p. 79).

The Shifting Phases of Globalization

For some, the concept of globalization continues to redefine itself. In his *The Rise of the Region State*, Kenichi Ohmae (1993) argues that the nation-state has become an unnatural, even dysfunctional, unit for organizing human activity and managing economic behavior in a borderless world. He argues that on the global economic map the lines that now matter are those defining what may be called "region states" — the boundaries of which are imposed not by political fiat, but by the deft but invisible hand of the global market for goods and services. Region states are natural economic zones, and represent no threat to the political borders of any nation, nor does it require any taxpayer's money to defend such borders. Ohmae points to the North American Free Trade Area (NAFTA) between the United States, Canada, and Mexico, the Association of South East Asian Nations (ASEAN), Hong Kong and the Pearl River Delta, the special economic zones in China, the growth triangle of Singapore and her neighboring Indonesian islands, Japanese manufacturing and the Mississippi Valley in the United States, the distinct cross-border economic units such as those in northern Italy, Wales, Catalonia, Alsace-Lorraine, or Baden-Wurttemberg.

On the other hand, Richard Rosecrance (1996) sees globalization as evolving into what he calls a "virtual state" — a state that has downsized its territorially based production capability. The virtual state is a country whose economy is reliant on mobile factors of production. It is an agile entity operating in twin jurisdictions: abroad and at home. The state no longer commands resources as it did in mercantilist yesteryears, but negotiates with foreign and domestic capital and labor to lure them into its own economic sphere and stimulate its growth. Rather than amass land, capital, and labor, virtual states set strategy and invest in people. Hence, in formulating economic strategy, the virtual state recognizes that its own production does not have to take place at home; equally, it may play host to the capital and labor of other nations. Examples of virtual states are Hong Kong, Korea, Japan, Germany, Switzerland, Holland, Singapore, and to an extent England.

But in both cases of the "regional" and "virtual states," economics serves as the driving governance mechanism. Because international market competition still retains the inherent tensions between the quest for state supremacy and maintenance of a global order, states will be less reluctant to invoke protectionist policies to protect their domestic economy and their relative position in the structure of the international economy. To the extent that domestic politics lacks the jurisdiction to alleviate global problems, states are more likely to strike out on their own when national interests collide with the collective interest of the global community. Hence, the credibility of any global governance mechanism must be seen in relation to how each state views it as advancing its own interest while limiting that of others in the system.

Conclusion: After Globalization, Then What?

Globalization raises many diverse issues, including culture, national identity, and the structure and governance of international economic organizations. But as increasing levels of interdependence are sought either through commerce, technology and communications, or through bilateral and multilateral regimes, there are still lingering questions as to the ultimate benefit of globalization, and if so, to whom and how much? Like any powerful movement for change, globalization encounters resistance — from religious fundamentalists to labor unions and their allies, anti-Americanists, and everywhere from cultural traditionalists (Waltz, 2000, p. 47).

It may be true that economic interdependence, cultural and environmental interdependence can bring states and societies closer, but in the same way that this could be beneficial, it could also be detrimental. "Economic growth that states seek in order to enhance the well-being of their people often leads to environmental degradation and loss of biodiversity that endangers everyone" (Payne & Nassar 2003, p. 112). Although economic interdependence essentially reinforces the asymmetrical nature of trade relations between rich and poor nations, it also has not abated the rise in relative poverty and deprivation among many nations in the developing world. On the cultural level, many societies in the developing world have begun to see aspects of economic interdependence as subtle forms of cultural hegemony and Westernization, as they seek overt steps to reaffirm their authentic native culture. Even in the developed countries of Europe and the Americas, the sudden rise in immigration from the developing countries has generated tensions that resonate both ethnic and religious overtones. Whereas the long-term consequences for the preservation of Western civilization are becoming more obvious, yet the arguments remain muted.

The jury is still out as to what globalization means and what it will lead to many years from now. While the world is far away from a perfect integration of markets, services, and factors of production, sometimes the simple existence of borders slows down and can even paralyze this integration, or at best give it "flavors" and "colors" of the dominant state (Hoffman, 2002, p. 108). In an ironic way, globalization involves everything around us, from the dissemination of Hollywood movies, the role of international news media, multinational national banking institutions, mega-international manufacturing corporations, international educational institutions, international airline conglomerates, are all agencies of globalization. Due to the essential differences in the nature and role of these agents, we are more often than not confronted with a sense of ambiguity in our understanding of globalization, hence the possibility for its regulation and governance.

But among the most critical challenges to globalization is cross-national immigration and how it can be managed. For the past few decades, there has been an increasing level of emigration from Asia and the Middle East to Western and Eastern Europe, and from Central and South America to the United States and Canada. Because modern immigrants seek to define and maintain their cultural identities in their host countries, they seek adaptation rather than assimilation. Over time, as the host culture is slowly undermined and made to accommodate itself to an "alien" culture, the possibility for the evolution of hybrid cultures in many host countries and the disappearance of authentic native cultures becomes more real than imagined. Because this has remained at the core of state sovereignty and national identity, what makes a person German, French, Swiss, Dutch, Polish, Slovak, Italian, or Canadian may be in danger of being lost. Hybrid cultures will continue to evolve over time, and could essentially, represent the last stage of globalization.

As new immigrants refuse to completely abandon their heritage to the attraction of Western civilization, their insistence on remaining true to their tradition and faith will emerge as the new source of global conflict — but this time not between states but within states. As their population increase, they will over time acquire enough voting power to reshape the political fate of their host countries in fundamental ways that can only provoke greater resistance and a sense of cultural loss and ambiguity in the host populations. Globalization may, in fact, lead to more conflicts among and within societies. The current cultural tension in France as it struggles to maintain its secularity in the face of Muslim advocacy for religious preferences has sent shock waves to other countries in Western Europe of the impending crisis they will face with an increasing Muslim population. Rising unemployment in many industrial countries has also led to resentment against immigrant populations who flock these countries for employment and other economic and welfare opportunities. The choice for governments and public administrators is to device methods for managing the assimilation or coexistence of immigrant cultures into their societies or to seek their integration in such a way that inherent tensions are not manifested in overt backlash and cultural conflict between native and foreigner.

It is rather premature when some of the literature (Ohmae, 1993; Rosecrance, 1996; Friedman, 1999) seeks to celebrate the presumed demise of the nation-state. Even if such an eventuality becomes real, it should be a source of concern for the world. The simple fact is that state institutions have historically provided the foundations for the governance mechanisms needed to bring societies and economies together. "The sovereign state with fixed borders has proved to be the best (as well as enduring) organization for keeping peace internally and fostering the conditions for economic well-being. States perform essential political, social, and economic functions (macroeconomic and regulatory policies) than other forms of organizations; national politics, not international markets, account for many international economic developments" (Waltz, 2000, p. 51). In an ironic way, "while the age of globalization may well be defined in part by challenges to the nation-state, but it is still states and government — by the practices they adopt, the arrangements they enter into, and the safety nets they provide — that will determine whether we exploit or squander the potential of this era" (Haass & Litan, 1998, p. 5). It is true that there have been various benefits credited to globalization, but like every other revolutionary change, and at some point, it will generate its own critical mass as it reaches a state of diminishing returns, and only then, will the triumphs and failures become more manifest. In the absence of any other sovereign authority and without the central role of the state and its institutions, globalization would be ungovernable.

References

Birdsall, N. 1998. Life is Unfair: Inequality in the World. *Foreign Policy* 111, Summer, pp. 76–93.

Davis, L.E. and J. Shapiro. 2003. Introduction. In: L.E. Davis and J. Shapiro, eds. *The U.S. Army and the New National Security Strategy*. Santa Monica, CA: Rand, pp. 1–5.

Friedman, T.L. 1999. *The Lexus and the Olive Tree*. New York: Farrar, Straus & Giroux.

Gaddis, J.L. 2003. Assessing the Bush Doctrine. http://www.pbs.org/wgbg/pages/frontline/shows/iraq/themes/assess.html

Haass, R.N. and R.E. Litan. 1998. Globalization and Its Discontents: Navigating the Dangers of a Tangled World. *Foreign Affairs* 77(3): 2–5.

Hoffman, S. 2002. Clash of Globalizations. *Foreign Affairs* 81(14): 104–113.

Kaplan, R.J. 1994. The Coming Anarchy. *The Atlantic Monthly* 273(2): 44–76.

Kettl, D.F. 2000. The Transformation of Governance: Globalization, Devolution, and the Role of Government. *Public Administration Review* 60(6): 488–497.

Link, A.S. 1979. *Woodrow Wilson: Revolution, War, and Peace*. Arlington Heights, IL: AHM Publishing Co.

Mansbach, R.W. 2000. *The Global Puzzle: Issues and Actors in World Politics*. Boston, MA: Houghton-Mifflin.

Mansbach, R.W. and E. Rhodes. 2003. *Global Politics in a Changing World: A Reader*. Boston, MA: Houghton-Mifflin.

Mearsheimer, J.J. 2002. Why We Will Soon Miss the Cold War. In: R.K. Betts, ed. *Conflict After the Cold War: Arguments on Causes of War and Peace*. New York: Longmans, pp. 17–23.

Nicholas, H.G. 1968. Building on the Wilsonian Heritage. In: A.S. Link, ed. *Woodrow Wilson: A Profile*. New York: Hill & Wang, pp. 178–192.

Ohmae, K. 1993. The Rise of the Region State. *Foreign Affairs* 72(2): 78–98.

Payne, R.J. and J.R. Nassar. 2003. *Politics and Culture in the Developing World: The Impact of Globalization*. New York: Longman/Pearson Education.

Pollard, A.F. 1918. *The League of Nations: An Historical Argument*. Oxford, UK: The Clarendon Press.

Rodrik, D. 1997. Sense and Nonsense in the Globalization Debate. *Foreign Policy* 107 (Summer): 19–37.

Rosecrance, R. 1996. The Rise of the Virtual State. *Foreign Affairs* 75(4): 45–61.

Waltz, K.W. 1999. Globalization and Governance. 1999 James Madison Lecture, PS Online (American Political Science Association). http://www.apsanet.org/PS/dec99/waltz.cfm

Waltz, K.W. 2000. Globalization and American Power. *The National Interest*, Spring: 46–56.

Wendt, A. and D. Friedheim. 1995. Hierarchy Under Anarchy: Informal Empire and the East German State. *International Organization* 49(4): 689–721.

Wilson, W. 1956. *Congressional Government*. New York: Meridian Books. Also Boston, MA: Houghton-Mifflin, 1885.

Ziegler, D.W. 2000. *War, Peace, and International Politics*. New York: Addison Wesley Longman, Inc.

Chapter 16

Good Governance: Its Theory and Practice in India

S.R. Maheshwari

CONTENTS

Governance is essentially a value-laden normative concept, defined as "how well do governments govern" or "does the government serve us well"? The *Oxford English Dictionary* defines it as "the action or manner of governing"; according to the same source, the term refers to the contents. The Webster's Encyclopedic Unabridged Dictionary of the English Language defines governance as a method or system of government or management. Good governance has become an exciting theme in India since the 1990s, having been originally popularized by international donor agencies like the

World Bank and the International Monetary Fund. Today, no discussion of contemporary public administration in the country is expected to be complete without a reference of good governance though the word has been in usage for a much longer time. The concept of good governance was known to India since ancient times. Good governance found its articulation in the world's oldest full treatise on public administration. In *Arthasashtra*, written about three to four centuries before Christ, Kautilya writes:

> In the happiness of his subjects lies his happiness in their welfare his welfare, whatever pleases himself he shall not consider as good, but whatever pleases his subjects he shall consider as good.[1]

The precise term "governance" is said to have entered the English language as early as 1628.[2] What is more, a distinction, though subtle, was made between government and governance which is underlined in the observation made as far back as in the year 1701: "Wise princes ought not to be admired for their government but governance." Governance is a qualitative concept whereas government is a physical entity to say so. The difference between the two can be conveyed more sharply by an observation like "India should have less of government but more of governance." Governance claims a complex of traits and includes both procedural and substantive formulations.

Good Governance Defined

The concept of good governance was exported to India by the international donor agencies like the World Bank and the International Monetary Fund which virtually made it a precondition for the monetary aid that India was desperately seeking in the 1980s and the 1990s even though it was implicit in the Indian social milieu.

Good governance must necessarily seek its base in a set of formally proclaimed structural attributes such as written constitution, rule of law, judicial review, natural justice, limited government — the familiar armoury of western liberal thought incorporated in India's system of governance as defined in their own imperial style by the British colonial rulers and later championed by the nationalist freedom movement. The list enumerating the components of good governance is not static.

More recent items co-opted in the concept of good governance include judicial reform, simplification of laws, and their subsidiary creations, namely

---

[1] R. Shamasastry; *Kautilya's Arthasashtra*, Mission Press, Mysore, 1929, Chapter xix, sloka 39, p. 38.
[2] The *Oxford English Dictionary*, Vol. IV.

subordinate legislation, property rights, contract enforcement, etc. Potentially, good governance covers the entire public sector reform — "all its aspects".[3] Because the structural adjustment program was underway since the 1990s, good governance incorporates reform in the private sector as well. It is not confined to the central government in New Delhi but extends to state and local governments as well, the country having a federal constitution.

Good governance legitimately takes its place within the ordering framework of the supreme document of the land, namely the Constitution. The Constitution of India, enforced in 1950, and in operation ever since can be properly understood only in the context of the long-drawn national freedom movement under the leadership of Mahatma Gandhi (1869–1948). To mobilize all sections of the society and to keep the national movement in momentum the fight for political freedom had to be made broad-based and comprehensive by articulating wide-ranging programs of economic and social reform. The various pledges made to the society, some of them apparently inconsistent but effectively overlooked in the overriding national urge for unity, essential for waging the struggle against the most powerful colonial power in human history, found their way into the Constitution. The ideology articulated during the freedom struggle may be said to broadly fall into three categories — liberal, socialistic, and Gandhian. The liberal articulations laid stress on rule of law, parliamentary democracy, secularism, freedom of the press, federalism, fundamental rights, etc. The socialist ideology was reflected in the demand for public ownership of means of production, planning as the mode of national development, and prevention of concentration of wealth in the society. The Gandhian philosophy also influenced the freedom movement and its mobilizational devices, with its principal ingredients like village panchayats, village and cottage industry, prohibition, crusade against untouchability, etc. All these streams of ideology were contending for inclusion and recognition in the Constitution of India, though in practice the Gandhian ideology proved to be a minor symphony in the overall orchestra with its dominant note on liberalism. At the time of constitution-making no one realized the contradiction in the ideological baggage fondly believing that the essential nobility of man would be the effective solution to any problems encountered.

The elaborate scale on which the ideological baggage has been spelled out must not allow one to think that the Constitution of India conditions the society to one particular ideology whether capitalistic, socialistic, or Gandhian. The ideology orchestrated in the Constitution's preamble,

---

[3]International Monetary Fund: *Good Governance: The IMF's Role*, International Monetary Fund, 1997, Washington, D.C., p. v.

fundamental rights, directive principles of state policy, and its other parts, to put it crudely, is very much like a cafeteria with enough options to pick and choose from, thus capable of accommodating all political parties whatever be their ideological persuasion. The goal of the state occupying the commanding heights of the economy was promoted by this Constitution as it is presently fulfilling the goal of market capitalism.

The concept of governance was thus not unknown to the nationalist leadership in India. Mahatma Gandhi used to talk about *swaraj* (independence) as well as "*suraj*" (good governance) as the twin goals of freedom movement. However, the term "governance" was not much in use when the Constitution was in the making. The Constitution has not used the term even once in its preamble. Indeed, the Constitution has used "governance" only once — in its directive principles of state policy. Article 37 says: "The provisions contained in this part shall not be enforceable by any court, but the principles therein laid down are nevertheless fundamental in the governance of the country and it shall be the duty of the state to apply these principles in making laws." The major components of good governance enumerated in the directive principles of state policy are:

1. Right to an adequate means of livelihood (Article 39(1))
2. The ownership and control of the material resources of the community are so distributed as best to subserve the common good (Article 39)
3. The operation of the economic system does not result in the concentration of wealth and means of production to the common detriment
4. Equal pay for equal work for both men and women is ensured
5. The health and strength of workers, men and women, and the children of tender age are not abused and the citizens are not forced by economic necessity to enter avocations unsuited to their age or strength
6. Children are given opportunities and facilities to grow in a healthy manner and in conditions of freedom and dignity and that childhood and youth are protected against exploitation and against moral and material abandonment (Article 39 of the Constitution)

The directive principles of the state policy emphasize the "content" part of good governance. It must be noted that in 1977 one additional item was added to the list of these parameters of governance — the item on child.[4]

A discussion of the constitutional provisions about good governance would remain incomplete without a mention of the fundamental duties[4] though not a part of the Constitution as originally drafted and was inserted

[4]Article 51A of the Constitution of India.

in it by the Constitution (42nd Amendment) Act, 1976. Good governance enjoins duties on citizens to renounce practices derogatory to the dignity of women, to protect environment, to have compassion for living creatures, and to safeguard public property and abjure violence, to name a few. Good governance includes transparency, accountability, citizens' responsiveness, and participation; the list is only illustrative. Good governance is a holistic concept and a shortfall in one area of administrative life is enough to nullify the otherwise adorable work done in other larger spheres. Good governance is an indivisible exercise precisely because life itself is indivisible. Regular electricity — electricity failure a common experience in modern times — for instance, is apt to negate good governance, leaving jarring notes in the society. The weakest link in administration determines the strength of the chain.

Additional Agenda of Good Governance

The notion of governance was for a long time restricted to the exclusive domain of government. Since the 1980s, the state started baring its fundamental inadequacies and limitations — a discovery which has led to a serious search for alternative and complementary institutions and processes of governance. Non-governmental organizations (NGOs), including people's organizations, the business sector, etc., are perceived as being alternatives to the career bureaucracy and indeed many of them have begun playing varying levels of roles particularly in the delivery of basic services to the citizens. Most conspicuous in this search has been the entry of the private sector. Privatization is a favored direction of structural reform that is increasingly advocated since the 1990s. Thus, there are many partners in the process of governance today and its dimensions have been steadily enlarging. Since 1990s India is leaning less and less on direct government intervention. This must not make one conclude that government is left with virtually no brief. It cannot fold up and leave those below the poverty line — who constitute nearly 30 to 40 percent (estimates vary) of the country's population — to their unenviable fate. About 250 million people consume less than three fourths of the needed calories whereas another 59 million take less than half of their daily calorie requirement.[5]

Unemployment in the country is another acute problem. India has a backlog of nearly 18.7 million unemployed and another 125 million people likely to enter the labor market between 1996 and 2010.[6] The employment opportunities are severally limited, posing a serious problem

[5]Report of the Fifth Central Pay Commission, 1997, p. 91.
[6]Ibid., p. 91.

to governance. It will continue to have an interventionist role for the deprived sections of the society. Liberalization also necessitates considerable strengthening of the regulatory role of the state. India will need a large regulatory bureaucracy on the broad pattern of independent regulatory commissions of the United States. The country has already set up multi-member bodies like the Telecommunication Regulatory Authority of India, Competition Commission, etc., and more such bodies are likely to be set up in the years to come. Also, the state in India has a significant role in ensuring wider diffusion of technologies developed elsewhere. This is especially true for small- and medium-sized enterprises, which have limited access to such technologies. For this, information systems at their disposal must be used to permit their diffusion to domestic industries.

History of Good Governance in India

It is pertinent to assert that it is not for the first time that the subject of good governance is examined in India. The problem of good governance (read administrative reform) is discussed in each five-year plan as well as by parliamentary committees. Besides, the Government of India has appointed no less than 34 committees[7] devoted to good governance making a large number of recommendations. The Administrative Reforms Commission, set up in 1966 and which worked till 1970, carried out a comprehensive examination of Indian administration in its various sectors and at various levels making as many as 581 recommendations. What is frustrating about

[7]These Administrative Reforms Committees are as follows:

1. The Reorganization of Central Government (Richard Tottenham) 1945–1946. (It visualizes independent India; hence its inclusion)
2. The Advisory Planning Board (K.C. Neogi), 1949
3. The Secretariat Reorganization Committee (Girja Shankar Bajpai), 1947
4. The Central Pay Commission (Varadachariar)
5. The Economy Committee (Kasturbhai Lalbhai)
6. The Reorganization of Machinery Government (Gopalswami Ayyangar), 1949
7. Estimates Committee's Second Report on Reorganization of the Secretariat and Departments of the Government of India (First Lok Sabha), 1950–1951
8. Report on Public Administration (A.D. Gorwala), 1951
9. Report on the Efficient Conduct of State Enterprises (Gorwala), 1951
10. The Machinery of Government — improvement of Efficiency (R.A. Gopalaswamy), 1952
11. Public Administration in India — Report of a survey (Paul H. Appeleby), 1953
12. Estimates Committee's Ninth Report on Administration, Financial and other Reforms (First Lok Sabha), 1953–1958
13. Re-examination of India's administrative System with special reference to administration of Government's Industrial Commercial Enterprises (Paul H. Appleby), 1956; The Railway Corruption Enquiry Committee (J.B. Kripalani), 1955; The Public Service (Qualification for Recruitment) Committee (A. Ramaswami Mudaliar), 1956

India's quest for good governance is not dearth of solutions — recommendations on good governance are as numerous as are leaves in Vallombrosa — but a paralytic reluctance to act on them. Indian story of efforts toward good governance enjoys notoriously low credibility, precisely, because of a low level of implementation.

Prerequisite to Good Governance

Good governance presupposes a wide-ranging package of administrative reform. This must make the reader think about the prerequisites of good governance. In order to be effective, quest for good governance must seek the prior fulfillment of certain conditions, some of which are referred to briefly here. Foremost is the assured availability of sustained political support by the Prime Minister and his cabinet. The reform effort, moreover, must be led by most competent persons: it must be led by star performers possessing clear vision and familiar with objectives of reform and its priorities. As the agenda of good governance is new, even novel in nature, it requires undivided attention of its managers. The portfolio of good governance must become the full time job of carefully selected public functionaries. Equally, such persons must stay in their job for a fairly long time and must not be transferred out quickly. They should also be given a

---

14. The Commission of Enquiry on Emoluments and Conditions of service of Central Government Employees (Jagannath Das), 1959
15. The Staff Welfare Review Committee (Fate Singh), 1961
16. Indian and State Administrative Services and Problems of District Administration (V.T. Krishnamachari), 1952
17. The Committee on Prevention of Corruption (K.Santhanman), 1964
18. Estimates Committee's 93rd Report on Public Services (Third Lok Sabha), 1966
19. The Administrative Reform Commission, 1966–1970. (it submitted 20 reports. Besides, there were study team reports)
20. The Third Pay Commission, 1973
21. The Committee on Recruitment and Selection (D.S. Kothari)
22. The Economic Reform Commission (L.K. Jha), 1983
23. The Fourth Central Pay Commission, (P.N. Shinghal), 1986
24. The National Police Commission (Dharma Vira), 1979
25. The Commission on Centre–State Relation (Justice K.S. Sarkaria), 1987
26. The Committee to Review the Scheme of the Civil Service Examination (Satish Chandra), 1989
27. The NDC Committee on Austerity (Biju Patnaik), 1990
28. The Tax Reforms Committee (Raja J. Chelliah), 1991
29. The Central Fifth Pay Commission (Pandian), 1993
30. The Strategic Management Group Task Force, 1997
31. The Central Expenditure Commission (Geetakrishnan), 2001
32. The Committee to Review in-service Training of the IAS Officers (Alagh), 2003
33. The Surendre Nath Committee on Assesment of Performance Evaluation in Civil Service, (2003)
34. The Committee on the Civil Service Reform (P.C. Hota), 2004

certain measure of flexibility, in action. Reform efforts must secure high-level employees' participation, and even support. It would prove the feasibility of reform if the reform proposals are first tested in pilot situations and then adopted all over the social space. Most importantly, good governance would remain a mere dream if it is not accompanied by appropriate attitudinal and behavioral change on the part of all the players engaged in the exercise. Also, governance cannot be strengthened merely by the reform of the career civil service. This must be underlined. It requires political revamping as an essential requisite of good governance of which an important component is a minimum political stability in the country. Since 1990s, India has entered an era of coalitional polities with Damocles' sword hanging over the executive, which inclines the government of the day to make all kinds of compromises detrimental to the cause of good governance. To save the country from political instability, India should borrow from the German constitution the concept of constructive vote of no confidence under which the legislature must elect the successor prime minister while dismissing a ministry. One must equally consider whether it is not prudent to delink membership of the council of ministers from legislative membership as in France. This would ensure at least two very powerful advantages. One, the chief executive would have greater freedom to choose his political crew and secondly, there would not be a high-pitch scramble for the legislative seats as at present. To clarify further, this measure would not in the least undermine the role and place of parliament in essential matters. Parliament would continue to control the public purse and legislation. What is proposed is the assertion and acceptance of the principle of incompatibility between the legislative membership and ministerial office. When these prerequisites have been fulfilled and the required mental discipline assured, ground is ready to initiate the reform exercise. It must be made absolutely clear that reform proposals made here constitute a package, constituting a single unbreakable unit traveling together.

Barriers to Good Governance

The Constitution, it is our firm conviction, is a noble document. Fifty-four years of its functioning show certain shortcomings, inadequacies, and gaps, which must be attended to. India's main worry is that those who are operating the Constitution — both the elected and the selected — lack proper skills, attitudes, and behavioral orientation. The human material operating the Constitution is not up to the mark to fulfil the dreams of the constitution-makers, which is perhaps India's saddest shame. No constitution is a shade better than the men and women operating it. The most disturbing problem confronting Indian politics is its criminalization confirmed by the Vohra Committee Report. The growing nexus between the bureaucracy, the politician, the businessman, and the criminal poses the greatest threat to both democracy and good governance in the society today. The country's legislative chambers are for some time showing signs of becoming the sanctuaries of criminals. The criminal-turned politician — or criminal-cum-politician — poses a direct threat to good governance, for under the latter's supremacy his rightful place should be the jail. He, therefore, leaves no stone unturned in frustrating its installation despite the occasional rhetoric he indulges in. Politicians in India constitute the country's elite, locally known as the VIPs ("very important personalities"). By definition, the VIPs — India's ruling class — are ideally placed because of their political status to carry out the necessary reform and ensure good governance but they are ensconced in preferential treatment and already get well served by the *status quo*, leaving them with little motivation, incentive, or provocation to work for good governance. They are above the law of the land — beyond its catch — although they formally enact laws under which the country is governed. Potential change agents are thus seen in practice to get co-opted by the target system. They become the staunchest critics of the country's public administration once out of power: alas, they wake up too late! The widely prevalent perception in the society that the country's public funds are the object of loot must be changed. Politicians must thus reorient their values and must seek to serve the society, not corner its resources.

Another barrier to reform toward good governance is the prevalent corruption in administration. Corruption is rampant in India: nearly all points of public dealings are bristling with corruption. Many laws and rules in India are too rigid and complicated, which the emerging middle class overcomes by bribing the local bureaucracy. In other words, members of the middle class are induced to view corruption as the local instant reformer of administration: corruption is thus perceived as functional in want of good governance. Good governance is sorely demanded by the inarticulate wretched of the Earth — the god-forsaken children of the land. Corruption is antipoor and the agency for administering plans and programs of good governance is not competent enough for the task. The civil service is politicized, career-seeking, corrupt, and weak in professionalism. Things in India are going deeply wrong: "... the reason will not be that we had a bad Constitution. What we will have to say is that man was vile."[8] These are the prophetic words of B.R. Ambedkar, regarded as the architect of the Indian Constitution.

---

[8]Quoted in M.P. Sharma: *The Government of the Indian Republic*, Allahabad, Kitab Mahal, 1951, p. 39.

Concluding Observation

Under liberalization the state increasingly finds itself on the defensive. Distrust of public bureaucracy deeply marks the modern administrative thinking and search is on for market-based solutions to social problems. Governance is, therefore, to be examined in the larger context of a shift away from the public sector to the private sector, privatization and deregulation are the highly courted components of the emerging system of governance. Free market economy underpinned by globalization is sweeping the world and India is also a willing partner, even active, in the emerging arrangement. As a result, the state is presently under disenchantment and its alternatives, namely market and NGOs are in growing demand. Reformers at the international level are becoming more active and assertive. What is more, the emerging challenges are likely to be more and more unprogramed, demanding novel solutions. New solution mechanisms will have to be devised to ensure good governance. Equally, sharing of tasks and responsibilities through partnership between the state and private groups is a notable shift from doing them alone either by the state or the private sector. These are among the new patterns of interaction between the public bureaucracy and the civil society, constituting altogether new ways of managing new problems. Public administration thus finds itself subjected to unexpected and powerful forces of novel nature.

Profession and practice seldom match but mismatch is a cause for embarrassment in a developing country like India. Education, as universally argued, has a vital role in promoting good governance but the country's rate of literacy in the year 2001 was 65 percent. Even the Supreme Court of India has taken the view that the right to education is an extension of the right to life. Yet, nearly 60 million children have not attended schools and are thus doomed to illiteracy. The directive principle of state policy elevates the child in the social hierarchy. But this apparently means precious little: gestures are recklessly made in India but these are cosmetic exercises. At the same time, articulations about good governance must not overlook administration's capacity to absorb and internalize them. Otherwise, such strategies would look like sheer decoration pieces that are not meant for implementation, thus enlarging the gap between the professed and the practiced. The civil society in India showing signs of emergence since the 1990s is unevenly developed and occasionally moving in opposite directions, providing no clear direction and leadership to the national quest for good governance. The state, still the prime mover though liberalization seeks broad basing of governance, appears to be unevenly developed and is weak in social skills and values. So are the other sectors engaged in the task of governance. The existing forms of governance in the country including its alternatives — or supplements — like NGOs and the market are presently weak to meet the challenge. What is called for is the innovative redesigning of governance. Governance also entails, among others, formulation of long-term views on national problems and concerns. This is important because most governments seem to lack vision, remaining absorbed in only day-to-day problems. This results in heavy discounting of the future — a neglect, which may cost a nation dearly. This is an apt warning in the case of India of today. Political parties of the land are presently engaged in fomenting what may be called competitive populism in a bid to create vote banks on the basis of caste, religion, or every other ascriptive base. Cheap popularity and good governance do not rhyme with each other and what India seeks or should seek is sustainable good governance.

A core area of good governance is where the execution of public policies takes place, which is the country's public delivery system. In the year 2002, India's Planning Commission in collaboration with the United Nations Development Program (UNDP) brought out *Successful Governance Initiatives and Best Practices: Experiences from Indian States*. The work narrates success stories of development depicting strategy of intervention in the delivery of social services. The key to success according to this study lies in the community empowerment marking a paradigm shift from a supply-driven model of service delivery to a demand-driven approach, leading to transparency and flexibility in operation.

A prerequisite to good governance is downsizing of the government — or the right sizing. This implies that the government should perform core functions, leaving noncore functions for the market. Government today is a major user of electronic computers and management information systems. Improvement has been made particularly in revenue collection, financial management and accounting, and interdepartmental communication system. Customer care programs are regularly organized by many government departments to impart a customer or client orientation to those engaged in public delivery system. The message sought to be conveyed is that the citizens are not mere passive recipients of monopolistically provided services. A large number of public organizations having direct dealings with the citizens have adopted citizens' charters, with the aim to promote openness, citizens' participation, and improved customer service in the public sector. But they have not been very effective for want of follow up. The much needed right to information is in operation since October 2005.

Instaling new institutions and processes is obviously vital to promote good governance. But even more crucial is the urgency for attitudinal and behavioral retuning. Instruments promoting responsiveness and accountability in administration like the citizens' charters need to be reinforced. But good governance demands, first and foremost, a mental revolution in the career bureaucracy in all sectors and levels. An example in this regard has to be set by the top political and administrative leadership of the land along with the strict enforcement of the necessary provisions of laws and other pronouncements. The reward and punishment armoury of the state must, without fear and favor, be activated and invoked more widely as part of the larger process of reform and rejuvenation. Civil society has a definite role to play in exacting a suitable behavioral change in the public functionaries. The babu (the clerical functionary in government) is presently the shame of Indian administration, and he has to be reinvented. In this respect, the classical mechanisms of control like regular inspection and supervision have a definite role to play in the path of good governance.

Indeed, administrative reinventing would be a constant need of good governance. Any passive role for India in the matter of ensuring a good governance is apt to transfer this task to bodies like the World Bank, which would not be a very wholesome development for the country. Citizens' charters that have been adopted to empower the citizens also entail a risk — formally announced measures seeking good governance may get distanced from groundlevel realities and dynamics of local life. India ought to discover its own solutions to its problems including problems of good governance.

Chapter 17

Globalization and Governance in the Former East Germany: The European Union Factor

Jean-Claude Garcia-Zamor

CONTENTS

The former German Democratic Republic's (GDR) present predicament is similar to that faced by many countries across Europe: How to deal with globalization and demographic change? Financial globalization may put the former GDR at greater risk of slipping into crisis than the western part of Germany. Its economy has been trailing that of the rest of the country since reunification in 1990. With unemployment rate in the former GDR much higher than in the western part of the country, many Easterners do not clearly understand why globalization does mean a sharing of jobs and goods within the national boundaries of unified Germany. An examination of the separate bureaucratic experience of the divided country will help understand why it is still so difficult for the East to share the benefits of globalization. After the separation of Germany, a wide gap developed between the bureaucracies of the GDR in the East and the Federal Republic in the West. Whereas the West German bureaucrats were selected because of their qualifications and continued to form a conservative, honest, and conscientious civil service, the East German bureaucrats were recruited primarily because of their political and ideological loyalty. Gravier (2003a,b) has argued that the loyalty factor has offered an important framework for civil service recruitment even after 1990 because it rooted the selection of East Germans in a legal procedure that had been elaborated over the years and could not be considered as an *ad hoc* solution to purge unwelcome personnel. But before 1990, East German bureaucrats had to work according to the principles of socialist morality and ethics. They also had to demonstrate their capacity to transform the general resolutions of the Communist Party — known as the Socialist Unity Party (SED) — into concrete administrative actions. One of the main principles of the GDR civil service was the blind observance of a socialist law and order. The disparity between the two bureaucracies added to the socioeconomic and political problems that became evident at the time of reunification in 1990. It has been argued that those who steered the processes of reunification failed to design institutions of sound governance that fit the circumstances of the governed.

However, it is important to point out that many of the bureaucrats who served the Western administration after 1950 had a Nazi past. They were allowed to return to the civil service only after the need for an efficient and effective administration started to threaten the Western (and especially American) efforts to build up a strong Federal Republic as a centerpiece of the Cold War architecture. This is another illustration of the importance administrative "know-how" has in a modern society. Some people were allowed to work for a democratic government often without a thorough investigation of their potentially criminal past. The key for the different situation in the two Germanies was the ideological configuration. In the East, it was impossible to employ former NS-officials because of the role "antifascism" played as a legitimizing state doctrine. This enabled the GDR propaganda machine to claim that the East represented the "good Germans," the Communists and Social Democrats, who had fought Fascism. But the West was more interested in establishing itself as a "free world," starting in the late 1940s, that meant: anticommunism. This made it possible to put criteria like efficiency ahead of questions of guilt. Yet, the quick transfer of Western political, judicial, and economic institutions to the East without any major modifications turned out to be problematic. It was clear that this radical system change would have a shock-like impact, but the majority of politicians overestimated the capacity of the Western institutions to solve problems under East German circumstances.

The sophisticated system elements of the Federal Republic had been developed gradually to meet the specific requirements of its society. Its complexity, overregulated aspects, and transparency became obstacles to the process of rebuilding in East Germany, especially in light of the fact that in 1980s the institutions of the West German welfare state were criticized heavily by protagonists of "Reaganomics" and "Thatcherism." Thus, the outdated Western laws and rules were used to solve problems in an even more complicated and fundamentally different context. Glaessner (1997, p. 97) wrote "fundamental differences between the Western and Eastern political cultures are the main obstacles to uniting the two parts of Germany socially and culturally in the foreseable future." A major problem in the GDR was the overstaffing of the bureaucracy. Because the objective of the Communist government was to have zero unemployment, not only the civil service, but also the bureaucracies of all universities and factories were grossly overstaffed. In addition, the federal government of the newly unified country has been demanding from the civil servants of the former East Germany a new adaptability and creativity that was never promoted in the GDR bureaucracy.

The chapter analyzes the state of the bureaucracy in the East prior to reunification and discusses the changes that occurred after 1990, whereas the country was moving from communism to democracy. It shows that despite some original difficulties in adapting the new Western norms, the Eastern bureaucracy has been able to develop some goal-oriented activities that are typical of good governance in Western bureaucracies. Its recent performance in a variety of public sectors reveals a new efficiency and professionalism. It has developed a sense of the necessities of the time, including globalization. The chapter analyzes the impact of the European Union (EU) on both governance and transparency in the former East Germany. In essence, EU has put some restraints in the freedom of its member countries to formulate policies unilaterally. It has also established a standard of administrative ethics that cannot be ignored by the bureaucracies of the member countries. The chapter is also about bureaucratic culture and the influences of external political, economic, legal, and social systems upon it, and shows the relationship of bureaucratic culture to organizational performance under different conditions (Garcia-Zamor, 2003). It also reviews two types of bureaucratic cultures over time — GDR and West Germany. In the GDR, there were transitions from "real existing socialism" to democracy and from democracy to reunification; In the West Germany there were transitions from a unified federal democracy to an enlarged geopolitical and bureaucratic structure. Each transition marked a change in laws, norms, structure, etc. In addition, reunification meant that the two separate cultures had to unify, resulting in yet another transition that is still taking place. At each step of transition, culture influences the behavior of individual bureaucrats and the culture of the bureaucratic organization.

The Political and Bureaucratic Transition

The GDR's first (and last) freely elected government after the March 1990 election explicitly rejected the idea of a professional civil service and its "traditional principles" that can be found in Article 33 of the Basic Law. However, this decision quickly became meaningless. The overwhelming victory of the Alliance for Germany in the 1990 election effectively put the German state professional civil service in the GDR's future, regardless of the immediate will of the newly elected East German government (Kvistad, 1999). In June 1990 the last democratic government in the GDR began to restructure state and administration. Reunification was imminent, so creating compatible administrative institutions was the main goal. Work began on the level of the old *Bezirke* (districts), the regional level, on which the reestablishment of the *Länder* would be based. Parallel to this activity, local self-government was reintroduced to towns and cities. It was at that time that the first administrative reform aid was provided by the West. Two overlapping phases can be identified: in the beginning, acting administrators were sent to the East for a limited period of time. It quickly became clear however, that a "permanent elite-transfer" was necessary, Because the East German administration would depend on the professional knowledge of Western experts for a very long time (König, 1999, p. 87). Limited time consultants were not seen as a long-term solution, it was necessary to keep them in the East. They were hoping that they could develop more empathy for the people and local conditions.

Western personnel went East for a variety of reasons. Some wanted an adventure in the "wild East," whereas others had ancestral roots there and wanted to rediscover a lost past. For others, monetary rewards certainly played a role. An American expert in East German studies wrote the following:

> Western elites received *Buschgeld*, or bush money to go east, and some also received free weekly flights home. While many of the imported personnel were fully committed to furthering German unity and planned to make the east their home, the behavior of other western imports created resentment among some eastern Germans who perceived they were being colonized by second-rate bureaucrats and carpet-baggers.
>
> Yoder (1999, p. 92)

For a variety of reasons, the approval of Western civil servants was not unanimous. For some of these expatriates, the East was formerly a distant and unknown world. Problems of integration and little interest in becoming familiar with Eastern problems were common. Staab (1998) mentioned that the mentality and living standards of East and West were too diverse to allow for a smooth integration, and friction was hard to avoid. He added that:

> The persistent post-unification rhetoric of denunciation of the SED regime — not only for its political failures and shortcomings but in general for every aspect of life in the GDR — helped to establish the notion of the victorious West in the fight for systematic supremacy between Capitalism and Communism. As a result, the perception of a political takeover was complemented by notions of an administrative subordination of the East.
>
> Staab (1998, p. 85)

Yoder also wrote that this development introduced a hierarchy in the new administrative institutions, which instantly put Easterners in a subordinate position. Western elites went East with the purpose of retraining indigenous personnel. The existence of a blueprint for administrative institutions, complete with the transfer of West German programs and routines, left little or no room for substantive contributions from the past experiences of Eastern Germany (Yoder, 1999). Although the adaptation to the Western system did not seem to present an overwhelming problem for some Eastern professionals, on the whole, many of them suffered severe setbacks in their careers. Those who were "taken over" by the West German system (public administrators and teachers) experienced the least disruption. Educational certificates functioned as a safety net for most of them (Kupferberg, 2002). So during 1991, the legal framework was created to transfer these Western *Beamte* to the East (with the new laws protecting their *status quo* and hierarchical rank). This situation prompted a German scholar to ask if German unification was not a watershed of institutional reform (Helms, 2000). Another European scholar, who has published widely on Germany, made the point that reform in Germany is typically incremental, painstaking, and legalistic (Flockton, 2001). After reunification, the German public sector seems to have been stabilized by minor adjustments rather than far-reaching reforms. The federalized nature of the institutional system played a decisive role in explaining this outcome. But up until today, West German civil servants hold many leading positions and therefore play a key role in Eastern administrative processes, although they only account for a small percentage of the total staff.

The shortage of trained experts could be bridged that way, but the question whether to keep or to lay off old cadre did not become obsolete. On the one hand, local staff was necessary, and on the other hand it was impossible, for political reasons, to keep the old structures. A quantitative problem added further pressure: overstaffing. 7 percent of the working population in the West and 12 percent in the East were employed in the public sector. Although most of the top positions were cleared of old nomenklaturists on October 3, 1990, the staff restructuring was an unsolved question at the time of reunification and had to be analyzed as an element of the general system transformation. Remaining administrative institutions had to be remodeled, obsolete ones shut down, and new ones created. There was one basic principle for remaining institutions: "in the interest both of administrative continuity and the civil service, public employees would not lose their job" (König, 1999, p. 88). In case they worked for a structure that is no longer necessary, the employees were "placed on hold." Some of them found a new position at a different administration, often they had to accept a lower rank. However, several criteria could be used to lay off the staff:

- *Stasi* activities
- Violations of (internationally recognized) human rights and the rule of law
- Lack of qualification
- Overstaffing
- Dissolving of an institution

It was still a tremendous task to move the old socialist administration to the principles of "classical administration" with its specific elements like professionalism, efficiency, and effectiveness. The Unification Treaty (*Einigungsvertrag*) specifically demanded public obligations to be performed by *Beamte* (civil servants). The practical solution of the problem consisted to entitle East German civil servants as *Beamte auf Probe* — on probation (König, 1999, p. 89). Furthermore, the specific educational degrees usually necessary to become a civil servant were not required. Instead, individual performance on the job was evaluated. Also, while on probation, everybody had to take part in further training classes organized by a network of West German educational institutions. This way of transforming the East

German administration basically accepted staff continuity and resulted in longer transitional period.

However, the transition took place within the new legal framework of the 1990 Unification Treaty. Chapter V of the Treaty dealt with public administration and the administration of justice and Article 19 affirmed the validity of decisions taken by GDR administrative bodies. It declared that all the administrative acts of the GDR performed before the accession took effect should remain valid. They could be revoked only if they were incompatible with the principles of the rule of law or with the provisions of the Treaty. In all other respects the rules on the validity of administrative acts should remain unaffected. But Article 20 on the legal status of persons in the public service merely stated that the exercise of public responsibilities should be entrusted as soon as possible to professional civil servants (Glaessner, 1992). Still, reunification altered significantly the process of policy making. It soon became apparent that policies aiming at equalizing living conditions between East and West could be successful only if these two factors were met: the transformation of the former GDR economy from state socialism to a market economy, and the adaptation of political and administrative structures to the Western model.[1] An immediate aim of the decision makers was to institutionalize joint responsibilities between different levels of government. However, after reunification the new *Länder* placed more emphasis on working together to pursue their specifically East German interests than on trying to work in concert with the Western *Länder*. They have in some cases, notably in education policy, pursued a policy agenda clearly different from that of the Western *Länder*, although they were willing to accept a high degree of federal influence over their affairs in return for extra financial assistance from the Federation (Jeffery, 1995). Policy making in Germany is highly interconnected. In addition to the coordination of decision making between the *Länder*, a wide range of tasks are jointly financed by the *Länder* and the federal government, sometimes with the involvement of European and local actors (Sturm, 1996).

The end of communism in the GDR created a host of new and unexpected challenges for West German government and public administration. As far as the public sector is concerned, stability and continuity seem to have prevailed (Benz & Goetz, 1996). Unlike the other Central and Eastern European countries where the building of new political and administrative

---

[1]Philip Zelikow and Condoleezza Rice, who were members of the U.S. National Security Council staff of the first Bush presidency, participated in some of the negotiations that led to the reunification of Germany. They later told their story from the U.S. perspective, while looking in detail at the other international actors and Washington's efforts to bring them in line with America's priorities (Zelikow & Rice, 1995).

institutions evolved in an almost incremental and partly erratic manner (Garcia-Zamor, 1994), institution building in the former GDR was shaped by a massive institutions transfer in which the entire readymade legal and administrative model of West Germany was literally exported overnight and implanted in the new eastern part of the country. This was a unique task: the transformation of the "real-existing socialist" state and its administration was part of a fundamental system change. Because any socialist economy was part of the state administration, one of the main challenges (and transformation starting points) was the necessary "re-differentiation" of state and economy—a crucial aspect to any capitalist, liberal, and democratic society. And this process itself was subject to political influence (by the new political power of course), as the different ways to approach that task in Eastern Europe show (with Germany choosing the *Treuhand* model of privatization). The whole process could be analyzed as "re-modernization," after communism had "de-modernized" Central and Eastern European States.

According to Luhmann system theory, modern societies are characterized by "functional differentiation": relatively independent subsystems with specific system rationalities (e.g., the economic sphere with private property, free markets, and competition, etc.) are separated from the political–administrative sphere featuring democracy, civil liberties, rule of law, separation of powers, etc. The Marxist ideology implemented in the GDR meant a "counter-modernization" because the level of differentiation reached in Eastern Europe was lowered back to "democratic Centralism" as it was called (König, 1999, p. 74). Holding this perspective, Meuschel (1992) argues that specific subsystems (especially the economic one) and their system requirements were dominated by the power of the political structure symbolized by the fact that the party always had the last word, thus, destroying the very conditions of specific system rationalities. A good example is the politically motivated East German welfare program, started in the early 1970s, which was far too generous relative to economic capacity. As a result, foreign debt rose sharply in the 1980s and, among other inefficiencies, infrastructure, equipment, and research investments declined, further diminishing the economic capacity. Meuschel pointed out the fact that party power in East Germany was based not only in society's "de-differentiation," but also in specific German traditions of being apolitical as a citizen, an attitude that prevented the development of an opposing civil society. Instead, the people showed a lack of participation or resistance and the majority simply accepted the system in an old authoritarian fashion (*ibid.*). The "re-differentiation" therefore included two major goals: the transformation from a centrally planned economy to a market economy and from an authoritarian to a democratic system.

This was made possible by the political, administrative, financial, and economic might and will of West Germany. In addition, a significant number of West Germans were transferred to the East to occupy high-level political and bureaucratic positions. These factors made the bureaucratic transition in East Germany a unique case in the spectrum of former socialist countries (Wollmann, 1996). The orderly disappearance of the GDR left no institutional void. The dissolution of the East German state and the transfer of West German political institutions were managed with remarkable efficiency as far as the legal groundwork and the merger of organizations were concerned. Some analysts mentioned the crucial role that time played during this period. It would have been impossible, they argued, to design a completely new set of rules quickly. The political pressure of the East's collapse created the need for fast solutions, which was to use Article 23 of the Basic Law to reunite Germany. Article 23 of the Basic Law simply extended the West German constitutional framework to East Germany.

During this period, a political rationality clearly dominated the decision-making process (including some competing economic rationalities). The most controversial one was the introduction of the West Deutsche Mark in the East in July 1990 against the advice of the Bundesbank and many economists. Whether the economic evaluation of the East German transformation process dominate the public discussion relative to questions like *Stasi* past, bureaucracies, or general democratic progress depended on whether West Germany or former communist countries were used as a comparison. The problem was twofold: not only did the SED with its multilevel party organization influenced state and bureaucracy, but also there was a net of party members within the administration, or as König wrote "both a 'party-pyramid' over the 'state-pyramid' and a 'party-pyramid' within the 'state-pyramid' existed" (König, 1999, p. 82). Thus political transformation had to deal with several problems: potential informal communication networks of the old cadre, the reestablishment of the horizontal separation of power (legislative, executive, and judicial), and the vertical separation of power, which was supposed to create a decentralized administration like the German federalism model, including the principle of local self-government by villages, towns, and cities — all in a sharp contrast to "democratic Centralism." However, as was to be expected, political and administrative integration after reunification have met with a host of obstacles that derive from the legacy of socialism, a lack of resources in the East, and differences in East and West German mentalities. The highly intrusive, demanding political regime of the GDR had forged a very real sense of "GDR identity" among its citizens. The GDR did not collapse because of a nationalist quest for reunification. The quest for reunification arose as a result, not a cause, of the collapse of communist rule in the GDR (Fulbrook, 1999).

One measure of bureaucratic performance is often the administrative capability of the civil servants in the economic sector. In case of the former

East Germany, the slow development of the economy could be traced to several obstacles. However, it has also been proven that when some very efficient technocrats took control of the management of certain economic sectors, they were able to overcome some of these obstacles (Garcia-Zamor, 2002, 2004). Among some of the mistakes that were made during the unification period was the federal government's goal to equalize East and West German wages, even though Eastern workers were only a quarter to a third as productive as their Western counterparts. Samuelson wrote that:

> East Germany's currency (and wages) were converted into West German marks at an unrealistic exchange rate of one to one; then, East German wages were raised more than 50 percent from 1991 to 1995. Instantly, high labor costs made many firms uncompetitive and rendered East Germany unattractive for new factories. Massive unemployment resulted; it still exceeds 18 percent.
>
> Samuelson (2002, p. 59)

In addition, Samuelson also pointed to the fact that huge payments (3 to 4 percent of GDP) from West Germany have been made to the East to pay unemployment and welfare benefits. The cost of unification has had a negative impact on the German economy. Work was what made somebody a valuable member of society in both parts of Germany, but the orientation toward work as the central aspect of life was more pronounced in the East than in the West, a difference that could probably be attributed in part to the threat of unemployment in the East. Unemployment is even more dramatic to Easterners as they were raised in a Communist society where every member of the society had a job (Glaeser, 2000).[2] For them, unification marked the beginning of a transformation that would radically alter their lives. As workers and firms were subjected to the rigors of market forces, the situation that had created the ironic GDR quip, according to which "they pretend to pay us, and we pretend to work," also passed into history (Keithly, 1999, p. 188). But after reunification, many of the jobs that people assumed to be guaranteed for life began to disappear. Professional qualifications were downgraded, and much of previous work experience counted

[2]In socialist countries, work is a central institution in the technical order of economic production. It is also central to the social structure and to individual motivation, and thus the central point at which the individual relates to society. Peattie (1981) explored the implications of social planning by looking at the transformation of Cuba in the course of the Revolution. She found that the country was organized around "moral incentives" just as — in the alternative model — around material ones. The Cubans developed a complex system of nonmaterial incentives that resembles in part the former East Germans' one (public praise by the leaders, medals, buttons, diplomas, plaques, certificates of communist work, and honorable mention in factory bulletins, etc.). These prizes and honors are the equivalent of the paper currency in the moral incentive system.

for little. East Germans became disillusioned with the new situation and were shocked by the unexpected burdens and the impact of unification on their personal lives. Many started looking back to the "good old days" of "real existing socialism" in the GDR. Staab (1998, p. 97) wrote: "Repressing the inhuman aspects of the oppressive regime resulted in a selective memory that disproportionately remembered the positive aspects — for instance, social welfare or job security." This remarkable phenomenon soon earned a name in the media: "GDR nostalgia" (Kapferer, 2000).

Before 1989, many East Germans thought that socialism was a far better system than capitalism, despite the fact that they were aware of the West Germans having a higher standard of living. They blamed party officials for the failure to achieve greater economic development, not the system of government. Despite the fact that the policies of *glasnost* or openness begun by Soviet President Mikhail Gorbachev rushed across eastern and central Europe like waters from a burst dam, most East Germans were not really pro-reunification. They had great hope that *perestroika* would only open the system and make it more transparent. It is sometime hard for people who have chosen to leave for the West, or for some Westerners who have always lived in a democratic system, to fully comprehend or to accept this fact (an interesting similarity with the case of Cuba) (Garcia-Zamor, 2001). König wrote a very interesting chapter in his book that might contribute to a greater understanding of this phenomenon. He analyzed the aspect of how to transform the *Kader-Verwaltung*. The specific East German situation was characterized by the classical question of any regime change: How many of the old faces will remain in power? Is it possible (both by political and professional standards) to keep at least some of them? What about the need to recruit new personnel? This classical situation was further complicated by the "dualism of East- and West-German administrators" (König, 1999, p. 86). It was clear from the beginning that a transformation to democracy could not work with the old *nomenklaturists* in charge. The consequences of their political incompetence could be observed everywhere (*ibid.*). After it became clear that the system would collapse, they did not put up relevant resistance to the change, but tried to use the time between November 1989 and the reunification in 1990 to "clean" their personal files or to transfer to a different, potentially safe, and unsuspicious position. In any case, they were no longer able to use their former power as administrators.

The European Union Factor

Although in Germany ideas for new policies formally originate from government ministries, parliament, or the Chancellor's office, pressure groups, new social movements, and even public opinion at home and abroad do have some influence on policy initiation. A very important new source of influence, which has stimulated many policy changes, has been the EU, especially after the member states agreed on the aim of the post-1992 Single Market with the Single European Act of 1986 (Sturm, 1996). Numerous new German laws are also influenced by the EU. German unification had presented great challenges for European integration. It bound the larger Germany into a deeper form of EU integration, while providing part of the architecture for a wider Europe, following the end of the Iron Curtain (Flockton, 2000). This factor became an important element in the complexity of the integration of the former GDR bureaucracy into the federal system and relates to patterns of external interaction with regard to Germany's participation in the EU. Benz and Goetz describe this as an important new development in the German public sector:

> As regards the contextualization of the German administrative system within the European legal, political and administrative framework, it is becoming increasingly impossible to understand the workings of German public administration without constant and systematic reference to its embeddedness in the European order. The scope and content of administrative action, the national institutional setting, administrative procedures and personnel policy are influenced by European integration to an extent where it is becoming increasingly problematic to conceptualize integration as an external force affecting domestically defined administrative arrangements. Already the interactive ties between the national administrative system and its European environment are of such variety and intensity that they constitute a decisive new element in Germany's administrative history.
>
> Benz and Goetz (1996, p. 22)

The EU is presently influencing policy making in all its member countries through a series of treaties that sometimes draw out struggle for power between the big and small member states. Some people view EU as a challenge and a threat to national governance Because it dictates norms to be followed in different bureaucratic sectors. In the economic area, the crucial challenge for Germany — and for most other EU members — is to promote sustainable growth. After several years of economic stagnation the German government has launched a comprehensive growth and modernization strategy called Agenda 2010. In the defense area, Germany wants to implement an EU plan to allow it, France, and Great Britain to set up a small military planning unit capable of overseeing operations independently of North Atlantic Treaty Organization (NATO). Many of these initiatives do not include EU's smaller states. At a December 2000 summit in Nice, a complex voting formula was adopted to preserve a better balance of power in the EU. Under this formula, accepted by German Chancellor Gerhard Schröder, Germany has 29 votes — the same as less populous Britain, France, and Italy. Poland and Spain both have 27 votes under this arrangement, even though they have populations half the size of Germany. Both argue this formula maintains the balance needed to stop Europe being run by a directorate of big member states. The new formula favored by Germany is a "double majority" voting system in the Council of Ministers where decisions would require the votes of a majority of states representing a majority of the population. However, a constitutional treaty that included these changes was not ratified at a meeting that took place in December 2003. Although the constitutional treaty was aimed to streamline the EU and sharpen its role on the world stage after it enlarges to 25 members in May 2004, failure at resolving the voting issue doomed the meeting.[3] That failure represents a big slowdown in the European integration process. Six of EU's biggest paymasters already are calling for a freeze in the EU budget until 2013 — a move that could cut aid to poorer countries, including Spain and Poland. The leaders of Germany, Britain, France, the Netherlands, Sweden, and Austria, all net contributors to the EU, said the union's budget should be subject to the same "painful consolidation" as national budgets (Parker, 2003, p. 4).

There were other major areas of conflict in the ratification of the new European constitution. Parts of the constitution, such as the provision that employees shall not be dismissed without due cause, have the potential to inflict economic damage. Several European countries have tried to open up their labor markets by granting exemptions from dismissal laws. These laws are now at risk of becoming unconstitutional on grounds of unfair discrimination — Why should some employees enjoy constitutional rights that others do not? At present the 16 million people from the former East Germany might have the most to lose when Germany fully adheres to the new constitutional treaty. The level of unemployment is higher there than in the western part of the country and the competition from the new EU member states where unemployment is even higher will possibly have negative effects on them. In addition, East Germans come from an

[3]The president of Rand Corporation, James A. Thompson, wrote that the collapse of the EU's efforts to agree on a constitution primarily over the issue of voting power, mirrors what happened in America more than 200 years ago. Like Europe today, the original states of the United States were in a weak union when they met in 1787 to strengthen their links to better manage the federal economy and provide for the common security. As in Brussels in December 2003, the vital issue dividing the delegates was the distribution of voting power among the states. The "Great Compromise," which created the two chambers of Congress, broke the deadlock: One house — the Senate — provides equal strength to each state. The other — the House of Representatives — is based on population (Thompson, 2003).

anti-Western culture and most recently have been exhibiting a sentiment referred to as *Ostalgie*, the sadness of not being able to go back to the "good old days" of their socialist past. New movies, TV shows, and publications depicting the past inaccurately seem to soften the bitterness felt by Eastern Germans over the alienation and high unemployment that have accompanied unification. To most of them, the integration into the EU seems hardly a solution to their problems.

The debate about EU in terms of Germany's interest as a nation is not a new issue. It came up soon after reunification and usually focuses on (a) how Germany should treat the question of participation in military operations and (b) what role the larger Germany should play in the process of European integration. In these debates, there are no substantial differences between Eastern and Western politicians. Although there remain "cultural" differences between East and West, such as a higher percentage of people in the East supporting pacifism, and more people there seems to have a critical attitude toward the United States and NATO, the former East Germany is solidly beyond the participation of Germany in EU. With regards to European Integration, there is almost a consensus among all major German parties that this is a good thing to do, although the left tends to point out to the democratic problems of the EU (transparency, participation, etc.). As the EU becomes more and more powerful (as pointed out earlier, the number of laws and regulations depending on EU legislature is constantly growing), nobody seems to know how to make it more transparent. Transparency, however, is a crucial factor in any democracy because it is necessary to know who is responsible for what and who should be held accountable. It is almost impossible for the ordinary German citizen to understand what is going on the European level. After all, the German political system is already so highly intertwined, that every political actor can deny responsibility by pointing to another institution or to a higher level. In that way, the EU, all too often, might be just another useful victim when playing the "blame game." But the only thing the East is constantly demanding is a permanent flow of financial aid. And so far, that has been no problem, although it is changing right now, as the richest Eastern regions or cities perform better than the poorest Western regions, especially in the Ruhr-Area (Gelsenkirchen, Duisburg, and Dortmund all have higher unemployment than Dresden, for example). So there is pressure building up to reduce the amount of money going to the East. This pressure will probably increase with the admission of the ten new countries from central and Eastern Europe. Most of these ten countries still have enormous domestic difficulties and a serious shortage of administrative staff. German policy makers worry that the Union may become unmanageable when these new small member states join the EU. In addition, their membership might shift the geographical center of Europe from Brussels to Prague.

Thus, after 2004, Eastern Europe might become Central Europe — as it has been for centuries until the Iron Curtain appeared after World War II. Although the rationale for Germany's former policy of support for European integration remains as valid as ever, some German politicians think that the EU is a bureaucratic hindrance.[4] They are tempted to use Brussels as a scapegoat for the failure of national politics.

A very ambivalent situation exists in the former East Germany. Although the anxiety over the arrival in EU of the new small Eastern countries is rather high in all of Germany, it is especially so in parts of East Germany. Some people there think that they might lose more jobs to countries like Poland, and that a wave of new immigrants and an increase of the crime rate might occur. These fears seem to be rather unsubstantiated. The process of moving jobs to Eastern Europe is more than ten years old and will probably not accelerate too much because the disadvantages of the East remain quite numerous. Also, immigrants will probably not flow in large numbers into East Germany because Germany negotiated a seven-year period during which the free movement of labor will not be possible. In addition, the new immigrants will probably not go to East Germany due to high unemployment there. On the other hand, those fears are compensated by the positive attitude toward the process of European integration by other East Germans. Not only political parties, but also many citizens agree that this is something necessary to eventually overcome the Cold War separation and to prevent deep conflicts like the ones that preceded World War II. The political parties have been telling people that their fears are unsubstantiated and that they should see the integration of the Eastern countries as a big advantage and an opportunity for them. East Germany will no longer be a border region and trade could grow more easily (trade between Germany and Poland, for example, grew by 98 percent between 1997 and 2002). East German companies could start new joint ventures with the East (especially the Czech Republic), something that is already happening, especially in Saxony. However, despite the reassurance of the politicians, most East Germans do not see the EU integration scheme as a helpful process for solving unemployment in the former East Germany. This ambivalence is something quite common in all of Germany. In general, the EU is viewed by many East Germans as a welcome additional source of money: billions have been directed to the East and East Germany has especially been taking advantage of the EU's principle to help underdeveloped member regions. Countless projects are financed by the EU (80 percent of Leipzig's new subway tunnel, for example, the Autobahn from Dresden to Prague, etc.)

---

[4]The EU enlargement will be a very hard bureaucratic task. It will need to put 80,000 pages of EU rules into domestic law and free movement of goods, services, money, and people.

Also, everybody enjoys traveling all over Europe without border controls or money exchange problems. Great portion of the public hardly realizes to what extend the EU is already influencing their lives.

Regarding the bureaucracy, the EU is a big challenge because it is a new, powerful player. After all, essential sovereignty rights have been transferred to that institution and the problems arising from this can be observed every day. Right now the Deficit and Stability Pact issue shows every one that the old nation-state has no longer unlimited budget power. All of a sudden there is someone in a foreign city telling the German finance minister what to do. This is quite remarkable and new. At the state and local levels, bureaucrats have to be trained so they would know how to apply for EU money. They have to implement countless new regulations, especially in the environmental sector (sewage plant standards are a big problem, Because the costs for modernization are enormous). They have to know what kind of subsidies to companies can be handed out without risking EU intervention. At the present time, the biggest fear of East German politicians and bureaucrats is the possible loss of the so called "Target One" status, which designates East Germany as an area eligible for receiving the highest level of EU aid and also allows the East Germans to hand out money to companies that plan to invest there. The negotiations in this area are still going on.

So, a brief assessment would be that on a political and bureaucratic level, the perception of EU integration in East Germany is positive. Problems are seen as natural and do not undermine the belief that integration is good. Among the electorate (both East and West), the perception is similar, although problems tend to frighten people, some people in a strong way because their knowledge about the process is limited. The scientific debate often stresses the fact that EU integration is undermining the nation-state, but is strengthening both the new supranational and local levels. This is a very slow but continuing process. The integration process at the local level is at least as interesting as the one on the supranational level. There are countless projects and network initiatives between European regions and cities focusing on all sorts of problems. This could be an important democratic fundament that will sustain integration from the local level, so both a "bottom-up" and a "top-down" process would push the project ahead — slowly, but with persistence. This is a unique process, and the fact that after a century of war and separation Europe is becoming one again is absolutely spectacular. To the present generation it means a big opportunity and only through the process of EU integration could the continent's problems be solved. There is no certainty that the current pace can be sustained. Probably everything will be much slower than expected. The ten new states will have to adjust to the big changes they will face in the coming years. Then there is also the problem of integrating the Balkan countries, Romania, and last but not least the big issue of what to do with Turkey. At the end, if the EU is going to survive and prosper, it can do so only on the basis of solidarity. The rich countries must help the poor ones.

Changes for More Integrity in Governance

A new generation of administrators is being educated at new schools for public administration that have been established everywhere on *Länder* level to gradually replace the old ones. After the Revolution of 1989 there was no relevant (quantitative or qualitative) counter-elite, which could have filled open positions (König, 1999). The reasons for that can be found in the perfect system of oppression, which usually excluded dissidents from higher schools and universities, thus preventing educational careers.

Prof. Dr. Dieter Schimanke who in 2000 was *Staatssekretär* (state secretary, the second highest rank in a ministry, right below the minister) in the Ministry for Work, Social Affairs and Health of Sachsen–Anhalt, Magdeburg wrote an interesting article describing his experience in his ministry. He found that even after thorough further education, Eastern civil servants continued to surprise their Western trainers. When it came to implementing new rules, specific behavior patterns came back to life, based on Eastern experience and socialization. Schimanke especially highlights what he calls "GDR-pragmatism," which meant that each individual case was decided in a discretionary way. If a decision turned out to be a mistake, it was possible to correct it, regardless of what the rule (the abstract norm) demanded. This behavior of course was not compatible with the standards of the rule of law. This pattern corresponds to the informal *Eingaben* (petition system) common in the former GDR. Whenever people had a problem, usually on the local and individual level (need for a new playground, problems with the distribution of consumer products, etc.), they wrote a letter to the administration complaining about what bothered them. Although there was no legal framework for this, these petitions were taken extremely seriously because they were considered to be an indicator of discontent and therefore important with regards to system stability. In a way, this was a method to control the administration, because whenever "Berlin" demanded a report, these letters and petitions usually revealed problems to the disadvantage of the local or district authorities. So the instrument of correcting administrative decisions in order to achieve "individual case justice" was widely used in the GDR.

Schimanke (2001, p. 185) describes his observation of the transformation process "interim results" as follows.

Professional Quality

Parts of the East German administration meet the requirements, especially if there is a stable authority with skilled civil servants (for example, infrastructure authorities). A general quality problem is a lack of professionalism when it comes to the legal framework. Very often mistakes are made because authorities exceed their competencies. There are too many incorrect or inadequate decisions that can cause significant damage for administrative authorities.

Independent Work

Very often civil servants wait for orders from a higher level, although they could act independently. And if they do, it is a different way of acting independently (Eastern behavior patterns) compared to Western standards.

Problem-Solving Capacities

Especially on the level of state ministries there are deficits in this field. Strategic thinking and "intelligent" modern administrative practices are not found often enough. Schimanke stresses the fact that this is a problem also characteristic for West German *Beamte* who settled in the East.

Budget and Overstaffing

Room for personnel policies and promotions is very limited, because of the need to reduce staff. Also, top positions are filled with a relatively young and homogeneous (with regards to age) Western group, which will block career opportunities for younger Easterners for the next years.

Further Education and Training

There is a lack of strategies and concepts to deal with the unique situation. Also, even if they were available, there are motivational problems: if you know that chances for a promotion are very small, the will to obtain more skills might not be very developed.

A Summing-Up: Governance, Ethics, and Bureaucratic Culture

In the transitory period between the opening of the wall in October 1989 and the unification of the two Germanies in October 1990, many people believed in the illusion that only the wall separated the Germans.

> Initially preoccupied with the enormous legal and financial burdens of Eastern reconstruction, federal officials devoted little energy to the equally formidable task of reforging a sense of national identity from within, beyond a reinvocation of national symbols. United Germany's health as a nation will depend upon the extent to which its predominantly Western leadership succeeds not in 'Kohlonizing' but in grafting Eastern political culture on to its own.
>
> Mushaben (1998, p. 374)

As the disparate citizens' groups that had provided the intellectual and spiritual rationale for the 1989 revolution were unable to present themselves as credible spokesmen for the population of East Germany, political power drained out of the few remaining centers of authority that still existed in the East. A disillusioned one-liner read: "The Revolution had won, the revolutionaries had lost." The mayor of Dresden observed: "Power is up for grabs, yet no one picks it up" (Peterson, 2002, p. 251). The GDR regime had permitted limited protests as long as the system was not generally questioned. The boundaries of criticism allowed by the party sometimes appeared to be far drawn. But the government made sure that the majority of citizens would respect these boundaries. Anyone trying to test the limits of the system by crossing the prescribed lines would incur great personal disadvantages, and most GDR citizens did not take the risk. The dissidents were no exception in this regard. And because they did not truly want a revolution, they never demanded power. They wanted only reforms and focused their entire political energy on defeating the *Stasi*. For them the *Stasi* was the root evil of GDR socialism. Yet they either did not perceive or did not react to the new tendencies turning up at the demonstrations. They neither expressed opinions on the question of reunification, nor put their objective in concrete terms, nor did they provide any revolutionary program (Voss & Opp, 1995). These two scholars concluded by writing that:

> There were no groups in the GDR that played an outstanding role in the revolution. There was no revolutionary class and no revolutionary party. There was also no charismatic personality who motivated the 'masses' to revolutionary actions. One reason for this lack was that the members of opposition groups, who were particularly active in the protests, were also

> prisoners of the ruling socialist ideology and thus could not offer 'the people' any basic alternatives.
>
> Voss and Opp (1995, p. 165)

The lack of dominant personalities, in the government as well as the opposition, made post-communist East German politics look very different from those of Poland and Czechoslovakia, where personality cults have formed around Lech Walesa and Vaclav Havel, respectively (Darnton, 1992). Contrary to the common view that the dissidents and intellectuals were the leaders of the revolution, at no point did they possess the decisive initiative. They were the reluctant revolutionaries and outsiders in a process that they neither initiated nor desired. Their prominence was more an effect than a cause of events during the autumn of 1989 (Ross, 2002). They remained a minority not only in Germany as a whole, but also within East Germany. West Germans took little interest in their claims. Moreover, they ended up feeling like the real losers of the democratization process (Müller, 2001).

The burden of GDR's absorption into the Federal Republic practically fell onto the shoulders of West Germany's policy makers. These policy makers were overburdened at the time. Thus, the federal administration had to hand over responsibilities to the *Länder* bureaucracies; in other cases it had to take over responsibilities normally vested in the federal units. But because the *Länder*, in cultural policy for instance, did not want to spend scarce resources on East Germany, the Federation took over. The process became a kind of "Keynesianism of Reunification" — against the will of the actors involved (von Beyme, 1998, p. 117). Another important reason for West German politicians' early interest and involvement was the fact that the Basic Law required federal elections in 1990 and the largest political parties in the West were to compete in an all-German vote for the first time. In early 1990, several of these political parties sought to take advantage of their existing or possible counterparts in the East by utilizing them as vehicles for reaching out to new voters (McAdams, 1993).

After reunification, public administration in the East could not simply be adjusted to accommodate the methods of the West. It had to be significantly modified to eliminate the structural incompatibility that existed between the two models of public administration. The centralized administration of the socialist state, which was subject to strict control by the SED hierarchy, was replaced by a differentiated system in accordance with the tenets of federalism and municipal self-government. An authoritarian and often arbitrary administration lacking many features of efficient bureaucratic and legal organization, such as administrative records, had to be transformed into a service-oriented administration mindful of the protection of citizens' rights, which are provided by administrative courts (Kreile, 1992).

In addition to analyzing the interaction of sound governance and administrative ethics in the former East Germany during the difficult transition of the GDR bureaucracy from communism to democracy, the paper sought to highlight bureaucratic culture and the influences of external political, economic, legal, and social systems on bureaucratic behavior. It illustrated the relationship of bureaucratic culture to organizational performance under different conditions. It also analyzed how two types of bureaucratic cultures (GDR and West Germany) have coped with a series of changes that involved fundamental ideological adjustments in the political systems of the two countries. The bureaucracies of the East and the West had to operate under changing laws, norms, and structures that were designed to maximize the control of the political leaders who were in power at different times. When reunification came in 1990, the two bureaucracies were merged according to plans that were not negotiated between them. West Germany had the sole control over the retention and recruitment of the Eastern civil servants who eventually joined the federal bureaucracy. Although problems still exist in the reunification process, they are neither unsurmountable nor influencing only the bureaucratic transition. As shown in the chapter, they are also affecting the social, political, and economic integration of the two parts of Germany. It is not easy to determine how long it will take before the former GDR bureaucracy can fully absorb the Western norms and values of sound governance, administrative ethics, and globalization that are being imposed by unification. At the federal level, the ruling SED party has seen the departure of 130,000 members during the years Gerhard Schröder was the German chancellor. These defections were partly prompted by the voters' rejection of the globalization policies of the government. However, it is safe to say that such integration of globalization values in the former GDR, even if it takes time, is inevitable.

A report of the global commission on the social dimensions of globalization issued in February 2004 showed dramatically how the debate on globalization has changed in recent years. The commission was established in 2002 by the International Labor Organization (ILO) and had 24 members chosen from diverse interest groups, intellectual persuasions, and nationalities. Its mission was to look carefully at the social dimensions of globalization that had been often neglected in policy discussions. Joseph E. Stiglitz, a professor of economics at Columbia University and a Nobel Prize winner for economics in 2001, was a member of the commission. He stated that the economic and financial volatility — and hence insecurity — associated with globalization is the result of an agenda driven by interests and ideology (Stiglitz, 2004). His comments seem to describe quite well the situation in the former East Germany where capital market liberalization has contributed little to full economic and societal growth.

References

Benz, A. and Goetz, K.H. (1996). *A New German Public Sector? Reform, Adaptation and Stability*. Brookfield, Vermont: Dartmouth Publishing Company.

Darnton, R. (1992). *Stasi* Besieged. In R.E. Long (Ed.), *The Reunification of Germany*. New York: The H.W. Wilson Company. pp. 57–62.

Flockton, C. (2000). Policy agendas and the economy in Germany and Europe. In C. Flockton, E. Kolinsky and R. Pritchard (Eds.), *The New Germany in the East. Policy Agendas and Social Developments since Unification*. London: Frank Cass Publishers. pp. 61–83.

Flockton, C. (2001). The German economy since 1989/90: problems and prospects. In K. Larres (Ed.), *Germany since Unification: The Development of the Berlin Republic*. 2nd Edition. London: Palgrave. pp. 63–87.

Fulbrook, M. (1999). *German National Identity after the Holocaust*. Cambridge, UK: Polity Press.

Garcia-Zamor, J.C. (1994). Neoteric theories for development administration in the new world order. In J.C. Garcia-Zamor and R. Khator (Eds.), *Public Administration in the Global Village*. Westport, Connecticut: Praeger. pp. 101–120.

Garcia-Zamor, J.C. (2001). Conundrums of urban planning in a global context: the case of the Frankfurt Airport. *Public Organization Review: A Global Journal*, 1: 415–435.

Garcia-Zamor, J.C. (2002). Ethics revisited in a society in transition: the case of the former East Germany. *Public Administration and Development*, 22: 235–248.

Garcia-Zamor, J.C. (2003). Workplace spirituality in the United States and the former East Germany. In R.A. Giacalone and C.L. Jurkiewicz (Eds.), *The Handbook of Workplace Spirituality and Organizational Performance*. New York: M.E. Sharpe, Inc. pp. 314–335.

Garcia-Zamor, J.C. (2004). Justice expectations and redress to human rights violations in the former East Germany. In J.C. Garcia–Zamor (Ed.), *Bureaucratic, Societal, and Ethical Transformation of the Former East Germany*.New York: University Press of America. pp. 121–145.

Glaeser, A. (2000). *Divided in Unity. Identity, Germany, and the Berlin Police*. Chicago: The University of Chicago Press.

Glaessner, G.-J. (1992). *The Unification Process in Germany from Dictatorship to Democracy*. Translated from the German by C.B. Grant. New York: St. Martin's Press.

Glaessner, G.-J. (1997). Political culture in Germany and the legacies of the GDR. In M. Zimmer (Ed.), *Germany: Phoenix in Trouble?* Edmonton, Canada: The University of Alberta Press. pp. 83–104.

Gravier, M. (2003a). Entrer dans l'Administration de l'Allemagne Unifiée: Une Approche Anthropologique d'un Rituel d'Intégration (1990–1999). In *Revue Française de Science Politique*. Paris: Presses de Sciences Po. pp. 323–350.

Gravier, M. (2003b). Recruiting East-Germans in the post-unification civil service: the role of political loyalty in a transition towards democracy. Paper Presented at the 19th World Congress of the International Political Science Association (IPSA) in Durban, South Africa, June 29th–July 4th.

Helms, L. (2000). *Institutions and Institutional Change in the Federal Republic of Germany*. London: Macmillan Press Ltd.

Jeffery, C. (1995). The changing framework of German politics since unification. In D. Lewis and J.R.P. Mckenzie (Eds.), *The New Germany. Social, Political and Cultural Challenges of Unification*. Exeter, England: University of Exeter Press. pp. 101–126.

Kapferer, N. (2000). 'Nostalgia' in Germany's new federal states as a political and cultural phenomenon of the transformation process. In H. Williams, C. Wight and N. Kapferer (Eds.), *Political Thought and German Reunification. The New German Ideology?* New York: St. Martin's Press. pp. 28–40.

Keithly, D.M. (1999). The German economy: shocks to the system. In M.N. Hampton and C. Søe (Eds.), *Between Bonn and Berlin. German Politics Adrift?* Lanham, Maryland: Rowman & Littlefield Publishers, Inc. pp. 171–199.

König, K. (1999). *Verwaltungsstaat im Übergang. Transformation, Entwicklung, Modernisierung*. Baden-Baden: Nomos Verlagsgesellschaft.

Kreile, M. (1992). The political economy of the new Germany. In P.B. Stares (Ed.), *The New Germany and the New Europe*. Washington, D.C.: The Brookings Institution. pp. 55–92.

Kupferberg, F. (2002). *The Rise and Fall of the German Democratic Republic*. New Brunswick, New Jersey: Transaction Publishers.

Kvistad, G.O. (1999). *The Rise and Demise of German Statism. Loyalty and Political Membership*. Oxford: Berghahn Books.

McAdams, A.J. (1993). *Germany Divided from the Wall to Reunification*. Princeton, New Jersey: Princeton University Press.

Meuschel, S. (1992). *Legitimation und Parteiherrschaft*. Frankfurt am Main: Suhrkamp.

Müller, J.-W. (2001). East Germany: incorporation, tainted truth, and the double division. In A.B. de Brito, C. González-Enríquez and P. Aguilar (Eds.), *The Politics of Memory: Transitional Justice in Democratizing Societies*. Oxford: Oxford University Press. pp. 248–274.

Mushaben, J.M. (1998). *From Post-War to Post-Wall Generations: Changing Attitudes toward the National Question and NATO in the Federal Republic of Germany*. Boulder, Colorado: Westview Press.

Parker, G. (2003). Europe big six call for freeze on EU budget. In *Financial Times*, December 16, 2003.

Peattie, L. (1981). *Thinking about Development*. London: Plenum Press.

Peterson, E.N. (2002). *The Secret Police and the Revolution: The Fall of the German Democratic Republic*. Westport, Connecticut: Praeger Publishers.

Ross, C. (2002). *The East German Dictatorship: Problems and Perspectives in the Interpretation of the GDR*. London: Arnold, a member of the Hodder Headline Group.

Samuelson, R.J. (2002). The (new) sick man of Europe. In *Newsweek*. New York: Newsweek, Inc., November 18, 2002. p. 59.

Schimanke, D. (2001). Dilemmata der Personalpolitik. In H. Derlien (Ed.), *Zehn Jahre Verwaltungsaufbau Ost – eine Evaluation*. Baden-Baden: Nomos Verlagsgesellschaft. pp. 179–187.

Staab, A. (1998). *National Identity in Eastern Germany: Inner Unification or Continued Separation?* Westport, Connecticut: Praeger Publishers.

Stiglitz, J.E. (2004). The social costs of globalization. In *Financial Times*, February 25, 2004, p. 13.

Sturm, R. (1996). Continuity and change in the policy-making process. In G. Smith, W.E. Paterson and S. Padgett (Eds.), *Developments in German Politics 2*. Durham, North Carolina: Duke University Press. pp. 117–132.

Thompson, J.A. (2003). Why US history holds a lesson for Europe. In *Financial Times*, December 19, 2003, p. 13.

von Beyme, K. (1998). *The Legislator: German Parliament as a Centre of Political Decision-Making*. Aldershot Hants, England: Ashgate Publishing Limited.

Voss, P. and Opp, K.-D. (1995). "We are the people!" A revolution without revolutionaries. In K.-D. Opp, P. Voss and C. Gern (Eds.), *Origins of a Spontaneous Revolution: East Germany, 1989*. Ann Arbor: The University of Michigan Press. pp. 155–166.

Wollmann, H. (1996). Rupture and transformation: local government in East Germany. In N. Ben-Elia (Ed.), *Strategic Changes and Organizational Reorientations in Local Government: A Cross-National Perspective*. New York: St. Martin's Press. pp. 109–123.

Yoder, J.A. (1999). *From East Germans to Germans? The New Postcommunist Elites*. Durham, North Carolina: Duke University Press.

Zelikow, P. and Rice, C. (1995). *Germany Unified and Europe Transformed: A Study in Statecraft*. Cambridge, Massachusetts: Harvard University Press.

IV

GLOBALIZATION AND ADMINISTRATIVE REFORM AND REORGANIZATION

Chapter 18

Global Administrative Reforms and Transformation of Governance and Public Administration

Ali Farazmand

CONTENTS

Introduction

The global waves of administrative reform of the last 25 years or so have produced intense political and administrative debates, monumental volumes of scholarly research and publication, and fundamental changes in directions and outcomes that have captured much of the discourse on governance and public administration, on the role and size of government in economy and society, and on how public management should be organized. New paradigmatic changes have developed and as a result of these changes, new trends have surfaced with new ideological claims, and new organizational patterns have been prescribed with theoretical and practical applications worldwide.

Much of these global waves of change have pointed to directions that challenge the traditional ways of thinking and refute the conventional wisdom on governance, administration, and public management. The premises and underlying assumptions of what was practiced in government and public administration have been questioned, rejected, and, in most countries around the world, replaced by new concepts and ideas, new models, and new perspectives. At the same time, a monumentally growing body of literature has surfaced on the discourse of globalization, which is the hallmark of many of these global waves of change and transformation that have affected governments, economies, citizens, administration, and public management. The dimensions of these changes and transformation are many and encompass the political, social, cultural, administrative, managerial, organizational, and administrative spheres; they cover all the spheres of public and private life, at local, national, and global levels.

Implications of these new trends in thought and action in the realms of government and administration are far too many to enumerate here, and they have had profound impacts on governance and administration, on the enterprise of public administration as a field of study and as a professional field of practice in public management. Within the scope of government and governance, the concepts of new governance, market-based governance, and good governance have replaced the traditional concepts of government and governance. Reinventing, reengineering, and reform have filled the literature. Similarly, in public administration, the concepts of new public management, public administration by proxy, outsourcing, and public–private partnerships, as well as through privatization and contracting out have captured much of the literature. Today, it is safe to say that the field of public administration has been profoundly transformed in both theory and practice across the world. Indeed, a new orthodoxy has captured the field with much strength, momentum, and lasting power.

Many of these transformational changes have been structural and systemic, producing fundamental transformation of the fields of public administration and governance, whereas the others have been both cultural and process oriented. Of these three categories, the structural–systemic changes and transformation are the hardest to reverse in the face of challenging opposition, although the cultural and process transformations are more flexible, trendy, and adaptive.

Yet, there is a discerning fragility in the premises of these changes and transformation, a problem that the critics have all along warned about; this fragility was expected and reported from the onset. Therefore, as expected, reports of failure of these new structural, cultural, and process transformation are appearing increasingly out of the fields of practice and experimentations across the globe. Although it is very early to assess comprehensively the impacts of these new global administrative reforms and the new public management orthodoxy, studies are now proving its critics' key challenges that have consistently been reported in the literature, including the studies of this author. It is beyond the scope of this chapter to address an evaluation of these impact studies, but a brief discussion of this important point is presented at the end of this chapter.

This chapter addresses these global waves of change and transformation that has ensued in the theory and practice of governance, public administration, and public management. Specifically, the paper is organized into four sections. The section "Structural Reorganization and Reconfiguration: A Theoretical Framework" presents a theoretical framework of structural reorganization and sectoral reconfiguration in governance and administration, including structural changes of privatization, contracting out, and outsourcing. The section "Administrative Reform and Reorganization: A Theoretical Analysis" addresses a theoretical analysis of administrative reform and reorganization, putting the issue of reforms in three perspectives that cut across several disciplines of organization theory, political science, economics, and management. The section "Global Reforms and Transformation: Dynamics and Outcomes" outlines an analysis of the dynamics and outcomes of the global reforms and transformation that have transpired worldwide since the 1980s. Here, a more focused discussion (1) puts the issues of globalization and global reforms in perspective, particularly, the relationship between systemic and structural privatization and other structural reforms that have tended to redefine the role and size of government as well as the ways in which governance administration and public management are organized and performed, including the rise of the new global orthodoxy of new public management (NPM) as an intellectual arm of globalization of corporate capitalism; (2) analyzes the process of global transformation of government and public administration as we enter the new millennium; and (3) presents a brief report on the failure of NPM based on some of the most recent studies, legislative actions in different countries, and scholarly reports of implementation from around the world. The final section concludes the chapter with a few final notes on the positive and the negative consequences of structural reforms such as sweeping privatization.

Structural Reorganization and Reconfiguration: A Theoretical Framework

The structural reorganization and reconfiguration here refer to two major types or forms of reform that have appeared in both theory and practice of governance and public administration. In order to understand these two developments, we need some clarifications on the meaning of the terms reform, reorganization, and revolution, on the one hand, and reconfiguration and restructuration, on the other. Let me proceed with these distinctions first, and then identify some of the key elements of structural changes, via a brief theoretical analysis that would help put the reforms in perspective.

Reform and Reorganization

First, on reform: Reform refers to intended or designed changes into established or routine ways of life, of the ways organizations perform, of governance, administration, and management. Reform may be profound fundamental alteration of the existing order, or it may simply be a surgical alteration in the system of organization and administration, government, and politics.

A reform with fundamental changes may at the ultimate level invoke radical changes with significant transformation of a system, and as such can produce revolutionary alteration of the existing order considered no longer desirable or acceptable. Outcomes of radical and revolutionary changes are often unpredictable and they produce uncertainties, at least in the short run. Most revolutionary changes demand popularly expected radical reforms or alteration in the system that are no longer legitimate or acceptable. Examples of this sort include changes in the entire system of governance and administration after the Iranian revolution of 1979, the Cuban revolution of 1959, and the Russian revolution of 1917 (Farazmand, 1989).

Less revolutionary reforms may also be expected when a system is in malfunction, disorder, or stagnation. Such reforms could either (1) serve and maintain the system by injecting new ideas and revitalizing it or (2) cause severe disruption, implosion, and uncontrollable events that may lead the system to the edge of chaos and breakdown. An example of this sort is Gorbachev's *perestroika* of the 1980s that caused the ensuing events, leading to the collapse of the Soviet system in the USSR. Such major reforms may also be launched as demanded by the external forces, a requirement for funding, legitimacy and support, and economic and political reasons, as a condition for receiving foreign aid. Most of the global reforms of the last 25 years have been of this sort, namely the Structural Adjustment Programs (SAPs), required and demanded of developing nations by global and supranational institutions such as the World Bank, the International Monetary Fund (IMF), the World Trade Organization (WTO), and transnational corporations that have had profound transformational impacts on most developing nations worldwide. However, many of these changes have also been carried out, with mixed results, in developed nations of the West, including the United States, Europe, and Japan.

On the other hand, surgical reforms are often embarked on for the purposes of: (1) system preservation and enhancement as well as reform for the sake of reform (e.g., Shah's reform in Iran in the 1960s); (2) improvement in the administrative and system capacities (e.g., most ongoing reforms in governance and organizational operations in business and public administration, including some of the reforms in postrevolutionary situations, and managerial reforms in the United States); and (3) simply following the trends of reform, as done by many organizations. Although some of these reforms may in the long run produce unexpected consequences, as in the case of the failures of the Shah's reforms and the eventual Iranian revolution in 1978 and 1979 that led to the system's destruction (Farazmand, 1998), other reforms simply tend to perpetuate or marginally improve the existing system; or they may also be resisted effectively and become irrelevant, and even lose credibility and be forgotten with changes in political masters. Examples of the latter are found everywhere, not only in the developing and less developed countries where the problem is most severe, but also in advanced countries of the United States and Europe, where changes in partisan leadership or regimes also change reform agendas. The result is a cycle of change and continuity, or "change of change" (Peters, 2001b).

In short, reform may range from surgical, minimal changes to radical and fundamental alterations in the system of government, administration, and management. Reform, as such, could be structural, process, and value or cultural oriented. Structural changes are prone to produce fundamental and radical changes, whereas process and value changes may or may not be profound changes with long lasting assumptions. In either case, reforms can serve as powerful forces of change and are important tools of governance, administrative, and managerial systems in both theory and practice. The more genuine and realistic the reforms, the more likelihood of their successful implementation and legitimate perception among the citizens, hence acceptance and effectiveness. This point explains why so many reforms fail so often, and why new reforms are always promised by new political and administrative leaders.

Second, on reorganization: Reorganization refers to structural rearrangement, reconfiguration, reordering, and reformation. By structure I mean three concepts: one is the skeletal formation, meaning either hierarchical, or flat and horizontal structuration of an organization, administration, and governance, where the flow of authority, decision making, communication, and coordination is structured by design. This concept may work very well, or may simply serve as a facade structure. Both terms facade and skeletal structures serve one meaning of reorganization as a way of restructuration to an existing structure of government, organization, administration, and management.

The second meaning of reorganization refers to the rescuing of an otherwise disorganized and chaotic system, government, organization, and administration. It is a way of bringing in a new structure, a new organization, and a new order; hence the concept of reorganization.

The third meaning of structure refers to the rules, procedures, and regulations that govern the process and functions of a system of government, organization, administration, and management; hence structuration by design. However, informal rules, regulations, and values very often form an informal and cultural structuration that can positively or negatively affect the formal structure of an organization; hence the concept of double structuration (Farazmand, forthcoming).

Thus, to reorganize means to restructure; hence structural rearrangement and reorganization. Reorganization therefore refers to skeletal, functional, regulatory, organizational, administrative, and managerial restructuration from an undesirable to an intended and desired structural system in governance and administration. Rearrangement and reorganization, therefore, mean, for example, consolidation of several organizations or agencies into a single structural organization with a combined or a new name or title. Examples include consolidation of several security agencies and organizations such as Central Intellegence Agency (CIA), Federal Bureau of Investigation (FBI), into the Homeland Security Administration (HSA) with a brand new cabinet level name in the post-9/11 United States' federal government. Or the recent consolidation of the former Plan and Budget Organization (PBO) with the State Organization for Administrative and Employment Affairs (SOAEA) into a single national agency in Iran, namely the Planning and Management Organization (PMO). Reorganization also occurs through restructuration of the rules, regulations, and procedures that govern the new or the same organizations. Reorganization also means re-prioritization of organizational and administrative structures to facilitate leadership function by signifying certain policy or issue preferences; it redefines new structuration. Most presidents of the United States have since the early 20th century, after election, exercised this constitutional power of reorganization of administrative structure to signify new policy directions. Structuration clarifies expectations and provides road maps to achieve expected goals and missions.

Therefore, like reform, reorganization may have structural, process, and value dimensions and orientations. However, unlike most reforms, reorganizations contain broader and macroscope dimensions of change that may also carry reform programs. Reorganization is a powerful tool of governments and most political leaders engage in some sorts of reorganizations to restructure their preferences and the organizational ways through which they intend to strive to achieve their missions.

Structural Reconfiguration

By structural reconfiguration I mean rearranging and resorting the functions, responsibilities, rights, and duties of government and public administration in the management of economy, society, and politics both domestically and internationally. Reconfiguration in the realm of governance and administration can mean many things with many areas, but two major realms are in mind here: One relates to the fundamental questions of governance: "What should and should not governments do?" This is a big question of philosophy, ideology, and political economy that affects every citizen and sector of society and economy.

The second realm refers to the big questions of "how, when, and who should do what that is to be done." Discussion of these two realms of governance and administration is beyond the scope and limits of this chapter. I briefly note here that, however, they address the functions and responsibilities of government in the management of the economy, society's resources, and in the provision of goods and services as well as in the distribution of national income. They are macro questions with far more political and economic consequences and outcomes.

Nevertheless, reconfiguration here refers to the sectoral redefinition of what government should do and how should it be done in the wide range of functions a society performs as an open system. Here, sectoral redefinition refers to: (a) revision of the traditional functions of government — what governments have done and how they have done it; (b) bringing into the plain field an expanded role of the private sector in performing what governments used to do; (c) emergence of new sectoral structures such as nonprofit organizations (NPOs) and non-governmental organizations (NGOs); and in some societies, especially in developing nations, (d) the cooperative organizations and associations (Cos/As) that serve to enhance a sector of the society and economy with characteristics of self-organization and self-governance. Together, these and other peripheral organizational restructurations help shape a reconfiguration in a wide range of the fields in which government and society function, including the fields of service delivery, security and social control, market performance, domestic and foreign relations, education, health, labor, etc.

Thus, sectoral reconfiguration here refers to the sectoral restructuration of governance administration in the last 25 years, leading to more pluralized, multisectoral, and multiactor structures in which the governance administration has been transformed from a more traditionally unilateral organizational arrangement to more dispersed, multisectoral, and pluralistic structural arrangements (Wise, 2002). This new structural reconfiguration in governance administration and public administration has not only created opportunities for some, but it has also created many new challenges and constraints for others. For example, massive privatization, contracting out, outsourcing, and workforce downsizing have been the key elements of structural reorganization and reform of the economy and society, and, in governance administration, they have served as powerful tools in the structural reconfiguration process. They have provided enormous amounts of opportunities to some, especially corporations and big business in the private market sectors. However, they have also created enormous challenges to governance administration and public management, as well as enormous amounts of adverse impacts and constraints on many citizens and groups, especially among the lower- and middle-working class people around the world. Additionally, with this massive restructuration, contract management has become a big challenge that most governments are ill-equipped to handle due to the lack of trained personnel and operational mechanisms.

Administrative Reform and Reorganization: A Theoretical Analysis

Administrative reforms reflect the nature of leadership decisions, content or substance of reforms, target populations or recipients of reforms, mode of operation; organizational arrangements for implementation, budgetary issues or funding the reforms, leadership support, continuity or disruptions in the reform programs, and politics as well as economics of reforms. Each of these issues demands comprehensive treatment of analysis, a task beyond the scope of this chapter.

Theoretically speaking, three broad approaches to administrative reform may explain some of the intricacies of reforms, including who starts and who benefits, who implements and who decides, how reforms take shape and how they are implemented, what makes reforms successful or failures, and a host of other questions. These three broad approaches are top-down, bottom-up or environmentally induced, and institutional or hybrid; each of these approaches cuts across several disciplinary fields of inquiry, namely organization theory and behavior, political science, economics, management, and public administration, each explaining the approaches from a distinct point of view (see, Farazmand, 2002d).

Top-Down Reforms

This approach to reform and change generally starts from the top leadership of organization, governing elites, administrative and bureaucratic elites or leaders, executive managers of an enterprise, and chief executive officer (CEO) of a corporation. Problems are detected, needs are identified, and issues are developed by top leadership — as a group, as an individual, or as a committee — who then decide to launch reform or change programs. Announcements are made and perhaps deliberations are sought, but leadership decisions are final on change and reform. Generally, it is perceived that top leadership has full knowledge of the whole organization, system, and government, and therefore knows well what the problems are and what changes would solve them. Also, it is argued that top leadership has a full view of the big picture, has the command of authority to make reform and change happen, and has the financial capacity to fund the implementation of reforms (Peters, 2002; Farazmand, 2002b).

If perceived to be a genuine reform, the change will have a great chance to be accepted by those below the leadership — organizational members, citizens, etc. — and the legitimacy will enhance the chance of implementation. Sound as it may be, this approach has a key drawback, namely, its blind ignorance of the real needs, expectations, and preferences of those below the leadership: citizens, employees, workers, and the like. It is very easy to misread people's preferences, and it is certainly very difficult to understand them if there is a lack of legitimacy and close communication between the leaders and the led or followers. Throughout the history, politicians and administrators have committed this basic mistake over and over again, and they are still making these mistakes as we read from this chapter. It guarantees failure.

Bottom-Up Reforms

The opposite to the top-down, elitist approach to reforms is the bottom-up reform approach that emphasizes not only marginal inputs or participation from rank-and-file employees in organizations, and, by extension, from citizens in decision making regarding changes and reforms, but also the spontaneously developed movements from the environment of an organization or political system. This means changing dynamics, pressures, demands, and expectations from people, constituencies in a governing system, and, of course, employees or workers of an organization within and from outside the system. That is why the environmental approach is used as a way to signify what a system or an organization and its leadership need to know on a constant basis, what they must understand by accurate reading of their surrounding changes, and what courses of action are needed to appropriately respond to those preferences, demands, and expectations. Otherwise, the leadership's position is no longer in capacity to lead.

External forces of change driving organizational leadership to perform can lead to three possible forms of responses: The first is the leadership adaptation of those changes and demands from the environment by reflecting in decision making and implementation via reforms and changes that would be responsive and adaptive. The second way to respond is to adopt as few as possible the environmentally induced changes in the leadership programs of reform; and this will be mainly a reactive and passive approach to respond to the environmental demands for change. There is a third possibility, and that is, in face of realization by those below that leadership — political or organizational — are not genuinely interested in reforms and changes that would reflect their interests, a full take over of the entire system of leadership may be contemplated.

This is of course a rare possibility, but it is a potent possibility once considered as an option; most revolutionary changes are of these sorts of action for change, and once happened, it would be too late to think of reforms, for the entire system is now up for grabs, and revolutionary changes are expected to sweep away the old, ancient regime of order. In such cases, reforms will not satisfy those from below, the citizens. Examples include the revolutions of Iran, Cuba, Russia, and Nicaragua around the world (Farazmand, 1989, 2002b).

One potential drawback of the bottom-up approach to reform and change is the possibility of missing the big picture by those from below — citizens and organizational members — who may see the trees well but do not have a full view of the forest system from above; they may be short-sighted.

Institutional or Hybrid Reforms

The institutional approach to change and reform is often viewed, in scholarly research, as a more realistic, more comprehensive model for change and reform. It is viewed as a superior approach because it combines the advantages of both the top-down and bottom-up approaches to reform and change. It is a hybrid approach.

The argument is that, from an institutional perspective, there are at least three key elements that require close attention: structure, process, and values. The first element of this approach is the structural dimension. Changing structures is fairly easy (not to be confused with structural changes) to pursue by a top-down approach, and the second element is process dimension, and process changes require cooperation of the bottom-up approach because it has a better chance of promoting an understanding of what the reforms and changes are all about, and how they can be implemented without threatening the people involved. The third element of this approach is the value or cultural dimension, which is embedded in the institution, in its environment, and in the basic assumptions that form and reform the organization, system of government, and society at large. In short, the institutional approach is considered a more comprehensive model to pursue change and reform, because changing institutionalized orders require institutional approaches (Farazmand, 2002c).

A drawback of this model is its potential resistance to reforms and changes that may threaten its basic assumptions as well as its structural foundation. For example, capitalism resists revolutionary changes and reforms that tend to challenge its basic assumptions or to bring in the ideas of socialism and nationalization of major properties. Similarly, organizations resist changes that threaten their core foundation. Even revolutionary leaders often find themselves having to go slowly and gradually to transform the already institutionalized systems of old government, bureaucracy, and administration. In short, the institutional theory explains why some reforms fail miserably while others succeed in modern public administration. It has roots in organization theory, economics, political science, and management, with the concept of neo-institutional theory that has a currency hold in scholarship and practice. (For more details on this, see Farazmand, 2002a, chapter 3; Farazmand, forthcoming; Peters, 2001a, 2002.)

Global Reforms and Transformation: Dynamics and Outcomes

The dynamics of administrative reforms of the last 25 years that have characterized major changes in the governance and administration of the public sector around the world have had many dimensions and produced significant transformation in the ways systems of government and public administration have traditionally worked for a long time. Indeed, one may argue that perhaps the world has turned upside down, and that time and the world have changed very dramatically. For example, Fukuyama (1992) spoke of "the end of the history and of the last man," Handy (1997) noted of the "age of unreason" in which doing unthinkable and thinking unlikely were possible, and Rifkin (1996) warned of the "end of work." There is a great deal of truth to the above assertions and statements, as the world has indeed changed and big turns of historical magnitude are unfolding with worldwide impacts.

This brief section addresses four components of this global trend of big turns (my own term, see Farazmand, forthcoming): First is the phenomenon of globalization of corporate capitalism; the second relates to the sweeping privatization of the state and public administration and other global administrative reforms in that line; third is the massive transformation, or rather, re-transformation of governance and public administration in both theory and practice. Fourth is the trend of disappointment and a turn away from these transformations, with still a search for new models as well as a return back to the good old ones in governance and administration. The future of governing and governance are given in detail elsewhere (see Peters, 2002; and Farazmand, 2004), and instead our focus here is on the key reforms and transformation of public administration.

Globalization and Global Reforms

The 20th century was a witness to several trends of administrative reform around the world. First came the big structural reforms of the post-World War II on nation-building followed by institution-building in the 1960s, both motivated by the necessity of the time — postcolonialism and national independence movements — and structural capacity-building for governance and administration in a new world characterized by Cold War dynamics. The world was divided and also were the theories of development, governance, and public administration equally divided.

The capitalist world led by the United States and Europe launched massive programs of aids, technical assistance programs, and projects that were intended to deter the appeals of socialism and the growing global power of the USSR, to westernize the third world countries, and to maintain culturally and institutionally similar, or replica of, capitalist models of government and administration with the private sector playing a key or dominant role.

The postwar nation-building and institution-building were coincided with the global quest of multinational corporations, now mainly controlled and dominated by the United States; the United States since World War II began a relentless global quest to outdo its rivals, including the Great Britain, and to claim global leadership of the Western capitalism. In this process, empowering the state as the key institutional player in the realms of economic and politics was essential, not only in advanced countries but also in developing and less developed nations. The state provided the most important basis of security for financial capital investments in developing countries; it was the grantor and guarantor of investment returns.

It was more profitable and secure for multinational corporations to enter into financial agreements with the states through which cheap labor and resources could be secured along with the state-led market opening to international or foreign imports. As a consequence, nationalization became a key policy tool in developing countries with a massive growth of public enterprise management, as was the growth of public enterprise management in the advanced countries for at least two centuries (see Farazmand, 2001b, 1996, for details on the rationales and factors contributing to the growth of government and public enterprise management worldwide).

Interestingly, nationalization and public enterprise management gained momentum and grew dramatically during the 1960s and even the 1970s. Governments and public management played a fundamental role in economic growth, infrastructure development, national development, and national income distribution and redistribution of national wealth. The state had become a moderator of inequality, and the so-called welfare state became a powerful institution of class and income gap moderation. The Western quest for globalization of corporate capitalism was checked and restrained by global socialism and the USSR that, as a superpower, had played a key role in international arena and significantly influenced the shaping of world politics. The rise of the welfare state in the West was primarily, it may be argued, a reaction and deterrent to the growing appeal of global socialism, with the USSR championing its leadership role for the working class worldwide.

The decline and the stagnation of capitalism in the West accompanied by the continuous rise in expenditures on arms race, on the one hand, and the growing pressures inwards — for higher wages and participation in management, emerging power of the women workforce, and unions, etc. — inside the industrialized countries of the West, on the other, pushed multinational corporations to go further outward in search of cheap labor, open markets, and cheap resources. This time, new technologies aided them to move faster, and to enter into joint ventures with former enemies, such as China and later the USSR. The fall of the USSR gave a golden opportunity to the global corporate capitalist elites to dismantle the welfare state, to turn back the decades of achievements in administrative and social reforms on labor and environmental regulations, to keep the working class and average people quiet at home, to move out and outsource jobs to cheap places with little or no regulations, and to exploit new markets in former socialist countries.

With the fall of the USSR, there was no longer a compelling rationale for the welfare state. The idea that every one must fend for himself or herself in the new world with "one market under God" (Frank, 2000) became the new global slogan of corporate capitalism. The ideological underpinning that market is superior to all other forms of social and economic organization (Lindblom, 2001) was coupled with the purported Western supremacy. As a result, many changes began to flow worldwide, affecting the lives of billions of people. Advancement in technological innovations, almost overnight, also added rapid pace to these changes, and transformation began to take place, some naturally and others by design. Consequently, epochal changes began as humanity entered the new millennium. Yet, these changes must be considered a part, or in a context, of continuity in historical quest of world capitalism for absolute profits or accumulation drive, and the changes only reinforce the horse power of global capitalism.

The hallmark of all these changes has been globalization, a term that has captured the topics and subjects of books and publications too many to count. Globalization has been the transcending force that recognizes no national boundaries, no space, no time, and no limit in its process of action. Globalization is a process "through which worldwide transcendence and integration are taking place" (Farazmand, 1999a, 2004), enclosing the entire globe under the banner of global capitalism with a self-declared ideological supremacy of market capitalism led by the globalizing corporate hegemony (Dugger, 1989). Discussion of globalization, its causes and consequences, and implications for public management is beyond the limits of this chapter. I have done this elsewhere (see, Farazamand, 1999a,b for details).

The fundamental points of relevance to administrative reform are several, the most important of which is a globally implemented comprehensive set of reforms that would: (1) facilitate the process of change and continuity in world capitalism toward a more cohesive and well-coordinated global organization of corporate capitalism; (2) shrink the size and reduce the functions of the state and governments worldwide, whereas at the same time, expand the role, functions, and scope of activities of the business–private sector dominated by the corporate organizational arrangements; (3) position the societies or countries for favorable operations of the global corporate capitalist systems by deregulations of environment, relaxation of labor laws, and deregulation of workplaces; (4) dismantle the welfare administrative state and replace it with a corporate welfare state that supports and promotes, both politically and financially, the corporate sector; (5) establish a system of global corporate dependency through "agencification" of national economies and promotion of the so-called subsidiarity concept through outsourcing and contracting out functions around the world; and finally, (6) establish a global corporate hegemony with concentrated global power centered in the West, especially the United States and Western Europe, with Japan as a key ally. Yet, interglobalization, rivalry, and competition are also developing via Western Europe, Japan, and now China which also has entered this new era of capitalist globalization.

The bottom line of all these changes — linear, nonlinear, and chaotic — is the continuity and expansion of global capitalism with the corporations positioning themselves toward a global hegemony (see also Korten, 2001). Therefore, the close correlation has already been established between globalization and its demands for sweeping structural reforms around the world (see Farazmand, 2002b,d; Korten, 2001; Mander & Goldsmith, 1996 for more details). Sweeping privatization has functioned as an instrument of implementing the goals of global corporate capitalism. Accompanied by a set of deregulations, devolution, and agencification, sweeping privatization and contracting out have been the most important and structurally comprehensive administrative reforms that have been carried out worldwide. Sweeping privatization reforms have taken place in several forms and resulted in the reorganization and the structural reconfiguration of public–private sectors, which is detailed earlier in this chapter.

Sweeping Privatization

Privatization reforms have been in at least three forms: tactical, pragmatic, and systemic. Tactical privatization and contracting out is not a new idea, and in fact it has been used by almost all governments worldwide, from local to national levels for thousands of years. It is a way of getting things done through other private or nonprofit organizations. Pragmatic privatization is applied to areas in which governments decide where and what areas to privatize on pragmatic grounds and for the reasons of efficiency, effectiveness, and economy, as well as for matters of priorities in policy and performance. Systemic privatization is the most comprehensive form of privatization, with profound structural changes in governance and administration. Together, these and other reforms produce a structural reorganization of governance administration, with a new public management philosophy that has served as an intellectual arm of corporate globalization; together, they serve as a driving engine of globalization of corporate culture.

The approaches used in launching and implementing reforms, right from the initial to the most transformational stages, have been predominantly top-down, with some environmentally induced models serving for justifications for change. The processes of radical, systemic as well as pragmatic and tactical privatization from introduction to implementation in most countries, including industrially advanced countries of the West, but especially developing and less developed countries, have been a response to two fundamental forces of change: one internal and the other external. Internally, the initial policy design of the Reagan and Thatcher regimes in the United States and the Great Britain set the whole motion of massive privatization in the early 1980s, a macro organizational redesign of the government–society–private sector relations. Reagan and Thatcher were the key governmental instruments of initiating and implementing by design the privatization policies to achieve the goals of the globalizing corporate power elites. Both regimes represented the core of the globalizing corporate elites and their interests using the institutional channels and budgetary powers of the state to accomplish the goals of global capitalism.

Subsequently, the international or foreign arms of these two governments of the North expanded the deliberate policy of globalizing restructuration into the developing and less developed countries, most of whom are highly dependent on them and had no choice but to adopt the reform policy. Foreign aid and other economic and technological exports accompanied the new conditions of structural reforms. These external forces to reform were also reinforced by a host of other international and globalizing institutions such as the United Nations and its strategic organizational entities, namely, the International Monetary Fund (IMF), the World Bank (WB), and the World Trade Organization (WTO), and others that have systematically pushed for fundamental structural reforms of the public sector with privatization and devolution as a key condition for technical assistance and financial aid. The key words of the 1980s were structural adjustment programs (SAPs) supplemented by the words good governance and public–private partnerships of the 1990s that have entered the new millennium. Today, a true transformation has taken place in governance, administration, and public management.

Global Transformation of Public Administration: A New Orthodoxy

The sweeping global privatization of the public sector has gone far beyond its initial rationale and ideological claim of inefficiency in certain public enterprises and other government corporations as a burden on national government treasury and citizen tax payers. The privatization policies that have been pursued during the last two decades or so have covered almost every function and activity, including those always considered the core and heart, of governments around the world for millennia. The entire public sphere has been taken over for profit and capital accumulation by the corporate business organizations.

Therefore, a fundamental structural reconfiguration has taken place in public–private sector relations worldwide; everything in society has been claimed by the business corporations for profit purpose, including prisons, mental hospitals, healthcare, and security areas. There has been a fundamental restructruation in public–private sector relations, and the structural reconfiguration has resulted in macro-reorganization of the ways in which economy, society, and governance administration function.

The role of government and society has been redefined by the new ideological reform of capitalist organization and philosophy. The role of the state has been pulled back, or forced to retreat (Strange, 1996), and reduced to providing law and order (system maintenance) for social control to promote the goals of capital accumulation and facilitation of corporate sector ideals. Structural and systemic privatization has been accompanied by massive deregulation, devolution, and deconcentration of some functions while centralizing others, especially the commanding ones. Therefore, although there are many paradoxes in the reforms movement, the overall structural changes are a reality that has taken place to position the corporate sector in a commanding status of governance, administration, and management, as well as of policy and economy worldwide. This has been accomplished by a top-down approach with the appearance of some bottom-up or environmentally induced changes. Although the forms of privatization have also varied — from partial privatization to contracting out, and outsourcing — systemic privatization has been the most dominant form, especially in developing nations, with tactical and pragmatic privatization to follow. Systemic privatization has structurally altered the public–private sectors' configuration as a macro public policy, with profound implications for governance, administration, and citizens.

Concurrent with the sweeping privatization reforms that resulted in structural changes in the public sector, a new ideological-oriented managerial theory has been developed. Dubbed as new public management, this new theory is constructed on business management models, with the conservative neoclassical economic theory of public choice of the 1960s (see Buchanan & Tullock, 1962), updated by transaction-cost and principal–agent theories. These theoretical underpinnings consider citizens as consumers, public managers as agents serving consumer principals, and business models as the best and only best models of managing any organization anywhere around the world; hence the ideological concepts of managerialism, subsidiarity, agencification, and principal–agent relations (see Hood, 1991; Jensen, 1983; Williamson, 1985) of modern public administration.

The initial idea of public choice theory — already discredited in the age of globalization of large-scale corporate organizational systems due to the concept of "voting on foot" and efficiency achieved through small-scale, overlapping jurisdictions — was now supplanted by the freshly supplied and refined models of transaction-cost and principal–agent in organization theory with a root in sociology (Williamson, 1985). This new ideological, managerialist, and entrepreneurial model of organization in public management has since the 1990s been on the forefront of governmental reforms to run governments and public organizations and programs like private enterprises, with maximum managerial flexibility. The traditional models of public administration and management have been rejected as inefficient, inflexible, and too regulatory and procedure-oriented. Efficiency and cost cutting imperatives have replaced concerns for equity, equality, and fairness. The concept of managerialism, therefore, is claimed to have the capacity of an ideal model for all organizations (see, for example, Hood, 1991; Barzelay, 2001).

This new public management therefore represents a new orthodoxy of "one size fits all" in public management and governance administration. Ironically, this so-called new public management is claimed by its proponents as a response to the failing and discredited old orthodoxy of the bureaucratic models of governance administration. Subsequently, what we have in hand today is a new ideological-oriented, neoconservative political–economic model of organization and management that purports to solve old problems, although it has become a new orthodoxy in itself, with too many promises and few achievements, as we will see further in the chapter. This new "one size fits all" model of public management is in fact more rigid and inflexible than any previous model, so much so that it allows no tolerance of any alternatives to its market-oriented supremacy in theory and practice. The reason for this self-declared supreme model of managerialism is its attachment to the globalization of corporate capitalism discussed earlier.

Therefore, the new ideological-oriented model of public management has risen as an intellectual arm of corporate globalization of capitalism serving its goals of profit maximization and accumulation of capital. It is this global transformation of governance administration and public management that the sweeping structural reforms and reorganization — through systemic privatization — and propagation of new managerialism and new public management have transpired worldwide as we enter the 21st century.

There are many features of this new global transformation in public management, with implications for education and training in public administration and for public policy. Aside from the structural transference of government functions, including its core functions, to the corporate sector and reducing the role of governments to agents of global corporate governance, there are cultural and value transformations that are also taking place. This new market-based, corporate organizations, and ideological-oriented definition of citizens as consumers will have serious ramifications for societies, human values, and cultures as well as for governance administration and public management.

It is beyond the limit of this chapter to go over the features of this new global transformation, but an outline of such listing would include the following:

- Replacement of public bureaucracy with giant, corporate bureaucracies without human face (e.g., dealing with 800 numbers and minimally trained and cheap corporate organizational workers, whom I call corporate soldiers)
- Private use of public assets for profit purposes
- Reducing citizens to market-place consumers
- Empowerment of corporate elites and elevating them to idols of success
- Emphasis on social control and fighting terrorism to provide security and peace worldwide and promote corporate goals of capital accumulation
- Viewing human beings as commodities to be exchanged in the marketplace
- Loss of control over public service delivery due to lack of capacity to monitor privatized functions
- Lack or loss of accountability and transparency
- Abuse of outsourced public authority (prisons, mental hospitals, children, and other institutions)
- Loss of quality and efficiency
- Loss of public funds in privatized organizations and services
- Loss of concern or value for human beings and viewing them as exchangeable commodities in the global marketplace. There are also other contradictions and paradoxes that have also characterized the public management and governance administration both institutionally and organizationally. For example, decentralization, empowerment, and diversity are preached by this new movement, although in reality the facts of centralization, disempowerment, and conformity are stressed in public organizations as well as in privatized enterprises.

Failure of NPM and Privatization?

Critics of NPM, this author included, have from its inception warned against the flaws of this new orthodoxy that range from promising too much to its impracticability, antidemocratic, and inequality-driven premises, as well as ethical and accountability problems that it carries both in theory and practice. Reports of the failures of administrative reforms — with privatization and adoption of NPM as their key features — in Latin America have been presented at the CLAD conferences (Latin American Conferences on Public Administration Reforms) since the mid-1990s. As a result, many Latin American countries have either abandoned NMP or modified its application to the point that it has become almost irrelevant to public management. The overriding concern of these countries has been the issues concerning fairness, equity, and equality, as well as accountability that NMP cares less about. In fact, NMP's overriding interest is managerial flexibility and cost efficiency without concern for fairness, equity, transparency and accountability. Ironically, much of the failure of the sweeping privatization and NMP reforms have been reported in Latin American countries, a region which is highly dependent on, and influenced by, the globalizing corporate forces of North America, namely the United States.

Similar evidence of failures of NPM and sweeping privatization have been documented by the United Nations documents and other international conference reports (see, for example, Argyriades, 2001). Other scholars (see, for example, Wettenhall, 2001, 2003) have also warned against the serious flaws of sweeping privatization, public–private partnerships, and NPM.

The most recent reports of NPM's failures have been documented in two European countries of Switzerland and the Netherlands (see Noordhoek & Saner, 2005). In both cases, local legislators (parliaments) have voted against NMP's application in local government administration, and a key overriding concern in both countries has been expressed regarding the loss of democratic control, accountability, and fairness, as well as lack of promised efficiency. Even in the birthplace of NPM, which is New Zealand, newly elected government recently reversed the NMP's adoption and decided to either abandon it or modify its application.

Despite the increasing failures of NMP and privatization, this new global orthodoxy continues to capture the attention and interest of many developing countries and scholars who have limited knowledge of it but are fascinated by its so-called new notion. One would wonder why? I have already given my answer to this key question, and that is, the intimate relationship between globalization and systemic privatization and similar reforms, with NMP acting as an intellectual arm of globalization promoting its goals in both academia and governments. Most governments in developing countries are under a heavy burden of financial, political, and military dependency on global capitalism and powers of the North. They have little or no choice but to accept what is dictated to them by the globalizing corporations, powerful governments of the North, and the international financial institutions such as IMF, WB, WTO, and the United Nations that tries to help achieve developmental goals. Others, like Iran, are following suit to meet the conditions of joining the WTO.

Conclusion

The global administrative reforms of the last two decades or so have had profound impacts on public administration, governance administration, and government–society relations all over the world. Through structural reforms of the public sector, implemented by sweeping privatization and its managerial ideology of NPM to achieve the goals of globalization of corporate capitalism, a fundamental transformation has taken place in governance administration and public management, a process that is still in progress.

Impacts of this global transformation are many and will likely last for a long time, though the reports of its failure are being documented worldwide. This chapter cautions against blind adoption of NMP, sweeping privatization, and promotion of the goals of globalization at the expense of national sovereignty, national development goals, independent growth, and development of a country. Example for this is Iran that has needed almost all natural resources as well as financial and organizational capacity to govern its society and manage its economy. Cooperation, partnership building, and other forms of regional and international governance relations are important issues in an increasingly interdependent world that is rapidly globalized, but this globalization is mostly driven by the powerful North, and the South on the receiving side. The receiving South must be very careful in its approach to the issues of globalization and its structural reforms.

Elsewhere (Farazmand, 2001a), I have discussed in detail some policy recommendations of globalization for developmental states in developing countries, including Iran, with some implications for public management education and training in another study (see Farazmand, 2002a). Is privatization all bad? No, and not necessarily; in fact, privatization has produced some positive as well as negative consequences (see Farazmand, 2001b, 2002a, b for details on these consequences). On the positive side, privatization may free governments from becoming shopkeepers involved in details of microeconomic issues of a society. Also, "privatization and globalization have made public administrators and managers appreciate what they have had and not to take things for granted" (Farazmand, 2002a, p. 365). There is a wake-up call for all in governance administration and public management. The idea of "thinking globally and acting locally" has also linked local problems to global ones and vice versa, and this is good.

On the negative side, globalization and sweeping privatization have posed serious threat to democratic self-determination, to state sovereignty and governability, reduced the ability to manage in government and administration, producing problems of corruption, unethical conducts as well as loss of accountability, fairness, and equity, and this means more problems for developing countries already in deep trouble. Globalization and spread of NPM as well as sweeping privatization and other structural reforms in administration and governance means Americanization of the world, with all its negative consequences such as the rise of the police state for social control and security, loss of personal liberty due to increasing concern of the states over terrorism, and a lot more (there are some positive ones too, including making people aware and understand the true nature of what globalization is, including globalization by violence can bring to their countries, their people, and their resources). What does all this mean for public management education and training? There are several, but this question calls for a separate paper presentation, beyond the limits of this chapter.

References

Argyriades, D. (2001). "Final Report on Governance and Public Administration in the 21st Century: New Trends and New Techniques." International Congress of Administrative Sciences, Athens, July 9–13.

Barzelay, M. (2001). *The New Public Management*. Berkeley, CA: University of California Press.

Buchanan, J. and G. Tullock (1962). *The Calculus of Consent*. Ann Arbor, MI: University of Michigan Press.

Dugger, W. (1989). *Corporate Hegemony*. New York: Greenwood Press.

Farazmand, A. (1989). *The State, Bureaucracy, and Revolution in Modern Iran: Agrarian Reforms and Regime Politics*. New York: Praeger.

Farazmand, A. (1996). *Public Enterprise Management*. Westport, CT: Greenwood Press.

Farazmand, A. (1998). "Failure of Administrative Reform and the Revolution of 1978–79 in Iran: A Contextual and Comparative Analysis." *Korean Review of Public Administration* 3 (2): 93–123.

Farazmand, A. (1999a). "Globalization and Public Administration." *Public Administration Review* 59 (6): 509–522.

Farazmand, A. (1999b). "Privatization or Reform: Public Enterprise Management in Transition." *International Review of Administrative Science* 65 (4): 551–567.

Farazmand, A. (2001a). "Globalization, the State, and Public Administration: A Theoretical Analysis with Implications for Developmental States." *Public Organization Review: A Global Journal* 1 (1): 437–464.

Farazmand, A. (2001b). *Privatization or Public Enterprise Reform?: Implications for Public Management*. Westport, CT: Greenwood Press.

Farazmand, A. (2002a). "Privatization and Globalization: A Critical Analysis with Implications for Public Management Education and Training." *International Review of Administrative Sciences* 68 (3): 355–371.

Farazmand, A. (2002b). "Globalization, Privatization and the Future of Governance: A Critical Assessment." *Public Finance and Management* 2 (1): 125–153.

Farazmand, A. (2002c). *Modern Organizations: Theory and Practice*, 2nd edition, expanded. Westport, CT: Praeger.

Farazmand, A. (2002d). *Administrative Reform in Developing Nations*. Westport, CT: Greenwood.

Farazmand, A. (2004). *Sound Governance: Policy and Administrative Innovations.* Westport, CT: Praeger.

Farazmand, A. (Forthcoming). *Globalization, Governance, and Administration.*

Farazmand, A. (Forthcoming). *Transformation of the U.S. Administrative State: Institutionalization and Globalization.*

Frank, T. (2000). *One Market Under God: Extreme Capitalism, Market Populism, and the End of Economic Democracy.* New York: Doubleday.

Fukuyama, F. (1992). *The End of History and of Man.* New York: Free Press.

Handy, C. (1997). *Age of Unreason.* New York: Harvard Business Press.

Hood, C. (1991). "A Public Management for All Seasons?" *Public Administration* 69 (3): 3–19.

Jensen, M. (1983). "Organization Theory and Methodology." *The Accounting Review* 8 (2): 319–337.

Korten, D. (2001). *When Corporations Rule the World,* 2nd edition. West Hartford, CT: Kumarian Press.

Lindblom, C. (2001). *The Market Systems.* New Haven, CT: Yale University Press.

Mander, J. and E. Goldsmith (eds.) (1996). *The Case Against the Global Economy and for a turn to the Local.* San Francisco, CA: Sierra Club Books.

Noordhoek, P. and R. Saner, (2005). "Beyond New Public Management: Answering the Claims of Politics and Society." *Public Organization Review: A Global Journal* 5 (1): 35–54.

Peters, G. (2001a). *The Future of Governing,* 2nd edition. Lawrence, KS: University Press of Kansas.

Peters, G. (2001b). "From Change to Change: Patterns of Continuing Administrative Reform." *Public Organization Review: A Global Journal* 1 (1): 41–54.

Peters, G. (2002). "Government Reorganization: Theory and Practice." In *Modern Organizations: Theory and Practice,* 2nd edition. A. Farazmand (ed.), Westport, CT: Praeger, pp. 159–180.

Rifkin, J. (1996). *The End of Work.* New York: G.P. Putnam's Press.

Strange, S. (1996). *The Retreat of the State: Diffusion of Power in the World Economy.* Cambridge, UK: Cambridge University Press.

Wettenhall, R. (2001). "Public or Private? Public Corporations, Companies, and the Decline of the Middle Ground." *Public Organization Review: A Global Journal* 1 (1): 13–36.

Wettenhall, R. (2003). "The Rhetoric and Reality of Public–Private Partnerships." *Public Organization Review: A Global Journal* 3 (1): 77–108.

Williamson, O. (1985). *The Economic Institutions of Capitalism.* New York: The Free Press.

Wise, C. (2002). "The Public Service Configuration Problem: Designing Public Organizations in a Pluralistic Public Service." In *Modern Organizations: Theory and Practice,* 2nd edition. A. Farzmand (ed.), Westport, CT: Praeger, pp. 135–158.

Chapter 19

Globalization of Administrative Reforms: The Dilemmas of Combining Political Control and Increased Institutional Autonomy

Tom Christensen and Per Lægreid

CONTENTS

Introduction

New public management (NPM) as a model for public-sector reform has spread rapidly to many countries over the past two decades. Spearheaded by reform entrepreneurs such as the Organization for Economic Co-operation and Development (OECD) and some Anglo-Saxon trailblazers (Pollitt & Bouckaert, 2004), the reform wave has, with varying degrees of intensity, encompassed mainly Western democracies but also affected some developing countries via the influence of the International Monetary Fund and the World Bank (2000). Although NPM now seems to have peaked and have been modified in countries that might be regarded as NPM pioneers, such as New Zealand (Gregory, 2003), it is still having a major impact on the structure and functioning of the public sector in many countries. In many cases a previously integrated state structure has become considerably more diffuse or even fragmented. Although this is the main picture, there is a considerable degree of national variation resulting from differences in the existing structural apparatus prior to reform and in historical–cultural traditions and determined by the extent of external pressure for reform (Christensen & Lægreid, 2001).

The main structural changes made in NPM reforms have been not only structural devolution or increased vertical specialization, giving agencies and state-owned companies more autonomy, but also increased horizontal specialization according to the principle of "single-purpose organizations," creating more narrow and nonoverlapping roles or functions as public owner, administrator, regulator, purchaser, provider, etc. (Boston et al., 1996). The effects of these reforms seem to have been more complex and bureaucratic organizations, not less as promised, more problems of political control, more influential administrative and commercial state leaders, etc. (Pollitt & Bouckaert, 2004). This again has created attempts at regaining some of the political control lost.

With this background, this chapter will address the following questions:

- What are some of the most crucial dilemmas and challenges of balancing political control and increased institutional autonomy in NPM reforms, and what characterize some of the attempts at solving or influencing these dilemmas and challenges?

- How can we explain similarities and varieties in the way governments handle these dilemmas and challenges in different countries?
- What may be the future prospects and trends in governments balancing political control and institutional autonomy?

We will have a broad transformation perspective as a point of departure, encompassing and combining theories about environmental pressure, cultural factors and path dependency, and instrumentally oriented theory digging into the importance of the actions of political executive leaders, top administrative executives, and CEOs of state-owned companies (Christensen & Lægreid, 2001; Pollitt & Bouckaert, 2004). We will mainly discuss the dilemmas mentioned on the central political–administrative level by utilizing broad comparative studies of these questions.

A Transformative Perspective

The theoretical perspective used to analyze governmental reform in general, and dilemmas of balancing political control and increased institutional autonomy in particular, is a broad institutional one, looking at the interaction between structural and instrumental features (national polity), cultural features (historical administrative traditions), and external constraints (the technical and institutional environments) (Christensen & Lægreid, 2001). This approach focuses on the complex and dynamic interplay between different internal and external factors as a way of understanding the organizational transformation, occurring in the public sector generally and in the civil service specifically, and its effects.

One school of thought regards the implementation of NPM-related reforms and the creation of a fragmented state primarily as a response to external pressure. This environmental determinism (Olsen, 1992) can be of two kinds. In the first instance, a country may adopt internationally based norms and ideas about how a civil service system should be organized and run simply because these have become the prevailing doctrine. NPM has its origins in certain Anglo-Saxon countries and international organizations like the OECD, where a kind of reform myth has taken hold, has become ideologically dominant, and has spread all over the world (Czarniawska & Sevón, 1996; Meyer & Rowan, 1977; Scott, 1995). This process of dissemination may imply isomorphic elements — i.e., it may create pressure for similar reforms and structural changes in many countries all over the world (DiMaggio & Powell, 1983 Boli & Thomas, 1999;). Isomorphism can be seen as a deterministic, decontextualized, natural process engendered by common dominating norms and values in a globalized world society (Drori et al., 2003; Kettl, 2000). In the second instance, NPM may genuinely be seen as the optimal solution to widespread technical problems — i.e., it may be adopted to solve problems created by lack of instrumental performance or by economic competition and market pressure. In this instance NPM reforms are adopted not because of their ideological hegemony but because of their perceived technical efficiency. The two lines of argument treat the environment as institutional or technical, respectively.

Another view of NPM holds that reforms are primarily a product of the national historical–institutional context. Different countries have different historical–cultural traditions and their reforms are "path dependent," meaning that national reforms have unique features and trajectories (Krasner, 1988; March & Olsen, 1989; Selznick, 1957). The reform roads taken reflect the main features of national institutional processes, where institutional "roots" determine the path followed in a gradual adaptation to internal and external pressure. The greater the consistency between the values underlying the NPM reforms and the values on which the existing administrative system is based, the more likely the reforms are to be successful (Brunsson & Olsen, 1993), for a high degree of compatibility furthers adaptation and implementation.

A third view emphasizes national differences in constitutional features and political–administrative structures and contends that these factors go some way to explaining how countries handle national problems and reform processes (Olsen & Peters, 1996; Weaver & Rockman, 1993). The main features of the polity, the form of government, and the formal structure of decision making within the political–administrative system may all affect a country's capacity to realize administrative reforms. Westminster-style "electoral dictatorships" and homogeneous administrative systems are potentially more conducive to reform than non-Westminster systems with complex party structures, changing parliamentary majorities, and a heterogeneous bureaucracy (Hood, 1996). And Westminster systems are more reform-prone than Presidential system with checks and balances, even though the latter system also opens up for reform entrepreneurs.

Within the constraints outlined, political leaders also have varying amounts of leeway to launch and implement NPM reforms via administrative design and an active administrative policy. Their identities, resources, and capacity for rational calculation and political control (Dahl & Lindblom, 1953; March & Olsen, 1995) are to a great extent constrained by the complex interplay of environmental, historical–institutional, and polity features. Thus, adaptation to external pressure is not only about environmental determinism but may also have intentional elements ensuing from the actions of the political–administrative leadership, the professionals or consulting firms that certify certain prescriptions or reforms, or else represent systematic double-talk or hypocrisy (Brunsson, 1989). Conscious national handling of internationally inspired reforms can, however, also lead to the imitation of only selected reform elements instead of whole reform packages and as such create variation between countries (Røvik, 1996). Furthermore, political ability to control reform processes can be enhanced by polity and structural factors increasing the capacity and attention of the political leadership or hindered by negotiation processes or by a lack of compatibility with historical–institutional norms (Christensen & Peters, 1999 Brunsson & Olsen, 1993;). Such features will probably also make political–administrative systems more vulnerable to pressure for reform from the environment.

A transformative perspective emerges when we combine internal and environmental reform features to explain why the content, effects, and implications of NPM may be different in different countries (Christensen & Lægreid, 1998). This perspective denies both the optimistic position that willful political reform actors have full, comprehensive insight into and power over reform processes, and the fatalistic position that they have no possibility of influencing reforms through political choice (Lægreid & Roness, 1999; Olsen, 1992). Instead, the transformative perspective offers an intermediate position, whereby political leaders are assured a degree of maneuverability whereas their influence is constrained by environmental factors, polity features, and the historical–institutional context.

At one extreme, international environmental pressure to adopt NPM reforms, whether through international organizations or economic crises, may have profound effects on national systems, if the reforms are simultaneously furthered by the political–administrative leadership and are compatible with historical–cultural traditions. At the other extreme, environmental pressure for reform may produce few changes and effects, if political and administrative leaders consciously try to hinder or avoid reforms owing to their lack of compatibility with traditional norms and values and with national reform models (Brunsson & Olsen, 1993). These extremes correspond, respectively, to a contextualization process — which emphasizes where environmental change concepts and internal needs match — and a decontextualization process, which stresses the uniqueness of national systems and the lack of compatibility between their values and norms and reforms of external origin (Røvik, 1996).

In reality it is likely that when externally generated reform concepts and processes are transferred to national political–administrative systems, they will become more complex and have more varied and ambiguous effects and implications than the extremes outlined above. In practice political leaders can use certain elements of externally generated reforms or try to redefine ambiguous reform elements and situations in a national context to match instrumental goals and national culture. Or they might deliberately manipulate the reforms as myths and symbols, pretending to implement them, but actually having little intention of doing so, and try to further their legitimacy through double-talk or by separating talk, decisions, and actions (Brunsson, 1989). In yet another scenario political leaders might accept the reforms, leaving their implementation to administrative leaders and thus allowing for adjustment, translation, and editing to fit institutional–cultural features (Jacobsson et al., 2003; Røvik, 1998; Sahlin-Andersson, 1996).

The effects of NPM-related reforms on political control may in principle, given the potential complexity shown by the transformation perspective, point in different directions. Politicians may intend to retain or strengthen their power and control by consciously using the reform measures. But they may also lose control by accepting reform elements that undermine their leadership. The effects of NPM reforms on political–democratic control may be related to how managers define or redefine their roles and implement reforms. Negotiation processes may also be evident, making political leaders accept compromises or culturally based resistance.

NPM as a reform wave consists of some main ideas, ideology, and theories on the one hand, and a variety of more practical reform measures on the other (Christensen & Lægreid, 2001; Politt & Bouckaert, 2004). This means that the dilemmas and challenges faced by public leaders, confronted with NPM reforms, may be of different kinds. First, they may be related to a confrontation of ideologies and main thoughts about how to organize the central government, i.e., related more to the big picture. This includes also a potential more fundamental tension between old and new political–administrative cultures, i.e., a conflict between different broader informal norms and values (Selznick, 1957). Second, they may be connected to more middle-range theories about how to organize government, i.e., particularly new institutional economy theories and management theories in the case of NPM reforms (Boston et al., 1996). Third, the dilemmas and challenges are also, on the practical side, connected to the specific organizational reforms made, i.e., to alternative ways of organizing political–administrative systems in reality. Fourth, the effects of NPM reforms, whether on political control, efficiency, consumers, or broader societal factors, are also significant in analyzing these dilemmas and challenges. The two first points are related to the world of ideas, ideology, and theories, whereas the last two encompass central elements of practice.

We will now address the dilemmas and challenges of balancing political control and increased institutional autonomy by first focusing on the world of ideas and then on the world of practice.

Balancing Political Control and Agency Autonomy: The World of Ideas

Confrontation of Governance Models

A traditional view, in parliamentarian countries, is that democracy and political–administrative control are defined according to the "parliamentary chain of governance" and the mandate given by the population to political leaders through the election channel (Olsen, 1983).[1] The people select representatives to political bodies in elections, executive power is based on the political majority in these bodies and the executive has at his disposal a neutral civil service with a wealth of professional expertise, who prepares and implements public policy, including reforms. This perspective on the role of the bureaucracy is still relevant and important, but it has been modified in a number of ways. Olsen (1988) labels this model of governance "the sovereign, rationality-bounded state," meaning a centralized state with a large public sector in which standardization and equality are prominent features. The model emphasizes the collective and integrative features of the political–administrative system, the common heritage and the role of the citizen (March & Olsen, 1989). The role of the civil service in such a state can be seen as rather complex, relating to considerations of political control, to decision effectiveness, responsiveness, professional competence, and to "Rechtsstaat" values (March & Olsen, 1983). This complexity is said to enhance the flexibility and political sensitivity of civil servants and is therefore perceived as more of a strength than a weakness (Christensen, 1991).

In accordance with this state model, change and reform processes in a political–administrative system are hierarchical and dominated by political and administrative leaders, i.e., the decision processes are closed and have an exclusive group of participants (Hood, 1998; March & Olsen, 1983). Within the limits of bounded rationality, leaders score high on rational calculation by consistent goal formulation and conscious organizational means–end thinking (Dahl & Lindblom, 1953; Simon, 1957). As indicated, this ideal is difficult to fulfill in a complex and fragmented state.

This traditional model has been supplemented by a variety of others, among them the corporatist state model (Olsen, 1988; Peters, 1996). But the one closely related to NPM, and the focus of our attention here, has been labeled by Olsen (1988) "the supermarket state." In this alternative model of democracy and political–administrative control, the state is

[1]Many of the basic features described here of course also apply in presidential and more mixed systems, but the difference is that in such systems the people have more than one set of representatives or agents.

perceived as a service provider, with an emphasis on efficiency and good quality, and the people as consumers, users, or clients (Hood, 1998). In this model the hierarchy is in a sense turned upside down — i.e., rather than the state controlling society on the basis of a democratic mandate from the people, society controls the state more directly through market mechanisms. The supermarket state primarily attends to economic values and norms, meaning that other values and considerations from the centralized state model must be downgraded, making this model more one-dimensional (Nagel, 1997). Furthermore, public reform processes are primarily a result of changes in market processes and user demand and hence environmental-deterministic in nature (Olsen, 1992). This model is not new in one sense, because its elements have been represented in Anglo-American countries over a long period of time, but has through NPM been revitalized, extended, and spread worldwide as a reinvented and generic model (Hood, 1996; Self, 2000).

Administrative reforms, according to this model, appear to be apolitical or even antipolitical in nature (Fredrickson, 1996). Thus, political bodies and politicians tend to be seen almost as illegitimate actors who obstruct efficiency, and the centralized state as overloaded and inefficient at the central level (Boston et al., 1996; Gustafsson & Svensson, 1999). What the model lacks is a perspective on the relationship between the influence of voters or citizens on politicians through the election channel, on the one hand, and their more direct influence on public bodies as clients and consumers on the other. And although the model may be said to contain some elements of an alternative view of democracy — namely, a direct, individually oriented democracy with economic overtones — it is not easy to see how atomized actors making choices in a market can participate in creating a stable and responsible democratic system and give political leaders unambiguous political constraints. One might indeed argue that their potential to influence services is also ambiguous and debatable.

To sum up, the supermarket state seems to represent a one-dimensional view of the public sector, where the economic factor predominates, whereas the society-controlling state is more preoccupied with a complex balancing of a variety of legitimate considerations. The two state models presented have normative-political implications traditionally associated with a left–right spectrum. Socialist and social democratic parties have defended the sovereign state model, whereas conservative and liberal parties have supported the supermarket state model (Nagel, 1997). The attitudes of interest groups have also followed the same cleavage, exemplified by resistance among trade unions and civil servants' unions associated with the labor parties to the supermarket model (Castles et al., 1996; Lægreid & Roness, 2003). However, an electoral shift to the right in Western countries during the last 20 years has led to a breakthrough for the supermarket model, such that now even many socialist and social democratic parties have come to accept some elements from it. Although these are seen by some as highly controversial, others view them as a political necessity or as a "third way" (Giddens, 1998), thus generally paving the way for a wider implementation of NPM. But still there are different trajectories in public sector reforms, ranging from families of states representing the more traditional and reluctant maintainers to the more radical countries enhancing a marketize or minimize strategy (Pollitt & Bouckaert, 2004).

NPM Representing New Models for Organizing Government

The political-normative debate about the development of the public sector has been accompanied by a parallel debate among scholars around the world. Some economists and management scholars have pointed to the inefficiency of the public sector and called for a leaner and more efficient state (Boston et al., 1996). These people have played an active role in reform processes, both as producers of models and ideologies and as entrepreneurs in the civil service, as exemplified in New Zealand (Goldfinch, 1998). They have seen NPM as a "window of opportunity" to further their own predefined model (Aberbach & Christensen, 2001; Kingdon, 1984). At the same time, political scientists have often defended a public sector model based on collective and institutional arguments.

When NPM reforms are said to be typically theoretical, as in New Zealand, this often means that economic theories dominate. Examples are public choice theories, principal–agent models, and transaction cost models (Boston et al., 1991; Boston et al., 1996). In these models activities in the political–administrative system are seen as strategic games between rational actors whose goal is to make the system more efficient, streamlined, and consistent (Evans et al., 1996). Such economic models seem to regard the ambiguous goals, complicated formal structures, and composite cultural norms of a complex civil service as signs of "disease" and not as fundamental distinctive features of a heterogeneous public sector. Critics of such models emphasize that this way of thinking is simplistic and plays down the importance of public-sector ethics and institutional–cultural constraints; they also point out that it has not proven as fruitful as anticipated when confronted with everyday life in the public sector.

Even if NPM espouses economic values and objectives, the concept is loose and multifaceted and offers a kind of "shopping basket" of different elements for reformers of public administration (Hood, 1991; Pollitt, 1995). The main components of NPM are hands-on professional management — which is said to allow active, visible, discretionary control of an organization by people who are free to manage — explicit standards of performance, a greater emphasis on output control, increased competition, contracts, devolution, disaggregation of units, and private-sector management techniques. The main hypothesis in the NPM reforms is that more market, more management, and greater autonomy will produce more efficiency without having negative side effects on other public-sector values, such as political control. We argue that this hypothesis is contested and that it has yet to be confirmed as a general finding. The effects of NPM are often promised or expected but seldom very well documented, as will be discussed later (Christensen & Lægreid, 2001; Pollitt & Bouckaert, 2004).

Tension arises from the hybrid character of NPM, which combines economic organization theory and management theory (Aucoin, 1990; Hood, 1991). This tension results from the contradiction between the centralizing tendencies inherent in contractualism and the devolutionary tendencies of managerialism. The first set of ideas comes from economic organization theory and focuses on the primacy of representative government over the bureaucracy (Boston et al., 1996). A lesson from this paradigm is that the power of political leaders must be reinforced against the bureaucracy. This concentration of power requires attention to centralization, coordination, and control, objectives that are to be achieved primarily via contractual arrangements. The question, however, is to what extent this actually happens in practice. The second set of ideas comes from the managerialist school of thought, which focuses on the need to reestablish the primacy of managerial principles in the bureaucracy (Kettl, 1997). However, enhancing the capacity of managers to take action requires attention to decentralization, devolution, and delegation, which, of course, potentially undermines the very political control prescribed by economic organization theory. Thus, by advocating both centralization and devolution, NPM contains an inherent contradiction or dilemma, creating different types of challenges for political and administrative executive leaders.

Summing up, the new economical and management-oriented theories of government, imitated from the private sector, are connected in many countries to the growing ideological dominance of the supermarket state model. In NPM their dominance is also connected to strong, and not always well-founded, opinions about the implications of economic values for the formal organization of the public sector, for administrative procedures, for the expertise needed, and for its relationship with the private sector (Self, 2000). These opinions have often been characterized by symbolic features. These features, creating several dilemmas and challenges for NPM reforms, seem to result from the ambiguities and inconsistencies of the new theories of government mentioned that they are underdeveloped concerning organizational implications and effects, and that they confront traditional complex governmental systems with elaborated cultures that cannot easily be substituted by new simple structures and values (Boston et al., 1996).

Balancing Political Control and Agency Autonomy: The World of Practice

Main Structural Elements of NPM — Structural Devolution and Horizontal Specialization

Vertical structural devolution entails a transfer of authority downwards in the hierarchy between different organizational forms, either between existing organizations or to new subordinate governmental organizations, like traditional multifunctional agencies, regulatory agencies, or state-owned companies (Pollitt & Bouckaert, 2004). Horizontal specialization, on the other hand, implies separating administrative functions within the same organization or between public organizations (for example, ownership in one ministry and regulatory functions in another), something that under NPM has often gone hand in hand with increased vertical structural specialization, creating a more disintegrated or fragmental formal structure of government.

In many countries structural vertical devolution or specialization occurs when they change their main organizational political–administrative arrangements by moving units to organizational forms that are further away from the central political leadership, in some cases still within the governmental administrative organization, and in other cases, not (Pollitt & Talbot, 2004, Pollitt et al., 2005). One well-known example is the next step reform in United Kingdom establishing a number of new semiautonomous agencies (James, 2003). Arguments in favor of the more internal kind of structural devolution, involving greater autonomy either for ordinary agencies or for regulatory agencies, are that the former can be more efficient in delivering services and that the latter have a special need for professional autonomy (Christensen & Lægreid, 2003). Arguments against the tendency to move agencies out of the government administration are the problems of decoupling policy control and development from service delivery, the potential importance of political control of many of these units, and from a democratic perspective, the problematic implications of elevating professional autonomy to the most important feature of the regulatory function.

Economic arguments for this structural devolution, particularly the more external kind of structural devolution, are based on a kind of deterministic logic. Global pressure to cooperate and compete in new ways is pointing in the direction of more market competition and vast change processes (Self, 2000). To adjust to this development, so the argument goes, more structural devolution of commercial functions is needed to handle the increased competition. This is a reflection also of the axiom that politics and business should be separated and that private actors make better market actors than public ones. Accordingly, the most effective way of doing business for the public sector is either to create organizational forms that attend more systematically to commercial functions or to let private actors take over some public commercial functions (Boston et al., 1996). The argument is that state monopolies should be deregulated and transferred to open market competition. Often this process is accompanied by a reregulation by building up quasiautonomous regulatory agencies to guarantee free and equal competition in the market. The nature of political considerations is also changing. Traditional public policy considerations of a broad societal character or sectorial considerations are now seen as either irrelevant or noncommercial functions that have to be paid for separately (Self, 2000).

In many countries that have implemented NPM-related reforms an increase in horizontal differentiation between administrative functions is evident. Functions that were traditionally organized together, such as policy advice, regulative tasks, ownership functions, control functions, and purchaser and provider functions, have now been separated into distinct units. New Zealand has been the most typical example of this type of structural change, having adopted the principle of single-purpose or single-mission organizations (Boston et al., 1996). Arguments for this solution are that it enhances effectiveness and efficiency by clarifying administrative functions and avoiding overlap and ambiguous coupling of functions that blur the lines of command and authority. One possible effect of such strong administrative specialization of functions is an increase in the need for horizontal coordination, because there is more fragmentation in the system (Gregory, 2003). Another effect could be that the new specialized units will grow by adding tasks they have lost through specialization — e.g., purchaser units might add policy advice functions. All this could potentially lead to an increase in the number of civil servants and resources used — i.e., in a more complex rather than a simplified bureaucracy.

Modern NPM-related reforms have combined vertical and horizontal specializations, thus creating a state that is more fragmented than the traditional integrated governmental model (Christensen & Lægreid, 2001). The transformational nature of these changes is of course more evident in parliamentarian systems than more fragmented system like the U.S. system, but even systems like the latter face many of the same dilemmas and challenges as exemplified in the Reinvention Government program (Aberbach & Rockman, 2000). The effects of this development will be analyzed in the next section.

The Effects of Increased Structural Devolution and Horizontal Specialization

Evaluating results of reforms may focus the main effects of the reforms and the side effects (Hesse et al., 2003). The ideal reforms are the ones reaching their main goals and also fulfilling side effects, or at least not creating negative side effects. According to the idea and theories behind NPM, reflected in the supermarket model, the main goals and effects focused are the ones related to efficiency (Boston et al., 1996). NPM is not that preoccupied with other effects, but seems to promise that effects on factors like political control should not be negative, without arguing much for why. Other effects like social effects are mostly ignored. Based on the ideas connected to the centralized state model, the main goals of public reform are related to their effects on political-democratic control, and culturally connected to effects on social factors like equality and equity, although efficiency is mostly de-emphasized. So it is obviously a tension concerning what effects to focus, showing quite clearly the general dilemmas and challenges of balancing political control and increased institutional autonomy.

The aim of structural devolution is to devolve functions that do not need to be controlled politically and to keep politically important tasks under central control. Together with greater transparency the aim of this process is said to allow "more steering in big issues and less steering in small issues" (Boston et al., 1996). We argue that this is easier in theory than in practice and that the result might easily be less political control, both formally and in reality. What is politically important may be difficult to define or controversial, or may change over time, and keeping central control through increasing institutional autonomy may be an illusion.

Devolution is inspired by the slogan "let the managers manage," meaning discretion for managers and boards and not too much daily interference from political leaders. The implication of this slogan is that chief executives are better at managing and therefore should be given the discretion and opportunity to do so, thereby reducing the burden on the political leadership, and through a sharp division between politics and administration, increase political control (Dunn, 1997; Weller et al., 1997). But one could also argue that the slogan reflects an antipolitical trend, potentially undermining political control. "Let the managers manage" may mean that managers gain more resources, tasks, and responsibility, making it less legitimate for politicians to interfere in their business. Moreover, structural devolution often means less capacity for central political control. One potential effect of increased structural devolution of commercial functions is both a slimmer core and generally a slimmer public sector, as experienced in New Zealand, due to cuts in the workforce in public enterprises and due to privatization (Gregory, 1998a). Adding to this is the fact that NPM narrows the definition of politics concerning public companies to only commercial aspects, from a broad societal and sectorial definition typical for traditional control of the companies. Another effect is growing structural complexity or hybrid forms, because there are new combinations of political and commercial interests built into new public units, showing both innovation and ambiguity in control relations.

But does increased structural devolution in reality undermine political control, regardless of whether it is efficient? The balance between control and autonomy varies according to a number of factors, such as how extensive and radical the devolution is, the starting situation, and polity features like whether it is a Westminster system or not. Political–administrative culture and stage of reform has also to be taken into consideration (Yesilkagit, 2004). Strategic constraints and control could mean different things in different countries, ranging from "hands-off" to relatively more "hands-on" activities from the political leadership. And there might be a "zone of indifference" in which managers might operate with great autonomy in the shadow of the politicians. If, however, they exceed a certain limit, politicians might tighten up political control. This means that the relationship between political and administrative executives might be more of an ebb-and-flow pattern than a linear development toward less political control. This being said, one main argument for decreased political control, and one dominant argument in several comparative studies, is that structural devolution changes the instruments of control and increases the distance between the political leadership and subordinate units and lower levels of management (Christensen & Lægreid, 2001; Egeberg, 1989). This logic is based on the notion of erecting new structural barriers or limits. The main lesson is, therefore, that structural devolution means a decrease in the central capacity for control and in the authority to exercise control and less attention to political considerations in subordinate units, especially market-oriented units (Mascarenhas, 1996; Pollitt & Bouckaert, 2004). There is a tendency to define political involvement in public enterprises as "inappropriate" interference in business matters, reflecting a confrontation between new and old public culture. A study of the top political and administrative leadership in Norway shows this development (Christensen & Lægreid, 2002a).

The more limited form of structural devolution is the internal procedural one, meaning a transfer of authority from ministries to agencies. This gives the agencies more autonomy, responsibility, and leeway in using allocated resources while keeping the main form of structural affiliation stable. This weak version of autonomization has generally not aroused much controversy, even though it potentially undermines political control. It is associated in many countries with various new systems of control, encompassing management by objectives and results (MBOR), performance budgeting, performance management and auditing, a formal "steering dialogue," an annual letter of objectives and resource allocation from the ministries to the agencies, performance reports from the agencies to the ministries, and formal meetings. When asked what they thought of the new system, Norwegian ministers and agency leaders generally expressed satisfaction (Christensen & Lægreid, 2002a). The main problem seems to be at the interface between politicians and administrators. The ministers expend little time and energy on the new steering techniques and leave them to a great extent to the administrative leaders, thus in practice transferring power and influence to them.

Another type of devolution, potentially combining the internal and external type, is the establishment of new regulatory agencies or supervisory authorities, often a reflection of increased structural devolution of public companies and service-producing agencies (Pollitt & Talbot, 2004). Whereas the regulatory function has always existed side by side with administrative and commercial tasks, it is now often located in specific regulatory bodies with the formal status of agencies, showing increased interorganizational horizontal specialization. This development, which has a long tradition in the United States and has been adopted more recently in other NPM countries, has proved to be more controversial for a number of reasons. One central issue is whether these regulatory agencies should have more autonomy than other agencies. Cabinet members in the Norwegian study mentioned are the most skeptical toward autonomy, their main argument was that some of the regulatory agencies cover policy areas that require political control and that there is no reason to give them extra autonomy (Christensen & Lægreid, 2002a). They also sense a whiff of antipolitical sentiment in the argument that regulatory agencies should have special autonomy in general or more professional autonomy in particular.

Another controversial question concerning the regulatory agencies is whether the ownership and regulation of state-owned companies should be located within the same ministry. The main argument in OECD and leading NPM countries is that these functions should be kept separate (OECD, 2003). But one argument in favor of having the regulatory agency in the corresponding sector ministry, often supported by political executives, is that this arrangement maintains and strengthens sectoral competence.

To sum up: although the single-purpose organization seems to have emerged as the new administrative orthodoxy, there is disagreement and institutional confusion and ambiguity among political and administrative leaders about how to organize the central agencies and supervisory authorities horizontally, vertically, and also geographically.

New Zealand is a kind of extreme case regarding complex structural devolution, because it chose to combine strong horizontal specialization with strong vertical specialization. Boston et al. (1996) argue that in New Zealand devolution has had a certain dual effect. On the one hand, the separation of noncommercial and commercial functions, highlighted in the establishment of public enterprises, is said to be efficient and to secure accountability, even though it is designed to weaken political control (Evans et al., 1996). On the other hand, some Crown entities, in competition with private actors, have made political control and coordination more problematic and lines of authority more ambiguous, and this has made it more difficult to secure collective interests. The current political leadership seems, however, to think that overall structural devolution has created problems of political control and the control is now tightened, whereas effects of horizontal specialization are met by increased coordination efforts (Gregory, 2003).

Australia has had a similar profile concerning structural devolution, but chose another much more integrated horizontal solution as a way of organizing the machinery of government. Sixteen core departments were established in the early 1980s, so-called mega departments, and this feature supported Hawke's policy of strengthening the integrative features of the cabinet (Campbell & Halligan, 1992). Compared with a more fragmented solution this probably strengthened the influence of the political leadership, both with regard to top civil servants in the central agencies and departments, and as a counterbalance to the subordinate institutions and commercial entities. But structural devolution, commercialization, and privatization, especially in the 1990s, and even more so now, under the Howard cabinet, generally have weakened the central political leadership, even though its control over the core of the public sector is still rather strong.

Norway, typical for some European countries showing traditional reluctance toward NPM reforms, chose a structural reform path more similar to Australia's than to New Zealand's in the 1980s, with the emphasis on moderate horizontal specialization of ministries — though it created nothing resembling Australia's mega departments — and moderate vertical specialization. Over the last 5–10 years the reforms have been more reminiscent of New Zealand in the 1980s, including transforming old public enterprises into new state-owned companies, giving ordinary agencies more autonomy, and establishing new regulatory agencies (Lægreid et al., 2003). Several studies have shown that this trend undermines central political leadership and creates increased complexity and confusion. It is some kind of paradox that imitation of NPM reforms from NPM trailblazers primarily digs into the reported successes, often exaggerated, although learning from problems, like New Zealand has experienced, is much more difficult.

Effects on Efficiency and Social Conditions

As NPM introduced a large number of reform elements at the same time, some of which point in different directions, it is clearly impossible to make a general analysis of the effects of reform on efficiency. Instead, the effects of different reform elements need to be analyzed individually. NPM aimed to produce more efficiency via several structural changes, like increased structural devolution (vertical differentiation) and increased horizontal specialization (single-purpose organizations) (Boston et al., 1996; Christensen & Lægreid, 2001). NPM has probably simplified the jobs of leaders of subordinate organizations, like agencies and state-owned companies, because they have fewer considerations to attend to, but at the same time the roles of top leaders have become more complex and potentially inefficient (Pollitt & Bouckaert, 2004). In a few countries, like New Zealand and United Kingdom, there has been a conscious attempt to reduce personnel, but this is not the main picture and attempts like there are often not lasting long (Gregory, 2001).

The most likely area for efficiency gains is public service provision, particularly where competitive tendering is used. Several studies have been conducted in this area, mainly by economists. Their overall conclusion is that NPM leads to savings and efficiency gains, often of around 20 percent or more (Domberger & Rimmer, 1994). More sophisticated studies put this figure rather lower, however (Hodge, 1999). There are also problems of measurement, and savings will vary according to the type of service, the market situation, and "purchaser competence." The main finding seems to be that savings result from increased competition as such, irrespective of whether the service is public or private, but this is disputed (Hodge, 2000; Savas, 2000).

A general finding is that the efficiency effect is not as significant as promised by the reform agents (Pollitt & Bouckaert, 2004). A study from United Kingdom on reforms in healthcare, housing, and schools shows that there are some efficiency gains of devolution and contracting out in the first two policy areas but less in education. Responsiveness toward users has been improved in the fields of housing and schools, but not for hospitals. For all three fields there have been enhanced equality and equity problems (Boyne et al., 2003). This tendency of positive effects on efficiency and responsiveness and negative effects on equity is also found in a Swedish study of NPM reforms in schools and hospitals (Blomquist & Rothstein, 2000).

Thus, one crucial question is whether increased efficiency through competitive tendering has been obtained at the expense of other goals and considerations. In the old public administration many considerations other than purely commercial ones were coupled to service provision, such as more general societal considerations or issues of sector policy. Many of these involved additional expense and have now been removed from the services. They are often defined as noncommercial and as something that has to be paid extra for making them vulnerable in budget processes (Christensen & Lægreid, 2003; Self, 2000). Clearly a narrower and commercial definition of a public service potentially may make it more efficient. Examples of this are when regional considerations in communications policy are weakened by the introduction of competition, or when the interests of weak clients in educational, health, or social services are formally de-emphasized or taken care of in other ways. In this latter respect NPM understandably increases social differences, a feature that is accepted to a very varied degree in different countries (Podder & Chatterjee, 1998; Stephens, 2000).

Another broader socioeconomic perspective on efficiency in public service provision concerns the fate of the workforce under NPM. In many countries, particularly Australia and New Zealand, efficiency gains were obtained by reducing the number of people working in public services, particularly in telecommunications and transport (Mascarenhas, 1996). Where the workforce is rather old or unskilled, these people may well end up in various pension programs, casting doubt on the overall economic gains of NPM.

It is often said that the increased consumer orientation of NPM will eventually lead to increase in both quality and efficiency. The argument is that the consumer knows best how to improve services and that increased consumer participation and influence will enhance service provision (McKevitt, 1998). There are few studies showing this in reality. One factor undermining this argument is that consumer's experience of and hence attitudes to public service provision vary considerably, so increased efficiency and quality for one set of consumers may run counter to the interests of others (Aberbach & Rockman, 2000).

Another question is whether consumers really influence public service provision under NPM. Although certain strong and coordinated groups of consumers may do so, possibly to the detriment of others, the overall picture is that service providers think primarily about profit. Allowing consumers too much participation or influence takes time and resources and is therefore not efficient (Fountain, 2001). In this respect the consumer-orientation of NPM may have symbolic overtones. Nevertheless, certain consumer-oriented structural reform efforts look more promising in terms of efficiency than others. One example is the "one-stop shop" or "one-window" programs established first in Australia (Centrelink) (Halligan, 2004; Vardon, 2000) and later in Western Europe (Hagen & Kubicel, 2000). They seem to make a difference for users with a complex problem profile and represent potential administrative efficiency gains, but may also create cultural conflicts and increased organizational complexity.

The Challenges of Accountability

A last effect to mention, involving both structural and cultural elements, is the effects of NPM on the accountability question, involving the challenges of balancing political control and managerial accountability. With its principles of accountability based on output, competition, transparency, and contractual relations, NPM represents a departure from "old public administration," where accountability was based upon process, hierarchical control, trust, and cultural traditions. There has been a shift from simple to complex models of accountability (Day & Klein, 1987). The traditional notion of accountability, namely, top-down authority responsible to the people through elected policy makers, is challenged by the twin emphasis on customers and results, which in some cases makes administrators focus downwards, toward citizens, rather than upwards toward elected officials. In administrative reforms such as NPM, much attention has been paid to managerial accountability with sparse consideration of political responsibility (Christensen & Lægreid, 2002b).

March and Olsen (1989) emphasize this difference by making a distinction between aggregative and integrative processes in public organizations. Civil servants will in integrative processes have a feeling of belonging, a shared history, and traditions that make it easier to have a sense of integration, obligations, and common purpose and to act appropriately (March, 1994). In aggregative processes actors are more atomized and do not have a sense of integration; they need incentives to act in certain ways. Instead of being socialized into an administrative culture and a code of ethics, they are disciplined to change their behavior by various kinds of formal motivation (Lægreid & Olsen, 1984). We see here the contrast between the logic of appropriateness (culturally related) and the logic of consequence (instrumentally related).

Although managerial accountability may have improved, as shown in the New Zealand government, the reforms have also led to fragmentation of the public sector and the acceptance of political responsibility by ministers has been attenuated, as shown by Weller et al. (1997) in a comparative study of the executive in several countries. The problem of "many hands" (Thompson, 1980) has grown. The conceptual distinctions drawn by the reform with regard to the roles of minister and chief executive are amply clear on paper, but they fail in practice. The ambiguity of responsibility becomes especially clear when things go wrong (Gregory, 1998b). This means that the reduction in political responsibility would need to be balanced against possible gains in effectiveness and efficiency (Boston et al., 1996). A preoccupation with efficiency tends to overvalue the need for managerial accountability rather than promoting political responsibility. Efficiency is no guarantor of good political and social judgment, which is essential in securing genuine political responsibility and legitimacy (Gregory, 1998b).

There is an underlying tension between the accountability standards of traditional public administration and contemporary public management (Shergold, 1997 Minson, 1998;). NPM challenges two main features of traditional public administration: anonymity and permanence of top civil servants (Stark, 2002). This raises new accountability problems. In Australia public-sector reforms have caused worries over accountability, with a special focus on the distinctive character of public accountability and on the role of the public's interest in the world of Australian public administration (Uhr, 1999). In Norway and New Zealand there has traditionally been a doctrine of ministerial responsibility, which states that the minister takes the political blame, as well as the credit, for the actions of administrators, who must remain anonymous and beyond credit or blame. The administrative reforms have enhanced public knowledge of the identity and policy obligations of many senior civil servants and separated ministers further from the administrative process, thus challenging this doctrine. In New Zealand the administrative reforms may have altered the doctrine of ministerial responsibility, though a new version of accountability has developed based on contractual relationships between ministers and their chief executives (McLeay, 1995). Accountability by contracts is based on the idea of opportunistic behavior, whereby people learn to distrust each other. This may make control more visible but it is an open question whether this is a better form of control than the old internal control based on trust.

The Handling of Dilemmas and Challenges

During 20 years of NPM reforms all over the world there have been some striking similarities between different political–administrative systems, primarily in the ideas, ideologies, and theories used. Based on the increasing pressure on the welfare states in many countries, earlier it was taken for granted that they had efficiency problems and that NPM was the solution to these problems. This was more a domination of neoliberal ideology and new institutional economic and management theories than spreading of similar specific NPM reform measures, reflecting a trend to decontextualize the reforms (Røvik, 1996). It was important for the reform entrepreneurs, whether OECD or central Anglo-American countries, to argue instrumentally — saying that different countries had the same technical efficiency problems — but in reality they relied very much on using broad reform myths and symbols to drum up support (Sahlin-Andersson, 2001). In their world there were not much of dilemmas balancing political control and institutional autonomy, because the NPM was the generic solution, pointing in a one-dimensional way toward more efficiency and autonomy.

Concerning the more practical reform measures, different countries have showed a lot of variety during the last two decades, even though the rhetoric often has been the same, reflecting some kind of belief in the legitimacy-enhancing effects of "double-talk" (Brunsson, 1989). The variety is rather easily explained by the three main elements in the transformative perspective outlines. The more reform-happy countries have been the Anglo-American countries, characterized by a strong neoliberal ideology, more accommodating historical traditions, political systems more easily allowing reform entrepreneurs, more pressure — both technically and institutionally — from the environment, etc. (Christensen & Lægreid 2001; Pollitt & Bouckaert, 2004). And the more reform-skeptical countries — the laggards — like Germany, France, Spain, Japan, and most Nordic countries, because they have developed less of an NPM ideology, have had cultures with less compatibility with NPM values, and have had a parliamentary complexity making it more difficult to implement reforms. The distinction between the two groups has not been that unambiguous concerning preconditions, as Labor parties implemented the reforms in Australia and New Zealand, and the United Sates has had better economic conditions than the other countries in the group and also a polity system of checks and balances, and there has also been variety in the group of reluctant reforms.

Over time — during the two decades of NPM reforms — there seems to have been a combination of two tendencies. One is characterized by some trailblazers moving even further in the direction of structural devolution, the emphasis on efficiency, the use of contracts, competitive tendering, and different market mechanisms, followed by many laggards, often more on the local than central level, showing the latter group moving closer to the practical reform measures of the front-runners. The other tendency is an overall tendency to modify at least some aspects of the NPM reforms in both groups, making it less obvious that NPM is moving continuously in a linear way, and one can even argue that the pendulum is partly swinging back. This does by no means, however, imply that the NPM is over (Pollitt, 2003). Two concepts may be used to explain these seemingly inconsistent tendencies: feasibility and desirability (March & Olsen, 1983; Pollitt & Bouckaert, 2004). Feasibility concerns the quality of the organizational thinking behind NPM and the potential for controlling the reform process and its implementation. Desirability is about normative questions and what kind of society and political–administrative system is preferable.

Feasibility may be connected to what Dahl and Lindblom (1953) labeled rational calculation, i.e., the quality of the organizational or means–end thinking. Do the main ideas of NPM draw a strong enough connection between economic and management ideas and organizational solutions to secure desired effects? Boston et al. (1996) show that the basic economic ideas in NPM may translate into a number of different organizational forms — i.e., contrary to the arguments of many reform entrepreneurs, the ideas of NPM do not offer one "best solution." A reasonable conclusion is, therefore, that the theories and ideas behind NPM are underdeveloped and do not provide a satisfactory basis for organizational solutions and concrete reform efforts. This seems to have translated further into the effects of the reforms, where NPM has had problems of delivering what has been promised, something that increases both elite and popular skepticism. The NPM-related thinking has not easily led to increased overall efficiency and effectiveness, particularly when reforms are broad ranging and ambitious. NPM has been too undifferentiated, not emphasizing enough that it is more feasible when a reform is narrow, related to one sector, public institution, or function, or if it is related to functions that inherently are easy to quantify (for example, technical functions) or targeted by elites as quantifiable (Christensen & Lægreid, 2001).

A second aspect of the feasibility question concerns political, administrative, or social control (Dahl & Lindblom, 1953). How easily will different stakeholders, inside and outside the public apparatus, accept the organizational thinking behind the reforms, the efforts to implement them, and the effects? As shown through the transformative perspective, the preconditions for control of reforms are much better in Anglo-American countries than in the groups of laggards. But if the organizational thinking behind the reforms is seen as unsatisfactory and particularly the effect seen as problematic or negative, it could also be quite easy to change course as seen in New Zealand during the last years (Gregory, 2003). This tendency seems to influence the traditional laggards increasingly and also more eager reformers now. Tensions now more often exist between and inside different governmental levels, international level, and societal actors. And the media seems more easily to dig into popular discontent with the NPM reforms, weakening their support for the elite actions.

The question of desirability is at the heart of the normative issue. NPM reforms may be feasible, but whether they should be furthered or implemented depends on basic ideological and cultural norms (Self, 2000). Does NPM represent a normative trend with the potential to create new types of leaders, citizens, public systems, and societies, or is it a less fundamental reform model, aimed at modifying only certain aspects of traditional public sector models? And another fundamental question is whether the magic of NPM is about to evaporate.

The debate about NPM reform processes often takes place at the symbolic or ideological level (Brunsson, 1989). Advocates of NPM gather support for reforms by stressing all the worst things about the traditional centralized state, particularly its legitimacy and efficiency problems. Myths and symbols are used to convince people that NPM-related reforms have all the instrumental answers to the pressing problems of a modern state (Christensen & Lægreid, 2003). Skeptics and opponents of NPM see this primarily as a neoliberal crusade, undermining and destroying traditional and well-functioning public systems. NPM ideas are presented as highly problematic and their potentially negative effects exaggerated, although the old public administration is held up as heroic and flawless. The result is normative polarization. Although supporters of NPM often claim that there are objective reasons to say that the old public administration has failed concerning efficiency and caring for clients or users, opponents deny this and underline that empirical evidence for this is loose and that if it isn't broken, don't fix it. Democracy is however an open project and in the long run the NPM reform project has to pass the test of citizens' assessment. If the general public is moving toward more individualization and neoliberal values then NPM reforms might fit well into their general attitudes and beliefs. But if negative effects are in the forefront, less popular support is expected.

There seems to be a certain change in many countries during the last few years that the ideological debate is less fierce, both because the supporters are less cocky and because the opponents are more pragmatic. And the supporters of the NPM seem to be somewhat more on the defensive rhetorically, partly because of problematic effects of the reforms and more problems of control, resulting in modifications of the reforms and even right out U-turns like in New Zealand (Gregory, 2003).

Future Prospects and Trends in Balancing Control and Autonomy

One possible scenario is efforts at regaining political control, now more and more emerging, connected to the tendency that the political executives are losing control while still getting the blame, something that is seen as increasingly problematic, even in NPM-eager countries (Brunsson, 1989). Structural devolution makes it more difficult for the political executives to obtain information about what is going on at lower levels in the systems, the administrative and commercial leaders may more easily engage in blame-games, something that is increasingly demanding the capacity and attention of the political executives. Therefore, there are now emerging different strategies of regaining political control.

The most obvious strategy for executive politicians to regain policy capacity and control is simply to reorganize to win back their influence. This depends primarily on two preconditions: there must be a winning coalition in favor of regaining control, and the negative effects of autonomization must be so obvious that there would be much to lose politically if nothing were done. The latest developments in New Zealand demonstrate a number of ways in which political influence can be regained (Gregory, 2003): the political–administrative center can be strengthened again by employing more people to perform control functions (Wise, 2002); control of agencies and state companies can be strengthened; contracts can be drawn up that clearly delineate the accountability of subordinate leaders; and programs and projects can be launched to strengthen coordination in a fragmented governmental structure. In several of the most radical NPM countries like the United Kingdom, New Zealand, and Canada, the governments have over the past few years established "joined-up-government" programs to regain coordination power (Bakvis, 2002; Gregory, 2003; Richards & Smith, 2002).

Another strategy to regain control is for political executives to reassert themselves by using the existing and reformed levers of control more actively. The advantage of this strategy is to "take back" more influence by being more proactive and to try to decrease the importance of the power vacuum that emerged when the executive political leaders withdrew from strong control and the parliaments are stepping in. The disadvantage is that they can end up in "double-bind" situations. The danger is that politicians will try to delegate blame but not credit, whereas the administration accepts credit but not blame. Such attempts by the politicians to have their cake and eat it by making credit flow upwards and blame flow downwards are likely to lead to conflicts and deadlock situations and ultimately probably to blame sharing (Hood, 2002).

Another way for executive political leaders to try to regain some control is to propose new reform programs. The best way to get rid of a reform is to launch a new reform. Reforms always look better *ex ante* than *ex post* (Brunsson & Olsen, 1993). Typical for these programs, which seem to be more frequent than before, is that they have strong symbolic features. They are important for developing meaning and interpreting experience (Lægreid & Roness, 1999). Thus, an important task for political leaders is to launch reform ideas, formulate visions of the public sector, and talk about what constitutes relevant questions and proper solutions.

One option for political leaders to regain political control is to put more effort into procedural rather than substantive planning of reforms. Focusing on procedure elements tends to transfer an increasing number of control tasks to the politicians. But because of limited capacity, control may be more formal than real. Stronger procedural focus includes increasing decision-making arenas, establishing access rules for people, problems, and solutions, and drawing up rules for the ways in which attention should be organized and decisions made (Lægreid & Roness, 1999). Procedural planning means controlling certain premises for future decisions rather than controlling the decisions themselves. The implication is that political leaders should pay attention to their role as organizers as well as to their role as substantive policy makers (Lægreid & Olsen, 1984).

Another fruitful strategy for politicians, who lack time and attention capacity, is to exert control by measures of random intervention (Hood, 1998; Lægreid & Roness, 1999). It is important to distinguish between political engagement in any matter and political engagement in all matters. In practice limited capacity and attention mean that they may only involve themselves in a limited number of matters. An element of contrived randomness or deliberate unpredictability with regard to when and how politicians intervene, oversee, and control the reform process can compensate for lack of capacity and attention and give them more influence over the policy process. Building an element of randomness into the reform process can be a feature of organizational design that gives participants with the largest attention deficit an opportunity to increase their control over the reform process.

The second possible scenario is that there will be increasing differences again in how political control and institutional autonomy are handled in the groups of traditional, eager, and reluctant NPM countries. This may be the result of increasing differentiation in these groups. In the Anglo-American group Australia, after Howard's last election victory, seems to continue to head down the extreme NPM path, and Bush's recent victory may also be seen as a mandate to pursue an even more neoliberal course, even though his reform policy in the first period was not having a clear profile (Aberbach, 2003). But in this group New Zealand is, as mentioned, following a path clearly modifying NPM, and there are also signs of Blair being more reluctant and pursuing more the third way and joined-up government (Pollitt, 2003). In the group of traditional laggards, recently more eager reformers, future prospects are also more mixed. Denmark and Norway, both headed by right-leaning governments, seem to be different in some ways and similar in others. A conservative hard-liner minister for the interior in Norway succeeded, for example, in strengthening the control of the immigration policy, modifying reforms that some few years ago allowed much more autonomy to the agency and appeal board in this sector. Denmark seems generally to follow a path more similar to Howard in Australia, and some social democratic parties in Europe are increasingly and openly talking about the apparent negative effects of NPM, often to regain voters or to soften their stands before elections.

A third possible scenario is that the main NPM path will still be the dominant one in the near future, but less clear-cut and more complex and differentiated. One argument for this is that the effects and implications of NPM have had that learning effect that the reform measures are more relevant at some levels and institutions, and connected to some roles and functions, than to others. This will make the government more multistructured and hybrid, i.e., it is not feasible to use "one size fits all" concerning reforms. A comparable development seems to emerge concerning the cultural trends, i.e., in some areas new cultural elements of autonomy will succeed, although in others there is an increasing need for stable and traditional cultural norms, making the political–administrative more differentiated and hybrid.

Over the past years there has been a rediscovery of historical–institutional context (Olsen, 2003). The need for in-depth understanding of the special situation in individual countries is now underlined to a greater extent. Priorities have shifted form a drive to create autonomous agencies to a striving to find the right balance between accountability and autonomy by focusing on weak coordination devices, lack of governing capacity, and weak accountability mechanisms (OECD, 2002).

A fourth scenario, probably overlapping the other three, concerns the increased attention to evaluation processes. Evaluation has become much more popular and is used by reform advocates, who often have the upper hand in the modern reform processes, as a political-symbolic instrument to brand most reforms as successes, and to underline the need for continued reforms (Boyne et al., 2003; Christensen et al., 2003). The opponents of NPM have tried to come up with countersymbols and counterexpertise to undermine the reform process, and seem increasingly to succeed with these strategies, partly supported by the media in many countries. The future of NPM-related reforms is therefore also probably increasingly a tug-of-war concerning impression management.

References

Aberbach, J.D. (2003). The U.S. federal executive in an era of change, *Governance*, 16(3): 373–399.

Aberbach, J. and Christensen, T. (2001). Radical reform in New Zealand: crisis, windows of opportunity and rational actors, *Public Administration*, 79(2): 404–422.

Aberbach, J.D. and Rockman, B.A. (2000). *In the Web of Politics: Three Decades of the U.S. Federal Executive*. Washington, D.C.: The Brookings Institution Press.

Aucoin, P. (1990). Administrative reform in public management: paradigms, principles, paradoxes and pendulums, *Governance*, 3(2): 115–137.

Bakvis, H. (2002). Pulling against gravity? Horizontal management in the Canadian federal service. Paper Presented at the SOG Conference Knowledge, Networks and Joined-up Government, Melbourne, 3–5 June 2002.

Blomquist, P. and Rothstein, B. (2000). *Velferdsstatens nya ansikte (The New Faces of the Welfare State)*. Stockholm: Agora.

Boli, J. and Thomas, G.M. (eds) (1999). *Constructing World Culture*. Stanford: Stanford University Press.

Boston, J., J. Martin, J. Pallot, and P. Walsh (eds) (1991). *Reshaping the State: New Zealand's Bureaucratic Revolution*. Auckland: Oxford University Press.

Boston, J., J. Martin, J. Pallot, and P. Walsh (1996). *Public Management: The New Zealand Model.* Auckland: Oxford University Press.

Boyne, G.A., C. Farrell, J. Law, M. Powell, and R.M. Walker (2003). *Evaluating Public Service Reforms.* Buckingham: Open University Press.

Brunsson, N. (1989). *The Organization of Hypocrisy. Talk, Decisions and Actions in Organizations.* Chichester: Wiley.

Brunsson, N. and Olsen, J.P. (1993). *The Reforming Organization.* London and New York: Routledge.

Campbell, C. and Halligan, J. (1992). *Political Leadership in an Age of Constraint: The Experience of Australia.* Pittsburgh: University of Pittsburgh Press.

Castles, F., R. Gerritsen, and J. Vowles (1996). Introduction: setting the scene for economic and political change, In F. Castles, R. Gerritsen, and J. Vowles (eds) *The Great Experiment: Labour Parties and Public Policy Transformation in Australia and New Zealand.* Auckland: Auckland University Press. pp. 1–21.

Christensen, T. (1991). Bureaucratic roles: political loyalty and professional autonomy, *Scandinavian Political Studies*, 14(4): 303–320.

Christensen, T. and Lægreid, P. (1998). Administrative reform policy: the case of Norway, *International Review of Administrative Sciences*, 64(3): 457–475.

Christensen, T. and Lægreid, P. (eds) (2001). *New Public Management: The Transformation of Ideas and Practice.* Aldershot: Ashgate.

Christensen, T. and Lægreid, P. (2002a). *Reformer og lederskap. Omstillinger i den utøvende makt (Reforms and Leadership. Renewal in the Executive Power).* Oslo: Scandinavian University Press.

Christensen T. and Lægreid, P. (2002b). New public management — puzzles of democracy and the influence of citizens, *Journal of Political Philosophy*, 10(3): 267–296.

Christensen, T. and Lægreid, P. (2003). Governmental autonomization and control — the Norwegian way. Paper Presented at the 7th International Research Symposium on Public Management, Hong Kong, 2–4 October 2003.

Christensen, T. and Peters, B.G. (1999). *Structure, Culture and Governance: A Comparative Analysis of Norway and the United States.* Maryland: Rowman & Littlefield.

Christensen, T., P. Lægreid, and L.C. Wise (2003). Evaluating public management reform in government: Norway, Sweden and the United States. In H. Wollman (ed.) *Evaluation in Public-Sector Reform: Concepts and Practice in International Perspective.* Cheltenham, UK: Edward Elgar.

Czarniawska, B. and Sevón, G. (eds) (1996). *Translating Organizational Change.* New York: de Gruyter.

Dahl, R.A. and Lindblom, C.E. (1953). *Politics, Economics, and Welfare.* New York: Harper & Row.

Day, P. and Klein, R. (1987). *Accountability: Five Public Services.* London: Tavistock Publishers.

DiMaggio, P.J. and Powell, W.W. (1983). The iron cage revisited: institutional isomorphism and collective rationality in organizational fields, *American Sociological Review*, 48(2): 147–160.

Domberger, S. and Rimmer, S. (1994). Competitive tendering and contracting in the public sector: a survey. *International Journal of the Economics of Business*, 1(3): 439–453.

Drori, G., J. Meyer, F. Ramirez, and E. Schofer (2003). *Science in the Modern World Polity*. Stanford: Stanford University Press.

Dunn, D.D. (1997). *Politics and Administration at the Top: Lessons from Down Under*. Pittsburgh: University of Pittsburgh Press.

Egeberg, M. (1989). Effekter av organisasjonsendring i forvaltningen (Effects of organizational change in the civil service). In M. Egeberg (ed.) *Institusjonspolitikk og forvaltningsutvikling. Bidrag til en anvendt statsvitenskap (Institutional Policy and Development of the Civil Service. Contribution to an Applied Political Science)*. Oslo: TANO. pp. 75–93.

Evans, L., A. Grimes, B. Wilkinson, and D. Teece (1996). Economic reform in New Zealand 1984–95: the pursuit of efficiency, *Journal of Economic Literature*, XXXIV(December): 1856–1902.

Fountain, J.E. (2001). Paradoxes of public sector customer service, *Governance*, 14: 55–73.

Fredrickson, H.G. (1996). Comparing the reinventing movement with the new public administration, *Public Administration Review*, 56(3): 263–270.

Giddens, A. (1998). *The Third Way: The Renewal of Social Democracy*. Oxford: Polity Press.

Goldfinch, S. (1998). Remarking New Zealand's economic policy: institutional elites as radical innovators 1984–1993, *Governance*, 11(2): 177–207.

Gregory, R. (1998a). The changing face of the state in New Zealand: rolling back the public service? Paper Presented at the Annual Meeting of the American Political Science Association, Boston, September 3–6, 1998.

Gregory, R. (1998b). Political responsibility for bureaucratic incompetence: tragedy at Cave Creek, *Public Administration*, 76(Autumn): 519–538.

Gregory, R. (2003). All the King's horses and all the King's men: putting the New Zealand public sector together again, *International Public Management Review*, 4(2): 41–58.

Gustafsson, L. and Svensson, A. (1999). *Public Sector Reform in Sweden*. Lund: Liber Ekonomi.

Hagen, M. and Kubicel, H. (eds) (2000). *One-Stop Government in Europe: Results from 11 National Surveys*. Bremen: University of Bremen.

Halligan, J. (2004). Advocacy and innovation in inter-agency management: the case of Centrelink. Paper Presented at the 20th Anniversary Conference of the Structure and Organization of Government Research Committee of the International Political Science Association, Smart Practices Toward Innovation in Pubic Management, Vancouver, June 15–17, 2004.

Hesse, J.J., C. Hood, and B.G. Peters (eds) (2003). *Paradoxes in Public Sector Reform*. Berlin: Duncker & Humblot.

Hodge, G.A. (1999). Competitive tendering and contracting out: rhetoric or reality? *Public Productivity and Management Review*, 22(4): 455–469.

Hodge, G.A. (2000). *Privatization: An International Review of Performance*. Boulder, CO: Westview Press.

Hood, C. (1991). A public management for all seasons? *Public Administration*, 69(Spring): 3–19.

Hood, C. (1996). Exploring variations in public management reform of the 1980s. In H.A.G.M. Bekke, J.L. Perry, and T.A.J. Toonen (eds) *Civil Service Systems*. Bloomington: Indiana University Press.

Hood, C. (1998). *The Art of the State: Culture, Rhetoric and Public Management*. Oxford: Clarendon Press.

Hood, C. (2002). The risk game and the blame game, *Government and Opposition*, 37(1): 15–37.

Jacobsson, B., P. Lægreid, and O.K. Pedersen (2003). *Europeanization and Transnational States: Comparing Nordic Central Government*. London: Routledge.

James, O. (2003). *The Executive Revolution in Whitehall*. London: Palgrave.

Kettl, D.F. (1997). The global revolution in public management: driving themes, missing links, *Journal of Policy Analysis and Management*, 16(3): 446–462.

Kettl, D.F. (2000). *The Global Public Management Revolution*. Washington: Brookings.

Kingdon, J. (1984). *Agendas, Alternatives, and Public Policies*, Boston: Little, Brown.

Krasner, S. (1988). Sovereignty: an institutional perspective, *Comparative Political Studies*, 21: 66–94.

Lægreid, P. and Olsen, J.P. (1984). Top civil servants in Norway: key players on different teams. In E.N. Suleiman (ed.) *Bureaucrats and Policy Making*. New York: Holmes & Meier. pp. 206–242.

Lægreid, P. and Olsen, J.P. (eds) (1993). *Organisering av offentlig sektor* (*Organizing the Public Sector*). Oslo: TANO.

Lægreid, P. and Roness, P.G. (1999). Administrative reform as organized attention. In M. Egeberg and P. Lægreid (eds) *Organizing Political Institutions: Essays for Johan P. Olsen*. Oslo: Scandinavian University Press. pp. 301–329.

Lægreid, P. and Roness, P.G. (2003). Administrative reform programs and institutional response in Norwegian central government. In J.J. Hesse, C. Hood, and B.G. Peters (eds) *Paradox of Civil Service Reform*. Berlin: Duncker & Humblot.

Lægreid, P., Rolland, V.W., Roness, P.G. and Ågotnes, J.-E. (2003). The structural anatomy of the Norwegian state 1947–2003. Paper Presented at the Workshop on the Study of Public Sector Organization, University of Leuven, May 2–3, 2003.

March, J.G. (1994). *A Primer on Decision-Making*, New York: The Free Press.

March, J.G. and Olsen, J.P. (1983). Organizing political life: what administrative reorganization tells us about government, *American Political Science Review*, 77(2): 281–296.

March, J.G. and Olsen, J.P. (1989). *Rediscovering Institutions: The Organizational Basis of Politics*. New York: The Free Press.

March, J.G. and Olsen, J.P. (1995). *Democratic Governance*. The Free Press, New York.

Martin, J. (1997). Changing accountability relations: politics, customers and the market. Paris: OECD, PUMA/PAC (97): 1.

Mascarenhas, R.C. (1996). The evolution of public enterprise organisation: a critique. In J. Halligan (ed.) *Public Administration under Scrutiny: Essays in Honour of Roger Wettenhall*, Centre for Research in Public Sector Management, University of Canberra, Institute of Public Administration Australia. pp. 59–76.

McKevitt, D. (1998). *Managing Public Services*. Oxford: Blackwell.

McLeay, E. (1995). *The Cabinet and Political Power*. Auckland: Oxford University Press.

Meyer, J.W. and Rowan, B. (1977). Institutionalized organizations: formal structure as myth and ceremony, *American Journal of Sociology*, 83(September): 340–363.

Minson, J. (1998). Ethics in the service of the state. In M. Dean and B. Hindess (eds) *Governing Australia. Studies in Contemporary Rationalities of Government*. Cambridge: Cambridge University Press. pp. 47–69.

Nagel, J.H. (1997). Radically reinventing government: editor's introduction, *Journal of Policy Analysis and Management*, 16(3): 349–356.

OECD (2002). *Distributed Public Governance: Agencies, Authorities and Other Government* Bodies. Paris: OECD.

OECD (2003). *Norway: Preparing for the Future Now*. Paris: OECD.

Olsen, J.P. (1983). The dilemmas of organizational integration in government. In J.P. Olsen (ed.) *Organized Democracy: Political Institutions in a Welfare State — The Case of Norway*. Bergen: Scandinavian University Press. pp. 148–187.

Olsen, J.P. (1988). Administrative reform and theories of organization. In C. Campbell and B. Guy Peters (eds) *Organizing Governance: Governing Organizations*. Pittsburgh: University of Pittsburgh Press. pp. 233–254.

Olsen, J.P. (1992). Analyzing institutional dynamics, *Staatswissenschaften und Staatspraxis*, 3(2): 247–271.

Olsen, J.P. (2003). Citizens, public adminsitration and the search for theoretical foundations. The 17th Annual John Gauss Lecture, American Political Science Asociation, Philadelphia, 29 August 2003.

Olsen, J.P. and Peters, B.G. (eds) (1996). *Lessons from Experience*. Oslo: Scandinavian University Press.

Peters, B.G. (1996). *The Future of Governing: Four Emerging Models*. Lawrence: University Press of Kansas.

Podder, N. and Chatterjee S. (1998). Sharing the national cake in post-reform New Zealand: income inequality in terms of income sources. Paper Presented to the New Zealand Association of Economists Conference, August 1998.

Pollitt, C. (1995). Justification by works or by faith, *Evaluation*, 2(2): 133–154.

Pollitt, C. (2003). *The Essential Public Manager*. Maidenhead: Open University Press.

Pollitt, C. and Bouckaert, G. (2004). *Public Management Reform: A Comparative Analysis*, 2nd edition. Oxford: Oxford University Press.

Pollitt, C. and Talbot, C. (eds) (2004). *Unbundled Government*. London: Routledge.

Pollitt, C., C. Talbot, J. Caulfield, and A. Smullen (2005). *Agencies: How Government Do Things Through Semi-autonomous Organizations*. London: Palgrave.

Richards, D. and Smith, M.J. (2002). The paradoxes of governance and policy coordination. Britain — a case of study in Joined-up Government. Paper Presented at the SOG Conference Knowledge, Networks and Joined-Up Government, Melbourne 3–5 June 2002.

Røvik, K.A. (1996). Deinstitutionalization and the logic of fashion. In B. Czarniawska and G. Sevón (eds) *Translating Organizational Change*. Berlin: de Gruyter. pp. 139–172.

Røvik, K.A. (1998). *Moderne organisasjoner. Trender i organisasjonstenkningen ved tusenårsskiftet (Modern Organizations: Trends in the Organizational Thinking at the Turn of the Millennium)*, Bergen: Fagbokforlaget.

Sahlin-Andersson, K. (1996). Imitating by editing success: the construction of organizational fields. In B. Czarniawska and G. Sevón (eds) *Translating Organizational Change*. New York: de Gruyter. pp. 69–92.

Sahlin-Andersson, K. (2001). National, international and transnational construction of New Public Management. In T. Christensen and P. Lægreid (eds) *New Public Management: The Transformation of Ideas and Practice*. Aldershot: Ashgate.

Savas, E.S. (2000). *Privatization and Public Private Partnership*. New York: Chatham House.

Scott, W.R. (1995). *Institutions and Organizations*. Thousand Oaks: Sage.

Self, P. (2000). *Rolling Back the Market: Economic Dogma and Political Choice*. New York: St. Martin's Press.

Selznick. P. (1957). *Leadership in Administration*. New York: Harper & Row.

Shergold, P. (1997). The colour purple: prescriptions of accountability across the Tasman, *Public Administration and Development*, 17(3): 293–306.

Simon, H. (1957). *Administrative Behavior*, 2nd edition. New York: Free Press.

Stark, A. (2002). What is the New Public Management? *Journal of Public Administration Theory and Research*, 12(1): 137–151.

Stephens, R. (2000). The social impact of reform: poverty in Aotearoa/New Zealand, *Social Policy and Administration*, 4(1): 64–86.

Thompson, D.F. (1980). Moral responsibility of public officials: the problem of many hands, *American Political Science Review*, 74: 905–916.

Uhr, J. (1999). Three accountability anxieties: a conclusion to the symposium, *Australian Journal of Public Administration*, 58(1): 98–101.

Vardon, S. (2000). Centrelink: a three-stage evolution. In G. Singleton (ed.) *The Howard Government*. Sydney: University of New South Wales Press.

Weaver, R.K. and Rockman, B.A. (eds) (1993). *Do Institutions Matter?* Washington, D.C. Brookings.

Weller, P., H. Bakvis, and R.A.W. Rhodes (1997). *The Hollow Crown: Countervailing Trends in Core Executives*. Basingstoke: Macmillan.

Wise, C.R. (2002). Organization for homeland security, *Public Administration Review*, 62(2): 131–144.

World Bank (2000). Reforming public institutions and strengthening governance: a World Bank strategy 2000. Washington, D.C. The World Bank.

Yesilkagit, K. (2004). Bureaucratic autonomy, organizational culture and habituation, *Administration and Society*, 36 (5): 528–552.

Chapter 20

Globalization, Regulatory Regimes, and Administrative Modernization in Developing Nations: Toward a Theoretical Framework

Robert F. Durant

CONTENTS

Scholars increasingly appreciate the impact of the global policy environment on administrative and policy processes and outcomes in both developed and developing nations worldwide (e.g., Cleveland, 1993; Haas et al., 1995; Jackson, 1990; Litfin, 1998; Wapner, 1996). As Welch and Wong (1998, p. 43) argue, "governments and their bureaucracies are not only [acutely] aware of global pressures for change and reform, they are increasingly making decisions that incorporate global constraints and opportunities into their own domestic agendas." Indeed, some scholars argue that in various policy areas, global agreements, institutions, and regulatory regimes (e.g., the General Agreement on Tariffs and Trade, the Convention on Biological Diversity, and Agenda 21) "may have even greater influence on a country's economy than any of the domestic economic institutions in each individual country" (Welch & Wong, 1998, p. 45). They aver, as well, that global policy pressures like these can "create more tension [in nations] between administration and democracy, and pose serious questions [regarding] the foundation of legitimacy in public administration" (Welch & Wong, 1998, p. 45). At the same time, however, they also demonstrate in subsequent research on the impact of global technology that domestic context has a powerful mediating effect on global pressures (Welch & Wong, 2001).

Illustrative of these global policy pressures for administrative modernization in recent years have been efforts to ensconce the precautionary principle as the animating principle of national and international regulatory regimes worldwide. As a meta policy, the precautionary principle "presumes that in situations where there are threats of serious or irreversible damage, lack of full scientific certainty should not be used as reason for postponing cost-effective measures to prevent environmental degradation" (Sampson, 2002, p. 60; also see Sunstein, 2002). In effect, activities or products are presumed harmful to public health, safety, or the environment until proven otherwise, if the magnitude of risk they afford is adjudged too great.

Despite its otherwise intuitive appeal, the precautionary principle has proven quite controversial. After all, it turns traditional regulatory approaches on their heads, shifting the burden of proof away from opponents of technoscientific advances to prove their harm and toward proponents to prove their safety. Moreover, critics such as Sunstein (2002, p. 103) argue that although "there is some inherent truth in the precautionary principle," it fails to consider that regulation itself can cause harm (e.g., if lives are lost in the interim as regulators await assurances of safety). Adds Sunstein, "[i]f we take costly steps to address all risks, however improbable they are, we will quickly impoverish ourselves."

Perhaps nowhere have these precautionary politics proven more intractable, volatile, and problematic for proponents of technoscientific advances in a global economy than in the application of modern agricultural biotechnology advances in the production of genetically modified food, feed, and fiber [henceforth referred to as GMOs (genetically modified organisms)]. Proponents of these products argue that agricultural biotechnology has the potential to meet the spiraling food, nutrition, and health needs of burgeoning and impoverished populations in the developing world in environmentally sustainable ways.[1] Their optimism is fueled by three types of GMO trait technologies under development that proponents argue will increase crop yields, at lower net costs to farmers, with greater health benefits to consumers, and in more environmentally benign ways. The first, input trait technology, promises to reduce substantially the use of environmentally harmful pesticides (e.g., by giving herbicide tolerance, disease resistance, and insect resistance). The second, output trait technology, promises to improve farm productivity and yields (both generally and on marginal lands in developing countries), nutrition, quality, appearance, and shelf life. For example, many scientists speak of GM plants becoming "microfactories" in the near future, producing "neutra-ceuticals" to deal with malnutrition in developing countries (Sriwatanapongse, 2002). The third, agronomic trait technology, promises to afford protection against natural conditions and disasters that devastate the livelihood of farmers on marginal lands in developing countries (by affording salt tolerance, drought tolerance, and water submergence tolerance).

Unpersuaded, anti-GMO campaigners worldwide tout the cataclysmic risks to public health, safety, and environment that they claim are inherent in GMO research, production, and commercialization. Most prominent among these risks for humans are the disruption or silencing of existing genes, activation of silent genes, modification in the expression of existing genes, and formation of new or altered patterns of metabolites. The creation of new allergies or harmful toxins is hypothesized, as well, for which the body is ill-prepared to deal, causing sickness and death among vulnerable populations. Anti-GMO activists also allege that a rise in antibiotic resistance in humans could occur because of the use of antibiotic resisters in gene-splicing.

---

[1]Supporters by late 2003 include six national academies of science, the Third World Academy of Sciences, 20 Nobel Prize winners, the World Bank, the World Health Organization (WHO), the Rockefeller and Ford foundations, the American Medical Association, the American Dietetic Association, the American Society of Toxicologists, and the United Nations (UN) Development and Environment programs.

In terms of ecological threats, GM food critics tout a miscellany of intolerable risks as genetically engineered genes "drift" to nearby locations, cross-pollinating with wild relatives and competing with other species. These risks include killing off otherwise useful natural pests and predators, introducing destructive alien species, enhancing the ecological fitness of genetically engineered plants at the expense of native species, creating "super weeds" that will damage crops, and inducing pathogen resistance in plants by using antibiotic resisters in gene-splicing.

The most notable manifestation of the polarized politics driving debates over the application of the precautionary principle to GMOs has been the European Union's (EU) reaction to them. Since 1997, for example, the EU has required mandatory labeling of foods containing GMOs. Moreover, since 1998, six nations led by France (and including Belgium, Ireland, Italy, Portugal, and Spain) have prompted and sustained a *de facto* EU moratorium on the approval of new GM crops. Then, in June of 2003, the European Parliament approved new, broader, and more stringent regulations on GM food labeling and traceability that it argued paved the way for ending the then five-year moratorium on approvals of new GM foods. Producing nations such as the United States, Australia, and Canada vehemently disputed the EU's claims as inaccurate, "onerous" to GMO-producing nations, scientifically unjustified, and constituting an illegal nontariff barrier to trade. Indeed, the United States filed a case against the EU at the World Trade Organization (WTO), an ultimately successful protest aimed at restarting testing of GM foods.

In May and July of 2004, the EU Commission effectively ended the moratorium on new biotech foods by allowing the selling of Syngenta's GM sweet corn and GM maize (NK603) developed by Monsanto for import, feed use, and industrial processing. But this occurred only after 13 other nations had approved them (e.g., Korea, Japan, South Africa, and the Philippines), and after Monsanto decided to delay (others say "cancel") development of GM wheat and halted plans for GM canola development in Australia in the face of regulatory restrictions and state bans. Moreover, because Syngenta's corn is considered less controversial than some of the other strains (33 applications are presently pending) that the EU is considering, rapid approvals on a wide-scale basis are unlikely. In fact, the approval of Syngenta's application occurred only after EU farm ministers deadlocked on Syngenta's application, allowing the more biotech-friendly EU Commission to approve it.

Meanwhile, a 2004 report by the UN Food and Agriculture Organization (FAO) supported agricultural biotechnology as a tool for meeting "the needs of the poor and undernourished" worldwide. The FAO report conceded that biotechnology is "associated with certain environmental and health risks, so that effective biosafety and food safety regulations have to be integral components of responsible biotechnology development and utilization. Yet, the evidence so far suggests that environmental and health risks can be managed, so that there is no reason for an outright rejection of GM crops based on safety concerns." The FAO also highlighted major areas where biotech applications are needed to bring the "gene revolution" to greater numbers of the poor (Scientists Support FAO Biotech Report, 2004).

Nations in the developing world are caught in the middle of these often roiling, acrimonious, and polarized debates over applying the precautionary principle to GM foods. First, with the EU–U.S. battle over GM foods at loggerheads for the last six years, multinational corporations (e.g., Aventis, Bayer Crop Science, and Monsanto) aggressively eyed developing world markets (especially in Africa, China, India, and Latin America) as both laboratories for GMO research and development (R&D) and as markets for their products. Second, many developing nations fear that if they eschew the modernization of their agricultural biotechnology capacity, they will lose both domestic and foreign market shares for their products if the promise of GMO pans out. Third, and conversely, they worry that if they do modernize their GMO biotechnology capabilities and if consumers at home and abroad view their GMO regulatory regimes as inadequate, they will lose markets to nations like the EU with stricter regulatory regimes.

What is the impact of global policy pressures like these on administrative modernization in developing nations? What is the pattern of politics informing their responses? And how can researchers best account for them? A growing and insightful literature addressing these questions has developed in recent years on larger questions of state sovereignty, and most especially regarding the impact of international environmental regimes (e.g., Haas et al., 1995; Litfin, 1998). Yet, as Welch and Wong (1998) argue, our understanding of the relationship between global policy pressures and administrative modernization still remains rudimentary and begs refinement in future research.

This chapter seeks to test, elaborate, and extend a model and theoretical framework for assessing the dynamics offered by Welch and Wong (1998). Its analytical focus is Thailand's efforts over the past decade to cope simultaneously with global cross-pressures to develop, pursue, and commercialize agricultural biotechnology amid raging conflicts within the nation and among its trade partners over the application of the precautionary principle to GMOs. Using a longitudinal case study design, the chapter's purposes are threefold. First, it seeks to describe how these global cross-pressures have affected R&D and regulatory modernization in Thailand. Second, the article offers and tests a theoretical framework for understanding these dynamics in cross-national settings that integrates and tests Wilson and Wong's framework as elaborated and extended with insights from comparative state-building, historical institutionalist, and international relations theorists. Third, it culls from this analysis lessons for advancing theory building on the impact of global policy pressures on administrative modernization more generally.[2]

Precautionary Politics, Administrative Modernization, and the Developing World: A Theoretical Framework

As Paarlberg (2001) argues, developing nations confronted by global pressures in this policy arena have five critical sets of decisions to make that have major implications for administrative modernization. First, they must make controversial decisions about how much institutional protection of intellectual property rights (IPRs) (i.e., patents) they will afford to multinational companies investing in GMO R&D in their countries. Second, they must determine to what extent regulatory regimes will screen for biosafety risk when GMOs are involved (i.e., will GMO seeds and products be screened differently). Third, they must specify the extent to which regulators will encourage or discourage the import or export of GMO products. Fourth, they must determine if, and at what levels, GMOs in food will trigger the labeling of these products to give consumers choice over whether to purchase them or not. Finally, nations must decide how much public research investment in GMOs they will allow or permit others to make within their borders, either unilaterally or in partnership.

How can practitioners and scholars best anticipate and understand cross-national variations in how, why, and with what patterns of politics developing nations respond to these types of global policy pressures? And going beyond immediate technocratic implications of these pressures, what implications do they hold for national sovereignty, the relationship between democracy and administration, and the legitimacy of public administration in developing nations? Arguably, Welch and Wong's model of global pressures on public bureaucracy offers an important point of departure for addressing these questions, and it does so in three unprecedented ways in the literature.

First, it synthesizes (as per the work of Dwivedi and Henderson, 1990) what they call the "traditionalist" model (e.g., Heady, 1995; Riggs, 1994) and "revisionist" model (e.g., Aberbach & Rockman, 1987; Peters, 1988) of administrative modernization. Second, it directs researchers' attention to both the "direct" impacts of globalization on bureaucracy and its "indirect"

[2]The data informing the analysis is the product of extensive archival research undertaken in Thailand in 2002; a content analysis of Thai newspapers from 1995 to 2003; and 30 semistructured interviews conducted in Thailand with indigenous and international representatives of NGOs, government R&D and regulatory officials, university agro-biotechnology scientists, international trade consultants, and the U.S. State Department from June through September of 2002.

effects through the changes it can have on the social, economic, and political systems of nations. Finally, their model directs attention to the specific attributes of bureaucracy that global pressures can affect: (1) centralization versus decentralization of structures, (2) the scope or breadth of bureaucracy's service responsibilities, (3) the relative autonomy of the national bureaucracy to make policy decisions, and (4) the type of bureaucratic accountability pursued.

From their model, Welch and Wong offer three hypotheses suitable for testing, elaborating, and refining when adapted to the GMO policy arena:

1. H_1: The greater the pursuit of GMO R&D in a nation, the greater the degree of bureaucratic centralization in making modernization decisions.
2. H_2: The greater the number and degree of formalization of global institutions attempting to affect GMO policy in a nation, the lower the policy-making autonomy of the bureaucracy in making modernization decisions.
3. H_3: The greater the number and types of GMO-related modernization efforts undertaken in other nations, the greater the number of initiatives undertaken in a specific developing nation and the more these initiatives mimic those taken by other nations.

As noted, Welch and Wong urge scholars to test, elaborate, and extend their model, theoretical framework, and hypotheses in future research. This enterprise, in turn, requires a set of analytical tools capable of "opening up" the black box of as yet unspecified political, social, and economic dynamics affecting and affected by the bureaucracies under pressure. I argue that the rudiments of such a theoretical framework lie in adapting and integrating insights from the comparative state-building literature, from historical institutionalist scholars, and from scholars studying the diffusion of policy in a globally interdependent world.

As comparative state-building theorists recognize, external "shocks" like battles over the precautionary principle or potentially revolutionary breakthroughs in agricultural biotechnology do not mean that nations (even those in the developed world) are capable of or willing to respond. Instead, a pattern of precautionary politics adapted from Skowronek's (1982) work on nation building is likely to emerge. First, a structural–historical mismatch arises between existing administrative structures and the strategies necessary to cope with environmental pressures (e.g., multinational corporations seeking permits for field testing in Thailand, or the EU issuing labeling requirements or imposing a *de facto* moratorium on GMOs). Proponents of GMO modernization are likely to go on the offensive to resolve this mismatch, with political leadership a key to success and with realignment of existing political coalitions a potentially critical variable. But even these efforts are conditioned initially by leaders' perceptions of the existing opportunities, incentives, risks, and constraints involved in advancing a modernization agenda. And if neoinstitutionalists and international relations scholars studying diffusion of global policy innovations are correct, the substance of the reforms proposed is likely to take one of two forms: policy emulation (imitating without analysis what other nations are doing) and policy learning (imitating and adapting on the basis of understanding what works, and thus is appropriate for one's circumstances) (DiMaggio & Powell, 1983).

Even when these circumstances are most favorable (i.e., opportunities to advance modernization exist, the political risks involved are minimal, the political incentives for doing so are high, and resource constraints are minimal), modernization efforts are likely to run pell-mell into a counteroffensive by opponents of the technology in question. Here, the work of comparativists and international relation scholars portends that a battle will be joined among actors from the international (e.g., transnational nongovernmental organizations (NGOs), multinational corporations, or business associations), domestic (e.g., local NGOs, elected officials, or producer associations), and bureaucratic (e.g., across public agencies and within single public agencies) realms. Indeed, as Haas et al. (1995) note, the most powerful impact that international regimes can make is in stimulating, supporting (with technical capacity and information), and focusing the attention of networks of local and transnational NGOs who, in turn, put grassroots and international pressures on governments for redress.

Following most likely as a consequence, however, is what Skowronek calls a "crisis of authority." This occurs as domestic actors within and outside the government — and even among pro- and antidevelopment elements within the same domestic and international ministries — vie for ascendancy. They wish to see either their positions ratified in policy, or their favored issues linked to others in ways that advance their causes (e.g., antiglobalization), or their jurisdictions expanded, contracted, or protected. The legacy of these crises of authority are accommodations among interests that leave compromised and implementation-challenged administrative systems in their wake. As such, rather than resolve conflicts over GMOs, these accommodations are more likely to institutionalize the abilities of the antagonists to "fight" another day within "halting, halfway, and patchworked" administrative structures.

Relatedly, a final insight applicable to these battles over modernization involves the reciprocal relationship that historical institutionalist scholars posit among politics, structural reforms, and policies (Skocpol, 1992). Based on their logic, longitudinal research on GMOs and administrative modernization in developing nations should, on the one hand, chronicle how changes in internal and international political, social, and economic forces lead to changes in administrative capacity building and policies pursued. Conversely, analysis also should reveal how changes in GMO-related policies and administrative structures lead, in turn, to changes in the nature of the politics that take place within a developing nation.

Expecting these patterns of modernization politics to unfold in this way over time, however, still offers little guidance about what attributes of these decision processes to study to ascertain "tensions between administration and democracy" and the "serious questions [regarding] the foundation of legitimacy in public administration" that arise in the process (Welch & Wong, 1998, p. 45). Arguably, adapting the five attributes that Cohen et al. (1972) suggest, informed decision making in "organized anarchies" affords a useful analytical framework for assessing these dynamics. "Entry times" refer to the pace at which GMO problems and decision opportunities confront Thai decision makers, whereas decision structures identify who has the legitimacy to participate in these GMO decisions by virtue of their position in formal hierarchies. Decision structures, in turn, differ in terms of how hierarchical (or nonhierarchical), specialized (closed or open to nonspecialists), and segmented (greater or fewer agencies or actors within the decision structure) they are. Access structures refer to the extent to which and to how readily other problems and decision opportunities get linked to GMO issues. Relatedly, energy loads refer to the nature and ratio of agency resources (e.g., financial, personnel, time) to agency responsibilities and, hence, to GMO decisions that must be made. Finally, energy distributions refer to who has the resources to deal with GMO issues, their institutional predisposition to make choices in certain directions, and their comparative strength relative to each other.

All this, in turn, suggests several interrelated hypotheses suitable for testing, elaborating, and refining when adapted to the GMO policy arena:

1. H_4: The more numerous, rapid, complex, or contentious the issues involved, the less adequate existing energy loads of bureaucracies will be, the greater the pressure to modernize them, and the more dependent developing nations become on global institutions for support.
2. H_5: The greater the disagreement among formal global institutions and subnational actors about the ends of policy both among subnational actors and formalized global institutions:
    a. The more open decision structures and access structures will become.
    b. The more likely modernization issues will get entangled with other issues related to domestic politics and globalization (access structures).
    c. The greater the amount of disagreement within decision structures.

   d. The less autonomy and centralization of decision power that accrues to national bureaucracies.
   e. The more halting, halfway, and patchworked (or prismatic — see Riggs, 1966) bureaucratic modernization becomes.
   f. The more likely that future conflicts over modernization are institutionalized within the bureaucracy.
3. H_6: The more halting, halfway, and patchworked administrative modernization becomes, the more modernization decisions depend either on power differentials among the bureaucratic actors involved in decision structures or on the larger political concerns of elected sovereigns.

GMOs, Precautionary Politics, and Administrative Modernization in Thailand

To test the utility of this more elaborated model, as well as the various hypotheses derived from it, this section assesses changes in the pattern of precautionary politics that have driven the five areas of modernization, which Paarlberg identifies as critical for developing nations. They are assessed in terms of the pre-1997 and post-1997 modernization of these GMO R&D and regulatory regimes in Thailand. This breakdown is used because 1997 was the year that the EU enacted its labeling law predicated on the precautionary principle (followed, of course, by the EU moratorium the next year).

As the following vignettes will describe, each of the five areas is characterized by a significantly quickened pace of GMO choice opportunities (i.e., entry times) in the post-1997 era, which in turn made access structures decidedly more amenable to linking GMO issues with nonscientific issues. The latter involves a more culturally based, redistributive, and conflict-enhancing "return-to-localism" discourse that is decidedly antiglobalization in outlook. Both responding to and affecting these pressures, Thai decision structures in all five areas became more open, less hierarchical, and specialized (i.e., there was more international, subnational, local, and cross-agency coordination needed), with each more vulnerable to the influence of pro- and anti-GMO forces alike.

In each case as well, these dynamics led to a decided imbalance in the energy loads of the bureaucracies involved, with modernization demands producing results but far outstripping the administrative capacities of these organizations. Rampant, as well, were both cross-agency and within-agency internecine conflicts as various actors in pro-GMO-development and regulatory bureaucracies struggled for power, access, and influence over the direction of Thai R&D and regulatory policy. Amid all this, as Zahariadis

(2003, p. 156) predicts, the antagonists used "framing" (i.e., taking advantage of people's tendencies to be more worried about losing something of value than gaining something new that might be of value) and the "strategic use of symbols" (i.e., biasing choice through emotive appeals) to advance their competing agendas. Left in the wake of these struggles in all five decision areas is a patchworked, halfway, and halting modernization structure that has institutionalized rather than resolved GMO disputes within these structures.

Public Research Investment

Thailand's stance on public research investment in agricultural biotechnology has leaned heavily toward the supportive end of the scale throughout both the pre- and post-1997 eras. Various Thai governments have invested scarce resources in GMO R&D, encouraged substantial support from international foundations (e.g., the Rockefeller Foundation), and partnered with different nations in the enterprise. What is more, they have consistently sought investments in both genetic transformation and post-transformation genetic capacity across the two eras (albeit to levels nowhere near commensurate with their aims because of financial constraints). What has changed in the post-1997 era, however, is the accelerated pace of the entry times of GMO-related modernization issues, accompanied by a heightened degree of caution in making these investments as they have gotten linked by GMO opponents to larger and more conflictual livelihood, antiglobalization, and anticorporate issues.

Thailand launched its campaign to create a biotechnology program in 1983. Albeit never funded on the same scale as China's formidable program, this beginning was still two years before Communist Party chairman Deng Xiaoping began funding the training of Chinese students abroad in biotechnology, and seven years before China opened its first bioengineering laboratory staffed by these scientists. The Thai campaign began with the founding of the National Center for Genetic Engineering and Biotechnology (known as BIOTEC today) under the Ministry for Science, Technology, and Energy. In 1991, BIOTEC was incorporated into a new National Science and Technology Development Agency (NSTDA) as a quasigovernmental center.

Operating outside the Thai civil service and state enterprise system to give it necessary flexibility, BIOTEC's mission ever since has been to support and transfer biotechnology R&D to the private and public sector to advance the social and economic welfare of the nation through development of industry and agriculture. Yet it also has been charged simultaneously with developing biotechnology to protect the environment and natural resources, a mission that frequently was marginalized in agency deliberations by Thailand's emphasis on economic development throughout the pre-1997 period. Since that time, BIOTEC, the Department of Agriculture (DoA), and the Ministry of Science and Technology — with strong support from the Commerce and Trade ministries — have led the development of GM food, feed, and fiber in Thailand. They have been joined most recently by several private Thai companies doing some (although not intensive) genetic R&D (e.g., the giant CP Group's work on flour).

With BIOTEC the first to enter the field with any R&D capacity at all, however, every subsequent extension of R&D capacity in the pre-1997 era was initiated and controlled tightly by scientists in these decidedly pro-GMO development agency. During this era, for example, BIOTEC launched a satellite laboratory — the Plant Genetic Engineering Unit (PGEU) at Kasetsart University in Bangkok — that pioneered GMO research in this area. PGEU, in turn, has been joined (either independently or collaboratively) in the post-1997 era by Mahidol University in GMO R&D ventures on cotton, papaya, and rice (focusing on both input trait technologies for pest and viral resistance, and agronomic trait technology for salt tolerance and delayed ripening). Output trait technologies also have been launched by Chulalongkorn University in Bangkok for vaccines against poultry diseases. PGEU additionally worked in the pre-1997 era with the Ministry of Agriculture and Cooperatives in the DoA on large-scale field testing of transgenic plants developed in Thailand, including GM papayas. And when the government established its first DNA Technology Laboratory in 1999 for testing GM content, it did so as an extension of BIOTEC operations. Thus, as the distributor of research grants, with the most developed institutional capacity, and the holder of the longest institutional memory on the subject, BIOTEC has operated with "energy distributions" in its favor — at least among other Thai government agencies. It has, as such, held a "first mortgage" on GMO research decisions, benefited from powerful constituencies in research universities dependent on its largesse, and enjoyed an institutional leg up on other agencies engaged in GMO research (but with decidedly less expertise in the genetic area).

What BIOTEC, the Ministry of Agriculture and Cooperatives in the DoA, and the Ministry of Science and Technology have *not* had over the years are sufficient technoscientific expertise, finances, and laboratories (energy loads) of their own to keep up with advances in the developed world, and even with those of some of Thailand's neighbors in the developing world. The UN estimates, for example, that the ratio of scientists to population is one-per-ten-thousand in Thailand. This ratio is in contrast to comparative ratios in biotechnology-bent regional competitors like Korea, Taiwan, and Japan of 26-, 23-, and 60-per-ten-thousand, respectively (UNDP Human Development Report 1997, cited in Sriwatanapongse, 2002, p. 9). Moreover, in 2002 the Thailand Research Fund (TRF) estimated that the country needed to invest annually at least five times (50 million baht) what it is investing presently (9 million baht) to realize its development potential. TRF also estimated that meeting Thailand's development needs requires a tenfold increase in the number of researchers in coming years, lamenting in the process Thailand's shortage of "strong research institutions" (Thailand Research Fund, 2002).

With energy loads so lacking in comparison to those of their economic competitors, and with GMO expertise lodged in private corporations rather than public research institutes worldwide (unlike during the Green Revolution) in the pre-1997 era, the Thai government began allowing foreign multinational corporations (viz., Calgene, Monsanto, and Novartis) to set up GMO field trials in the country for various crops (in particular, the Flavr Savr tomato and Bt cotton). As one BIOTEC researcher describes the results of this policy, by the late 1990s, "streams of GMOs" were entering the nation in the form of "finished food products, feed ingredients, and raw material for production of food-related products such as vegetable oils" (Damrongchai, 2002).

Also in the pre-1997 era, resource-strapped Thai agencies began searching for R&D partnerships with other nations and international organizations. For example, PGEU joined in collaborative GMO R&D ventures on cotton, papaya, and rice with CIRAD (a French company), Cornell University (United States), and the Rockefeller Foundation (Valyasevi et al., 2003). These public–private–nonprofit ventures also focused on developing pest, viral, and salt resistance, as well as delayed ripening. All this picked up in the late 1990s as Thailand began partnering with, among others, the Consultive Group on International Agricultural Research (CGIAR) and its International Rice Research Institute (IRRI), as well as with nine other nations in the International Rice Genome Research Consortium (IRGRC) and the Papaya Biotechnology Network of Southeast Asia (including Indonesia, Malaysia, the Philippines, and Vietnam).

Venturing into collaborative agreements with multinational corporations and institutions was not without its consequences, however. First, and as dependency theory predicts, external Thai actors began having enhanced control over the pace of GMO entry times, energy distributions, and formal influence in Thai decision structures. Second, Thailand gave anti-GMO activists an opening to link the (still even today) esoteric technology with another larger issue that was becoming salient to developing nations: concerns about the impact of globalization on their finances, culture, and economic livelihoods. As political scientist Robyn Eckersley (1994) argues, the end of the Cold War wrought the rise of environmentalism as a galvanizing force for opponents of capitalism and the state. More precisely, "environmentalism [and use of the precautionary principle as a driving force within it] has emerged as a powerful challenge to dominant industrial capitalism," generally, and, in particular, to the so-called "Washington consensus" for attaining economic development in the developing world (i.e., through financial market liberalization) (Eckersley, 1994, p. 5; also see Stiglitz, 2002).

Proffered instead is an alternative development model dramatically in opposition to what recent Thai governments and their business constituencies see as the way for Thailand to modernize its economy. This "softer" development model is predicated on a return-to-localism discourse that some Thai scholars have linked to a "culture at risk" discourse that is "a form of guerilla resistance to the peripheralization" of communities that they see globalization promoting (Phongpaichit & Baker, 2002). This alternative development model is premised on non-Western scientific models and thus eschews large-scale, high-technology farming in preference for small community-based tracts informed by the "traditional wisdom" of farmers, a traditional wisdom that they want to see protected from patenting by multinational corporations. Proponents also reject the Western penchant for consumerism and maximizing productivity in favor of "self-reliance" (i.e., producing enough only for one's family and to share with one's village).

Significant enough in its own right, personal and village self-reliance morphed into a philosophy of national "self-reliance" in the aftermath of the Asian financial crisis of 1997. Calls mounted for rejecting ties with global financial and trade markets, especially when less free-market-exposed nations like Korea and Malaysia did not fare anywhere near as badly as Thailand. Also linking GMOs to these antiglobalization sentiments were two indigenous networks established in 1995: the Assembly of the Poor (a coalition of over 100 people's organizations and NGOs, including 35 farmer groups) and a Bangkok-based NGO called BIOTHAI (Biodiversity Action Thailand; previously the Thai Network on Community Rights and Biodiversity).

Following rapidly on the heels of these events were a series of public–private–nonprofit partnering-related embarrassments in Thailand. For example, in 1999 antiglobalization elements exploited a ham-handed effort by Monsanto to use a microcredit system to pay farmers in northeast Thailand to buy the company's pesticides and to train them to use herbicides and GM seeds. Involved in this venture were the Thai DoA, a Thai NGO (the Population and Community Development Association), the Kenan Institute of Asia (KIAsia), and the IRRI in the Philippines. With the World Bank financing the IRRI, with Monsanto's project director a former high-level employee of IRRI, with KIAsia funded by the U.S. Agency for International Development, and with the head of the NGO on the IRRI board of directors, it was an easy "sell" for anti-GM campaigners to arouse "cultural imperialism" fears. Nor was this situation helped when, a year later, an internal Monsanto report was leaked to anti-GMO campaigners outlining the company's efforts to have pro-GMO scientists appointed by governments in developing nations (including Thailand's government) to international scientific committees reviewing these issues (see, for example, GeneWatch UK Press Release, 2000; Third World Network, 2000).

In response, the agricultural biotechnology industry launched concerted pressures globally to offset the "localism discourse" in developing nations like Thailand with pro-GMO campaigns of their own. For example, after Greenpeace Southeast Asia established its headquarters in Bangkok in 2001 to coordinate its anti-GMO campaign, the U.S.-based International Service for the Acquisition of Agri-Biotech Applications (ISAAA) opened an office in Bangkok. As ISAAA-Thailand director Panatta Junchai explained, her organization's immediate aims in Thailand were to counteract "biased and unsound" information about GMOs propagated by NGOs (led by Greenpeace), and to work closely with Thai scientists from the Science and Technology Development Agency to develop these technologies (Samabuddhi, 2002a). But to BIOTHAI director Witoon Lianchamroon, the ISAAA was only a tool of the biotech industry: "ISAAA's goal, to eliminate Asian farmers' poverty by using biotechnology, will make conditions worse for small farmers because the technology is controlled by multination agribusiness whose interests are contrary to farmer needs" (Samabuddhi, 2002a).

Still, in late 2003 the Thaksin government's commitment to improving the nation's biotechnology advances became clear, as did its commitment to building the capacity to protect them from pilfering by other countries. Thailand's National Biotechnology Committee on Agriculture released a draft of an eight-year R&D development plan for Thailand that the government approved. Included among its aims for the 2004–2012 era were improving the input, output, and agronomic traits of 11 commodities (including jasmine rice, commercial fruits, commercial woods, tapioca, rubber, and sugarcane). To these ends, the Agriculture and Cooperatives Ministry set up a new Biotechnology Research and Development Office. Yet even in opening Thai R&D decision structures even more broadly by including representatives of the NGO opponents, committee chairman Sutat Sriwatanapongse noted serious capacity-related (i.e., energy-load-related) challenges that constrained these efforts, most notably a lack of Thai experts in biotechnology fields (Changyawa, 2003a). And wrought in the process was the institutionalization of conflict over future GMO R&D decisions.

IPRs, Biosafety, and Trade

Not unlike the R&D modernization effort, over the past two decades Thai governments have cobbled together a variegated, fragmented, and resource-challenged biosafety, IPR, and trade regulatory regime. In the pre-1997 era, decision structures related to each of the three areas were relatively hierarchical and specialized. In the area of biosafety, BIOTEC in 1986 commissioned a status report on agricultural biotechnology. The agency's fear was that the promise of GMO research in Thailand could never be realized if the nation failed to develop trusted biosafety guidelines for testing. Not until 1990, however, did BIOTEC form a biosafety subcommittee to develop those guidelines, and not until 1992 did it release laboratory and field testing guidelines (rather than rules).

While making Thailand one of the first Southeast Asian nations to adopt national guidelines for GMO laboratory work, field testing, and release into the environment, these remained only guidelines. Moreover, they were guidelines developed in hierarchical and specialized decision structures by an avowedly pro-GMO development agency. The following year, Thailand expanded this decision structure somewhat by creating a National Biosafety Committee (NBC) to do technical assessments on GMOs and to advise the government on GMO safety issues. However, the Committee still reported to the secretariat of BIOTEC, which made final decisions. At the same time, the government created Institutional Biosafety Committees (IBCs) at research centers to approve all GMO research at these institutions, IBCs that still reported to BIOTEC (and that in 2003 totaled 23 in number).

Thailand's GMO regulatory responsibilities in the areas of trade and IPRs also were shared among several largely pro-development and pro-commercial government ministries. Of those most relevant to GMO food, feed, and fiber in Thailand, the DoA has to approve all imports, testing, and releases of GMOs into the environment (as per Thailand's Plant Quarantine Act of 1964 as amended in 1999 and the Plant Variety Act of 1975). In turn, the Department of Livestock Development in the DoA handles petitions for commercial release of GMO-containing animal feed, regulates rDNA-derived and biotechnological products, and is responsible for general environmental protection regarding GMOs. Meanwhile, the Department of Justice and, most importantly, the Department of Intellectual Property Rights in the Department of Commerce is responsible for regulating GMO technology transfers dealing with IPRs.

The pace of the entry times of issues related to all three areas began to accelerate dramatically in the post-1997 era, however. Spawned in their wake were significantly less hierarchical and specialized decision structures than those afforded historically by Thai statutes, as well as a more precautionary approach to GMOs. As noted, GMOs of foreign origin were first introduced for field testing into Thailand in 1994. As more requests for field testing for research came in, however, so too did controversy. In 1999, for example, Monsanto became involved in yet another scandal regarding the legality of its actions, this time related to Bt cotton seeds.

The Thai government had given Monsanto permission to conduct Bt cotton research experiments in four provinces (Lopburi, Nakhon Ratchasima, Phetchabun, and Ratchaburi), with the understanding that all Bt seeds would be burned after the experiments ended. Yet prompted by Thai NGOs led by BIOTHAI and Technology for Rural and Ecological Enrichment, BIOTEC testing found that GM seeds were still used by farmers, Bt cotton seeds that villagers claimed "were provided by a cotton company" (Bt cotton found in two provinces, 1999). As the group's leader, Daycha Siripatra charged caustically, "only the Department of Agriculture and Monsanto don't know" that GM seeds are sold illegally in Thailand to farmers anxious to improve their yields (Bt cotton found in two provinces, 1999).

Nor was the situation helped when Thai plant quarantine inspection officials confessed that genetically modified soybean and corn had been imported illegally into Thailand since 1994 with their full knowledge. Under the Plant Quarantine Act of 1994 (originally banning the import of 40 plant species and subsequently amended in 1999 to require the banning of all possible GM plant varieties unless imported for research and experimentation), inspections were done by the pro-industry Commerce department. As one inspector put it in the late 1990s, his inspection station had never tested products for GMOs: "We can prohibit GM produce imports only in the law. In reality, the authorities can hardly do anything with the transgenic [i.e., GMO-containing] produce brought in for consumption for fear that the food industry would be harmed" (Atthakor & Noikorn, 1999).

Meanwhile, in the post-1997 era, foreign concerns about GMOs picked up the pace of issue entry times in Thailand. For example, several supermarket chains in Austria, France, and Great Britain banned GM products from their shelves; the EU's Scientific Committee on Plants advised against the release of GMO potatoes containing antibiotic resisters; the British Medical Association warned that GMOs could lead to new allergies and resistance to antibiotics; Greece banned the import of GE rapeseed; a Brazilian court outlawed cultivation of GM soybeans; national bans on planting GM crops were enacted by the Danish and Norwegian governments; South Korean students blockaded state-funded greenhouses used in biotechnology; and over a million Japanese supported a "No GMO Food" campaign. In short order, and with Europe's *de facto* moratorium beginning in 1998, Thai exports also were caught in the crosshairs of these international regulatory debates with, for example, canned tuna and several other exports (e.g., soybean flower in Germany) returned to Thai exporters or detained from entry by several EU trade partners and (later) Middle East countries.

Not surprisingly under these circumstances, business groups like the Thai Food Processors' Association and the Thai Tuna Packers' Group began demanding that BIOTEC's capacity to screen food samples be improved (Atthakor, 1999). This, in turn, produced demands on agency capacity that quickly outstripped available Thai regulatory capacities (i.e., their energy loads). When in 1999, for example, exporters submitted over 200 food samples for testing and certification as GMO-free during the first month his agency opened a new DNA testing center for screening, the director of BIOTEC, Somwong Tragoonrung, averred that BIOTEC was not qualified to issue GMO-free certificates: "We simply produce laboratory results. We will be able to give certification only when ... we know exactly whether the tested samples are really used in production. And we [can do] this only on a random basis" (Atthakor, 1999). Nor, he averred, did BIOTEC have the capacity to test all kinds of oils for GMOs.

Nonetheless, as a result of these internally generated demands to cope with these externally generated global policy pressures, GMO decision structures (i.e., those with formal authority to address GMO issues) that had historically been dominated by technocrats at BIOTEC expanded to include Thailand's nonscientific Committee on International Economic Policy and its National Biotechnology Committee on Agriculture. The latter was comprised of nonscientific ministries and a few NGO representatives. Meanwhile, splits in attitudes toward GMOs among administrators arose even within the same Thai R&D and regulatory agencies. Deputy agriculture minister Newin Chidchob, for example, said he would set up a committee that would include NGO representatives to investigate contamination charges. But before these studies were done, Agriculture Department head Ananta Dalodom denied the allegations, saying that "field trials are transparent and all procedures [already] are strictly controlled" (Bt cotton found in two provinces, 1999).

Against this leitmotif of internecine warfare, and despite the representation of some NGOs in decision structures, grassroots NGO actions to stymie GMOs did not let up. Indeed, the 1999–2001 era saw a variety of NGO efforts in Thailand to halt field trials of Bt cotton in particular and GMO testing and experimentation more generally. In late 1999, for example, a network of eight agricultural organizations formally petitioned the Thai government for a ban on imports and field testing of GMOs. Veerapol Sopa, representing this network, plied with virtuosity indigenous anticorporate and antiglobalization feelings. Farmers, he argued, would be forced to buy seeds at higher prices from the multinational corporations and GMOs also would cause mutation of local produce. To which a prodevelopment commerce ministry official responded that "relaxation [of rigorous GMO standards is] in the public interest [because] ... denying GM produce access would result in a string of problems affecting producers and consumers" (Atthakor, 1999).

Conceding, however, that smuggling of GM seeds and lax inspection at Thailand's borders were occurring, deputy agriculture minister Newin

Chidchob announced in late 1999 that the government would try to set up a GMO-free zone in the country to allow Thai organic farmers to access organic markets globally (Bid for plainly grown food, 1999). Chidchob, however, made no pretense that a totally GMO-free Thailand was possible in light of Thailand's inadequate administrative capacities. Not only did Thai farmers in any prospective zone have to be registered and certified as not using GMO seeds, but also at least one DoA laboratory had to be added to the one already operated by BIOTEC to guarantee that imported seeds were non-GMO (and thus would not contaminate organic plants in non-GMO areas).

In quick order, however, the anti-GMO campaign was rejuvenated again after Mr. Newin Chidchob approved the import into Thailand of 30 tons of potato seeds by the U.S.-based Frito-Lay company for field testing near Chiang Mai without prior testing for GMO content (Noikorn, 2000). In a now-familiar tactic, anti-GMO campaigners also deftly linked biotechnology on Jasmine rice to both health concerns and pockets of resentment against globalization and the Green Revolution. The latter was particularly effective with Thai farmers who had gone deeper into debt, lost farms to finance continuing rounds of pesticides, or lost traditional rice varieties because of the green revolution's emphasis on "high yield with high [fertilizer] input" (Siripetra, 2000). Wrought in the process was a widely publicized rice forum and a "long march" of farmers in September 2000 across six northern Thai farm provinces.

Confronted by this grassroots opposition and the administrative capacity challenges it wrought, in April 2001 the Thai cabinet announced that it would suspend GMO field trials and reconsider field testing once adequate biosafety standards were legislated. And to these ends, another expansion of Thai regulatory decision structures occurred: although the National Biosafety Committee convened to develop those standards was led by the largely prodevelopment Agriculture Department, vocal anti-GMO activist Witoon Lianchamroon of BIOTHAI was added to the committee as well.

After nearly two years of deliberation, the biosafety committee announced, first, in February 2003 that large-scale open field trials of GMOs still would be banned. However, limited field trials involving Monsanto and overseen in DoA laboratories would be allowed (Samabuddhi, 2003). Perceived by NGOs as a relaxation of the ban in favor of their perennial GMO nemesis, this proposal was quickly denounced by Varoonvarn Svangsophakul of Greenpeace Southeast Asia as both nonimplementable and dangerous because Thailand lacked an adequate monitoring system to ensure leakage or drift of GM seeds (Samabuddhi, 2003). What is more, these comments were indirectly supported by some careerists within Thai bureaucracies and by some in the Thai cabinet who were split over the issue.

For example, Hiran Hiranpradit, a senior career civil servant in the DoA, was decidedly less sanguine about GMO plants and seeds than his political superiors. Urging caution and worrying about avoiding untoward effects of

GMOs on the "natural production of crops" (i.e., traditional farming and conventional breeding), Hiranpradit asked in a public forum, "How can we be sure that transgenic [i.e., GMO-containing] crops are 100% safe?" (Samabuddhi, 2003). Likewise, two deputy agriculture and cooperatives ministers (Prapat Panyachartraksa and Natee Klipthong) made public their concerns about purely government testing. To which deputy agriculture permanent secretary Ampon Kittampon warned that keeping the testing ban meant that agricultural biotechnology industries would not transfer badly needed and desired genetic technology to Thai agencies (a *quid pro quo* they had been offering) (Samabuddhi, 2003).

Significantly, however, this internecine GMO biosafety debate between and within regulatory and pro-development agencies was won by historically weaker proponents of precaution (albeit with some concessions). Responding positively to continuing pressures from the Assembly of the Poor, biodiversity advocates, regulatory agencies, and transnational NGOs, the Thaksin government decided to keep the full ban in place (Changyawa & Kongrut, 2003). Thus, as of late 2003, neither third parties like Monsanto nor civil servants could field test GMOs, even if international market competitors were selling the same GMO-derived crops commercially.

According to Thai deputy prime minister Suvit Khunkitti, the total ban on field testing of GMOs would not be lifted until the National Environment Board (NEB) decided that GM crops were not a threat to the nation's ecology. However, the comments of Lianchamroon of BIOTHAI and the biosafety committee foreshadowed the direction of future conflict: even then, lifting the ban would be too risky because Thailand would still be "without a code of practice dealing with biosafety, patent protection, benefit-sharing, and liabilities for [GMO] contamination."[3]

Food Safety and Consumer Choice

As with the other R&D and regulatory regimes discussed in this chapter, the pace of the entry times of GMO consumer choice issues increased dramatically in the post-1997 era, especially as labeling laws were linked to other international pressures (i.e., access structures grew more open, less hierarchical, and more unsegmented). Global and internal pressures began mounting for a GMO food labeling law in late 1999 as concern grew over Thailand's export markets and as drift from GMO field testing continued.

---

[3]Moreover, as Langkarpint (2003, p. 7) notes more generally, capacity problems plague the operation of the NEB, sorely limiting its ability to carry out responsibilities like these. The NEB, for example, cannot directly monitor and enforce its findings unless business agrees, and its focus has remained on urban rather than rural issues.

However, labeling initially was opposed successfully by a coalition of Thai food processors and feed mill operators, a coalition that would later come to support it to protect their export business.

Appealing directly to consumer concerns over pocketbook issues, they argued that labeling would prove expensive to consumers because suppliers would charge more for separating GMO products from non-GMO products. They also argued that Thailand's fallible GMO testing processes rendered labeling problematic. Moreover, even were this not the case, labeling was not necessary because GMOs had not been scientifically proven harmful. Still, the Thai Food and Drug Administration (FDA) — an organization within the Ministry of Health with lead responsibilities for regulating food safety — announced that it did not rule out labeling laws. At the same time, however, deputy FDA administrator Siriwat Tiptharadol also noted how a labeling law would place complex and capacity-challenging demands on his agency that could not be met if European standards (preferred by NGOs) were used (see Bhatiasevi, 1999).

But with labeling requirements of varying stringency and breadth spreading across Europe, Australia, Hong Kong, Japan, Korea, and New Zealand in the post-1997 era, the anti-GMO BIOTHAI mounted an aggressive public campaign to prod the industry ministry to promote a GMO labeling law for Thailand. Premising their arguments on the right of consumers to know what they were eating, BIOTHAI, other NGOs, and many university academics simultaneously pointed out the benefit that Thai farmers could reap by selling GMO-free foods abroad (Pressure up for labelling of products, 1999). Labeling proponents also got an unexpected boost for their cause when word spread of a meeting that deputy agriculture permanent secretary Ampon Kittampon held with a three-member delegation from the United States, including Senator Christopher Bond (R-MS) and Monsanto scientists (based in St. Louis). They came to Thailand both to press their antilabeling case on Thai officials and to dissuade Thai regulators from embracing the precautionary principle (Pressure up for labelling of products, 1999). Once announced, however, this meeting quickly became a focusing event, linking health and environmental concerns about GMOs to indigenous antiglobalization, anticorporate, and return-to-localism sentiments (i.e., as access structures opened).

Nor was the pro-GMO movement helped in early 2001 when Greenpeace Southeast Asia shipped 30 corn-, soy-, and potato-related products already in Thai grocery stores to an independent laboratory in Hong Kong to see if they contained GMOs. Despite government assurances that all the products sold in Thailand were GMO-free, seven of those tested contained GMOs: Nestle baby food (Baby Cerelac), Unilever's Knorr soups, Pringles potato crisps, Nissin Cup Noodle, Vita-Tofu soybean curd, Good Time cereal beverage, and Lay's potato products. Moreover, by late 2002, the

Hong Kong laboratory found a variety of other products that contained Monsanto's GMO-Roundup-Ready soybean, including Nestle's Nesvita and Leader Price's soy products (Samabuddhi, 2002b).

Not surprisingly, labeling opponents quickly went on the offensive. For example, senior officials at BIOTEC caustically indicted the integrity of both Greenpeace and the tests themselves. "I wonder," asked Sakarindr Bhumiratana of BIOTEC, "why Greenpeace avoided stating there are no scientific data on health problems due to consumption of GM foods" (Samabuddhi, 2001a). In addition, when Greenpeace forwarded another batch of baby foods for GMO-testing in mid-2001, the head of BIOTEC's DNA technology laboratory argued that transparency was lacking in the testing: "to be fair, every sample taken for testing should be countersigned by the manufacturers" since contamination might be occurring during the sampling process itself (Atthakor, 2001a).

This counteroffensive by labeling opponents notwithstanding, Greenpeace and local NGOs adroitly turned the Nestle baby food findings into the centerpiece of their anti-GMO campaign. Moreover, they framed the GMO issue more broadly as cultural bias promoted by immoral globalization forces: multinational corporations were using Thais—and, especially, Thai babies—as "guinea pigs in what is a massive experiment with potentially far-reaching and irreversible [health and safety] consequences" (Atthakor, 2001b). Noting how Nestle had, since 1996, committed to not using GMOs in baby foods in Germany, Greenpeace campaigner Auaiporn Suthonthanyakorn said the company was nonetheless "feeding [Thai] children GE baby food without even informing mothers about GE ingredients" (Atthakor, 2001b).

How soon would the Thai FDA respond to these calls for action, and in what form? As one manufacturer characterized the realpolitik of the pre-1997 situation, "it is known fact that the [Thai] Food and Drug Administration was reluctant about labeling because that move would have a critical impact on Thai industries, especially small-scale manufacturers" (Atthakor, 2001b). But with the entry times of labeling-related issues mounting, Thai decision structures that were once dominated by pro-GMO development agencies grew less hierarchical and segmented (Samabuddhi, 2001b). For example, a subcommittee was established to inform the FDA's deliberations over labeling laws (which involved the medical science department in the Ministry of public health). Moreover, membership on the subcommittee included not only pro-GMO representatives like BIOTEC and the DoA, but also representatives of Greenpeace and other consumer groups (Samabuddhi, 2001c). In turn, whatever recommendation the subcommittee eventually made was subject to public comment, then subsequent review by a newly constituted National Food Commission with broadened representation.

Drafted in July 2001 and subject to public comment in August, the subcommittee's recommendations reflected a combination of tactical positioning vis-à-vis trade competitors, Thailand's administrative shortcomings, and Thai electoral politics. To the chagrin of Greenpeace campaigners and local NGOs, for example, the subcommittee recommended limiting labeling to only 22 specific food products made from GMO corn or soybean. Moreover, labeling on these products was necessary only if one of their three primary ingredients (rather than any ingredient or overall ingredients) contained more than 5 percent GM materials. Thus, the subcommittee decisively rejected the EU's 1 percent content standard in favor of positioning the nation tactically with its neighboring market competitors. More precisely, the law was not as stringent as Korea's labeling law with its 3 percent content standard, and no more stringent than Japan's 5 percent rule (Changyawa, 2003b).

The FDA's secretary-general Vichai Chokeviwat readily admitted that further limiting the stringency of the labeling law was the inability of Thai laboratories to test for GMO content in products other than corn and soybean (Bhatiasevi, 2001a). Nor would testing and labeling of raw materials be pursued, as these were very costly and complex and would be infeasible in light of the thousands of corn and soy products already requiring testing. Likewise, decisions to categorize cooking oils as GMO-free were made because analyzing their transgenic content was too difficult, given existing Thai capacity (Bhatiasevi, 2000).

Finally, the proposed labeling law sought to assuage both multinational corporate concerns and those of Thai small businesses and street vendor interests. As the corporations urged, labels could not be stigmatizing (i.e., could not imply that GMOs were harmful), and they could not be written in red (as this color is typically used for "warnings" and the FDA was not saying the product is dangerous). Moreover, the Thai cabinet gave manufacturers six months from final approval of the law to clear their shelves of GMO products before they could be punished for not labeling them. Finally, "small food producers" and street vendors selling fresh corn or soybeans did not have to worry about labeling their products.

This compromise satisfied no one, of course, thus engendering conflict over the timing and terms of the labeling law during the next year. According to Ms. Svangsophakul of Greenpeace, "to continue using the present [5 percent] rule is to continue lying to consumers .... Products which Greenpeace already knows contain GM materials, such as Nestle's baby food Cerelac, do not need a special label under the rule" (Changyawa, 2003b). Likewise, Saree Ongsomwang of the Thai Foundation for Consumers said that labeling should begin immediately and be premised less on laboratory testing and specific content than on whether or not products were made from raw materials containing GMOs (Bhatiasevi, 2001b). In the end, however, the Thai government embraced the original recommendations with minor amendments. For example, producers and sellers of products (e.g., grocery chains) with GMO content were granted more time to find reliable alternative suppliers of non-GMO raw materials (i.e., the labeling law did not go into effect until May 2003). In response, Thai NGOs and transnational NGOs refused to endorse the document. This set the stage for further conflict.

Conclusions

The preceding discussion has used the Thai GMO experience over the past decade as a policy "window" for testing, elaborating, and refining the insights of Welch and Wong's theoretical framework for understanding how global policy pressures affect administrative modernization in the developing world. Revealed in the process are the strengths of their framework; the importance of incorporating within their model the insights of comparative state-building, historical institutionalism, and international relations theorists; and the utility of Cohen and his associates' parameters of decision making in organized anarchies. Combined, these help ascertain "tensions between administration and democracy" and the "serious questions [regarding] the foundation of legitimacy in public administration" that arise in the process (Welch & Wong, 1998, p. 45).

Turning first to the components and posited direction of the relationships in Welch and Wong's original synthesis model, the Thai experience suggests that researchers pay special attention to the impact of three key attributes of the global policy environment on administrative modernization: (1) the heterogeneity of the pressures it affords and the level of conflict these produce (e.g., the competing pressures applied by pro- and anti-GMO forces internally and transnationally); (2) the instability of the pressures exerted (e.g., the volatility and rapidity of the entry times of GMO-related issues); and (3) the level of turbulence, whereby pressures in one part of the environment affect other parts, reverberate, and spread (e.g., the opening of access structures leading to less hierarchical and specialized decision structures as GMO health and safety issues were linked to livelihood and anti-globalization feelings).

At the same time, the Thai experience also points to the utility of conceptualizing the direction of influence in the global policy arena as reciprocal rather than unidirectional. To be sure, global policy pressures affect bureaucratic modernization both directly and indirectly (through the political, economic, and social systems). Yet the historical and existing decision structures, energy loads, and energy distributions of the bureaucracy in a given nation also structure today's patterns of access, influence, and relative advantage of political actors (national, subnational, intrabureaucratic, transnational, and international). These in turn define the nature, pace, and scope of administrative modernization and the policies produced.

So, too, does the state of administrative capacity in a nation's ministries help to shape the nature of the global policy initiatives, pressures, and inducements offered for change in GMO R&D and regulatory capacity exist and thwart corporate, scientific, and trade interests in the developed world, the major antagonists in the GMO battle — the United States and the EU — have linked (implicitly or explicitly) technical assistance to particular regulatory structures. In the case of GMOs, for example, the United States offers financial and technical assistance to these countries that are linked to their adopting GMO regulatory regimes that eschew the precautionary principle. In contrast, and in addition to direct threats of GMO product boycotts, the EU tries indirectly to advance regulatory regimes based on the precautionary principle through its more generous foreign assistance to developing nations and its more ready engagement (than the United States) in international regulatory regimes. This gives greater influence than the United States when these entities are making GMO R&D and regulatory decisions.

Likewise, the internecine dissensus and conflict occasioned by global pressures in this policy arena both across and within Thai ministries demonstrate the wisdom of not treating the bureaucracy as a unified and opaque "black box" in future research. Revealed in the process is how historical differences in agency power among these bureaucratic entities actively confront the present. For example, agencies such as BIOTEC no longer dominate in increasingly more open and less specialized decision structures, but they are still relatively advantaged by virtue of their accumulated expertise and ability to distribute R&D resources.

In terms of testing the validity of the hypotheses proffered earlier, the Thai experience offers both support and areas for refinement. In Thailand's case, for example, conflicting global policy pressures produced a decidedly mixed result. To be sure, a diminution of political autonomy for national bureaucracies occurred (H_1 and H_2), and greater numbers of initiatives were taken in other nations (e.g., labeling laws). At the same time, conflicting global policy pressures had diffuse impacts on access structures and decision structures that simple categories like decentralization versus centralization fail to capture.

Decision structures did decentralize in terms of becoming more open to indigenous actors and NGO associations in all five of Paarlberg's modernization areas (H_5·a, b, c). Currently, and in distinct contrast to the pre-1997 era, the GMO regulatory structure alone is comprised of four disparate policy bodies, with memberships and subcommittees chaired or cochaired by institutional representatives that both embrace and have strong reservations about GMOs. These include: (1) the Committee on International Economic Policy (chaired by a deputy prime minister, and with a subcommittee on biotechnology policy chaired by the permanent secretary of agriculture); (2) the Committee on Conservation and Utilization of Biodiversity (chaired by another deputy prime minister, with a subcommittee on national biosafety policy chaired by the chairman of the National Biodiversity Committee); (3) the Committee on Solving the Problems of the Assembly of the Poor (chaired by another deputy prime minister, with a subcommittee on biosafety law chaired by the Agriculture minister); and (4) the National Food Committee (chaired by the permanent secretary of public health, with a subcommittee on safety review of GM food and a workgroup on GM food labeling, both chaired by the FDA secretary). But decision structures also expanded vertically to include corporations and international foundations offering funding and technology assistance, as well as to include interagency coordinating committees in an effort to accommodate more open access structures and more political control by the prime minister's representatives. By the same token, they also expanded horizontally to include other nations and international entities, like the Rice Genome Project and the ISAAA, in cooperative ventures.

Relatedly, evidence from Thailand supports to a degree the hypotheses (H_2 and H_5·d) that the greater numbers and degrees of formalization of global institutions that evolved during this era would lessen the autonomy of national bureaucracies. But again, the process by which this occurred was not exclusively driven from top downward. Nor did it necessarily erode the legal sovereignty of the nation, as "state erosion" theorists like Falk (1971), Ophuls (1977), and Jackson (1990) predict. Discerned instead, as other scholars predict (e.g., Haas et al., 1995), was a modification of operational sovereignty, but one in which international actors are just as likely to be at the mercy of states for success. As Haas et al. (1995) point out more generally, international regimes depend for their success on the concern, credible commitments to regulate, and capacity of nation states.

Relatedly, as the Thai case illustrates, when conflict over international norms like the precautionary principle are involved, a pattern of politics is likely to emerge that is driven simultaneously by the interaction of top–down pressures (e.g., international influences like producer and trade associations and transnational NGOs), bottom–up pressures (e.g., domestic interests like national trade associations and indigenous NGOs), and horizontal pressures (e.g., cross-organizational "mimesis," as well as cross-agency conflict). Moreover, the specific form of any administrative modernization that does emerge from these multidirectional pressure points need not be a function solely of policy emulation or policy learning (H_3). It also can be a function of political, capacity-building, and tactically driven considerations (e.g., the setting of the content standards of the Thai labeling law).

In sum, the Thai experience suggests that developing nations' dependence on others for resources is growing, but this does not mean that they inevitably get drawn disadvantageously into a resource dependency relationship with international donors or multinational corporations (H_2 and H_4). As in Thailand, for example, savvy domestic and international opponents can reframe biotechnology advances to their advantage by linking them to antiglobalization, anticorporate, and return-to-localism discourses in the post-Cold War era (H_5·b). Neither does it mean, however, that domestic or transnational GMO opponents necessarily will get their way. Recall, for example, how Thailand's biosafety, trade, and labeling laws were distinctly limited in scope and substance by existing R&D and regulatory capacity in the country, as well as by local political realities and by the actions of regional (rather than transnational) market competitors.

All this leads, in turn, to a major conceptual refinement for researchers to consider in their work. Theoretical frameworks accounting for responses of developing nations to global policy pressures must take into consideration the return-to-localism cultural discourse that exists in many of these nations. As the pace of GMO-related "choices" confronting Thai decision makers accelerated in the post-1997 era, GMO issues increasingly were linked to even more cleavage-ridden issues with redistributive implications like globalization, discomfort with Western technoscientific models, and cultural imperialism (access structure). In the process, greater numbers of more diversified, less specialized, and often polarizing actors from the domestic and transnational realms drove GMO precautionary politics in Thailand as decision structures grew less hierarchical, less specialized, and more unsegmented.

At the same time, the Thai experience shows how efforts to respond and shape global policy pressures do not end conflicts over the introduction of technoscientific advances (H_6). Rather, and as comparative state-building theorists suggest, they tend largely to institutionalize them in the resulting administrative structures created (e.g., incorporating dissident NGO groups and agencies with competing interests in coordinating groups in Thai decision structures). Indeed, a pattern of politics described by Skowronek tends largely to emerge: a structural–historical mismatch arises between existing structures and the strategies necessary to cope with environmental change (e.g., multinational corporations seeking permits for field testing in Thailand or the EU issuing labeling requirements or its *de facto* moratorium). Proponents then go on the offensive to try to resolve this mismatch, but quickly run into a counteroffensive by opponents of the technology in question — some from the international realm (e.g., transnational NGOs, multinational corporations, or business associations), some from domestic political actors (e.g., local NGOs, elected officials, or producer associations), and some from within the government (e.g., across public agencies and within single public agencies).

As a consequence, a "crisis of authority" follows as these domestic actors vie to see: (1) their positions ratified in policy (e.g., BIOTEC, the Thai Biodiversity Center, and the FDA); (2) their jurisdictions expanded, contracted, or protected (e.g., BIOTEC and the FDA); or (3) their favored issues linked to others (e.g., Buddhist economics or protectionism) in ways that advance their causes. What follows from these crises of authority is an accommodation among interests that leaves in its wake fragmented and implementation-challenged administrative systems (e.g., at Thai agricultural inspection stations, DNA laboratories, and FDA certifiers). Moreover, rather than resolve policy problems, this accommodation institutionalizes the abilities of the protagonists to "fight" another day within the four patchworked, halting, and halfway structures noted above.

Writing in the mid-1960s, Riggs (1966, p. 382) characterized Thailand as a prismatic society. "[A]s economic growth and industrialization take place," he observed, "the required level of governmental outputs — the 'infrastructure' — increases ... but not as rapidly as the need ...." As this study of R&D and regulatory modernization has described, nearly four decades later no more apt characterization exists of Thailand's evolving response to the global cross-pressures on its administrative capacities occasioned by the precautionary politics of GMOs. Are these and other global policy pressures having the same effect in developing nations worldwide? Much empirical and comparative work is needed before definitive answers to this question are known. Arguably, the theoretical framework afforded in this chapter can help inform this cross-national research agenda. But regardless of the framework used, such analyses are timely, important, and overdue as globalization proceeds apace in the early 21st century.

References

Aberbach, J.D. and Rockman, B.A. (1987). Comparative administration methods, muddles, and models. *Administration and Society*, 18(4): 473–506.

Atthakor, P. (1999). Food exporters anxious to have samples tested. *Bangkok Post*, 30 September. Available at http://www.bangkokpost.com/issues/gmo/300999.html

Atthakor, P. (2001a). Greenpeace sends more items for GMO tests in Hong Kong. *Bangkok Post*, 3 June. Available at http://www.bangkokpost.com/issues/gmo/030601a.html

Atthakor, P. (2001b). GMO food giants unmasked. *Bangkok Post*, 11 April. Available at http://www.bangkokpost.com/issues/gmo/110401a.html

Atthakor, P. and Noikorn, U. (1999). Transgenic laws flouted for years. *Bangkok Post*, 26 October. Available at http://www.bangkokpost.com/issues/gmo/261099a.html

Bhatiasevi, A. (1999). No FDA licences for any GMO products. *Bangkok Post*, 24 October. Available at http://www.bangkokpost.com/issues/gmo/241099.html

Bhatiasevi, A. (2000). GM labeling rule soon to be drafted. *Bangkok Post*, 8 April. Available at http://www.bangkokpost.com/issues/gmo/080400.html

Bhatiasevi, A. (2001a). FDA decides GM food must be labeled. *Bangkok Post*, 4 July. Available at http://www.bangkokpost.com/issues/gmo/040701a.html

Bhatiasevi, A. (2001b). Consumers in call for compulsory labelling. *Bangkok Post*, 25 April. Available at http://www.bangkokpost.com/issues/gmo/250401a.html

Bid for plainly grown food. (1999). *Bangkok Post*, 28 September. Available at http://www.bangkokpost.com/issues/gmo/280999a.html

Bt cotton found in two provinces. (1999). *Bangkok Post*, 19 October. Available at http://www.bangkokpost.com/issues/gmo/161099.html

Changyawa, P. (2003a). Biotech to be harnessed for growth. *Bangkok Post*, 21 August. Available at http://www.bangkokpost.com/News/21Aug2003_news18.html

Changyawa, P. (2003b). Labels unchanged despite new rules. *Bangkok Post*, 12 May. Available at http://search.bangkokpost.co.th/bkkpost/2003/may2003/bp20030512/news/12May2003_news

Changyawa, P. and Kongrut, A. (2003). Ministry to promote exports of GMO-free food products. *Bangkok Post*, 6 March. Available at http://search.bangkokpost.co.th/bkkpost/2003/mar2003/bp20030306/news/06Mar2003_news....

Cleveland, H. (1993). *Birth of a New World: An Open Moment for International Leadership*. San Francisco: Jossey-Bass.

Cohen, M.D., J.G. March and J.P. Olsen (1972). A garbage can model of organizational choice. *Administrative Sciences Quarterly*, 17: 1–25.

Damrongchai, N. (2002). Thailand's dilemma: The policy issues of genetically modified organisms (GMOs). A Paper Presented at the Study Meeting on the Use and Regulation of Genetically Modified Organisms, 18–23 November, Republic of China.

DiMaggio, P. and Powell, W. (1983). The iron cage revisited: institutional isomorphism and collective rationality in organizational fields. *American Sociological Review*, 48: 147–160.

Dwivedi, O.P. and Henderson, K.M. (1990). State of the art: comparative public administration and development administration. In O.P. Dwivedi and K.M. Henderson, *Public Administration in World Perspective*. Ames, IA: Iowa State University Press.

Eckersley, R. (1994). *Environmentalism and Political Theory: Toward an Ecocentric Approach*. London: University College Press.

Falk, R. (1971). *This Endangered Planet: Prospects and Proposals for Human Survival*. New York: Vintage Press.

GeneWatch UK Press Release. (2000). Monsanto's 'desperate' propaganda campaign reaches global proportions. 6 September. Available at The Campaign to Label Genetically Engineered Foods, http://www.thecampaign.org/news-updates/sept00b.htm

Haas, P.M., R.O. Keohane and M.A. Levy (1995). *Institutions for the Earth: Sources of Effective International Environmental Protection*. Cambridge, MA: The MIT Press.

Heady, F. (1995). *Public Administration in Comparative Perspective*, 5th edition. New York: Marcel Dekker.

Jackson, R. (1990). *Quasi-States: Sovereignty, International Relations, and the Third World*. Cambridge: Cambridge University Press.

Langkarpint, K. (2003). The evolution of environmental law in Thailand and the way forward. Unpublished paper (available from author).

Litfin, K. ed. (1998). *The Greening of Sovereignty in World Politics*. Cambridge, MA: The MIT Press.

Noikorn, U. (2000). Newin approaches Frito-Lay import plan. *Bangkok Post*, 6 September. Available at http://www.bangkokpost.net/issues/gmo/060900.html

Ophuls, W. (1977). *Ecology and the Politics of Scarcity*. San Francisco: W.H. Freeman.

Paarlberg, R.L. (2001). *The Politics of Precaution: Genetically Modified Crops in Developing Countries*. Baltimore, MD: Johns Hopkins University Press.

Peters, B.G. (1988). *Comparing Public Bureaucracies: Problems of Theory and Method*. Tuscaloosa: The University of Alabama Press.

Phongpaichit, P. and Baker, C. (2002). *Thailand's Crisis*. Chiang Mai, Thailand: Silkworm Books.

Pressure up for labelling of products. (1999). *Bangkok Post*, 24 November. Available at http://www.bangkokpost.com/issues/gmo/241199.html

Riggs, F.W. (1966). *Thailand: The Modernization of a Bureaucratic Polity*. Honolulu: East-West Center Press.

Riggs, F.W. (1994). Global forces and the discipline of public administration. In J.-C. Garcia-Zamor and R. Khator, *Public Administration in the Global Village*. Westport, CT: Praeger.

Samabuddhi, K. (2001a). Public told not to panic over GMO report. *Bangkok Post*, 12 April. Available at http://www.bangkokpost.com/issues/gmo/120401d.html

Samabuddhi, K. (2001b). Food to be labeled to show it's GM-free. *Bangkok Post*, 22 April. Available at http://www.bangkokpost.com/issues/gmo/220401a.html

Samabuddhi, K. (2001c). Labeling 'will make prices soar.' *Bangkok Post*, 6 September. Available at http://www.bangkokpost.net/issues/gmo/060901a.html

Samabuddhi, K. (2002a). U.S.-based group to counter 'NGO bias.' *Bangkok Post*, 6 April. Available at http://scoop.bangkokpost.co.th/bkkpost/2002/apr2002/BP20020406/. . ./06Apr2002_news24.htm.

Samabuddhi, K. (2002b). Public urged not to put GMO food in New Year gift baskets. *Bangkok Post*, 12 December. Available at http://search.bangkokpost.co.th/bkkpost/2002/dec2002/bp20021212/news/12Dec2002_news14.html

Samabuddhi, K. (2003). Farm officials plan GM field experiments. *Bangkok Post*, 8 February. Available at http://search.bangkokpost.co.th/bkkpost/2003/feb2003/bp20030208/news/08Feb2003_news10.html

Sampson, G.P. (2002). The environmentalist paradox: The World Trade Organization's challenges. *Harvard International Review*, 23(4): 56–61.

Scientists Support FAO Biotech Report. (2004). *CropBiotech Update*, 23 July. Cited in Agbioworld Listserve, agbioworld@yahoo.com. Accessed 23 July, 2004.

Siripetra, D. (2000). Khoaw Kwan (or Rice Spirit) Foundation in speech at a Rice Forum, Kasetsart University, Bangkok, Thailand, 15 August.

Skocpol, T. (1992). *Protecting Soldiers and Mothers: The Political Origins of Social Policy in the United States*. Cambridge, MA: Belknap Press.

Skowronek, S. (1982). *Building a New American State: The Expansion of National Administrative Capacities, 1877–1920*. Cambridge, UK: Cambridge University Press.

Sriwatanapongse, S. (2002). Biotechnology development in Asia and food security. A Paper Presented at the Export–Import Bank of India, National Conference on Agricultural Product Export, 21–22 January, Pune, India.

Stiglitz, J.E. (2002). *Globalization and Its Discontents*. New York: W.W. Norton & Company.

Sunstein, C.R. (2002). *Risk and Reason: Safety, Law, and the Environment*. Cambridge: Cambridge University Press.

Thailand Research Fund (2002). Corporate overview. Document provided to author by Dr. Arworn, Regional Director of TRF, interviewed at Chiang Mai University, Chiang Mai, Thailand, 28 August.

Third World Network. (2000). Monsanto project in Thailand assailed. Available at www.twnside.org.sg/title/1887-cn.htm.

Valyasevi, R., M. Tanticharoen and S. Bhumiratana (2003). Current status of biosafety of genetic modified foods in Thailand. Bangkok, Thailand: National Center for Genetic Engineering and Biotechnology, National Science and Technology Development Agency. 18 February, p. 7.

Wapner, P. (1996). *Environmental Activism and World Civic Politics*. Albany, NY: State University of New York Press.

Welch, E. and W. Wong (1998). Public administration in a global context: Bridging the gaps of theory and practice between Western and non-Western nations. *Public Administration Review*, 58(1): 40–49.

Welch, E. and W. Wong (2001). Global information technology pressure and government accountability: The mediating effect of domestic context on website openness. *Journal of Public Administration Research and Theory*, 11(4): 509–538.

Zahariadis, N. (2003). *Ambiguity and Choice in Public Policy*. Washington: Georgetown University Press.

Chapter 21

Promising the Future or Just Empty Promises? The Paradoxes and Perils of Human Resource Management Reform in a Global Context

Heather Getha-Taylor

CONTENTS

Introduction

According to Schultz (2002), two factors dominate the history of the U.S. civil service: "first, the pursuit of merit; second, the desire for reform." That desire for reform is not confined by U.S. borders, though. Because of the concerns and criticisms about the structure and performance of public service delivery, "many countries embarked on comprehensive reform of their public services" (Bissessar, 2001). Leaders of nations around the world are searching for the best ways to reform their bureaucracies to meet their governmental needs (policy) and the needs of their citizens (service provision). Reform is such a popular topic that Cayer (1995) notes that "reform is virtually a national pastime," and from Bissessar's work, we can infer it is a worldwide pastime as well. This preoccupation, says Cayer, is often due to competing values. For instance, the tension that exists between the values of democracy and the values of bureaucracy can create value trade-offs. Nachmias and Rosenbloom (1980) suggest that democracy embraces plurality, diversity, equal access, liberty, dispersion of power, freedom, election, openness, and participation although bureaucracy demands unity, hierarchy, command, control, appointment, and long tenure of members. It is because that the ill-fitting bureaucracy is used to serve mismatched democratic objectives that the conflicts occur (Cayer, 1995). "Much of reform is an attempt to resolve the conflict."

Although public sector reform is not a new topic, interest in reforming the public human resource function is a fairly recent phenomenon. According to Bissessar (2001), around the world, until the late 1980s there was "little to no concern to increase output in the public sector and little or no attempt was made to link resources, especially human resources to output or productivity." It is surprising that this interest began so late considering that according to Schiavo-Campo et al. (1997), "a competent and motivated civil service is a prerequisite for maintenance of good governance, production and distribution of public goods and services, fiscal management and sustainability, and efficient and effective performance of government."

The information presented in this chapter is the result of scholarly literature review and practitioner document analysis. Throughout the research, there appeared ongoing references to the merits of private sector human resource management when considering public sector reforms. "In the race to reinvent government and to develop a new public management (NPM), government leaders, both elected and administrative, have excitedly drawn on the popular strategies of the private sector to guide change" (Hays & Plagens, 2002). However, according to these authors, the sectors do not confront the same problems in an age of globalization and as a result, the worldwide public sector suffers if it relies on private sector advice alone. According to the authors,

> Assaults on public personnel systems strike us as particularly counterproductive at a time when most of society's problems transcend jurisdictional borders. Our primary argument is that the major thrusts of reinvention and NPM — decentralization, decreased reliance on government, privatization, and managerialism — swim upstream from what the demands of globalization would otherwise suggest.
>
> Hays and Plagens (2002)

According to Hays and Plagens (2002), globalization and administrative human resource reform "spring from a remote yet common gene pool." And although sweeping global generalizations taken from country-specific reforms are not appropriate based on cultural, geographic and economic, variations, it should be noted that all the countries are increasingly becoming a part of the global reform scene. "While the general purpose of reform may be similar — citizens and policy makers want public sector workforces that meet citizen needs better and more efficiently — the specific needs of individual governments vary" (Selden, 2003).

HRM Reform: Drivers and Promises

Human resource management (HRM) reform often finds its worst critics in its target audience: members of the civil service. Such reform is often viewed as either thinly veiled or blatant criticism of the ways in which the members of the bureaucracy are doing their jobs, and for civil servants, this can be a personal blow. Civil servant morale and motivation can suffer, which is ironic, because many reforms seek to invigorate the men and the women of the bureaucracy. According to Ingraham (1995), during the implementation of the U.S. Civil Service Reform Act of 1978, "the members of the civil service being attacked in the selling of reform were the same people who would be revitalized public servants once the reforms were in place."

The risk of potential losses in motivation and morale requires that HRM reform be well-founded. Although much of reform (particularly private sector models) is based on the "bottom-line", Wise (2002) reminds us that not all drivers for government reform are market-based. In addition, there can be multiple driving factors that spur the reform as well as several promises that will hopefully become tangible following implementation of the reform plan. Wise argues that there is a balance to be found between competing drivers of change, and understanding that balance is instrumental for "interpreting both contemporary and future administrative reform."

Driver: Economics

In the case of Paraguay's attempts to reform the bureaucracy, as presented by Nickson and Lambert (2002), international financial institutions exerted pressure on the nation to engage in civil service reform to both "improve the provision of basic services and to avoid a growing fiscal deficit." Marked by rampant corruption and inconsistent personnel practices, Paraguay officials faced huge obstacles in enacting a reform plan. However, the financial push was enough to spur the public sector to action.

Adamolekun (1993) provides the example of sub-Saharan Africa where public sector employees were forced to engage in outside employment to supplement their inadequate paychecks. As a result, says Adamolekun, this economic stimulus was one that could not be ignored. The sector had to be reformed to remedy this imbalance because the civil servants in this case could not "be relied upon to respect the norms of loyalty, fairness, and impartiality." In other words, they could not serve the state efficiently because they were unfocused.

In the case of Jamaica and Trinidad and Tobago, as chronicled by Bissessar (2001), both countries faced severe, unprecedented economic hardship in the 1970s and 1980s. Both countries approached the World Bank for loans. In this case, one of the stipulations for granting the loans was centered on civil service reform. Says Bissessar: "they were to be accompanied by comprehensive reform of the public services." Both the countries accepted the loans with the stipulations and began on a comprehensive reform plan, although both countries adopted different provisions of the plan.

Driver: Privatization/Democratization

Denhardt and Denhardt (2000) discuss the ways in which the public sector is changing to be more responsive to citizens, or more in line with the democratic ideals of access and equity. In this way, reforming the civil service for this purpose builds "public institutions marked by integrity and responsiveness." The tenets of the New Public Service, as advocated by Denhardt and Denhardt (2000) and King and Stivers (1998), are greater responsiveness and an increase in citizen trust, as opposed to greater managerial control and efficiency. The authors cite the contributions of Osborne and Gaebler (1992), who remind us that "the kind of governments that developed during the industrial era, with their sluggish, centralized bureaucracies, their preoccupation with rules and regulations, and their hierarchical chains of command, no longer work very well."

One of the lessons learned from New Public Service, as offered by Denhardt and Denhardt (2000), is that *people* should be valued just as much as productivity. Under the values of the New Public Service, "rational attempts to control human behavior are likely to fail in the long term if, at the same time, insufficient attention is paid to the values and interests of individual members of an organization." The authors do not agree that values such as efficiency and productivity should be sacrificed, "but should be placed in the larger context of democracy, community, and the public interest."

In the case study of civil service reform in Paraguay, as presented by Nickson and Lambert (2002), privatization and democratization were both essential components of implementing the reform plan. Because of the unique features of the nation including its small size, low levels of both efficiency and effectiveness, high levels of politicization and an "endemic level of corruption," Paraguay presents an interesting case for examining the importance of these principles for HRM reforms to take root. Paraguay's public sector was marked by poorly qualified employees, inconsistency in salary levels, extremely high rotation of senior staff, no transparent recruitment system, promotion based solely on political and personal loyalty, and no performance evaluation of staff. By privatizing many of the state's enterprises, the nation was able to introduce a measure of competitiveness to revitalize the public service.

Driver: Political Agendas

According to Green (1998), growth of the civil service via reform is fundamentally a public policy issue.

> It is often argued that Civil Servants wish to expand their departments to signify their success, politicians want their hobby horse supported, customers want more and better quality in provision of services, and the ageing population and high levels of unemployment increase the demand for social services and benefits. Whether through the increasing complexity of society of through the power of public officials to grow their empires, the public service is seen to have an inexorable tendency to grow, to graft on new initiatives without replacing older ones.
>
> Green (1998)

From Cheng's 1998 study of civil service reform in Korea and Taiwan, we learn that in both the cases, "political leaders had an interest in reforming the civil service to carry out their programmatic initiatives." Although the two nations implemented separate paths to reform (Korea faced an overall reform of the civil service by the military, Taiwan relied on special career tracks to transform the civil service), Cheng notes that in both cases, there was a common interest in building state capacity by strengthening the civil service. This, says Cheng, "is a clear reminder that policy and institutional reform go hand in hand."

Promise: Merit over Patronage

In the United States, the Pendleton Act of 1883 serves as the benchmark for obliterating patronage, or hiring based on personal or political ties, and replacing it with hiring based on merit, or qualifications. However, "patronage continues to adversely affect the efficiency of the public service" around the world (Daniel, 1993). Patronage, says Daniel, stifles the efforts of public organizations as they become more complex, more professionalized, and foster mission-oriented cultures. The process by which employees are selected or promoted sends "strong signals about real priorities, be they mission fulfillment, cronyism, or supporting campaigns."

Promise: Control of the Bureaucracy

Some scholars have suggested that reforms are simply attempts to exert more control over the bureaucracy. The U.S. Civil Service Reform Act of 1978, the first major reform of federal personnel practices since the Pendleton Act of 1883, has been both critiqued and applauded. According to Ingraham (1995), the Act included provisions for the creation of the Senior Executive Service, performance appraisal, merit pay and pay for performance, and the abolition of the Civil Service Commission. Although these measures were meant to professionalize the civil service, they could also be interpreted as means to elicit greater accountability from bureaucrats.

In the case of China's reforms, as documented by Ding and Warner (2001), the reforms, which removed the "three irons" of public employment (lifetime employment, centrally administered wages, and state-controlled appointment and promotion), sought to improve employee motivation and morale. Under the "three irons" system, workers were not held to performance standards. Further, their work lives were inextricably tied to their personal lives. Employees had to receive permission to marry and were prohibited from relocating to another area. In this case, new reform measures will result in additional control over professional tasks via performance measurement, but the component of personal control will be relaxed.

Promise: Efficiency

According to Hays and Plagens (2002), civil servants have served as "scapegoats for many of society's problems." Public servants often feel the brunt of that criticism directed at perceived inefficiency and waste in the government. For many, it is all about numbers. In one example documented by Fifield (1998), government officials determined it was paramount to transform the South African public service, based, at least partially, on the fact that there seemed to be a great deal of duplication and overlap. This was clearly evidenced by the fact that before the implementation of the Public Service Act of 1994, there were "no less than ten pension funds in existence."

In another example, Gaertner et al. (1984) noted concern among the U.S. employees who worried that after HRM reforms took effect, the "quantity rather than quality of work" would be emphasized for the purposes of pay and promotion. For those workers, more work seemed better. But for Jim King, less was more. When King took over as the director of the

Office of Personnel Management in 1993, he promised to downsize the organization. By his definition, efficiency equalled a smaller, more streamlined organization (Marshall, 1998).

Promise: Responsiveness

Again, the influence of private enterprise is felt in this promise of reform. According to Green (1998), in today's culture that embraces the "customer is king" principle, governments must follow suit or lose favor in the public eye. Public services, like markets, says Green, must be "more responsive to the needs and preferences of their users." The reinventing government movement of the early 1990s, which utilized principles of total quality management, was viewed not only as a way to reduce government costs, but also as a way to make government more responsive to citizens (Cayer, 1995). This new direction in service may be due to many factors, including party politics and citizen preferences. According to Ingraham (1997), "intensely ideological politics captured citizen dissatisfaction and translated it into demands for leaner, more focused, more responsive government."

Promise: Comparative Lessons Learned

By analyzing reports on multinational attempts at implementing HRM reform, learning is a priority. Even if the reform is not deemed effective, the nations' representatives seem willing to share those failures in addition to the successes for the purposes of learning. According to Shim (2001), HRM reform has become a priority for Organization for Economic Cooperation and Development (OECD) countries seeking to enhance the productivity of the civil service and its customer service orientation. The author's study of reforms during the 1980s and 1990s in OECD countries identified four common reform trends that were shared (see below). It should be noted that "the pace and scope of the HRM reforms are very different from country to country, depending on their overall reform strategies, cultural and historical backgrounds, and the degree of economic recessions."

HRM Reform Trends: OECD Countries (Shim, 2001)

1. Reducing the gap between public and private HR management
2. Decentralization and flexibility of HR management
3. Securing Managerial and organizational accountability
4. Maintaining a "good model employer"

In addition, Shim identifies leadership development as a critical issue for further study for all OECD countries in the context of human resource management reform.

Reflection on HRM Reform Paradoxes

Certainly, drivers of reform can be misinterpreted, thereby leading countries to respond incorrectly to a stimulus for change. Also, the promises reformers seek may not always come to fruition just as a result of trying. In addition to these potential disappointments, there are additional considerations that must be weighed before, during, and even after a reform is implemented. By learning from the experiences of others, reformers can glean new lessons to apply to their own circumstances. Below are some common paradoxes identified through the literature review on global HRM reform.

Ethical Issues

Crow (1998) provides a look into the Polish civil service reforms, from the point of view of the female government employees. In an effort to overcome past problems such as low productivity and low morale, the Polish government introduced changes and innovations in the 1990s. Part of that reform included rebuilding a civil service that emphasizes education, experiences, knowledge, and competencies rather than "communist party membership and political reliability." In order to retain only the best employees, reform leaders implemented "labor-shedding programs," which targeted employees who were considered "redundant." Women, says Crow, feel threatened as a result of these reforms, because of their dual roles as wife or mother and employee. Because these women have family responsibilities, the organization views them as both expensive and unreliable, and therefore, expendable workers. In the case of this Polish case study, women have had to bear the negative effects of reform. Crow identifies three barriers for women that should be dealt with in future reforms to improve the working conditions for women in this Polish organization: access to training, perception of management as a masculine domain, and mentorship in the workplace.

Divergent Reform Plans

In Chan's 2003 analysis of China's "one nation, two systems" approach to civil service reform, we learn that even within nations we might find separate civil service systems to meet different needs. According to Chan, in post-handover Hong Kong, the high level of institutionalization within the civil service was viewed as "an obstacle to the assertion of political leadership." The reform efforts therefore set politically appointed leaders apart from civil servants in order to "centralize political authority." However, in China, the civil service framework reinforces "political authority over the civil service" and greater institutionalization is seen as a reform option. According to Chan, "the institutions of China's and Hong Kong's civil services point to two logical extremes: Hong Kong has chosen to strengthen political authority over the civil service, which promotes deinstitutionalization. By contrast, China has opted to strengthen the institutionalization of its civil service. What appears to be a problem for one actually can be seen as a solution for another."

Diversity Effects

Anderson et al. (2002) document Australia's experience with a NPM initiative: the implementation of the Public Service Act of 1999. According to the authors, NPM is based on a greater reliance on market forces and a reduced role for government, which is believed to result in better economic and societal outcomes. The Public Service Act of 1999, which was meant to (1) "maintain public service integrity and professionalism," (2) "continue the traditional notions of a career service," and (3) reinforce "the merit principle and notions of equity and fairness," actually resulted in negative HR workforce development effects. Primarily, as a result of the Act, the civil service was indeed reduced in size — keeping with NPM tenets. However, following the implementation of the Act, workforce diversity has been negatively affected. "The composition of the APS [Australian Public Service] has been characterized by a decreasing proportion of people with a disability and people from racially or ethnically diverse backgrounds" (Anderson et al., 2002). A similar example comes from Fifield's 1998 study of South African reform efforts. Although considerable progress has been made in South Africa in improving the level of representativeness "especially as regards the variables gender, color, and race," little has been done to address the imbalances in representation of disabled individuals. To investigate this matter, however, the author notes that efforts must first be made to make sure that the government buildings are accessible for disabled clients and employees. Returning to Australia as an example, Patrickson and Hartmann (1995) present the case in which the restructuring of the Australian civil service has negatively affected senior adult employees by highlighting "the vulnerability of the over 50s" and it has "helped validate negative stereotypes concerning their competence." Reform efforts must not sabotage other HRM provisions, such as equal opportunity regulations that are protected by law.

Rhetoric, Not Reality

"Political leadership, in short, is clearly important. Political rhetoric is not" (Ingraham, 1997). To many, the reform efforts around the world have more to do with rhetoric than results. "One of the essential competencies of the Civil Service is its ability to draft elegant prose which dresses up the ordinary into the exceptional. Creating a hubbub and a lot of noise about change can create the illusion of change without the substance" (Green, 1998). In addition, Green adds, many reform efforts might just be cleverly wrapped boxes containing the same old ingredients — "indeed a subtle way of gaining more time to carry on as in the past." There are many examples in which rhetoric prevailed over results in the scholarly and practitioner literature. Anderson et al. (2002) report that following the implementation of the Australian Public Service Act of 1999, there were large gaps in government rhetoric between successful implementation and the actual flaws of the implementation such as unclear reporting standards and unfair remuneration. In South Africa, although a lot of work has been invested in developing goals and policy frameworks over the past decade, little has actually been done toward drafting strategies for change and implementing plans for change (Fifield, 1998). According to Gabris et al. (1998), it is common for governments to formulate strategic plans for reform "that are little more than sophisticated and, in some instances, unsophisticated wish lists with very little probability of implementation. It is easy to formulate a plan, even fun. The difficulty arises in its implementation."

In the case of Barbados' HRM reform efforts, adherence to the guidelines of implementation lagged behind other management reform efforts for a decade. According to Khan and Charles-Soverall (1993), "a great deal of verbiage and rhetoric permeated organizational reform." The case of Paraguay also provides a fascinating tale in the use of rhetoric rather than reform. In 1970, a civil service law was passed to establish a professional civil service, complete with merit-based recruitment, promotion based on qualification and performance evaluation. However, the law was not implemented and both patronage and corruption continued to reign until 1996, when a consensus rose to replace rather than implement the sound law. Nickson and Lambert (2002) view this as the "highly rhetorical content of the reform discourse" rather than healthy political participation.

Even in the United States, the reinventing government movement of the 1990s, which was spurred by the work of Osborne and Gaebler (1992) and spearheaded by Vice President Al Gore, provided politicians "with a means to at least symbolically respond to the widely-shared cynicism people hold toward government" (Thompson & Ingraham, 1996). Ban (1998) provides the example of the publicity stunt in which the lengthy Federal Personnel Manual (FPM) was discarded to much fanfare under the tenets of deregulation that the National Performance Review ushered into federal personnel management. In fact, this was simply a symbolic event: many personnel managers continued to use the regulations to guide their activities. According to one federal employee, "without changing the fundamental rules, you've not helped them by eliminating the FPM."

Reversal of Expectations

In the case of the National Performance Review, it was expected that the initiative would result in a trimmer, less regulated, decentralized human resources function. However, as a result of the drastic cuts in personnel specialists (18 percent between 1992 and 1996), agencies responded by centralizing the personnel function of the organization (Ban, 1998). Also, in the case of New Zealand's civil service reform efforts, Green (1998) notes that the public organizations are actually on the increase — like business firms. In this trend, "there is continuing pressure to drive costs down and efficiency up, managers routinely manage against plans, and they are more responsive to external conditions and customer expectations. There is more emphasis on team work and more pressure for conformity and groupthink." The end result is felt most strongly in the individual employees, and that result is negative. "All this can make for more productive organizations and more stressed employees" (Green, 1998).

Absence of Theoretical Frameworks to Guide Reform

One U.S. initiative, GeorgiaGain, profiled by Facer (1998) implemented the tenets of the reinventing government movement by dissolving the merit system and implementing pay-for-performance among civil servants in the state of Georgia. Facer notes that the initiative could have been helped with the insights from scholarly literature on government reform efforts, but has missed several "critical lessons." According to Facer, the GeorgiaGain pay-for-performance provision "was theoretically bankrupt." A similar incident was mirrored in the Caribbean in the case of Barbados' reform efforts. In the absence of theoretical insights to supplement practical experience, Khan and Charles-Soverall (1993) claim that it is unlikely that the reform will have "any significant and sustained impact on the public sector." The closest thing that academics have to really do is roll up their sleeves, put their theories to work, and "test" human resource reforms to evaluate the results of the U.S.-based demonstration projects of the past 20 years. These projects, which were approved under the U.S. Civil Service Reform Act of 1978, serve as experiments to test reforms under specific guidelines provided by the Office of Personnel Management. One such project was chronicled by Gilbert (1991). This demonstration, known as Project Pacer Share (PPS), was implemented at McClellan Air Force Base in Sacramento, California. According to Gilbert, PPS was unique "in its focus on HRM reform in order to demonstrate improved quality in government."

Breaking the Promises of Reform

Even under the best circumstances, successful reform can be elusive due to a number of factors. Based on scholarly literature and practitioner accounts, below are some of the most frequent reasons for HRM reform failure.

Resource Deficiencies

For a government to reform the human resource function, it must first have human resource managers and structures in place. As governments "attempt to develop more coherence in their strategic role and aims, they turn increasingly to their own agencies to do the planning and coordinate the implementation" (Green, 1998). In the case of Tanzania, personnel employees were unable to carry out the reform initiatives due to a lack of basic amenities. According to McCourt and Sola (1999), the employees were unable to process disciplinary cases "for want of the necessary official forms." In addition, their filing proved sporadic and unreliable. Records were often lost. Unreliability, says the authors, "enables corruption: it is too easy for ages to be falsified, ghosts to be created, and so on." Although the failure in Tanzania can be attributed to human resource failure, in the case of Nigeria, the country was unable to sustain the reform effort because of the high price tag. According to Sekwat (2002), there were insufficient financial resources to maintain the necessary training, recruitment, and retention activities. "The impact of inadequate fiscal resources is manifested by the steady decline of civil servant salaries, pensions, and other benefits; deteriorating physical conditions of public facilities including office buildings, machinery, and equipment; and increased incidence of corruption in the civil service." Last, a study by Randma (2001) indicated that small nations, such as Estonia, face considerable amount of difficulty in achieving reform success in large part due to the scarcity of resources available — both financial and human.

Improper Preparation

Branine (1996) provides evidence that for reforms to be implemented properly, managers must be trained effectively. In the case of China's reform efforts, Branine notes that there remains a gap between the abilities of Chinese managers and what is expected of them when implementing reform. "Expectations run higher than what could be actually achieved." This mismatch is due to three factors directly related to training deficiencies: limited resources, inadequate means, and ideological restrictions. According to Green (1998), organizations must first engage in some self-assessment before beginning the reform process. Even with detailed plans for reform implementation, "there is little assessment of the skills, organizational and cultural capabilities and learning that may be required to enable the organization to meet its performance objectives or broader political outcomes." We learn from Wescott's (1999) account of civil service reform in Uganda, in which the cart went much too far before the horse, that the nation's effort to downsize the civil service was unsuccessful in large part because the infrastructure was not ready to handle the redistribution of activity once the reform was set in motion.

Selective or Creeping Implementation

In the case of China, during the mid-1980s when the "three old irons" system was replaced with one that was centered on employee performance, reform scholar Warner (1996) noted a phenomenon referred to as "one factory, two systems." In this case, says Warner, incumbent permanent workers continued to enjoy the benefits of the old system in which salary was guaranteed. The new employees, however, were contractual employees who would be evaluated based on their performance. "When contractual workers are working, permanent workers are just looking." In another example, Gaertner et al. (1984) found that employees of some U.S. agencies responded in a very lukewarm way to the Civil Service Reform Act of 1978. The Mine Safety and Health Administration (MSHA) had a hard time being convinced "that there are any benefits to the new [performance appraisal and merit pay] system," and managers at MSHA felt that the reforms "were not seen as providing a tool for management." As a result, the agency devoted few resources to implementing the reform initiatives and made minimal efforts to integrate the reforms with their other management systems.

Resistance to Reform

In the case of China's human capital reforms, where the nation broke away from the traditional "three old irons" system of lifetime employment, centrally administered wages, and state-controlled appointment and promotion, it was a struggle to change the attitudes associated with these systems. "If there was an economic rationale involved here, there was also a psychological one as well" (Ding and Warner, 2001). Nigeria confronted a similar situation when attempting civil service reform in the 1990s. Attitudinal changes are perhaps one of the most important changes that would have been necessary to sustain the reform effort. Unfortunately, in the case of Nigeria, there were no leaders to advocate for reform and stand against the rampant corruption in the country by issuing tough sanctions for offenders (Sekwat, 2002). In addition, Bissessar (2001) notes that the lack of success in reforming the public sector in Trinidad was due to "resistance by public servants," who were unmotivated to implement reform perhaps primarily due to what they perceived as "veiled threats by the government" that seemed to nearly guarantee their removal from the public employment.

Finding Themes in Global Human Resource Management (HRM) Reform

Considering the vast variations in experiences, cultural influences, economic realities, and geographical space among nations implementing HRM reform, can we find themes or lessons from these cases? From the literature reviewed, indeed, six themes were identified that crossed individual national reform efforts and served as lessons for future reform efforts.

Trust Matters

- Gaertner et al. (1984) found in their study of organizational reactions to the U.S. Civil Service Reform Act that employees at the Environmental Protection Agency welcomed the reforms because they would create accountability and lower "suspicions" from outsiders of their agency activities.
- Gilbert (1991) reports that in the case of the demonstration project known as Project Pacer Share (PPS), "most employees in the host agency were overtly distrustful" of the initiative. One way to move from distrust to trust, says Gilbert, is to provide workforce education and training to inform the workforce and quell rumors.
- A lack of trust between supervisors and workers can be magnified under reform conditions. Especially for older workers, who may view reforms as means to make them accept a form of "voluntary early retirement" (Patrickson & Hartmann 1995).
- According to Peters and Savoie (1994), the constant bureaucracy bashing issued by political leaders during the 1980s "constituted a hostile environment for civil servants." The constant references to

the practices of the private sector "served to underscore the lack of trust in bureaucrats and in traditional public administration." This lack of trust resulted in a severely demoralized civil service across the globe as evidenced in the United Kingdom, Canada, and the United States. The Volcker Commission (1989) commented on the sad state of affairs: "it is evident that the public service is neither as attractive as it once was nor as effective in meeting perceived needs."

Values Matter

According to Kellough and Selden (2003), personnel administration in the public sector "sits at the intersection of competing values." Nearly every case study reviewed for this chapter overtly presented a set of values that were used as guiding principles for reform efforts, which are summarized below.

Setting	*HRM Reform Values*
South Africa (Fifield, 1998)	Efficiency, effectiveness, economy, fairness, merit, equity, accountability, transparency, accessibility, quality service delivery
Ireland, Northern Ireland, Australia, New Zealand (Green, 1998)	Culture, excellence, vision, core competencies, learning, empowerment, transformation, sustainable competitive advantage
United Kingdom (Green, 1998)	Privatization, deregulation, strategic management initiatives, efficiency audits, senior management reviews, devolved budgeting, merit pay, enhanced communication
Singapore (Jones, 2001)	Output volume, service quality, efficiency, effectiveness, accountability, accuracy
Barbados (Khan & Charles-Soverall, 1993)	Delegation of authority, public accountability, decentralization of recruitment, succession planning, and performance appraisal, effectiveness, efficiency, productivity
Korea (Kim, 1997)	Flexibility, fairness, effectiveness, democracy, ending corruption, eliminating fraud
China (Liou, 1997)	Decentralization, professionalization, accountability, efficiency
Tanzania (McCourt & Sola, 1999)	Efficiency, effectiveness, reducing public sector employment, building capacity, retraining
Paraguay (Nickson & Lambert, 2002)	Transparency, accountability, performance evaluation, efficiency, compulsory retirement

Setting	*HRM Reform Values*
Nigeria (Sekwat, 2002)	Simplification, accountability, professionalization, transparency, efficiency, effectiveness, reorganization
Estonia (Randma, 2001)	Merit, competition, decentralization, security of tenure, professionalization

Culture Matters

- When the government officials of Barbados recognized a need to reform the Caribbean nation in 1986, they did so in response to "low motivation and morale, declining productivity and efficiency, poor measurements, widespread centralization, lack of mission statements and articulated policies, structural rigidities, unsatisfactory communications and indecisive leadership" (Khan & Charles-Soverall, 1993). To address these concerns, government officials looked to other Caribbean countries to find "the most relevant structures and tools" to match their cultural needs.
- "Even in countries that share a number of basic underlying values and traditions and where political and administrative institutions are similar, the kind of systems or mechanisms that may be implemented may vary due to factors such as ethnicity, political culture, party dominance or level of economic development" (Bissessar, 2001). According to Hood (1996), no one tenet or principle of NPM has been consistently applied in any two countries. Similarly, according to Selden et al. (2001), it seems there may not be one best way to personnel reform. Each nation is likely to adopt the most appropriate form based on their own culture and needs.

Competencies Matter

- Kamoche's 1997 study of civil service reform in Africa highlights the importance of competency development for successful implementation. "Ultimately, the effectiveness of the public sector product and service delivery will depend not only on economic and financial parameters but also on the availability of sufficiently skilled personnel." Although Kamoche notes that human resources are valued as organizational assets in the reform process, "this view quickly turns into an empty platitude if little effort is made to develop and realize the full potential of the human resources." To meet reform objectives, it is important to identify the necessary competencies that will be needed to implement the reform "and then institute efforts to develop and cultivate a stock of expertise."

- In the case of Barbados' public human resources reform experience, Khan and Charles-Soverall (1993) found that the effort was stunted due to the fact that they did not have trained personnel to carry out the functions of interviewing, grievance handling, people management, counseling, and performance appraisal.
- In the failed case of reform implementation in Nigeria as chronicled by Sekwat (2002), we find that the lack of employee competencies in policy formation and service delivery served as a blow to the effort.

Long-Term Goals and Vision Matter

- In the case of Jamaica and Trinidad and Tobago as described by Bissessar (2001), reform was imminent because of duplication of tasks, incoherent personnel policy implementation, lack of coordination between departments, there was "little or no attention" paid to developing competencies, and there was no planning for future needs. "Essentially, human resource agencies were reacting to crisis phenomena instead of adapting to changing needs or long term plans."
- According to Kamoche (1997), for organizations to meet long-term strategic goals such as the implementation of HRM reform, it is critical that they develop a long-term plan that includes the skills and competencies that will be necessary to meet the organization's goals.

HRM Professionals Matter

- According to Gilbert (1991), the implications of human resource reform for HRM professionals are great. One of the implications the author references is that "the HR manager needs to identify impediments to quality in the personnel system and take the lead to reform them."
- According to Ban (1998), reforms that call for "delayering," or that reduce the workforce, actually put more pressure on those remaining human resource managers. Those managers must take on greater responsibilities and accept a greater span of control.
- For successful civil service reform, Wescott (1999) emphasizes the importance of support for the initiatives — not just from top-level politicos, but from administrative leaders and rank and file employees. HRM professionals can play an important role in garnering this support. In the case of the Nigerian efforts at civil service reform as

reported by Sekwat (2002), the partial implementation of the reform was in part due to a lack of committed leaders, both political and interorganizational leaders.

Future Directions

Based on this research, I offer the following suggestions for further exploration.

Develop a Consistent HRM Reform Vocabulary

Separating HRM reforms from general public management reforms can be a challenge. The vocabulary used when referring to values, personnel, and so forth, is inconsistent across the board. It would be a useful endeavor to work and develop a more consistent language for comparing and contrasting HRM reforms.

Find Measures for Reform Outcomes

In 1998, Ban noted that with regard to the Government Performance and Results Act (GPRA), agencies were required to provide five-year strategic plans linked to annual performance plans with objective, quantifiable outcome measures. However, says Ban, "there appears to be little if any centralized effort to develop standards that could be applied across agencies." Similarly, as noted in Jones' 2001 study of the civil service reform efforts in Singapore, there was great difficulty in developing indicators of effectiveness "which go further than measure outputs and efficiency, and measure ultimate outcomes." By giving attention to consistent, valid measures, we are giving attention to our desire for standardization that will allow for better comparisons and more relevant lessons learned.

Give More Thought to Demonstration Projects

Gilbert's comprehensive overview of Project Pacer Share is a rich account, but unfortunately, it is only one of barely a handful of similar studies. Demonstration projects require time, effort, and money. Not concentrating more scholarly effort in the evaluation and discussion of these projects seems to be a great waste. Although each project is required to submit evaluation reports, these reports are not widely circulated. Gilbert (1991) notes that in the case of PPS, the RAND corporation was unable to "identify relationships between specific changes in the Civil Service system (e.g. gainsharing, pay banding, etc.) under demonstration and overall organizational performance improvement." However, the finding is not unusual in this type of measurement that is often difficult. Although evaluating each project is a useful exercise, the application of those lessons from the projects to broader contexts would be even more useful. However, Ban (1998) notes the dismal prospects when it comes to applying demo projects' successes to the rest of the bureaucracy. "In the complex political environment of federal personnel management, no demonstration project has led to systemwide reform." Although demonstration projects have not yet transformed the civil service system in the United States, they remain an important topic for scholarly research. "Just as Congress and agencies are building on the lessons from 20th century demonstration projects to reform today's civil service, so tomorrow's policy makers will look to the next civil service demonstration projects for breakthrough ideas that take human capital management to the next level" (Beecher, 2003).

Conclusion

In an age when the world is getting smaller, thanks to instant communication, and the expanse of national government authority is no longer limited by national boundaries, we must even consider the impacts and lessons of human resource reform in a global context. "We suspect that long-term solutions to such crises as populations migrations, deadly communicable diseases, malnutrition, income maldistribution, terrorism, and stateless crime syndicates can only be found through the cooperation and collaboration of governments" (Hays & Plagens, 2002). So also, the global community should work together to determine the best ways to support and sustain the men and women who comprise the bureaucracy. Based on this literature review, it is clear that reform is not always successful and can, in fact, result in unitended negative consequences. For instance, the psychological effect that reforms have on public employees needs to be investigated further. "The so-called 'quiet crisis' in public employment," says Hays and Plagens (2002), has now "evolved into a loud chorus of complaints and concerns about governments' inability to recruit, retain, and motivate the next generation of civil servants." Perhaps the best way to prepare for the future is to look in the rear-view mirror, which is what I hope is the contribution of this research. When thinking about these reforms, says Schultz (2002), the real challenges "are carefully defining the goals, taking sufficient account of the environmental context, and learning from the lessons of the past."

References

Adamolekun, L. (1993). A Note on Civil Service Personnel Policy Reform in Sub-Saharan Africa. *The International Journal of Public Sector Management* 6(3), 38–46.

Anderson, E., Griffin, G., and Teicher, J. (2002). Managerialism and the Australian Public Service: Valuing Efficiency and Equity? *New Zealand Journal of Industrial Relations* 27(1), 13–31.

Ban, C. (1998). Reinventing the Federal Civil Service: Drivers of Change. *Public Administration Quarterly* 22(1), 21–34.

Beecher, D.D. (2003). The Next Wave of Civil Service Reform. *Public Personnel Management* 32(4), 457.

Bissessar, A.M. (2001). Differential Approaches to Human Resource Management Reform in the Public Services of Jamaica and Trinidad and Tobago. *Public Personnel Management* 30(4), 531–548.

Branine, M. (1996). The Perception of Training and Development for a High Performance Economy in the People's Republic of China. *Management Research News* 19(4/5), 50–51.

Cayer, N.J. (1995). Merit System Reform in the States. In S.W. Hays and R.C. Kearney (eds.) *Public Personnel Administration: Problems and Prospects,* Third Edition, Englewood Cliffs: Prentice Hall.

Chan, H.S. (2003). The Civil Service under One Country, Two Systems: The Cases of Hong Kong and the People's Republic of China. *Public Administration Review* 63(4), 405.

Cheng, T.J., Haggard, S., and Kang, D. (1998). Institutions and Growth in Korea and Taiwan: The Bureaucracy. *The Journal of Development Studies* 34(6), 87–111.

Crow, M. (1998). Personnel in Transition: The Case of Polish Women Personnel Managers. *Personnel Review* 27(3), 243.

Daniel, C. (1993). Curbing Patronage without Paperasserie. *Public Administration Review* 53(4), 387–391.

Denhardt, R.B., and Denhardt, J.V. (2000). The New Public Service: Serving Rather than Steering. *Public Administration Review* 60(6), 549–559.

Ding, D.Z., and Warner, M. (2001). China's Labour-Management System Reforms: Breaking the 'Three Old Irons' (1978–1999). *Asia Pacific Journal of Management* 18(3), 315.

Facer, R.L., II. (1998). Reinventing Public Administration: Reform in the Georgia Civil Service. *Public Administration Quarterly* 22(1), 58–73.

Fifield, G. (1998). The Transformation of the South African Public Service, 1994–1997. *Public Personnel Management* 27(3), 385–405.

Gabris, G.T., Grenell, K.D., and Kaatz, J. (1998). Reinventing Local Government Human Services Management: A Conceptual Analysis. *Public Administration Quarterly* 22(1), 74–97.

Gaertner, G.H., Gaertner, K.N., and Akinnusi, D.M. (1984). Environment, Strategy, and the Implementation of Administrative Change: The Case of Civil Service Reform. *Academy of Management Journal* 27(3), 525–543.

Gilbert, G.R. (1991). Human Resource Management Practices to Improve Quality: A Case Example of Human Resource Management Intervention in Government. *Human Resource Management* 30(2), 183–198.

Green, S. (1998). Strategic Management Initiatives in the Civil Service: A Cross-Cultural Comparison. *The International Journal of Public Sector Management* 11(7), 536.

Hays, S.W., and Plagens, G.K. (2002). Human Resource Management Best Practices and Globalization: The Universality of Common Sense. *Public Organization Review* 2(4), 327–348.

Hood, C. (1996). Exploring Variations in Public Management Reform. In H.A.G.M. Bekke, J.L. Perry, and T.A.J. Toonen (eds.) *Civil Service Systems in Comparative Perspective*. Bloomington: Indiana University Press.

Ingraham, P.W. (1995). *The Foundation of Merit*. Baltimore and London: The Johns Hopkins University Press.

Ingraham, P.W. (1997). Play it Again, Sam; It's Still not Right: Searching for the Right Notes in Administrative Reform. *Public Administration Review* 57(4), 325–331.

Jones, D.S. (2001). Performance Measurement and Budgetary Reform in the Singapore Civil Service. *Journal of Public Budgeting, Accounting & Financial Management* 13(4), 485–511.

Kamoche, K. (1997). Competence-Creation in the African Public Sector. *The International Journal of Public Sector Management* 10(4), 268.

Kellough, J.E., and Selden, S.C. (2003). The Reinvention of Public Personnel Administration: An Analysis of the Diffusion of Personnel Management Reforms in the States. *Public Administration Review* 63(2), 165–176.

Khan, J., and Charles-Soverall, W. (1993). Human Resource Development in the Public Sector: A Developing-Country Experience. *The International Journal of Public Sector Management* 6(1), 48–58.

Kim, J.Y. (1997). Direction for Developing the Korean Civil Service System. *Public Personnel Management* 26(1), 89–107.

King, C., and Stivers, C. (1998). *Government is Us: Public Administration in an Anti-Government Era*. Thousand Oaks, CA: Sage Publications.

Liou, K.T. (1997). Issues and Lessons of Chinese Civil Service Reform. *Public Personnel Management* 26(4), 505–514.

Marshall, G.S. (1998). Whither (or Wither) OPM? *Public Administration Review* 58(3), 280–282.

McCourt, W., and Sola, N. (1999). Using Training to Promote Civil Service Reform: A Tanzanian Local Government Case Study. *Public Administration & Development* 19(1), 63–75.

Nachmias, D., and Rosenbloom, D.H. (1980). *Bureaucratic Government USA*. New York: St. Martin's Press.

National Commission on the Public Service (Volcker Commission). (1989). Leadership for America: Rebuilding the Public Service. Washington, D.C.

Nickson, A., and Lambert, P. (2002). State Reform and the "Privatized State" in Paraguay. *Public Administration & Developmen* 22(2), 163–174.

Osborne, D., and Gaebler, T. (1992). *Reinventing Government.* Reading, MA: Addison-Wesley.

Patrickson, M., and Hartmann, L. (1995). Australia's Ageing Population: Implications for Human Resource Management. *International Journal of Manpower* 16(5) 34–46.

Peters, B.G., and Savoie, D.J. (1994). Civil Service Reform: Misdiagnosing the Patient. *Public Administration Review* 54(5), 418–426.

Randma, T. (2001). A Small Civil Service in Transition: The Case of Estonia. *Public Administration & Development* 21(1), 41–51.

Schiavo-Campo, S., de Tommaso, G., and Mukheriee, A. (1997). Government Employment and Pay in Global Perspective: A Selective Synthesis of International Facts, Policies and Experience." Background Report for the 1997 World Bank Development Report. Policy Research Working Paper No. 1771.

Sekwat, A. (2002). Civil Service Reform in Post-Independence Nigeria: Issues and Challenges. *Public Administration Quarterly* 25(3/4), 498–517.

Selden, S.C. (2003). Innovations and Global Trends in Human Resource Management Practices. In B.G. Peters and J. Pierre (eds.) *Handbook of Public Administration.* Thousand Oaks, CA: Sage publications, 62–71.

Selden, S.C., Ingraham, P.W., and Jacobson, W. (2001). Human Resource Practices in State Governments: Findings from a National Survey. *Public Administration Review* 61(5): 598–607.

Shim, D.S. (2001). Recent Human Resources Developments in OECD Member Countries. *Public Personnel Management* 30(3), 323–347.

Schultz, D. (2002). Civil Service Reform. *Public Administration Review* 62(5), 634–637.

Thompson, J.R., and Ingraham, P.W. (1996). The Reinvention Game. *Public Administration Review* 56, 291–298.

Warner, M. (1996). Economic Reforms, Industrial Relations and Human Resources in the People's Republic of China: An Overview. *Industrial Relations* 27, 195–210.

Wescott, C. (1999). Guiding Principles on Civil Service Reform in Africa: An Empirical Review. *The International Journal of Public Sector Management* 12(2), 145.

Wise, L.R. (2002). Public Management Reform: Competing Drivers of Change. *Public Administration Review* 62(5), 555–567.

Chapter 22

Deconstructing the Nation-State Bureaucracies: Supranationalization and Regionalization as Polarizing Forces in the New Europe

Lon S. Felker and Platon N. Rigos

CONTENTS

Introduction

By the end of the millennium, evidence abounded that the nation-state was in trouble. With the rise of a new Europe out of the ashes of the old in the phoenix-form, what we call the European Community[1] or EU, it is becoming ever clearer that the nation-state, at least in Europe, is being deconstructed into a mere member in a federation and weakened by regionalist movements and units as in Belgium or Italy. It is ironic that the nation-state is in the process of deconstruction in the very world region that gave birth to it. But this is not entirely surprising, as the elements of supranationalism and regionalism have always been present in Europe (Newman, 1996, pp. 109–137). What, after all, was the Holy Roman Empire if not an early form of loose supranationalism? Or to go to the other extreme, what are the regional movements from Scotland to Belgium (Newman, 1996, pp. 112–113)? Evidence surely that there is nothing new under the European sun.

The signing of the Maastricht Treaty in 1992 (Agence Europe, 1991) more formally known as the "Treaty of European Union," marked the establishment of a new supranational governmental entity in Europe. Under its terms, the Union established under Maastricht was founded at the time on three pillars: amendments to the treaties that founded the original European Coal and Steel Community (ECSC), the European Eco-

[1]We will use the term EU to stand for European Union or the term EC to stand for European Community interchangeably. The Europa site (see http://europa.euint/) uses the term EU in its main page, but also refers to European Community in other instances.

nomic Community (EEC), and the European Atomic Energy Community (Euratom),[2] a Common Foreign and Security Policy; and cooperation in the areas of justice and domestic affairs (Dinan, 1998, pp. 1–2). More recently we have seen the emergence of a new entity: the European Monetary Union (EMU) and its select number of states. Dinan (1998, p. 2) observes that the European Community's (EC) "pervasiveness tends to obscure its uniqueness and relative newness." The ever closer union envisioned in the movement toward a common currency is unprecedented in modern history.

However, the view of a federalizing Europe, the integration of many individual nations into one big super federal system, is not an uncontested view. In fact some see only two alternatives to Europe's future, as summarized by Schmitt and Thomassen (1999: p. 16): "(1) as pure intergovernmental cooperation among sovereign states; (2) as a federal entity that would take the form of a supranational sovereign European state." It is the latter view that is offered here as a form of deconstruction — the view that as the EC evolves further politically (the use of the Veto in the Council of Ministers), economically (the EMU), and socially (i.e. common labor standards), it might erode the sovereignty base of the individual nation-states. Within this second view there is also awareness that within a federalizing Europe, regional movements and units can gain more autonomy and recognition,[3] whereas the state still controls the important tools of power and authority like an army and taxation.

The force of regionalism, long suppressed by the individual nation-states but never entirely destroyed, is the other factor in the deconstruction. At present, across the face of Europe, subnational groups are claiming their birthright and making bids for sovereignty unparalleled in 20th century history. Scotland, which has often thought of itself as a "nation," not a region gained a lot of autonomy (Bulmer, et al., 2002 pp 1–2) as we shall see later in this chapter. Even in Germany, which is struggling to integrate the eastern Laender of the former German Democratic Republic into the Federal Republic, there had already been substantial strengthening in the status of the old Laender. They used the Maastricht Treaty to recover lost rights and have gained strong constitutional guarantees to maintain them (Newman, 1996, pp. 112–113). This is a fascinating time to view European politics. Never have Europe's

---

[2]Some names of institutions have changed and some new institutions have been added (see http://europa.euint) *op. cit*; The Council of Ministers is now called Council of the European Union, there is still the European Commission. Along with the Court of Justice which has not changed name, there is a Court of Auditors. Among other important institutions are The European Central Bank, the Committee on Regions, the European Ombudsman and the European Investment Bank.

[3]Devolution like the one in Spain resulted in 17 provinces in Spain; 6 units in Belgium and the more recently empowered 20 regional governments of Italy. The Laender of the German State have increased their powers and the French units are the weakest.

stakes been so high and the risks so great. Yet the story becomes more complex as ten new states were admitted in 2004 and the issue of Turkish membership looms large in the near future. But this is not a part of this study.

What we propose to do here is to present some new ways of looking at the EU and its relationships with member nation-states and their bureaucratic and political systems. A general examination of the EC in terms of several different theoretical perspectives is offered, along with some possible scenarios as to the likely futures of the EC. Finally, we will propose a poststructuralist analysis of the EC.

Deconstruction — Its Origins and Significance

Deconstruction is a term attributed to Jacques Derrida (1984), a French philosopher. As used here, it connotes a major change in the form and nature of European government and bureaucracy. This change, it is proposed, will be in the direction of destruction or transfiguration of the nation-state. Deconstruction is associated with linguistic analysis as a methodology in the determination of meaning. In applying Derrida's mode of analysis to the changing nature of government within the EC, some light may be shed on recent developments. The results of such an analysis are presented later in this chapter.

Deconstruction is a postmodern approach that seeks to unmask hidden assumptions and contradictions in "texts." Deconstruction is sometimes literally the taking apart of an argument or theory to reveal hidden, previously unanalyzed dimensions (Lye, 1996). The approach is now extended to other fields, including public administration (see Denhardt, 2000, pp. 176–180). Deconstruction sometimes takes the form of discovering "differance" (a combination of the concepts of difference and deferral) that signifies a system in which meaning is conveyed by means of the contrast of differences between signs, but in which ultimate meaning, or presence, is always deferred. This occurs because each sign is only a referent to another sign, and so on. Meaning is never truly present except by the virtue of the recognition of its absence.

As practiced by Derrida and others, deconstruction offers a potent tool in getting beneath the skin of otherwise commonly accepted dichotomies. Rooted in postmodern skepticism, deconstruction shares postmodern writer Francois Lyotard's idea that the term "modern" designates any science that legitimates itself with reference to a metadiscourse...(that makes) explicit appeal to some grand narrative" (quoted in Fox & Miller, 1995, p. 44).

We argue that the fields of public administration and to a larger extent, its parent discipline, political science make such claims. Indeed, within the larger "texts" of Western social science literature and research is the underlying assumption that progress lies in certain directions, institutions, and procedures. Postmodernism adds that they cannot be understood without apprehending their opposite or nonexistence. And by the same token, regression, lack of progress, and decay lie in the reverse direction.

The "grand narrative" here is the idea of a United State of Europe, the notion of an "every closer union," and other appeals to the vision of progress as cooperation and integration of nation-states into one political entity with fervent and active regionalist movements that sometime take on formal attributes like Parliaments. Let us begin with an examination of the history of European federalism, for this structure lies at the root of that remarkable project, the EC.

Federalism in Europe

The modern history of European federalism is relatively short, and largely German. The only successful European nation-state to implement a federal system for a long time is Germany. It did so under the aegis of Bismarckian *realpolitik*.

Recognizing the significant differences that pervaded the Germany of the 1800s, Otto von Bismarck created a union of states directed from Berlin, but one that recognized local institutions and political traditions. This broke the mainstream trend in political state organization at that time: all European states were unitary in nature.

It is telling that the system survived the World War I and the Weimar Republic. Hitler, of course, centralized most of the state power in the hands of the National Socialist Party, but the federal system remained intact, at least on paper. Again, in the post–World War II period, West Germany adopted the same federalist model as in previous eras.

The Federal Republic was born with a system of national and local political organization roughly modeled on the American constitution, with most of the prewar states or Laender having territorial readjustments. Even so, the new republic retained the old system of provincial control and local tradition. The ghost of Prussian hegemony was laid to rest. In East Germany, the boundaries and governments were also retained, albeit in the service of a Communist centralizing party.

This long retention of federalism bespeaks a deep commitment to this form of governance in Germany. It also served as a basis for German willingness to experiment with a European-wide federalism. As the largest nation-state within the EC, this long relationship with federal systems is not an insignificant factor. More recently, federal structures have appeared in

Spain and Belgium. France and Italy have created provinces. The federal idea seems to be spreading even to some of the most centralized nation-states.

Supranationalism — The Force from Above: A Brief History

The First Period: The Birth of Institutions

The father of a "United States of Europe" is Jean Monnet, a senior official in the French government, who introduced and championed the concept of sectoral economic integration. Today, French foreign minister Robert Schuman is also acknowledged just as much the founder of the EC on May 9, 1950.[4] The European Coal and Steel Community, the first tentative step toward European integration, was "never viewed as an end in itself but [as] part of a process that would culminate in a European federation transcending the nation-state" (Dinan, 1998, p. 3).

Monnet's "selling" of his idea for a unified control of German–French coal and steel to Robert Schuman was premised as much on French national interest in economic recovery following a devastating war, as it was on altruistic notions of international cooperation (Monnet, 1978). Dinan (1998, p. 9) observes that, in accepting West Germany as an equal in partnership with France, and in turning over the responsibility of both nations' coal and steel production to a supranational entity, the Schuman Plan "gave substance to the hitherto vague notion of European unity and integration."

Equally important were the other institutional entities created to manage the ECSC and resolve disagreements (http://europa.eiint, scadplus/log/en/lob/133080.htm). First, the High Authority (which would become the EU High Commission) was tasked with economic planning and implementation. Because of its small size, it was essential that the High Authority work closely with the national bureaucracies to coordinate the implementation of ECSC legislation. The Court of Justice was established as a judicial body established to adjudicate intracommunity disputes and underwrite member states' compliance with the treaty's terms. Against Monnet's judgment, a council of ministers of member states was also created to represent the individual member states' wishes and interests. The latter was to take on extraordinary importance, as nothing gets done without approval from the

[4]It is now acknowledged as Europe Day (see http://europa.euint) *op. cit.*

council. Finally, a Common Assembly (later renamed the European Parliament) consisting of delegates from national legislative and parliamentary bodies would provide the element of popular democratic accountability.

The European Commission has extraordinary powers as an executive body (Haas, 1958). It is empowered to table most legislative proposals. The Commission is furthermore empowered to implement most of the legislation of the Parliament. Following the Amsterdam Treaty (1997), the European Parliament has the power of codetermination in areas roughly comprising half the legislation (Duff, 1997), whereas the council of ministers, comprised as it is of representatives of the member-state governments, still is the most powerful actor in the EC's governing process. Unfortunately that power is limited by the need for unanimity in the council's voting, which frequently proves elusive (Pinder, 1998, 27ff.).

The Second Period: The Gaullist Challenge, 1958–1969

The imposing figure of Charles de Gaulle assumed a major role as an opponent of the intergovernmental aspects of the ECSC, and as an opponent of the expansion of the Community by admission of Great Britain. For de Gaulle, supranationalism posed a threat to France's sovereignty and her chances for leadership in postwar Europe.

De Gaulle successfully exploited divisions within British party councils over Common Market membership, and publicly questioned Britain's commitment to the Community (see, for example, Dinan, 1998, Chap. 2; Pinder, 1998, pp. 59–60, 216). De Gaulle used the Common Market's common tariff as another weapon, challenging Britain's call for a free trade zone (EFTA: European Free Trade Association, which still exists) within what was then termed the Common Market.

Within the Community itself, de Gaulle was equally confrontational; attempting successfully to limit the powers of the Commission and the Parliament. Dinan (1998, p. 41) suggests that admission of Great Britain on the terms she demanded might very well have made the Common Market ineffectual as a policymaking body, as it would have turned Europe into a free trade zone.

This would have "thwarted the CAP (Common Agricultural Policy), would have also undermined the Community, and turned the customs union into a broad free trade zone" (Dinan, 1998). In short, Dinan sees de Gaulle as a guarantor of the integrity of the EU, albeit for motives that had little to do with protecting the principles of supranationalism. De Gaulle's rejection of Britain's bid for membership in the Common Market in 1963 constituted the gravest crisis in this second era of EU history.

The Third Period: The International Challenge, 1969–1979

The period was christened one of "completion, deepening and enlargement" by French president Pompidou at the Meeting of the Six at the Hague summit of 1969 (Dinan, 1998, p. 68). International events outside Europe, such as the Arab oil embargo of the mid-1970s, had a negative effect on the EC's ability to pursue new initiatives such as the Economic and Monetary Union (EMU).

Georges Pompidou was more of a political realist. France's worsened economic fortunes dictated another course of action in the 1970s. After currency devaluation, Pompidou tacitly acknowledged that the German mark — not the French franc — had become the dominant currency in the Common Market. He called for a coordination of the member states' economic policies. This was primarily directed at securing the Common Agricultural Policy, a policy very essential to French interests.

On the other hand, German chancellor Wily Brandt was eager to launch his *Ostpolitik* toward East Germany. He recognized that any territorial settlement with the East would awaken fears of resurgent German nationalism in France and other nations in Western Europe. Therefore he sought to balance his rapprochement with East Germany with a *Westpolitik*: a broadening of the Community to include Great Britain (Pinder, 1998, pp. 148–153).

In Great Britain, Prime Minister Edward Heath had long concluded that membership in the Community made sense for Britain. After winning an electoral victory in June 1970, Britain under Heath renewed its application for membership. The White Paper, which Heath submitted to Parliament, stressed the competitive advantages and efficiency that Britain sorely needed (Pinder, 1998, p. 62).

These personalities and events led up to the first expansion of the EC to include Great Britain, Ireland, and Denmark. The major obstacle for the new members was the Common Agricultural Policy (CAP), which had been designed largely for the six founding members. With a small agricultural sector, and a major importer of foodstuffs, the British consumer paid a high price for Britain's accession to the EC.

Another sore point was the surrender of sovereignty, an issue that the House of Commons took up periodically. Heath's White Paper had repeated assurances that there would be "no question of any erosion of essential national sovereignty" although there was to be a "sharing and an enlargement of individual national sovereignties in the general interest" (Heath, 1971, p. 16). British public opinion has not been completely mollified by such assurances — then or now.

The major impression that one carries from an examination of this period of EC history is that the expansion from the Inner Six to include

Britain, Ireland, and Denmark resulted in a widening, but not necessarily a deepening, sense of EC (Pinder, 1998, p. 63). Important signs of progress were an agreement for the first direct elections to the European Parliament and the inception of the European Monetary System (EMS). But overall there hung an atmosphere of stagnation and delay, if not deliberate obstruction. Britain and Denmark resisted most efforts to limit national sovereignty, and Heath's party, facing a more critical attitude toward the EC within the British voting public, became at best lukewarm in its embrace of EC membership. In 1975, a referendum was held on the membership question, with a two-to-one favorable response by the voters. Still some of the old British elites were far from mollified.

There were other events and crises that deepened the sense of EC malaise. The contentious admission of Greece, Spain, and Portugal to membership was one of these. The three new nations had considerably underdeveloped economies in comparison to the other states in the EC. Another issue was the continued dilatory behavior of the Council on the question of agricultural reform. All the three new countries had large agricultural sectors that were undermechanized and undermodernized. By the end of the 1970s, The EC's CAP had resulted in large agricultural overproduction in many of the member states. Although the problem was acknowledged by the Mansholt Plan, which was calculated to reduce the number of laborers in the EC's agricultural sector by roughly half, the political will to do something about it was lacking. A principal stumbling block was the need for "guidance" from the top, and for a considerable surrender of authority if the Mansholt Plan were to succeed. As Pinder (1998, p. 104) summarizes:

> All, and not least the Germans, were influenced by the lobbies; and the French government, still strongly Gaullist, was keenly opposed to the enhancement of the Commission's role that the proposed policy would imply. . . . The result was the attrition of the Mansholt Plan over more than three years of discussions, until the Council decided in April 1972, to provide only some modest finance for development loans to farmers, incentives for early retirement, and assistance for information and training intended to raise efficiency.
>
> Pinder (1998)

This was a case of too little, too late. The EC's inadequate handling of the CAP would haunt it well into the 1980s.

The Fourth Period: Revival

If the 1970s were years of stagnation for the EC, the 1980s might be called a period of revival and renewal, a third period starting with unauspicious beginnings. To start with, the problems besetting the EC in the early 1980s were considerable: an inadequate agricultural policy (CAP), a new French president (Mitterand) committed to a revitalized French economy at any price, and a new British prime minister (Thatcher), who was stridently demanding a rebate of Britain's contribution to the EC budget (Dinan, 1998, pp. 99–100). In December 1983 at Athens, the European Council concluded its summit without agreeing on a concluding communiqué. The future of the EC looked bleak, indeed.

There were many factors that helped the EC turn the corner in the early 1980s, many of these having started earlier, but bearing fruition in 1980s: (1) the previous establishment of the EMU; (2) the earlier direct elections to the European Parliament, thus adding a popular and democratic dimension to an otherwise elitist panoply of EC institutions; (3) the satisfactory resolution of the British budget contribution dispute at Fontainebleau in June 1984, and probably most significantly; (4) the leadership of Roy Jenkins, who had become president of the European Commission in 1977.

Jenkins's chief contribution to the EC was the championing and the implementation of the EMU (Jenkins, 1989). Drawing on support from the Belgians, Jenkins got a recommitment to the concept of an EMU from the Council of Ministers. Furthermore, he got unexpected help from German chancellor Helmut Schmidt, whose concerns about the increasing burden West Germany was assuming in assuring global economic stability led him to attempt to share that burden with other EC member states. This led to the establishment of a European Economic System in 1978, complete with an Exchange Rate Mechanism (EMR), which supplanted the so-called "snake in the tunnel" exchange rate system that had earlier proved problematic.

Pinder (1998, p. 159) credits the ERM with stabilizing the EC participants' exchange rates in the 1980s. Both exchange rates and interest rates reduced in variability, and the 1980s saw a much brighter economic picture. These events opened the door to further macroeconomic convergence by EC members, leading to the creation of the EMU and the Single European Act, which established the goal of a common European currency.

If the EMU counts as one of Jenkins's triumphs, the other major conundrum of the early 1980s was the settling of the British Budget Question (BBQ) under pressure from Margaret Thatcher (Thatcher, 1988). Her complaints that the U.K.'s budgetary contribution was excessive led to a major crisis that Jenkins sought to head off. Thatcher had additional ideological reservations to the whole notion of supranational European governance. According to Jenkins's account, the Strasbourg summit of June 21–22, 1979 saw Thatcher engage in major histrionics over the budget issue, ultimately alienating not only Giscard D'Estaing and other representatives from the Netherlands, Ireland, and Denmark, but also Schmidt, whose cooperation was crucial (Jenkins, 1991, p. 494).

Eventually it took several more diplomatic efforts and the good offices of Lord Carrington, as well as a formal cabinet vote, to convince Thatcher that the offer on the table was the best that Britain was going to get. At the Brussels summit of the European Council, March 19–21, 1984, the budget issue was finally laid to rest with an agreement that Great Britain would receive a rebate of her contribution to the common budget based on a fixed percentage (66 percent) of Britain's net contribution each year (Dinan, 1998, pp. 111–115).

With the BBQ (Jenkins quipped it had become the "Bloody British Question") resolved, the Brussels summit proved to be surprisingly cordial. Thatcher's insistence on fiscal adjustment paid off in other respects. It stressed the need for budgetary restraint in EC expenditures, and underscored the problems with the CAP as well as contributing to the decision to implement an *ad valorem* tax (effective in 1986), from 1.0 to 1.4 percent of the value-added tax revenues collected in the member states (Dinan, 1998, p. 115).

More progress was made throughout the remainder of the 1980s in terms of the single market agenda, as well as the improvement of EC cooperation in industrial policy. The wave of deregulation that begun in the United States had a profound impact on economic thinking within the EC. After a failed attempt at renewed state intervention, protectionism, and regulation in the early 1980s, the socialist Mitterand government of France embarked on a radical change, of course, embracing to the possible extent a number of free market policies, resulting in a remarkable turn-around in the French economy.

In this period we see a new resolve of interests within the EC to chart an independent course between the superpowers, and to lessen dependence on the United States for technology. Within the EC itself, a major obstacle was the use of the veto by members of the Council of Ministers. Specifically, France called for restricted use of the veto in the Council, which had proven a stumbling block to agreement on policy.

Mitterand noted that the Luxembourg compromise, which was France's 1966 assertion that it would exercise the right of veto in the Council "when very important interests were at stake," had proven more a curse than a blessing (Pinder, 1998, p. 15). The logic for abandoning the veto was persuasive: the EC was due to undergo an enlargement to include Spain and Portugal, and unanimity with a body of 10 had been difficult in the best of times; with 12 it might be insurmountable. In fact, the Council had been moving toward majority voting on an informal basis for some time; Mitterand's plea merely served to move matters along (Mazey and

Newman, 1987). Belgium challenged Britain on a veto over farm prices in May 1982, and successfully managed to get a vote despite Britain's stated intent to veto.[5]

Of equal note was the emergence of the European Parliament as an active institution in EC affairs. In the years from 1980 to 1982, the European Parliament passed eight resolutions for institutional reform and progress on political and economic integration in the EC (Dinan, 1998, p. 122). The work of Altiero Spinelli and the Crocodile Club are worthy of special note here. This led in time to a parliamentary-based Committee on Institutional Affairs, which met in parliamentary chambers to consider a reaffirmation of the EC's fundamental principles. And gradually there emerged out of these discussions a sensed need for a new treaty and a new union to replace the ones that existed. These developments served to heighten the sense of urgency that the European economic crisis and the concerns over the institutional viability of the EC's institutions as voiced by Mitterand and others.

The Fifth Period: Challenges and Progress

The 1990s proved to be an era of transformation, in which many of the reform initiatives of the 1980s bore fruit. The word "irreversible" began to be heard in the discourse over EC future policy by the late 1980s. It signaled the sense that the single market and all it symbolized for the EC was now inevitable, and it was only a matter of time and political will before it manifested itself (Dinan, 1998, pp. 149–150).

The decade of the 1990s also brought changes in the size of the EC, with the applications of eastern European states such as Hungary and the Czech Republic after the end of the cold war. These eastward expansions (made official in 2004) brought complications, and the integration of nation-states having economies crippled by years of socialist economic policy could prove problematic. Much more troublesome were the new Balkans wars in the former Yugoslavia, which strained many facets of the EC's foreign policy and reawakened fears of German hegemony as a unified Germany backed the Croatians in their war against Serbia. North Atlantic Treaty Organization's (NATO) eventual involvement in peace keeping and the containment of Serbia also renewed questions of whether a common EC foreign and military policy without NATO was politically feasible.

Despite the ominous developments in southern Europe, the overall impression of the 1990s in terms of EC economic, political, and social policy

---

[5]The subject of the veto is looming even larger today with the entrance of the new states. Still it is felt that some matters should be still protected by veto.

was positive. With the Maastricht summit of December 9–10, 1991, there was a marked change in direction for the Community. On the one hand, there was Britain's opposition to greater EC involvement in domestic social policy. This rejection by Britain nearly precipitated a dumping of the social policy chapter from the Maastricht treaty. Had the other 11 states of the Community decided to proceed without the U.K., this would have been a serious change in terms of furthering the intergovernmental nature of the EC. Progress was made in the direction of a common currency (EMU), and the stage was set for intensive political reaction to the Treaty (Dinan, 1998, pp. 182–183).

On the other hand, at the national level, there was the Danish Parliament's rejection of the Treaty following a referendum defeat by Danish voters. Then Ireland's high court issued an opinion judging the Treaty unconstitutional. The surprising aspect of both of these decisions by national governments was that at no time was there any serious mention of a "crisis in the Community" (Dinan, 1998, p. 184). The Danish referendum vote, however, signaled a serious challenge to the EC's future. Despite the actions of Denmark, Great Britain, and France — where referendums were called for — all the other member states ratified the Treaty by the target date of December 1992, thus giving the forces of unity a strong vote of confidence (Nugent, 1999).

By the end of the 1990s, despite the Danish "opt-out," ratification was a reality, and the EC was becoming a fixture in European politics. Its four primary institutions — the Council, the Parliament, the Court, and the Commission — had over a period of 40 years developed a series of protocols and relations that suggested a mature institutional setup.

But is the old Europe truly "deconstructing?" Are national interests and identities being subsumed within the larger framework of the EC? More specifically, are the EC's institutions absorbing the sovereignty of the member state governments and furthering the deconstruction process? Before attempting a response to these questions, it is necessary to provide another perspective on the EC and its operations.

Problems and Public Policy in the European Union

A continuing problem in many Western European economies is recurrent unemployment. However, an opposing view holds that long-term unemployment might be because of overregulation at the supranational level, exposing national economies to international competition (Scharpf, 1989). This view locates the problem in the nature of the EC and its tariff structure. According to this view, long-term low employment is an artifact of the "unfair regulatory competition" that prevails between nation-state and the EC. Scharpf discusses this in terms of "negative integration" within the Union (Scharpf, 1999, pp. 4–5).

Regulatory policy coordination within the EC seems to be one sore point between national and suprantional governments. Regulatory competition contributes to lack of flexibility in adjusting national to supranational regulatory targets, where the latter have precedence over the former. As more of the individual member states' regulatory policies are set in Brussels rather than the nation-state capitals, it follows that there will be a corresponding loss of legitimacy and sovereignty of national regulatory bureaucracies.

Another source of potential conflict is the question of how national bureaucracies have been integrated and coordinated with one another. Since the inception of the EC the pattern for national bureaucracies has been to be coordinated through Brussels and the highly focused bureaucracy of the Commission. But the question of nation-to-nation coordination and cooperation seems to be the one seldom addressed in the literature.

An example of the sort of problem that can result when such cooperation is lacking, arose in a recent Internet discussion site (Reading Room; www.pathfinder.com/time/reports/visions/judt1.html). One voice in protest over Brussels's hegemony was that of Dr. Drude Dahlerup, a professor of political science at the University of Aarhus, Denmark:

> ... The transfer of so much decision-making power to Brussels benefits two sets of people: bureaucrats and large corporations. The losers are elected politicians, smaller organizations like unions, and ordinary people, who feel more powerless than ever. The democratic connection is cut. Why aren't there more referenda? Why don't the European elites dare ask people for their opinions? What are they afraid of?
>
> Dr. Drude Dahlerup

From a "street-level bureaucrat's" perspective, there is also a mild dissent. Werner Thiel, a custom officer in Trier, Germany (http://www.pathfinder.com/time/reports/visions/Thiel.html) remarks:

> I believe in the idea of a united, borderless Europe. But from my experience as a customs officer, the participating countries first have to reconcile their differences if Europe is to work.
>
> Werner Thiel

Differences in legislation and in the labor market are just two of the many problems Europe will face on its way to unity. Since the Schengen

Agreement (which in March 1995 eliminated border controls between certain countries inside the EC) was put into action, there has been a huge increase in the number of people traveling to the Netherlands to buy soft drugs, which are forbidden in Germany. Naturally, those who are seized with soft drugs do not understand the German procedures. Such discontent indicates that political and bureaucratic *Gleichschaltung* (integration) has yet to be fully achieved between the bureaucracies of member states and the overarching EC bureaucracy (Weidenfeld, 1994).

Regionalization: The Force from Below

In studying how regionalization and governance have manifested themselves in Europe, Budge and associates (1997) distinguish two distinct models, the federal and the differentiated models. The second has a number of variations (Budge and associates, 1997, pp. 295–303). The first one is the Germanic model said to exist in Switzerland also. We can also add Belgium because it has a well-recognized federal system (Hooghe, 1995, pp. 134–165). All units in the federation have the same standing.[6] The *Laender* and Cantons do the field administration. The local civil services carry out legislation of the Federal or *Laender* governments on one hand and legislation is usually pretty uniform. On the other hand, the regions have power over what the Federal Government wants to do. In Germany the *Laender* nominates delegations to the *Bundesrat,* the second chamber (like the U.S. States used to do in the 19th century with Senators). This gives them a lot of political power. This is how they have extracted out the central government, specific articles that have gone into the Basic Law. These stipulate that the further integration into the EU will not undercut any of their prerogatives.

We will not deal with Switzerland since it is not within the EC. But Belgium deserves our scrutiny. In 1989, six Belgian regions and communities were federalized; and, they have acquired so much autonomy that they can deal directly with the EC. The Belgian model provides an alternative that would allow regions to go directly to the EC's agency for some problems, bypassing the state. Scotland and Northern Ireland have also asked for that power. The constitutional revisions of May 1993 gave final status to the changes of 1989 that recognized the formal change of a unitary state into "a federal state, composed of Communities and Regions" (see Article 1 of the [New] Constitution), (Hooghe, 1995, p. 135). There are two regions, Flanders and Walloonia. The regions and communities can, as we stated

[6]The German states have closer intergovernmental relations than in the USA.

above, deal directly with other nation-states. Only an "elaborate machinery of co-ordination, ensures coherence in Belgian Foreign policy" (Hooghe, 1995, p. 136). The Flemish and Walloon administrations have proved that they can organize society as well as the Belgian state. The Belgian case is particularly unique because of the sharp linguistic differences. These are not duplicated to the same intensity elsewhere.

The second model is labeled the "differentiated model" in Budge et al. (1997, pp. 298–299). This "second type of European Federalism" is designed to manage minority nationalism. It varies with the intensity of the minority movements in some regions. It also varies between the formal recognition of movements and the creation of semiautonomous provinces in Spain, to the creation of regions in highly centralized France where Corsica is given a separate parliament.

In 1986, France has created some 22 regions and given them the right to elect their own council members. Before that date, they existed purely as administrative subdivisions. France has the weakest form of regionalism. The status of French regions was diminished when it became impossible (Balme, 1995, p. 177) for regional council members to be members of the national Parliament, something that is allowed to mayors of cities. The regions were created by Francois Mitterand in 1982, as part of the fulfillment of a campaign promise, but have been dominated by conservative parties, even before Jacque Chirac came to power. Regions have a large say in environmental politics (Balme, 1995, p. 171), but have few other powers except those delegated to them by Paris. Yet they are playing a significant role in the national policy, because they have attracted a lot of the new technocrats and professionals who seem to be more attuned with modern governance concepts (Balme, 1995, p. 176) than most French politicians.

Parliaments have been created in Scotland, Wales, and Northern Ireland (Bulmer et al., 2002 ch. 1). The Scottish one is the most evolved. After Tony Blair's accession to power, Scotland and Wales were given a lot of autonomy through acts of Parliament. Scotland is effectively self-governing through a Scottish Executive.[7] The Executive was established in 1999, following the first elections to the Scottish Parliament. It is a coalition between the Scottish Labor Party and the Scottish Liberal Democrat Party. A First Minister, who is nominated by the Parliament and in turn appoints the other Scottish Ministers, leads the Executive (http://scotland.gov.uk). Northern Ireland is too mired in the fight between the Catholics and the

[7]The Scottish Executive is the devolved government for Scotland. It is responsible for health, education, justice and police, rural affairs, and transport. It manages an annual budget of more than £20 billion in the financial year 2002–2003. Executive civil servants are accountable to Scottish Ministers, who are in turn accountable to the Scottish Parliament. http://scotland.gov.uk

Protestants to make much of an impact as a region, but it has had an Assembly which has been dissolved once, but is back in business. Britain's devolution is more advanced than in France simply because of its history and the ascendancy of the Labor party that has always had a strong position in the localities. Under Thatcher in the 1980s, the local governments were actually punished for being pro-Labor by losing autonomy and were asked to raise additional taxes (Keating & Jones, 1995, pp. 91–95). Under Thatcher, conservatism's belief in local government in most nations took a second place to political expedience.

Italy has given special status to Alto Adige (near the Austrian border), Val d'Aosta, Sardinia, and Sicily. The activities of the Northern League (*Il lega*) in the 1990s did not result in special status for Lombardia because it was seeking outright secession. But the Northern League came back in September 2004 under the leadership of Roberto Calderoli and was able to extract more autonomy for all of northern Italy, which then was translated into more autonomy for all 20 regions in the country. They acquired new powers over health, education, and law and order (Barber, 2004).

In Spain, following the death of Franco and the accession of King Juan Carlos, the bitter conflict between the central government and the Basque terrorist movement (ETA), set in a province called Euzkadi (local name for the Basque Area), was gradually resolved as efforts to provide true regional expression for the Basque, Catalonian, and other Spanish national regions were implemented. Regionalization not only proved to be an instrument for local development planning, but also strengthened the Spanish state as well (Budge and associates, 1995, p. 302).

Although regionalization is significant as a development within the context of the nation-state, it has not totally modified the power relationships in all European countries (except Belgium), or in even those with significant regional council systems. What it has accomplished, however, is a serious rethinking of centralized "*etatisme*," and provided a viable model of what a "Europe of the regions" might look like. Another aspect of this is the degree to which modern Europeans, whether in the EC or not, are coming to regard themselves not just as Frenchmen, Germans, or Italians, but also, and perhaps just as meaningfully, as Gascons, Rhinelanders, and Sicilians. In other words, they can be members of subnational groups having real political identity, as well as a cultural or linguistic *personae*.

Among the more recent additions to the institutions of the EC is the Committee on Regions. As the EC's youngest institution, it reflects "the member states' strong desire not only to respect regional and local identities and prerogatives but also to involve them in the development and implementation of EC policies" (http://europa.eu.int/inst-en.html). As an expression of the EC's recognition of a Europe "of the regions," the

Committee could take on greater importance as regional identity and regional issues begin to generate more interest and controversy. At present, it mainly seems to be a discussion group.

Supranational and Regional Forces "Deconstructing" Europe

Deconstruction is a term widely attributed to the French philosopher Jacques Derrida. Here it connotes a major change in the form and nature of European government and bureaucracy. This change, it is proposed, will be in the direction of destruction or transfiguration of the nation-state, to such an extent that it will be virtually unrecognizable. Applying Derrida's mode of analysis to the changing nature of government and its meaning within the EC might shed some light on recent developments. More immediately however, we present four scenarios of EC development that range from the rosy to the dark and the dreary.

Scenario One: A Europe of States That Are "Withering Away"

Within this scenario, the trends are toward eventual devolution of the nation-state into federal units similar to state governments in the United States but with fewer functions and an EC bureaucracy as large of the U.S. Federal government today. The major operative force in Scenario One is the continued ability of the EC to regenerate itself in ever more profound and extensive ("deepening and widening") iterations. Some of these would be moving toward a common foreign and social policy. Labor standards will have to be set so as to satisfy the very generous states with those that would like a greater freedom for market forces. Ireland has achieved such a compromise, often called "the third way." Other areas of deepening would be the policies toward unemployment. In terms of internal forces, the EC is successful in developing functional governmental machinery that successfully integrates all the institutional elements and provides a framework for incorporating the various ethnic, linguistic, and cultural entities of the EC into a mosaic of meaningful and manageable proportions. The Council, Commission, Parliament, and Court all function in an institutional atmosphere of checks and balance, with the overall policymaking process a reflection of the original intent of Jean Monnet. Regions will exist in an *ad hoc* way, not challenging the states, but playing a constructive role buttressed by the EC's Committee on Regions. The security system of

Europe might provide a better defensive umbrella than the present European Force, making NATO an historical artifact.

A Europe dominated by a supranational government, with regional expression permitted and encouraged, may strike some as overoptimistic at best, particularly in the light of past European history. But the forces now at work within the EC seem to offer optimistic grounds as well as the alternative. Britain's commerce is 60 percent with Europe. Even though Britain seems reluctant to go down that road, economic self-interest often prevails.

Scenario Two: Regionalization Weakens the States

This scenario posits that the regional movement now progressing in a number of European countries will eventually develop more legitimacy by bypassing the states and getting recognition and funds from the EC. Regions will emerge as primary local decision-making venues in the light of the continued expansion of participatory decision making at all levels. Frustration with the regulatory competition between the EC and nation-states will provide a window of opportunity for the regional subgovernments to express themselves as local representatives of the popular will. This will create a cascade effect, eroding the sovereignty of the nation-state even further.

The nation-state does not disappear, but it remains a legal entity with lesser meaning. This will vary from nation to nation. Some of the small nations like Greece, Slovakia, the Czech Republic, Denmark, and the Netherlands may not experience any regionalist upsurge. But even in France under that scenario, some of its old division will reassert themselves. Alsace, Britany, the Basque area, Corsica, the Rhone Corridor (increasingly the center of hi-tech activity), and Marseilles are just a few among many units ready to stake their claim. Germany's *Laenders* will start playing a role internationally, as will Scotland and Northern Ireland. Some regions will start reaching across boundaries, the Spanish Basques and Catalans reaching out to their homologues in France. The Rhinelanders will reach out to Alsace; parts of Slovenia will reach out to southern Austria; and parts of northern France may reach out to Wallonia as the Belgian state becomes the first to disappear.

It is unlikely that Frieslanders will ever demand autonomy from the Netherlands. But even in this example, the future is not so foreseeable. The Friesian Islands extend over German as well as Dutch territory. Is not a transnational Friesian independence movement possible as Dutch and German nationalism in the larger states lose their attraction? Much of this scenario depends on what Europe becomes if and when Turkey is accepted. Romania, Bulgaria, and Croatia are also in the wings. But all these are problematic states.

Scenario Three: The EC at Two or Three Speeds

In this scenario, some portions of the New Europe like Great Britain, Poland, Denmark, and the new states (such as the Czech Republic and the Latvian) may seek to give no further powers to the EU than what they feel they have already given to Brussels. This means no monetary union and no deepening of the Union, and no labor policy (see Scenario One). For these countries, the EC will remain nothing more than a glorified set of intergovernmental agreements useful for economic development and trade.

But another part of the EC may proceed to some of the ideals described in Scenario One. Among the core of those nations will be France, Germany, and Belgium (at least Wallonnia). Italy, the Netherlands, and Spain are also members of that group despite some doubts mentioned above. Portugal and Greece are also the likely members of the club that believes that Europe is more than an intergovernmental agreement. Agricultural subsidies play a role for the southern European states, like Malta, Cyprus, Slovenia, Slovakia, and soon Croatia. The latter three's linkages to Germany will keep them on track toward a stronger EU. The same applies to Austria. Some of the new states that want to stay on a course toward full membership may get a time of adjustment to join the EMU.[8]

Spain and Italy particularly will be split. A lot will depend on their internal politics and their links to the United States. They may join a third set of nations. The third set will be made up of states like Spain and Italy and all those who are pressured by the United States to follow Great Britain, yet cannot have full separation from the EC institutions. Spain and Italy are in the EMU. Would they want to give that up? In this scenario some of the EU institutions (the Court of Justice, the Parliament etc.) will weaken but still survive albeit with reduced membership. The Council of Ministers will remain the main decision body.

Scenario Four: The EC as an Intergovernmental System

Scenario Four may include larger membership and stronger nations-states. It is in some ways the "doom and gloom" scenario. Here the forces unleashed within the EU create its own destruction. The EC expands to unmanageable proportions, and the Eastern European nations, unwilling to sacrifice the level of national sovereignty and national identity that membership will require, revolt, and spark a general reassessment of supranational governance. This turn of events is encouraged by Great Britain and Denmark that resent any loss of sovereignty and with the help of the United

---

[8]This would be similar to the period of adjustment granted to Greece before it could join the EMU in 2001.

States seek to neutralize any supranational Europe led by France and Germany, which may threaten NATO.

According to this scenario, there is no deconstruction. National governments and bureaucracies engage in "win back" strategies that beggar the EC. Furthermore, regional movements are reduced to pipe dreams and hard nationalist agendas resurface. The recent electoral victory of the Freedom Party in Austria, a political party with an avowedly antiimmigrant and antiforeign platform, has raised a number of questions about Austria's domestic political situation within the context of the EC. The inclusion of this party, whose ideology and program violate much of the EC's governing philosophy, brought threats of pushing Austria out of the EU. This type of conflict may become more common, if immigration issues are not resolved to the satisfaction of voters in states on the periphery of the EC's borders. The influx of new immigrants into established nation-states may well provide the catalyst to bring about a version of Scenario Four, especially given the related factors of high youth unemployment rates in many West European nations, and the attraction of unemployed youth to extremist movements.

However, there is perhaps another way of viewing this scenario. Europeans of all nations may in time come to see the EC as an institutional arrangement that served a specific period of European history. The reassertion of nationalism may take on a less destructive course than its 19th and 20th century history might portend.

Game Theoretical Perspective of the European Union

Game theory offers some notions of how the EC has succeeded in the past, and may continue to do so into the future. The EC resembles a nonzero-sum game. It has aspects of a cooperative game in which side payments and cooperative strategies are possible. Moreover, the EC is a game in which resources are not divisible, and the gains of one player do not represent losses to the other players.

Recollecting the brief summary of EC history offered above, it is important to recall that the initial ECSC was a success because it offered both initial partners, Germany and France, rewards for engaging in cooperative strategies. France wanted economic growth; Germany desired rehabilitation in the community of nations and a sharing of natural and industrial resources. Both found the ECSC a win–win strategy.

The EC expanded from this base because it offered potential member-states opportunities for larger markets and access to more resources, not the least of these a larger labor pool. It gave individual European countries a firmer base from which to deal with superpower entities such as the United

States (in farming and export/import policies) and the Soviet Union (military/diplomatic policy) when it was a credible threat.

Game theory further offers at least one idea about EC success. Strategies of member states that at one time may have destroyed the EC do not have that outcome now. These developments instead point to the viability of the EC as an ongoing game, and the degree to which side payments and selective incentives may motivate member-states to continue their support in other areas of EC policy, despite profound differences in other areas. The Baltic states, Poland, Hungary, and the Czech Republic may still harbor fears of the Russia. Side payments may help in their cases.

Conclusions — Deconstructing Europe: Some Postmodern Thoughts

It is simple to identify ongoing dichotomies in the history of the EC since its inception. The long-standing debate as to whether the EC represents a federal system of weakened states or just a large system of intergovernmental agreements between sovereign states (see Schmitt & Thomassen, 1999) is still even more urgent after the French and Dutch rejections of the European Constitution in June 2005. This sort of dichotomy is the very meat of deconstruction and poststructuralism, for it makes the unstated assumption that structure is the essence of the thing.

Do the nation-states represent the "building blocks" of an ever-growing intergovernmental system, or are they being "chipped away" in a more centralized federal structure? Which model — federal or intergovernmental — represents the "true face" of the EC? Each group of advocates would muster arguments for one view or the other in terms of more structural "signs" — institutional arrangements, voting procedures, policymaking processes — that serve to refer to other signs. The play here (to use Derrida's term for this manipulation of symbols) serves only to lead the argument away from an examination of other data and signs that point to possible other interpretations of the EC's nature, or presence.

What other signs and which alternative interpretation depend as much on the values and interests of the observer/analyst as anything else. One interpretation presented in this chapter, for example, is that the rise of regionalism and regionalist subgovernments in Western European nations signals a shift away from the nation-state toward a government with a recognizable human face (or at least a local face). Furthermore, it can be argued that such regionalist phenomena not only challenge the nation-state, but also suggest that another possible dialectic in European politics may be that of a supranational federal EC versus a series of regional subgovernments.

In support of this alternative interpretation offered signs are — evolving regionalist institutional arrangements, the shifts in decision-making power away from the national bureaucracies and toward the European Commission and the regionalist governments — all perfectly real phenomena and all referring to one another in a sort of argument daisy chain. Structures, as Derrida and others have stated, are "historical, temporary, contingent, operating through differentiation and displacement" (www.brocku.ca/english/courses/4F70/deconstruction.htlm). All "texts" are so constituted so as to be different from other texts, but any text includes that which it excludes, hence the similarity with other texts. One merely reaches for the appropriate signage and constructs according to the intended structure.

There are vehement dissenters like Stephen J. Korbin (1999) who attacks the EMU. He argues "whether E.M.U. was born an anachronism, a 20th century innovation that will become increasingly irrelevant in the 21st century." Britain and Denmark still oppose it, and it is a question whether the new states admitted in 2004 will be able to qualify for the EMU. Already discussion is proceeding as to whether the strict standards should be relaxed because not a single member of the EC is able to meet them.

Examining the issue of democratic participation within the EC, one can again employ a poststructural view on the available information. Previously we have seen that certain observers of the EC have less than sanguine views of the degree to which democratic participation will flourish under EC hegemony. The essential dichotomy here is one of elitism (EC) versus democratic participation. The discontents of Euro-federalism see the panoply of Euro institutions as window dressing for elitist supranationalism, a venue for peak organizations in Europe to subvert the sovereignty of national governments, and a superstate run for and by Eurobureaucrats. Yet many ethnic, linguistic, or religious minorities might find in the EU and its courts and agencies an additional bulwark against encroachment against the existing European nation-states.

There have been recent developments in a few European countries that suggest not only an emerging tolerance of such minorities but also a "new deal" for ethnic and linguistic regions within the nation-state. The Union criteria demand more than lip service, and the absence of a free press, free elections, and other "democratic" standards poses a high barrier to EC membership for a nation-state in which minority oppression has been a major feature of domestic politics.

In ensuring democratic governance and regional semiautonomy, is not the EC establishing a "meta-discourse" with many of the regional entities heretofore submerged within existing nation-states? In establishing a Committee on Regions and encouraging regional identity, is not the EC moving toward a "Europe of the Regions" rather than a Europe of the nation-states?

The play here seems to be underway and the players seem to be changing. The various scenarios adumbrated above may be by no means exhaustive, and the nature of the game may well change early in this millennium. Definitely there are signs and portents that signal a change of course and a new set of realities in European politics, and not all of them are emanating from the EC. Much of the tolerance and even encouragement of regionalist phenomena could, and perhaps should, be attributed to a new confidence in the EC. Deconstruction is afoot, but precisely where the fracture lines will run is mostly a matter of historical guesswork. The attitudes of Britain, the United States, and some of the new countries will have a major impact.

References

Agence Europe. 1991. Treaty on European Union: Final draft by the Dutch presidency as modified by the Masstricht summit. 13 December (Article W.2) Europe Documents, No. 1750/1751; http://www.agenceurope.com/EN/GobalFrameset.html. Accessed October 2000.

Balme, R. 1995. "French regionalization and European integration: Territorial adaptation and change in a unitary state." In B. Jones and M. Keating (eds.) *The European Union and the Regions*. Oxford, U.K.: Clarendon Press, pp. 167–188.

Barber, T. 2004. "Northern League" rising star scores victory for regional rule: Self Government in Italy. *The Financial Times*, London Edition 1, Extracted from LexisNexis Academic (p. 8). Accessed September 30.

Budge, I.N.K. and associates. 1997. Regions and localities: Power sharing with the periphery. In B. Jones and M. Keating (eds.) *The Politics of the New Europe*. London: Longman, pp. 91–313.

Bulmer, S., B. Martin, C. Carter, P. Hogwood and A. Scott (eds.) 2002. *British Devolution and European Policy-Making: Transforming Britain to Multi-Level Governance*. New York: Palgrave Macmillan.

Denhardt, R.B. 2000. *Theories of Public Organization*, 3rd ed. Fort Worth, TX: Harcourt Brace.

Derrida, J. 1984. "Psyche: Invention of the Other," cited in J. Lye, "Deconstruction: Some Assumptions." http://brucku.ca/englishj/courses/4f70/deconstruction.html. Accessed October 2, 2004.

Dinan, D. 1998. *Ever Closer Union: An Introduction to the European Community*, 2nd ed. London: Macmillan.

Duff, A. (ed.) 1997. "The Treaty of Amsterdam," in *The Treaty of Amsterdam: Text and Commentary*. London: Collins.

Fox, C.J. and H. Miller 1995. *Postmodern Public Administration*. Thousand Oaks, CA: Sage Publications.

http://europa.euint/scadplus/log/en/lvb/133080.htm. "Area of Freedom, Security and Justice: Action plan." Accessed November 17, 2004.

http://www.ecsanet.org/whoswho/who95int.htm. "Who's Who in European Integration: EU States." Accessed in May 1999.

http://scotland.gov.uk. Accessed November 22, 2004.

http://europa.euint. Accessed November 22, 2004.

Haas, E.B. 1958. *The Uniting of Europe: Political, Social and Economical Forces, 1950–57*. London: Macmillan.

Heath, E. 1971. *The United Kingdom and the European Communities*. London: Macmillan.

Hooghe, L. 1995. Belgian federalism and the European community. In B. Jones and Keating M. (eds.) *The European Union and The Regions*. Oxford, U.K.: Clarendon Press, pp. 135–167.

Jenkins, R. 1989. *European Diary: 1977–1981*. London: Collins

Jenkins, R. 1991. *Life at the Centre*. London: Macmillan.

Keating, M. and B. Jones. 1995. Nations, Regions and Europe: The UK Experience. In B. Jones and M. Keating (eds.) *The European Union and the Regions*. Oxford, U.K.: Clarendon Press, pp. 89–113.

Korbin, S.J. 1999. "Back to the Future." www.pathfinder.com/time/reports/visions/korbin.html. Accessed November 7, 2000.

Lye, J. 1996. "Deconstruction: Some Assumptions." URL: http://www.brocku.ca/courses.brocku.ca/courses/4F70//english/courses/4F70/deconstruction.html. Accessed January 1997.

Mazey S. and M. Newman. 1987. *Mitterrand's France*, London: Croom Helm.

Monnet, J. 1978. *Memoirs*, translated by R. Mayne. London: Macmillan.

Newman, M. 1996. *Democracy, Sovereignty and the European Union*. New York: St. Martin's Press.

Nugent, N. 1999. *The Government and Politics of the European Union*, 5th ed. London: Macmillan.

Pinder, J. 1998. *The Building of the European Union*, 3rd ed. New York: Oxford University Press.

Scharpf, F.W. 1995. *Negative and Positive Integration in the Political Economy of European Welfare States*. Florence: Jean Monnet Chair Papers, European University Institute.

Scharpf, F.W. 1999. *Governing in Europe: Effective and Democratic?* Oxford: Oxford University Press.

Schmitt, H. and J. Thomassen (eds.) 1999. *Political Representation and Legitimacy in the European Union*. Oxford: Oxford University Press.

Thatcher, M. 1988. *Britain in the European Community*. London: Conservative Political Centre.

Weidenfeld, W. (ed.) 1994. *Europe, 96, Reforming the European Union*. Guetershoh: Bertelsmann Foundation Publishers.

www.pathfinder.com/time/reports/visions/judt1.html. Accessed May 1999.

www.pathfinder.com/time/reports/visions/Thiel.html. Accessed May 1999.

V

ADMINISTRATIVE REFORM AND REORGANIZATION IN THE ASIA–PACIFIC REGION

Chapter 23

Adapting Asia and the Asia–Pacific Public Administration to a Globalizing World: Some Lessons from Experience

Clay G. Wescott[a]

CONTENTS

---

[a]This is a personal view, and not necessarily the view of the ADB. An earlier version was published.[2]

Background

Since 1995, the Asian Development Bank (ADB) has increased its attention to governance issues. Building on a notion that sound development management is needed for effective development performance in a globalizing world, the ADB became the first international finance institution (IFI) to adopt a Board-approved, governance policy.[1] This work was carried out in close coordination with the World Bank, which subsequently issued a similar commitment at the highest level.[b] To support this emerging consensus, Transparency International was launched in 1993 by a former World Bank staff to mobilize pressure from civil society on the governance agenda.

ADB has since broadened its definition of good governance to include a cluster of policies and strategies, including procurement, law and policy reform, participation of civil society, gender, anticorruption, and money laundering. This cluster helps member countries adopt institutional and policy reforms to adapt to an increasingly competitive regional and global economy by building sound macroeconomic and legal frameworks that strengthen markets and individual choice, and in turn economic growth and poverty reduction. Although internationally accepted tools, concepts,

[b]Cf. Wolfensohn.[3] This policy commitment to good governance by the World Bank's President followed a series of analytical reports.[4–6]

and notions of good practice broadly influence the goals and strategies of reforms,[c] there are significant differences among Asian countries in how they choose to implement their reforms.

The ADB defines governance as "the manner in which power is exercised in the management of a country's social and economic resources for development." Within ADB's governance policy, support to public administration reform is a key component:

> Civil service reform is perhaps the most elusive transformation facing a government.... A professional and accountable civil service that can administer rules, maintain standards and competition, and respect property rights is critical for private sector confidence in the government's efforts at economic reform. What is needed, therefore, is to move progressively towards public administration systems that provide clear career paths, adequate compensation and benefits, and incentives that tie advancement in the civil service more closely to staff performance and productivity. While downsizing operations should facilitate such improvements, [they] will not by [themselves] obviate the requirement for more sophisticated management and control systems.[1]

By contributing to sound governance, public administration reform also contributes to reducing poverty because it

(i) supports participatory, pro-poor policies and sound macroeconomic management,
(ii) ensures adequacy, predictability, transparency, and accountability in use of public funds for pro-poor budget priorities,
(iii) encourages private sector initiatives,
(iv) promotes effective delivery of public services by a capable, motivated civil service,
(v) disseminates basic performance data and provides client feedback to monitor service delivery, and
(vi) helps establish and maintain the rule of law.[11]

Although ADB and other IFIs use terms such as "participation," "transparency," "accountability," and "rule of law" in describing their governance support, they do not explicitly promote democratic political processes as is done by other development agencies. Article 36 of the ADB's Charter states that the ADB "shall not interfere in the political affairs of any member nor shall they be influenced in their decisions by the political character of the member

---

[c]For example, "Washington Consensus," cf. Williamson[7]; "new public management," cf. Mathiasen[8]; "total quality management," cf. Sharma and Hoque[9]; "performance–based management," cf. Jones.[10]

concerned. Only economic considerations shall be relevant to their decisions. . . .” Similar restrictions in other IFI charters also apply. However, this has proved less of a hindrance to supporting good governance than might be expected. One reason is that the United Nations (UN) and bilateral development agencies have been active in promoting democratic political processes, based on their different mandates and comparative advantage. A second reason, particularly evident in the Asia region, is that some countries have achieved economic growth and poverty reduction with less attention to democratic freedoms than has been the case elsewhere. Recent surveys[12] show, for example, that People’s Republic of China, Vietnam, Malaysia, and Singapore have higher competitiveness ratings than the Philippines and Indonesia, despite lower rankings in civil liberties and political rights.

With this conceptual foundation in mind, the following will draw from recent experience in the Asia–Pacific region to examine some conditions that are needed for administrative reforms to take hold, some lessons, and two approaches to reform. It will then give a brief overview of some key reform priorities, with examples from the region. This typology is drawn from a framework recently developed by the ADB.[13] Although experience with reform has improved our understanding of what works, more in-depth research is needed on how to achieve high performance in the public sector.

Conditions Needed for Reforms to Take Hold

There are five conditions that are generally met when public administration reforms start to take hold: (i) leadership; (ii) vision; (iii) selectivity; (iv) sensitivity; and (v) stamina.

Leadership

Barzelay[14] points out that heads of state and other top officials have a crucial role in putting reforms on the policy agenda and in determining how important reforms are relative to other priorities, with the decisive factors being maximizing political advantage and minimizing political risk. For many leaders, the politically opportune time for launching reforms is shortly after forming a government.

For example, in Vanuatu, inheriting fiscal uncertainties and a weak governance structure, the government that assumed office in October 1996 introduced the Comprehensive Reform Program. This was a broad initiative to reform the public service sector and public enterprises, and improve the enabling environment for private sector development. A participative and consultative process was adopted from the very beginning, which included extensive media coverage, and convening annual summits to provide citizens an opportunity to monitor progress in the implementation of reforms. However, a weakness of the program is that there are not enough senior lawyers, engineers, accountants, and capable managers. As a result, service delivery has not improved, and may have gotten worse in some sectors such as in agriculture.[15,16]

In Pakistan, the new Government taking power in 1999 launched a process of decentralization reforms to "(i) break the political and administrative hold of traditional elites, (ii) pass effective political and fiscal power from the federal and provincial levels to newly empowered local governments, and (iii) make local governments accountable to the Public."[17] The reforms were formally instituted following the conclusion of local government elections in 2001. Among the reasons for slower than expected implementation since then has been the challenge of ownership. Although the reforms have the full support of the Head of State and the powerful National Reconstruction Board, they were not initially fully supported by key officials at the provincial levels. Since then, extensive consultation has taken place with the concerned officials, and as a result implementation progress is improving.

In the case of Vietnam, a reform-minded prime minister appointed in 1997 was initially responding to demands from "war veterans" (who carried out unprecedented protests against corrupt local officials, punitive tax demands, etc., in two provinces in 1997), some party elites, investors, and donors for cleaner, more effective implementation of party policy to better regulate a fast growing economy. To ensure effective coordination in designing a reform program, the Vietnam National Public Administrative Reform (PAR) Committee, chaired by the prime minister, was constituted in 1998. It included two former deputy prime ministers, Nguyen Khanh, who effectively chaired meetings, and Nguyen Tan Dung, responsible for financial reform. Other members were ministers responsible for the Government Committee on Personnel, the Office of the Government, and the Ministry of Justice.[18]

Although authentic national leadership and ownership are crucial to reform success, one must be careful in aid-dependent economies not to confuse it with merely placating donors.[19] Donors can play a supportive role, but successful reforming leaders generally have more important, domestic political reasons for reform.

Vision

Comprehensive reforms that take hold are founded on a coherent vision of goals, broad objectives, and notional timetables for bringing about improved public administration. For example, Vietnam's PAR Program approved by the prime minister in 2002 outlines a work plan for the period 2001–2010, and it proposes to reform the entire public administration system by the end of that period. This is in line with Vietnam's overriding goal to accelerate the transition from a centrally planned to a socialist oriented market economy, with a state governed by the rule of law.

The program's agenda is broad. It includes replacing cumbersome administrative procedures with more simplified and transparent ones; reducing red tape and corruption; better defining the mandates and functions of institutions; reducing, during the period up to 2010, the number of ministries and consolidating within these the number of agencies; reforming provincial and other subnational administrations and redefining their relations with one another and the center; streamlining and rightsizing the organizational structures of ministries and other government agencies; reforming and rationalizing the relationship between ministries and other administrative bodies, and service delivery organizations and enterprises; raising the quality, standards, and skills of civil servants and other public sector workers; undertaking salary reform for public employees; reforming public financial management; and modernizing the public administrative system, notably through computerization and the introduction of e-government.[20]

Selectivity

Reforms take hold when they are important, and have a good potential to be carried out in a timely manner and to be a catalyst for additional reforms. Selectivity means filling in the reform timetable in a pragmatic way, while supporting the long-term vision. It does not mean pushing ahead with *ad hoc* reforms, or with isolated project implementation units (PIUs) or other privileged enclaves isolated from the mainstream. For example, the state government of Andhra Pradesh, India, has in recent years begun implementing its "Vision 2020" reforms. One part of the reform agenda that has captured global attention has been a number of e-government initiatives. For example, about 214 land registration offices have been completely computerized since April 1998. Deeds are registered in one hour and other services like the issue of encumbrance certificates and valuation certificates in 15 minutes. As of February 2000, about 700,000 documents had been registered under CARD. Middlemen are no longer needed, and time consuming manual copying and indexing of documents, and storage in paper forms have all been replaced.[21] There has also been some progress in the state in human resource management and public enterprise reforms. However, politically sensitive reforms on reducing staffing, streamlining investment approvals, and reducing corruption have moved at a slower pace. For example, the government has only been able to get public employee union approval for e-government projects by promising that no jobs would be lost.[22]

Sensitivity

Each country has its own unique historical, political, and cultural context that needs to be factored in. For example, Cambodia has experienced frequent changes in its political and economic regimes, which have been somewhat influenced by regional (e.g., Vietnam) and nonregional countries (e.g., France). The evolutionary process of the legal system includes a French-based civil code and judiciary before 1953; a Vietnamese communist model from 1979 to 1989; and now back to the French-based civil code combined with common law in certain sectors. The economic system similarly changed from a colonial system, to market-based, to Soviet-style central planning; and now back to a market-based economy.[23] In addition to the plethora of economic and administrative models, there are postconflict issues including reconciliation, rebuilding institutions, skills and trust, and demobilizing combatants. The Royal Government of Cambodia's Governance Action Plan has been designed with this complex array of issues in mind.

Stamina

Any fundamental reform takes time to take hold, and needs to be sustained across changes in governments and changes in donor funding. Because of the range of administrative problems, and the economic and political urgency of solving them, governments need a comprehensive vision and timetable for reform. However, because of the enormity and political sensitivity of the task, and the severe limitations on capacity to manage reform, such a framework may take 10 to 20 years to achieve significant impact. Take the case of ICT reforms in Vietnam. The story begins at least as far back as 1993, when a National Information Technology Program was initiated. The new prime minister appointed in 1997 continued implementing the program, including a government information network, and considerable application development, training, and awareness raising. Next, the prime minister approved the PAR Master Program mentioned above with seven action programs, one on modernizing state administration with a major role for e-government. Next, the Government made a landmark policy decision in September 2001 for State Administrative Management Computerization (SAMCom), which was a far more comprehensive strategy than the earlier 1993 program. Based on this, the prime minister requested ADB support through the policy loan for support to PAR action program 4 (training) and program 7 (e-government). In addition to the loan approved in 2003, two additional ADB loans are provisionally planned to ensure successful implementation through 2010.

The slow progress of administrative reform in the Russian Federation also shows the need for stamina. In 1989, a group drafted a civil service law that was not adopted. Spurred on by the dramatic political changes of 1991, some modestly effective laws and regulations were enacted, and progress made on modernizing human resource management and training. In 1996, work began on designing more significant reforms toward a merit-based, efficient, effective, corruption-free public sector, based on surveys and analysis by a number of expert working groups. Although a comprehensive design was presented to the new prime minister in 1997, and summarized in President Yeltsin's annual message to the National Assembly of 1998, the detailed design was never published nor implemented. However, the initial effort did help to raise awareness among some senior officials of the need for reforms, and thus helped pave the way for a recent wave of reform launched by President Putin in 2002. The new reforms are reinforced by extensive diagnostic and comparative analytical work, initially led by the Center for Strategic Studies, including a functional review of 5600 functions of 60 federal agencies. Achievements include launch of significant pay reform for senior-level civil servants, enactment of a code of conduct for civil servants and other relevant decrees, laws, and regulations, and launching of pilots projects in ministries and regions on pay reform and performance budgeting, with support from the World Bank[24,25] and other donors.

Broad Lessons from Experience

Improving public administration is one of the most difficult challenges facing governments and their development partners because of the complexity of the processes, the wide variation in context, and the difficulties in measuring reform outputs and outcomes. Still, there are four broad lessons to consider: (i) begin with diagnostic work; (ii) test for readiness; (iii) move at the right speed; and (iv) implement effectively.

Begin with Diagnostic Work

Broad diagnostic work can be useful as a first step. Governments, development agencies, and other stakeholders are often not fully aware of the administrative challenges faced.

For example, ADB carries out Country Governance Assessments (CGAs) to systematically assess the quality of governance for borrowers, and to strengthen the linkage between the quality of governance and levels and composition of assistance. ADB has completed CGAs in six countries, and they are underway in an additional 22.[26] Results of CGAs have been incorporated or are being incorporated into Country Strategy and Programs, and Poverty Partnership Agreements. Internal reviews of CGAs have found that there needs to be better linking of governance support and poverty reduction. CGAs often highlight the "absorptive capacity" of the country to pursue market-oriented reforms and utilize external assistance as a reoccurring governance challenge. Within strategic sectors of the country's economy, such as agriculture and transportation, governance was repeatedly discussed as an underlying issue essential to the sectors' overall development and performance. Other development partners such as the World Bank,[27] the European Bank for Reconstruction and Development, and the U.K. Department for International Development, along with private consultancies such as Political & Economic Risk Consultancy, Ltd. also support governance diagnostic work in the region.

In addition, political assessment tools can help stakeholders to better understand the array of interests lining up for and against specific reforms, and the opportunities for mobilizing decisive coalitions of interests to speed up reform.[28–30] One analyst suggests focusing on "where does the shoe pinch," or what aspects of governance offend government stakeholders and clients, how durable is the support for change, how much division is there among stakeholders, and what are the lessons of similar attempts to change in the past.[31]

Test for Readiness

Even when conditions may not be right for fundamental reforms, governments may be willing to carry out detailed surveys, functional reviews, and nonsensitive improvements in areas such as information systems. These pilot initiatives can test the readiness of the government and society for more fundamental reforms, and help to increase the demand for reform from a range of stakeholders. For example, in Nepal the Ministry of General Administration (MOGA), with support from ADB, has put civil service personnel records online linked to approved positions, and is in the process of linking this system to payroll. In addition, some vacant positions have been eliminated, the creation of new civil service posts frozen, and agreement reached to stop new recruitment in vacant posts in lower positions constituting about 33 percent of total civil service positions. The government has also approved a contracting out directive, which will allow subcontracting of certain positions and functions to the private sector.[32] These initial reforms may help to build up support for deeper reforms in the future.

Move at the Right Speed

Some stress the need for a "top-down," politically driven, all-encompassing reform process to address such problems. Thus Werlin,[33] citing the example of countries such as Korea, argues that reforming central bureaucracies is primarily a problem of political will and government capacity to effectively use persuasive and manipulative (rather than coercive and corrupting) forms of power.

Esman,[34] on the other hand, advocates a "bottom-up" approach. He claims that systemwide reforms disrupt familiar routines and threaten established centers of powers without demonstrating convincingly their effectiveness. He prescribes, instead, incremental, confidence-building measures, such as training, new technologies (e.g., e-government), introduced with staff participation and focused at the level of individual programs or organizations. Brautigam[35] makes a related argument that reforms should concentrate on a few critical functions, shifting politically important patronage opportunities to less vital agencies.

Both viewpoints are correct, assuming that in either case a coherent vision is being broadly followed. Reforms need to move "...as fast as possible when circumstances permit, and as slow as necessary when accountability needs to catch up, absorptive capacity to grow, or public tolerance to be rebuilt...."[13] Implementation may need to proceed in many small stages. Some of these can be planned, and scheduled based on priorities and complementarities. Others will proceed based on targets of opportunity.

ADB's policy-based lending to the Kyrgyz Republic in corporate governance and enterprise reform points out the risks of trying to move too fast in the regulatory area. Although regulatory changes were needed to improve performance of key, state-owned enterprises (SOEs), there was only limited success in implementing the changes because of corruption and weak governance in public administration, the financial sector, and the judiciary. Targeted support to address selected aspects of these problems might have helped to build the foundation for broader, more successful SOE reforms at a later stage.[36]

Implement Effectively

Outputs at the early stages of reform may include vision statements, strategies, action plans, frameworks, sectorwide adjustment programs, commitments agreed on at international meetings, reorganizations, and new laws and procedures. However, these are of little value if not properly resourced and implemented. Both development agencies and governments sometimes take such outputs as indications that a challenge has been solved, rather than as a step along the way.[37] For example, Philippine leaders periodically boast of their strong stance against corruption, citing the seven laws and 13 anticorruption agencies instituted to fight graft since the 1950s. Yet because of the overlapping mandates and accountabilities of these agencies, low salaries for public officials, red tape, inconsistent policing, nepotism, and lack of political will, these laws, institutions, and related action plans have not been effective.[38]

Approaches to Reform

Building on the conditions and lessons outlined above, there are two operational approaches that have been successful in some countries: (i) assessing and strengthening capacity, including interagency linkages and (ii) empowering agents of change.

Assessing and Strengthening Capacity, Including Interagency Linkages[d]

Many capabilities are needed for effective public administration and to design and implement reforms, and capacity assessments are key components of the diagnostic work needed. Competitive pay and incentives are necessary, but not sufficient, conditions for building capacity to effectively perform critical tasks. Improving the performance of a task needs to begin with mapping the organizations involved in performing it.[39] The organizational map is the picture of the task network: the organizations with primary responsibility for carrying out the task, those that are less central but still play a role, and those that provide various kinds of support to the performance of the task. The description of interactions between these organizations is important, as is analysis of whether the interactions among the institutions are effective or are an area of capacity weakness. Questions of relationships and coordination among organizations are important here. All the dimensions of capacity need to be viewed from the perspective of the performance of the task.

[d]This draws from conceptual work in Wescott.[40]

The second step involves looking outward from the task network. What contextual factors play a significant role regarding the capacity to perform these tasks, and how do they affect how — and how well — the tasks are performed? At the level just above the task network, the impact of the institutions of the public sector needs to be considered, along with the broader economic, political, and social environment.

The third step focuses on each organization and its human resources. These are closely interwoven, with the human resources a principal component of an organization's capacity, but only as brought together, structured, and utilized by the organization. A profile of the human resource dimension should focus on the recruitment, training, and retention of skilled managerial, professional, and technical personnel. What impact does the organization's human resource profile have on its ability to perform its assigned tasks and reach its goals? What are the human resource strengths and weaknesses?

Whereas the human resource profile of an organization is very important, whether those skilled personnel are effectively utilized is frequently the key to an organization's level of capacity to perform its assigned tasks and reach its goals. This issue focuses analysis on the organizational level, where such factors as the structure of work and authority relations, appraisal and incentive systems, formal and informal behavioral norms, management practices, and leadership influence whether skilled personnel are willing or able to contribute fully to performing the task.

In addition, there are other capacity issues. Does the organization have adequate financial and physical resources to function effectively? Is it organized to use these resources effectively and efficiently to reach its goals? Is it able to interact with other organizations, clients, and other stakeholders?

Capacity strengthening is most effective when it is designed based on a thorough assessment covering the above issues. Evaluations of ADB[41] and other donor agency support to capacity strengthening show that such assessments are often not carried out, and thus the support is less effective than desired. To address these concerns, ADB supported an extensive capacity assessment in 2003 of elected commune councils in Cambodia, and key organizations they work with at national, provincial, and commune levels, prior to making investments in capacity building. Elected commune councils have relatively little decision-making power, and are subject to bureaucratic control from their governor, and from central ministries. Although citizen participation is minimal in commune affairs, survey results suggest that citizens have a favorable impression of their performance. Since commune council members are mainly elderly, conservative men with relatively low levels of education, most have limited capacity for absorbing training. However, commune clerks need enhanced skills to deal with complex programming requirements. Training is also needed to support civil registration of 95 percent of Cambodia's citizens not presently registered. This exercise requires close coordination with commune council chiefs, provincial and district staff, and the Office of Civil Registration and Department of Local Administration (DOLA) of the Ministry of Interior.

DOLA is considering the following priority steps for building capacity: competitive staff incentives, clear strategic direction, new organizational structure aligned with this, and a professional human resource function. Without these, any training provided will mainly contribute to the personal development of staff, and not to the achievement of organizational goals.

Empowering Agents of Change

One element of capacity strengthening deserves special mention: for reforms to take hold, there need to be change agents strategically located in key functional areas to spread new ways of working throughout the public administration system. Such staff need to be carefully selected, provided good working facilities, flexible procedures, and other incentives, good at teaching others on the job, and at networking across organizations.

Such agents of change and their organizational units are different from the "project implementation units" often set up by donor agencies. The latter are set up to be insulated from mainstream administrative systems, on the assumption that this is the best way to prevent corruption and ensure effective delivery of donor support. By contrast, agents of change emerge within existing structures, and work to change them from within, and to spread innovations across government.

For example, the Royal Government of Cambodia began implementing Priority Mission Groups (PMGs) in 2003 as a means of motivating a group of initially 1000 carefully selected officials to facilitate key reform initiatives whereas longer-term civil service reforms were taking hold. PMGs were meant to replace the previous practice of donor agencies topping up the salaries of counterpart officials working on their projects.[42]

In another type of example, the Hyderabad (India) Metropolitan Water Supply & Sewerage Board uses its single window cell (SWC) to reduce corruption for new connections. Previously, applications were made to one of 120 section offices, and then forwarded to 14 other staff before approval, each requiring "speed payments." Under the SWC, the application process is centralized in one, public place, with applications recorded on computers that are difficult for corrupt officials to alter. Staff are motivated to provide good service with distinctive uniforms, modern offices, and individual computer terminals. The service improvement has been praised extensively in the media, which further improves staff motivation.[43]

Key Reform Priorities

With these conditions, lessons, and approaches in mind, one can now review some key reform priorities that have emerged in the region, and have a better basis for analyzing how to tackle them in a given country. This list is not complete, but gives an indication of some leading reform challenges in Asia–Pacific countries.

Government Machinery and Organization

Central Government Organization

Governments need a structure at the center that ensures both coordination and accountability. When there are trade-offs between the two, emphasis should be placed on assigning clear roles and accountabilities. For example, public administration reforms in People's Republic of China since the late 1980s have initially focused on aligning government structures and practices with the needs of a market economy. This has included corporatizing government departments producing goods for the market, and reducing the number of State Council ministries and commissions from 40 to 29 between 1998 and 2001. New personnel practices have also reduced the average age and raised the educational level of cadres, and made the selection process more competitive. Downsizing efforts have not been as successful during this phase, with the number of public employees increasing by 16 percent from 1991 to 1999.[44] By another measure, between 1980 and 1996, administrative costs increased 14.6 times, whereas revenues increased by 5.5 times, thus giving an impetus for future reform.[45]

Central agencies are normally responsible for the regulatory framework covering, *inter alia*, banking, capital markets, utilities, environment, labor, and pensions. The central issue in most countries is not the quality of regulations, but the weaknesses in implementation. Take, for example, ADB's recent support to pension reform in Bangladesh, India, Indonesia, Thailand, and Uzbekistan. Governments drew on this support in the hope that the growth of privately managed pension funds would spur the development of capital markets, and reduce the burden on publicly funded, pay-as-you-go systems. However, an evaluation found that vital preconditions were missing such as qualified regulators, an independent judiciary, capital markets too thin to give reasonable assurance of adequate returns, and fiscal constraints. Initial work should have focused in these areas.[46]

Subnational Government Organization and Decentralization[e]

Decentralization means transferring fiscal, political, and administrative functions from higher to lower levels of government, and can take on different forms depending on the degree to which independence of action is assigned to lower levels of authority. Deconcentration involves central agencies assigning certain functions to lower-level branch offices, and is appropriate when the national government wants to retain control. Delegation takes place when authority for defined tasks is transferred from one public agency to another agency or service provider that is accountable to the former, but not wholly controlled by it, and is appropriate for certain technical functions. Devolution takes place when authority for defined tasks is transferred from a public agency to autonomous, local-level units of elected leadership holding corporate status, granted, for example, under legislation,[f] and is appropriate for functions that are local in scope.

Decentralization is not necessarily a spatial concept requiring reassignment of service delivery responsibilities from higher to lower orders of administration, though this often is the case. Cohen and Peterson[50] emphasize that it is rather the broadening of institutions producing and providing needed goods and services at efficient cost, wherever they are located and whether they are public, quasipublic, or private. A related trend is that many governments are contracting out public services, which gives rise to debate about the consequences for efficiency, through competition and accountability, and through unclear, overlapping mandates.[51]

It is fallacious to presume decentralization indicates an inexorable policy progression from "more" to "less" centralized governance structures, but by conventional measures, decentralization is in its early stages of adoption in the region, despite common commitment in most countries to intensify it and the fact that various "decentralizations" are underway.

A key issue in the region is ensuring that subnational units have sufficient skills and capacity to exercise essential functions. Weak capacity is not a reason for keeping functions at the center that should be decentralized, although it can mean avoiding hasty decentralization until sufficient capacities are in place. For example, ADB is supporting district governments in

---

[e]This section draws from Wescott and Porter[47] (2004).

[f]This categorization as defined by Rondinelli,[48] Leonard and Marshall,[49] and others, is the most widely accepted in the recent literature, although Cohen and Peterson[50] list a long array of alternative definitions.

Indonesia to raise their operational capability. Each participating district is preparing a capacity-building action plan (CB-AP), strengthening service providers (CB-AP) to help implement the plan, and using information and communications technology to support coordination and management. Initial implementation was slow due to the uncertainty whether the project falls under the provision of finance minister decree no. 35/2003 on the channeling of international aid to the regions, which was issued in January 2003 one month after the loan was approved by ADB Board. After a six-month consultation between ADB, Ministry of Home Affairs, and Ministry of Finance, it was agreed that the project should be the responsibility of the central Government (Ministry of Home Affairs), not regional governments. Article 112 of Law no. 22/1999 stipulates that the empowerment of regional government under decentralization (such as capacity building) is the responsibility of central government.

By mid-2004, it is expected that 14 district CB-APs will be approved by their regional parliaments. Procurement of service providers to implement the CB-APs will start immediately and 14 contracts are expected to be awarded at the fourth quarter of 2004. The formulation of CB-AP will be done through a participatory process involving media, civil society, and private sector. The project will also support a change to the focus of government personnel training from structural into technical- and competency-based training.[g]

In Vietnam, as part of the ADB-supported PAR program, processing and clearing procedures for ships using the Ho Chi Minh City Sea Port are now handled by one agency rather than six, and require only nine rather than 36 documents, reducing clearance time from 6 hours per agency to only 30–60 minutes per ship. Likewise, in Quang Tri Province, the time for issuing land tenure certificates has been reduced from 91 to 23 days for urban land and from 90 to 13 days for rural land. One-stop-shop systems have been set up in 35 out of 64 provinces to allow citizens and businesses better access to government, and expansion to all provinces is planned.[52] A sample survey of citizens and officials in 20 districts and 40 communes reveals that there have been widespread benefits from simplification of administrative procedures through similar, "one-stop, one-door" models. Citizens benefit by spending less time waiting and traveling, and having better information provided to them. However, progress has been uneven; more prosperous jurisdictions have benefited more than poor ones, and poor and vulnerable groups, ethnic minorities and women benefit less than other groups. For example, even though more efficient local administrations can now deliver

---

[g]Personal communication from Syahrul Luddin, ADB Jakarta.

birth and land use right certificates, and other documents faster than before, poor people still cannot afford the charge.

Managing Public Sector Resources

Central Government

Sound public expenditure management (PEM) aims to control expenditures with available revenues, to allocate funds so that policies and programs are adequately funded, and to ensure efficient and effective implementation. Budgets should be comprehensive, and given adequate time for preparation, transparent consultation, and due process. Reliable revenue forecasts are crucial for ensuring budget realism. Adequate accounting and other systems should be in place to facilitate good budget execution and audit.

ADB supports this process at both core and sector levels. For example, in Mongolia, ADB helped set up an outcome-based PEM system to provide the needed backbone for planned public administration reforms. The system (i) links medium-term planning with annual budgeting, (ii) establishes credible hard budget constraints on aggregate and sectoral spending, and (iii) incorporates contingent liabilities as an integral part of the annual budget. In PRC, ADB supported the formulation and adoption of auditing standards and procedures that conform to PRC's Audit Law and international auditing standards. Auditors from China's National Audit Office (CNAO) were trained in the application of audit standards through courses and study tours to various private audit firms and supreme audit institutions in the region. They also learned about risk-based audit methods, planning processes, and evaluation of internal controls. The audit training programs developed will continue to be used to improve adherence by CNAO auditors to the revised government auditing standards and procedures. The auditors also introduced measures to ensure continued compliance. These measures comprised establishing systems for accountability, quality review, and incentives. CNAO reported that effective results could be seen and are drawing increasing public attention.

An example at the sector level is ADB's support to Royal Government of Cambodia in managing its comprehensive sectorwide education reform program. To support a doubling of government spending over the period 2001–2003, ADB provided technical support to ensure improved spending effectiveness, including: (i) systemic and targeted programs aimed at the poorest families and communes; (ii) targeted facilities development programs in underserved areas; (iii) new financial planning processes that directly link policy priorities to annual budget allocations; and (iv) introduction of new accounting and audit procedures covering 15 programs across around 250 budget holding institutions and departments. As part of this process, procedures have been developed to underpin delegated spending authority to over 6500 primary and secondary schools. An annual financial performance review process has been introduced in 2003 to identify future capacity-building gaps and staff development programs.

Subnational Government

The benefits of decentralization can only be achieved if local authorities have clear fiscal responsibilities, and the means to carry them out. Careful consideration is also needed for the impact of fiscal decentralization on poverty and regional balance, and appropriate measures instituted as necessary to ensure adequate service standards across all jurisdictions.

For example, following the election of over 126,000 new councilors in Pakistan in 2001, district governments are responsible for elementary and secondary education, and primary and secondary health. They can raise some additional revenues, whereas Provincial Finance Commissions authorize transfers from provincial funds. Improving access to justice has been a priority, with additional funding provided to subordinate courts and police services. Although these reforms are significant, there are still many remaining challenges, including cumbersome budget execution procedures and uneven provincial cash flow.[53]

Since the enactment of the 1991 Local Government Code, intergovernmental transfers in the Philippines from central to local authorities have increased from about 3 to 18 percent of the total government budget. Over 70,000 personnel were transferred from central to local agencies, including 60 percent of personnel of the Ministries of Agriculture and Health. Many services were transferred to local authorities, including agricultural extension and research, health, social welfare, and local infrastructure provision. However, the outcome has been mixed. On the plus side, local governments have more predictable and transparent financing than in the past, allowing them to pursue a range of innovative reforms, some of which have won international awards.[h] However, there has been no comprehensive effort to assess local government performance, so the overall record is unknown. The generous revenue allotments have contributed to an unsustainably high national budget deficit, and possibly allowed many local authorities to avoid collecting local taxes.[54]

---

[h]Mayor Jesse M. Robredo of Naga City won the Magsaysay award in 2000 "for his giving credence to the promise of democracy by demonstrating that effective city management is compatible with yielding power to the people." See http://www.rmaf.org.ph/FRAMES.HTML

Procurement

Systems work best when they are simple and transparent, and managed by competent officials and clear organizational arrangements. Many countries in the region have centralized, overly complex systems that often only exacerbate the corrupt practices they are intended to control. Government agencies with such procedures need to go through a lengthy process of securing funds, seeking competitive tenders, and awarding contracts. This lengthy process leads to different problems concerning, for example, procurement of ICT systems. To prevent undue influence of any one official, many decisions along the way are made by committees, which can lead to an unclear focus as compromises are made. In addition, a result of the lengthy process is that when acquisitions are made, the technology has often moved far beyond where it was when the project was first conceived. Thus, governments often install outdated systems. They also pay excessive prices, because new products may have come to the market during the long tender review that can deliver the same ICT power for much less money. The difference between the outdated tender price and the market price is also an arbitrage opportunity for corrupt officials.[55]

A study[56] of procurement practices in the Philippines allows one to estimate the exposure of ADB projects to potential losses from corruption. The prequalification stage is the most subjective, and therefore an area at great risk to corruption. Payments are made by bidders to be prequalified. Bidders also agree at this stage who will win the bid, with others stepping aside in return for payment. Bidders may also collude with public officials to have competitors disqualified on false grounds. In the civil works area, foreign consultants reportedly pay 5–10 percent of the contract value to "buy" a contract. This increases the cost of the contract, and reduces quality by discouraging many qualified bidders. Contractors may also have to pay to expedite permits, licenses and approvals, certification for payment, contract revisions or variations, quarry royalties over and above those officially negotiated, to the consultants' site staff for approval of work done, to expedite progress and escalation payments, to help agreement on the final measurement, and to approve the final handover. Although specific payments can rarely be proven, the wide consensus that they do helps explain the low quality of work frequently observed. Table 23.1 provides estimates of exposure for ADB civil works projects and goods procurement.

To address such problems, Mongolia instituted a Public Procurement Law in 2000. Bidders usually have 4–6 weeks to prepare bids, and evaluation and selection usually take another month. For domestically financed projects, the total process rarely lasts longer than 2 or 3 months. The results of major tenders are made public and unsuccessful bidders are informed of

Table 23.1 Exposure to Graft of ADB-Financed Projects in the Philippines in Civil Works and Procurement of Goods

	Percent of Project Cost	
Area	*Civil Works*	*Supply of Goods*
Project selection	0	0
Bidding stage		
Prequalification	5	5
Evaluation, negotiation, and award	5	0
Conduct of works and delivery of goods		
Permits, licenses, approvals	10	5
Contract administration	10	5
Financial management	0	0
Total	30	15

Source: ADB.[56]

results. Most tender exercises to date have generated a good deal of interest and multiple bids, which one hopes is leading to price competitiveness.

Pay and Employment

Governments need a workforce of the right size and skills, which is motivated, honest, accountable, efficient, effective, and responsive. This is a challenge for developed countries, and more so for developing ones in Asia–Pacific. Internal accountability mechanisms may not be sufficient when officials collude with each other and with politicians, whereas outward accountability faces challenges of weak democratic traditions and systems. Public sectors are overstaffed and underpaid, thus limiting motivation and further encouraging graft. Personnel management systems are politicized and without a strong emphasis on merit or performance. Training is not well targeted, and often granted as a political favor rather than to build capacity.

Despite these formidable challenges, some countries in the region are making headway. The Republic of the Marshall Islands reduced the unsustainable size of its civil service by 30 percent with ADB support between 1996 and 2000, although it subsequently increased by 20 percent. Because of other personnel issues remaining to be addressed, the quality of public services has declined.[57,58] The Federated States of Micronesia also reduced the size of its civil service by 22 percent during FY1997 and 1998, and a 28 percent savings in wage bill costs.[59] This helped to reverse a situation of economic decline (4.5 percent in 1997 to 6 percent growth in 2000). Public services have weakened in some areas (education) but not in others (health).

Improving Performance

Although improving the performance of public services is a goal widely supported across many different stakeholders in the region, determining how to achieve it is not easy. There are many ways to improve performance, including use of quantitative and qualitative indicators, dialogue, report cards, peer pressure, incentives, and sanctions. Performance measures should be simple and normally brought in without disrupting normal administrative and budgetary systems.

Take, for example, the road sector in Cambodia. Since the end of hostilities in the early 1990s, Cambodia and its development partners have improved about one third of primary and secondary roads to a point where they can be maintained, and about two fifth of tertiary roads. Yet survey results indicate that while 40.7 percent of primary roads were in good or better condition in 2001, only 7.7 percent of secondary national roads were at this standard, and 6.5 percent of provincial and urban roads, because of poor maintenance. To improve this performance, development partners have recommended a unified planning and budgeting process, use of analytical tools in making inputs to the planning and budgeting process, greater transparency in investment and procurement decisions. Although these recommendations make sense in principle, the reality on the ground is that many transport planning and strategy documents are prepared only in the local Khymer language, and thus not fully understood by donors. Before donors push Cambodia toward new administrative systems, they themselves need a better understanding of the local systems already in place, and their strengths and weaknesses.

An approach to productivity improvement being adopted in some regional countries is results-based management (RBM),[i] which typically includes the following elements: (i) a focus on desired results; (ii) indicators to measure progress made toward these results; (iii) the ability to use information on results to manage operations and resources to improve future performance; (iv) holding relevant staff accountable for results; (v) recruitment and promotion of staff based on merit; and (vi) staff awareness and ownership.[60] For example, since 1999, 49 agencies in Thailand have adopted RBM to improve performance.[61] Notions of improving performance by measuring results originated in the private sector. Yet both private and public organizations have found it difficult to adopt this approach.[62,63]

---

[i]See footnote c for some related approaches.

ADB has been facilitating education ministries in Cambodia and Mongolia to develop result-oriented sector performance management capacity-building plans. In Cambodia, a key aspect of results-based monitoring has been the development of a joint annual sector review process, including the involvement of a recently formed non-government organization (NGO) education partnership to formally participate in the process. The annual review includes formation of joint ministry, donor, or NGO working groups who jointly assess performance and make recommendations for improving sector results. A follow-up Education Forum involves a range of stakeholders, including provincial governors and National Assembly officials.

In Mongolia, the focus of ADB-supported, RBM development is the introduction of performance agreements at central, aimag, and school levels. The objective of these agreements is to develop an inclusive process for results-oriented planning, management, and monitoring. The leadership of the process by the minister and provincial governors is designed to ensure accountability to a range of stakeholders. In particular, the school performance agreements directly involve communities and parents in annual target setting, development planning, and monitoring, using the results of the year's work, as a basis for revising school development plans.[j]

In a more developed example, the system of program agreements adopted in Malaysia, starting in 1990 provides contracts between implementing agencies and the Treasury. Agency performance is evaluated at the end of each year against targets for output and impact; substandard performance necessitates preparation of an "exception report." Agencies are given flexibility to move spending within their budget ceiling. The system has some shortcomings: it does not set priorities among results achieved, it does not vary penalties depending on the extent to which the target is missed, and it does not cover non-Treasury funded areas. Still, the system has reportedly improved efficiency and client satisfaction.[64]

However, such measures need to be used carefully. In the quest to achieve measurable results, there is a risk of quick fixes that are not sustainable, attaining measurable targets of questionable benefit (e.g., downsizing staff and rehiring the same staff as consultants), and setting up unreasonable expectations for change that cannot be met.[65] There is also the risk that perception will diverge from reality.

Laws and regulations enacted may not be enforced. Anticorruption units may focus on eliminating political opponents. Policy makers may ventriloquize commitment to donor-supported policy changes, giving the impression of local ownership of reforms; yet their actual views may be directly opposite. Expatriate advisors may be used not to train counterparts, but to

[j]Personal communication from Dr. Claudia Buentjen, ADB.

carry out policy formulation and coordination roles, thus sidelining counterparts, who are seen by insecure rulers as potential threats if they know too much. Staff given specialized training may be transferred to assignments where the training is irrelevant for the same reason, thus perpetuating problems of low government effectiveness. Thus, one needs to be careful what results one measures, and what inferences are drawn.[66]

Conclusion

Drawing from ADB's experience since 1995 in the Asia–Pacific region, we have examined five conditions that are needed for administrative reforms to take hold: (i) leadership; (ii) vision; (iii) selectivity; (iv) sensitivity; and (v) stamina, with examples of each. Improving public administration is one of the most difficult challenges facing governments and their development partners, because of the complexity of the processes, the wide variation in context, and the difficulties in measuring reform outputs and outcomes. The paper considers four broad lessons: (i) begin with diagnostic work; (ii) test for readiness; (iii) move at the right speed; and (iv) implement effectively.

Building on the conditions and lessons outlined above, there are two operational approaches that have been successful in some countries: (i) assessing and strengthening capacity including interagency linkages; and (ii) empowering agents of change. With these conditions, lessons, and approaches in mind, this chapter reviews examples of two administrative reform priorities in the region: (i) strengthening government machinery and organization (e.g., central government organization, subnational government organization and decentralization, and other government bodies); and (ii) managing public sector resources (e.g., central government, subnational government, procurement, pay and employment, and improving performance).

The public administration reform experiences in Asia–Pacific and other regions have improved our understanding of what works and what does not, what practices are transferable, and under what conditions. The successes and failures of reforms are better understood than in the past with the help of cross-border reform networks, international agencies, think tanks, consultants, media, and scholars. However, genuine evaluation of reforms using rigorous social science techniques is rare. Reasons include the difficulties of proving cause-and-effect relationships because of problems of multiple attribution, lack of baseline data, lack of robust, experimental designs, lack of agreed conceptual frameworks and language for reform, methodological difficulties of comparing reform outcomes with counterfactuals, and the tradition of public management research focusing on prescription rather than explanation and analysis.[67,68] Fully cognizant of the methodological challenges, greater investment is needed in more rigorous research on how to achieve high performance by the public sector in Asia–Pacific. Such research would lead to better prescriptions, and a better return on the considerable investment in reform by governments and international agencies.

References[k]

1. ADB (1995). *Governance: Sound Development Management.* Manila: ADB. pp. R151–R195.
2. Wescott, C. (2004). "Improving public administration in the ASIA-Pacific region: lessons, approaches and reform priorities." *International Public Management Review*, 5(2): 78–102.
3. Wolfensohn, J.D. (1996). "People and development." World Bank–IMF Annual Meetings Address. October 1, 1996. Washington, D.C.
4. World Bank (1991). *Managing Development: The Governance Dimension.* Washington, D.C.: World Bank.
5. World Bank (1992). *Governance and Development.* Washington, D.C.: World Bank.
6. World Bank (1994). *Governance: The World Bank's Experience.* Washington, D.C.: World Bank.
7. Williamson, J. (2003). "From reform agenda to damaged brand name: a short history of the Washington consensus and suggestions for what to do next." *Finance and Development*, 40(3): 10–13.
8. Mathiasen, D.G. (1999). "The new public management and its critics." *International Public Management Journal*, 2(1): 90–111.
9. Sharma, U. and Hoque, Z. (2002). "TQM implementation in a public sector entity in Fiji." *The International Journal of Public Sector Management*, 15(5): 340–360.
10. Jones, L.R. (2002). "A comparative analysis of the development of performance-based management systems in Dutch and Norwegian local government." *International Public Management Journal*, 5(1): 15–53.
11. ADB (2003). "A progress report on implementation of ADB's governance action plan in ADF borrowers," March 2003. Technical Document Prepared for ADF VIII Midterm Review Meeting, 14–15 April 2003, Washington, D.C.
12. Political & Economic Risk Consultancy (PERC) (2004). "Civil liberties & political rights in Asia." *Asian Intelligence*, vol 650. Hong Kong: Political & Economic Risk Consultancy Ltd.
13. Schiavo-Campo, S. and Sundaram, P. (2001) *To Serve and to Preserve: Improving Public Administration in the Competitive World.* Manila: ADB (online). Available: http://www.adb.org/documents/manuals/serve_and_preserve/default.asp
14. Barzelay, M. (2003). "Introduction: the process dynamics of public management policymaking." *International Public Management Journal*, 6(3): 251–282.

[k]Web sites accessed February 2005.

15. ADB (1999). "Republic of Vanuatu." In Kapman, B. and Saldanha, C. (eds.) *Reforms in the Pacific*. Manila: ADB. pp. 143–168 (online). Available: http://www.adb.org/Documents/Books/Reforms_Pacific/chap7.pdf
16. ADB (2002). *Country Strategy and Program Update (2003–2005) Vanuatu*. Manila: ADB (online). Available: http://adb.org/Documents/CSPs/VAN/2002/CSP_VAN_2002.pdf
17. ADB (2000). *Technical Assistance to the Islamic Republic of Pakistan for Fiscal Decentralization*. Manila: ADB.
18. Wescott, C. (2003). "Hierarchies, networks and local government in Viet Nam." *International Public Management Review*, 4(2) (online). Available: www.ipmr.net
19. Hirschmann, D. (2003). "Aid dependence, sustainability and technical assistance." *Public Management Review*, 5(2): 225–244.
20. ADB (2002). Support Implementation of the Public Administration Reform master program. Manila: ADB (online). available http://adb.org/Documents/RRPs/VIE/rrp_vie_35343.pdf
21. Bhatnagar, S. (2000). *Land/Property Registration IN Andhra Pradesh*. Washington: World Bank (online). Available: http://www1.worldbank.org/publicsector/egov/cardcs.htm
22. Beschell, R.P. (2003). "Civil service reform in India." In Howes, S., Lahiri, A. and Stern, N. (eds.) *State-Level Reforms in India: Towards More Effective Government*. New Delhi: Macmillan India. pp. 233–255.
23. ADB and Cambodia Development Resources Institute (2000). *Cambodia: Enhancing Governance for Sustainable Development*. Manila: ADB. (online) Available: http://www.adb.org/Documents/Books/Cambodia_Enhancing_Governance/default.asp?p = govpub
24. World Bank (2002). *Russian Civil Service Reform (History of Reform Attempts from 1992 to 2000)*. Moscow: World Bank (online). Available: http://www.worldbank.org.ru/ECA/Russia.nsf/ECADocByUnid/460CDD2633162966C3256E24004BC004
25. World Bank (2004). "Russia: programmatic TA/ESW support to administrative and civil service reform," February, Progress Report.
26. ADB (2005). *Country Governance Assessments*. (online). Available: http://www.adb.org/governance/gov_publications.asp#country_governance
27. Kaufmann, D. (2004). "Rethinking governance: empirical lessons challenge orthodoxy," Discussion Draft, World Bank.
28. Nunberg, B. and Nellis, J. (1995). *Civil Service Reform and the World Bank*, World Bank Discussion Paper, no. 161, Washington, D.C.: The World Bank.
29. Reich, M.R. and Cooper, D.M. (1995). *Political Mapping*, version 1.2, software for windows, Boston: Harvard School of Public Health.
30. Gillespie, P. et al. (1996). "This great evil: anticipating political obstacles to development." *Public Administration and Development*, 16(5): 431–453.
31. Montgomery, J. (1996). "Bureaucrat, heal thyself! lessons from three administrative reforms." *World Development*, 24(5): 953–960.
32. ADB (2003). *Country Strategy and Program Update 2004–2006 Nepal*. Manila: ADB (online). Available: http://adb.org/Documents/CSPs/NEP/2003/CSP_NEP_2003.pdf

33. Werlin, H. (1992). "Linking decentralization and centralization: a critique of the new development administration." *Public Administration and Development*, 12(October): 223–235.
34. Esman (1991). *Management Dimensions of Development — Perspectives and Strategies.* West Hartford, CT: Kumarian Press, Inc.
35. Brautigam, D. (1996). "State capacity and effective governance." In Ndulu, B. and Walle, N. (eds.) *Agenda for Africa's Economic Renewal.* Washington, D.C.: Transaction Publishers for the Overseas Development Council.
36. ADB (2003). *Program Performance Audit Report on the Corporate Governance and Enterprise Reform Program in the Kyrgyz Republic.* Manila: ADB (online). Available: http://adb.org/Documents/PPARs/KGZ/ppar_kyr_IN17–04.pdf
37. Easterly, W. (2002). "The cartel of good intentions: bureaucracy versus markets in foreign aid." Washington: Center for Global Development, Institute for International Economics. March.
38. Quah, J.S.T. (2003). *Curbing Corruption in Asia: A Comparative Study of Six Countries.* Singapore: Eastern Universities Press.
39. Hilderbrand, M.E. and Grindle, M.S. (1995). "Building sustainable capacity in the public sector: what can be done?" *Public Administration and Development*, 155: 441–463.
40. Wescott, C. (1999). "Guiding principles on civil service reform in Africa: an empirical review." *The International Journal of Public Sector Management*, 12(2): 145–170.
41. ADB (1997). *Review of the Bank's Technical Assistance Operations.* Manila: ADB.
42. World Bank and ADB (2003). *Enhanced Service Delivery through Improved Resource Allocation and Institutional Reform.* Washington and Manila: World Bank and ADB.
43. Davis, J. (2004). "Corruption in public service delivery: experience from South Asia's water and sanitation sector." *World Development*, 32(1): 53–72.
44. ADB (2003). *Development Management: Progress and Challenges in the People's Republic of China.* Manila: ADB.
45. Straussman, J.D. and Zhang, M. (2001). "Chinese administrative reforms in international perspective." *International Journal of Public Sector Management*, 14(5): 411–422.
46. ADB (2003). *Technical Assistance Performance Audit Report on the Reform of Pension and Provident Funds in Selected Developing Member Countries.* Manila: ADB (online). Available: http://adb.org/Documents/TPARS/REG/tpar_-reg_2003-31.pdf
47. Wescott, C. and Porter, D. (2004). "Fiscal Decentralization and Citizen Participation in East Asia." In Licha, I. (ed.) *Citizens in Charge: Managing Local Budgets in East Asia and Latin America.* Washington: Inter-American Development Bank (online). Available: http://www.adb.org/Governance/fiscal_decentralization.pdf
48. Rondinelli, D.A., Nellis, J.R. and Cheema, G.S. (1983). *Decentralization in Developing Countries: A Review of the Experience.* Washington, D.C.: World Bank, Staff Working Paper no. 581.

49. Leonard, D. and Marshall, D.R. (eds.) (1982). *Institutions of Rural Development for the Poor.* Berkeley: University of California, Institute of International Studies.
50. Cohen, J. and Peterson, S. (1999). *Beyond Administrative Decentralization Strategies for Developing Countries.* West Hartford, CT: Kumarian Press.
51. Milward, H.B. and Provan, K.G. (2003). "Managing the hollow state: collaboration and contracting." *Public Management Review*, 5(1): 1–18.
52. ADB (2004). *Country Strategy and Program Update 2005–2007 Viet Nam.* Manila: ADB.
53. Manning, N., Porter, D., Charlton, J., Cyan, M. and Hasnain, Z. (2003) "Devolution in Pakistan — preparing for service delivery improvements," A Working Paper Prepared for the Forum on Intergovernmental Relations and Service Delivery in Pakistan, 27–29 June.
54. Diokno, B. (2003). "Decentralization in the Philippines after ten years: what have we learned? what have I learned?" Paper Presented at the Asian Development Conference, Kitakyushu City, Fukuoka Prefecture, Japan, November 10–11.
55. Wescott, C. (2003). "E-Government: supporting public sector reform and poverty reduction in the Asia-Pacific region." In Howes, S., Lahiri, A. and Stern, N. (eds.) *State-Level Reforms in India: Towards More Effective Government.* New Delhi: Macmillan India.
56. ADB (2002). *Philippine Project Implementation Report.* ADB: Manila.
57. ADB (2002). *Country Strategy and Program Update (2003–2005). The Marshall Islands.* Manila: ADB.
58. ADB (2004). *Program Completion Report: Fiscal and Financial Management Program (Marshall Islands).* Manila: ADB.
59. ADB (2003). *Program Performance Audit Report on the Public Sector Reform Program (Loan 1520-FSM[SF]) in the Federated States of Micronesia.* Manila: ADB (online). Available: http://adb.org/Documents/PPARs/FSM/ppar_fsm_29657.pdf
60. ADB (2003). "Enhancing effectiveness: managing for development results." Discussion Paper. Manila: ADB.
61. World Bank (2003). *Thailand Economic Monitor.* Bangkok: World Bank.
62. Ittner, C.D. and Larcker, D.F. (2003). "Coming up short on non-financial performance measurement." *Harvard Business Review*, November: 88–95.
63. De Bruijn, H. (2002). "Performance measurement in the public sector: strategies to cope with the risks of performance measurement." *International Journal of Public Sector Management*, 15(7): 578–594.
64. Trivedi, P. (2004). "Program agreements in Malaysia: instrument for enhancing government performance and accountability," World Bank, Draft Paper.
65. Brinkerhoff, D. (2000). "Democratic governance and sectoral policy reform: tracing linkages and exploring synergies." *World Development*, 28(4): 601–615.
66. Wescott, C. (2001). Measuring governance in developing Asia. In Jones, L., Guthrie, J. and Steane, P. (eds.) *Learning from International Public Management Reform.* Oxford: JAI — Elsevier Science.

67. Kelman, S., Thompson, F., Jones, L.R. and Schedler, K. (2003). "Dialogue on definition and evolution of the field of public management." *International Public Management Review*, 4(2): 1–19. (online). Available: www.ipmr.net
68. Jones, L.R. and Kettl, D.F. (2003). "Assessing public management reform in an international context." *International Public Management Review*, 4(1): 1–19. (online). Available: www.ipmr.net

Chapter 24

Recent Major Administrative Reforms: Japan's Response to Global and Domestic Challenges

Yuko Kaneko and Itoko Suzuki

CONTENTS

Introduction

Japanese government has recently organized major administrative reforms to adapt its public administration to the emerging challenges both from international and domestic communities. The reform agenda included the areas of restructuring, privatization, decentralization, strengthening of the local government, creation of incorporated administrative agencies, civil service improvement, promotion of e-governance, etc. The reforms are directed at strengthening the leadership of the government, central and local, to promote accountability, transparency, and participation of the civil society, and to make public administration responsive and responsible to new issues of social equity, efficiency, and effectiveness. This chapter will focus on these current reform efforts that began in 1996 in Japan, analyze the several factors that make these the most comprehensive and drastic major administrative reforms a reality, and draw innovations of administrative reform undertakings as lessons of experiences that may be of use to the future major administrative reforms in Japan and elsewhere.

Administrative State and Administrative Reforms as Social Innovations in Japan

As late Prof. Yasuo Watanabe, an eminent Japanese scholar in public administration, asserted, administrative reform is a continuing process as long as civilization unfolds. In more specific terms, Herbert Emmerich (1950, pp. 1–3) once stated that administrative reform would take place whenever there is a change in the size, the distribution and the nature of the executive functions, or their staffing and financing. Administrative reforms comprise both major administrative reforms and continuing changes in functions and structure brought about by less generalized and less comprehensive reforms. It could be used synonymously with administrative improvements that are taking place on a daily basis. Administrative improvement is a long-range and continuing undertaking. Some administrative improvement efforts organized in the name of administrative management may be integrated in its broad sense as part of administrative reform. These continuous efforts may be reinforced by landmark activities, which may be called major administrative reform, defined as a normative undertaking of a comprehensive nature deliberately organized to bridge the gap between desirability and reality in public administration, usually, with the establishment of an extra-bureaucratic investigation or review organ.[1]

Public administration inherently suffers from time lag. In an administrative state such as Japan, because of the importance of public administration systems in the national and local governments as well as their impact on individual people's lives, many governments have strived to remove this time lag to accelerate administrative improvement. Such efforts include

[1]Suzuki, I. (1980). Administrative Reforms in Japan, 1962–1964, Ph.D. dissertation, US Microfilm, Inc., New York, in which the references are cited on definition of administrative reform, UN ESA, *Interregional Seminar on Major Administrative Reforms in Developing Countries*, Report (ST/TAO/M/62). p. 10; Leemans, A.F. ed. (1976) *The Management of Change in Government*. The Hague: Maritinus Nijhoff. p. 61 and pp. 64–65.

major administrative reforms. In fact, according to one of our founding fathers of modern public administration (Mosher, 1978) one important feature of public administration in the 20th century was administrative reform. Japan was not an exception.

In Japan, public administration has in fact been dominant in the country's governance system which initiated modernization and economic development during the 1868 Meiji Restoration. It was particularly so when the government clearly selected industrialization and strong armament as national objectives in the prewar era, and when Japan adopted accelerated economic growth without arms and military expenditures after World War II, especially after 1960. Japanese public administration's initiatives and roles in the national modernization and development process may have been incomparable to those of other countries.

It is often said that the entire modernization and industrialization process of Japan occurred under the leadership of so-called modernizing elites or higher civil servants as technocrats. Whereas the postwar Japanese governance system is based on a parliamentary democracy, and it has market economy, the system has been strikingly involved in administrative leadership and guidance in its operations. Up until the mid-1980s, an important characteristic of the Japanese government in the last century was the increased role and size of the public sector. Bureaucracy and public administration systems had expanded with the advent of new technological changes, increasing complexity of political and social systems, and adoption of national planning. When the national goals are clear and shared by the majority of the people and the political process is stable, the governance can be left to the public administration as the more important influencing mechanism of quality and outcome of national activities. It has also influenced the existence of government. In Japan, the security of political power in a particular regime had become increasingly dependent on the content of public policies formulated by public administration, rather than the representatives of the political power (Suzuki, 1980).

It is only in recent years that administrative guidance has become weakened, and instead, citizens and the private sector have now required vigorous evaluation of what public administration and government are doing. At least until the collapse of the bubble economy in the middle of the last decade, the Japanese governance system was more generally characterized in a trilateral cooperative system of higher civil servants, political leaders, and big business leaders. In this axiomatic relationship, higher civil servants and their bureaucratic organizations had played a significant role to pursue the national goal. Foreign critique used to call this system "Japan Incorporated".[2]

---

[2]Kaplan, E.J. (1972). *Japan: the Government–Business Relationship.* Washington D.C.: U.S. Government Printing.

Due to a leading role of the bureaucracy in managing national resources and the opportunities of society, administrative reform meant a great deal to not only public administration, but also private sector management. Bureaucracy served, though indirectly, other economic and social institutions in Japan in addition to public sector institutions. Many major administrative reforms have taken place in Japan since the end of World War II. These administrative reforms constantly generated not only administrative innovations such as constant review of the range and level of government activities, abolishing or transforming government regulations, and changing the central–local government relations but also social innovations such as a more competitive market and the development of nonprofit organizations.[3]

Background for the Hashimoto Major Administrative Reforms

The major administrative reforms that are discussed in this chapter are also indicative of the administrative and social innovations that occurred during a particular time in Japan. Before the cessation of the Cold War, Japan has become one of the world's most affluent countries under the postwar world order. When Japan was rising upward in economic success and when the state aim was to catch up with the rest of world, politicians could leave their steering to the bureaucracy, as because of the end of the war, there was no other ideology other than the economic development and promoting market-oriented society. In the past 50 years, living standards have improved remarkably. Then the people's attitude toward the government started to change and began to demand more and in increasingly diversified areas, such as customers seeking efficiency and responsiveness in government and public administration as that enjoyed in the economic sector management.

Japan became an aging society in 1970 and turned into an aged society in 1994, where the elder citizens (65 years old and over) accounted for more than 14 percent of the population. Now the population is continuously aging although the people's needs for public services are increasingly getting more diversified. In 2004, Japanese population in age of 65 years and above accounted for 20 percent, and will soon reach 25 percent. Domestic challenges coupled with the cessation of the bubbly economy that features bankruptcies, big ban, and the end of the lifetime employment, and these domestic predicaments are coupled with the international challenges of globalization.

---

[3]Gerald Caiden examined relations between social change and administrative reforms in his book, *Administrative Reform*. Chicago: Aldine. 1969, pp. 43–71.

After the Cold War ended, the political and ideological confrontation, which once existed among countries and hindered free economic activities, was destroyed. International money flow evolved greatly and money began to move almost freely to more lucrative markets seeking financial gains beyond the national borders. With the deepening of such economic globalization, every government is forced to examine and reform economic structures and systems, and government functions and organizations.

At the same time, technological development in every field has been changing the world greatly. Recently, technological innovations in the fields of transportation and telecommunication, in particular, have been facilitating globalization. Information and communication technologies are advancing rapidly and with the development of the Internet, it has become much easier for the ordinary citizens to explore, transmit, and distribute information across the world. E-government and transparency of government operations are now making different sets of government and public administration process.

These are the circumstances in which the Hashimoto major administrative reforms were organized, which paralleled with the other streams of governance reforms — local, economic, and social. In September 1996, Prime Minister Hashimoto propagated that 23 ministries and agencies were to be reorganized into about half the number of ministries. He asserted that the current government structure was so compartmentalized that appropriate allocation of tasks and coordination became difficult, when the challenges for the emerging needs for public administration were so much diversified.

During the general election of the House of Representatives held in October 1996, the reform of ministries and agencies was put on every political party's election platform and these party pledges had become a major contesting issue in the national election. After winning this election, in November 1996, Prime Minister Hashimoto established the Administrative Reform Council as an advisory body, a usual procedure to undertake the major administrative reform in Japan since 1962, but this time, under the direct control of the prime minister himself. The council started its deliberation to study the roles and functions of the government to be suitable for the 21st century to examine how the central government ministries and agencies should be reorganized, and to consider how to strengthen the functions of the prime minister and the cabinet to empower political authorities than the then still strong bureaucratic power.

In December 1997, about a year after its establishment, the council made its final report on the major administrative reform. The contemplated reform indicated that the Japanese government would, at the turn of the century, carry out the most radical government reform in these 50 years, to cope up with the new challenges that resulted from the economic and social development, which took place over many years, from the emerging aging population society, and from the continuing globalization and instability of the world.

This chapter deals with not only the content of these major administrative reforms, but also the procedures of the reform that have taken place from planning to implementation that is still continuing. The various initiatives have been interlinked and function complementarily, involving comprehensive administrative reform of the central and local government reforms, and other decentralization movements, as well as various economic and social reforms. The comprehensive governance reforms have been put in place in parallel efforts with the administrative reforms in Japan of which 1996 Hashimoto major administrative reform was the most significant part that has been inherited and followed up by the current Prime Minister Koizumi.

Procedures of the Hashimoto Major Administrative Reforms

Firstly, the procedures that took place for the Hashimoto reforms will be analyzed. Prime Minister Hashimoto is a ranking politician of the government party, who has a long experience with government systems, organizations, and practices, and already had rich experience in administrative reforms. Before he became the prime minister, he had been convinced of the need for a very drastic restructuring of the central government bureaucracy including restructuring of ministries and agencies. Notably, the following events took place for the Hashimoto major administrative reforms.

Major Administrative Reforms as an Election Pledge

Before and during the election campaign for the House of Representatives in 1996, Prime Minister Hashimoto made pledges to overhaul the central government machinery.

Creation of an Advisory Body by Cabinet Order

After winning the general election, Prime Minister Hashimoto created the Administrative Reform Council as an advisory body for the prime minister. Different from previously organized advisory bodies for administrative reforms, which were created by law, the cabinet order this time established the Administrative Reform Council. The prime minister himself became the chairman of the council, and the Minister for Administrative Reform (the Director-General of the Management and Coordination Agency[4]) was appointed as the vice-chairman.

Prime Minister Hashimoto took the leadership during the deliberations of the Council. It was very rare in Japan for a prime minister himself to chair his advisory body and to take active leadership in it. Because ex-government officials were not included in the council members this time, Prime Minister Hashimoto himself was the most knowledgeable about the systems and operations of the central government among the council members. Former chairman of the Headquarters for the Promotion of Administrative Reform of the Liberal Democratic Party (government party) became the prime minister's assistant in charge of the administrative reform, and was appointed as a member of the Administrative Reform Council and also as the director of the secretariat for the Administrative Reform Council. Even though core members of the secretariat were seconded from the Management and Coordination Agency and other government agencies, young professional staff was also recruited from outside the bureaucracy.

Creating the Administrative Reform Council by the cabinet order allowed the prime minister to start the deliberation as early as possible and to choose members as freely as possible. The choice of the council members including the prime minister and the minister for administrative reform as core members of the council, appeared accelerating the decision-making process of the council even on controversial issues and critical points, obviously also facilitated the earlier transition of reform process from a deliberating stage to an implementing stage.

Accelerated Process of Council Report Preparation

About nine months after it began its work, the Administrative Reform Council issued an interim report, which was made public. Three months later, a final report was issued. During the period between the issuance of the interim report and the final report, intensive discussions and negotiations were carried out between the Administrative Reform Council and the government party. About one year after the Administrative Reform Council started its activities, the final report was issued.

---

[4]The Management and Coordination Agency was one of the Agencies whose heads were the ministers of state established under the Prime Minister's Office. It was responsible for promoting and coordinating administrative reform efforts. It was merged with the other two ministries (Ministry of Home Affairs and Ministry of Posts and Telecommunications) to become the Ministry of Internal Affairs and Communications in 7 January 2001.

Enactment of the Basic Law Incorporating All Reform Measures

One day after the final report was issued, a cabinet decision was made to respect the final report to the maximum extent. After this cabinet decision, different from the previous cases of major administrative reforms, the government immediately prepared a bill to enact all the reform contents included in the final report as well as the schedule for their implementation. This bill included the creation of the Headquarters for the Promotion of the Reform of Ministries and Agencies. Two and a half months after the issuance of the final report, the Basic Bill for the Reform of Ministries and Agencies was submitted to the parliament and enacted in June. This means that not only the government (ministries and agencies), but also the parliament made the commitment to implement the administrative reforms, as they were stipulated in this Basic Law. The drastic restructuring of ministries and agencies became the law, although the political momentum and the strong support of the general public still existed. Even though other legislations were necessary to implement restructuring and other reforms, the implementation became easier, politically speaking, because the Basic Law was enacted. The Basic Law also stipulated the schedule for the implementation. Unlike the previous time, in which the schedule of implementation was left to the cabinet and each ministry, this time the schedule for actual reforms could not be postponed as stipulated by law.

Creation of Implementation Monitoring Office

According to the Basic Law, the Headquarters for the Promotion of the Reform of Ministries and Agencies was to be created in July 1998. The prime minister headed the headquarters that had the executive office with more than 100 staff. The director and most of the core staff members were seconded from the Management and Coordination Agency and other ministries. Because each ministry or agency was made responsible for implementing reform of its own, it was very rare to create an *ad hoc* administrative body in charge of implementing reforms with the executive office composed of a large number of professional staff from the government offices.

This implementation monitoring office had the following functions and authorities:

— Drafting bills and cabinet orders necessary to implement restructuring ministries and agencies and other reform programs

- — Making basic plans for downsizing government organizations and improving the efficiency of their operations
- — Overall coordination for a smooth transition to the new government structure.

Governmentwide restructuring of ministries and agencies required many parallel and well-coordinated preparatory works of interrelated organizations based on the same principles and rules to be applied uniformly to all the organizations that are to be affected. This *ad hoc* body with the professional secretariat turned out to be extremely effective and it also enabled to promote the large-scale governmentwide restructuring in accordance with the implementing schedule stipulated by law.

Content of the Hashimoto Major Administrative Reforms

With the above procedures, the following major reforms were undertaken in the Hashimoto major administrative reforms, some of which are in fact followed by the current Prime Minister Koizumi.

Reduction of Number and Amalgamation of Ministries and Agencies

In accordance with the Hashimoto major administrative reforms, in 2003, the former 23 ministerial-level organizations were actually restructured into one cabinet office and 12 ministries, and agencies. The basic idea of this reorganization was to break the organizational walls among ministries and agencies and to integrate interrelated or similar functions. Under the Japanese cabinet system, any decision at the cabinet meeting must be made unanimously; therefore the cabinet cannot decide anything if one Minister of State objects. When interrelated or similar functions among ministries are merged into a single ministry with wider jurisdiction, one Minister of State can coordinate interrelated functions more efficiently and also reduce the duplication and redundancies of similar programs within one single ministry. This makes the cabinet to decide its policy with speed.

Two ministries and two agencies, including the Ministry of Transport, the Ministry of Construction, the National Land Agency, and the Hokkaido Development Agency were merged into one ministry called the Ministry of Land, Infrastructure, and Transport. The new ministry is now promoting the thorough and systematic exploitation, development, and preservation of national land; constructing social infrastructures in a more coordinated way, and establishing a unitary traffic system including road, air, and marine traffic facilities and services.

Two ministries, the Ministry of Health and Welfare and the Ministry of Labor merged as a new Ministry of Health, Labor, and Welfare. This merger, for instance, enabled consolidation of three different programmers under one ministry, including job and child rearing support measures; job and social welfare measures for the handicapped; and job and social participation measures for the elderly.

The Science and Technology Agency and the Ministry of Education were consolidated to become the Ministry of Education, Culture, Sports, and Science and Technology. The new ministry is making efforts to upgrade research and development programs by integrating basic research projects with applied and development research projects. It is also promoting to integrate the science and technology measures with the education measures.

The Environment Agency was upgraded to the Ministry of Environment, symbolizing the more emphasis and importance of environment administration, and the new ministry took over responsibilities of waste treatment from the former Ministry of Health and Welfare.

The most prominent merger was the creation of a new Ministry of Internal Affairs and Communications, integrating three ministerial-level organizations (Management and Coordination Agency, Ministry of Home Affairs, and Ministry of Posts and Telecommunications) into one. Later, postal service functions were separated from the internal organs of the new ministry, and the Postal Services Agency was created to carry out these services as an external organ of the ministry. In 2003, the Postal Services Agency was abolished, and the Japan Post was newly established as a public corporation to deliver postal services. Simultaneously, the internal organization of the ministry was restructured, and the size of the bureau in charge of supervising postal services became much smaller than before.

Introduction of the Incorporated Administrative Agency System[5]

The reform item to be described next is the introduction of the incorporated administrative agency (IAA) system. This system was introduced to establish a separate and independent legal entity outside a ministry and to entrust the entity with certain public functions to be carried out. The basic idea of this system is to separate, as much as possible, policy or program implementing

[5]"Incorporated administrative agency" is the formal English translation decided by the Ministry of Internal Affairs and Communications in July 2003. It is the same entity as "independent administrative institution" described in the papers by Yuko Kaneko in 1999, 2000 and 2002 and by Yuko Kaneko and Masahiro Horie in 2003 and by Toshiaki Matsuda in 1999.

functions from policy-formulation functions of the government and to allow more flexible, business-like, autonomous management for policy implementation, and to ensure efficiency and effectiveness. The concept is close to the application of "Management by Objectives" in the public sector. In April 2001, 57 incorporated administrative agencies were for the first time established to carry out functions previously conducted by the ministerial-level government organizations.

The characteristics of the IAA are summarized as below:

- IAAs are corporate bodies independent of the government; the employees may or may not have the status of civil servants.
- To promote flexibility and autonomy, the executives of IAAs are given more discretion in implementing the projects and programs, and in management of the institutions. The chief executive can appoint members of the board of directors and employees without approval of supervising minister. It can be said that the responsibilities and decision-making authorities of the executives have been strengthened. They now do not have to report to the supervising ministries as frequent as their predecessors (before incorporation) used to do.
- To ensure more effective and efficient operations of IAAs in a more autonomous way, IAAs must prepare medium-term business plans covering a three-to-five-year period according to the medium-term business goals set by the supervising ministers. These medium-term business plans are to be submitted to the supervising ministers for approval. IAAs are not subject to annual approval of business plans by the ministers.
- To promote transparency in accounting, IAAs must comply with the corporate accounting principles and must have their accounts audited by certified public accountants.
- To promote result-oriented operations, IAAs must submit annual reports as well as medium-term reports to the evaluation committees, established in the supervising ministries. Evaluation committees will conduct evaluations of performance and achievements based on these reports and other related information.
- As a high-level evaluation body with governmentwide responsibility and perspective, the Evaluation Council of the Ministry of Internal Affairs and Communications is to be reported by the individual evaluation committees concerning the individual evaluation results. The Council has the authority to submit its opinions to the evaluation committees and to recommend necessary measures on IAA's projects and programs, and organizations, including the abolition of IAAs to the supervising ministers.

Strengthening the Cabinet Office and Leadership of the Prime Minister (Augmented Capacities of Political Leaders vis-à-vis Bureaucratic Leaders)

Numerous reform measures were implemented by the Hashimoto Reforms to strengthen the cabinet functions and the leadership of the prime minister. To operate the cabinet with speed, flexibility, and better coordination, the number of the ministers was reduced from 20 to 14 (up to 17 is allowed) on one hand. On the other hand, the number of ministries and agencies was reduced to 12. Therefore, the prime minister can appoint Ministers of State without portfolio more freely than before to accommodate the emerging needs for special tasks and responsibilities that may arise from time to time.

To ensure stronger leadership of the prime minister and the cabinet, the cabinet secretariat is now given the authority not only to coordinate ministries and agencies but also to initiate basic policymaking. The cabinet office was newly established with several hundred staff in its head office to support the prime minister, the cabinet, and the cabinet secretariat. The prime minister may appoint his supporting staff more freely on his own initiative not only from within the government but also from outside.

As one of the measures of restructuring ministries and agencies, highly authoritative advisory councils such as the Council on Economic and Fiscal Policy and the Council for Science and Technology Policy were created in January 2001, in the cabinet office, to strengthen the political leadership of the prime minister and the cabinet. Because the prime minister himself heads these councils and the other members of these councils are the Ministers of State in charge of relevant policies and programs (in addition to relevant experts and distinguished figures from the outside), the decisions hitherto made by the relevant ministries are now made by the leadership of the prime minister with the support of fresh blood from outside the bureaucracy. These councils are becoming the *de facto* decision-making bodies of the cabinet (rather than the ministries). The relative strength of the cabinet and hence the prime minister is now secured substantially by this new device.

Especially, the Council on Economic and Fiscal Policy now plays an important role in deliberating various challenges that Japan faces today. The law gives the council the responsibilities of investigating and deliberating crucial matters such as basic policies on economic and fiscal management of the state, and structural reforms upon the request from the prime minister. Issues of vital importance such as strategies for structural reforms (the most important parcel of the Koizumi reform, which was the pledge of the national elections that he won twice) including regulatory reform, taxation system reform, and social security reform were put on the agenda and deliberated intensively in this council.

For instance, Prime Minister Koizumi has been advocating (as another important pledge of the national election and an important pillar of his strategies) the privatization of the Japan Post (now existing as the public corporation in charge of postal services); he brought the agenda of the postal reform to this council and asked the council to prepare a basic policy on privatization of the Japan Post. There was certain opposition expressed against the privatization of the Japan Post in the ruling parties, but the cabinet decided the basic policy on privatization of the Japan Post in September 2004, taking into account the deliberation results of the council.

It is evident that Prime Minister Koizumi takes advantage of the Council on Economic and Fiscal Policy as he chairs it. The council as a capable deliberating authority of every important area of national economy and societal agenda, having in its members, prominent and reliable (to the prime minister) personalities from the big businesses and the academic fields has so far proven to be useful to the prime minister. It appears that the outcomes of the previous reforms have equipped strong institutional capabilities for Prime Minister Koizumi to effectively promote his structural reforms.

December 2000 Cabinet Decision to Reinforce Hashimoto Reform with a New Deadline of 2005

To ensure the successful outcome from the Hashimoto major administrative reforms as well as to promote the continuous governmentwide reform efforts, a cabinet decision was made in December 2000 just before the initiation day of the government restructuring that was included in the Hashimoto Reform as of January 2001. The present reform efforts are carried out mainly based on this cabinet decision, "Fundamental Principles of Administrative Reform." In this cabinet decision, the basic direction of the reforms and a deadline of 2005 is prescribed so that the progress is to be timely monitored and a follow-up approach is to be taken appropriately.

The main reform items included in this cabinet decision are:

- Fundamental reform of government organizations and operations such as the reforms of public corporations and civil service system, and the introduction of policy evaluation system
- Further promotion of decentralization
- Regulatory reform

- Realization of electronic government
- Other items to improve the effectiveness and efficiencies of the government.

The following reforms scheduled from January 2001 have been actually put in place as of today.

Reform of the Public Corporations

Public corporations were established directly by law or through the special procedure provided by specific laws to meet specific policy needs of the time. There were 77 public corporations as of June 2001. They carried out programs of public nature based on their establishment laws, and substantial public funds were allocated to them. There existed 86 government-authorized corporations as of June 2001. They are private entities but are authorized by the relevant ministries to carry out certain government programs. Therefore, their functions are quite similar to those of the public corporations so that they have been treated almost in the same manner as the public corporations by the government.

As society and economy change, the policy needs will change accordingly. The reform of public corporations and government-authorized corporations became the top priority reform item. These reform needs included the abolition and transferring of the corporation programs to the private sector along with cutting down the government subsidies.

To promote the deliberation of reform plans, the Framework Law on Public Corporation Reform was enacted and took effect in June 2001. Based on the law, the Headquarters for Promoting Public Corporation Reform headed by the prime minister was established and an executive office comprising about 20 staff was set up in the cabinet secretariat.

During the period from June to December, the executive office carried out a complete review of the respective public corporations and government-authorized corporations. In December 2001, the Cabinet decided the Program for Streamlining and Rationalization of Public Corporations. This program included specific organizational reform measures as well as rationalization plans of projects and programs of public corporations and government-authorized corporations.

Based on the program, some corporations have already been or will be abolished; some corporations are to be privatized. Public corporations and government-authorized corporations whose major functions were decided to be continued as public projects and programs are allowed to survive. Many of them were required to be transformed into incorporated administrative agencies. By October 2004, 36 public or government-authorized corporations were transformed into incorporated administrative agencies.

Privatization of the Japan Post

As for the privatization of the Japan Post (until 2003 it was the part of the ministry and it became a public corporation in April 2003), which was the top priority reform item of Prime Minister Koizumi, the lessons learned in the past reform efforts seem to be utilized for the necessary preparation. For example, in the basic policy of privatization of the Japan Post, it is stipulated that the Headquarters for the Promotion of Privatization of the Japan Post is to be established with members consisting of all cabinet members and with the prime minister as chairman. This headquarters is in charge of conducting preparatory work such as drafting bills related to privatization, making overall coordination for a smooth transition from a public corporation to private companies as well as the transitional process. This arrangement followed the exact practice as what Prime Minister Hashimoto created for the Headquarters for the Promotion of the Reform of Ministries and Agencies.

Reform of the Civil Service System

The reform of civil service system was investigated in the Hashimoto Reform but the deliberation was set aside until the completion of restructuring of ministries and agencies. The Fundamental Principles of Administrative Reform of December 2000 stipulated that reform of the civil service system should be carried out with a view to restore the confidence of the people toward civil service as well as to make better use of the capabilities of the civil service. Basic policy directions included the introduction of a performance-based personnel system, rational and strict control of ex-officials' reemployment, and promotion of personnel interchange among the ministries and between the government and the private sector.

Fundamental Principles for the Civil Service Reform were adopted at the cabinet meeting in December 2001. The major points of this decision included:

- Establishment of a new framework of personnel/organization management for comprehensive and strategic policy planning and swift and efficient delivery of public services
- Introduction of a new civil service system including a new capability appraisal system, a performance-based pay system, a new impartial capability/performance evaluation system, etc.

- Reform of the recruitment examination system
- Establishment of fair reemployment rules for ex-officials.

Some issues of civil service system are so controversial and complicated that further reviews and deliberation may be required before the government prepares for the necessary bills and regulations.

Introduction of Policy Evaluation System

Under the new structure of the central government, each ministry established a unit responsible for policy evaluation, so that the evaluation results would be properly fed back to the policy-planning units. The ministerial evaluation unit was also meant to improve the transparency of the administration by disclosing the evaluation results to the public. In addition, a policy evaluation committee, a third party organ consisting of outside experts, was created in each ministry to review and examine the evaluation results conducted by the ministry. The Policy Evaluation Council was also established in the Ministry of Internal Affairs and Communications for an overall examination and coordination of government policy evaluation activities.

In January 2001, a Guideline for Policy Evaluation was adopted at the Liaison Conference for Policy Evaluation, members of which were the heads of policy evaluation units in all the ministries. The guideline obliged all the ministries to make their own directives for implementing policy evaluation activities; and such directives were prepared and made public by July 2001.

To make the policy evaluation system more effective and to improve the accountability concerning policy evaluation, the Policy Evaluation Law was enacted in June 2001 and took effect in April 2002. Based on the stipulation of the law, the fundamental principles on policy evaluation were adopted at the cabinet meeting in December 2001.

From April 2002, under the framework of the Policy Evaluation Law and the fundamental principles on policy evaluation, each ministry prepares its own policy evaluation plan comprising a three-to-five-year basic plan and an annual plan, and duly implements evaluation of its projects and programs, compiles the evaluation results, and prepares and releases the evaluation report.

The Ministry of Internal Affairs and Communications, as an office specialized in policy evaluation with a governmentwide viewpoint, monitors the policy evaluation activities, compiles and publishes an annual report including the evaluation results by the ministries, and provides governmentwide training in policy evaluation. It also carries out additional evaluations for securing coherence of policies as well as for ensuring objectivity and strictness of policy evaluations conducted by the ministries.

Promotion of Decentralization and Strengthening Local Governments

Japanese governance has been shared by the central and local governments. Before and during the Hashimoto major administrative reforms, parallel major reforms toward decentralization were undertaken, and a series of decentralization acts took effect in 2000. In these reforms, the division of responsibilities between the central government and the local governments was changed. Before the reform, some government affairs were delegated by each ministry to local governments as agency-delegated affairs. These affairs amounted about 30–40 percent of the work of the local governments. In this practice, the heads of the local governments had to deal with the central government ministries as their subordinates. The ministers retained the authorities for these affairs and the governors or mayors of the local governments carried out these affairs under the supervision of the ministers.

In the new system, the central government can only entrust the local governments to deal with the affairs of the central government by stipulation of laws. Thus, the relationship between the central government and the local governments became on equal footing, as trustees. When a dispute arises between the ministers and the heads of local governments, the committee on intergovernmental disputes, a third party organ newly established in the Ministry of Internal Affairs and Communications, would act, as it is in charge of examining the contents of the dispute, making recommendations and mediating the dispute.

Local Government Mergers

To further promote decentralization, encouraging the merger of second tier of local governments (cities, towns, and villages) is highly recommended, as the merger would strengthen the organizational infrastructure of the local governments. There were 3218 municipalities in Japan as of April 2002, when a special law for promoting merger of the municipalities was enacted. Based on the law, the government has been promoting voluntary merger of municipalities. As of 6 December 2004, the number of municipalities is 2927. The special affirmative treatments (getting some subsidies, if merged and attained certain population size) for the merged local governments will be applicable if they merge by the end of March

2005. Therefore, the intensive efforts are being taken at the local government level. The ruling party suggests the goal to be 1000 local governments in the second tier. But some local governments, even small ones, may not wish to merge with the neighboring entities although the number of merged local governments has been increasing.

Trinity Reforms for Local Governments: Subsidies, Equalization Tax, and Tax Authorities

The so-called "Trinity Reform," to undertake simultaneously (1) changing subsidies and grants-in-aid and (2) the local allocation tax, as well as (3) the transfer of the tax sources to local governments is another important priority of the current Koizumi cabinet. The financial self-responsibilities of the local governments are acutely called for to improve local public finance system from that of huge debts to a sound system. The Japanese government, both central and local, holds huge financial deficits of about 700 trillion yen.

Currently the revenue of the local government largely consists of three major sources: the local tax revenue, the local allocation tax revenue, and the subsidies and grants-in-aid from the individual ministries. The local government itself collects the local tax revenue. The local allocation tax revenue is the tax money allocated by the central government. The Local Allocation Tax Law stipulates the amount of total local allocation tax as a certain percentage of specific national tax revenue. The Ministry of Internal Affairs and Communications distributes the local allocation tax fund to the local governments taking into account the financial situation as well as the public service needs of the individual local governments. These funds have certain effects for equitable provision of public services among the local communities, whether they are richer or poorer communities.

The percentage of local tax revenue to the total revenue of the local governments is 33.3 percent, that of the local allocation tax revenue is 19.0 percent, and that of the subsidies and grants-in-aid is 13.5 percent, as of fiscal year 2001. Thus, the local government collects only one third of the total revenue and more than 30 percent of the total revenue is provided by the central government. In this practice, local governments cannot exercise their own initiatives based on the local needs or else dependent local governments may waste their allocated funds as they are not borne by themselves. At the same time, because the central government financial deficits became so huge, it is now forced to cut government expenditures including the subsidies to the local governments as much as the local government must also streamline their activities to reduce their own financial debts. To restore balance to the public finances and improve the efficiency and effectiveness of public administration, both central and local, financial decentralization and the reduction of the subsidies were chosen by both the central and the local governments.

With a view to strengthen the financial independency of the local governments as well as to reconstruct a sound central and local government finance system, the central government is now deliberating how to curtail the subsidies and grants-in-aid and the local allocation tax, and how to transfer tax sources (authorities) involving the governors and mayors of the local governments. Some ministries are not ready to reduce the subsidies and grants-in-aids as they are afraid of not performing their responsibilities mandated by law without these resources. Some local governments are also resisting the Trinity Reform, as the delegation of tax sources may not always be an effective solution to rectify the local government's finance system.

Regulatory Reform

In coping with liberalization of economies to open them to transnational spheres, deregulation is one of the most important policies including simplifying the government organizations and functions. The basic framework is to decide a three-year action program, to revise it at the end of the first year and to revise it again at the end of the second year, and to adopt a new program at the end of the final year, of the three-year term. The government has been carrying out deregulation measures based on a series of action programs since 1995. In promoting the action programs, an advisory body which was established to assist the prime minister monitored the progress of regulatory reform, deliberated future regulatory reform measures, and prepared its recommendations to be submitted to the prime minister. The government prepared its regulatory reform measures by taking into account these recommendations. The 2001–2003 action programs for regulatory reform were adopted in March 2001 and revised in March 2002 and 2003.

The Council for Regulatory Reform, an advisory body established in April 2001, included in its members, prominent experts and distinguished figures from the private sector. As an example of the measures deliberated by the council, an idea of special zones for structural reform was presented in March 2002. The Council of Economic and Fiscal Policy materialized this idea. The Law on Special Zones for Structural Reform was enacted and put into effect in December 2002. The law aims at promoting socioeconomic structural reform and regional development in fields such as education, retail trade, agriculture, social welfare, and research and development, through establishing special zones for structural reform. The Headquarters for the Promotion of Special Zones for Structural Reform headed by the prime minister was established in December 2002, based on this law, for the purpose of setting special zones, where exceptions to government regulations are permitted corresponding to the proposals by the local governments. Each local government can propose a unique special zone program for revitalizing local economy.

The activities of the Council for Regulatory Reform ended in March 2004, when a new three-year regulatory reform program was adopted at the cabinet meeting. In April 2004, the Headquarters for Regulatory Reform and Opening the Doors to the Private Sector headed by the prime minister was newly established together with the Council for Regulatory Reform and Opening the Doors to the Private Sector, which inherited the work of the Council for Regulatory Reform.

Now the Headquarters for the Promotion of Special Zones for Structural Reform, the Headquarters for Regulatory Reform and Opening the Doors to the Private Sector, and the Council for Regulatory Reform and Opening the Doors to the Private Sector are promoting regulatory reforms in parallel under the leadership of the prime minister. The council is currently deliberating reform measures to be recommended in December 2004. One of the major proposals discussed at the council is to introduce market testing of public service functions.

Realization of Electronic Government

Recent Efforts

To promote comprehensive measures aimed at developing Japan into an internationally competitive IT nation, the Basic Law on the Formation of Advanced Information and Telecommunication Network Society (The IT Basic Law) was enacted and came into force in January 2001. Realization of electronic government is one of the basic policy measures stipulated by the IT Basic Law.

Based on the stipulations of the IT Basic Law, an e-Japan Strategy was adopted at the first meeting of the IT Strategic Headquarters in January 2001. To implement the e-Japan Strategy, an e-Japan Priority Policy Program was approved in March 2001. The program is a specific blueprint for achieving the national goal of becoming the world's most advanced IT nation and includes details of the government actions that need to be implemented expeditiously and intensively, as well as the target date.

The Priority Policy Program was reviewed and amended once every year. The latest version was adopted in June 2004.

A Ministerial Chief Information Officers Council (CIO Council) was established in September 2002 as a subordinate organization to the IT Strategic Headquarters. The council is expected to play an important role of promoting the use of information and communication technologies

(ICTs) in the government as well as making the public administration more streamlined, efficient, trustworthy, and transparent.

The CIO council adopted a Program for the Creation of Next-Generation Electronic Government in July 2003. The program is a three-year plan from fiscal 2003 to fiscal 2005. The program targets at realizing user-oriented public services and high budget efficiency.

The following three objectives are identified in the program:

- Enhancing the convenience and service standards to the people
- Operational reform in response to the use of ICTs
- Building common frameworks for promoting next-generation e-government.

The Program for the Creation of Next-Generation Electronic Government was reviewed and amended in June 2004. Now the Japanese government is implementing specific measures described in the program and is expected to realize user-oriented streamlined public administration by March 2006.

Major Achievements to Date

The major achievements of the government's actions toward the e-government up to date are listed as follows.

Provision of Government Information over the Internet

A government portal site (http://www.e-gov.go.jp) has been developed to allow anyone access to government information easily and comprehensively. The site has been accessible since April 2003. Services that are offered include a search engine for the websites of the government organizations, appropriate guidance for the use of government-built databases and relevant links to basic information on the government websites.

Online Filing of Administrative Procedures

All the foundations for online filing of administrative procedures have been developed. Currently the following services are available online:

- The Government Public Key Infrastructure Services were started in April 2001.
- A group of laws to enable online filing of administrative procedures, enacted in December 2002, were enforced in February 2003.

- Online application acceptance systems were developed and the services became available in March 2003.
- The electronic revenue payment services became available in January 2004.
- The local governments started the public individual authentication services in March 2004.

Promoting Outsourcing to Improve Effectiveness and Efficiency

The government has been making as much use as possible of the private sector capabilities to process the following affairs:

- Statistical affairs such as tabulation, database construction, and field survey operation
- Public works
- Maintenance of housing for government employees
- Communication affairs of local branch offices of the National Police Agency
- Management and maintenance of jails
- Security services for immigration control offices
- Consulting functions for part-time job seekers
- Maintenance of air traffic control offices and national park management offices.

National Hospitals Now as IAAs

To improve the efficiency and quality of public services as well as to downsize the government, the government has tried as much as possible to transform existing government organizations into incorporated administrative agencies.

National hospitals, which had been part of the Ministry of Health, Labor, and Welfare, were transformed into incorporated administrative agencies, as the National Hospital Organizations in April 2004.

Transforming National Universities into National University Institutions

Likewise, National Universities were removed from the Ministry of Education, Culture, Sports, Science and Technology and became national university institutions, similar entities as the incorporated administrative agencies, as of April 2004.

Reduction of Staff

The five-year staff control plan under the new structure of central government was adopted at the cabinet meeting of July 2000. According to the new plan, the number of full-time employees of ministries and agencies including postal service personnel should be reduced by a minimum of 10 percent over a ten-year period starting from January 2001 (the total number of these employees is 840,691). It also stipulated that the government should make every effort to reduce personnel by creating incorporated administrative agencies, and by other methods of outsourcing and privatization, so that the final goal of 25 percent reduction (this reduction goal is to be applied to the employees excluding postal service personnel, i.e., 543,665 employees) would be attained in ten years.

It is expected that the government will be able to achieve this final goal by the end of fiscal year 2004 (March 2005).

Reform Procedures and Institutions as Innovations of Japanese Major Administrative Reforms

Overall Frameworks for Reform Undertaking

It is uncertain whether the above major administrative reforms are really successful undertakings or not. We still have to wait for yet a number of evaluations needed from various perspectives. However, as described earlier, these reforms have actually been put in place; the new government structure of "the cabinet office plus 12 ministries and agencies" (much reduced in number) is now in operation and other key reform measures have also been implemented. Some of the enabling factors are endogenous to the Japanese innovations, which had been created over years in many administrative reform undertakings. Through the experience of decades, mechanisms and procedures for governmentwide reform have been built up.

In promoting administrative reform and realizing successful outcomes, two of the most crucial elements are how to make effective reform plans, and how to get the commitment of all concerned. Administrative reforms are essentially changing the vested interests in the existing system. Reform plans must be convincing and resistance must be removed, by providing good plans and by obtaining commitment of leaders and public support.

The Japanese innovations created out of diverse and rich experiences accumulated over the years can be seen in some procedural frameworks of the administrative reforms from the very initiation stage to the end of the realization stages: firstly, the initiation of reform efforts; secondly, examination of reform agenda and deliberation of reform plans; thirdly, implementing reform plans; and lastly, monitoring the reform implementation.

Institutions such as a central management office, advisory committees on administrative reform, and *ad hoc* headquarters headed by the prime minister assisted by a sizable staff, all proved to be substantially effective to carry out comprehensive major administrative reforms. These institutional innovations are outlined below as these were also made available during the Hashimoto major administrative reform undertaking, and the subsequent follow-ups organized by the current prime minister Koizumi.

Initiation Stage: Availability of Central Administrative Management Office

In Japan, primary responsibilities for changing policies or programs and improving organizations or operations belong to each ministry concerned. A central management office, now called as the Ministry of Internal Affairs and Communications, played an important role to promote such changes and reforms and also governmentwide reform efforts.

This ministry is given the responsibilities of planning, making, and coordinating measures with regard to organizations, personnel, and management of administrative organs by its establishment law. Its mission is to restructure the government organizations based on the requests from the ministries as well as to control the number of government employees by setting up a personnel reduction plan and examining the requests of personnel increase from the ministries.

It is mandated to make constant efforts to investigate the actual situations, collect facts and figures, identify the challenges the government faces, and study and prepare necessary reform strategies. Such continuous day to day work is contributed substantially to implement the reforms. The previous experiences of reform have been embedded as innovations in the central management office, from which core members of the executive office to the advisory committees on administrative reform were seconded.

At the reform initiation stage, it is indispensable to have a strong support of the prime minister even though the ministry is given authorities to promote the reform. After all, whether it is active or passive, the commitment of the prime minister is essential to initiate major administrative reforms.

Deliberation on Necessity and Measures

Establishing an Advisory Committee

An *ad hoc* advisory committee on administrative reform is always organized for the prime minister. Such an advisory committee on administrative reform is usually composed of prominent scholars, journalists, ex-government officials, leaders of the business world, trade unions, and so on. It is not only a place to deliberate on the necessity and measures of administrative reform, taking into consideration various views and opinions of different backgrounds and interests, but also a place to involve concerned parties in the process of administrative reform. Creating such an authoritative advisory committee can symbolically appeal to the public and attract the attention of the public whose support is essential for the success of reforms.

Legal Framework for the Advisory Committee

The creation of an above-mentioned advisory committee is by stipulation of law, which requires the prime minister to get the approval of Parliament in appointing members of the committee and also requires the prime minister to respect the report and recommendations of the committee. In the case of the Hashimoto major administrative reforms, as mentioned earlier, Prime Minister Hashimoto created the Administrative Reform Council after winning the general election in 1996 not by law but, at this time, by a cabinet order. By avoiding the time-consuming enactment process, this method of creating the advisory body enabled the speedy deliberations and finalization of the needed reforms.

Supporting Staff for the Advisory Committee

When an advisory committee is established, it is assisted by the secretariat. Before the Hashimoto Reform, core members of the secretariat were "professional reformers" seconded from the Management and Coordination Agency of the Prime Minister's Office. Because the committee must cover many areas during its fixed term of office, usually two or three years, subcommittees are normally set up and members including experts are commissioned to participate in the deliberations of subcommittees. In the case of the Hashimoto Reform, as stated earlier, the procedure itself was streamlined, and his close aide who was a minister-level politician was placed in the reform center, together with the professional experts from the government office. A reliable plan for the prime minister was thus created smoothly for speedy operations.

Deliberation on the Necessities of Reform and Reform Measures

The advisory committee and subcommittees invite government agencies and private sector organizations as well as individual citizens to express their views and opinions. Based on the reports of subcommittees, the committee prepares its reports and recommendations to the prime minister. The committee may make reports and recommendations several times during its term. In the case of the Hashimoto major administrative reforms, within a year, the final report of reforms of the advisory committee was issued in public. By the time the report was issued, commitment of all parties for implementation had already been attained. The pattern of membership and the procedure accelerated the decision-making process and also the transition of reform process from a deliberating stage to an implementing stage.

Adopting and Implementing Reform Plans and Programs

Usual Process from 1980s to 1996

In the case of the advisory committees established by law, the prime minister is required by law to pay serious attention to their reports and recommendations on administrative reform, and the government has to decide how to deal with them. Usually the first action of the government is to make a cabinet decision to give serious consideration of the report and recommendations to the maximum extent. Making a cabinet decision by a unanimous agreement among ministers means ensuring the commitment of ministers, and thereby the commitment of ministries and agencies they head. However, "to pay serious attention to the reports and recommendations to the maximum extent" does not necessarily mean that all the ministries and agencies agree on all parts of the reports and recommendations, and more often than that there remain many parts in recommendations which need further elaboration and deliberations before concrete reform programs of the government are made. Therefore, the central management office has to persistently pressure the ministries and agencies to make further reform efforts and to take necessary steps in accordance with recommendations.

For this purpose, the central management office usually prepares another cabinet decision on administrative reform platform including specific reform items. Ministries and agencies are required to take necessary reform measures, such as amending existing laws or enacting new legislation, in accordance with an administrative reform platform. The central management office monitors the progress of implementation and thus promotes the reform efforts to the fullest extent.

In the Case of the Hashimoto Reform: 1998 Enactment of the Basic Law Forbade Changes and Hence Enabled Implementation

In the case of Hashimoto major administrative reforms, about one year after the Administrative Reform Council started its activities, the final report was already issued. Different from the previous cases of administrative reform, as analyzed earlier, the early enactment of the contents of the final report enabled the actual implementation of reform measures without much resistance.

Conclusion: A Dozen Points as Enabling Factors for the Hashimoto Reforms

In any country, it is difficult to abolish or consolidate government organizations. It is particularly so, when reorganization involves abolition or consolidation of the central government ministerial-level organizations that requires enactment of a law. In Japan, on the one hand, these administrative reforms take a legislative process that may provoke resistance of many vested interests of concerned parties in parliament, government, bureaucracy, and the private sector. This factor alone tells us the difficulty of reorganizing government organizations.

On the other hand, government structures such as ministries and agencies, and the allocation of functions and responsibilities among them, provide the basic framework of government activities. Therefore, organizational changes, especially ministerial-level reorganization, as well as personnel changes are expected to result in changes in the framework and the process of decision making. Such changes, in turn, are expected to result in changes in the content of decisions as well as in the speed of decision making. Administrative reforms are meant to realize these changes.

Current major administrative reforms went through many difficulties to attain consensus and agreement on specific reform programs. Many resisting and opposing factors existing in the bureaucracy and political process have been overcome to start implementation. This chapter did not deal with the stories of the difficult process. It rather simply tried to explore what was proposed and implemented, and through what procedures. Our mission was to highlight the procedures that have been established for many major administrative reforms over the past decades in Japan, and to make available the undertaking of the current reforms with additional innovations that have been created by the current political leaders with the assistance of the administrative reform professionals.

On the basis of our review of the reforms that took place and analysis of the Japanese innovations of administrative reform procedures, which were employed by the Hashimoto major administrative reforms, the following 12 points can be summarized without order, as factors that have enabled the current reforms in Japan. These synopses may be of some positive reference to the future undertaking of the major administrative reforms in Japan and elsewhere.

- Time was ripe for comprehensive administrative reforms as evidenced by the emergence of the circumstances under which even the opposition parties submitted administrative reform bills
- Timely appearance of one of the most experienced prime ministers, who had knowledge and experiences in government operations and a strong conviction and will for government reform
- Victory of the government party headed by the leader in 1996 general election, who had pledges of major administrative reforms in election campaign
- Creation of the Administrative Reform Council not by enactment of a law (avoiding legislative procedure) but as a cabinet order under the leadership of the winning prime minister (Hashimoto)
- Immediate start of the implementing process of the key administrative reform measures proposed in the final report of the Administrative Reform Council
- Prompt enactment of the Basic Law for the Reform of Ministries and Agencies, which stipulated detailed reform measures proposed in the final report of the Administrative Reform Council
- The stipulation of reform implementation schedule by the Basic Law
- Creation of the Headquarters for the Promotion of the Reform of Ministries and Agencies with a sizable secretariat. The secretariat reports directly to the prime minister and is given the authority of drafting necessary bills and cabinet orders for the reform
- Stationing influential and politically powerful members of the Diet around the prime minister, namely the cabinet secretary, the deputy cabinet secretaries, and the minister of state in charge of administrative reform
- Weakening of the resistance from the senior bureaucracy because of repeated reports of scandals
- Changing positioning of the private sector from government-dependent to more independent, and self-responsible
- Empowered citizens' watching of government affairs and vocal opinions becoming a most important criterion for continuing the current regime.

Addendum for the Present and Prognosis

In concluding this chapter, we would like to provide some thoughts that may be considered as a reference to the future major administrative reforms to be undertaken. We are repeatedly reminded that major administrative reforms cannot be carried out without overcoming resistance. For each major administrative reform, change in the bureaucracy's mentality and attitudes is always called for, as it is difficult to change their patterns of behavior, and the administrative reform always aims at changing the ongoing patterns.

In Japan, strong resistance was exerted particularly from inside the bureaucracy in the cases of many previous major administrative reforms. The existence of such a strong resistance was due to the fact (1) that the prime minister and his cabinet were highly dependent on the ministerial bureaucracies for policy making and coordination functions; (2) that the senior civil servants of ministry bureaucracies successfully mobilized major power groups of society to prevent implementation of reform programs that might jeopardize their vested interests; and (3) that it was the senior bureaucrats themselves who actually formulated concrete administrative reform programs to implement the reforms recommended by an advisory committee on reform (Suzuki, 1980).

Until this system was abolished a few years ago in Japan, senior civil servants were often appointed as government members to respond to the questions that occurred in the parliamentary debates on behalf of the cabinet ministers. In addition to the fact that they were potential candidates for members of the parliament, their participation in parliamentary sessions had blurred the relationships between public administration and politics under the parliamentary cabinet system. On the other hand, the parliament's dependence on the bureaucracy in policy planning had deteriorated the parliamentary power and the control of the bureaucracy.

This portrait of the bureaucratic power and the situation has nonetheless been changed significantly these days. For instance, the parliamentary debates must now be addressed only to the ministers and his deputies who are the members of the parliament. This means that these political figures must be capable of responding to parliamentary debates by themselves, although that capacity had been in the past performed by senior bureaucrats. These changes are only a part of many others as a result of the Hashimoto major administrative reforms as well as the current follow-ups that are institutionalized by the Koizumi Cabinet. At present, only highly qualified and learned politicians who understand how to perform in professional capacities can only survive in the cabinet or as successful parliamentarians. However, it is still largely the bureaucracy where the expertise is available in such an administrative state as in Japan. A harmonious and adequate level of role division between the political and administrative processes yet needs to be attained.

It is encouraging to note that Hashimoto major administrative reforms have been producing some results in enhancing the public knowledge and watch on the government undertaking, which in turn can ensure the support of the public toward the reforms. The strong public support is after all most essential to the success of major administrative reform undertaking.

Bibliography

Articles and Papers

Horie, M. (2000). Significance of Restructuring the Ministries and Agencies by the Hashimoto Reform Program and the Future Challenges. In: Proceedings Annual Conference of the Public Policy Studies Association of Japan. Tokyo, Japan, June 10.

Horie, M. (2000). Administrative Reform in Japan: Recollection and Future Perspective. In: Proceedings Symposium of the Fudan University. Shanghai, China, April.

Imamura, T. (1999). Administrative Reform in the Central Government. *Annals of the Japanese Society for Public Administration* 24–41.

Ito, D. (1999). Administrative Reform in the Context of Legitimacy. *Annals of the Japanese Society for Public Administration* 3–23.

Kaneko, Y. (1999). Government Reform in Japan. In: Proceedings IIAS First Specialized International Conference. London, United Kingdom, July 12–15.

Kaneko, Y. (2000). Globalization and Public Administration in Japan — Centering on Deregulation Efforts. In: Proceedings IIAS First Regional International Conference. Bologna, Italy, June 19–22.

Kaneko, Y. (2001). Promoting "Electronic Government" with a Focus on Statistical Activities. In: Proceedings 25th International Congress of Administrative Sciences. Athens, Greece, July 9–13.

Kaneko, Y. (2002). Downsizing the Japanese Government. In: Proceedings IIAS Second Specialized International Conference. New Delhi, India, November 5–9.

Kaneko, Y. (2004a). Realization of the E-Government: Japan's Strength and Challenges. In: Proceedings OECD E-Government Symposium — Making Change Happen. Seoul, Korea, July 14–15.

Kaneko, Y. (2004b). ICTs and a Rejuvenated Japan Post — Ensuring Diverse Services for Local Communities. In: Proceedings 26th International Congress of Administrative Sciences. Seoul, Korea, July 14–18.

Kaneko, Y. (2004c). Administrative Reform and Its Legal Framework in Japan. In: Proceedings Sino-France International Conference on Public Administration Reform. Beijing, China, October 29–31.

Kaneko, Y. and M. Horie (2000). Reinventing the Japanese Government. In: Proceedings IIAS Seminar on Administrative Reform in Asia. Beijing, China, July 14–15.

Kaneko, Y. and M. Horie (2003). Independent Administrative Institution: Innovation of Public Organizations in Japan. In: Proceedings International Conference on the Reform of Chinese Public Institutions and Construction of NPOs. Beijing, China, October 23–24.

Matsuda, T. (1999). Some Points for Independent Administrative Corporation System. In: Proceedings IIAS First Specialized International Conference. London, United Kingdom, July 12–15.

Nakamura, A. (1999). Administrative Reform in the Age of Governance. *Annals of the Japanese Society for Public Administration* 42–62.

Tanaka, K. (1999). Conditions for Meaningful Restructuring of the Ministries and Agencies. Intellectual Cabinet. pp. 2–3.
Watanabe, Y. (1966). Rincho Commission and Political Parties. Japan Society of Public Administration. Vol. 5. Gyousei Kenkyu, ed., Tokyo: Keiso Shob.

Books

Caiden, G.E. (1969). *Administrative Reform*. Chicago: Aldine Publishing Co.
Dimock, M.E. (1968). *The Japanese Technocracy: Management and Government of Japan*. New York: Walker/Weatherhill.
Eda, K. (1999). *By Whom We Lose the Fight for Reform*. Tokyo: Shincho-sha.
Emmerich, H. (1950). *Essays on Federal Reorganization*. Alabama: University of Alabama Press.
Former Staff Organization of the Executive Office of the Administrative Reform Council (1998). *Japanese Public Administration in the 21st Century*. Tokyo: Institute of Administrative Management.
Inuzuka, S. and N. Hoshi (1999). *Systemic Reforms in Japan*. Tokyo: Yushindo-Koubunsha.
Inoguchi, T. (1994). *Perspective for Changing World*. Tokyo: Chikuma Shobou.
Institute of Administrative Management (2004). *Japan's Government and Administration at a Glance 2004*. Tokyo: Institute of Administrative Management.
Kaplan, E.J. (1972). *Japan: The Government–Business Relationship*. Washington, D.C.: U.S. Government Printing.
Kusano, A. (1993). *Coalition Government in Japan*. Tokyo: Bungei-shunju.
Leemans, A.F. ed. (1976). *The Management of Change in Government*. Institute of Social Studies Series on the Development of Societies. Vol. l. The Hague: Martinus Nijhoff.
Masujima, T. (1996). *Perspectives of Administrative Reform*. Tokyo: Ryousho-Hukyukai.
Masujima, T. (2003). *Perspectives on Administrative Reform and its Evolution*. Tokyo: Gyosei.
Masujima, T. and M. O'uchi eds. (1995). *The Management and Reform of the Japanese Government*. 2nd ed. Tokyo: Institute of Administrative Management.
Morita, A. ed. (1998). *Basics of Public Administration*. Tokyo: Iwanami-shoten.
Morita, A. (2000). Contemporary Public Administration. Tokyo: University of the Air Education Promotion Society.
Mosher, F.C. (1978). *Current Issues in Public Administration*. New York: St. Martin Press.
Muramatsu, M. (1994). *Public Administration in Japan*. Tokyo: Chuoukouron-shinsha.
Muramatsu, M. (2001). *Text on Public Administration*. Tokyo: Yuuhikaku.
Nishio, M. (2001). *Study of Public Administration*. Tokyo: Yuuhikaku.
Research Project on Restructuring of the Ministries and Agencies (2000). Five Recommendations for Realizing the Expected Reform of the Ministries and Agencies. Tokyo: Tokyo Foundation.
Tanaka, K. (1996). *Administrative Reform*. Tokyo: Gyosei.

Tanaka, K. and A. Okada, eds. (2000). *Reforms of Central Government Ministries and Agencies.* Tokyo: Nihon-Hyoron-Sha.

Tsuji, K. (1968). *Bureaucracy of Japan.* Tokyo: University of Tokyo Press.

United Nations (1988). National Management Consultancy Services for Administrative Development (Administrative Innovations Series III). New York: United Nations.

United Nations Department of Economic and Social Affairs in Cooperation with the International Institute of Administrative Sciences and Institute of Administrative Management, Japan (1997). Administrative Reforms: Country Profiles of Five Asian Countries. New York: United Nations.

Watanabe, Y., et al. (1966). *Introduction to Public Administration.* Tokyo: Yuhikaku.

Government Documents

Administrative Reform Council (1997). Final Report.

Government of Japan (1998). Decentralization Promotion Program. Cabinet Decision.

Government of Japan (1999a). Second Decentralization Promotion Program. Cabinet Decision.

Government of Japan (1999b). Basic Plan of Slimming and Streamlining Government Organizations and Operations. Decision by the Headquarters for the Promotion of the Reform of Ministries and Agencies.

Government of Japan (2000). Fundamental Principles of Administrative Reform. Cabinet Decision.

Government of Japan (2001a). Program for Streamlining and Rationalization of Public Corporations. Cabinet Decision.

Government of Japan (2001b). E-Japan Strategy. Decision by the IT Strategic Headquarters.

Government of Japan (2001c). Fundamental Principles for Civil Service Reform. Cabinet Decision.

Government of Japan (2001d). Decision on the Establishment of the Municipality Merger Back-up Headquarter. Cabinet Decision.

Government of Japan (2002). Follow-up Report of Fundamental Principles of Administrative Reform in Fiscal 2001.

Government of Japan (2003). Follow-up Report of Fundamental Principles of Administrative Reform in Fiscal 2002.

Government of Japan (2004a). Follow-up Report of Fundamental Principles of Administrative Reform in Fiscal 2003.

Government of Japan (2004b). Three-year Action Plan for Regulatory Reform and Opening the Doors to the Private Sector. Cabinet Decision.

Government of Japan (2004c). Basic Principles for the Privatization of the Japan Post. Cabinet Decision.

Rincho Commission (1964). Report of the Rincho Commission: General Guidelines.

Dissertations

Suzuki, I. (1980). Administrative Reform in Japan during 1962–1964. Ph.D. dissertation, US Microfilm, Inc., New York.

Chapter 25

Administrative Reforms in China: Globalization or Localization?

Mengzhong Zhang

CONTENTS

Introduction

Most countries all over the world have implemented administrative reforms in one form or another since early 1960s, and during this time, a number of formerly colonial countries attained independence. As different countries were in different historical, political, social, and economic stages, their reforms bore distinct features in terms of causes, purposes, and approaches. Nevertheless, careful studies have found out that many of these administrative reforms share certain common traits.

How can this phenomenon be accounted for? One explanation is that the forces of globalization are at work. As the world entered into the "global village" era in the latter half of the 20th century, no country ever since is immune from influence from the other parts of the globe. However, the impact is not uniform, i.e., not every country is influenced to the similar degree and of the same scope by globalization. Each independent country had its unique hallmark of social, economic, and political circumstances and was at a different historical starting point in the first place. Therefore, it is interesting to observe the two seemingly contradictory phenomena: convergence on the one hand and divergence on the other.

Conventional studies of comparative administration focus on borrowing the lessons and experiences from the first world (more developed societies) and giving to the third world (less-developed societies). Although comparative study of public administration has its ebb and flow, it has never been a full-fledged academic discipline of learning. Less attention is paid to the aspect of administrative reforms in socialist countries in general, and to that of China in particular, by the mainstream public administration community. Even less energy is spent on comparative study of administrative reforms between socialist China and the rest of the world, despite a few recent efforts (Straussman & Zhang, 2001; Zhang & Straussman, 2003; Zhang & Zhang, 2005).

This chapter attempts to fill this gap in public administration literature by putting Chinese administrative reforms under the microscope of global government innovation in general and the New Public Management (NPM) movement in particular. The purpose is to identify the common traits shared by Chinese administrative reforms and those of NPM-labeled countries, as well as distill distinct characteristics of Chinese administrative reforms.

To accomplish the aforementioned task, this chapter first reviews public administration literature from three dimensions: globalization and its impact on public administration; NPM; and policy transfer. Second, a brief description and analysis of Chinese administrative reforms are presented. Third, the author analyzes the impact of globalization on Chinese administrative reforms and identifies the common features of administrative reforms shared by China and other countries. Fourth, unique characteristics of Chinese administrative reforms are demonstrated. Finally, concluding thoughts and future prospects are presented.

Literature Review

The detailed accounts of globalization, NPM, and policy transfer literature can be found elsewhere. The purpose of this section is to lay a concise international background of Chinese administrative reforms and to conceptualize policy transfer. Thus it serves as a foundation to analyze the common as well as unique characteristics of Chinese administrative reforms.

Globalization and Its Impact on Public Administration

As other academic terminologies, globalization defies simple definition. The essential understanding of globalization is that economic globalization is a necessary trend of world economic development. Globalization means that economic resources (capital, technology, products, and labor) flow across national boundaries over the globe. In this process, the economy of each country becomes increasingly open and interdependent. One country's economy is shaped and constrained by other country's economy, and vice versa. Thus, an integrated global economy is formed.

Accompanied by the recent revolution of science and technology, especially the rapid growth of information and communication technology and network technology, information can be freely delivered over space, thus accelerating the progress of globalization. Human beings can overcome space obstacles and social barriers, such as institutional and cultural aspects, to realize adequate communication and achieve more concerted actions. Under the influence of globalization, world economy, politics, culture, science and technology, education, and even the thinking modes have had profound and ongoing changes. As a result, countries and societies are more interconnected and more interdependent.

Globalization can be traced back to the 16th century, and the spread of imperialism and capitalism across the globe are essential (Amin et al., 1994, pp. 2–3; Halliday, 1994, p. 2). As capitalism was boosted by the two world wars and reached new heights in the Cold War era, the process of globalization also speeded up. With the collapse of Soviet communism, the pace of globalization in the 1990s was further hastened. Globalization refers to "quantitative and qualitative increase in the scope and intensity of the processes of internationalization" (Cope et al., 1997, p. 446).

Farazmand (1999) highlights the challenges facing public administration and offers 12 suggestions for public administrators across the world. Five aspects of impact of globalization on public administration are briefly presented here.

First, there are multiple public administration subjects under globalization. The traditional notion of nation-state is challenged and weakened. Supranational agencies such as United Nations and its affiliated organizations, like the World Bank, the International Monetary Fund (IMF), and the World Trade Organization (WTO), are playing increasingly important roles, and these organizations are dictated by the Trilaterals (the United States, some West European governments, and Japan) (Farazmand, 1999). In addition, there are other international non-governmental organizations (NGOs) and multinationals and transnational corporations as the governance bodies (Farazmand, 1999).

Second, in the age of globalization, the means of public administration has become more computer-based, digitalized, and networked. E-government, e-commerce, e-education, e-mail, and other information communication modes are deeply transforming the traditional administration instruments and methods. These changes are enhancing public productivity (Zhou, 2000).

Third, although the process of globalization has boosted the world economy and societal development, many new problems are generated in the meantime. These problems include environmental pollution, endangered species, deforestation, desertification, and scarcity of resources. In the social aspect, the problems are demonstrated in population growth, an increasing gap between rich and poor, financial crisis, and ethnic and religious conflicts. Other than that, drug trafficking, smuggling, international prostitution, organized crime, and international terrorism are all challenging the public administration community. Therefore, concerted effort and coordinated resolution are needed.

Fourth, globalization requires a higher qualification of civil servants. Public employees are expected to have the awareness of reform and innovation of the traditional institution and administrative systems.

Fifth, there are a number of negative consequences of globalization. "They include the diminished or lost sovereignty of states, constraints on democracy, loss of community, concentration of the global power structure, increased centralization of corporate and government organizational elites, and increased dependency among less-developed nations on globalizing powers" (Farazmand, 1999, p. 515). It is imperative that the public administration community fight against such changes.

New Public Management

According to Hughes (1998, p. 1489), NPM is "a concerted program of public sector reform aimed at replacing administration by management, replacing formal bureaucracy by markets or contracts as far as possible, and reducing the size and scale of the public sector."

Hood (1991), who popularized the term NPM, stated seven aspects of the managerial program. First, there should be hands-on professional management in the public sector. This indicates that the focus on management is the manager. Or in other words, the frontline administrator should be empowered. Second, there should be explicit standards and measures of performance. Third, there should be a greater emphasis on output controls instead of input controls. Fourth, there is a need to separate units in the public sector and establish some sorts of quasi-independent organizations as executive agencies. Fifth, there is a shift to greater competition in the public sector, including public tendering procedure. Sixth, there is a stress on bringing the private-sector style of management practice into the public sector. Seventh, there is a stress on reducing resource use in the public sector to minimize the public expenditure.

In short, the concept of NPM movement started from the early 1980s, originating from New Zealand (later became the "New Zealand Model"), Australia, and the United Kingdom, and later disseminated to the United States and a number of other countries. The essence of NPM is borrowing and applying the concepts and techniques of private-sector management into public-sector management, thus reducing the functions of the public sector through contracting out and privatizing. The theoretical foundations of NPM are the new institutional economics and public choice theory, which assumes that human beings are rational and economic and believe that maximizing budgeting provides the biggest incentive for public officials. Thus rational choice is supplanting government and other public sectors with market mechanisms (Zhang & Straussman, 2003). To be more concrete, these NPM ideas cover the retrenchment of public employees, reducing the scale of public expenditure, privatizing, contracting out, shifting out government service to the outside, importing private-sector instruments to the public sector, decentralization, deregulation and reregulation, fostering a culture based on performance, utilizing quality as measuring instruments, emphasizing results and outcomes instead of process, as well as emphasizing the priority of customers (Masser, 1998).

There might be multiple causes that triggered NPM style of administrative reforms in recent two decades. From late 1970s to early 1980s, many countries initiated reform programs in the public sector, many of which had economic downturns. Moreover, there was political pressure requiring reform endeavor. "Bureaucracy bashing" is a typical phenomenon. Bureaucrats were accused of self-expanding, trouble making, lack of initiative, and insensitivity (Savoie, 1994). The sentiment of anti-state was vividly demonstrated in the late President Ronald Reagan's various quotes: "In this present crisis, government is not the solution to our problem. Government is the problem" (Ronald Reagan, January 20, 1981, http://joshbotts.-com/pdf/tnr-sullivan-crisisoffaith.pdf: accessed on May 20, 2005); "Outside of its legitimate function, government does nothing as well or..."; "The federal government has taken too much tax money from the people,..."; "As government expands, liberty contracts"; "Government is like a baby. An alimentary canal with a big appetite at..."; "A government bureau is the nearest thing to eternal life we'll ever..."; "No government ever voluntarily reduces itself in size" (quoted from: http://www.quotedb.com/categories/government: accessed on May 20, 2005). With its long-term guidelines of administrative reforms in the United Kingdom, Thatcherism originated from the ideological influence of the right. It pursued the stance of antistatism. Thatcher argues that overarching government suffocates the creativity of individuals, families, and social groups. She maintains that big government generates and distributes public goods without efficiency, that big government twists the market mechanism and is insensitive to the quality requirements from the consumer, that uniform provision ignores the diversity of public service. Thatcher also believed that political appointees had become the captives and conspirators of the bureaucracy. In the aspect of executive function, the criticism of Thatcherism focused on its rigid hierarchical structure that lacked flexibility and creativity. Therefore, the bureaucracy could not follow the rapid pace of economic and technological development (Zhou, 1999).

The core of the Thatcherism public management tenet is reform based on market orientation, which has four dimensions. First, Thatcherism admires market mechanisms and market forces, arguing for reducing government intervention to the minimum. Second, Thatcherism advocates cheap and small government. Thus, cost savings and tax reductions are believed to have the incentive to motivate private capital investment that results in economic prosperity. Third, Thatcherism suspects that bureaucratic government will lead to low efficiency and waste, thus it is imperative to strengthen the control of senior political appointees and downsize the scale of the civil service force. Fourth, Thatcherism distrusts government and all public sectors. In contrast, Thatcherism appreciates the methods and means of private-sector management (Greenwood & Wilson, 1989).

Policy Transfer

Although literature on policy transfer is not scant, a recent comprehensive effort to review the literature on policy transfer is an article titled "Policy Transfer as a Form of Prospective Evaluation: Challenges and Recommendations" by Mossberger and Wolman (2003). As early as the Civil War era, the United States borrowed the idea of a national income tax system from the British to finance the army (Waltman, 1980, p. 16). Social security and unemployment insurance were examples of cross-national policy transfer during the period between the end of the 19th century and the early 20th century (Collier & Messick, 1975; Waltman, 1980). Although the use of entrance examinations for the employment of competent civil servants in the United States was distinctly British in origin (Carter, 1998), the root of this practice could be traced to the practice of ancient China's civil service. The United Kingdom actually benefited from Chinese intellectual sources in the civil service system. Immediately after World War II, the administrative reform in Japan borrowed ideas and practices from the United States (Pempel, 1982).

With the advancement of communications and the accelerated pace of globalization, cross-national policy transfer has the potential to increase in frequency and scope. In the field of public administration over the past two decades or so, ideas of administrative reforms such as privatization, decentralization, and market orientation witnessed transnational diffusion not only between developed countries, but also penetrated the thinking and practice of many developing countries (Lam, 1997; Zhang & Straussman, 2003).

One aspect of the policy diffusion literature is the chronological and geographic patterns of the adoption of policy innovation across government units. It tries to explain the determining factors of which units are early, more innovative adopters, or factors that distinguish adopters from nonadopters in particular policy fields (Seely, 2003). The other aspect of the policy diffusion literature seeks the sources of diffusion: cue-taking patterns among the states and the role of national governments, professional organizations, policy communities, and policy entrepreneurs in promoting diffusions (Seely, 2003). Although many factors played significant roles in promoting policy diffusion across national boundaries, cross-national case studies showed that at least five factors are important in the process. These are: (i) geographic proximity (Rose, 1991); (ii) policy entrepreneurs (Dolowitz and Marsh, 2000; Wolman, 1992); (iii) informal policy communities (Haas, 1989); (iv) federal government involvement (Welch & Thompson, 1980); and (v) international organization assistance (Haas, 1989).

There is a plethora of individual case studies for cross-national policy transfer. Most of them have built theoretical constructs based on a few cases. These studies examine a variety of concerns, including the reasons that the recipient government engages in policy transfer, the roles that policy transfer plays in the political process, the characteristics of the decision process, and reasons for the success or failure of the effort (Seely, 2003).

In recent years, the study of policy transfer garnered further momentum. For example, New Zealand collected ideas from Australia and several other countries in its NPM reforms (Boston, 1996). The U.S. government used the results of the Organization for Economic Cooperation and Development's (OECD) research on performance management in a few countries, and especially the practice of Australia to form its Government Performance and Results Act (Breul, 1996). A few new book titles also suggest the popularity of policy transfer. These are: *Policy Transfer and British Social Policy: Learning from the USA* (Dolowitz et al., 1999); *Public Management & Policy Transfer in Southeast Asia* (Common, 2000); and *Policy Transfer, New Public Management and Globalization: Mexico and the Caribbean* (Bissessar, 2002).

Administrative Reforms in China

In this section, I sketch the main outlines of Chinese administrative reforms. While detailed accounts may take book length, this part attempts to distill the prominent features of Chinese administrative reforms. From a historical point of view, commentators and observers would agree that the People's Republic of China's (PRC) history could be divided into two parts: the Mao era (1949–1976) and the post-Mao era (1977 onwards), for each era has some unique characteristics. The two eras also present a natural comparison of similarity and difference of the reform effort.

The Mao Era (1949–1976)

The Formation of Chinese Governance

When the Chinese Communist Party (CCP) came to power in 1949, it did not have many alternatives for economic development. Its priority task was to rehabilitate the war-torn economy and the immediate implementation of some form of land redistribution. The most important program enacted by the PRC, from 1950 to 1953, was agrarian reform. In 1949, when the CCP took over the country, some 500 million people were living in the countryside. The 1950 Agrarian Reform Law was basically a mild reform measure that permitted "rich" peasants and landlords to retain their land. The land redistribution was completed in 1952. It soon became obvious that land redistribution was not going to solve the basic agrarian problem. The millions of new landowning peasants realized very quickly that their plots were too small to produce enough to feed even their families. Having committed themselves to the party's cause by participating in the land redistribution, the peasants had to accept the party's new appeal for mutual aid teams, which pooled together draft animals, implements, and shared labor. In 1953–1954, the mutual aid teams gave away to more complicated cooperative ventures, the mandatory agricultural producers' cooperatives (APCs). The individual peasants pooled their productive resources (land, draft animals, implements, and houses) in return for shares in the enterprise. Although the movement was voluntary, the party conducted massive campaigns to persuade and to coerce peasants to join the APCs.

The APCs made the peasants utilize resources and labor better. During the slack seasons, surplus labor could be mobilized easily to carry on small-scale irrigation works, such as making ditches, ponds, and dams. Combined surplus labor could reclaim land through irrigation and reforestation. By 1953, the regime had completed the immediate tasks of rehabilitating the war-torn economy and consolidating its control over the nation. With the end the Korean War, the regime was confident enough to embark on a rapid industrialization program. The approach adopted was the Stalinist strategy of long-term centralized planning that was approved to be the successful socialistic model emerging from World War II.

Fundamental to the Stalinist model was the rapid buildup of the heavy industry sector through the concentrated allocation of investment into capital goods industries. The model demanded highly centralized decision making by the top politicians to determine targets and quotas to be fulfilled by the different economic sectors (Theen & Wilson, 1996).

First Three Rounds of Administrative Reforms

Unlike the U.S. political system, which has three branches of government, in the PRC, there are a number of branches of governance. These include: the Executive branch (State Council, formerly known as Political Council from 1949 to 1953); the Central Military Commission of People's Revolution; The Supreme People's Court; and The Supreme People's Procuratorate. In addition, The Central Political Bureau and Its Central Committee of Chinese Communist Party, the National People's Congress and the Chinese People's

Political Consulting Conference have been playing an essential role in Chinese governance.

The First Round of Administrative Reform (1949–1956)

Within the Political Council, there were 35 working organs (ministries and commissions) in 1949. Although there were some minor adjustments, the total number of central administrative organs remained the same by 1951, i.e., 35. To implement the first five-year plan, it was perceived necessary to strengthen the centralization of central government and to increase the number of central administrative organs within the Political Council. By 1953, the total central administrative organs increased to 42, largely responding to the increased economic functions of the government. In 1954, the State Council was established, replacing the former Political Council. By 1954, there were altogether 64 Central Administrative Organs (hereafter CAOs, ministries, commissions, and other working offices under the State Council). Among them are 35 CAOs in charge of economic function. In 1955–1956, the State Council was further adjusted and there were 81 CAOs; the first round of administrative reform was completed. The main feature was increasing the central administrative organs, largely responding to the need for economic development of socialist construction (Liu, 1998, pp. 290–294).

Within the first administrative reform, there were a couple of attempts to downsize the number of administrative organizations and personnel. For example, the central government had promulgated directives to downsize personnel and administrative organs in 1951. By June 1954, 152,000 public employees had been downsized from central and provincial governments. The second attempt was conducted in 1956 that downsized 36,270 personnel, accounting for 40.1 percent of the total number, and eliminated 2198 divisions and sections of administrative organs (about 38 percent of the total number) (Song, 2001).

The Second Round of Administrative Reform (1956–1959)

Accompanied by the completion of the measures of the first five-year plan and socialist reformation, some problems appeared out of the overall concentration of the central authority. These included the bloating of administrative organs, low efficiency of administration, and complaints of local authority. Because the central government was taking care on a basis that was too wide, the local government had no discretion and incentive to produce public goods and deliver effective public service. Under such circumstances, Chairman Mao Zedong said in his well-known "On the Ten Major Relations" in 1956:

> At present, under the premise of consolidating the leadership of central government, we should expand the power of local government, permit them more independence to construct a powerful socialist country. The territory of our country is so huge, and the circumstances are so complex, that it is much better to have the independent initiatives of both the center and the locality. We should not follow the path of the Soviet Union, centralizing everything to the central government, in the process strangling the flexibility and motivation of local government.
>
> Mao (1999a, p. 31)

Following Mao's article, the central government began to delegate some authority to local governments. In particular, some of the state-owned enterprises (SOEs) previously controlled by the central government went to the hands of local governments. It was no longer necessary for the central government to have so many ministry-level units. CAOs had downsized from 81 in 1956 to 60 at the end of 1959 (Liu, 1998). Among these downsized departments, those in charge of economic functions occupy 50 percent or more (Song, 2001).

The Third Round of Administrative Reform (1959–1976)

The "1959 downsize" brought about chaos and anarchy partly because of the "Great Leap Forward" movement and the influence of "left" ideology. At the Mount Lu Conference in July 1959, Mao said, "we have delegated too much of the Four Powers (referring to Personnel, Finance, Commerce, and Industry) to the local government too quickly. Chaos and confusion are in existence. Now we are in a situation of semi-anarchy. We should emphasize unified leadership and centralize power again. The delegated powers should be claimed back to the central and provincial governments" (Mao, 1999b, p. 80).

To comply with Mao's opinion, the central government began to emphasize unified leadership and concentration of authority. In 1961, many of the previously eliminated organs came back and new organs were also created. Thus, by the end of 1965, there were 79 working organs under the State Council. Nevertheless, downsizing also occurred in this period. Between July 1960 and September 1961, central government downsized 16,000 public sector employees (15 percent) and service institutions (Shiye Danwei) downsized 65,000 employees (26 percent). From February of 1962 to 1964, central government further downsized 10,000 public sector employees and local government nationwide downsized about 800,000 public sector employees (Liu, 1998, p. 297). This downsizing was a response to the "three difficulty years" from 1959 to 1961. It was estimated that about 20 to 30 million people died in the period of the Great Leap

Forward (1958–1960) (http://www.boxun.com/freethinking/freetxt/lishi/ls011.htm: accessed on March 5, 2005). The hardship can be compared to the Great Depression periods from 1929 to 1933 in the capitalist world. As a result, not only government employees were downsized, but also workers in the factory. From early 1961 to June 1963, about 20,000,000 workers were downsized (Song, 2001, pp. 338–339). Many of them were sent to the rural areas, losing their urban residency.

In 1966, the "cultural revolution" movement began and the normal operation of State agencies was affected. As a result, many government agencies were trapped into stagnation. By the end of 1970, there were 32 administrative organs under State Council. In reality, the State Council only led 19 organs (Liu, 1998, p. 298). In 1975, Premier Zhou Enlai (or Chou En-lai) stated that China would realize four modernizations (industry, agriculture, science and technology, and defense) by the end of 20th century. In the meantime, the central government determined that Deng Xiaoping would be in charge of the State Council, reflecting an emphasis on economic development. By 1975, the number of ministry-level units increased to 52.

Recent Four Rounds of Administrative Reforms in the Post-Mao Era (May 25, 1977)

The Fourth Round of Administrative Reform (1977–1987)

With the fall of the "gang of four" and the end of the "cultural revolution" in 1976, there was profound underpinning of political and economic logic for the administrative reform. To correct the problems created by the ten-year turmoil, it is natural to increase agencies and personnel to solve a number of urgent issues. In December 1978, the Third Plenum of the Eleventh Central Committee of the CCP was held, which decided the overall "reform and open" grand policy of the PRC. This is indicative of the focus change from previous priority of class struggle to the current economic development.

From 1977 to 1981, the State Council had recovered and created 48 administrative organs. Thus, by the end of 1981, there were 100 administrative organs altogether under the State Council. Administrative personnel also increased to 51,000 in the central government. From 1978, a number of SOEs previously delegated to the subnational government had been claimed back by the central government. The number of SOEs and service institutions affiliated with the central government jumped from 1260 in 1978 to 2680 in 1981. Correspondingly, fiscal administration, tax power, and materials authority was withdrawn to the central government. There were several prominent features of the administrative system in this period. First, the number of administrative agencies rocketed. Second, government employees became more aged. Third, overlapping of agencies was a predominant phenomenon. For example, there was a ministry of agriculture, a ministry of agricultural reclamation, and a ministry of agricultural machinery. Above these ministries, there was a higher layer called the National Agricultural Commission. Fourth, deputy positions were mushroomed. For the Ministry of Metallurgy, there were 19 deputy ministers (Ren, 1998).

Against such a backdrop, Deng Xiaoping, the actual paramount leader of China from 1978 to 1997, presented his view for the necessity of further administrative reforms. A few of which are quoted here: "Now (December 1978), in our economic work, there were overbloated and overlapping agencies. Red tape is rampant and leading to low efficiency. Exaggerated rhetoric overwhelmed other issues. It is not the responsibility of certain cadres, but is the problem of not raising the issue of reforms in time" (Deng, 1998, p. 76); "...but now (July 1979), the executives at every level of government are too old and they do not possess adequate energy...it is certain there are other problems in organization lines, such as how to solve the problem of the bloat of agencies and retirement. The temple is fixed and the number of Buddhas cannot be increased. Therefore, the younger employees cannot enter the public service if the elders do not retire. This is a simple reason" (Deng, 1998, pp. 191–193). In January 1982, Deng further stated that "Downsizing administrative organs is a revolution." He argued that "administrative agencies overbloating and overlapping, duties are not clear. Many people are not qualified. They are not accountable. They lack vitality, knowledge and efficiency...the situation has been reaching to an intolerable degree. The public will not tolerate it and our party will not tolerate it either" (Deng, 1998, p. 396).

In the wake of Deng's speech, the fourth administrative reform proposal was passed in March 1982. The effect of the reform was demonstrated in three levels: central, provincial, and county governments. At the central level, administrative organs were reduced from 100 to 61, government employees were reduced from 51,000 to 32,000. At the provincial level, administrative agencies were reduced from previous 50–60 to 30–40, government employees were reduced from 180,000 to 120,000. At the county level, government employees were downsized by about 20 percent. The average age of minister-level leaders was reduced from 64 to 60 and the average age of bureau (juji) level leaders was reduced from 58 to 54. In addition to the above changes, the education length of the leaders increased (Liu, 1998, pp. 301–302). All these reflected a trait of revolution, professional, knowledgeable, and younger age, which are required for the cadres.

Nevertheless, not long after, the expanding incentive showed its power again; there were 65 administrative organs and by the end of 1986 this number increased to 72. This situation heralds a new round of administrative reform.

The Fifth Round of Administrative Reform (1988–1992)

The 1982 administrative reform reduced administrative organs at the ministry level from 72 to 65. The number of central government employees downsized was 9700. However, the main character of the 1982 reform was the transformation of government function. The reform proposal of the State Council in 1988 had the following callings. It is necessary to establish an administrative system with comprehensive functions, reasonable structure, coordinated operation, and flexible and high efficiency. It is also important to separate the function of government from the CCP; separate the function of government from enterprise and service institutions. So the targets are: transforming the government functions, downsizing agencies and personnel, enhancing administrative efficiency, overcoming the bureaucratic style of doing business, and strengthening the vigor and vitality of agencies. That is, trying to create conditions to smooth the relation between government-enterprise and between government units and between central and local governments (Liu, 1998; Song, 2001).

The Sixth Round of Administrative Reform (1993–1997)

By the end of 1991, the number of public employees in the government and party system reached a new height at 9.2 million. The administrative expenditure of the government was 37 billion yuan RMB, plus the expenditure of service institution (Shiye Danwei) of 140 billion yuan RMB; these two items account for 37 percent of the government fiscal expenditure. The year 1993 started another round of administrative reform, the focus of which was to adapt the socialist market economy. The emphasis was still transforming the government functions. The avenue to do that was to separate the function of the enterprises from that of the government. The 1993 reform had reduced the administrative organs from 86 to 59, and downsized central government employees from 36,700 to 29,200.

In 1994, reform efforts continued in three aspects. First, returning the discretion of enterprise management to enterprises (from government); second, transferring the basic functions of adjusting resources to the market; and third, shifting the social service function and monitoring functions to the market intermediate organizations. By the end of 1994, there were 1.3 million service institutions with 26 million employees (Liu, 1998, pp. 306–309).

The Seventh Round of Administrative Reform (1998–2002)

In March 1998, the First Session of the Ninth People's Congress ratified the organizational reform proposed by the State Council. The number of ministries and commissions was reduced from 40 to 29. Sizeable cuts in government employment were planned and targeted at downsizing 50 percent of government employees. Gan Luo, the General Secretary of the State Council put forth the following "principles" to justify the seventh administrative reform in the PRC:

1. According to the requirements of developing socialist market economy, transforming government functions, realizing the separation of enterprise from government, it is imperative that government's function should be transformed to macro-adjustment and control, social management and public service, and to return the power of producing and operating to enterprises.
2. According to the principles of retrenchment, unification and efficacy, adjusting the organizational structure of the government is needed realizing downsizing of personnel and simplifying government agencies. Strengthening the macro-economic adjust and control agencies, adjusting and reducing the professional economic agencies, appropriately adjusting social service agencies, strengthening law-enforcement and regulation agencies, and developing social intermediate organization.
3. According to the principle of harmony of power and duty, adjusting the boundary of position and duty is needed to clarify the division between different government units.
4. Strengthening the rule of law is needed (Liu, 1998).

The seventh reform efforts sought to transform government functions. In clarifying the relationship between government and enterprise, the State Council had shifted out 280 functions to the enterprises, social intermediate organizations, and local governments. It aimed at creating clear functional divisions between different sectors and organizations; downsizing organizations and personnel, and strengthening the rule of law. Gains were made in all of these areas (Song, 2001, pp. 375–376).

Impact of Globalization on Chinese Administrative Reforms

In this section, I further abstract and conceptualize the characteristics of Chinese administrative reforms, compare and contrast the similar features with other NPM and non-NPM type countries, and analyze the avenues and resources of international impact on Chinese administrative reforms.

Administrative Reforms in the Mao Era (1949–1976)

Prominent Features

The fluctuation between downsizing and expanding central government agencies and employees could be observed throughout the Mao era (1949–1976). The objective was to search for a proper balance in the relationship between the center and locality. Yet, the pendulum constantly swung between the central and local governments without ever finding a proper equilibrium. In examining administrative reforms in China, Lan (2001) correctly observed that the central–local government relationship was not the only issue troubling the leadership. Also entangled in the mix were the issues of party–government relationship and government–business relationship. For instance, Dong Biwu once said at the Eighth Party's Congress, "The Party should lead government organizations through its party members and party organizations, not by taking their place" (Lan, 2001, p. 447). As early as November 6, 1956, an article titled "Allowing More Autonomous Power for the Enterprise" appeared in the *People's Daily*, the premier newspaper in the PRC. The Eighth Party over the Congress also reported that government agencies exercise too much control over enterprises, severely hindering the initiatives and flexibility of enterprises. These perplexing issues would again enter the lexicon of administrative reforms in the post-Mao era (after 1976).

One prominent feature of administrative reforms in this period is a top-down approach where top politicians are decision makers. In particular, the authority was concentrated to one person. The paramount leader Mao's words were obeyed as absolute truth. It was a time of blind obedience, for Mao gradually enjoyed a status as the "God" of the country. It is against such a political background that decentralization and centralization decisions were made in a seemingly *ad hoc* manner.

These decisions sometimes influenced the destiny of millions of people. A bad decision could be lethal to the whole country, such as the case of "Great Leap Forward" that was a disaster for the entire nation. It is also noticeable that the swing of the pendulum between the central and local governments mainly concerns who is in charge of what SOEs. This is indicative of a command economy where the government controls every facet of the enterprise and the national economy. Literally, there was no private industry, which reflects the essential character of collectiveness of a typical socialist country.

In short, the reform efforts in the Mao era were partly a response to the economic development and partly a response to the political incentives of class struggle and continued revolution under the proletariat dictatorship (perceived by Mao). On the surface, an evil cycle of "downsizing–swelling–downsizing–swelling (of government organizations and public employees at every level)" was easily observable. The Stalinist model that China adopted demanded highly centralized decision making by the top politicians for the political, economic, and social development of the country.

Why did the PRC adopt the Stalinist model of governance instead of other models? What global forces influenced China's direction in the Mao era? To address and appreciate these issues, we have to look at the international environment and examine China's foreign policy.

PRC in the Cold War Era

From the early days of the PRC in 1949, Mao Zedong tried to break the bipolar system and enable China to become an independent and important strategic power. In the Mao era, the foci of Chinese foreign relations strategy alternated between the Soviet Union and the United States: the *yibiandao* (leaning to one side) strategy in the 1950s, the *liangge quantou daren* (fighting with two fists) strategy in the 1960s, and the *yitiaoxian* (one united front) strategy in the 1970s (Zhang, 1998).

The "leaning to one side" strategy was adopted by the Common Program of the Chinese People's Political Consultative Conference in September 1949 and embodied in the Sino-Soviet Treaty of Friendship, Alliance, and Mutual Assistance in 1950. China cooperated with the Soviet Union against the United States, thus positioning China as a key member of the socialist bloc against the Capitalist camp in the bipolar Cold War era. "Of course, *yibiandao* was constructed on the basis of independence, equality and mutual benefit, not fell into the Soviet Union's arms" (Qian Qichen, 1994, pp. 40–44). *Yibiandao* is a strategy for survival, which was expected to guarantee China's security, sovereignty, and independence.

By the end of 1950s, Nikita Khrushchev was perceived to be ready to cooperate with the United States in controlling the world and imposing many unreasonable demands on China's sovereignty. Moscow adopted a number of steps to threaten China politically, economically, and militarily (Zhang, 1998). Although the United States welcomed the Sino-Soviet split, Washington continued to isolate China. The latter became the key target of the U.S. strategy of "containment" pursued since the end of World War II.

In such unfavorable international environment, China adopted an anti-imperialist (the United States) and anti-revisionist (the Soviet Union) international united front strategy in the 1960s, which was known in China as the *liangge quantou daren* (fighting with two fists) strategy, or the *liangtiao xian* (two united fronts) strategy, or the *shijie geming* (world revolution) strategy.

In view of the deterioration of Sino-Soviet relations, especially the armed conflicts along the Sino-Soviet border in 1969, the Chinese leadership realized that China's biggest threat came from the Sino-Soviet relationship. China's very survival was at stake.

While looking for allies to deter the Soviet Union, China's best choice obviously was the United States. In February 1972, President Richard Nixon visited China, which presented a chance of cooperation between China and the United States. Mao explained his *yitiaoxian* strategy (1973): "I talked with a foreign friend and indicated that I want to draw a line, i.e., the latitude lining up the U.S., Japan, China, Pakistan, Iran, Turkey and Europe" (Mu, 1994, pp. 172–180). The essence of this strategy was to unite all the forces that could be united, including the United States, to struggle against Soviet hegemony. The *yitiaoxian* strategy continued until 1982–1983 (Zhang, 1998).

By and large, Chinese governance was greatly influenced by the Stalinist model of command economy where market force plays a minimal role. As for the administrative reforms, no perceivable forces were coming from abroad. The Chinese economy was quite a closed model in the Mao era. China seldom, if ever, had contact from outside other than the brotherly friendship with the Soviet Union and socialist blocs in the 1950s. The interaction of China with socialist countries in this period did not exert any incentive and pressure over administrative reforms in China. Thus, administrative reforms in the Mao era were quite a matter of internal affairs in terms of cause, approaches, contents, and consequence.

Administrative Reforms in the Post-Mao Era (1977–2002)

Prominent Features

It is apparent that in the post-Mao era, the cyclical trend of downsizing and expanding of organizations and personnel has been repeated. However, it was not a simple replication of the previous efforts. As for adjustment in the relationship between the center and the locality, for example, the Mao era reforms were, in some sense, a swing between centralization and decentralization to locate an "optimal point" for the expediency of internal management. In the post-Mao era, the adjustment of central–local relations reflected more of the decentralization trend, a phenomenon called "playing to the provinces" (Solinger, 1996) from which local governments benefit. This trend is irreversible if the PRC wishes to continue harvesting the vitality and creativity of local governments in economic development, the key concern of the Chinese government in the post-Mao era. On the path to a market economy, more authority was delegated from the central to local governments, and from government to enterprises. Although there was resistance in the bureaucracy to "surrendering" their power to enterprises and the phenomenon of "two steps forward and one step backward" did exist, the overall trend has favored decentralization and delegation.

The post-Mao reform is not a simple repetition of the Maoist reforms. Superficially, it is somewhat similar in its focus on downsizing organization and personnel. But under scrutiny, the market-oriented economy is not only changing the relationship between central and local government, and the government and enterprises, but it is also a driving force in adjusting the relationship between the government and society and the government and the party. From this perspective, Chinese administrative reforms are surely moving down a one-way path.

Among others, prominent features of administrative reforms in this period at least include the following aspects: (i) transforming the functions of government to macro-adjustment and control, social management and public service, and to return the power of producing and operating to enterprises; (ii) adjusting the boundary of position and duty to clarify the division between different government units; (iii) strengthening the rule of law; (iv) separating the functions of enterprises from that of government; (v) decentralization and centralization trends in the fiscal relation between central and local governments; (vi) building an open and transparent government; and (vii) emphasizing grass root democratic participation.

Possible Avenues of Policy Transfer

We can safely say that administrative reform in the Mao era was largely an activity within a comparatively closed society, given the focus of the country on class struggle under a command economy. The administrative reforms in the post-Mao era were different in the sense that the country implemented an opening policy and gradually built a market economy.

New ways of thinking and means of governance filtered in from the outside world. For example, when China was considering building a modern civil service system, the government held a conference jointly with the United Nations (United Nations, 1985) and sponsored numerous visits to learn from the experiences of Western societies. In the area of public administration, the Chinese Public Administration Society was established in 1988 as a semiofficial association, and the National School of Administration was founded in 1994 to train PRC's high-level officials. A number of academic journals were created to reflect the theory development and the conduct of practice in public administration around the world.

A specific case in point is the introduction of the Master of Public Administration (MPA) program in China in 2001 that in some ways reflects the American model. At the beginning, there were 24 MPA programs in

China that recruited more than 3000 students in 2001 and 2002. Now there are 83 MPA programs in China.

Although hard evidence is yet to be found regarding the details of how Western NPM ideas influenced Chinese administrative reform initiatives, it is clear that there has been some influence. Osborne and Gaebler's (1992) best-seller *Reinventing Government; How the Entrepreneurial Spirit is Transforming the Public Sector* was translated into Chinese soon after its publication, while the Chinese version of Hughes's (1994) *Public Management and Administration* became a best-seller, as well as hundreds of other books in the field. Visits to the Western countries, scholar exchange programs, conferences, workshops, seminars, book and journal publications, and specific consultant reports have all helped to shape Chinese administrative reform ideas. This situation is in sharp contrast to the Mao era when the aforementioned channels of knowledge transfer and dissemination virtually did not exist due to the PRC's closed-door policy at the time. What we are arguing here is that administrative reform initiatives in the post-Mao era reflect both China's distinct characteristics and the influence of Western NPM thought (Zhang & Straussman, 2003).

Common NPM Features of Chinese Administrative Reforms

Does China share some of the features that are typical in NPM countries? Zhang and Straussman's probe provide a preliminary answer (See Table 25.1).

Bashing the bureaucrats was a phenomenon common to all four countries compared. In the United Kingdom, this was prominent during the Thatcher administration. Margaret Thatcher took a stance of antistatism and

Table 25.1 Similar Features of Administrative Reforms in Japan, the United Kingdom, the United States, and the PRC

A. Phenomenon	1. Bashing the bureaucrats
	2. Economic concern
B. Reasons	3. Restoring the trust and confidence in government
	4. Top politician support
	5. Downsizing government organization and employees
	6. Decentralization of government function and authority to lower levels of government
	7. Privatization
C. Contents	8. Market-orientation
	9. Contracting-out
	10. Minimal state orientation
	11. Promoting transparency of administrative procedure
	12. Improving public service

Source: Zhang, M. and Straussman, J. (2003). *Public Administration and Policy*, 12(2): 142–179.

was very critical of conventional bureaucracy (Zhou, 1999). From that posture, administrative reform in the United Kingdom was generally regarded as benchmark of NPM movement. In the United States, both Reagan and Clinton used this strategy for political advantage. Ronald Reagan, surely unsympathetic to bureaucrats, declared "In this present crisis, government is not the solution to our problem. Government is the problem" (Ronald Reagan, January 20, 1981, http://joshbotts.com/pdf/tnr-sullivan-crisisoffaith.pdf, accessed on May 20, 2005). In Japan, although bureaucrats were highly respected for centuries, a recent survey revealed that almost half of the respondents did not trust them in the 1990s. In the PRC, the bureaucracy was seen as inefficient and irresponsible by the public. Corruption was rampant in the 1980s and especially in the 1990s and the 21st century.

Although economic downturn in the 1970s was perceived as a driving force for administrative reforms in the United Kingdom, the United States, and Japan, in China it was a different scenario. Based on a poor foundation in 1970s, the growth of Chinese economy was strong in the 1980s and well into the 21st century. The fast pace of economic development demands a corresponding administrative system that can further facilitate economic growth. This situation requires a changing of traditional structure, instruments, functions, and ideology of administration. The pressure for administrative reforms to match the economic reform and development was high over the past two decades or so.

In all the countries listed, governments were conceived as overbloated, inefficient, unproductive, and generally not responsive. Therefore restoring trust and confidence in government was a major concern that compelled the governments to go to reform. To win back the public trust and confidence in the governments, and to rebuild the legitimacy of governance, top politicians (Mao, Deng, and Jiang Zemin in the PRC, Thatcher and Blair in the United Kingdom, Reagan and Clinton in the United States, and a number of prime ministers in Japan) have supported somewhat similar administrative reform initiatives.

In their efforts of administrative reforms in the recent two decades, all four countries (PRC, United Kingdom, United States, and Japan) have downsized government organizations and employees to a certain degree. Under the banner of "decentralization," Japan, the United Kingdom, and the United States focused more on empowering the frontline managers "to manage." This operation contrasts with the practice of PRC, where the focus was on shifting power and authority to the lower levels of government, and transferring economic functions to enterprises from the government.

Careful observers would notice that under the same rubric there exists the nuanced differences. For example, privatization in Japan, the United Kingdom, and the United States took place in an economy in which private capital dominated. Thus, privatization in these developed capitalist countries privatized the state-operated company. In the PRC, the private economy virtually ceased to exist in the Mao era (1949–1976). Thus the post-Mao reforms concentrated on both stimulating the growth of the private sector and privatizing SOEs.

Although Japan, the United Kingdom, and the United States adopted an approach more pro-market, in the PRC market-oriented reform gradually took place in the early 1990s, though with Chinese socialist characteristics. Contracting out of some government services to the private sector and nonprofit sector is not dominant in the PRC, but it is not unthinkable. However, other NPM countries used the strategy more frequently.

Minimal state orientation echoed each other in these countries to rebuild the image of government as efficient and productive. In Japan, the United Kingdom, and the United States the effort focuses on cutting public expenditure. In China, the emphasis is on downsizing government organizations and employees. It is ironic to notice that the government expenditure over gross domestic product (GDP) has been steadily increasing since 1994 (Zhang, 2003).

Constructing a transparent government is an objective shared by all the four governments. In the United Kingdom, the Citizen's Charter movement is dubbed as the "the core element of government reforms in the 1990s" by Prime Minister John Major (Zhou, 1999). The Citizen's Charter requires that all information related to the public service must be open and transparent, including the content and operating status of service, expenditure and cost of specific service, management organization and operating agencies, and the standards and quality information of the latter institution (Zhou, 1999). In the United States, the reinventing government movement also presented similar requirements by the National Performance Review. Japan's broad postwar administrative history can be summarized as repeated efforts to control the growth of government, to develop a policy of fiscal conservatism, to pursue deregulation, and to make the elite civil service more transparent and accountable (Terasawa & Gates, 1998). In China, there are a number of initiatives to make the government more transparent. The buildup of a public hearing system in China is a recent demonstration of such an endeavor (Peng et al., 2004).

Although improving public service is an umbrella term matching all the government reforms, in China, this characteristic is more obvious. City governments in Chengdu, ZhongQing, Nanjing, and Guangzhou have piloted service-oriented government in recent years. Public service is no longer a lip-service, but a practical action serving the public, both individuals and organization, especially the "one-stop shops" for the enterprise.

Common Features with Nontypical NPM Countries

By presenting the NPM features of Chinese administrative reforms, I am not saying that administrative reforms for the rest of countries do not look alike.

Far from that point of view, Lam (1997) actually suggested that administrative reforms all over the world share some sort of NPM traits. In his understanding, the NPM movement not only is restricted to developed countries such as United Kingdom, New Zealand, Australia, and Canada, but also found its way to developing and transitional societies in Asia, Latin America, and Africa. Countries like Singapore, Malaysia, India, the Philippines, Ghana, and Malta all adopted NPM ideas and practices (Lam, 1997).

Elaine Kamarck, of the JFK School of Government of Harvard University, once the advisor of National Performance Review, recently reviewed government innovation around the world (2004). She identifies six universal components of government reform. They are: government that costs less; quality government; professional government; digital government; better-regulated government; and honest and transparent government. Chinese reforms also have this content.

As countries around the globe have attempted to reduce government cost to stimulate economic development and attract more foreign direct investment, public sectors have resorted to various forms of budget innovations. In every round of administrative reform in China, efforts were made to downsize government agencies and personnel to reduce administrative cost. In the recent two decades, the incentive of building a small government is strong in China.

In a reform age, every nation is trying to construct a quality government. Although quality can mean a lot of things, many reformers regard quality as reforms that attempt to improve service delivery (Kamarck, 2004). Borrowing the idea of Citizen Charters that originated in Great Britain, the leader of a government department in Yantai municipality in 1994 introduced a pathbreaking new system, called the "Service Promise System" (*fuwu chengnuo zhi*), designed to enable his agency to do a better job of providing public services (Foster, 2004). In 1999, the Chinese Customs agency cooperated with the United States Customs agency to begin the Shanghai Model Port Project. The project will give Shanghai Customs a capacity to process clearance 24 hours a day, seven days a week. It serves as a model for customs modernization (Kamarck, 2004). In 2002, the city government of Chengdu piloted the standardized service-oriented government in three agencies but is now applied to all government-wide agencies in the city. In the same period, city governments of Zhong Qing, Nanjing, and Guangzhou all adopted similar efforts in constructing service-oriented government. In China, to serve the joint venture better, the increased proliferation of public administration service centers or "one-stop-shops" started around 2000. Now, there are hundreds of such one-stop-shops all over the country (Li, 2004b).

As for a professional government, China adopted a tentative regulation of civil service on August 14, 1993, which initiated the contemporary civil service system. The law of PRC civil service was formally approved by the

Tenth National Congress on April 27, 2005. The promulgation of the law is an indication that China is on the way toward a professional government. Starting from 2001, China started its first MPA program, now there are 83 such programs. Other than that, China built a system of public administration schools at national, provincial, and municipal levels. At the national level, China Pudong Cadre School, China Jinggangshan Cadre School, and China Yanan Cadre School began to recruit trainees from 2005. Many Chinese public employees have been sent abroad (United States, Canada, Europe, Singapore, etc.) for advanced learning. These initiatives are only a part of a concerted effort to build a professional government in China.

China is not a laggard for digital government building. The earliest effort could be traced to 1985. At that time, Chinese government started a domestic project targeted at government information (Wu, 2004). By January 2001, the total number of domain names ending with "gov.cn" had reached 4722. Starting in 1993, the Chinese government attempted to build a series of "golden" projects such as Golden Bridge Project (aimed at economic information communication), Golden Customs Project, Golden Credit Card Project, Golden Wisdom Project, and so forth. The effort of building digital government is along two lines: one is a vertical line which is a top-down approach to facilitate online government functions such as finance, tax, civil affairs, customs; and the other is a horizontal line which is targeted at facilitating cross-regional cooperation such as the "digitalized Beijing" and "digitalized Shanghai" (Wu, 2004).

Whereas many developed economies are on the track of deregulation to provide incentive for entrepreneurship and reduce the chance of corruption, the developing world is working toward more and better regulations. In China, the main trend is making more regulations for related professions. The recent official promulgation of civil service law is a case in point. Because China has been transforming from a planned economy to a market economy, it is necessary to establish a number of laws and regulations. Parallel to the economic development, China has been strengthening the rule of law, from rule by man, over the past decades. Thus, deregulation is not a major current in China. This is not to say that deregulation does not happen in China.

For example, in 2002 alone, the State Council eliminated administrative approval of 789 items and correspondingly would make an impact on the function of adjustment of related administrative agencies.

To build an honest and transparent government is not easy but it is not impossible. In Changsha (China), the opening of government affairs was initiated in the late 1980s and up to 1996, the party's Committee and Municipal Government of Changsha jointly decided to expand the system of opening government affairs citywide. This innovation has won back confidence in the government from the public (Yu, 2002). In Guizhou province, China, the city of Guiyang won the Innovations and Excellence in Local Chinese Government award in 2002 for opening up the standing committee of the People's Congress to citizen attendance and citizen participation (Kamarck, 2004). As a matter of fact, many local governments in China take similar actions to make their governance more open and transparent.

Thus, with the above comparison and analysis, we can say for sure that the forces of globalization are at work. In the post-Mao era (1977 onwards), China is hardly immune from outside influence. In the area of administrative reforms, China shares a number of universal traits that were identified in other countries, either NPM or non-NPM ones.

Unique Characteristics of Chinese Administrative Reforms

In the last section, we have seen that administrative reforms in China share a number of characteristics with other countries. Then, are there any features unique to China?

As we know, administrative reforms in the Mao era demonstrated a vicious strange cycle of "swelling–downsizing–swelling–downsizing," reflecting a centralization and decentralization swing. When the administrative power was centralized, the central government was in charge of too many enterprises and directly participated in the micromanagement process of planning, production, circulation, and consumption of industrial products. When this happened, the central government was swelled and the subnational governments lacked the initiative for economic development. In return, when decentralization took hold, many of the enterprises previously affiliated to central government now became the turf of the local governments. Then, the central government had the incentive to claim back the lost authority. Compared with the Western developed countries, the recurring of such centralization and decentralization phenomenon is unique to China.

In the post-Mao era, the adjustment of several pairs of relations in China is not familiar to other countries, especially to those developed countries. First is the adjustment of the relation between the government and the CCP. Traditionally, the government and the CCP are regarded as the same integrated entity by the public, because they have overlapping functions and more often than not, they have the same personnel working for the two units. Even nowadays, in some circumstances, one set of personnel carries two titles. For example, one set of personnel serves a local School of Administration and a local CCP School simultaneously; these two schools have the same locality and are staffed with the same faculty.

The direction of the reform is to separate the functions of the party from that of the government. The second approach is the separation of enterprise from that of government. Government should focus on macro-management, coordination, and control, whereas enterprise should be responsible for its own planning, production, circulation, and sale of its products and services. Thus, government and enterprise have their different domains of business, and government should not interfere with the affairs of enterprises. In the past two decades reform has largely adjusted the relationship between the government and the enterprise. Still, governments occasionally try to intervene with the business of enterprises. In this regard, the transformation of government functions has yet a long way to go. The third approach is to adjust the relationship between government and the social intermediate organizations. In the past, government took over all the social issues under its wings. Now, it is recognized that a strong nonprofit sector is the requirement of developing a civil society. The last, but not the least, approach is the adjustment of the relationship between the government and the individual. Government in China conventionally played such important roles in personal life as to influence individuals' private life. Now, it is recognized that there must be a boundary between government and citizen, and that individual freedom, liberty, and privacy should be protected. In a word, human rights are more appreciated. Although some other countries may have similar adjustment of these relationships, the adjustment of these relations is essential to the Chinese society in the post-Mao era.

One focus of administrative reforms in the recent two decades is the transformation of government functions. This is basically the adjustment of relationship between government and enterprises as just described. This transformation of government function is an ongoing business in China.

As discussed earlier, China has been on the way toward strengthening the rule of law and promulgating more regulations in related professions. This feature may be in sharp contrast with many developed countries where the efforts are spent on deregulation. However, better-regulated government is a target for many developing countries (Kamarck, 2004).

In developed countries, it is not difficult to locate an organization that is in charge of reform initiatives. In the United States, for example, we know that the Grace Commission was responsible for the reform design of the Reagan Administration, whereas the National Performance Review was the leading force for the reinventing government movement during the Clinton Administration. In Great Britain, the Efficiency Unit was in charge of the NPM style of reform initiatives. This is in contrast to the administrative reform in China, where to identify the institution in charge of reform initiative is like entering a labyrinth. Although we understand that the State Council proposed the reform bills, we have no idea who prepared them.

It is ironic that China is striding toward the rule of law on the one hand, whereas on the other hand, each round of administrative reform had no accompanying laws to guarantee the enforcement. Instead, there were only administrative directives to guide the reform efforts. Thus, more often than not, there was no performance measurement and no corresponding mechanism of awards and punishment. It is not surprising to know that the outcome of the reform frequently falls short of accomplishing the promised targets. For example, the seventh round of administrative reform was targeted at reducing 50 percent of civil servants. There were reports about the actual downsizing in the central and provincial level government, but it is not clear how many public employees were actually downsized in the city, county, and township level, where most public employees are located. In the end, no one knows how many personnel were downsized nationwide.

There is no budget constraint for each administrative reform exercise in China. Thus, the targeted governments (and agencies) have no incentive to reduce their personnel and associated power, authority, and prestige. This may result in the failure of administrative reform.

Although borrowing ideas and techniques from the private sector is a typical strategy of many NPM style reforms, in China, such a notion is alien to the reformers. In China, there is a growing awareness of serving the public and achieving high performance. Nevertheless, in each of the former seven rounds of administrative reform, the issues of customer orientation and performance orientation did not appear to surface.

Concluding Thoughts and Future Prospects

From previous discussions, we observe that Chinese administrative reforms share a number of common features with NPM style of reforms in terms of phenomenon, reasons, and contents. At least in the following eight areas, Chinese administrative reforms have similar characteristics with those of NPM movement countries: downsizing government organizations and personnel; decentralization of government function and authority to lower levels of government; privatization; market-orientation; contracting out; minimal state orientation; promoting transparency of governance; and improving public service. Compared with nontypical NPM movement countries, the six universal components of government reform identified by Kamarck (2004) are also hallmarks of Chinese reforms: government that costs less; quality government; professional government; digital government; better-regulated government; and honest and transparent government.

For those "unique" characteristics of Chinese administrative reforms, we have to understand them in a relative sense. The vicious cycles of "swelling–downsizing–swelling–downsizing" in the Mao era reflected the requirements of internal management, though the globalization forces were somehow irrelevant to Chinese reforms in this period. In the post-Mao era, the evil cycle repeated, but it was not a simple replication, because factors counted in. The transformation of the government functions is essential to Chinese reforms and the adjustment of several pairs of relationships is the key to understanding recent changes of the Chinese governance. From rule by man to rule of law is a core feature of Chinese society striding toward modernity. For the area of Chinese administrative reforms, the future attention should be paid to promulgating corresponding laws and regulations for each specific effort. A stringent budget constraint is necessary as a mechanism to ensure the reform results for each targeted government agency. Performance measurement for the government organization is an effective instrument for administrative reform. Ultimately, the most important question is the purpose of the reform endeavor. In this regard, future reforms should be focused on customer orientation. There are encouraging signs that Chinese reformers have gradually emphasized the issue from the abstract concept of "serving the people" toward the concrete construction of a service-oriented government with detailed standards and procedures.

Administrative reforms have been shaped by and would shape the changing society. The average annual growth rate of Chinese economy was 9.5 percent over the past 26 years. This achievement is a miracle comparable to the four mini-dragons (South Korea, Hong Kong, Taiwan, and Singapore). Assuming that China can maintain an annual growth rate at 8 percent, then the per capita GDP of China will reach the 2004 U.S. level — US$ 38,000 in 2031 (http://news.creaders.net/headline/newsPool/11A237493.html: accessed on April 12, 2005). What are the outlooks of China for the future? Wang Mengkui, the Director of the State Council Development and the Research Center of China, provided some clues. According to his understanding, for the next five to fifteen years, China will be on the track of industrialization, urbanization, marketization, and internationalization. In the same period, China needs to grasp the megatrend of social economic development, purposefully adopting some grand policy measures. Wang raised four concerns to be addressed. First, how to alternate the manner of economic growth? Second, how to combine the issue of facilitating urbanization with the issue of "agriculture, peasants, and rural development?" Third, focusing on solving social problems, and realizing a harmonious development between economy and society. Fourth, enhancing the level of opening to the outside, and participating international cooperation and competition in larger scope, scale, and higher level. The essence of these concerns is industrialization, urbanization (with Chinese characteristics), marketization (complementing socialist market economy system), and internationalization (merge to world economy and trade system), as well as realizing the coordinated development between societal stability and economic growth (http://news.yam.com/cna/china/200505/20050527183752.html: accessed on May 28, 2005).

The future prospects of Chinese governance thus lie in a broad political, social, historical, economic, and cultural context. Both domestic and international forces will exert great influence on Chinese public sector management in general and government reform and innovation in particular. With China's entry into the WTO in 2001, China faces serious challenges at least in the following facets: government system, law system, mindset and ideology, civil service workforce, market system, and industrial system (Ruan, 2001). At present, many Chinese local governments are in a fad of building up service-oriented government, which not only serves the people and various organizations better, but also has a responsibility to construct a government to be more responsive, accountable, legitimate, fair, and equitable. Li (2004a) stated that a service-oriented government is also a public, limited, rule of law, accountable, entrepreneurship, and digital government. One of the necessary means is performance measurement and management.

Although nobody can predict precisely the features of Chinese administrative reforms in the future, it is for sure that both domestic and international forces will play important roles in the process. Despite the fact that Chinese reforms emerged from a radically different starting point in the early years (relatively underdeveloped, centrally planned, and ruled by a one-party monopoly) (Burns, 2001), in the long run, Chinese governance will bear more global than local characteristics. In other words, in the area of administrative reforms in China, the force of convergence is stronger than the force of divergence.

References

Amin, A., Gills, B., Palan, R., and Taylor, P. (1994). "Editorial: forum for heterodox international political economy." *Review of International Political Economy*, 1(1): 1–12.

Bissessar, A.M. (2002). *Policy Transfer, New Public Management and Globalization: Mexico and the Caribbean*. Lanham, MD: Rowman & Littlefield.

Boston, J. (1996). *Public Management: The New Zealand Model*. Oxford: Oxford University Press.

Breul, J. (1996). "Borrowing experiences from other countries." In G. Davis and P. Weller (eds.) *New Ideas, Better Government*. Brisbane: Allen and Unwin. pp. 74–82.

Burns, J.P. (2001). "Public sector reform and the state: the case of China." *Public Administration Quarterly*, 24(4): 419–436.

Carter, L.F. (1998). "Public personnel administration in the 20th century." In R. Jack, W.B. Hildreth and G.J. Miller (eds.) *Handbook of Public Administration*, 2nd edition. New York: Marcel Dekker.

Collier, D. and Messick, R. (1975). "Prerequisites vs. diffusion." In G. Davis and P. Weller (eds.) *New Ideas, Better Government*. Brisbane, Australia: Allen and Unwin. pp. 74–82.

Common, R. (2000). *Public Management & Policy Transfer in Southeast Asia*. London: Ashgate Publishing Company. 300 pp.

Cope, S., Leishman, F., and Starie, P. (1997). "Globalization, new public management and the enabling state: futures of police management." *International Journal of Public Sector Management*, 10(6): 444–460.

Deng, X. (1998). *Selected Articles of Deng Xiaoping II*. Beijing: People's Press (Chinese).

Dolowitz, D.P. and Marsh, D. (2000). "Learning from abroad: the role of policy transfer in contemporary policy-making." *Governance: An International Journal of Policy and Administration*, 13(1): 5–24.

Dolowitz, D.P., Hulme, R., Nellis, M., and O'Neill, F. (1999). *Policy Transfer and British Social Policy: Learning from the USA*. Buckingham and New York: Open University Press. 176 pp.

Farazmand, A. (1999). "Globalization and public administration." *Public Administration Review*, 59(6): 509–522.

Foster, K.W. (2004). "Chinese public policy innovation and the diffusion of innovations: an initial exploration." Paper Prepared for Presentation at the 2nd Sino-U.S. International Conference on Public Administration, People's University, Beijing, China, May 24–25, 2004.

Greenwood, J. and Wilson, D. (1989). *Public Administration in Britain Today*. London: Unwin Hyman.

Haas, P.M. (1989). "Do regimes matter? Epistemic communities and Mediterranean pollution control." *International Organization*, 3(3): 377–403.

Halliday, F. (1994). *Rethinking International Relations*. Basingstoke: Macmillan.

Hood, C. (1991). "A public management for all season?" *Public Administration*, 69(1): 3–19.

Hughes, O.E. (1994). *Public Management and Administration: An Introduction*. New York: St. Martin's Press.

Hughes, O.E. (1998). "New public management." In J.M. Shafritz (ed.) *International Encyclopedia of Public Policy and Administration*. Boulder, CO: Westview Press.

Kamarck, E. (2004). "Government innovation around the world." Faculty Research Working Papers Series. John F. Kennedy School of Government. Harvard University. RWP04–010.

Lam, J.T.M. (1997). "Transformation from public administration to management: success and challenges of public sector reform in Hong Kong." *Public Productivity & Management Review*, 20(4): 405–418.

Lan, Z. (2001). "Understanding China's administrative reform." *Public Administration Quarterly*, 24(4): 437–468.

Li, J. (2004a). *Public Service Oriented Government.* Beijing: Beijing University Press. (Chinese).

Li, X. (2004b). "Recreating China's public service: reality and improvement of public administrative service centers." Paper Presented at the Effective Public Service Delivery Workshop, Launching Conference: Network of Asia-Pacific Schools and Institutes of Public Administration and Governance (NAPSIPAG), 6–8 December 2004, Kuala Lumpur, Malaysia. National Institute of Public Administration (INTAN)–Malaysia and Asian Development Bank.

Liu, Z. (1998). *The Seventh Revolution — Memorandum of 1998 Reform on Chinese Government Organization.* Beijing: The Economic Daily Publishing Company (Chinese).

Mao, Z. (1999a). "On the ten major relations." *Selected Works of Mao Zedong*, VII. Beijing: People's Press (Chinese).

Mao, Z. (1999b). "Eighteen issues discussed at Mount Lu Conference." *Selected Works of Mao Zedong*, VIII. Beijing: People's Press (Chinese).

Masser, K. (1998). "Public sector administrative reforms." In J.M. Shafritz (ed.) *International Encyclopedia of Public Policy and Administration.* Boulder, CO: Westview Press.

Mossberger, K. and Wolman, H. (2003). "Policy transfer as a form of prospective policy evaluation: challenges and recommendations." *Public Administration and Review*, 63(4): 428–440.

Mu, J. (1994). "An important historical decision — on Mao Zedong's strategic decision and tactical thinking on achieving a breakthrough in Sino-U.S. Relation." In P. Jianzhang (ed.) *Study of the Diplomatic Thought of Mao Zedong.* Beijing: World Affairs Press (Chinese).

Osborne, D. and Gaebler, T. (1992). *Reinventing Government; How the Entrepreneurial Spirit is Transforming the Public Sector.* Reading, MA: Addison-Wesley.

Pempel, T.J. (1982). *Policy and Politics in Japan: Creative Conservatism.* Philadelphia, PA: Temple University press.

Peng, Z., Xue, L., and Kan, K. (2004). *Public Hearing Systems in China: Transparent Policy-making & Public Governance.* Beijing: Qinghua University Press (Chinese).

Qian, Q. (1994). "Study Mao Zedong's diplomatic thought and perform the diplomatic work well in the new era." In P. Jianzhang (ed.) *Study of the Diplomatic Thought of Mao Zedong.* Beijing: World Affairs Press (Chinese).

Ren, X. (1998). *Administrative Reforms in China.* Hangzhou: Zhejiang People's Press (Chinese).

Rose, R. (1991). "What is lesson-drawing?" *Journal of Public Policy*, 11(1): 3–30.

Ruan, C. (2001). *WTO and Government Reforms.* Beijing: Economic Daily Press (Chinese).

Savoie, D.J. (1994). *Thatcher, Reagan, Mulroney: In Search of a New Bureaucracy.* Pittsburg and London: University of Pittsburgh Press.

Seely, B.E. (2003). "Historical patterns in the scholarship of technology transfer." *Comparative Technology and Society*, 1(1): 7–48.

Solinger, D.J. (1996). "Despite decentralization: disadvantages, dependence and ongoing central power in the inland — the case of Wuhan." *The China Quarterly*, 145: 1–34.

Song, D. (ed.) (2001). *Chinese Government Management and Reform*. Beijing: Chinese Law Press.

Straussman, J.D. and Zhang, M. (2001). "Chinese administrative reforms in international perspective." *International Journal of Public Sector Management*, 14(4): 411–422.

Terasawa, K.L. and Gates, W.R. (1998). "Relationships between government size and economic growth: Japan's government reforms and evidence from OECD." *International Public Management Journal*, 1(2): 195–223.

Theen, R.H.W. and Wilson, F.L. (1996). *Comparative Politics: An Introduction to Seven Countries*, 3rd edition. Upper Saddle River, NJ: Prentice Hall.

Waltman, J.L. (1980). *Copying Other Nation's Policies: Two American Case Studies*. Cambridge, MA: Schenkman Publishing Company.

Welch, S. and Thompson, K. (1980). "The impact of federal incentives on state policy innovation." *American Journal of Political Science*, 24(4): 715–729.

Wolman, H. (1992). "Understanding cross-national policy transfers: the case of Britain and the U.S." *Governance: An International Journal of Policy and Administration*, 5(1): 27–45.

Wu, A. (2004). *Public Management: Theories and Practice*. Taiyuan: Shanxi People Press (Chinese).

Yu, K. (2002). "Four-tier joint action in opening government affair in Changsha municipality, Hunan province." In K. Yu (ed.) *Innovations and Excellence in Local Chinese Governance*. Beijing: Social Science Literature Press.

Zhang, W.F. (1998). "China's foreign relations strategies under Mao and Deng: a systematic comparative analysis." *Department of Public and Social Administration*, City University of Hong Kong, Working Paper Series.

Zhang, M. (2003)."Assessing the China's 1994 Fiscal Reform: An Intermediate Report." From September 18 to 20, 2003, at the ABFM (Association of Budgeting and Financial Management) conference in Washington, D.C.

Zhang, M. and Straussman, J. (2003). "Chinese administrative reforms with British, American and Japanese characteristics?" *Public Administration and Policy*, 12(2): 142–179.

Zhang, C. and Zhang, M. (2005). *Public Administration and Administrative Reform in China for the 21st Century: From State-Center Governance to the Citizen-Center Governance*. Genesis: A Caravan. Spring.

Zhou, Z. (1999). *Comparative Study of Contemporary Foreign Administrative Reforms*. Beijing: National School of Administration Press (Chinese).

Zhou, D. (2000). "Globalization and administrative reforms in developing countries." *Forum of Party and Government Cadres*, 10: 21–23 (Chinese).

Chapter 26

Globalization, Bureaucracy, and Administrative Reform in Hong Kong

Ahmed Shafiqul Huque

CONTENTS

Introduction

Hong Kong has gone through remarkable changes over the past four decades, first as a British colony and then as an autonomous region of the People's Republic of China. The exceptional performance of the Hong Kong economy was the first to catch the attention of scholars and observers across the world. Economic prosperity was a major catalyst in the formulation and implementation of a wide range of reforms in social policy. However, in the absence of an effective political authority, leadership was provided by the bureaucracy, which was acknowledged to be one of the key driving forces behind the success of Hong Kong in the late 20th century. Thus, by default, the bureaucracy has been a key institution in responding to the challenge of reforming the administrative system for integration with the globalized world.

A series of reforms in the administrative system have helped Hong Kong deal with the turning points in its pursuit of economic miracle and manage the social tensions triggered by major changes in the economy and society. The unique political structure and administrative arrangements in Hong Kong have contributed to the closest approximation of Weberian bureaucracy in the contemporary world. This chapter seeks to draw parallels between the ideal construct of Weberian bureaucracy and the nature of changes taking place in the Hong Kong administrative system to argue that the traditional approach to public administration can be applied to circumstances where the conditions are appropriate. However, subsequent changes in the international arena have influenced recent reform endeavors, and finally, the inadequacies of a Weberian style of bureaucracy are becoming evident.

The chapter begins with an attempt to develop a portrait of the bureaucracy in Hong Kong and draw parallels with the ideal construct postulated by Weber. An overview of the background and evolution of the administrative system in Hong Kong will further substantiate the unique features of the bureaucracy and its special position in the society. This is followed by a discussion of the reform attempts made during the British rule as well as after the reversal of sovereignty to China, to identify the main themes and directions of changes. An interesting paradox can be noted in the divergence from the approaches followed by Britain and China in structuring and operating administrative organizations. The British rulers of Hong Kong established and reinforced the classical bureaucratic format, although the approach in the United Kingdom has been more open and flexible. The Chinese government adheres strictly to the classical approach in its administrative system, but has allowed Hong Kong to proceed along different directions that are consistent with the international trend.

Classical Bureaucracy and Administrative Reform

Administrative reforms are influenced by numerous considerations. The literature is replete with cases of reforms initiating from the changes in government, ideology, financial and political capability of countries, as well as demands from the internal and the external environments. Reforms often aim to balance the needs of the time, the pressures from the environment, and the intention and capability of the system (see Szanton, 1981; Caiden, 1991).

Globalization has brought to the fore another source of reform ideas that emanate from international trends. Influential countries, powerful financial institutions, and international agencies offer ideas and agenda on the direction of changes they would like to see for strengthening the global efforts to promote development. The essence of administrative reforms in the Western industrialized countries are generally considered appropriate. In addition, governments learn from the experience of other countries and seek to introduce changes for emulating success achieved in their efforts to improve management and living conditions.

Generally, reforms are carried out with the stated objective of enhancing the capacity of the government and the bureaucracy by simplifying procedures, restructuring the organization, rearranging personnel, or streamlining the administrative process, of which many appear to have a common objective of cost-cutting (Huque, 2002, p. 8). In the final analysis, political considerations play an extremely important role in the process. In the absence of strong political authority in a country, the bureaucracy may be able to assume a strong position and set the agenda for the reform process. In most cases, administrative reforms are aimed at serving the interest of the government in cutting costs, improving services, and enhancing the acceptability of its programs to the electorate.

The public bureaucracy is a key institution in Hong Kong, and has played a central role in all aspects of change and development in the territory. Bureaucracies take various forms with differing degrees of emphasis on the structure, function, relationship with other institutions and place in the system. Although bureaucratic structures in one form or another have existed for a long time, Max Weber was the first to attempt to discuss the features of the bureaucratic form of organization and constructed a list of its key features:

1. Fixed authority and official jurisdictions based upon a specific grant of power to the official office
2. Written, formal rules as the basis of management of the bureau
3. Impersonality and bureaucrats to apply rules without regard to their own interests, special features of the case, status of the clientele, bestowals of favor, or traditional value

4. A hierarchy of offices in which the relationships between officials are regulated by the rule of hierarchy
5. Career services in which bureaucrats are expected to be loyal to their office[1]
6. Permanence, as it provides continuous service and its web of power is impossible to destroy (Weber, 1946).

McCurdy pointed out that all public organizations cannot be considered as bureaucratic, and succinctly summed up Weber's views: "An organization is not bureaucratic unless, by definition, it possesses special structural characteristics designed to maximize efficiency in pursuit of established goals. The most important structural characteristics are a permanent class of civil servants with clearly defined duties, whose authority is officially fixed by law, and record keeping, so that past decisions can be used as the basis for future administrative actions. The result is a system of administration that can provide routine, uninterrupted services where officials are prone to emphasize operational effectiveness and rational behavior over other organizational values" (McCurdy, 1977, p. 71).

It is understandable that classical bureaucracy is not easily amenable to change and is likely to resist efforts to alter distribution of power and patterns of relationships. It will be interesting to examine the response of the bureaucracy — a powerful institution in Hong Kong — to the efforts to introduce reforms and initiate changes to keep abreast of developments in the contemporary world.

Globalization and Administrative Reform

One of the most potent developments in the contemporary world has been the enigma of globalization. The move toward an integrated world economy began, as major business corporations sought to expand their markets — and subsequently, operations — across national boundaries. Globalization is thus a consequence of the liberalization of states and the opening up of economies, and the process took off in a big way after the cessation of the Cold War. It was facilitated by the remarkable progress achieved in information technology (IT), and the net result has been the free movement of capital, commodities, services, people, and ideas across national borders. It can be said that globalization has succeeded, to a considerable extent, in opening up societies and standardizing rules of governance.

---

[1]The bureaucrats receive a fixed salary based on the rank, permanency in office, pension, and prospect of promotion on the basis of seniority.

There are implications for administrative reform. A common tendency is to introduce similar programs for all countries, regardless of indigenous needs. One of the most common problems confronting most nations has been the diminishing pool of resources and rapidly rising demands from the public for better and new services. As the 20th century drew to a close, a changed macroeconomic environment and expectations on the part of the citizens led to a challenging environment, and these were further compounded by "a changed international context, the change in organizational paradigm in the private sector, and the modernization policies being pursued in competitor countries" (Naschold and von Otter, 1996, pp. 57–60).

The impact of the forces of globalization on administrative reform in Hong Kong was relatively easier to handle as the territory had already been a participant in the global economy. Administrative institutions and their regulations had to be consistent with global standards, and positive reports from influential international agencies indicated that the reform agenda was consistent with the trend. The principles, values, procedures, and practices of public administration are increasingly becoming similar across the globe, and Hong Kong has followed the trend to respond to the strong influence of globalization.

One of the most striking impacts of globalization has been the exertion of pressure — direct or indirect — on countries to converge toward a common system of governance. This calls for, among other prerequisites, mature political and economic institutions, as well as a system of public administration that emphasizes economy, efficiency, and effectiveness. Although many countries seek to introduce reforms along these lines after succumbing to external pressures, problems arise if there are strong internal pressures that are ignored in the process.

Administrative Reforms in Hong Kong

In many ways, Hong Kong has been a unique entity in terms of administrative arrangements. It was described as an "administrative state" in which administrative organizations and operations were particularly prominent in spite of the presence of legislative and judicial organs (Harris, 1978, p. 55). A large number of expatriate officials occupied the key positions in the bureaucracy and they were under the direct control of the governor and the chief secretary. Strict hierarchical authority and a simple pyramidal structure in a colonial setting provided the ideal condition for implementing Weberian principles. Weber believed that bureaucracy was critical not only in achieving the optimum level of rationality for overcoming chaos but also for the achievement of social justice (Weber, 1946, p. 260).

As a British colony for over a century and a half, the natural choice for Hong Kong was to emulate the British model that emphasized a system led by administrative generalists. Understandably, the style of administration in the public sector was modeled on the British system, and some of the reforms introduced there in the late 1970s and 1980s were emulated in Hong Kong. However, before the new culture emphasizing service to the public and stronger customer orientation could take root, Hong Kong was returned to China.

Administrative reforms in Hong Kong have been influenced by its internal as well as external influences, mainly from the United Kingdom. Under a simple structure of the administrative system, a colonial governor appointed by the British Crown exercised full control. A bureaucracy, led mainly by British officials, provided strong support with senior public servants running the administrative machinery. The executive council, a body of officials and advisers appointed by the governor, was the key forum for discussing policies and making decisions. The executive branch of the government dominated policy initiation, formulation, and implementation (Lee and Lam, 1992, p. 45). As the global wave of democratization influenced Hong Kong, the legislature did acquire some power in the 1990s.

There was practically no attempt to introduce changes in the administrative system of Hong Kong for a long time after the British assumed control of the territory. Riots and social disturbances in the late 1960s drew attention to the fact that the classical bureaucratic approach had resulted in a vast distance between the citizens and the government. A report on the social disturbances revealed that the cause of the riots was alienation of citizens, which resulted from the rigid and nonpublic nature of the system, and suggested strengthening the channels of communication between the government and the public and making service delivery more proactive (Commission of Inquiry, 1967).

The government sought to identify the source of the weaknesses in the administrative system that may have contributed to the disturbances by appointing a consulting firm — McKinsey and Company — to review the machinery of the central government in 1973. This was the first attempt to undertake a review of the system and was the first concrete step toward administrative reform in Hong Kong. It should be noted that advice from senior bureaucrats played a central role in selecting the consulting firm as well as determining the terms of reference.

Since the 1970s, Hong Kong began its transformation from a manufacturing and trading center toward a thriving and modern emerging economy in the region. The government tried to cope with the changes by introducing plans to expand a range of social services in the areas of health, welfare, education, and municipal services. These steps were expected to promote social stability. McKinsey and Company had identified work overload at the highest level as a major problem, and a group of policy secretaries were appointed within the central secretariat to support the bureaucrats at the highest level. This resulted in the establishment of a highly centralized system, which ensured that the governor received complete information and remained in full control (Miners, 1995, p. 88). The main features of the administrative system could be described in terms of minimal government, deference to authority, and high degree of centralization (Lee and Huque, 1996, p. 14). "The government was essentially an administrative structure and the bureaucracy strictly Weberian in nature" (Huque and Yep, 2003, p. 147). The Hong Kong government thus embarked on the path of modernization with a fully entrenched classical bureaucracy.

As a result of spectacular economic growth in Hong Kong during the 1980s, new challenges were encountered and administrative reforms were needed to deal with them. The size and scope of administrative organizations expanded rapidly as the government became involved in additional responsibilities. Some of the new responsibilities were a consequence of major changes ushered in the form of "new public management." Rhodes listed its main features: "a focus on management, not policy, and on performance appraisal and efficiency; the disaggregation of public bureaucracies into agencies which deal with each other on user-pay basis; the use of quasi-markets and contracting out to foster competition; cost cutting; and a style of management which emphasizes, amongst other things, output targets, limited term contracts, monetary incentives and freedom to manage" (Rhodes, 1991, p. 1).

New public management encompassed a common set of responses to problems of oversized bureaucracies, expensive public services, and demands to a transparent and responsive public service. Hong Kong government responded to the changing circumstances by publishing plans in 1989 to initiate major changes. The aim was "to improve the quality of management within the civil service by promoting an increased awareness of what results are actually being achieved by the government and at what cost" (Finance Branch, Hong Kong Government, 1989, p. 1). The same classical bureaucracy was able to implement the new public management-oriented reforms with similar effectiveness. A small public sector and the dominant influence of business interests were conducive to the introduction of private sector practices to the public sector.

These proposals continued to be implemented over the 1990s through a series of reforms, reorganizations, and reorientations. In 1992, an efficiency unit was established to plan, guide, and assess the implementation of reforms. The government departments were required to develop performance pledges, and senior public officials emphasized service to the community in their statements.[2] The composition of the legislative council was gradually changed to make it fully representative with directly elected members for the first time in Hong Kong's history. The process was helped by an enthusiastic media, which acted as an important catalyst in transforming the administrative philosophy, approaches, and strategies. However, with the withdrawal of British control over Hong Kong, the initiatives of opening up the government's administrative process to intense legislative scrutiny lost momentum as the composition of the legislature underwent changes.

Worldwide, there was a clear shift in the values to be accorded prominence in administrative principles and practices. Economy, efficiency, and effectiveness as well as increased care in using financial resources became the predominant theme. In Hong Kong, institutional arrangements were in the process of consolidation after government responses to perceived and actual problems helped chart the courses of actions to be taken, particularly drawing lessons from the experience of other countries across the world.

The basic structure of the political and administrative systems remained largely unchanged with the reversal of sovereignty to the People's Republic of China. Under the current system, a chief executive holds widespread power similar to the former British governor, and the executive council continues as the key unit in making important political and administrative decisions. Led by the key officials — the chief secretary for administration, the financial secretary, and the secretary for justice — the civil service retains most of the power and privileges it has enjoyed over the past century. Yet, changes have taken place in the society and the government had to respond to them.

Hong Kong sought to retain the advantages it had carved out for itself in the world system, and these advantages were considered in the negotiations to determine the terms and conditions of handover to China. The capitalist system and the way of life in Hong Kong were to remain unchanged for 50 years (Basic Law Article 5), and there was to be no interference from the central government except in the clearly specified areas of defense and foreign affairs (Basic Law Articles 13, 14). The region was to be administered autonomously, and the concept of "one country, two systems" allowed the coexistence of different economic and political systems to function within greater China.

External Influences and Local Challenges

For several decades, Hong Kong flourished as a financial and commercial center due to its natural as well as strategic advantages and achieved a high

[2]For example, see Anson Chan (1996), based on a speech delivered by her as the chief secretary for administration, Hong Kong government.

standard of living for the population. Hong Kong has been exposed to the vagaries of international competition for many years as the territory earned the reputation of being the "freest" economy and a major financial center for successive years in the 1990s. This has facilitated the integration of Hong Kong with the global system, which has been substantially affected by the phenomenon of globalization. The move toward an integrated world economy was a consequence of the liberalization of states and the opening up of economies after the cessation of the Cold War. The process was facilitated by remarkable progress achieved in IT, and the net result has been the free movement of capital, commodities, services, people, and ideas across national borders. It can be said that globalization has succeeded, to a considerable extent, in opening up societies and standardizing rules of governance.

Globalization has been a major force pushing toward the tendency to perceive problems facing governments in similar ways and to develop solutions within internationally accepted frameworks. One of the most common problems confronting most nations has been the diminishing pool of resources and rapidly rising demands from the public for better and new services. The private sector served as a point of inspiration, and governments have sought to change established practices and procedures, revise priorities, and reassess the values of outcome and efforts undertaking and managing the public sector (see, for example, Hood, 1991; OECD, 1995).

Hong Kong's small size and simple administrative structure had helped avoid many problems faced by states across the world. There is a strong pressure — direct as well as indirect — on countries to converge toward a common system of governance. This requires mature political and economic institutions, as well as administrative arrangements that emphasize economy, efficiency, and effectiveness. Although many countries seek to introduce reforms along these lines in accordance with external pressure, problems arise if there are strong internal pressures that are ignored. Hong Kong has been moving in that direction with its Weberian bureaucracy in the driving seat, and has overcome many of the impediments to reforms that exist in political systems with democratic institutions and effective political control over the administrative apparatus. Internal pressures have forced the government to strengthen the economy and the capacity of the government, as well as respond to the social needs of health, housing, education, and employment for the local population.

The composition of the bureaucracy began to undergo changes with the termination of British rule in 1997. The Basic Law (1990) stipulated that "only Chinese citizens among permanent residents of the Region with no right of abode in any foreign country may fill the following posts: the Secretaries and Deputy Secretaries of Departments, Directors of Bureaux,

Commissioner Against Corruption, Director of Audit, Commissioner of Police, Director of Immigration, and Commissioner of Customs and Excise" (Article 101). This provision has significant implication, as many non-Chinese bureaucrats with extensive experience were no longer eligible to rise to the top echelon.

The emergence of a middle class and economic and social progress achieved over the previous three decades resulted in high citizen expectations in Hong Kong. The standard of living was on the rise, and many local citizens were exposed to overseas administrative systems and practices as they traveled or emigrated. The underlying current of a democratic movement encouraged effective scrutiny of the government's operation, management, performance, and efficient use of financial resources. A strong and independent media was encouraged by these circumstances, and emerged as a facilitator of such changes.

Administrative reforms were introduced in line with changes taking place worldwide. The basic principles of the reforms emphasized regular and systematic review of public expenditure as well as a proper system of management of resources and policies. There should be clearly defined and delegated responsibilities for formulating policies and implementing them. Moreover, public bureaucrats were to be made aware of resources used in pursuing policy objectives, and they were to be held accountable for the outcome. Finally, services were to be provided through an appropriate framework of organization and management that was conducive to the nature of each service (Finance Branch, Hong Kong Government, 1989, pp. 1–2).

A key initiative has been the establishment and inculcation of a culture of service in the framework of public administration. The efficiency unit served as the engine behind the changes aimed at improving the quality of service, enhancing efficiency, and ensuring customer orientation. Over a short period of time, there were evidences of increased awareness of customer needs and preferences, and senior bureaucrats emphasized the importance of service to the community (see Chan, 1996; Lee and Huque, 1996).

By way of implementation of the reforms initiated in the 1990s, agencification, corporatization, contracting out, and privatization were in progress when British rule ended in Hong Kong.[3] The handing over of Hong Kong to China coincided with a number of problems related to the avian (bird) flu and an increase in microalgae (red tide) in the coastal water of Hong Kong, indicating a weakening of the capability of the bureaucracy, and system

[3]For example, certain transportation services were handed over to public corporations, contracts were awarded to build and operate transportation tunnels and public housing, and a number of government departments were designated as self-financing trading funds.

failures on the day of opening Hong Kong's expensive new airport attracted severe criticism from the public, media, and observers (see Huque and Lee, 2000). These events seemed to highlight a declining level of efficiency of the bureaucracy. Hong Kong government responded by drawing up reform plans for introducing substantial changes with special emphasis on the areas of personnel management, performance and pay, and a result-oriented management culture (Huque, 2002, p. 14).

Under British colonial rule, the administrative system of Hong Kong developed and underwent reforms that were intended to respond to local needs and challenges. The organizational structure and distribution of power reflected a high degree of centralization, quite unlike the United Kingdom, which adopted a parliamentary democratic system with an effective system of checks and balances. So the structure was British in orientation, whereas the spirit was quite the opposite. Under Chinese sovereignty, Hong Kong has been allowed a high degree of autonomy, and hence the structure and spirit remain basically unchanged. This is in contrast with the administrative system in China, which has strong centralizing tendencies.

Classical Bureaucracy and Change in Hong Kong

Common emphasized the resemblance of the Hong Kong civil service to the classical bureaucracy. He highlighted the support of a strong hierarchy by Chinese values, and the lack of expectation for junior officials to become involved in problem-solving or employing discretion (Common, 1999, p. 49). This feature has, in fact, contributed to higher cohesion as there is no scope of misinterpretation or distortion of ideas or information flowing up or down the hierarchy.

How does a stable, permanent, and neutral bureaucracy respond to circumstances involving flexibility, transition, and rapid turnover of program and personnel? Hong Kong's interest has been served well for several decades by its classical bureaucracy. The key tasks have been dealing with the routine problems of management and development of human resources to manage Hong Kong and provide adequate support to the fast-growing economy. A number of factors made it convenient for the bureaucracy to respond to changing circumstances and implement decisions speedily without encountering strong opposition from within its ranks.

Unity of Values

The concentration of power of the chief executive (earlier governor) and his executive council has been a facilitator. The small body of decision makers included the key officials from the bureaucracy and they were able to represent the interest of the bureaucracy. The elitist nature of the executive council has helped in fostering a spirit of camaraderie, and there is not much possibility of disagreement among the members. Therefore, it has been comparatively easier for the decision makers in Hong Kong, with active participation by the bureaucracy to determine the nature and scope of administrative reforms.

Speedy Decision Mechanism

The small size and simple structure of the administrative system and the pattern of power distribution has resulted in an efficient decision-making arrangement. The executive council meets regularly and follows a simple method of discussing issues and providing directions that is worked upon by the bureaucracy to put them into action. Potential concerns of the bureaucracy can be dispelled at the decision-making stage because the key administrative officials participate in the process.

Easy Implementation of Decisions

In many countries, the gap between decisions on administrative reforms and their implementation is a matter of concern. Many reforms are unsuccessful as implementation plans are vague and, more commonly, the bureaucracy may resist them for several reasons. Bureaucratic resistance is common in cases where the reform initiatives come from the political leadership, with little input from the institution that will be responsible for implementing them. In the case of Hong Kong, these problems were minimized as key officials of the bureaucracy are active participants in the decision process, and often the initiators of reform plans.

The simple hierarchical structure and strict discipline assist in the quick dissemination of reform plans and programs. The small size of Hong Kong and its bureaucracy makes it possible to make uniform arrangements for informing and instructing officials and motivate them in the spirit of the reforms.

Support from Society

The bureaucracy enjoys the confidence of the public as an efficient and reliable institution in Hong Kong. Leading members of the bureaucracy often top the list of the popular public personalities in opinion polls, and frequently are ahead of political leaders. Prolonged period of colonial rule during which Hong Kong achieved remarkable progress under the competent leadership of the bureaucracy has led to such a mindset. Strict adherence to the rule of law and effective anticorruption measures have succeeded in establishing a fair and efficient image of the bureaucracy among the public. This helps the bureaucracy to function as a trusted agency that operates with the best interest of the community in mind, and enables it to secure the support of the citizens, which is critical in implementing administrative reforms.

Security of the Bureaucracy

There are various reasons that make the bureaucracy arguably the best institution to work for in Hong Kong. Traditionally, public officials have enjoyed excellent compensation packages, and attractive perks were offered to entice the best and the brightest to public service. Proximity to the power center and full cooperation from the governor and the executive council boosted the image further and the bureaucrats were highly satisfied with the terms and conditions of the job. These factors encouraged the bureaucracy to be proactive and anticipate changes in the society that would require prompt response. While making adjustments to the existing system to deal with changing circumstances, the bureaucracy was cautious to protect its own interests, and thus a classical rigid bureaucracy was able to dictate the directions of administrative reforms.

There may be undesirable effects and issues of concern emanating from these reforms. For example, programs aimed at diminishing the role of the state, contraction of the public sector and the government's activities, privatization, and reduction of public expenditure have some beneficial outcome. But in some cases, these "policies increased the gap between rich and poor, the powerful and the weak, the well connected and the isolated, the skilled and the unskilled; multiplied worldwide the poverty-stricken and underprivileged; aggravated crime, violence and corruption; and degraded the environment" (Caiden and Caiden, 2002, p. 41). Hong Kong was able to avoid such effects due to the strong influence of a classical bureaucratic model, which worked on the basis of clear rules oriented toward definite goals.

Conclusion

Over a century of British rule has left Hong Kong typically colonial in nature, and the governor and his executive council exercised absolute control. Several modifications were made to the administrative system to adjust to societal and economic changes and also address the political aspirations of the citizens. Reform programs were in line with the core values of classical bureaucratic ideals with hierarchical structure, rationality, efficiency, and devotion to rules acquiring prominence.

A strong bureaucratic institution was effective in serving the government well and, at the same time, protecting and promoting its own interests. The bureaucracy was an active participant in all public activities and was able to plan and design administrative reform programs. Unlike other societies where conflicts between the executive and legislature result in obstacles to formulation of meaningful reform programs and effective implementation, Hong Kong bureaucracy was in sync with the decisions of the government.

The power structure of Hong Kong facilitated value consensus at the top, and the simple administrative arrangement allowed the making of quick decisions and their implementation. Strict discipline and extremely attractive compensation packages elicited a high degree of loyalty and the bureaucrats considered their positions valuable. The bureaucracy was cautious to protect its own interests, and obviously a classical rigid bureaucracy was able to dictate the directions of administrative reforms. Thus, the absence of strong political leadership and the existence of a weak state provide a context in which classical bureaucracy can be a useful tool for designing and implementing administrative reforms. Hong Kong's bureaucracy has demonstrated the advantages of the traditional model by highlighting its efficiency, rationality, cohesiveness, and capacity to adopt and implement hard choices under the right circumstances.

References

Basic Law of the Hong Kong Special Administrative Region of the People's Republic of China. 1990. Hong Kong: Consultative Committee for the Basic Law of the Hong Kong Special Administrative Region of the People's Republic of China.

Caiden, G. 1991. *Administrative Reform Comes of Age*. Berlin: Walter de Gruyter.

Caiden, G. and N. Caiden. 2002. "Towards More Democratic Governance: Modernizing the Administrative State in Australia, Canada, the United Kingdom, and the United States." In E. Vigoda (ed.), *Public Administration: An Interdisciplinary Critical Analysis*. New York: Marcel Dekker.

Chan, A. 1996. Serving the Community. *Hong Kong Public Administration* 5:55–80.

Commission of Inquiry. 1967. *Kowloon Disturbances 1966, Report of Commission of Inquiry*. Hong Kong: Government Printer.

Common, R. 1999. Civil Service Reform in Hong: Conforming to the Global Trend? *Public Administration and Policy* 8:37–56.

Finance Branch, Hong Kong Government. 1989. *Public Sector Reform*. Hong Kong: Government Printer.

Harris, P. 1978. *Hong Kong: A Study of Bureaucratic Politics.* Hong Kong: Heinemann.

Hood, C. 1991. A Public Management for All Seasons. *Public Administration* 69:3–19.

Huque, A.S. 2002. Government–Society Relations and the Politics of Administrative Reform in Hong Kong. *Public Policy and Administration* 17:5–20.

Huque, A.S. and G. Lee. 2000. *Managing Public Services: Crises and Lessons from Hong Kong.* Aldershot, UK: Ashgate Publications.

Huque, A.S. and R. Yep. 2003. Globalization and Reunification: Administrative Reforms and the China–Hong Kong Convergence Challenge. *Public Administration Review* 63:141–152.

Lee, G. and A.S. Huque. 1996. Hong Kong: Administrative Reform and Recent Public Sector Changes. *Australian Journal of Public Administration* 55: 13–21.

Lee, J. and J. Lam. 1992. The Changing Public Administration: Issues in Hong Kong Transition. *Teaching Public Administration* 12:45–52.

McCurdy, H. 1977. *Public Administration: A Synthesis.* Menlo Park, CA: Cummings Publishing Company.

Miners, N. 1995. *The Government and Politics of Hong Kong.* 5th ed. Hong Kong: Oxford University Press.

Naschold, F. and C. von Otter. 1996. *Public Sector Transformation: Rethinking Markets and Hierarchies in Government.* Amsterdam/Philadelphia: John Benjamins Publishing Company.

OECD, Organization for Economic Co-operation and Development. 1995. *Governance in Transition: Public Management Reforms in OECD Countries.* Paris: OECD.

Rhodes, R. 1991. Introduction. *Public Administration* 69:1–2.

Szanton, P. 1981. "So You Want to Reorganize the Governments?" In P. Szanton (ed.), *Federal Reorganization: What Have We Learned?* Chatham, NJ: Chatham House, pp. 1–24.

Weber, M. 1946. *From Max Weber: Essays in Sociology.* Translated, edited, and with an introduction by H.H. Gerth and C.W. Mills. New York: Oxford University Press.

Chapter 27

Chinese Administrative Reform: A Genie in a Bottle

Barbara L. Neuby

CONTENTS

Introduction

China has embarked on perhaps the greatest, most rapid economic expansion of any nation in history. China's gross domestic product (GDP) has risen about 8 percent each year for the last 25 years and can be compared to the relatively modest growth in the GDP of the United States at 4 percent (Mandel, 2004). China's purchasing power parity was 6.4 trillion dollars in 2004, or perhaps more, when considering the current decline of the U.S. dollar (CIA, 2004). China's share of the global GDP rose from 3.2 percent in 1980 to 13 percent in 2004 (Mandel, 2004). E-commerce growth was 100 percent in 2004 (Gardner & Gardner, 2004). China's economy is red hot and is a focal point for multinational corporations, journalists, scholars, and governments around the world. Economic and administrative reforms over the last 20 years have changed the relationship between the State and the citizens and have paved the way for one of the most massive levels of private investment and capitalism ever recorded (Sappenfield, 2004). Party leaders and scholars agree that growth and economic reform is predicated on administrative reform (Lai, 2003; Tong & Straussman, 2003; Chen, 2002; Deng, 1985a). For China to truly modernize and develop their economy, gain entrance into the World Trade Organization (WTO), and successfully host the 2008 Olympics, China's bureaucracy must become more effective and efficient — almost overnight (Lim, 2004; Fewsmith, 2003; Lai, 2003; Ma, 1999; Morey, 1993; Whyte, 1980).

To pave the way for continued investment as well as improve administrative effectiveness, eliminate corruption, and generally improve their overall position throughout the world, China has, in part, rested her economic growth upon modernization of bureaucratic structure and procedures. Although considering her thousand-year experience in bureaucracy, China has embarked on an interesting reform movement to modernize while retaining her uniqueness and addressing her problems particularly in building administrative capacity. This chapter highlights Chinese structural reforms, administrative developments, discusses the challenges that China faces, and analyzes the consequences of these changes for the administrative field and the global community.

Background

China has one of the longest recorded histories and longevity of any nation as a discrete political unit. Combine that history and tradition with a wealth of experience administering a tremendously diverse region and it is obvious that China has made lasting contributions in many fields. During imperial dynastic rule, China's bureaucracy was considered efficient and effective and even as a model for others. As China transitioned into communism although she remained unique in her culture, advancement in administration halted. Under the planned economy, collectivization alienated the peasants and exposed the poor management by various party cadres regarding the local production of goods (Ogden, 2004; Ruan, 1994; Kirby, 1985).

Concerns over the Soviet Union's activities and China's experience in the Korean War showed Chinese leaders that she must increase production and quality of all manner of goods and services. The commune system, by and large, was not achieving this goal. During the 1960s rural experiments with a peasant-initiated system of household contracts and local control over production produced stronger outputs across the agricultural sector. Commodity surpluses improved the State's situation and the door of peasant autonomy was nudged open (Unger, 2002). This "responsibility" system that linked production of food and livestock to the individual's efforts, (and less to the State's) introduced some degree of local control although ultimate control still rested within the party cadre system. As the notion of a market economy got its foot in the door, farmers were happier and wealthier and the State had a surplus of goods (Ogden, 2004; Ruan, 1994).

On the promise of technological exchange, foreign multinationals were allowed to invest on a small scale in Chinese markets bringing with them new products and an entirely different set of values than those held by the Chinese for thousands of years. The door to modernization was nudged open a little further. Continued State control of production resulted in low outputs of poor quality military and industrial goods not easily salable in world markets. Changes were obviously needed, even though resisted by many conservative Chinese leaders, if China was to prosper (Ogden, 2004; Ruan, 1994; Morey, 1993; Lee, 1989). Decentralization of economic decision making and the idea of local autonomy had taken hold and demonstrated the positive results that could be produced.

Although this modest experiment in "capitalism" was occurring, Mao halted the development of Chinese bureaucracy. Seeking to rid the State of her negative influences, Mao criticized the bureaucracy for its corruption and limited its intellectual advancement (Tong & Straussman, 2003; Whyte, 1980). Other nations pressed forward in administrative science — paving the way for their continued socioeconomic development. China fell further behind in administrative and economic reforms. When Mao died in 1976, a vacuum of leadership and encroachment of Western values (in part from foreign firms and in part from the media) had eroded China's traditional value system. By the time Deng Xiaoping survived the intraparty politics and rose to become the Party leader in 1979, China lagged behind most nations in administration, democratic reforms, and various socioeconomic indices (Ogden, 2004; Tong & Straussman, 2003). Realizing that China's economic status would not improve and she would be shut out of the emerging global economy, Deng and most of Chinese Communist Party (CCP) leaders instituted reforms that included private incentive systems for entrepreneurship, wealth, and private property. China began the long march toward streamlined bureaucratic structures and procedures as well as a reorganization of the methods of production involving state-owned enterprises (Nathan, 1990; Tsai, 1989). Streamlined administrative policy and procedures would help make China competitive. Deng believed that political reform would follow economic reform and that economic reform rested upon sound administration (Tong & Straussman, 2003; Ruan, 1994; Tsai, 1989). Hu Jintao carries forward Deng's reforms to usher China into the 21st century (Hu Urges, 2004). Indeed, China's percentage of nonstate-owned enterprises has increased from 24 percent in 1980 to 72 percent in 1996 (Jefferson & Rawski, 1999). Her technological growth is unparalleled (Ramstad, 2004). The GDP has risen to 1.4 trillion dollars in 2003 and the per capita incomes have quadrupled since 1979 (Kuhn, 2004). Her exports as a percentage of GDP rose from 23 percent in 1985 to 44 percent in 2000; and in 2002, China is the third largest world market, only behind the United States and Germany (Nation Now No. 3, 2005). It is to those reforms that we now turn.

Structural and Procedural Reforms

Over the last 20 years, structural and procedural changes in the Chinese administration have paved the way for economic development, membership in the WTO, and acceptance of the bid to host the 2008 Olympics. These opportunities mandate reorganization of relationships between the State and private business, elimination of bureaucratic inefficiencies, strengthening the rule of law, and modernizing the military, healthcare, and education.

"Rationalization" and administrative capacity building are now the policies for growth and development. Since 1995, the number of Chinese ministries has been reduced from 86 to 29. Millions of employees have been forced to find other jobs. Functional areas have been reviewed and agencies merged to eliminate redundancies. The state council, the highest administrative body overseeing all ministries and agencies, has been reorganized to focus on managing the new market economy (China, 2004). Ministries that suffered the largest reorganization were those responsible for industrial and energy planning. Many were subsumed under the new State Economic and Trade Commission charged with overseeing and regulating China's industrial and energy output. One exception is the creation of a new ministry of information that replaces the ministry of electronics and telecommunications. The state planning commission formerly known for its production quotas has been renamed The State Development Planning

Commission and is now charged with estimating growth targets instead of planning outputs. These ministerial changes are designed to break up some of the older state-owned enterprises and promote competition among them. Other ministries and agencies were demoted to a lower level status or brought up to the position of vice ministry all in an attempt to transition from a planned state economy to a market oriented one. In addition, the central government staff has been reduced by nearly 50 percent, thereby reducing the layers of bureaucrats, through which a business or a citizen must go to receive service (Yang, 2002).

It was those very redundancies and excessive bureaucratic "red tape" at the local level that prevented many foreign businesses from investing in China (Ogden, 2004; Lai, 2003; Yang, 2002). The local level serves as the interface between foreign firms and a Chinese entrepreneur; and when regulations, lost paperwork, and corruption stand in the way, corporations are likely to go elsewhere. It is easy to see why foreign and particularly American and European firms would be interested in China. In 2002, the average wage of an industrial worker was $21.11 in the United States and $14.22 in other countries (Coy, 2004). The average Chinese factory laborer earns 64 cents per hour, is younger, is willing to work 12-hour shifts, and does not expect a wide range of benefits (Engardio et al., 2004). Indigenous Chinese manufacturers can produce goods far more cheaply than almost any other manufacturer in an industrialized nation. The "China price" (about 30 percent lower than other manufacturing prices) is the new benchmark signifying to all large manufacturers that they either have to match this price or beat it, or else they will lose business (Engardio et al., 2004; Fishman, 2004). Furthermore, few environmental regulations exist to hinder business in China, though everyone knows that the *status quo* is destined to change.

Many of these reforms were directly linked to China's 15-year effort to gain entrance to the WTO. When China emerges as a full partner she will experience a 30 billion dollar increase in her trade surplus and an 8–11 percent increase in the GDP (Adhikari & Yang, 2002). As part of the membership, China agreed to eliminate or change its business licensing and locating procedures, regulations on business scope, and open their telecommunications and financial services markets as well as promote private ownership of industrial property (Adhikari & Yang, 2002; Jefferson & Rawski, 1999). Zoning regulations will change and China also agreed to eliminate *ex post facto* regulations, subsidies to certain State-owned enterprises, and reduce other import tariffs by 50 percent (Adhikari & Yang, 2002). To accomplish these changes, radical shifts in the bureaucratic structure and procedure will be necessary (World Bank, 2002; Deng, 1985a). New missions, new policies, procedures, routines, and employees will reinvigorate bureaucracies once geared to a state-planned economy.

Position classifications, facilities, procedures, and agency structures — all need to change to implement these sweeping reforms successfully. But when this happens, and most China watchers believe it will, there will be global shifts in trade, production, and employment as the full thrust of 1 billion workers and an efficient bureaucracy impact the world's markets (Sappenfield, 2004).

As both a structural and a procedural reform, China's banking sector adopted friendlier policies toward private capital investment. Grants for state-owned enterprises were gradually replaced by loans linked to production. Special enterprise zones (SEZs) were created to facilitate private investment. New state banks and credit cooperatives were established at the local level to further the investment. The market was also opened to branches of foreign banks in the mid-1990s (Jefferson et al., 1999). One holdover of planned socialist banking is the "policy loan" designed to further the planned economy model even when it is known that the state sector is performing poorly. Few expect these loans will be repaid, hence, allowing inefficiency into the banking market (Jefferson & Rawski, 1999). China's state-owned banks are also replete with nonperforming loans, as much as 40 percent in some sectors (Bremner, 2004; Cheng, 2000). What is interesting is the fact that lending decisions are centrally less determined and focused not on a planned socialist economic model but, rather, on the capitalist paradigm.

Decentralization and Devolution

Decentralization of power and functions is bringing newfound autonomy to local levels. An experiment in Guandong province brought reduced agency size and payrolls and allowed local agency directors to make decisions about business policy. State-owned enterprises are also enjoying increased autonomy, and horizontal relations between the governments are replacing strict vertical relations in which the province once determined everything for local governments. A new tax-sharing arrangement, which cuts approximately 23 percent of provincial and cadres staff, has furthered this devolution of powers (State Council, 2004; Chen, 2002). Within Guandong province is the city of Shenzen in which a SEZ has been created. Elimination of taxes and other hindrances to investment have been removed, resulting in a 34-fold increase in Shenzen's GDP (Chen, 2002). This decentralizing pattern has emerged in other provinces as well. Many argue that decentralization must include democratic reforms for a truly free-market economy to work (Cai, 2002). Yet the economic boost to the city and province cannot be denied. Others argue economic decision making may prompt more openness in political decision making

(Jin & Qian, 2001). Some villages elect their local leaders though there is dispute as to whether the party controls these elections. At minimum, decentralization or devolution strengthens the institutional capacity at the local level. Some of these changes almost resemble federalism — "with Chinese characteristics."

Tensions over decentralization persist. Although some view the movement as the central government relinquishing control (Zhong, 2003) others point out that the central government still appoints provincial leaders and the provinces still set local budgets (Saich & Yang, 2003; Yang, 2002). A system of rewards and punishments remains in effect for failing to meet production quotas. If the government really wants a free-market economy could they get out of the game altogether (Lee, 2001; Saich & Yang, 2003; Cai, 2002; Unger, 2002)? Although the public is generally regarded as obedient and, for the most part trusts the central government, the thousands of mass demonstrations since 1999 may signal an emboldened citizenry willing to get involved politically (Wong, 2004a; Yang, 2002; Cheng 2000). Moving 1.3 billion people from a planned to a market economy cannot be done overnight and is certain to pose some dislocations in society. Incrementalism is probably the only way. Deng Xiaoping focused on small steps (1985b). An elephant runs a slower race but moves everything out of its way.

Law

China is developing its civil legal codes. Criminal law is fairly well established, but leaders and scholars insist that rule of law in all areas including matters affecting government become the norm in China. Most insist on an independent judiciary based on precedent (Qi, 2004; Cai, 2002; Wang & Gu, 2002; Ma, 1999; Lam & Chan, 1996; Tsao & Worthley, 1995). Noting that China has a 1000-year history based on moral law, an independent judiciary would go far toward, creating a branch of government with a greater degree of separation from the party and the government thus limiting the state power. Over reliance on legal statutes has been the norm, the judiciary having been controlled by the government. Law is the foundation for most administrative systems and a stable administrative system contributes to steady economic growth because it tends to produce more predictable, fair outcomes and therefore certainty (Qi, 2004). Business desires a fair and impartial forum that settles disputes that inevitably arise in a foreign investment arena. Recently, in a significant event, a private firm won a trademark dispute with a government agency. An administrative law ruling based upon interpretation of statute provided that victory and of course, business is watching (Manacling the Mandarins, 2004). This development will be even more important as China becomes a full partner in the WTO and learns to operate under international law. Ministries and agencies, once again need to facilitate procedures for business to prosper, having an administrative law system, provide a mechanism by which to do that (CIA, 2004; Manacling the Mandarins, 2004; Fewsmith, 2003). If civil and administrative law evolves such that private business can rely on a body of known common law and the use of precedent, further investment will continue.

Public Administration

The Practice

Essential to and simultaneous with economic, structural, and procedural reforms is the reinvigoration of Chinese public administration as a science and a discipline. Deng believed and also most other scholars believe that forward progress in science and technology and hence economy, rest on proper management (Fewsmith, 2003; Cai, 2002; Ma, 1999; Deng, 1985a). Two parallel developments ignited scholarly efforts. One, the CCP officially sanctioned efforts toward professional management of state workers and party cadres; and two, universities are planning to offer degrees in public administration that will actually inform administration and develop the discipline. The goals are many and questions remain. For administration to prosper, the criteria for a Chinese public administration must be determined. What Chinese characteristics or values should be the framework of this effort (Lan, 2003; Cai, 2002; Wang, 2002; Zhang, 2002; Guo & Zhang, 2001)? What sort of management system or paradigm should operate (Wang & Gu, 2002; Wang, 2002; Lam & Chan, 1996)? Who should control this huge reformed bureaucracy — the party or a separate organization (Aufrecht & Bun, 1995; Tsao & Worthley, 1995; Lam, 1994)? How should theory structure efforts toward administrative reform and what is that theory (Lan, 2003; Wang, 2002)? How should public administration curricula be formed (Ding, 2004; Hayhoe & Zha, 2004; Wang, 2002; Xu, 2002; Guo & Zhang, 2001)?

What characteristics typify 1.3 billion people? Are there commonalities among them that amply describe what they are about? A few are clear. The Chinese people have been ruled by a strong central government for thousands of years and are basically obedient and trusting, in general. From Mao and Communist ideology the good of the state is a more important focus than the individual. There are signs in demonstrations and attitudes that this may be changing. Rule of man has been more prevalent than rule by law or position. The size of the nation indicates rapid sweeping change that must give way to slower, more incremental change.

A number of aphorisms also mark the Chinese society. "Right title, proper words," "Open and aboveboard," and "the world as one community" serve as reminders of what is important (Zhang, 2002). Chinese public administration should be valid, stable, public, and universal (Zhang, 2002). Newer ideals include capitalism for the collectivity and collective leadership (Wang, 2002). The Chinese system is also characterized as patriarchal and redundant (Tong & Straussman, 2003) and is based on politics and not science (Cai, 2002; Zhang, 2002; Ma, 1999). The Chinese boast some of the best tailors in the world. Can they fashion their unique brand of administrative science?

They are also searching for theory. It has been suggested that Marxist theory does not provide guidance for new administrative efforts (Lan, 2003; Wang, 2002). This difficulty suggests that the good of the state and the capitalist paradigm have not yet been blended to produce one or more guiding principles on which to base reform. Yet reform proceeds. The current president and leader of the CCP, Hu Jintao, realizes as Deng earlier realized, that inconsistencies remain between modern theories of administrative reform, a market economy, and earlier ideologies (Fewsmith, 2003; Lan, 2003). Some say China should borrow from Woodrow Wilson, the individual whom most consider as the father of American public administration. Others suggest Weber's focus on "efficiency" provides the priority paradigm (Ma, 1999). The autocratic rule by minority based on Machiavelli and Hobbes may have played a role in the traditional theory of state administration that focuses on control. As reform continues scholars see the other possibilities for China (Wang & Gu, 2002). After 100 plus years of experience with the Wilson–Weber model, Chinese scholars point to ill effects. This model tends to produce institutionalization, bureaucratic rigidity, opacity, and separates politics from administration (Wang & Gu, 2002). The new public management paradigm focuses on streamlined, downsized, and democratized administration and this focus may be, in part, better suited to the current reform movement (Wang & Gu, 2002). Building theory takes time; and, given China's history it is likely that they will borrow eclectically from existing theories as well as create their own theories quite in line with Chinese characteristics.

Ideas represented in the 1993 civil service reform may indicate the direction the Chinese scholars are leaning with respect to theory. One of the crucial questions is what operating system or paradigm is best for China? The 1993 Regulations on State Functionaries Act advances pillars of the Wilson–Weber paradigm in that power and legitimacy is placed in the office, title, or institution, rather than in the person as it has been in the past. Changing a 40-million person bureaucracy is no mean feat. Clearer demarcation of job duties, types of positions, merit examinations for recruitment, and promotion and pay as enumerated in the Act, indicate that the Chinese are focusing on objectivity, a big change from the traditional rule by human (Tsao & Worthley, 1995). Penalties for malfeasance and the right spirit and attitudes one should possess to perform one's state job are also spelled out. A code of ethics identifies 14 ideals and the penalties for nonperformance to eliminate alleged administrative corruption and ineptitude (Ma, 1999; Lam & Chan, 1996; Tsao & Worthley, 1995). Debates on important management issues have been held throughout the country and have included many levels of state, provincial and local managers, and party cadres. The role of the cadres within a professionalized management system is also reviewed. Currently, the new ministry of personnel governs the state workers whereas the central organization department controls the cadres. Affirmative action provisions are also included in the Act of 1993. These moves suggest that China is evolving its administration by implementing some aspects of the Wilson–Weber model and incorporating elements of participatory democracy.

The Military and Public Order

Technocratization marks the changes found in China's military forces. Replacement of obsolescent equipment with advanced, electronic technology and a more mobile, leaner force advances China's conventional military power around the world (National Defense in 2004). Reduction in personnel, the purchase of modern fighter jets, naval carriers, and destroyers has brought China on par with the United States and Russian capabilities (Lim, 2004; Gregor, 1989). The party feels that the military must remain under their control for the party to remain in power therefore it is in the party's best interest to make the military as efficient and effective as possible (Lim, 2004; Cossa, 1996; Jencks, 1996). The development of rapid deployment forces is underway and younger technocrats with engineering and science degrees replace the older, and the more conventional military elites. Professionalization of military ranks vaults this essential branch to "reformed" status much like other bureaucracies.

The public perception of the police has declined to an all-time low (Wong, 2004a). As evidence of this angst, citizens have taken the lives of 443 policemen in 2001 (Wong, 2004a). This serious statistic is mirrored by the number of investigations against police officers for corruption, an increase in crime, and the occurrence of new crimes like cybercrime and drug trafficking for which the Chinese police are totally unprepared for (Let a Hundred…, 2004; Gill et al., 2002). New regulations governing police behavior were promulgated; and, in 1995 the Police Law was passed to bring police regulations under one comprehensive structure thereby hoping to provide coherence and continuity to the reform effort.

Healthcare and Social Policy

Social welfare policy is a fairly new focal point for the Chinese government (Fewsmith, 2003; Wong & Cheng, 2003; Zhang, 2002). Unemployment, socioeconomic differentiation, maldistribution of resources, migration, healthcare inequities, and police brutality have contributed to a general feeling of public dissatisfaction with government policy and service (Gill et al., 2002). Huge disparities exist between the urban and rural healthcare systems and funding for preventive measures dropped off considerably until the severe acute respiratory syndrome (SARS) epidemic hit (Hsiao, 2004). Many in rural areas remain with no care or ineffective and intermittent care. Forty-three percent of urban dwellers had insurance but only three percent of rural dwellers enjoyed this coverage (Hsiao, 2004). With the recognition of the SARS and HIV problems, a new health minister and conferences on health modernization, most think China has ushered in a new era of openness (Kuhn, 2004).

The United Nations, the WHO, and the U.S. government have praised China's recent efforts to combat HIV. Predicting 10 million HIV victims by 2010 unless something was done, the Chinese government has begun several programs to combat the spread including needle distribution, condom education, and free HIV testing (Let a Hundred..., 2004). Other reforms include a renewed preventative effort. Noting that too much is spent on curative services, Chinese reformers urge the public not to adopt a Western diet, to exercise regularly, stop smoking, and are working with the WHO to develop a healthcare reform plan (Bekedam, 2004).

Education

The rebirth of the study of public administration parallels the radical development in the structure and procedure of administration. In 1980, Deng authorized a reincarnation of the public administration field as a discipline. "We have overlooked the study of political science, law, sociology, and world politics, and we need to catch up" (Guo & Zhang, 2001). For further development, conferences and seminars were held throughout China and a new journal, *Chinese Public Administration Review* published its maiden issue in 1985. In 1988, the Society for Public Administration was created and the state council recommended adoption of its various suggestions. At its founding conference Premier Li Peng wrote the inscription for the society that symbolized its mission: "Government administration must focus on science, pursue efficiency, follow the law and emphasize uprightness" (Guo & Zhang, 2001). The charter defines the agenda. The society's purpose is to study theories and practices of public administration, provide suggestions for reform, promote the development of administration with Chinese characteristics, conduct research, and academic exchange (Guo & Zhang, 2001). The stage was set.

There are four types of universities in China: (1) research universities; (2) provincial universities; (3) public short-term colleges; and (4) private schools. Enrollment in higher education, in general, increased from 15 percent in 2001 to 18 percent in 2003 (Hayhoe & Zha, 2004). Public administration degrees are now being approved, and, given that career mobility now requires an advanced degree, a steady stream of willing bureaucrat-students seems certain. Will China be able to keep up with this new academic demand (Ding, 2004)? With the reduction in size of most bureaucratic agencies, where will all these new graduates be employed (Cheng, 2004)?

As Ding (2004) points out, development of the field of administration as a discipline will do several things for China. One, increased enrollments may alleviate unemployment, currently about 10 percent in urban and rural areas (CIA, 2004). Two, an intellectual class of administrators is certain to promote change in administration. Finally, the direction of that change is not clear, and however may depend upon the paradigms and theories adopted or the Chinese characteristics identified as ideal.

Practical matters are also open for discussion. Class size, manner of instruction, curricula, methods of examination are all debated as Chinese scholars search the world for what works the best. Noting that the American system is itself a hybrid, with its own particular problems, China is not necessarily eager to adopt "all things west." An interesting program began in 2003 to send Chinese administrators to American institutions for fast-track masters in public administration degrees (Wang & Gu, 2002). It is too soon to understand what impact an American Master of Public Administration (MPA) degree has on administrative reform and the discipline, however, this author is one of the professors in such a program. My preliminary assessment shows that the Chinese student-bureaucrats possess managerial capability but are learning how to be creative and flexible and adapting to the facts in each situation.

Dilemmas and Contradictions

China has much to show for its supreme economic effort. They have significantly reformed their administration and revived the discipline. Despite these successes, there are dilemmas and contradictions worth noting. Can administrative reform with democratic precepts flourish alongside Chinese communism? What will a new class of highly educated bureaucrats, or "supercrats," mean for Chinese society? How does rule of law impact the party? Is administrative reform part of the military's game plan? The degree of growth and change has produced anxiety in society. Is there concern about human rights? Does economic power segue into political power? Can China repair its health system and avoid larger problems? Finally, will the Chinese allow the imagination and creativity to flexibly manage, what will probably be in a few years, the largest economy on earth? What do answers to these questions mean?

Conflicting Values

Scholars say that the Chinese modernization produces two contradictory values, control versus autonomy and believe that they cannot coexist indefinitely (Lan, 2003; Wang & Gu, 2002; Falkenheim, 1981; Nathan, 1990). Some miss the point. The dilemma is one of not only how to maintain control but also what type of control to maintain and who is doing the maintaining? For the last 25 years, elements of democracy have coexisted alongside a ruling Communist party while the dramatic reforms have taken place. The Chinese have never had total democracy, as the West has known it. Why should they? Democracy is not an easy thing to put into practice. Witness Russia's attempts and failures. Could the CCP and the National People's Congress state policy goals, through the new class of educated bureaucrats, implement the changes to meet those goals? The model is not Western but one based on Chinese characteristics. Deng saw no contradiction between the party's ideology and the market economy (1985b).

China is in much the same position as the United States was at the turn of the 20th century. A booming economy in the industrial revolution produced a whole new range of tasks for government. There was societal dislocation, immigration, broad economic and social change, health problems, etc. America had no administrative science on which to base her reforms. Woodrow Wilson argued for eclecticism. "But where has this science grown up? Surely not on this side of the sea." "If we would employ it, we must Americanize it (Wilson, 2000)." This is no different than reform with "Chinese characteristics." Wilson borrowed from German sociologist, Max Weber, and reluctantly factored in the democratic aspect of administration. Wilson and Weber thought little of the collective mass wisdom. Can China adopt democratic reforms on an incremental basis? Indeed, can she do otherwise? Another issue is whether, as Wilson desired, politics will be separate from administration? A difficult road to walk and almost nowhere evident among nations is the complete divorce of the two concepts. Reform and progress can continue despite seeming contradictions.

"Supercrats" and the Rule of Law

An unanswered question is what power and status do the newly educated bureaucrats have? It is often said that knowledge is power. How will new knowledge transform these new "supercrats?" Will they form an elite class similar to their Hong Kong counterparts and thus be a counterweight to the party's modernization plans? At the heart of this debate is the question of who will make policy? If the bureaucrats are allowed freedom to implement laws on the basis of a rule of law, then they will have established their own power base and serve as a check on the party.

Article V of the 1982 Constitution of the People's Republic of China places all parties and governments under the law, but thus far, it is not clear what sort of limitation actually exists. Scholars call for rule of law but conveniently sidestep the issue of the party's position. At issue is the concept of limited power and the party has never known such limits. Will law be the required framework for other governmental sectors including the bureaucracy? If the judiciary is allowed to issue opinions based on precedent, another independent power base may be established. A public held to legal standards will likely expect that the government will be held to the same standard. A freewheeling government loses legitimacy and contributes to the growing public sense of dissatisfaction.

Public Safety and Welfare

Capable militaries and effective police forces are definite power bases but, if not used well, will likely ignite more dissatisfaction in a public that already feels emboldened, prone to protest, and refuse direction. In turn, this may bring stricter controls on the public and reform efforts could stall. Is there any degree of independence in the military's new technological ability? Health-care and socioeconomic challenges also remain. Improvements in rural health and incomes must occur for growth patterns to continue. Action toward a cleaner environment will bring more worldwide investment and the threat of bank failures looms large over the financial scene.

Conclusion

Checks to party rule are emerging. Village self-control, provincial self-determination, encroaching Western materialism, independent branches of government, and a democratizing administration are all signs of change in action and attitude. The once very tightly held parameters of public life are loosening by encroachments from the economic, political, and social sectors. As Kaifeng Yang (2001) asks, will the public body in China develop a new "*danwei*" or spirit to move them forward and faster and, is the party's position powerful enough to stop them? China can continue for the foreseeable future to grow very, very fast but only if it walks a fine line between control of the mammoth movements it has begun, and limited freedom. The genie is part way out of the bottle. If the party can keep its distance and direct administrative and economic reform whereas provincial and local levels and the public enjoy some degree of autonomy and betterment in the quality of life then there is every reason to believe that the economic trend will continue. China is now, and will likely continue to be, a player in all realms. In offering a new model of government and administration to the world, in which seeming contradictions can, in fact coexist to produce a new force to be reckoned with, China's genie may cause many to scratch their heads and go back to the drawing board.

References

Adhikari, R. and Yang, Y. (2002). What Will WTO Membership Mean for China and Its Trading Partners. *Finance and Development*. 39(39). Accessed January 5, 2005: www.imf.org

Aufrecht, S.E. and Bun, L.S. (1995). Reform with Chinese Characteristics: The Context of Chinese Civil Service. *Public Administration Review*. 55(2): 175–183.

Bekedam, H. (2004). Speech: At Peking University Health Economics and Management Forum, December 8, 2004, Beijing, PRC. Accessed: www.chn.wpro.who.int/news

Bremner, B. (2004). Asia Needs Seats at World Tables. *Business Week Online*. September 28, 2004: Accessed January 4, 2005: www.businessweek.com

Cai, L. (2002). Public Administration in China's Transitional Period and the Analysis of Its Reform. *Chinese Public Administration Review*. 1(1): 101–110: http://www.andromeda.rutgers.eddu/cpar

Central Intelligence Agency (CIA) (2004). *World Fact Book: China*. Accessed: January 4, 2005: www.cia.gov

Chen, R. (2002). Administrative Reform in Guandong Province and Its Characteristics. *Chinese Public Administration Review*. 1(1): 17–24: http://www.andromeda.rutgers.eddu/cpar

Cheng, L. (2000). China in 1999. *Asian Survey*. 40(1): 112–129.

Cheng, K. (2004). Expansion of Higher Education in China and Then What? *Harvard China Review*. 5(1): 82–86.

China (2004). *Encyclopedia Britannica*. Accessed January 4, 2005: www.eb.com

Constitution of the People's Republic of China (1982). Accessed January 5, 2005: http://www.chinatoday.com/law/no1law.htm

Cossa, R. (1996). The PRC's National Security Objectives in the Post-Cold War Era and the Role of the PLA. In Lin, B.J. and Meyers, J.T. (Eds.) *Contemporary China in the Post-Cold War Era*. Charleston, SC: University of South Carolina Press, pp. 199–224.

Coy, P. (2004). Just How Cheap Is Chinese Labor? *Business Week*. December 13, 2004.

Deng, X. (1985a). Reform is the Only Way for China to Develop its Productive Forces. *China People's Daily*. August 28, 1985. Accessed January 6, 2005: http://english.peopledaily.com.cn/

Deng, X. (1985b). There is No Fundamental Contradiction between Socialism and a Market Economy. *China People's Daily*. October 23, 1985. Accessed January 6, 2005: http://english.peopledaily.com.cn

Ding, X. (2004). The Challenges Faced by Chinese Higher Education as It Expands in Scale. *Chinese Education and Society* 37(1): 36–53.

Engardio, P., Roberts, D., and Bremner, B. (2004). The China Price. *Business Week*. December 6, 2004, pp. 102–112.

Falkenheim, V.C. (1981). Autonomy and Control in Chinese Organization: Dilemmas of Rural Administrative Reform. In Greenblatt, S.L., Wilson, R.W., and Wilson, A.A. (Eds.) *Organizational Behavior in Chinese Society*. New York: Praeger Publishing, 1981 pp. 190–208.

Fewsmith, J. (2003). Chinese Politics under Hu Jintao—Riding the Tiger of Politics and Public Health. *Problems of Post-Communism* 50(5): 14–21.

Fishman, T.C. (2004). The Chinese Century. *New Yorker Magazine* July 4, 2004, pp. 25–47.

Gardner, T. and Gardner, D. (2004). Tapping China's Newfound Wealth. *Motley Fool Stock Advisor*. Accessed January 2, 2005: www.fool.com

Gill, B., Chang, J., and Palmer, S. (2002). China's HIV Crisis. *Foreign Affairs* 81(2): 96–110.

Gregor, A.J. (1989). Military Modernization and Defense Policy in the People's Republic of China. In Leng, S.C. (Ed.) *Changes in China — Party, State and Society*. Lanham, MD: University Press of America, pp. 247–268.

Guo, J. and Zhang, M. (2001). The Development of the Chinese Public Administration Society. *Chinese Public Administration Review* 1(1): 1–11. Accessed December 20, 2004: http://www.andromeda.rutgers.eddu/cpar

Hayhoe, R. and Zha, Q. (2004). Becoming World-Class: Chinese Universities Facing Globalization and Internationalization. *Harvard China Review* 5(1): 87–92.

Hsiao, W.C. (2004). Disparity in Health: The Underbelly of China's Economic Development. *Harvard China Review* 5(1): 64–70.

Hu Urges CPPCC to Improve Advisory Capacity. (2004). *China Daily*. Accessed January 2, 2005: www.chinadaily.com.cn/english. *Chronicle of Higher Education* 48(47): 33–35.

Jefferson, G.H. and Rawski, T.G. (1999). China's Industrial Innovation Ladder: A Model of Endogenous Reform. In Jefferson, G.H. and Singh, I. (Eds.) *Enterprise Reform in China*. New York: Oxford University Press, pp. 65–88.

Jefferson, G.H., Hu, A.G.Z., and Singh, I. (1999). Industrial Investment, Finance, and Enterprise Performance in Chinese Industry. In Jefferson, G.H. and Singh, I. (Eds.) *Enterprise Reform in China*. New York: Oxford University Press, pp. 217–239.

Jencks, H.W. (1996). The PRC's Military and Security Policy. In Lin, B.J. and Meyers, J.T. (Eds.) *Contemporary China in the Post-Cold War Era*. Charleston, SC: University of South Carolina Press, pp. 225–259.

Jin, T. and Qian, Z. (2001). The Construction of an Institutionalized Relationship of Chinese Central and Local Government in the New Century. *Chinese Public Administration Review*. 1(1). Accessed December 19, 2004: http://www.andromeda.rutgers.eddu/cpar

Kirby, J.K. (1985). *Urbanization in China-Town and Country in a Developing Economy*. New York: Columbia University Press.

Kuhn, A. (2004). The Death of Growth at Any Cost. *Far Eastern Economic Review*. 167(13): 28–32.

Lai, H.H. (2003). Local Governments and China's Entry in WTO. *American Asian Review*. 21(3): 153–186.

Lam, J.T.M. (1994). Administrative Culture and Democracy in Hong Kong. *Asian American Review*. 21(3): 166–181.

Lam, T.C. and Chan, H.S. (1996). China's New Civil Service: What the Emperor is Wearing and Why. *Public Administration Review*. 56(5): 479–485.

Lan, Z. (2003). Disciplinary Rationale and Public Administration Field Development. *Chinese Public Administration Review*. 2(2): 1–11. Accessed December 20, 2004: http://www.andromeda.rutgers.eddu/cpar

Lee, H.Y. (1989). China's Future Leaders: The Third Echelon Cadres. In Leng, S.C. (Ed.) *Changes in China — Party, State and Society*. Lanham, MD: University Press of America, pp. 61–88.

Lee, P.N. (2001). Issues in Public Management Reform in China. *Policy Studies Review* 18(1): 8–15.

Let a Hundred Flowers Bloom. (2004). *New Internationalist*. 371. September, 2004, pp. 26–28. Accessed January 9, 2005: www.newint.org

Lim, T.W. (2004). Implications of the People's Liberation Army's Technocratization for U.S. Power in East Asia. *Asian Affairs: An American Review*. 31(1): 30–39.

Ma, S. (1999). Man of Efficiency and Man of Ethics: Can China's Administrative Reform Produce Both for Her Economic Development? *Policy Studies Review*. 16(2): 133–146.

Manacling the Mandarins. (2004). *The Economist* August 19, 2004, pp. 31–32.

Mandel, M.J. (2004). Does It Matter if China Catches Up? *Business Week*. December 6, 2004, Special Report.

Morey, R.D. (1993). A Letter from Beijing on Reform of China's Public Institutions. *PS: Political Science and Politics* 26(1): 17–19.

Nathan, A.J. (1990). *China's Crisis: Dilemmas of Reform and Prospects for Democracy*. New York: Colombia University Press.

National Defense in 2004. (2004). *China Daily*. Accessed January 2, 2005: http://english.peopledaily.com.cn/

Nation Now No. 3 Global Trader. (2005). *China Daily*. Accessed January 12, 2005: http://english.peopledaily.com.cn/

Ogden, S. (2004). *Global Studies: China*. 10th ed. Guilford, CT: McGraw-Hill/Dushkin.

Qi, Z. (2004). Towards a Precedent System in China — One Way of Institutionalization of the Rule of Law in China. *Harvard China Review* 5(1): 60–65.

Ramstad, E. (2004). The Technological Rise of China Was Speedy and Is Just the Beginning. *Wall Street Journal* December 20, 2004. pp. B1.

Ruan, M. (1994). *Den Xiaoping: Chronicle of an Empire.* Boulder, CO: Westview Press.

Saich, T. and Yang, X. (2003). Innovation in China's Local Governance: Open Recommendation and Selection. *Pacific Affairs* 76(2): 185–220.

Sappenfield, M. (2004). A Landmark Move for China. *The Christian Science Monitor.* December 9, 2004. pp. A1.

State Council. (2004). Circular Transmitting the State Administration of Taxation's Request for Directives Concerning Regulations Relevant to the Conscientious Implementation of Division of Work among Central and Local Tax Institutions on Tax Levying and Management. *Chinese Law and Government* 37(2): 61–63.

Tong, C.H. and Straussman, J.D. (2003). A Master of Public Administration Degree with Chinese Characteristics. *Journal of Public Affairs Education* 9(2): 105–115.

Tsai, W.H. (1989). New Trends in Marriage and Family in Mainland China: Impacts from the Four Modernizations Campaign. In Leng, S.C. (Ed.) *Changes in China — Party, State and Society.* Lanham, MD: University Press of America. pp. 225–246.

Tsao, K.K. and Worthley, J.A. (1995). Chinese Public Administration: Change with Continuity during Political and Economic Development. *Public Administration Review* 55(2): 169–175.

Unger, J. (2002). *The Transformation of Rural China.* New York: M.E. Sharpe.

Wang, L. (2002). A Probe into China's Public Administration Education and the Construction of the Subject of Public Administration. *Chinese Public Administration Review* 1(1): 31–36. Accessed December 20, 2004: http://www.andromeda.rutgers.eddu/cpar

Wang, B. and Gu, Y. (2002). Three Paradigms of Public Administration: An Analysis of the Current Status of Public Administration in China. *Chinese Public Administration Review* 1(3/4): 199–208. Accessed December 20, 2004: http://www.andromeda.rutgers.eddu/cpar

Whyte, M.K. (1980). Bureaucracy and Anti-Bureaucracy in the People's Republic of China. In Britan, G. R. and Cohen, R. (Eds.) *Hierarchy and Society: Anthropological Perspectives on Bureaucracy.* pp. 123–141. Philadelphia, PA: Institute for the Study of Human Issues.

Wilson, W. (2000). The Study of Administration. In Stillman, R.J. (Ed.) *Public Administration: Concepts and Cases.* pp. 6–16. Boston, MA: Houghton-Mifflin Co.

Wong, K. (2004a). The Police Legitimacy Crisis and Police Law Reform in China: Part I. *International Journal of Police Science and Management* 6(4): 199–218.

Wong, L. (2004b). Market Reforms, Globalization and Social Justice in China. *Journal of Contemporary China* 13(38): 151–171.

Wong, J. and Cheng, T.-J. (2003). Introduction to Social Policy in Asia. *American Asian Review* 21(2): 23–24.

World Bank (2002). Development Data Bank—China. Accessed Janauary 6, 2005: www.worldbank.org

Xu, X. (2002). On MPA Education Engineering in China. *Chinese Public Administration Review* 1(3/4): 261–265. Accessed December 20, 2004: http://www.andromeda.rutgers.eddu/cpar

Yang, D.M. (2002). Can the Chinese State Meet Its WTO Obligations? Government Reforms, Regulatory Capacity, and WTO Membership. *American Asian Review* 20(2): 191–221.

Yang, K. (2001). From Danwei Society to New Community Building: Opportunities and Challenges for Citizen Participation in Chinese Cities. *Chinese Public Administration Review*. 1(1). Accessed December 21, 2004: http://www.andromeda.rutgers.eddu/cpar

Zhang, G. (2002). Establishing the Criteria for Public Administration: An Evaluation of Chinese Government in the New Era. *Chinese Public Administration Review*. 1(3/4): 221–229. Accessed December 20, 2004: http://www.andromeda.rutgers.eddu/cpar

Zhong, (2003). *Local Government and Politics in China: Challenges from Below*. Armonk, NY: M.E. Sharpe.

VI

ADMINISTRATIVE REFORM AND REORGANIZATION IN AFRICA–INDIA

Chapter 28

Privatization in Africa: The Case of Botswana

Keshav C. Sharma

CONTENTS

Introduction

Soon after their independence, a large number of countries on the African continent earmarked a central role to the public sector for economic development. Public sector continued to expand not only as a result of creation of new public enterprises but also due to large-scale nationalization of private enterprises (indigenous, foreign, and multinational) motivated by ideological, political, or preferred development policy and development planning considerations. Toward the end of the past century, as a result of continued poor performance of public enterprises, the collapse of communism, and advocacy of structural adjustment programs (SAPs) by donor agencies, the state and the public-sector agencies in these countries started rolling back and we started witnessing a shift of emphasis from public sector to private sector. A significantly different approach toward the private sector was noticeable. The private sector that was earlier considered to be an instrument of exploitation and creator of disparities between the rich and the poor was then recognized as an engine of growth. Divestiture and privatization in different forms became common. The governments of different countries started encouraging private and even foreign investments. New forms of partnership between public and private sector started developing (Nellis, 1986; Ramanadham, 1989; Shirley and Nellis, 1991; Rasheed et al., 1994).

Poor Performance of Public Sector Enterprises in Africa and Efforts for Reforms

The performance of public enterprises in African countries has been disappointing. Many of these are incurring huge losses, have not been able to meet the objectives for which these were set up, and have been a drain on the national exchequer. Corruption, nepotism, political manipulation, inefficiency, and mismanagement have plagued many public enterprises. In many countries, rigid adherence to the ideology of socialism after independence resulted in large-scale nationalization and all pervasive public sectors. Private enterprise was shunned as it benefited a few entrepreneurs and created a gap between the rich and the poor. Public sector overexpanded beyond its capacities and even started undertaking activities, which should have been the domain of the private sector (Fadahunsi, 1996; Grosh and Mukandala, 1994). The United Nations Economic Commission for Africa (UNECA) (1991) identified the following factors as contributing to the failure or poor performance of public enterprises in Africa: excessive control and political interference; managerial incompetence; poor financial base; low integrity and incompetence of boards of directors; managerial corruption; poor personnel policies and practices; unclear objectives; and poor industrial relations. With limited and overstretched administrative capacity, the performance of public enterprises continued to deteriorate (Jefferies, 1998).

Public enterprise reform became a major concern of African countries when the overexpanded public sector undertakings were running a loss and were not meeting the objectives for their creation. Wide-ranging reforms related to structural reorganization and management were advocated and adopted as problems continued to surface. Realistic appraisal of managerial capabilities, reduced political controls, greater managerial autonomy, sound composition of boards of directors, improved personnel and financial management practices, downsizing of staff, cordial industrial relations, workers' participation in management, management development and training of staff at different levels, appraisal of performance-measuring techniques, effective financial controls, and cordial consumer relations were advocated. Efforts undertaken in all these aspects did not make a significant difference in the performance of a large number of public enterprises. These could not be turned around and made productive (AAPAM, 1987). Gradually it was realized that essentially it was the public policy framework that needed change. The large public sector had to roll back. Many of the nationalized public undertakings had to be sold back to the private sector where they appropriately belonged and could be better managed. A consensus started developing that apart from the national security, the state should primarily be concerned with those activities that the private sector is either unwilling or incapable of doing. Privatization was also visualized as an aspect of wide-ranging public-sector reforms needed for enhanced productivity and more efficient service delivery. Thus in Botswana other reforms such as performance management system (PMS), performance-based reward system (PBRS), computerization and decentralization in the civil service became significant components of public-sector reforms. Privatization became significant not only with regard to the public enterprise management but also for the entire public service as it was realized that the governments could deliver public service more efficiently in some cases by using the private sector, by contracting-out and outsourcing instead of relying on and expanding public bureaucracy.

The experience of many countries indicates that privatization is more effective when it is accompanied by other reform programs that create an enabling environment for efficient private enterprises (Abu Shair, 1997). The public sector plays a critical role in creating and supporting a market-friendly policy framework. Privatization and public-sector reform must therefore go hand in hand (Republic of Botswana, Draft White Paper, 1988, p. 39).

Reforming the Botswana public sector would require paying greater attention to maintaining lean and efficient public institutions; relating inputs (i.e., public expenditure) to outputs (i.e., provision of goods and services); avoiding redundant, conflicting, or overlapping powers, responsibilities, and departmental operations; rationalizing or terminating public services that are not cost-effective; and monitoring more closely and evaluating the performance of government ministries on a continuous basis. The application of commercial principles in running government operations (commercialization) would be one way of reducing waste and improving the efficiency of allocation and utilization of economic resources (BOCCIM, 1996). The Task Force on Privatization emphasized the need to modernize the country's public enterprises and make them operate in a business-like manner. It recommended measures such as managerial autonomy, appointment of boards of directors exclusively on grounds of merit, performance contracts for the CEO and senior staff, and performance targets (Republic of Botswana, Draft White Paper, 1998, pp. 39–40).

Expansion and Performance of Public Enterprises in Botswana

The creation and expansion of public enterprises in Botswana was not due to the ideology of socialism as was the case in many other African countries. The Government of Botswana never adopted a policy of nationalization. On the contrary, the government was against the policy of nationalization all along and its development plans assured the private sector investors in this regard. Botswana, right from the time of independence in 1966, was not restrictive of the private enterprise and welcomed foreign investments. Where feasible, the government was interested in joint ventures. The largest (diamond mining) company Debswana, a 50–50 joint venture between De Beers and the Government of Botswana is an example of that policy. Botswana Development Corporation (BDC) holds shares in a variety of firms across the economy. The creation and expansion of existing public enterprises in Botswana was a result of the positive role assumed by the government after independence for developing the country's poor economy. As the private sector was not developed at the time of independence, the state had to come forward and undertake activities that were considered essential for economic development and social welfare. Development plans and economic policies operating in a mixed economy were governed by pragmatic considerations. Some public enterprises (e.g., Botswana Power Corporation (BPC), Water Utilities Corporation (WUC)) were considered essential, as these were public utilities. Some public enterprises (e.g., National Development Bank

(NDB), BDC) were created to induce or facilitate private enterprise. Mass urban housing in the capital city was to be provided by the Botswana Housing Corporation (BHC). Other public enterprises were created to help the agriculture (Farmers Marketing Board), telecommunications (Botswana Telecommunications Corporation (BTC)), and transport network (Botswana Railways (BR)). Bank of Botswana came into existence as the central bank. Botswana Building Society as a housing finance institution and the Botswana Savings Bank (BSB) as a successor to the Post Office Savings Bank were among other public enterprises. Botswana's public enterprises were not to restrict or inhibit the growth of private enterprises. The public enterprise sector as a whole in Botswana is rather smaller than is typical in Africa.

With regard to the performance of public enterprises, the general view is that African public enterprises have yielded a very low rate of return on the large amount of resources invested in them. Botswana's record is better than that of most public enterprises in Africa. Presenting his budget speech to the National Assembly in 2004, the minister of finance and development planning B. Gaolathe observed "financial performance of majority of public enterprises was satisfactory for the year 2002/2003 although there is ample scope for improvement." More specifically, "the Botswana Telecommunications Authority (BTA), the Botswana Power Corporation (BPC), the Water Utilities Corporation (WUC), the Botswana Development Corporation (BDC), the National Development Bank (NDB), the Botswana Vaccine Institute (BVI), Air Botswana (AB), the Botswana Housing Corporation (BHC), the Botswana Savings Bank (BSB), and Banyana have all recorded operating as well as net profits for the year 2002/2003 ... However, the Botswana Telecommunications Corporation (BTC), the Botswana Railways (BR), the Botswana Meat Commission (BMC), the Botswana Post (BP), and the Botswana Agricultural Marketing Board (BAMB) made losses in 2002/2003" (budget speech, Republic of Botswana, 2004, p. 6). In 2005 the same minister reported to the National Assembly in his budget speech that "the financial performance of the majority of public enterprises was relatively satisfactory for the year 2003/2004. Some public enterprises that recorded losses during 2002/2003 have now recorded net profits and positive return on capital employed. These include the Botswana Telecommunications Corporation, the Botswana Agricultural Marketing Board, the Botswana Post.... Despite the good performance of most parastatals, there has been no noticeable improvement in the performance of the Botswana Meat Commission, as it continued to make losses in 2003/2004.... The Botswana Development Corporation continued its good performance in the past year with a profit before tax of P65.5 million" (budget speech, Republic of Botswana, 2005, p. 6). The performance of public enterprises has fluctuated during the past years. BMC, for instance, was a profit-making public enterprise in the 1990s and was even identified by UNECA as a model of success (Sharma, 1994). A mixed picture of this kind and fluctuating performance, although not too depressing, establishes a need for reforms and privatization for enhanced productivity.

Reasons for Privatization

Disappointing performance of public enterprises, failure of different measures for improving performance, and structural adjustment measures recommended by donor agencies have resulted in the adoption of different forms of privatization in various African countries. The collapse of communism in the Soviet block of nations and pursuance of privatization policies in the Western world have given further impetus to the privatization drive all over Africa. It has been suggested that as the state with its limited administrative capacities has overextended and overloaded itself, it should reduce and curtail the scope of its activities and contract. Increased scope of activities has resulted in inefficiency, mismanagement, and corruption. With political control and interference, it has been difficult to operate these enterprises on business lines. Weak management has been difficult to develop and the environment has not been conducive for the successful operation of public enterprises. Privatization policy in African countries is an outcome of these reasons (UNECA, 1990; 1991).

Botswana's reasons for privatization are somewhat different from those of other African countries. The government has not been pressurized to follow SAPs by international financial institutions to privatize its public enterprises. This policy in Botswana has also not been driven by budgetary constraints as in some other African countries. The impetus for privatization in Botswana has come from a desire to improve efficiency in the delivery of service, to attract direct foreign investment, and to create further opportunities for the citizen business sector. It is expected to create greater business development opportunities for the private sector as a whole. The private sector in Botswana has grown during the past years. It is now capable of delivering services both in competition with and in place of government. The financial sector is also more developed. The government realizes that the private sector could undertake some functions more efficiently and the government could be left primarily with the tasks that cannot be performed by the private sector. The National Development Plan (Republic of Botswana, 2003, NDP 9) follows this policy and Vision 2016 also suggests that the government must become better at costing its activities and must feel free to contract for services from the private sector to achieve its objectives more economically.

The privatization policy for Botswana is a product of extensive nationwide consultation undertaken by the task force set up to prepare the draft White paper on privatization in 1998 (Republic of Botswana, 1998). The report of the task force culminated in the adoption of the Privatization Policy for Botswana by the government in 2000 (Republic of Botswana, 2000, Government Paper No. (GP) 1).

Meaning of Privatization

Defined narrowly, privatization means transferring the ownership of public enterprises to private buyers. The transfer of ownership from public to private hands is usually through selling all or some of the assets of public enterprises or other public entities to the private sector. This particular form of privatization is often termed divestiture, which may also be done by liquidation of assets. Defined broadly, privatization is much more than that; privatization encompasses all measures and policies aimed at strengthening the role of the private sector in the economy. The government of Botswana has adopted the latter definition where privatization covers a very wide range of different policy actions, resulting in private sector involvement in economic activities that have been previously undertaken by the public sector (Republic of Botswana, 2000, GP 1, p. 7). According to the CEO of PEEPA, "privatization is not an end in itself but is a tool to shape economic policy. Privatization is a journey, not a destination, and must be understood in that context" (Galeforolwe, 2004, p. 4).

Objectives of Privatization

Privatization policy has been advocated as the means to enforce market discipline and promote efficient allocation and use of economic resources. Although the reasons for privatization differ from one country to another, the objectives of privatization have often been very similar. These objectives include: promoting competition, improving efficiency, and increasing productivity of enterprises; increasing direct citizen participation in the ownership of national assets; accelerating the rate of economic growth by stimulating entrepreneurship and investment; withdrawing from commercial activities that no longer need to be undertaken by the public sector; reducing the size of public sector; relieving the financial and administrative burden of the government in undertaking and maintaining a constantly expanding network of services and investments in infrastructure; and broadening and deepening the capital market (Republic of Botswana, 2000, GP 1, pp. 8–9).

Forms and Methods of Privatization

There are many alternative forms or methods of privatization such as commercialization, corporatization, contracting-out, management contracts, franchises, leases, concessions, and stock market floatation. The choice of privatization modalities depends upon the objectives to be achieved. Commercialization will mean bringing the public enterprise activities to the market place, putting them on a fee for service basis, and managing them like any other business enterprise. The main requirements of corporatization are: the establishment of clear and nonconflicting objectives; the appointment of board members, management, and staff based on merit; managerial autonomy; effective performance monitoring; remuneration and terms of service according to market conditions; effective rewards and sanctions related to performance; establishment of competitive environment; tax liability like private enterprises; commercial accounting practices; eliminating subsidies; and adoption of consumer- and market-oriented approach. In some cases, commercialization and corporatization may be an appropriate privatization method. In other cases, they are regarded as the prelude to outright divestiture. Under the contracting-out method, the government maintains control of the activity but contracts out the production of goods or services to the private sector. Instead of using government employees and equipment, private firms are paid from government funds to perform specific tasks or supply specific goods. The contracting-out of services to the private sector is carried out through competitive tendering. Under a management contract arrangement, the government retains ownership of business and its assets but hires an operator who manages them for a fee (common in hotels, airlines, etc.). Franchise involves the government granting a private firm an exclusive franchise to supply a particular service in a given locality. The government may maintain control over the price of goods or services to be sold by the private firm. Under a lease arrangement, the government concerned retains the ownership of the property and other assets and simply leases them to an operator who runs the business for his own account. The private party pays the government a fee to use the assets. For some types of property or activity (for example, a forest, wildlife management, or a mining prospect) a concession arrangement may be considered appropriate as it specifies the precise use that can be made of the property and the nature of charges to be levied (Republic of Botswana, 2000, GP 1).

Public–Private Sector Participation

The government realizes that the public sector and private sector have to play complementary roles and do not have to be seen as substitutes for each other. Government and markets both play an indispensable role in economic development. Markets are not always perfect and government intervention is needed to offset market limitations and failures. Governments cannot replace markets as evidenced by the collapse of centrally planned economies. The government believes that "the question should not be what activities should be carried out by the government and which activities should be undertaken by the private sector. Rather, it should be how best to balance the strengths and limitations of markets and governments and how best they can complement each other" (Republic of Botswana, 2000, GP 1, p. 1).

In a mixed economy, the government has a number of responsibilities. This includes the designing of public policies and legal framework for operation of private sector, giving property rights, facilitating the provision of basic needs of its population, establishing conditions for enforcement of contracts, ensuring social justice, and providing equitable access to economic opportunities. The government intervention in the market has been justified on the grounds of public interest. This includes defense and security services, looking after the interests of vulnerable and marginalized sections of society, creating and maintaining a social safety net, building of infrastructure, protecting environment, and promoting universally accessible education. Increasingly the role of government is expected to be concerned primarily with the creation of enabling environment for the operation of the private sector so that it can operate as an engine of growth, operate within the framework of public policies and legal framework of the country, and contribute to the realization of vision and mission of the government in partnership with the government.

Machinery for Implementation of Privatization

Realizing that the management and implementation of the privatization process requires an autonomous organization that has the authority, resources, and technical skills to undertake the task, the government has established "Public Enterprise Evaluation and Privatization Agency (PEEPA)." This entity is mandated to perform the twin tasks of effective evaluation of the performance of parastatals and advice on the commercialization and privatization processes. PEEPA is at present attached to the ministry of finance and development planning, but it is expected to be an autonomous entity. The government would like it to be a company with a board of directors drawn mainly from the private sector. Those chosen from the public sector will serve in their personal capacities. Members of the board will have diversified backgrounds and experiences (i.e., a lawyer, a banker, an economist, an accountant, an engineer, a businessman).

The responsibilities of PEEPA are: to identify candidates for privatization or commercialization/corporatization and decide on the appropriate course of action; to prepare a privatization master plan; to oversee all aspects of implementation of commercialization and privatization on behalf of the government; to review objectives of existing parastatals and set objectives for entities to be commercialized or corporatized; to assist the government in setting performance targets for parastatals and other public entities; to monitor the performance of these entities in meeting their objectives and targets; to advise the government on the appointment of directors of public companies and parastatals; to monitor the performance of those directors and boards; to hire and supervise consultants on privatization and performance evaluation; to publicize its activities; and to develop and execute public education programs (Republic of Botswana, 2000, GP 1, pp. 21–22).

Process of Implementation

Principles

The Government of Botswana has adopted the following principles for implementing the policy of privatization: privatization will be conducted for the benefit of all, not for the privileged few; privatization will be selective and, where implemented, the process will be transparent and equitable; privatization will be conducted in a way that will stimulate the development of local financial and capital markets and citizen-owned businesses; different modalities of privatization will be considered as appropriate for improving the efficiency of different enterprises; measures will be taken to safeguard employee interests; the government will drive the privatization process but also hire in the expertise of different kinds required for the task (Republic of Botswana, 2000, GP 1, pp. 9–10).

Selecting Candidates for Privatization and Action Plans

The criteria to be adopted by the government for considering candidates for privatization include: potential of the enterprise for improvements in efficiency and productivity; advantage of acquiring foreign participation to produce new technology and management and international link-up; the opportunity it could afford for domestic private sector growth and for citizen empowerment; contribution to stock market development; introducing competition into an otherwise monopolistic market; and extent of private sector interest in purchase and capacity for quicker investment. Action plans prepared by PEEPA will guide the process and determine the kinds of safety nets and other support programs that will be developed on a case-by-case basis to ensure success of commercialization and privatization process. The privatization master plan prepared by PEEPA outlines how privatization of different activities and entities can be structured, sequenced, and implemented.

The Task Force (1998) recommended that the following list could be considered for privatization or commercialization: refuse collection, catering services, security services, cleaning services, landscaping and gardening, laundry services, medical equipment maintenance, mechanical and electrical maintenance, ambulance and transport services in public hospitals, debt collection, tax collection, road maintenance, administration of selected tourism, management of national parks and game reserves, bore-hole drilling and maintenance, and organization of international conferences.

Public enterprises listed by the Task Force (1998) as serious candidates for privatization include: BDC, NDB, Botswana Building Society, BSB, Botswana Motor Vehicles Insurance Fund, BPC, WUC, BTC, BHC, AB, BMC, Botswana Livestock Development Corporation, BAMB, BR, Botswana Postal Services, BVI, municipal abattoirs, and government ranches.

The Task Force (1998) also listed the government departments and other public entities, which could be considered for commercialization and corporatization. These include entities like Department of Architecture and Building Services, Registrar of Companies, Government Printer, Botswana Institute of Administration and Commerce (BIAC), Institute of Development Management (IDM), Botswana National Productivity Center (BNPC), Department of Supplies, Title Deeds Office, Surveys and Mapping, Department of Information and Broadcasting, Customs Department, Department of Transport (Motor Vehicles Registration), Roads Department, Birth/Death Registration, Veterinary Services, Geological Department, Department of Water Affairs, Immigration Department, Department of Civil Aviation, Central Sterilizing Unit, Department of Student Placement and Welfare, Botswana Wildlife Training Institute, Central Transport Organization (CTO), Computer Bureau, Rural Industries Promotion, Botswana Technology Center, and Food Technology Research Service.

Citizen Empowerment

To facilitate citizen empowerment the government will promote shareholding by citizens and special access to the shares by management and employees. The government will also set up an "Investment Trust Fund" to purchase a certain percentage of shares of privatized enterprises on behalf of citizens. These shares will later be sold to citizens in small tranches over a given period. Government will also extend the small, medium, and macro Enterprises (SMME) "credit scheme" to small citizen investors, in order to facilitate citizen ownership of privatized enterprises. Some services (cleaning, catering, gardening, maintenance, etc.) currently produced in the public sector would provide opportunities to start many small business ventures by the same people who are presently government employees (Republic of Botswana, 2000, GP 1, pp. 11–12).

Foreign Participation

The government realizes that there may not be enough local corporate investors with the financial resources and management expertise to acquire large state-owned enterprises. In such cases foreign participation would be necessary. As limiting foreign participation to very low levels could deter foreign investors, the government plans to adopt liberal rules for encouraging foreign participation and investment. The government's policy is not to exclude foreign investors outright and not to impose across-the-board fixed restriction on foreign participation but to consider these on case-by-case basis. This is in keeping with government's policy to project Botswana as an investor-friendly country. Where practicable, government will encourage and enable Botswana investors to acquire majority control. If citizen investors do not come forward to own majority of shares, concessions such as build–operate–transfer (BOT) or build–own–operate–transfer (BOOT) will also be considered in cases where international expertise and technology are needed (Republic of Botswana, 2000, GP 1, pp. 12–13).

Safeguards and Safety Nets

Lay-off of some workers could be inevitable in the interest of efficiency and productivity as some of these enterprises to be privatized have been overstaffed. In such cases, the government would award negotiated redundancy packages to the affected employees within the established laws and policies. A program of training and skill reorientation will be launched to facilitate the absorption of employees in other trades.

Measures for Public Education

Government realizes that privatization will be successful only when it respects and informs the public. The public needs to be regularly informed about each activity and how it will affect them. Government intends to disseminate information to the public through workshops and seminars, brochures and articles in newspapers, television and radio panel discussions, public speeches and special activities in rural areas. A national stakeholders' conference on privatization organized by PEEPA in April 2004 was an effort in that regard.

Apprehensions

Successful implementation of privatization policy will depend upon the extent to which it will be able to address adequately the anxieties and apprehensions of the people. It will have to be understood and appreciated by the public that privatization will not be a panacea for all the problems of ailing public enterprises. These enterprises may not become productive overnight simply as a result of change of ownership. In many cases competitive environment and commercialization may be an essential prerequisite for successful operation of privatized enterprises (UN, 1989). Privatized enterprises may not become productive if these remain monopolies. The public may be subjected to inefficient and unproductive operations and may not be able to exercise control over these enterprises due to their diminished public accountability as a part of private sector. Because of underdeveloped private sector and dearth of local entrepreneurs, privatization may result in domination of foreign enterprises, multinationals, or local business elite when these are offered for sale. The interests of the poor and vulnerable may not be adequately guarded when these enterprises are owned by the private entrepreneurs or when the government starts applying cost recovery principles for the services rendered by the public sector. Lay-offs, retrenchment, and downsizing exercises might increase unemployment and unrest. Haphazard implementation of privatization policy without adequate preparation and consultation with stakeholders and appropriate administrative machinery for implementation of the task could result in an unexpected outcome. The objectives of privatization may not be realized. Privatization could also create room for corruption, in identifying the clients for buying the enterprise, fixing the price, settling the terms and conditions, etc. The experience of Zambia during the last few years demonstrates how economic liberalization and privatization could increase corruption. In that country, a widespread privatization program undertaken during 1992–1997, hailed by Western donor countries as a model of success, revealed widespread corruption as documented by Chikulo (2000): "Indeed, although there is no evidence to suggest an economic turn around, privatization of the economy has, instead, opened up opportunities for rampant corruption and allowed the ruling political elite to amass enormous wealth . . . small scale companies which have been bought at almost give away prices by locals, have been monopolized by politicians and their associates . . . only the well connected few reap any benefits from the government's privatization and economic liberalization program" (pp. 168–169).

The Government of Botswana appears to be mindful of such apprehensions and anxieties and proposes to undertake measures (some of these have been discussed above) to preempt such possibilities. Botswana has been cautious and proposes to be selective in identifying the candidates for privatization or for resorting to a particular form of privatization. The country took time to deliberate extensively on the privatization policy before it was adopted. The recommendations of the task force on privatization submitted in 1998 were widely discussed and the government adopted the policy in 2000. PEEPA, established as an administrative machinery after the adoption of the policy, has taken time to produce the action plan for privatization. This will be debated in the National Assembly and by the public before approval and implementation. Public discussion and transparency will hopefully check the undesirable practices and corrupt practices.

Monitoring, Evaluation, and Follow-Up

An effective system of regulation, continuous evaluation, and close monitoring are essential to the success of the privatization process. Regulation may be required to intervene to influence the economic decisions of an enterprise and continuous evaluation will be required to draw conclusions and make judgments on the outcomes or impact of the reform program. Similarly, monitoring will be essential for systematically appraising progress during the process and after privatization and to check that the objectives of privatization are being achieved. The government has entrusted PEEPA to be responsible for these tasks with assistance from the public enterprise monitoring unit (PEMU) of the ministry of finance and development planning.

Critical Factors for Success of Policy

The government recognizes that the success of privatization is contingent upon a number of factors: a strong political commitment to policy implementation; an appropriate legal framework; an effective supervisory or regulatory authority; reformed management systems; support of public servants and public enterprise employees; public support and transparency. It is widely recognized that privatization is a political process as well as a commercial and economic process. Therefore, public support is a major consideration in any privatization program.

Postprivatization Phase: Changed Role of the State

The role of government will not end after the implementation of privatization plans, but it will only change. The government will have to continue to safeguard public interest and monitor the performance of private sector generally and privatized undertakings in particular. The government realizes that its role will continue to change as the economy changes. The determination and commitment of the government will have to be matched by readiness and cooperation from the private sector. "The interaction between government and the private sector will be transformed into a "smart partnership" of cooperation and complementarily that emphasizes "win–win" situations. The drive toward diversified growth must be led by the private sector, which is expected to display the qualities of good corporate citizenship, including the promotion of citizen empowerment. The public sector will progressively diminish its role in the provision of marketable goods and services and will rather seek to facilitate and, where necessary, regulate the operation of business by the private sector" (Republic of Botswana, 2000, GP 1, p. 3). One could derive some satisfaction in this regard from the statement made to the National Assembly by the minister of finance and development planning, Baledzi Gaolathe, when presenting the draft privatization policy for Botswana. He made it clear to the country that the privatization should not entail government discarding any of its core responsibilities, which include good governance, safety, and welfare of its citizens. He assured the house that the process will be carried out with a human face and efforts will be made to safeguard national interests (*Mmegi*, 2000). To what extent these assurances will be honored; only the time will tell.

References

AAPAM. 1987. *Public Enterprise Performance and Privatization Debate: A Review of Options for Africa*. New Delhi: Vikas.

Abu Shair, Osama J.A.R. 1997. *Privatization and Development*. London: Macmillan Press.

Botswana Confederation of Commerce, Industry and Manpower (BOCCIM). 1996. *Privatization in Botswana*. Gaborone.

Chikulo, B.C. 2000. "Corruption and Accumulation in Zambia," in K.R. Hope Sr. and B.C. Chikulo (eds.), *Corruption and Development in Africa: Lessons from Country Case Studies*. New York: Pelgrave.

Fadahunsi, O. (ed.) 1996. *Privatization in Africa: The Way Forward*. Nairobi: AAPAM.

Galeforolwe, J.B. 2004. "Privatization Policy for Botswana," Paper Presented at a National Stakeholders Conference on Privatization, "Making Privatization Everyone's Business," Gaborone.

Grosh, B. and R.S. Mukandala. (eds.) 1994. *State Owned Enterprises in Africa.* Boulder, CO: Lynne Rienner.

Jefferies, K. 1998. "Botswana's Public Enterprises," in W.A. Edge and M. Lekorwe (eds.), *Botswana Politics and Society.* Pretoria: Van Schaik Publishers.

Mmegi. 2000. 31 March–06 April.

Nellis, J.R. 1986. *Public Enterprises in Sub-Saharan Africa.* Washington, D.C.: World Bank.

Ramanadham, V.V. (ed.) 1989. *Privatization in Developing Countries.* London: Routledge.

Rasheed S., Asmelash, B., and E.E. Otobo. (eds.) 1994. *Public Enterprise in Africa: Lessons from Country Case-Studies.* Ljubjana: ICPE and UNECA.

Republic of Botswana. 1998. *Draft White Paper on a Privatization Policy for Botswana.* Gaborone: Government Printer.

Republic of Botswana. 2000. *Privatization Policy for Botswana.* Government Paper No. 1 of 2000, Ministry of Finance and Development Planning, Government Printer. (Referred in the paper as GP 1).

Republic of Botswana. 2003. *National Development Plan 9: 2003/04 – 2008/09.* Gaborone: Ministry of Finance and Development Planning.

Republic of Botswana. 2004. *Budget Speech 2004 Delivered to the National Assembly on 9th February, 2004, by Hon. B. Gaolathe.* Gaborone: Government Printer.

Republic of Botswana. 2005. *Budget Speech 2005 Delivered to the National Assembly on 7th February 2005 by Hon. B. Gaolathe, Minister of Finance and Development Planning.* Gaborone: Government Printer.

Sharma, K.C. 1994. "Botswana Meat Commission: A Success Story?" in S. Rasheed, A. Beyene, and E.E. Otobo. (eds.), *Public Enterprises in Africa: Lessons from Country Case-Studies.* Ljubjana: ICPE and UNECA.

Shirley, M. and J. Nellis. 1991. *Public Enterprise in Africa.* Washington, D.C.: World Bank.

UN. 1989. *Role and Extent of Competition in Improving the Performance of Public Enterprises.* New York.

UNECA. 1990. *Improving the Performance of Public Enterprises in Africa.* Addis Ababa: Report of a Senior Policy Workshop.

UNECA. 1991. *Improving Performance of Public Enterprise Management in Africa: Lessons from Country Experiences.* Dakar.

Chapter 29

Globalization and Administrative Reforms: A Case Study of a Globalizing City (Gurgaon) in India

Amita Singh

CONTENTS

Introduction

This chapter attempts to investigate the impact of globalization on administrative reforms brought about in the area of local governance. This happens to be a formidable assignment especially at this juncture when studies on globalization have developed a high level of proficiency in administrative research and legitimization on parameters of democracy. In public administration studies it could be understood as the second tide of introspective analysis to clear its own jungle, the first being in 1961 when comparative studies evoked three dynamic trends in administrative studies.[1] Through the case study methods, these trends affirmed that the institutions cannot be abstracted from their environments. The present genre of administrative research moves still further to state that the inner contradictions of the processes which implant globalization-induced reforms in local governance fail the test of sustainability. Yet it cannot be denied that although the intellectual roots of the Comparative Administration Group (CAG) were located in American positivism and structural–functional approach, the impetus to present analysis is indigenous and completes the onerous research undertaken by CAG in explaining the ecology of governance relationships. This second tide of investigating reforms relocates the "community" at the center of local governance, which sets at rest the illusion of a passive society in a developing country and also provides answers to the anxious query which Ford Foundation's George Gant had made to CAG, "With all this theorizing and all this study what are you going to do about it?" One would concede that it is for three reasons that public administration can now provide incisive answers to such a query. First, the focus is now on the analysis of microlevel institutions that have a greater capacity than the state to prescribe and proscribe local norms and practices in public policies. Second, there is a better understanding of regulatory changes and policy implementation processes due to generous inputs from anthropological and economic data in public administration. Third, due to a resurgence of civil society and rise of environmental movements there is better understanding of resource distribution issues that substantiate claims on ecology as the driving force of governance today.

Public administration is now asserting a different domain outside that of "American exceptionalism" (Lipset, 1996). Globalization has unfolded the perceived monoliths of Eastern and Western societies into dispersed community structures that represent completely self-governed but unique ecosystems. These ecosystems also generate discourses and carve out

[1]Riggs identified three trends in comparative study of public administration (1962, pp. 9–15). The first was a movement from normative toward empirical approaches, the second from idiographic tonomothetic approaches, and the third from nonecological to ecological modes of thought.

channels for deliberations on issues that cause discomfort in a transitional society. They are also knowledge centers as they possess resources and information about resources not known to any outside developmental agent. Because these ecosystems have become areas of frenetic activity of global multinational partners in development this assignment has identifiable arena for research and is therefore not likely to end up into a road less traveled, which had become the bane of CAG.

The study highlights the process of growth and expansion toward urbanization and market expansion that has subdued or silenced local voices and institutional resonance.[2] This has accelerated the process of market fundamentalism taking over radical civil society movements like peasant uprisings or student and trade union protests on regulatory changes, which restrict thier deliberative institutions by governments. Even erstwhile radical women's movements have been confining themselves to a safe corner in which they could avoid a direct confrontation with the state. Issues that inspire international attention such as rape, amniocentesis, and HIV have taken over more widespread pathologies affecting women such as measuring household income, sale and acquisition of village commons, slaughtering of milch cattle, flesh trade involving smuggling poor women across international frontiers, and changing property and inheritance laws. Thus local governance has become an arena of corporate campaigns for establishing control over the local body. A corporate friendly candidate in it would help the multinational seize over village resources like land, wetlands, and cheap labor. This hypothesis is backed by evidences from this study on Gurgaon.

This chapter has focused upon three main sections: local governance in Gurgaon within the wider frame of local governance in India, local governance and its interdependence with ecosystems which generate local occupations, and lastly the delinking of governance reforms with the ecology of a village during global integration of a village economy creates not only unsustainability of programs but also brings irretrievable loss to local institutions. In the end the rationale of reforms ought to be derived from local concerns rather than the global glitter of efficiency-based organizations which may pass the test of cost-effective governance but may fail on implantation in rural India.

The study is built around three indicators: changes in the regulatory mechanism, land acquisition, and developmental programs that compensate for the land that they lose to global companies in terms of other

---

[2]'Institutional resonance' is a form of reverberation in institutional structures that synchronizes with the voice of its people and this is one of those characteristics of institutions which gives a meaningful existence to the institution. The 1989 Minnowbrook II Conference rediscovered the significance of institutional resonance in administrative reforms.

opportunities. These indicators are accepted as fundamental to the assessment of deliberative bodies that help clear people's access to the benefits of globalization. Other factors such as that of service delivery improvements, which include variables like speed, cost of transactions, corruption in public offices, etc., are treated as spillovers from the previous indicators. Democratic institutions are taken as dependent variables of global investments in terms of foreign direct investment (FDI) and foreign institutional investors (FIIs).

Local Governance in India

India is a vast country of diversities and is divided into 28 states and 7 union territories. States are divided into administrative districts that are the centers of local governance activities. Local government has been one of the most integral components of Indian democracy as it is the only direct interface with people and so better equipped to deal diversities at local level. It is of two types: *Panchayati raj* is the name given to local governance in rural areas and *Nagarpalika* for urban areas. For explaining the processes that disaggregate community structures over land this chapter would only focus on the former, nevertheless this is also true that globalizing cities have obliterated the divide between the two while at the same time deepening further the gulf between. Although its valuable role in providing sustainable economic regeneration had been recognized from preindependence era, yet it has subsequently been sidelined in the planning processes of post-independent India. The first five-year plan introduced the community development program (CDS) in 1952 but the system worked through a centralized system of monitoring and control that reduced local deliberative spaces and hence the initiatives of grassroots dwellers. The CDS model also failed to work out a reasonable people–resources relationship and in fact the centralized state was so obsessed with structural modifications that it completely ignored the substantive rationality of the existing structures. Balwant Rai Mehta Committee Report of 1957 suggested a three-tier system of panchayati raj institutions (PRIs) in rural areas but in the absence of a constitutional status to this level of governance it remained under part IV of the constitution, which contained "directive principles of state policy." This led the local governance system to develop differently in different states. Thus the CDS model of postindependence reforms ended up as a futile exercise, which could neither inspire participation nor bring development in the poverty-stricken rural areas.

The consistent failure of all the five-year plans till the eighth five-year plan in 1992 led to a rethinking of the processes of development in a manner that would contain exclusion and alienation in local communities.

It was also recognized that by merely changing structures, local bodies only develop excessive formalism,[3] which weaken the implementation of reforms. Despite early attempts of Balwant Rai Mehta Committee in 1957 until 1992 these local government bodies continued to be plagued by political apathy and corruption, which prevented their growth as responsible constitutional bodies at local levels. This was however overcome in 1992 when the 73rd Constitutional Amendment was brought about to provide a constitutional status to PRIs. This made them both welfare as well as service delivery bodies. The three tiers are, the gram sabha and the gram panchayat, which compose the grassroots body over which stands the panchayat samiti as the middle-level link between the village and the district administration, and zila parishad, the topmost district level body that composed of both elected members and district administrators. This system has historical roots in village governance patterns in India. Although service delivery obligation under the 11th schedule of the Act was a British perspective, where local bodies are seen more as an agency of service delivery rather than a political institution, yet the political element introduced into a forgotten institution almost 40 years after independence required much more than just an introduction of regular elections. As John Stewart (1996, p. 41) observes, "In so far as there is scope for local choice and local voice, the case remains but it is a weaker case, leading to a weaker approach to local democracy. A different conception of local government is possible as the community governing itself — which is a stronger concept of local government." Little research was fed into the process of integrating community governance systems with local governance model of 1992. Thus the value of an ecosystem-based existence of agricultural communities in Indian villages was not realized in policy changes at grassroots. This also cut through the ability of the panchayats in overcoming the insurmountable jungle of governance embedded into institutions controlled by landowning upper castes. The 1996 Panchayats Extension to Scheduled Areas Act (PESA) tried to overcome the weaknesses of the 1992 Act but because it was introduced only in nine states that contained a dominant percentage of tribal population, therefore it could not provide a comprehensive solution to the problem. It also conveyed a highly mischievous impression that only villages with tribal population are natural resources dependent and others can be dispensed of them, thereby clearing the way for multinational corporations (MNCs) to enter their domain, and use their resources under a viel of legitimacy.

---

[3]Riggs defines formalism as "a degree of discrepancy or congruence between the formally prescribed and effectively practised, between norms and realities. The greater the congruence, the more realistic the situation; the greater the discrepancy the more formalistic" (1967, pp. 415–416).

Thus the market reforms based on new public management (NPM) approaches also influenced policies toward village resources like land, water, forests, and grazing grounds. The 73rd Amendment Act in 1992 diverted attention from their just distribution, management, and control to a democratic election thereby throwing the onus of solutions to historically subdued and dependent mass of people who were never trained to mobilize for a just cause like their counterparts in West Bengal and Kerala. Also, no effort was made to neutralize the corrupt nexus of revenue administration with landowning classes controlling local government. In West Bengal programmes such as *Operation Banga* could help strengthen the voice of poor and few years later these voices became change agents in local programmes. Most local governance institutions have been embedded historically into these resources that generate a management regime of reciprocity and substantive democracy[4] in contrast to the representative democracy. Once this element is removed, local governance inflates into a narrow platform for representative democracy but composed of dispirited communities estranged from their ecosystem and have nowhere to go. The wilting of those ecosystems, which had made face to face deliberations and debates on common issues possible, is a prelude to the MNC takeover of an area.

The Gurgaon Phenomenon

This chapter is mainly a study of the impact of globalization on a city called Gurgaon (a district in the Indian state of Haryana), an erstwhile small village on the outskirts of Delhi. In the last ten years Gurgaon has become one of the top three silicon valley regions in India, the destination for main software companies, and a hub of business process outsourcing (BPO) companies and so it is named as the millennium city, a medicity, or a cybercity. Its skyscrapers and malls of international standard may leave any non resident Indian not residing in India awestruck for the progress that India has made out of globalization, which has seeped into the social fabric of this city and manifests into branded lifestyles where San Jose is better known than the streets of Agra where the Taj Mahal is. Gurgaon has been one of the four cities in India, other three being Bangalore, Hyderabad, and Chennai, and has been quick enough to catch up and keep pace with the global upswing of the Indian market. The 2004 Global Retail Development Index of A.T. Kearney titled as the *Emerging Market* reveals that on the basis of attractiveness among global retailers India rises to the second position whereas even the "Asian Powerhouse," that China is known as, remains at

[4]"It encourages the citizen to see in the local authority not one agency among many carrying out administrative tasks, but the corporate manifestation of the local community (collective locale), which is the first resort in case of local difficulty" Blair (1991, p. 51).

the third position. But it further says that this attractiveness is high on the scales of retail per capita, which have increased by one third between 1999 and 2003 (2004, pp. 7–8) Thus a large number of foreign retailers seek land in India for setting up their shopping malls. Two out of the top five are the Hong Kong based Dairy Farm and Metro AG. There are many retailers such as the African retailer Shoprite, Wal-Mart, and Carrefour waiting for the FDI regulations to ease. As the report states, "until reforms pass, successful global retailers will have to adapt and enter using different formats" and these include local collaborations on a temporary basis (Kearney, 2004, p. 8). The BPO and IT companies are another thrust to Gurgaon's boom. In the next five years, 3.5 million new jobs and 200 million sq. ft. of additional real estate space are required (NAI Report 2004).[5] This has led MNCs to place expatriate employees in India who look for serviced apartments and recreational areas that match the global standards, thereby creating a construction boom. This however is dependent upon the acquisition of land, which comes from the villages. In 1991, when MNCs had not started their operations in this area, it composed a total of 730 villages but in 2001 their number reduced to 726 villages.[6] So villages are gradually being sucked into frantic infrastuctural expansion for chaste globalization being brought as science turns to MNCs. In a densely populated country and a saturated inhabitation possibility in Delhi, Gurgaon was looked upon as the most appropriate site for this expansion. The decade of 1990s was a period for rapid urban expansion and in the post-2000 period there is a mutual dependence of the FDI investment and land acquired. Till 2000, the telecom sector alone invited Rs. 9576.40 crores[7] of FDI, and in 2004, these IT companies acquired more than 85,000 sq. ft. of residential space in Delhi (including Gurgaon) and the Mumbai region in one month alone[8] and the BPO companies are set to create 200 million sq. ft. of additional real estate space in the country over the next five years.

The U.S.-based North American International (NAI) in its global market report predicted that the Gurgaon region has been the hotspot for commercial expansion and residential relocation.

Thus the main pressure of global integration in India is upon villages which are the repositories of "land" be it agricultural land, land under forests, wastelands, wetlands, or land under the control of the panchayats. In every-way this has not only affected lives of villagers but has also disintegrated community bondings and weakened ecosystems. During the course of this work a survey was made of the top 14 villages in Gurgaon that were adopted for urbanization by Haryana Urban Development Authority (HUDA),

---

[5] "The Gurgaon region has been the hotspot for commercial expansion and residential relocations. This region has seen capital values appreciate in the excess of 40–50 percent" NAI Report 2004.

[6] Table 3.4, p. 40. Statistical Abstract of Haryana. 2004. Chandigarh.

[7] 95,764 million.

[8] http://www.rediff.com/news/2003/aug/22ariban.htm

which meant that their land would be acquired and plots would be finally measured and sold out to developers and infrastructural builders. The 14 villages in Gurgaon (Table 29.1), which were adopted for urbanization, are some of the oldest historical villages dating back to the times of Mahabharata and the period of Dronacharya, the guru of Pandavas.[9]

A further investigation reveals that the situation is much worse in the villages that were given to private developers. No record was available about the money spent on developmental works nor on the land acquired. These areas have police, district, town, and country planner working in tandem to apply stringent disciplinary laws on villagers. They were centers of electoral fallacies, caste divisions, and the greatest democratic deficits. Most of these private colonizers are working in connivance with land-owners to provide work spaces, residential townships, and recreational centers for MNCs by transferring village resources to them. There are many cases lying in the High Court of Chandigarh against these colonizers. Colonizers have their own bureaucracy that lacks accountability and transparency in any form.

In March 2004 HUDA came up with the second round of "urbanization of village programme" in which any "gram panchayat" having more than 15 acres of land would be selected for this block development work. HUDA planned to cut plots of the size of 250, 300, and 500 yd to be sold to developers for residential purposes. It was able to quickly implement it in Rangla, Rajour, and Pinghava where it acquired 16.8 and 16.10 acres, respectively (Tiwari, 2004, p. 6). However with the defeat of Om Prakash Chautala, the globalizing chief minister of Haryana, in the March 2005 State Assembly elections this plan has slowed down.

The history of Gurgaon has been a history of an intricate relationship of people to their land. This historic fact has been ignored in the process of globalizing this area. Being an arid region, the majority of people living here have been dependent upon cattle and other animal-rearing occupations or potters who survived on clay they obtained from a pond, which was very sacred to them. Wells have been very well protected and were used not just for water but as a meeting space for village women. A large majority had served in the Indian Army from earlier times and their aggressive control of land kept any administrator in the past from acquiring their land. They have also been highly emotional in fighting injustices of the State starting from the mutiny against the East India Company in 1857 and later for

---

[9]Mahabharata was written in around 2500 BC which narrates the historic battle between the Pandavas and the Kauravas. Dronacharya was the great teacher who taught Arjuna, one of the Pandavas, the strategic master archery but also took away the thumb of a poor dalit boy who revered him for the fear that he may be a threat to Arjuna's position. Gurgaon is named after the so-called great guru and one of the villages here is the home of the dalit boy Eklavya.

Table 29.1 Land Acquisition in Villages Adopted by HUDA for Urbanization Process between July 1999–September/2004

Number of Villages	*Names of Villages*	*Years of Existence*	*Land Acquired (in acres)*	*Amount Spent on Developmental Work (in lakhs)*	*Population[a] 1991 Census*
1	Kadipur	500	500	82.81	3310
2	Basai	1000–1500	[b]	47.44	6767
3	Sukhrali	500	total	29.42	5538
4	Daulatpur–Nasirabad (Carterpur)	500	[b]	59.89	2602
5	Mulahera	500	2000	30.28	3589
6	Islampur	900	60	36.14	2436
7	Jharsa	500–1000	600	211.30	8480
8	Dundahera	500	[b]	60.17	6767
9	Naharpur	500	1000 + 60	2.74	1586
10	Gurgaon			108.45	14398
11	Khandsa (Eklavya's village)	2500	[b]	79.28	4634
12	Dhanwapur Dalit village	500	[b]	110.35	6767
13	Kanhai	1000–1500	[b]	33.35	2995
14	Sarhole	500+	[b]	51.17	2638

[a]This does not include a population increase in these villages @ 2 percent per year between 1991 Census and 2001. This also does not include a four times growth of migrant population of workers from outside states.

[b]Indicates that clear records of land acquired were not made available in HUDA/HSIDC office in Gurgaon.

laying their lives in the freedom movement led by Mahatma Gandhi. They also served in the Indian National Army led by Subhash Chandra Bose against the British regime.[10] It was only once in history that their land was acquired forcibly by the British government under Acts XXV of 1857 and 1858 "for their failure to extend any help to British at the time of sore need.'[11] The British had perceived that this would act as a capital punishment for them but it ultimately turned out to be harmful to even the British as these people sank into complete inactivity and anarchy till a sensitive Indian Civil Service (ICS) officer, F.L. Brayne, developed programmes to bring them out of this crisis. Brayne was posted as a deputy commissioner of Gurgaon district in 1920. In trying to rectify this he launched his famous "Gurgaon Experiment," focussing upon improved techniques of farming. Because economic betterment targeted an area that sent strongest signals for participation to the local mind the experiment did succeed in its objective "to jerk the villager out of his old groove, convince him that improvement is possible, and kill his fatalism by demonstrating that both climate, disease and pests can be successfully fought." (Gurgaon gazette, 1984, p. 398). Although this experiment fizzled out once Brayne was posted out of Gurgaon, its message left behind was completely ignored by policy makers of the globalization decade. The MNC requirement ignored the balance sheet of land acquisition. The population of these villages was largely dependent on two main sources of income. First, upon agriculture as they enjoyed a healthy existence on rich agricultural produce over their land. Second, upon those common property resources made available from land such as ancient wells, ponds, forests, and grazing grounds raised and conserved by few committed village personalities in the course of historical evolution like Sadhu Baba, Sukhpal Maharaj, and Yadavs of Nuni–Rasunpur (Narnaul).

Tanks, wells, and ponds are now the dumping grounds for urban wastes. Many villages such as Narsimhapur and Daulatabad have become dumping stations and suffer effluent discharges from chemical factories and medical wastes on their agricultural land (Yadav, 2004, p. 6). The grazing grounds and forests are gone cattle roam on the streets and pigs feed on residential area garbage. There is a deepening divide between the land owners, who have got rich compensation for their land and now act as local help for land acquisition authorities in tandem with colonizers and developers, and the landless who survive on animal dependent or wetland-based occupations. Many village chiefs called *sarpanchas* came out openly to express their woes when this survey was taking place. One Ramprasad

[10]Gazette of Gurgaon 1984 mentions, "According to records maintained by Capt. Mehtab Singh, President, INA Association, Rohtak, 1317 persons (233 officers and 1094 other ranks) belonged to the Gurgaon District." p. 72.

[11]File/R/194, pp. 240–241; Statement of the landed property confiscated during the Mutiny.

complained of the spread of allergic diseases about which they are kept in complete dark by the district authorities. Another sarpanch, Ramzan, expressed the threat posed by severe fall in water table and the drying land. Many others like Sarpanch Mukhtiar Singh of Dundahera feels tired running after district authorities for preventing the destruction of their forest land and water bodies but there is nobody to listen to them. The only gain for villagers' source of income has been the large number of migrant workers in BPO companies and low-wage laborers from the poor states of Bihar, Orissa, and West Bengal who have taken sheds and rooms in the villages on rent. In a village called Nathupur, which has the prestigious Microsoft, Convergys, GE, and Sony Erickson's offices on its land, the per month income rise for ten sample households has been 1000 percent and two of them have only the rent as their source of income from more than 250 dilapidated rooms with common toilets. In some of these villages sewer lines have been put in promised, but they lead to nowhere and end up within the village as a result of which these globalizing villages are an island in the midst of sewer water. The worst complaint that the villagers expressed aggressively was that none of the companies have employed local people as promised by them when the land was being acquired. Not even the security services employ any local villager for fear of an uprising on their wage exploitation, which most companies are doing for their unorganized labor (survey made between March and September 2004). Some of the basic facilities like a primary health center, a school, a computer training center, self-help programme, or an infrastructure like a metaled road and clean drainage system remain what they were prior to 1995 in the preglobalization era. The water table has dropped to a scary low, setting at naught all the borewells and handpumps for irrigation and drinking water. Whatever water remains is first served to the rich residential areas and MNCs rather than to the people in the villages. Within the village also the dalit areas often get their water blocked for failing to comply with some unjustified electoral demand. The younger boys from Nathupur village came out openly to a local newspaper *Amar Ujala* in February 2004 in protest against a local candidate belonging to the ruling party of the state. It shows that village residents have neither benefited from the spread of MNC clusters on village land nor their local deliberative structures gained in empowering themselves democratically.

These areas also generate electoral fallacies which create a smokescreen of democracy to conceal the increasing exclusion of the ordinary Indian from social security systems governed by the market.[12] These villages have

---

[12]"— Although democracy has never been more widely established in the world as a system of government it is increasingly seen as subordinate to and invaded by the market, to such an extent that its distinctive character as an institutional order separate from the market is being lost. Democracy is being hollowed out" Gamble (1996, p. 127).

witnessed great instabilities in their elected bodies. The post of sarpanch has been the worst affected. Basai village for example had six sarpanchas in four years and one village sarpanch, Satish Yadav, admitted that HUDA's land acquisition and urbanization program has broken homes and has destroyed bonds of trust and affection among villagers. In Bangalore also, which is another city undergoing rapid globalization and FDI investment, during the last elections to the panchayats, as a report revealed, there has been an auction of seats in the 2001 panchayat elections (Vyasulu, 2001). Most of the intermediate local bodies are elected under donor pressure. Government departments are given targets to set up self-help groups and other people's organizations for better participation of peoples. There have been allegations on government by Bellandur gram panchayat and surrounding villages that were selected for the proposed IT corridor project in the city. The exogenous pulls of reforms bring in structures of governance, which are neither understood by people nor do they gel with their experience. "All of a sudden, an electoral system arises in a country so the government can get some aid, credits or most-favored-nation trading status," Karl Terry said. "I call this electoralism; that is, having the procedures of democracy without deeper internal roots" (1986, pp. 9–36). This suggests that the postsocialistic transformation of Indian state would need a reinvestigation of democratic ideals in administrative reforms with an ecological perspective.

Local Institutions as Ecosystems for Meaningful Discourses

Any analysis of local institutions has a contextual and epistemological relationship to its sociological and anthropological origin. Institutions emerge to regulate a reciprocative way of communitarian life. Durkheim may call this a reciprocative function or a social obligation. Thus their task is to constrain individual behavior in accordance with the requirement of community welfare. In this way they are largely composed of informal rules (Lijphart, 1984, p. 3). This chapter inclines to accept the Durkheimian conceptualization, which suggests that institutions are shaped by social realities that determine the patterns of possible behavior. This sociological realism forms the basis of institutional analysis in Durkheim. "The bottomline is that institutions are not only effect producing but also distinct 'realities' that mould patterns of behaviour of groups and organizations" (Keman, 1996, p. 8).

Therefore institutional analysis is based upon three key questions: The first is about rules, be they formal or informal, the second is about the relationship between behavior and action, and the third question is about how do rules affect political processes. An analysis of local institutions in a globalizing city is supported by the cultural theory of institutions. It provides some important "paradigmatic" answers to market fundamentalism and NPM reforms in a third world country. It explains "cultural biases" and the nature of "social relations." The degree of congruence between the two is then expressed in "ways of life" or "culture" (Keman, 1996, p. 13). Thus it assumes that every institution has a cultural context or it is a unique ecosystem like entity, self-governed, stable, and sturdier pattern of interaction rooted into its evolutionary history, and experience-based good practices. Douglas North sums it up as, "institutions provide the participants with classifications, logical operations and guiding metaphors" that function as a cognitive window with a view at reality (1986, p. 10). This cultural theory of institutions in the larger mold of critical theory is like a time bomb under the globalization-induced reforms such as NPM and provides a framework for explaining the qualitative weakening of local institutions while the overall growth rate of the economic index of the nation rises.

Globalizing cities are undergoing a process of public sector reform based on the economic theory of democracy. It pushes through and instills the aggregating strategies into society so that public policies could balance people's expectations from reforms. It implies pure deductive reasoning, which is free of value systems and therefore gains legitimacy through elections. This however reduces what Habermas (1992) referred to as a "deliberative perspective of politics," in which people participate, confront, and debate in local institutions to solve common problems and also shape a collective identity (Erikson, 1995). Most ethical and moral questions that fail to feature in large national legislatures become important issues for local bodies. Solutions are where problems emerge. Thus the essence of discourse model is that it ties legitimacy to a free and open debate in public forum (Christensen & Laegreid, 2001, p. 294).

Globalization in India as in other third world countries has come as a reaction to the centralized socialist and protectionist state. An emboldening of market theorists in the present era has pushed reinvention exercises in which democratic institutions have been reduced to a provider of services. This has serious consequences for the role of politician and that of bureaucracy but the most discernable impact is that on the lives of citizens. The deliberative aspect of local institutions shrinks as the most difficult questions are kept out of the political arena. "By replacing democratic procedures of consensus building by such other method of conflict resolutions, government elites avoid the 'official' institutions of politics in a constant search for nonpolitical forms of decision making" (Offe, 1984, p. 168).

Panchayats have been sacrosanct to villages in India even before they were constitutionally recognized in the 73rd Constitutional Amendment Act of 1992. This amendment was a new milestone in the democratic evolution of India because it was a landmark in the direction of decentralized decision making. Panchayati raj institutions (PRIs, which are the rural governance structures) and municipal bodies (urban structures) ensured people's participation in planning, decision making, implementation, and delivery. This chapter would work on the logic that reforms have to resonate people's habits and value systems and for that reason it is imperative for reforms to originate from people because administrative practices cannot divert from established habits and norms of society (see Box, 1997, pp. 84–100).

The "freedom to govern their own problems" has been the core of local institutions in Haryana as the panchayats are historic bodies governed by customary laws, which have evolved within the village community. This aspect gets weakened as globalization spreads on their land in the form of a master plan prepared for the city as it is mandatory for every city to prepare a developmental plan. This master plan sets in motion the task of land acquisition for developmental purposes in accordance with the prospective problems, which the city may encounter as it grows. The problem begins when the core component of development, that is "land," is the scarcest commodity within the municipal limits. So this land would have to be acquired from the surrounding villages. Thus agricultural fields, land under panchayats, and the village community resources such as ponds, wells, village forests, and watershed areas, which are cherished as common property of all village inhabitants suddenly become commodities to be sold in the market. This process of acquiring land from villages has been going on for ages, but HUDA records in Gurgaon reveal that earlier they were being acquired for laying a railway line, a road, an electric line, or an industry that in many ways compensated the loss of land through the ethical argument of capacity development of villagers. In present times globalization pushes multinationals into the market as a result of which government acquires land and passes it on to the developer who finally becomes the major beneficiary.

The ability to enter a meaningful discourse or deliberate on policy issues has been reduced with the loss of the main occupations in the villages. Many farmers cherished their local innovations in the field and now feel amputated and as secondary citizens in their own village. The region as a whole indicates that growth has not been sustainable. Since the village governance became the center of policy deliberation in a globalizing city there has been systematic decrease in the number of villages in Gurgaon. In the 1991 census Gurgaon had 688 inhabited villages, which increased to 700 villages in the 2001 census because of the massive explosion of 44.64 percent increase in its population, mostly migrants from poorer states like Bihar, Orissa, and West Bengal, but the number of so-called "uninhabited villages" mentioned in the Director of Census Operations records fell from

42 in 1991 to 26 in 2001. This is reflected in the creation of a new town in Gurgaon district as the number of towns increased from 11 to 12 during this period. These so-called uninhabited villages were the grazing grounds of cattle and sheep rearing rural inhabitants who gained little out of a global spread of BPO companies. Gurgaon being a district with a dominant rural population,[13] the workforce largely arrived from cities outside Gurgaon. The massive housing and construction boom that followed took place over the land acquired from villages.

Although foodgrain production has gone down in Gurgaon from 71.02 percent in 1970–1971 to 49.01 in 2001–2002 as percentage of gross value of agricultural output at current prices (Economic and Statistical Organization, Haryana, 2004, p. 768) even the area under forests has been drastically reduced from 4.62 percent in 1980–1981 to a mere 1 percent in 2004 (Statistical Abstracts of Haryana 1980–81 and 2004) and therefore Gurgaon has a pathetically low forest area, that is just 2.56 percent of forest area to the total geographical area of the district (Forest Department, Haryana, 2004:332). These factors have also led to a loss of state credibility and legitimacy, and this is evident in decreasing people's contribution to the developmental programs and their participation in state programs. The community development statistics of Haryana (2004, pp. 346–347) reveal that people's contribution to the community development programs in Haryana, which rose from Rs. 648.19 lakhs in 1967 to Rs. 763.44 lakhs in 1981 shows a sharp downturn in the period of global shift in which it has fallen to a mere Rs. 75 lakhs in 2002–2003. There is also a startling revelation that the globalizing industrial states when compared to the less globalized industrial states have more working population for the simple reason that these small states offer more diversified and community-based options available to every class of citizen whereas the globalizing townships are straightline trajectories of urbanized middle-class growth marginalizing the rural poor.[14] This is adding on to the burgeoning numbers of unemployed people in Haryana. The director of the Employment of Haryana Statistics Department shows that the number of unemployed persons has almost

---

[13]The 2001 census of Gurgaon shows rural and urban populations as 1,288,365 and 369,304 as compared to 913,386 and 135,884 in 1991 census. The maximum increase of population has occurred in the central Gurgaon town where urban population in 2001 shows a substantial rise to 249,403 of the total of 369,304. This part of Gurgaon, which forms the industrial region, is contiguous to Delhi and therefore is the hub of MNCs expansion (Director of Census Operations, Haryana. Statistical Abstracts of Haryana, Economic and Statistical Advisor, Planning Department, Government of Haryana, 2004, pp. 36, 40, 51).

[14]The 2001 Statistical Abstract of Haryana shows that the percentage of main workers out of total population is 28.03 and 28.32 in Gurgaon and Faridabad, respectively, the top globalizing districts of Haryana but is 32.57 and 32.47 in Sirsa and Fatehabad, respectively, which are trailing far behind in the rush for global companies.

doubled from 486,706 persons in 1985 to 802,581 persons in 2002 even though the market has opened up but the state capacity for placement has decreased from 17,253 persons to 4764 persons in 2002.

Thus globalization has brought reforms that have weakened people's participation in meaningful discourses for their empowerment. In this manner the obsolescence of local governance continues to disempower local people.

Global Integration through Administrative Reforms

Many legal and structural reforms have been brought about to rationalize the process of global integration in Haryana. In the early era of liberalization most of the state governments did not have the requisite money to compensate villagers for their acquired land. This anomaly was partly rectified in 1996 when urban development plans formulation and implementation (UDPFI), the government of India rationalized the problems of land acquisition so that the benefits of adequate compensation reach out straight to the owner and the predictability of developmental programs for the city are also assured.

UDPFI defined "transfer of development rights" (TDR) as "development right to transfer the potential of a plot designated for a public purpose in a plan, expressed in terms of total permissible built space calculated on the basis of Floor Space Index or Floor Area Ratio allowable for that plot, for utilization by the owner himself or by way of transfer by him to someone else from the present location to a specified area in the plan, as additional built up space over and above the permissible limit in lieu of compensation for the surrender of the concerned plot free from all encumbrances to the planning and Development Authority." This system helped the real estate developers and thus the total land cost flows from the developer to the landowner. It also got a shot in the arm when government notified in November 2003 that it would permit 100 percent FDI, on a case to case basis, in the development of integrated townships. This would permit FDI into housing, commercial premises, hotels, resorts, city, and regional level urban infrastructure facilities such as roads and bridges, and mass rapid transport systems. Two Malaysian companies — Feedback Integrated Infrastructure Development Corporation and IJM Infrastructure Ltd. — have already entered into an agreement in development of townships at Gurgaon in Haryana and Kukatpally in Hyderabad. Reforms that have reduced bureaucracy and liberalized laws have also helped in reducing the democratic imperative of local institutions.

The developments mentioned above have made rural areas and their local bodies such as the panchayats vulnerable to the pressures of real estate developers. The role of the panchayats in protecting and generating income for the poor, the landless, the animal-rearing tribes, and the dalits in the village by protecting most of their resources such as land, water bodies, and forests including the common property resources has decreased and mostly subdued. The planning commission has also noticed this lacuna of planning in which the higher administrative bodies of the country have failed to relate the people's problems to their policies. The Report of the Task Force on the Panchayats, constituted in 2001 under the chairmanship of K.B. Saxena had pointed out certain grave factors that prevented people's access to the planning process. "It is observed that a number of Ministries of Central Government have not taken any concrete steps to integrate PRIs in their strategy of planning and implementation of various programmes which essentially fall in their jurisdiction" (2001:1). This problem has also been exacerbated due to the direct nongovernmental organization (NGO) access to relevant ministries. The shocking fact discovered in the report is that "PRIs do not really figure in this strategy of implementation and in fact there is not even a conceptual recognition of it. That, NGOs are operating in areas and on subjects which belong to the PRIs and therefore are expected to work in tandem with them" (2001, p. 1). The report further admitted that because the ministries undertake internationally funded projects, they tend to implement them directly without any involvement of PRIs. Ironically, the ministry of rural development has failed to bridge this gap. In 2001 annual report (2001 column 5) there were 232,278 panchayats at the village level, 6022 at the intermediate level, and 535 at the district level. These panchayats were manned by 29.2 million elected representatives at all levels out of which one third were women. Ironically this huge deliberative framework has been ignored in the process of planning and the NGO-led decentralization has brought in experts who are delinked from the anthropological history of that region.

This part of the chapter mainly looks into the process of globalization and the reforms undertaken to facilitate it. To understand reforms in the local governance of Gurgaon, it would be interesting to begin from the panchayats of the capital city Delhi, in the neighborhood, where the panchayati raj continues to be suspended by the state government and no effective steps have been taken to revive PRIs. Much of the illegal activity of land mafia continues over a large juridically overlapping area of rural–urban governance also called the "lal dora land." The Delhi Development Authority controls most of the development over the land. Bangalore had also set up Bangalore Development Authority and now has the Bangalore agenda task force as a catalyst in realizing the city's potential. Gurgaon has HUDA, which until 1996, was acquiring land and then giving it to Haryana State Industrial Development Corporation (HSIDC) for demarcating plots for developmental activities. It is a paradox that in these cities no specific body has come up to look into these irregularities of globalization-led land acquisition from rural communities. This has helped the state government acquire the benefits of centralizing city plans including the financial flows.

It is imperative to study the process of development and urbanization in globalizing areas and seek ways to measure the democratic deficit of such townships. The most important administrative and political strategy is that of acquiring land from adjoining villages. It involves a number of interrelated measures. First comes the most essential ingredient, a developer-friendly legal framework, which ensures that land can be easily bought and sold. Second is the administration-friendly procedures and regulations to ensure that the development of land is at an affordable cost. Third measure is that of a legitimacy in which land taxation system is designed to promote equity and efficiency in land use. This process also includes an installation of a transparent and corruption-free local administration that may not really push up the reforms to improve people's access to these measures.

The legal framework, which was reformed, included the laws protecting land in villages and to smoothen their acquisition. The district town and country planner (DTCP) claims that the controlled areas that fall at the rural–urban fringes are real centers of planning for further industrialization. In Gurgaon alone it comprises something of one third of the total land in the district out of which only 9.5 percent of the areas are urban areas, thereby leaving more than 90 percent area of the state free from any of the controls of Acts enforced by the Government. There has been a substantial amount of infrastructural mismanagement considering the fact that the municipal committee and the panchayats are not obliged to function within this area and the town and country planner (TCP) cannot undertake work without an officially declared plan for that area. They may more reasonably be termed as the "areas of diluted governance." The land purchased within the controlled areas needs a change of land use (CLU) certificate from the DTCP that the land purchased outside the controlled areas does not require. Because the industrial townships have not been able to develop plots, these industries have started buying plots directly from the farmers and managing to obtain CLU certificates from the directorate of town and country planning (TCPD). This process was guided by a colonial legal system defined under Land Acquisition Act of 1894. In 1995, on February 9th, government constituted a committee comprising of the following officers as a process to decentralize the power hereby concentrated in the development corporation (DC):

- Divisional commissioner as the chairman
- Deputy commissioner as the member secretary
- Representative of the concerned member department
- District revenue officer as the concerned member

This also restricted the District Commission's (DC) discretion to determine the market price of land not on the basis of five years sales average but only on the basis of one year's sales average. Section 5A of this New Land Acquisition Act 1995 also enabled the land owner to refer to the court under Section 18 of the Act. At the peak of this globalizing exercise in Gurgaon another amendment was undertaken on September 8, 2003. Section 22 of the Punjab Scheduled Roads and Controlled Areas Restriction of Unregulated Development Act, 1963 after clause (a) an amendment (aa) clause was added to increase the "abadi deh areas" (or the inhabited areas within the village) and reduce the controlled areas in which there are numerous restrictions on constructive activities. The explanation to the amendment given in the statement of objects and reason given by the town and country planning minister of Haryana was the need to exempt construction activity in abadi deh areas to prevent unnecessary harassment of villagers but it implied that a larger part of village land was liberated from official controls. The impact of this change is evident in at least one important case in the Supreme Court involving the former prime minister of India, Chandrashekhar.[15] His huge farmhouse and luxury villa was built on village land belonging to the panchayat. The issue of a village panchayat gifting land to the person in power violated Section 5A and 15(2) (ff) of Punjab Village Common Land (Regulations) Act, 1961 and Rules 3(2), 3(10), 13, and 13 A of Punjab Village Common Land (Regulation) Rules 1964. The issue also brought to light a violation of Forest Conservation Act 1980, Section 2.

Parallel to liberalizing the process of laws related to ceiling on agricultural land, acquisition and disposal of surplus area,[16] there has also been a systemic restraining of decision-making autonomy of local bodies. The 73rd Panchayat (Amendment) Act 1992 had given a constitutional status to the panchayats and the Haryana Panchayati Raj Act 1994 had adopted this provision for better administration of rural areas. With the globalization of market there are certain amendments made to the state act, which raise questions about the democratic imperative of these local bodies. Three provisions may be mentioned here. First the Act of 1994 contains that, "If the whole of the sabha area is included in a municipality or a cantonment, the Gram Panchayat shall cease to exist and the assets and liabilities of it

[15]B.L. Wadhera versus Union of India 2002SOLCase No. 242/decision date April 19, 2002.

[16]Haryana Ceiling of Land Holdings Act 1972 (Act 26 of 1972) through which surplus land was assessed and automatically vested in the State on the pretext of "unutilized" (*Kehar Singh and another versus State of Haryana and others 1995* (2) RRR 654 (P&H) even though the family of the landowner grows bigger he is not entitled to have surplus area case reopened for recomputation under the 1972 Act (*Bhagwanti Devi versus State of Haryana* 1994 (2) RRR 358 (SC).

shall vest in the municipality or cantonment as the case may be." (Part II, 7[4]). Taking cue from this, the developers constructed urban areas on village lands and thus were given the benefit of not having any such taxation regime of cities. But the price for this anomaly is extremely high as these villages are on the verge of extermination by real estate developers in business here such as DLF city, Unitech city, Ansal city, Ardee city, etc. These areas exempted from the restrictions imposed by the 1963 Act mentioned above have not been included in the municipal council of Gurgaon for fear of losing a vote bank because their inclusion into a municipality would mean their subjection to a taxation system on property and land transfer deeds. But besides this tax exemption these residents of MNC-led urban areas also become entitled to vote in the panchayat elections without being the residents of villages either physically, historically, or emotionally. This is a total turnaround to the very idea of the panchayats as a system of self-governing institution for village communities and as recognized by the Constitution of India (Article 243G). The urban voters almost outnumber the rural communities living in these village areas who have lost their land, occupations as well as access to their community governance systems.

Second are the series of amendments to the 1994 Act that have systematically weakened the checks and balance system embedded into the Act. Part II Article 8(2b) of the Act which provided for 6 to 20 *panches* (deputy village headmen) from wards in a panchayat area in the manner prescribed so that the despotism of the headman or the sarpanch could be restrained has been omitted vide Haryana Act No. 10 of 1999. This has abolished the power of the panches to call a special meeting with notice to the sarpanch and have also led to the Haryana Act No. 14 of 2003 in which the obligation upon the panchayats for having a circle supervisor from amongst the existing gram sachivs to supervise the work of gram vikas sahayaks (village development supervisor) was substituted vide Haryana Act No. 14 of 2003.

The third concern is that it also raises questions of constitutional propriety of such measures becoming common in India. In a case pending in Haryana high court against a major colonizer in this area it has been recognized that there exists a clear violation of Articles 243 X and 243 W read with Schedule 12 in which the developer was to undertake the responsibility of maintenance under agreement between DLF and DTCP. The contesting Qutab enclave resident welfare association (QERWA) of urban settlers charges it as the "biggest land scam in the country" (QERWA press release, August 2003). People's awakening in villages led to the demise of the regime of former chief minister of Haryana Om Prakash Chautala and his sons in the last Assembly elections of 2004 who were instrumental in chaperoning an uncontested rule of colonizers and land mafia in the district of Gurgaon (*Amar Ujala*, September 29, 2003). In Bangalore, Janata Dal (secular) secretary-general C. Narayanswamy demanded a high-level inquiry into land grabbing by private land developers and influential persons.[17] It has been reported that influential persons, middlemen, and private land developers have cheated the farmers by paying them less than the actual market value for their lands and then selling the acquired lands at prevailing market rates to IT companies like Intel, despite preliminary notification for land acquisition by the Bangalore Development Authority and the Karnataka Industrial Area Development Board (KIADB).

Globalization and Epistemic Bondings in Local Governance

Globalization has traumatized local communities by imposing policies that contrasts with their norms and modes of living. New unidentifiable actors have come into the fray to steal their resources and benefit out of their ignorance. A question arises as to what constitutes sustainable governance in which people participate in the policy process without fear or obligation. This model of epistemic bonding suggests a relationship that merges well in a sustainable process of growth, which would be reciprocative and therefore egalitarian and more economic. But this cannot be represented in the form of a structural functional model based upon subject–object approach but a spherical system in which each member of a community is bonded to the center (which represents their most commonly used natural resources, could be land, water, common grazing areas, animals, forests, etc.) and their distance from the center builds the degree of motivation to participate in a program. Communities are composed of people who have compatible roles and contrasting tasks that are mutually fulfilling. The use of resources may generate a set of relationships and a network of exchanges, which may be hierarchically arranged and it keeps solidifying their bonds on a continuous basis. Collection of a large number of bonds in a particular geographical region may form a community. Community has a regular crystalline structure representing a natural hierarchy of valuable ecological relationships for economic and social governance (see Figure 29.1). This creates a niche of autonomy for each community system within which they survive in equilibrium with their ecological domain. When development is exogenous these ecological relationships are disturbed and as a result community spaces start shrinking (see Figure 29.2).

Quantum mechanics offers a method to understand the structures of society and about the ecological bonds, which may be referred to as

[17]"Janata Dal seeks probe into land acquisition" *Deccan Herald*, September 23, 2004.

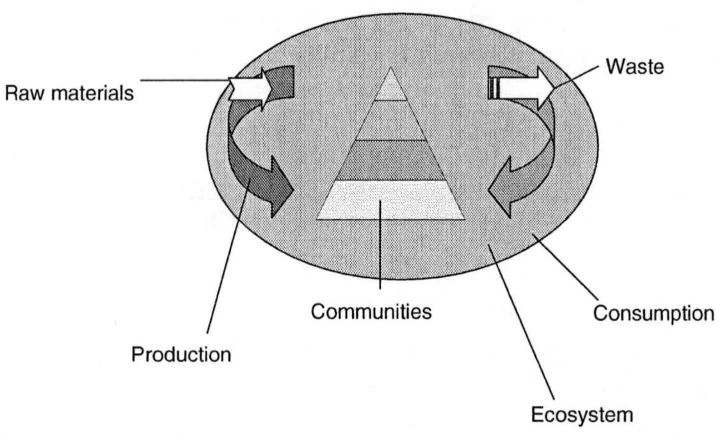

Figure 29.1 Ecological existence of community structures.

epistemic bonds (EB), which bring people together and sustain them into a common mode of beliefs, values, and culture or more appropriately in an ecosystem. Thus EB is a "strong attractive force" composed of a set of relationships between the resources and the resource-dependent community. These bonds also provide stability and security of habitation and of the availability of needed resources from the ecosystem. All this is assured due to internal governance systems nurtured and sustained over a long period of history within the framework of ecological relationships, which an exogenous mode of development fails to visualize.

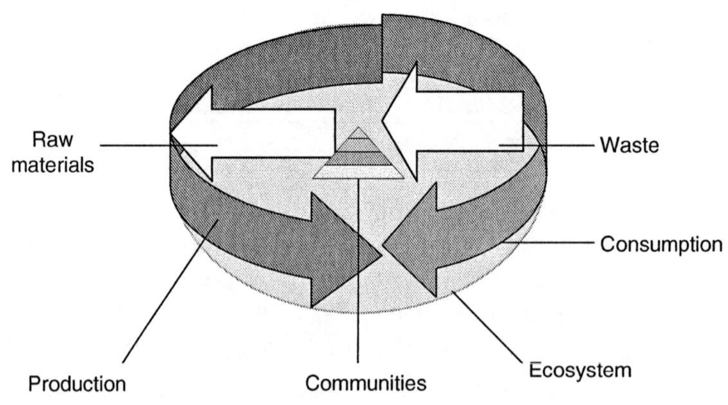

Figure 29.2 Ecosystem stress and reduced community space.

Conclusion

Gurgaon, like most other globalizing cities in India has strengthened the hypothesis about the nature of administrative reforms undertaken during the period of globalization. These reforms have mostly been undertaken in haste and failed to absorb related research findings from their society and ecosystem usages. The sole criteria of reforms has been to find access to local resources in land and the process of liberalization and infrastructural advancement of cities has been directed to serve this." In the process they have once again failed to consider the intangibles that contain embedded realities of development in a third world country. Land acquisition has been the prime requirement of spreading MNC operations in India, which are looked upon as the main providers of FDI and FII to the host country. The issue of sustainable prosperity has not been considered effectively as state governments have used their own ways, which are legitimized by a reform mechanism through democratic elections and rationalized through FDI returns. People living in villages have been the worst affected because their land has been taken away but adequate developmental tasks that were promised to them have not been undertaken.

Gurgaon as a sample district in the state of Haryana has been selected because of the paradoxes of development emerging in its growth from a small sleepy village to a global city in a small period of ten years. It contains some of the most ancient villages where governance and agricultural practices have been based on customary laws. Even after government spending into their developmental process these villages have become a den of corruption, exploitation, and a most medieval form of power play.

This study asserts that communities are rooted into ecological systems and are an ecosystem themselves. Once they are estranged from their land their intracommunity bonds are broken, they disaggregate and succumb to a highly opaque, criminal, and undemocratic regime. Any form of governance that aspires for sustainability has to link itself with the realities of community bondings. It not only reduces the cost of state spending on developmental work but also generates entrepreneurship and participation in the democratic process.

Acknowledgements

The author acknowledges support of a brave journalist and rural reporter, Mayank Jewari, and his city bureau chief, Malik Asgar Hashmi, of local daily news *Amar Ujala* for extending support at field work and media surveys of troubled Gurgaon.

Bibliography

Amar Ujala, September 29, 2003.

Benjamin, S. and Bhuvneshwari, R. (2001) "Democracy, Inclusive Governance and Poverty in Bangalore," Working Paper 26, International Development Department, University of Birmingham.

"Bhumafia," *Amar Ujala*, September 29, 2003, Gurgaon Edition.

Box, R.C. (1997) "The Institutional Legacy of Community Governance," *Administrative Theory and Praxis*, 18(2): 84–100.

Bambaci, J., Saront, T., and Tommasi, M. (2002) "The Political Economy of Economic Reforms in Argentina," *Journal of Policy Reform*, 5(2): 75–88.

Christensen, T., Lægreid, P. (Eds.) (2001), *New Public Management: The Transformation of Ideas and Practice*, Ashgate, Aldershot.

Deccan Herald, (2004) "Janata Dal Seeks Probe into Land Acquisition," September 23.

Economic and Statistical Organization (2004) *Statistical Abstract of Haryana 2002–03*, Economic and Statistical Advisor, Planning Department, Publication No. 758. Government of Haryana.

Erikson, E.O. (1994) "Deliberate Democracy and the Politics of a Pluralist Society," Working Paper No. 6, Oslo: Arena.

Forest Department (2004) *Statistical Abstract of Haryana 2002–03*, Economic and Statistical Advisor, Planning Department, Publication No. 758. Government of Haryana.

Fung, A. and Wright, E.O. (2003) "Thinking about Empowered Participatory Governance" in *Deepening Democracy, Institutional Innovations in Empowered Participatory Governance*, London: Verso.

Gupta D. (2000) *Culture, Space and Nation State*, Delhi: Sage Publications.

Gutmann, A. and Thompson, D. (2003) "Deliberate Democracy beyond Process," in J.S. Fishkin and P. Lasslett (eds.) *Debating Deliberate Democracy*, Malden, MA: Blackwell.

Hardin, R. (2003):165, "Street Level Epistemology and Democratic Participation," in J.S. Fishkin, and P. Lasslett (eds.) *Debating Deliberate Democracy*, Malden, MA: Blackwell.

Habermas, J. (1992) *Between Facts and Norms*, Cambridge: Polity Press.

Haryana Panchayati Raj Act 1994, Chandigarh, Haryana: Chawla Publications.

Inbanathan, A. (2000) "Power, Percentage, and Accountability in the Panchayats of Karnataka," Institute for Social and Economic Change, Bangalore, Working Paper: 68.

Issac, T.T.M. and Heller, P. (2003) "Decentralization, Democracy and Development: People's Campaign for Decentralized Planning in Kerela," in A. Fung and E.O. Wright (eds.) *Deepening Democracy: Institutional Innovations in Empowered Participatory Governance*. Verso Books: London.

Karl, T. (1986) "Imposing Consent? Electoralism vs. Democratization in El Salvador," in P.W. Drake and E. Silva (eds.) *Elections and Democratization in Latin America, 1980–1985*. San Diego, CA: Centre for Iberian and Latin American Studies, University of California, San Diego.

Kearney, A.T. (2004), "The 2004 Retail Development Index," *Emerging Market for Global Retailers* Chicago, IL: A.T. Kearney.

Keman, H. (1996) *The Politics of Problem-Solving in Postwar Democracies*, London: Macmillan.

Kothari, R. (1991) "Human Rights: A Movement in Search of a Theory," in S. Kothari and H. Sethi (eds.) *Human Rights Challenges for Theory and Action*, New York: New Horizon Press.

Lijphart, A. (1984) *Democracies: Patterns of Majoritarian and Consensus Government in 21 Countries*. New Haven and London: Yale University Press.

Lipset, S.M. (1996). *American Exceptionalism*. New York: Norton.

Lipset, S.M. (1999). "The End of Political Exceptionalism". In W. Merkel & A. Busch (eds.). *Demokratie Ost und West*. Frankfurt am Main: Suhrkamp. 183–209.

Long, N.E. (1976) "The Three Citizenships," *Publius*, Spring.

Mill, J.S. (1991) *Considerations on Representative Government*, New York: Prometheus Books.

Moe, T.M. (1997) "The Positive Theory of Public Bureaucracy," in Mueller, D.C. (ed.) *Perspectives on Public Choice*, New York: Cambridge University Press.

Neale, W.C. (1957) "Reciprocity and Redistribution in the Indian Village," in A. Polanyi and H.W. Pearson (eds.) *Trade and Market in the Early Empires*, Glencoe, IL: The Free Press.

North, D. (1986) "The New Institutional Economics," *Journal of Institutional and Theoretical Economics*, 142: 230–237.

OFFE, C. 1984: Contradictions of the Welfare State. Hutchinson.

Paul, S. and Gopa Kumar, K. (2002) *India Infrastructure Report*, Oxford: Oxford University Press, p. 72.

Polanyi, K. (1957) *The Great Transformation*, Boston, MA: Beacon Press.

Riggs, F.W. (1960) "The Use of Models for Administrative Analysis: Confusion or Clarity?" *Indian Journal of Public Administration*, 6(3): 225–242.

Riggs, F.W. (1962) "Trend in the Comparative Study of Public Administration," *International Review of Administrative Sciences*, 28: 9–15.

Riggs, F.W. (1973) *Prismatic Society Revisited*, Morristown, NJ: General Learning Press.

Riggs, F.W. (1978) *Applied Prismatics*, Kathmandu, Nepal: Centre for Economic Development and Administration, Tribhuvan University.

Rosenbloom (Constitutionalism and Public Bureaucrat), *The Bureaucrat*, Fall 1982, p. 54.)

Report of the Task Force Constituted in 2001 *Task Force on Panchayati Raj Institutions*, vide Notification No. P–12025/5/98-RD dated December 20, 1998.

Sharma, S. (2004) "Outsourcing is a Big Factor in Driving India's Current Real Estate Boom," Gurgaon Scoop Community Portal, http://www.gurgaonscoop.com/story/2004.

Satish Chandran, T.R. (2000) "Status of Panchayati Raj in India 2000: Karnataka," In G. Mathew (ed.) *Status of Panchayati Raj in India's States and Union Territories*, New Delhi: Concept Publications.

Statistical Abstract of Haryana (2002–03), "Economic and Statistical Advisor," Planning Department, Publication No. 758. Government of Haryana.

Strange, S. (1996) *The Retreat of the State*, Cambridge: Cambridge University Press.

Tiwari, M. (2004) "Gaon Ke Sharikaran Ka Prayog Raas Aya," *Amar Ujala*, August 28, 2004, Gurgaon, India.

Tommasi, M. (2004) "Crisis, Political Institutions, and Policy Reform: The Good, the Bad, and the Ugly," in B. Tungodden, I. Kolstad, and N. Stern (eds.), *Towards Pro-Poor Policies*, The International Bank for Reconstruction and Development, World Bank, Washington.

Vyasulu, V. (2001) Decentralization, Democratization, Finances and the Constitution, Reflections Based upon Local Realities, Centre for Budget and Policy Studies, Bangalore.

Walsham, G. (1993) Interpretativism in IS Research: Past, Present, and Future, Research Papers in Management Studies, Paper No. 6. Judge Institute of Management Studies, Cambridge: Cambridge University.

Williamson, O.E. (1964) *The Economics of Discretionary Behaviour*, Englewood Cliffs, NJ: Prentice-Hall.

Yadav, D. (2004) "Udyogon Ke Chemical Se Vishela Hua Jal," *Amar Ujala*, May 10, 2004, p. 18, Gurgaon, India.

Chapter 30

The Effect of the African Growth and Opportunity Act on the Textile and Apparel Industry in South Africa

Pan G. Yatrakis, Leslie Cauthen Tworoger, and Helen K. Simon

CONTENTS

Introduction

The Bush administration is hoping that its economic policy in sub-Saharan Africa will serve as a model for its broader approach to development, one that emphasizes trade over foreign aid (Alden, 2002, p. 10).

On May 18, 2000, the U.S. president Bill Clinton signed into law the Trade and Development Act of 2000, Title II of which is the African Growth and Opportunity Act (AGOA). The stated purpose of AGOA is to facilitate economic development in sub-Saharan Africa through trade and the development of open markets. Similar in scope to the Caribbean Basin Initiative, AGOA is intended to encourage the nations of sub-Saharan Africa to open up their markets, accelerate the privatization of their economies, tackle corruption, and implement democratic and human rights reforms. In return, the Act facilitates access to the U.S. market by eliminating or reducing tariff barriers for countries that implement the desired reforms (Office of the U.S. Trade Representative, 2001).

Countries potentially eligible for preferential treatment of their exports to the United States under AGOA are the 48 nations of sub-Saharan Africa. However, only those countries that are certified by the president of the United States as meeting the criteria set forth in AGOA can actually receive this preferential treatment of their exports. These criteria include:

1. Progress toward a market-based economy that respects private property and minimizes government interference
2. Democratic institutions, political pluralism, due process and respect for the law
3. Elimination of barriers to U.S. exports and investment and protection of intellectual property
4. Economic policies to reduce poverty, increase healthcare and education opportunities, expand infrastructure, promote private enterprise, and encourage capital formation
5. A system to combat corruption and bribery
6. Protection of worker rights, including a minimum age for the employment of children, minimum wages, hours of work, and occupational safety and health (AGOA, Section 104 (a), 2000).

There are additional provisions in the Act that prevent or curtail preferential treatment for countries which support international terrorism or international communism and, interestingly, which participate in cartels that withhold vital commodity resources or raise their prices to "unreasonable levels" (AGOA, Sections 502 (b) and (c), 2000). On December 30, 2003, the U.S. president George W. Bush approved the continued eligibility of 37 sub-Saharan African countries for the tariff preferences allotted under AGOA (see Table 30.1) (Statement of the Deputy Press Secretary, 2003).

Eight countries do not meet AGOA eligibility requirements at this time because of their failure to meet one or more of the AGOA criteria. A list of these countries, together with the reasons for failure to qualify is provided (see Table 30.2). The countries of Comoros, Sudan, and Somalia were not reviewed, because they did not formally request to be considered for AGOA benefits (Feldman, 2003).

Preferences provided to the sub-Saharan countries that are certified to comply with the Act's criteria include:

1. Duty-free access for about 95 percent of exports under the generalized system of preferences (GSP) program, with the major exception of apparel
2. Duty-free and quota-free access for apparel produced in the qualifying countries from fabric or yarn made in the United States
3. Duty-free and quota-free access for apparel produced in the qualifying countries from types of fabric or yarn not produced in commercial quantities in the United States, such as silk, velvet, and linen, as well as for knit sweaters made from cashmere and merino wool
4. Duty-free, but not quota-free, access for apparel produced in all but the most developed sub-Saharan countries (Botswana, Gabon, Mauritius, Namibia, Seychelles, and South Africa) from input materials made anywhere in sub-Saharan Africa (Office of the U.S. Trade Representative, 2001).

Two years after AGOA was enacted, early reports indicated that the effects have been immediate and fairly dramatic: "in the first 11 months of 2001 U.S. imports of AGOA-covered products, excluding oil and other

Table 30.1 AGOA Beneficiary Countries as of December 30, 2003

Angola	Gabon	Namibia
Benin	The Gambia	Niger
Botswana	Ghana	Nigeria
Cameroon	Guinea	Rwanda
Cape Verde	Guinea-Bissau	Sao Tome and Principe
Central African Republic	Kenya	Senegal
Chad	Lesotho	Seychelles
Republic of the Congo	Madagascar	Sierra Leone
Cote d'Ivoire	Malawi	South Africa
Democratic Republic of the Congo	Mali	Swaziland
Djibouti	Mauritania	Tanzania
Eritrea	Mauritius	Uganda
Ethiopia	Mozambique	Zambia

Table 30.2 Nonbeneficiary Countries

Country	*Reasons for Failure to Qualify*
Burkina Faso	Undermining U.S. foreign policy; dealing in contraband diamonds
Burundi	Civil war; economic mismanagement; corruption; child labor; human rights
Central African Republic	Military coup
Equatorial Guinea	Government interference in private sector; corruption; child labor; arbitrary behavior by government security forces
Eritrea	Deteriorating human rights conditions
Liberia	Corruption; virtually no social services; interfered in Sierra Leone's civil war; forced child labor; inhumane prisons
Togo	Corruption; no fair elections; privatization stalled; labor rights; abuses by security forces
Zimbabwe	Intimidation of political opponents; illegal seizures of private property; corruption

mineral fuels, rose by 96 percent to $1.2 billion" (Alden, 2002, p. 11). Additionally, the area has become attractive for investors from Asia hoping to take advantage of both the low-cost labor and trade preferences under AGOA (Alden, 2002).

South Africa is particularly well suited to take advantage of AGOA. Statistics from the Embassy of South Africa's ministerial meeting on AGOA indicated that from January to June 2001, South Africa realized benefits of $135.5 million. "Excluding the benefits accrued to participating oil-producing African countries, South Africa accounts for some 72 percent of total benefits accrued through AGOA" (Embassy of South Africa, 2001).

The Economy of South Africa

The U.S. Trade Representative Robert Zoellick observed that if sub-Saharan Africa had been able to continue the level of world trade it had in 1980, its exports to the global marketplace would be more than double their current levels (Alden, 2002). Indeed, after more than 22 years of isolation from the world's markets, South Africa is taking advantage of liberalized trade with the United States. What economic and governmental policies are in place that enabled South Africa to benefit from AGOA?

South Africa stands to gain for a number of reasons. The government has reduced the national budget deficit. In 2001, the deficit was a planned

1.9 percent, down from 8 percent in 1994. Inflation is under control and has fallen from 9 percent in 1994 to 6 percent in 2001. Furthermore, this commitment to sound fiscal policy has resulted in South Africa being given investment grade status by Moody's and Standard & Poor's (*The Economist*, 2001). South Africa's currency, the rand (R), has been one of the strongest in the developing world (Mead, 2001). In addition, the government is reasonably free from corruption and has a competent central bank headed by a fine administrator. Further, it has a stable government, an adequate transportation system, and a legal system comparable to first world countries (*The Economist*, 2001).

The government's policies should continue to attract foreign direct investment (FDI). Auto manufacturers, such as Mercedes, BMW, Fiat, Volkswagen, and Ford have factories in South Africa. However, "by the standards of other countries, South Africa has lured relatively little FDI: \$32 per head in 1994–1999, compared with \$106 for Brazil, \$252 for Argentina, and \$333 for Chile" (*The Economist*, 2001).

Despite this optimistic picture, however, many obstacles must still have to be overcome if progress is to continue. Privatization of large, government-controlled enterprises has begun and must move forward. "When the African National Congress came to power in 1994, it inherited big debts and a bunch of public utilities that guzzled subsidies . . . and offered rotten service at extortionate prices" (*The Economist*, 1999). Furthermore, these firms are overstaffed and in debt. At least 27,000 jobs must be eliminated, a difficult move for the government when the unemployment rate hovers between 30 and 40 percent (*The Economist*, 1999). At least 500,000 jobs were lost in various industries in South Africa from 1995 to 2000 (Swarms, 2000). Further complicating the labor picture is the strength of the labor unions. Their demands for higher wages, coupled with declining productivity, discourage investors (*The Economist*, 1999).

Health and human services issues need to be addressed, as HIV/AIDS is rampant: 3 million people need housing, 7.5 million people do not have running water, and 21 million people have no access to sanitation services (Swarms, 2000). Approximately one half of the population of South Africa gets by on less than \$200 a month, and many suffer from hunger and malnutrition (Mead, 2001).

Political Background

Despite widespread recognition of Africa's economic problems on the part of congressional lawmakers, there was nevertheless considerable opposition to the passage of the AGOA from those with NAFTA-like concerns with regard to American jobs and worries about the exploitation of African workers

(Boyer, 1999). The House rollcall vote taken on July 16, 1999 showed 234 in favor, but 163 opposed (*Washington Post*, 1999). Despite considerable arm-twisting by the Clinton administration, many Democrats failed to support their party's leadership, and voted 99 to 98 against AGOA. Among Republicans, the Act passed by 136 to 63, with most of the "nay" votes coming from those representing districts with textile-manufacturing plants.

Opposition to the bill was orchestrated by an unlikely coalition of apparel and textile companies, labor unions, environmental groups, antifree traders, and some black clergy. Neither party affiliation nor loyalty to a specific caucus or interest group mattered in the end. Charles Rangel of New York, a liberal Democrat and a member of the Congressional Black Caucus, teamed up with the conservative Republican Tom DeLay of Texas to support the bill; other Black Caucus members such as Maxine Waters (D-CA) and Jesse Jackson III (D-IL) joined southern Republicans in vocal opposition (*Washington Post*, 1999).

Conservatives opposed to the bill argued the protectionist point of view that AGOA would undermine America's textile industry by facilitating the entry of inexpensive imports. Liberal opponents argued that the Act failed to provide sufficient protections for human rights and against labor and environmental abuses, and did nothing to provide debt relief for Africa's poorest nations. Rep. Waters argued that the bill would reward corporations that had done business in the past with South Africa's apartheid government.

In answer to the protectionist argument, proponents of AGOA pointed out that African textiles comprised less than 1 percent of all textiles imported into the United States and that, even under AGOA, this total was not expected to rise much above 1 percent. Responding to the arguments from the left, Rep. Rangel expressed the view that AGOA would help level the playing field and give Africans the opportunity to enter the game of international trade (*Washington Post*, 1999).

The change of administrations in Washington did not diminish official support for AGOA. In October 2001, Secretary of State Colin Powell expressed the Bush administration's resolve to help African nations to participate in and benefit from the global economy, and to utilize trade to achieve self-propelled economic development (*Africa News Service*, 2001). Elsewhere, the Bush administration has been quick to publicize AGOA success stories, such as the 126 percent increase in Madagascar's exports to the United States and the $100 million investment in Lesotho by a Taiwan denim factory, which will eventually create 5000 new jobs (*Financial Times*, 2001).

Trade Liberalization

There is ample evidence in the literature that trade liberalization can have a positive impact on economic development, precisely as intended in the

AGOA. Levinsohn (1992) outlined the ways in which trade liberalization can affect growth:

1. By promoting investment in export-oriented capital goods, which increase productivity and economic growth throughout the economy
2. By facilitating acquisition of technology developed outside the country through FDI in export-oriented industries
3. By broadening consumer choice, leading to an increase in consumer expenditures
4. By increasing competition, thereby improving the efficiency with which resources are used.

Several of these effects were demonstrated empirically during the last decade. Dollar (1992) and Sachs and Warner (1995) examined the relationship between trade and growth in the output across countries and identified positive correlation between trade and economic growth. Coe et al. (1997) and Edwards (1998) focused on economic growth through increased productivity. They, too, used cross-section analysis and concluded that trade is positively correlated with increases in total factor productivity. In one of the few time-series studies of this relationship, Coe and Moghadam (1993) found a robust long-run association among growth, factor inputs, and openness in the economy of France.

In the *IMF Staff Papers*, perhaps most relevant to the present study, Jonsson and Subramanian (2001) presented the empirical relationship between trade and total factor productivity in South Africa. Using data across manufacturing sectors, they demonstrated that trade liberalization during the last decade had a positive effect on productivity. An interesting twist on the direction of causality was put forth by Bernard and Jensen (1999); they suggested that firms that are already efficient tend to take advantage of open markets and thereby contribute to increased trade, rather than market openness, and increased trade further contributing to the higher efficiency of firms.

Finally, Rodriguez and Rodrik (2001) questioned a number of studies that show relationships between trade and productivity, on conceptual and technical grounds. They criticized some for endogeneity of outcomes and for failing to specify the mechanisms through which trade affects growth; others were cited for measurement problems, lack of robustness to alternative specifications, or multicollinearity of their trade data with other variables such as macroeconomic stability and regional dummies.

Even if the main premise of AGOA, the relationship between trade and economic growth, is accepted, there still remain doubts about the efficacy of this specific legislation in facilitating investment in sub-Saharan Africa.

The South Africa Foundation summarizes the criticism of AGOA in this context as follows:

In light of World Trade Organization (WTO) commitments to eliminate completely the tariffs on textiles and other manufactured goods over the next eight years, AGOA provides only a short-run advantage, which may limit investment to cheap, nonproductivity-enhancing sweatshops that will close or relocate once their preferential treatment in U.S. markets is eroded. Without substantial debt relief, the ability of many African countries to direct resources toward basic services and infrastructures is limited; lacking such basics (e.g., roads, communications, a healthy and educated work force, etc.), businesses will be severely constrained in implementing new investment (South Africa Foundation, 2001).

In a similar vein, Khor (2000) criticizes AGOA for providing "slim benefits" to African exporters while improving substantially the access of American companies to domestic markets in sub-Saharan Africa. Reinforcing this argument, the South Africa Foundation (2001) points out that countries of sub-Saharan Africa have not taken substantial advantage of benefits already available to them under the U.S. GSP, or under the Lome Agreement for preferential access to markets in the European Union.

Although AGOA provides opportunities for firms in qualifying countries, there is some skepticism in the literature as to whether these opportunities will actually translate into an acceleration of textile and apparel exports from the countries of sub-Saharan Africa to the United States, and whether such a trend will be powerful enough to generate a wave of investment and productivity-led growth in their domestic economies. Although several years of data will be required to answer the second question, it should now be possible to gain at least some initial insight into the first two full years, as relevant data has now been released by the U.S. International Trade Commission.

This chapter reports on a descriptive analysis of these data by the authors, along with the current literature. We have also relied upon the correspondence with textile and apparel industry officials and interviews with officials from two large apparel and textile enterprises, in which they shared their thoughts regarding AGOA's impact on exports from South Africa and other qualifying sub-Saharan countries to the United States.

AGOA's Impact on the Apparel and Textile Industry

AGOA comes at a time when the beleaguered textile industry is on its knees. The retail industry is suffering under light recession, and there has been a change in consumer spending. The market is flooded with illegal textile imports. The local situation was dismal, but AGOA has brought new hope (BharatTextile.com, 2001).

The textile and apparel industries comprise the sixth largest manufacturing sector and are the eleventh largest exporters of manufactured goods in South Africa. Furthermore, this industry provides 430,000 direct and indirect jobs and is the second most significant source of tax dollars (Clothing Federation of South Africa, 2000).

These industries are recovering after a devastating period that initially began in 1992. At that time, the South African government began a program to significantly lower tariffs over a 12-year period (Clothing Federation of South Africa, 2002). This reduction in tariff protection, which opened up the South African marketplace to worldwide competition, coupled with the Asian financial crisis resulted in a wave of low-cost imports. By 1995, Pakistan, China, and India, all low-cost producers, contributed to imports going up by 225 percent. After years of protection by the South African government, the domestic textile and apparel industries found themselves unable to compete. They were overstaffed and saddled with factories whose technology was out of date (Roberts and Thoburn, 2004).

AGOA Progression

In the first full calendar year of implementation, AGOA has proved to be a vital tool for economic growth and development that is stimulating trading opportunities for African businesses, empowering local entrepreneurs, delivering much-needed investments, and creating jobs (Shine, 2002).

During the fourth quarter of 2001, AGOA enabled 92 percent of beneficiary country exports to enter the United States duty-free. In addition, indications are that nearly $1 billion of new investment has been realized (Shine, 2002). Sub-Saharan countries' exports to the United States in 2001 included more than 4000 products under a GSP, plus 1800 items that were added through AGOA (BBC, 2002).

Janet Labudda of the Division of U.S. Customs, speaking in Africa on July 2, 2002, indicated that AGOA will not serve as a protection for African goods, but will simply provide producers the opportunity to compete in the American marketplace. She further indicated that many requirements need to be met by African governments to comply with the Act, and that having strong export associations to help monitor compliance is crucial. To enable sub-Saharan countries to realize the full benefits of AGOA, she indicated that the Act is likely to be extended past its original 2008 termination date (newafrica.com, 2002a,b).

Data from South Africa's Textile Industry, provided by textile federation economist Helena Claassens and covering the period 1999–2002, is presented (see Table 30.3) and indicates that textile jobs were still lost as late as 2001 (Textile Federation, 2003). In 2002, employment in the spinning,

Table 30.3 South African Textile[a,b] Industry — Summary Statistics 1999–2002

	1999	*2000*	*2001*	*2002*
General				
Employment — total (average)	56,486	55,475	53,372	54,538
Spin, weave, and finish	26,278	25,379	25,203	26,634
Sales — total (million rand)	9,774	10,164	10,470	13,412
Spin, weave, and finish of text	6,304	6,440	7,023	8,632
Imports (million rand)	4,023	4,656	5,192	6,929
Exports (million rand)	2,618	2,888	3,372	4,517
Contribution to GDP (percent)	2	1.5	1.2	
Consumption per capita	R280	R298	R307	R400
Index of physical volume of production 1995 = 100	91.2	93.5	94.8	104.9
Utilization of production capacity (percent)	83.6	80	81	82
Fabric production (mill m2):				
Wovens	415	420	386	408
Knitted	165	136	139	138
Fabrics — total	580	556	525	546
Spun yarn production (thousand tons)	90	93	93	100
Exports of garments to the United States. (million rand)	474.05	790.77	1194.26	1646.8
Exchange rate: **US$1 = R**	6.1131	6.3953	8.6031	10.5165

[a]"Employment in the spinning, weaving, and finishing industry has increased. Ex-factory sales have increased. Index of physical volume of production has increased. Utilization of production capacity has increased. The existing textile mills have geared themselves to be compliant to the AGOA rules" (Claassens, 2003).
[b]Excludes knitting.

weaving, and finishing industries increased. Capital expenditures on new technology and plant upgrades were made before AGOA, and were forced by the increasingly competitive marketplace after tariff protection was phased out in 1995 (Claassens, 2003).

Roberts and Thoburn (2004) postulate that the greatest employment losses have been in the large textile-manufacturing firms. These are the firms that process the fabric to prepare it for garment manufacturing. This may be attributed to the fact that the machinery purchased by these firms in recent years has much greater throughput than the units they replaced. This equates to increased productivity and lower unit labor costs, and finally reductions in the workforce. "Even if the textile sector were significantly to increase production and exports, it is evident that it would not create significant amounts of new employment relative to the jobs that they have lost" (p. 135). However, they believe that greater employment creation is possible at the relatively labor-intensive level of garment manufacturing.

Claassens pointed out that, at present, some companies are producing at full capacity, but in general the local textile industry's capacity utilization is still only about 82 percent, just slightly up from 80 percent in 2000 (see Table 30.4). Currently, there are no real signs of major investment in manufacturing facilities as a result of AGOA (Claassens, 2002). Wendy Wilson of Credit Guarantee indicated that capital expenditures have to be considered in relation to the margins that have been sought by American companies (Textile Sector Makes Risky Stretch to Fill AGOA Orders, 2001).

Claassens indicates that apparel exports to the United States have nearly tripled from 1999 to 2001, an increase that can be directly attributed to AGOA. Even though the Act did not come into existence until 2000, there was a sharp level of investment prior to its enactment as firms prepared to "meet the increased demand for textiles from garment producers taking up export opportunities under the AGOA bill" (Roberts and Thoburn, 2004, pp. 129–131).

Exports of fabrics to Mauritius have also increased; however, many other sub-Saharan countries have received least developed country (LDC) status and can also import fabrics from other countries for a period of four years (Claassens, 2002). A direct benefit of AGOA has been the enhanced relationships between the South African textile industry and the suppliers elsewhere in Africa. Raw materials are sourced throughout Africa and woven in South Africa and Lesotho (Textile Sector Makes Risky Stretch to Fill AGOA Orders, 2001). AGOA II will be particularly helpful to the textile industry if the list of applicable products includes household linens in addition to apparel (Claassens, 2002).

AGOA and the Individual Enterprises

Sherco Group

Sherco Group is a producer of fashion and commodity products, with three business divisions encompassing the entire product process from the spinning of yarn to knitting, dyeing, printing of fabrics, cutting, and the manufacture of finished apparel. The company is owned by a German investor, who also owns 52 other South African enterprises ranging from mining to apparel.

According to Alf Hartzenburg, sales and marketing director of Sherco Group, "AGOA has been a lifeline for the textile industry. South Africans have had an insular nature for 22 years, and it has helped us to lift our heads and look at the rest of the world" (Hartzenburg, 2002). Revenue increases

Table 30.4 South Africa Garments

Production Price Index

2000 = 100	*Manufacturing*	*Textiles*	*Clothing*
PPI for total output			
1998	88.2	94.9	93.1
1999	92.9	96.7	95.2
2000	100	100	100
2001	107.2	105.5	105.3
2002	121.4	118.9	114.6

Source: Stats SA.

Index of Physical Volume of Production

1995 = 100	*1998*	*1999*	*2000*	*2001*	*2002*
Manufacturing	101.2	101.2	106	109.4	114.1
Textiles	91.4	91.2	93.5	94.8	104.9
Clothing	87.3	88.7	82.7	78.8	86.9

Source: Stats SA.

Employment and Remuneration

Number of Employees Average per Annum	*1998* No.	*1999* No.	*2000* No.	*2001* No.	*2002* No.
Manufacturing ('000)	1,360	1,308	1,284	1,261	1,270
Textiles (total — excluding knitting)	58,267	53,997	55,476	53,372	54,538
Spin, weave, and finish	29,585	26,278	25,379	25,203	26,634
Other	28,682	27,719	30,097	28,169	27,904
Knitting mills (fabrics and garments)	14,569	11,661	11,150	10,701	10,913
Clothing	11,9657	12,2380	12,5237	12,2513	12,2531

Remuneration (Total/Annum) Gross Salaries and Wages	*1998* R (million)	*1999* R (million)	*2000* R (million)	*2001* R (million)	*2002* R (million)
Manufacturing	65,358	67,798	70,867	76,031	84,435
Textiles (total)	2,357	2,265	2,290	2,305	2,472
Spin, weave, and finish	1,338	1,272	1,181	1,152	1,273
Other	1,019	993	1,109	1,153	1,198
Knitting mills (fabrics and garments)	364	380	311	365	374
Clothing	2,899	3,199	2,452	3,043	3,383

Source: Stats SA.

Percentage	*1998*	*1999*	*2000*	*2001*	*2002*
Manufacturing	80.1	80.4	79.5	81	81
Textiles	79	83.6	80	81	82
Clothing	83.8	87.4	86.3	86	87

Source: Stats SA.

Value of Sales (Ex-Factory)

R'Million	*1998*	*1999*	*2000*	*2001*	*2002*
Manufacturing	366,798	397,715	448,704	502,200	613,940
Textiles – total	9,615	9,774	10,164	10,763	13,412
Spin, weave, and finish of text	6,544	6,304	6,440	7,023	8,632
Other textiles	3,070	3,470	3,724	3,740	4,780
Clothing – total	9,650	10,983	10,544	11,065	12,407
Wearing apparel	8,191	9,101	8,853	9,217	10,220
Knitting mills (fabrics and articles)	1,459	1,882	1,690	1,848	2,187

Source: Stats SA.

Retail Trade Sales (at Constant 1995 Prices)

R'Million	*1998*	*1999*	*2000*	*2001*	*2002*
Total — RSA	12,7377	12,7797	13,2530	13,7794	14,4226
Men's and boys' clothing	8,589	8,966	9,556	10,425	12,604
Ladies's, girl's, and infant's clothing	14,487	13,916	15,375	16,815	18,978
Textiles (household and haberdashery)	2,879	2,969	3,056	3,178	3,186

Source: Stats SA.

Garment Imports

	1998 R'000	*1999 R'000*	*2000 R'000*	*2001 R'000*	*2002 R'000*
Garments	930,700	1,042,500	1,337,100	145,7400	1,858,800
Knitted	376,200	395,900	512,200	601,400	728,700
Woven	554,500	646,600	824,900	856,000	1,130,100

Source: SARS (Customs and Excise).

Garment Exports

	1998 R'000	*1999 R'000*	*2000 R'000*	*2001 R'000*	*2002 R'000*
Garments — total	771,500	1,027,300	1,415,300	1,912,900	2,570,600
Knitted	319,000	465,400	733,200	1,048,600	1,233,300
Woven	452,500	561,900	682,100	864,300	1,337,300

Source: SARS (Customs and Excise).

have been dramatic. Five years ago, Sherco's revenues were 75 million rand. In 2002, revenues reached 140 million rand, and projections for 2004 are at 190 million rand.

Sherco has chosen to recapitalize, and this recapitalization was funded by the aforementioned German investor. They have upgraded their technology and begun to replace their aging plant and equipment. This has lead to greater savings in manpower and allowed for new types of fabrication. Any future capital improvements will be funded out of operations, although Sherco has no further expansion plans due to the temporary nature of AGOA. Further expansion in the industry will likely come from investments by the Asian companies that want to take advantage of AGOA (Hartzenburg, 2002).

Another major benefit of AGOA for Sherco has been the opportunity to work with blue-chip American firms, such as The Gap, Abercrombie & Fitch, Mast, Express, and Nordstrom. Sherco has stopped shipping to the United Kingdom (60 percent of Sherco capacity went to the United Kingdom five years ago) in favor of developing its American markets. Hartzenburg said that Americans played hardball on prices initially, but have "held our hand, worked with us, and been a part of our team." They have set up offices inside Sherco plants and are very careful about compliance issues. "They have made us better at what we do" (Hartzenburg, 2002).

Hartzenburg cited a shortage of spun yarn in the region as a cause of supply bottlenecks affecting exports. To find supplies of spun yarn, Hartzenburg will be traveling to the United States in the Fall to meet with companies that may be able to supply yarn to Sherco for finishing in South Africa. The finished goods will then be reexported back to the United States. He sees this as a "win–win" situation for both the United States and South Africa, and a way to increase support in the United States for the eventual renewal of AGOA beyond its original eight-year time frame (Hartzenburg, 2002).

Finally, AGOA has forced Sherco to begin working with South Africa's neighbors, particularly Kenya, Uganda, Zambia, Madagascar, and Mauritius, to develop export markets (Hartzenburg, 2002).

Dyefin Textiles

Dyefin Textiles is the largest dyehouse in South Africa, specializing in finishing and dyeing for the textile industry. The company was founded in 1989 and employs 110 people. It is privately held by South African interests.

Volker Gundert, technical director of Dyefin, stated that exports by Dyefin had risen because of AGOA from 0 to 30 percent of capacity since

September 2001. The company is anticipating "huge growth" due to AGOA, and will continue to expand capacity by upgrading technology and developing new business processes. Efficiencies realized through investment in new technology have enabled the company to reduce the number of employees by almost one third since 1997. They are currently looking to a business partner from Singapore to possibly double the plant size. However, Dyefin, like Sherco, is fearful of the risk of expansion because "AGOA has an eight-year time horizon and the world economic and political environment is unstable" (Gundert, 2002). In addition, strict environmental laws in South Africa make it extremely difficult to build new factories. Unless these laws are made more flexible or technological advances help resolve issues of pollution, building new plants in South Africa will remain difficult. Ramatex, a large Asian textile firm, was set to build a new factory in South Africa, but environmental laws led the project to be moved to another African country (Gundert, 2002).

Working with American business such as The Gap, Knight Athletics, Hot Source, and FUBU has helped Dyefin become increasingly competitive. These customers are looking for "quality, high standards, and compliance and have stirred us up and taken us out of our downward spiral" (Gundert, 2002).

Furthermore, Gundert credits the steady hand of the finance minister of South Africa in "creating a miracle since 1994 when apartheid ended" (Gundert, 2002). He stated that the investment community applauds the minister's efforts to keep inflation under control and stabilize the currency.

Conclusions and Recommendations

Manufacturers have to quickly get to grips with costly machine upgrades, demanding new specifications, heightened expectations from workers, and vastly larger raw materials orders . . . these expenses must be weighed carefully against the tight margins American buyers have negotiated. In fact, there still seems significant uncertainty about the extent to which these margins will filter down to the bottom line (Textile Sector Makes Risky Stretch to Fill AGOA Orders, 2001, p. 1).

The results of this research provide a first glimpse into the effects of AGOA on the textile and apparel industry of the Act's beneficiary countries in sub-Saharan Africa, and in particular in the largest of these economies, South Africa. In general, the data demonstrates that the South African apparel industry's exports to the United States have increased tremendously since AGOA's implementation. However, the overall effects on South Africa's textile industry may take several years to determine, although data for 2002 provided by the Textile Federation indicates that employment, sales, exports, consumption per capita, the index of physical volume production, and utilization of production capacity all increased over 2001 (see Table 30.3).

Based on the qualitative research conducted with the executives of leading South African apparel and textile firms, there appears to be substantial benefits that may not have not been reflected in the previous research on AGOA. They are the following:

- The opportunity for South African firms to work in concert with top American companies, which have set high standards and are, in turn, helping make their South African counterparts more competitive
- Increased networking and cooperation among textile firms in the sub-Saharan nations impacted by AGOA
- Increased interest by other nations in investing in South African industries to take advantage of AGOA.

Numerous factors will determine how effectively South Africa will be able to take advantage of AGOA: political climate, labor relations, training of workers, investment in new technology and equipment, and cost of money. For South Africa to fully realize the potential of AGOA, the authors recommend the following:

- South Africa's government must continue to work to make the country attractive to investors by providing sound economic management, effective governance, enhanced infrastructure, and improved health and human services.
- The temporary nature of AGOA has made companies hesitant to expand capacity to take full advantage of the Act. Lobbying should continue in the United States to obtain an extension of AGOA and expand the items covered. Adding household linens to the list of goods would be of immediate and enormous benefit to South Africa's textile industry.
- When possible, South African textile and apparel manufacturers should be encouraged to purchase equipment, raw materials, and yarn from producers in the United States. As the dollar declines, this source becomes increasingly attractive to South Africa's textile firms, and will make allies of U.S. manufacturers in the quest to increase bilateral trade.
- Job creation in South Africa is vital. The number of jobs in the textile industry increased slightly in 2002; however, it is still well below 1999's level. Even though sales and exports are up significantly in the apparel industry, there is still a net loss of jobs since 2000 (see

Table 30.3). South Africa's textile industry has been realizing efficiencies with new processes and technologies, but its capacity utilization rate is still just 82 percent. According to Roberts and Thoburn (2004), the garment industry is the most likely to create new jobs because it is very labor-intensive.

- Only new capital investment will create these much-needed jobs; however, very strict environmental laws are hindering new plant construction. The government must work with private industry to review South Africa's environmental laws and to investigate technologies that will facilitate new construction while protecting the environment.

References

Africa News Service. 2001. "Remarks of Secretary Colin Powell to the African Growth and Opportunity Act Forum," Washington, October 29.

Alden, E. February 13, 2002. "Zoellick Take Trade Path to Africa: The U.S. Trade Representative's Visit Aims to Extol the Virtues of a Supply-Side Approach to Development," *Financial Times*, London. Retrieved September 12, 2004 from: http://0-web.lexis-nexis.com.novacat.nova.edu/universe/document?_m =c605ac95283b4f4e 87711476e5c7ee85&_docnum=10&wchp=dGLbVtbzSk VA&_md5=aa52fa853389d7f08938399dbbfd0d26.

BBC. June 7, 2002. "South Africa: Exports to USA for First Quarter in 2002 Amount to 69.5m Dollars," *BBC Monitoring Africa*.

Bernard, A.B. and J.B. Jensen. 1999. "Exporting and Productivity," *NBER Working Paper No. 6198*, National Bureau of Economic Research.

BharatTextile.com. 2001. Retrieved September 12, 2004 from: http://www.bharattextile.com/newsitems.

Boyer, D. July 16, 1999. "African Trade Bill Opens Rift in Congressional Black Caucus," *Washington Times*, p. a3.

Claassens, H. July 8, 2002. Personal communication, Economist, Textile Federation of South Africa.

Claassens, H. May 20, 2003. Personal communication, Economist, Textile Federation of South Africa.

Clothing Federation of South Africa. July 2, 2002. Textile Industry in South Africa, http://www.infomat.com/information/research/industry/Reports/SouthAfrica_Textiles.html.

Coe, D.T. and R. Moghadam. 1993 "Capital and Trade as Engines of Growth in France," *IMF Staff Papers*, 40: 542–566.

Coe, D.T., E. Helpman, and A.W. Hoffmaister. 1997. "North-South R&D Spillovers," *Economic Journal*, 107: 134–149.

Dollar, D. 1992. "Outward-Oriented Developing Economies Really Do Grow More Rapidly: Evidence from 95 LDCs, 1976–85," *Economic Development and Cultural Change*, 40: 523–544.

Edwards, S. 1998. "Openness, Productivity and Growth: What Do We Really Know?" *Economic Journal*, 108: 383–398.

"Embassy of South Africa Statement on African Growth and Opportunity Act Ministerial Meeting," *U.S. Newswire*. Washington, D.C., October 29, 2001.

Feldman, G. 2003. "U.S.–African Trade Profile," *United States Department of Commerce, International Trade Administration*, March.

Financial Times. 2001. "Lesotho Seen as Gateway to U.S. Market," London Edition, August 23.

Gundert, V. July 11, 2002. Personal communication, Technical Director, Dyefin Textiles.

Hartzenburg, A. July 9, 2002. Personal communication, Sales and Marketing Director, Sherco Group.

Jonsson, G. and A. Subramanian. 2001. "Dynamic Gains from Trade: Evidence from South Africa," *IMF Staff Papers*, 48.

Khor, M. 2000. "The U.S. Trade and Development Act, 2000: Implications for Africa," *Third World Network*.

Levinsohn, J. 1992. "Testing the Imports-as-Market Discipline Hypothesis," *Journal of International Economics*, 35: 1–22.

Mead, W. July 22, 2001. "South Africa: A New Leader Emerges," *The Los Angeles Times*.

newafrica.com: Business News. May 9, 2002a. "South Africa: Business Confidence Increases Slightly." Retrieved September 6, 2003 from: http://www.newafrica.com/news/business/articlepg1.asp?ID=46517.

newafrica.com: Business News. June 14, 2002b. "AGOA Benefits Elude African Companies." Retrieved September 6, 2003 from http://www.newafrica.com /news/business/articlepg1.asp?ID=48133.

Office of the U.S. Trade Representative. 2001. *U.S. Trade and Investment Policy Toward Sub-Saharan Africa and Implementation of the African Growth and Opportunity Act*. Washington, D.C., May.

Roberts, S. and J. Thoburn. 2004. "Globalization and the South African Textiles Industry: Impacts on Firms and Workers," *Journal of International Development*, 16: 125–139.

Rodriguez, F. and D. Rodrik. 2001. "Trade Policy and Economic Growth: A Skeptic's Guide to the Cross-National Evidence," In B. Bernanke and K. Rogoff, (eds.) *NBER Macroeconomic Annual 2000*. Cambridge, MA: MIT Press, pp 261–324.

Sachs, J. and A. Warner. 1995. "Economic Reform and the Process of Global Integration," *Brookings Papers on Economic Activity*.

Shine, J. June 10, 2002. "US Program is Boosting Trade with Africa," *Financial Times*.

South Africa Foundation. June, 2001. "The Impact of the African Growth and Opportunity Act on African Exports to the USA," Johannesburg.

Statement by the Deputy Press Secretary, The White House. December 30, 2003. "White House Statement on 2004 AGOA Eligibility for 37 Countries." Retrieved September 13, 2004 from http://www.whitehouse.gov/news/releases/2003/12/2003 1230–8.html.

Swarms, R. February 5, 2000. "South African Leader Warns Unions Not to Impede Development," *The New York Times*.

Textile Federation. May 19, 2003. "News Clip — African Growth and Opportunity Act." Retrieved May 19, 2003 from http://www.texfed.co.za/main.htm.

Textile Sector Makes Risky Stretch to Fill AGOA Orders. December 5, 2001. Business Report. Retrieved September 13, 2004 from http://www.agoa.info/news.php?story=12.

The Economist. 1999. "International: The Painful Privatization of South Africa." London, September 11.

The Economist. 2001. "Survey: Jobless and Joyless." London, February 24.

Washington Post. 1999. "House Passes Measure on Trade with Africa." July 17.

Chapter 31

Nature of Decentralized Governance in Africa: Obstacles and Measures for Strengthening Decentralization for Good Governance

Keshav C. Sharma

CONTENTS

New Objectives of Good Governance in Africa and Significance of Decentralization

Democracy, decentralization, public participation, and accountability have been considered to be the major objectives of good governance globally. During the past few years, the forces of change toward democratization and decentralization have emerged on the African continent. Demands for public participation in government and its fair share in development activities have increased all over Africa. Efforts to strengthen democracy and good governance in Africa have to be complemented by invigorating the institutions and process of decentralization. Local-level governance assumes special significance in this context. The role of local government as an instrument of democratic decentralization, development, and good governance is realized increasingly. Throughout Africa, moves are made to give more power to the people at the grassroots (AAPAM, 1996; IIAS, 1996; Mawhood, 1983).

The governments adopt decentralization (which is a process of sharing of authority and decision making) due to geographical, political, economic, social, and administrative advantages (Sharma, 1992a,b). The government cannot manage all its activities from the center and needs to delegate some tasks to the lower level organizations. Certain geographical features of the country such as the size of its territory or underdeveloped infrastructure and communication facilities create the need for decentralization. Decentralization becomes a necessity for political reasons. It can be a means for accommodating diverse groups of population in plural and heterogeneous societies, and for giving them a sense of participation in governance. It could promote national unity by accommodating the demands for autonomy and power sharing. In the form of local government it becomes a training ground for democracy. It facilitates administration of societies with cultural and social heterogeneity with different customs, traditions, or languages (Sharma, 1999a, 2003a). It could facilitate the formulation and implementation of development plans by securing people's participation so that greater attention could be given to the felt needs and priorities of local population. Better use of locally available resources and self-help could be promoted this way and economic reforms related to deregulation or privatization could also be facilitated. Administratively, decentralization reduces the concentration of authority at the center, promotes decongestion of activities at the headquarters of government ministries, relieves the central government bureaucracy from involvement in purely local issues, checks excessive and uniform prescription from the center, and encourages speed in decision making.

A system of democratic decentralization has to be so organized that the relations between the central and the local government are characterized by a balance between centralization and decentralization of authority and functions. Although the central government has to delegate some of its authority and encourage autonomy of local authorities, it has to continue to retain some responsibilities relating to control, direction, supervision, and guidance, particularly during the infant stage of development of local authorities. Central government has to retain the functions, which the local government may not be able to undertake due to the magnitude of resources or expertise required. It may have to provide the local government with financial and manpower resources and technical assistance of different kinds without which these bodies may not be able to perform their functions. It may have to guide these bodies on the nationally defined priorities for utilization of scarce resources. Some central controls may be needed for maintaining nationally accepted standards of performance and integrity and for sound management of finances. Over and above all, the center may have to play a role in developing the administrative capacities of local-level institutions through various measures, which could include training, manpower development, and gradually increasing autonomy.

This ideal balance between centralization and decentralization has been difficult to realize in practice, and centralization has been a dominant feature of the nature of governance in African countries. In many of these countries, democracy has been a luxury and the people have not been able to live in dignity or enjoy basic or fundamental rights and freedoms. Although it is difficult to visualize democracy without decentralization and effective participation of people in the governance of the country, the system of government remains highly centralized even when formal political framework of democracy is adopted in many countries. In some cases decentralization is more of rhetoric than a reality.

Obstacles to Meaningful Decentralization

Effectiveness of decentralization in African countries has been limited due to several factors. Some of these include: absence of enabling environment for decentralization; limited financial resources of local authorities; scarcity of qualified personnel; centralized mechanisms of decision making for development planning; nature of political leadership; dependence of local authorities on the central government ministries; weak vertical and horizontal linkages; and ineffective grassroots participation (Sharma, 1997, 1999b, 2003b, 2004).

One of the serious constraints in the realization of desired objectives of decentralization is the absence of enabling environment in Africa. African countries have not been able to establish firmly the rule of law and democratic political framework for governance. A number of these countries are faced with one or the other or multiple of problems relating to the legitimacy of the government, enforcement of law and order, tribal violence, political instability, coups and counter coups. Their limited resources and energies are diverted from development purposes to the handling of such problems. The political, economic, and social environment therefore has created serious obstacles in the promotion of good governance (Wunsch and Olowu, 1990; Reddy, 1999).

Limited financial strength of local authorities has been another limiting factor in the effectiveness of decentralization. The local authorities in African countries do not have their own sources of revenue and depend very heavily on the central government for their needs. The central government not only meets their capital or development expenditure but also their recurrent expenditure. In such a situation, the local government remains weak. In a country like Botswana, although the recurrent expenditure of local authorities has been growing steadily, their own independent sources of revenue have remained limited. The difference between their expenditure and revenue is financed by the central government, through increased contributions from the central government budget (Reddy et al., 2003).

Scarcity of qualified staff has been a major constraint of local authorities. Due to this scarcity, local authorities have faced problems in planning for development. Particular bottlenecks have been caused by shortage of qualified professional and technical personnel such as engineers, architects, and accountants. In some countries the local authorities have been heavily dependent on the administrative staff provided by the central government. This dependence limits their autonomy. In Botswana, when the local authorities did not have the capacity to attract, remunerate, and train qualified staff, the central government decided to provide them with such staff by creating a separate service called unified local government service. Through this service, all the permanent and contract staff in the local authorities are provided to them. In Botswana, the establishment secretary based at the headquarters is responsible for recruitment, training, promotions, postings, transfers, discipline, and conditions of service of all employees belonging to the local government service. This arrangement has some advantages but it limits the autonomy of local authorities. Through a unified service such as this one, the local authorities are able to get qualified staff at salaries they could not pay independently. The staff belonging to this pool of service could have better training opportunities and promotion prospects and better conditions of service generally. The staff is also insulated from local politics. However, this arrangement strengthens the central control over the local authorities and limits their autonomy. Due to this arrangement local authorities have little control over their own staff, which is accountable to and has its loyalty to the establishment secretary at the center instead of the collective body of councillors representing the local population. The autonomy of the councils and their capacity to make their own policies or to take independent decisions is limited as they receive explicit or implicit approval, direction, control, or guidance from above.

The morale of local government staff in African countries is not high. Their conditions of service do not compare favorably with those of the central government employees. Their training opportunities and promotion prospects are limited and they are held in lower esteem compared to the central civil service. Attracting and retaining competent staff continues to remain a difficult problem due to likely postings in rural or remote areas. Greater incentives are required to attract and retain the university graduates in local authorities.

The local government organizations are expected to make a significant input into the decentralized district level development planning through their own projects, which have to be prioritized, elaborated, accepted, and implemented through the various mechanisms involving horizontal and vertical linkages. Effectiveness of decentralization and capacities of local-level organizations with regard to development planning are limited due to the problems related to formulation, implementation, monitoring, guidance, and vertical–horizontal two-way communication.

The nature of development planning in Africa, in spite of the declared intentions for "bottom–up planning" continues to be what is generally known as "top–down planning." The policies are determined at the central government level and major decisions for resource allocation are also taken there. The contribution of local-level organizations remains limited. The district plans are coordinated in many countries under the umbrella of bodies like the District Development Committee chaired by the district commissioner of Botswana, but their successful operation depends on effective coordination of activities of different district-level organizations participating in the exercise. This coordination means harmonization of activities for the purposes of ensuring the optimum collective contribution to the achievement of a common end and required eradication of duplication, conflict, friction, overlapping, and ambiguity as well as development of team spirit, complementarity, and mutual support. The existing situation in African countries needs to be improved in these respects (Sharma, 2004).

Consultation between the central government and the district-level organizations generally takes the form of explanation of policies and elaboration of plans formulated at higher levels. The link and communication between the center and the districts is somewhat ineffective, as the district-level staff do not receive adequate, satisfactory, timely information required. Professional caliber and training of concerned staff need to be strengthened as well as their commitment. The central government needs to display greater sensitivity for the problems, needs, and priorities of districts and give them guidance with positive interest.

The nature of political leadership in local government has a bearing on the capabilities of councils and their effectiveness. The caliber of elected politicians has often been a target of criticism. The caliber of many local-level politicians is not encouraging. As local authorities in Africa are in their infant stage, it may be unrealistic to expect high standards of qualifications found elsewhere in well-established institutions in other countries; nevertheless, the level of their caliber has a bearing on the existing capacities of local government. One hopes that with passage of time and experience, leadership roles of local-level politicians in these organizations will improve. Prescription of minimum qualifications for councillors, as has been suggested by some, can go against the spirit of democracy. It will be more appropriate if the political parties exercise their discretion in nominating candidates for election who at least have some elementary education.

The limited capacity of local government is evidenced from their dependence on the central government ministries for the performance of their statutory responsibilities such as primary education, primary healthcare, construction and maintenance of rural roads, and construction and maintenance of water supplies in rural areas. The experience of Botswana illustrates the point. The district councils are responsible for the administration of primary schools but the ministry of education provides the salaries to teachers administered under unified teaching service (UTS) operating under the director based in the ministry of education. The contribution of the ministry of health to the provision of health services by the councils is quite significant. The ministry has provided nurses and doctors to the councils and also provided drugs and equipment. The district councils have limited capacities to discharge their responsibilities for construction and maintenance of rural roads or construction and maintenance of water supplies in rural areas on their own without the support of the ministry of works, transport, and communications and the department of water affairs. These central government ministries/departments provide the equipment, machinery, and services of their staff to assist the district councils.

The local authorities cannot operate in isolation of the various organs of government in the center as well as in the districts. Vertical and horizontal linkages therefore assume significance. Effective two-way communication mechanisms are required for building a healthy partnership between the center and the periphery. In order that the national development plans and rural development policies are in keeping with the felt needs, problems, and priorities of the people, the center has to establish mechanisms of communication with the masses and the organizations such as district councils, which are close to them. The organizations such as district councils operating in rural areas have to remain informed about nationally determined strategy, resource position, national priorities and constraints so that they can organize their own efforts accordingly and make a worthwhile input into the formulation and implementation of rural development programs. Although some countries such as Botswana have developed mechanisms and procedures for promoting healthy relationship between the center and the periphery, there are many weaknesses that need to be remedied. The local-level mechanisms require greater commitment from political and bureaucratic leadership and the central authorities need to take more positive interest in giving guidance to the lower level organizations.

Public participation in rural development and planning is important, as it is a means of obtaining information about local conditions, needs, and attitudes. People are more likely to be committed to a development project or program if they are involved in its planning and preparation, because they could then identify with it and see it as their project. And it is also important for getting local assistance in the construction and maintenance of projects. Local contributions in cash or kind may be easier to get for "self-help" projects if people see these as something they have helped to initiate. For increasing people's participation, greater and more genuine decentralization is required from the center to the districts, but the process of decentralization will have to be taken down further below the district level to the subdistricts and the villages. The districts have often complained about the lack of adequate decentralization from the center to the districts but the district level has done very little to promote further decentralization, which could result in strengthening the lower level organizations like village development committees (VDCs). Decentralization is incomplete if it stops at the district level. Village-level organizations like the VDCs need greater attention from district councils and increased participation in development activities. The VDCs whose effectiveness has varied in different villages need to be taken more seriously by the governments, the masses, and the members themselves (Sharma, 2000a,b).

Measures for Strengthening Decentralized Governance

The earlier discussion leads us to the conclusion that the strength of decentralized governance will first of all depend upon the existence of an enabling environment with peace, stability, legitimate political authority, and democratic political framework. Apart from such an environment, strengthened human and financial resources will be essential prerequisites for effective decentralized governance, so also an accountable, responsible, and responsive public bureaucracy.

Qualified manpower is a scarce resource in Africa. There is a widespread concern about continuing and growing shortages of technical personnel and the quality of the training available to them. Governments in

African countries accept that they have a primary responsibility for human resource development. Various efforts have been made by the governments in these countries to develop human resources by strengthening different educational programs and training courses of different kinds. There has been a large expansion in education at primary, secondary, and tertiary levels and preservice and in-service training programs of different kinds have been introduced or strengthened. More concentrated efforts are, however, needed for human resource development in local authorities.

Effectiveness of decentralization and autonomy of local government will depend to a significant extent upon the financial strength of the local authorities. Unless these local authorities have their own-source revenues and reduce their exorbitantly high dependence upon the revenue-support grants given by the central government, decentralization will not be meaningful. The experience of Botswana in this context might be of interest to other countries. In this country, the entire development and capital expenditure of local authorities is met by the central government. About 90 percent of the recurrent expenditure of district councils in the rural areas is met by the central government. Although urban councils generate some revenue, in their case also the central government provides for more than 60 percent of their recurrent expenditure. The situation in other African countries is not very different as local authorities continue to depend on revenue support from the central government. Realizing the need for raising the basis of local government finance, the government of Botswana has agreed to establish firstly "a revenue formula which automatically allocates to the Local Authorities a specified share of designated national revenues" that would put them on a "predictable revenue path." Secondly, certain own-source income targets (i.e., own-source revenues) have been approved that, if achieved, will reduce the growth of recurrent grants. To facilitate the achievement of these own-source revenue targets, the government has announced its intention to expand the revenue base of local authorities. In addition, the government appreciates that to undertake meaningful budget planning, councils must know well in advance not only the recurrent grants that they will receive in the budget planning period but also the fees, charges, rates, and levies that they will be authorized to impose. The government is considering authorizing local authorities to introduce petroleum fuel tax, utilities tax (on monthly water, power, telephone bills), tax on gross sales revenues of commercially licensed businesses, tax on real property improvements, and borehole tax.

Realization of democracy, decentralization, and good governance will require a responsible, responsive, sensitive, and caring public bureaucracy, with characteristics of accountability to the community it serves. Responsible behavior of public bureaucracy implies adequate understanding by public servants of their roles, functions, and authority. It also requires appreciation of problems of the public whom they are expected to serve. Taking right action and decisions at the right place and time is a feature of responsible behavior. Democratic political framework also has its demands. Public bureaucracy in such a setup has to be answerable to the public through its representatives. It has also to be responsive to the needs, expectations, priorities, and felt needs of the population. Public policies and development plans have to be formulated with consultation and participation of the people for greater realism, acceptability, legitimacy, and implementability (Sharma, 2004). The development plans, policies, and projects imposed from above may fail to get the enthusiastic support of the people.

The public bureaucracy in African countries has undergone considerable reorientation since independence in its attitude toward the public, and the gap between the government and the public has been narrowed. Nevertheless, the administration, particularly at the grassroots level, has to be more humane and sensitive to the problems of the poor, the underprivileged, and the ignorant. The masses in the rural areas need to be treated with adequate respect and consideration by the urbanized and educated public servants. Arrogance, indifference, apathy, officiousness, and rigidity are unethical and the public bureaucracy in African countries has to get rid of such behavior wherever it exists.

Public bureaucracy is not an autonomous institution. It is accountable to the people and its representatives. In theory, the public keeps the bureaucracy accountable for its actions (or inaction) through legislative, executive, and judicial controls. Opposition political parties, communication media, press, and public opinion act as checks on the bureaucracy. In spite of the existence of such controls, the power of public bureaucracy has grown so much in different political and economic systems that it has become a matter of concern. The various control mechanisms, countervailing forces, and political institutions are not strong enough to curtail the power of public bureaucracy. It keeps growing due to its knowledge, expertise, and experience. Countries with different political systems and levels of economic development have been faced with the ineffectiveness of mechanisms of control over public bureaucracy. This kind of situation establishes rule by officials and undermines democracy and elected government. The public bureaucracy usurps the power that should legitimately be enjoyed by the representatives of the people. Increased power of bureaucracy gets worse when the public has limited access to the information related to public service activities and the public service remains withdrawn into its own shell. Lack of transparency could give rise to mismanagement.

The problem of accountability and transparency of the type outlined earlier manifest themselves in Africa, due to the weakness of mechanisms of control and accountability. Even in countries such as Botswana, which is a parliamentary democracy, its political institutions like parliament or local authorities are still in their infancy and they have their limitations in performing the roles that are normally expected of them. The parliament exercises control over the public bureaucracy but the limitations of knowledge, expertise, information, time, and interest are major constraints on the effectiveness of the parliament. The dominance of public bureaucracy at the local level is much more evident due to inadequate leadership provided by local politicians.

Local government is entrusted with public moneys for use in accordance with the laws, prescribed authorities, instructions, and directions. The government bureaucracy is expected to exercise reasonable precautions to safeguard the collection, custody, and disbursement of public moneys under proper authority. In order that the local government machinery raises and spends money according to the prescribed authority, various controls and accountability mechanisms have been devised. At the central government level, the parliament as custodian of public finances, maintains public accountability through the approval of annual budget, which outlines the proposed income and expenditure of the government. All the sources of revenue from taxes, loans, etc. have to be approved by the parliament so also all the items of public expenditure. No money can be raised or spent without the explicit or delegated authority of the parliament. To ensure that the government ministries operate strictly in accordance with the given authority, the parliament also relies on the control mechanisms like its public accounts committee and the independent office of the auditor general.

The machineries and mechanisms for financial control and accountability for financial administration that exist are instrumental in promoting sound financial management at central and local government levels. Their effectiveness, however, remains limited. Most of the members of the parliament are laypersons and do not understand the intricate budget details. The councillors in urban and rural councils understand much less. Auditor general's office is significant as an instrument of control and accountability. It is an independent office established by the constitution. In order that he can act without fear or favor, once appointed he can be removed only by the parliament after following an intricate procedure and establishing a charge of incapacity or incompetence. He has wide-ranging authority to call for evidence from any public servant or examine any public document. The annual reports of the auditor general of Botswana have exposed the weaknesses of financial administration without reservations. It is from these reports that one notices the nature and extent of loss of public moneys, stock loss, misappropriation, over or under or unauthorized expenditure, violation of prescribed authority and procedures, accidents of public vehicles, cases of fraud or thefts, embezzlements, incorrect record keeping, etc. The effectiveness of auditor general's contribution for financial control is limited, not because of lack of freedom or authority but due to the continuing shortage of qualified staff in his office. Furthermore due to the fact that the public servants as well as the parliament have not taken this office as seriously as one would expect. This can be discerned from the fact that the reports of the auditor general point out the same weaknesses every year repeatedly reporting the loss of public money, accidents of public vehicles, violation of proper procedures, failures in retiring imprests, etc. Public Accounts Committee of the parliament also serves as an instrument of control. This committee is assisted by the report of the auditor general and reports cases of financial impropriety to the parliament. It has a wide mandate and authority to examine documents and calls for evidence from public servants. The permanent secretaries of ministries appear before it with their finance officers to answer the queries. The auditor general and public accounts committee need to be taken more seriously by the African countries. The parliaments in these countries should explore ways and means to ensure that the public service takes concrete measures to attend to the weaknesses pointed out repeatedly by these bodies. A separate public accounts committee for local authorities as established in Botswana could be instrumental in strengthening local government financial management and accountability (Sharma, 2003b).

Corruption, which is a worldwide problem, has inflicted African countries in all spheres of life and is another major concern for developing high ethical standards of performance in the governance of these countries at central and local levels. African countries need to give serious attention to this malaise. One of the concrete measures undertaken by the government of Botswana for checking the growth of corruption in the country includes the Directorate on Corruption and Economic Crime established by a statute of parliament in 1994. This directorate, headed by a director of permanent secretary's level, is authorized to receive and investigate any complaints alleging corruption in any public body. The director has the authority to require any person to produce all books, records, reports, data, and documents relating to functions of any public or private body. He may require any person to provide any information or to answer any questions considered necessary in connection with any investigation. Different African countries have established machineries of this nature and have adopted codes of conduct for promoting ethical standards in public life. The effectiveness of these measures remains limited. Measures for eradication of corruption and promotion of higher standards of integrity have to be based on a deeper understanding of the social, economic, and political factors that have resulted in the decline of ethical standards and values.

Another measure undertaken for checking maladministration and enhancing the accountability of government bureaucracy to the public is the establishment of the office of ombudsman. This office exists in some African countries and was established in Botswana in 1995 by a statute of parliament. The ombudsman is authorized to investigate any administrative action of a government organization due to which a member of public might have sustained injustice. The ombudsman is not authorized to conduct an investigation into an action in respect of which the person aggrieved has or had a remedy in any court of law. The ombudsman is to be appointed by the president, and once appointed, he can be removed only in the way a high court judge can be removed following the constitutional provisions and only on the grounds of infirmity of body or mind or misbehavior. The ombudsman can require any minister or officer of any department or any other person to furnish information or produce documents relevant to the investigation. After conducting the investigation, if he thinks that some injustice has been done to an aggrieved party as a result of maladministration he can make recommendations to the department concerned to remedy the injustice caused. If no action is taken following his recommendation or the action taken is not adequate, he may submit a special report to the National Assembly. Every year the ombudsman submits a report to the president concerning the discharge of his functions to be placed before the National Assembly. In the discharge of his functions, the ombudsman is not subjected to the direction or control of any other person or authority and no proceedings of the ombudsman can be called in question in any court of law. Thus ombudsman has been given considerable authority and independence. Establishment of such mechanisms can be instrumental in enhancing the accountability of public service in Africa at central as well as local government levels (Ayeni and Sharma, 2000).

Although these measures are devised for developing a responsible, responsive, and accountable public bureaucracy at central and local government levels, these could not be a substitute for controls that can be exercised by informed public opinion and strong organs of civil society, which will take some time to grow in Africa (World Bank, 1989).

In the present state of development of local authorities, although the central government has to assist in building their administrative capacities, the local authorities also have to try to do whatever they can to strengthen themselves. Associations of local authorities could play some role in this regard. These could serve as a common platform for articulating the views and problems of local authorities and could be instrumental in strengthening decentralization.

Conclusion

The discussion above reveals that the effectiveness of decentralization in African countries remains limited. Even in those countries that are expressing their interest in decentralization, their governments remain centralized and the local governments in these countries remain underdeveloped. A strong and dominant center with limited autonomy of the local government characterizes the central–local government relations in these countries. The capacities of local government remain limited due to several factors which include: their dependence on the central government for financial resources and manpower; nature of financial and personnel management; limited autonomy of local government in decentralized development planning; inadequate local-level political leadership; dependence of the local government on the contribution of central government ministries for the performance of their essential functions; ineffective vertical and horizontal linkages; inadequate grassroots participation; and inadequate commitment of political and bureaucratic leadership in the central government for promoting decentralization. Limited capacities of local government have also been a constraint to further strengthening of democratic decentralization. Effective local government remains a distant objective. It could be noted that the nature and the extent of decentralization of authority and functions should be commensurate with the capacities of local-level institutions involved. The effort of the central government needs to be concentrated on capacity building of local authorities in the initial stages of their development.

Capacity building will imply that the local authorities strengthen their financial resource base by sharing revenue with the central (or provincial) government as constitutional or statutory right and do not continue to depend on central government's discretionary deficit grants. The autonomy of local government will continue to remain limited unless they strengthen their own sources of revenue. More important than increased revenue will be the increased capacity for sound financial management and adequate measures for control, accountability, and transparency. Greater professional competence in their staff, effective control over recruitment, promotions and discipline, and vigorous training efforts for different kinds of bureaucrats as well as politicians will be needed for strengthening self-government at local level. Effective decentralized participatory development planning at local level will require sensitivity on the part of central government for the problems, needs, aspirations, and priorities of the grassroots, guidance with positive interest, meaningful consultation with people, and effective coordination of different governmental and non-governmental organizations (NGOs). Finally, high standards of integrity and commitment on the part of bureaucratic and political leadership at central as well as local levels will be crucial for developing sound central–local government relations, democratic decentralization, bureaucratic accountability, and good governance (Jones et al., 1996).

References

African Association of Public Administration and Management (AAPAM). 1996. Report of the Expert Group Meeting on Decentralization Programme for Africa. Nairobi.

Ayeni, V. and K.C. Sharma. 2000. *Ombudsman in Botswana*. London: Commonwealth Secretariat.

International Institute of Administrative Sciences (IIAS). 1996. *New Challenges for Public Administration in the 21st Century: Efficient Civil Service and Decentralized Administration*. Brussels.

Jones Merrick, L., B. Peter, and K.C. Sharma. 1996. "Managerial Perception of Leadership and Management in an African Public Service Organization," *Public Administration and Development*, 16(4): 455–467.

Mawhood, P. (ed.) 1993. *Local Government in the Third World: The Experience of Tropical Africa*. Pretoria: Africa Institute of South Africa.

Reddy, P.S. (ed.) 1999. *Local Government Democratization and Decentralization: A Review of the Southern African Region*. Kenwyn: Juta & Co.

Reddy, P.S., D. Sing and S. Moodley (eds.) 2003. *Local Government Financing and Development in Southern Africa*. Cape Town: Oxford University Press.

Sharma, K.C. 1992a. "Bureaucracy and Coordination of Rural Development Policies at the District Level in Botswana," in H.K. Asmerom, R. Hoppe and R.B. Jain (eds.), *Bureaucracy and Development Policies in the Third World*. Amsterdam: Free University Press.

Sharma, K.C. 1992b. "Role of Local Government and Decentralized Institutions in Botswana," *African Journal of Public Administration and Management*, I(2): 1–19.

Sharma, K.C. 1997. "The Capacity, Autonomy, and Accountability of Local Government in Local-Level Governance," in *Regional Development Dialogue*, UNCRD, Japan, Vol. 18, No. 2.

Sharma, K.C. 1999a. "Traditional Leadership and Contemporary Public Administration," in E.H. Valsan (ed.), *Democracy, Decentralization and Development*. Brussels: IASIA.

Sharma, K.C. 1999b. "Botswana: Decentralization for Democratization and Strengthening of Local Government," in P.S. Reddy (ed.), *Local Government, Democratization and Decentralization: A Review of Southern African Region*. Kenwyn: Juta & Co.

Sharma, K.C. 2000a. "Popular Participation for Good Governance and Development at the Local Level," in *Regional Development Dialogue*, UNCRD, Japan, Vol. 21, No. 1.

Sharma, K.C. 2000b. "Decentralized District Development Planning and Management in Botswana," in P.O. Alila and W.O. Kosura (eds.), *Regional Development Policy and Practices in Africa and Asia: A Comparative Study*. UNCRD, Nairobi.

Sharma, K.C. 2003a. "Traditional Leadership and Rural Local Government in Botswana," in D.I. Ray and P.S. Reddy (eds.), *Grass-Roots Governance? Chiefs in Africa and the Afro-Caribbean*. Calgary: University of Calgary Press.

Sharma, K.C. 2003b. "Local Government Finance and Management: A Critical Factor in the Development of Local Government in Botswana," in P.S. Reddy et al. (eds.), *Local Government Financing and Development in Southern Africa*. Cape Town: Oxford University Press.

Sharma, K.C. 2004. "Good Governance in Africa: Decentralized Planning and Means of Participation in Development in Botswana," in G.M. Mudacumura and M.S. Haque (eds.), *Handbook of Development Studies*. New York: Marcel Dekker.

World Bank. 1989. "Strengthening Local Government in Sub-Saharan Africa," EDI Policy Seminar Report No. 21, Washington, D.C.

Wunsch, J. and D. Olowu. 1990. *The Failure of the Centralized State: Institutions and Self Governance in Africa*. New York: Westview Press.

Chapter 32

Good Governance: A Model for India*

O.P. Dwivedi and D.S. Mishra

CONTENTS

---

*An earlier version of this paper was published in the *Indian Journal of Public Administration*, Volume L1, no. 4, Oct–Dec. 2005, pp 719–758.

Introduction

The concept of governance is as old as human civilization. In essence it means the process of decision making and the procedure by which such decisions are implemented (or not implemented). The term is used in different contexts and varies in perspective among those who govern and those who are being governed. Good governance is a subset of this process, and is based on such fundamental values as accountability, transparency, fairness, equity, and ethics, which are essential ingredients for the sustenance of liberal democratic polity. "Good governance" or "good administration" is a necessity for any government to achieve the best quality of life for its public. However, what constitutes good governance and how it could be achieved are matters of debate in the public administration literature. On the other hand, corruption and mismanagement are impediments to good governance.

United Nations (UN) recognized corruption as the biggest impediment to development and authorized Secretary-General through General Assembly's resolution dated January 28, 1997 to help states design strategies to prevent and control this (United Nations General Assembly, 1997). Pioneering work has been done to identify the causes and remedies of corruption that not only prevents a country from deriving optimum benefit from its resources in nation-building but also endangers national security and is known to be disproportionately harmful toward the most vulnerable, including the poor and deprived. If caught in a "corruption trap," i.e., where corruption feeds on itself breeding more corruption, the economy of a country may collapse, leading to civil strife. The Transparency International's annual report 2003 highlights the magnitude of devastation caused by corruption on the governing process of the developing world and calls for an urgent need to arrest its growth (Transparency International Report, 2003).

This chapter discusses the process and strategies of governance with special reference to India. The authors examine, specifically, the cardinal values essential for good governance and within this context the exhortations and directions originating from classical times, a number of impediments responsible for poor governance, widespread corruption including its symptoms and possible remedies, and a search for good governance by suggesting a good governance strategy for India drawing upon its diversity, local experiences, and global best practices as a template suitable to its needs, heritage, tried practices, dominant culture, and values. We have argued that the country can use its core strength or unique selling proposition (USP) of spirituality, strong value system, British legacy, and cultural heritage to pioneer a sustainable change in the society including its politico-administrative system by ushering a strong and effective leadership at the top and a network of clean-administration champions to bring about positive changes and move India toward good governance with greater transparency, accountability, and equity, leading to all-round growth and development.

Governance

Governance as a process is of recent origin that goes beyond the classical functions of the government. Different schools of thoughts derive different meanings from the term governance, depending upon the role of process versus activity and control versus rules (Hyden & Court, 2002). In this chapter, we use a widely acceptable concept of governance involving all such governmental measures that guide, steer, control, or manage society. In essence, whereas the term government, as an institution, refers to a set of instruments through which people living in a state, believing and sharing a common core of values, govern themselves by means of laws, rules, and regulations enforced by the state apparatus (Dwivedi, 2001), the term governance includes a range of activities involving all cultural communities and various stakeholders in the country, all government institutions (legislative, executive, administrative, judicial, and parastatal bodies), political parties, interest groups, non-governmental organizations (including civil societies), the private sector, and the public at large (Frederickson, 1997, p. 86). The concept is also viewed as the exercise of political power to manage a nation's affairs (World Bank, 1992), as well as "the manner in which power is exercised in the management of a country's economic and social development" (World Bank, 1994, p. vii).

Motivated by the developments in modern day management principles and private business enterprise, specially the transnational corporations, the Western public administration academicians came up with a paradigm of new public management (NPM) movement, prescribing a leaner and meaner state in the 1990s (Dwivedi, 2002a). This was different from the classical Weberian concept of bureaucracy, which stressed on anonymity, meritocracy, and procedures. The new concept emphasized training, professionalism, customer orientation, ethics, productivity, responsiveness to the changing demands of business, and global mindedness. Briefly, the public services were to be given business orientation and better remuneration to improve their efficiency and effectiveness in the public domain and fast changing deregulated society with private service providers. The efforts were to reduce dependency on the government and inculcate entrepreneurship. Whereas the West celebrated the retreat of the state (Dwivedi, 2002a), the developing nations faced deprivation, corruption, and retardation in social capital formation. This could be because the symbols of the West were not married to the local culture and traditions and therefore did not bear the expected fruits. Administrative reforms must, in the end, be carried out in the local context and cannot be imposed or imported from outside. Unlike the laws of physical sciences, norms in the domain of public administration do not, usually, have universal applicability.

Good governance has become a catchphrase being used widely by various international agencies such as the UN, the World Bank, and International Monetary Fund (IMF). It means governing well, i.e., clean governance to achieve the anticipated goals and objectives of the public and the government. In essence, the concept incorporates the following ten values as necessary ingredients: (i) *democratic pluralism*, which is essential to maintain cultural sensitivity in a pluralistic society to ensure empathy and tolerance toward diversity, fundamental freedom and equality for all, and universal participation in the governing process; (ii) "legitimacy" in the eyes of the public under the law of the land, i.e., through the constitutional instruments, for example, free and fair elections; (iii) "consensus" among competing interests and "equity" in approach; (iv) "public participation" in decision making; (v) "rule of law" to ensure fairness and nonpartisanship; (vi) "responsiveness" of the governing systems toward the needs of the various stakeholders; (vii) "efficient and effective accountability" of the institutions responsible for the governance so that power is not misused and outcomes as anticipated or planned are delivered; (viii) "transparency" in action so as to build confidence in the state or other institutions; (ix) "moral governance," which refers to public service ethics and moral accountability in the process of governance; and (x) "a strategic vision" for sustainable long-term human development (Dwivedi, 2002c; UNESCAP, 2004).

In summary, good governance refers to not only the government but also all the players involved in the process of governance, namely, all five organs discussed earlier. Accountability, incorruptibility, sensitivity, and ethical conduct are the key factors of good governance. Who is accountable to whom varies depending on whether decisions or actions taken are internal or external to an organization or institution. As a fundamental principle, various instruments of governance are accountable to those who will be directly or indirectly affected by the decisions or actions. Transparency and rule of law are prerequisites for ensuring accountability. Moral or ethical behavior is essential for sustainability of the dynamic relationships formed during the conduct of the governance. A good example of this is the Biblical teaching "do not do unto others what you would not have others do unto you." This simple, universal principle is as valid for the institutions or groups as it is for the individuals. Incorruptibility requires clean conscience and keeping the public good above the private. This is more pertinent in the resource starved developing world, where corruption further impoverishes the state, impacting the poorest of the poor.

The Context

At the time of independence, the divided British India was faced overnight with the movement of millions of refugees across the border, perhaps the largest exodus of people at any one time anywhere on the Earth. This posed the problem not only of relief and rehabilitation, but also of welding the various communities divided by language, culture, religion, caste, and creed into the working cohesion of one united country. In addition to wars with its neighbors, the nation faced some perennial problems of poverty, disasters (both economic and natural), inflation, and food shortage. These problems put the inherited and emergent administrative structure and governing process to a severe test (Dwivedi et al., 1985). Over the years, there have been changes in administrative institutions, structures, styles, and cultures in postindependence India; however, India's administrative development can be best understood only in the context of the totality of this nation's economic development, sociopolitical and administrative environment.

At independence, India inherited from the British a monolithic, highly stratified, and strictly hierarchical administrative structure. The line of command ran unimpeded from the viceroy and governor-general in New Delhi to the farthest village head. The administrative system evolved during the time of Warren Hastings and Lord Cornwallis had four distinguishing features: (i) the district as the basic unit of administration, with the district collector or deputy commissioner acting as the alter ego of the vice-regal authority, controlling, directing, and coordinating all administrative activity in his district; (ii) centralization of authority, as the recognized principle of administration both territorially and functionally, with centralization of decision making in almost all policy areas; (iii) a single dominating civil service, with the Indian Civil Service (ICS) an elite generalist service, occupying the top policy and management position in the country; and (iv) a system of elaborate rules and regulations designed by the British to control their large number of Indian subordinates, dispersed far away from the administrative capitals of the central and provincial governments. Such a system of administration suited the British colonial system of law and order. It maintained and preserved the broad structure of society in India, particularly the large proportion of the rural society, as it then existed.

The constitution of India laid the foundation of the welfare state, guaranteeing all citizens the fundamental right to realize oneself within the prescribed framework outlined in the constitution. The statutes passed by the legislature are the expressions of the society to govern itself within the framework of the constitution. Supreme Court is the watchdog that ensures that the basic character of this document is not violated. The conflicting interests and activities of the different organs of governance are balanced in a way that ensures that the integrity of the Indian constitution, which is based on the principles of equity, fairness, and rule of law, is maintained. (Hardgrave & Kochanek, 2000) Competition, negotiation, and various forms of conflict resolution methods are among the tools that facilitate this process.

The attainment of independence and its aftermath gave an opportunity for political leaders to usher in momentous changes. A number of revolutions were tried. First, a political revolution began, which resulted in transition from a colonial system of government to a full-fledged parliamentary democracy with a federal structure of government. Second, an economic revolution started with a commitment toward welfare state, caused by transforming a semisubsistence economy into a modern industrializing community to solve the problems of poverty, unemployment, and want. Third, a social revolution, changing the caste-ridden stratified society into a progressive community oriented toward social justice. Finally, a scientific–technological revolution came in, which had an enormous impact on the traditional ways of conservative people. To usher in these revolutions, various strategies and development models were adopted by the Indian political leadership, especially its prime ministers, such as: (i) political integration; (ii) the framing and amending the new constitutions; (iii) the adoption of adult franchise; (iv) creation of the welfare state and an independent judiciary; (v) state intervention in the economy through five-year plans, with emphasis on agro-industrial growth; (vi) the policy of equal opportunity and protective discrimination for providing social justice to backward groups; and (vii) a number of administrative reforms.

To fulfill the objectives of a welfare state and promote rapid economic growth, India adapted five-year plans as a major instrument of its economic policy, based on the principle of mixed economy. Attempts to formulate and implement development plans were accompanied by a vast expansion of various administrative institutions and agencies, and proliferation of rules and regulations. Of course, the adoption of planned economic development inevitably led to an increase in the size of the bureaucracy. The planning system placed heavier responsibilities on the district, a traditional unit of administration in India. However, the British-devised administrative system could not carry on, and eventually suffered from: (i) the rigid adherence to, and inflexible dependence upon rules; (ii) focus on top–down decision making with a lack of delegation of authority and a generalized rigidity that prevented the organization from adapting readily to the changing demands placed upon it; and (iii) a lack of trust and reluctance on the part of the senior echelon to delegate authority, and the structuring of human reactions in rigid hierarchical terms, a tendency encouraged by the caste system and by the tradition of deference toward authority (Taub, 1969). It was no surprise that in a few years' time, the administrative system adopted *ad hocism*, both in the governing and administrative sectors, resulting in low levels of efficiency, integrity, and public trust. Perhaps the political leaders of India tried to govern too much, when compared to the Britishers who governed too little and did not concern themselves enough with changes in the social and the economic order. Perhaps it was inevitable, partly because the political leaders were in a great hurry to reach to the level of industrialization akin to the West, and partly because they had a great deal to make up to relative to other nations of the world. Nevertheless, this seeming haste resulted in a snowballing influence on the political culture and administrative process, especially its efficiency, effectiveness, and standard of conduct. The Indian government became more intensively involved in regulating, planning, stimulating, and placing under direct government control many economic, commercial, and banking activities, thereby stifling market forces that became dependent on government control and licensing. Over time, citizens also became overly dependent upon the initiative and the bestowal of governmental largesse in all spheres of their lives.

A number of visible changes in the administrative system and style became evident since the British rule. The district, the fundamental unit of administration, underwent a metamorphosis in terms of the importance, position, and stature of its chief executive. The importance of both the district and district officer was reduced due to the fragmented expansion of governmental activities on the one hand, and to the growth of "mafia" politics on the other. Much of a district officer's time was being simply wasted on listening, persuading, and arguing with a host of political leaders, including some antisocial elements, whereas the regular official work remained unattended. Along with the decline in the performance of the district level of administration, there had been a simultaneous weakening of in the strength and morale of the government service in general. Although the Indian Administrative Service (IAS) cadre tried to maintain its dominant position in policy making and governance, and consequently its power and prestige suffered due to constant political interference, caste and tribal politics, money, prejudices, and related matters. Coupled with political expediency and amoralism exhibited by politicians and businessmen, the public service ethics has declined to the point that practically all aspects of public life appears to have been engulfed in unethical activities. Politicians, officials, and even those who act as brokers between government and public have acquired dual personalities; their private actions ill match their public pronouncements. This has contributed to the emergence of an amoral politico-administrative culture with the arrival of a new breed of political leaders for whom the main tenets of a merit-based, secular, and politically neutral bureaucracy had been an obstacle. Soon, politicians emerged as the most important actors, as they acquired supremacy in all decision-making matters.

With this shift in the power base, particularly in civil service appointments, promotions and the use of discretionary decision-making authority, certain side effects were inevitable. For example, politicians would be found acting as brokers between business and commercial interests and government departments; the interpretation and enforcement of laws was politicized; interference in normal personnel administration to secure the appointments of friends or supporters, or the promotion of local civil servants became commonplace; the sale of government property and the issuing of contracts and licenses came under political influence; police, paramilitary, and military forces were used improperly in the normal functioning of society's affairs; there was political manipulation and intervention in the purchase of machinery, property, equipment, and services for government departments; official and confidential information was misused by politicians for private gain; and the concentration of extra-constitutional and legal authority was placed in the hands of favored individuals who did not hold any elected position. Naturally, such an environment influences the conduct and attitudes of public servants who, by and large, saw the benefit of accommodating to the prevailing winds. Slowly, a new trait of administrative culture had emerged; the existence of a parallel "black administration" where influence, favors, money, privileges, misuse of public funds, falsifying records, and the bending of rules and regulations play the crucial role (Dwivedi, 1988c, p. 249). This insidious subculture does not encourage citizens even to attempt to seek what is legally due to them; instead of facing the ordeal, such citizens employ the services of agents to lobby and get the work done, for which a fee must be paid. To make matters worse, the lower echelon of employees seems to have become insensitive to their public duties, and unresponsive to protect public good.

Here, the public good refers to a comprehensive set of goods in which the entire civil society participates (Symon, 1993). This is quite different from a common good, which could be contextual to the party it is referred to. For example, election manifesto may be a common good to the members of a political party but alleviation of poverty or eradication of corruption from public life is the public good of all those who are responsible players in governance. Every stakeholder in the process of governance pursues their own agenda but the public good deserves to be the universal commitment of all these parties. India, with over one billion population comprising of diverse religions, castes, creeds, beliefs, ethnicity, languages, cultures, food habits, dresses, local histories, etc., represents unity in diversity. Common governance through single constitution provides a strong bond. The challenge is how to bring together the individual needs and aspirations within the overarching domain of the public good.

Governing Style

Earlier, the nature of colonial administrative style was discussed. Taking that discussion further, as an interpretative exploration, some general propositions concerning the style of governance, can be offered:

1. The style of governance and the administrative culture of India, as well as other Asian nations, reflect the distinctiveness and complexity of the various national realities. These include persistent dependence, the perpetuation of rigid and particularistic social structures, chronic economic vulnerability, weak and unstable growth, marginalization, low institutionalization, and acute social polarization. The above translates into high levels of ambiguity and uncertainty.
2. The outer layers of the region's style of governance are directly affected by current circumstances, as well as the pressures of globalization and changes. The paradox is that, while demands on the public sector to provide more services are growing, the state apparatus is forced to shrink.

3. The culture of governance in India has been distinctively derivative. As a reflection of an entrenched center–periphery regional and global order, it has tended to follow vogues in the industrialized nations. In this sense, it has been exogenous in its motivations, definition of problems, and prescriptions.
4. Any profound administrative reform entails significant attitudinal and value changes. Thus, efforts at administrative restructuring, modernization, and other reforms must address first, either directly or indirectly to the question of the style and culture of governance. This culture is heterogeneous, and dynamic: syncretism, continuities, and discontinuities are part and parcel of its fabric and texture (Nef, 1998).
5. Historically, especially during the last half of the 20th century, the governing style of India in particular, has been molded by numerous failed attempts at modernization and cyclical economic and governance crises. The end result of crises and failed modernizations is a continuing condition of underdevelopment. It has also contributed to perpetuating a self-fulfilling prophecy of immobility.

Governance in Classic India

The *Rig Veda*[1] states *Atmano mokshartham jagat hitayacha*, i.e., the dual purposes of our life are emancipation of the soul and welfare of the world. Thus the public good should be the welfare of the society; or in other words, the private good or self-promotion should be subservient to the greatest good of all.

Kautilya's *Arthshastra*, written in the 4th century B.C., is the first known Indian treatise on public administration. Vishnugupta, also known as Chanakya or Kautilya, was the architect of Mauryan empire during the reign of Chandragupta Maurya in the 4th century B.C. He positioned the state as an institutional necessity for human advancement (Maheshwari, 2000, p. 3). On the basis of this premise, he outlined almost everything that the state should do and described how it should be managed for the maximum happiness of its citizens. He prescribed the following to the ruler:

> *Praja sukhe sukham rajyaha prajanamcha hitehitam,*
> *Natma priyyam hitam rajanaha prajanam cha hitam priyam.*
>
> Kautilya's *Arthashastra*

> [In the happiness of his public rests the king's happiness, in their welfare his welfare. He shall not consider as good only that which pleases him but treat as beneficial to him whatever pleases his public.]

[1] *Rig Veda* is the oldest of the four main scriptures of the Hindu religion.

Truly, the commonly believed Hindu philosophy is expressed in the words: *bahujan sukhaya bahujan hitaya*, i.e., public welfare lies in the happiness of the masses. Therefore, not only the king but also all individuals and institutions should keep the happiness and welfare of the society in proper perspective in all their deeds or decisions. This also highlights the prominence of public good over private good. Mahatma Gandhi, who led India to freedom, through *Satyagraha*, emphasized the importance of means, stating that the means are as much or even more important than the end. He laid the foundation of moral and ethical conduct in political and public life. His concept of trusteeship is pertinent to the concept of good governance. He maintained that those in position of power hold the trust of the subject and the future generations and, therefore, should conduct themselves in incorruptible and nonexploitative manner. In the *Bhagavad Gita*, a major religious scripture, Lord Krishna prescribes the following as the virtuous path:

> *Pravrittim cha nivrittim cha karyaakarye bhayaabhaye,*
> *Bandham moksham cha yaa vetti, buddhim saa Partha saattviki.*
>
> *Bhagavad Gita*, Verse 30, Chapter 18
>
> [*O Partha*! That understanding by which one knows what ought to be done and what is not, what is to be feared and what is not, what one can do and what is prohibited, leads to the virtuous path.]

In *Mahabharata*, the great Indian epic, which narrates the victory of good over evil, Bhishma Pitamaha, who had mastered the art of governance and had dedicated himself to the throne of his kingdom, Hastinapur, says: "the foundation for good governance is righteousness in public affairs. The king, his son — including relatives — his ministers, and the State employees who have taken the oath of their offices to uphold Dharma and to take care of the public needs, must not act unjustly or unethically because if they do so, they will not only destroy the moral basis of governance but will also turn the State into a hell" (*Mahabharata, Shanti Parva*). *Brihadaranya upanishad* lays the king's duty as follows:

> *Tadetat kshatrasya kshatram yaddharmaha tasmaddharmatparam nasti,*
> *Atho abliyan baliyamsamanshamsate dharmena yatha ragna evam.*
>
> *Brihadaranya upanishad*
>
> [It is the responsibility of the king to protect dharma, the public good, so that all citizens get equal opportunity and that the weak are not exploited and harassed by the strong.]

Dharma, in Sanskrit, means that which sustains the righteous path. This has been explained in Verse 58, Chapter 59, *Karna Parva* of Mahabharata as below:

> *Dharanat dharma mityahu dharmo dharayate prajaha, Yat syad dharanasamyuktam sa dharma iti nischayaha.*
>
> *Mahabharata*, Verse 58, Chapter 59
>
> [Dharma sustains the society, Dharma maintains social order, Dharma ensures well-being and progress of humanity, and Dharma is surely that which fulfills these objectives.]

Governance in Indian scriptures is called *rajdharma*, i.e., righteous duty of the king. Thus, as defined above, the conduct of those involved in governance requires adhering to righteousness, which calls for exhibiting the highest standards of morality and ethical behavior. Hindu scriptures suggest that as kings have been bestowed divine authority they are duty bound to rule only under God's command and by providing clean and ethical administration. Moreover, a king is obligated to do justice to the public by treating them as if they were his own children, and punish any corrupt behavior in the society. Unethical conduct, therefore, amounts to doing disservice to God, because the king acts only as God's viceroy or a deputy. In a nutshell, the Indian philosophy lays emphasis on the premise that inner spirituality and character must govern the conduct and behavior of the leaders in the society.

Inspired by these values, the architects of India's constitution laid down the foundation of effective governance for the country by declaring the nation as a sovereign, socialist, democratic, secular, and federal republic.[2] The basic characteristics of the constitution emerge from the ideals of participatory democracy, guaranteed fundamental rights to the citizens, secularism, cooperative federalism, and independent judiciary empowered to review the action and inaction of legislatures and the executives to achieve the objectives of socioeconomic and political justice (Narang, 1996). The constitution recognizes the diversity in the Indian society and provides opportunities for all citizens, irrespective of caste, creed, religion, gender, etc., to realize their true potential in a multicultural environment. This includes affirmative actions in favor of those who have been deprived by incorporating need-based accelerated growth for their mainstreaming. It casts responsibilities on all the three organs of the government to implement these values enshrined in the constitution.

[2]Socialist and secular added through 42nd Amendment of the Constitution of India in 1976.

Although it does not specifically use the term good government as in the Canadian constitution (1867), in effect the mandate amounts to the same.

The concern for clean and good government has been a major challenge not only for India but also for all developing nations. That challenge was recognized by India's first prime minister Jawaharlal Nehru as mentioned earlier. Over the years, many impediments emerged such as lower level of (and in some cases no) accountability, lack of transparency, unethical behavior, lack of sensitivity toward public concerns, uneconomic use or misappropriation of state resources, or plundering of natural resources with no concern for society or future generations. These impediments along with many related factors have caused public concern about the effectiveness of existing system of governance in India.

Impediments to Good Governance

Among major impediments to good governance, corruption and corrupt behavior among public officials constitute the most insidious challenge; this aspect is examined in detail in the following section; however, a few relevant impediments are discussed below.

Erosion of the Classical Nature of Politically Neutral to Politicized Public Service

Traditionally, the public service is expected to be politically neutral so that public servants may perform their tasks objectively, efficiently, impartially, and without fear of being punished when rendering advice against prevailing political winds. The convention of ministerial responsibility (as developed in the Great Britain and subsequently adapted in various countries with the British administrative heritage) meant that the ministers are accountable to parliament or a state legislative assembly for acts done by public servants of their department whether they personally directed the act or personally did it or not. However, this 19th century doctrine became partially ineffective when the state assumed enormous tasks, though ministers were unable to have any prior knowledge and conduct of hundreds of government employees working in their ministry or department. That classical theory of individual responsibility of ministers for each and every act of public servants gave way to a modified convention, which limited ministers' responsibility to only those actions that were done at their behest directly and personally. Of course, ministers continued being answerable at parliament and assemblies for various matters related to their charges, but not being legally responsible for each and every act unless directly involved in the decision making. Nevertheless, the convention remained intact with respect to noninterference of politicians into the regular administrative process and procedures (Dwivedi, 1982).

Direct form of partisan control has been considered improper for maintaining a responsible and accountable administration. But politicization occurs whenever political criteria is substituted for the merit-based standards used in the selection, transfer, promotion, rewards, and punishment of members of the public service. The process includes attempts by politicians to control policy enforcement or implementation, regulatory control, distribution of state resources through grants or contracts, and fixing jobs to party-faithful or family members. Another reason why politicians wish to control governmental apparatus is their fear that the decisions made by them might simply disappear into the quicksand of administrative jungle of norms and procedures, as they have a much shorter span of time to implement their electoral promises and related policy changes. They also hold a negative view of the long service tenure held by public servants whom ministers are unable to remove because a slow, delayed, or nonperformance of assigned tasks is rarely a punishable action. It is a view held by some that most government officers can produce alibis for nonperformance; and that there is no cost either to an officer or to the government for the harm caused by such indecision (Saxena, 2004). All these perspectives have caused to create an atmosphere of either mutual distrust among ministers who are in a rush, and seasoned but honest officers who still believe in old civil service tradition of integrity, political neutrality, accountability, and ethics, or a situation of mutual gain where ministers and civil servants help each other to exploit state resources by amassing wealth through corrupt practices.

Although politicization of administration started earlier in many developing nations immediately after gaining independence, countries like the United Kingdom, Canada, Australia, etc., remained wedded to the concept of civil service neutrality. However, during the Thatcher years in the United Kingdom, it was argued that politicization as blamed was not towards making government employees adhere to new allegiance to the Conservative Party but was more to ensure that employees showed appropriate and rapid commitment to policy changes. Sausman and Locke (2004, p. 103) state that Mrs. Thatcher participated proactively in the appointment of senior civil servants, and that there emerged a personalization of the appointment procedures for senior civil service posts.

Institutional Impediments

The biggest challenge faced by India is the administration and implementation of various policy programs and effective delivery of service. Although the country has adequate legal mandates to solve problems, the gaps in policy implementation mechanisms indicate that enforcement of policies is rather weak, and at times nonexistent. Three of such gaps and impediments are discussed below.

Structural Impediments or Administrative Hurdles

Structural impediments or administrative hurdles relate to the rigidity of existing watertight division of various ministries who are desperate to safeguard their jurisdictions; and so policies and program enthusiastically initiated by one ministry may be slowed to be embraced by others. Despite its posturing, the planning commission, which has a national vision has been unable to create the same foresight among individual ministries. What is needed is a concept of "super coordinating ministry" structure, which discourages interministerial competition, is able to overcome sectoral issues, and makes efforts to ensure that there exists cooperation within interministerial agencies, public sector undertakings, and boards or commissions; and furthermore, to remove any administrative hiccups or wrinkles, a mechanism is in place to iron out issues both at the senior administrative level, as well as at the ministers level. For example, J.B. D'Souza, a former Municipal Commissioner of Bombay remarked: "If the quality of the urban environment in India is determined by the number of laws on the matter and the rate at which we add to the laws, the city life in India would easily create envy the world over. Instead the condition of our cities is an eternal source of lament. India's readiness to equate legislation on a problem with its solution ... there are a profusion of laws that do not serve their purpose and eventually create many new problems. In India, it is said that 'problems are found for every solution' " (D'Souza, 1992, p. 54).

Weak Compliance and Inadequate Enforcement

The Organization for Economic Coordination and Development has noted that many developing nations have legislated various laws concerning social welfare, environmental protection, and economic development, but such legislation is rarely enforced due to lack of sufficient technical and administrative resources, and also because powerful groups are able to influence the regulatory system or bypass compliance measures in place (OECD, 1982). Furthermore, many government departments and ministries suffer from lack of not only necessary research tools and intelligence gathering for their respective functions but also appropriate financial and human management capabilities thereby unable to properly enforce measures outlined in those laws. As mentioned earlier, it is not the lack of laws which appear adequate on the surface, but the necessary infrastructure to support these laws is missing, thereby rendering institution mechanisms ineffective; and then it is no surprise that such inadequate infrastructure for implementation of legislation creates negative implications. For example, in the field of environmental protection, "chemicals already banned or obsolete in other countries are still being produced in India. In other cases, relatively dirty industries or processes which find themselves under considerable economic and environmental pressure in developed nations, have been installed in India, exacerbating the environmental problems associated with industrial sources" (India, 1993, p. 186).

This inadequacy has resulted largely because of human resource and financial limitations affecting the management, routine operation, maintenance of existing infrastructures, and application of various regulatory provisions. There is also a view among the federal government officers that due to lethargy on the part of state government officials, appropriate enforcement is not done in those programs in which the central government is also a partner. Perhaps, it is not realized that one of the major impediments to the effective enforcement of any regulation such as pollution control at a provincial level is the enormity of the task in relation to the human and financial resources available. Finally, lower level bureaucrats are not free from political and social pressures either. They are often undercut by powerful economic and social interests. For example, it is a common practice for an industry to approach a higher-up connection if lower level bureaucrats fail to adhere to their whims and fancies (Dwivedi & Jain, 1985). Finally, for government regulators, the cost of enforcement in time and resources to be invested is higher than the cost of nonenforcement. Government officials lack a political constituency, and furthermore, they lack public credibility due to their negative image. Under such circumstances, no decision appears to be a better way out compared to be seen over enthusiastic if they wish to escape from political interference discussed earlier.

Overemphasis on Command and Control

There is a tendency in India to "legislate away" problems. This curative approach avoids tackling the root causes of problems. For example, in the realm of industrial pollution control, there exist barriers to the movement away from the curative "command and control" approach and toward the implementation of a more preventative "polluter pays" alternative. But a polluter pays system requires the formulation of a schedule to determine the rates that polluters will pay in accordance with, for example, the toxicity of their waste or type of industrial activity. This process is considered too cumbersome and complex by authorities who would rather deal with the issue through the formulation of new laws. The problem, of course, is that with increased regulation there is also an increased regulatory burden and enforcement challenge (Dwivedi, 1997, p. 127). However, offending industries and individuals, instead of obeying compliance, obtain a court injunction (called stay order) and continue operating in their usual fashion by virtue of their access to sophisticated legal mechanisms and knowing fully well that due to an enormous backlog of court cases, it might take years before anything happens.

Summary

Each nation has its own way of handling a crisis. The institutional and cultural context of India makes the implementation of its various developmental and nation-building programs uniquely Indian. Of course, examples from other countries are studied and used in the Indian context; however, the process of implementation remains Indian. One may find that resources get diverted, that there is direct political interference in the administrative and enforcement process, that policy goals are deflected and responsibilities for achieving policy mandates are evaded, and that the tokenism may appear to be employed by government administration; nevertheless, the tenacity of some administrators and political leaders (albeit a very few) is such that they are able to keep the system functioning. And so, it would be erroneous to conclude that institutional impediments facing India are such that it is hopeless to expect fast results; instead, one should take the view that Indians have developed their own style of governance and management, and that things get done in their own time.

Corruption: The Most Insidious Impediment to Good Governance

Through five-year plans, which started in 1951, India began its journey as a welfare and development-oriented nation. The national extension program in 1952 and the foundation of panchayati raj institutions in 1957 initiated the process of participatory governance. India inherited two legacies from its immediate past: the concept of a clean and spiritual politics from Mahatma Gandhi and an essentially honest public administration led by officers of ICS, who stood out for their impeccable integrity and devotion to duty (Maheshwari, 2000, p. 362). However, the industrial orientation of the second five-year plan (1957–1962) with large-scale investments and commencement of the license-permit-quota *raj* polluted both the political and the bureaucratic atmosphere forcing the government to institute K. Santhanam committee on prevention of corruption in 1962. Further, Justice

S.R. Das enquiry commission was set up in 1964 to inquire into the charges of corruption against the then chief minister of Punjab Pratap Singh Kairon. Both the reports confirmed the existence of widespread and deep-rooted corruption of politico-administrative nature. Consequently, Central Vigilance Commission (CVC) was instituted by the government to look into charges of corruption in the bureaucracy. Kairon was forced to resign from the public office. This marked the beginning of the malaise in the Indian system of governance. The disease has grown so much over the years that in their latest report declared in October 2003, after carrying out a detailed study of 133 countries, Transparency International has placed India at the 83rd position with corruption perception index (CPI)[3] of 2.8 (Transparency International Report, 2003). Finland with CPI of 9.7 is on the first position and Bangladesh with 1.3 on the 133rd.

Corruption has emerged as the greatest threat to the democracy and development of India. It undermines the efforts of governance. It is becoming all-pervasive and encompasses within itself all the five organs of governance discussed earlier. Indian newspapers are full of scandals; and corrupt practices are becoming a way of life even at lower levels of bureaucracy. This adversely affects the very tenets of democracy: equity, fairness, and rule of law. In 1984, the then Indian prime minister Rajiv Gandhi's comment that out of every rupee released for antipoverty programs only 15 paise (Indian currency: 1 rupee is divided into 100 paise) reached the real beneficiary became very famous. An efficient system of delivery may require 30 paise on the establishment, but considering overwhelming employment in the Indian bureaucratic set up, even if 45 paise is earmarked for managing the delivery system, 40 paise seems to be leaking out of the system. In this way he quantified the extent of corruption in the government and society in general.

Corruption in public life adversely affects human development. Various resources are underutilized or inefficiently utilized and public morale, at large, is low. Personal gains take prominence over public good, leading to favoritism, inequity, and unfair treatment by those holding positions of power. This leads to human deprivation. Figure 32.1 depicts interlinkages between corruption and poor governance.

Figure 32.1 shows how corruption adversely affects the human development as well as economic growth of the country. This is even more dangerous for developing countries like India, which is scarce in resources and has to make optimal use of the limited resources to improve the quality of life of the people. This self-perpetuating vicious circle of corruption must be broken by conscious efforts of those who provide

[3]CPI of 10 is the ideal score representing public perception of no corruption in the country.

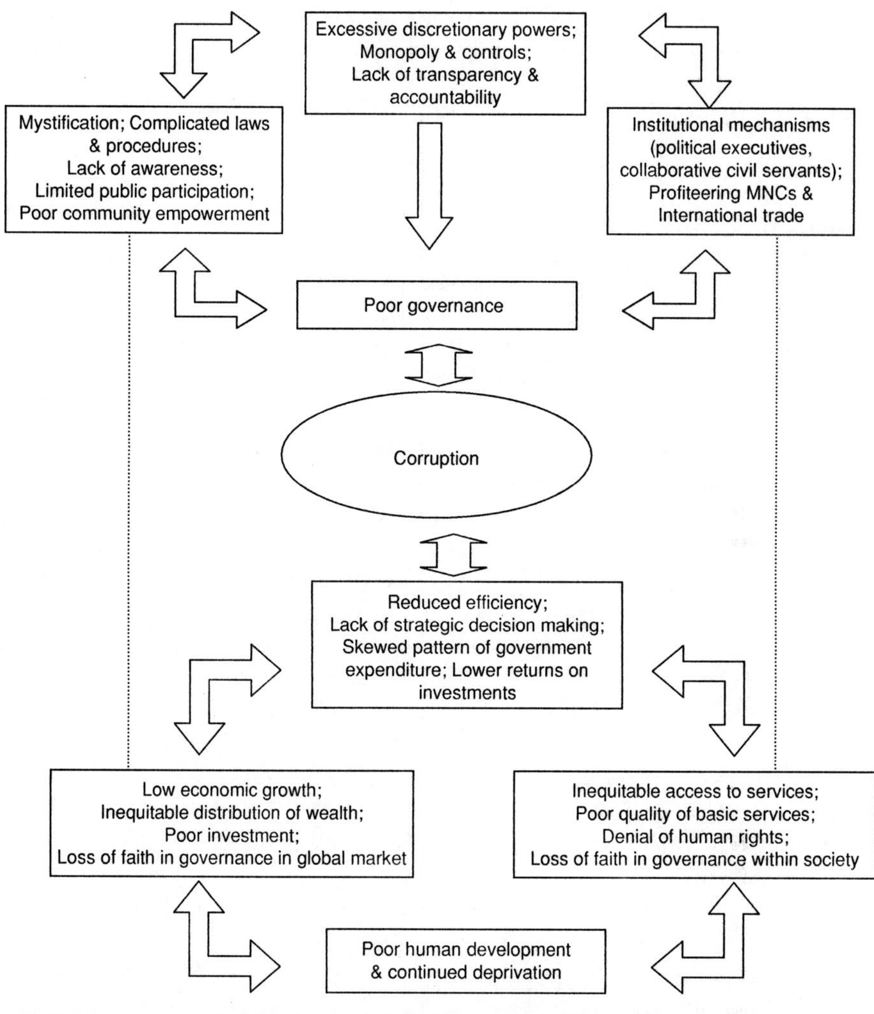

Figure 32.1 Corruption: human deprivation chain.

leadership in governance. The next few sections are devoted to understanding the dimensions of corruption within India so that a model of good governance could be developed with the aim to prevent its proliferation further and curb the existing level to the extent possible. Findings in public administration indicate that corruption can be reduced and contained through appropriate counter measures, but as long as the underlying causes persist, corruption is unlikely to be eliminated altogether. Indeed, as long as human beings are imperfect, corruption will persist (Caiden, 2001, p. 19). According to Indian philosophy, human beings can attempt to be perfect; if they reach the stage of perfection they would be devoid of any imperfection and could be close to divinity. The same is true of nations, as is evident from the CPI of some of the developed countries like Singapore, Australia, and Canada that have indices of 9.4, 8.8, and 8.7, respectively. (Transparency International Report, 2003). None of the countries has a perfect CPI of 10.

Symptoms of Corruption

Corruption means influencing the due process from inside or outside the system for expediting, modifying, or winning a favorable outcome, or depriving the deserving party for a personal gain by those who are in or have access to those in positions of power to take decisions. In a corrupt governing system, the rule of law is substituted by unscrupulous performance, personal whims, fancy, or gratification, serving the private ends of individuals. Caiden has defined corruption as a behavior that deviates from the formal duties of a public role because of private — regarding (personal, close family, private clique) pecuniary or status gains; or that violates rules against the exercise of certain types of private — regarding influence (Caiden, 2001, p. 20). This includes bribery, nepotism, patronage, cronyism, influence peddling, and misappropriation; all of which have an element of intentional deviation from the rule of law for personal gains.

Corruption in public life manifests in different forms at different levels. Major kickbacks in government deals for purchase of items from within or outside the country, *hawala* transactions, money laundering, institutionalized percentage cuts in contracts, seeking free hospitality or accepting valuable gifts or cash as bribe, institutionalized payoffs in lieu of services rendered as a part of government duty, gratifications by different gatekeepers of the institutions, e.g., customs or excise clearances, financial considerations for tax exemptions and reduction, etc., are quite common. Academic institutions, hospitals, other basic services in the government, or otherwise are no exceptions — corruption has impacted all walks of life in India to a greater or lesser degree. From the days of Santhanam committee, it has deepened its roots and expanded its coverage to the extent that a major overhaul of the politico-administrative set up is long overdue. Recruitments, transfers, postings, promotions, and other personnel issues in government service have become major sources of corruption in the state governments. Even the judiciary has been caught in the whirlpool of corruption to the extent that the process of impeachment was initiated against a Supreme Court Judge on charges of corruption. Charges have also been framed against many high court and subordinate court judges. Media and the civil society organizations, the fourth and the fifth organs of governance, have their own share of corruption as well. Possibly, the evil has taken deep roots in the society and is noticeable in different organs of the governance with varying degrees.

Corruption at the cutting edge level is most harmful for the common public. Their day-to-day activities like seeking basic services or amenities are adversely affected. There is often an underhand deal between officials who have the authority to do a job and the touts who take service charge from ordinary men and women to get their job done. It must be noted that the service charge is usually not for a favor but for a legitimate piece of work and is undertaken on a turnkey basis. Unfortunately this has become a way of life, often unquestioned. Whether dealing with development authorities, transport offices, passport offices, police department, or banks, it is the same story for the ordinary citizens, unless they have so-called influence or contacts in the right places. False billing or depriving the government of revenue by collusive sharing of the dues is also common practice. Blackmailing and harassment of the guilty, and sometimes even the innocent by the media or press is another form of corruption. Like cancer, the disease of corruption has spread all over the body of governance.

Causes of Corruption

No country or society allows or promotes corruption in public life as this may put a question mark on the very existence or sustenance of the society. This is why efforts are made to curb corruption. This leads to formation of public institutions and promulgation of statutes to control corruption. For example, CVC in the central government and vigilance cells in the states and union territories (UTs) have been instituted as watchdogs of bureaucracy. Similarly, institutions of Lok Pal in the center and Lokayukta in the state governments have been set up to oversee political corruption. Central Bureau of Investigation (CBI) in the central government and anticorruption cells of the police department in the state governments have been formed to investigate serious charges of corruption by the respective governments. However, despite these institutional arrangements and the statute regarding prevention of corruption, it continues to prosper in the public offices and governance systems. This may be attributed to the "low-risk and high gain" situation offered in the Indian context.

This phenomenon has been explained in Figure 32.2. Risk stands for chances of being caught, and severity of ultimate punishment and gains pertain to the fortunes one makes by involvement in corruption. In low-risk high gain countries like India, where, one, chances of being caught is low, and, two, there are many loopholes and escape routes to get out of the mess if caught, corruption becomes institutionalized and all-pervasive. The limited cases of noncorrupt behavior may be credited more to the individual's moral strength rather than to the institutional control. In a country like Singapore, which is high-risk low gain, incidents of corruption

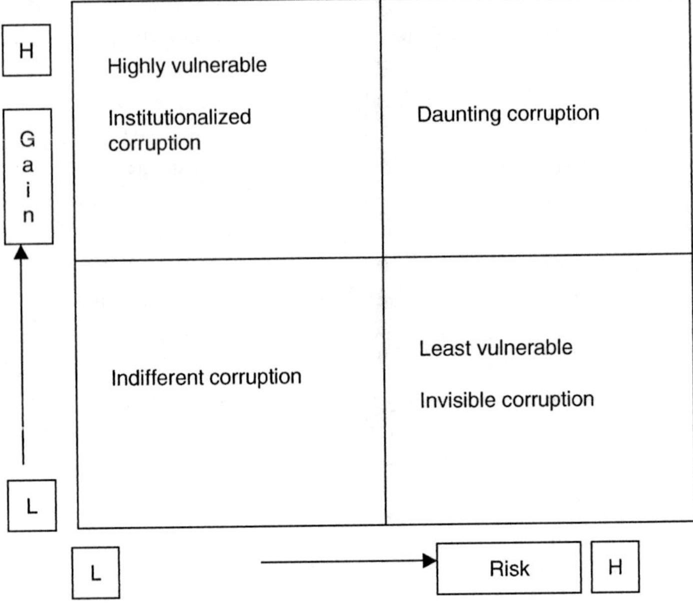

Figure 32.2 Risk versus gain corruption model.

are rare. In high-risk high-gain countries like United States, it is daunting to engage in corruption, and in low-risk low-gain countries like some of sub-Saharan countries, people may become indifferent to corruption, as the stakes are very low.

The major causes of corruption, as discussed in the literature, are presented in the context of India as below.

Economic Causes

Government through its various instruments manages the distribution of valuable economic benefits and imposition of onerous costs to its citizens. Those who are involved in such responsibilities at different levels have wide discretionary powers. This leads to rise of corruption when private gains of those in position of power take precedence over the public good. These causes have been argued very well in the discussion paper on "Corruption and Good Governance" (UNDP, 1997) and have been summarized as under:

1. Payments to equate supply and demand, when state follows dual pricing policy, e.g., through fair price shops, the shopkeepers sell the

products at higher free market price to share the gains with managers of lower price supplies; when the supply and services are scarce, e.g., domestic gas connection, then premium in terms of bribe may allow one to jump the line and get priority service; when supply is in abundance, e.g., issuance of passport or driving license, inordinate delay in delivery breeds corruption; and when the beneficiary is ineligible, gratification is the key consideration for awarding benefit.
2. Payment as incentive to the bureaucracy to get quicker service so that the outcome brings benefits to the citizen.
3. Payment that reduces cost of taxation, levy, or any legal dues by sharing the government dues collusively between the customer and the service provider.
4. Payment to win contracts and concessions from the government.
5. Payment to buy political vote and influences.
6. Payment for favorable judicial decisions.

Sociocultural Causes

In terms of Hofstede's study of sociocultural classifications, the countries with high degree of power distance between public and government and collectivistic culture (rather than individualistic of the West) are more prone to corruption. Societies, which lay high premium on the government service and have less job mobility or have high level of income variations and low per capita income may experience higher level of corruption. Also, sociological changes with the acquisitive consumerist culture gradually engulfing the erstwhile values of austerity, "simple living high thinking"; disappearing social sanctions and ostracism against those who earn fortunes overnight; growing dowry demands; and higher costs of education for children are other driving factors for corruption (Muhar, 1997).

Political Causes

Democratic representative forms of governments have periodic or mid-term elections to get the people's mandate for governance. Electioneering process involves large-scale expenditure and is a breeding ground for corruption. The electorate or those who may win votes are bribed by the politicians to assure electoral victory. Short tenure of legislatures due to unstable coalition governments and quick successive elections in states and center in last two decades has made it worse. Further, the process of governance is by the majority, and, therefore, instances have surfaced where the legislatures have been bribed to vote in favor or abstain from voting on floor of the parliament house.

Ethico-Religious Causes

Corruption is seen as an ethical mistake for which one may be exonerated by bribing gods through donations to temples, offerings, and other services. This provides not only rationalization for those engaged in corruption but also justification to those who seek favors from the demigods or representatives of power, to bypass institutional arrangements by unfair means.

Administrative Causes

The cumbersome procedures leading to red tape and unreasonable delays, high level of individual discretion, lack of transparency, lack of awareness among citizens, mysticism of government processes and procedures, and low level of fear of delayed disciplinary proceedings with various loopholes and escape routes are some of the major administrative causes of corruption.

Psychological Causes

Human beings are fallible. In a corrupt environment it takes lot of courage and moral strength to avoid temptation. Some may give up to the peer pressure as they do not want to appear as losers in the eyes of their family or friends. They are sucked into corrupt conduct against their will and better judgment simply because there seems no advantage to sticking it out (Caiden, 2001, p. 23).

All the above causes are quite pertinent in the context of India and needs to be pondered for designing a model for good governance. Briefly, the causes can be condensed into the following mathematical formulation:

$$\text{Corruption} = \text{Discretion} + \text{Mystification} - \text{Accountability}$$

Here, accountability means answerability for one's actions or behavior (Dwivedi, 2002b, p. 20) in terms of constitutional, legal, institutional procedural rules and regulations, or other instruments of public governance. This constitutes five elements: efficiency, effectiveness, economy, equity, and ethics. More the accountability, less the corruption but more the discretion and mystification (i.e., long drawn procedures with lack of clarity or scope for multiple interpretations), more the corruption.

Impact of Corruption

Unchecked corruption leads to "softness of the state" (Nossiter, 1970) comprising of all manners of social indiscipline that prevents effective governance and obstructs national development (Myrdal, 1970). The impacts may be briefly described under the following heads:

Reduced Economic Growth

Corruption bypasses competition and merit and leads to less than the best for the economy. It drains the exchequer of scarce financial resources as the kickbacks and payoffs are accounted for as hidden cost in the contract. Even the quality is compromised. The world has witnessed the so-called growing tigers or south-east Asian economies collapsing in mid-1997 as a result of corruption and crony capitalism. N. Mittal, the then Chief Vigilance Commissioner of India, has quoted 1999 human development report for South Asia saying that if India's corruption level comes down to that of Scandinavian countries, then India's GDP growth rate will grow by 1.5 percent and FDI will grow by 12 percent (Mittal, 2002). For a developing country like India, which has to muster resources to provide minimum essential services to its population for better quality of life, the resources drained out of the system through corrupt means cause a very heavy burden, for which the price is paid by the poor. Figure 32.3 illustrates how effective plugging of leakages may result in enhanced resources, and therefore may reduce costs on loan repayments.

Lower Social Development

Investments in social sectors like education, health, social security, etc., are less rewarding to those involved in corruption than the ones in business, commerce, industry, defense, or infrastructure. This affects adversely not only the allocations on the social sector but also the so-called public image in terms of job-seeking behavior of politicians and bureaucrats. The consequences are poor development of social infrastructure and, therefore, poor human development. The chairman of Transparency International, in his report, dated October 7, 2003, mentions that if corruption is allowed to

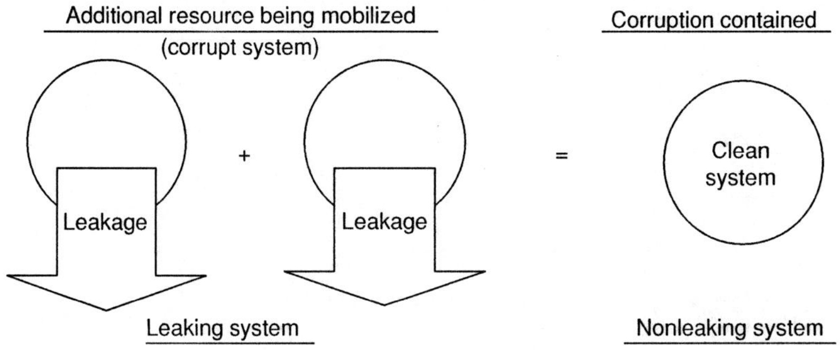

Figure 32.3 Illustration of stopping corruption means adding resources.

flourish unchecked, more children will suffer from lack of clean water and lack of medicines, and will go to schools with no books (Transparency International Report, 2003).

Increased Crime

Corruption allows immunity for criminal acts so much so that the law is for sale to the higher bidder (Sherman, 1978). Criminals are able to defy the legal consequences of their action by intimidating the public, who are the sufferers or influencing the law enforcing agencies by means of corruption. Links have been uncovered of *hawala* transactions being utilized for terrorist or other antisocial activities. Criminals seek patronage of those in positions of power and perpetrate crimes and acts of terror that harm the common people. Studies show nexus between criminals, politicians, and bureaucrats, which is dangerous for all-round development of a country.

Increased Poverty

Corruption impacts the poor the most. Those who are rich, are able to reduce their burden of direct taxes through collusive sharing of dues with the tax collecting authorities, leading to increased indirect taxes, which are shared by the poor. This has been illustrated in Figure 32.4.

Therefore, the poor are affected adversely not only by poor social and economic development but also by the transfer of burden of taxes from the rich to them.

How to Control Corruption

Many strategies have been attempted and recorded in literature with varying degrees of success. Because of human weaknesses, corruption cannot

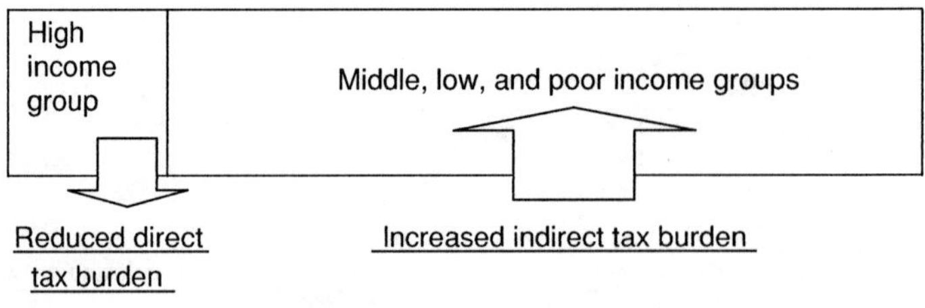

Figure 32.4 Transfer of tax burden from rich to poor due to corruption.

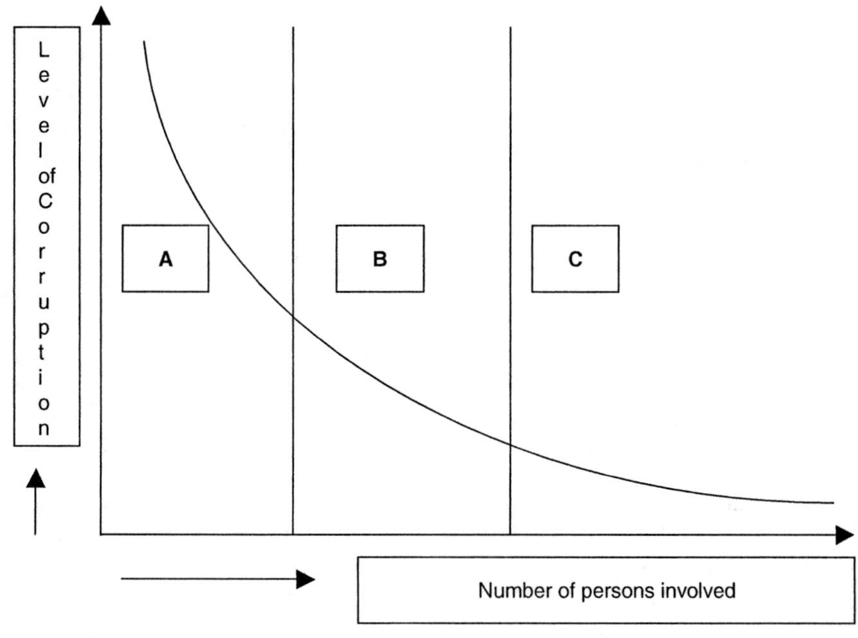

Figure 32.5 Pareto's ABC analysis.

be rooted out altogether but can be contained to a great extent so that it neither retards growth and development of the country nor pinches the citizens in their daily life. Wherever corruption has expanded its roots deep down in the system and has become all pervasive, the strategy should be to focus on eradication of corruption from the A class deceivers of the systems before the other classes are touched upon. According to Pareto's principle (illustrated in Figure 32.5), 15–20 percent of corrupt people, categorized as A, are responsible for 60–70 percent of the corruption; 60–70 percent of such people, categorized as C, are responsible for 15–20 percent of the corruption; and 20–30 percent, categorized as B, are responsible for 20–30 percent of corruption. Targeting category A yields best results as not only major corrupters are cleansed, but also the efforts have salutary effect on B and C, as they may withdraw from corrupt practices out of fear.

Government policy can control the risks and benefits of corruption. The anticorruption policy can increase the benefits of being honest, increase the probability of detection, provide safety to whistle blowers, enhance the speed of punishing the guilty, and make heavy punishments and penalties to reduce and eradicate opportunities of corrupt behavior from governance. The following include key methodologies for combating corruption.

Political Will

In a democratic system of governance, political will from the highest level is absolutely critical for the success of anticorruption campaign. This will cleanse the political setup and will have moral strength to deal with bureaucratic corruption. This will also break the politico-administrative collusion to plunder the state with low risk. High-morality based politics of Mahatma Gandhi could be a motivator. This can make the institutions like CBI, CVC, Lok Pal, Lokayukta, and other anticorruption bodies more effective. The tenants of Gandhi's teachings should be emphasized at all levels of trainings for the bureaucrats.

Judicial Activism

Even though judiciary has not been left untouched by corruption, higher-level judiciary, which has constitutional protection, may set the motion to deal with corruption heavily through public interest litigations (PIL) or other ways. Indian system of governance gives prominence to judiciary with their authority to interpret constitution and review the decisions of legislatures and executives. They can be instrumental in bringing probity in public life of all organs of governance including themselves.

Procedural Simplification

Too many laws, complicated procedures, multiple levels of clearances, multilevel approvals, and no set time limit and accountability provide enough scope to harass and extract private gains from the public. Under ongoing administrative reforms many things have been simplified and power of information technology (IT) has been utilized to bring transparency in the system, yet this is the beginning, and a long journey has to be covered to ensure compliance with Citizens' Charter and full transparency in all government and non-government dealings with public. Computerization of railway reservation system is a major success story in India and has given great relief to the public. Some of the institutions have improved competitiveness by incorporating web-based tendering system with open procedures and availability of status online. Such good practices must be documented and shared widely.

Accountability of Executives

Strengthening institutional checks and balances, improving vigilance enforcement measures, reforming civil services at different levels with emphasis on moral content, recognizing integrity and honesty as virtues in service, enhancing compensation package to make it lucrative to retain honest personnel, etc., may bring accountability at all levels. A sense of vocation and public service must be instilled unequivocally among the civil servants with proper carrot and stick policy. The belief holds that government is a public trust and working for the government is public service that demands highest level of integrity and behavior that exhibit such virtues as honesty, impartiality, sincerity, and justice. Further, it is equally desirable that the conduct of public administrators should be beyond reproach; that they should perform their duties loyally, efficiently, and economically (Dwivedi, 1995). Speedy disposal of disciplinary proceedings and severity of punishment may bring fear among defaulters.

Role of Media

Media can play a double-edged role. On the one hand, the press can expose the corrupt and guilty bureaucrats and politicians, and on the other, it may get involved in yellow journalism and help corruption prosper through collusive blackmailing. A vigilant judicial system may keep a check on this.

Role of Social Activists and Civil Society Organizations

Social activists and civil society organizations (CSOs) may play an important role in educating the public of their rights and legal status on different matters so that public may demand the services with authority rather than with fear or servility. Such individuals and organizations may expose the corrupt and create public pressure or initiate judicial action against the guilty. Recently a large-scale collusive government stamps scandal in many states in India was busted on behest of Baba Amte, a social activist in Maharastra. This led to resignation of political personalities, arrests of senior police officers, including the police commissioner of Mumbai and officers of other central and state governments. CBI is investigating the widespread corruption trail.

Demystification and Public Awareness

Opening of the system to bring transparency in dealings and improving public awareness is crucial for arresting corruption. Holding government agencies accountable to the public is to some extent a matter of institutional design and internal checks and balances, but ultimately, it is the people whom government supposedly serves who are responsible for monitoring its performance and demanding responsive behavior (Fukuyama, 2004,

p. 30). The introduction of Citizen's Charter to help change the mindset of the public officials from someone with power over the public to someone with a care of duty toward them (*A Guide to Developing and Implementing a Citizen's Charter*, 2003), and information communication technology (ICT) based transparent provision of services may help in limiting corrupt practices.

Strategic Targets

As discussed earlier, the efforts should be concentrated on A-class corrupters, who may include politicians, senior level bureaucrats, and law enforcers. Sometimes, when a new government takes over, being very enthusiastic and concerned about its electoral promises of clean government, it may initiate action against corruption but, in the process, all its energy gets wasted on C-class corrupters, which does not yield any perceptible change and any improvement is short-lived. Targeting the strategic component may put the law enforcement agencies on guard, leading to protection of law-compliant citizens, and uniform, fearless, and unprejudiced enforcement. This may do much to clean the rest of the governance system and bring sustainable changes in attitude and practice.

India is a very large country with wide-ranging regional and intraregional variations. Therefore, it may not be possible to conceive of one single universally applicable model of good governance for the entire country. Attempts have been made by different wings and institutions of the government in different states as well as by the central governments to incorporate best practices in governance with varying results. The country has many successes in public administration reforms, which may be shared within the country as well as with the outside world. Computerization of railways and airlines reservation system has shown the path of how intervention of IT can make a big difference in public convenience and help reduce malpractices. The introduction of electronic voting machines (EVMs) and photo identity cards, i.e., use of technology, for elections has brought major reforms in the electioneering process. Civil services reforms have been introduced to catch up with the western NPM model, but such reforms did not yield expected results. Administrative restructuring and reforms must address first, either directly or indirectly, the question of indigenous style, values, and culture of governance (Nef, 1998).

In Search of Good Governance

In India, concern for good governance and effectiveness of the state machinery has a long tradition as exemplified in an earlier section. The federal government has been keenly aware of such a need by appointing several committees and commissions of administrative reforms. Immediately after two years of India becoming a democratic federal republic, the first prime minister, Jawaharlal Nehru, wrote a letter to all his provincial chief ministers in March 1951 advising them that the objectives of nation-building can be achieved only when there is "a clean, impartial and efficient administration in every sector of public activity" (Nehru, 1986, p. 353). Even the first five-year plan (1952–1957) with Nehru as its chairman, recognized that there has been the "decline in the standards of administration which has taken place during the past few years" (Nehru, 1986, p. 113), and the nurturing of democratic institutions "call for a consciousness of social purpose, courage to stand by principles, and restraint in the exercise of authority (India, 1952, p. 123). Thus, it was no surprise when the tenth five-year plan (2002–2007) devoted a special place on the topic of good governance.

Federal Government Plan for Good Governance — The Tenth Five-Year Plan

Chapter 6 of Tenth Five-Year Plan (2002–07) document is devoted to governance and implementation (India, 2002). The opening paragraph mentions that "the issue of governance has in the recent times emerged at the forefront of the development agenda. Good governance is one of the most crucial factors required if the targets of the tenth plan are to be achieved. It is also this factor, or rather lack of it, which could be the cause of missed development opportunities." After listing few instances of poor governance and describing the current global dynamic scenario, the plan document proposes an alternate model of governance wherein the stress is on three elements: institutions, formal or informal to bring about predictability, stability, and efficiency in managing social, economic, or political transactions; delivery mechanisms, including the executive apparatus adopted or evolved to achieve the objectives of the institutions; and supportive and subordinate framework of legislations, rules, and procedures, for efficient implementation of the goals set for the institutions. The model stresses on continuous improvement and adaptation to the latest global changes. It also proposes bringing in synergy in the system so that resources are utilized optimally and the benefits are maximized.

The document stresses that corruption is the most endemic and entrenched manifestation of poor governance in the Indian society, so much so that it has almost become an accepted reality and a way of life. Public servants, who enjoy monopoly and discretionary power without any or limited accountability, seek and charge any price for the services rendered by them. The plan outlines 16 strategies for improving the Indian governance system. These strategies incorporate measures for systems reforms, people's empowerment, activation of civil societies, civil services reforms, adoption of project approach, bringing synergy through effective monitoring and coordination, judicial reforms, and effective use of IT in bringing transparency in the process of governance. Through the next few paragraphs, the authors propose two approaches in search of good governance for India.

Beyond Corruption: Approaches Needed in Search of Good Governance

India is a multireligious and multicultural society. Irrespective of cultural, ethnic, or religious backgrounds austerity, penance, renunciation of worldly goods, simple living high thinking, etc., were cherished values in the Indian system. Elderly, knowledgeable, and wise people were highly respected in the society — for their worth and not physical possession. Those who made quick fortunes were suspected and ostracized if it was known that they adopted unethical means. With economic transition and growing consumerism such virtues have gradually lost value and material acquisitions have gained much more significance than in the past.

A prevalent belief especially among the Hindus has been that a life of austerity and good values not only improves the prospect for the next birth but also may help in achieving salvation or emancipation from the cycle of birth, death, and rebirth. These values are fast getting forgotten by an emerging generation that lives for the now and are much more concerned about the comforts of this life than the next, which they rationalize, may not even exist. Although the Hindu religion is much less organized than many other popular religions of the world, its presence in the day-to-day life of men, women, and even children has been significant. With a change in lifestyle, aspirations and values, as spiritual values lose their significance, the feeling of guilt is strong, often reflected in the newfound obsession with religious symbolism and ritualism even among the educated. Religion has suddenly moved out from the private domain to the public as the need to be seen as spiritual and religious is paramount. There is, however, little attempt to purify the soul, which is considered part of the *Brahman*, the ultimate God.

The revival of the deep-rooted values, which once governed the lives and choices that people made, is critical. It is high time those values are resurrected but with suitable modifications that make them acceptable and relevant today. Living in the past and consistent reference to the good old days may yield no result. Religious institutions and schools can take a lead role in inculcating these ethical standards in the Indian population using modern approaches and methods. The process may take time but may yield lasting results.

There is growing cynicism that corruption has become a way of life and is inevitable. The situation and the feeling among masses today is well captured in the *Ramcharitmanas,* a great epic of India written by Tulsidass as, "*Kou nrip hou hamahi kaa haanii, Cheri chhari aba hoba ki ranii,*" i.e., it does not matter who governs because my status as a servant will never change to a queen (Tulsidas, *Shri Ramcharitamanasa*, Book 2, Ayodhya-Kanda, Doha 16). This kind of public apathy may be a harbinger of the death of democracy. However, this also shows that such phases of public indifference and unhappiness have existed in the past but have subsequently undergone change. One way to effectively countering this kind of cynicism is to support those in the society who are called champions of good governance. As is well known, the inevitable becomes intolerable, the moment it is perceived to be no more inevitable. A movement led by champions can have a multiplier cascading effect reviving optimism in the society. A strong political leadership constituted of leaders who are and look real and therefore worthy of being emulated is, no doubt, the need of the hour. Leaders, who can promote a strong value system contextualized to the realities of the everyday life of people and who can practice exemplary behavior themselves, can spearhead a change toward *rajdharma* or dharmic government, as was envisaged by the framers of Indian constitution. To usher good governance, the governmental administration and its officials (including elected members of government), two basic approaches are needed: the ethical and spirituality or deontology-based governance.

Educating Public Servants to Serve — The Ethical Approach

Conflicts of responsibility that individuals experience within public organizations should not be resolved in an idiosyncratic fashion. For an organization to keep the bureaucratic machine in the service of the public, rather than to itself or to special interests, values, and principles essential to democratic political community must provide constant points of reference from beyond the boundaries. If public administrators are to behave in a manner that is responsive to the wishes of a democratic citizenry, it is essential that policies be established that guide their general course of conduct toward the serving of the public interest. These policies should enforce and reenforce prescribed public service values (Cooper, 1982, p. xiv).

The basis of moral, legitimate, and effective government is public trust and confidence. This is based on the belief that the state is a moral entity whose actions and policies are, and should be, liable to ethical and moral judgment. Government is a public trust, and public service is a noble calling for persons who should know how to behave morally. However, this assertion has certain implications. Are public officials aware of the ethical implications of the power they exercise? What values should they choose in the exercise of their responsibilities? It is essential that policies be established which guide, and ultimately control, their general course of conduct toward the serving of the public interest. These policies should enforce and reenforce prescribed public service values. There must be enough control from outside the individual to discourage those inclinations toward indulgence of self-interest, but enough internal control to encourage the most socially constructive idealistic, altruistic, and creative impulses to flourish. The balance of controls is essential for the fully responsible conduct of the public sector (Dwivedi, 1988b, p. 237).

The implication of the difficulty in defining ethical issues for training sessions or classroom instructions is that it is essential to spend considerable time working on it in a variety of ways before asking participants to develop the full range of steps leading to a final resolution of the issues as discussed. A course on public service ethics should be approached from three dimensions: (a) classical; (b) legal; and (c) environmental. The classical approach emphasizes drawing from the philosophical and cultural traditions of a nation. The legal approach focuses on laws, rules and regulations, and constraints on individuals to regulate their administrative power and authority. The environmental approach aims as sensitizing public servants to the need to act as guardians of the state, somewhat akin to Plato's philosopher kings. In addition, the approach drawing from the administrative culture and bureaucratic morality of a nation focuses on case studies and actual problems (Dwivedi, 1988a, pp. 124–125).

Educating the officials of public sector is the first step; however, one must keep in mind that moral ambiguities are going to remain because no one can formulate policies that are morally justified under all circumstances. It is important, therefore, that those formulating, implementing, and evaluating policies be made aware of these ambiguities and be ethically sensitive so as to act in a responsible manner. Ambiguity does not diminish the importance of the issue; the moral dimension of governance represents a concern for the quality of public service and governmental conduct. Otherwise how can citizens trust that their affairs are justly managed and that they have not surrendered rights and freedoms to an irresponsible administrative state?

Morality in the public service does not mean that one should exhibit negative obligations such as to do no harm, or to keep out of trouble; on the contrary, the notions of governmental ethics suggest that administrators actively undertake acts that are socially just. Only by proactively pursuing social justice can the official and the government be moral and just. Administrators need personally to exercise positive moral judgment in their duties by demonstrating the highest standards of personal integrity, honesty, fairness, and justice, public officials can inspire confidence and trust which are the key ingredients of a moral government (Dwivedi, 1987b, p. 318).

All government acts, if they are to serve the present and future generations well, must be measured against some higher law. That law cannot be secular law because it is limited in vision as it is framed by imperfect people in their limited capacities and therefore limited in vision. The law has to be, perforce, based on the principles of higher spiritual and philosophical foundations. Administrative theology is one such foundation that can provide an important base to a moral and responsible statecraft (Dwivedi, 1987a, p. 708).

The Spirituality-Based Approach

Spirituality can lead to mastery over our basic impulses such as greed, exploitation, abuse of power, and mistreatment of people. It requires self-discipline, humility, and above all, the absence of arrogance in holding public office. Furthermore, it enables people to center their values on the notion that there is a cosmic ordinance and divine law, which must be maintained. Spirituality serves as both a model and an operative strategy for the transformation of human character by strengthening the genuine, substantive will to serve the common people. Spiritually oriented public officials know that their duties enable them to serve others. In so doing, spirituality will be fulfilling two duties: one to the self, whereby one seeks inner strength through spiritual action, and the other to the community-at-large, whereby one works for the common good. As such, personal spirituality and character regulate human conduct and cast individuals into the right character mold by inculcating them with spiritual, social, and moral virtues, and thereby strengthening the ethos that hold the social and moral fabric of a society together, by maintaining order in society, building individual and group character, and giving rise to harmony and understanding (Dwivedi, 2002a, p. 48).

As has been documented in India's tenth five-year plan, corruption has emerged as major concern in the development of the country. As human beings are fallible, it may not be realistic to think that this can be eradicated altogether but it can be contained to a great extent to allow the gains of rapid growth and development to percolate to the masses in rural as well as urban areas. The administrative and political system needs chemotherapy to get rid of this cancerous disease. A concerted effort and strong political will may be required from the leadership at various levels of the society but specially those at the top. Many electoral reforms have been introduced in the last decade to cleanse the political set up, but still a long journey has to be covered before the country witnesses morally strong and nationally committed leadership inspired by the Gandhian philosophy.

Dwivedi (2005) has discussed four models: (i) public service model, the classical concept of civil services reforms; (ii) judicial model, the approach of improving enforcement; (iii) NPM model, the approach of introducing business management principles in governance; and (iv) deontological or morality-driven model, based on inculcating highest values of public service with spiritual and ethical drives like sacrifice, compassion, justice, etc. In the case of India a mix of these models as has been discussed earlier could be suitable. The country has a deep-rooted culture inspired by spiritualism that could become a via media for reversal of societal degradation. As has been argued, spiritual and educational content may make the job of a reformer easier and give sustenance to the change. On the basis of this, a model for good governance is being proposed as shown in Figure 32.6.

Under this model, judiciary has to play a vital role in cleaning up political as well as executive system and also to keep an eye on the other two organs of governance. Mass media, civil society, and a network of champions may play major roles in developing public awareness and controlling corruption. The system will ensure ten core values of democratic governance and will be driven by spiritualism and ethical behavior. For achieving this, a strong benevolent and charismatic effective leader with strategic vision such as Lee Kuan Yew, ex-premier of Singapore, may be needed to lead from the front. Alternatively all political parties may shed their differences on this nationally important issue and take a conscious decision to launch a national campaign against corruption from public life and that may be effective under the present-day era of coalition politics. The current level of public indifference to the governance is due to long drawn fatigue and any change would be welcome. Fed up with bad governance and the nuisance of corruption, the public at large may be willing to join or support any realistic movement against it led by worthy leaders.

Concluding Observations

Governance involves mechanisms, processes, and institutions, through which people articulate their interests, exercise their rights, meet their obligations, and mediate their differences. The characteristics of good governance include core values of rule of law, fairness, equity, participation, transparency, responsiveness, consensus, economy, efficiency and effectiveness, and above all impeccable accountability. As people are the source of all power in a democracy, accountability to people is the hallmark of democratic governance (Mohanty et al., 2004). Corruption in public

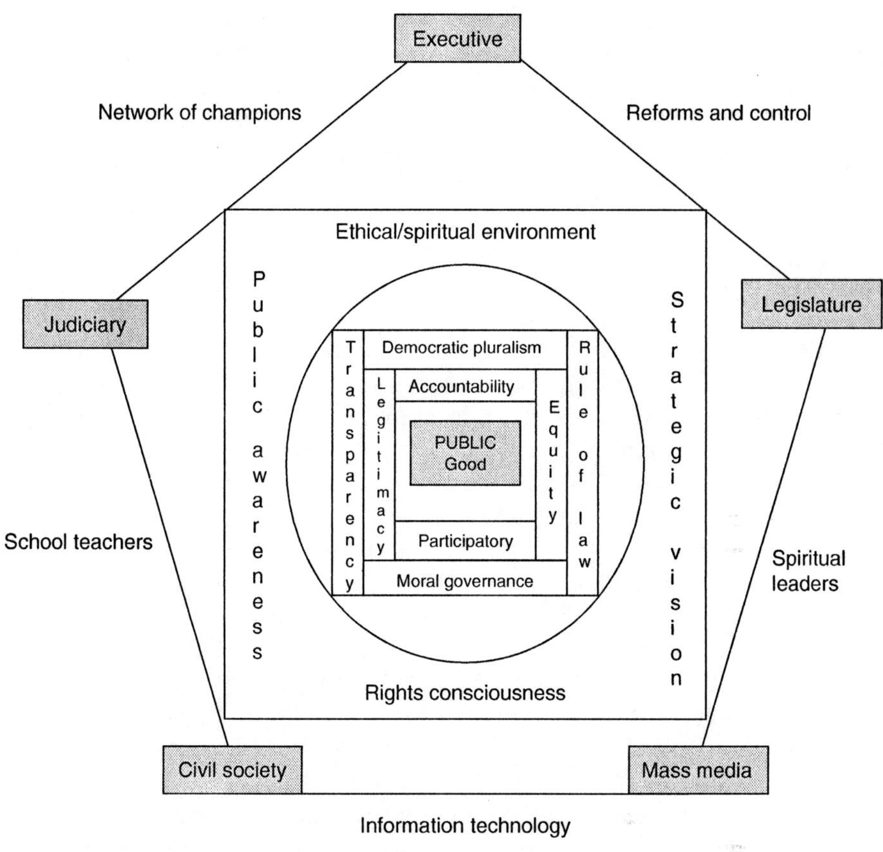

Figure 32.6 A model of good governance for India.

institutions has adversely affected good governance. Human beings have weaknesses; and it can be argued that no system can be free of human-made vices; yet many countries have shown successful transition from poor governance to good governance. Singapore is one such example in India's vicinity. With strong dedicated leadership, the country has covered a long journey to attain the CPI of 9.4 with fifth rank among 133 countries globally (Transparency International Report, 2003).

Because of a range of diversities in the Indian society, there cannot be one single model of good governance for the entire country. The Western concept of "only one size fits all" may not work well in the domain of public administration. The approach will have to be suitably married to local administrative as well as societal practices, culture, and values. However, spiritualism and deep-rooted cultural values are the core strengths of the society and a common thread across social, economic, and religious groups. The model discussed in the paper draws its concept from this and uses modern day developments in technology, especially ICT to bring transparency and accountability in the system. The present Finance Minister of India, P. Chidambaram, called upon the states the union territories to improve their governance and share the best practices with each other in the conclave of "the state of States" organized by *India Today* group, a leading media house (*India Today*, 2004, p. 82). He said, "we produce the best teachers and doctors and yet we have high dropouts and poor medical care. Only good governance can be the answer to this riddle."

India can improve its CPI with a multipronged approach wherein conscious efforts for cleansing of the society as well as politico-administrative system may bring dividends. It is important that the holders of public offices take up moral responsibility for all the wrongs under their commands and are accountable for all their actions. By deflecting responsibilities, consequences cannot disappear. Nothing is more damaging to the public trust than justifying fraud and deception in the name of national security, public interest, government's needs, or nation-building. Such moral leadership must start from the top and percolate downwards. Its absence breeds cynicism, and generates tolerance of hypocrisy, greed, and self-indulgence (Dwivedi, 2005). The external control methods may yield temporary results; but unless the fear of consequences for indulging in corruption is very high compared to expected gains, and the same persists for long time to make attitudinal changes, the tenacity of corruption will bring it back to the same level quickly. No matter how comprehensive the rules and procedures to check the abuse of power and authority are made, corrupt people will invent the means to bend the rules or use legal loopholes to engage in unethical activities (Dwivedi, 2002b, p. 21). This is precisely the reason why longlasting changes in the society and governing systems through emphasis on core cultural strengths of the country has been argued in the model for India. The call by the president of India, A.P.J. Abdul Kalam, in his address to the conclave on "the state of States" organized by *India Today* group in Delhi, for "having the conviction that nation is above all" (*India Today*, 2004, p. 82) is crucial for the country to progress and make a difference in the world.

References

A Guide to Developing and Implementing a Citizen's Charter (2003). Hyderabad, India: Centre for Good Governance.

Caiden, G.E. (2001). "Corruption and governance." In G.E. Caiden, O.P. Dwivedi and J. Jabbra (eds.) *Where Corruption Lives*. Connecticut: Kumarian Press, 19 pp.

Cooper, T.L. (1982). The responsible administrator: an approach to ethics for the administrative role. Port Washington, NY: Kennikat Press.

D'Souza, J.B. (1992). "Urban rules, regulations: myth and reality." *Survey of the Environment 1992. The Hindu*, pp. 54–55.

Dwivedi, O.P. (1982). "On holding public servants accountable." In O.P. Dwivedi (ed.) *The Administrative State in Canada.* Toronto, Canada: University of Toronto Press, pp. 151–175.

Dwivedi, O.P. (1987a). "Moral dimensions of statecraft: a plea for an administrative theology." *Canadian Journal of Political Science*, 20(4): 699–709.

Dwivedi, O.P. (1987b). "A comparative analysis of ethics, public policy, and the public service." In J. Bowman and F. Elliston (eds.) *Ethics Government and Public Policy: A Reference Guide.* New York: Greenwood Press, pp. 307–318.

Dwivedi, O.P. (1988a). "Teaching ethics in public administration courses." *International Review of Administrative Studies*, 54: 115–130.

Dwivedi, O.P. (1988b) "Bureaucratic morality: concluding comments." *International Political Science Review*, 9(3): 231–239.

Dwivedi, O.P. (1988c). "Where the future begins." Convocation Address by O.P. Dwivedi on the Occasion of the Award of the Honorary LL.D. University of Lethbridge, Alberta, May 27, 1988.

Dwivedi O.P. (1995). "Reflections on moral government and public service as a vocation." *Indian Journal of Public Administration*, 41(3): 296–306.

Dwivedi, O.P. (1997). *India's Environmental Policies, Programmes and Stewardship.* London: Macmillan Press.

Dwivedi, O.P. (2001). "The challenges of cultural diversity for good governance." A Presentation Made at the *ad hoc* Expert Group Meeting of the United Nations, New York, May 3–4, 2001.

Dwivedi, O.P. (2002a). "Challenges in public administration in developing nations." In G. Bertucci and M. Duggett (eds.) *Turning World: Globalization and Governance at the Start of the 21*st *Century.* Amsterdam: OS Press , pp. 47–48.

Dwivedi, O.P. (2002b). "The challenges of cultural diversity for good governance." *The Indian Journal of Public Administration*, XLVIII(1): 14–28.

Dwivedi, O.P. (2002c). "On common good and good governance: an alternative approach." In D. Olowu and S. Sako (eds.) *Better Governance and Public Policy.* Bloomfield, CT: Kumarian Press, p. 43.

Dwivedi, O.P. (2005). "Good governance in a multi-cultural world: oceans apart yet world together." In J.G. Jabbra and O.P. Dwivedi (eds.) *Administrative Culture in a Global Context.* Toronto, Canada: de Sitters Publishers, pp. 271–290.

Dwivedi, O.P. and Jain, R.B. (1985). *India's Administrative State.* New Delhi: Gitanjali Publishing House.

Frederickson, H.G. (1997). *The Spirit of Public Administration*, San Francisco, CA: Jossey-Bass Publishers, p. 86.

Fukuyama, F. (2004). *State Building: Governance and World Order in the 21st Century.* New York: Cornell University Press, p. 30.

Hardgrave, R.L. and Kochanek, S.A. (2000). *India: Government and Politics in a Developing Nation*, 6th edition. Fort Worth, TX: Harcourt College Publishers, p. 106.

Hyden, G. and Court, J. (2002). "Comparing governance across countries and over time: conceptual challenges." In D. Olowu and S. Sako (eds.) *Better Governance and Public Policy*. Bloomfield, CT: Kumarian Press, pp. 13–33.

India (1993). *Environment Action Programme: India*. New Delhi, Ministry of Environment and Forests.

India Today (August 23, 2004). Published in Delhi, India.

India, Planning Commission (1952). *The First Five Year Plan (1952–57)*. New Delhi: Publication Division, Government of India.

India, Planning Commission (2002). *Tenth Five-Year Plan (2002–07)*. New Delhi: Publication Division, Government of India.

Mahabharata, Shanti Parva, Rajdharmanushasan, Chapter 85, Verses 16–17, Gorakhpur, India: Gita Press.

Maheshwari, S.R. (2000). *Public Administration in India*. Delhi: Macmillan India.

Mittal, N. (2002). "Corruption in public life: steps to improve India's image." Text of the Speech of the Chief Vigilance Commissioner of India delivered on February 14, 2002, at BASF, Mumbai, India.

Mohanty, P.K., Jones, K. and Rao, S.J. (2004). *Good Governance Initiatives in Andhra Pradesh 2003*, Hyderabad, India: Centre for Good Governance.

Muhar, P.S. (1997). "Corruption in public services in India." In V. Grover (ed.) *Indian Political System: Trends and Challenges*. New Delhi: Deep & Deep Publications, pp. 240–241.

Myrdal, G. (1970). *The Challenge of World Poverty: A World Anti-Poverty Programme in Outline*. New York: Pantheon Books.

Narang, A.S. (1996). *Indian Government and Politics*. New Delhi: Gitanjali Publishing House, p. 42.

Nef, J. (1998). "Administrative culture in Latin America: historical and structural outline." *Africanus, Journal of Development Administration*, 28(2): 19–32.

Nehru, J. (1986). In G. Parthasarathi (ed.) *Jawaharlal Nehru — Letters to Chief Ministers: 1947–1964*, vol. 2. New Delhi: Publications Division, Government of India.

Nossiter, B.D. (1970). *Soft State: A Newspaperman's Chronicle of India*. New York: Harper and Row.

OECD (1982). *Aid and Environment Protection: Ten Years after Stockholm*, Paris: OECD Development Committee.

Sausman, C. and Locke, R. (2004). "The British civil service: examining the question of politicization." In B. Guy Peters and J. Pierre (eds.) *Politicization of Civil Service in Comparative Perspective*. London: Routledge, pp. 101–138.

Saxena, N.C. (2004). "Improving programme delivery." Seminar (New Delhi, India), (541): 49–54.

Sherman, L.W. (1978). *Scandal and Reform: Controlling Police Corruption*. Berkeley, CA: University of California Press.

Symon, Y.R. (1993). *Philosophy of Democratic Government*. Notre Dame: University of Notre Dame Press.

Taub, Richard P. (1969). Bureaucrats under stress: administrators and administration in an Indian state Berkley, CA: University of California Press.

Transparency International Report (2003). http://www.transparency.org/cpi/index.html, the Web site of Transparency International.

UNDP (1997) Discussion Paper 3 on "Corruption and good governance" prepared by Management Development and Governance Division, Bureau of Public Policy and Programme Support, New York: UNDP, July 1997.

UNESCAP (2004). http://www.unescap.org, the Web site of United Nations Economic and Social Commission for Asia & Pacific (UNESCAP), Bangkok, Thailand.

United Nations General Assembly (1997). "Resolution 51/58: Action Against Corruption," A/RES/59, January 28, 1997.

World Bank (1992). *Governance and Development: The World Development Report.* Washington, D.C.: The World Bank.

World Bank (1994). *The World Development Report.* Washington, D.C.: The World Bank.

VII

GLOBALIZATION: COMPARATIVE, DEVELOPMENT AND GLOBAL PUBLIC ADMINISTRATION

Chapter 33

Transnational Corporations, Development, and Underdevelopment

Bjørn Letnes[1]

CONTENTS

Corporations became increasingly transnational — even global — in reach as today's advanced industrialized countries (the first world) gradually developed from national economies into one global economy. Many late

[1]I thank Jonathon Moses for his extensive comments and support, and I would also like to thank the participants of the Ph.D. and the IPE forum at NTNU for their annotations.

developers (the third world) faced — and still face — the prospect of a similar development in an environment where the corporations of the first world are penetrating their economies to varying degrees. A question that has divided development theorists for decades is whether the activity of transnational corporations (TNCs) breeds development or underdevelopment in the third world. Two rich and vibrant theoretical traditions with a contradictory view on the effect of TNC investment have argued their case for decades. However, there is a sign of reconsolidation in the literature, as a synthesized theoretical framework is emerging — one based on the implicit assumptions of conflicting traditions in development theory. This literature highlights the importance of context, and stress that both development and underdevelopment are plausible outcomes. The activities of some TNCs are conducive to development whereas the activities of others are not, and some host countries have characteristics favorable to development whereas others do not.

The two more historically rooted traditions are still very much alive among theorists, policymakers, and activists. Nevertheless, the humble undertaking of this chapter is to trace the maturation of the synthesized argument from the implicit statements of classical liberalism and modernization theory to the explicit thinking of contemporary scholars. In so doing, the basic arguments of the contradictory traditions are also illuminated. The aim is, however, not to give a detailed account of the history of the TNC-development debate; rather it is to sketch out — from a bird's eye view — those events and theoretical developments that can help us understand today's discourse.

Before this enterprise can be initiated, it is essential to define what is meant by development. Development has often been equated with economic development or even — in the more contracted form — with growth in gross domestic product (GDP) per capita. In such a narrow perspective many facets of human development are ignored. Economic development or growth need say nothing about distribution of wealth or of the costs of wealth in terms of human suffering. A more fruitful concept — for the population at large — encompasses a broader human rights dimension as well as an economic dimension: a perspective best put forward by Amartya Sen in *Development as Freedom* (1999). In this tradition development cannot take place without economic growth, and cannot be sustained if economic growth does not lead to developments in human rights for the population at large. Sen's argument introduces a dimension of mutual dependence to Lipset's economic development–democracy thesis, which states that economic development must prevail before human rights in general and democracy in particular can be achieved. The position of this chapter is, therefore, that development (and underdevelopment) should be treated as the complex interaction of economic development and human rights, and not as mere economic development. Hence, TNCs can affect the development of the economy and human rights not only directly through its day-to-day operations but also indirectly — through the effects of economic development (in the host country) on human rights. Now let us turn to classical economic liberalism, to see how it all began.

The Initial Thesis: An Engine of Development

Until the 1960s, there was no distinct theory of the TNC as such. Its initial reputation, therefore, has to be extracted from theories of capitalism (in general) and from applied development policies (in particular). After World War II, structuralism and modernization theory also shed some light on the role of TNC in those early years of development theory. Although challenging in their perception of capitalism, these sources of information all believed that the TNC — through different processes — had a positive role to play in development *per se*.

Classical liberalism was the dominant ideology in Western economies before World War I. It emphasized free markets and minimum state interference (see e.g., Smith, 1776). As the growth of corporations that transcended national borders at the turn of the 20th century was in its infancy, classical liberal theory highlighted national corporations and trade rather than corporate investments in foreign countries. The underlying logic, however, remained the same: individuals and corporations are much more efficient allocators of resources (than states). State intervention only stifles investment and, hence, reduces the wealth of nations. For the benefit of both the individuals and the market, though, the state had to maintain rule of law and provide public goods like physical infrastructure.

Marx — and later Lenin — also foresaw a progressive role for capitalism, albeit only in a long-term perspective (Jenkins, 1996; Marx & Engels, 1996). The inevitable growth of the proletariat and the destruction of precapitalist social structures were ensured as capitalism needed to continually conquer new markets to halt its inherent recurring crises. Short-term influence, on the contrary, was harsh for the labor force with working conditions intended to satisfy nothing but the bottom-line interests of the bourgeoisie. Lenin also stressed the monopolistic nature of capitalism, which tended toward economic stagnation and decay. These Marxist thoughts would prove to have great impact on the post-World War II neo-Marxist and Marxist-inspired literature. For contemporary policymakers, however, events rather than Marxist theory initiated a greater role for the state in the economy.

The first half of the 20th century witnessed two events or currents that had a major impact on applied development policies: nationalism and economic stagnation. The Spanish and Portuguese retreat in Latin America and the collapse of the Ottoman Empire in the Middle East had left behind new nation states that sought to roll back the influence of their former masters — and the threatening weight of the great powers — through greater economic independence. The Great Depression paralleled this nationalist current and revealed the vulnerability of international market dependence. These developments — coupled with Keynesian theory that rose in the aftermath of the Depression — all added momentum to a shift from market-led toward state-led development. State-stimulated industrialization, or more precisely import substitution industrialization (ISI), was now the dominant development strategy for those who had previously been reduced to resource sites for their colonial masters. This strategy became increasingly attractive as decolonization spread in the 1950s and 1960s. State-led development was particularly appealing to the new nation states because colonialism had left behind a limited industrial base and an immature capitalist class that alone could not push them into the industrial age (Rapley, 2002). The strategy of ISI partly gave birth to and was partly justified by new ideas in the theory of development: modernization theory.

Although there are many variants and contentions, modernization theory held that underdevelopment was only an initial stage for all countries. This initial state would be overcome by following the route laid open by the first world. It was the traditional structures and values that had to be modernized, and industrialization was the key to this process as it had been for the early developers of the first world. The advantage of the third world, however, was that this process could be accelerated by access to first world know-how and capital. Moreover, modernization theory shared one of the basic notions of the Marxist imperialistic literature that TNCs also helped to undermine development-blocking traditional features found in the developing countries (Törnquist, 1999; Le Roux & Graaff, 2001; Rostow, 2003). Thus, TNC investments were attractive and had a positive contribution to make. This view was even shared by those third world policymakers who were skeptical of capitalism, as access to foreign capital could speed up development without necessarily giving rise to a local capitalist class (Rapley, 2002).

A more sophisticated theoretical argument for pursuing an ISI strategy — what became known as the Prebish–Singer thesis — was based on the concept of declining terms of trade. That is, over time, the value of primary commodity exports will decline compared to that of finished imports. This thesis rested on the assumption that prices in more advanced industrialized societies would rise quicker due to the differences in income elasticities of demand and due to the search for primary commodity substitutes. As a result, developing countries have to export more of their primary commodities just to maintain their level of imports of finished goods from the developed countries. The solution to this accelerating problem was obvious at the time: developing countries had to rely more on the industry for their wealth and less on the primary sector; they had to industrialize (Prebisch, 1950; Singer, 1950). Even though these structural theorists were more skeptical of the role of capitalism in third world development, they nevertheless favored the role of foreign investment in the ISI strategy (Rapley, 2002).

Hence, the diverse set of theories and applied policies that colored development theory in the first half or so of the last century all proclaimed a positive role for TNCs: a role as an engine of development. However, certain arguments and assumptions had implicit flaws that became explicit through failed policies. Marxist theories on imperialism and modernization theory both assumed that capitalism would break down precapitalist structures in developing countries as they had in developed countries; and third world policymakers, modernization theorists, and structuralists alike assumed that foreign capital would aid an ISI strategy that would ensure development as well as economic independence from the former colonial masters. What this first notion failed to see — what dependency theory and world system theory later would emphasize — was that some third world precapitalist structures would be strengthened through alliances with first world capitalism. Moreover, what both notions failed to realize was one implicit assumption vital to both modernization and structural theory: that industry-related foreign direct investment (FDI) had a more positive linkage to the host country economies than primary sector–related FDI. This assumption would later be made explicit by the synthesized theoretical framework.

The failures of state-led development policies became apparent throughout the 1960s and 1970s. The role of capitalism in general and the TNC in particular, thus, became scrutinized as theoretical assumptions proved not to hold. More radical forms of structuralism — dependency theory and world system theory — provided a reaction: the TNC should be regarded as a tool of exploitation.

The Antithesis: A Tool of Exploitation

For years, the post-World War II economic boom hid the flaws of the ISI strategy. However, critics surfaced as the failure of third world countries to develop became more and more evident. On the Left, blame rested with the market system as such. Dependency theorists argued that development and underdevelopment were interlinked. First world development depended on third world underdevelopment for access to markets, raw materials, and a cheap labor supply. The first world drained the third world of resources, and whatever development occurred in the third world depended on first world capitalism (Frank, 1978; Sunkel, 1979; Törnquist, 1999).

World system theorists also pointed to unfavorable market structures and emphasized a core–periphery distinction between and within first and third world countries. There was an implicit alliance between the core and the periphery in the first world and the core in the third world that led to a dual development both at the world system level (where developed countries could be separated from underdeveloped) and within the peripheral countries (development as well as underdevelopment was the result) (Galtung, 1971; Wallerstein, 1974; Hymer, 1979).

As a consequence, the TNC was no longer seen as a partner in development, but rather as a tool used by developed countries to extract resources from the underdeveloped ones. Few jobs and linkages to other producers in the economy were created, as capitalism would not spread beyond the foreign corporations. Local firms could even be displaced, rather than supplemented, by TNCs. Moreover, surplus capital was shipped back home — through tax-avoiding arrangements like transfer pricing — rather than reinvesting locally (Gilpin, 1987; Jenkins, 1996). From a human rights perspective, dual development created a need to control the masses in order for the TNC to maintain its momentum. Instruments of control entailed repression and denials of civil and political rights for residents of the third world (Hymer, 1979).

The antithesis — the tools of exploitation school — prescribed a break away from the international market as the solution to failed development policies. A mere political break from the former colonists would not suffice. A full economic break with autonomous national development policies was necessary to break free of dependence and poverty (Gilpin, 1987). However, a major dilemma was facing the policy prescriptions of this radical Left: development occurred in some third world countries, and for none more than for the East Asian tiger economies of Taiwan, Singapore, Hong Kong, and South Korea. It appeared as capitalism — at some level or another — had a positive contribution to make after all. Nevertheless, the ISI strategy had discredited state-led development policies, and therefore dependency theory and world system theory proved to be of little importance in applied development policies. Many of their notions about TNC influence, though, would be picked up by the synthesized theoretical framework. However, for the 1980s and on, less — not more — statism was the prescription as a renewed Right called for a rolling back of the state.

A Retreat to the Initial Thesis: More Market, Less State

The market supremacy of classical liberalism foresaw a minimal role of the state. The failures of the third world to catch up were not due to the market as such, but to obstacles to economic development in the third world countries themselves (Gilpin, 1987). State-led development policies had been too optimistic about human nature. Neoclassical theorists argued that the same selfish behavior that prevailed in the marketplace would also prevail in the public sector, only with more damaging effects. Although ISI had proven successful in building factories and infrastructure, its export and agricultural performance was poor. Moreover, the bureaucratic mechanisms needed to pursue the strategy of ISI was a breeding ground for inefficiency, corruption, and rent-seeking behavior (Rapley, 2002).

In the early 1980s, the free market economy was back as the dominating state-market ideology, and eventually found its way back into the Bretton Woods institutions — the World Bank (WB) and the International Monetary Fund (IMF). Even some third world policymakers began to be influenced by neoclassical theory as it seemed to offer solutions to the practical problems they faced. Nevertheless, the debt crises — resulting from OPEC oil shocks, liberal lending practices to questionable development projects, and economic stagflation — gave these institutions the leverage they needed to alter development policies in third world countries. In exchange for loans to manage their debt, third world countries had to agree to structural adjustment programs (SAPs), aimed at rolling back the state and removing structural blockages to the (assumed) efficient operation of markets. Moreover, export industrialization — exploiting comparative advantage — was recommended over the failed ISI strategy (Rapley, 2002).

As far as the TNCs were concerned, neoclassical writers also criticized rules that restricted foreign investment. The TNC was back as an engine of development. Not only did TNCs have a direct positive effect on economic development but also through economic development they indirectly supported the development of political and civil rights (Meyer, 1998). The latter indirect relationship could be traced back to Lipset's economic development–democracy thesis (1959), whereas the former direct relationship rested on TNC's capacity to transfer capital, know-how, and technology (Balasubramanyam et al., 1999; Gelleny & Sacko, 2001), as well as by the greater efficiency of its internal market (Jenkins, 1996). However, like the ISI strategy of the supporters of state-led development policies before them, neoclassical theory in general and SAPs in particular ran into problems when facing the complexity of real-life conditions. At some level its prescriptions failed the test of universalism. Perhaps the question was not whether capitalism was good for development or not, but rather when (or in which context) it was good and when it was not.

The Synthesis: It All Depends

Although partly successful in some Latin American and Asian countries, Rapley (2002) criticized the neoliberal paradigm for being too optimistic about the market's ability to generate wealth and too pessimistic about the state's ability to play a positive role in development. For instance, where neoclassical theory speaks of static comparative advantage (ignoring the inelasticity of primary commodities), the successful developmental-state policies of the East Asian tigers speak of dynamic comparative advantage, i.e., advantage developed by the state in selected export-oriented industries; where neoclassical theory prescribes openness to attract FDI, capital itself tends to pursue those opportunities that — more often than not — are created by government policies. Moreover, neoclassical reforms seem to be most effective in societies that have already attained a relatively advanced level of development, and that to reach this level a high degree of state guidance is needed. This more nuanced view of the capabilities or limitations of capitalism is also argued by others (see e.g., de Soto, 2000; Lindblom, 2001), and it is — as we shall see — also paralleled by a more nuanced view of the impact of TNCs on third world economic development as well as its development of human rights.

Throughout the 1990s a theoretical framework has emerged that represents a synthesis of the arguments presented by — structural, modernization, and neoclassical theory on the one hand, and dependency theory and world system theory on the other hand. Methodological as well as theoretical notions can help explain the emergence of this framework. Methodologically, the two opposing research traditions seem to find support at different levels of analysis. Although anti-TNC theorists generally find their empirical evidence in numerous examples of human rights' malpractices in corporate and country case studies, pro-TNC theorists have generally applied statistical analyses at the national level to support their argument (Meyer, 1998). However, evidence of the opposite exists, and in statistical analysis the choice of proxy and timespan can determine the outcome (de Soysa & Oneal, 1999; Firebaugh, 2003; Kentor, 2003; Letnes, 2004). This highlights the importance of context, and theoretical notions help to settle when TNCs are good for development and when they are not.

Corporate and host country characteristics help bridge the gap between the two conflicting views on TNC influence. Despite conflicting objectives and the fact that TNCs outweigh many of the smaller economies in bargaining power (Walters & Blake, 1992), TNCs can engage in a positive dialogue with respect to host countries' development (out of either a genuine sense of social responsibility or out of respect for the market force of bad publicity) (Madely, 1999; Spar, 1999). However, no business can survive without paying attention to its immediate bottom-line interests. Thus, the motives of the TNCs — beyond those of profit maximization *per se* — are likely to have a greater influence on host country human rights' conditions than any well-intended policies, whether genuine or imposed. The motives and interests of TNCs, however, will change according to the type of activity undertaken

(Dunning, 1993; Spar, 1999). Corporations engaged in primary-sector activities will have different motivations than corporations engaged in secondary- or tertiary-sector activities (Spar, 1999). Therefore, as the composition of FDI shifts from the primary to secondary and tertiary sectors (Lall, 1997; Spar, 1999; UNCTAD, 1999; Letnes, 2002), it should bring a shift in the motives and interests of the TNC. The emerging argument is that this shift — in general — has resulted in a more positive impact of TNC activity on host country's development (see e.g., Spar, 1999; Narula & Dunning, 2000). TNCs become less dependent on development-blocking host government ties when the composition of FDI is located in the secondary and tertiary sectors, as resource sites do not limit them, and they have a wider range of possible investment sites of choice. Motivated more by the search for low-cost skilled labor and expanded markets, the implication for host countries also change. Now bottom-line interests, not moral obligations, argue for maintaining the health, training, and pay of workers to increase their productivity and the quality of their output (Spar, 1999). Moreover, the higher value-adding TNC activities in the secondary and tertiary sectors are considered as a means for promoting technological upgrading in the host countries (Narula & Dunning, 2000). However, motives alone do not tell a complete story: host country conditions matter too.

A central argument in the emerging synthesized framework is that the positive impact of TNCs on host countries' development is conditional on a range of host country characteristics. Different authors have emphasized the role of the TNC–host country's balance of bargaining power (Moran, 1996; Evans, 1998; Panic, 1998), the composition of FDI (Dunning, 1993; Spar, 1999), and the host countries' level of created assets (Narula, 1996; Borenzstein et al., 1998; Narula & Dunning, 1999; Xu, 2000; Letnes, 2002) as important determinants in this regard. Also, the host countries' level of natural and created assets are not to be regarded as independent because resource abundance has been seen as a curse to institutional development and the general development of human capital (Shafer, 1994; Sachs & Warner, 1995; Karl, 1997; Ross, 1999).

When fused with the strong tradition that argues the importance of economic development to democracy, and hence human rights (Lipset, 1959; Moore, 1966; Rueschmeyer et al., 1992), this literature on the host country characteristics emphasizes the importance of the host countries' stage of development (Dunning, 1993). That is, the more economically developed a host country is, and the more created assets (e.g., human capital and high-quality institutions) it possesses, the more likely it is to benefit from the presence of TNCs and the more likely it is to develop and sustain democratic values. We might even speak of a virtuous cycle as far as investments in the secondary and tertiary sector is concerned, as corporate investments, human capital, economic development, and democratic values seem to mutually reinforce each other. However, corporate investment is not the likely trigger here as TNCs are more likely to invest in host countries where the other variables are already well developed (Narula & Dunning, 1999). Host countries, therefore, seem to face a two-edged dilemma: on the one hand, TNCs can provide assets like human capital and technology and on the other hand, TNCs are more likely to invest in host countries where these assets already exist. Narula and Dunning refer to this phenomenon as "the danger of falling behind," and some areas are falling farther behind than others, especially sub-Saharan Africa (Lall, 1997; Narula & Dunning, 1999; UNDP, 2000).

The synthesized theoretical framework embraces arguments from both the pro-TNC and the anti-TNC thesis. Many of the underlying assumptions of the two opposing schools have matured over the years. Empiricism from applied development policies have erased their most incompatible arguments and highlight the conditional nature of the relationships in question. Both the state and the market are seen as important contributors to development, and the TNC can be seen as both an engine of development and a tool of exploitation.

Conclusion

The central argument of this chapter is that our view of the relationship between TNCs and development has developed — over time — as a synthesis of opposing theories. This view sees the TNC as capable of breeding development as well as underdevelopment, depending on both TNC and host country characteristics. For instance, primary-sector investments are poor linkages compared to secondary- and tertiary-sector investments, and host countries with high-quality institutions and a high level of human capital are more likely to benefit from the presence of TNCs. As a result, the relationship is not as unambiguous as proclaimed by advocates from the orthodox Left or the orthodox Right.

However, the synthesized theoretical framework has not displaced the neoclassical paradigm. The neoclassical paradigm — speaking of the supremacy of the market in general and the TNC in particular — is very much alive in the literature and in applied development policies. Moreover, the Left is not dead. To some extent it has influenced the synthesized framework presented here and to a larger extent inspired the discontents of globalization in general (see e.g., Stiglitz, 2002). The complexity of TNC–host country relationship is far from unraveled, and future literature is likely to benefit from an open eye toward all traditions in the debate.

References

Balasubramanyam, V.N., M. Salisu, and D. Sapsford. 1999. "Foreign Direct Investment as an Engine of Growth," *The Journal of International Trade and Economic Development*, 8(1): 27–40.

Borenzstein, E., J. de Gregorio, and J.-W. Lee. 1998. "How Does Foreign Direct Investment Affect Economic Growth?" *Journal of International Economics*, 45: 115–135.

de Soto, H. 2000. *The Mystery of Capital: Why Capitalism Triumphs in the West and Fails Everywhere Else*. London: Bantam Press.

de Soysa, I. and J.R. Oneal. 1999. "Boon or Bane? Reassessing the Productivity of Foreign Direct Investment," *American Sociological Review*, 64(October): 766–782.

Dunning, J.H. 1993. *Multinational Enterprises and the Global Economy*. Wokingham: Addison-Wesley.

Evans, P. 1998. *Transnational Corporations and Third World States: From the Old Internationalization to the New*. London: Macmillan.

Firebaugh, G. 2003. "Growth Effects of Foreign and Domestic Investment," in M.A. Seligson and J.T. Passe-Smith (eds.), *Development and Underdevelopment: The Political Economy of Global Inequality*. Boulder, CO: Lynne Rienner Publishers, pp. 327–344.

Frank, A.G. 1978. *Dependent Accumulation and Underdevelopment*. London: Macmillan.

Galtung, J. 1971. "A Structural Theory of Imperialism," *Journal of Peace Research*, 8(2): 81–117.

Gelleny, R.D. and D.H. Sacko. 2001. "Money with a Mean Streak? Foreign Economic Penetration and Government Respect for Human Rights in Developing Countries," *International Studies Quarterly*, 45: 219–239.

Gilpin, R. 1987. *The Political Economy of International Relations*. Princeton, NJ: Princeton University Press.

Hymer, S. 1979. *The Multinational Corporation and the Law of Uneven Development*. New York: W.H. Freeman and Company.

Jenkins, R. 1996. "Theoretical Perspectives on the Transnational Corporation," in C.R. Goddard, J.T. Passe-Smith, and J.G. Conklin (eds.), *International Political Economy: State–Market Relations in the Changing Global Order*. Boulder, CO: Lynne Rienner Publishers.

Karl, T.L. 1997. *The Paradox of Plenty: Oil Booms and Petro-States*. Berkeley, CA: University of California Press.

Kentor, J. 2003. "The Long-Term Effects of Foreign Investment Dependence on Economic Growth, 1940–1990," in M.A. Seligson and J.T. Passe-Smith (eds.), *Development and Underdevelopment: The Political Economy of Global Inequality*. Boulder, CO: Lynne Rienner Publishers, pp. 345–356.

Lall, S. 1997. "TNCs: The New Custodians of Development?" in R. Culpeper, A. Berry, and F. Stewart (eds.), *Global Development Fifty Years after Bretton Woods*. London: Macmillan, pp. 169–191.

Le Roux, P. and J. Graaff. 2001. "Evolutionist Thinking," in J.K. Coetzee, J. Graaff, F. Hendricks, and G. Wood (eds.), *Development: Theory, Policy, and Practice.* Oxford: Oxford University Press.

Letnes, B. 2002. "Foreign Direct Investment and Human Rights: An Ambiguous Relationship," *Forum for Development Studies,* 29(1): 33–61.

Letnes, B. 2004. "Transnational Corporations and Human Rights: Silencing the Ontological Controversy," *Public Organization Review: A Global Journal,* 4(3): 259–277.

Lindblom, C.E. 2001. *The Market System: What It Is, How It Works and What to Make of It.* New Haven, CT: Yale University Press.

Lipset, S.M. 1959. "Some Social Requisites of Democracy: Economic Development and Political Legitimacy," *American Political Science Review,* 53: 69–105.

Madely, J. 1999. *Big Business, Poor Peoples: The Impact of Transnational Corporations on the World's Poor.* London: Zed Books.

Marx, K. and F. Engels. 1996. "Excerpts from Capital and Communist Manifesto," in C.R. Goddard, J.T. Passe-Smith, and J.G. Conklin (eds.), *International Political Economy: State-Market Relations in the Changing Global Order.* Boulder, CO: Lynne Rienner Publishers.

Meyer, W.H. 1998. *Human Rights and International Political Economy in Third World Nations: Multinational Corporations, Foreign Aid, and Repression.* Westport, CT: Praeger.

Moore, B. 1966. *Social Origins of Dictatorship and Democracy: Lords and Peasants in the Making of the Modern World.* Boston, MA: Beacon Press.

Moran, T.H. 1996. "Governments and Transnational Corporations," in UNCTAD (ed.), *Transnational Corporations and World Development.* New York: International Thomson Business Press.

Narula, R. 1996. *Multinational Investment and Economic Structure: Globalisation and Competitiveness.* London: Routledge.

Narula, R. and J.H. Dunning. 1999. "Developing Countries versus Multinational Enterprises in a Globalising World: The Dangers of Falling Behind," *Forum for Development Studies,* (2): 261–287.

Narula, R. and J.H. Dunning. 2000. "Industrial Development, Globalization and Multinational Enterprises: New Realities for Developing Countries," *Oxford Development Studies,* 28(2): 141–167.

Panic, M. 1998. "Transnational Corporations and the Nation State," in R. Kozul-Wright and R. Rowthorn (eds.), *Transnational Corporations and the Global Economy.* The United Nations University, WIDER: Macmillan, pp. 244–276.

Prebisch, R. 1950. *The Economic Development of Latin America and its Principal Problems.* New York: United Nations.

Rapley, J. 2002. *Understanding Development: Theory and Practice in the Third World.* Boulder, CO: Lynne Rienner Publishers.

Ross, M. 1999. "The Political Economy of the Resource Curse," *World Politics,* 51: 297–332.

Rostow, W.W. 2003. "The Five Stages of Growth," in M.A. Seligson and J.T. Passe-Smith (eds.), *Development and Underdevelopment: The Political Economy of Global Inequality.* Boulder, CO: Lynne Rienner Publishers.

Rueschmeyer, D., E.H. Stephens, and J.D. Stephens. 1992. *Capitalist Development and Democracy*. Chicago, IL: The University of Chicago Press.

Sachs, J.D. and A. Warner. 1995. *Natural Resource Abundance and Economic Growth* (No. NBER Working Paper # 5318). Cambridge, MA: National Bureau of Economic Research.

Sen, A. 1999. *Development as Freedom*. New York: Alfred A. Knopf.

Shafer, M.D. 1994. *Winners and Losers: How Sectors Shape the Developmental Prospects of States*. Ithaca, NY: Cornell University Press.

Singer, H.W. 1950. "The Distribution of Gains Between Investing and Borrowing Countries," *American Economic Review*, 40(2): 473–485.

Smith, A. 1776. *The Wealth of Nations* (reprinted 1999 edn. Vol. I–III). London: Penguin Books.

Spar, D. 1999. "Foreign Investment and Human Rights," *Challenge*, 42(1), 55–80.

Stiglitz, J.E. 2002. *Globalization and Its Discontents*. London: W.W. Norton.

Sunkel, O. 1979. *Big Business and "Dependencia."* New York: W.H. Freeman and Company.

Törnquist, O. 1999. *Politics and Development: A Critical Introduction*. London: Sage Publications.

UNCTAD. 1999. *World Investment Report: Foreign Direct Investment and the Challenge of Development*. New York: United Nations Publication.

UNDP. 2000. *Human Development Report*. Oxford: Oxford University Press, for UNDP.

Wallerstein, I. 1974. "The Rise and Future Demise of the World Capitalist System: Concepts for Comparative Analysis," *Comparative Studies in Society and History*, 16: 387–415.

Walters, R.S. and D.H. Blake. 1992. *The Politics of Global Economic Relations*, 4 edn. London: Prentice-Hall.

Xu, B. 2000. "Multinational Enterprises, Technology Diffusion, and Host Country Productivity Growth," *Journal of Development Economics*, 62: 477–493.

Chapter 34

New Views on North–South Relations of Imperialism

Keith Kelly

CONTENTS

Introduction

Imperialism is a topic frequently outside the purview of American public administration discourse. First, mainstream discourse tends to address topics that are normative (improvement in bureaucratic systems, civic government, and the like) versus politically critical discourse (which is the general tenor of studies on imperialism). Secondly, the discourse within public administration has tended toward domestic administration, with discussions and theories of globalization becoming more popular over the past few decades. Finally, imperialism is a topic that deals with the projection of power of advanced nation-states toward relatively weaker geopolitical regions of the globe. Interests often conflict, and there is less in the way of addressing this conflict using standard theoretical paradigms. As Howard and King (2000, p. 19) note, "while the reality of imperialism has rarely been denied, it has been widely thought to be outside the boundaries of orthodox economic analysis, which limits itself to the logic of rationally acquisitive action." One might add, too, that imperialism has also been beyond the realm of orthodox or conservative political analyses.

The discipline of public administration, as most administrative disciplines, now addresses globalization and its effects. This is important, as the issues surrounding globalization and imperialism — issues of social justice, military policy, international political policy, economic policy, and national interests — are very important for both domestic and foreign policy. The impacts of trade negotiations, economic agreements, military actions, and other power brokering activities also have vital consequences for social groups and communities, and as such have been given increased attention across the social and administrative disciplines.

This chapter considers imperialism in the context of globalization. Imperialism refers to a specific relationship that exists within globalization, and is taken to mean the extension of a core state's power to gain or enhance control over resources or resource flows within another state's geopolitical range of sovereignty or jurisdiction, or to preempt another core state from controlling such resources.[1] Although some concepts of globalization indeed do exclude or minimize the possibility of imperialism, the inclusion of imperialism here provides a specific perspective on power relationships between the entities within the global system. It follows that the concept of globalization is quite variegated in the literature, and this is the case whether or not it includes the possibility of imperialism. Harris (2002, p. 5) notes that "[t]he contemporary literature and ideological debates on 'globalization' involve a highly contested, complex, and multidimensional discourse on the nature of the present world order and its historical antecedents, underlying causative forces, and future evolution." Guillén (2001, p. 235) declares at the outset of one of his articles that "[g]lobalization is one of the most contested topics in the social sciences." Burbach and Robinson (1999, pp. 10–11) note that "[g]lobalization, it seems, has become the 'fin de siecle' debate. Ardent controversies over the extent and significance of globalization are taking place in a number of publications and forums. Not even established economists and defenders of the current neoliberal world order seem to agree on how to assess the current era, as demonstrated in the pages of *Business Week* and *The Economist*."

As a preface to this discussion, it is beneficial to briefly examine some of the perspectives that inform the globalization literature. Farazmand (1999, pp. 511–512) discusses several perspectives on globalization. First, globalization is seen as the trans-state relations between communities and other entities across national borders. This pattern is an old one, however it has been facilitated by international organizations and agencies, such as the United Nations. A second perspective centers more on the openness of national borders through liberalization — with economic and perhaps other activities that traverse national borders being less impeded by the removal of protectionist regulations and legislation. Another perspective examines globalization in terms of the processes of the event. Globalization represents a continuation of capitalism in the modern expansion of accumulation processes, allowed for by technology and other factors. Capitalism therefore has become more widespread and also has more deeply entrenched in national economies throughout the globe. In another perspective, globalization is also seen as the promulgation of an ideology that reflects the political values of mainstream Western industrial nations in the form of democratic capitalism, as that ideology is spread to other nations through support of political and economic practices consistent with this thinking. Yet

[1]For a detailed and formal definition of imperialism, the reader is referred to Richard Koebner's "The Concept of Economic Imperialism," in Boulding, K.E. and Murkerjee, T. (Eds.), *Economic Imperialism: A Book of Readings*, pp. 60–94, (1972, Ann Arbor: The University of Michigan Press) and Patrick Wolfe's "History and Imperialism: A Century of Theory from Marx to Postcolonialism," *American Historical Review*, 102, 388–402 (1997).

another perspective sees globalization as a type of phenomenon that pervades space without respect to national borders or boundaries. The globe itself becomes the "global village" where states and institutions are significantly affected by a globalization that crosscuts their spheres of authority. This new global space is inherent in capitalism's search for greater market penetration and capital accumulation. Although these perspectives provide considerable explanatory power, they also possess explanatory gaps (variously, the impact on the state, and role of the state and public administration in globalization). Lastly, Farazmand considers a hybrid of two approaches, one that holds globalization to be a process, but also a phenomenon. He states "[s]haring with and building upon the previous meanings, this perspective considers globalization to be a process of accumulation by global capitalism — a constant process of expansion into new frontiers and opportunities for increasing capital accumulation at the global level. It also views globalization as a phenomenon caused by the process of global capital accumulation — a phenomenon that has manifested its negative and positive effects almost everywhere" (Farazmand, 1999, p. 512). This perspective sees the state and public administration at once affected by globalization, and at the same time an active partner in globalization. Other factors contribute to globalization as well. These include "surplus accumulation of corporate capital, the role of the dominant states and their bureaucracies, domestic constraints, rising human expectations, international institutions, and technological innovations" (Farazmand, 1999, p. 512).

At this point, it is also important to understand what the globalization literature itself aims for. Guillén (2001) gives five questions that the globalization literature attempts to address: (1) Is globalization really occurring? (2) Is it occurring in an integrated way? (3) Is it affecting the role of the nation-state? (4) Does it make its mark on the human experience and distinguish itself from previous forms of organization? (5) Is it resulting in cultural characteristics that are truly global, for example global consumerism, global politics, or a global system?[2] Here it is neither the intention, nor is there the space, to delve into each of these questions in detail.

In this chapter, we examine two bodies of studies at the outset that focus on globalization. These studies do not specifically have the designation of being the definitive works in their respective areas, however they serve well as representative works that have generated a fair amount of discussion about globalization and imperialism. The first is the popular book by Hardt

[2]See Mauro F. Guillén's article "Is Globalization Civilizing, Destructive, or Feeble? A Critique of Five Key Debates in the Social Science Literature," *Annual Review of Sociology*, 27, 235–260 (2001), for an excellent (though far from exhaustive) compendium of what scholars answer "yes" and "no" to each of these questions.

and Negri, entitled *Empire* (2000). This study has achieved considerable popular attention in the press and to a lesser degree among academic audiences. The second is a body of literature, largely associated with the work of Robinson, which discusses the development of a transnational ruling class. This literature has also generated considerable discussion.

After reviewing these perspectives, we turn to their critiques. We then look at the realities of imperialism, economic issues in globalization and imperialism, perspectives on the role of the state, interimperialist rivalries and American hegemony, and then bring together some concepts germane to a fuller understanding of the topic.

The Globalization Thesis: A Look at Two Representative Perspectives

Hardt and Negri's Empire

In their book simply entitled *Empire*, Hardt and Negri have set off a lively debate about the new shape of global relations. Hardt and Negri, both neo-Marxists, posit the end to the era of state-sponsored imperialism. This comes about because the geopolitical space itself that contained imperialism, in their view, has ceased to exist. It is their claim that the nation-state can no longer control the global influx of exogenous cultural and economic influences and powers. Although this tended to be the case for subservient states under imperialism, they are careful to underscore their assertion that they are not describing imperialism. Instead, the entire globe has now blended together under the single rubric of spaceless empire (Hardt & Negri, 2000, p. xii).

The new empire is thus not identified by boundaries or designated political space. This is because communication networks bridge the gaps that previously divided. Hardt and Negri (2000, pp. 32, 33) also make the claim that

> The development of communication networks has an organic relationship to the emergence of the new world order — it is, in other words, effect and cause, product and producer. Communication not only expresses but also organizes the movement of globalization.... Language, as it communicates, produces commodities but moreover creates subjectivities, puts them in relation, and orders them. The communications industries integrate the imaginary and the symbolic with the biopolitical fabric, not merely putting them at the service of power but actually integrating them into its very functioning.
>
> Hardt & Negri (2000, pp. 32, 33)

Bridging this previously existing communication gap, in fact, yields a landscape marked by no specific operational centers. The forces within the system are ubiquitous. In the new order, economic possibilities and constrains in the system relate directly to changes in the processes of production. In the new era of the information economy, the locales of production themselves are displaced by production networks, with these networks tying together the diffuse production processes of discrete production locales. Previously the locations of production existed to a much greater extent *sui generis*, although periodically open to outside processes or manipulation, such as from actions of core states on the periphery. Now, however, the prominence of new networks in the organization of production effectively bypasses the locational factors that played into global organization under the previous system of nation-states (cf. Hardt & Negri, 2000, p. 295). This has occurred to the extent that "the spatial division of the three Worlds (First, Second, and Third) have been scrambled so that we continually find the First World in the Third, the Third in the First, and the Second almost nowhere at all" (Hardt & Negri, 2000, p. xiii).

The role of production and the political and cultural reproduction of life become the postmodern dynamic that sustains, or at least characterizes, the empire (Hardt & Negri, 2000, p. xiii). This empire is judicially tied together with power relations that attempt to order the system — a system that necessarily experiences crisis from time to time and is affected heavily by the interplay of the demands of the system itself and the conflicts from the local manifestations of power within the system (Hardt & Negri, 2000, p. 20).

So when did the era of imperialism end? Hardt and Negri date the end of the United States imperialism to the January 1968 Tet offensive in Vietnam, stating that this event "marked the irreversible military defeat of the U.S. imperialist adventures" (Hardt & Negri, 2000, p. 179). They claim that now "*[t]he United States does not, and indeed no nation-state can today, form the center of an imperialist project.* Imperialism is over" (Hardt & Negri, 2000, pp. xiii–xiv).

Far from being optimistic capitalists who herald the era of global capitalism, Hardt and Negri are espousing a new Leftist version of international relations, or one that may not truly be international, but transnational. This spaceless and smooth-to-capital world of the modern networked global economy leaves no room for something like imperialism. However all is not well in this new world. Exploitation still exists, yet it is difficult to locate the specific source of the exploitation. And, also there is no geographical haven for retreat so as to avoid the perils of the new system. They also claim that the

> imperial power can no longer discipline the powers of the multitude; it can only impose control over their general social and productive capacities. From the economic point of view, the wage regime is replaced, as a function of

> regulation, by a flexible and global monetary system; normative command is replaced by the procedures of control and the police; and the exercise of domination is formed through communicative networks. This is how exploitation and domination constitute a general non-place on the imperial terrain.
>
> Hardt & Negri (2000, p. 211)

Hardt and Negri therefore see exploitation as being systemic in the new order, and no less immune to occurrence than in the previous order. The new era is marked not only by exploitation, but also by corruption, leaving the "multitude," in Hardt and Negri's parlance, in a struggle to fend for their place in the Empire (Hardt & Negri, 2000, pp. 389–391).

Others have commented that Hardt and Negri express a certain optimism for the advent of Empire. Giovanni Arrighi, for example, notes that "[t]his is probably the most optimistic picture of the nature and consequences of globalization proposed thus far by the radical left," as the *Empire* team express a hope that the dispossessed will attain a place in the new global order (Arrighi, 2003, pp. 29, 32). According to Hardt and Negri, imperialism no longer defines geopolitical relationships, but the multitude is nonetheless left with the prospect of struggle. This struggle entails the right of global citizenship, so that the rights and needs of citizens to relocate in following the flows of capital are recognized, or alternatively the "right also to stay still and enjoy one place rather than being forced constantly to be on the move" (Hardt & Negri, 2000, p. 400). To this they add the right to a social wage, or a wage is tantamount to a guaranteed income, and also devoid of the discrimination that alienates women as in the current wage structure (Hardt & Negri, 2000, p. 403). Finally, there is the issue of the "right to reappropriation" inherent in the class struggle and that occurs in the context of the new global communication network (Hardt & Negri, 2000, pp. 403–407). Telling, however, is the observation that the outcome and form of these struggles are indeterminate, and Hardt and Negri lack concrete recommendations.

Such is the world that we now live in, according to Hardt and Negri. It is a world where we are increasingly immersed in global networks, changing social and work arrangements, disintegrating traditional structures of jurisprudence, and one marked by a social, political, and economic landscape, where production ceases to be fundamentally associated with space. It is also a world of struggle, where the masses attempt to find their place in newly aligned dimensions of space and nonplace.

The Transnational Capitalist Ruling Class

A second perspective on globalization that has sparked debate among scholars is the concept of the transnational ruling class. This topic has been variously explored by a number of researchers, notably "neo-Marxist scholars like Kees Van der Pijl, Leslie Sklair, Robert Cox, Barry Gill and others..." (Mann, 2001, pp. 464–465). Here, however, we look at the representative work of Robinson and his associates for an introduction to the topic (cf. Burbach & Robinson, 1999; Robinson 1996, 1998, 2002a,b, 2004; Robinson & Harris, 2000).

Burbach and Robinson examine the epochs of capitalism, arguing that globalization represents capitalism's fourth epoch. They date capitalism's first epoch from European emergence to the Industrial Revolution, the second from the Industrial Revolution to an era of monopoly capitalism in the early 20th century, and the third from monopoly capitalism to the global era. They claim that although these categorizations are "somewhat arbitrary," the reality of the new era is not. The fourth epoch is simply not a continuation of capitalism, but an emergence of a form characterized by distinct features of networking technology, power arrangements, and transformed institutions (Burbach & Robinson, 1999, pp. 11–12).

Beginning around the 1970s and into the 1980s, a transnational ruling class began to vie for power of state apparatuses, in competition with state elites. This transnational class threw off Keynesian policy approaches, instead championing neoliberalism, the liberalization of markets, and a polyarchy of institutions and groups on multiple levels within and beyond the state realm, designed to coordinate transnational globalization. Coordination among key financial and political institutions within states and between such states, and through the agency of international financial organizations, was promoted to foster the growth of global capitalism among this upcoming transnational ruling class (Burbach & Robinson, 1999; Robinson, 2002a, p. 225, 2002b, pp. 1055–1056; Robinson & Harris, 2000, p. 23).

One change with the advent of the global era is the diffusion of production. In the previous nation-state centered production, the circuit involving money, capital, and production yielded a circuit of M–C–P–C′–M′, with M–C–P–C′ largely taking place within the nation. Commodity production was engaged in for export, but profits were repatriated into the national cycle. Now, the circuit is not as heavily associated as with a specific center. Profits may very well find their incidence throughout the system instead of finding their way back to the location of their origin, or necessarily back into the production circuit (Robinson & Harris, 2000, pp. 19–20). So for Robinson and Harris, globalization has come about because of the changes in the organization of production as well as the concurrent rise of new technologies that facilitate the process. They state "[t]he globalization of production has entailed the fragmentation and decentralization of complex production chains and the worldwide dispersal and functional integration of the different segments in these chains" (Robinson & Harris, 2000, p. 19).

Burbach and Robinson (1999, pp. 16–17) also claim that we are in a computerized age as well as an age marked by the collapse of a number of socialist states. And while we continue to be in the era of capitalism, it is indeed a very different sort of capitalism. There are increased rates of foreign direct investment (FDI) with economic peripheral nations receiving increased shares of FDI. Burbach and Robinson (1999, pp. 18, 19) state that by the 1990s "the transition from the internationalization to the transnationalization of capital, which involved in the first instance the horizontal integration of the Triad [United States, Western Europe, and Japan], is being complemented by North–South vertical integration." This is possible by the transnationalization of the ownership of production, which corresponds to a transnationalized class that exercises power in ordering the global economy. And this has, in ways now familiar within this chapter, scrambled the meanings of conventional terms that related nation-states or regions to one another — such as "core," "periphery," "North," and "South." Burbach and Robinson (1999, p. 28) note that "[t]he concepts of core and periphery, or North and South, are increasingly not geographic *per se*, as much as they are social class in character, as the global economy creates new variation, specialization, and asymmetries that cut across nations and regions." The members of the new transnational ruling class come from both the North and the South (Robinson & Harris, 2000, p. 12).

Thus, this marks the beginning of the transnational ruling class and the current process of globalization. This globalization has changed the long-standing international relationships and economic and production processes. Robinson (2002a, p. 224) also claims that globalization has decimated the character and traditional functions of the nation-state. He states that

> Globalization has increasingly eroded these national boundaries and made it structurally impossible for individual nations to sustain independent, or even autonomous, economies, polities, and social structures. A key feature of the current epoch is the supersession of the nation-state as the organizing principle of capitalism and with in, of the inter-state system as the institutional framework of capitalist development. Globalization, in the process of creating a single and increasingly undifferentiated field for work capitalism, integrates the various polities, cultures and institutions of national societies into an emergent transnational or global society.
>
> Robinson (2002a, p. 224)

Robinson calls for the substitution of analyses based on the concept of the nation-state, instead of focusing on the new dynamic of globalization that is headed up by the transnational rulers. In his work, globalization is the complete penetration of global capitalism. It is the transition from national production processes that newly articulate with the global market and are thus transformed by the process, displacing many traditional nation-based processes and organizational dynamics. This means "[t]he essence of globalization is global capitalism, which has superceded the nation-state stage of capitalism" (Robinson, 1998, p. 563).

The state does not simply disappear, however. Instead globalization has produced a profound impact on the state. The members of the transnational ruling class have now fostered the creation of a new form of organization in the globalized economy — the transnational state. The transnational ruling class accomplished this by utilizing the new configurations of power within the state and the state's institutions. The newly formulated state power structures articulate more closely with the structures of the global network and come to reflect the exigencies of the global transnational system (cf. Robinson & Harris, 2000, pp. 26–28). Robinson notes that internal to nation-states, this is also accomplished by the transnationalist class grasping power of state institutions, stating that

> Class fractionation is occurring along a new national/transnational axis. Transnational fractions of local elites have ascended politically in countries around the world, clashing in their bid for hegemony with nationally-based class fractions. They have increasingly captured local states — or key institutions within those states, such as central banks and foreign ministries — and used national state apparatuses to advance globalization.
>
> Robinson (2002a, p. 225)

The transnational state subsequently articulates with other transnationalized states and transnational organizations as well, yet to date it does not have a "centralized institutional form." Its work is currently achieved through the transnationalized state system, international agreements, and international organizations such as the International Monetary Fund (IMF) and the World Bank, the central banks, and the World Trade Organization (WTO) on multiple levels to forge a transnational core of global capitalist influence and power (Robinson & Harris, 2000, pp. 27–29).

This process, of course, is not without considerable conflict. Political and military interventions on behalf of the transnationalists will still occur. Robinson (2004, p. 137) notes that "[g]lobal capitalism requires an apparatus of direct coercion to open up zones that may fall under renegade control, to impose order, and to repress rebellion when it threatens the stability or security of the system. There are no transnational capitalist armed forces, and there may not be for many years to come." He also sees recent interventions by the United States not to be of the older imperialist character, but a newer type of intervention that paves the way to greater resource and market access for the transnational capitalist class and transnational corporations. This has been accomplished by the United

States by participating in interventions that essentially shift the power base from the local or regional elites to the transnationalist elites (Robinson, 2004, pp. 137, 139, 140).

Yet the United States' role as hegemonic state has also changed. According to the transnational ruling class view, this phenomenon marks the decline of the U.S. hegemony in important ways, as the United States ultimately cedes authority to the transnational class and its institutions and agencies (Burbach & Robinson, 1999, p. 37). These are the propositions that we shall critique in subsequent sections.

In Robinson's view, the development of transnational ruling class administration also is not neutral in terms of uniform economic growth or protection of interests. The transnationalization results in a new global division of labor (Robinson, 2002a, p. 226), and this new sociopolitical–economic arrangement is "profoundly antidemocratic" (Robinson, 1996, p. 20). Robinson's sixth thesis on globalization holds that "the dramatic growth under globalisation of socioeconomic inequalities and of human misery, a consequence of the unbridled operation of transnational capital, is worldwide, and generalized" (Robinson, 1996, p. 21). Interestingly, this uniformity of global production and administrative processes will correspond to a lack of uniformity in socioeconomic statuses of people, as the gap between the rich and the poor increases on a national basis, as well as between the North and the South (Robinson, 1996, pp. 21–22). In Robinson's (1996, p. 23) words "[t]he North–South divide is growing and should not be understated." In fact, the North–South divide is counted as one of the greatest and devastating economic schisms of the new era. Although the per capita global income tripled from 1960 to 1994, it has shown a tremendously uneven distribution among regions and nations. In the decade of the 1990s, over 100 nations had a per capita income that was lower than in the 1980s. There are also instances where such per capita income was lower than in the decades of the 1970s or 1960s. Robinson also cites a 2000 IMF report that claims a faltering position for almost 20 percent of the world's population over the past few decades. The growing gap between the world's rich and poor is what Robinson calls apartheid on a global level (Robinson, 2004, pp. 152–153, 157).

Also problematic is the increasing plight of women in the global division of labor, in addition to growing racial and ethnic disparities (Robinson, 1996, p. 24). In the strongest statement on this state of affairs, Robinson claims that "[t]he worldwide inequality in the distribution of wealth and power is a form of permanent structural violence against the world's majority" (Robinson, 1996, p. 22).

Moreover, the problems take root in the capitalist crisis of underconsumption (to which Robinson also adds overproduction, either or both creating overaccumulation). This leads to the struggle to find new markets and cycles of speculative investment. These, in conjunction with the crisis of state power and the disparities previously discussed, give rise to conflict in the new global era (Robinson, 2004, pp. 147–150).

Critiques of the New Globalization Literature

Empire *and Its Critics*

Hardt and Negri's study has received copious and swift criticism. The purpose here is not to cover each point of critique, but to highlight the most salient criticisms in the literature. One criticism is that the book, largely in a narrative style and using ill-defined images of "multitudes," "networks," and the like, lacks sufficient analytical depth and empirical support of its arguments (Bartolovich, 2003, pp. 178–179; Callinicos, 2002, p. 320; Petras, 2002b). The book is neither seen as an economics treatise, nor is it a convincing historical treatise, and it leaves several conceptual gaps uncovered.

The first gap we address relates to the use of history, or rather a lack of it. Hardt and Negri do not discuss the nature of the discontinuity between imperialism, and the transition to empire (Barkawi & Laffey, 2002, pp. 111, 118). The transition, as it were, from imperialism to empire goes from a condition where there are historical agents to a condition where these agents occupy a vastly different world, with their role and place in the world obscured. It is suddenly as if "Empire did it" (Bartolovich, 2003, p. 194). Critics such as Bartolovich (2003), Barkawi and Laffey (2002), and Petras (2002b) appear to be somewhat disconcerted that political economy is performed without history — one of its chief pillars. If perhaps the transition is not the topic Hardt and Negri wish to directly address, there are still problems with the connection of history and explanation. Their promotion of the January 1968 Tet offensive in Vietnam as the benchmark for military imperialism's demise, for example, leaves questions of how this is so and what it is about that event that makes it such. This is especially problematic in light of the U.S. military expansion throughout the world subsequent to that event (Barkawi & Laffey, 2002, p. 124).

Secondly, critics take issue with the portrayal of economic (and related institutional) explanations in *Empire*. Petras claims that the role of economic institutions and economic actions on the part of the state is much different than portrayed in the world described by Hardt and Negri. According to Petras, it is the state that is the senior partner in the relationship between the state and international financial institutions (IFIs). Petras (2002b, p. 142) notes that "[a]ll major internationally-binding trade agreements, liberalizing trade and establishing new trade regulations, are negotiated by states, enforced by states and subject to state modification." He notes that major arrangements and organizations such as General Agreement on Tariffs and Trade (GATT), the WTO, and the Loma Convention were all established by states. Further, IFI officers are frequently appointed by states, and work closely with the state's financial institutions in decision making and operations of the agency (Petras, 2002b, p. 145). Likewise, Aronowitz (2003, p. 24) makes the point that Hardt and Negri give very little discussion to these financial institutions or institutional arrangements at all, save their rather broad discussion of the nature of jurisprudence of the new order.

Hardt and Negri also inadequately address the role of multinational corporations. Petras points out that these corporations are also dependent on the states to facilitate their business in the host state. Whereas Hardt and Negri focus on the development of communication networks and technology in the growth of global capitalism, Petras claims that there is a close connection between military expansion that facilitates and protects the expansion of the multinationals (cf. Petras, 2002b, pp. 143–144). The more powerful nation-states also play a senior role to the multinationals in other ways. The states step in to prevent effects of the chaos of financial collapse and provide succor to the ailing corporations, as well as provide subsidies to export sectors and other forms of trade intervention (Petras, 2002b, pp. 140–141). Finally, he notes that decisions of the multinational corporations are headquartered entities, with decisions being largely made at the corporation's headquarters (Petras, 2002b, p. 144). To sum up, the tenor of some of the criticism can be found in Petras' observation, that

> [a]t a time when the US is the only superpower, when almost 50 percent of the 500 biggest multinationals are US owned and headquartered, and Washington is leading a war of intervention against the peasants and workers of Afghanistan — after previous wars of intervention against peasants and workers in the Balkans, Central America (Panama), the Caribbean (Grenada) and proxy wars in Columbia (Plan Columbia) and earlier Angola, Mozambique, Nicaragua — the authors of this widely-praised book tell us that imperialism is a thing of the past.
>
> Petras (2002b, p. 137)

Petras also takes issue with the claim that information technology (IT) occupies the critical role assigned to it by Hardt and Negri. He notes that Japan has highly automated the production processes, but however has lingered at a very slow growth rate for more than a decade. Studies are also cited that indicate that productivity rates and profitability have very little to do with the use of information and computer technology. Despite the fanfare, computerization has had little real impact on profit and growth, and the IT industry itself has suffered from a lack of robust growth in recent years (Petras, 2002b, pp. 146–148).

Crystal Bartolovich sees another gap in the economic landscape portrayed in Hardt and Negri's *Empire*. Here we will simply allude to one of her main issues — consumerism and consumption. Whereas most critics focus on production and production processes, Bartolovich sees the lack of attention to consumption as problematic. Consumption is bound to affect other aspects of an economy in a regional sense. She points out that the North has a consumption rate that is not possible in other parts of the world, making them the equivalent of "gated communities," noting that "every 5 per cent unit of the world's population can't use one quarter of the oil" (Bartolovich, 2003, p. 183). The role of the conflict over resources therefore occupies an important place in the nature of globalization that Hardt and Negri fail to articulate in their discussion of the Empire (cf. Bartolovich, 2003, pp. 188–189).

Arrighi criticizes Hardt and Negri's characterization of the smoothness of global economic space and hence the North–South divide, noting that the divide is continuing and persistent. Arrighi suggests that there is neither the evidence of significant narrowing of the gap between the North and South, nor of the development of unprecedented capital or labor flows that the authors describe (Arrighi, 2003, pp. 32–33).

The use of force is an important topic that is omitted from *Empire*. The prospect of the use of nuclear weapons by a state is a security issue that does not find its way into *Empire*'s pages (Barkawi & Laffey, 2002, p. 125; Callinicos, 2002, pp. 325–326). Apart from the threat of nuclear weapons, the prospect of nonnuclear warfare among states is omitted from Hardt and Negri's globalized world, and must be taken into account as well (Barkawi & Laffey, 2002, p. 126).

Criticism of the Transnational Ruling Class Approach

A good deal of comment and criticism on the transnational ruling class literature is addressed by a symposium in the Winter 2001–2002 issue of the journal *Science and Society*, containing nearly 36 pages of critique followed by a 9-page response from Robinson. Many of the criticisms directed toward the transnational class literature are very similar to those directed toward *Empire*. Although it is beyond the scope of this chapter to cover the details of the criticisms, we here highlight a few of the most relevant and critical points.

First, there are critiques regarding methodology and the use of historical method. Mann argues that Robinson and Harris' work tends toward conjecture, omitting empirical evidence and data to support their arguments (2001, pp. 466–467). Specifically, the question arises as to the omission of how the new global order arises from past conditions, i.e., how the transition to a global order based on a transnational class has occurred (cf. Moore, 2001, p. 481). Further, the Robinson and Harris' conceptualization of the stages of capitalism is troubling to Moore (2001, pp. 478–479), as "how one periodizes capitalism has an awful lot to do with how one defines it." Again, Moore takes issue with a rather sudden appearance of the new global capitalism and the lacuna in how capitalism and state have evolved to meet the interests of both global capitalists and transnational state interests (Moore, 2001, p. 479). Robinson and Harris' lack of strong consideration of intricacies that national class relations have on the transnational class condition is another criticism (Van der Pijl, 2001, pp. 492–494), as well as the lack of engagement with opposing theoretical frameworks (e.g., world systems theory) (Mann, 2001, p. 465). Moore (2001, pp. 481–483) calls for the use of a world-reaching historical approach to further understand the roles of history, geographies, and class in understanding changes in the regimen of capitalist accumulation and the processes that regulate it. Overall, it is the analysis of many of the authors that although there is more of a transnational character to global capitalism, it is still in an incipient form and is prone to rapid changes and unpredictable developments.

There are considerable questions not only about the nature, but also about the extent of transnationalization as described by Robinson and his associates. Mann (2001, p. 468) sees the prospect for a number of complex interactions and events between various global actors — frequently indeterminate interactions that preclude what could truly be called a global system. Arrighi (2001, p. 474) claims that a true transition from nation-state capitalism to transnational capitalism could take a century or even centuries. Likewise, Went (2001, pp. 487–490) sees a long period of "trial-and-error" in the unfolding of the new order, given disparate interests among actors, who frequently pursue competing interests. In addition to what may be considered "ultra-imperialism," or an imperialism based on the convergence of financial and state interests, Went holds that a global outcome could very well be "super-imperialism," or an hegemony characterized by the financial and military strength of a single nation-state, or alternately the "continuing competition among blocks" of imperialist state groupings that shape the landscape of the global system. The role of force in establishing and maintaining a transnational system and the physical location of production also cannot be overlooked or minimized (Mann, 2001, pp. 477–478).

Critics also question the claim of a weakened nation-state function, as offered in the transnational ruling class approach. With so much of global economic organization in flux, there is a tendency for many theorists to see the nation-state, and the economic production that occurs within nation-states or a region of nation-states, as a defining element within global economic organization. States provide the source of regulation for production that finds its way on the global trading field, and states coordinate well with IFIs because their staff share a "dual identity" in their work within these institutions (Mann, 2001, pp. 466–467). States still provide essential and unduplicated functions within the international system (Went, 2001, pp. 486–487). Much economic production remains tied to a specific location within states or regions (Moore, 2001, p. 480). This is not to say that the nation-state is "watertight" or "fully compartmentalized." To the contrary, it is the state that provides the economic and political basis for cross-border labor and capital flows (Van der Pijl, 2001, p. 494). In sum most critics argue that there are indeed emerging transnational trends in the new global landscape, to be sure, however these are overstated in the works of Robinson and Harris (2000) and Burbach and Robinson (1999). Further, the current horizon prevents easy seeing or predicting eventual outcomes related to transnationalization or the role of a transnational ruling class.

Robinson's response to critiques of his and his associates' work also features discussions of methods and, to use an overworked catchword, paradigm. Here we do not focus on some of the more technical points of his argument, which are necessarily variegated as they represent a response to several critiques, but again focus on the most salient points. Robinson responds that his works are "early approximations" of transnationalization, and that "the transnationalization of capitalism *by definition* involves the transnationalization of classes" (Robinson, 2001, pp. 500–501). His concern is that the analysis of some of his critics is centered on the nation-state, and this perspective confounds the recognition and understanding of transnational patterns. Robinson (2001, p. 502) notes in discussing gross national product (GNP) that

> GNP per capital is nation-state-centric data that in fact *disguises* the processes involved in transnational class formation, such as the rise of new capitalist groups and high consumption sectors that participate in the global economy in countries where GNP per capita may well be in relative decline. And vice-versa: GNP per capita masks rising "third-worldization" in the North.
>
> Robinson (2001, p. 502)

Not only does GNP as a national indicator confound understanding the transnationalization process, but the Weberian concept of dual states and markets is a framework that can no longer be used to understand current realities. It is not nation-states themselves, but variously the social groups contained within those states that have the economic interests. In this process, the terms "core" and "periphery" cannot refer simply to territories or physical political geographies, but nonspatial social places within the transnational system (Robinson, 2001, pp. 503, 502). This does not mean, however, that space ceases to be relevant, and capitalism has not become devoid of space. Robinson attempts to clarify his position by asserting that

> *Nowhere* have I ever suggested, for instance, that global capitalism is "placeless." My argument is that the changes involved in globalization compel us to reconsider the relationship between territory, power, and accumulation. It is *not* that space becomes irrelevant under globalization. Instead, the social configuration of space can no longer be conceived in nation-state terms but rather as processes of uneven accumulation denoted primarily by social group rather than territorial differentiation. The question is *not*, does space still matter?, but how may we reconceive space?, and is there any justification to continue to privilege *nation-state space*? (italics in original)
>
> Robinson (2001, p. 505)

Thus, Robinson's paradigm is different than that of Hardt and Negri, as he views the transnationalization through a different prism. It is to be noted also that Robinson has recognized the role of force in his previous writings (Moore, 2001, p. 478), and analyzed the role of the U.S. hegemony in globalization (Chilcote, 2002, p. 81).

So Is It Globalization or Is It Still Imperialism?

We have sketched a picture of two perspectives on the new global order — one featuring the death of imperialism as in Hardt and Negri's *Empire*; the other the demise of the traditional nation-state, as in Robinson's work. We have also looked briefly at the critique of these ideas. Here we move into specific subtopics, but do not attempt to address the globalization/imperialism debate *vis-à-vis* each of Guillén's five questions about globalization. Indeed, some topics would be questions that depend upon the answers to other questions, for example questions regarding homogeneous convergence are germane only after an affirmative affirmation that globalization exists. In this introductory study we will instead look at five areas of the debate: the reality of imperialism, the economics of imperialism/globalization, the role and function of the nation-state, international (some would say imperialist) rivalries, and the global role of the United States.

Arguments for the Reality of Imperialism

Many scholars claim that the evidence presented in the case for globalization is misleading, and that we are still in an era of imperialism. Many in this camp, such as Vilas (2002), Petras (2002a,b), and numerous others contend that the new globalization is in reality a continuation of the old imperialism in updated raiment. Vilas points out that globalization entails new instruments, methods, and roles for institutions, however these are the new ways of pursuing the same goals of dominant capitalism — accumulation and profit — in the context of changing circumstances (Vilas, 2002, pp. 71, 73). Petras (2002a,b) and Petras and Veltmeyer (2001) have explicitly extended this critique to question the very technological basis of globalization by questioning the impact of a scientific–technological revolution and computerization, and indeed labels the new ideologically driven discourse on globalization as "globaloney." Kleinknecht and ter Wengel (1998) also refer to economic globalization as a myth, citing their findings on trade and financial patterns. Again globalization, in this view, does not exist — at least not in a sufficiently different form than an enhanced stage of imperialism.

The concept of imperialism has a spotted history. In the decades of the 1960s and 1970s the concept was overshadowed by other theories of development, and the subsequent two decades have seen it wane with the rise of globalization theories (Chicote, 2002, p. 83). It can easily be argued, however, that the argument for imperialism is strong, notwithstanding sociocultural propositions to the contrary. It would seem, given the popular political discourse at a given time (at least in the United States), that imperialism has rarely existed in the present tense. History delivers a different interpretation of the imperialist situation in retrospect, however. For example, although the United States has championed itself as a defender of human rights, it has also played the role of world tyrant in support of business interests and political manipulation. One only needs to look at the once-covert overthrows of democratically elected governments and the subsequent establishment of dictatorships in their place by the United States as facilitated by the Central Intelligence Agency (CIA) — such as the 1954 overthrow of Arbenz in Guatemala (Galeano, 1973, pp. 127–128; Jonas, 1974, pp. 155–169), the 1964 overthrow of Goulart in Brazil (Dos Santos, 1974, pp. 455–486; Galeano, 1973, pp. 232–233), and the 1973 overthrow of Allende in Chile (Cavarozzi & Petras, 1974, pp. 542–560) — among others.[3] Interestingly, the 1973 event is five and one-half years after Hardt and Negri's demarcation of imperialism's 1968 demise.

Moreover, the policy of intervention has extended into the 1980s, 1990s, and into the present primarily, though not exclusively, through U.S. involvement within the global theater (Petras 2002b, pp. 137, 143–144). In these more recent decades, along with military interventions and support of insurgencies, the United States has also instituted a policy over the past two decades described by Robinson as "democracy promotion." Although Robinson describes the policy in the context of his theory of transnational capitalism, imperialism scholars can apply this theory as well. Robinson argues that the United States has instituted a polyarchy to assert control over the political and

[3]Items that have recently been declassified on the 1973 Chilean coup and the U.S. involvement in it can be accessed from a link on the National Security Archive Electronic Briefing Book No. 8 web page of George Washington University at www.gwu.edu/~nsarchiv/NSAEBB/NSAEBB8/nsaebb8i.htm

economic affairs of host nations. He states that this "involves the use of political aid as a new foreign policy instrument, in conjunction with the panoply of established U.S. foreign policy instruments, including economic and military aid, traditional diplomacy, and so forth." In asserting hegemonic control through this polyarchy (including Chile in the 1980s):

> U.S. funding and political guidance for political parties, trade unions, business groups, mass media, and civic organizations have been broadly introduced and integrated into multidimensional U.S. "democracy promotion" undertakings. These "democracy promotion" programs support existing groups, or create new groups entirely from scratch, in the civil society of the target country, in synchronization with U.S. state operations at the level of political society. Complex and multilayered nexuses develop between the civil and political society of target countries and the organs of the U.S. state and civil society operating in conjunction. These operations became most prominent in the 1980s and early 1990s in those countries where social movements, scattered protests and pressures for democratic change had begun to coalesce into mass national democratization movements, such as in the Philippines, Chile, and Haiti.
>
> Robinson (1995, p. 5)[4]

In addition to asserting American control through democracy promotion practices, current events that mark the invasion of Iraq to rid that country of weapons of mass destruction do not set well for arguing that either the imperialism or the nation-state are in functional decline (cf. Harvey, 2003). An interpretation of these current events might otherwise hold that military action and other action is taking place on behalf of a transnational class (cf. Robinson, 2004, p. 137), however this is a proposition critiqued later in discussing interimperialist rivalries.

Global hegemonic relationships exist, to be sure, however are these best understood in terms of globalization and transnationalization or the more classical analysis provided by imperialism studies? For further insight, we turn to the economic arguments that relate to the globalization/imperialism debate.

Economic Issues in Globalization and Imperialism

There is much support to the claim that certain economic events and conditions are global. This is not to say that in discussing global events,

---

[4]While Robinson makes these observations about the polyarchy, such purposeful engagement is not new. For example, one of the arguments about foreign aid provided by Western industrialized nations is that provides continuity for colonial or colonial-like influence and control (Goulet & Hudson, 1971; Sallnow, 1990).

one must therefore preclude the possibility of imperialism, as conceptualizations of globalization can vary. Only that as a matter of observation there are economic conditions that are indeed globally present and interconnected. International trade has significantly increased. Over a 30-year period, from 1960 to 1990, exports as a percentage of gross domestic product (GDP) doubled from 10 to 20 percent in Organization for Economic Cooperation and Development (OECD) nations. In the decade from 1980 to 1990 alone, bank lending rose from 4 to 44 percent of the GDP among those nations (Tabb, 1997, pp. 20–21). There is also evidence that various macroeconomic variables move together among some nation-states over time, that is they simultaneously covary. Such effects have been observed particularly among countries in Europe and East Asia, as shocks produce covariance effects through current account transactions and capital markets (Loayza et al., 2001). Changes in production patterns and displacement of agricultural production because of product price differentials and trade are also observed, frequently causing acute social, political, and domestic livelihood disruptions (Petras, 2000, p. 187). Beginning in the 1980s, macroeconomic policy itself has become globalized through neoliberalism and associated austerity and structural adjustment programs (Went, 1996, pp. 52–53). It is not unreasonable to suppose that the commonalities in policy might produce commonalities in outcomes in many cases.

Yet the relatively weak patterns observed in global trade and investment flows lead some to conclude that globalization, as measured by these indicators, might be close to being a myth. To support the counterthesis against globalization, there are arguments that net trade flows have not appreciably changed over the past century. Incredibly, it is argued that patterns of trade and investment as a percentage of GNP do not vary significantly today from what they were in 1913. Kleinknecht and ter Wengel (1998, p. 638) observe that two world wars and the Great Depression in the 20th century stymied the growth of trade, with international trade then registering a mildly accelerated growth rate in the 1950s. Yet by 1973 most nations experienced a lower level of trade than they did in 1913, and some nations had not even reached their 1913 level of trade as a percentage of GNP by as late as 1994. Weiss (1997, p. 7) concurs, stating that "for a range of industrialized nations, the ratios of export trade to GDP in 1913 may actually have exceeded the level reached in 1973. As late as 1991, the OECD shares of exports in terms of GDP (17.9 per cent) did not enormously outweigh those estimated for 1913 (16 per cent)." Moreover, to the extent that international trade has increased, it tends to be a highly regionalized trade between a few nations or national clusters. Kleinknecht and ter Wengel, for example, state that Europe's trade with non-European nations as a percentage of GDP has actually declined since 1960. Overall, the low volume (less than 10 percent of GDP) of European trade occurring outside the European Union (EU) further signals that the region is an identifiable and highly concentrated trading block (Kleinknecht & ter Wengel, 1988, p. 641). Likewise, Went (1996, p. 39) (who is not a strong antiglobalization thesis proponent but still retains a place for the nation-state) cites ter Wengel's assertion that that most production and financial transactions take place between the Triad, which is the European Union, the member nations of North American Free Trade Agreement (NAFTA), and Japan.

There may be some confounds in understanding trade patterns, however. One confound might be the changing economic mix in modern economies. One must consider the changing industrial mix between the manufacturing and the physical production industries versus service industries in accounting for changes of trade patterns as a percentage of GDP. The more services become a part of the productive mix, the less trade will become a part of GDP (Kleinknecht & ter Wengel, 1998, pp. 638–639; Went, 1996, p. 41). This is especially the case until recently when significantly more goods were traded than services. Hoogvelt (2001, p. 70), who supports the globalization thesis, also notes that in 1945 the world recognized 50 countries. Now, however, borders arising out of newly formed sovereign nations proliferate. In 2000, the number of nations is closer to 200, a fact that must be taken into consideration in analyzing the actual trade between and among the regions. This is further complicated, of course, by the decline of formal colonial relationships and associated dynamics.

We now turn to considering FDI. FDI has flowed heavily into the United States and Europe (Wade, 1996, p. 70). By 1991, 81 percent of the world's FDI was in "high wage — and relatively high tax — countries: principally the US, followed by the UK, Germany, and Canada. Moreover, this figure represents an increase of 12 points since 1967" (Weiss, 1997, p. 10). Such a concentration in FDI, and in trade, as prompted some to speak of "Europeanization" instead of "globalization" (Kleinknecht & ter Wengel, 1998, p. 644). Since 1990, the United States had a positive net holding of FDI, as its workers labor under the employment of other nation's firms (Tabb, 1997, p. 22). Meanwhile China, Taiwan, South Korea, Hong Kong, and Singapore have become important sources of FDI (Wade, 1996, p. 71).

Similar patterns of concentration hold for other investing as well. In Latin America, for example, investments have been highly concentrated. Beginning in the 1990s, liberalization allowed increases in the amount of portfolio investments in the form of stocks, bonds, and other portfolio investments, and that these were concentrated in more industrialized countries such as Brazil, and not surprisingly, Mexico. Since the 1990s the shift in capital flows has gravitated toward FDI or equity investment *vis-à-vis* portfolio investment. Portfolio investment has grown, however not at the rate of FDI. FDI, however, has grown precipitously. In Brazil, FDI has grown from $3 billion in 1997 to $17 billion, for example, with deficits in that country's current accounts increasing from $1.2 billion to $33 billion in the period from 1994 to 1997. In the 1990s, FDI worldwide increased 223 percent. The increase registered in Latin America is closer to 600 percent, however, with Brazil, Argentina, and Mexico absorbing 62 percent of this increase (Petras & Veltmeyer, 2001, pp. 79–81). FDI and other investment appear to be very much on the rise, however that increase is highly concentrated on the global level.

We now turn to the topic of the location of multinational corporate production, and this is also a story of regionalization and centralization. Some globalization theorists make a strong claim to the transnationalization of production. Production processes or production for various market segments increasingly transcend the national borders, however there are questions as to the degree of transnationalism among these transnational operations. It seems that relatively few transnational or multinational corporations are globalized in terms of not having a distinct national headquarters, having independence from their home national government, having persons (or very many) of other nationalities on their boards, or having truly internationalized R&D or technology producing operations (Patel & Pavitt, 1991; Ruigrok & van Tulder, 1995, pp. 152–169; Wade, 1996, pp. 78–82). This appears to be the case because of concentrations of skilled workers, the proximity of resources available in certain industrial clusters, and the various logistical, organizational, and technical advantages of proximity (Kleinknecht & ter Wengel, 1998, p. 645). Advantages also arise from tacit "person-to-person" knowledge, knowledge that cannot be learned apart from experience with a given technology, and knowledge that can be quite costly to acquire (Kleinknecht & ter Wengel, 1998, p. 645; Wade, 1996, p. 85).

What does the foregoing mean for globalization? Although Hardt and Negri have attempted to describe globalization as negating the dimension of space, we see that globalization features heavy concentrations of trade, investment, and technology development in space — it is far from spaceless. There are also those who would argue that globalization is so concentrated in given spaces that it hardly merits being called global. However levels of economic activity across national borders are much higher, even given that they are relatively concentrated, and the world is much more open to outsourcing and privatization. These and other changes (e.g., electronic communications) characterize the global economy, and given the continued expansion of capitalism any comparison with 1913 calls for considerable qualification. High concentrations of economic activity also do not themselves preclude the existence of a transnational class, but one would likely need to suggest that the concentration of such economic activity over respective regions of the globe mirrors the concentrated presence of such a class. This is consistent with Robinson's (2001, pp. 500–501) own approach, that "the transnationalization of capitalism by *definition* involves the transnationalization of classes" (italics in original), only this could be the case over selected regions of capitalist space. Further, those that hail the demise of capitalist geographical space, claiming that this *ipso facto* precludes the possibility of imperialism, lack a sufficient argument.

We can see here, however, that these propositions are based on a number of contingencies, and we must proceed further to understand the dynamics of the system. We therefore turn to the topic of the state and the state power.

Bringing the State In or Ushering It Out?

Sassen (1999, p. 410) stresses the importance of accounting for other factors than merely the economic ones in understanding globalization. The function of the nation-state is important as well, and to this we might add that it is likewise important for understanding arguments pertaining to the globalization/imperialism debate. Sassen states that "[w]e cannot understand globalisation by focusing merely on international trade and investment and other cross-border flows. This type of focus easily leads to the notion that globalization comes simply from the outside."

It seems not terribly long ago that Evans, Skocpol, and others were calling for "bringing the state back in" for analyzing the complexities of political and economic events and policies (Evans et al., 1985). Evens outlined several possibilities for the effects of transnational transactions on state power. Evans (1985, pp. 193–194) cites Barnet and Müller's (1974) *Global Reach* as one perspective that holds that the state cedes some of its power to the transnational parties as transnational exchanges or flows increase. Another perspective of dependency theorists and world system theorists is that increasing the transnational flows increases the core state power, while decreasing the power of peripheral states. A third perspective is that the governance required for formulating, regulating, and monitoring policy responses actually enhances state apparatuses as they engage the requirements of the new transaction environment. Finally, Evan's own perspective, surprisingly, is somewhat the reverse of that of the dependency and world system theorists — increased transnational transactions enhances the functions of peripheral states in some cases while limiting the functions of core states. The rationale for this position is that multinationals might prefer working with more powerful host states, thus supporting this development, and the relatively advanced development of state structures to accommodate transnational guests would necessarily strengthen what were previously relatively weak state mechanisms. As for core states, the stronger and more active the transnationals become within them, the more they encroach upon the economic and financial roles of the state.

The first position, previously discussed, corresponds to the arguments of those who promote the rise of a transnational class, although this position now requires further modification given the rise of the knowledge-based information economy. The second proposition is commonly associated with the position of most scholars who argue that we are still firmly in an age of imperialism. The third proposition is similar to that espoused by Sassen, with some qualifications that we will address. The fourth proposition is Evans' own, and there seems to not be a large body of literature to date that addresses this perspective.

We have discussed the first and second position, and now examine the third. Sassen acknowledges the impact of global events on the state, but retains a place for state power in her thinking. The position of Sassen (1996, 1999) is that while the state retains power, its power has nonetheless been "reconfigured." The United States' intervention in the 1994 financial crisis of Mexico, for example, was handled by the Department of the Treasury that was headed up by a financier, instead of being managed by the State Department. Changes go far beyond shifts in departmental responsibilities. Much attention is also focused on keeping the peace among international players. Organizations have come into existence to affect this (e.g., the WTO), and not without significant debate as to their role in administering international agreements. Interestingly enough, the state has reconfigured power, but this power is in part directed toward, and simultaneously shaped, by political exigencies beyond its borders. It is power that is indeed state power, but power that interfaces in a relationship with global forces. Sassen explains that

> While the national state was and remains in many ways the guarantor of the social, political, and civil rights of a nation's people, from the 1970s on we see a significant transformation in this area. Human rights codes have become a somewhat autonomous source of authority that can delegitimize a state's particular actions if it violates such codes. Thus both the global capital market and human rights codes can extract accountability from the state, but they do so with very different agendas. Both have gained a kind of legitimacy.
>
> It is clear that defining the nation-state and the global economy as mutually exclusive operations is, in my analysis, highly problematic. The strategic spaces where many global processes take place are often national; the mechanisms through which the new legal forms necessary for globalization are implemented are often part of state institutions; the infrastructure that makes possible the hypermobility of financial capital at the global scale is

> situated in various national territories. The condition of the nation state, in my view, cannot be reduced to one of declining significance.
>
> Sassen (1996, pp. 27–28)

Along similar lines, Biersteker (1990, p. 480) delineates several tasks assumed by states in a global economy. These include influencing private sector actors; regulating business and financial actors behavior; mediating conflicts between parties; providing a distribution function through transfer payments, subsidies, and the like; actually producing goods and services, whether by production, parastatals, contract, or subsidy; and planning. Beirsteker (1990, p. 481) contends that "[e]very state intervenes in its economy, and nearly all intervene in each of the ways identified above."

Others see the role of the nation-state as under transformation and reconfiguration, but feel many state functions are being displaced as the state becomes more transnational in nature. The interface of states with global institutions such as the IMF is a case in point. Not only do states work with the IMF in obtaining development funding (primarily loans), but the IMF can also serve as a central banking function, as it did when it managed the debt repayments during the 1980s debt crisis in Eastern Europe and some developing nations (McMichael, 1995, pp. 38, 42, 44–45).

Interimperialist Rivalry and the Globalization/Imperialism Debate: American Hegemony at the Turn of the Century

We have gotten a little further in the debate, if only by clarifying whether or not the state retains power — and it appears that in many ways it does — but still there is the issue of what this means for specific types of states and under certain conditions. We turn now, however, to what imperialism theorists term interimperialism rivalries, in further probing the global landscape and deciphering its contours. There is considerable literature regarding the nature and meaning of such rivalries.

After World War II and throughout the 1960s, the United States' investments abroad grew. U.S. FDI more than doubled over the decade of the 1960s, tripled during the decade of the 1970s (going from a 1970 level of $75.5 billion to a 1980 level of $213.5 billion), and reached $1.4 trillion in 2000 (Berberoglu, 2003, p. 66). U.S. FDI specifically in the manufacturing sector in 2000 was $254 billion, and $89.7 billion in the less developed countries for that same year. As expected, investment was heavily concentrated in the developed nations of Canada, Britain, Germany, France, and the Netherlands, and the developing nations of Mexico, Brazil, and Singapore (Berberoglu, 2003, p. 66).

However there was another development. The decade of the 1970s also saw the rise of Western Europe (we should not forget Japan) as a contender for world economic leadership, and at a time when the United States began to loosen its absolute grip on the position of economic frontrunner (Wallerstein, 2003, p. 24). Another event for setting the stage for greater rivalry between Western capitalist nations is the subsequent fall of the Soviet Union. The Soviet Union unified capitalist nations behind the United States and facilitated a political cohesion (Gowan, 2003, p. 31; Wallerstein, 2003, p. 24). Its demise did not create rivalry on its own, but it did mean that less clarity of purpose and cooperation was necessary than in the Cold War era.

This has cleared the way for greater interimperialist rivalry, and the existence of such strong leadership among frontrunners has become less a matter of doubt and more a matter of interpretation. One interpretation relates to imperialism. The use of the term "imperialism" was considered unacademic for most of the 20th century. Suddenly, however, this is a word that has become prominent among political figures and the established press (Foster, 2002, p. 1). Wallerstein (2003, p. 23) agrees with this observation, with penetrating insight. He asks

> How come at the moment we are living through a particularly aggressive and egregious form of imperialism, which for the first time in over a hundred years has been ready to use the words "imperial," and "imperialism?" Why should they do that? Now, the answer most people give in one word is U.S. *strength*. And the answer I will give in one word is U.S. *weakness* (italics in original).
>
> Wallerstein (2003, p. 23)

It can just as well be said here that the practice of imperialism is balanced lopsidedly toward the United States. But why is this the case? The answer, in part, is that the United States is the superpower that has access to a strong military foundation as well as the absence of popular protest in its use. The idea that came to the fore with the demise of the neoliberal-based Washington consensus was that the United States would use its military power to preserve its status in the world as the world superpower. This strategy entails substantial increases in defense expenditures, the use of the military as an instrument of persuasion with other nations with respect to its political and economic goals, and "selling" the need for a strong military to a national audience as necessary to enhance national security (Block, 2003, pp. 443–444). Underscoring the position that the current war in Iraq is based on the struggle for power, Wallerstein (2003, p. 27) states that the United States

> needed [the war] to show the United States could do it, and they needed that demonstration in order to intimidate two groups of people: (1) any-

> body in the third world who thinks that they should engage in nuclear proliferation; and (2) Europe. This was an attack on Europe, and that is why Europe responded the way it did.
>
> Wallerstein (2003, p. 27)

There is debate, however, about the degree to which the war is over oil. Wallerstein (2003, p. 27) thinks that the aim was the ability to garner more leveraging power, not controlling oil itself. Others, although agreeing that the war was an affront to Europe, nonetheless contend that it was also to trump Europe's hand in that region and compete with non-Anglo Europe over region's oil resources (Berberoglu, 2003, p. 81; Foster, 2003, p. 6; Gowan, 2003, p. 48; Klare, 2003, p. 53). Consequently, there is little in the way of core European support for postwar reconstruction and institution-building in Iraq, outside Britain. Harvey is the most pointed about the matter. He states that the question can be framed in light of oil: "whoever controls the Middle East controls the global oil spigot and whoever controls the global oil spigot can control the global economy, at least for the near future" (Harvey, 2003, p. 19). Whatever the motivations, it appears that the case is a strong one for inter-imperialist rivalry, and arises out of addressing certain vulnerabilities regarding the United State's place in the global system. Pronouncements that Iraq did not have weapons of mass destruction by Bush administration officials before the policy shift appear to be correct, and as this is written, the U.S. president is struggling with an explanation of how the war fits into his antiterrorism agenda, at least as far as the United States is concerned.[5]

This presence of rivalry between the nation-states has important implications for thinking about the global transnational class. In circumstances of rivalry, and over the past few years these have been great, one can ask what the status of such a class is and just how it relates to the nation-state. That this class quietly operates above the level of national rivalries seems untenable. That nation-states act consistently with and for the interests of the financial and manufacturing interests (and class) within their own borders, on the face of it, seems more reasonable. Yet another possibility is that

---

[5]There are other topics not regularly and directly addressed in the globalization debate, or that receive only scant attention. Such topics include structural adjustment programs, IMF conditionality that frequently is the source of structural adjustment and other austerity measures, debt and debt servicing, and the like. A fuller analysis calls for these to be addressed, however much of the debate regarding the IMF and structural adjustment has been well aired, with several decades of criticism of the IMF and its sister institution and the effects of their recommended (or forced) economic policies. This has been further updated by no less than a former Chief Economist of the World Bank, with the publication of Joseph E. Stiglitz's *Globalization and Its Discontents* (2003, New York: W.W. Norton & Company). The reader is also referred to Cheryl Payer's *The Debt Trap: The International Monetary Fund and the Third World* (1974, New York: Monthly Review Press), and *The Debt Boomerang: How Third World Debt Harms Us All*, by Susan George (1992, London: Pluto Press).

interimperialist rivalries are themselves contradictions in a global economic and political balancing act. There may be interdependence and cooperation in the market, however this may be tenuous. Albo (2004, p. 95), in his discussion of the new imperialism, best expresses this when he states that

> To the extent that the circuits of capital in states are internationalized, and thus dependent on the world market for their self-expansion and realization, both increased international competition and interdependency will be present. Inter-imperialist relations will register this contradiction. But only in particular historical moments will inter-firm and inter-state competitive rivalries spill over into imperial rivalry in the sense of conflict over political leadership of the imperialist block.
>
> Albo (2004, p. 95)

Now, much of what has just been discussed relates to relations between the core nations. The topic here is North–South relations, or for shorthand relations between the core states and the noncore states. The interimperialist rivalries considered here have a significant impact on the core's realignment not only among the core states, but also among noncore states as well. And this dual realignment, occurring simultaneously, has re-fanned the cinders of imperialism as a topic of discussion. These discussions shed new light on the topic of globalization, and allow for conceptual reformulation of the role of the nation-state.

The Complex Tapestry: Reweaving Some Threads in 12 Propositions

So what is the verdict from the debates on the organization of the global economic system and North–South relations of imperialism? Many of the globalization theories are serious attempts to understand new realities. Others, however, tend to center heavily on the spectacular and on the newness of the modern era: impressive space-transcending cases of new production processes, business and political arrangements, technology development, and the proliferation of knowledge, information, and communication. This is likely the reason that those theories tend toward grossly overstated propositions, and are voraciously consumed by the popular press, as in the case of *Empire*. As such, many of these theories are not in a position to mount a successful argument against the reality of imperialism. Some of the new developments that inspire such narratives are impressive, to be sure, however focusing too heavily upon "limelight developments" within the new global economic landscape provides a distraction from a complete consideration of its contours. We are in interesting times, however there are continuities. New knowledge and technology do not in themselves have to imply new goals among the class elements, the new organizational paths, or the like. They may very well point to better ways of achieving established goals, such as capitalist accumulation.

Here we briefly cite some propositions related to continuities, many already supported in this chapter. These are built upon or are related to central points developed here, and are fruitful areas for further study in the areas of governance and public administration.

The Nation-State

It is not particularly a good time to claim that there is a form that resolutely displaces the nation-state as a form of global political organization. The nation-state may certainly be reconfigured and certain elements of its function may therefore lessen, or even increase, however, the nation-state — and core nation-states more than others — have considerable power to interface with, affect, and otherwise influence global conditions. To no small degree, core nations are a party to creating and fostering global conditions. From interimperialist rivalries, to the use of economic and political power, especially the core states are formidable entities. Nation-states of less developed countries will also have important functions to perform in the changing economic and organizational milieu of global influences.

Imperialism

It is also not a good time to announce the death of imperialism. Imperialism is not only accomplished militarily, but also by applying political and economic levers. Before the collapse of the Soviet Union, imperialism was fueled by the Cold War and was struggling to obtain access to and control of resources. Today, the remaining superpower, the United States, attempts to retain a position of dominance. Already having military dominance, the focus shifts primarily to economic and resource dominance. This also colors its strategy for political dominance. Imperialism, although justified (and simultaneously denied) in the present tense, remains both a present and a historical reality.

The Transnational Ruling Class

In responding to his critics' complaints that his work lacks the solid empirical bases that they seek, Robinson (2001, p. 500) acknowledged that his work represents "early approximations in an ongoing research agenda." Tacit understanding of the world economy, however, would support a theory that suggests some cooperation among global transnational capitalists. Such cooperation is evident in agreements, processes for adjudicating trade disputes, and transnational financial management. As noted, much investment and trade is concentrated where the wealth of capital is concentrated. However, this cooperation can be tenuous, as noted above by Albo (2004), and interstate rivalries among capitalists do emerge. The Iraq war provides a good example of such rivalry. This is why many see the development of a truly transnational form of global organization as trial-and-error, as just in the formation stages, very distant, or even without the necessity that it must eventually form. It is suggested here that interstate imperialist rivalries poses a strong challenge to the concept of a truly transnational ruling class.

Business and National Government

In piecing together an important piece of the tapestry, here we also accept Veblen's (1904, pp. 285–286) proposition that there is a close association between government and business interests. The specification between a clear dichotomy between the two, as is sometimes observed in the literature on the relationship between government and business interests, runs the risk of being specious. On the other hand it is important to understand that institutions (governmental and financial) develop a functional existence of their own, but one that consists of their relationships to one another and to the context of the situations they operate within (Neale, 1988, pp. 231–235, 245–247). Business never purely leads, but provides strong influence in the negotiation of political direction.

The Uneven Landscape of Statehood

Regarding global geopolitics, a state is not simple a state, but is endowed with the power and functions of a state. In the very uneven global landscape, there are different types of states. World system theory attempted to deal with this by positing core, semiperipheral, and peripheral states (Wallerstein, 1974). States are highly differentiated and many are dwarfed by the size of corporations. The imbalances of economic power are important in thinking about the global landscape. Exxon Mobil, Wal-Mart, Ford Motors, or General Motors (in descending order of size) each have greater annual sales revenue and earnings than the Netherlands, Brazil, or Canada have GDP. Daimler-Chrysler, Royal Dutch/Shell, BP, General Electric, or Mitsubishi each have annual sales revenue and earnings that exceed the

GDP of Canada, Belgium, Spain, or Sweden. The economic resources of smaller nation-states are dwarfed by the world's large corporations, and especially by the world's top core states, as the sales revenues and earnings of those corporations are composed within the top core nations' GDP (cf. Sklair, 2002, p. 37 for a diagram; Munkirs, 1985, pp. 194–195 for a more complete but dated listing of 1977 standings of national GDPs and corporate annual sales revenues). As discussed above, the business influence upon some domestic states can be quite powerful and influence the role of state-to-state relations. This, as all statements, must be qualified. However this is a topic for consideration and study.

Internal Capitalist Class Dynamics

Piecing together the above discussed two sections, we consider the studies that highlight the nature of class within the nation-state that articulate with a larger, transnational base. Such classes within less developed countries have been termed the "comprodorial class" (Turner, 1980) or as in Frank's (1972) work, the "lumpenbourgeoisie." These concepts point to a peripheral state's ruling class that serves as a junior partner with elites in core states in the task of capitalist exploitation. Both senior and junior partners benefit and have considerable political power within their own borders. This concept does not itself eliminate the role of state functions, but many aspects of the state functions are directed toward class purposes. This, of course, in many ways carries very strong similarities with Robinson's (1995) thesis on the United States' "democracy promotion" discussed above, except Robinson sees the balance favoring a truly transnationalized class as opposed to ruling opportunistic elements within the state that have specific relationships with actors external to the state. Likewise Sunkel, although not ignoring the external and the imperialist relationships, also focused on the internal dynamics of transnational processes within the less developed states, and the dynamic between the internal and the external (Blomström & Hettne, 1984, pp. 49–50, 59–61).

Uneven Economic Space

Patterns of investment, trade, finance, and other capital and resource flows remain regionalized and concentrated for a number of reasons. In some cases, this relates overtly to political or economic strategies, i.e., strategies that could be identified as imperialistic. However in other cases, as we have seen, it relates to the operational benefits of proximity that are less directly associated with political strategies. In some cases, it may relate to institutions or even tacit knowledge. These various factors, however, create a global landscape that is far from spaceless, heavily riveting economic and political processes to space.

Certain areas of the globe also show improved growth. East Asia and the Pacific region have experienced positive economic and agricultural growth over the few decades, interrupted for a time by the 1997 Asian financial crisis. Oil shocks, among other factors, are projected to somewhat dampen this growth (Chatterjee et al., 2004; World Bank, 2004). Overall, the gap between the North and the South has widened and is considerable, as Robinson (2004, pp. 152–153) states.

The Uneven Landscape of Global Production and Transactions

The dynamics of above three sections variously interact in different circumstances to create an uneven global landscape of production and transactions. Global production and transaction patterns may yield disastrous or beneficial results. In the Philippines, Uruguay Round trade agreement under General Agreement on Tariffs and Trade (GATT) threatened the livelihood of over a million poor corn farmers, with subsidized grain from the United States and grain from Thailand being cheaper to import and process than domestically produced corn (Oxfam, 1996; McMichael, 1998). Such an example highlights the need for checking neoliberal trade policies. Trade liberalization is credited for facilitating the import of rice to Bangladesh from India, however, during the former country's 1997 harvest failure (Dorosh, 2001). Unevenness in both the economic landscape and domestic economic effects of policy is a critical factor in transnational relations.

The Need to Study Economic Structures

In-depth studies of the structure of economic relations can help elucidate the nature of relationships, or at a minimum clarify the debates about those relationships. In the previous era of dependency studies, contributions on the nature and mechanisms of trade and exchange were provided in the works of and Prebisch (1950), Dos Santos (1970), Frank (1970), Galtung (1971), and Balogh (1972). These works represented a major accomplishment in understanding the nature of dependency. All of these works are nation-state-centric, however. Here it is agreed with Robinson that new directions must be explored to fully understand the dynamics that lie behind the trade, financial, and production statistics that are collected on the level of the nation-state. This does not in any way discount the role of the state and state dynamics, however the totality of capitalist processes and dynamics must be searched out. This new task represents a challenge. As Mann (2001, p. 465) observes, capitalists and their behavior are very difficult to study, as there is limited access to data on their behavior. The more the behavior of capitalists is studied, however, the better is our understanding of the dynamics of capitalism.

Globalization and Ideology

Although the purported globalization may be highly concentrated over an uneven global landscape, and highly concentrated within discrete regions themselves, it seems to have no lack of an ideological component. Overstatements (some would say mythology) about the great trek and triumph of the neoliberal capitalist order are muffled by the emergence of alternate realities in many cases. Privatization has frequently lacked an adequate basis in planning, or alternatively provided the basis, in tandem with other neoliberal policy formulations, for economic chaos (cf. Stiglitz, 2003, pp. 54–59, 142–165). Neoliberal policies of liberalization and privatization have done well for capitalist accumulation, but have worked havoc on the mass segment of populations that are out of the social and economic limelight (Petras & Veltmeyer, 2001, pp. 69–73). The demise of communism and rise of capitalism in the former Soviet Union, which supposedly required mainly the difficult mastering of the capitalist learning cure to achieve market economy success, has resulted in a GDP that is 66 percent of what it was in 1989. Ukraine's GDP in 2000 was only one third of what it was a decade earlier. It seems that only a few former Eastern Block nations, such as Poland, Slovenia, Slovakia, and Hungary, have managed to regain a GDP of about the same level as a decade earlier (Stiglitz, 2003, pp. 142–165). This is the celebrated "transition" from communism to capitalism in the opening of the former Soviet economy to global economic and political participation.

Secular Trends

Trends, such as demographic patterns and transitions, will likely have a tremendous impact on the globe. The aging of Europe (Grant et al., 2004), for example, will produce profound economic and productivity effects and will impact the conditions described in other propositions here. Immigration will also play a greater role in an increasingly global economy (cf. Sassen, 1996, pp. 59–99).

The Tenuous Balance

With increased globalization, or what Petras and Veltmeyer (2001, pp. 69–71) call a "new imperial order," there may be reason to argue that there already are periods of social and organizational upheaval among the nation-states (Berberoglu, 2003, pp. 65–86), within the nation-states (Petras, 2000, p. 187), or within international global financial networks (Block, 2003, pp. 453–454). There appear, however, to be few current strong responses to this on the level of the nation-state. In Brazil, President Lula has embarked upon a path of guarded engagement with globalization forces. One of the strongest stands against unbridled power of extranational capitalist control (chiefly of the United States) is seen in the popular presidency of Hugo Chávez (cf. Ellner, 2002, pp. 88–93). One would expect both further postures of control and resistance, bolstered by economic and ideological stands, as respective parties stake out their claim in the new order.

Implications for the Future

At the outset, we lamented that there is not a high level of attention given to the important topic of globalization and discussions of imperialism across the discipline of public administration. We now might be willing to excuse that there is not. The new economic realities appear to be sweeping the globe in such a way so as to appear unstoppable, creating vast pockets of wealth and at the same time precipitous drops in some national GDPs and a gap between the rich and poor of historical proportions. Yet there is no lack of precedent for understanding such changes. In the previous section, we looked at the older threads, threads that can be rewoven to provide a reliable understanding of present realities. We concur with Petras and Veltmeyer (2001, p. 61) that there is a considerable continuity with conditions of the past, and the new era (of globalization) is best understood as a new condition of the past state economic and political power within the global core (imperialism). The rise of certain Asian nations to international prominence has changed the equation in important ways. Nonetheless the supremacy (although weakened) of the United States as the sole superpower and the omnipresence and power of the American dollar cannot be ignored.

This study is primarily a study of political economy. However there are important implications for public administration. The role of government and public administration is contextualized by the historical development of institutions and emerging economic realities. This has created an increased management task for government and governmental entities, which lead to new decisions that governments or government entities make, but not defined solely by them. The ability among some nations — particularly in the core — to define the new order is unique, but there will nonetheless be anticipated and less anticipated changes in adapting to new economic, social, and political realities.

This will also continue to be the struggle for administrative and political control within and among governments, governmental entities, and transnational organizations, however this will be set in the context of other struggles. These other struggles are the struggles of Hardt and Negri's multitude, the struggles between established rival states, newly emerging rival states, between states that have lost their global fortunes, and the other states that are intent upon keeping and enhancing theirs. And we cannot discount that there will be the exercise of power by alliances that are not specifically tied directly to the instrument of the national state government, i.e., transnational alliances and organizations. These will likely function, however, with the blessing of advanced states and with the support of those states.

These events are events that point to a considerable amount of work to be done in the arena of public administration studies. The discipline of public administration will continue to be equipped to address these issues by those that investigate them, and at the same time the discipline will continue to be challenged to forge understandings and values germane to the ever-changing global society.

References

Aronowitz, S. (2003). The New World Order. In Balakrishnan, G. (Ed.), *Debating Empire.* London: Verso, pp. 19–25.

Albo, G. (2004). The Old and New Economics of Imperialism. In Panitch, L. and Leys, C. (Eds.), *Socialist Register 2004: The New Imperial Challenge.* London: The Merlin Press Ltd., pp. 88–113.

Arrighi, G. (2001). Global Capitalism and the Persistence of the North–South Divide. *Science and Society* 65: 469–476.

Arrighi, G. (2003). Lineages of Empire. In Balakrishnan, G. (Ed.), *Debating Empire.* London: Verso, pp. 29–42.

Balogh, T.P. (1972). The Mechanism of Neo-Imperialism. In Boulding, K.E. and Mukerjee, T. (Eds.), *Economic Imperialism: A Book of Readings.* Ann Arbor, MI: The University of Michigan Press, pp. 275–294.

Barkawi, T. and Laffey, M. (2002). Retrieving the Imperial: *Empire* and International Relations. *Millennium: Journal of International Studies* 31: 109–127.

Bartolovich, C. (2003). Post-Imperialism or New Imperialism? The Eleventh September of George Bush: Fortress U.S. and the Global Politics of Consumption. *Interventions* 5: 177–199.

Berberolgu, B. (2003). *Globalization of Capital and the Nation-State: Imperialism, Class Struggle, and the State in the Age of Global Capitalism.* Lanham: Rowman & Littlefield Publishers.

Biersteker, T. J. (1990). Reducing the Role of the State in the Economy: A Conceptual Exploration of IMF and World Bank Prescriptions. *International Studies Quarterly* 34: 477–492.

Block, F. (2003). The Global Economy in the Bush Era. *Socio-Economic Review* 1: 439–456.

Blomström, M. and Hettne, B. (1984). *Development Theory in Transition: The Dependency Debate and Beyond.* London: Zed Books.

Burbach, R. and Robinson, W.I. (1999). The fin de siecle debate: Globalization as Epochal Shift. *Science and Society* 63: 10–39.

Callinicos, A. (2002). The Actuality of Imperialism. *Millennium: Journal of International Studies* 31: 319–326.

Cavarozzi, M.J. and Petras, J.F. (1974). Chile. In Chilcote, R.H. and Edelstein, J.C. (Eds.), *Latin America: The Struggle with Dependency and Beyond.* New York: John Wiley, pp. 495–578.

Chatterjee, S., Prakash, B., and Tabor, S.R. (2004). *Income, Poverty and Hunger in Asia: The Role of Information.* International Conference on Agriculture Statistics (ICAS III), Cancun, QR, Mexico.

Chilcote, R.H. (2002). Globalism or Imperialism? *Latin American Perspectives* 29: 80–84.

Dorosh, P.A. (2001). Trade Liberalization and National Food Security: Rice Trade between Bangladesh and India. *World Development* 19: 673–689.

Dos Santos, T. (1970). The Structure of Dependence. *American Economic Review* 60: 231–236.

Dos Santos, T. (1974). Brazil: The Origins of a Crisis. In Chilcote, R.H. and Edelstein, J.C. (Eds.), *Latin America: The Stuggle with Dependency and Beyond.* New York: John Wiley, pp. 415–490.

Ellner, S. (2002). The "Radical" Thesis on Globalization and the Case of Venezuela's Hugo Chávez. *Latin American Perspectives* 29: 88–93.

Evans, P.B. (1985). Transnational Linkages and the Economic Role of the State: An Analysis of Developing and Industrialized Nations in the Post-World War II Period. In Evans, P.B., Rueschemeyer, D., and Skocpol, T. (Eds.), *Bringing the State Back in.* Cambridge, England: Cambridge University Press, pp. 192–226.

Evans, P.B., Rueschemeyer, D., and Skocpol, T. (Eds.) (1985). *Bringing the State Back In.* Cambridge, England: Cambridge University Press.

Farazmand, A. (1999). Globalization and Public Administration. *Public Administration Review* 59: 509–522.

Foster, J.B. (2002). The Rediscovery of Imperialism. *Monthly Review* 54: 1–16.

Foster, J.B. (2003). The New Age of Imperialism. *Monthly Review* 55: 1–14.

Frank, A.G. (1970). On the Mechanisms of Imperialism: The Case of Brazil. In Rhodes, R.I. (Ed.), *Imperialism and Underdevelopment: A Reader.* New York: Monthly Review Press, pp. 89–100.

Frank, A.G. (1972). *Lumpenbourgeoisie: Lumpendevelopment: Dependence, Class, and Politics in Latin America.* New York: Monthly Review Press.

Galeano, E. (1973). *Open Veins of Latin America: Five Centuries of the Pillage of a Continent.* New York: Monthly Review Press.

Galtung, J. (1971). A Structural Theory of Imperialism. *Journal of Peace Research*. 8: 81–117.

George, S. (1992). *The Debt Boomerang: How Third World Debt Harms Us All*. London: Pluto Press.

Goulet, D. and Hudson, M. (1971). *The Myth of Aid: The Hidden Agenda of the Development Reports*. New York: IDOC North America.

Gowan, P. (2003). U.S. Hegemony Today. *Monthly Review* 5: 30–50.

Grant, J., Hoorens, S., Sivadasan, S., van het Loo, M., DaVanzo, J., Hale, L., Gibson, S., and Butz, W. (2004). *Low Fertility and Population Ageing: Causes, Consequences, and Policy Options*. Santa Monica, CA: Rand.

Guillén, M.F. (2001). Is Globalization Civilizing, Destructive, or Feeble? A Critique of Five Key Debates in the Social Science Literature. *Annual Review of Sociology* 27: 235–260.

Hardt, M. and Negri, A. (2000). *Empire*. Cambridge, MA: Harvard University Press.

Harris, R.L. (2002). Globalization and Globalism in Latin America: Contending Perspectives. *Latin American Perspectives* 29: 5–23.

Harvey, D. (2003). *The New Imperialism*. Oxford, England: Oxford University Press.

Hoogvelt, A. (2001). *Globalization and the Postcolonial World: The New Political Economy of Development*. 2nd Edn. Baltimore: The Johns Hopkins University Press.

Howard, M.C. and King, J.E. (2000). Whatever Happened to Imperialism? In Chilcote, R.H. (Ed.), *The Political Economy of Imperialism: Critical Appraisals*. Lanham, MD: Rowman & Littlefield Publishers, pp. 19–40.

Jonas, S. (1974). Guatemala: Land of Eternal Struggle. In Chilcote, R.H. and Edelstein, J.C. (Eds.), *Latin America: the Struggle with Dependency and Beyond*. New York: John Wiley, pp. 93–219.

Klare, M. (2003). The New Geopolitics. *Monthly Review* 5: 51–56.

Kleinknecht, A. and ter Wegnel, J. (1998). The Myth of Economic Globalization. *Cambridge Journal of Economics* 22: 637–647.

Loayza, N.V., Lopez, H., and Ubide, A. (2001). Comovement and Macroeconomic Interdependence: Evidence from Latin America, East Asia, and Europe. *International Monetary Fund Staff Papers* 48: 367–396.

Mann, M. (2001). Globalization is (Among Other Things) Transnational, International, and American. *Science and Society* 65: 464–469.

McMichael, P. (1995). The New Colonialism: Global regulation and the Restructuring of the Interstate System. In Smith, D.A. and Böröcz, J. (Eds.), *A New World Order? Global Transformations in the Late Twentieth Century*. Westport, CT: Greenwood Press, pp. 37–55.

McMichael, P. (1998). Global Food Politics. *Monthly Review* 50: 97–111.

Moore, J.W. (2001). Capital, Territory, and Hegemony Over the Longue Duree. *Science and Society*. 65: 476–484.

Munkirs, J.R. (1985). *The Transformation of American Capitalism: From Competitive Market Structures to Centralized Private Sector Planning*. Armonk, NY: M.E. Sharpe.

Neale, W.C. (1988). Institutions. In Tool, M.R. (Ed.), *Evolutionary Economics, Vol. I: Foundations of Institutionalist Thought*. Armonk, NY: M.E. Sharpe.

Oxfam (1996). *Trade Liberalisation as a Threat to Livelihoods: The Corn Sector in the Philippines*. Oxford, England: Oxfam.

Patel, P. and Pavitt, K. (1991). Large Firms in the Production of the World's Technology: An Important Vase of Non-Globalisation. *Journal of International Business Studies* 22: 1–21.

Payer, C. (1974). *The Debt Trap: The International Monetary Fund and the Third World*. New York: Monthly Review Press.

Petras, J. (2000). Globalization: A Critical Analysis. In Chilcote, R.H. (Ed.), *The Political Economy of Imperialism: Critical Appraisals*. Lanham, MD: Rowman & Littlefield Publishers, pp. 181–213.

Petras, J. (2002a). The Myth of the Third Scientific-Technological Revolution in the Era of Neo-Mercantilist Empires. *Latin American Perspectives* 29: 44–58.

Petras, J. (2002b). A Rose by Any Other Name? The Fragrance of Imperialism. *The Journal of Peasant Studies*. 29: 135–160.

Petras, J. and Veltmeyer, H. (2001). *Globalization Unmasked: Imperialism in the 21st Century*. London: Zed Books Ltd.

Prebisch, R. (1950). *The Economic Development of Latin America and Its Principle Problems*. New York: United Nations.

Robinson, W.I. (1995). Transnational Politics and Global Social Order: A Reassessment of the Chilean Transition in Light of U.S. Intervention. *Journal of Political and Military Sociology* 24: 1–30.

Robinson, W.I. (1996). Globalization: Nine Theses on Our Epoch. *Race and Class*. 38: 13–31.

Robinson, W.I. (1998). Beyond Nation-State Paradigms: Globalization, Sociology, and the Challenge of Transnational Studies. *Sociological Forum* 13: 561–594.

Robinson, W.I. (2001). Global Capitalism and Nation-State-Centric Thinking — What We *Don't* See When We *Do* See Nation-States: Response to Critics. *Science and Society* 65: 500–508.

Robinson, W.I. (2002a). Globalization as a Macro-Structural-Historical Framework of Analysis: The Case of Central America. *New Political Economy* 7: 221–250.

Robinson, W.I. (2002b). Remapping Development in Light of Globalization: From a Territorial to a Social Cartography. *Third World Quarterly* 23: 1047–1071.

Robinson, W.I. (2004). *A Theory of Global Capitalism: Production, Class, and State in a Transnational World*. Baltimore: Johns Hopkins University Press.

Robinson, W.I. and Harris, J. (2000). Towards a Global Ruling Class? Globalization and the Transnational Capitalist Class. *Science and Society* 64: 11–54.

Ruigrok, W. and van Tulder, R. (1995). *The Logic of International Restructuring*. London: Routledge.

Sallnow, J. (1990). Is It Aid or Is It Neocolonialism? *Economic Geography* 62: 30–35.

Sassen, S. (1996). *Losing Control? Sovereignty in an Age of Globalization*. New York: Columbia University Press.

Sassen, S. (1999). Making the Global Economy Run: The Role of Nation States and Private Agents. *International Social Science Journal* 161: 409–416.

Sklair, L. (2002). *Globalization: Capitalism & Its Alternatives*. 3rd Edn. Oxford: Oxford University Press.

Stiglitz, J.E. (2002). *Globalization and Its Discontents.* New York: W.W. Norton & Company.

Tabb, W.K. (1997). Globalization is *an* Issue, the Power of Capital is *the* Issue. *Monthly Review* 49: 20–30.

Turner, T. (1980). Nigeria: Imperialism, Oil Technology, and the Comprador State. In Nore, P. and Turner, T. (Eds.), *Oil and Class Struggle.* London: Zed Press, pp. 119–223.

Van der Pijl, K. (2001). Globalization or Class Society in Transition? *Science and Society* 65: 492–500.

Veblen, T. (1904). *The Theory of Business Enterprise.* New York: Charles Scribner's Sons.

Vilas, C.M. (2002). Globalism or Imperialism? *Latin American Perspectives* 29: 70–79.

Wade, R. (1996). Globalization and Its Limits: Reports of the Death of the National Economy are Greatly Exaggerated. In Berger, S. and Dore, R. (Eds.), *National Diversity and Global Capitalism.* Ithaca, NY: Cornell University Press, pp. 60–88.

Wallerstein, I. (1974). The Rise and Future Demise of the World-Capitalist System: Concepts for Comparative Analysis. *Comparative Studies in Society and History* 16: 387–415.

Wallerstein, I. (2003). U.S. Weakness and the Struggle for Hegemony. *Monthly Review* 55: 23–29.

Weiss, L. (1997). Globalization and the Myth of the Powerless State. *New Left Review* 225: 3–27.

Went, R. (1996). Globalization: Myths, Reality, and Ideology. *International Journal of Political Economy* 26: 39–59.

Went, R. (2001). Globalization: Towards a Transnational State? A Skeptical Note. *Science and Society* 65: 484–491.

World Bank (2004). *Steering a Steady Course. Special Focus: Strengthening the Investment Climate in East Asia.* New York: World Bank.

Chapter 35

Assessing Sustainable Development Administration: A Framework and Implications for Organizational Structure

Tina Nabatchi

CONTENTS

Introduction

In 1972, the United Nations sponsored the Stockholm Conference and released the Stockholm Declaration on the subject of sustainable development. In the decades since, the forces of globalization have continued to swell. The global economy has expanded and become more integrated, profoundly reshaping the social, cultural, and political landscape of the world, as well as the base of natural resources that support human society. In turn, these changes have helped produce a global awareness of the impact that humanity has on the Earth. Likewise, as humanity has come to realize its impact on the global environment, there has been a shift in the way we think about development, whereas development was once viewed almost entirely in economic terms, we are now beginning to think about the concept of sustainable development.

Many have observed that although sustainable development is a wonderful concept in general, its particulars can be difficult to implement (Cooper, 1995; Cooper & Vargas, 2004). However, that is exactly what many public administrators at all levels of government throughout the world are expected to do: work with other governments, non-governmental organizations, and the private sector to implement sustainable development on a day-to-day basis in specific settings, in response to particular problems, and in an increasingly complex political, social, cultural, and economic environment (Cooper, 1995). What follows is the realization that sustainable development projects are implemented within a highly complex, multidimensional environment.

Despite the prominence of calls for sustainable development, there have been few systematic and comprehensive research efforts surrounding sustainable development administration. Most research has taken the form of individual or comparative case studies. There has been even less research about the organizational structures that support sustainable development administration, which is somewhat surprising given the continued calls for contributions from the organizational sciences. The lack of research on sustainable development administration is likely a function of the fuzziness of the term; the definition is vague, and there is no clear blueprint for organization and administration.

In an effort to spark research on this subject, this chapter outlines three perspectives that contribute to our understanding of sustainable development administration. The first perspective examines base assumptions about policy domain coordination. The second perspective examines macrolevel assumptions about intergovernmental and intersectoral relationships. The third perspective examines microlevel assumptions about project feasibility. Although each perspective is valuable in and of itself, when used together, they constitute a multidimensional framework for assessing the numerous elements of sustainable development administration. Thus, the framework could be used to generate comprehensive studies useful to both scholars and practitioners about the development, implementation, and management of sustainable development efforts.

To this end, the chapter first briefly reviews the history of development theories and highlights the differences between traditional notions of development and the newer concerns of sustainable development. It then explores the multidimensional framework for assessing sustainable development administration, discussing each of the three perspectives in detail. The chapter concludes with a brief discussion about the implications of this framework for the organizational dimensions of sustainable development.

Theories of Development

Although development administration can be traced to ancient times (Farazmand, 2001), the systematic study of development as a separate subdiscipline of economics is a relatively new, post-World War II enterprise (Backhouse, 1991; Farazmand, 2001; Photiades, 1998). The field emerged in the postwar period as nations and former colonies attempted to implement national economic plans (Farazmand, 2001). Thus, after World War II and throughout the 1950s, the dominant development paradigm focused almost exclusively on the ideas of economic growth. Various international economic institutions, such as the International Monetary Fund, the World Bank, and the General Agreement on Tariffs and Trade, were established to provide stability and capital for international development efforts.

One of the earliest thinkers about economic development was W.W. Rostow (1960), who proposed the stages of economic growth model. He suggested that all societies develop in a linear fashion toward modernity, and that the economic dimensions of all societies fall within one of five categories: the traditional society, the preconditions for take-off, the take-off, the drive to maturity, and the age of high mass consumption. With this foundation, the primary goal of economic development became the creation and implementation of growth strategies for the attainment of a mass consumption society (Photiades, 1998). The idea was to create structural changes in economic systems such that the capabilities of people were expanded (Griffin & Knight, 1992; Sen, 1983), living standards increased, and more goods and services were supplied to an expanding population (Clark et al., 1995; Harris & Goodwin, 2001). In addition to these explicit goals, the paradigm also included the more implicit goal of containing Communism (Harris & Goodwin, 2001). Economic development, as defined by the West, was in essence an alternative to Communism, a model of development through central planning (Harris & Goodwin, 2001). For example, as Harris and Goodwin (2001) point out that the complete title of Rostow's (1960) influential book is *The Stages of Economic Growth: A Non-Communist Manifesto*. When viewed in this light, the impetus for early theories about economic development was borne of the Cold War between the West and the East (Harris & Goodwin, 2001).

Traditionally, the Western model of economic development utilized measures of gross national product (GNP) or gross domestic product (GDP) to evaluate the progress of countries toward economic development. With these measures, progress meant raising GNP or GDP with a "big push" of large investments in infrastructural development and industry (Rosentein-Rodan, 1963), "balanced growth" through the simultaneous planning and investment in complementary products (Nurkse, 1959), or "unbalanced growth" with the concentration of investments in key, existing industries (Hirschman, 1958). Economic growth strategies also tended to stress import substitution, the replacement of goods and services purchased outside a region with goods and services produced within the region; however, Japan's successes since the 1960s, and those of the little dragons or Asian Tigers since the 1970s, encouraged the acceptance of international trade as an essential partner to economic growth (Photiades, 1998).

During the 1960s and 1970s, development was recharacterized as economic growth plus social change. It became clear that the singular focus of development efforts on capital formation and accumulation was inadequate; economic development did not necessarily trickle down from the wealthy to the poor as was theorized (Harris & Goodwin, 2001). Thus, scholars began to emphasize the need for human capital formation (e.g., Schultz, 1971, 1972), and began to view development as a social phenomenon that involved more than increasing per capita output (e.g., Seers, 1969). Theorists emphasized the need to focus on basic needs as a paramount goal of development (Streeten et al., 1981; ul Haq, 1976). A new emphasis was placed on healthcare, education, family planning, nutrition, water, sanitation, and shelter (Streeten et al., 1981). The broad sharing of benefits, the redistribution of land assets, and access to education and income were often set as first priorities (Adelman, 1975; Myrdal, 1968; Stewart and Streeten, 1976).

Building on the disparities in access to basic needs, scholars began to critique ideas of development from a North–South perspective and formulated the dependency theory of economic development (Prebisch, 1976, 1978). In this theory, the decolonization that followed World War II produced greater disparities between the industrialized countries of the North and the developing countries of the South. These disparities had developed into a core–periphery relationship among nations, where the countries in the periphery of the third world were being actively underdeveloped by structural relationships with core nations in the first world. These structural relationships forced periphery nations into being the producers of raw materials and other resources for first world manufacturers, and thus, were condemned to a dependent role in the world economy (Amin, 1980; Frank 1967, 1978; Prebisch, 1976, 1978). To break the controlling influences of the first world, scholars argued that nations had to engage in some degree of protectionism, preferably through import substitution and government tariff policies (Prebisch, 1976, 1978).

Similarly, the mid-1970s also heard calls for the new international economic order, a broad model for restructuring the world economy that focused on the relationships between developing and industrialized countries. The new international economic order became an official part of the United Nations' concept of development (Photiades, 1998), and was supposed to include the transfer of basic foreign-owned assets to national control, technology and financial transfers, the creation of new patterns for production and trade, a new system of international commodity agreements, and reforms in the global economic institutions.

The emphasis on social factors and economic growth continued throughout the 1980s, as discussions gradually extended to include the concept of human development. The human development paradigm emerged from the basic needs approach to development (e.g., Streeten et al., 1981; ul Haq, 1976), as well as from the work of Amartya Sen (1981, 1983, 1992, 1999), who advocated a shift from incomes to outcomes and from per capita income growth to quality of life outcomes (Wise, 2001). The human development index (HDI) was created in 1990 by the United Nations Development Program (UNDP) to respond to these new concerns. The HDI defined and assessed human priority areas for immediate attention in development initiatives (United Nations Human Development Program, 1994), and uses health and education measures together with GDP to calculate an overall index of development success.

The 1980s also witness a global debt crisis, prompting many international lending agencies to promote and pursue structural adjustment programs. The goals of structural adjustment programs were to tame bureaucracies, balance budgets, and reduce debt, by adopting a strategy based on the promotion of export-oriented growth, the privatization of state-owned industry, the elimination of barriers to international trade and investment, the reduction of the role of the state as an economic agent, and the deregulation of domestic markets (Gallagher, 2001). Critics have found structural adjustment programs to be at odds not only with basic needs priorities but also with the concept of human development, as they often have deleterious effects on poverty, equality, gender relations, education, health, and the natural environment (Gallagher, 2001).

The failures of structural adjustment programs resulted in harsh critiques of international lending agencies and their policies. Hancock (1989) suggests that the primary beneficiaries of foreign aid are the local elites in the recipient countries, special interest groups in the developed counties, and the aid industry itself, and that the chief losers are the first world taxpayers and the poverty-stricken in the third world. Korten (1990) argues that the "development industry . . . is in a state of disarray. The landscape is littered with evidence of the failures of the official development efforts to reach the poor" (Korten, 1990, p. ix). He asserts that "the processes of economic globalization are not only spreading mass poverty, environmental devastation and social disintegration, they are also weakening our capacity for constructive social and cultural innovation at a time when such innovation is needed as never before" (Korten, 1995, p. 269). This leads him to conclude that "real development cannot be purchased with foreign aid monies. Development depends on people's ability to gain control of and use effectively the real resources of the localities . . . to meet their own needs" (Korten, 1995, p. 5).

In the relatively short history of development theories, the majority of research has emphasized economic growth through a restructuring of economic policies. Only in the last couple of decades has there been a focus on human development and social policy, and it was not until the 1970s that there was discussion about the environment vis-à-vis development (Photiades, 1998). Rachel Carson's *Silent Spring*, Paul Ehrlich's *The Population Bomb*, the Club of Rome's *Limits to Growth*, and other seminal works helped introduce environmental concerns to development theories. The only recent emergence of environmental concerns in development theories demonstrates that "there has been a rather dangerous political economy of development that has historically had little regard for sustainability" (Cooper, 1995, p. 11).

In 1980, the notion of sustainability made a modest appearance in the developmental literature with the publication of Lester R. Brown's *Building a Sustainable Society*:

> A sustainable society will differ from the one we now know in several respects. Population size will be more or less stationary, energy will be used far more efficiently, and the economy will be fueled largely with renewable sources of energy. As a result, people and industrial activity will be more widely dispersed, far less concentrated in urban agglomerations than they are in a petroleum-fueled economy.
>
> Brown (1981, p. 247)

The concept of sustainable development has received a lot of attention since then, and numerous definitions of the term have been offered. Most of these definitions accept that any form of development "involves a progressive transformation of economy and society" (World Commission on Environment and Development, 1987, p. 43). Thus, sustainability is related to the quality of life in a community — whether the economic, social, and environmental systems in a community are providing a healthy, productive, and meaningful life for all community residents, present and future.

The most frequently cited definition of sustainable development comes from the World Commission on Environment and Development (also known as the Brundtland Commission) report, *Our Common Future* (1987). This report drove home "the fundamental importance of sustainable development as a concept and as an essential public policy" (Cooper, 1995, p. 4). It defines sustainable development as "development that meets the needs of the present, without compromising the ability of future generations to meet their own needs" (World Commission on Environment and Development, 1987, p. 43). Cooper and Vargas (2004) suggest that this definition contains three core elements. First, it recognizes that human beings affect and are affected by the environment. Second, it acknowledges that human interactions with the environment must be sustainable in the long term if we are to ensure the well-being of our families and communities. Finally, the definition implicitly accepts the interconnections among the environment, social development, and economic development.

During the 1990s, sustainable development became a vogue term, because it "succinctly reflected the key aspiration of contemporary society: how to maintain or achieve acceptable standards of living and quality of life without depleting the stock of environmental resources on which biospheric integrity depends" (Selman & Wragg, 1999, p. 330). However, "the expression is very general and is susceptible to a range of interpretations, some of which would allow for a stable but ecologically impoverished world" (Caldwell, 1990, p. ix). One of the reasons for this is that although we have a definition for the concept of sustainable development, there is not agreement about how to organize for sustainable development administration. Intrinsic to the concept are complex and unique conditions, multiple factors, and varying normative beliefs, which make it difficult to operationalize in any uniform manner. Despite this, there is general agreement that "sustainable development is a process of change in which the exploitation of resources, the direction of investments, the orientation of technological development, and institutional change are all in harmony and enhance both current and future potential to meet human needs and aspirations" (World Commission on Environment and Development, 1987, p. 46).

A Multidimensional Framework for Assessing Sustainable Development Administration

Although only some argue that sustainable development is an immediate concern necessary for continued human survival, nearly everyone agrees that sustainable development requires remarkable feats of administration. Although there is not a clear blueprint (indeed the creation of a uniform plan for sustainable development is probably impossible given the variety of unique circumstances throughout the world), this chapter outlines three perspectives that can be used to gain insight about sustainable development administration. These perspectives focus on base assumptions about policy domain coordination, macrolevel assumptions about intergovernmental and intersectoral relationships, and microlevel assumptions about project feasibility. Individually, each perspective contributes to our understanding of sustainable development administration; but taken together, the perspectives create various levels of analysis that constitute a multidimensional framework for assessing sustainable development administration. This framework can contribute to systematic and comprehensive research that will deepen our understanding about the processes of sustainable development administration.

Policy Domain Coordination

The first perspective for understanding sustainable development administration concerns base assumptions about policy domain coordination. As noted above, traditional development theory focused primarily on economic policy. With growing concern about human and environmental development, the policy focus shifted; however, policy fields were still viewed and worked on largely independently of each other. Measures of development focused on only one particular policy domain at a time, without showing the many links between various policy spheres (Goldberg, 1989). Just as policy domains were seen as separate from one another, so too were policy problems viewed as isolated issues, related to only one of the policy domains. Sustainable development theorists frown upon such a piecemeal approach. Instead, they push for an approach that accounts for the many links among the economy, society, and environment (see for example, Cooper, 1995; Cooper & Vargas, 2004; Goldberg, 1989; World Commission on Environment and Development, 1987). Indeed, the basic, overarching theme of sustainable development is that these policy issues are not separate challenges, but are rather inexorably linked in a complex web of causes and effects.

The policy domain coordination perspective suggests that sustainable development is contingent on linking environmental, social, and economic policy with a holistic approach focused on integration. In this perspective, the various policy domains are no longer separate, but are instead interconnected and understood as simultaneously affecting and being affected by the others. Thus, for example, environmental sustainability requires changing policies such that they do not adversely impact the natural resources and ecological systems vital for economic and social development. Social sustainability requires tackling policy issues such as health and education, so that the economy and environment remain healthy. Economic sustainability requires policies that eradicate poverty and inequality and promote trade and industry to secure social and environmental health. In short, this perspective assumes that sustainable development administration requires transcending the boundaries of traditional policy domains such that environmental, social, and economic policies are coordinated and integrated.

Intergovernmental and Intersectoral Relationships

The second perspective for understanding sustainable development administration concerns macrolevel assumptions about intergovernmental and intersectoral relationships. Responsibility for development was once characterized as a purely national government activity. Although international support was readily available, the onus for implementing development activities fell squarely on the shoulders of national governments. With sustainable development, this is no longer true; sustainable development has "a hybrid locus of action, with responsibility for different types of problems resting at different levels" (Cooper, 1995, p. 13). Therefore, in addition to the coordination of policy domains, sustainable development theorists call for both intergovernmental and intersectoral cooperation.

Intergovernmental relations used to refer to the relationship among public administrators at the national, regional, state, and local levels; in sustainable development, this definition must broaden (Cooper, 1995).

Although national governments are still responsible for a tremendous amount of coordination, execution, funding, and so on, the essential requirements of sustainable development necessitate actions that transcend the boundaries of the nation-state. Sustainable development requires cooperation not only across national, state, and local jurisdictional lines, but also across international and regional levels. In addition to transcending intergovernmental boundaries, sustainable development initiatives must also be intersectoral, involving both the private and public sectors (Mangun & Henning, 1999), including international organizations and supranational regional institutions (Cooper, 1995; Cooper & Vargas, 2004). Thus, successful administration likely requires the engagement of the government agencies, businesses, institutions of civil society, and non-governmental organizations addressing the full range of environmental, economic, social, and other issues that impact sustainable development (Raskin et al., 2000). In short, this perspective assumes that successful sustainable development administration will involve international, national, subnational, and regional governments acting in partnership with each other, as well as with, private and non-governmental organizations. In other words, this perspective assumes that sustainable development administration requires intergovernmental and intersectoral cooperation and relationships that transcend geopolitical boundaries.

Project Feasibility

A base assumption of sustainable development focuses on the coordination of policy domains. Taken in a macro context, this must occur at the international, national, subnational, and community levels, incorporating the work of government, private, and non-governmental organizations. However, sustainable development administration ultimately occurs at the microlevel: the day-to-day tasks of sustainable development are accomplished by work on various projects, carried out by individuals within and across organizations.[1] Therefore, the third perspective for understanding sustainable development administration recognizes that effective sustainable development projects require managers to consider a multitude of factors that shape implementation efforts from both within and outside of their organizations. As Cooper and Vargas (2004, p. 15) have astutely noted, "If politics is the art of the possible, then implementation is the art of the

[1]One might argue that individuals working on projects through organizations accomplish the day-to-day tasks of sustainable development. For example, Goldberg (1989) asserts that sustainable development will be accomplished only if society and individuals change in tandem, as each composes the other. Exploring these arguments, however, is beyond the scope of this chapter.

feasible." As such, this third perspective for sustainable development administration focuses on microlevel assumptions about project feasibility.

Although Cooper (1995) and Cooper and Vargas (2004) are largely responsible for developing this "feasibility framework," additional areas of feasibility analysis have been suggested by Abaza (1993) and are included herein. In the project feasibility perspective, project managers must scan the environment for numerous indicators of project feasibility, including its administrative and institutional, informational, environmental, legal, technical, fiscal and economic, political, social and cultural, and ethical aspects (Abaza, 1993; Cooper, 1995; Cooper & Vargas, 2004). It is important to note that these aspects of feasibility are neither mutually exclusive nor exhaustive. Moreover, given the assumptions about policy domain coordination and intergovernmental and intersectoral relationships, feasibility assessments will likely be conducted by multiple persons in multiple organizations, and may require the participation of experts from multiple disciplines. The major aspects of the feasibility analysis are discussed below.

Administrative and Institutional

Administrative and institutional capacities are an extremely important area of feasibility analysis. Adequate institutional arrangements are the primary means of ensuring the efficiency and effectiveness of project implementation and are significant determinants of project success (Abaza, 1993; Baum & Tolbert, 1987; Cooper, 1995; Cooper & Vargas, 2004). An assessment of administrative and institutional feasibility will examine whether the agency has the range of capacities necessary to implement projects, whether there is an appropriate infrastructural system, and how relationships among technical and scientific, legal, and administrative staff will be developed (Cooper, 1995; Cooper & Vargas, 2004). It should also assess project management, indigenous capabilities, and the integration of project activities (Abaza, 1993). This aspect of project feasibility also facilitates (or impedes) the analyses of other elements of project feasibility.

Information

The first step in assessing project feasibility is conducting an information analysis, where relevant information is gathered at the start so that the project is designed on the basis of a realistic appraisal of existing local conditions, including the socioeconomic and political environment existing in the country (Abaza, 1993). Information is "among the most essential resources" for sustainable development administration and can provide important initial insights about project feasibility (Cooper, 1995, p. 22).

Environmental

The purpose of an environmental analysis is to devise methods to ensure that environmental damage is avoided or reduced so that the project initiatives and benefits are sustainable (Abaza, 1993). The objective of environmental management is the achievement of the greatest benefit possible from the use of natural resources without reducing their potential to meet future needs and the carrying capacity of the environment (Baum & Tolbert, 1987). Therefore, some projects, despite possible potential benefits, may be deemed unfeasible after an environmental investigation.

Legal

Avenues for sustainable development are paved by the rule of law: administrators are constrained by the boundaries, jurisdictions, and powers that are available to them. Agencies or officials wishing to undertake a project must assess whether the legal infrastructure can support that project and whether they have the legal authority to act. Judgments about the legal feasibility of a project can be particularly complex because of national sovereignty issues, disputes among subnational units of government, and issues regarding separation of powers (Cooper, 1995; Cooper & Vargas, 2004). Thus, sustainable development is generally thought to require what is termed "merged sovereignty," because only international bodies can claim authority over issues of the global commons, and to act effectively, efforts must be undertaken in concert with others (Cooper, 1995).

Technical

The primary concern of technical feasibility is the availability or potential to develop the technology and technological capacity needed for a project (Cooper, 1995; Cooper & Vargas, 2004). A technical analysis requires a multidisciplinary approach that takes into account the technical, environmental, socioeconomic, and institutional aspects of project development (Abaza, 1993). This may be more difficult in developing countries that lack technological expertise (Cooper, 1995; Cooper & Vargas, 2004). Although each project context may be unique, there are some broad technical issues that can be identified, including size, location, timing, and technology; therefore, a technical analysis may provide insight about appropriate technologies that suit local conditions, use the available skills and training, and are within the financial means of the population (Abaza, 1993).

Fiscal and Economic

Every project requires a financial plan that ensures the availability of funds necessary for development, operation, maintenance, and completion of the project (Abaza, 1993). Appraisals of the fiscal and economic aspects of a project have heightened significance given that governments around the world are increasingly facing budgetary cuts and few ministries have financial support adequate to conduct their assigned responsibilities (Cooper, 1995). If project funds are not available from traditional budgetary means, other potential options for financial support, such as international or regional support and non-government organization consultation, can be considered (Cooper, 1995; Cooper & Vargas, 2004). To assess the economic aspects of a sustainable development project, a cost–benefit analysis that includes environmental considerations, a risk assessment, and valuation of environmental goods and services can be conducted (Abaza, 1993).

Political

Sustainable development projects are impacted by the amount of political independence accorded to administrators and their agencies, how actions will affect relations among units of government, and if and how the public will support the actions. Thus, understanding the politics of development efforts, the rationale for public intervention, the sources and consequences of political decisions, and organizational structures and the politics therein, are important aspects of assessing the political feasibility of projects (Staudt, 1991). Moreover, the political feasibility of a sustainable development project is, at least in part, defined by the cultural and political values of the country involved (Mangun & Henning, 1999; Dahlberg, 1985); since sustainable development means that there are limits to growth, "the political and cultural norms that govern the country dictate where the lines shall be drawn" (Cooper, 1995, p. 9).

Social and Cultural

Culture affects the meaning of development for people and nations, as well as the values that guide people's actions and the behavior of administrators (Staudt, 1991); thus the elements of social and cultural feasibility directly relate to sustainable development project administration. A project that ignores the traditions, values, and social organization of its intended beneficiaries has little chance of success (Baum & Tolbert, 1987). A social analysis that examines how cultural expectations influence agency actions, identifies the project beneficiaries, establishes levels of public participation, and develops appropriate training for all those involved can contribute to the success of the project (Abaza, 1993). Public participation can help ensure the transparency of projects and is regarded as critical to sustainable development administration (Cooper, 1995).

Ethical

There are several dimensions to ethical feasibility. First, there are ethical challenges surrounding the administrator's responsibility to the public (Cooper, 1995). For example, failure to include citizens in critical decisions or failure to inform affected citizens about projects can present administrators with ethical dilemmas. Likewise, problems such as gender inequality, racial disparity, or other participatory flaws are other critical ethical issues that must be addressed for each sustainable development project. There are also ethical stresses imposed on personnel working on sustainable development projects or relevant agencies (Cooper, 1995). These stresses arise from the normative goals and principles on which sustainable development is based, and may be aggravated when an individual's social or cultural norms diverge from the legal and political frameworks that foster sustainable development projects (Hempel, 1996).

In sum, this third perspective of sustainable development administration assumes that project managers are "practitioner[s] of the art of the feasible" (Cooper, 1995, p. 23). It suggests that administrators must analyze the administrative and institutional capacity to engage in a sustainable development project and take a multidisciplinary approach to analyzing the feasibility of various project elements, including, but perhaps not limited to its informational, environmental, legal, technical, fiscal and economic, political, social and cultural, and ethical aspects. Moreover, as suggested by the other perspectives on sustainable development, most feasibility analyses will transcend policy domains, as well as governmental and sectoral boundaries.

The discussion of these three perspectives highlights the fact that sustainable development projects are carried out within a highly complex and multidimensional environment.

Individually, each perspective offers insights about sustainable development administration; however, taken in sum, the perspectives form a multidimensional framework for assessing sustainable development administration. The framework is sufficiently narrow so as to provide boundaries and context to a nebulous area of study, yet broad enough to allow for interdisciplinary analyses at multiple levels.

Moreover, the framework has implications for research in the organizational sciences. The framework suggests that organizations involved in sustainable development activities engage in a broad range of transcendence activities: they work within and across the social, economic, and environmental policy domains; they coordinate projects that are multisectoral and span geopolitical boundaries; and they engage in the analyses of several feasibility elements that contribute to project success. Given these perspectives about sustainable development, the question arises, what type of organizational structure will best facilitate the ability of organizations to engage in these transcendence activities? It is to the subject of organizational structures that this chapter now turns.

The Organizational Dimensions of Sustainable Development

Until recently, the institutional dimensions of sustainable development have received less attention than the environmental, economic, technical, and financial ones (Abaza, 1993). However, there is growing concern about institutional inadequacies for sustainable development, such as a shortage of skilled manpower and experienced staff, a lack of training and staff incentives, overloaded facilities, low salaries, and counterproductive government policies and legislation (Baum & Tolbert, 1987). Thus, there are calls for the birth of new organizational arrangements that allow for the closing of what some have called the institutional gap — the dichotomy between organizations born of the modern bureaucratic eras of the past several centuries and the new demands of a postmodern, supranational, globally linked world system of change (Cooperrider & Dutton, 1999).

Theorists suggest that modern organizations, those resembling Weber's conception of bureaucracy, are authoritarian, hierarchical, and formal, and have fewer degrees of complexity, and as such are less able to function effectively in this globalized world: "the global expansion of the modern organization is also accompanied by range of new challenges and adjustments, each of which undermines it viability" and "as the modern organization globalizes, its capacity for effective functioning is also diminished" (Gergen, 1999, p. 261). It has been suggested that new organizational structures are needed, and that these structures will take a postmodern form that focuses on relational processes, where the primary concern is not with recognizable units (e.g., headquarters, subsidiaries, the marketing division) and their structural arrangements, but with continuous processes of relationship (Gergen, 1999). This view calls attention to the domains of interdependence and the forms of coordinated activity that are necessary for managing global change in terms of sustainable development.

Organizational research on networks (see for example, Agranoff & McGuire, 2001; La Porte, 1996; Milward & Provan, 2000; O'Toole, 1997; Powell, 1990) provides a basis for beginning to understand these relational processes; however, the organizational sciences can contribute more to the understanding about how the empirical forms of organizational life operate to promote or impede sustainable development administration (Bouwen & Steyaert, 1999). These claims prompt the following discussion about elements organizational structure and the organizational dimensions of sustainable development. Using the framework for assessing sustainable development administration, the discussion culminates in the assertion that an organic organizational structure (as opposed to a mechanistic organizational structure) is likely to be more successful in fostering effective sustainable development administration.

As noted earlier, there is not a uniform blueprint for sustainable development administration. Despite this, there are many details of organizational structure that can inform sustainable development administration. Organizational structure is defined as "the way a purposive entity (for example, a private firm, a government agency, a development project, or a program) is set up to accomplish its missions and goals — that is, the choices it makes in (a) dividing up its tasks into various work groups and (b) specifying how the activities of the work groups are coordinated" (Binkerhoff, 1991, p. 102). Two basic elements of organizational structure include differentiation and integration (Lawrence & Lorsch, 1967). Differentiation is the division of functional units within an organization. Integration is the pattern of relationships among those units. These two elements of organizational structure can be disaggregated into smaller facets, including authority, hierarchy, formality, and complexity.

Authority encompasses the extent of reliance on power in relationships and the basis on which that power rests (Binkerhoff, 1991). The framework for assessing sustainable development administration suggests that organizations involved in sustainable development activities will be less authoritarian. The transcendence activities of sustainable development require a dispersal of power among administrators in the various policy domains, as well as among administrators in different organizational and geopolitical sectors. It also requires experts from multiple disciplines working together to assess various aspects of project feasibility. A concentration of authority within an organization or an authoritarian organizational structure would likely hinder the dispersal of responsibility among these multiple actors, thereby impeding the ability of administrators to effectively engage in the transcendence activities of sustainable development.

Hierarchy refers to the construction of an organization in terms of the number of levels in the organizational pyramid, the span of control of supervisory units over subordinate units, and the intensity of that supervision. Modern organizations have tended to be rather hierarchical in structure; however, over the last few decades, there has been movement toward more horizontal or flat organizational arrangements (Agranoff, 2003; Agranoff & McGuire, 2001, 2003; Berry et al., 2004; Powell, 1990). The framework for assessing sustainable development administration suggests that organizations involved in sustainable development activities will have less hierarchical structures. This assertion flows from the same dynamic that suggests less authoritarian structures. Sustainable development activities will have multiple loci of action: they will occur within and across policy domains; they will be multisectoral and span geopolitical boundaries; and they will require the input of administrators, scientists, technicians, and other experts from various backgrounds and disciplines. This suggests that a hierarchical structure with vertical supervisory configurations could prevent the development of arrangements that facilitate the transcendence activities of sustainable development, and that a less hierarchical structure with horizontal configurations would be better suited to the requirements of sustainable development administration.

Formality is "the extent to which the structure is described by formal, written rules that detail missions, objectives, differentiation among units and subunits, integrating relationships among them, and characteristics of the roles of unit and subunit incumbents (job descriptions)" (Binkerhoff, 1991, p. 103). The framework suggests that successful sustainable development administration requires organizational structures to be more informal, iterative, and evolving because of the interconnections between policies and organizations, the changing nature of problems and metaproblems, and the dynamics of politics and culture. An organization with high levels of formality would be less able to respond to the dynamics of uncertainty in sustainable development administration. It would be hindered in its ability to move across policy domains, organizational boundaries, and relevant disciplines, and therefore would be less able to effectively engage in the transcendence activities of sustainable development.

Complexity concerns the number of sites where work is done, the number of units and subunits involved in that work, the types of experts or specialists used in the work, and the overall differentiation and integration of these units and subunits (Binkerhoff, 1991). The framework for assessing sustainable development administration suggests that such work, by its very nature, will create tremendous amounts of organizational complexity. The issues of sustainable development administration can be characterized as contested, nonlinear metaproblems with long lead times, unintended side effects, unclear cause–effect structures, and consequences that are often irreversible (Weick, 1999; Cooperrider & Dutton, 1999). Sustainable development administrators confront a continuous tension between the need for risk management and demands for predictability that require the acquisition and use of analytic tools to help administrators estimate risk, as well as administrative institutions that are capable of operating under conditions of uncertainty (Cooper, 1995).

In short, the transcendence activities of sustainable development suggest that organizations involved in such work will have structures that are less authoritarian, less hierarchical, informal, and complex. This organic form of organizational structure is likely to be more successful than a mechanistic form of organizational structure in fostering effective sustainable development administration. The framework proposed here suggests that organizations with a sustainable development agenda should engage in transcendence activities that integrate the economic, social, and environmental policy domains, generate multisectoral involvement that spans geopolitical boundaries, and facilitate a multidisciplinary investigation of project feasibility. An organization with an organic structure that is less authoritarian, less hierarchical, informal, and complex will be more likely to effectively engage in these transcendence activities; high degrees of authority, hierarchy, and formality, coupled with low degrees of complexity would impede an organization's ability to work within and across the multiple policy domains, impair the development of interorganizational and multisectoral relationships, and hinder a multidisciplinary feasibility analysis. In turn, engaging in these transcendence activities may help promote the development of an organic organizational structure for those involved in sustainable development work. In other words, there is likely a cyclical relationship between the structure of the organization and its ability to engage in the transcendence activities of sustainable development.

Conclusion

Calls for sustainable development efforts have increased dramatically in the past decade, yet there have been few systematic and comprehensive research efforts about sustainable development administration and the organizational structures necessary to support that work. The few individual and comparative case studies that exist do not provide the methodological and inclusive research that is needed. One goal of this chapter was to help fill that gap in research by outlining three perspectives that contribute to our understanding of sustainable development administration. The first perspective focuses on base assumptions about policy domain coordination, the second explores macrolevel assumptions about intergovernmental and intersectoral relationships, and the third considers microlevel assumptions about project feasibility. Taken together, these perspectives form a multidimensional framework for assessing sustainable development administration that can be used to generate comprehensive studies about the development, implementation, and management of sustainable development efforts.

The framework also provides insights about the organizational structures necessary to support sustainable development efforts. It suggests that an organic organizational structure that is less authoritarian, less hierarchical, informal, and complex is more likely to engage in effective sustainable development administration than the mechanistic organizational structures of modern bureaucracies. Hopefully, this chapter will prompt researchers to test and improve this framework, and contribute to our knowledge about sustainable development administration and the organizational structures necessary to support such efforts.

References

Abaza, H. (1993). "Appraisal methodology for sustainable development projects." In M. Mohan (ed.) *Environmental Economics and Natural Resource Management in Developing Countries*. Washington, D.C.: The World Bank Committee of International Development Institutions on the Environment.

Adelman, I. (1975). "Growth, income distribution, and equity-oriented development strategies." In *World Development*. New York: Pergamon Press.

Agranoff, R. (2003). *Leveraging Networks: A Guide for Public Managers Working across Organizations*. Arlington, VA: IBM Endowment for the Business of Government.

Agranoff, R. and M. McGuire (2001). "Big questions in public network management research." *Journal of Public Administration Research and Theory*, 11(3): 295–326.

Agranoff, R. and M. McGuire (2003). *Collaborative Public Management: New Strategies for Local Governments*. Washington, D.C.: Georgetown University Press.

Amin, S. (1980). *Class and Nation*. New York: Monthly Review Press.

Backhouse, R. (1991). *A History of Modern Economic Analysis*. Oxford: Blackwell.

Baum, W. and S. Tolbert (1987). *Investing in Development: Lessons of World Bank Experience*. New York: Oxford University Press.

Berry, F.S., S.O. Choi, W.X. Goa, H.-S. Jang, M. Kwon, and J. Word. (2004). "Three traditions of network research: what the public management research agenda can learn from other research communities." *Public Administration Review*, 64(5): 539–552.

Binkerhoff, D.W. (1991). *Improving Development Program Performance: Guidelines for Managers*. Boulder, CO: Lynne Rienner Publishers.

Bouwen, R. and C. Steyaert (1999). "From a dominant voice toward multivoiced cooperation." In D.L. Cooperrider and J.E. Dutton (eds.), *Organizational Dimensions of Global Change: No Limits to Cooperation*. Thousand Oaks: Sage Publications.

Brown, L.R. (1981). *Building a Sustainable Society*. New York: W.W. Norton.

Caldwell, L.K. (1990). *Between Two Worlds: Science, the Environmental Movement and Policy Choice*. New York: Cambridge University Press.

Clark, N., F. Perez-Trejo, and P. Allen (1995). *Evolutionary Dynamics and Sustainable Development: A Systems Approach*. Brookfield, Vermont: Edward Elgar Publishing Limited.

Cooper, P.J. (1995). "Inside–outside management: public administration, sustainable development, and environmental policy." In P.J. Cooper and C.M. Vargas (eds.), *Implementing Sustainable Development*. New York: United Nations.

Cooper, P.J. and C.M. Vargas (2004). *Implementing Sustainable Development: From Global Policy to Local Action*. Lanham, MD: Rowman & Littlefield Publishers.

Cooperrider, D.L. and J.E. Dutton (1999). "No limits to cooperation: an introduction to the organizational dimensions of global change." In D.L. Cooperrider and J.E. Dutton (eds.), *Organizational Dimensions of Global Change: No Limits to Cooperation*. Thousand Oaks: Sage Publications.

Dahlberg, K.A. (1985). *Environment and the Global Arena: Actors, Values, Policies, and Futures*. Durham, NC: Duke University Press.

Farazmand, A. (2001). "Comparative development administration: past, present and future." In A. Farazmand (ed.) *Handbook of Comparative and Development Public Administration*. New York: Marcel Dekker, pp. 9–22.

Frank, A.G. (1967). *Capitalism and Underdevelopment in Latin America*. New York: Monthly Review Press.

Frank, A.G. (1978). *Dependent Accumulation and Underdevelopment*. New York: Monthly Review Press.

Gallagher, K.P. (2001). "Globalization and sustainability: overview essay." In J.M. Harris, T.A. Wise, K.P. Gallagher, and N.R. Goodwin (eds.), *A Survey of Sustainable Development: Social and Economic Dimensions*. Washington, D.C.: Island Press, pp. 223–229.

Gergen, K.J. (1999). "Global organization and the potential for ethical inspiration." In D.L. Cooperrider and J.E. Dutton (eds.), *Organizational Dimensions of Global Change: No Limits to Cooperation*. Thousand Oaks: Sage Publications.

Goldberg, M.A. (1989). *On Systemic Balance: Flexibility and Stability in Social, Economic, and Environmental Systems*. New York: Prager.

Griffin, K. and J. Knight (1992). "Human development: the case for renewed emphasis." In C.K. Wilber and K. Jameson (eds.), *The Political Economy of Development and Underdevelopment*, 5th edition. New York: McGraw-Hill.

Hancock, G. (1989). *Lords of Poverty: The Power, Prestige, and Corruption of the International Aid Business*. New York: Atlantic Monthly Press.

Harris, J.M. and N.R. Goodwin (2001). "Volume introduction." In J.M. Harris, T.A. Wise, K.P. Gallagher, and N.R. Goodwin (eds.), *A Survey of Sustainable Development: Social and Economic Dimensions*. Washington, D.C.: Island Press, pp. xxi–xxxvii.

Hempel, L.C. (1996). *Environmental Governance: The Global Challenge*. Washington, D.C.: Island Press.

Hirschman, A.O. (1958). *The Strategy of Economic Development*. New Haven: Yale University Press.

Korten, D.C. (1990). *Getting to the 21st Century: Voluntary Action and the Global Agenda.* Hartford, CT: Kumarian Press.

Korten, D.C. (1995). *When Corporations Rule the World.* Hartford, CT: Kumarian Press.

La Porte, T.R. (1996). "Shifting vantage and conceptual puzzles in understanding public organization networks." *Journal of Public Administration Research and Theory*, 6: 49–74.

Lawrence, P.R. and J.W. Lorsch (1967). *Organization and Environment: Managing Differentiation and Integration.* Homewood, IL: Richard D. Irwin.

Mangun, W.R. and D.H. Henning (1999). *Managing the Environmental Crisis: Incorporating Competing Values in Natural Resource Administration.* Durham, NC: Duke University Press.

Milward, H.B. and K.G. Provan (2000). "Governing the hollow state." *Journal of Public Administration Research and Theory*, 10: 359–380.

Myrdal, G. (1968). *Asian Drama: An Inquiry into the Poverty of Nations.* New York: Twentieth Century Fund.

Nurkse, R. (1959). *Patterns of Trade and Development.* Stockholm: Almqvist and Wiksell.

O'Toole, L.J. (1997). "Treating networks seriously: practical and research-based agendas in public administration." *Public Administration Review*, 57: 45–52.

Photiades, J.G. (1998). "Notions of development, past and present." In A.G. McQuillan and A.L. Preston (eds.), *Globally and Locally: Seeking a Middle Path to Sustainable Development.* Lanham, MD: University Press of America.

Powell, W.W. (1990). "Neither market nor hierarchy: network forms of organization." *Research in Organizational Behavior*, 12: 295–336.

Prebisch, R. (1976). *A Critique of Peripheral Capitalism.* New York: United Nations Commission for Latin America.

Prebisch, R. (1978). *Socioeconomic Structure and Crisis of Peripheral Capitalism.* New York: United Nations Commission for Latin America.

Raskin, P., G. Gallopin, P. Gutman, A. Hammond, and R. Swart (2000). "Bending the curve: toward global sustainability." http://www.gsg.org/btcsum.html

Rosenstein-Rodan, P.N. (1963). "Problems of industrialization of eastern and southeastern Europe." In A.N. Agarwala and S.P. Singh (eds.), *The Economics of Underdevelopment.* New York: Oxford University Press.

Rostow, W.W. (1960). *The Stages of Economic Growth: A Non-Communist Manifesto.* Cambridge: Cambridge University Press.

Schultz, T.W. (1971). *Investment in Human Capital: The Role of Education and of Research.* New York: Free Press.

Schultz, T.W. (1972). *Human Resources (Human Capital: Policy Issues and Research Opportunities).* New York: National Bureau of Economic Research.

Seers, D. (1969). "The meaning of development." *International Development Review*, 11(4): 3–4.

Selman, P. and P. Wragg (1999). "Local sustainability planning: from interest-driven networks to vision-driven super-networks." *Planning and Practice Research*, 14(3): 329–341.

Sen, A. (1981). *Poverty and Famines.* Oxford: Oxford University Press.

Sen, A. (1983). "Development: which way now? *Economic Journal*, 745–762. Reprinted In C.K. Wilber and K. Jameson (eds.), *The Political Economy of Development and Underdevelopment*, 5th edition. New York: McGraw-Hill, 1992.

Sen, A. (1992). *Inequality Reexamined.* Cambridge, MA: Harvard University Press.

Sen, A. (1999). *Development as Freedom.* New York: Alfred A. Knopf.

Staudt, K. (1991). *Managing Development: State, Society and International Contexts.* Newbury Park: Sage.

Stewart, F. and P. Streeten (1976). "New strategies for development: poverty, income distribution, and growth." *Oxford Economic Papers*, 28(3): 381–405.

Streeten, P., S.J. Burki, M. ul Haq, N. Hicks, and F. Stewart (1981). *First Things First: Meeting Basic Human Needs in the Developing Countries.* Published for the World Bank. New York and Oxford: Oxford University Press.

ul Haq, M. (1976). "The third world and the international economic order." Development Paper No. 22. Washington, D.C.: Overseas Development Council.

United Nations Human Development Program (1994). Human Development Report, 1994. New York: Oxford University Press.

Weick, K.E. (1999). "Sensemaking and global change." In D.L. Cooperrider and J.E. Dutton (eds.), *Organizational Dimensions of Global Change: No Limits to Cooperation.* Thousand Oaks: Sage Publications.

Wise, T.A. (2001). "Economics of sustainability the social dimension." An overview essay In J.M. Harris, T.A. Wise, K.P. Gallagher, and N.R. Goodwin (eds.), *A Survey of Sustainable Development: Social and Economic Dimensions.* Washington, D.C.: Island Press, pp. 47–57.

World Commission on Environment and Development (1987). *Our Common Future.* Oxford: Oxford University Press.

Chapter 36

International Development Management: Definitions, Debates, and Dilemmas

Derick W. Brinkerhoff and Jennifer M. Brinkerhoff

CONTENTS

Introduction

Scholars and practitioners have long grappled with identifying the best policies and approaches to promoting socioeconomic development. Since World War II, the international development field has been marked by an evolution of approaches to understanding and addressing development challenges.[1] Policies, approaches, and strategies need to be implemented to lead to results and real improvements in people's lives; this is where international development management comes to the fore. This chapter presents a framework for defining development management, and reviews the major debates that make a simple definition difficult to craft. In conclusion, this chapter highlights some of the ongoing dilemmas that face development managers.[2]

In the early post–World War II era, development theory and practice was mainly concerned with economics. Experience soon revealed that economics and a focus on industrialization was insufficient, and analysts and practitioners in developing countries and in international donor agencies expanded their focus beyond production to distribution, politics, basic human needs, and cultural values. So a primary change over time has been increased recognition of the complexity of promoting development, replacing simpler notions of economic "takeoff" or "big push" modernization. Other changes in the field have emerged as a function of shifts in values, such as a movement away from Western-centric modernization agendas toward an emphasis on human development that embraces the inherent and functional value of local knowledge and culture. Although variations in emphasis can be found, today there is a relatively broad consensus that besides economic growth, development includes equity, capacity, empowerment, self-determination, and sustainability. Development terminology is descriptive both of societal patterns and of processes found in many countries around the world (poverty, economic and social deprivation, lack of capacity) and of aspirational goals (having more and being more).

---

[1]For an informative overview of the history of international development see Rist (1997).

[2]Over the years, an extensive stream of literature has reflected upon development management, where it has been, and where it might go. We draw on our previous efforts at elaborating a definition (Brinkerhoff & Coston, 1999), and build on earlier work. See Riggs (1998), Heady (1998), Esman (1980, 1988, 1991), Korten and Klauss (1984), Rondinelli (1987), Nicholson and Connerley (1989), Brinkerhoff (1991, 1997), and Brinkerhoff and Ingle (1989).

From Development Administration to Development Management

Along with the evolution of the concept of development have been changes in thinking regarding how to achieve it. The primary trajectory here has been along a path that began with centrally planned, state-dominated strategies to market-led polycentric approaches with the state as coordinator and regulator rather than as the sole or predominant actor. This shift corresponds with a change in the terminology to describe these processes, from development administration to development management. The term "development administration" has been the traditional label for the subfield of public administration in developing/transitional countries. However, this has in many circles been gradually supplanted by the term "development management." The replacement of administration with management signifies an emphasis on nimble organizations, flexible strategies, and proactive managerial styles, as opposed to the tasks and tools of routine administration in bureaucracies. Also, flowing from the polycentric concept, where numerous actors are actively engaged in the tasks of improving people's lives and generating socioeconomic benefits, development management is not restricted to the public sector. Development managers can be staff of non-governmental organizations (NGOs), members of community groups, entrepreneurs and business people, as well as civil servants.

Development management encompasses the set of theory and practice that concentrates upon organizational and managerial problems, issues, and practices in the developing countries of Africa, Asia, and Latin America, and in the transitional economies of Eastern Europe and the former Soviet Union. However, as a variety of observers have pointed out, the same types of problems that confront the developing/transitional world can be found in pockets of poverty, marginalization, and inequality in industrialized countries as well. This overlap suggests that development management has applicability to poverty alleviation and community organizing in the industrialized world.

The evolution of development management, as an applied discipline like its parent field, public administration, has shifted along with the changes in development strategies mentioned earlier. To oversimplify slightly, the trend has been away from techno-rational, universalist, public sector administrative models toward context-specific, politically infused, multisectoral, multi-organizational models. From its initial focus on institution building for central-level public bureaucracies and capacity-building for economic and project planning, development management has gradually expanded to encompass bureaucratic reform and restructuring to enhance democratic governance and responsiveness to citizens, including the poor; the integration of politics and culture into management improvement; participatory and performance-based service delivery and program management; community and NGO capacity building; and policy reform and implementation.[3] In short, the trend in development management has been away from:

- Sole reliance on the technical-rational "fix": concentrating on improving so-called hard systems (e.g., budgeting/accounting and personnel) and structures, to the exclusion of "soft" systems (people)
- Universalist solutions: one size fits all, good for any situation
- Focus on reactive administrative models: fulfilling routine functions and paying attention to day-to-day routine.

Development management has moved toward:

- Context specificity, recognizing that while solutions in various settings will share some features, they must be adapted to the particular features that make each context unique
- Recognition that any change, even if it appears to be just a "neutral" technical modification, is in fact politically infused (i.e., somebody wins and somebody loses, and power matters)
- Multisectoral solutions: no single discipline or perspective has a corner on "the truth"; the best solutions emerge when the insights of many viewpoints and sources of expertise are brought to bear
- Strategic perspectives merged with operational administration: paying attention to the "big picture" and long-term direction while not neglecting the details of how to get there
- Multiorganizational models: the complex problems of development almost always require the attention and intervention of numerous agencies, even if one organization is nominally "in charge."

A Framework for Defining Development Management

The conceptual and operational threads we have just outlined weave a confusing definitional tapestry. How can we make sense of the numerous and disparate elements that reside within the development management term? Perhaps the most straightforward distinction is that of Alan Thomas

[3]This overview obviously does not do justice to the evolution of development and development management. See the introductory chapters of Bryant and White (1982), the thematic overview of the development management field by one of its founders (Esman, 1991), the history of development management and U.S. foreign assistance (Rondinelli, 1987), the review of approaches to institutional development in Brinkerhoff (1986), the retrospective on policy analysis in Brinkerhoff (1997), and the framework-building effort in Thomas (1996, 1999).

(1999): development management can be viewed as management of development or management for development. This is akin to Warren Bennis' distinction between a narrow managerialist emphasis on doing things right versus a leader's doing the right things (Bennis & Goldsmith, 1997). Management of development focuses on applying the rules and procedures governing the mechanics of foreign assistance to achieve planned outcomes through projects and programs. Management for development encompasses a broader view of development as involving progressive improvements in societal well-being, and looks at the politics of donor agencies, whether poor people actually benefit from assistance, and the power imbalances inherent in development assistance relationships.

A more complex, though consistent, framework outlines four facets of development management (Brinkerhoff & Coston, 1999). First, development has an explicitly interventionist orientation; it is a means to promoting institutional agendas. This facet most closely corresponds with Thomas' notion of "management of development": the emphasis of this dimension is to enhance the efficiency and effectiveness of sponsoring institutional actors' plans and objectives. Most often, these agendas are those of international donor agencies; but alongside this driver, other institutional agendas compete or complement, including those of NGOs, private firms, and recipient governments. Second, development management is a toolkit consisting of a range of management and analytical tools adapted from a variety of social science disciplines, including strategic management, organization development, political science, and psychology. Third, development management is a process intervention, where the application of tools in pursuit of objectives is undertaken in ways that self-consciously address political and values, issues. This dimension emphasizes process consultation and contingency approaches. Finally, development management encompasses a values dimension that emphasizes self-determination, empowerment, and an equitable distribution of benefits. This dimension also recognizes the inherent political nature of development, acknowledging winners and losers, and working with rather than assuming away the political aspects of development. Taken together, these four facets encompass both aspects of Thomas' and Bennis' distinctions: doing things right and doing the right things.

Each of these four facets represents one essential aspect of development management as a field of theory and practice, and collectively they constitute a complete definition. However, there are inherent tensions among them and they can be contradictory. For example, although it is fairly straightforward to understand how development management's tools can promote foreign assistance agendas, less clear is whether or not their application in this context will promote espoused values of empowerment and self-determination, and whether or not the donor agency and its procedures can adequately support a genuine process approach. Such contradictions imply that development management means different things to different actors. Emphasizing one facet as primary can blur the tensions and contradictions among the four facets, exacerbating the challenge of specifying a unified definition for development management. The choice of balance among its four facets varies, contributing to development management's ambiguity. An examination of each of the facets of development management further clarifies the framework, illustrates their interdependencies, and illuminates the debates surrounding them.

Development Management as Means to Institutional Agendas

Development management is most often sponsored by international donor agencies, all of which have their own priorities and corresponding agendas. Typically, development management professionals enter the scene upon request from a donor agency for a predetermined task.[4] It is not always clear if the need for, and the design of, a task represent priorities of the ultimate client, a developing — country actor. In this sense, development management is a means to enhancing the effectiveness and efficiency of projects and programs determined and designed by outside actors (see, for example, Rondinelli, 1987). Cooke (2003) takes a more radical position, arguing that this facet of development management reveals a connection to the imperialist agendas of colonialism, and that today's development management is the instrument of donor-imposed priorities just as colonial administration enabled Western imperialists to rule their acquired territories for their own purposes.

This facet of development management is perhaps the most problematic to reconcile with its other facets. First and most obviously, institutional agendas, particularly those of international donor agencies, at a minimum compromise some degree of self-determination in pursuit of socioeconomic reforms. Sometimes these externally derived reform agendas strongly limit the ability of countries to modify the reform package in ways that would support local empowerment. Second, donor programming requirements and incentives — such as loan disbursement schedules, project timetables, and compliance with predetermined indicators — can further inhibit the ability of groups in the recipient country, whether inside or outside of the government, to play an active role in tailoring the assistance provided to their needs and pace of change.

[4]Development management practitioners also reflect the agendas of the organizations they work for, which may or may not be aligned with international donor agencies. For example, they may work in NGOs, which may or may not be recipients of donor funds, and in some cases pursue missions that are opposed to donor policies and practices. See for example, Fowler (1997).

Multilateral and bilateral foreign assistance programs, despite espoused policies regarding country participation and adaptation to local priorities and needs, share a common set of principles and objectives.[5] Most donor policy frameworks incorporate a combination of market liberalization, privatization, state downsizing, democratic governance, equitable delivery of basic services, and poverty reduction. They take a comprehensive approach to country-level planning, such as for example, the World Bank's comprehensive development framework (CDF) and poverty reduction strategy papers (PRSPs); the development assistance committee's strategy, shaping the 21st century; or the United Nation's common country framework. All donor agencies, whether multilateral or bilateral, incorporate performance-based management into their agendas and practice and, by extension, so do the private sector contractors — firms and NGOs — with whom they work. The latest translation of this performance agenda into policy is the Bush administration's establishment of the millennium challenge account (MCA), which offers foreign assistance to a select group of countries deemed to be high performers according to 16 indicators.

These frameworks make it difficult (although not impossible) to accommodate local political realities or to take a process approach. What if, for example, the process leads to identified priorities and targets that significantly modify or contradict the priorities of the foreign assistance funder? A well-documented response is for recipient country governments to accept reforms for which there is significant reticence or opposition to get the funds, leading to superficial commitment to reform and proforma meeting of targets.[6] For example, development clients may go through the motions of complying with requirements and making changes without internalizing them. Development management specialists have pointed out the difficulties in implementing reforms that ignore process considerations and the failure to identify and support policy champions committed to change (see Brinkerhoff and Crosby, 2002).

However, in today's world of scarce international assistance resources and expanding competition for those resources, development management is enlisted in the service of foreign assistance programs that largely assert the primacy of the donors' agenda. As noted, the policies embodied in CDFs, PRSPs, and the MCA promote a particular development agenda related to economic liberalization, privatization, governance, service

---

[5]These are what are termed variously the Washington consensus (Gore, 2000), neoliberal modernization (Cooke, 2004), or the international development orthodoxy (Landes, 1999; Easterly, 2001).

[6]The literature on the politics of reform is vast. See for example, Haggard and Kaufman (1992) or Bates and Krueger (1994). Cooke (2004) argues that donor-planning frameworks in essence impose an externally determined set of priorities and practices and leave little space for local accommodation.

delivery, and democratization. Although the successful implementation of these agendas involves attention to process and values, these facets of development management tend to serve the donors' priorities and values first, and those of people in the recipient countries second or third. Thus, as Cooke (2004) points out, the relationship among the four facets of development management in practice often resembles something of a hierarchy, where development management's role in achieving foreign assistance agendas trumps the others. However, not all development management takes place within the context of foreign assistance, some NGOs and community groups operate independent of (to greater or lesser degrees) external resources and imposed priorities and pursue their own agendas. In these cases the interface among development management's facets may be less dominated by the foreign assistance instrumentality.

Development Management as Toolkit

Development management promotes the application of a range of management and analytical tools adapted from a variety of disciplines, including strategic management, public policy, public administration, organization development, psychology, anthropology, and political science. These tools assist in mapping the terrain in which policy reforms, programs, and projects are designed and implemented, that is the political, sociocultural, and organizational contexts of interventions. For example, strategic policy management might begin with SWOT analysis (identifying internal strengths and weaknesses and external opportunities and threats), which would then be followed by other tools to assess the actors involved. These latter tools include stakeholder analysis and political mapping (Lindenberg & Crosby, 1981; Brinkerhoff & Crosby, 2002). The results of these exercises feed into the elaboration of potential response strategies that incorporate flexibility and adaptation.

Development management tools merge policy and program analytics with action. It is precisely the blending of the process and value facets with the tools that accounts for the distinctiveness of development management as toolkit. On the analytic side, this means tools that explore the institutional and organizational incentive aspects of achieving results (see Bryant, 1996; Brinkerhoff, 1997, 2002a), and that examine the psychology of change efforts (see Hubbard, 1997), focusing on individual incentives and motivation. On the operational side, the toolkit includes tools and approaches that focus on data gathering, such as participatory rural appraisal (e.g., Kumar, 1993; Blackburn with Holland, 1998); flexible and adaptive design and planning (e.g., Delp et al., 1977; Brinkerhoff and Ingle, 1989); and action learning and experimentation (e.g., Rondinelli, 1983; Kerrigan and Luke, 1987).

An important consideration in terms of the connection between this facet of development management and the others is the issue of who is acquiring the toolkit. Both the process and the values facets are explicit in their attention to assuring that tools and expertise do not remain the sole province of outsiders, donor agencies, international NGOs, and consulting firms, or other technocratic elites. Acquiring the appropriate tools and expertise is important, but transferring them to others is also important. The dimension of development management as toolkit thus responds to development as being more and having more, in this instance having more in one's own toolkit and being capable of using those skills.

Development Management as Process

The process facet of development management is most closely related to development management as values, both politics and empowerment. Development management as process operates on several levels. In terms of the individual actors involved, it builds on organizational development and process consultation; that is, starting with the client's priorities, needs, and values, development management specialists help to: "initiate and sustain a process of change and continuous learning for systemic improvement" (UNDP, 1994 quoted in Joy, 1997, p. 456). Because the process is client-driven, development management serves as handmaiden to: (1) empowering individual actors to assert and maintain control and (2) building their capacity to sustain the process into the future and in other situations. Development management's process facet holds important lessons to help move from analysis to action, beginning at the individual level with its emphasis on client-driven change efforts (e.g., Joy, 1997), and extending to the organizational and sectoral levels with its concentration on understanding and building linkages and system-wide capacity (e.g., White, 1987; Brinkerhoff, 1996).

This facet of development management is largely based on the process consultation model of organization development (see, for example, Bell, 1997; Blunt, 1997; Cooke, 1997, 1998). Among others, Thomas (1999) confirms that development management means doing things with people, not for them. This statement encapsulates the core principles of process consultation:

- Clients know more about their own situation than the consultant ever will
- A consultancy process needs to engender psychological ownership of the activities

- The consultant should seek to develop clients' capabilities to solve their own problems (Cooke, 1997).

Consistent with the tension among development management's four facets, these principles are complicated in their application. As Burkey (1993, p. 102) puts it, "The successful practice of the development practitioner is responsive, disciplined, flexible but constrained by the parameters of development itself." Those parameters concern each of the four development management facets: the institutional agendas at play, the conflicting values and political context of the intervention, the particular tools selected and their feasibility, all of which influence the strategy and effectiveness of the process.

At the organizational level — whether inside an individual agency or multiple organizations working together — development management as process is concerned with the interplay between policy, program, project plans and objectives, and the organizational structures and procedures through which plans are implemented and objectives achieved. Here development managers look for a balance among these factors and the broader setting where development intervention takes place. This is the contingency notion; that is, the best managerial solutions are context-specific and emerge from a process of searching for a fit among programmatic, organizational, and environmental factors.[7]

At the organizational level, tools also come into play. Particular tools may be required or standardized in ways that have implications for process. For example, the logical framework (and its variations) is a tool designed by the international development industry for program design, performance measurement, and evaluation.[8] It has been criticized on several fronts, most of which are really about the process of its implementation than the tool itself. It was originally intended to be a tool for participation and consensus building. Instead it is often applied as a blueprint, usually with a top–down approach that locks implementers and constituents into specific activities, results, and sometimes timelines. In fact, one development scholar has warned that it can be a "lockframe" rather than a logframe (Gasper, 2000). In that sense, it has become more of an auditing and enforcement device than a learning tool. In their application, these types of tools confirm one of the universal features of life in organizations: what gets measured gets done.

---

[7]The contingency approach has been widely applied in development management analysis and practice. See Brinkerhoff (1991), Fowler (1997), Hage and Finsterbusch (1987), and Israel (1987).

[8]Most donors continue to use the logical framework, or logframe, but the United States Agency for International Development (USAID) has modified it into what it calls the results framework. The underlying program logic is the same, and both tools have faced similar criticisms.

At the sector level — public, civil society, and private — development management as process addresses broader governance issues such as participation, accountability, transparency, responsiveness, and the role of the state. This brings in empowerment in its societal and political dimension, looking at how various sociopolitical groups interact in the policy and program implementation process. Again, there are implications for the application of tools like the logical framework. Who gets to decide what the objectives and the activities of a program will be? Who gets to participate in the process of identifying indicators for what success means? And if "beneficiaries" are consulted, which ones? Can we assume that community leaders represent the aspirations of the community as a whole? More broadly, development management's process facet considers the following types of illustrative questions: Who has a place at the policy table? What process mechanisms allow which groups to play a role, or exclude others? What managerial practices and capacities are required for effective democratic governance and socioeconomic development? How can public sector agencies and NGOs best cooperate to achieve joint objectives?[9] As these questions imply, the process facet of development management is intimately linked with the tool and foreign assistance agenda facets. An important place in the toolkit is accorded to process tools, those that facilitate consultation, joint problem and solution identification, ownership and commitment building, participatory strategy development, and so on. Further, many of these questions arise in the context of pursuing institutional agendas.

Whereas development management's process approaches can be cost-efficient in the longer term through contributing to the design of more feasible policies and programs and building commitment among stakeholders for their implementation, in the short term these approaches can prove costly and time-consuming. An important consideration is the cost-benefit analysis — broadly construed — of participatory process approaches. Development management has pursued questions that explore and clarify the connection between process inputs and policy and service delivery outputs (see, for example, Brinkerhoff, 1997; Blackburn with Holland, 1998; Brinkerhoff and Crosby, 2002).

Development Management as Values

The values, facet of development management recognizes that development-promoting activities of any sort constitute interventions in the *status quo*, and that any intervention advances some particular set of interests and objectives at the expense of others. Helping to implement a policy reform

[9]See for example, Brinkerhoff (2002a,b), Brinkerhoff (2000), Coston (1998), Fowler (1997).

or program more effectively or building managerial capacity in a particular agency or organization is a value-laden endeavor. Development management involves tools and approaches that: (1) illuminate goal trade-offs and conflicts, (2) clarify who participates in decisions and who does not, and (3) build capacity for empowering managerial and decision processes. Hence, it can contribute to incorporating equity and sustainability into socioeconomic development.

Development management as values is expressed in two ways. First, development management acknowledges that managing is infused with politics; successful management takes account of this fact and therefore is both contextual and strategic (see, for example, Lindenberg and Crosby, 1981; White, 1987; Brinkerhoff and Crosby, 2002). Part of this acknowledgment extends to the recognition that managers, whether the local managers in a particular country or the external providers of technical or managerial assistance, are "carriers" of values, and hence are inherently political whether they recognize it or not (see Grammig, 2002). However, providers of international technical assistance often don a mantle of neutrality, assumed as a function of their scientific and professional expertise. However, knowledge and expertise cannot be separated from the values context in which they are developed and applied.[10]

Second, development management takes a normative stance on empowerment and supporting groups, particularly the poor and marginalized, to take an active role in determining and fulfilling their own needs. Development management should enhance the capacity of development actors to effectively pursue their own development: it should be people-centered (see, for example, Bryant and White, 1982; Korten and Klauss, 1984; Thomas, 1996).

Another, more subtle, aspect of the values facet is that whether intended or not development managers bring their own values to the work and these inform the decisions they make, including whose view counts, how resources are allocated, and what they choose to do and why. Values cannot be avoided. This aspect of development management as values is closely linked to work on development ethics, and the ethics of inquiry and intervention more generally. In the development field, scholars and promoters of development ethics argue that because values inevitably inform behavior and interactions with others (including those with whom and for whom development managers perceive they are working), there is an obligation to make those values explicit (see, for example, Crocker, 1991). Although values are an inherent component of development management, they are most often discussed only in terms of how they relate to

[10]The classic reference here is Burger and Luckmann (1966).

programmatic objectives. For example, implementers may link to values when discussing political feasibility and winners and losers of policy and program initiatives. Or, initiatives targeted to capacity building may specifically refer to empowerment and participation. Beyond that, values may not often be openly discussed.

Development management's values, facet is closely related to development management as process. The values orientation also links to tools and the donor-funded provision of external assistance. Management tools and technologies are meant to combine external expertise with local knowledge and skills in a process that employs outside resources in the service of indigenously directed endeavors (see Spector and Cooley, 1997). Thus, development management blends local, indigenous knowledge and norms as it seeks to promote sustainable change, whose contours are developed through a participatory dialog incorporating multiple perspectives (Joy, 1997).

An important implication for development management specialists in regard to values is how to deal with the ethics of development intervention. This dilemma surfaces most starkly as a potential conflict between development management as an instrument of external institutional agendas versus the agendas of groups within developing/transitional countries, and in the conflicts among developing country groups. This is often a contest among unequal actors, with predominant power residing with the international donors in the case of negotiations between international funders and national governments. Internal to the recipient country, power tends to be concentrated in political and economic elites, whose agendas overrule those of the poor and marginalized.

One response, related to development management's process facet, is to be very explicit about who the client is for any change intervention (see Cooke, 1997; Joy, 1997). In this regard, some development management professionals have shifted their efforts away from working with international donors or the public sector to focus on independent NGOs and civil society, and to opt for challenging existing power structures and policy elites (Thomas, 1996).[11]

---

[11]Perhaps the most well-known "defector" is David Korten, whose early work on bureaucratic reorientation, learning-process organizations, and people-centered development has been very influential in shaping the development management subfield (see for example, Korten, 1984; Korten and Klauss, 1984). Korten sees development management professionals who work with international donor agencies or developing/transitional country governments as contributors to "the problem," not "the solution." His reasoning is laid out in Korten (1995) and in the various publications of the advocacy NGO he founded, the People-Centered Development Forum (http://iisd1.iisd.ca/pcdf). Bill Cooke (2003, 2004) similarly argues that development management's value and process dimensions have been co-opted by their subservience to the interests of the dominant foreign assistance orthodoxy.

Development management has traditionally acknowledged the importance of community self-determination and locally driven development (Esman, 1988, 1991). The interdependence inherent in the global economy suggests that the challenge for the future will be how to manage an appropriate degree of integration and linkage such that local, regional, national, and international priorities and interests can be balanced and some measure of local empowerment and autonomy maintained.[12]

Development management is crucial in helping governments build the capacity to respond to citizen expectations and to put in place the institutional structures that allow democracy to function effectively. The promotion of democratization and its associated values is among the agendas of a number of foreign assistance agencies, but those values are frequently translated into a relatively narrow view of what constitutes democracy (see Carothers, 1999). Traditional village governance structures in Africa, for example, are not considered "democratic" due to perceived limits in representation in their consensual model. The notion of traditional benevolent leaders runs counter to Western ideals of democracy. Development management, as Riggs (1998, 2000) points out, has not always been at the forefront of exploring various institutional options for democratization that fit with particular country circumstances, and of recognizing that the U.S. model is but one path among many.

Conclusion

Our four-faceted framework for defining development management has unpacked the term to expose both the complexity and the tensions contained within it. Development management is inextricably connected to the applied arena of intervention and change. The conundrum inherent in development management lies in the disconnect (potential and actual) between the two facets that concern doing things right (serving donor agency agendas and the toolkit) and the two that relate to doing the right things (process and values). There is increasing recognition that the process facet is also important to doing things right (i.e., effectively), though these considerations are often overwhelmed by concerns for

[12]Uphoff and Esman (1974) were among the first to demonstrate that local communities could not develop without linkages to larger administrative and economic entities. The same principle of linkages applies today in the larger sphere of nations and the global economy. Bogason (2000) elaborates on the complex interplay among the forces pushing for economic and social integration, globalization, and capitalist production on the one hand, and those of decentralization, differentiation, individualism, and pluralism on the other hand.

immediate efficiency. In the ideal, the four facets reinforce and complement each other: development management serving to do the right things in the right way. However, in the real world, the practice of development management often falls short of this ideal, or approaches it only at the margins. As Thomas concludes in his article on "good" development management, it "will often remain an ideal rather than a description of what takes place" (1999, p. 17).

For development management and managers, the most fundamental contradictions and fiercest debates emerge around the determination of the answer to what is the right thing to do. The political economy of international development places predominant power to answer that question in the hands of the international donor community. For example, the U.S. government's launch of the MCA seeks to reward countries that are doing the right things. The World Bank's PRSP process argues for the importance of local ownership, all the while mandating participation and adherence to a set of investment priorities that closely resemble the Bank and the International Monetary Fund's (IMF) preferred policy agenda.

The debates in development management also extend to doing things right. Beyond macro-level planning, such as that embodied in the CDF and PRSPs, the project remains the donor modality of choice. Consonant with that emphasis is the continuing assumption that development can be "packaged" in discrete blocks of time and effort. The emphasis is also on the results of these short-term efforts, as is consistent with logframe and the more general donor performance-based management agenda. Here, many development scholars argue that donor assistance as currently practiced is not conducive to development as a process of empowered self-determination (see, for example, Cooke, 2004; Holcombe et al., 2004, Kilby, 2004).

New analytic frameworks may assist in resolving some of the tensions and contradictions among development management's four dimensions, but their usefulness will be contingent, to a large extent, on whether they can, first, encourage a more explicit recognition of the skewed power relations that affect what development activities are undertaken, and for whom; and second, make any inroads in rebalancing those power relations. The disconnect within development management will persist as long as there are multiple actors with competing values. In short, the tensions are inevitable. Like political processes more generally, the resolution of these tensions in a particular context will reflect the compromises and power brokering of the actors involved. The ideal for development management may be unattainable in the messy real world, but that does not mean that analysts and practitioners should cease their efforts to move in that direction.

References

Bates, R.H. and A.O. Krueger. 1994. "Political and Economic Interactions in Economic Policy Reform: Evidence from Eight Countries," Cambridge, MA: Basil Blackwell Publishers.

Bell, S. 1997. "Not in Isolation: The Necessity of Systemic Heuristic Devices in All Development Practice," *Public Administration and Development*, 17(3): 449–452.

Bennis, W. and J. Goldsmith. 1997. *Learning to Lead: A Workbook on Becoming a Leader*. Boulder, CO: Perseus Books.

Blackburn, J. with J. Holland (eds.) 1998. *Who Changes? Institutionalizing Participation in Development*. London: Intermediate Technology Publications.

Blunt, P. 1997. "Prisoners of the Paradigm: Process Consultants and 'Clinical' Development Practitioners," *Public Administration and Development*, 17(3): 341–349.

Bogason, P. 2000. *Public Policy and Local Governance: Institutions in Postmodern Society*. Cheltenham, UK: Edward Elgar Publishing.

Brinkerhoff, D.W. 1986. "The Evolution of Current Perspectives on Institutional Development: An Organizational Focus," in D.W. Brinkerhoff and J.-C. Garcia-Zamor (eds.), *Politics, Projects, and People: Institutional Development in Haiti*. New York: Praeger Publishers, pp. 11–63.

Brinkerhoff, D.W. 1991. *Improving Development Management Program Performance: Guidelines for Managers*. Boulder, CO: Lynne Rienner Publishers.

Brinkerhoff, D.W. 1996. "Process Perspectives on Policy Change: Highlighting Implementation," *World Development*, 24(9): 1395–1403.

Brinkerhoff, D.W. 1997. "Integrating Institutional and Implementation Issues into Policy Decisions: An Introduction and Overview," in D.W. Brinkerhoff (ed.), *Policy Analysis Concepts and Methods: An Institutional and Implementation Focus*. Greenwich, CT: JAI Press, Policy Studies in Developing Nations Series, Vol. 5, pp. 1–18.

Brinkerhoff, D.W. 2000. "Democratic Governance and Sectoral Policy Reform: Tracing Linkages and Exploring Synergies," *World Development*, 28(4): 601–615.

Brinkerhoff, J.M. 2002a. "Assessing and Improving Partnership Relationships and Outcomes: A Proposed Framework," *Evaluation and Program Planning*, 25(3): 215–231.

Brinkerhoff, J.M. 2002b. *Partnership for International Development: Rhetoric or Results?* Boulder, CO: Lynne Rienner Publishers.

Brinkerhoff, D.W. and J.M. Coston. 1999. "International Development Management in a Globalized World," *Public Administration Review*, 59(4): 346–361.

Brinkerhoff, D.W. and B.L. Crosby. 2002. *Managing Policy Reform: Concepts and Tools for Decision-Makers in Developing and Transitioning Countries*. Bloomfield, CT: Kumarian Press.

Brinkerhoff, D.W. and M.D. Ingle. 1989. "Between Blueprint and Process: A Structured Flexibility Approach to Development Management," *Public Administration and Development*, 9(5): 487–503.

Bryant, C. 1996. "Strategic Change Through Sensible Projects," *World Development*, 24(9): 1539–1551.

Bryant, C. and L.G. White. 1982. *Managing Development in the Third World*. Boulder, CO: Westview Press.

Burger, P.L. and T. Luckmann. 1966. *The Social Construction of Reality: A Treatise on the Sociology of Knowledge*. New York: Doubleday and Company.

Burkey, S. 1993. *People First: A Guide to Self-Reliant, Participatory Rural Development*. London: Zed Books.

Carothers, T. 1999. *Aiding Democracy Abroad: The Learning Curve*. Washington, D.C.: Carnegie Endowment for International Peace.

Cooke, B. 1997. "From Process Consultation to a Clinical Model of Development Practice," *Public Administration and Development*, 17(3): 325–340.

Cooke, B. 1998. "Participation, 'Process' and Management: Lessons for Development in the History of Organization Development," *Journal of International Development*, 10(1): 35–54.

Cooke, B. 2003. "A New Continuity with Colonial Administration: Participation in Development Management," *Third World Quarterly*, 24(1): 47–61.

Cooke, B. 2004. "The Managing of the (Third) World," *Organization*, 11(5): 603–629.

Coston, J.M. 1998. "A Model and Typology of Government–NGO Relationships," *Nonprofit and Voluntary Sector Quarterly*, 27(3): 358–383.

Crocker, D.A. 1991. "Toward Development Ethics," *World Development*, 19(5): 457–483.

Delp, P., A. Thesen, J. Motiwalla, and N. Seshadri. 1977. *Systems Tools for Project Planning*. Bloomington: Indiana University, Program of Advanced Studies in Institution Building and Technical Assistance Methodologies.

Easterly, W. 2001. *The Elusive Quest for Growth: Economists' Adventures and Misadventures in the Tropics*. Cambridge, MA: MIT Press.

Esman, M.J. 1980. "Development Assistance in Public Administration: Requiem or Renewal?" *Public Administration Review*, 40(5): 426–431.

Esman, M.J. 1988. "The Maturing of Development Administration," *Public Administration and Development*, 8(2): 125–134.

Esman, M.J. 1991. *Management Dimensions of Development: Perspectives and Strategies*. West Hartford, CT: Kumarian Press.

Fowler, A. 1997. *Striking a Balance: A Guide to Enhancing the Effectiveness of Non-Governmental Organisations in International Development*. London: Earthscan Publications.

Gasper, D. 2000. "Evaluating the 'Logical Framework Approach': Towards Learning-Oriented Development Evaluation," *Public Administration and Development*, 20(1): 17–28.

Gore, C. 2000. "The Rise and Fall of the Washington Consensus as a Paradigm for Developing Countries," *World Development*, 28(5): 789–804.

Grammig, T. 2002. *Technical Knowledge and Development: Observing Aid Projects and Processes*. New York: Routledge.

Hage, J. and K. Finsterbusch. 1987. *Organizational Change as a Development Strategy: Models and Tactics for Improving Third World Organizations*. Boulder, CO: Lynne Rienner Publishers.

Haggard, S. and R.R. Kaufman (eds.) 1992. *The Politics of Economic Adjustment: International Constraints, Distributive Conflicts, and the State*. Princeton, NJ: Princeton University Press.

Heady, F. 1998. "Comparative and International Public Administration: Building Intellectual Bridges," *Public Administration Review*, 58(1): 32–40.

Holcombe S.H., S.A. Nawaz, A. Kamwendo, and K. Ba. 2004. "Managing Development: For What and For Whom?" *International Public Management Journal*, 7(2): 187–205.

Hubbard, R. 1997. "People – Hearts and Minds Towards Rebirth of the Public Service," *Public Administration and Development*, 17(1): 109–114.

Israel, A. 1987. *Institutional Development: Incentives to Performance*. Baltimore, MD: Johns Hopkins University Press.

Joy, L. 1997. "Developing a Development Practice: A Commentary in Response to Cooke," *Public Administration and Development*, 17(4): 453–477.

Kerrigan, J.E. and J.S. Luke. 1987. *Management Training Strategies for Developing Countries*. Boulder, CO: Lynne Rienner Publishers.

Kilby, P. 2004. "Empowerment in a Results-Based Project Environment: Is it an Impossible Task?" *International Public Management Journal*, 7(2): 207–225.

Korten, D.C. 1984. "Strategic Organization for People-Centered Development," *Public Administration Review*, 44(4): 341–352.

Korten, D.C. 1995. *When Corporations Rule the World*. West Hartford, CT and San Francisco, CA: Kumarian Press and Berrett-Koehler Publishers.

Korten, D.C. and R. Klauss (eds.) 1984. *People-Centered Development: Contributions toward Theory and Planning Frameworks*. West Hartford, CT: Kumarian Press.

Kumar, K. (ed.) 1993. *Rapid Appraisal Methods*. Washington, D.C.: World Bank.

Landes, D.S. 1999. *The Wealth and Poverty of Nations: Why Some are so Rich and Some so Poor*. New York: W.W. Norton & Company.

Lindenberg, M. and B. Crosby. 1981. *Managing Development: The Political Dimension*. West Hartford, CT: Kumarian Press.

Nicholson, N.K. and E.F. Connerley. 1989. "The Impending Crisis in Development Administration," *International Journal of Public Administration*, 12(3): 385–426.

Riggs, F.W. 1998. "Public Administration in America: Why Our Uniqueness is Exceptional and Important," *Public Administration Review*, 58(1): 22–32.

Riggs, F.W. 2000. "Exporting Government?" Leiden, Netherlands: Association for Law and Administration in Developing and Transitional Countries, Conference paper, June 23.

Rist, G. 1997. *The History of Development: From Western Origins to Global Faith*. London and New York: Zed Books.

Rondinelli, D.A. 1983. *Development Projects as Policy Experiments: An Adaptive Approach to Development Administration*. New York: Methuen and Company.

Rondinelli, D.A. 1987. *Development Administration and U.S. Foreign Aid Policy.* Boulder, CO: Lynne Rienner Publishers.

Spector, B.I. and L. Cooley. 1997. *Consultant Roles in the Strategic Management of Policy Change.* Washington, D.C.: U.S. Agency for International Development, Center for Democracy and Governance, Implementing Policy Change Project, Technical Note No. 8.

Thomas, A. 1996. "What is Development Management?" *Journal of International Development,* 8(1): 95–110.

Thomas, A. 1999. "What Makes Good Development Management?" *Development in Practice,* 9(1–2): 9–17.

United Nations Development Programme (UNDP). 1994. *Process Consultation for Systemic Improvement of Public Sector Management.* New York: Author.

Uphoff, N. and M. Esman. 1974. *Local Organization for Development: Analysis of Asian Experience.* Ithaca, NY: Cornell University, Center for International Studies.

White, L.G. 1987. *Creating Opportunities for Change: Approaches to Managing Development Programs.* Boulder, CO: Lynne Rienner Publishers.

Chapter 37

The World Bank and Postconflict Reconstruction

Leon Newton

CONTENTS

The World Bank Group was established to support the reconstruction of Europe following World War II. The post-Cold War era brought a proliferation of intrastate conflicts. These intrastate conflicts are undermining development in a wide range of countries, threatening national and regional stability in some areas and diverting international attention and scarce resources from pressing development problems. This chapter considers an array of issues that arises during postconflict reconstruction and how the Bank seeks to assist countries emerging from conflicts. Postconflict reconstruction supports the transition from conflict to peace in a war-torn nation through "the rebuilding of the social economics framework of the society" (World Bank, 1999, p. 14). Some of the problems with postconflict reconstruction projects the Bank helps with are: widespread population displacement; damaged infrastructure, including schools, health facilities, housing and other buildings; reduced productive capacity; a devastated government revenue base; an erosion of human and social capital; greatly reduced security; and an increased proportion of people needing social assistance (World Bank, 1999, p. 15). Among the goals of postconflict reconstruction projects are to create the conditions to jumpstart the economy by restoring key financial, legal, and regulatory institutions; to reestablish a framework for governance so that civil society can work freely; and to repair physical infrastructure. The Bank supports health and educational needs through reintegration of internally displaced people as well to demobilize soldiers and combatants.

In addition, there has been a renewed focus on specific issues such as the emergence of violence as a result of the criminalization of many postconflict settings in the absence of public security. Gender- and age-related issues in conflict are surfacing as new challenges to development projects as is the fate of child soldiers, who are among the youngest victims of conflict. The Bank emphasizes the impact that respect for human rights has on judicial reform. Projects that address these issues can be used to support reconstruction. The Bank, like any other large institution, has restraints placed on it by their charter that defines which projects it can engage and which projects it cannot engage. The Bank's Articles of Agreement have constrained any type of engagement in political conduct; in particular, section 10, article IV, provides that only economic considerations shall be relevant in the Bank's dealing with its members. The Bank has begun to define performance criteria for countries emerging from conflict (World Bank, 1995, p. 20).

The World Bank has enhanced their policies and instruments for helping postconflict countries. In September 1998, the Bank explored options for enhancing assistance to postconflict countries, including those with high debt levels (Mascat, 1995, p. 10). These options were developed in subsequent powers discussed by the Boards of the Bank and Fund and were considered by ministers at the spring meeting in 1999. An eligible country has to establish a satisfactory track record of sound economic policies and performance to qualify for Bank assistance that will effectively be used for poverty reductions. Normally, this requires three years of satisfactory performance under Bank-supported projects, of which one year should immediately precede the decision to fund. Conflict is the main obstacle to development and poverty reduction in many countries, and has impact on all parts of society. The international community has recognized that, unless contained, conflicts will prevent some countries from making progress toward development without the help of the Bank. These countries may as a result face serious difficulty to both consolidate peace by adequately funding recovery efforts, and to use resources to normalize relations with creditors and remain current on external debt service.

In these situations, early access to debt relief may be a critical component of the successful transition to peace and resumption of sustainable development.

Countries emerging from conflict have suffered violence to their population and damage to their economic and social capital. Often, the administrative capacity of key economic institutions has been compromised; the ability of the authorities to provide basic services is limited or nonexistent; there are unsustainable financial and economic imbalances; and regulatory and institutional environment for private sector activity, especially investment, is significantly undermined. Once security conditions have improved, conflict-affected countries need substantial support for economic and social recovery, in parallel with the continued provision of humanitarian assistance to meet urgent needs. Especially for countries that have had a major domestic conflict, the recovery process is often lengthy and complex, and prone to frequent setbacks, and sometimes resumption of conflict. Success is aided by the direct participation in, and ownership of, the reconstruction effort by the country's communities and government at all levels, and also by broad and coordinated participation of key international actors, including United Nations (UN) agencies, bilateral donors, non-governmental organizations (NGOs), and the international financial investors (IFIs). These broad partnerships can be critically important because the magnitude and diversity of the problems are frequently beyond the capability of any single institution to address.

The World Bank and International Monetary Fund usually become involved in postconflict situations at an early stage, as soon as the security conditions permit a credible political authority to be established, and their involvement can be productive. In this work, the Fund takes the lead on macroeconomic issues whereas the Bank focuses on reconstructive efforts and on helping the government define priorities for structural reforms. The Bank and the Fund both play a key role in mobilizing support from bilateral donors, who look to the Bank and Fund to guide their involvement (United Nations Development Program [UNDP]). Effective coordination of postconflict assistance efforts is especially important to avoid the imposition of unnecessary burdens on government capacity, which is frequently especially fragile in postconflict environments, and to ensure that available resources are channeled to the priorities set out in the national recovery plan. Coordination should include the preparation of damage and needs assessments, and of national recovery plans, which should clearly prioritize actions and investments. While the particular priorities will depend on the specific circumstances of each country, the key objectives will generally be to facilitate the transition to sustainable peace, and to support rapid economic and social development. To this end, the following may need to be considered: jump-starting the economy; re-establishing a framework of governance; rehabilitating social services;

repairing key physical infrastructure; and helping war-affected populations and communities, including programs in support of reintegration, income generation and other support for vulnerable groups such as orphans and female-headed households (United Nations Development Program, "Assistance to Post-Conflict Countries: Progress Report" paper prepared by Bank and Fund for the Interim and Development Committees, April 21, 1999.)

The World Bank objectives for postconflict reconstruction for the development of war-torn nations are twofold: one, to facilitate the ease of transition to sustainable peace after the conflict has ended and two, for social and economic development. To obtain these goals the bank has set up programs to support these developments:

- Jump-start the economy through investments in key productive sections; create the necessary conditions for domestic and foreign investment; and promote macroeconomic stabilization, rehabilitation of financial institutions, and restoration of appropriate legal and regulatory framework of governance by strengthening government institutions, restoring law and enabling the organization of civil society to work effectively
- Repair important physical infrastructure, including key transport, communication, and utility networks
- Rebuild and maintain key social infrastructure; that is, financing education and health, including recurrent costs
- Target assistance to those affected by war through reintegration of displaced populations, demobilization and reintegration of excombatants, revitalization of the local communities most disrupted by conflict through such means as credit lines to subsistence agriculture and microenterprise, and support for vulnerable groups such as female-headed households
- Support landmine action programs, where relevant, including mine surveys and determining of key infrastructure, as part of comprehensive development strategies for supporting a return to normal life of populations living in mine-polluted areas
- Normalize financial borrowing arrangements by planning a work out of arrears, debt rescheduling, and the longer-term path to financial normalization (World Bank, 1999, pp. 4–5).

Postconflict reconstruction supports the transition from conflict to peace in order to help rebuild countries torn by conflict after the conflict has stopped. Postconflict includes not just the physical infrastructure but the rebuilding of the socioeconomic system. The Bank's projects support the maintaining of key social factors such as health, education, school building, women programs, nutrition, and populations living in mine-polluted areas. The cause of conflict differs for each nation. The Bank tries to bridge its knowledge with the links to development assistance and conflict. The Bank's work in a situation of conflict is to increase the understanding of the cause of the conflict in order to prepare for postconflict recovery. The focus is on the environmental causes and consequences of conflict.

The Bank has a conflict analysis unit that is based on the awareness of the possibility of the success of the development assistance to war-torn nations that has ended their violent conflicts. The conflict analysis uses seven variables to determine the way it relates to conflict and poverty for development:

- History/changes: how the issue has evolved over a pertinent time span
- Dynamics/trends: what is determining the future path of the issue, and how it is likely to develop
- Public perceptions: public attitudes and biases regarding the issue
- Politicization: how the issue is used politically by different groups
- Organization: the extent to which the issue has led to the establishment of interest groups, or has influenced political parties and militant organizations
- Link to conflict and intensity: how the factor contributes to conflict and the current level of intensity
- Link to poverty: how the issue relates to poverty (World Bank, 2002, *Conflict Prevention and Reconstruction Unit*, p. 1).

In conclusion, the Bank's objective is to help nations that have experienced violent conflicts and are on their way to recovery. The Bank's work on postconflict reconstruction eases the transition to sustainable peace after hostilities have ceased and supports social and economic development. The Bank uses multilateral donors. The Bank helps in the development of a nation's staff and with their operational support staff and client governments. The Bank tries to structure a loan program that is fair and will help war-torn nations on the road to recovery, including social and economic development. The Bank normalizes financial borrowing arrangements by planning debt rescheduling.

The Bank's conflict prevention and reconstruction unit supports activities that are making more nations become more resilient to the start and escalation of violent conflict. The concept of conflict analysis with its seven variables as indicators is used to assess the outbreak, escalation, or the restart of a conflict. The Bank seeks to establish peaceful and stable political institutions so that nations that were once involved in violent conflicts can develop and contribute to world peace.

References

Mascat, R. (1995). *Conflict and Reconstruction: Roles for the World Bank*, OED: Washington, D.C., pp. 1–50.

UNDP (United Nations Development Program) (1996). *Building Bridges between Relief and Development: A Compendium of the UNDP Record in Crisis Countries*. New York: United Nations.

World Bank (1995). The Bank's Role in Conflict Prevention and Post-Conflict Reconstruction: A 1–10.

World Bank (1999). *Post-Conflict Reconstruction: The Role of the World Bank*. Washington, D.C.: World Bank Publication, pp. 1–69.

World Bank (2002). *Conflict Prevention and Reconstruction Unit*. Washington, D.C.: World Bank Publication, pp. 1–4.

Chapter 38

The Effects of Governance on Competitiveness in India, China, and Mexico

Susan Scott and Jack Pinkowski

CONTENTS

Introduction

Transnational corporations (TNCs) have created global supply chains that span the world in their quest to service their markets. Developing nations compete to be part of these supply chains to advance trade, gain technology, and grow their economies. For that reason, government policy should have a demonstrable effect on the competitiveness of the country. The competitiveness of a developing nation in this environment has traditionally been measured relating to the four dimensions: the nation's macroeconomic situation — namely its financial and educational institutions; its enforcement of law; the number of administrative barriers impeding commerce or competition of firms; and its labor and industrial policies. Increasing importance has been attributed to technology in the development process and the country's technological readiness. This chapter will review and compare the effect of these dimensions of governance on the competitiveness of China, India, and Mexico that are striving to capture a spot in the global supply chain through their attractiveness to TNCs. These countries were selected for comparison because they are popular outsourcing markets for U.S. firms that are attracted to their low-wage rates and ample labor pool with corresponding influence on the country's domestic markets and governmental policy.

National Competitiveness

When questions arise concerning the increase of prosperity in one nation versus the economic decline of another, the explanation usually involves the concept of national competitiveness. For over 20 years the World Economic Forum, in addition to studying national data, has conducted executive opinion surveys of key representatives of the business world including senior government policymakers in more than 100 countries to make country-to-country comparisons. The World Economic Forum includes in their analysis technology integration, government policies such as the tax and regulatory environment, labor market legislation, and educational and financial institutional development in addition to other factors such as quality of the country's infrastructure, the macroeconomic environment, and prevalence of corruption or other irregular practices in the economy. It interprets competitiveness through growth in exports and foreign direct investment (FDI) as well as by an increase in per capita gross domestic product (GDP). GDP is an estimate of the value of all of the goods and services produced in a nation in a given year using standardized international dollar price weights for the comparison of the economic strength between countries. The GDP real growth rate reflects an annual adjustment for inflation. The result is an annual ranking of the competitiveness of nations titled *The Global Competitiveness Report*.

In the 2004 World Economic Forum's growth competitiveness index rankings and 2003 comparisons, mainland China was ranked 46th, down from 44th in the previous year. Mexico was ranked 48th (47th in 2003) and India was ranked 55th compared to 56th in the year before (World Economic Forum, 2004). India may be penalized in the World Economic Forum methodology by virtue of its large budget deficits, which amounted to 4.4 percent of its GDP in the fiscal year 2005 (Reuters, 2005). In ranking countries based just on the year's results, according to the International Institute for Management Development in the *IMD World Competitiveness Yearbook* (2005), China ranks 31st, India 39th, and Mexico 56th.

Traditional trade theory, espoused by leaders of many developing countries, posits that increased international trade will bring greater prosperity. To snare such trade, a nation needs to be "competitive" in its markets, which is usually interpreted as having low costs and liberalized trade policies. However, several studies have demonstrated that there is no conclusive evidence that liberal trade policies alone are enough to ensure competitiveness and growth (Rusek, 2004). Nonetheless, one indication of a nation's competitiveness is the number of its firms that are part of the global supply chain (also called the global value chain (GVC)). These supply chains are controlled by large TNCs that source production and services from all regions of the world in order to deliver their offerings to market in the most profitable and efficient manner possible. Developing countries seek to attract the TNCs with local suppliers offering lower cost labor, favorable financing, or abundant natural resources (Lall, 1995). Expenditures by TNCs in the developing world are growing. TNCs provide a way for a country to adopt technology from abroad through technology transfer that is necessary to serve the needs of the TNCs.

China, India, and Mexico have all succeeded in joining the global supply chain. Although their exports have risen, FDI increasingly is flowing into activities requiring higher technology, "disciplined and productive labor, high skill levels, world class infrastructure and a supportive network of suppliers" (Lall, 1995, p. 522). This suggests that competitiveness is not static, that a nation must advance up the GVC to ensure continued growth and prosperity. According to a U.K. Cabinet white paper,

> Improving competitiveness is central to raising the underlying rate of growth of the economy and enhancing living standards. The need to improve our competitiveness is not imposed by government but by changes in the world economy. Improving competitiveness is not about driving down living standards. It is about creating a high skills, high productivity and therefore

> high wage economy where enterprise can flourish and where we can find opportunities rather than threats in changes we cannot avoid.
>
> UNCTAD (2002, p. 210)

A nation's government, culture, and trade policies combine to strongly influence its place in the GVC.

The most commonly cited economic measures of global competitiveness are export levels, FDI and GDP growth (Thompson, 2004). Table 38.1 lists the relative status of China, Mexico, and India on these dimensions using the United States as a frame of reference. Using these measures to determine the level of participation in the global supply chain, China leads the three nations under comparison. Its 2004 exports and its 2003 FDI are well ahead of those of India and Mexico. China currently offers costs low enough to offset market risks. Mexico, burdened by heavy foreign debt, must shore up its finances and increase technology integration to bring conditions up to a point where cost and risk are both attractive. Although India has succeeded in creating a successful software-related specialization, other sectors, such as energy, still lag. Excellence in a single sector is not enough to propel the nation to prosperity without significant progress in others.

FDI and exports should be correlated because investment by TNCs is linked to the global supply chain. A country, such as the United States, the largest direct investor abroad, would likely see TNCs manufacturing products in countries wherever lower production and labor costs could be capitalized upon. Then finished goods would be shipped back to the United States. The trade would show as U.S. imports and the foreign land's exports when in reality they are U.S. products sourced worldwide as a consequence of globalization. This now relates to 20 to 25 percent of U.S. imports (Garelli, 2005).

Mexico has achieved a place in the supply chain, but the skills, technology, and employment generated by its foreign trade are not increasing its domestic prosperity. This seems to support the assertions of De Matteis that

Table 38.1 Relative Status on Global Economic Competitiveness Measure

Country	*Real GDP Growth Rate (%)*	*Estimated 2004 Exports in Billions (US$)*	*FDI 2003 Inflows in Billions (US$)*
China	9.1	583.1	447.9
India	6.2	69.2	25.4
Mexico	4.1	182.4	154.0
United States	4.4	795.0	2 trillion

trade liberalization inhibits industrialization, due to the comparative advantage of low-income countries in the export-oriented production of primary products (De Matteis, 2004). The explanation for a country's competitiveness relates to its structural or governmental action, including sound monetary policy, inflationary controls; coordinated labor and industrial policies that foster the formation of industrial clusters to promote specialization and worker training; reduction of administrative barriers to business creation and investment; and enforcement of law, especially business law such as patents, copyrights, and contracts. These are the realm of government policy and help determine national competitiveness in the globalization context.

Government Influence on National Competitiveness

Government's actions effect national competitiveness by assisting the finance markets in setting borrowing rates and providing data and information that corporate marketing requires in support of competition. They establish or modify institutions that are necessary for markets to function. And they have to coordinate investment decisions across activities where market forces by themselves are unable to provide adequate information.

Markets sometimes require government intervention to advance their competitiveness (Pook & Pence, 2004). Governments do well to intervene in supplying those "public needs and wants" that the markets are not able to provide satisfactorily (Meso, 1999). Far-East economies such as Hong Kong and Taiwan have demonstrated the success of the concept of government working with labor and business to help advance efficiency in industry by creating policies that foster international competitiveness. China is proceeding in the same manner. By lowering or removing tariffs on Chinese goods, the World Trade Organization (WTO) effectively increased the competitiveness of Chinese firms bidding for business with the TNCs. Both India and Mexico joined the WTO years ago and the advantage it brought them in world trade has been neutralized to some extent by China's ability to provide many of the same items at a lower cost.

Removing Administrative Barriers to Competitiveness

Many forms of trade barriers are created more by practice than by policy. Thomas and Grosse concluded that cultural dimensions are important "because foreign investment requires interface on many levels including state and local competitors, and at least some elements of a foreign work force. FDI levels may be higher... where similarity eases the cultural dimensions of business relations" (Thomas & Grosse, 2001).

Although a country may be a signatory to the General Agreement on Tariffs and Trade (GATT) and tariff regulation policy, internal or country-specific rules and customs may present barriers to trade. For example, since India joined GATT, the Bureau of Indian Standards has developed 17,248 Indian standards that must be met for companies serving various sectors (WTO, 2002, p. 179). These standards act as nontariff barriers to foreign trade. Moreover, wading through the bureaucracy to find information on standards or on regulations can be very daunting for foreign investors. Because the Indian government is the biggest employer in the world, it may hinder rather than advance ease of trade (Patnaik, 1997). India needs legislation "guaranteeing freedom of information on what the government is doing" both for administrative as well as legislative policies (Patnaik, 1997, p. 173).

Lack of free and open disclosure by governments is another barrier to trade. Chinese enterprises trying to comprehend India's trade rules complain about the lack of transparency (WTO, 2002, p.179). A large bureaucracy allows India to track imports closely and use antidumping legislation frequently. Between 1992 and 2002, India initiated 51 cases against Chinese products such as textiles and appliances. Yet India is hardly blameless in its adherence to export rules. The use of antidumping tariffs is perceived by the Chinese as a major barrier to trade with India (UNCTAD, 2002) and nontariff barriers exist in agriculture and in the health industry. India is currently the recipient of 40 antidumping suits and 13 countervailing measures according to the WTO (2002, p. 53). The policies of India and China reflect the idea that governments who want their nations to remain competitive are forced to behave like "strategic oligopolists" to protect certain industries that will advance their national interests (Dunning, 1998).

Unlike India, Mexico has removed almost all of its tariff barriers. Recent pacts with Central America, added to their previous agreements under the North American Free Trade Agreement (NAFTA) and the WTO, remove trade restrictions on over 90 percent of their foreign commerce (CIA, 2003). Mexico has also removed most restrictions on foreign investment in the telecommunications sector and the natural gas industry. Its exports, mainly to NAFTA nations, increased steadily from 1995 to 2000, in concert with wages (Walden, 2002). Mexico's reliance on trade with the United States, however, makes it more vulnerable than China or India to the U.S. cycles of prosperity despite its own administrative facilitation of trade.

Financial Systems and Monetary Controls

In the "new economy" we see the increasing emphasis on entrepreneurialism, innovation, and risk taking. These are often characteristics of emerging industries. Such industries are financially riskier than many banks are willing to accept as business partners, with the result that venture capital firms often fill the finance gap by accepting a percentage of the company to compensate for their greater investment risk (Rusek, 2004). None of the three countries, India, China, or Mexico, has an established venture capital system. In all these economies, the government has at times chosen to underwrite loans for firms or industries that are inherently risky but vital to future economic growth. China still does this today in order to advance its climb up the supply chain. As an outcome of government policy to aid their banking sector in accepting the risks associated with entrepreneurial start-ups, both China and India's banking sectors have an unhealthy amount of nonperforming loans, which has required government bailout of the largest state-owned commercial banks in China using billions of foreign exchange reserves to boost their capital adequacy ratios.

In terms of the overall financial sector, creating a strong financial system is still a work in progress for both Mexico and China. Mexico has had significant problems with its monetary policies, as evidenced by the peso's debacle of 1994. The huge influx of dollars that followed NAFTA raised the standard of living, but loose fiscal policy led to a foreign debt level that reached 35 percent of GDP in 1999 and caused a diversion of funds to pay down debt that might otherwise have been invested in infrastructure or technology. China is still hindered by a lack of transparency in its financial system (CIA, 2004) and by restrictions on currency repatriation. China's central government has strict monetary controls and manipulates its currency's value to ensure increasing foreign investment. This is one of the reasons that China kept the value of its currency pegged to the dollar. This, coupled with the loan problems, is reminiscent of the position Mexico found itself in during the early 1990s. A sharp boost in exports and foreign investment lifted the currency beyond a sustainable level, while the business boom was fueled by easy lending.

Mexican monetary policy is controlled by the minister of finance and administrative development, with influence from the president. Recently Mexico's central bank has pursued an anti-inflation policy in order to bring rates to parity with the United States, its major trading partner. This has been successful. Part of this policy was to use interest rate incentives to increase national savings (and thus fund investment). This has not proven effective (Walden, 2002). Recently a tighter monetary policy has been used to ensure that fundamentals are sound enough to foster fiscal and exchange rate stability. The need for more foreign currency to service its huge foreign debt pushes Mexico to keep trade open and foreign investment flowing. Unlike China, Mexico has reduced its problems with transparency and financial corruption sufficiently to attract foreign banks in partnerships.

The banking sector has evolved enough to force weaker banks to merge with stronger players rather than rely on government bailouts.

In India, the parliament has jurisdiction on all international trade issues. In its 2002/2003 session the government introduced a bill to strengthen creditor rights of foreclosure for banks and financial institutions (WTO, 2002, p. 125). Banking sector reform recently included raising capital adequacy ratios as part of India's effort to reduce the level of nonperforming loans in the sector. According to the report from the United Nations Conference on Trade and Development (UNCTAD), "the insurance industry has been opened to competition from the private sector [although] foreign equity is restricted to 26 percent of the total" (WTO, 2002, p. xxi). These moves, which parallel those made by the Mexican government, seem to confirm that as a developing nation grows its economy and its value chain beyond the primary products stage into more technological realms, it will be forced to improve financial controls and allow competition in the financial markets in order to remain competitive. It may be for this reason that both India and Mexico have stock markets that have performed well in comparison to the other nations of their regions.

India's central bank policy is rated 9th in the world, compared to 30th and 36th for China and Mexico, respectively (IMD, 2005). This makes India more attractive than China for many investors. Moreover India's immense population growth continues to offset any gains in economic prosperity, which will for the foreseeable future ensure that comparative wage levels will remain lower than those in Mexico or China, whose populations have much slower growth rates.

Although the world is eager to consume new, innovative products, as well as established technology if it can be made cheaper, rapid development of industrial activities should not mask the importance of developing in parallel a sophisticated financial system that can provide appropriate financial resources and corporate governance (Garelli, 2005). When industrial competitiveness becomes disconnected from a weak financial system, countries can collapse under the burden of nonperforming loans, loan guarantees, and illegal practices. This has resulted in financial crisis in Japan previously and may be on the horizon for China due to its financial system and policies.

The Legal Structure and the Rule of Law

Both India and Mexico, with federalist systems, have achieved enough political maturity that the legislative branch of government acts as a check on the executive branch. The judicial branch is still insufficiently independent in Mexico and is severely troubled by corruption. China still operates as much from custom as by law and needs further legal development before its judicial system can be independent. It too has issues with corruption that undermine the confidence of foreign investors. Enforcement of contracts in China is uncertain, especially because local business does not operate on the basis of formal, written contracts, but rather in the context of long-term relationships.

China is instituting and enforcing laws to protect intellectual property. In the early stages of growth, it may have been considered wiser for the emerging economy to copy and absorb any knowledge that could be gained from trading partners, regardless of alleged proprietary rights. However, as learning is institutionalized and confidence grows in the skills of the native workers, respecting intellectual property becomes critical to gaining trading partners for design work, cutting edge manufacturing or technology (Rodrigues, 2002). India is in much the same position, with a high incidence of political corruption and poor enforcement of intellectual property laws. Enforcement of copyright law is the responsibility of the state governments. Directives to crack down on intellectual property law enforcement have been issued in the last few years. Mexico is more advanced at enforcement of patents and copyrights, but because it is not attracting the level of investment in technology and software that China and India do, little competitive advantage is gained.

Impact of Labor Laws and Industrial Policies on Competitiveness

In all the three countries, there is interaction between business and government policymakers to improve national competitiveness. It has been noted that most TNCs do not transfer their latest technologies to their trading partners in circumstances where they do not have full control of its use and benefit (Lall, 1995). Some countries, such as China, have tried to change this by creating FDI performance requirements for use of local suppliers, sharing of research and development (R&D), and equity participation. In India, the Department of Commerce frequently interacts with trade and industry groups such as the Confederation of Indian Industries. The Board of Trade also interacts with business (WTO, 2002). The Chinese government has underwritten construction funding for entire cities to increase foreign trade, whereas in Mexico the state makes regular concessions to labor to head off demands that could lead to strikes.

Neither Mexico nor India has sufficient institutional checks and balances to prevent exploitation of its workers. Labor unions are weak. Business interests are well organized whereas legal mechanisms for those harmed by the corporate world are few. China has no nonpolitical workers' organizations and even fewer laws for worker protection compared to Mexico or India. Further development of institutions such as the United States' Occupational Safety and Health Administration (OSHA) is needed to balance economic development in these nations.

According to Howes and Singh (2000), "market share growth is better explained by relative productivity growth (and the associated growth of investment) than by falling relative unit labor costs." As prosperity increases, wages will rise and take away one source of competitive advantage. UNCTAD reported in 2002 that,

> While low cost labour provides an excellent launching pad for the initial export of simple manufactures by developing countries, countries cannot grow if their competitive edge remains low-wage, unskilled labour. . . . Thus competitiveness over time means upgrading simple labour-intensive activities to make higher-quality products that yield greater value-added and so sustain higher wages. It means deepening local technological and organizational skills over time to handle more advanced functions, say, from simple assembly to . . . new product design, innovation and basic research.
>
> UNCTAD (2002, p. 3)

Telecommunications and information technologies show a close relationship to national economic output measured by per capita GDP (Pook & Pence, 2004, p. 77). To progress up the supply chain, a labor force that is skilled in these areas will be needed. In terms of education, India ranks 1st in the world on its professionals' education level (IPS, 2001), compared to 43rd place for China and 26th for Mexico. Public spending on education in India is 3.4 percent of GDP, 4.9 percent in Mexico, and 2.3 percent in China. India also ranks 3rd in the world on the presence of information technology (IT) skills in its populace, which is currently fueling their success as a major source of software for developed nations. Mexico ranks far behind in 54th place and China ranks 58th. India leads both the other countries on the application of technology as well (IMD, 2004). The fact that English is the historic language of trade for India makes it more attractive to the large economies of the United States, Great Britain, and Canada and gives them a further edge on technological development involving the Internet, which is predominantly in English.

Conclusions

There seems to be agreement among policymakers, scholars, and corporate executives that the integration of computer technology into a nation's government, businesses, financial sector, and institutional services is critical to that nation's ability to advance its economy. "A nation's standard of living is determined by its own long-term productivity growth rather than its productivity growth relative to others" (Howes & Singh, 2000). Patnaik carries this further by saying,

> Many major developing countries such as India, Brazil, Mexico and China have been undergoing restructuring in their economies that will offer increased access. The vast markets in these countries are highly attractive to foreign investment and trade. This will offer not only the opportunity to expand the volume of trade, it will also enable the developing countries to integrate fully into the world market.
>
> Patnaik (1997, p. 167)

Therefore, as multiple countries compete for foreign investment, raising competitiveness is essential to improving the nation's standard of living in the long term.

In addition to liberalizing trade, internal institutions and business practices need to be revamped. Governmental administrative barriers must be removed to facilitate FDI and reciprocal trade (Kim, 2004). This is possible regardless of the form of government. Singapore has a one-party, tightly controlled government and yet it has excelled at remaining competitive for over a decade. Nontariff barriers such as complex commercial standards or industry subsidies should be only temporary measures and used sparingly. India's decision not to tax information technology services allowed that sector to grow and prosper. It can now afford the imposition of taxes without floundering. India exported US$4 billion in 1999/2000 of software services and US$1.1 billion of communications services. Interestingly, absolute investment in FDI has not increased, but rather shifted as computer-related exports increased to 16 percent in 2000/2001 from 3.7 percent in 1995/1996, whereas other segments declined (WTO, 2002, p. 13). Output from the service sector now accounts for 49 percent of India's GDP (WTO, 2002, p. 181), a significantly higher ratio than in China or Mexico.

New worker education practices are needed to progress up the supply chain. Specialization and advanced technology skills increase in importance as a nation develops. Integration into the large value chains of the TNCs now requires use of computerized communications, logistics, accounting, banking, and design. In countries where electricity is not always in adequate supply, state-of-the-art communication systems pose a challenge that must be overcome. Intellectual property laws must be passed and, more importantly, enforced. Worker protection laws are needed to force firms to pursue productivity gains in a safe and legal manner. The competition among firms engendered by high demand for skilled workers may help this cause.

Financial controls must be put in place to police the banking sector, followed by encouragement of competition. Adequate capital ratios must be maintained and free market movement of the exchange rate should be encouraged. As a developing nation grows its value chain beyond the primary products stage into more technological realms, it must improve financial controls and allow competition in the financial markets to remain competitive. Those governments that continue to bailout ailing financial institutions deprive healthy new firms of valuable funding needed for growth.

Progress on these fronts can be measured by the three metrics mentioned previously: FDI levels, export levels, and percentage of real growth of GDP. Mexico has raised the first two metrics quite successfully. China has made remarkable progress on all three fronts. However, as the WTO noted in its report, India's "FDI has not increased, and indeed has declined slightly since the mid-1990s despite further liberalization of foreign investment policies, [which] may indicate the need for further regulatory reform" (WTO, 2002, p. 13). Many administrative and structural barriers still remain in the form of "unusual rigidity of labor laws, weakness of infrastructure, and slow and cumbersome administrative processes" (WTO, 2002, p. 14).

In China, the public administration continues to work with industry to increase investment in education and technology in order to advance knowledge and move further up the value chain. In this way, states and industries work in partnership to foster growth. The government's willingness to invest in technology by granting no-interest loans for equipment purchases and by sending students abroad for technical education has already paid dividends. China has improved its universities and now graduates twice as many mechanical engineers per year as the United States.

Of the three nations, India currently resides highest on the supply chain by operating successfully in the knowledge economy, despite the extreme poverty of the masses. Mexico is determinedly pushing into the middle range as it concentrates on engineering and design of those components it was merely assembling a few years ago. Mexico has been able to successfully utilize its domestic market to help expand the skills of its workforce. Its rank in 54th place for technology skills must be corrected before further progress can be made. According to Pook and Pence (2004, p. 79), in order for nations to conquer the "digital divide" created by the computer, "emphasis must be placed on the effective integration of information and e-commerce technologies into all levels of their societies, governments, commerce, and institutions."

Comparing the four aspects of competitiveness exhibited by these three countries, it would appear that China is the most competitive today, by virtue of its very low costs (both labor and financing), which offset the other risks it poses to investors. It seems likely however, that it is their workers' technology skills that will be the differentiator for tomorrow.

The real engine for competitiveness and economic success for nations ultimately is not to be the workshop with the lowest wages for the rest of the world. It is scientific advancement, innovation, technology, and education amidst a scientific culture that promotes entrepreneurship. China and India are among those nations that are building its intellectual base intertwined with industrialization, as evidenced by its applications for patents. Bridging the gap between applied research and new, innovative business applications will result in long-term and lasting competitiveness.

References

CIA (2003). *The World Factbook.* Washington, D.C.: Central Intelligence Agency, Supt. of Docs., U.S. GPO.

CIA (2004). *The World Factbook.* Washington, D.C.: Central Intelligence Agency, Supt. of Docs., U.S. GPO.

De Matteis, A. 2004. "International Trade and Economic Growth in a Global Environment." *Journal of International Development*, 16: 575–588.

Dunning, J.H. 1998. "An Overview of Relations with National Governments." *New Political Economy*, 3(2): 282.

Garelli, S. 2005. "The World Competitiveness Landscape in 2005: A Higher Degree of Risk." *IMD World Competitiveness Yearbook.* Lausanne, Switzerland: International Institute for Management Development, pp. 40–46.

Howes, C. and A. Singh. (eds.) (2000). *Competitiveness Matters: Industry and Economic Performance.* Ann Arbor, MI: University of Michigan Press, p. 5.

IMD (2005). *IMD World Competitiveness Yearbook.* Lausanne, Switzerland: International Institute for Management Development.

IPS (2001). *IPS National Competitiveness Report.* Seoul, Korea: Institute of Industrial Policy Studies.

Kim, Z.K. (2004). "The Allocation and Motivation of Japanese and U.S. Foreign Direct Investment in an Economically Integrated Area: The Case of the European Union." *S.A.M. Advanced Management Journal*, 69(2): 47–58.

Lall, S. (1995). "Employment and Foreign Investment: Policy Options for Developing Countries." *International Labour Review*, 134(4–5): 521–541.

Meso, P. (1999). "Can National Information Infrastructures Enhance Social Development in the Least Developed Countries?" *Journal of Global Information Management*, 8(4): 30–42.

Patnaik, J.K. (1997). *India and the GATT: Origin, Growth and Development.* New Delhi, India: A.P.H. Publishing Corporation.

Pook, L.A. and N.E. Pence. (2004). "Evaluation of Information Infrastructures and Social Development among the Visegrad-Four Countries of Central Europe." *Journal of Global Information Management*, 12(2): 63–83.

Reuters (2005). FACTBOX — India's 05/06 Annual Budget — What to Expect. *Yahoo! India News*, March 4, http://in/news.yahoo.com/050218/137/2jp6r.html.

Rodrigues, M.J. (ed.) (2002). *The New Knowledge Economy in Europe: A Strategy for International Competitiveness*. Cheltenham, UK: Edward Elgar Publishing.

Rusek, A. (2004). "Economic Growth in the New Era." *Atlantic Economic Journal*, 32(1): 68.

Thomas, D.E. and R. Grosse. (2001). "Country of Origin Determinants of Foreign Direct Investment in an Emerging Market: the Case of Mexico." *Journal of International Management*, 7: 66.

Thompson, E. (2004). "The Political Economy of National Competitiveness." *Review of International Political Economy*, II(February): 62.

UNCTAD (2002). *The Competitiveness Challenge: Transnational Corporations and Industrial Restructuring in Developing Countries*. United Nations Conference on Trade and Development (UNCTAD). NY and Geneva: United Nations.

World Economic Forum (2004). *The Global Competitiveness Report 2004*. NY and Oxford: Oxford University Press.

Walden (2002). World of Information Business Intelligence Reports — Mexico, ISSN 1364–4572. Essex, UK: Walden Publishing.

WTO (2002). *Trade Policy Review — India*. World Trade Organization. NY: World Trade Organization.

Chapter 39

The Globalization of Public Administration: Rhetoric, Reality, and Reason in Ghana

Peter Fuseini Haruna

CONTENTS

Introduction

From the decolonization period, descriptions of public administration in Africa have focused on development and modernization, citing cross-cultural concepts and theories arising from the first wave of globalization that brought Africans into contact with other nations, peoples, cultures, politics, and economics (Jackson & Rosberg, 1994; Dzorgbo, 2001). These descriptions attempt to explain Africa's affiliation with Westernized forms of public administration, broadly characterized as concern with state-led development anchored by bureaucracy and a rationality that emphasizes economic growth. Despite the widespread discourse generated and the nationalism fired by these descriptions, this initial wave of globalization through colonialism passed over the heads of the majority of Africans and thereby failed to promote the public interest (Hyden, 1983; Leys & Berman, 1994; Ake, 1996).

However, since the 1980s a different set of concepts and theories of public administration have emerged that define a new wave of globalization, shifting the focus to market principles and neoliberal thought, but they have similarly failed to lead to institutional transformation in Africa (Werlin, 2003; Haruna, 2004). Public administration has been construed mainly as an economic transaction, and efforts by African governments and their development partners (multilateral corporations, Western nations, and international non-governmental organizations (NGOs)) to institutionalize shared governance and liberalized politics have been oriented toward economics and managerialism. In spite of the rhetoric and normative claims, these concepts and theories have failed to make an impact because they are decontextualized. It can be argued then that the recent wave of globalization rooted in market principles lacks robustness to connect to the reality and reason through which Africans construct the meaning of their shared environment.

The purpose of this chapter is to provide a detailed, critical analysis of the conditions under which globalization, whether based on development logic or neoliberalism, has functioned in an African nation, Ghana. This is important because although a variety of studies on how globalization affects developing nation-states abounds, there is a dearth of critical literature on how the evolution of such a globalization has been accelerated by ideology-driven reforms in individual nations. Much of the recent writing tends to take not only a general perspective but also to accept the foundation of the instrumentalist philosophy of public administration, prioritizing liberalization, democratization, and managerialism (Olowu, 2002; Rondinelli & Cheema, 2003). Such writing suggests that globalization leads to, if not encourages, "a convergence of Western and non-Western systems both economically and politically" (Minogue, 2001, p. 1). Nonetheless, this assumption has been questioned on the basis that the latest globalization is a continuation of the "modernizing project" that began in the 20th century, even though Western institutions are no longer that authoritative.

In this chapter, a critical-pragmatist perspective to examine how globalization has affected, and is reflected in, public administration thought and practice in Ghana is applied. The argument holds that in pursuing the global public administration model, particularly "new public management" (NPM) reforms, Ghana responded mainly to the pressures of exogenous forces at the expense of its unique historical, social, cultural, and political specificity: Ghana sacrificed its local institutional demands and variations in favor of the global model. As a result, public administration has focused on globally and internationally recognized standards, and public administrators are expected to possess generic managerial expertise and an entrepreneurial value system comparable to those of their counterparts in Anglo-American society (Office of the Head of the Civil Service, 1993, *Civil Service Management Handbook*; The University of Ghana Corporate Strategic Plan, 2002).

Taking advantage of the body of comparative public administration literature (Box, 1998; Jun, 2000; Haque, 2002; Hoppe, 2002; Johnston, 2004; Luton, 2004; Rutgers, 2004), the wholesale transferability of concepts, theories, and governance ideas across national and regional cultures as portrayed by the global public administration model is questioned. In analyzing the relevance of U.S. public administration theory to former Soviet Russia, Luton argues that "the unique historical and cultural experiences of each nation-state pose a great source of challenge" to a globalized or universalized public administration (p. 229). The question of intellectual interest is how well does the global model fit Ghana's unique historical legacies, moral experiences, and social, cultural, and political conditions to make it legitimately acceptable. In a critical response to the globalization thesis, it is contended that although human problems are of course human (reasonably generalizable), they are invariably contextualized because they arise in, or out of, certain historical and cultural conditions. This being the case, the approach to solving such problems need not be the same across regions; different ideas and therapies may be required from locale to locale and the global approach, therefore, cannot be unqualifiedly tenable.

If so, public administration in Ghana might benefit from a blend of education and knowledge based on the depth understanding of local dynamics with the changing institutional patterns, resulting from the processes of globalization of politics, policy, and administration. This will allow Ghana to exploit the ideas, values, and institutions of other peoples and cultures where necessary, relevant, beneficial, and practicable for addressing its own problems — consistent with the idea of cross-cultural borrowing when contacts between peoples of different cultures occur. The blend or composite model, if well managed, can serve as the basis for developing a legitimate public administration system capable of responding to both global and local needs.

The chapter begins with a brief account of the uniqueness of Ghana, emphasizing how its historicity and specificity condition public administration. Then it provides a summary that analyzes and critiques the rhetoric and normative claims of the global model. It is argued that although globalization might have created a variety of opportunities for Ghana to tap into the world economy and become a part of the so-called "global village," it has generated dilemmas and problems that obstruct public administration from connecting to reality and reason in the context of its uniqueness. The chapter concludes by discussing the implication of this analysis for future research and institutional reform policy for achieving a truly "glocalized" public administration system.

Context of Politics, Policy, and Administration

Scholars do recognize that nation-states are either successful or not successful in large part because of the structure of the society within which they work, and they relentlessly seek ways to make society their focal point of analysis (Box, 1998; King & Stivers, 1998; Putnam, 2000). Putnam's work, *Bowling Alone*, points to the importance of social organization in facilitating democratic governance in the United States. In public administration, there is a growing scholarly interest in communitarian and nonbureaucratic approaches to public service through contracting, outsourcing, and non-governmental production and provision of services (Provan & Milward, 1995; Bogason et al., 2002). Although all of this work indicates clearly the indispensable role that the civil society plays in public administration, scant attention has been paid to the African society and its impact on administrative thought and practice, especially the fabric and bonds of its communities. With the exception of a handful of studies (Riggs, 1964; Ayittey, 1992; Ayee, 1994), little is known about the endogenous forces that historically condition politics, policy, and administration in African societies.

Several key features of Ghanaian society are either misunderstood or misinterpreted or ignored altogether in the quest for economic development and social progress. At the core of this kind of society lies the communo-ethnic diversity and a strong sense of localism with a potential for enhancing community governance — the idea of promoting local participation in the shared pursuit of the communal good. It is estimated that Ghana's population of 20.1 million people comprises of over 90 communo-ethnic groups each with its distinct cultural practices and social norms (Ayittey, 1992; Boamah-Wiafe, 1993; Brydon & Legge, 1996; Gyekye, 1997; Ayee, 1999; World Bank, 2003). Although four broad communo-ethnic groups are often distinguished (Akan, Mole-Dagomba, Ewe, and Ga-Adangbe), there are several others scattered around the country that do not fit neatly into these categories. In fact, most civil society organizations — local NGOs — are communo-ethnic in character.

An outstanding characteristic of communo-ethnicity is the sense of community that pervades social relations among individuals in African societies, including Ghana (Mbiti, 1970; Dickson, 1977; Gyekye, 1997). In other words, community takes precedence over the individual. As Mbiti (1970, p. 141) states, "I am, because we are; and since we are, therefore I am." This suggests that cultural community life is not optional for the individual. Indeed, the individual is born into an existing human society and therefore into a specific human culture of which they have no choice. This is reflected in the daily routine, which is intertwined with political, economic, social, and cultural activities often conducted along communo-ethnic lines: religious and spiritual observances, music, art and craft, games and sports, microfinance, policy advocacy, to mention but a few.

The directory of non-governmental organizations in Ghana (GAPVOD/ISODEC Initiative, 1999) provides useful insights about local, regional, or national civil society organizations and associations that illustrate the richness and the significance of cultural community life. First, like NGOs elsewhere in Africa, their potential lies in generating self-help initiatives and to serve as vehicles for support, education, and development. Second, they give voices to popular demands because of their accessibility to, and representation of, both rural and urban people. Finally, they bring together individuals of a similar ethnic group, community, area, or region under the banner of common issues or for the provision of services — credit, music, art, and many more. Their unique contribution is that they bring people face-to-face with their neighbors, which helps to sustain social connectedness and to build what Putnam (2000, p. 19) sees as "social capital."

The commonest type of these organizations are: Ga Mansaamo Kpee, La Mansaamo Kpee, Osu Welfare Association, and Abossey Okai Youth Club; Jamasiman Nkosoo Kuo, Kwadaso Men's Club, Asunafo Educational Complex, and Yonso Development Association; Dunenyo Women Club, Mafi Akyenfo Agroforestry, Wli Afegame Miwoenenyo Cooperative Society, and GboxomeYouth Multipurpose Cooperative; and Zuuri Organic Vegetable Farmers Association, Tuma Kavi Women Group, Biu Farmers Association, and Agobisa Women's Association. Parliamentary constituencies, administrative regions, and local authorities have been demarcated on the basis of, and in response to, communo-ethnic cohesion, identity, and concerns.

These community-based organizations have coexisted and, in many instances, collaborated across communo-ethnic lines in the overall public interest. For example, regional and national interethnic organizations and associations include Concerned Citizens Association of Ghana, Concerned Youth Development, Consumers Association of Ghana, Countrylife Development Agency, Companions of Environment and Development, and many more. To the extent that these organizations are active and functional, they form the framework for understanding and building community capacity in Ghana. Thus a multicultural society need not involve conflict, although the potential for such conflict exists like in any body-politic.

Such ethnic plurality is equally matched by climatic and geographical diversity in Ghana. The northern half consists of open grasslands with moderate rainfall that is drained mainly by two rivers: The Black Volta and the White Volta. The land contains light soils, and apart from its huge potential for cereals such as rice, sorghum, and millet, it also supports livestock rearing and animal husbandry. On the other hand, the south has a lot more rainfall and is more endowed with greener vegetation. The midsection of the country, in particular, has thick rain forests with rich minerals, as well as soils suitable for cultivating timber, coffee, and cocoa. The extreme coastal and trans-Volta regions are a mixture of undulating scrub or grassland. Although the settlement pattern is pretty much agreed upon, historically the land was arbitrarily demarcated without due regard paid to sociocultural cohesion and communo-cultural identity. Moreover, these lands became a part of Ghana at different times and under different circumstances (Agbodeka, 1972). As a result, they not only differ socioculturally and geographically, but also have been administered differently historically, leading to wide regional and social disparities, which tend to be either ignored or conveniently glossed over (Bening, 1990).

The livelihood of the majority of Ghanaians (70 percent) either derives from, or is connected to, subsistence agriculture and other closely related activities: mostly small-scale crop farming, livestock keeping, fishing, food processing and trading, textile manufacturing and trading, art and craft work, and more. About 66 percent of local NGOs are engaged in crop farming, agroforestry and environment, and food security (GAPVOD/ISODEC Initiative, 1999, pp. 243–247). Overall, the agricultural sector is the largest contributor (41 percent) to the gross domestic product (GDP) (Institute of Statistical, Social, and Economic Research, 1999, p. 77). Most agricultural activities are owned and carried out by families and micro socioeconomic groups for domestic purposes (Brydon & Legge, 1996, pp. 57–74). Even employees engaged in formal employment with regular wages and salaries are involved in agriculture by either directly sponsoring their own farms or indirectly funding the cultivation of family-owned farms. Brydon and Legge found that, "All the government employees . . . in the rural areas cited farming or some other 'informal' activity as a second source of income" (p. 151). To the extent that the economy is predominantly agrarian and not controlled by entrepreneurial organizations seeking massive profits, the society is traditional, a *gemeinschaft* or one bound by mostly kinship obligations.

In such a society, the philosophy of work and public service, as well as public expectations about the government, are completely different. There is little distinction between public and private domain or work and home. Work is carried out often as a sense of personal, family, or community obligation. The fulfillment of social, economic, and political duties depends on everybody working cooperatively and relying exclusively on experience, not expertise. There are no systematic written rules describing work, although private and public conduct is regulated according to informal codes of behavior. Responsibilities may be delegated but hardly systematically, and they may be subject to change. The absence of standardized rules in many communities makes it difficult to find a uniform application of laws and the existence of the same economic conditions. Much of the understanding of government is rooted in community (local control or small responsible government close to home). As some scholars argue, community is indeed the organic unit of cultural, social, economic, and political organization in Ghana (Ayittey, 1992; Boamah-Wiafe, 1993). Thus ideas about government, public service, and work constitute avenues for helping kith and kin, ethnic groups, and regions. As a result, community loyalty exerts a strong influence on public employees most of whom are first generation government workers (Haruna, 1999). These employees are often identified by their formal grades or ranks and by ethnic and regional origins. Government workers are expected to be of help to relatives and to protect ethnic and regional interests in matters of national policy.

In addition to these characteristics, the demographic composition of Ghana is unique. As already explained, the majority of the population lives in rural areas with "poor sanitation, inaccessible roads, polluted water, unhygienic markets, and dilapidated school buildings" (Ayee, 1997, p. 51; World Bank, 2002). Despite the expansion of education, average adult literacy (age 15 and above) is only about 71.5 percent, making it impossible for a good proportion of the population to participate in, and contribute to, the formal, political, judicial, and legal processes. Substantial proportions of the population have always been children (40.9 percent), illiterate (30 percent), and poor (31.4 percent). As high as 7 percent of the population is considered as desperately poor, i.e., subsisting on about US$ 8 per annum (Ayee, 1999, pp. 250–251). This tends to put pressure on services and raises questions of service quality, effectiveness, and accountability in conducting public administration. As the economy operates increasingly in a global capitalist market system, Ghana has to compete with other nations for scarce resources often with little or no success.

On gender differences, women's roles remain underrecognized in public service (Women in Public Life in Ghana Report, 1998). Although women's workforce participation has improved since the introduction of the Industrial Relations Act (Ghana Government, 1965) and the Equal Pay Act (Ghana Government, 1967), biased cultural attitudes toward women persist. The Women in Public Life in Ghana Report (p. 4) found that public institutions are inclined toward "masculine" work environments, where women are underrepresented, less educated, and less competitive: "women constitute only a fraction of the management and leadership of their organizations." In fact, women form a paltry 18 percent of the middle-to-top public sector executives (Haruna, 1999), a situation inconsistent with efforts to improve the political, economic, and social status of women (Proceedings of the International Conference on Women, 1995).

Like in many parts of Africa, infrastructural development in Ghana is still rudimentary. Means of communication and transportation are poor. For example, several communities are inaccessible whereas interregional and interdistrict connectivity is inadequate or totally lacking (Ayee, 1997). Road networks remain largely in a deplorable state, especially trunk and feeder roads leading to the hinterland and raw material–producing areas (Institute of Statistical, Social, and Economic Research, 1999, p. 146). By 1999, the National Communications Authority had licensed only 56 communication service providers: 3 internet providers, 3 mobile cellular operators, 25 privately owned radio stations, and 3 national network providers, 5 pager providers, 4 public data providers, 4 free-to-air stations, 7 pay-per-view cable, and 2 dispute resolutions. Although this is a positive development, overall it falls below national need. The cost of social services such as preschool, education, and health puts them beyond the reach of millions of people. Rural schools are not only underenrolled, but also children tend to be left in the mercy of untrained and inexperienced teachers. In short, Ghana indicates a certain uniqueness that deserves to be taken into account in considering ideas about public administration and governance, a reality based on its own beliefs and value systems, socioeconomic conditions, moral experiences, and historical legacies.

Waves of Globalization and Their Impact

Given the reality of the unique circumstances outlined above, how has globalization affected, and reflected in, Ghanaian public administration? The next three sections provide a summary of waves of "globalizations" that brought Ghana into contact with the people of other nations, most notably, Anglo-American democracies (United States and United Kingdom). Globalization is seen as the all-embracing process of internationalization, interconnection, and integration of the world. To that extent, Ghana's administrative history largely concerns efforts to link Anglo-American philosophies, theories, ideas, and concepts to the fate of the human condition there. Although it is not correct to say that the efforts to globalize are in vain, it can be argued that globalization must consider the concrete realities on the ground. After all and as scholars posit, to be legitimate and effective, public administration should derive from and be in conformity with the people's vision of how they want to be administered (Esman, 1974). Yet, globalization ignores or pays little attention to the so-called "traditional way of life," thereby creating a credibility gap between public institutions and the daily lifeworld of Ghanaians. Before analyzing the implication of this for research and institutional reform policy, a sketch of the notion of globalization is first provided.

Ideas of Globalization

There is considerable consensus among social scientists that globalization comprises a variety of processes entangling nation-states, their peoples, politics, economies, and cultures in global affairs (Knight, 1989; McGrew, 1992; Schlesinger, 1997; *The Economist*, 2001; MacDonald, 2002). Included in these processes are ideology, administration, managerialism, international trade, migration, global financial markets, telecommunications, science, and technology. MacDonald argues that "these processes bring diverse parts of the world together, making the world smaller" (p. 31) and integrating it thereby into Marshall McLuhan's proverbial "global village." This typically implies a "borderless world" in which states and national economies fade, giving rise to an integrated world market (Jilberto & Mommen, 1998, p. 2). Beyond this underlying commonality, the literature shows little or no agreement and is in fact polarized. Those advocating greater social, economic, and political integration across borders view it as "a great force for good," while others perceive it as a march toward unfettered international capitalism and "a force for oppression, exploitation, and injustice" (*The Economist*, 2001, p. 3). Nonetheless, with the collapse of the Soviet Union and the weakening of centrally planned economies in Eastern Europe and China, there has been a rapid transformation into a global economy, the "new political economy" (Haque, 2002, p. 103).

As a result, there is emerging a single dominant mindset of public administration and governance based on the culture of the market, neoliberalism, and managerialism. In this perspective, public sectors across the world emphasize efficiency, flexibility, and enhanced performance through downsizing, outsourcing, and performance measurement (Osborne & Gaebler, 1992; Haque, 2002). However, public administration theorists remain critical of, and indeed have questioned, the appropriateness of such a market-driven administrative model for public service (Stivers, 2000). Those interested involved with comparative and international public administration and raise questions about the transferability of concepts and theories across regions and national borders (Minogue, 2001; Luton, 2004, pp. 213–232; Rutgers, 2004, pp. 150–168; Werlin, 2003, pp. 329–342). Such questions are relevant when one considers sharp differences between industrialized and nonindustrialized societies, particularly in terms of histories, sociocultural conditions, organizational limitations, and political regime restrictions. Regardless, globalization is neither new nor do we live in a totally integrated world. Even if we are living in a "digital globe," there is a distinct "digital divide" that separates the majority of Ghanaians from the world economy.

First Wave of Globalization

Although it is true that globalization intensified with the information and communication technological revolution of the 20th century, it certainly has a longer and deeper history than is often portrayed. For several waves of globalization have brought Africans into contact with other nations, peoples, cultures, politics, and economics since 639 AD, when Arabs wrestled Egypt from Byzantium (Apter, 1965; Ayittey, 1992). Ayittey has argued that the Arabs advanced to the Maghreb region and "effectively established their rule by the second half of the seventh century and imposed Islam on the Berbers" (p. 4). Likewise, the contact with Europe is equally long and deep-rooted, starting from the 15th century when Europeans "enjoyed fruitful relationships with Africans for over 400 years" (p. 75). These early communications and interactions laid the foundation for the globalization of ideas about governance, public administration, and human relationships in Africa from the trans-Atlantic slave trade through the period of the Berlin International Conference (1884–1885) to decades of European colonialism and imperialism.

For practical reasons, the first major wave of globalization in Ghana occurred in the 19th century, following the industrial revolution and economic expansion of Europe (Ayittey, 1992; Dzorgbo, 2001). Three forces propelled such a globalization: (1) the need for new markets beyond European borders, (2) the industrial competition for the control of sources of raw material, and (3) the search for avenues to invest accumulated surplus capital. In this regard, the Portuguese, Danes, Dutch, Germans, and British took turns at different times to influence and even control both the economy and the society in Ghana. However, the British outcompeted the others and emerged as the sole imperial power, initially engaging in business along the coastal areas and subsequently gaining absolute political control over Ghana (then Gold Coast Colony). The people were receptive to British control of their economy and society because of their hospitality and, more important, the protection it offered against antagonisms from outside.

To consolidate its rule, British colonial government passed imperial orders-in-council (1901 and 1906) that created the Gold Coast Colony and laid the foundation of the state, its mode of governance, and public administration (Adu, 1965; Ayee, 1994). This is not to suggest that there were no public institutions before British colonial rule was imposed. Quite to the contrary, Ayittey (1991, Chapters 2 and 3) provides a comprehensive description and an analysis of indigenous African institutions and sociopolitical systems in existence before the historical contact and interaction with Europe. Of course, as he points out (p. 71), the organizational structures and objectives of these institutions and systems "were generally based upon kinship, ancestry, and survival..." rather than upon an all-embracing phenomenon such as the colonial state. The purpose of the imperial orders was to legitimize British domination and also bring the people of the four regions of the colony under one umbrella government for the first time in their history. With the establishment of British-style political and administrative institutions — civil service, executive, and legislative councils — the foundations of the first major wave of globalization of governance and public administration were firmly erected in Ghana.

The building blocks of these Westernized forms and ideas of public administration were anchored by bureaucracy, centralization, and a rationality that emphasized economic growth. The bureaucratic framework ensured that agencies were functionally related, each reinforcing the other in what Adu (1965) described as a countrywide grid-like public administration and governing system. The grid interlinked the hierarchy of offices and officeholders and provided the political and administrative context "to prosecute the imperial policies in Africa" and to bring the "Pax Britannica to all the dependent territories overseas" (Adu, 1965, pp. 14–15). The sole purpose was to establish and sustain law and order, regulate individual and collective behavior, and provide basic infrastructure for advancing the interests of the colonial government (Adu, 1965; Greenstreet, 1971; Ayee, 1994). Underlying law, order, and regulation were two sets of values centering on integrity, impartiality, and loyalty on one hand, and control, efficiency, and economy on the other. These values have since remained as the enduring concerns of public administration and governance throughout the nation-building experience in Ghana.

Six institutions of colonial public administration made a lasting imprint on Ghana: governorship, colonial secretariat, executive council, legislative council, provincial council, and local administration in the order of hierarchy of authority (Ayee, 1994). The governor was the ultimate source of power, accountable not to Ghanaians but to the British Crown. With the support of both executive and legislative councils the governor made policies, whereas the lower levels of authority, including provincial councils and local administrations implemented them. The colonial secretary — governor's executive officer — coordinated policy formulation and execution and maintained a secretariat that operated as a technical departmental establishment with divisional heads coordinating the functions of the government (Greenstreet, 1971, p. 17).

Although the legislative council provided for the representation of indigenous taxpayers, colonial structures employed mainly British nationals until public employment was totally Africanized. Provincial councils and local administration had limited representation: only Accra, Cape Coast, and Sekondi had one representation each in 1850. From the inception, then, colonial administration reflected three administrative tenets: centralization, bureaucratization, and limited representation, which continued to dominate administrative thought in Ghana (Ayee, 1994). State intervention in the economy was restricted and the public sector remained small because of the prevailing belief that "government is best that governs least." Accordingly, indirect rule became the key administrative tool, whereby indigenous political institutions, such as chieftaincy worked alongside the superimposed colonial structures. Without question, this served colonial interests well, limiting fiscal commitments to the colony and generating support among the colonists for the colonial administration (Hodder-Williams, 1984, p. 33).

Despite the *laissez-faire* approach to governance, the direct wave of globalization through colonialism has had enduring influences in Ghana. The foundation of how to organize and run government based on Westernized philosophies and ideas were laid. In particular, the seeds of rationalization, bureaucratization, legalization, quantification, and formalization of society were sown, even if little positive policy toward political, social, and economic development occurred. Sure, colonialism sought to provide mainly the Hobbesian political framework for British capital to flourish. Much economic activity lay in the hands of private businesses and foreign merchants interested only in securing raw materials, selling finished products, and repatriating huge profits to European metropolitan centers. Likewise, colonialism failed to promote democratic traditions, with the result that after independence, Ghana adopted a parliamentary system about for which it was least prepared. Even then, by the independence period in 1957 Western-style education and development planning had begun to blossom that would launch the colony on to the path of modernization (Kay, 1972, p. 32; Hopkins, 1988, p. 190; Dzorgbo, 2001, p. 123).

Second Wave of Globalization

Although it is true that the first wave of globalization laid the rudiments of public administration and governance in Ghana, it is equally true that colonialism possessed neither the moral fiber nor the legitimacy to administer. As Murungi (2004, p. 11) argues, "colonialism was and remains a classic example of catastrophe of governance." The basis of governance and public administration was narrow and limited in both structure and function, which required reform in the transition from a colony to a constitutional, self-governing, and democratic republic (Adu, 1965; Amonoo, 1981). Although Adu (1965) considered this transition as a "revolution," ministries, departments, state-owned enterprises, and regional or district authorities were merely grafted on the colonial structures. On the surface, the change marked a departure from the *laissez-faire* approach of the colonial state, emphasizing self-government, representation, nationalism, statism, and development (Rasheed & Luke, 1995). However, the change reinforced the bureaucratic values of rationality, neutrality, and efficiency. Colonial agencies continued to carry on as before with the new ministries and departments replacing the colonial secretariat. In other words, this change reflected and sustained the ideals of the first wave of globalization in Ghana.

The second major wave of globalization occurred in the last two decades of the 20th century when Ghana adopted two major policy initiatives that the World Bank and the International Monetary Fund (IMF) jointly sponsored: economic recovery and structural adjustment (World Bank, 1996; Konadu-Agyemang, 2001; Haque, 2002). Originating from Anglo-American society, this latest wave resulted in a global governance and administration model based on managerialism, neoliberalism, and market principles. This perspective sought to make a break from the past by creating an enabling environment, developing consensus-building and collaboration in policy implementation, and increasing institutional capacity for improved performance. The effect has been the replacement of the state-centered and development-oriented logic pursued three decades earlier with policies, including democratization, managerialism, decentralization, and liberalization, to mention but a few (Minogue, 2001). In particular, these changes can be found in public sectors around the world under the general rubric of the NPM, whereby public agencies and institutions have been expected to reinvent or reengineer themselves following private-sector or market-based models of reform.

Launching the latest global model of governance and public administration in Ghana has involved implementing several interrelated policies and programs derived from the World Bank and the IMF that limit the intervention of the state in the economy, thereby moving away from bureaucratic controls (Gyimah-Boadi, 1990; Rasheed & Luke, 1995; Hutchful, 1996; Mohan, 1996). This chapter focuses only on the NPM, an important aspect of the global model that emphasizes, "a smaller policy core, overseeing a flatter, less hierarchical, more fragmented implementing periphery" (Minogue, 2001, p. 28). Public sector reform has comprised of two aspects: redeploying excess labor and improving managerial capacity. Redeployment involved the identification of redundant and underemployed workers as well as nonexistent employees on government payrolls. This resulted in downsizing 44,838 employees, i.e., 30 percent labor reduction between 1986 and 1993 (ODA, 1993).

On improving public sector managerial capacity, several new legislations have been introduced alongside the implementation of institutional support programs, such as training, new equipment, and materials to strengthen analytical capability. For example, the new Civil Service Act (PNDC Law 327) has provided the legal framework and ethical code for guiding civil service reform and improvement. The law enhanced political control and supervision over civil service employees. Civil service reform also involved training personnel in new management techniques, reassigning responsibility, and providing infrastructure (copiers, computers, and typewriters) to improve information processing and decision making. In terms of performance, reform emphasized a mission-driven, entrepreneurial, and result-oriented appraisal system based on measurable goals, participatory decision making, and provision of feedback.

Structural requirements of reform have involved restructuring, rationalizing, and decentralizing the functions of ministries, departments, and agencies. Ministries have four functional areas (policy planning, programming, budgeting, monitoring, and evaluation; research, statistics, and manpower development; information management, computer support, and public relations; and general and financial administration). Management reviews and job inspections have been established along with computer training for junior and middle-level employees. Decentralization has devolved fiscal, political, and administrative authority to local jurisdictions, as well as rationalized the functional relationship between ministries and other public agencies.

Critique of the Global Approach

The argument in the two previous sections is that globalization of public administration is not new and has deep roots in Ghana. If so, is there anything wrong that makes the global approach unsuitable or unworkable there? At both practical and theoretical levels, globalization has been defended mainly on the basis that free market leads to a better quality of life by stimulating economic growth and promoting governance (Hyden & Court, 2002; Rondinelli & Cheema, 2003). However, much of this scholarship tends to overemphasize restrictive economistic perspectives that ignore the ecology in which public administration is immersed. For example, the IMF has focused on "ensuring the rule of law, improving the efficiency and accountability of the public sector, and tackling corruption, as essential elements of a framework within which economies can prosper" (Camdessus, 1999, p. 1). This section digs deeper and argues that the problem with administrative globalization and governance is the failure to take into account historical legacies and sociocultural conditions unique to Ghana.

Critiques targeting the global model in Ghana are either narrowly construed or skewed toward the macroeconomic perspective. On the one hand, critiques of the first wave of globalization seem to accept the bureaucratic approach, while making suggestions for fine-tuning and adjusting it to improve public administration performance (Riggs, 1964; Adu, 1965; Hyden, 1983; Huq, 1989; Indome, 1991; Haruna, 1999). In his pioneering work on public administration reform, Adu seeks to clarify the role of the civil service in developing societies for which he recommends appropriate structures, functions, and processes. He explains that the role of the civil service is to offer advice to the government based on professionalism, expertise, loyalty, and neutrality. However, his emphasis on structure and function is too restrictive, overlooking, and taking for granted the larger context in which public administration operates. Indome (1991) writes about "lethargy and apathy" affecting the civil service and identifies political intrusion and threats to tenure of office as some of the factors contributing to low productivity and poor performance. In interviews conducted with mid-to-top-level Ghanaian public-sector executives, Haruna (1999) finds that politicization of the civil service is one of the sources of concern for public administrators. Hyden (1983) blames the dysfunction of the bureaucracy and describes the postcolonial state as "soft" because of its incapacity to address the problems of development. He laments the absence of a bourgeois class and the prevalence of a peasant mode with an "economy of affection." In light of Ghana's increasing population, urbanization, and growing complexity of the society, these critiques represent a narrow approach to public administration and are unable to meet challenges of the 21st century.

On the other hand, critiques of the second wave of globalization anchored by the market focus attention on economic growth and development. Werlin (2003) and Huq (1989) point to the bright start Ghana made in the 1960s, especially with 6 percent economic growth. The Institute of Statistical, Social, and Economic Research (2000) provides annual historical data that suggests a steady macroeconomic performance since the introduction of structural reforms. Mohan (1996) focuses attention on national development planning and argues that decentralization is used "to deflect pressure from lenders and domestic political forces." Although the macroeconomic perspective offers insights about material conditions among Ghanaians, it does not portray the full potential of families, groups, and communities populating rural, urban, and semiurban landscapes. It fails to capture the daily routine of the majority of people based on sharing, collaboration, and consensus (Ayittey, 1992). This uniqueness constitutes social capital, facilitating cooperation for pursuing public purposes, which the macroeconomic perspective misses entirely.

Another shortcoming of the macroeconomic perspective is the failure to recognize the centrality of the environment in public administration (Hutchful, 1996; Deng, 1998; Akuffo, 2000). Akuffo asserts that Ghana's Environmental Protection Agency (EPA) operates "at the fringes and not in the main arena of environmental management." According to Hutchful, public-sector reform did not focus attention on the environment until recently, ignoring the symbiotic relationship between the human endeavor and the environment to ensure ecological harmony and sustainable development (Riddell, 1981; United Nations Environment Program (UNEP), 1994). Nonetheless, because the goals of the global approach is to achieve linear economic growth and development, they have contributed in a large measure to the total neglect of the unique local conditions in which public administration and governance take place. Overall the global approaches, whether from the perspective of the first or the second wave, tend to espouse similar assumptions, particularly the shared view on economic rationality and material condition.

As a result, theorizing about Ghana and Africa in general has been too unilateral, narrow, and inadequate for gaining understanding of, and empowering Africans, at all levels of social life.

Toward a Composite Model

The argument so far is this: the two major waves of globalization that hit Ghana resulted in a restrictive, straight, and narrow definition of public administration and governance, focusing on economic rationality at the expense of other equally important public interest concerns — historical legacies, socioeconomic conditions, and value or belief systems. Globalization has sought "right" answers to modernization and progress, drawing exclusively from concepts, theories, and philosophies originating from

Anglo-American society. The means for attaining such a unilinear economic growth has been managerialism, the classical administrative doctrine that says there is one best way for accomplishing a given task. Because globalization takes the ecology of public administration for granted and assumes that modernization and progress can happen in a social, cultural, economic, political, and historical vacuum, the phenomenon Joseph (2003) describes as "catastrophic governance" is slowly but steadily creeping into Ghana. This concluding section attempts to sketch an alternative approach to public administration, a composite embracing historical and social realities, as well as moral and political experiences of Ghana. It builds on ideas drawn mainly from critical pragmatist and comparative public administration thought.

For this undertaking to be fruitful, the meaning of public administration as employed in this essay must first be clarified. Against the narrow conceptualization of public administration that globalization has provided, pioneering scholars have considered the possibility of a broader conceptualization encompassing the economic, social, cultural, and political concerns of the society. Such a broad-based approach has its intellectual roots in scholarship seeking to legitimate the political role of public administration in democratic societies (Waldo, 1948; Marini, 1971; Stivers, 1993; Box, 1998). Waldo questions the restrictive notion of public administration and advocates a broader perspective inclusive of normative concerns. He argues that public administration theory privileges concerns of expertise, economy, and efficiency at the expense of the democratic values of participation in government. Thus he conceives of public administration not as a narrow policy instrument but also as an ongoing process to harmonize the norms of democracy and efficiency: public administration should concern both thinking and valuing.

More contemporary scholars have sustained and developed the theme of democratic public administration even further; they emphasize active community, citizenship, participation, and collaboration in a body of literature that Denhardt and Denhardt (2000) characterize as the new public service perspective. Several theorists of citizenship, community and civil society, and organizational humanism provide ideas for theorizing about public administration and lessons for practitioners. At the core of this strand of literature are concerns for citizenship and democracy, which advocate more active and involved citizenship (Sandel, 1996; Stivers, 2000). Stivers directly addresses care and relationship as the basis of public administration study and practice, and argues that:

> What makes public life public is irreducible differences, out of which we must as a people find a way to live together. Workable answers to public questions grow out of daily, lived experience and a posture of caring

> toward one another, rather than out of transcendental principles and tested hypotheses.

She emphasizes "daily, lived experience" and "a posture of caring toward one another" as important to public administration. Dennard (1995) speaks of "recognizing the human other" in the person with whom they are dealing because pathologies of communication are alleviated and democratic governance is enhanced. Wamsley and Wolf (1996) assert that people have an innate desire to find meaning in their lives and be in community with others, and that the relationship between public administrators and citizens is "potentially transformative for all concerned."

Consistent with this broad-based approach, some scholars argue that efforts should be made to weave public administration and governance thought into the political and social fabric of society (Gaus, 1947; Box, 1998; Stillman, 2000). As Stillman (p. 80) argues, "the study of public administration must include its ecology," a concept Gaus introduced to describe the intertwining of administration and the environment, including "the people who live there — their numbers and ages and knowledge, and the ways of physical and social technology by which from the place and in relationships with one another, they get their living" (pp. 6–19).

How can this broad-based approach be appropriated and applied to enrich understanding of, and appreciation for, public administration in Ghana? First, the people's history, their core philosophy of work, expectations about government, and public service values are not irrelevant to, but indeed important for, theorizing about public administration. The Berlin Conference historically gave birth to the state, an "overarching" concept that is both alien and incomprehensible to the people. Because such a state was constituted without due consideration given to social cohesion and the value of communo-cultural identity, it failed to create an environment conducive to, and deserving of, cooperation from the widest range of social and political actors (Mengisteab, 2004). Despite the state's potential viability, it is perceived largely as a colonial historical relic. Hyden (1983) rightly argues that the state bears no structural relationship to society, which raises questions about the legitimacy and integrity of public administration. As a result, public organizations and institutions supposedly designed to work for the public interest have little or no grounding in society. If so, administrative theorizing should consider and incorporate this historical experience into administrative infrastructure capable of drawing societywide support and promoting broad public ownership of governance.

Second, a composite model ought to shed light on and embrace the structure of Ghana, not as a monolithic but as a heterogeneous society comprising of disparate elements at different stages of social, economic, and political development. The national bureaucracy established under colonial rule and reinforced by administrative practices tends to favor the so-called "golden triangle" or the urbanized southern regions at the expense of rural areas, where over 70 percent of the population lives and works (Konadu-Agyemang, 1998; Werlin, 2003). Despite globalization, Ayee (1997, p. 51) argues that the quality of life is worse in the rural than urban communities: those benefiting from globalization include urban residents, not the majority rural people to whom the global administrative model remains irrelevant. This not only raises the concerns of equity, ethics, and morality in public administration and governance but also exposes a fatal flaw in and a failure of the global approach that incorrectly equates economic growth with good governance.

Third, a composite approach should show sensitivity to, and grapple with, Ghana's diverse and multicultural populations whose sentiments and aspirations must reflect in, and sustain public administration. *Accra Daily Mail* (November 14, 2003, p. 1) laments, "ethnic rivalry and deep-seated ethnic prejudice run deep among all the various groupings in the country." As well as being politicized, sociocultural ties tend to influence resource allocation and create suspicions that public administration is not treating all groups equitably. Because a few majority ethnic groups dominate politics, policy, and administration, this undermines the public trust and constrains the capacity of public institutions to have their decisions and activities accepted as legitimate by all segments of the society. This tendency denies the state and its internal administrative arrangements the capacity to nurture a cohesive, all-inclusive political community.

Fourth, in contrast to a global model fixated on economy, efficiency, and effectiveness, a composite approach should pay attention to values underlying the "traditional way of life" that the people cherish — community, kinship, and complex systems of rights and obligations. Boamah-Wiafe (1993), Ayittey (1992), and Gyekye (1997) point out the centrality of community as the basic organic unit. Ayittey (1992, p. 38) argues that community is "the most powerful and effective force for unity and stability," which finds expression in various forms of political participation, consultation, and consensus. Although this notion of community may be different, it is relevant because community-based administrative reform has been justified on the basis that it meets both practical and theoretical demands at least in American society (Box & Sagen, 1998; King & Stivers, 1998). Community is not only a means for realizing social justice but also for anchoring the values of participatory democracy. The logic of community therefore is significant for, and relevant to, administrative thought that can be linked to the lived experiences of the majority of people, their value or belief systems, and assumptions about governance.

Finally, the normative theme of this chapter is the need to create a public administration system appropriate to, and useful for, Ghana, one that empowers people across the full spectrum of social life. The goal is to sketch a composite theoretical framework, emphasizing the building of administrative thought and practice from the bottom–up, or at least making some compromises between global needs and local conditions to achieve a "transcultural ethos" (Gyekye, 1997, p. 280). The impetus is not cynicism about administrative globalization, but the recognition that such a model with its focus on economic, instrumental, and substantive rationality is not nearly as global as it appears to be. Because public problems are "wicked," as Weick (1979, p. 12) pointed out, there can be no quick fixes and the global model is no exception. Given existing material conditions and an emerging participatory society, implementing an administrative system with a universally imposed rationality seems fruitless. However, none of this should imply that public administration ought to be parochially construed without due regard to global and international influence. In framing the composite model, then, one should not throw away the baby with the bathwater: professional competence and economic efficiency, two of the key values associated with administrative globalization are worth saving, if they can be creatively integrated into the composite model to safeguard the common good.

Implications

What does this study in globalization of public administration imply for future research and institutional reform policy? In terms of research, the notorious problem is mainly that the understanding and knowledge of developing society is both obsolete and inadequate. The worn-out mechanisms for studying Africa as a continent in crises of poverty, disease, conflict, squalor, and corruption are hardly tenable. A major research task is to clarify the context of politics, policy, and administration by investigating the people's core values of government and public service without preconceived notions, theories, and mindsets of development. This must mean going beyond formal frameworks and acquiring insights into the medium through which the people construct the meaning of their shared environment. The goal should be to systematically determine how to tap into Africa's sociocultural networks and creatively build on such capacities to ensure sustainable progress. As an interdisciplinary field, public administration can draw from a variety of methodologies and tools to undertake this effort and create a legitimate "globalization" of public administration.

A broad-based institutional reform policy informed by local conditions and sensitive to global and international awareness should be sought: a global–local interplay should be required. Such a policy should be crafted primarily on the assumption that the government's primary responsibility is to promote public discourse and collaboration with citizens. In other words, institutional capacity development and utilization should be made a legitimately public enterprise, involving not only experts and expertise but also experience-based knowledge (Hummel & Stivers, 1998). Clearly, developing a culture of collaboration will help to bridge the gap between theory and practice and test new possibilities for a better understanding of comparative and international public administration.

References

Accra Daily Mail, November 14, 2003, p. 1.

Adu, A.L. 1965. *The Civil Service in New African States*. London: Allen & Unwin.

Agbodeka, F. 1972. *Ghana in the Twentieth Century*. Accra: Ghana Universities Press.

Ake, C. 1996. *Democracy and Development in Africa*. Washington, D.C.: The Brookings Institution.

Akuffo, S.B. 2000. "Restructuring the Ministry of Environment," *The Accra Mail Online*, 2(100), December 21.

Amonoo, B. 1981. *Ghana 1957–1966: The Politics of Institutional Dualism*. London: Allen & Unwin.

Apter, D. 1965. The Politics of Modernization. Chicago: University of Chicago Press.

Ayee, J.R. 1994. *Anatomy of Public Policy Implementation: The Case of Decentralization Policies in Ghana*. Aldershot: Avebury.

Ayee, J.R. 1997. "The Adjustment of Central Bodies to Decentralization: The Case of the Ghanaian Bureaucracy," *African Studies Review*, 40(2): 37–57.

Ayee, J.R. 1999. "Ghana," in L. Adamolekun (ed.), *Public Administration in Africa: Main Issues and Selected Country Studies*. Boulder, CO: Westview Press, pp. 250–274.

Ayittey, G.B. 1991. *Indigenous African Institutions*. New York: St. Martin's Press.

Ayittey, G.B. 1992. *Africa Betrayed*. New York: St. Martin's Press.

Bening, R.B. 1990. A History of Education in Northern Ghana 1907–1976. Accra: Ghana Universities Press.

Boamah-Wiafe, D. 1993. *Africa: The Land, People, and Cultural Institutions*. Omaha: Wisdom Publications.

Bogason, P., S. Kensen, and H. Miller. 2002. "Pragmatic, Extra Formal Democracy," *Administrative Theory & Praxis*, 24(4): 675–692.

Box, R.C. 1998. *Citizen Governance: Leading American Communities into the 21st Century*. Thousand Oaks, CA: Sage Publications.

Box, R.C. and D.A. Sagen. 1998. "Working with Citizens: Breaking Down Barriers to Citizen Self-Governance," in C.S. King and C. Stivers (eds.), *Government Is Us: Public Administration in an Anti-Government Era*. Thousand Oaks, CA: Sage Publications, pp. 158–172.

Brydon, L. and K. Legge. 1996. *Adjusting Society: The World Bank, the IMF, and Ghana*. London: I.B. Tauris Publishers.

Camdessus, M. 1999. "Second Generation Reforms: Reflections and New Challenges," in *Opening Remarks to IMF Conference on Second Generation Reforms*. Washington, D.C., USA, November 8.

Deng, L.A. 1998. *Rethinking African Development: Toward a Framework for Social Integration and Ecological Harmony*. Trenton, NJ: African World Press.

Denhardt, R.B. and J.V. Denhardt, 2000. "The New Public Service: Serving Rather than Steering," *Public Administration Review*, 60(6): 549–559.

Dennard, L. 1995. "Neo-Darwinism and Simon's Bureaucratic Antihero," *Administration & Society*, 26(4): 464–467.

Dickson, K.A. 1977. *Aspects of Religion and Life in Africa*. Accra: Ghana Academy of Arts and Sciences.

Dzorgbo, D.S. 2001. *Ghana in Search of Development: The Challenge of Governance, Economic Management and Institution Building*. Aldershot: Ashgate.

Esman, M.J. 1974. "Administrative Doctrine and Developmental Needs," in P.E. Morgan (ed.), *The Administration of Change in Africa: Essays in the Theory and Practice of Development Administration in Africa*. New York/London: Dunellen, pp. 3–26.

GAPVOD/ISODEC Initiative. 1999. *Directory of Non-Governmental Organizations in Ghana*. Accra.

Gaus, J.M. 1947. *Reflections on Public Administration*. University of Alabama: The University of Alabama Press.

Ghana Government. 1965. Industrial Relations Act. Accra, Ghana.

Ghana Government. 1967. Equal Pay Act. Accra, Ghana.

Greenstreet, D.K. 1971. "The Post-World War II Integration of Departments with Ministries in the Commonwealth States of Africa," *Journal of Management Studies*, 5(1): 15–22.

Gyekye, K. 1997. *Tradition and Modernity: Philosophical Reflections on the African Experience*. Oxford: Oxford University Press.

Gyimah-Boadi, E. 1990. "Economic Recovery and Politics in PNDC's Ghana," *Journal of Commonwealth and Comparative Studies*, 28(3): 328–343.

Haque, M.S. 2002. "Globalization, New Political Economy, and Governance: A Third World Viewpoint," *Administrative Theory & Praxis*, 24(1): 102–124.

Haruna, P.F. 1999. "An Empirical Analysis of Motivation and Leadership Among Career Public Administrators: The Case of Ghana," Ph.D. Dissertation, The University of Akron, Akron, Ohio.

Haruna, P.F. 2004. "Rethinking Administrative Globalization: Promises, Dilemmas, and Lessons in Ghana," *Administrative Theory & Praxis*, 26(2): 185–212.

Hodder-Williams, R. 1984. *An Introduction to the Politics of Tropical Africa*. London: Urwin Hyman.

Hopkins, A.G. 1988. *An Economic History of West Africa*. New York: Longman.

Hoppe, R. 2002. "Co-Evolution of Modes of Governance and Rationality: A Diagnosis and Research Agenda," *Administrative Theory & Praxis*, 24(4): 763–780.

Hummel, R. and C. Stivers. 1998. "Government Isn't Us: The Possibility of Democratic Knowledge in Representative Government," in C.S. King and C. Stivers (eds.), *Government Is Us: Public Administration in Anti-Government Era*. Thousand Oaks, London, New Delhi: Sage Publications, pp. 28–48.

Huq, M.M. 1989. *The Economy of Ghana.* London: Macmillan.

Hutchful, E. 1996. "Ghana: 1983–94," in P. Engberg-Pederson, P. Gibson, P. Raikes, and L. Udsholt (eds.), *Limits of Adjustment in Africa: The Effects of Economic Liberalization, 1986–1994.* Copenhagen: Center for Development Research, pp. 144–214.

Hyden, G. 1983. *No Shortcuts to Progress: African Development Management in Perspective.* Berkeley and Los Angeles, CA: University of California Press.

Hyden, G. and J. Court. 2002. "Comparing Governance across Countries and Over Time: Conceptual Challenges," in D. Olowu and S. Sako (eds.), *Better Governance and Public Policy: Capacity Building and Democratic Renewal in Africa.* Bloomfield, CT: Kumarian Press, pp. 13–33.

Indome, J.A. 1991. "Apathy and Lethargy in the Ghana Civil Service," in Address delivered at the Ghana Military Academy & Staff College on the Ghana Civil Service. Accra, Ghana, July 11.

Institute of Statistical, Social, and Economic Research. 1999. *The State of the Ghanaian Economy in 1998.* Legon, Ghana: ISSER.

Jackson, R.H. and C.G. Rosberg. 1994. "The Political Economy of Personal Rule," in D.E. Apter, and C.G. Rosberg (eds.), *Political Development and the New Realism in Sub-Saharan Africa.* Charlottesville, VA: University Press of Virginia.

Jilberto, F.E. and A. Mommen. 1998. "Globalization vs. Regionalization," in F.E. Jilberto and A. Mommen (eds.), *Regionalization and Globalization in the Modern World Economy: Perspectives on the Third World and Transitional Economies.* London and New York: Rutledge Studies in Development Economies, pp. 1–26.

Johnston, J. 2004. "An Australian Perspective on Global Public Administration Theory: 'Westington' Influences, Antipodean Responses and Pragmatism?" *Administrative Theory & Praxis*, 26(2): 169–184.

Joseph, R.A. 2003. Facing Africa's Predicament: Academe Needs to Play a Stronger Role," *The Chronicle of Higher Education*, March 7, 2003.

Jun, J.S. 2000. "Transcending the Limits of Comparative Administration: A New Internationalism in the Making," *Administrative Theory & Praxis*, 22(2): 273–286.

Kay, G.B. 1972. *The Political Economy of Colonialism in Ghana: A Collection of Documents and Statistics 1900–1960.* Cambridge: Cambridge University Press.

King, C. and C. Stivers. 1998. "Conclusion: Strategies for an Anti-Government Era," *Government is Us: Public Administration in an Anti-Government Era.* Thousand Oaks, CA: Sage Publications, pp. 195–204.

Knight, R.V. 1989. "Introduction: Redefining Cities," in R.V. Knight and G. Gappert (eds.), *Cities in a Global Society.* Newbury Park: Sage Publications, pp. 15–23.

Konadu-Agyemang, K. 1998. "Structural Adjustment Programs and the Perpetuating of Poverty and Underdevelopment in Africa: Ghana's Experience," *Scandinavian Journal of Development Alternatives and Area Studies*, 17(2&3): 127–143.

Konadu-Agyemang, K. 2001. "An Overview of Structural Adjustment Programs in Africa," in K. Konadu-Agyemang (ed.), *IMF and World Bank Sponsored Structural Adjustment Programs in Africa: Ghana's Experience 1983–1999.* Aldershot: Ashgate, pp. 1–15.

Leys, C. and C. Berman. 1994. "Introduction," in B.J. Berman and C. Leys (eds.), *African Capitalist in African Development.* Boulder, CO: Lynne Rienner Publishers.

Luton, L.S. 2004. "The Relevance of U.S. Public Administration Theory for Russian Public Administration," *Administrative Theory & Praxis*, 26(2): 213–232.

MacDonald, S.H. 2002. "Globalization and Risk: A Contingent Response for Democratic Governance," *Administrative Theory & Praxis*, 24(1): 31–54.

Marini, F. 1971. *Toward a New Public Administration: The Minnowbrook Perspective.* Scranton, PA: Chandler.

Mbiti, J.S. 1970. *African Religion and Philosophy.* New York: Doubleday, Anchor Books.

McGrew. A.G. 1992. "Conceptualizing Global Politics," in A.G. McGrew and P.G. Lewis (eds.), *Global Politics: Globalization and the Nation State.* Cambridge: The Policy Press, pp. 23–32.

Mengisteab, K. 2004. "Africa's Intrastate Conflicts: Relevance and Limitations of Diplomacy," *African Issues*, XXXII(1&2): 25–39.

Minogue, M. 2001. "The Internationalization of New Public Management," in W. McCourt and M. Minogue (eds.), *The Internationalization of Public Management: Reinventing the Third World State.* Cheltenham, UK: Edward Elgar, pp. 1–19.

Mohan, G. 1996. "Neoliberalism and Decentralized Development Planning in Ghana," *Third World Planning Review*, 18: 433–455.

Murungi, J. 2004. "The Academy and the Crisis of African Governance," *African Issues*, XXXII(1&2): 9–23.

Office of the Head of the Civil Service. 1993. *The Civil Service Management Handbook*, Vol. 1. Accra: Universal Printers.

Olowu, D. 2002. "Introduction: Governance and Policy Management Capacity in Africa," in D. Olowu and S. Sako (eds.), *Better Governance and Public Policy: Capacity Building and Democratic Renewal.* Bloomfield, CT: Kumarian Press, pp. 1–9.

Osborne, D. and T. Gaebler. 1992. *Reinventing Government.* New York: Plume.

Overseas Development Administration (ODA). 1993. *Evaluation of ODA Project in Support of the Ghana Civil Service Reform Programme.* London: HMSO.

Proceedings of the International Conference on Women. 1995. Beijing, China.

Provan, K. and H.B. Milward. 1995. "Institutional-Level Norms and Organizational Involvement in a Service Implementation Network," *Journal of Public Administration Research and Theory*, 1: 391–417.

Putnam, R. 2000. *Bowling Alone: The Collapse and Revival of American Community.* New York: Simon & Schuster.

Rasheed, S. and F. Luke. 1995. *Development Management in Africa: Toward Dynamism, Empowerment, and Entrepreneurship.* Boulder, CO: Westview Press.

Riddell, R. 1981. *Ecodevelopment: Economics, Ecology and Development.* Hampshire, England: Gower.

Riggs, F.W. 1964. *Administration in Developing Countries: The Theory of Prismatic Society.* Boston, MA: Houghton Mifflin.

Rondinelli, D.A. and G.S. Cheema. 2003. "Reinventing Government for the Twenty-First Century: An Introduction," in D.A. Rondinelli and G.S. Cheema (eds.), *Reinventing Government for the Twenty-First Century: State Capacity in a Globalizing Society.* Bloomfield, CT: Kumarian Press, pp. 1–31.

Rutgers, M.R. 2004. "Comparative Public Administration: Navigating Scylla and Charybdis Global Comparison as a Translation Problem," *Administrative Theory & Praxis*, 26(2): 150–168.

Sandel, M. 1996. Democracy's Discontent. Cambridge, MA: Belknap Press.

Schlesinger, A., Jr. 1997. "Has Democracy a Future?" *Foreign Affairs*, 5: 10.

Stillman, R.J., II. 2000. *Public Administration: Concepts and Cases.* Boston, MA: Houghton Mifflin.

Stivers, C. 1993. Gender Image in Public Administration Legitimacy and the Administrative State. Newburg Park. Sage Publications.

Stivers, C. 2000. "Resisting the Ascendancy of Public Management: Normative Theory and Public Administration," *Administrative Theory & Praxis*, 22(1): 10–23.

The Economist, September 29, 2001.

The University of Ghana Corporate Strategic Plan. January 29, 2002. www.ghanaweb.com

United Nations Environment Program. (UNEP). 1994. *An Environmental Impact Assessment Framework for Africa.* Nairobi: Environment and Economics Unit.

Waldo, D. 1948. *The Administrative State: A Study of the Political Theory of American Public Administration.* New York: Ronald Press.

Wamsley, G. and J. Wolf. 1996. *Refounding Democratic Public Administration: Modern Paradoxes, Postmodern Challenges.* Thousand Oaks, CA: Sage Publications.

Weick, K. 1979. *The Social Psychology of Organizing.* Reading, MA: Addison-Wesley.

Werlin, H.H. 2003. "Poor Nations: A Theory of Governance," *Public Administration Review*, 63(3): 329–342.

Women in Public Life in Ghana. 1998. Research Report Submitted to the Department for International Development (DFID). Development and Project Planning Center, University of Bradford, UK.

World Bank. 1996. *Reports on Ongoing Operational, Economic and Sector Work.* Washington, D.C.: Knowledge Networks.

World Bank 2002. *World Development Report.* New York: Oxford University Press.

World Bank. 2003. *World Development Report.* New York: Oxford University Press.

GLOBALIZATION: ISSUES IN PUBLIC MANAGEMENT

VIII

Chapter 40

New Public Management: Theory, Ideology, and Practice

Naim Kapucu

CONTENTS

Introduction

Reform of public administration is now a worldwide phenomenon, as governments grapple with rapid social, economic, and technological change, including the effects of globalization. Several countries have implemented radical and comprehensive public-sector reforms since the mid-1980s. These reforms have established objectives and set incentives for productive performance and involve greater transparency. The opening of government agencies to competition, greater privatization, and accountability standards contributed to improved government performance. These reforms have reduced the governments' market involvement relative to the total economy.

This chapter briefly discusses new public management (NPM) in terms of its theory, ideology, and practice. In this chapter, NPM and its reforms are conceived as deliberate policies and actions to alter organizational structures, process, and behavior to improve administrative capacity for efficient and effective public-sector performance. The advantage of this definition is its operational thrust compared with the view of administrative reform as "artificial inducement of administrative transformation against resistance" (Caiden, 1969, p. 8). The legitimate authority of the system usually sanctions substantive reforms whether induced by internal organizational influences (pull factors) or external environmental forces (push factors). There have been too many changes in the structure of governments and relations that the states have with society since the 1970s and early 1990s. "New right" Reagan revolution and Thatcherism in the United Kingdom are well-known examples. Also there have been serious administrative reforms mostly known in centralized governments like France and Sweden (Peters, 1996, Lane, 1997).

A number of countries have been putting the NPM into practice. The implementation of the NPM not only is restricted to develop countries, but also has extended to developing and transitional societies in Asia, Latin America, and Africa. Some academics and practitioners believe that there is a new global paradigm in public management and that the rise of NPM is inevitable (Osborne & Geabler, 1992). Aucoin (1990, p. 134) observes that "an internationalization of public management is taking place in every government of developed countries. A good deal of comparative learning is thus attempted, this internationalization of public management parallels the internationalization of public and private-sector economies." Nevertheless, another school of thought treats the universal application of NPM and the administrative reform movement with skepticism and reservation. Hood (1995, p. 109) points out that "the movement away from progressive public administration in the 1980s was in fact far from universal," and that "it does not necessarily follow that administrative reforms were undertaken for the same reasons or will automatically have the same results in different countries." Even though Hood (1991, p. 8) denies the universality of NPM, he does not reject the applicability of NPM to a number of countries. According to Hood, "like many other philosophies, NPM was presented as a framework of general applicability of 'a public management for all seasons'."

The 1980s and 1990s have seen a plethora of reinventing, rationalizing, reengineering, and reforming initiatives designed to improve the organizational efficiency and effectiveness of the public service. Collectively, these initiatives represent a substantial shift away from the traditional bureaucratic paradigm toward a postbureaucratic paradigm. Although clearly offering a number of benefits to the public service, these reforms have also contributed to an environment of turmoil, a largely disillusioned and cynical public service, and almost pervasive strain between competing values and goals (Aucoin, 1990; Boston et al., 1996, Lane, 1997). The need to move toward a value-driven public administration that incorporates improved management but more fundamentally addresses the right and entitlement of clients, taxpayers, and citizens is clear. Given the challenge ahead, this will require the development of strong policy community that works together horizontally to gather, share, and process information, as well as coordinate solutions (March & Olsen, 1995; Moore, 1995).

Each country should address the specifics of the problems it has encountered, and not import a set of reforms designed initially for one country and adopted by another one. In fact, NPM has been implemented selectively, some countries have adopted some parts and not others, or adopted and then adapted the reforms in a variety of ways, while others such as China have focused on their immediate needs, such as providing agencies a single estimate of revenue for the year, and South Africa, which is focusing intensively on accountability issues as part of the effort of nation building. Those who considered NPM as a consistent and ready-to-use concept to reform the public sector never understood that there is no NPM that has been used as a single concept in any country. Most NPM-related contributions have been made out of an Anglo-Saxon, in the beginning, mostly British perspective (which is, in fact, closer to a U.S. perspective than it is to Continental Europe, Scandinavia, or developing countries) (Kosecik & Kapucu, 2003).

What is New Public Management?

Is NPM just another management fad, a fashion, another thing promising everything? NPM is nothing more than a set of almost every management tool found to be suitable for the public sector. NPM is the practical result of the 1980s normative idea of "private is better than public." The basic idea was that instrument used in the private sector must be successful in the public-sector. And the opponents of the past, as well as those of today, usually evaluate any change in public-sector with a highly normative and idealistic view of public sector. NPM is by far more than management systems or performance measurement. Excessive customer orientation also raised concerns about democratic accountability and control.

Several people have considered NPM as a set of tools, but some have seen it as a political theory. NPM tries to realign the relationship between expert managers and their political superiors. Particularly, it seeks to set the relationship closer to parallel, allowing the expert manager to have greater discretion than in the immediately preceding paradigm. The curious fact about the bureaucratic paradigm is that it, too, expanded the expert manager's discretion through the political theory of the politics–administration dichotomy. NPM looks more like an echo than a rejection of the bureaucratic paradigm.

Cross-National Communications and NPM

The cluster of reform ideas dominant in international discourse during the 1980s provided a global diagnosis and a standard medicine for the ills of the public sector around the globe. It was suggested that the medicine would have beneficial effects whether used in established democracies, in the former Warsaw Pact countries or in third world, less-developed countries. Trust of market and NPM were the key aspects of the doctrine (Olsen & Peters, 1996). The old public administration emphasizing due process and rules was declared old-fashioned and dysfunctional. Reformers advocated replacing old public administration with NPM focusing on goals and results and getting lessons from private-sector techniques in public sector reform. These ideas are primarily developed in the Anglo-American context, and diffused by international organizations such as Organization for Economic Co-operation and Development (OECD), International Monetary Fund (IMF), and World Bank. As Peters explains:

> The ideas of reform have served as a relatively common stimulus to which the countries have responded, and the responses provide valuable insight into their administrative and political systems. Most of the examples of reforms provided in text books are derived from the Anglo-American parts of the world, but similar changes are being implemented in other developed, developing, and less-developed countries. The Anglo-American countries have been home to much of the advocacy of free enterprise and the market while the continental Europe has opted for a more restrained form of mixed-economy welfare state even when conservative political parties have been in power. Governments in Anglo-American countries have been more subject to influence from private-management consultants

> and other purveyors of reform ideas. Many of the reform techniques, such as TQM and strategic planning, have been imported directly from the private sector into government.
>
> Peters (1996, p. 115)

The ideas of NPM have become the gold standard for administrative reforms around the world (Hood, 1991). Most of these ideas for reform are based implicitly on the assumption that government will function better if it is managed more as if it were a private-sector organization guided by the market, instead of by the hierarchy (Peters, 1996). To achieve better results in the public-sector, governments should run like business. Although the influence of NPM varies across Western democratic regimes, everywhere there is recognition of the need to reduce the micromanagement of government operations by legislatures, the executives, and central administrative agencies (OECD, 1993). It is difficult to find any country where there have not been some efforts to promote significant change in the public sector. This is even true for countries of the third world who are being required to implement administrative reform as a condition of receiving assistance from organizations like the World Bank or IMF (Peters, 1996).

The bureaucratic model of management worked exceedingly well for its time, but times have changed and a new approach to management, emphasizing teams and customer service, has emerged to challenge the traditional model of public administration. Peters (1996) mentions some of the major characteristics of the old or traditional public administration as follows: an apolitical civil service, the job at the civil service was to "implement the decision made by the political masters and to do without questioning the sagacity of the decision," hierarchy and rules, permanence and stability, an institutionalized civil service, and political control over public bureaucracy. There were several reasons to think "reinventing governments." First, "significant shifts in economy forced governments to respond" (Peters, 1996, p. 13). Then there is a need for more efficient government that "works better costs less." Second, demographic change (increasing social political heterogeneity among population) and decline in government's capacity to regulate society effectively is another reason that causes rethinking of governance (Peters, 1996, p. 15). The market models of reforms take places against the traditional models of public administration as alternative models.

NPM: The Need for Managerial Reforms

The economic recession after the 1970s resulted in an unaffordable budget deficit for the Western states. There were three ways to deal with deficit.

First is by restricting public expenditures and terminating some public tasks, and second is by raising taxes. These two ways seem to be unrealistic alternatives from a political perspective. That leaves us with "a third way," according to the subtitle of the National Performance Review (Gore, 1993) "work better cost less." Therefore the "third way almost logically forces the public-sector to move towards public management that the golden age of administrative reform apparently resulted particularly in managerial reforms, this logically follows from cause and effect" (Kickert, 1997, p. 17). The universal administrative reform movements in public management of past years have been driven in large part by the government's response to the fiscal crises brought by changes in the international economic crises and by the demands for government services and regulations in national political systems. These financial crises have led to budgetary restraint and downsizing of public employees, as well as attempts to privatize government operations and to deregulate private economic initiatives (Aucoin, 1990; Peters, 1996).

There has been a discussion about "making government work better and cost less" in almost every government around the world. What is especially remarkable about the contemporary NPM movement is the similarity of the changes implemented, and the similarity of the discourse about change in the public sector occurring in many of those settings. The expectations from NPM are the same for all the governments: more efficient, more effective, small, transparent, and less expensive government (Peters, 1997; World Bank, 1997). According to Kickert, "public sector reform is in fashion and no self-respecting government can afford to ignore it. How a fashion is established is one of the most intriguing questions of public policy. Part of the answer lies in policy diffusion brought about by the activities of international officials, by meetings of public administrators, and so-called policy entrepreneurs" (Kickert, 1997, p. 15).

Major Characteristics of NPM Reforms

In all the leading Western democracies, the reforms of the 1980s and early 1990s drew upon previous dissatisfaction with government and upon the work of previous commissions or groups that studied the problem. Britain's Fulton Report in 1968 argued that members of the British higher service lacked management skills. Australia's Coomb's Commission Report argued that financial and management systems needed greater simplicity and more integration. Canada's Glassco Commission argued for decentralization and greater managerial discretion. The Grace Commission in the United States simply argued that government should be operated like a business (Ingraham, 1997). In all these cases, the message was the same: NPM is an important policy tool in improved governmental performance; it is a subset of all policy performance, not a separable set of technical efforts. As a result, the reforms that eventually ensued emphasized not only significant downsizing, but also significantly improved management capabilities.

NPM is accepted as "gold standard for administrative reform" for almost all countries. The main idea for reforming government was if government guided private-sector principles rather than (Weberian) rigid hierarchical bureaucracy, it would work more efficiently and more effectively. Surveys conducted by the OECD (1993, 1990) attempted to categorize the most important initiatives in the various OECD countries. These surveys clearly demonstrate the extent and depth of recent administrative reform initiatives. The OECD surveys arrive at a number of trends that seem to be common to all countries, such as increased result and cost consciousness, service provision and customer orientation, performance budgeting, human resources management, performance control, and evaluation of results.

The shift from bureaucratic administration to business-like professional management with NPM was promoted as a strategy fitting for all levels, and branches of the public-sector, local as well as central governments, and every kind of administrative culture in any country whatsoever. NPM has been presented as a remedy to cure management ills in various organizational contexts, as well as in various areas of policy making, from education to healthcare.

According to its general applicability in various settings, the style of NPM obviously differs depending on the political and historical conditions of the administrative cultures under which it has to operate. Therefore, it should be obvious that NPM is not a monolithic administrative reform doctrine that operates similarly in all countries, governmental levels, and agencies (OECD, 1993). At the very least, differences in the state and administration need to be considered before an idea of public management is transferred to another country. According to specific (political) goals or national administrative cultures, NPM approaches differ in two main respects. First, there are substantial differences in the role the states take on in the reform process, and second, there are essential differences in the orientation of reforms: the targeted subject matters with which to improve efficiency and goal attainment in public service.

It is obvious that Anglo-American countries have tended to be the leaders in NPM reforms. "This is true for market reforms, but also true for some of the other styles of change as well. This appears to be a function of the approach to public administration taken in these regimes" (Peters, 1997, p. 81). As Kaboolian points out, "[c]ommon to reform movement in all countries is the use of the economic market as a model for political and administrative relationships.... While the reform movements vary in depth, scope, and success by country, they are remarkably similar in the goals they pursue and technologies they utilize" (Kaboolian, 1998, p. 190). The core reform ideas and principles included in most national efforts of the past three decades are frequently put up with the term managerialism. Managerialism relies on an essentially private-sector set of techniques and practices, largely raised by public choice and market theories (Aucion, 1990; Peters, 1997; Flynn, 1999). Greater efficiency is a primary objective of managerialist reforms: decentralized, privatized, or otherwise off-loaded government services are also central to the managerialist strategy. In the Westminster systems, the separation of policy advising from service delivery was common. In virtually all cases, the senior civil service was a target of reform with the use of performance contracts, often in combination with greater authority and discretion in budgetary and personnel matters, as a common feature. "Governments around the globe adopted management reforms to squeeze extra efficiency out of the public-sector to produce more goods and services for lower taxes" (Kettl, 1997, p. 446).

Since the early- to mid-1980s, the search for smarter as well as smaller government has led numerous countries to launch major public sector reforms. In Britain, the "Next Steps" initiative has radically overhauled the structure and operations of much of the civil service. In Australia, there have been important financial management reforms and machinery of government changes at the federal, state, and local government levels. And in the United States, the Clinton administration has made the quest for a government that "works better and costs less" one of its top priorities. Although the rhetoric might have varied around the world, most of the recent efforts at governmental reinvention, restructuring, and renewal have shared similar goals. The major goals are to improve the effectiveness and efficiency of the public sector, enhance the responsiveness of public agencies to their clients and customers, reduce public expenditure, and improve managerial accountability (Halligan, 1995; Kettl, 1997). The choice of policy instruments has also been remarkably similar: commercialization, corporatization, and privatization; the devolution of management responsibilities; a shift from input controls to output and outcome measures; tighter performance specification; and more extensive contracting-out (Holmes, 1992; Boston et al., 1996).

National NPM Programs

There are some trends in public-sector modernization (in terms of changing processes and structures) and in state modernization (in terms of institutional changes of the system, and nationwide policy changes). Usually, these trends have been named internal modernization, marketization, and democracy and participation. Most of the terms seem to be the smallest common ground of OECD reforms. These general categories are not cross-country trends that embrace all public-sector reforms. It can be found useful to form groups of countries. In addition, the composition of the trends is different in almost every country, and different emphasis is given to some elements even in so-called "coherent" countries like Scandinavia. Speed is also different, as well as the approaches. For example, in Britain — at least until the very early 2000s — democracy and participation were mostly a managerial driven customer orientation in public sector modernization. It was not based on democracy. However, it would be wrong to conclude that British modernization efforts were only management based — at least after the Conservative era. Changes in the political structure — devolution in Scotland and Wales, the regional debate in England, the introduction of cabinets on the local level, etc. — should also not be regarded isolated (Kosecik & Kapucu, 2003).

In public sector reform in developing countries, the large donors relied heavily on deregulation, instruments, and promoted leadership. The context in which these necessary deregulations took place, the misunderstanding between "goal" and "instrument," and the often missing civil society with subsequent fatal outcomes on leadership led to no better public service. This is especially true for sub-Saharan Africa, to some extent to South America, and to Asian countries as well. The structural adjustment programs had a severe impact on stability, and the failure in democratic terms encouraged large donor organizations to formulate joining programs. The missing success of NPM-related reforms in developing countries is a logical consequence of its missing institutional and path dependency perspective.

Although many ascribe the adoption of NPM-oriented methods as responses to economic and fiscal stress and global trends, drawing on research on Spain, Mexico, Brazil, Thailand, and the United States, Barzelay and his colleagues show that reform agenda setting is sensitive to a number of context-specific political and other variables. The influences of traveling ideas and economic policy over public management policy making are overdrawn. NPM ideas have created a distinctive legacy that prompts continuous adjustments. Public-sector managers now take for granted private-sector-like routines that are more the exception than the rule internationally. Effective public services stem ultimately from effective routines, the following are the really important legacies: decentralized authority for financial management (within central budget limits), backed by information about assets and liabilities, which put constant pressure on managers to consider the best mix of capital and staffing, and decentralized authority for human resource management, meaning that managers have considerable discretion over who they can hire and how they manage performance.

Routines of planning now place more emphasis on outcomes and "strategic intent" rather than tightly specified outputs. Although annual planning at times has become ritualized, it ensures organizations keep focused on purpose and value creation — particularly given the potential for serious scrutiny through parliamentary select committees. Considerably more information is available for scrutiny than was the case prior to 1988, a healthy development for democratic debate. Of course managing by results is a very old idea, closely tied to managing by performance, which seemed new back in the Kennedy administration, but even then was just the upswing of an older cycle.

Performance has always been a significant concern of students of public administration (Downs & Larkey, 1986). That was as true of its founders in the progressive era as it is of the most dedicated contemporary managerialists. The main issue that divides students of public administration goes to this issue of administrative control. Conventional study of control treats control as technical process related to inputs (resources, including employee behavior) and desired outputs (specific organizational goals and economic efficiency generally) (Ouchi, 1977; Peterson, 1984). If there is anything consistent about NPM, it is the mantra — let the managers manage; make the managers manage, which is usually translated to say: give them the flexibility to acquire and deploy resources and then hold them accountable for results. Of course, the efficacy of this prescription depends not only on several variables, at a minimum the specification of organizational purpose, but also effective mechanisms for central handling of accounts payable and perhaps also an appropriate structure of accounts. Many if not most developing nations lack these minimum conditions. NPM should be and has been implemented as a reaction of (local, regional, national) problems perceived by decision makers — and its success should be measured by its ability to solve these problems. In many cases, severe existing problems have been solved by methods of the NPM.

New Zealand and Australia have acted as a testing ground for a set of reforms intended for widespread implementation. The rhetoric might differ in different countries, but emerging research suggests that the basic set of NPM reforms is essentially the same (Norman, 2003). This is suggested by OECD, Public Management and Governance (PUMA) documents, for example, which suggest that the underlying intent was always to "maintain the momentum" of privatization initiatives, but to do so through largely hidden budgeting and financial management process, thus avoiding political debate.

In many developing countries, the public sector is an optimal place where the political class can situate its clientele and the bureaucratic class its relatives, and nobody wants to give it up. The managerial public teams possess almost absolute ignorance about managerial tools and the public administration personnel grows in number and inadequacy of profiles to duties to be performed despite the public rhetoric. Control is focused on procedures and not in results. There is always a way to elude restrictive measures and controls. The managerial aspects of the reform are systematically put aside because they can drive to let the political and bureaucratic classes with less power and nobody has interest in such a scenario.

NPM is indeed a set of tools rather than a consistent program to be applied to all countries in all circumstances. It is a set of tools based on the use of markets instead of bureaucracy — i.e., choice rather than force, to use Ostrom's typology. The institutional frameworks of countries differ and this is what conditions the utility of using NPM or any other model to signal the failure of formal bureaucracy. So rather than saying NPM is all bad and formal bureaucracy all good, there needs to be some appreciation of the circumstances in which one, and not the other, might work and in which direction. It is patronizing to say that developing countries must stick to the bureaucratic model when they are developing markets and other institutions to assist their people.

Conclusions

NPM reforms, if they are to be effectively implemented, require a holistic approach, integrating the multiple human resources, financial, technical, and structural factors involved within a dynamic environment (OECD, 1995). Kaul (1996, p. 136) emphasizes the "importance of securing highest level of political authority to reform programs. Equally important is the institutionalization within the government machine of the skills necessary for the continuation and development of good management in government." Kaul also points out another very important issue related to success of administrative reform in any country by drawing lesson from Commonwealth experience. "The Commonwealth experiences have demonstrated that most successful reforms are politically driven at the highest level. There should be sufficient political will to implement such reforms" (Kaul, 1996, p. 149).

Countries with no firmly established principles of the rule of law, "neutral" bureaucracy and political accountability should think twice before attempting implementation of "modern management practices." Poorly thought out, rash, and mechanical application of approaches borrowed from the practices of the business sector may have a counterproductive effect. A country with huge pressing problems of corruption or lack of work ethic among public employees is probably not matured for more frontline empowerment reforms, and it probably needs to get its house in order before it can start in a serious way worrying about the quality of public-sector results. Conversely, we should not impose hypercontrol and rule boundedness on public-sector organizations where these are less serious issues, and where the costs of a lack of result-orientation are much greater (Kelman, 1990).

Nations around the world have been and are continuing to apply different methods contingent upon the nature of their problems and contexts. It is useful to think of NPM not as a management reform ideology, movement or trend but rather as a set of tools, any of which may be applied (or not) in specific settings. With respect to application of these tools or methods in developing nations caution is advised. Without a sound infrastructure of governance and government, efforts to implement some methods probably will not produce the results desired.

The wider international experience of public sector reform, suggests that the origins of ideas of public administrative reform and policies to which they give rise are multiple and diverse. Although other aspects of NPM such as privatization, the separation of policy and delivery agencies, and the creation of quasimarkets have been wound back since 1999, the core routines remain firmly in place. The result, in my assessment, is a public sector that is more capable of continuous improvement than was previously the case.

Each new generation of theory accretes a new layer on the old rather than displacing it. If a theory (like NPM) lies around long enough, it gets accreted upon. In its new sedimentary environment, it just does not look the same. The wider international experience of public sector reform suggests that the origins of ideas of public administrative reform and policies to which they give rise are multiple and diverse. It is rare for a set of reforms to be taken straight from a management textbook or transplanted directly from another country. The process is actually much more complex and dynamic. Ideas are continuously generated, rediscovered, refined, rejected, borrowed, and transferred across boundaries. Thus, no single formula would work for every country; rather the ideas should be tailored to specific countries and regions.

References

Aucoin, P. (1990). "Administrative reform in public management: paradigms, principles, paradoxes and pendulums," *Governance*, 3(2): 115–137.

Boston, J., J. Martin, J. Pallot, and P. Walsh (1996). *Public Management: The New Zealand Model*. Auckland, New Zealand: Oxford University Press.

Caiden, G. (1969). *Administrative Reform*. Chicago: Aldine.

Downs, G. and P.D. Larkey (1986). *The Search for Governmental Efficiency: From Hubris to Helplessness*. New York: Random House.

Flynn, R. (1999). "Managerialism, professionalism, and quasi-market," in M. Exworthy and S. Falford (eds.) *Professionals and the New Managerialism in the Public Sector*. Philadelphia, PA: Open University Press.

Gore, A. (1993). Report of the national performance review: creating a government that works better and costs less, Washington, September 7, 1993.

Halligan, J. (1995). "Policy advice and the public service," In B.G. Peters and D.J. Savoie (eds.) *Governance in a Changing Environment.* Montreal, Canada: McGill-Queens University Press, pp. 138–172.

Holmes, M. (1992). "Public sector management reform: convergence or divergence?" *Governance,* 5(4): 472–483.

Hood, C. (1991). "A public management for all seasons?" *Public Administration,* 69(Spring): 3–19.

Hood, C. (1995). "Contemporary public management: a new global paradigm," *Public Policy and Administration,* 10(2): 104–117.

Ingraham, P.W. (1997). "Play it again, Sam; it's still not right: searching for the right notes in administrative reform," *Public Administration Review,* 57(4): 325–331.

Kaboolian, L. (1998). "The new public management: challenging the boundaries of the management versus administration debate," *Public Administration Review,* 58(3): 189–193.

Kaul, M. (1996). "Civil service reform: learning from commonwealth experience" in Adamolekun, L., De Lusignan, G. and Atomate, A. (eds.) *Civil Service Reform in Francophone Africa.* Washington, D.C.: The World Bank.

Kelman, S. (1990). *Procurement and Public Management.* Washington, D.C.: American Enterprise Institute Press.

Kettl, D. (1997). "The global revolution in public management: driving themes, missing links," *Journal of Policy Analysis and Management,* 16(3): 446–462.

Kickert, W.J.M. (1997). *Public Management and Administrative Reform in Western Europe,* Northampton, MA: Edward Elgar.

Kosecik, M. and N. Kapucu (2003). "Conservative reform of metropolitan councils: abolition of the GLC and MCCs in retrospect," *Contemporary British History,* 17(3): 71–94.

Lane, J.-E. (1997). *Public Sector Reform: Rationale, Trends, and Problems.* Thousand Oaks, CA: Sage Publications.

March, J.G. and J.P. Olsen (1995). *Democratic Governance.* New York: The Free Press.

Moore, M. (1995). *Creating Public Value: Strategic Management in Government.* Cambridge: Harvard University Press.

Norman, R. (2003). *Obedient Servants? Management Freedoms and Accountabilities in the New Zealand Public Sector.* Wellington: Victoria University Press.

OECD (1990). *Public Management Development Survey.* Paris: OECD.

OECD (1993). *Public Management Development Survey.* Paris: OECD.

OECD (1995). *Governance in Transition: Public Management Reforms in OECD Countries.* Paris: OECD.

Olsen, J.P. and G.B. Peters (eds.) (1996). *Lessons from Experience: Experiential Learning in Administrative Reforms in Eight Democracies.* Boston: Scandinavian University Press.

Osborne, D. and T. Geabler (1992). *Reinventing Government.* Reading, MA: Addison-Wesley.

Ouchi, W.G. (1977). "The relationship between organizational structure and organizational control," *Administrative Science Quarterly,* 22: 95–113.

Peters, B.G. (1996). *The Future of the Governing: Four Emerging Models.* Lawrence, Kansas: University Press of Kansas.

Peters, B.G. (1997). "Policy transfers between governments: the case of administrative reforms," *West European Politics*, 20(4): 71–88.

Peterson, K.D. (1984). "Mechanisms of administrative control over managers in educational organizations," *Administrative Science Quarterly*, 29: 573–597.

World Bank (1997). *World Development Report.* Washington, D.C.: World Bank. World Competitiveness Yearbook. 1997. IMD.

Chapter 41

Global Ethics in the 21st Century: An Alternative Approach

Thomas D. Lynch, Cynthia E. Lynch, and Peter L. Cruise

CONTENTS

Introduction

At the beginning of the 21st century, there continues to be disagreement over the application of ethics in the public sector. In this chapter, we argue that the current approaches to ethics used in public administration are inadequate, and we are suggesting an alternative that is more useful for public administrators. For example, elsewhere we have discussed how many current approaches to public-sector ethics lead to an increase in organizational bureaucracy and a subsequent reduction in organizational productivity (Lynch et al., 2002). Our suggested approach to ethics is not new; in fact, it builds on the common spiritual wisdom found in the five current largest religious traditions, and it directly flows out of the work on ethics by Aristotle.

In discussing professional ethics, Windt et al. (1989) note that there are three basic types of ethical theories. The first, "deontological," is based on fundamental principles of right and wrong with the moral person asked to apply a rational process to those principles. The Ten Commandments and many of the common professional codes of ethics are examples of this theoretical approach. Immanuel Kant is a noted philosopher associated with this approach. The second set, "consequential or teleological," is based on asking the moral person to think through the consequences of his or her decision. Jeremy Bentham is one of the most noted philosophers associated with this approach. The best-known version of consequential ethics is "utilitarianism" that largely underpins modern democratic thought and various well-known analytical methods such as cost–benefit analysis. Utilitarians define human happiness, pleasure, and satisfaction as good and conversely human unhappiness, suffering, and dissatisfaction as bad.

The third basic type is called "virtue ethics" by Windt et al. (1989), "human nature ethics" by Donaldson and Werhane (1983), and "spiritual wisdom ethics" by Lynch and Lynch (1998). It is based on having the moral person seek and develop an inward looking ethical view by cultivating virtuous character traits and conversely transforming or eliminating nonvirtuous character traits. A good person is a moral person who acts in that way for the sake of morality itself. Rather than asking the good person to apply a rational reasoning process to moral decisions, this approach expects the good person to not only intelligently apply reason to the moral problem, but also exhibit a developed intuitive understanding of what is essentially right and wrong. Aristotle is the philosopher most associated with this set of theories. If this ethical theory is to be followed, professionals must cultivate a virtuous character within them and then exhibit that character in their everyday behavior. An example would be the U.S. military officer who observes the concepts of duty, honor, and country taught in the military academies. Each officer must bring those values into their very being, and then exhibit them in their everyday work activities.

Although in this chapter we argue in favor of the third approach, we recognize the importance of the other two approaches, especially in understanding how individuals and collective sets of people can and do go about justifying decisions in terms of right and wrong. We disagree with the use of deontological theories in many, but not all, normative decision-making situations, because rules or principles seem too often to not capture fully all the details and require multiple exceptions to seemingly sound principles. For example, few can argue with the principle of not killing people, but our statute books are filled with exceptions and mitigating circumstances that never seem to fit every situation that arise in our life experience. We also disagree with consequential theories that evolved out of the enlightenment that placed humankind as our focus rather than God. Our reason for disagreement is simple. Humankind is not God and therefore any collection of people such as a legislature or a bureaucracy is not omnipotent, omniscient, and omnipresent. Thus any major decision of a group of humankind, regardless of what rational technique is used, is always flawed.

The failure of the consequential theories can be seen in the way scholars treat them. For example, Herbert Simon advocates the suboptimizing or settling decision-making theory called "satisficing." This theory accepts the inherent impossibility of a utilitarian rational model to make the correct decision in a practical environment and says you should just settle for the best decision you can make within the given time constraint. The impossibility of consequential theories leads to impossible professional processes like planning programming and budgeting, and political systems such as communism that assume rational planning can correctly direct a whole human society. As a result of these theories used well beyond their practical limitations, reforms are created that cannot work and professionals and political leaders must face the consequences of trying to do the impossible. The result in society is massive frustration, disillusionment, and cynicism as professional and political leaders discover the realities of applying finite reasoning processes to infinite challenges.

With spiritual wisdom ethics, life is seen as a stream of opportunities to move toward and gain in spiritual wisdom within the individual. As the individual grows, his new insight is manifested in his actions and deeds. Thus, professional administrators should become more and more balanced and harmonious as they learn from each life situation, gaining greater virtue within them. In turn, the gained virtue is merely a reflection of the gained spirituality within the person that is manifested in their deeds and actions. With these ethical theories, each individual is able to exercise free choice in their professional decision making. Certainly such individuals have more choice options than the deontologicalist with their rules and principles and the consequentialist with their endless calculations of results (Windt et al., 1989, p. 15). A spiritual wisdom ethics creates a professional who has a special consciousness that is always growing and guiding their professional life.

What does spiritual wisdom ethics bring to the table that is new? In the first place, it is really not so much new but rather a totally different orientation in making ethical choices that go beyond deductive reasoning and calculating alternative consequences for our choices. Secondly, spiritual wisdom ethics has a totally different concept of what is good in that it values morality for its own sake, seeks a good life not in terms of pleasure seeking but rather self-actualization, and uses the wisdom of the ages to always refine and improve its applied ethics. Thirdly, with spiritual wisdom ethics, the implementer of ethical decision making views the process as not a single-step but rather a two-step effort. You first consciously refine and create your virtue characteristics, and then primarily make your ethical decisions through your unconscious, but created habits. Fourthly, spiritual wisdom ethics permits the ethically concerned person to search out the accumulated wisdom of the world, which is often found in the spiritual wisdom literature of the various religions, and use them to develop within the person the best virtue characteristics possible.

After this introduction, this chapter develops the case for spiritual wisdom ethics. First, Aristotle's *Nicomachean Ethics* is explained. The chapter then shows the relationship of the spiritual wisdom ethics to Aristotle's ethics. The next section refutes the common arguments that are made against the use of spiritual wisdom ethics. The following two sections explain the roots of the ethics and the interrelationship of ethics and God. Finally, we offer some conclusions.

Nicomachean Ethics

Aristotle (384–322 BC) wrote two treatises on ethics called Eudeman and Nicomachean after his first editor and pupil, Eudeman, and his son, Nicomachean. Aristotle probably wrote *The Nichomachean Ethics* when he was in his fifties or sixties. He directed his inquiry toward discovering how we can achieve our highest ideal of a fulfilled life, which he called the *telos*. His answer was the virtue of the soul, achieved by deliberate choice of action, and based on a worked out plan using his famous Golden Mean (Aristotle, 1925, p. v).

Aristotle viewed individuals achieving ethics not so much through intellectual reasoning, but by the character of their person. He said, "the virtue of man also will be the state of character which makes a man good and which makes him do his own work well" (Aristotle, 1925, p. 37). Achieving a high morality is no easy task because it requires a person to live the Golden Mean between excess and deficiency. Like the Buddha, Aristotle said we should aim at what is intermediate or the middle path in our passions and actions. The aim is to perform the right action, with the right person, to the right extent, at the right time, and in the right way. Although this is the objective, Aristotle considered achieving this goodness as rare, laudable, and noble (Aristotle, 1925, p. 45; Rahula, 1974).

Aristotle saw two potentials for humankind. We can let our passions and desires rule us or we can be free from them by acting with our ethics and morality. He said, "we feel anger and fear without choice, but the virtues are modes of choice or involve choice" (Aristotle, 1925, p. 36). The more developed our virtue, the more choices we, in fact, have because we are able to apply a wider range of tools in making our choices. Virtues have nothing to do with passions or faculties, but rather they are a state of character. Morality is a state of mind or consciousness that each of us must develop with effort and perseverance (Aristotle, 1925, pp. 36, 37). To be moral, you must exercise your morality in your daily life as you exercise to develop your muscles. It is not something that can easily be comprehended and then applied by logic or reason. It is something that must be lived spontaneously. He said, "without these no one would have ever a prospect of becoming good" (Aristotle, 1925, p. 35). Aristotle believed we can all be moral, but most of us fail because we believe that merely knowing about ethics will result in our being good. There is a wide gulf between knowing and being. He argued this self-delusion is much like the physician's patient who listens carefully to the doctor, but follows none of the advice. He says, "As the latter will not be made well in body by such course of treatment, the former will not be made well in soul by such a course of philosophy" (Aristotle, 1925, p. 35).

Aristotle believed that we must each create morality within ourselves. Leading a life pursuing pleasure or avoiding pain is a fundamental mistake. Morality comes from the avoidance and abstention from excess indulgences and bravely confronting life's difficulties. He said, "it is by reason of pleasures and pain that men become bad" (Aristotle, 1925, p. 32). The road to morality involves lifelong learning, beginning with early childhood education and continuing throughout our lives. He said, "Hence we ought to have been brought up in a particular way from our very youth, as Plato says, so as both to delight in and to be pained by the things that we ought; this is the right education" (Aristotle, 1925, p. 32).

Unlike deontological and teleological theorists, Aristotle saw no predictable clear moral answer that anyone can generalize before a situation requires a moral judgment. On the contrary, he believed that, "matters concerned with conduct and question of what is good for us have no fixity" (Aristotle, 1925, p. 30). He went on to say, "the account of particular cases is yet more lacking in exactness; for they do not fall under any art or precept, but the agents themselves must in each case consider what is appropriate to the occasion." He continued, "matters of conduct must be given in outline and not precisely" (Aristotle, 1925, p. 130).

To achieve the ability to be moral requires developing the proper character. To develop the proper character requires developing virtues. To develop virtues requires creating and living with moral habits (Aristotle, 1925, p. 29). Aristotle said, "so too is it with the virtues: by abstaining from pleasures we become temperate, and it is when we have become so that we are most able to abstain from them" (Aristotle, 1925, p. 31). What begins as a great effort to give up in time and with effort and practice becomes quite normal and is no effort at all. He also said, "we learn by doing them… states of character arise out of like activities. …It makes no small difference, then, we form habits of one kind or of another from our very youth; it makes a very great difference, or rather all the difference" (Aristotle, 1925, p. 29). If we learn by doing as children, and behavior is the result of repeated actions, we are going to form habits anyway. Therefore, they might as well be good ones.

Each of us must develop virtues that apply to us as individuals but also apply within the context of our life situation such as our profession. Intellectual virtue comes from being taught. Moral virtue results from developing proper habits. Neither arises without our active intervention and participation over nature. Aristotle said, "we first acquire the potentiality and later exhibit the activity" (Aristotle, 1925, p. 28). We develop virtues by practicing them much like we learn the arts and music. We learn by doing them repeatedly and forming the correct habits then by exercising them as a young musician learning a new instrument. To Aristotle, the soul is where virtue exists. The body is what moves us astray from virtue (Aristotle, 1925, p. 26).

God was a central part of Aristotle's vision of ethics because to him proper morality was considered divine and highly prized (Aristotle, 1925, p. 24). Aristotle reasoned the best things are to be described as blessed and happy because this was the status of God and the most godlike men (Aristotle, 1925, p. 23). Animals could not attain this status but only humans who properly develop their souls can achieve that status (Aristotle, 1925, pp. 18, 23).

Aristotle felt that happiness was not a state of feeling, enjoyment, or pleasure, but rather it was the definition of that which is the most desirable and satisfying of life. Aristotle did not believe that God provided us with such a life, but rather we had to earn it as a result of our good actions. Our good actions were the result of our acquired virtues we developed through learning, training, and cultivation of proper habits. If we did this, he believed, we then acquired the most godlike blessed prize that a human could achieve in the world. To Aristotle, critical thought and application over time created virtue, which was the greatest and most noble accomplishment of any human being (Aristotle, 1925, p. 18).

Human good is the activity of exhibiting excellence. To Aristotle, the good man is one who performs nobly (Aristotle, 1925, p. 13). Each person should seek the good because it is desirable in and of itself and never for the sake of something else (Aristotle, 1925, p. 11). He said, "The Pythagoreans seem to give a more plausible account of the good, when they place the One in the column of good" (Aristotle, 1925, p. 9). He argued that we should pursue the universal good in spite of how difficult it is for us to achieve (Aristotle, 1925, p. 7). Aristotle believed the masses of humankind are slaves to their senses and desires, which makes their lives essentially beastlike. He recognized some led superficial lives that some might call sophisticated and noble living, but that are really no better than their beastlike counterparts (Aristotle, 1925, p. 6). His ethics calls us to be truly noble, because the potential exists within us. If successful, we would reach the universal divine good that would be the highest of any life.

What is Spiritual Wisdom Ethics?

Spiritual wisdom ethics is not based on a set of deontological rules or reasoning about consequences, but rather on a state of being that is a transformational consciousness. A person using spiritual wisdom ethics is in a constant dialogue between the mind and the intuitive conscious that we label here the EGO and the SELF, respectively. The EGO is a perceptually sentient being that is a system of habitual reflexes that we so commonly address in the behavioral sciences. The environment, culture, history, economics, desires, genetic makeup, and other factors push, pull, and reshape the EGO. Thus, it is always the dependent variable governed by a variety of interacting independent variables. In other words, the EGO may think it has freedom of choice but totally lacks it (Lockhart, 1997, p. 315). In contrast, SELF is our conscious consideration, our gut feeling, and our intuitive awareness. The SELF gives us guidance but it is rarely more than a whispered suggestion.

With spiritual wisdom ethics, invoking our choice, which we create with a dialogue between the EGO and the SELF, gives us freedom based on our critical thinking processes. The first step in freedom is to understand the EGO or the "me, my, mine." This is possible because each of us has a SELF that can observe the EGO as it takes possession of us. The second step in freedom is restraining the EGO. These are the simple two steps that constitute the beginning of spiritual wisdom ethics in each of us. The individual soul, and not the mind, is the user of spiritual wisdom because that is where the individual waking consciousness exists (Lockhart, 1997, p. 317). To develop and advance the soul's spiritual wisdom, each of us must look simultaneously to the balanced tension between our SELF that provides our inner gyroscope and our outer experiences that are constantly challenging us and even trying to reprogram our inner gyroscope. With spiritual wisdom ethics, we must realize that often this tension is not in balance with the result we ignore developing the soul and have our lives dominated by the EGO. We must force ourselves to wake up out of our dreamlike ignorance and assert our potential freedom over the independent influencing variables in our lives (Lockhart, 1997, p. 323).

In spiritual wisdom ethics, the goal is to uncover the complete soul and then develop and sustain that condition through the person's actions and deeds. The challenge is to free the person's soul from the bonds of the EGO consciousness that normally blinds each of us from seeing what proper human behavior really means. This is an ethics based on awareness, freedom from desires, and controlling our wayward emotions. This ethical theory intentionally brings to bear the SELF's heightened awareness into every moment of our existence. We see ourselves existing both as a perceived part of the universe, but also as a complex and meaningful interrelationship to the oneness, which is often beyond our ability to understand (Lockhart, 1997, pp. 328–338).

Human development is the struggle for self-actualization or more accurately allowing the inherent perfect divine nature to exist in spite of the various influencing independent behavioral variables. The goal of each of us is to let the soul become completely free. Using this theory is seeing humankind as a mixture of good and bad much like what James Madison did when he wrote the U.S. Constitution. Inherent in each of us is the good or the so-called divine. The challenge is to reach that good that we sometimes bury deep within us and to free it to direct our decisions and actions, rather than those many determining EGO variables described by modern behavioral science. Spiritual wisdom ethics is predicated on using the SELF to develop the individual soul in a manner consistent with what we intuitively call a person of good heart. If that heart is properly developed to care for the oneness of all, then spiritual wisdom will enhance the soul. When that occurs, the SELF can first restrain the harmful desires and emotional reactions of the EGO, and second cultivate beneficial habits and traits that further give us true free choice (Lockhart, 1997, pp. 533–534).

Learning spiritual wisdom ethics is waking up to our freedom and recognizing that some emotions masquerade as feelings (e.g., sexual desires) and some compulsive behaviors masquerade as our conscious mind (e.g., smoking). When we wake up and stay awake, we defeat the dream-like influence of the EGO and our decisions become based on our free will because we are no longer at the mercy of our desires channeled through our EGO. With this freedom comes an increased awareness of the soul and its part in the larger oneness of everything. This in turn leads us to a better understanding of why loving one's neighbor is wise and even helps us to comprehend the true meaning of the word neighbor. The core problem of humankind is the submerged awareness of SELF and its inherent nonassociation with the larger meaning of oneness. Spiritual wisdom ethics is a process of waking up to the core problem (Lockhart, 1997, pp. 338–340).

Spiritual wisdom ethics is meant to be a life transforming process. For example, it teaches the professional public administrator about the abrasive effect of holding in anger and resentment. We should not boil inside ourselves and bottle-up our emotions. However, neither should we indulge our egos by engaging in wild emotional outbursts. At a minimum, we should allow the pain to be felt through consulting with others (e.g., talking a problem out with a friend) but better, yet, we should allow such feeling to pass through us without affect (e.g., not let someone get to us). Above all spiritual wisdom ethics teaches us not to let such emotions that are masquerading as feelings control our movements and thoughts. We must allow ourselves to be free. If we do, we have transformed ourselves and morality serves intelligence, attention, awareness, and change. Spiritual wisdom ethics is real growth and development of real substance. It is not stoic indifference or self-congratulatory perfection (Lockhart, 1997, p. 341).

Spiritual wisdom ethics is freeing the possibilities and escaping the imprisonment of the EGO forces (Lockhart, 1997, p. 343). This goes beyond superficially knowing the SELF, but it is engaging us in bare bones self-realization (Lockhart, 1997, p. 341). Spiritual wisdom ethics is being what you can be.

Refutation of the Opposition

Donaldson and Werhane (1983) identified the following three common arguments made against spiritual wisdom ethics:

1. All humans do not have any specific inherent capabilities.
2. Humans are not basically good.
3. This theory lacks clear-cut rules and principles for those making moral decisions and thus this theory is not practical (Windt et al., 1989, p. 534).

The first argument is predicated on questioning the spiritual wisdom ethics assumption that all humans have some inherent potentialities that humans can bring forth and perfect. Certainly, we can find individuals that are near death or have very little intelligence. To all intents and purposes they appear to not be able to be developed further. However, those in opposition to the argument declare that most of us have significant inherent capabilities that we can develop (Cooper, 1982, p. 114). Spiritual wisdom ethics asks only that each of us assume the responsibility for taking what inherent capabilities we have and develop them to their maximum extent. Certainly, those capabilities will vary widely from person to person. The first argument against spiritual wisdom ethics is merely the common debate ploy of the straw man. Create a false description and then argue against the proposition based on the wrong description. Spiritual wisdom ethics asks each of us to develop ourselves to our fullest potential. As public administration professionals, if we all do that or even if only some of us do that, then we can improve the political and bureaucratic arena by our cumulative action.

The second argument should be familiar to students of philosophy, as many important philosophers have held that humankind is not good. Certainly, Thomas Hobbes comes to mind immediately and American history students should be aware of Alexander Hamilton's views that influenced the U.S. Constitution. Not all people are good, and there are certainly many examples that anyone can cite such as Hitler. However, philosophers like Jean-Jacques Rousseau and early American leaders such as Thomas Jefferson also hold the converse. In other words, the argument is false, as each of us can cite at least some altruistic actions of others and ourselves. The pessimistic argument about the nature of humankind is wrong. The correct view is the Madison perspective that humankind is a mix of altruistic and ego- and materialistic-centered people (Cooper, 1982, p. 128; Fredrickson, 1993, p. 247).

The third negative argument relates to the practical nature of spiritual wisdom ethics. How can anyone apply it? Given a moral decision situation, what clear-cut criteria can we use to make the correct decision? Kant's categorical imperative gives us guidance by asking the question: "Could I wish that everyone in the world would follow this principle under relatively similar conditions?" Spiritual wisdom ethics offers no formula way such as the categorical imperative to look at moral decision-making challenges because to do so would immediately limit our abilities to make good moral decisions. If we look at the categorical imperative more closely, we can easily agree that the holocaust was evil, but Hitler could argue that he believed the world would be better by his policy. A thief might rationalize that stealing whenever you have the opportunity is a perfectly reasonable general policy for everyone. In other words, if the soul of the person using the categorical imperative is not developed, then he will have flawed conclusions. Another problem is that strict interpretations of deontological ethical reasoning can easily lead to moral rigidity and failure to accommodate a complex moral situation. In other words, on the surface deontological theories appear to have practical application, but closer examination shows they do not (Windt et al., 1989, p. 532).

Consequential theories also fail largely because its advocates cannot account for justice. The utilitarian focuses on the consequences for the majority (the greatest good for the greatest number), and this leads to injustice for the minority such as the underclass. Under utilitarian thinking, is injustice to a minority wrong regardless of the consequences? How does one properly identify and rank the so-called good that utilitarianism should maximize? What is the basis for selecting what is good and what is the proper weight the utilitarian analysts is to give the various goods in the utilitarian calculation? Those are all serious questions that address the practical working ability of consequential theories (Windt et al., 1989, p. 529).

Additional examples of the practical limitations of deontological and consequential theories have been noted in attempts to improve the ethical climate in healthcare organizations. Cruise (2002) described the inadequacy of consequential and deontological approaches to strengthen voluntary accreditation standards for hospitals to combat medicare and medicaid fraud and abuse. For example, hospital accreditation standards that become more consequential in their approach and specify exactly what constitutes fraud and abuse will only draw lines in the sand — lines that some will cross, others will step up to (but not cross) and still others will stay well behind. This is approximately the current state in healthcare organizations — and fraud and abuse persist. In hospital accreditation, fraud and abuse standards were to become more deontological (or process-focused), although better than the current consequential approaches, shortcomings will still exist. To effectively address fraud and abuse issues, deontological approaches to hospital accreditation would have to focus on individual behavior and actions, and not on organizational behavior and actions — as individuals, not organizations, act ethically or unethically. However, deontology is not a practical approach in this instance as hospitals, not individuals, seek accreditation (Cruise, 2002).

Of course, saying the argument of practicality defeats other ethical theories is not addressing the question raised by the critics of spiritual wisdom ethics, but we wanted to first establish that the argument itself is not reasonable. Moral decisions are sometimes easy for us to make, but they are also sometimes very complex decision challenges. Spiritual wisdom ethics allows each professional to maximize their potential and apply a more developed ethical insight to their daily moral challenges. The end result is that there is no one right answer, but rather the best answer possible. Is there more we can ask of any ethical theory?

Roots in Spiritual Wisdom

The literature of spiritual wisdom is helpful in addressing the question of ethics. For example, we can find deontological examples such as the Ten Commandments and the Golden Rule. However, spiritual wisdom also uses a form of ethics similar to Aristotle's and that is why we selected the term "spiritual wisdom ethics" for use in this article. The spiritual wisdom literature of almost all religious traditions can sometimes provide useful insight as to how to better approach our life's challenges. For example, in the Christian tradition, the New Testament uses the metaphors "kingdom of heaven" and "kingdom of God" as an ideal construct much like the famous sociologist Max Weber used the ideal construct of bureaucracy. The "kingdom of man" represents the bad ideal and the New Testament uses it as a counterpoint to the kingdom of God, which is the good ideal. Rather than representing physical places, the kingdom of man and the kingdom of God are states of consciousness for individuals that guide their behavior — that is, they are means to express an ethical theory.

The best way to explain this sophisticated concept is to quote the New Testament. It says, "And when he was demanded of the Pharisees, when the kingdom of God should come, he answered them and said, the kingdom of God cometh not with observation: Neither shall they say, Lo here! or lo there! for behold, the kingdom of God is within you" (Gospel of Luke, 17, pp. 20–21). This simple metaphor tells us to search within ourselves and through our inquiry come to comprehend exactly what are good works. This ideal consciousness must originate within each person, but each of us must manifest it outside the person. In other words, learn and then apply spiritual wisdom ethics. The reader can see this same ideal construct in the following Hindu quote:

> Free from desire,
> immortal,
> wise and self-existent,
> With [its own] savior satisfied,
> and nothing lacking,
> — Who so knows him,
> the SELF,
> — wise, ageless, [ever] young, —
> Of death will have no fear.
>
> (*Atharvana-Veda* 10, 8:44, in Zaehner, 1992)

In this quotation, the saying places stress on looking within to find a higher consciousness to give us the wisdom to act in our daily lives. Another example to help us understand the ideal construct is the following quote:

> Descry It in its Oneness,
> Immeasurable,
> firm,
> Transcending space,
> immaculate,
> Unborn,
> abiding,
> great, —
> [This is] SELF!
>
> (*Brihadaranyaka Upanishad* 4, 4:20, in Zaehner, 1992)

Note the similarities of the last two quotes to Aristotle's *Nicomachean Ethics*. These traditions are telling us about spiritual wisdom ethics. The answer to ethics is within the person and not through a convoluted mental process of deductive logic or a complicated calculation of consequences. The answer is freedom from the kingdom of man and this means freedom to associate with the higher concepts associated with the divine. The so-called intuitive mind or SELF is central to spiritual wisdom because it is our linkage to the larger oneness of everything. With the SELF, we develop our soul. Possibly, the following words from the Hebrew Bible are helpful to understand this point:

> Neither is it beyond the sea,
> that thou shouldest say,
> Who shall go over the sea for us,
> and bring it unto us,
> that we may hear it,
> and do it?
> But the word is very nigh unto thee,
> in thy mouth,
> and in thy heart,
> that thou mayest do it.
>
> (Deuteronomy 30:11–14)

The common spiritual wisdom of the various traditions tells us that by knowing the SELF we know the kingdom of God and knowledge of the SELF can be found in the heart, not the mind. Conversely, if we do not know the SELF, we remain in the kingdom of man (that is in "me, my, mine" perspective) with all its desires and other dependent variables that dictate what we do in our lives without thought or consideration on our part. To be truly free, we must select the kingdom of God (that is "thee, thy, thine" perspective) with its consciousness that allows us to govern ourselves and be in harmony with those around our environment and us.

God and Ethics

Modernism and postmodernism, which are the two streams of intellectual thought that dominate contemporary thinking in public administration (Lynch et al., 1997), are producing a marginalized, relative, or absence of faith and ethics (Lynch & Lynch, 1998). Given the current and likely future human condition, this is dysfunctional (Küng, 1996). We share the following views of Socrates who said, "He who would be dear to God must, as far as is possible, become like Him" (Plato, 1960). Socrates felt the fountainhead of ethics was God and ethics was essentially a process of becoming like Him. In his words, "The Ruler of the universe has ordered all things with a view to the excellence and preservation of the whole; and each part, as far as may be, does and suffers what is proper to it. And one of these portions of the universe is thine own, unhappy man, which infinitesimal though it be is ever striving towards the whole; and you do not seem to be aware that this and every creation is in order that the life of the whole may be blessed; and that you are created for the sake of the whole, and not the whole for the sake of you" (Plato, 1960). Socrates also said,

> ...This is that life above all others which man should live,...holding converse with the true Beauty, simple and divine. In that communion only beholding Beauty with the eye of the mind, he will be enabled to bring forth, not images of beauty, but Reality [Itself];...and bring forth and nourishing true virtue, to become the friend of God and be immortal, if mortal man may. Would that be an ignoble life?
>
> (Plato, 1947)

Socrates believed deeply in God and saw that our lives should be about bringing forth and nourishing true virtue so that each of us would become like God. Socrates did not marginalize God, ignore, or declare God was dead. Instead, for Socrates the very reason for life was to exercise true virtue and thus bring forth God within each of us through the exercise of ethics. Socrates, himself, lived that life. In his fateful trial, he said the following in his own defense: "This I do assure you, is what my God commands; and it is by belief that no greater good has ever befallen you in this city than my service to my God; for I spend all my time going about trying to persuade you, young and old, to make your first and chief concern not for your bodies nor your possessions, but for the highest welfare of your souls" (Plato, 1947).

Ethics is about God. Spiritual wisdom ethics provides us a way to live our lives. On the basis of a belief in the transcendent, it motivates us to not live selfish lives, but generous lives by providing a continuous source of inspiration and guidance that allows us to function positively in the whole of society. It speaks of both an outer and inner life while stressing the importance of deepening and strengthening the inner life so that it can properly guide the outer life. The spiritual wisdom of most religious traditions inextricably intertwines God and us as individuals and as communities. To spiritual wisdom everyday life, with its pleasures and pains, is one of the two linked spheres that are united by God's creation. The other sphere is the life of faith that goes well beyond just believing in God's existence as it includes manifesting that belief constantly in our everyday thinking and actions toward others and the whole (O'Connor, 1990, pp. 14–16).

Conclusions

We offer three conclusions. First, spiritual wisdom ethics is a viable alternative and useful approach to ethical decision making in the public sector. Second, spiritual wisdom ethics is fundamentally different from the other two approaches. Although we can use the other two approaches to a limited extent with spiritual wisdom ethics, this third approach requires a uniquely different method of education if it is to become a commonly used ethical approach. Third, more scholarly research is needed to develop optimal use of this approach.

Spiritual wisdom ethics has the advantage that it does not impose a single right answer requirement to moral decision making. It relies greatly on our intuitive right-brain thinking processes and being an engaged critical thinker. The more complex moral decision-making challenges rarely have one clear right answer. Often a thinking person can eliminate wrong answers, but finding the one right or best moral answer is rarely obvious. Unfortunately, the other two approaches, deontological and consequential, often lead decision makers to the false conclusion that one need only apply the correct principle or make the calculations in the proper manner. As noted earlier, these false expectations are not functional in today's complex societies and create whole new sets of problems. We need to employ an ethical theoretical approach that expects us to do our best, to grow from each experience, and to at least avoid wrong answers. Spiritual wisdom ethics does that.

Humans have both intuitive and analytical abilities, but the other two approaches to ethical decision making stress only the importance of the decision maker's analytical capabilities. Deontological approach stresses deductive reasoning ability and consequential approach stresses the ability to calculate often with fairly complex math. With "spiritual wisdom ethics," the use of the other approaches is considered potentially useful, but its stress is on developing better intuitive decision-making skills largely by creating positive ethical habits and avoiding or transforming negative ones.

Spiritual wisdom ethics is fundamentally different from deontological and consequential ethics. The other approaches are extremely left brain-oriented. If a person is intelligent enough in terms of either deductive logic capabilities or the ability to calculate, then the two theories say we can make moral decisions. Spiritual wisdom ethics is predicated on a different holistic view of human nature. It assumes we make our moral decisions with both our intuition and our analytical minds or some combination. Therefore, we need to develop both to meet our moral challenges. Spiritual wisdom ethics requires developing judgmental skills. First, we must focus on our hearts by recognizing our own worth. Then we must extend our love to those immediately around us and continue our increasing regard for others until it extends to everybody and everything. Spiritual wisdom of almost every tradition includes versions of the Golden Rule because it is that important for the development of our morality.

With that awareness deep inside us, we can begin the process of learning intuitively. We need to understand why the kingdom of man (that is "me, my, mine") is so limited. We need to see the wisdom of the Golden Mean in helping us to properly deal with the kingdom of man. We need to see the value of the contrasted kingdom of God consciousness. We can achieve intellectual awareness of the kingdom of God consciousness only if we properly develop the heart. With or without such intellectual awareness, we need to create positive daily habits to reinforce our virtues and we need to transform our negative habits so that we operate better at the intuitive level of our being. This gaining and losing can occur differently for different people and different cultures. There is no one formula but there are key intuitive understandings that must exist if the habits are to be functionally useful to the person using spiritual wisdom ethics. Ideally, we need to start the education process as soon as possible in a person's life, but it can start at any point as soon as the person is willing to and wants to grow within him or herself.

Our third point in this conclusion is the need for scholarly research. Although there are no formulae, research will help identify better means to clarify spiritual wisdom lessons and teach moral virtues. Spiritual wisdom literature tells us what we need to know, but understanding it is difficult at best, and methods of teaching it are still largely established by traditions that do not accommodate for varying circumstances of time and space. One thing that careful research can do is establish what teaching methods of virtue ethics work best under what circumstances. This is a type of research that is well understood in the social sciences and can result in extremely important knowledge as we begin to apply spiritual wisdom ethics in public administration professional situations.

References

Aristotle (1925). *The Nicomachean Ethics*. Translated by David Ross. New York: Oxford University Press.

Bible (King James' version). Cleveland, OH: The World Publishing Company, First Published in 1611.

Cooper, T. (1982). *The Responsible Administrator*. Port Washington, New York: Kennikat Press.

Cruise, P.L. (2002)."Are there virtues in whistleblowing? Perspectives from health care organizations." *Public Administration Quarterly*, 25(4): 413–435.

Donaldson, T. and P. Werhane (1983). *Ethical Issues in Business: A Philosophical Approach*, 2nd edition. Englewood Cliffs, NJ: Prentice Hall.

Frederickson, H.G. (ed.) (1993). *Ethics and Public Administration.* Armonk, New York: M.E. Sharpe.

Küng, H. (1996). *Global Responsibility: In Search of a New World Ethic.* New York: Continuum.

Lockhart, D. (1997). *Jesus: The Heretic.* Rockport, MA: Element.

Lynch, T.D. and C.E. Lynch (1998). "Twenty-first century philosophy and public administration." In T.D. Lynch and T.J. Dicker (eds.) *Handbook of Organization Theory and Management: The Philosophical Approach.* New York: Marcel Dekker, pp. 463–478.

Lynch, T.D., R. Omdal, and P.L. Cruise (1997). "Secularization of public administration." *Journal of Public Administration Research and Theory*, 7(3): 473–488.

Lynch, T.D., C.E. Lynch, and P.L. Cruise (2002). "Productivity and the moral manager." *Administration & Society*, 34(4): 347–369.

O'Connor, K.M. (1990). *The Wisdom Literature.* Collegeville, Minnesota: The Liturgical Press.

Plato (1947). *Four Dialogues of Plato Including the Apology of Socrates.* Translated by John Stuart Mill. London, England: Watts.

Plato (1960). *The Laws.* Translated by A.E. Taylor. New York : Everyman's Library.

Rahula, W. (translator) (1974). *What the Buddha Taught.* New York: Grove Weidenfeld.

Windt, P.V., P.C. Appleby, M.P. Battin, L.P. Francis, and B.M. Landesman (1989). *Ethical Issues in the Profession.* Englewood Cliffs, NJ: Prentice Hall.

Zaehner, R.C. (translator) (1992). *Hindu Scriptures.* London, England: J.M. Dent and Sons Ltd.

Chapter 42

Subnational Governments and Globalization: The Changing Face of Federalism

Curtis Ventriss and Tina Nabatchi

CONTENTS

We live in an era where globalization is transforming the original meaning (and understanding) of governance (Sassen, 1997). This transformation is due, in part, to the ascendance of the information technologies, the mobility and the liquidity of capital, new patterns of immigration and technology transfer, and the marked blurring of the boundaries between international and domestic affairs in the United States and in other countries. Some have referred to this process as the "domestication" of international affairs (Hanrieder, 1978) and the "internationalizing of politics" (Czempiel, 1989). Manning (1977), for instance, has coined the term "intermestic politics" in referring to how international factors are also interlocal in that "disruption of particular trade flows can cause disproportionate concern and reaction in certain regions or among specific important groups, thereby creating the basis for a more concentrated political response" (cited in Kline, 1984, p. 53). In short, subnational governments — particularly in the last 25 years — have increasingly involved themselves in international affairs that has taken the form of "global microdiplomacy" whereby "states, willing or not, have been drawn into the global economy where they must fend for themselves with their own set of problems and mix of goods and services" (Luke & Ventriss, 1988, pp. 113–114).

In an effort to cope up with this increased global interdependence, record numbers of subnational governments have become active participants in the international arena ranging from the four regions in Europe called the Focus Motors (Baden-Württemberg, in southwest Germany; Catalonia, Spain; Lombardy province in northern Italy; and Rhone-Alps in southwest France), to the different provinces in Canada, and the federated systems of Mexico, Australia, and Switzerland (just to name a few). However, it can be argued that the involvement of the U.S. state and local governments in the global affairs has caused the most controversy given their high-profile, expansive activities, significant financial resources, and potential economic impacts. For the purpose of analysis, we will therefore focus our attention on the U.S. state and local subnational activity in the global arena and the challenges and dilemmas that it poses for federalism *vis-à-vis* globalization.

State and Local Involvement in the Global Arena

Although the word global is over 400 years old, the term globalization was not first mentioned until 1962, and, according to Robertson (1992), it did not emerge as a major scholarly interest until the early 1980s. Yet, it is worth noting, that U.S. subnational involvement in international affairs began as early as 1959, when Governor Luther Hodges of North Carolina traveled to Europe for the explicit purpose of attracting foreign direct investment to the state (Kincaid, 1984). Today it is widely recognized that both the state and the local economies are inexorably interwoven with the world economy, and international trade and business development have become central strategies for fostering local and regional economic growth (Luke & Ventriss, 1988).

For example, international business opportunities are particularly important to the U.S. state and local governments because one in six private sector jobs in the United States is linked to the global economy (Fry, 1998). Moreover, there are five million Americans working for foreign companies in the United States and foreign direct investment in the United States has quadrupled since 1981 (Fry, 1998). In response to these trends, over 40 governors undertake international missions in search of trade, investment, and tourism opportunities each year (Fry, 1998). Moreover, numerous states offer export outreach or counseling to local businesses, participate in "trade lead" matching programs and joint-venture agreements, sponsor trade development seminars and conferences, publish international newsletters, and provide export financing, all with the goal of becoming more involved in international commerce (Fry, 1998).

To handle this proliferation of international contact, many states have developed their own "foreign affairs" offices. In 1969, only 4 states operated overseas offices; by 1990, 43 states operated 160 offices abroad, four fifths of which were located either in East Asia or Western Europe (Kresl & Gappert, 1995). Today, state governments operate almost as many permanent overseas offices as the U.S. government operates embassies (Fry, 1998). Moreover, these state international offices are endowed with tremendous financial resources: between 1984 and 1990, state international budgets grew at a dramatic rate of 40 percent a year, rising from an average of $590,000 per state in 1984 to $2,025,000 in 1990 (Conway & Nothdurft, 1996). Presently, 47 states have 188 international offices with an average per office budget of over $200,000 (Ventriss, 2002). Counties and other municipalities are also becoming involved in international missions. Today, all the 50 states have the sister city programs in operation, linking more than 1000 U.S. communities with 1850 communities in 96 countries (Fry, 1998).

The growing importance of the world to the U.S. states has also meant a growing importance of the U.S. states to the world. This reciprocal importance is largely because of the tremendous financial resources U.S. subnational governments bring to the international economic arena. The U.S. states are major players in the international economy, spending over $92 million on international economic programs in 1990, excluding investment incentive programs (Kresl & Gappert, 1995). This state spending is roughly half of what the U.S. Department of Commerce spent on international trade promotion and development in that same year (Conway & Nothdurft, 1996). The wealth of subnational governments is not in question. If they stood as independent nations, seven American states would be counted among the top 25 countries in terms of GDP; even Vermont, with the smallest economy among the states, would outrank almost 100 nations (Fry, 1998). Moreover, state and local governments have tremendous procurement budgets: the annual expenditures of subnational governments exceed one trillion dollars (Fry, 1998). The annual budgets of California and New York each surpass $65 billion, as compared to about a $70 billion budget in Russia, a nation with almost 150 million people (Fry, 1998). Massachusetts, a considerably smaller state, has a procurement budget of over $2 billion.

Until recently in the United States, subnational activity in the international arena was seen primarily in economic terms: it increases competitiveness by generating revenues and creating healthy business environments. Indeed, it is widely recognized that the last few decades have seen significant transformations in the composition of the world economy, accompanied by the shift to the services and finance, which have renewed the importance of subnational locations for certain types of activities and functions. In short, it is precisely the combination of the global dispersal of economic activities and global integration under conditions of continued concentration of economic ownership and control that has contributed to the strategic importance of subnational entities.

Despite their economic importance and financial resources, subnational governments must still compensate for weak controls over their own economies and counteract the potential employment and economic opportunity losses derived from the free migration of industries and households among the cities and the states. To do so, subnational governments often subsidize industries to attract or retain them in their localities. For example, recent attempts to provide tax breaks and subsidies to hire auto plants to particular states have become a fairly costly matter. To cite just a few illustrations of this trend and the per cost to each state: "$16,667 for the Saturn plant in Tennessee; $49,900 for the Toyota plant in Kentucky; $65,000 for the BMW plant in South Carolina; $40,793 for Diamond-Star plant in Illinois; $50,588 for the Isuzu/Fuji Motors in Indiana; and finally a whopping $200,000+ for the Mercedes plant in Alabama" (Ventriss, 2002, p. 90). Despite the costs, forgone tax revenues, potential environmental degradation, and other opportunity costs, such "smokestack chasing" is generally portrayed as meeting the interests of the community in terms of more jobs and greater net tax revenues (Clarke & Gaile, 1998) and is celebrated as introducing a new era of free trade and democracy in the global economic system.

A new issue has recently evolved from this activity, generating critical attention and creating serious political divisions in both the domestic and the international arenas. The U.S. subnational governments have, with increasing frequency, used their international role to enact their own types of "foreign policy." Over the past three decades, state and local governments have entered into thousands of accords, compacts, and agreements (but not "treaties") with national and subnational governments around the world (Fry, 1998). States, counties, and cities have developed and employed a variety of trade sanction laws that some argue compete with federal foreign policy making and interfere with free trade in the global economic system. The international controversies generated by such laws are evidence that the U.S. state and the local governments are gaining importance in the international system, and that they can and do wield their international economic power in a manner that affects businesses and foreign nations alike.

We now turn our attention to the controversy surrounding the Massachusetts Burma Law. The passage of this law triggered a heated political debate with enormous implications for the U.S. subnational governments. At the heart of the controversy are uncertainties about the role of subnational governments in the international arena. This example provides support for John Kline's (1993, p. 218) observation that given the changing nature of governance in this era of globalization, perhaps we need to "rethink federalism in this new international environment."

The Massachusetts Burma Law and Subnational Involvement in International Affairs

A prominent example of an international controversy triggered by the involvement of a U.S. state in the international arena is the Massachusetts Burma Law, entitled: *Act Regulating State Contracts with Companies Doing Business with Burma (Myanmar)* (Act of June 25, 1996, Chapter 10, 1, 1006 Mass Acts 210, codified as Mass. Gen. Laws, ch. 7 §§ 22G–22M [hereinafter referred to as the "Massachusetts Burma Law"]). In 1996, the Commonwealth of Massachusetts passed a law penalizing companies that engage in trade and investment in Myanmar (formerly Burma)[1] by imposing a special tax on goods and services offered by such firms to the state government. The legislation was enacted as a protest against the Myanmar junta's crackdown on prodemocracy movements (Thurston, 2000). The junta, known as the State Peace and Development Council (SPDC), ignored the results of a 1990 general election in which the National League for Democracy (NLD)

---

[1]Burma changed its name to Myanmar in 1989; however, several of the documents used in this research, make a point of noting their reference to the country as "Burma." Among the reasons for this choice were conforming to the relevant literature and voicing opinions concerning the political legitimacy of the "Myanmar" government. This chapter adheres to that standard and refers to the country as "Burma."

won a landslide victory (Carvajal, 1998; Dhooge, 2000). The SPDC has been accused of abuses ranging from rape, forced labor, prostitution, drug smuggling, and arbitrary detentions, arrests, and executions, to restrictions on freedom of movement, speech, and assembly (for a more detailed discussion of the problems in Burma, see Carvajal, 1998; Dhooge, 2000). In 1998, there was a military crackdown on prodemocracy movements, which led to the house arrest of the Burmese prodemocracy leader and Nobel peace laureate Aung San Suu Kyi (Carvajal, 1998). These allegations received international attention and reinforced the resolve of the Massachusetts state legislature in enforcing this law.

The Massachusetts Burma Law effectively barred companies doing business with or in Burma from procuring state government contracts by levying a pricing penalty on their contract bids. The Massachusetts Secretary of Administration and Finance maintained a "restricted purchase list" that contained "the names of all persons currently doing business with Burma (Myanmar)" (Mass. Gen. Laws, ch. 7 § 22J, 1996). To prepare the list, the Secretary consulted "United Nations reports, resources of the Investor Responsibility Research Center and the Associates to Develop Democratic Burma, and other reliable resources" (Mass. Gen. Laws, ch. 7 § 22J, 1996). The restricted purchase list was then provided to "all state agencies and state authorities and to the House of Representatives and to the Senate" (Mass. Gen. Laws, ch. 7 § 22J, 1996).

In 1999, the restricted purchasing list consisted of 346 companies; 44 were U.S. companies, and 15 of those were Fortune 500 companies (Brief of the National Foreign Trade Council, 1999). This law also affected numerous European and Japanese companies. For example, Unilever (an Anglo-Dutch conglomerate) and Siemens (a German electronics giant) were denied contracts with the Massachusetts state government, and at least 13 other companies, including the U.S. multinational Apple Computers, withdrew from their business activity in Burma so as not to face action under the law (Lobe, 1998).

The Political Debate Surrounding State and Local Sanction Laws

State and local sanction laws typically forbid companies that conduct business with the targeted nation from bidding on state or local government contracts. Their purpose is to force companies to choose between consumers: companies can opt to do business with state and local governments, some of which award billions of dollars in contracts each year, or they can maintain ties with the targeted countries. In this case, companies could have foreclosed their access to the Massachusetts state government's $2 billion procurement market, or they could have turned their backs on the $2.3 billion in annual revenues generated by foreign trade with Burma.

In 2000, about 30 U.S. states and municipalities had similar "pricing penalty" or selective purchasing laws pending on the books against Burma and a multitude of other nations (USA Engage, 2004).

Selective purchasing laws were first launched during the antiapartheid movement in the late 1970s (Price & Hannah, 1998). Over 150 states, counties, and municipalities placed sanctions on U.S. and foreign businesses operating in South Africa, well before a Congressional set of national restrictions were implemented (Fry, 1998). These sanction laws are largely credited for helping dismantle the proapartheid government in Pretoria by pressuring dozens of U.S. companies to decide to withdraw from South Africa (Lobe, 1998).

Despite their historical significance, pricing penalty laws have recently come under international fire. The global climate of trade has changed dramatically since the late 1970s and early 1980s, and now such laws are often described as tools used to dismantle free trade (Price & Hannah, 1998). The Massachusetts Burma Law was the first of its kind in the United States under the new World Trade Organization (WTO) system (Price & Hannah, 1998), and it sparked fierce international reactions. Among the first and strongest international challengers of the law were the European Union (E.U.) and Japan.

The E.U. and Japan claimed that the law violated the WTO multilateral 1994 Agreement on Government Procurement (AGP). The 1999 report on the WTO consistency of trade policies by major trading partners took aim at the Massachusetts law, describing it as inconsistent with the government procurement agreement under the WTO (WTO Subcommittee of the Industrial Structure Council, 1999). Under the WTO regulations, countries are not allowed to let political considerations influence their decisions on granting access to national markets. As such, the E.U. and Japan insisted that the U.S. federal government bring the state government measure into conformity with the WTO rules. The U.S. State Department tried to persuade Massachusetts to repeal the law, but state officials, led by former Republican Governor William Weld, refused, asserting states' rights to control procurement practices (Aslam, 1997).

Both the U.S. and the E.U. already maintained strict sanctions against Burma and many governments with the E.U. moved to strengthen the bloc's existing sanctions, which comprised of an arms embargo and a visa ban on senior government officials (Dhooge, 2000). Moreover, several organizations including the International Confederation of Free Trade Unions (ICFTU), the International Federation of Chemical, Energy, Mine and General Workers' Union (ICEM), and the European Trade Union Confederation (ETUC) vocally supported the Massachusetts law (Aslam, 1997). Despite this support, the E.U. and the Japanese officials saw the Massachusetts law as part of a trend by U.S. federal, state, and local governments to impose their political goals on non-U.S. companies. They argued that these activities merely amounted to a new type of "gunboat diplomacy." In the summer of 1997, the E.U. and Japan requested talks with the United States to resolve the issues. When the joint talks failed, the E.U. and Japan threatened to ask the WTO to formally convene a three-person panel to rule on the Massachusetts Burma Law. This threat helped galvanize the National Foreign Trade Council's (NFTC) legal challenge to the Massachusetts legislation.

The NFTC was founded in 1914 with the support of President Woodrow Wilson. Since its inception, it has been an advocate for liberal trade policy, denouncing economic sanctions and encouraging foreign investment. The NFTC is a nonprofit interest group representing over 600 U.S. manufacturing corporations, financial institutions, and other firms with significant foreign economic interests. Members of the NFTC include AT&T, IBM, PepsiCo Food and Beverages International Ltd., The Chrysler Corporation, Bank of America, General Electric, and Texaco, to name a few. In its public profile release, the NFTC states that its fundamental goal is "to develop policies reflecting the interests and consensus of Council members, designed to expand exports, protect U.S. foreign investment, enhance the competitiveness and profitability of U.S. industry and promote and maintain a fair and equitable trading system" (National Foreign Trade Council, n.d.).

To support this goal, the NFTC began a campaign against unilateral sanctions, claiming that the Congressional enactment of economic sanctions against countries such as Iran, Cuba, Libya, and China were ineffective in achieving their aims and cost U.S. business about $20 billion a year in lost commerce (Lobe, 1998). The campaign, aimed primarily at Congress, received tacit support from key players in the Clinton administration. Prior to the threat of WTO action, the NFTC had focused minimal efforts on state and local jurisdictions; however, the possibility of a WTO ruling created an opportune time to challenge the constitutionality of the Massachusetts Burma Law and to levy additional pressure on states and municipalities to repeal or reject selective purchasing laws.

Congressional response to the NFTC lawsuit and the WTO challenge culminated in an unusual coalition of left-wing Democrats and right-wing Republicans, who mobilized to sponsor a constitutional amendment that would bar the federal government from challenging any local or state sanctions laws found by the WTO to violate international trade accords. In other words, the amendment served to block the federal government from taking legal action to enforce the WTO rulings. The Clinton administration opposed the amendment, arguing that it was "unnecessary and ill-advised" (Lobe, 1998). In a letter, former U.S. Trade Representative Charlene Barshefsky insisted that Washington was not obligated to conform to WTO rulings or to sue local or state jurisdictions to ensure compliance. She noted that the federal government had not sued a subnational body during the 50 years in which the General Agreement on Tariffs and Trade (GATT), the WTO's predecessor, had issued rulings (Lobe, 1998).

Passage of the amendment would have protected the Massachusetts Burma Law and similar state and local sanction laws; however, on August 5, 1998, the House of Representatives rejected the amendment 228–200, retaining the right of the U.S. federal government to challenge state and local sanction laws. The vote, which split both the Republicans and the Democrats, was representative of the heated debate about the appropriateness and the legality of U.S. states and municipalities enacting unilateral sanctions against foreign countries. On the other hand, supporters of states' rights argued that the WTO's rules requiring that government contracts be awarded only on the basis of economic considerations interferes with the constitutional right of subnational governments to act as market participants and to pursue economic development and other social objectives. For this reason, they asserted that the constitutional rights of subnational governments to exercise their purchasing power should be protected from WTO rules. On the other hand, many argued that selective purchasing laws were not only unconstitutional, but also interfered with the global economic system of free trade, and should therefore be forbidden. The Clinton administration supported this latter argument by discouraging other states from using selective purchasing laws as tools to oppose human rights violations. For example, in the spring of 1998, the administration actively lobbied the Maryland state legislature to not adopt a selective purchasing law against Nigeria (Wallach, 1999). The proposal subsequently lost by one vote, again, highlighting the great debate surrounding this issue.

Although there was tremendous concern about the role of subnational governments in foreign affairs, and the potential for consequent domestic and international political divisions, the legislative and executive branches of the government were constrained in their ability and willingness to deal with the issue. Some argue that this debate should not have been within the purview of legislators in the first place, because when faced with an issue of supporting (or nullifying) state activities, legislators and other elected officials may employ a normative or moral stance, or might be swayed by their personal interests in re-election, rather than consider broader foreign-policy objectives and issues of federalism (Schaefer, 1998). Thus, a greater deterrent to action was likely that neither the legislators nor the president wanted to take public action that would suppress subnational actors and activities, especially when those activities sought to promote human rights. As a result of these legislative and executive constraints, the issue was forced into the judicial arena. The issue, and the legal and political disputes that ensued, worked themselves through the judicial process to the U.S. Supreme Court. We now turn our attention to the various legal challenges and judicial opinions about the Massachusetts Burma Law.

The United States District Court of Massachusetts

In April 1998, the NFTC mounted a legal challenge in search of declaratory and injunctive relief against the Secretary of Administration and Finance and the State Purchasing Agency of the Commonwealth of Massachusetts.[2] The NFTC argued before the United States District Court of Massachusetts that the Massachusetts Burma Law was unconstitutional on three grounds. First, the NFTC asserted that the Massachusetts Burma Law infringed on the exclusive foreign affairs power of the federal government derived from Article I of the U.S. Constitution. The argument rested on the notion that foreign affairs should be conducted by those with the "legal competence to take international action" and those who "can make and keep [international] commitments" (Amicus Curiae Brief in Support of Plaintiff National Foreign Trade Council, 1998). Accordingly, foreign policy activities should be conducted between the federal governments of nations, and not among individual, subnational governments. Second, the NFTC argued that the Massachusetts Burma Law violated the Commerce Clause (Article I § 8) in the U.S. Constitution. Finally, the NFTC argued that by logic of the Supremacy Clause in Article VI of the Constitution, the Massachusetts Burma Law was preempted by the Omnibus Consolidated Appropriations Act of 1997 (see Federal Burma Law, Pub. L. No. 104–208), which authorized federal sanctions against Burma and was passed by the U.S. Congress three months after the passage of the Massachusetts Law. Thus, although the Massachusetts Burma Law took similar, albeit more severe, measures against Burma, the NFTC asserted that the federal law must take precedence.

On November 4, 1998, the District Court of Massachusetts decided *National Foreign Trade Council versus Baker* (26 F.Supp.2d 287 [D. Mass. 1998]). The opinion, written by the Chief Judge Tauro, enjoined enforcement of the Massachusetts Burma Law and found that it "unconstitutionally impinge[d] on the federal government's exclusive authority to regulate foreign affairs" (26 F.Supp.2d 287 [1998]). The District Court asserted that "states and municipalities must yield to the federal government when their actions affect significant issues of foreign policy" (26 F.Supp.2d 287 [1998], p. 291).

---

[2]The Secretary of Administration and Finance and the State Purchasing Agency of the Commonwealth of Massachusetts were the two primary officials responsible for the implementation and administration of the Massachusetts Burma Law. In 1998, those officials were Charles D. Baker and Philmore Anderson, III, respectively.

The United States First Circuit Court of Appeals

Massachusetts appealed the District Court's ruling, arguing the following points:

1. The law did not impede federal power to regulate foreign affairs
2. The law did not violate the foreign commerce clause and its alleged extraterritorial effects were not so profound and inevitable so as to invalidate the law on its face.
3. Congress had implicitly permitted the Law.
4. Massachusetts had a legitimate local purpose: to reflect the moral judgment of Massachusetts to not associate itself or its tax dollars with dictators and their works (Brief for the Defendants Appellants, 1999; Defendants' Memorandum in Support of their Motion for Summary Judgment, 1998).

The United States First Circuit Court of Appeals in Boston, Massachusetts, reviewed the case *de novo*, and affirmed the District Court ruling with *National Foreign Trade Council versus Natsios*[3] (181 F.3d 38 [1999]). This opinion provided a much more detailed analysis of the arguments and precedents than the district court ruling, and reached agreement with all the three NFTC arguments. The Circuit Court held that the Massachusetts Burma Law interfered with federal foreign affairs power, violated the Foreign Commerce Clause, and was preempted by the Omnibus Consolidated Appropriations Action of 1997.

The United States Supreme Court

Massachusetts again appealed this decision, and in November 1999, the Supreme Court agreed to review the lower courts' decisions and hear the appeal. The issue decided by the Supreme Court in *Crosby versus National Foreign Trade Council*[4] was:

> Whether the Burma law of the Commonwealth of Massachusetts, restricting the authority of its agencies to purchase goods or services from companies doing business with Burma, is invalid under the Supremacy Clause if the

---

[3]By the time of the hearing, Andrew S. Natsios had replaced Charles D. Baker as the Secretary of Administration and Finance for the Commonwealth of Massachusetts. During briefing of the appeal, Frederick Laskey was the acting Secretary of Administration and Finance for the Commonwealth of Massachusetts. Philmore Anderson, III was still the State Purchasing Agent for the Commonwealth.

[4]Stephen P. Crosby was the new Secretary of Administration and Finance of the Commonwealth of Massachusetts.

> National Constitution owing to its threat of frustrating federal statutory objectives (530 U.S. 363 [2000], p. 366).
>
> United States Supreme Court

Arguing that "a fundamental principle of the Constitution is that Congress has the power to preempt state law," (530 U.S. 363 [2000], p. 372), the Supreme Court found that the Massachusetts Burma Law was "an obstacle to the accomplishment of Congress's full objectives" under the Omnibus Consolidated Appropriations Act of 1997 (530 U.S. 363 [2000], p. 373). First, the Court reasoned, "Congress clearly intended the federal act to provide the President with flexible and effective authority over economic sanctions against Burma" (530 U.S. 363 [2000], p. 374) and that "this plentitude of Executive authority...controls the issue of preemption." (530 U.S. 363 [2000], p. 375). Second, "Congress manifestly intended to limit economic pressure against the Burmese Government to a specific range" (530 U.S. 363 [2000], p. 377) and the Massachusetts Burma Law "conflicts with federal law at a number of points by penalizing individuals and conduct that Congress has explicitly exempted or excluded from sanctions" (530 U.S. 363 [2000], p. 378). Third, the Court reasoned, "Congress's express command to the President to take the initiative for the United States among the international community invested him with the maximum authority of National Government" (530 U.S. 363 [2000], p. 381) and therefore, the Massachusetts Burma Law "undermines the President's capacity...for effective diplomacy" and "compromise[s] the very capacity of the President to speak for the Nation with one voice in dealing with other governments" (530 U.S. 363 [2000], p. 381). In short, the opinion authored by Justice Souter, and joined by Justices Rehnquist, Stevens, O'Connor, Kennedy, Ginsnburg, and Breyer, the Supreme Court held:

> Because the state Act's provisions conflict with Congress's specific delegation to the President of flexible discretion, with limitation of sanctions to a limited scope of actions and actors, and with direction to develop a comprehensive, multilateral strategy under the federal Act, it is preempted, and its application is unconstitutional, under the Supremacy Clause (530 U.S. 363 [2000], p. 388).
>
> Justice Souter

Justice Scalia, joined by Justice Thomas, concurred in the judgment, but noted that the conflicts and issues presented in the case were "perfectly obvious on the face of the [federal] statute" (530 U.S. 363 [2000], p. 388). Therefore, he rebuked the majority for its "invocations of legislative history" (530 U.S. 363 [2000], p. 390) to support their reasoning.

Regardless of this minor censure, the Supreme Court unanimously agreed that the Massachusetts Burma Law was preempted by federal law, and therefore unconstitutional.

The Supreme Court Decision, Subnational Sanctions, and U.S. Federalism in an Era of Globalization

In its opinion, the Court noted that it granted certiorari to resolve questions regarding the constitutionality of laws like the Massachusetts Burma Law. Many presumed that this decision would resolve issues concerning the constitutionality of the other state and local sanction laws; however, because the Supreme Court addressed only the preemption issue in declaring the Massachusetts Burma Law unconstitutional, the decision, and a unanimous one at that, perpetuates doubt about the constitutionality of such subnational legislation. Therefore, serious questions about states' rights with regard to foreign relations and free trade still remain, and the debate continues.

Both opponents and supporters of states' rights *vis-à-vis* sanction laws have compelling arguments. On the one hand, those who oppose subnational rights with regard to sanction laws assert that the power to engage in foreign relations activities should be limited to the federal arena because individual subnational action may harm other subnational entities, and the nation as a whole, in many ways (see for example, Price & Hannah, 1998; Amicus Curiae Brief of the Chamber of Commerce of the United States of America in Support of the National Foreign Trade Council, 1998; Amicus Curiae Brief of the Organization for International Investment in Support of the National Foreign Trade Council, 1998).

First, subnational decisions may not be consistent with the reality and objectives of federal foreign relation activities, and subnational governments are likely to ignore the broader trade-offs in pursuing their own particular objectives. Subnational governments may not understand the consequences of their actions for the nation as a whole, and may not take them into account during the decision-making process. Moreover, because subnational governments do not have to shoulder the consequences of their decisions, they are less likely, and have less incentive to understand what those consequences might be.

Second, as the magnitude of state and local activity in the international arena continues to grow, the number of disputes surrounding subnational government action would grow in tandem (Dhooge, 2000). The potential for subnational actions to disrupt and complicate foreign relations is evidenced by the persistent diplomatic controversies and litigation concerning state and local sanction laws. Moreover, despite the changing construction of global society to recognize subnational actors, subnational interests do not justify the potentially high costs of a disrupted national foreign policy. The importance of this point must be underscored, as international law has established that a nation is responsible for the misconduct of its subnational components. This is evidenced in the case of the Massachusetts Burma Law, as the E.U. and Japan did not retaliate against Massachusetts directly, but rather pursued the case at the national level. Thus, subnational measures have the potential for creating a negative impact on the nation and its foreign policy objectives.

Third, federal supervision over economic policies, such as those pertaining to NAFTA, GATT, and the WTO, has created and maintained a vibrant national market and sustained the national government's ability to pursue a consistent federal policy of encouraging and facilitating international free trade and investment (Amicus Curiae Brief of the Chamber of Commerce of the United States of America in Support of the National Foreign Trade Council, 1998; Amicus Curiae Brief of the Organization for International Investment in Support of the National Foreign Trade Council, 1998). Multiple state and local sanction laws blur the distinction between the nation and the state and create a plethora of state–foreign nation relations. The effect is a patchwork of subnational regulations that often diverge from federal strategy. Foreign investors already complain that when entering the U.S. market, they must deal with a fragmented banking system and with 50 sets of product liability laws and state regulations covering financial services, real estate, workers' compensation, professional and environmental standards, and a host of other issues that may impact the profitability of businesses (Fry, 1998). The complexities of compliance with dozens of inconsistent subnational regulations generate dizzying permutations that affect domestic, foreign, and world markets. The long-term result of such activities could be the balkanization of the U.S. market, the segregation of the U.S. and foreign markets, and denial of the U.S. access to parts of the world market (Amicus Curiae Brief of the Chamber of Commerce of the United States of America in Support of the National Foreign Trade Council, 1998; Amicus Curiae Brief of the Organization for International Investment in Support of the National Foreign Trade Council, 1998).

In short, opponents of state and local sanction laws conclude that such laws have a negative effect on interstate and foreign commerce and severely impair the ability of U.S. businesses to compete in the world market. These laws may not have the purpose, but certainly have the consequence, of disrupting and fragmenting domestic and foreign commerce in the United States. Not only do such subnational actions fracture the national and the international markets, but also usurp the federal authority and discretion over the foreign policy of the United States.

First, those who favor subnational rights begin with the premise that the context of global affairs is now dramatically divergent from the old-line rationalization provided to foreign relations. In other words, the very nature of international society and global affairs has changed, although reasoning about foreign relations has not (Bradley, 1999). Put bluntly, international relations no longer exclusively consist of relations among national governments (Bradley, 1999; Thurston, 2000). Instead, tremendous advances in information technology have allowed those channels to be disaggregated to lower levels including state and local governments, public and private organizations, and even individual persons. There is now a multitude of new international actors, including approximately 40,000 multinational corporations, that account for the bulk of international direct investment, global trade and jobs, tens of thousands of international non-governmental organizations, as well as the myriad of religious groups, labor unions, professional societies, and other organizations participating in the web of international interactions that go far beyond the purview of national governments (Fry, 1998; Thurston, 2000). This disaggregation has created a framework in which states are not only recognized as autonomous players in global politics, but also their territorial jurisdiction in international affairs is justified and encouraged (Thurston, 2000). For example, tourism, communications, and trade are valid reasons for state and local government contact with foreign nations. In fact, the dismantling of the U.S. Travel and Tourism Administration in 1996 sent a clear message to the subnational governments and to the private sector that they now bear the responsibility for enticing foreign visitors to the United States (Fry, 1998).

Second, because foreign nations recognize states as players in global economics, in this reciprocal relationship, states should be able to express their preferences on political–economic issues, especially when acting as market participants (Carvajal, 1998). Moreover, supporters argue that the state activity in foreign relations will force states to be accountable to the international community. The constraints of a reciprocal two-way economic relationship will facilitate competition among subnational actors as they vie for foreign investment, trade, and tourism dollars (Conway & Nothdurft, 1996; Clarke & Gaile, 1998). Globalization is a two-way street: not only do global forces shape local fortunes, but also localities actively engage in composing global practices and processes (Clarke & Gaile, 1998). Local officials do more then "mediate" global pressures; they make strategic choices about resistance, accommodation, and adaptation to these forces (Clarke & Gaile, 1998). Thus, although subnational governments may choose to implement legislation similar to the Massachusetts Burma Law, when faced with targeted retaliation by international actors and the prospect of losing foreign monies, the incentive for subnational entities to emerge and promote international activity would be great.

Finally, supporters of subnational sanction laws also assert that even when subnational actors opt for legislation that ultimately expresses their normative political preferences, as the Commonwealth of Massachusetts did with the Burma Law in seeking to promote human rights, such actions should be applauded. These sanction laws effectively recognize that the economic activities have consequences that stretch far beyond their intended financial implications, and almost always result in social, environmental, and other human effects, not all of which are positive. Thus, as long as the dynamic of global capitalism exists, then choice — the ability of market participants to select with whom they will do business with — must be offered to all consumers and producers of goods and services, regardless of whether those participants are national or subnational actors. In sum, those who support the rights of state and local governments to pass sanction laws argue that given the reality of the new world order, subnational entities should be viewed as demisovereigns that are accountable for their conduct in international affairs.

The Changing Face of Federalism in a Globalized World

Immediately after the Supreme Court decision, the New England Burma Roundtable began drafting new "Free Burma" legislation that does not conflict with the Massachusetts Burma Law decision. In addition, dozens of similar laws against a multitude of other countries remain on the books throughout the nation. Despite the fact that the Supreme Court issued an unanimous decision, because it addressed only the preemption issue in declaring the Massachusetts Burma Law unconstitutional, questions about the constitutionality of such subnational legislation persist. Do state and local governments have the right to pass sanction laws? Can they present political opinions about foreign nations through legislation? At the heart of these questions are serious and significant concerns about the functional form of U.S. federalism as it operates in this increasingly globalized world.

Globalization trends, especially global economic trends, frequently emerge in regional processes where subnational areas are important decision arenas and play a critical economic role (Clarke & Gaile, 1998). As Conlan and Sager (1998) have noted, although we are seeing a reinvigorated subnational involvement in international economic affairs, at the same time, we are observing the growing importance of NAFTA and the WTO that could change the dynamics of federalism substantially. In the next breath, they claim that such trends are barely unique to the United States: "Governments in federated systems throughout the world are renegotiating intergovernmental relationships as they confront internal pressures for regional autonomy, the external demands of a changing global economy . . . " (1998, p. 39). In an insightful analysis, Daniel Elazar (1988, p. 15) articulated the emergence of these new actors in global affairs:

> The transformation of the international system from one in which politically sovereign states under international law were the only legitimate actors to one in which other entities, particularly the constituent of federal systems, are also involved is one of the major developments of the post–World War II period.
>
> Elazar (1988, p. 15)

Within the U.S. context, the federal government has actually encouraged subnational involvement in global affairs in the promotion of cultural exchanges, reverse investment, and international trade. "This is based on the belief that subnational and national objectives are basically complementary even though nuanced differently" (Duchacek, 1984, p. 25). However, the somewhat declining problem-solving abilities of nation-states (which is not the same as saying that there is any serious negation of the inherent power of the nation-state in the global economy) has prompted subnational governments to increase their responsibilities and functions (Cohn & Smith, 1995). Cities and states are the new arenas for global competition; as such, the actual "work of globalization" transpires with the practices of multiple formal and informal enterprises at the subnational level (Clarke & Gaile, 1998).

Given the trends of globalization, there can be no doubt that the U.S. subnational governments will continue to occupy a strategic position in the global web and play an increasingly important and active role in international affairs. Often, their activities will occur as a matter of regular business; however, sometimes they will evolve into matters of heated debate over the respective roles and authority of subnational governments and the federal government. Subnational governments have and will continue to take actions that diverge from federal policy and kindle the federalism debate. For example, in addition to subnational sanction laws, there are dozens of instances where subnational governments have exercised voice in international affairs but where the Supreme Court has not (yet) become involved. States and cities have provided "sanctuary" for illegal immigrants, in direct violation of federal immigration laws (Fry, 1998). In addition, several city councils aired political views when forming sister-city relationships between the United States and Nicaragua at the height of tensions between the Reagan and Sandinista administrations (Fry, 1998). Likewise, in 1996, the mayor of Pasadena, California visited Cuba, where he stated that he and many of his constituents were opposed to the embargo on Cuba — a statement he later denied making (Fry, 1998). More than 120 cities and counties have passed resolutions banning nuclear weapons' productions within their boundaries, and by the end of the 1980s, more than 200 local governments had passed resolutions, supporting a comprehensive treaty banning the testing of nuclear weapons (Fry, 1998). Finally, state and local governments have exercised voice in the Arab League boycotts, issues involving Northern Ireland, and at the Organization of the Petroleum Exporting Countries (OPEC) meetings (Fry, 1998).

All of these examples place state and local governments in the middle of foreign affairs and produce questions about the role of subnational governments in the international arena. The real issue, therefore, can be posited, or recast, to make another point: "that it is not whether every state [government] should be involved in international affairs, given global interdependency, but rather the extent and scope of state [government] involvement congruent to the unique concerns of the state economy" (Ventriss, 1994, p. 19).

Interestingly, the Constitution places a few restrictions on the state engagement in foreign affairs, and is intended to give states a central role in foreign policy, via their representation in the U.S. Senate. Some interpretations of the Constitution argue that the original intent was for the direct engagement of individual states in foreign policy with the national government supervising, and only rarely forbidding such actions (Carvajal, 1998; Clarke & Gaile, 1998). As it has worked out, states now are probably much less active in foreign affairs than originally envisioned, and the federal government is much less attentive to what the states are doing. State and local jurisdiction have shaped policy in many areas important to economic development: banking, insurance, business subsidies, environmental regulations, highway safety, and government procurement; however, NAFTA, GATT, and the WTO now substantially affect these policies, and may have the power to limit the actions of subnational governments. Global trade has grown considerably over the decades and there is a new willingness to view regulations that are based on state and local values to be potentially unfair trade barriers. In short, what was once considered state turf — because foreign relations are inextricably linked to trade and other forms of economic development — is now being invaded. Yet, as one keen observer so aptly put it:

> A number of issues are now emerging in international negotiations . . . that raise questions about the possible preemption of state powers as pressures build for the development of a consistent national policy. Examples of areas where international policy interests and negotiations encounter overlapping national and state government authorities are environmental, telecommunications and product-labeling standards.
>
> Kline (1989, p. 17)

The wealth of subnational activity and its likelihood of increasing into the future, coupled with the continual devolution of authority and responsibilities to subnational governments, suggest that below the surface, the

U.S. federal system is in a state of flux. As such, this is an appropriate time for a reconsideration of federalism *vis-à-vis* globalization. Our current views about federalism are the product of the Cold War era; however, changes in the international system, including the end of the Cold War and the resulting demise of the Soviet Union, a rapid expansion of international trade, and the formalization of the international trading system, suggest that the old-line functional logic of federalism and the federal exclusivity with regard to foreign affairs must evolve for a new global dynamic. In short, the logic of federalism that guided us through the late 20th century does not function well within the conditions of the 21st century.

The context of global affairs is now dramatically divergent from the old-line rationalization provided to foreign relations. International relations no longer exclusively consist of relations among national governments. Instead, there is now a multitude of new international actors on the global stage (Keohane & Nye, 1977), and implicitly included among them are the state and the local governments. In this new global order, subnational governments are not only recognized as autonomous players in geopolitics, but also justified and encouraged to engage their territorial jurisdiction in international affairs. A more dynamic conception of co-operative federalism needs to be applied to cases and issues involving state and local government action in international affairs. The U.S. Constitutional conception of federalism does not treat the federal or state division of authority as unalterably fixed, but rather permits shifts and realignments in response to the political will of the U.S. citizenry. It could be argued that subnational activities that are implemented for normative purposes can be constitutionally permitted, especially if those activities are aligned with the principles of international law, such as those involving human rights.

We live now in an era of federalism where "although federal–state relations in domestic governance is often described as having evolved through three relatively clear and distinctive phases of federalism – from dual to cooperative to conflictual – intergovernmental relations in the international arena form a complex mixture of all three" (Colan and Sager, 1998, p. 40). Perhaps, what is needed is the perspective that federalism in the new geopolitical order requires that the principle of federal exclusivity be replaced by a more moderate principle of federal supremacy (or "limited federal exclusivity") that allows the federal government to have the final say in foreign affairs and provides subnational governments with broader international involvement. As such, it appears that the challenge to be resolved in the next federalism controversy is how to devise approaches that permit — or at least balance — greater subnational participation, protects national interests, and prevents absolute federal exclusivity. Such is the challenge before us in this era of globalization.

References

Amicus Curiae Brief in Support of Plaintiff National Foreign Trade Council (1998). *National Foreign Trade Council v. Baker* (1998). U.S. District Court of Massachusetts (Civil Action No. 98-CV-10757).

Amicus Curiae Brief of the Chamber of Commerce of the United States of America in Support of the National Foreign Trade Council (1998). *National Foreign Trade Council v. Baker* (1998). U.S. District Court of Massachusetts (Civil Action No. 98 10757-JLT).

Amicus Curiae Brief of the Organization for International Investment in Support of the National Foreign Trade Council (1998). *National Foreign Trade Council v. Baker* (1998). U.S. District Court of Massachusetts (Civil Action No. 98 10757-JLT).

Aslam, A. (1997). U.S.-Labor: Unions want Tough Action against Burma. *Inter Press Service*, August 12, 1997.

Bradley, C.A. (1999). Symposium Overview: A New American Foreign Affairs Law? *University of Colorado Law* Review, 70: 1089–1107.

Brief of the National Foreign Trade Council (1999). *National Foreign Trade Council v. Natsios* (1999). U.S. First Circuit Court of Appeals (No. 98–2304).

Brief for the Defendants Appellants (1999). *National Foreign Trade Council v. Natsios* (1999). U.S. First Circuit Court of Appeals (No. 98–2304).

Carvajal, A. (1998). State and Local "Free Burma" Laws: The Case for Sub-National Trade Sanctions. *Law and Policy in International Business*, 29: 257–274.

Clarke, S.E. and Gaile, G.L. (1998). *The Work of Cities*, Minneapolis. MN: University of Minnesota Press.

Cohn, T.H. and Smith, P.J. (1995). Developing Global Cities in the Pacific Northwest. In Kresl, P.K. and Gappert, G. (eds.), *North American Cities and the Global Economy: Challenges and Opportunities*, Thousand Oaks, CA: Sage Publications.

Colan, T.L. and Sager, M.A. 1998. International Dimensions of American Federalism: State Policy Response to a Changing Global Environment. Lexington, KY: Council of State Governments.

Conway, C. and Nothdurft, W.E. (1996). *The International State: Crafting a Statewide Trade Development System*, Washington, D.C.: The Aspen Institute, Rural Economic Policy Program.

Czempiel, E.-O. (1989). Internationalizing Politics: Some Answers to the Questions of Who Does What to Whom. In Czempiel, E.-O. and Rosenau, J.N. (eds.), *Global Changes and Theoretical Challenges: Approaches to World Politics for the 1990s*, Lexington, MA: Lexington Books.

Defendants' Memorandum in Support of Their Motion for Summary Judgment (1998). *National Foreign Trade Council v. Baker* (1998). U.S. District Court of Massachusetts (No. 98-CV-10757-JLT).

Dhooge, L.J. (2000). The Wrong Way to Mandalay: The Massachusetts Selective Purchasing Act and the Constitution. *American Business Law Journal*, 37: 387–484.

Duchacek, I.D. (1984). The International Dimension of Subnational Self-Government. *Publius*, 14(4): 5–32.

Elazar, D.J. (1988). Introduction. In Duchacek, I.D., Latouche, D., and Stevenson, G. (eds.), *Perforated Sovereignties and International Relations: Trans-Sovereign Contracts of Subnational Governments*, New York: Greenwood Press.

Fry, E.H. (1998). *The Expanding Role of State and Local Governments in U.S. Foreign Affairs*, New York: Council on Foreign Relations Press.

Hanrieder, W.F. (1978). Dissolving International Politics: Reflections on the National-State. *American Political Science Review*, 17(1): 1–30.

Kincaid, J. (1984). American Governors in International Affairs. *Publius*, 14(4): 95–114.

Keohane, R.O. and Nye, J.S. (1977). *Power and Interdependence: World Politics in Transition*, Boston, MA: Little Brown and Company.

Kline, J.M. (1984). The International Economic Interests of U.S. States. *Publius*, 14(4): 81–94.

Kline, J.M. (1989). The States and International Affairs. Policy Paper Prepared for the *U.S. Advisory Commission on Intergovernmental Relations*, December 4, 1989, Washington, D.C.

Kline, J.M. (1993). United States Federalizing and Foreign Policy. In Brown, D.M. and Fry, E. (eds.), Berkeley, CA: Institute of Governmental Studies Press.

Kresl, P.K. and Gappert, G. (1995). *North American Cities and the Global Economy: Challenges and Opportunities*, Thousand Oaks, CA: Sage Publications.

Lobe, J. (1998). Trade-U.S.: Clinton Manages to Avert Blow to WTO's Power. *Inter Press Service*, August 7, 1998.

Luke, J. and Ventriss, C. Reed, B.J. and Reed, C.M. (1988). *Managing Economic Development: A Guide to State and Local Leadership Strategies*, San Francisco: Jossey-Bass.

Manning, B. (1977). The Congress, the Executive and Intermestic Affairs. *Foreign Affairs*, 55: 306–324.

National Foreign Trade Council (n.d.) Profile of the National Foreign Trade Council, Inc. Retrieved October 18, 2004 from http://www.usaengage.org/archives/background/nftc.html

Price, D.M. and Hannah, J.P. (1998). The Constitutionality of United States State and Local Sanction Laws. *Harvard International Law Journal*, 39: 443–499.

Robertson, R. (1992). Globalization London: Sage Mass General Laws. ch. 7 22j, 1994.

Sassen, S. (1997). Cities, Foreign Policy, and the Global Economy. In Crahan, M.E. and Bush-Vourvoulias, A. (eds.), *The City and the World*, New York: Council on Foreign Relations.

Schaefer, M. (1998). Sovereignty Revisited: The "Grey Areas" and "Yellow Zones" of Split Sovereignty Exposed by Globalization: Choosing Among Strategies of Avoidance, Cooperation, and Intrusion to Escape an Era of Misguided "New Federalism.". *Canada–United States Law Journal*, 24: 35–72.

Thurston, P.J. (2000). National Foreign Trade Council versus Natsios and the Foreign Relations Effects Test: Searching for a Viable Approach. *Brigham Young University Law Review*, 2000: 749–800.

USA Engage (2004). State and Local Sanctions Watch List. Retrieved October 18, 2004 from http://www.usaengage.org/archives/news/status.html

Ventriss, C. (1994). The Impact of International Trade and Direct Foreign Investment on National and Subnational levels: An Overview. In Baker, R. (ed.), *Comparative Public Management*, Westport, CT: Praeger.

Ventriss, C. (2002). The Rise of the Entrepreneurial State Governments in the United States: The Dilemma of Public Governance in an Era of Globalization. *Administrative Theory and Praxis*, 24(1): 81–102.

Wallach, L. (1999). Prepared Testimony of Lori Wallach, Director, Public Citizen's Global Trade Watch. Testimony before the House Ways and Means Committee Trade Subcommittee. August 5, 1999.

WTO Subcommittee of the Industrial Structure Council (1999). *The 1999 Report on the WTO Consistency of Trade Policies by Major Trading Partners*, Geneva, Switzerland: World Trade Organization. Report available at http://www.meti.go.jp/english/report/data/gCT9913e.html

Chapter 43

Globalization and Energy

Catherine Horiuchi

CONTENTS

Before humans harnessed energy for everyday use, the sun and moon lit our days and nights, the sun's radiation and natural heat sources such as hot springs warmed our bodies. People lived only where the temperature range did not exceed our primitive housing and clothing. Western mythology extols Prometheus for stealing fire from the gods and reducing the misery of mankind by providing this first and constant source of controlled light and heat.

The expansion and refinement of the use of energy was essential to the migration and settling of large portions of the planet. Energy products make deserts inhabitable year round. They provide the light and heat required in far northern and southern regions to maintain a standard work schedule during long, dark winters.

In early civilizations, each family managed its own energy portfolio, which could be as simple as fuel for an open-flame fire for cooking and seasonal heating, with torches, candles, or lanterns used for lighting. Over time, as nearby sources of fuels were exhausted and specialized labor developed, families obtained their fuel from wood cutters and candle makers. Eventual shifts in technologies and fuels bring us to the present time, where a plethora of firms use a variety of fuels to create a range of energy products used in heating, lighting, transportation, and manufacturing. Governments very early became involved in energy production in the management of forests, the development of rivers, and coal mining. Governments also sponsor expanded access to affordable energy and establish rules to mitigate negative effects of energy usage, principally the waste products of combustion.

Energy production has been a local matter for most of our history. But our modern world depends on a global energy market, where producers of fossil fuels ship their natural resources to consumers worldwide. The energy created through use of these fuels allows us to produce the food and goods we desire, but negative externalities abound. The by-products of mining and drilling pollute the lands and seas where these activities are conducted. Exhaust from open fires and power plants, from automobiles, trucks, and locomotives compromise air quality. Hydropower dams destroy fish habitats and historic alluvial deposits. Nuclear power plant waste remains hazardous for tens of thousands of years, much longer than any government has ever prevailed.

Limited international consensus exists on the stewardship of finite energy resources such as fossil fuels. No obvious path with equal opportunities for all people leads to an environmentally and economically sustainable energy supply into the distant future. Managing energy in a global context requires a sense of shared history, good political instincts, optimism about the future, and a willingness to potentially trade some measure of present comforts for long-term global stability.

This chapter begins by providing a public administration lens through which energy matters might be examined. It then offers basic information on energy production and consumption. The problems inherent in these processes offer certain agreed-upon targets for improvements that are noted. But impediments exist, creating doubts about our capacity to meet these targets. This leads to consideration of possible incremental remedies.

Examining Energy Policies in the Global Context

Energy fuels the economic engine of globalization. Students of administrative theory bring their knowledge of fundamental decision-making frameworks to energy-related controversies. Practitioners are pragmatic about accomplishing goals and managing for public benefit, and should not shy away from energy-related discussions, lest the middle ground be unrepresented.

Public administration, as an interdisciplinary field of study, integrates research across the social sciences, from sociology to economics to political science. Theoretical insights about policy making and human behavior provide a public management context for determining how to appropriately administer our energy resources. One involves public policy making and the power inherent to the party setting the agenda (Kingdon, 1984). Another derives from the study of rationality (Simon, 1947) and game theory economic modeling. The acting out in self-interest leads to a third insight, acknowledging that stakeholders and industrial energy consumers tasked with creating markets must be expected to promote positions favorable to their interests. This expression of self-interest rightly understood is quintessentially American (Tocqueville, 1994) in the belief that this self-interest works within democratic self-governance, but it is equally relevant in the global context.

The model of public policy developed by Kingdon (1984) revolves around four processes. First, one or more of the parties set the agenda. Next, alternatives are developed. From exploration of the alternatives, an authoritative choice is made. Finally, the decision is implemented. While this appears to be a linear model, in practice many factors alter the progress of these processes. Public and interpersonal communications among parties alter alliances; the press and other media may choose to highlight certain implications or outcomes, affecting public perception. Misunderstandings regarding funding or technology may prevent consideration of feasible alternatives.

The concept of bounded rationality considers human nature as the limiting feature of decision making. Each individual person faces cognitive limits in thinking about what choice to make. Each has limited capacity to execute a chosen action. These limitations provide the boundaries that reduce rational thinking and action. Without time or knowledge for complete analysis, this is not a wholly irrational approach. At some point in time a decision must be made, action must be taken regardless of further information that might exist and would alter the choices selected.

Game theory, as developed by economists in the 1950s and 1960s, simplifies transactions to core elements and allows for exploration of what constitute winning and losing positions. Simulations of potential exchanges provide a low-risk method to explore how people might actually respond to opportunities that are presented (John, 2003; Ederington, 2003). "Prisoner's dilemma" and its derivative, "tit for tat," share elements of information asymmetry, bargaining, and deal making central to economic and political negotiations. In these games, uncertainties that can mask underlying behaviors do not exist. The number of players, the rules, and possible outcomes are fixed and known. Games can represent actions between two players or several players. They may be linear (each person takes a turn) or simultaneous. Although real-world bargaining moves far beyond these straightforward, rule-based systems, and reintroduces uncertainty of outcomes, the knowledge gained from study of theoretical models assists us in investigating what types of conditions can favor good ongoing relationships between nations.

Policy making on energy involves a collection of experts and special interests. No one person or firm holds complete knowledge regarding energy production, consumption, markets, and mitigation. Wall Street investment firms employ analysts whose sole specialization might be natural gas, oil, or coal, political analysts who monitor instability in producer nations, and financial experts who work on the capitalization of large projects. Oil exploration firms rely on technicians and scientists with specialized skills. Environmental public interest organizations focus on collateral effects of fuel extraction, transportation, and consumption. These various interests often disagree on the validity or relevance of data. Even when the data is clear, they may argue over valid interpretation. Interest groups share publicly available data, collect proprietary information, and purchase data from one another at times. The information may then be processed through proprietary models with opaque rules and assumptions prior to presentation before public officials and decision makers. Policy makers must assess the relevance and validity of data, balance competing desires of interested parties, and determine constraints or incentives that will dynamically adjust the behaviors of the various interests in changing circumstances.

The Energy Production Framework

Although energy has its genesis in local production and consumption, the quantity of energy now required for large-scale industrial processes and human comfort has resulted in a global, inherently closed system, comprising fuels, consumption, accounting for imbalance between consumers and producers, and remediation of undesirable externalities. These elements tie the world together while also creating categorical labels such as "industrialized" that separate national fortunes and futures. This

Table 43.1 Top Five Importers and Exporters of Fossil Fuels

Exporters	*Percent*	*Importers*	*Percent*
Saudi Arabia	11.6	United States	17.2
Russia	11.6	Japan	12.9
Canada	5.6	Germany	7.0
Norway	5.3	Italy	5.2
Iran	4.5	South Korea	4.6
Percentage of Total Exports	38.6	Percentage of Total Imports	46.9

Source: UN 1995 Energy Statistics Yearbook, cited in Smith (1999).

interconnection crosses time as well as national boundaries, as production decisions today will affect where future generations can live, and how comfortable those lives may be.

Energy can be created from combustible fossil fuel (oil, coal, and natural gas) or from natural forces that are considered renewable (primarily falling water, to a lesser degree wind and sunshine). Neither type of energy source is evenly distributed across the world. The top five exporters of fossil fuels in 1995 (Smith, 1999, pp. 96–97) were Saudi Arabia, Russia, Canada, Norway, and Iran, comprising over one third of all exports. The top five importers were the United States, Japan, Germany, Italy, and South Korea, comprising nearly half of the world's imports of fossil fuels. Table 43.1 details these exports and imports.

In 1995, China's total energy consumption was 10 percent of the total world consumption, second only to the United States (27 percent), supplied by its domestic energy production, mainly powered by coal. As China's economy has grown, so has its energy consumption and imports. In 2003, China surpassed Japan as the second largest consumer of crude oil (Cordier & Gross, 2004).

Great uncertainty surrounds predictions of the stability and longevity of our energy system. For instance, fossil fuel production and consumption are affected by growth in demand, regional political instability, price controls, the logistics of shipping coal, oil, or natural gas, and new technologies for exploration, extraction, transportation, and transformation. These uncontrolled factors result in questionable assessments of how much energy potential can be extracted from existing resources.

Most depictions of energy production or consumption are specific to a particular question, showing growth in consumption over time or a flat ratio between production and proved reserves (an indicator of how long the *status quo*, fossil fuel based economic order can last). Although these charts are essential for day-to-day management of the energy infrastructure and markets, they provide little guidance for high-level policy design. Fewer analyses develop the interconnections between production and emissions, producer and consumer nations, present-day conservation and future prosperity, as the substantial uncertainties make these analyses speculative.

The U.S. Department of Energy's Energy Information Administration (EIA) 2002 annual energy report graphically portrays the flow of fuel energy in by source and consumption out by function, as shown in Figure 43.1. This visualization offers specific information useful for public policy dialogue. The viewer can clearly assess the degree of consumption dependent on various fuel sources, and thereby can begin to consider trade-offs between consumption and production.

The 413-page EIA report also extensively references U.S. fuel imports and global emissions of greenhouse gases. This information is useful in conceptualizing energy use as a cycle from creation of fuel, transformation, consumption, and renewal. The mass of information cannot be comprehensively mastered, and this adds to its frequent presentation in fragmented form, with a loss of connective narrative. Energy policy is rarely handled as a whole.

Most of the energy used on Earth originates from solar energy; this includes fossil fuels. Coal, oil, and natural gas are the pressure-generated decayed remnants of ancient forests, representing a half-billion years of stored sunshine. Rapid consumption of this energy store means that at some future point it will no longer be available. Just how soon the planet will deplete its fossil fuel source varies, depending on how the rate of consumption might be altered by upward shifts in pricing. Proved reserves and consumption shifts may result in fossil fuels remaining the leading source of energy for another half-century (Smil, 2003, p. 211), though some estimates suggest much longer availability of certain fuels (Reardon (2004), suggests a 260-year supply of U.S. coal at current consumption rate).

In the mid-20th century, scientists and policy makers thought they had found the solution to the depletion of fossil fuel sources and the polluting by-products of combustion. Following the creation of atomic weapons and their role in concluding World War II, the United States sought to develop atomic energy for peacetime uses. In 1954, the chairman of the U.S. Atomic Energy Commission, Lewis L. Strauss, suggested in a speech to science writers that someday electric power would be "too cheap to meter" (Canadian Nuclear Society, 2004). Nuclear power, unlike fossil fuels, harnesses the internal energy of matter, freeing this source from the problems inherent in the finite amount of fossil material. Additionally, the immediate waste product from a nuclear power plant is heated water, something far more benign than the sulfurous rain that falls over much of the coal-powered industrialized world.

Unfortunately, nuclear combustion creates another waste product, spent nuclear fuel. Although not an immediate problem, this material requires

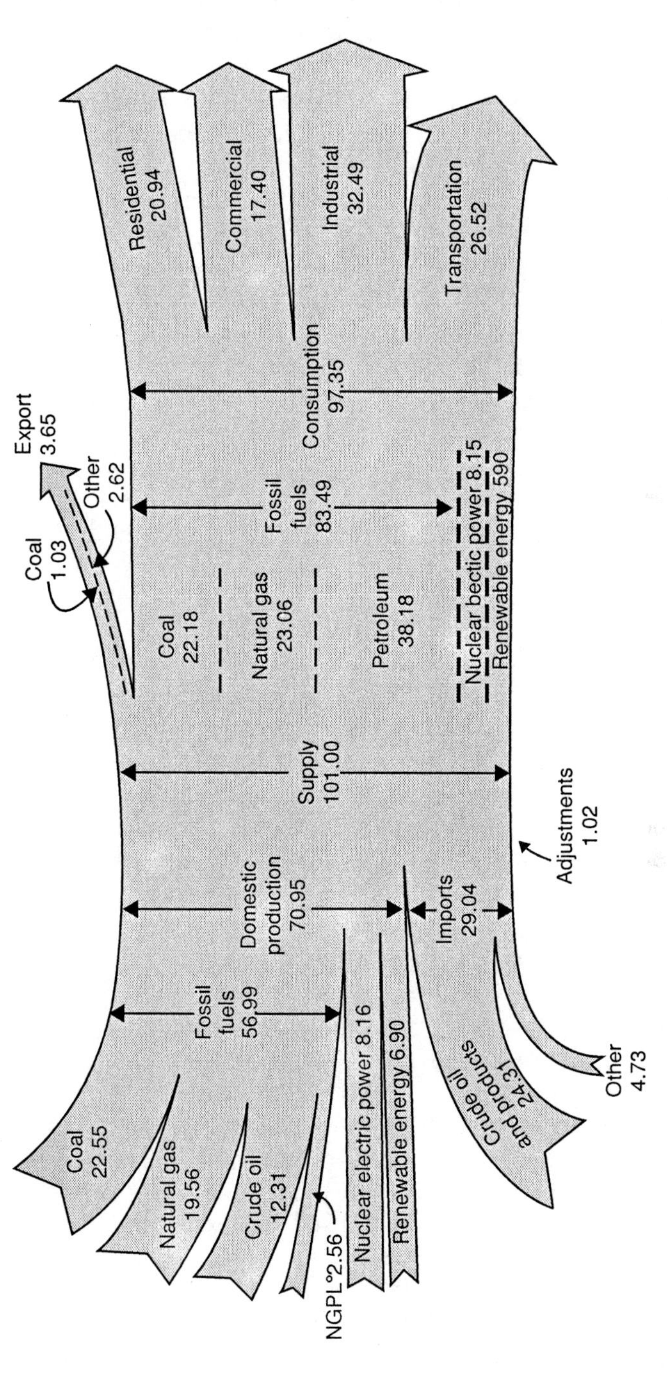

Figure 43.1 Energy production and consumption in the United States. (Energy Information Administration (2002)).

long-term secure storage. Spent fuel is one type of intergenerational problem in our global energy production model, adding to the long-term problem of the ultimate exhaustion of fossil fuels.

Equal access to energy sources implies equal opportunity for health and prosperity related to clean water, manufactured goods, adequate heat and lighting. But access to fuel sources does not eliminate imbalance in consumption benefits. In its 1997 report, the World Bank quantifies this imbalance. Even excluding low-efficiency traditional fuel sources such as firewood and dung in common use in developing nations, high-income economies receive three times the benefit per consumed fuel equivalent of low- or middle-income economies (World Bank, 1997, pp. 228–229). Consumption is the topic of our next section.

The Energy Consumption Framework

The value of fuels in their transformation into heat, light, and energy cannot be overstated. Ralph Waldo Emerson wrote in 1860 that "Coal is a portable climate" (Emerson, 2000; quoted widely, for example, Freese, 2003, p. 10) The consumption of fuel powers modern factories, personal and mass transportation, and allows us to make the most remote locations habitable. "Electricity is an essential of life. Electricity and water really do have life and death consequences." So said California governor Gray Davis in the midst of its energy crisis (Public Broadcasting System, 2001).

The amount of energy the California consumer may consume at the lowest rate is far more than what is allocated in other parts of the world. In the same interview, Governor Davis states "The rate increase I propose basically exempts 50 percent of the population because they're the most efficient users of power — using just their baseline amount." Baseline is a legal designation that does not require any frugality of consumption. Rather, it represents in summer "50 to 60 percent of average residential consumption" and in winter "60 to 70 percent of the average residential winter consumption" (California Public Utilities Commission, 2004). This translates to an average of approximately 12,000 kilowatt-hours per household per year, more than twice the world average, according to the Central Intelligence Agency (CIA) World Factbook (Central Intelligence Agency, 2004; also available with graphs at Nationmaster.com, 2004). The United States could cut its consumption in half, and still rank with other highly industrialized and prosperous nations from the United Kingdom to Russia to Hong Kong and South Korea.

For most consumers, two fuels dominate everyday life. The first is gasoline or diesel for personal and business vehicles and equipment. The second is electricity. Gasoline, diesel, and natural gas are all primary fuels modified to meet certain regulatory and technical constraints (such as adding a scent to natural gas). Electricity is not a primary fuel, but rather is a product created by generation equipment that consumes fuel and energizes the electric grid that runs to homes and businesses.

Marketing efforts for clean or green electric power popularize the notion that a consumer can choose to buy a particular type of energy. Consumers pay a surcharge on their bill, either a set fee or a price per kilowatt-hour. This surcharge is earmarked to defray the extra expense for the utility to either buy renewable energy power from a third party or construct its own renewable generation.

In practice, short of installing a fuel cell, heat pump, or solar panels, the consumer receives electrons no different than neighboring properties. All electrons are the same.

Consumption in the industrialized world, for commercial and private use, far outstrips that of the less developed nations. The economic value of this energy in industrialized countries is also multiples above that of less developed nations. The lack of adequate, affordable access to energy increases disparity and inequality between nations.

Daily consumption in the industrial world is far removed from its short- and long-term consequences. A person turning on a light may not know whether the moment's electricity is derived from gas, water, wind, or coal. Nor does the consumer experience a direct cost for the consumption. Energy is produced in bulk, often far from population centers. It may be bought and resold, then packaged by the utility with surcharges to cover transmission and distribution expenses, debt service, and many types of mandated or utility-specific programs. Further clouding the costs and consequences of consumption, the consumer may opt for levelized billing to smooth the peaks and valleys of seasonal demands. In this case, any action taken by the consumer to moderate use has no direct impact on his bill for many months. It is not surprising under these conditions that consumers make no connection between their individual life choices and the depletion of nonrenewable sources of energy and the creation of negative environmental impacts.

No apparent public value is derived from consumption beyond what is useful and necessary. Yet in a consumption-oriented society, nearly all incentives are geared toward increased consumption and very little thought is given to increasing use only when cost-effective, including the costs of mitigating externalities. As many of the increases are very small, the individual decisions do not face neutral examination. As an example, public washrooms in the United States are increasingly automated, with sensors that turn lights and faucets on and off as needed. Along with other objects in washrooms, paper towel dispensers are also automated; they now will dispense a few inches of toweling when a hand is waved in front of the device. This replaces the manual effort of pressing down a lever. A person's manual effort derives its energy from a renewable resource — food. The automated effort requires a reduction in our half-billion year carbon store.

Standard cost–benefit analysis cannot stop these types of mindless and arguably unnecessary projects that replace human-powered systems with fossil-fueled ones. Cost–benefit analysis fails because it considers only whether the benefits of the replacement exceed the direct cost of the project. At best they might include the anticipated cost of operating the new environment for the estimated life of the equipment. At worst, modifications like the towel dispenser are rolled into the overall project cost. Intangibles, such as the esthetic ambience of an environment, may carry more weight than a minor increase in a monthly energy bill. In no case are externalities included, especially if the externalities are not to be paid for by the project owner.

Motivating System Improvements

With this degree of disconnect between production and consumption, compelling motivation is required. The world risks rapidly consuming the remainder of fossil fuels, dealing with the consequences only after the opportunity to use them for the highest value has been lost. Two motivating factors are described here. Negative externalities, such as acid rain, global warming, and nuclear waste are obvious indicators that mankind must exercise more care in the creation and utilization of energy. Closer linkage between the cost of bulk production and end use payment for energy offers another signal to connect our individual use and quality of life issues worldwide.

Fuel combustion produces undesirable environmental impacts. Acid rain describes the polluted precipitation created when moisture combines with sulfur dioxide or nitrogen oxide emitted as by-products of coal-based electric generation or industrial smelting. These emissions travel far from the point of origin — acid rain in Canada is largely derived from U.S. operations. Studies suggest extensive forest damage from the acidic precipitation, from trout streams in Pennsylvania and sugar maples in Maine to the Black Forest in Germany.

All fossil fuels, including clean natural gas, produce carbon dioxide as a combustion by-product. "Climate change" is one of a set of terms — "greenhouse effect" and "global warming" are two alternatives — that describe a rise in average temperature of approximately one degree attributed in part to the atmospheric buildup of fossil fuel combustion gases (Desombre, 2004). The precise contribution to this warming from energy production is disputed, as are both the cost of reducing these emissions and the benefits to be gained from reducing them. U.S. emissions dwarf most other nations. The United States emits more than all of western Europe and exceeds the combined emissions of Africa, Central and South America, and the Middle East. Figure 43.2 graphically compares emissions since 1980.

Climate change is an impact endured globally whereas the benefits of energy use are experienced locally, creating an ethical imbalance (Gardiner, 2004). The Kyoto Protocol was developed to address this problem on a global basis.

Once considered the solution to the problems associated with fossil fuels, nuclear energy has stumbled in the United States with its substantial fossil fuel reserves. The early promise of nuclear technologies resulted in extensive commitments to build large reactors for steam-generated electricity. Technical problems emerged in managing large amounts of radioactive fuel, irradiated water, and other objects in contact with the fuel. An overheated reactor and shutdown of the nuclear plant at Three Mile Island in 1979 was followed by the explosion at Chernobyl in 1986 that irradiated the Ukraine, Belarus, a large area of eastern Europe and Scandinavia. In the 1980s, plant construction problems resulted in billions of dollars in cost overruns. Voters in Sacramento, California, convinced the municipal utility board to shutter their 900-MW nuclear power plant after a series of rate increases, all resulting from plant management problems. Despite these troubles, nuclear power still provides 20 percent of American electricity; worldwide, 441 generators in 30 countries produce 16 percent of electricity.

Beyond the costs and complexity of plant operations, nuclear fission creates highly radioactive waste: the degraded fuel, the water that cools fuel rods and other materials that come in contact with the fuel. The U.S. government has the task of managing waste from commercial and government reactors. It is also responsible, through its Atoms for Peace program, to bring back to the United States waste products from reactors overseas, as

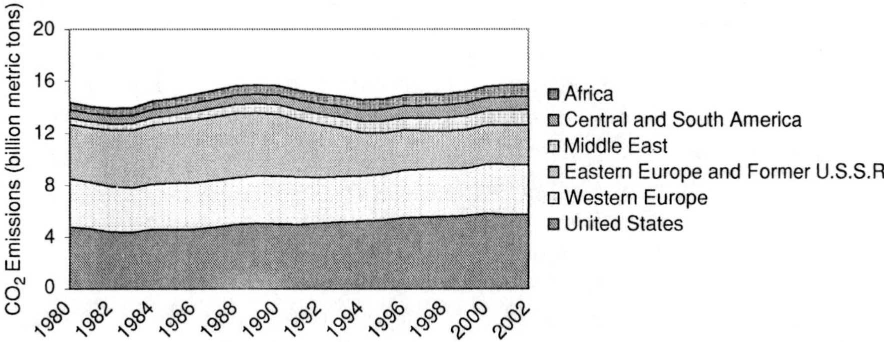

Figure 43.2 U.S. contribution to total carbon dioxide emissions, 1980–2002. (From Energy Information Administration (2002)).

part of efforts to prevent nuclear weapon proliferation. Yucca Mountain, Nevada has been selected as the site for the national high-level nuclear waste repository. Hardened steel and titanium casks filled with radioactive material will be placed end to end in chambers covering over 1000 acres up to 1600 feet underground; waste heat from atomic decay will raise the chamber temperature above the boiling point of water for hundreds to thousands of years. It will be filled to capacity — 70,000 metric tons of radioactive heavy metal — before 2035; at that time the site can be sealed or left open and actively managed (U.S. Department of Energy, 2001). In its technical analyses of the site, the Department of Energy has constructed a set of scenarios to evaluate risks to receptors on the surface. Only one scenario involves human intervention, and in that case it is inadvertent, the risk of drilling into the radioactive waste. A 2002 update to the plan estimates this scenario is unlikely for 10,000 years. The update did not address intentional efforts to breach the containment.

Challenges in Creating a Bright Energy Future

A bright and equitable energy future is possible. A social stigma against waste could significantly alter consumption patterns, especially in the United States. Government standards could increase fuel efficiency; incentives could be enhanced to speed replacement of aging power plants — ranging from 30 to 100 years old — with cleaner, high-efficiency generation. Prices could better reflect the cost of consumer choices. There are challenges to this future: regulatory co-optation by interested parties, ideological resistance to solutions, loss of public support through poor conceptualization of challenges and solutions, and resistance to the trade-offs required (Hoffert et al., 2002).

Co-optation is the subsumation of new external elements into policy-making processes to prevent those elements from becoming a threat to the organization (Selznick, 1948). In the context of energy and globalization, this is evident in producers desiring to continue operating their businesses as they see fit, and in consumers maintaining their existing habits. Recent efforts by the environmental community to increase vehicle fuel efficiency as part of an omnibus energy bill failed. Both producers (automakers) and affected consumers (owners of large sports utility vehicles or SUVs) lobbied Congress against the efficiency standard.

Ideological resistance takes many forms. In 1998, the United States signed the Kyoto Protocol, but later withdrew. President Bush stated "America's unwillingness to embrace a flawed treaty should not be read by our friends and allies as any abdication of responsibility" (White House, 2001). The Bush administration felt the protocol unfairly disadvantaged the

United States, and adopted instead a reduced set of voluntary goals focused on modest reductions less likely to have negative economic impact. For the United States to achieve the emissions goal of the protocol, the EIA estimated that coal generation would have to be cut somewhere between 18 and 77 percent; to pay for the changes in generation source fuel, the price of electricity would need to rise somewhere between 17 and 83 percent (Energy Information Administration, 1998). The EIA also noted that the 1990 emissions benchmark would provide for substantial economic growth opportunities in the former Soviet Union states since industrial operations were scaled back substantially after the Soviet dissolution and subsequent economic downturn. In the United States, meeting the reduction target would require major restrictions in energy production, negatively affecting the national economy of expensive purchase of emission permits from other nations.

The existing energy system persists in the absence of informed public interest and discourse. Virtual mountains of information on energy production and consumption are publicly available, but this data is difficult to understand. What has a person to think in seeing a statement such as this one from the 2002 Energy Information Administration, 2002 Annual Energy Report: "Renewable energy consumption rebounded . . . from a decade-low level of 5.3 quadrillion Btu in 2001." Does this statement suggest something good happened? How much is a quadrillion Btu, and what difference would it make if the number were 5.2 quadrillion? Is this renewable energy number up because all types of fuel consumption are up, and so it merely reflects increasing consumption in general? Obscure, opaque information advantages the special interests.

The Bush Administration reaction to the Kyoto Protocol demonstrates one challenge to developing a beneficial and sustainable energy future. Many of the consequences of decisions regarding energy production and consumption accrue to future generations. Many actions have uncertain outcomes. Should we conserve more today, to the degree we become uncomfortable, when we cannot guarantee that future generations will be equally frugal? Can we assume that future scientific knowledge and technological advances will solve the problems we cannot address today? If scientists calculate there is a 10 percent chance of a bad outcome, does this not suggest a 90 percent chance everything will be alright, so is optimism not warranted?

Some challenges involve unfathomable timeframes. Nuclear waste decays slowly; the Yucca Mountain repository scenarios attempt to estimate conditions for 30,000 years, a span three times as long as mankind's recorded history. The carbon stored in prehistoric forests represents a half-billion years of sunshine — we do not have any concept of sustainability on that scale.

Can Incremental Remedies Help?

Incrementalism offers an explanation of how policies are established (Lindblom, 1959) and how managers reach goals (Behn, 1988). Whether following a method of successive comparisons or groping along and using feedback to make adjustments, much international effort centers on small acts toward a larger goal. In the case of global energy policy, large acts abound, perhaps due to the scale of the problems. The Kyoto Protocol combines actions from scores of nations toward the same end. Deregulation of electric systems in many countries has resulted in international conglomerates.

Given the challenges in direct actions to reduce or even eliminate externalities (Wirth et al., 2003), can small changes result in major improvements? Evidence from past efforts provides mixed guidance on the potential of incremental changes to the energy system.

In the wake of the 1974 Organization of Petroleum Exporting Countries (OPEC) oil embargo, the United States passed the Energy Policy Conservation Act of 1975, which included the establishment of corporate average fuel economy (CAFE) standards. Efforts to update the CAFE standard to reflect a quarter century of energy efficiency research have not succeeded (Nadel, 2003, pp. 11–12). The standard has resulted in a constant supply of higher efficiency small vehicles; consumer demand is higher for larger cars, especially low-efficiency SUVs, so automakers must sell the small vehicles at reduced profit margin to meet the target overall fleet mileage. Unintended consequences include large disparities of weight between the two types of vehicles, resulting in the perception that the smaller cars are unreasonably unsafe.

The Public Utility Regulatory Policies Act of 1978 (PURPA) included a small section promoting the development of independent power. Between 1978 and 2000, a large portion of incremental generation was developed by independent power producers, reducing utilities' base expenditures on which rates are set and profits are guaranteed. The unexpected emergence of independent generation played a large role in the federal government decision to open up transmission lines so generators could sell directly to customers other than utilities, allowing large customers to substantially reduce their electric bills.

In California, the 1996 legislation that changed the electric system completely and suddenly rather than incrementally did not succeed. Multiple factors have been implicated in the crisis, among them reluctance by lawmakers and officials to incrementally alter the rules that had been established. Under the rules, several anticompetitive behaviors were allowable and companies that exploited these weaknesses were able to push the price for electricity so high that two of three investor-owned utilities became insolvent.

Effects of Energy Policy on Economic Globalization

Responses to environmental impacts of energy choices can range from the government-directed regulatory and tax strategy used in Germany, market mechanisms such as emission caps and trading favored by U.S. administrations, or the blend of these basic strategies adopted in Japan (Schreurs, 2003). In the United States, the federal government has also periodically set national standards, such as the CAFE standard for gasoline consumption, to spur innovative technological solutions.

Coordinating cross-national structures differ in structure from nation-states (O'Toole & Hanf, 2002). The United Nations, World Bank, European Union, the OPEC, each creates its own bureaucracy and rules. Multinational private corporations can move headquarters from the country of origin to an alternate state with more liberal rules and tax policies. Organizations and firms interact with traditional national interests and involve themselves in interlocking fashion. Functional initiatives such as the Kyoto Protocol include nations, intergovernmental organizations (IGOs), and non-governmental organizations (NGOs) as parties to the discussion (Kyoto Protocol, ND).

Conclusion

Under pressure or in crisis, governments and organizations can make substantial changes. Globalization and the shift of manufacturing operations around the world bring opportunities to upgrade the energy infrastructure of developing nations. Mismatch between production capacity and consumption requirements in these nations can disadvantage consumers over business interests, who often deal directly with large utilities, the government, or international organizations. The question is how much pressure will be required before the needs of the consumer are given adequate priority.

Beyond production and consumption, the negative externalities impact all nations. Whereas most nations actively support efforts to develop international consensus on solutions, other nations, particularly the United States, appear to face short-term losses in what looks like a zero-sum game, resulting in reluctance to participate fully. Rather than withdraw from the difficult bargaining and passively hope for the best or wait for system failure, iterative negotiating cycles also are possible. Past efforts show many different approaches can effect major shifts and incremental improvements.

References

Behn, R.D. (1988). "Management by groping along." *Journal of Policy Analysis and Management*, 7(4): 643–663.

BP (2004). *Statistical Review of World Energy*, 53rd edition. London: BP Distribution Services. Also online at http://www.bp.com/statisticalreview2004 (July 31, 2004).

California Public Utilities Commission (2004). "Baseline allowances for electricity and natural gas." Online at http://www.cpuc.ca.gov/static/industry/electric/faq/baseline.htm (July 31, 2004).

Canadian Nuclear Society (2004). "Too cheap to meter?" Online at http://www.cns-snc.ca/media/toocheap/toocheap.html (April 15, 2004).

Central Intelligence Agency (2004). *The World Factbook 2004*. Washington: Central Intelligence Agency.

Cordier, J. and M. Gross (2004). "China's heavy hand moving markets." *Futures*, 33(9): 42–45.

DeSombre, E.R. (2004). "Global warming: more common than tragic." *Ethics & International Affairs*, 18(1): 41–46.

Ederington, J. (2003). "Policy linkage and uncertainty in international agreements." *Economic Inquiry*, 41(2): 305–317.

Emerson, R.W. (2000). *The Essential Writings of Ralph Waldo Emerson*. New York: Modern Library.

Energy Information Administration (1998). "What does the Kyoto Protocol mean to U.S. energy markets and the U.S. economy?" Online at http://www.eia.doe.gov/oiaf/kyoto/kyotobtxt.html (February 28, 2004).

Energy Information Administration (2002). *Annual Energy Review*. Washington, D.C. Online at http://www.eia.doe.gov/cneaf/electricity/epa/epa_sum.html (July 29, 2004).

Freese, B. (2003). *Coal: A Human History*. Cambridge: Perseus Publishing.

Gardiner, S.M. (2004). "Ethics and global climate change." *Ethics*, 114(3): 555–600.

Hoffert, M.I., K. Caldeira, G. Benford, D.R. Criswell, C. Green, H. Herzog, A.K. Jain, H.S. Kheshgi, K.S. Lackner, J.S. Lewis, H.D. Lightfoot, W. Manheimer, J.C. Mankins, M.E. Mauel, L.J. Perkins, M.E. Schlesinger, T. Volk, and T.M.L. Wigley (2002). "Advanced technology paths to global climate stability: energy for a greenhouse planet." *Science*, 298: 981–987.

John, P. (2003). "Is there life after policy streams, advocacy coalitions, and punctuations: using evolutionary theory to explain policy change?" *Policy Studies Journal*, 31(4): 481–498.

Kingdon, J. (1984). *Agendas, Alternatives, and Public Policies*. Boston: Little, Brown.

Kyoto Protocol (ND). Online at http://unfccc.int/resource/convkp.html (April 15, 2004).

Lindblom, C. (1959). "The science of 'muddling through'." *Public Administration Review*, 19(2): 79–88.

Nadel, S. (2003). "The federal energy policy act of 2003 and its implications for energy efficiency program efforts." Washington, D.C.: American Council for an Energy-Efficient Economy.

Nationmaster.com (2004). Online at http://www.nationmaster.com/graph-T/ene_e-le_con_cap (July 31, 2004).

O'Toole, L.J., Jr. and K.I. Hanf (2002). "American public administration and impacts of international governance." *Public Administration Review*, 62(Special Issue): 158–169.

Public Broadcasting System (2001). "Frontline: blackout!" Broadcast June 5. Transcript and supplemental materials available online at http://www.pbs.org/wgbh/pages/frontline/shows/blackout (March 8, 2004).

Reardon, J. (2004). "An institutionalist critique of the Bush administration's energy policy." *Journal of Economic Issues*, 38(2): 449–457.

Schreurs, M.A. (2003). "Divergent paths: environmental policy in Germany, the United States, and Japan." *Environment*, 45(8): 9–17.

Selznick, P. (1948). "Foundations of the theory of organization." *American Sociological Review*, 13: 25–35.

Simon, H.A. (1947). *Administrative Behavior.* New York: Macmillan.

Smil, V. (2003). *Energy at the Crossroads: Global Perspectives and Uncertainties.* Cambridge: MIT Press.

Smith, D. (1999). *The State of the World Atlas*, 6th edition. London: Penguin Reference.

de Tocqueville, A. (1994). *Democracy in America.* New York: Alfred Knopf. Also online at http://xroads.virginia.edu/~HYPER/DETOC/toc_indx.html (July 29, 2004).

U.S. Department of Energy (2001). "Yucca Mountain science and engineering report: executive summary. DOE/RW-0539." Washington, D.C.: U.S. Department of Energy, Office of Civilian Radioactive Waste Management. Also online (2002 revision) at http://www.ocrwm.doe.gov/documents/ser_b/index.htm (July 7, 2004).

White House (2001). "President Bush discusses global climate change." Press Release, June 11. Online at http://www.whitehouse.gov/news/releases/2001/06/20010611-2.html (April 16, 2004).

Wirth, T.E., C.B. Gray, and J.D. Podesta (2003). "The future of energy policy." *Foreign Affairs*, 82(4): 132–155.

World Bank (1997). *World Development Report 1997: The State in a Changing World.* Oxford: Oxford University Press.

Chapter 44

Globalization within Countries in Conflict: The Energy Company Case

Mantha Vlahos Mehallis

CONTENTS

Introduction

All countries wrestle with the amount of international trade that is best for them. What are their competitive advantages? What and how much should they import and export? And with whom should they trade? Countries must foresee the potential profits in trading on a global scale to develop strategies in that direction. International opportunities must be perceived as greater than domestic ones, for companies to divert their resources to the foreign sector. Due to the Internet and modern telecommunications, business transactions can occur almost instantaneously around the world. In the 21st century, what happens economically in one region of the world has an impact on the economy of other regions of the world. It is virtually impossible for actions in one company in the economy not to have an impact on an entire business sector.

The chief executive officer (CEO) of Hewlett-Packard (HP), Carleton Fiorina, in the letter to shareholders, appearing in the Hewlett-Packard 2001 annual report to shareholders (2002), stated that the events of September 11th, which caused a recession in the United States along with economic declines in Europe and Japan, resulted in a global economic slowdown. This and the collapse of the dot-com sector in the United States caused a significant drop in information technology (IT) spending, and, subsequently, a major negative impact on HP's 2001 fiscal results. This demonstrates the impact of the global economy on a single company, albeit a company doing business in 120 countries throughout the world.

Traditional literature in the field of international business management has explicated the tenets of international business. In the context of the external business environment, the social aspects of the society are investigated in terms of values, ethics, religious beliefs, languages, and ethnic differences. Generally companies are cautioned to understand the societal aspects of the country into which they are going to conduct business. Companies must identify the "host country" (the one they are going into for international business) that appears to be most likely to provide the business opportunity to make considerable profit, beyond that made domestically.

Although the more recent literature (Weidenbaum, 2004, pp. 156–170) discusses the impact of crises (natural or human-made) on doing business, it has not paid much attention to the impact of internal conflicts among local populations that exist before the company goes into the region. This chapter outlines how globalization of companies is impacted when the company expands into countries with regional conflicts, which directly affect the ability to "do business." To analyze the factors that impinge upon the global expansion, the chapter addresses the concepts and definitions of country conflicts, dimensions of conflicts at the regional country level, and the factors creating such conflicts. As an example, two energy sector cases are analyzed: one in the Niger Delta and the other in Sudan. The impact is reviewed from the perspective of the government and the public administration, the global company, the competitors, the non-governmental organizations (NGOs), and the public, in general. The primary thesis espoused herein is that the business community must be in synchronization with the government and the public administration in the global context, especially in the realm of values and social responsibility.

The large multinational corporations (MNCs) and multilateral institutions have sometimes unwittingly contributed to the continuation and sometimes to the extension of strife in countries, particularly developing countries, by encouraging economic expansion while assuming that the social and human condition will improve as the companies and the governments become wealthier. To quote Farazmand (2001, p. 112), "Much of the historical progress toward the betterment of human conditions is now expected to be lost, and people everywhere have become disposable commodities or tools of the new globalization of capital in search of rapid growth in profits."

Specialized competitive advantages differ among countries. The Porter Diamond was developed as a model by Porter (1998) to identify the conditions that are important for competitive superiority: demand conditions; factor conditions; related and supporting industries; and firm strategy, structure, and rivalry. In most cases, all of the four dimensions must be favorable for an industry to attain global supremacy. Although sometimes entrepreneurs are able to be successful without having all four dimensions be positive, it is essential that companies develop and sustain a competitive advantage. To do so, they must have positive firm strategy and structure, and not much rivalry of any significance among competitors.

Dimensions of the Global Company

Since the classical study of management began with Taylor, the "father" of modern management, in the late 1800s with the Industrial Revolution, there have been several management models in place to define the organization. The models have evolved over time from the classical market approach to the managerial model, or to the one focused on social environment. The following is a brief description of them:

- Classical market model — This is the original concept of business organization based on the British economy of the 19th century. Competition was mainly concentrated on price (Marshall, 1949, pp. 240–313).
- Managerial model — This acknowledges the separation of ownership from management. It was the dominant business mode in the first half of the 20th century and is still on the business scene. The manager is viewed as a trustee for various groups of stakeholders;

shareholders, employees, customers, and local communities (Berle and Means, 1991).

- Social environmental model — This is the model where the company reacts to the total socioeconomic environment and not merely to markets. The corporation is affected by political forces, public opinion, and government pressures. Management is primarily concerned about shareholders as a group.

The social environmental model is the one in play with most of the companies in the energy sector. As a result, the large companies, or MNCs, seem to be "servants of multiple interests." These interests, including governments and special interest groups of NGOs, such as the aid organizations and some religious groups, usually have some claim against the company and the necessary power to pursue it. This is often done through "stockholder initiatives, collective bargaining, taxation, regulation, private litigation, public pressure, and marketplace influence." No company is in a position to ignore public opinion and expectations without suffering the loss of sales and consumer goodwill (Preston, 1986, pp. 25–26).

Organization for global business operations is another factor that must be taken into account. Often companies take their basic business model and use it like a "cookie cutter" in other regions of the world. Instead, they need to organize the company so that the international and global operations are managed from a multicultural perspective. For example, if a company considers itself to be a global company, it should not have a board of directors and top management team that are all comprised of individuals from the home country. Such segregation can often lead to a misinterpretation of events in the host country and an underestimation of the potential negative impact. Such was the experience of Talisman Energy Ltd. of Canada, which will be discussed later.

Causes and Consequences of Conflict

Cross-cultural friction is not unusual across country borders and between businesses. When dealing with cultures that are considerably different from the United States or North American culture, they can be vastly different and can lead to disastrous consequences. An example was detailed in *The Economist* (1984, p. 67). An American oil company had set up a drilling operation on a Pacific island and hired local labor. About a week later, all the foremen were found lined up on the floor with their throats slashed. Unfortunately for all involved, the company did not understand until it was too late that hiring younger men as foremen to boss older workers was not acceptable in a society where age indicates status. The company had used its own cultural criteria for recruitment without fully understanding the culture in which it was doing business.

Another, not so drastic, example was espoused by Leiber (1997, pp. 195–197) in *Fortune*. British Airways spent approximately $108 million to change the colors on its planes' tailfins from those depicting the British flag to the multiple ethnic designs from around the world. The international community seemed quite pleased with this gesture; however, British business passengers, who comprised the core customers of the airline, were outraged. Within two years, the company returned to the original British flag tailfins.

The management literature expresses concern for businesses that can possibly get affected with cultural clashes due to cross-border issues. The literature mentions that it is the manager's role to identify cross-cultural issues and to find out the cause of irritations. Schneider and Barsoux (2003, p. 10) state that, "To capture the potential benefits while limiting the potential misunderstanding, managers must be prepared to articulate how they see their own culture and to recognize how others may experience it." Further, they suggest that it is not only the behavior, values, and beliefs that differ across cultures but also the importance with which a particular value, belief, or behavior is perceived as sacred in one culture and yet considered irrelevant in another. The two examples given earlier depict this issue. Age and its seniority were considered sacred in the Pacific island culture, whereas in the United States older age is not revered and, often, not even respected. Similarly with the British flag on the plane tailfins, the British customers held this symbol of pride in their country at a much higher level than any attempt to patronize international constituencies.

Gladwin and Walter (1980) recommend that the importance of the stakes involved and the power should determine the degree of assertiveness, whereas the nature of the relationship and the interest should determine the amount of cooperativeness. In what are considered individualist countries, where power is unequal and not shared such as in France, Nigeria, and the Sudan, conflict is likely to be managed initially through avoidance and then by confrontation or force. This normally results in a violent reaction or counterforce. In countries where power is supposed to be shared equally and there is much concern for the quality of relationship and mutual gain, like Sweden, Canada, and the United States, conflict resolution is more likely to occur through collaboration. Accommodation is based on interdependence and mutual obligation. When perceived power is low, the subordinate either expects or is expected to submit to the boss. Japan is an example of such a culture wherein the buyer is obliged to take care of the seller. Avoidance of conflict is often used when power is low, not much if any mutual gain is perceived or where there is not very much interest in pursuing a relationship. In negotiations, Japanese will use silence (avoidance) as a tactic to get Americans to agree. They also find it very important to "save face" in any relationship and, so, will avoid any public conflict (Black and Mendenhall, 1993, pp. 49–59).

Individualist cultures are more likely to push for or assert their own ideas. They assume that conflict of interests is inherent in any negotiations. Specifically, negotiations are seen as a zero-sum game. There is a winner and a loser, i.e., this is distributive versus integrative which aims for mutual gain. The amount of resources available, or "the pie," is perceived as fixed with the prime objective to get as much of it as possible. The goal is to win at all costs rather than to be concerned about longer-range relationships (Schneider and Barsoux, 2003, pp. 236–237).

The causes and consequences of conflict have direct effect on the energy sector company cases discussed later. Specifically, in each case there is a collaborative, accommodating type culture as the heritage of Royal Dutch Shell and Talisman Energy. On the opposite side, there are countries as defined by the governments of Nigeria (the Niger Delta region) and the Sudan who are individualist cultures. These governments tend to avoid conflict, allow conflict and the apparent denial of it to fester, and then move directly to violence. The specific consequences to the companies and their respective globalization are discussed later.

Globalization of the Energy Sector

The demand for energy results from possession of wealth and from promoting and generating wealth. Thus, energy has become a strategic factor in global geopolitics (Weidenbaum, 2004, p. 231). Per capita consumption of energy in the United States is approximately 70 percent more than in other developed countries. Geographically there is an incongruity between the location of energy supplies and where the consumers live (demand). No nation, except for former Soviet Russia, is both a major oil exporter and a user. Energy is central to national power: political, economic, and military. Governments can fairly easily threaten the orderly process of producing, distributing, and using energy.

The degree to which major industrialized nations import energy from unstable regions globally is projected to increase in the future. The impact of regional conflicts is illustrated by examples in the recent past, such as the Organization of the Petroleum-Exporting Countries (OPEC) embargo in the 1970s and the Iran–Iraq war in the 1980s. Industrial production was reduced, inflation increased, and output and employment among the large industrial nations declined. The Gulf War in the 1990s demonstrated the geopolitical dimensions of the supply–demand situation in the energy sector. If Iraq was not pushed back out of Kuwait, it would have possibly moved into Saudi Arabia and changed the balance of political and economic power in the region (U.S. CIA, 2001). However, many of the Middle East countries are often at odds between what is best for them and their economies and what is strategically best for the United States. More often, the two are not synonymous.

Energy security is realized through measures that are taken to increase the economy's ability to be flexible and prepared to respond to supply shocks and volatile price changes. According to Toman (2002, pp. 20–27), some of the actions to reduce a nation's vulnerability to aggressive energy geopolitical pressures include the following:

1. Expansion of emergency stockpiles, such as strategic petroleum reserve
2. Reliance on a greater variety of standard as well as nonconventional energy sources to reduce vulnerability to supply disruptions in any individual region or production category
3. Developing the flexibility to switch quickly to alternative fuels
4. Maintaining an effective economic stabilization mechanism, comprising rapid adjustments to monetary and fiscal policies that can help to cope with large and disruptive shifts in energy prices

While discussing the geopolitical energy vulnerabilities, Weidenbaum (2004, p. 238) says, "Disrupting the oil shipped from Saudi Arabia, the top exporting nation, could provoke price increases and production shutdowns substantial enough to trigger a widespread recession. By 2020, one half of estimated global energy demand will be met from countries that pose a high risk of internal instability." Nunn et al. (2000, p. xvii) state that comprehensive energy policies need to be developed and, in so doing, nations should "recognize the domestic weaknesses and fragility of some of the major energy exploring nations."

The Impact of Conflict on Globalization of the Energy Sector

The Government and the Public Administration Perspective

Generally the countries with former colonial-style governments and dictatorships are the countries with command economies. A command economy exists in a country where all economic activity, including policies, is determined by the central government. In other words, the resources are owned and controlled by the public sector. In market economies, such as the

United States, resources are allocated and controlled by the consumers or the private sector. A mixed economy consists of different degrees of ownership and control, such as China that owns mostly everything but which is transitioning to a more market-oriented economy. In fact, economies are not generally mutually exclusive in terms of public versus private ownership, but they do have a preponderance of one or the other (Daniels et al., 2004, p. 115).

The Global Company Perspective

Companies conduct business internationally for access to production factors or demand conditions. Factor conditions (production factors) include resources (human, physical, and fiscal), knowledge, and infrastructure (Porter, 1988, pp. 74–75). Physical resources include transportation methods to get goods to and from the market (e.g., roads, waterways, ports, rail, and air), natural resources (minerals), weather, agricultural goods, energy, and communications. Demand conditions (market potential) include three dimensions: (1) the composition of home demand (or the nature of buyer needs); (2) the size and pattern of growth of home demand; and (3) the internationalization of demand (Porter, 1980, p. 86).

Composition of demand is defined as the "quality of demand," and the "quantity of demand" is defined by the size of the demand. Factor conditions are critical for investments made for the production of goods, but demand conditions are critical for market-seeking investments. Factor and demand conditions make up the location-specific advantage that a country has to offer the domestic and the foreign investors.

The size of demand is the gross national product (GNP), which is used to classify countries. Countries with high populations and high per capita GNP have the most desirable market potential. Those with low per capita GNP and low populations are least desirable. GNP is used in this manner, because the World Bank (www.worldbank.org) uses per capita GNP as the basis for its lending policies. The World Bank (2002) classifies economies into one of the following categories according to per capita GNP:

Developing countries: low income ($755 or less in 1999)
Middle income ($756–$9265)
Developed countries: high income ($9266 or more)

According to the World Bank, high-income countries generate 80 percent of the world's GNP; however, developing countries comprise about 75 percent of the total countries in the world and 85 percent of the total population. GNP is a macro measure of national income or the market value of final goods and services that are produced by factors of production that are owned domestically. Generally, the industrialization of the developed world has enabled a higher standard of living in those nations. In developed countries where there are established legal and institutional frameworks, there tends to be more international trade in an environment of public policies in which governments legislate to protect home industries, to encourage foreign direct investment (FDI), and to maintain civil order.

Besides classifying countries by income, they can be categorized by their type of economic system. The economic system is a determinant of the locus of control of business, i.e., who owns and controls resources. Societies with command systems, such as those within totalitarian governance, have their resources owned and controlled by the government. The emphasis is on the "whole." Everything that is done is done for the good of the entire society. Also, market economies have their resources owned and controlled by private sector companies and individuals. The emphasis is on the "individuals." Countries with open market systems exhibit higher economic growth, and the civil society generally appreciates a better quality of life within a stable, peaceful environment.

The International Monetary Fund (IMF) (1999) identified factors that lead to reform and economic progress. In countries where there is opposition to open-entry competition and full liberalization of trade, vested interests develop. Often these are interests entertained by the government or the political factions, which are not necessarily in the best interest of the private sector. This and the lack of adequate and appropriate public policies open the opportunity for corruption and the development of an underground economy. The result is a vicious cycle of reforms, revealing low growth and the decimation of financial stability. It has often been said that many of the developing countries are not poor, but the wealth and the control of that wealth are held in the hands of a few at the top who do not invest in public works or other activities that benefit the "whole" and raise the per capita GNP. How ironic that this occurs in many countries, with command economic systems and repression of the masses, that claim to be concerned for the "good of the whole." Unfortunately, accurate and credible market and social data are difficult to obtain in developing countries. Therefore, decision making required to enhance the economy is impaired.

According to Daniels et al. (2004, pp. 196–197), considerable government interference in international trade is motivated by political rather than economic concerns. In fact, political objectives of governments often oppose economic proposals to improve market efficiency and international competitiveness. Government officials are the ones who must resolve this, if they wish to develop.

Companies, who choose to do business in developing countries, should prepare an exit strategy for situations in which a government selects politics over economics and intervenes in the flow of imports and exports or in which the government participates in activities that do not reflect the moral, ethical, and social responsibility held by the company and its shareholders. As Drucker (2001, pp. 3–20) reminds one, the business system of the future is a developing institution with dynamic responses to a constantly changing external environment.

To summarize the global company perspective, the role of government appears to be stronger in the developing countries that have not had the opportunity to build their economic base. Therefore, it appears as though, in developing nations, the greater the direct role of the government in development, the greater the risk to the stakeholders and the more potential for conflict among their constituent groups.

Royal Dutch Shell and Conflict in Nigeria

Royal Dutch Shell (referred to here as Shell) invested $7.5 billion in oil and gas beginning in 2002 over a five-year period. Nigeria, which was a British colony until 1960, is the most populated country in Africa with more than 126 million people. These people comprise of 250 different ethnic and linguistic groups. Ethnic conflict has long existed in Nigeria with civil war between predominately Moslem Hausas and predominantly Christian Ibos. The latter group seceded to form the Republic of Biafra, which did not survive for very long. However, during the time of its existence, demands for royalty payments on Biafran oil were lodged against the oil companies from Nigeria and Biafra. Nigeria has been rampant with military coups and military dictatorships and elected a civilian government in 1998. The government established the Nigerian National Petroleum Corporation (NNPC), which serves as a joint venture partner in all Nigeria petroleum projects. Prior to this time, Shell enjoyed a joint venture with Britain, which gave it exclusive rights to explore for oil in Nigeria. It found oil for the first time in 1956 in Ogoniland and later in other parts of Nigeria. Ogoniland is at the edge of the Niger Delta where other oil reserves have been found. The Nigerian government has enjoyed a great deal of profits as a result of Shell's exploration; however, very little, if any, of the wealth has been redistributed back to Ogoniland (Adams et al., 1995).

Shell has been in Nigeria since the late 1920s and controls about half of Nigeria's output. These operations are significant for Shell and for the Nigerian central government. A group of Ogonis, starting in 1992, formed the Movement for the Survival of Ogoni People (MOSOP). They advocated for a greater share of oil revenues, compensation for losses from

Shell's activities, and restoration of the environment, especially the farmland and fishing areas. Further, MOSOP accused Shell of damaging public health tantamount to genocide of the Ogoni people. The Nigerian government reacted violently and used troops from other ethnic groups to shoot demonstrators and attack villages. Shell announced that it was not condoning the genocide and that the subsequent violence was not started by government troops but, rather, that various ethnic groups had a history of engaging in conflict with each other. Ogonis then struck back by sabotaging Shell's plants. In 1993, Shell suspended its operations in the Niger Delta region of Nigeria. The government arrested the organizers of MOSOP, accused them of inciting supporters to violence, and hung them in 1995. Although adequate, accurate, and credible information is not readily available from the government, aid groups and other NGOs claimed that the Ogonis were not initially violent but had to defend themselves through the government-sponsored genocide (Wallis, 1999).

The first shareholder resolution given to any company in the United Kingdom was given to Shell in 1997 demanding public accountability of the Nigerian operations. The resolution was supported by a number of NGOs: 18 public and private pension funds, 5 religious institutions, and 1 academic fund. This action led to a general "melt down." Protesters marched in Washington, D.C., for a boycott of Nigerian oil; $295 million in aid to Nigeria was frozen by the European Union (Lascelles, 1995); the World Bank said it would not invest $100 million in a gas plant if Shell was involved; and the United Kingdom was considering a consumer boycott of Shell (Hudson and Rose, 1995).

Shell's strategy for counteracting the negative impacts created by its acquiescence with the actions of the Nigerian government was to develop programs of social responsibility in Nigeria. It hired some of the Ijaw youth who had joined with the Ogonis and asked them merely to stay at home and not create trouble. This was identified as a management training program. Shell had hired social workers and invested more in Nigeria with the idea that expansion of its operations there shows that it supports the current civilian government and will provide the government with more funds to invest in public works. Also, Shell is shifting its operations to more natural gas production rather than oil as a way of quelling the environmental issues brought about by the oil seepage and spills. MOSOP, and now the Ijaw and Akassas who have joined them, believe that Shell is still insensitive to humans and their quality of life in the Niger Delta region (Daniels et al., 2004, pp. 405–407).

Even though Shell has begun some corrective actions, at issue is the speed with which those actions are taken. In terms of remediation, in 2001, 961 damaged areas (797 on land and 144 in swamps) were assessed with an additional 269 still waiting for assessments. To date, 305 sites have been identified as needing remedial action, and 120 of them are under treatment. This is a little more than one third of the sites treated within four years. Shell continues to claim that numerous sites cannot be remediated, "because the local community prevents access." They state that leaving these sites, "goes against all the principles of sustainable development" and that they are intensifying their efforts at negotiation. Shell continues to maintain that, "any future resumption of oil production in Ogoniland is contingent on the support of all Ogonis." Shell's Nigerian operations website (www.shellnigeria.com) refers to "issues and dilemmas" and says that, "There have been accusations of corrupt practices in relation to our Community Development Projects. Some of these issues are in the past, but many continue to be debated in the world press." The company seems to be suggesting that it has become a better corporate citizen by taking the types of corrective actions mentioned earlier. More recently in early 2004 Shell Nigeria Gas (SNG) signed its first Gas Sale and Purchase Agreement with an indigenous company in the Niger Delta (http://www.shell.com).

In summary, Shell has attempted to use publicity to make it appear as if it has a social environment-type model of management. In reality it is more oriented toward bringing in the profits at any human cost and appears to be using the social responsibility focus as a strategy for cleansing itself from all the negative publicity and subsequent actions against its operations in the Niger Delta region of Nigeria. The government of Nigeria, with Shell's attempt to avoid any appearance of complicity in the government's actions, is permeated in an individualistic culture where conflicts are initially ignored and then addressed with violence, rather than with negotiations and reconciliations. Shell has not admitted any wrongdoing in the human conflict resulting from its and the government's response to Nigerian people who wanted them to accept responsibility for the environmental degradation caused by Shell's oil operations. Compared to the wealth that Shell and the government are reaping from these lands, their socially responsible response is too little over too long a time. The situation continues with the NGOs taking a bigger role in applying pressure to Shell in other regions. Shell continues to avoid the conflict by not resuming Niger Delta operations and announcing that it will do so only when all Ogonis agree to support its operations. Because neither it nor the government is taking proactive steps to negotiate a resolution to the conflict, there appears to be a stalemate.

Talisman Energy Inc. and Conflict in the Sudan

Talisman Energy, Inc. is one of the largest independent Canadian energy companies working upstream in the oil and gas operations industry. Its main activities are exploration, development, productions, transporting, and marketing of crude oil, natural gas, and natural gas liquids. With 47 percent of its total operations in Canada and the United States, it decided to become a global company and extended its operations to the North Sea, Asia (Malaysia and Vietnam), Nigeria, Algeria, Trinidad, Peru, and Columbia. The company has generally experienced positive growth until its implication in the conflict with the Sudan (www.talisman-energy.com).

Canada, the home country of Talisman, established the International Code of Ethics for Canadian Business in 1997 as a result of confrontations which occurred among business, government, and various NGOs such as aid and religious groups, with regard to operations in regions such as the Niger River Delta in Nigeria. In this region many human rights abuses have taken place and been documented by the villagers and the international NGOs. Publicity concerning human rights abuses in the Sudan, where Talisman was operating, was even more critical due to the civil war between the north and the south and due to allegations of slavery and genocide. The result was a decrease in the price of stock. In an effort to reverse the downward spiral, the company, in late December 1999, decided to adopt the code of ethics. It also decided to participate in the Extractive Industries Transparency Initiative (EITI), which is aimed at improving transparency and accountability for oil and gas revenues. Signing on to the code and joining EITI, strategic business moves in and of themselves are good for publicity; however, public opinion in Canada and the United States is generally too sophisticated to be duped by publicity (the "spin") with no action to change behaviors. It became obvious to stakeholders that Talisman adopted the code to appease the Canadian government but did nothing to change its activities or its continued support of the Sudanese government (Chase, 1999).

Talisman Energy, Inc. had begun its exploration operations in the Sudan in October 1998 with support of the Canadian government to expand its business internationally. It purchased 25 percent of a Chinese company already doing business in the Sudan (www.talisman-energy.com). This action followed "good business" practices whereby partnering with a company already successful in a country provides the experience and knowledge of the local culture. In Talisman's situation partnering with the existing Chinese company gave it access to a potentially high yield oil field without a great deal of direct competition. This strategy basically can "jump start" a company's immersion in the local political and social conditions so that it can successfully manage its local workers and operations. However, in this case, it appears as though Talisman did not consider that both Sudan and China have continuing histories of human rights abuses, which do not fit with the corporate culture prevalent in North America (Mehallis, 2005).

Sudan is the largest African country but one of the least populated due to its desert and arid lands. The Nile flows from the south to the north with Khartoum, the country's capital, located at the intersection of the Blue and the White Niles. People living in the north are mostly Arab-Africans who are Muslims and Arabic-speaking. About one sixth of the population lives in the southern region, which tends to be Black Africans of Christian or local traditional tribal beliefs who speak local languages (mostly Nilotic) or English. Among the indigenous groups are at least three independent rebel groups. While the political power and most of the population are in the north, most resources, including gas and oil reserves, are in the south. From the 1800s slave trade has existed until today, with people from the south sold into slavery in the north of the Sudan, or historically, into parts of Europe. A civil war has been going on for almost 20 years between the north and the south. Approximately two million people have died or been killed due to this war. Another four million or more have become displaced refugees, some of whom have migrated to the United States. Sudan is considered one of the seven state sponsors of terrorism in the world by the United States. Sudan appears to be moving toward lowering its involvement in terrorist practices; however, it still supports Hamas (the Islamic Resistance Movement) and the Palestinian Islamic Jihad (PIJ) (World Bank, 2003).

If there was any thought given to the potential impact of the ongoing civil war conflict and other human rights considerations, Talisman seemed to have complete trust in the information given to it by the government. Generally in regions of conflict it is most difficult to obtain accurate, credible, and timely information for decision making, but Buckee, Talisman's president and CEO, has said that the company was not taking sides in the conflict (i.e., avoidance behavior) and denied that it was party to any of the abuses (Waldie and Gillis, 1999). He went on to say that Canada had encouraged businesses to get involved with China and that Talisman was singled out and unfairly treated among companies working in developing countries. Buckee said that Talisman was taking the Sudanese government at its word that it was not using oil revenue to fund its campaign against rebels in the south, and he blamed any atrocities against civilians on the civil war and not due to the need to remove people from the oil fields. Further he claimed to believe that the government would publish its budget and, thereby, prove that revenues from the oil field were used on agriculture (www.talisman-energy.com/corporate_responsibility/business_conduct.html).

Discovery of at least two billion barrels of oil in the region between the north and south of the Sudan resulted in the change in government tactics (The Rumbek Report, 2001). Whereas initially the government armed Arab militia groups from the north to raid the south for cattle and slaves, the government embarked on a campaign to remove southerners through ethnic cleansing. Christian Aid, a Britain-based charity, confirmed these allegations along with other aid and religious NGOs. The oil companies claim that they are fulfilling their social responsibility by providing food and shelter to victims of the conflict, but others, particularly the NGOs, blame them for contributing to the escalation of the conflict. Command economies, such as China, appear to function in much the same way. China's National Petroleum Corporation, which operates in the Sudan, seems to have continued its operations unscathed. However, the market economy with impetus toward the social responsibility mode of management in the United States resulted in the United States placing sanctions on the Sudan (Mehallis, 2005).

Negative publicity appearing in Canadian newspapers as well as in publications, such as *The Economist* and financial websites, resulted in a decrease in Talisman's stock, nearly 1 billion Canadian dollars of stock market value. Buckee and Talisman's management were very concerned about the impact on shareholders and so bought back significant amounts of stock to enhance the price. Specifics about the ethnic cleansing and Talisman's apparent role (at the very least standing by while the Sudan government directed the actions against its population in the south) reached the U.S. Congress. Actions were underway to bar Talisman from the U.S. markets. Thus, on November 1, 2002, the Sudan assets were made available for sale. Talisman used this strategy so that it could exit as gracefully as possible by divesting itself of any connection with Sudan without admitting to any wrongdoing. On March 12, 2003, Talisman sold its Sudan operations to an Indian company and had a gain on disposal of approximately US$200 million. Besides the profit, Talisman's risk was greatly reduced, and it began expansion into lower risk regions of the world, including upstate New York (Talisman Energy, 2003, 2004).

Whereas Talisman was occupied with its sale of the Sudanese assets and taking measures to increase stock price, the Sudanese-displaced refugees who went to the United States were encouraged by the U.S. Presbyterian Church to have the Sudan Presbyterian Church file a lawsuit against Talisman Energy, Inc. and the Republic of the Sudan for atrocious human rights violations including ethnic cleansing. An allegation exists that the president of Talisman, Buckee, sent a signed letter to the Sudanese government, requesting that people be removed from the oil field lands. This is a direct contradiction to Buckee's allegation that neither he nor the company has in any way encouraged or been complicit in the ethnic cleansing. The company's response may be to say that removing people from land is done in Canada and the United States (right to public domain). People are generally found housing at an equal level by the government and compensated for their move. In a country, like Sudan, where conflict and violence against humans is unchecked and often initiated and condoned by the government, it is extremely naïve for a CEO to request removal of people and not entertain the possibility that the methods for doing so might be unacceptable to the developed world. This and eyewitness accounts from survivors are included in the lawsuit as the cause for action. Until the case is adjudicated, there is no way to know if this, in fact, is true, whether someone in the Sudanese government forged such a letter or if there actually is such as letter.

The plaintiffs in the lawsuit allege that Talisman and the Republic of Sudan collaborated to commit gross human rights violations, including extrajudicial killing, forcible displacement, war crimes, confiscation and destruction of property, kidnapping, rape, and enslavement (Schwartz, 2004, p. 1). Talisman initially filed papers to have the case dismissed on the basis of the court's "lack of power to enforce an injunction against Talisman" and the fact that Talisman "does not conduct business in Sudan nor with its indirect subsidiary GNOPC" (the company with which it had partnered in Sudan). A recent ruling indicates that Talisman is accountable and will stand trial in the United States for its actions in Sudan (Schwartz, District Judge 10 Civ. 9882, AGS).

In summary, Talisman appears to have thought that by buying one quarter of a larger oil and gas exploration company, it would have been able to reap larger profits while keeping a low profile. It has not embraced the social environmental model of management until the last couple of years when its position was so tenuous that it was forced to sell its holdings. If it had continued to do business in Sudan, it would have been banned from U.S. markets, and public opinion in Canada would have been very damaging. The company entered a region with much intracultural conflict and allowed the command economic system of Sudan to determine how people were treated while removing them from the oil field lands. The CEO seems to believe that by saying that the company trusts the government when it claims no part in the genocide and other human rights abuses, and that any blame which may occur would be aimed at the government and not at the company. Talisman underestimated how much public opinion can sway the attitudes of shareholders. Even though the Sudan was a fairly small part of Talisman's portfolio, the outrage of NGOs and shareholders had a negative impact on all of Talisman's operations throughout the world. This is an example of how conflict in a single region, when not resolved, could create concerns that spill over to other regions of the operations. In North America, in particular, public opinion favors social responsibility and environmental concerns. The sooner the company internalizes this, the sooner it will be in harmony with its external environment. Stakeholders want to see deliberate action in this direction, not mere "lip service."

Conclusions and Implications

Globalization in developing countries where there is conflict has been slowed down by the conflict and its consequences. The energy sector cases described earlier have demonstrated two such impacts: (1) The conflict in the Niger Delta region of Nigeria resulted in a stoppage of Shell's operations. The company discontinued its exploration in the region and has not resumed its activities. (2) The conflict in Sudan created a barrier to the globalization of Talisman in the region. Talisman completely withdrew and sold its holdings to decrease the risk it faced in the southern region of the Sudan. This was because its shareholders, the U.S. Congress, and the Presbyterian Church of Sudan used public opinion against Talisman and its role in the ethnic cleansing.

Below are listed some conclusions and implications to globalization:

- Due to technology in the telecommunications networks, what happens in one region is communicated throughout the world and impacts all company operations.
- Each company, especially those entering known regions of conflict, should have an exit strategy developed and ready to use before making a final selection on location.
- Business schools should spend more time discussing conflicts and how to negotiate. They should teach about cultural definitions in doing business beyond understanding the local workers and external environment. They should partner with schools of public administration to teach how the culture of particular governments and their orientation to conflict affect the company's ability to be successful in other countries.
- Multilaterals, such as the World Bank, should expand their assistance programs in developing countries. In the last five years, the World Bank has developed a program of project development facilities (PDFs). These are similar to the small-business development centers designed by the commerce department in the United States. Their focus is to empower the support structure (lending organizations, local supply chain companies, etc.) so that companies will be able to be successful in "doing business" and be able to sustain that effort. The PDFs, or similar organizations, should include conflict resolution for governments and education in cross-cultural operations within the country.
- Companies should identify the amount of risk that is acceptable to the entire company when going into a region of conflict. They need to determine consciously the threshold for going into conflicted

regions when potential profits are high and fully understand the potential negative impact on the company in other global sites.

- Accommodating-type cultures do not synchronize with individualist ones, and management-type models of business do not embrace the social responsibility models. Placing energy sector companies in developing countries with command economies puts them in a precarious position; however, exploration for new energy resources will most likely continue to be in developing countries.
- The greater the access to communication technology, the less developed the country; and the more command-like the economy, the more possibility for conflict with a resulting slowdown on globalization.

Although the energy sector is used in two case examples herein, the globalization of any business sector depends on certain conditions both in the government and in the company. NGOs and public opinion play a much more central role in how companies become global than was initially realized. This is primarily true because of networks that extend all over the world. To expand globalization efforts, companies must understand the nuances of their own culture and that of others. Unfortunately in developing nations where conflict is prevalent, efforts to globalize are thwarted. This is a cycle that must be broken to improve the general quality of life in developing countries. Without the elevation of developing countries into viable economies that can alleviate poverty and reduce conflict, primarily between the "haves" and the "have nots" within their own country, conflict, violence, and terrorism will continue to thrive and impede the ability of developing countries to participate in the global economy. Both Royal Dutch Shell and Talisman Energy are examples where the company has continued to meet its own goal of globalization but where the company, as a result of intra-country conflict, has discontinued its economic activities in particular regions of developing countries and, thereby, reduced the country's efforts at globalization. MNCs, working with shareholders and NGOs, must embrace the social responsibility model of management into their business cultures so that they can become the vehicle for change and globalization in developing countries.

References

Adams, P. et al. 1995. "Shell Facing New Onslaught over Nigeria," *Financial Times*, December 15.

Berle, A. and G. Means. 1991. *The Modern Corporation and Private Property*. New Brunswick, NJ: Transaction Publishers.

Black, J. and M. Mendenhall. 1993. "Resolving Conflicts with the Japanese: Mission Impossible?" *Sloan Management Review*, Spring: 49–59.

Chase, S. 1999. "Talisman Bows to Ottawa, Adopts Business Code of Ethics," *Alberta Bureau*, Saturday, December 11.

Daniels, J., L. Radebaugh, and D. Sullivan. 2004. *International Business: Environments and Operations*. Upper Saddle River, NJ: Pearson, Prentice-Hall.

Drucker, P. 2001. "The Next Society," *The Economist*, November 3, pp. 3–20.

Farazmand, A. 2001. "Global Crisis in Public Service," in A. Farazmand (ed.), *Handbook of Crisis and Emergency Management*. New York: Marcel Dekker, pp. 111–130.

Gladwin, T. and I. Walter. 1980. *Multinationals under Fire*. New York: John Wiley.

Hewlett-Packard Annual Report 2001. 2002. http://www.hp.com/hpinfo/investor/financials/annual/2001/text_only_10k.pdf

Hudson, R. and M. Rose. 1995. "Shell is Pressured to Scrap its Plans for New Plant in Nigeria amid Protests." *Wall Street Journal*, November 14.

International Monetary Fund. 1999. *Finance & Development*, Vol. 36, No. 2.

Lascelles, D. 1995. "Shell under Pressure as EU Toughens Stance on Nigeria," *Financial Times*, November 14.

Leiber, R. 1997. "Flying High, Going Global," *Fortune*, July 7, pp. 195–197.

Lewis, W. 1997. "Shell Faces UK First in Investors' Resolution on Ethics," *Financial Times*, February 24.

Marshall, A. 1949. *Principles of Economics*, 8th edn. New York: Macmillan.

Mehallis, M. 2005. "Talisman Energy, Inc. Case: Working in Conflict in the Sudan," Unpublished paper, May 3.

Nunn, S. et al. 2000. *The Geopolitics of Energy into the 21st Century*, Vol. 1. Washington, D.C.: Center for Strategic and International Studies.

Porter, M.E. 1998. *The Competitive Advantage of Nations*. New York: Free Press, pp. 74–75.

Preston, L. 1986. *Social Issues and Public Policy in Business and Management*. College Park, MD: University of Maryland, Center for Business and Public Policy.

The Rumbek Report. 2001. "Sudan's Government has Adopted a Brutal New Policy of Clearing the Oil Areas," *The Economist*, April 12.

Schneider, S. and J. Barsoux. 2003. *Managing Across Cultures*. Essex, England: Prentice-Hall Financial Times.

Schwartz, 2004. District Judge 10 Civ. 9882, AGS.

Talisman Energy, Inc. 2003. *Annual Report 2003*.

Talisman Energy, Inc. 2004. *Annual Report 2004*.

The Economist. 1984. "Mad Dogs and Expatirates," March 3, p. 67.

The World Bank, Data, and Statistics. August, 2002. http://www.worldbank.com/data/databytopic/class.htm

Toman, M. 2002. "International Oil Security," *Brookings Review*, Spring: 20–27.

U.S. CIA. 2001. *Handbook of Economic Statistics*.

Waldie, P. and C. Gillis. 1999. "Talisman to Embark on Share Buyback," *National Post*, Wednesday, December 16.

Wallis, W. 1999. "Ethnic Fighting Flares in Nigerian Oil Delta," *Financial Times*, June 2.

Weidenbaum, M. 2004. *Business and Government in the Global Marketplace.* Upper Saddle River, NJ: Pearson, Prentice-Hall.

World Bank. 2003. Sudan: Stabilization and Reconstruction: Country Economic Memorandum Report No. 24620-SU. June 30 (Document) World Bank. www.worldbank.org.

www.talisman-energy.com

www.talisman-energy.com/corporate_responsibility/business_conduct.html

Chapter 45

Competitive Advantage and Market Organizations in the 21st Century: Market Driving or Market Driven

Bahaudin G. Mujtaba and Donovan A. McFarlane

CONTENTS

Market-Driving Concept and Characteristics

Businesses today are faced with many more difficult decisions than ever before, and the intricate dynamics of the global environment in which companies conduct their everyday activities and functions call for strategies and programs, which are constantly geared toward success, growth, competition, and survival. As a result of these strategies and programs, and the need to be overly competitive and economically–financially aggressive, two major types of business firms have emerged using the most effective and efficient combinations of technology, human resources, and other productive factors to achieve a unique balance between markets, economics, and superiority in customer satisfaction, profits, and sales. These two distinguished types of firms have been studied extensively by Kumar et al. (2000) and are referred to as market-driven and market-driving firms or businesses. Over the past years these two concepts have emerged to become the major line of classification for businesses driven by mass technological inputs and customer oriented success. Superior marketing management policies and techniques rather than organizational structure and traditional business leadership theories have become the standard method for ranking businesses according to these two categories.

According to Kumar et al. (2000), firms are constantly urged to become more market driven. However, they are better off being market driving in today's cut-throat competitive global business environment where getting information and the ability to diversify and enter new markets is easier than before. No clear and distinct definitions of the concepts have been universally posited thus far. However, most scholars on the subject along with management theorists seem to agree on "market-driven" firms being the ones in which growth, success, and competitive edge have been achieved through incremental innovation blended with the traditional market research. As a result, such firms lack revolutionary products, concepts, and technologies, but are still ahead of those firms that have remained overly traditional in market research and not embracing technological innovation and the application to marketing processes and trends. The lack of revolutionary products is just one disadvantage of being market driven. According to Zultowski (1992), a market-driven business begins with the needs of a market, decides on the best products to serve the market, then builds or acquires distribution systems to meet the market's needs. Zell (2001) believes that market-driven businesses are revenue driven and customer focused. Vervack (1993) states that market-driven companies develop products specifically to address the unmet needs of a certain group within their target markets. Zultowski (1992) seems to express concern regarding the competitive challenges market-driven firms face when they must live up to changing market demands as push factors in potential organizational breakdown. Accordingly, he states "Markets for our industry's products and services can emerge, change and disappear as a function of many external environmental factors: the economy, governmental actions, technology, changing social attitudes and demographics." (p. 48). Examples of market-driven firms are Nestle, Procter & Gamble, Unilever, L'Oreal, and American Airlines. Massing (2001) describes the media as one of the most highly market-driven businesses, and many companies seem to direct their strategies towards this end (Smith, 1997). Age Recycle, Inc. has been described by its president Castagnero as a business that is essentially market driven with a "marriage between appropriate technology and sensible management" (Anon, 2001). To be market driven entails much more than this however, as we will see in further discussions. "Market driving" firms, on the other hand, are those which have used radical business innovations, and are generally new entrants to the industry, delivering a leap in customer value through designing and utilizing unique business systems (Kumar et al., 2000). Examples of market-driving firms are Starbucks, Dell Computers, Swatch, Charles Schwab, Southwest Airlines, Wal-Mart, Amazon.com, and Sony. It is recognized that the differences are dependent on the degree of integration achieved with technology, innovation, business systems, and their effects upon creating and adding customer value, and hence generating absolute competitive advantage in the market place. Thus, becoming "market driving" is all about delivering superior value to the demanding and time-impoverished customers.

Jaworski et al. (2000) provide interesting and comprehensible definitions of market-driven and market-driving firms. According to these authors, "market driven" refers to a business orientation that is based on understanding and reacting to the preferences and behaviors of players within a given market structure (p. 45), whereas "Driving Markets [Market Driving] implies influencing the structure of the market and/or the behaviors of market players in a direction that enhances the competitive position of the business" (p. 45).

According to Kumar et al. (2000), there are seven major differences between "market-driven" and "market-driving" firms (discussed below), and these account for the competitive advantage that market-driving firms possess in the global business environment. Narasimhan (2003) seems to agree on the distinguishing features from his studies and essay on *The Market Driven Enterprise*. The authors state these differences by focusing on firms' reactions to, and approaches to markets and their outlays and processes. Figure 45.1 presents a summary of the market-driving characteristics that distinguish them from the market-driven firms.

The first distinguishing characteristic is that market-driving firms are guided by vision whereas market-driven firms are guided in majority by the traditional "market research" approach. Through unique vision that brings

Vision

Segmentation

Customization of offerings

Education of customers about products

Using diverse marketing channels to reach clients

Creating brand attachment and loyalty with existing products

Delightfully overwhelming customers with value-added products and services

Figure 45.1 Market-driving characteristics.

about revolutionary product ideas and concepts, utilizing the most up-to-date and cutting edge technologies, market-driving firms are able to surpass consumers' expectations and "wow" them into buying their products. Consumers have become more and more aware of the use of technology and innovation and how these result in greater efficiency and effectiveness in product and services use and value. Consumers seek added value with each dollar spent and technology and innovation seem to add to the total utility. According to Kumar et al. (2000), market-driving firms band together around visionaries who see opportunities where others do not, and in so doing use these opportunities to fill hidden, unsatisfied needs and to offer unprecedented levels of customer value. Market-driven firms, however, provide only incremental innovations and therefore add less value, and this is not enough to overwhelm consumers and win market shares. Market-driven firms are furthermore characterized by what Adawi (1989) seems to indicate as systems inadequacies and limitations resulting from the lack of vision.

The second distinguishing factor is that market-driving firms "redraw or redefine industry segmentation," while market-driven firms strive on retention strategies which prove to be ineffective at times. Market-driving firms attract customers from various market niches, which are strategically defined and manipulated to align around their product–service offerings. Although market-driven firms understand the need for change and demonstrate leadership commitment (Day, 2000), they lack the action and driving forces necessary to redefine markets, strategies, and apply these effectively in new marketing arenas.

The third difference between market-driving and market-driven firms is that market-driving firms create and offer value through new price points, which they obtain from adding superior customer value and satisfaction.

Kim and Mauborgne (1997) believe that value innovation is a strategy used by those companies which are ahead of the competition, and this is true of market drivers, because value innovation is considered as "the strategic logic of high growth." Market-driving firms have discovered new ways to offer quality and as a result set prices that put competitors under serious pressures, forcing them to make great changes in operations and product lines to survive. Many competitors are unable to meet such a challenge because of the inability and lack of know-how, the unavailability of customized business systems and experts to successfully and strategically replicate structures, which enable lower price points. Although "it is in vogue to aspire to become market-driven" (Day, 1998), the nature of today's competitive environment is the one in which companies are better off being market drivers. Market-driving firms are able to put forward unique value propositions that are more successful, convincing, and appealing than the alternatives offered by the market-driven firms and this makes all the difference.

The fourth difference between market-driving and market-driven firms lies in the superior ability of market-driving firms to increase sales growth and profits through customer education. According to Kumar et al. (2000), the radical new concept, the sales task for firms is not to sell, but rather to educate the customer on the existence, of and how to consume their radical value proposition. Market-driven firms are still using the old aggressive sales tactics that sell the customers a product rather than a value, especially failing to demonstrate the added value in the value paradigm.

The fifth distinguishing factor between market-driving and market-driven firms is the unique ability of the market drivers (market-driving firms) to redesign or reconfigure marketing channels to generate architectural innovations that result in the identification, use, and application of unique business systems to their markets and the creation of customer value. Market-driven firms, on the other hand, have mainly remained etched in the old channeling or distribution system that can be slow, inefficient, and ineffective in various market segments, and for various customer needs, given the factors that come into play in delivering products or services.

The sixth differentiating factor between those firms that are market drivers and those which are market followers (market-driven firms) is the fact that market drivers place greater reliance on what Kumar et al. (2000) refer to as "buzz network" to encourage brand attachment and drive their messages to the customers. According to Kotler, the customers become so delighted that they are motivated and eager to communicate their "finds" to the other customers. Capitalizing on the "buzz network" allows market drivers to depend less on traditional advertisement unlike market-driven firms that offer consumers their value propositions through the same old media. The "buzz network" has a greater impact as it represents value and utility communicated more directly from one product-service user to another; a more believable point of reference motivating others to try the product or service.

The final, or the seventh, factor that marketing management experts use to distinguish market drivers from market followers is the varying ability and success of the two to overwhelm customer expectations. Market-driving firms (market drivers) seek and develop new ways to constantly overwhelm the customers' expectations regarding their services and products, while market-driven firms (market followers) are resolved to satisfying standards and qualities that define the industry on an average customer's expectation on a whole. Market-driving businesses believe in delivering above and beyond what Johnson and Weinstein refer to as the unique value propositions. According to Johnson and Weinstein (2004), designing and delivering superior customer value are the keys to successful business strategies in the 21st century, and value reigns supreme in today's market place. They further state that innovative companies, which create maximum value for their customers, will survive and thrive; they will carve out sustainable competitive advantages in the marketplace. This is where market-driving firms excel, as they are able to better understand this act and implement programs, policies, and strategies to achieve the results they do. Of course, overwhelming the customers cannot be done just through internal resources but one must also align external resources toward the vision of the organization. When everyone in the value chain is jointly working toward a common goal of providing the best value for the customer, reaching there will become much easier because of the profound impact of synergy. Figure 45.2 provides the power for teamwork and synergy as demonstrated when geese fly in formation. Market drivers shape consumer behavior, transform the marketplace, and redefine all the rules of engagement with suppliers and competitors (Harris & Cai, 2002; Kumar, 1997). Whereas market-driven firms have understanding, attracting, and keeping valued customers as their goal (Landry, 1999; Maxwell, 1999; Maxwell & Steele, 1989), market-driving firms on the other hand create new customers through the creation of new services and products, which pull customers from all market niches.

There are many lessons that can be learned from the research done with the geese and can be applied with teams in the workplace. As each goose flaps its wings, it creates an "uplift" for the bird following. By flying in a "V" formation, the whole flock adds 71 percent more flying range than if each bird flew alone. The lesson here is that people who share a common direction and a sense of community can get the going quicker and easier because they are traveling on the thrust of one another.

Whenever a goose falls out of formation, it suddenly feels the drag and resistance of trying to fly alone, and quickly gets back into formation to take

When
geese fly
in formation
they travel 71
percent faster than
when they fly alone. Geese
share leadership. When the
lead goose tires, it rotates back into
the "V," and another flies forward to
become the leader. Geese keep company
with the fallen. When a sick or weak goose drops out
of the Flight's formation, at least one other goose joins to
help and protect.

Figure 45.2 Power of common vision and synergy.

advantage of the lifting power of the birds immediately in front. The lesson here is that if we have as much sense as a goose does, we will join in formation with those who are headed where we want to go.

When the lead goose gets tired, it rotates back into the formation and another goose flies at the point position. The lesson here is that it is beneficial to take turns doing the hard task and sharing leadership with people — as with geese, interdependent with one another.

The geese in formation honk from behind to encourage those up front to keep up their speed. The lesson here is that we need to make sure our honking from behind is encouraging, not something less helpful.

When a goose gets sick or wounded or shot down, two geese drop out of formation and follow their fellow member down to help and provide protection. They stay with this member of the flock until he or she is either able to fly again or dies. Then they launch out on their own, with another formation, or to catch up with their own flock. The lesson here is that if we have as much sense as geese, we will stand by one another like they do. These are principles of teamwork and synergy that must be demonstrated by everyone in the value chain for the organization to become a market-driving firm in the industry.

Principles of Becoming Market Driving

The distinguishing factors between market-driven and market-driving firms are not just casual, or the result of a perpetual growth process that all the firms in the global business environment experience. Firms have to make an extraordinary effort to experience the transition from being market driven to market driving, and there are certainly no magic formulas or established strategies and policies designed by management gurus to accomplish a transformation. Kumar et al. (2000) believe that business firms can become market driving rather than market driven in six ways. These include allowing space for serendipity or chance. Kotler and other marketing management experts believe that market-driving firms are what and where they are because of the ideas that they fostered at one point along the marketing continuum, and that such ideas were nonconformist in nature and process. They argue that market-driving firms were once companies that facilitated and fostered the creativity and generation of ideas from any level of the organization without seeing such ideas as negative or disruptive. This is argued to be unlike those companies arranged around the concept of efficiency in such a strict bureaucratic fashion that the generation of ideas, which would lead to spontaneous growth or divergence is not accepted. First strategy is that that the firms should become more flexible in their approach to generating and creating ideas and processes that may impact their marketing, products, and services, as well as their entire structures and processes. Theorists believe that market-driven firms pressure individuals to hide market-driving ideas as they "rebel against the prevailing industry and incumbent wisdom." As a result of this, such firms remain in a kind of traditional marketing and business environment structure, always responding to old situations, using old concepts and methods (Prahalad & Hamel, 1994). So, one strategy for becoming market driving is to be flexible in generating and implementing new ideas for delivering better value.

A second strategy that researchers suggest for market-driven firms to become market driving is through high-risk ventures in which firms empower latent entrepreneurs and offer multiple channels for new idea approval. Market-driving firms are those businesses that have successfully emerged from high risks in the global business environment. Such firms at one point in the past had undertaken radical innovation in the way they design products, offer services, carry out transactions or respond to customers' needs, etc. Their decisions at such points involved radical innovations in their value propositions and business systems and resulted in dramatic changes in both the way they approach the market and how customers view the value resulting from these changes.

A third strategy in which firms can become market driving, rather than market driven is through the establishment of competitive teams and "skunk networks." According to Kumar et al. (2000), when radical new concepts are introduced into market-driven firms they are not readily accepted and there are no clear-cut approaches to integrate them into existing business systems and processes or how to develop them into their ultimate success. This can pose a serious problem because the discordance can cause organization-wide dysfunctions. What experts suggest is that to overcome the organizational resistance and inertia, firms establish and set up "skunk networks" or physically and organizationally independent, self-contained entities with dedicated individuals to further develop and facilitate successful growth and maturation of new ideas into the firm's existing structures and processes. This is a good idea because new ideas can only become successful if they are translated into some form that can be understood by employees at all levels of the firm. According to Kumar et al. (2000), the established skunk works serve to bring a sense of urgency to new projects and ideas, harness the entrepreneurial zeal of members, and concentrate the effort of those involved, as well as protect the business from motives designed to suppress and discard such creative ideas for growth and expansion.

A fourth method that existing and market-driven organizations take to become market driving is the cannibalization of their own core competencies, services, and products. According to Kumar et al. (2000), the natural propensity of established market leaders to protect their core business makes it extremely difficult for them to voluntarily pursue avenues that threaten to undermine that core. To become market driving, however, such firms should subscribe to cannibalization, because market driving explicitly encourages cannibalization, with a belief that eventually some other firms will cannibalize that core business as a result of tough competition. Therefore, the firm owning such a core business, to maintain its post, and possibly develop new business opportunities, and eliminate threats and weaknesses, would be better off doing such an act of cannibalization.

A fifth method recommended by existing marketing experts for firms to become market drivers is to encourage experimentation and tolerate mistakes. There is a belief held by many firms and their management today that experimentation and mistakes are very damaging to the efficiency, and therefore must be discouraged at all costs. In many bureaucratic firms, mistakes are seen as very detrimental to organizational progress and structural function. Therefore, in such firms individuals are encouraged to strictly abide by the protocol on all levels to avoid costly mistakes to the organization. Such firms have limited experimentation, and creative solutions to problems are discouraged, especially at lower levels of the organization, where accountability is not transferred. Firms should probe and learn in the marketplace, improving with each successive generation (Kumar et al., 2000). In doing so firms may eventually discover novel methods of product design, marketing, customer response, value change and radical innovative techniques, which allow them to become market leaders. Firms that experiment are likely to find new means and methods to offer value and change product concepts and market niches. Firms should tolerate mistakes and encourage more experimentation at all levels to generate new ideas and use and implement radical technologies in meeting market needs in the competitive environment, while learning from their mistakes or failures.

A final or sixth method, which is recommended for firms to make the transition from market driven to market driving, is the selection and matching of employees for creativity. This can be rather difficult in some firms, especially those with all power and authority to make decisions and to monitor processes concentrated at the top of the organization. To generate new ideas, firms must allow employees the freedom to think creatively and contribute to the product and services, management decisions, strategic development, and organizational changes. For example, to generate new ideas, Nissan Design International promotes the "Creative Abrasion" by hiring people with different levels of creativity. Companies must have greater pools from which they can generate ideas, as the global market grows more competitive. Employees are the cheapest and most effective ways to generate market-driving ideas. Some firms attempt to use consultants and "inventions and ideas" businesses, which have no idea about their work processes and internal workings, and have failed miserably. Using employees to generate ideas is a wiser approach, because they spend their lives working with the firm's structures and processes and living within its culture and environment. Firms just do not become market driving overnight, it takes resources, high risks, errors and failures, radical ideas, and generation of unique business systems and solutions, vast leap in value offerings and propositions, capital investment, new concept application, organizational wide dedication, and vision. To become market driving, firms must consider their purpose and their existing locality within the business environment. Figure 45.3 presents some of the characteristics associated with market-driving organizational cultures.

The transition from being market driven to market drivers is not as subtle as current marketing management experts communicate. In fact, the above factors discussed as recommendations by these experts to initiate the transition are within themselves too simple and are based on a narrow approach to looking at the underlying differences between the market-driven and the market-driving firms. Allowing space for serendipity; selecting and matching employees for creativity; empowering latent entrepreneurs and offering multiple channels for new idea approvals; establishing competitive teams and skunk networks; cannibalizing its own and encouraging experimentation and tolerating mistakes are just too hypothetical and uncontrollable when it comes to organizational change, which will lead to the type of growth, expansion, and diversification under argument. The fact is that the idea of becoming market driving is a kind of growth orientation to be achieved, and therefore, measurable and manipulable

Flexibility
Risk and Innovation
Competitive teams and skunk works
Cannibalization of core business for new ones
Experimentation with innovative ideas and tolerance for mistakes
Employee empowerment and creativity for generation of market driving strategies

Figure 45.3 Market-driving cultures.

variables need to be coordinated into the goal and objectives required to reach this marketing utopia. It is the insufficiency of the factors and their lack of consideration concerning organizational contingencies, which have led the researchers to further develop and implement a series of new strategies for firms desiring to become market drivers.

Strategies for Achieving a Market-Driving Status

Based on the knowledge research has yielded thus far, variables influencing organizational scope, policies, strategies and operations, the global marketing environment, and current trends and development in management and marketing, the following strategies have been developed and recommended for implementation by firms determined to achieve a market-driving status. Firms desiring to become market drivers must have a unique understanding of the nature and functions of their businesses within the general market and industry. This requires assessing organizational mission and establishing a strategic vision centered on the market-driving concept. First of all a firm should ensure that its basic purpose and scope of operations are facilitative and tolerant of the opportunities and factors relevant for the transition from a market-driven approach to a market-driving command. Some firms may be too narrow in scope and operations to initiate and attain, as well as sustain the transitional factors that are relevant to encompass the type of innovation and changes which market driving requires. In such a case, firms will need to assess and perhaps change their organizational mission and establish a new strategic vision with the goal of market driving in mind. Firms that are unable to adapt to the radical innovations and concepts that market driving require will definitely fail in any attempt to achieve this status.

To become a market driver, a firm can develop and implement a plan of action that will carefully lay out the steps and approaches the company intends to take. This plan of action should include goals or plans and their continuum within operationally defined standards and measures. A plan of action to become market driving can be very difficult to generate and implement. However, an effective plan of action should include a series of activities formulated around the firm's marketing and product or service development innovation and standards. The firm must carefully decide the relevant variables in its marketing mix, product or service offerings, and overall general approach to doing business, and adequately combine and re-orient these to initiate and sustain innovation and build a competitive advantage to achieve market-driving power. A firm desiring to become a market driver may need to redefine marketing objectives and approach, and this can best be achieved through redefinition and refinement of the firm's value proposition. Differentiating oneself from the competitors might be the most viable solution for many firms desiring market-driving power. Exemplary companies have one thing different from the commoners, and that is their own unique identities attained through a carefully conceived and unmatched value proposition (Johnson & Weinstein, 2004). The value propositions of those firms that have emerged as market drivers are very much different and proven factors in their current status as market drivers.

Value-driven management, as suggested by Pohlman and Gardiner (2000), can be a powerful approach to cementing the changes and strategies that firms need to initiate the market-driving process. With the introduction of value-driven techniques and approaches to managing organizational resources, growth, and redirection, firms are able to experiment with and apply new processes, technologies, ideas, concepts, and forces into evolving as stimulators and leaders of industry trends. With value management techniques, a firm basically can initiate an organization-wide process orientation that affects service and product quality in such a way that it redefines the market. Some authors recommend the selection and matching of employees for creativity as a strategy for becoming market driving. This strategy is not wholly disagreed upon, but is seen as too narrow in terms of systems consideration. Therefore, it is recommended that rather than having this narrow focus, firms desiring to become market drivers develop and implement a human value management program to increase the entire people resources across all branches and departments of the organization. This is a very powerful statement. Human or people resources are the most powerful amongst organizational growth and transition factors. If an organization can get its people to focus on the same goal, in the same place, at the same time, with a great degree of accord, then the stage for creativity, ideas, innovation is well paved. With a united focus and increase in all employees' power for creative ideas and generation of solutions and concepts achieving market-driving status and power will become only a matter of how much, instead of how and when.

The idea of becoming a market driver becomes more realistic when firms understand that the greatest forces against which they struggle are themselves. Such realization can become evident if firms constantly carry out routine strategic audits. Firms must constantly assess their financial and operational activities and abilities as far as these can constrain and influence their growth patterns and abilities to compete. This will affect the degree to which factors relevant to the market reorientation and innovations are adaptable. If a firm is convinced that it can accommodate such factors based on strategic audit analyses, then it can carry out strategic maneuvering by consciously changing the boundaries of its task environment with identified capabilities and the resources available at its disposal. Firms desiring to become market drivers must also learn how to define and manage quality, whether it is product or service quality, and must utilize the best marketing relationship techniques to communicate their quality to customers. The management of quality and marketing relationships are crucial factors in the emergence of market drivers. Such firms have managed to redefine market perception of quality, while diversifying their approaches to marketing their products and handling customer transactions and interactions.

Firms desiring to become market drivers should reassess value factors using marketing research tools such as the customer value assessment tool (CVAT), as suggested by Johnson and Weinstein (2004). A tool such as the CVAT can allow a prospective market driver to ascertain its existing perceived image, service quality, product quality, and value-based pricing. With this, a firm will be able to determine where to implement radical innovation, and which factor or factors to concentrate on for developing or changing to attain competitive advantage and a core competency needed to establish market-driving power. Firms seeking to become market drivers must also manage for competitive advantage through costs, speed, quality, and innovation. These four factors are what management experts such as Bateman and Snell (1999) refer to as the foundations for building competitive advantage. Costs, speed, quality, and innovation have become four important words against which marketing success is gauged.

Finally, it is recommended that firms seeking to become market drivers rather than market driven understand and manage their internal and external environments through use and applications of the value chain and competitive forces models. Companies must constantly draw on competitive strategies from highly developed internal and external frameworks, which link all their opportunities and resources (Gedansky, 1985). As such, product development, supply chain management systems, and quality approach toward products and services creation become paramount. Though Narisimhan (2003) treats these as essential defining characteristics of market-driven firms, they have been factors that have rather distinguished the emergence of market drivers from market followers, especially when we consider the different degree of success between the two with regard to supply chain management systems, customer relationship systems, knowledge management systems, and information systems. The value chain model emphasizes the primary or the support activities that add a margin of value to a firm's products or services where information systems can best be utilized and applied to achieve a competitive advantage (Laudon & Laudon, 2004). Twenty-first century environment is an age where information systems play a definitive role in determining organizational success (Dries, 1997). Current firms with market-driving goals in mind must use information systems to enhance their production and distribution capabilities, as well as to coordinate their infrastructures, human resources, technology, and procurement into a functional unit. The competitive forces model developed by Porter (1985) to describe the interaction of external influences, particularly threats and opportunities affecting an organization's strategies and ability to compete, can be carefully applied to understand organizational factors interplaying to affect market position and power. Understanding the factors in this model will enhance the firm's ability to deal with customers, suppliers, new entrants to the market, substitute products and services, which can change the balance of power between the firm and other competitors in the industry in a favorable manner (Laudon & Laudon, 2004). Firms must constantly understand, adapt to, and respond to the changes in both the task and general environments in which they operate. This can be a critical factor in achieving sustained growth, competitive advantage, and becoming a market driver.

Strategies for Sustaining a Market-Driving Status

There is certainly a deficiency in the current body of knowledge, theory, and line of thought when it comes to examining and studying the market-driving firms and the concept. This is particularly noticeable when it comes to the question of sustainability. What exactly are the sustainability factors that account for the continued success and power of market-driving firms? So far, research has yielded little or no published or recommended readings on this particular division and avenue of the subject matter. Therefore, it is the researchers' aim to propose several sustainability factors, with a definitive assumption that market driving is sustainable. This assumption is based heavily on the fact that sustainability of competitive advantage is instrumental in attaining market-driving status. Competitive advantage is not achieved overnight and neither are the resulting market advantages. When firms have achieved market-driving status, this means that they have managed and sustained their competitive advantage with unmatched superiority.

Because the business environment is characterized by competition, markets, customers' expectations, and technological changes — globalization and progress have made such changes rapid and unpredictable. Market driving firms must therefore, grapple with these factors to remain on course. Competitors constantly modify their strategies and copy market leaders' strategic systems, and as a result will eventually affect the ability of the market-driving firms to maintain their influence and competitive advantage. With this in mind, market drivers need to consider factors that will sustain their market-driving powers or positions in the industry. These factors should include a combination of strategies and policies designed to constantly assess marketing strength and opportunities, gauging these against competitors' strategies and programs, and rerouting developmental processes.

Other sustainability factors that market-driving firms can use to maintain their power include constant generation of new ideas within the organization, conducting regular assessment on market assignment position, constant incremental changes in innovation and technology, value chain management and supervision, product planning and research, quality management assessment, trend-setting strategies, and definition and establishment of new marketing niches. According to Ghingold and Johnson (1998), the ability of business marketers to monitor, strategically adopt, and manage new technologies is an important predictor of long-term competitiveness. Sustaining market driving can be as difficult as achieving it, especially in an environment where change is the only certainty. Market-driving firms must recognize that management information must be of strategic and operational value in positioning themselves for continued success (Brooks, 1989).

What exactly are the functions of market-driving businesses, and how do they influence and affect the global marketing environment in which they operate? Do market-driving firms constrain or restrict marketing environment and factors, or do they just simply adapt and react? These are questions that are vital in examining the limitations of market-driving firms. After all, the laws of economics will hold under all circumstances, and therefore, the thought of having absolute market power, especially in the global capitalist market should be far from mind. Market-driving firms do have the same functions as other firms in the market, except that their influences are greater through their abilities to influence and affect the market with their radical ideas, innovative designs, new marketing techniques, unique value propositions, and leap in the value offer and perception, as well as value added services and products.

The fact is that market-driving firms can hardly constrain the marketing environment in terms of its growth, because supply and demand both remain superior in theory and real world application as far as capitalist approaches are concerned. However, as a result of their competitive advantages they do restrict markets, especially where entry barriers come into play to deter other firms that might be seeking market shares. Market-driving firms do not have absolute powers because markets do not exist in a vacuum. Market-driving firms must simply react and adapt to changes in the market that have been initiated by factors that do not operate under their control. Global economic, technological, legal, and political factors are included among these. Market drivers would have greater ability to affect market through competitor relations than attempting to influence global economic changes, and this alone makes them just like any other firm; react and adapt or perish.

Market-driving firms can find themselves more limited than market-driven firms in the global market environment because of the fact that their success, strategies, policies, and programs are more greatly influenced and affected by a variety of unstable factors such as emerging technological systems, international relations, and affairs. The market is not always "manageable" and this becomes very evident when several large-scale factors blend to affect global markets. Market-driving firms must acknowledge that they are on a risky road where constant competition is the norm and systems changes are required to sustain success. Markets are best seen as dynamic interactions of innumerable variables; controllable and uncontrollable, and these are operational at all levels, affecting all firms. Market-driving firms, although have acquired distinction on several levels, are not invisible hands within and by themselves. With this said, Rich (2000) advocates the careful focus of businesses on the direction of marketing relationships as they affect growth and performance.

There seems to be little doubt that there is a dynamic relationship taking place between the market-driving businesses and the global market. This dynamic relationship can be referred to as a facilitative exchange involving reciprocal variables of systems and processes, which coordinate and synchronize to engender sustained economic progress and technological growth and expansion. Market-driving businesses are currently those delivering on the demands of the global market with a high degree of success that enables globalization to be a process still in its growth. The relationship between strategies and market position should be carefully considered by firms (Piontek, 1983). Measures and variables of marketing success have been reoriented by global definitions, and market-driving businesses are well aware of this, and therefore have strategically positioned and maneuvered themselves to respond adequately to the new concepts of value, quality, and standards.

The global market requires businesses that can change at the speed of lightning; moving progressively with technology and trends in the industries and world economy. Market-driving businesses live up to this very elusive and ever-changing value proposition because value in the global market environment has no stability, but changes with emerging ideas and technologies oriented toward an uncertain future. This is where the risk characteristic of market drivers is seen as an inherent quality, because this uncertainty implies a degree of risk never before encountered in firms and industries. With the changing nature of economies, transformation into industrialized systems, the emergence of digital firms, transformation of enterprise, and globalization of industries, market-driving firms can sustain growth and performance by using the following factors to keep themselves in check. These factors (with modifications) were originally proposed by Norris (1991) as critical success factors in market-driven management, but can be applied to market drivers to ensure constant development: providing energetic leadership, engaging in sound strategic thinking, developing new marketing capabilities, utilizing market-driving management philosophy in all core processes, building infrastructure in accordance with technological advancement, and constantly adapting corporate culture to environment. Furthermore, market-driving businesses must capitalize upon knowledge-based and experienced-based marketing skills in sustaining their growth. According to Thomas (1994) knowledge-based and experience-based marketing will increasingly define the capabilities of a successful marketing organization.

The current interactions and exchanges existing between market-driving businesses and the global market are at their best evolutionary, and these firms like any other will have to adapt and respond correctly to changes in the general environment to sustain their growth and possibility. These firms will need to constantly develop and implement strategies to sustain this dynamic exchange and interaction on all levels or otherwise regress to being market driven and only relatively competitive. Some market-driving firms such as K-Mart and Sears have failed to adapt at the fast rate required by the global market and therefore, they have been unable to sustain their market power and influence. On the other side, firms like Wal-Mart might just simply adapt a culture of innovation and progress as far as the market will travel.

Wal-Mart as Market-Driving Example

Wal-Mart, a Delaware corporation, has its principal offices in Bentonville, Arkansas. In 1962, the first Wal-Mart Discount City store was opened. In 1984, the company opened its first three Sam's Clubs, and in 1988, its first Wal-Mart Super Center (combination of full-line supermarket and discount store). Wal-Mart sells more toys than Toys "R" Us, more clothes than the Gap and Limited combined, and more food than Kroger and many other supermarkets combined (Upbin, 2004). Upbin (2004), in his *Forbes* article, states that if Wal-Mart were its own economy, it would rank 30th right next to Saudi Arabia while growing at the rate of 11 percent each year. As of April 2004, Wal-Mart had over 3550 stores in the United States and has plans to add over 1000 supercenters nationally by the year 2009.

In 1992, the company began its first international initiative to provide the same value and low prices on a global scale. The company's international presence has continued to expand and is growing faster than ever across the globe. Jointly, the sales from the countries of Canada, Mexico, and the United Kingdom make up about 80 percent of its international revenues. Wal-Mart, with $47.5 billion in international sales making up one fifth of its overall revenues in 2004, has enjoyed an enormous success and does not seem to be losing momentum nationally or internationally, despite some temporary challenges and setbacks. With more than one million associates nationwide and over 400,000 employees internationally, Wal-Mart is the fastest growing and largest private employer in the United States. According to Upbin (2004), the Wal-Martization of the world is bringing about good and bad changes to commerce around the globe. Because of its relentless vision for low prices, more and more manufacturing jobs are moving to developing economies such as China, leaving U.S. workers unemployed. On the other hand, international commerce through Wal-Mart will create "over 800,000 jobs worldwide over the next several years, not to mention the labor needed to build the stores, parking lots and distribution centers" (Upbin, 2004). Wal-Mart is expected to be the first trillion-dollar retailer in the world. Wal-Mart has become what it is due to its national and international market-driving strategies and operations that show an organization, which is both effective and efficient in pursuit of providing low prices for customers. Wal-Mart has been consistently rated as the number one efficient retailer in the world (Biesada, 2004). The application and realization of their slogan "always low prices, always" is perhaps one of the main reasons for its success at home and abroad. Wal-Mart partners with efficient suppliers to provide consumers with quality goods at affordable prices in their stores (Moore, 2004).

Wal-Mart's founding philosophy and the implementation of successful leadership skills and management strategies have led to its global success. One can easily expand on some of the strategies that have brought them enormous success and opportunities in today's competitive world of retail business. Some of Wal-Mart's highlights are the following:

- Total sales at Wal-Mart were $256 billion with 68 percent from Wal-Mart Stores, 19 percent from its international operations, and 13 percent coming from its Sam's Club. Wal-Mart's annual profits are about $9 billion and they have a market value of $244 billion with assets worth over $105 billion during 2004.

- As of April 2004, in addition to its 3550 stores in the United States, Wal-Mart had 640 stores in Mexico, 404 stores in Japan, 267 stores in the United Kingdom, 236 stores in Canada, 92 stores in Germany, 53 stores in Puerto Rico, 34 stores in China, 25 stores in Brazil, 15 stores in South Korea, and 11 stores in Argentina while expanding into these countries on a continuous basis.
- Wal-Mart employs over one million people in the United States and nearly half million individuals internationally.
- It ranked tenth on *Forbes*' "Leading 2000 Companies in the World" based on a composite score for sales, profits, assets, and overall market value. As a matter of fact, Wal-Mart ranked first in sales, sixth in total market value, and eighth in overall profits through *Forbes*' ranking of world's 2000 leading companies in *Forbes*' April 12th issue.
- Wal-Mart is recognized as one of the leading employers of individuals with disabilities in the United States. In the 2002 annual poll by *Careers for the Disabled* magazine, it named Wal-Mart first among all the U.S. companies in providing opportunities and a positive work environment for people with disabilities.
- Wal-Mart is one of the leading employers of senior citizens in the United States, employing more than 170,000 associates who are 55 years of age and older.
- Wal-Mart received the Hispanic National Bar Association (HNBA) 2002 Corporate Partner of the Year Award for its consistent support and best practices in the area of diversity.
- Wal-Mart is the leading private employer of emerging groups in the United States. More than 160,000 African American associates and more than 105,000 Hispanic associates work for Wal-Mart.
- Wal-Mart received the 2002 Ron Brown Award, the highest presidential award recognizing outstanding achievement in employee relations and community initiatives.
- The National Action Network (NAN) presented Wal-Mart with the 2002 Community Commitment Corporate Award in recognition of community involvement and diversity practices.

Summary

Being and remaining a market-driving force in the 21st century's global and competitive environment requires strategic planning and effective execution. Although firms like Publix Super Market, Sears, and K-Mart have seen their share of market success in the past four decades, Wal-Mart has outpaced, outperformed, and outmaneuvered them and many others in the retail industry by effectively using market-driving strategies. Upbin (2004) stated that, for Wal-Mart, "Europe has proven at times adept, at times inept, at acquiring. In China, it struggles with a dauntingly primitive supply chain. In Japan it is taking rice-grain-size steps so as not to damage a powerful but backward retail ecosystem... it... stumbled among stronger competitors in the huge markets of Brazil and Argentina." Wal-Mart, to sustain its market-driving status and success, entered Hong Kong and two years later in 1996 left due to mistakes in merchandize selection and location. It left Indonesia in less than two years after its entry in 1996 because one of their stores in Jakarta was looted during the riots. Furthermore, Wal-Mart made mistakes in Germany, South Korea, Brazil, and other international locations but because of its distaste for repeating mistakes, Wal-Mart's marketing driving managers learn and adjust quickly. Wal-Mart is so massive that now it has a market capitalization as large as the gross domestic product of many developed countries.

Modern business is a study in perpetual motion — expansion, closures, bankruptcies, cost cutting, mergers, acquisitions, divestitures, turnarounds, and retreats. Organizations are in a constant state of flux as they reshape themselves to meet the demands of investors, employees, owners, and customers simultaneously. The companies that are built to last and grow are market driving as they change on all fronts nationally and internationally while increasing the value for all relevant stakeholders such as customers, employees, owners, and third parties by providing everyone great value. Wal-Mart has shown that it is keeping its momentum for creating superior value by offering an organizational culture that is passionate about market-driving strategies while remaining flexible to reduce cost and offer lower prices to sustain their industry success and status.

References

Adawi, N. (1989). Market Driven Systems. *Communications* 26(9): 146.

Anon., (2001). When Composters Manage "Market Driven" Companies. *BioCycle.* 42(9): 14.

Bateman, T. and Snell, S. (1999). *Management: Building Competitive Advantage*, 4th edition. Boston, MA: Irwin McGraw-Hill.

Biesada, A. (2004). Wal-Mart Stores, Inc. Hoover's On-Line. Retrieved January 18, 2004 from http://www.hoovers.com/wal-mart/ID_11600/free-co-factsheet.html

Brooks, N.A.L. (1989). Market Driven. *Banking Strategies* 65(11): 46.

Day, G.S. (1998). What Does It Mean to Be Market-Driven? *Business Strategy Review* 9(1): 1–14.

Day, G.S. (2000). The Market Driven Organization. *Direct Marketing*. Garden City. Jan. 2000, Vol 62(9) p. 32.

Day, G.S. (2000). The Market-Driven Organization. *Direct Marketing* 62(10): 20.

Dries, M. (1997). Becoming Market Driven. *The Business Journal* 14(34): 10.

Gedansky, M. (1985). Strategic Planning in the High-Tech Industry: A Market Driven Focus. *Managerial Planning* 33(6): 32.

Ghingold, M. and Johnson, B. (1998). Intrafirm Technical Knowledge and Competitive Advantage: A Framework for Superior Market Driven Performance. *The Journal of Business & Industrial Marketing* 13(1): 70.

Harris, L.C. and Cai, K.Y. (2002). Exploring Market Driving: A Case Study of De Beers in China. *Journal of Market-Focused Management* 5: 171–196.

Jaworski, B., Kohli, A., and Sahay, A. (2000). Market-Driven versus Driving Markets. *Journal of the Academy of Marketing Science* 28: 45–54.

Johnson, W.C. and Weinstein, A. (2004). *Superior Customer Value in the New Economy: Concepts and Cases,* 2nd Edition. St. Lucie, FL: CRC Press.

Kim, W.C. and Mauborgne, R. (1997). Value Innovation: The Strategic Logic of High Growth. *Harvard Business Review* 75(1): 102–112.

Kumar, N. (1997). Revolution in Retailing: From Market Driven to Market Driving. *Long Range Planning* 30(6): 830.

Kumar, N., Scheer, L., and Kotler, P. (2000). From Market Driven to Market Driving. *European Management Journal* 18(2): 129–142.

Landry, J.T. (1999). The Market Driven Organization: Understanding, Attracting, and Keeping Valuable Customers. *Harvard Business Review* 77(6): 171.

Laudon, K.C. and Laudon, J.P. (2004). *Management Information Systems: Managing the Digital Firm*, 8th edition. Upper Saddle River, NJ: Prentice Hall.

Massing, M. (2001). Market Driven. *Columbia Journalism Review* 39(6): 37.

Maxwell, L.M. (1999) The Market Driven Organization: Understanding, Attracting, and Keeping Valuable Customers. *Library Journal* 124(17): 80.

Maxwell, D.M. and Steele, J. (1989). Are You Truly Market Driven? *Telephony* 217(1): 24.

Moore, S. (2004). Beaumont, California Approves Wal-Mart; Critics Say Small Businesses Will Suffer. *Knight Ridder Tribune Business News*. Retrieved April 11, 2004 from ProQuest database. http://0-proquest.umi.com

Narasimhan, K. (2003). Market Driven Enterprise: Product Development, Supply Chains, and Manufacturing. *The TQM Magazine* 15(1): 61.

Norris, D.M. (1991). Market-Driven Success. *Association Management* 43(11): 32.

Prahalad, C.K. and Hamel, G. (1994). Strategy as a Field of Study: Why Search for a New Paradigm? *Strategic Management Journal* 15: 5.

Piontek, S. (1983). Are Products or Markets Driving Your Strategy? *National Underwriter* (Life & health/financial services ed.). Erlanger: Mar 5, Vol. 87, Iss. 10; p. 2.

Pohlman, R. and Gardiner, G. (2000). *Value Driven Management: How to Create and Maximize Value Over Time for Organizational Success*, New York: AMACOM.

Porter M.E. (1985). *Competitive Advantage: Creating and Sustaining Superior Performance.* New York: Free Press.

Rich, M.K. (2000). The Direction of Marketing Relationship. *The Journal of Business and Industrial Marketing* 15(2/3): p. 170.

Smith, J.S. (1997). Strategic Planning Is to Be Market Driven. *Transmission & Distribution World* 49(1): 39.

Thomas, M.J. (1994). Marketing — In Chaos or Transition? *European Journal of Marketing* 28(3): 55.

Upbin, B. (2004). Wall to Wall Wal-Mart: The Retailer Conquered America and Made it Look Easy. The Rest of the World is a Tougher Battleground. *Forbes: The World's 2000 Leading Companies.* April 12, 2004 issue.

Vervack, J.C. (1993). Market Driven — A Product of Change. *Broker World* 13(10): 40.

Zell, D. (2001). The Market-Driven Business School: Has the Pendulum Swung too Far? *Journal of Management Inquiry* 10(4): 324.

Zultowski, W.H. (1992). Driven by the Market. *Advisor Today* July 1992.

Chapter 46

Revenues and Expenditures in Russian Oblasts: The Changing Role of Financing State and Local Public Services

Jane Beckett-Camarata and Anna A. Anickeeva

CONTENTS

Introduction

The economic performance of the Russian economy is very different from the economic performance of other countries in Eastern Europe that have also undertaken market reforms. Yet real Russian gross domestic product (GDP) declined for eight years and stabilized for a period of time. Other countries such as Poland, for example, have benefited from continued high economic growth. This chapter explores oblast and federation intergovernmental fiscal relations as a possible reason as to why Russia lags behind in economic growth.

A unique dataset taken from Russian oblasts' budgets is used to show that any change in oblast revenues is almost entirely offset by an opposite change in shared revenues. Oblast revenues do not benefit from an increase in the federation tax base, and therefore lack an incentive to expand the tax base. A model is used to illustrate that if fiscal incentives are weak, the oblast's ability to increase marginal revenue by increasing its tax base is close to zero. Further, stronger fiscal incentives should lead to higher efficiency in provision of public goods, because a smaller portion of public expenditure is wasted.

The purpose of this study is to describe the financial base for stable, safe, and competitive development of a region. This analysis will be achieved through examining Russian regional budgets. First, we provide some evidence that shows that the spending at the oblast level increases with oblast fiscal incentives. For each oblast and each year, we gauge the strength of fiscal incentives by an indicator of the crowding out of changes in own revenues by changes in shared revenues. We estimate how the variation in the strength of incentives helps to predict the variation in outcome of public goods.

Literature Review

The theoretical basis for this study is the theory of "market-preserving federalism." This literature emphasizes the importance of fiscal and political incentives for economic growth (Monitola et al., 1995) and argues that some local governments have the incentive to pursue local-economic growth and possibly create a basis for a positive economic performance. The importance of these fiscal relationships is that they generate a positive relationship between the local revenue and the local-economic prosperity, thus providing an incentive to local officials. Because the Russian fiscal system contrasts with the literature on fiscal federalism, the system of intergovernmental relations in Russia could be called "market inhibiting federalism" because local revenues are independent of the local-economic prosperity.

Schleifer (1997) describes Russia's economic problems partly as a result of the government's failure to provide institutions that promote economic growth. There has been extensive previous research on Russian federal–regional fiscal relations. Triesman (1996a,b, 1997) established that federal grants are distributed purely according to the political negotiation and do not follow the economic objectives of the federation. Lavrov (1996) demonstrated that there is a vertical imbalance between the distribution of revenue and expenditure responsibility and a competition between and among the levels of government is generally accepted (Tiebout, 1956, 1961). Oates justified the need for decentralization of government functions. He argued that a requirement that central governments provide equal amounts of public goods to all citizens (regardless of their preferences or income levels), though it would meet certain equity objectives would fail to provide optimal levels of social welfare in a general equilibrium function. Oates decentralization theorem describes the situation where subnational fiscal autonomy provides local control over revenue and expenditure policy and tax administration. A general principle of fiscal federalism is that "each function of government should be provided at the lowest level of government in the fiscal hierarchy, consistent with the requirements of efficiency and effectiveness" (Tresch, 2002).

This study describes the revenues and expenditures variations in that context in selected Russian oblasts. There has been a void in our understanding of the effect of Russian federal–oblast intergovernmental fiscal relations on oblast revenue and expenditures. The focus of this chapter is on describing the effects of fiscal negotiation between the Russian federation and oblasts. The chapter is organized as follows: the next section compares the Russian government and the U.S. intergovernmental system. The section on "Discussion" describes the data and the empirical methodology. The section on "Empirical Evidence from Russian Oblasts" describes the model of fiscal incentives and the results. The final section presents the conclusion.

Russia versus U.S. Intergovernmental Relations

In this section, organizational structures of governments in the United States and Russia are compared and it is argued that although they have many differences, they have some similarities as well. They do differ substantially in revenue sharing processes and the incentives created by those processes. While Russia is a unitary federal state, the United States is a federal system that distributes authority among the various levels of federal, state, and local government. In Russia, there are five levels of government. The top three levels are authorized to collect their own revenue and make decisions on expenditures. In 1991, the first tier local governments became officially independent from the upper levels and since 1993, the independence of the first tier local governments has been guaranteed by the Constitution.

Expenditure Responsibilities

The distribution of expenditure responsibilities among levels of government is similar in the United States and Russia. In Russia, one third of the spending takes place on the local level. In the United States, approximately 60 percent of state and local spending takes place at the local level (U.S. Census, 2002) (www.uscensus.gov). Expenditure responsibilities between the different levels of government are poorly defined in Russia, whereas in the United States they are clearly defined. Oblasts and counties are responsible for providing some basic goods such as education and healthcare, public transportation, police protection, etc. In Russia, the largest share of expenditures at the oblast level is the subsidies to large industrial enterprises and utilities. In the United States, such subsidies constitute a smaller portion of the budget.

Oblast Revenue Sources

The sources and structure of revenue for Russian oblasts and U.S. counties are somewhat similar. Revenues in Russia consist of own and shared revenues. The oblast revenues consist mostly of *ad hoc* taxes, including licenses and fees, surcharges and fines, and some nontax revenues that come from private property leases, profits from municipal enterprises and TVEs, and privatization. The U.S. county's own source revenue consists mainly of property taxes and user fees. The Russian components of shared revenue are taxes shared with upper levels of government and transfers from upper levels of government. The Russian and the U.S. fiscal structures look somewhat similar. U.S. local governments have more autonomy in their decisions on taxation and expenditures than Russian oblasts do. There is one major difference between the U.S. and the Russian intergovernmental fiscal relations and that is the revenue sharing between the different levels of government.

Revenue Sharing

In the United States, there is wide diversity of revenue sharing arrangements. There are coordination mechanisms that accommodate more than one level of government using a single tax base. These coordination mechanisms include: (1) cooperative administration; (2) coordinated tax bases; (3) tax supplements; and (4) centralized administration (Mikesell, 2000). Cooperative administration involves continuous contact and information exchange among taxing units. With coordinated tax bases, one government links its tax to some point in the tax structure of another government. For example, several states key their individual income tax to federal adjusted gross income, and a number of localities begin their local sales tax ordinances with definitions taken from their state sales tax. Tax supplements provide more coordination, either through applying a lower-level rate on the base used by the higher level (many state sales taxes have supplements added by localities) or applying a lower-level rate that is a percentage of tax paid to the higher level (a few states define their income tax to be a percentage of federal liability. The last coordination system is central administration of a "piggy-back tax." A lower-government unit applies its own rate to the tax base used by a higher government unit. Fully piggybacking means higher unit doing all the administrative and the enforcement work, the taxpayer reports on a single form to the higher unit, which records for and remits collections to the lower unit (Mikesell, 2000).

The regional–local and federal–regional revenue sharing arrangements in Russia are frequently renegotiated. Thus, the revenues of the Russian government at subnational levels depend largely on the distribution of bargaining power. As a result of this bargaining, budget funds of oblasts and local governments are independent of their efforts to raise additional own revenues. Treisman (1996a,b, 1997) demonstrated that negotiation over the federal–regional sharing gives oblasts incentives to encourage separation and other forms of political revolt against the federation government. The components of shared revenues at the oblast level are determined through annual or biannual negotiations between oblast and federation officials. In most oblasts, the portions of shared taxes and amounts of transfers are not determined on the basis of a fixed formula, and they vary over time and across oblasts.

Federation authorities set target levels of expenditures for oblasts based on past experience. These targets serve as a basis for the amounts of shared revenue allocated regionally. Oblast officials estimate the "required level of expenditures" for each local government in the oblast, and the total amount of funds that are to be distributed among the localities in the form of shared revenues with the localities. This further results in large cities within oblasts having no incentive to maximize its own source revenue because additional revenue is taxed away by the oblast.

Discussion

In this section the data is described. We used a unique dataset of oblasts over a three-year period. This dataset includes oblasts in Russia for the time period of 1995–1997. To supplement the data, face-to-face interviews were conducted with selected oblast officials in the summer of 2002. Table 46.1 presents the expenditures and the revenues.

Astrakhan, Volgograd, Voronesh, Rostov, and Saratov regions and the Republic of Kalmykia represent interesting and important cases in the study of budgeting during the economic reform. Compared to other oblasts, Astrakhan, Volgograd, Voronesh, Rostov, and Saratov regions and the Republic of Kalmykia have had more budget stability and maintained fiscal balances through shared political norms.

Rapid budgetary change has been one of the most difficult challenges for Russia since the dramatic political changes in the 1980s and early 1990s. Russian oblasts have had to adapt to radical new budget policies while reinventing budgetary institutions to facilitate economic restructuring and democratization. In the recent years, budgeting has been increasingly recognized as one of the most critical, integrative processes in governing. This is especially true for Russian oblasts that are adapting from a command economy to a more decentralized resource allocation.

The Russian budget system is currently adapting to market conditions. This change means that a financial base for regional systems functioning is being formed and "rationally evaluated local revenues create the conditions for harmonious development of social and industrial infrastructures in separate regions and all over the country" (Povolzhye, 1999). At present, "the finance flows are primarily accumulated in the center, coming from the regions to Moscow, and then they return to the regions as transfers. The regions turn out to be beggars asking for their own money and depending on the federal authorities' grade" (Povolzhye, 1999). Thus, the regions are unlikely to provide their own self-financing and federal subsidies, so the transfers and subvention distribution methods are subjective in many respects, i.e., they depend on the federal authorities' decisions.

The same subjectivity can be observed in budget policies of all the countries. As Berge writes, "Not a single day passes without someone's demand for new budgetary credits to support some economy sectors experiencing difficulties, to buy equipment for schools and universities, or for computer science development; they constantly claim to increase banking crediting to create favorable conditions for capital construction, industrial investments, and even-if we consider some more particular matters, for energy conservation, or small enterprises creation" (Berge, 1993). Despite this situation, in the economically developed countries, the objective budgetary regulation methods based on normative approaches, which are fully described, should play the decisive role.

It is the subjective approach that prevails in Russia, and the approach "doesn't allow for leveling of social and industrial infrastructure disparities of the country's regions. Indeed, it doesn't create the necessary conditions for carrying out rational policy in this field" (Berge, 1993). The next section will describe the oblasts selected for this study.

Saratov Oblast

Saratov is located in the heart of the Volga River Valley region. It was once the capital of the lower Volga region and it is now the center of one of the biggest provinces in Russia. Saratov is located in the southeast of the East European plain in the lower Volga region. The oblast's area equals the total area of states such as Belgium, Switzerland, and Albania. Saratov has a size close to 380 sq. km and a population of about 900,000 people. An additional two million people live in the surrounding area.

Volgograd Oblast

The object of our analysis is Volgograd region, which includes the list of neighboring regions, economic entities, viewed together as an external competitive environment. Volgograd is known throughout the world for World War II's Battle of Stalingrad. It is the gateway to southern Russia. It is located 1073 km southeast of Moscow at the point where the Volga-Don Canal connects the two Russian rivers. Volgograd is the world's longest thinnest city. It stretches nearly 100 km along the Volga River and at places is often no more than 5 km wide. The Volgograd oblast has a population of 2.7 million; the city of Volgograd has a population of over one million people. There are 33 administrative districts, 18 towns, and 27 settlements in the region. Within the Volga River Basin, Volgograd ranks third in industrial output and industrially is among the top petrochemical and fuel industries. The region's agriculture is highly developed with high grain production and in total agricultural output it ranks among the best in the Volga River Basin. The region is rich in oil, natural gas, phosphorites, cooking and chlormagnesium (bischofite) salts, mineral water, mason's sand, and limestone.

Voronezh Oblast

Voronezh oblast, one of the most important industrial and agricultural centers of Russia, is actively participating in market reforms in the Russian Federation. The oblast is connected by rail, air, and water to all the major centers within Russia and abroad. The Voronezh oblast is about 600 km south of Moscow and has a population of about 2.5 million. The oblast has traditionally contributed a large part to Russia's total agricultural output; however, the economy is diverse because about 25 percent of the working population is employed in manufacturing. Voronezh-based industries are involved in synthetic, rubber, mechanical engineering, and chemical and electronics industries.

Rostov oblast is a regional subdivision. Rostov-on-Don is the capital of Rostov oblast in the northern Caucasus district of Russia, located at the Don River near the Sea of Azov. Rostov has a population of 1,012,300.

Republic of Kalmykia

The Republic of Kalmykia has its administrative center at the City of Elista. Kalmykia's region is situated in the steppe, semidesert, and desert zones and occupies 75,900 sq. km of territory. It exceeds the size of European nations such as Belgium, Denmark, Switzerland, and the Netherlands all together. The Republic is situated in the southeast of the European part of the Russian Federation. It verges on Rostov oblast on the west, Volgograd oblast on the north and northwest, Astrakhan oblast on the east, and Republic of Dagestan on the south and Stvaropol territory on the southwest.

The data on budget revenue and expenditure dynamics of Volgograd region and the neighboring regions (except the Republic of Kazakhstan) is the basis for the analysis. The result of the analysis will be the objective estimation of budgetary processes in the regions, including the characteristics of the Volgograd region financial plan in the developing competitive environment.

While using some separate budget revenue and expenditure indices of the region, we will show how financial provision changes their volume and rate. The analysis used is described in the Russian literature discussed previously. This chapter will analyze and describe the revenues and expenditures of regions in Volgograd Oblast. The initial budgetary revenue and expenditure indices of Astrakhan, Volgograd, Voronesh, Rostov, and Saratov regions and the Republic of Kalmykia are presented in Table 46.1 to Table 46.4.

Because the revenues and expenditures of the budgets are different in different regions, the influence of each one on the total result is estimated through the subindices of annual growth, average growth, and growth rate. In this case, the subindices are particular indices of different oblasts estimated with allowance for the share of receipts in total revenue and for the index characterizing the dynamics of budget revenue and expenditure volume.

Our analysis reveals the existence of conflict between regional finances. The Volgograd oblast is characterized by the lack of federal "guardianship" as compared to neighboring oblasts. The subsidy rates are decreasing several times and consequently the material base of the regional economic

Table 46.1 The Regional Budgetary Revenue and Expenditure Volume and Growth (billions of rubles)

	Revenues				*Expenditures*			
	1995	*1996*	*1997*	*Structure in percent*	*1995*	*1996*	*1997*	*Structure in percent*
Region								
Volgograd	3,749.7	4,449.2	4,532.6		3,826.3	4,695.1	4,830.1	
Voronezh	2,539.6	2,964.5	3,710.0		2,560.3	3,144.4	3,659.5	
Saratov	3,188.4	4,020.5	4,996.8		3,210.4	4,119.1	6,213.5	
Rostov	4,883.3	5,623.4	5,887.0		4,869.6	5,564.4	6,419.9	
Astrakhan	1,456.9	1,581.8	1,994.5		1,469.2	1,736.3	2,347.9	
Republic of Kalmykia	529.1	559.1	826.9		527.7	646.2	972.7	
Total	16,347.0	19,198.5	21,947.8		16,463.5	19,905.5	24,515.6	
Annual Growth								
Volgograd		699.5	83.4	24.5		868.8	135.0	25.2
Voronezh		424.9	745.5	14.9		584.1	515.1	17.0
Saratov		832.1	976.3	29.2		908.7	2,094.4	26.4
Rostov		740.1	263.6	26.0		694.8	927.5	20.2
Astrakhan		124.9	412.7	4.4		267.1	611.6	7.8
Republic of Kalmykia		30.0	267.8	1.1		118.5	326.5	3.4
Total		2,851.5	2,749.3	100		3,442.0	4,610.1	100
Average Revenue/ Expenditures								
Volgograd		4,099.5	4,490.9	23.1		4,260.7	4,762.6	23.4
Voronezh		2,752.1	3,337.3	15.5		2,852.4	3,402.0	15.7
Saratov		3,604.5	4,508.7	20.3		3,664.8	5,166.3	20.2
Rostov		5,253.4	5,755.2	29.6		5,217.0	6,028.2	28.7
Astrakhan		1,519.4	1,788.2	8.5		1,602.8	2,042.1	8.8

Table 46.1 The Regional Budgetary Revenue and Expenditure Volume and Growth (billions of rubles) (*Continued*)

	Revenues				*Expenditures*			
	1995	*1996*	*1997*	*Structure in percent*	*1995*	*1996*	*1997*	*Structure in percent*
Republic of Kalmykia		544.1	693.0	3.1		587.0	809.5	3.2
Total		17,772.8	20,573.2	100.0		18,184.5	22,210.6	100.0
Growth Rate								
Volgograd		0.1706	0.0186			0.2039	0.0283	
Voronezh		0.1544	0.2234			0.2048	0.1514	
Saratov		0.2309	0.2165			0.2480	0.4054	
Rostov		0.1409	0.0458			0.1332	0.1539	
Astrakhan		0.0822	0.2308			0.1667	0.2995	
Republic of Kalmykia		0.0551	0.3864			0.2019	0.4034	

The revenue (expenditure) changes are characterized in all their structural elements by the following indices: annual revenue (expenditure) growth of i-region estimated as the difference between annual receipts.

Table 46.2 Budgetary Revenue (Expenditure) of Selected Russian Federation Regions Revenue (Expenditures) 2002

Region	*Revenue*	*Expenditure*
Volgograd	0.1192	0.1554
Voronezh	1.7545	0.8819
Saratov	1.1733	2.3048
Rostov	0.3562	1.3349
Astrakhan	3.3042	2.2898
Republic of Kalmykia	8.9267	1.3394
Total Percent Revenue (Expenditure) of Region	15.6341	8.3062
Average Regional Percentage of Total	2.6057	1.3844

Table 46.3 Average Actual Growth (1997 compared to 2002) in Region Revenue (Expenditure)

Region	*Revenue*	*Expenditure*
Volgograd	1.0955	1.1178
Voronezh	1.2126	1.1927
Saratov	1.2509	1.4097
Rostov	1.0955	1.1555
Astrakhan	1.1769	1.2741
Republic of Kalmykia	1.2737	1.3791
Total Actual Growth	7.1051	7.5289
Average Actual Percentage Growth 1998 compared to 2002	1.1842	1.2548

Table 46.4 Average Expected Revenue (Expenditure) Growth Rate 1997 vs. 2002) Based on Population

Region	*Revenue*	*Expenditure*
Volgograd	0.1088	0.1390
Voronezh	1.4469	0.7394
Saratov	0.9380	1.6349
Rostov	0.3251	1.1553
Astrakhan	2.8075	1.7971
Republic of Kalmykia	7.0087	1.9979
Total Average Expected Percentage Revenue Growth	12.6350	7.4636
Average Expected Percentage Growth Based on Population	2.1058	1.2439

Note: Table 46.4 Growth Rate Index is calculated on what the percent revenue and expenditures should be based on population.

Authors' Computations Based on Russian Ministry of Finance State Budget for 1995, 1996, 1997 and 2002 documents in the authors' possession.

development is diminishing with all the corresponding results. The data confirms the previous finding that "the Ministry of Finance of the Russian Federation uses subjective methods when estimating the transfers, and as a result, the rate of financial assistance to regions such as Volgograd Region from the federal budget is several times smaller (both in absolute sums and in percentage) than that of its neighbors. (Povolzhye, 1999).

Empirical Evidence from Russian Oblasts

In this section, we present evidence that the fiscal incentives of Russian oblasts are very weak and we further show the absence of fiscal incentive. When the city collects more taxes on its own, the federation cuts transfers to certain oblasts and lowers the oblast portion of shared taxes. We also found evidence that the budget constraints for oblasts are soft, because the federation not only taxes away marginal own revenues, but also provides additional revenues if there is a shortfall in own revenues. Because Russian oblasts do not have a secure, independent source of revenue, which would not be subject to seizure by the regional governments, they never became independent fiscal entities. In addition, Russian oblasts and local governments tend to overregulate businesses whereas in the United States, we have relatively few regulations over private businesses. Extrabudgetary funds however are available at the federation and oblast level but generally do not exist at the local level. Moscow and St. Petersburg have the same status as a region or oblast so they do not have the same problems as other cities.

We can hypothesize that wealthier oblasts experience increases in revenues, have efficient public goods provision, and have profitable growing enterprises, so do not need subsidies. In contrast, poor oblasts have to spend a lot on subsidies and experience both decline in revenues and poor public goods provision. In that case, the results would be driven by the presence of wealthy oblasts in the group with good fiscal incentives.

Conclusion

One of Russia's major problems is its structure of intergovernmental relations. The preliminary finding of this chapter is that Russian oblasts are not financially independent on the federation and this chapter provides some evidence that revenue sharing relations between the federation and the oblasts hinders incentives for providing infrastructure for private business development. In addition, the dependency of oblasts on the federation has a negative effect on the efficiency of local public goods provision.

The central finding of this research is that Russian fiscal reform still needs to be coordinated between all the levels of government. This is particularly true at the oblast level. Transfers in expenditures to higher decentralization will not accomplish the anticipated benefits without a simultaneous shift in control to the oblasts over how much revenue can be collected.

Bibliography

Anickeeva, A.A. (1996). The Subject Analysis of Property Relations Realization within the Framework of the Government Enterprise. *Vestnik of VSU.* Series 3: Economics Law. See also Anickeeva (1986). *Index Analysis of Role of Tax Payment in Budget Formation.* Questions of Statistics, pp. 96–101.

Bahl, R. (1994). Revenues and Revenue Assignment: Intergovernmental Fiscal Relations in the Russian Federation. In C.I. Wallich (ed.), *Russia and the Challenge of Fiscal Federalism.* Washington, D.C.: The World Bank. pp. 129–180

Berge, P. (1993). *Money Mechanism M: Progress.* Universe. pp. 128–129.

Dorogov, N. (1998). The Approval of the Choice of the Regional Economic Strategy. In Y. Kaleta (ed.), *The Problems of Management Theory and Practice.*

Kaleta, Y. (1999). The Financial Reform within the Framework of System Transformation. *The Problems of Management Theory and Practice.*

Lavrov, A. (1996). Fiscal Federalism and Financial Stabilization. *Problems of Economic Transition.* 39(1), 83–94.

Mikesell, J. (2000). *Fiscal Administration: Analysis and Applications for the Public Sector.* Sixth Edition. Belmont: Wadsworth Publishing.

Montinola, G., Qian, Y., and Weingast, B.R. (1995). Federalism Chinese Style: The Political Basis for Economic Success in China. *World Politics.* 48(1), 50–81.

Povolzhye, D. (1999). *Volgograd Has Become a Victim of the Budgetary Revolution.* (10) 2

Qian, Y and Weingast, B.R. 1996. China: Transition to Markets: Market Preserving Federalism, Chinese Style. Journal of Policy Reform 1(2): 149–186.

Treisman, D. (1997). The Politics of Intergovernmental Transfers in Post-Soviet Russia. *British Journal of Political Science.* 26, 299–335.

Schleifer, A. (1997). Government in Transition. *European Economic Review.* 41(3), 385–410.

Semenov, G. (1995). Establishing More Rational Relations between Federal and Regional Budgets. *Russian Social Science Review.* (36)5, 3–21.

Tiebout, C. (1956). A Pure Theory of Local Expenditures. *Journal of Political Economy.* Vol 64(5): 416–424.

Tiebout, C. (1961). An Economic Theory of Fiscal Decentralization. In NBER, Public Finance Needs, Sources, and Utilization, Princeton Univ. Press: 79–96.

Tresch, R.W. (2002). Public Finance: A Normative Theory, 2nd Academic Press: San Diego.

Treisman, D. (1996a). The Politics of Intergovernmental Transfers in Post-Soviet Russia. *British Journal of Political Science.* (26)3, 299–336.

Treisman, D. (1996b). Fiscal Redistribution in a Fragile Federation: Moscow and the Regions in 1994. *British Journal of Political Science.* 28, 185–222.

Treisman, D. (1998). *Deciphering Russia's Federal Finance: Fiscal Appeasement in 1995 and 1996*. Europe-Asia Studies, 50(5) July: 893–906.

www.USCensus.gov. U.S. State and Local Finances 2002.

IX

GLOBALIZATION AND THE FUTURE OF GOVERNANCE AND PUBLIC ADMINISTRATION

Chapter 47

The Earth Charter: Toward a New Global Environmental Ethic

O.P. Dwivedi and Renu Khator

CONTENTS

Our Attitudes toward Nature

Humans are a species, albeit the ecologically dominant one in the ecosystem that we inhabit. Although we have the same needs as do all other species, such as heat, light, water, and food, humans alone possess those attributes that give us dominance over other living species, and thus we can compete more successfully than all other living creatures. Furthermore, humans have been able to manipulate natural forces in the ecosystem with an intensity unsurpassed by any other living being. This manipulation has given rise to the breakdown of the natural self-protective and self-perpetuating mechanisms built into nature, a situation made yet worse by our belief that we have the right to use the natural environment solely for our own designs and ends, without consideration for the consequences of our actions to the system. In the Western world, at least, this view has dominated our thinking with respect to the environment and, at the same time, has provided the justification for our actions toward nature and the ecosystem.

The subjugation of nature, along with the primary emphasis on the use of technology and machines, became the credo of the industrial revolution and the motto of modern humanity, which was helped constantly by many scientific discoveries and tremendous technological advances. It seems that by the 1960s, when the human journey to the moon became a reality, our hegemony over nature and the universe was complete. It was thought then by many in the West that there was nothing that science and technology could not solve or achieve. Pollution (but not "environmental crisis") was seen, at least until the late 1960s, as a necessary side effect of progress, which could be prevented and controlled just as dreaded diseases such as small pox and plague had been. It was only in the 1970s that the effects of our activity on the biosphere became obvious, and questions such as the following were raised: Did we have a right to continuously exploit nature in the name of economic development and material progress? Was not the belief in our superiority over nature and the myth that we are endowed with an abundance of natural resources, the cause of many environmental problems and even some natural disasters? What are those factors which have influenced our view of nature?

Factors Influencing Our View of Nature

Our attitudes toward nature, and how we treat it, depend largely upon certain values, norms, and beliefs, which we have acquired over the past centuries. These factors can be grouped into four major divisions: (1) a desire to dominate and control nature, (2) acquisitive materialism, (3) a blind faith in science and technology, and (4) an unconstrained growth ethic in a limited world (Dwivedi, 1988, p. 9).

Much of the blame for fostering such attitudes toward nature must lie with these values and attitudes, as well as in institutions (such as laws, regulatory mechanisms, political process, market forces, scientific and professional bodies, and political ideologies) that reinforce such ethics and values. And one of the paradoxes of the environmental protection movement is that it seeks solutions to problems from the very same institutions that are a part of the problem. For example, we are compelled to look to scientists and engineers to develop better technologies, and thereby increase our dependence on the "technological fix." We look to lawyers who have provided us with laws that favor the prodevelopment lobby, and who are so clever in manipulating legal mechanisms and judicial procedures in favor of industrial and business interests. We look to politicians for comprehensive, long-term oriented legislative mechanisms, "knowing full well that the short-term, reactive perspective of the political process impairs their view of the problem." We look to economists for better and efficient working of their economic plans, not realizing that most of them are great proponents of the philosophy of "acquisitive materialism." And then we blame all others for the mess that we are in. At the same time, each group, be they scientists, engineers, economists, lawyers, business leaders, and others, has come out with its own paradigm of environmental issues and solutions. It is, however, not being realized that the sum total of all parts does not constitute the complete whole.

There is no doubt that much good has come from the determined and vigorous pursuits of such values by our scientists, technicians, engineers, economists, lawyers, industrialists, and various types of entrepreneurs. In the industrial countries of the Organization for Economic Cooperation and Development (OECD) (including Japan), people enjoy the material benefits not even dreamed of by their ancestors two generations ago. Furthermore, great strides have been made to eradicate several diseases, and the quality of healthcare is at an all-time high. And the more the West secures better quality of life for its citizens, the more emulative policies are put in place by the leaders of the third world and others. But the same values and attitudes, which have given rise to these material benefits and political and social progress, have also led to a situation where the exploitation of nature was also taken for granted; the continuation of these pursuits in the present manner has resulted, and could result, in dire consequences for humankind, and even beyond our planet. Many of these consequences have been already documented in the stories of dying lakes, Minimata disease, and cancer deaths.

How then can we the people inhabiting this planet preserve, protect, and sustain the environment while maintaining the benefits thus accrued and yet lay a foundation for an appropriate relationship with nature? Such a foundation, if it is to become an effective, workable, and comprehensive paradigm, must be based on a holistic approach to the comprehension, study, research, and solution of environmental problems. Such an approach would have to be built on a paradigm, which includes at least the following main components: (a) our values and beliefs, which are based on our religions and cultures, (b) our scientific and technological capabilities, and limits to such innovations, (c) the pursuit of perpetual happiness, and material progress, and (d) our governing institutions, legal mechanisms, political process, and ideologies, which condition our socioeconomic and cultural behavior (Dwivedi, 1997). Thus, the paradigm for our understanding of environmental behavior would have to be, perforce, multidisciplinary, multidimensional, and holistic approach. Such a paradigm should consist of all kinds of human knowledge (including the spiritual and religious dimension) necessary to cover the variety of factors that influence the continuation and further deterioration of our precious environment.

Background

Every generation receives a natural and cultural legacy in trust from its ancestors, and is supposed to hold it in trust for future generations. This trust imposes upon each generation the obligation to not only conserve and protect the environment and that natural legacy, but also to enhance it so that the future generations can enjoy the fruits of such trust in a most appreciable manner. Of course, human beings as trustees are permitted to use the resources of that trust for purposes set down either in writing or enunciated through societal, cultural, and religious values. However, trustees do not have free rein to exploit the legacy in such a manner that a dwindling amount is left for the future generation of those trustees. It is from this perspective that we have to see how our actions (present as well as past) impose serious environmental burdens on future generations. These burdens can be divided into four groups: depletion of natural resources, degradation of environmental quality of specific areas, protection and enhancement of the natural legacy, and reparation for the exploitation and overuse of environmental resources by previous generations.

Renewable natural resources like forests, fish, and sand, get depleted faster when we consume them much faster than their rate of regeneration. We already have problems due to deforestation and overfishing in our seas. These stocks should be replenished and time and efforts should be invested toward this process; otherwise, our legacy to future generations will be hollow. Similarly, nonrenewable natural resources, such as minerals and heavy metals, ought to be used wisely; once these are exhausted, future generations will be unable to reap the same benefits as the present generation.

How we dispose of our wastes in the water and in the air affects not only us, but also our children and their children. Indeed, our system of waste disposal is life-threatening not only to human beings, but to all other animate and nonanimate creatures. That it why it is crucial for all human activities that degrade the environment be minimized, if not completely terminated. This can be possible only when each nation-state accepts some basic international convention (such as an Earth Charter) to modify its internal environmental protection laws and regulations with the aim of improving air, water, and soil quality within their boundaries.

Right to Environmental Quality

Humanity's role in manipulating our surroundings is enormous and ranges from the obvious — the damming of great rivers to the subtle — the effects of DDT on the reproduction of wildlife. This concern over environmental impacts generated a great deal of worry starting in the late 1960s. Many environmentalists, therefore, began to propose a "right" to environmental quality. Their proposals included decision-making tools primarily, such as environmental impact assessment, duties, and regulations imposed on private industries and corporations, and powers acquired by the state to monitor related activities, both in the public and private sectors. However, environmental impact does not stop at measuring pesticide residues and the amount of mercury in fish. It involves the quality of life on Earth, and indeed the ability of humans to interact with nature and survive in the long run. Soon it was realized that pollution, destruction of species and natural areas, and depletion of resources could not be placed second to our materialism and our unthinking belief in technological progress. To break out of past patterns, people's attitudes must be changed. The value of nature needs to stop being defined absolutely as either intrinsic or economic (Norton, 2000, p. 1039). Otherwise the same old solutions, although presented in new ways, will continue to crowd public perception as well as the public policy agenda. To bring about such an attitudinal change, one requires an environmental code of conduct, appropriately called the Earth Charter, which can be similar to the UN Universal Declaration of Human Rights. The World Commission on Environment and Development (WCED), established by the United Nations in 1983 through its report, *Our Common Future* (World Commission on Environment and Development, 1987) recommended that the UN General Assembly should "commit itself to prepare a universal Declaration" (p. 333) as well as to strengthen and extend the existing international conventions and agreements. Such a declaration should set forth "new norms for state and interstate behavior needed to maintain livelihoods and life on our shared planet" (p. 332). It is obvious that the commission's recommendation was based on the Universal Declaration of Human Rights. Since 1987, the movement to get the Earth Charter accepted by various international organizations gained momentum. Such efforts are discussed below.

The Earth Summit held in Rio de Janeiro in 1992 started a movement to consider the Earth Charter on the same lines as the UN Charter on Human Rights. It was felt by various environmental non-government organizations (NGOs) assembled in Rio that the world needs a Charter with a clear and integrated vision of the fundamental ethical values and practical guidelines for improving the quality of human life and protecting as well as restoring the health of Earth's ecosystem. At that Earth Summit, various governments and international organizations were asked to submit recommendations dealing with the Earth Charter. But the attempt at reaching a consensus by states and international organizations on endorsing such a Charter failed; instead there emerged a Rio Declaration on Environment and Development which showed a broad support for the Earth Charter (Taylor, 1999, p. 194). But, due to mounting pressure from NGOs and some organizations representing world religions, Agenda 21 included reference to the Earth Charter, and an Earth Council was created to follow up various recommendations made during the Summit. Although both the Rio Declaration and Earth Charter address sustainable development, their focus differs. The Rio declaration focuses on "human beings." The Earth Charter, on the other hand, focuses on "community of life," as reflected in its principles (Bosselman, 2004, p. 68).

In May 1995, an international workshop on the Earth Charter was held with participants from 30 nations and over 70 different organizations (Rockefeller, 1997, p. 71). The workshop drafted a Charter with six principles: (1) right to food security and clean and safe air, water, and soil; (2) reinforcement of the right to public participation in government decision making; (3) eradication of poverty; (4) affirmation of gender equality as a prerequisite to sustainable development; (5) securing of rights to sexual and reproductive health; and (6) global sharing of environmental costs (McChesney & Mueller, 1997, p. 14).

Many organizations took initiatives to prepare a draft Charter or environmental code of conduct. [As an example, we are attaching as an appendix one such document prepared by Professor Dwivedi in 1992.] Later, another initiative was taken at the Rio+5 Forum to work on such a Charter, which resulted in the establishment of the Earth Charter Commission in 1997. The Commission formed an international drafting committee, which met several times in different nations to create a worldwide dialogue on the draft Charter. Finally, in March 2000, at a meeting in UNESCO, Paris, the Commission approved a final version of the Earth Charter. But still, the United Nations was yet to formally consider the Charter. Another impetus came in 2002 at the time of the World Summit meeting in Johannesburg, South Africa when the matter of this Charter was endorsed by all. The result was that by 2003, 54 countries had constituted their own national committees about the Charter. In addition, the Charter has been translated into 27 languages

(UNDP, 2003). Despite these national and international efforts, the Charter (as of February 2005) is yet to be adopted by the UN General Assembly; consequently, it is yet to receive the same international status akin to the UN Declaration on Human Rights.

The Earth Charter — Main Features

The Earth Charter prepared by the Earth Commission and endorsed by UNESCO, consists of the following 16 principles, within four major themes (Earth Charter, 2000):

1. *Respect and Care for the Community of Life*: (a) respect Earth and life in all its diversity; (b) care for the community of life with understanding, compassion, and love; (c) build democratic societies that are just, participatory, sustainable, and peaceful; and (d) secure Earth's bounty and beauty for present and future generations.
2. *Ecological Integrity*: (a) protect and restore the integrity of Earth's ecological systems, with special concern for biological diversity and the natural processes that sustain life; (b) prevent harm as the best method of environmental protection and, when knowledge is limited, apply a precautionary approach; (c) adopt patterns of production, consumption, and reproduction that safeguard Earth's regenerative capacities, human rights, and community well-being; and (d) advance the study of ecological sustainability and promote the open exchange and wide application of the knowledge acquired.
3. *Social and Economic Justice*: (a) eradicate poverty as an ethical, social, and environmental imperative; (b) ensure that economic activities and institutions at all levels promote human development in an equitable and sustainable manner; (c) affirm gender equality and equity as prerequisites to sustainable development and ensure universal access to education, healthcare, and economic opportunity; and (d) uphold the right of all, without discrimination, to a natural and social environment supportive of human dignity, bodily health, and spiritual well-being, with special attention to the rights of indigenous peoples and minorities.
4. *Democracy, Nonviolence, and Peace*: (a) strengthen democratic institutions at all levels and provide transparency and accountability in governance, inclusive participation in decision making, and access to justice; (b) integrate into formal education and life-long learning the knowledge, values, and skills needed for a sustainable way of life; (c) treat all living beings with respect and consideration; and (d) promote a culture of tolerance, nonviolence, and peace.

In addition to these 16 major principles, the Charter refers to the Earth as people's home that is alive with a unique community of life. That community of life and its resilience as well as the well-being of humanity "depend upon preserving a healthy biosphere with all its ecological systems, a rich variety of plants and animals, fertile soils, pure waters, and clean air" (Earth Charter, 2000). Its preamble exhorts people to join together to bring forth a sustainable global society founded on respect for nature, universal human rights, economic justice, and a culture of peace. Furthermore, it calls for the people of the Earth "declare our responsibility to one another, to the greater community of life, and to future generations" (Earth Charter, 2000). That concept of a "greater community of life" is also expounded as *Vasudhaiv Kutumbakam* (the greater family of Mother Earth) in Hindu ecology.

The Earth Charter is set apart from many other international agreements in that it "recognizes the successful achievement of the goal of sustainable development requires not only international commitment and legal regulation, but also basic changes in attitudes, values, and behavior of people" (Taylor, 1999, p. 193). In addition to changes in attitudes, values, and behavior of people there are policy objectives that could be associated with such a Charter. Mackey (2004, p. 89) identified three such policy objectives: increased protection of ecological systems, through the creation of protected areas; an abatement of anthropogenic activities resulting in climate change; and the maintenance of natural resources, especially those in developing countries. Additionally, according to Norton (2000, p. 1030), the Earth Charter provides the political framework needed to develop environmental protection strategies on various scales: local, regional, national, and international. Finally, the Earth Charter provides optimism for the development of a political framework in line with its objectives of preserving nature for future generations. However, as the United Nations Development points out, the Earth Charter is not a policy making document, but can be used as a guide for a more sustainable way of life. The Charter is aimed at the citizens around the world, instead of governments as traditional attempts to preserve ecological integrity have been.

Despite the widespread support of NGOs and some organizations representing world religions, the principles of the Earth Charter have also drawn criticism. Though not a binding agreement, the legal status of a number of Earth Charter principles has been questioned (Bosselman, 2004, p. 71). An additional criticism is that the Earth Charter is not necessary to achieve the ideal of ecological integrity. Already there exist international agreements and laws, such as Stockholm's commitment, the Rio Commitment, and the World Charter for Nature, that present similar ethical considerations and therefore the ideas presented in the Charter offer no new hope (Mackey, 2004, p. 83). Furthermore, for the Earth Charter to be effective, nations around the world must embrace the attitudinal changes promoted by the Charter.

Some, however, are concerned that the changes proposed by the Charter will threaten their economic development. For instance, China and other G77 have argued that the Charter should pertain differently to developed and developing nations. Developed countries should be obligated to address their "unsustainable pattern of production and consumption," whereas developing countries should receive financial support to assist in their compliance with the principles of the Earth Charter (Timmerman, 1992, p. 155). Additionally, there is some concern that the acceptance of the Earth Charter principles will not occur evenly around the world. As of 2003, 41 developing countries have begun to implement some activities consistent with the Earth Charter. On the other hand, there have only been approximately 20 developed or transition countries to implement such activities (UNDP, 2003).

Respecting the Mother Earth: An Eastern Perspective

Stewardship of the environment requires that one considers the entire universe as his/her extended family with all living beings in this universe as the members of the household. This concept, also known as *Vasudhaiv Kutumbakam* (*Vasudhà* means this Earth, *Kutumba* means extended family consisting of human beings, animals, and all living beings), means that all human beings as well as other creatures living on Earth are the members of the same extended family of Devï Vasundharà. Only by considering the entire universe as a part of our extended family, can we (individually and collectively) develop the necessary maturity and respect for all other living beings.

On the concept of *Vasudhaiv Kutumbakam*, Dr. Karan Singh has said: "that the planet we inhabit and of which we are all citizens — Planet Earth — is a single, living, pulsating entity; that the human race, in the final analysis is an interlocking, extended family — *Vasudhaiv Kutumbakam* as the Veda has it . . . " (Singh, 1991, p. 123). We also know that members of the extended family do not wilfully endanger the lives and livelihood of others; instead, they first think in terms of caring for others before taking an action. That is why, to transmit this new global consciousness, it is essential that the concept of *Vasudhaiv Kutumbakam* is encouraged. For this, the world's great religions would have to cooperate with each other. The welfare and caring of all would be realized through the golden thread of spiritual understanding and cooperation at the global level. How to secure a development which brings welfare of all without harming others and destroying the environment is a challenge before India. Can there be a strategy which is practical and yet draws on the Hindu heritage for nature conservation and the appropriate respect for the extended family of our Mother Earth.

Environmental stewardship can lead to mastery over our base characteristics such as greed, exploitation, abuse, mistreatment, and defilement of nature. Before we can hope to change the exploitative tendencies of society, it is absolutely essential that we discipline our inner thoughts. This is where the role of environmental stewardship comes into play. Environmental stewardship can be a mechanism that creates respect for nature because it is devoid of institutional structures, bureaucracy, and rituals associated organized religions, thus enabling people to center their values upon the notion that there is a cosmic ordinance and a natural or divine law which must be maintained. Further, the environmental stewardship can provide new ways of valuing and acting. It can promote the preparation of policies of sustainable development and the introduction of environmental protection initiatives. Environmental stewardship, if globally manifested, can also provide the values necessary for an environmentally caring world and will not advance economic growth, creating in its wake greed, poverty, inequality, and environmental degradation. This may be a new focal point around which the concept of global stewardship for the environment aligned with the Earth Charter and respect for Mother Earth may develop; and in this way we may have new values in line with an environmentally caring world.

There exists a cosmic connection between the micro and the macro; and thus, there exists a harmonizing balance between the planet and the plants, animals, human beings, and birds (Dwivedi, 2000). They are all part of one big family. Consequently, people of all faiths as well as those belonging to other spiritual traditions should view the large existing in the small; and hence their every act has not just global but cosmic implications (Shiva, 1991, p. 3). For them, responsibilities, limits, and restraints must be self-directed rather than externalized. This is our global duty toward the environment; let us make it a part of not only our local culture and tradition but also an integral part of universal consciousness, vision, and acceptance. But, to raise the human spirit and create a worldwide family or community of ecologically sound and sustainable order, there is a need to subscribe to an Earth Charter. This may become an instrument through which a new universal consciousness for the healing of creation and a befitting understanding of divine purpose can be created to transform that human spirit, which unites material realities and spiritual imperatives. It is that conscience which could restore and nourish a harmonized world through trusteeship, stewardship, and accountability for present and future generations.

Each spiritual tradition on Earth has helped humanity. Those who see divinity in nature (or worship nature) have increased our sense of the light of beauty, the largeness and height of our life, and our aim at multidimensional perfection. Christianity has given us the vision of divine love and charity; Buddhism has shown us a noble way to be kinder, purer, and nobler; Judaism as well as Islam has shown us how to be devoted to God and be religiously faithful in following His command. Hinduism has given us the profound spiritual possibilities. Would it not be great if these God visions could be brought together for the care of the Earth? All religions as well as other spiritual traditions aim to save souls, but they have yet to spiritualize the humanity. Environmental crisis facing our universe has given all of us — belonging to various religions and cultures — an opportunity to come together and work for the protection and sustenance of the entire cosmos.

The Earth Charter: Toward a New Global Environmental Ethic

By the time we entered the third millennium, it became increasingly clear that many of our values were totally inadequate for long-term survival and sustainable development. This was evident from the emergence of a wide spectrum of challenges to the traditional materialistic view. For over millennia, guided by Western culture, people have had blind faith in the prowess of science and technology to bring material progress. It is only recently that we have come to understand that so-called material prosperity should not be an end in itself. Slowly, a realization is also emerging that spirituality and the control of one's desires can bring a more lasting happiness than acquisitive materialism. However, such a realization has yet to enter the domain of governmental policy or the corporate world, where spiritual perspectives are generally ignored. The economic criteria which place no value on the commons (the air, water, oceans, outer space, etc.), and which use concepts such as cost–benefit analysis, law of supply and demand, rate of return, land as commodity, etc. have been based on the delusion that has operated independently of the cultural and spiritual domains. Until now, we have taken a great deal from our Mother Earth. We have given little thought to putting limits on our plundering and ravaging instincts. Without a change in our current value system, there is little hope of correcting the present environmental problems we face today. Slowly, a heightened consciousness is emerging for the formation of new international environmental rights regime, including instilling respect for Mother Earth and care for all species in the Creation. The Earth Charter is a proper instrument for helping in empowering that consciousness.

Mikhail Gorbachev, one of the main proponents of the Earth Charter, continues to "advocate for a global value shift on how we handle Earth, a new sense of global interdependence, and a shared responsibility in humanity's relationship with nature. It is for these reasons that I helped draft the Earth Charter, a code of ethical principles now endorsed by over 8000 organizations representing more than 100 million people around the world" (Gorbachev, 2005). It is also clear that without a universally accepted regime of environmental protection, world resources will keep on depleting and the quality of life for the majority of people on Earth will remain questionable. For this reason, we urgently need a holistic vision of basic ethical principles supported by broadly accepted tenets and practical guidelines that should govern the behavior of people and states in their relations between each other and the Earth. This is not a new demand; it has been persistently called for by various environmental NGOs, international organizations, and reports such as *Our Common Future* by the WCED, and *Caring for the Earth* report by the International Union for Conservation of Nature and Natural Resources (IUCN).

The Earth Charter is a reminder of our moral duty to leave a healthy legacy for future generations by not only protecting the environment from the harmful ways of our activities, but also by attempting to restore the *status quo* of two generations ago. This is not going to be an easy task; nevertheless, attempts will have to be made. This requires an attitudinal change on the part of all of us, and undoubtedly, the industrialized countries that are consuming natural resources too quickly have a heavy burden to carry. Finally, it is a duty for us all to see that future generations receive appropriate reparations for the damage, which we visited upon them by our careless and exploitative tendencies.

There is no doubt that individual societies have to consider by what is best for them in the long run, rather than be told by outsiders. Codes of conduct and charters are helping tools for nations. For the leaders of various nations, the key to success will greatly depend on how these concerns are integrated in a systematic way to evolve a comprehensive vision for protecting the quality of life of humans as well as other species on Earth.

There is an urgent need to encourage cooperation among people of the world. This can probably be done best by fostering the convergence of one shared fundamental value: protection and enhancement of the environment. Of course, there are differences in lifestyle among nations. It is agreed that people do not want identical lives, cultures, and beliefs. Nevertheless, there are several mutually reinforcing values, which provide us with a point of reference to help us resolve the issue of environmental protection. Given the opportunity to express and act locally on these global issues, communities can respond to regional and global challenges. For this to occur, some institutional changes will have to be undertaken. Reforms will be needed in international laws and treaties, and attitudes of people would have to go through some fundamental changes. Flexibility, adaptability, and the ability to reconcile the needs of different communities and local interests will have to be carefully nurtured. The reality of our world, the central fact that we must take into account in the design of global environmental protection policy and programs, is not independence but interdependence. The complexity and scale of environmental problems no longer permit a "water-tight" division of environmental issues within nation-states and among sovereign states. The challenge before us is the reform and renewal of the existing world system, and securing a firm place for the rights of future generations. It is to this end — the care of our planet — that much of our efforts must now turn if we are to avoid further damage to the world ecosystem. This challenge affects everyone (rich and poor) and every where. The Mother Earth does not differentiate between rich and poor or strong and weak. If we all subscribe to the Earth Charter, our future will be safer, brighter, and better.

A Proposed Code of Conduct and Guiding Principles for Environmental Protection[1]

The Code

The role of a Code is to provide not only inner incentives so that individuals may act in a way which is conducive not only to their self-preservation but also external motivations in the form of laws, rules, and regulations so that individuals, groups, industries, and governments are impelled to care for the well-being of the environment. Such "inner incentives" become necessary when external inducements, either in the form of governmental directives, laws or regulations, are either unenforceable or unworkable. This Code may also act as an adaptive instrument that strengthens our obligation toward nature, which is seen as the provider and sustainer of our life support system.

The following are the basic principles which ought to govern the proposed Code:

- (a) Human beings have an obligation for the stewardship of the Earth and the planetary system.
- (b) Nations should aim for sustainable development, which is ecologically sound.
- (c) We must recognize that there is interdependence among all species on Earth, and that the obliteration of any one species may have disastrous consequences for all others.

[1]Drawn from Dwivedi, O.P. (1992). "An Ethical Approach to Environmental Protection: A Code of Conduct and Guiding Principles," *Canadian Public Administration*, 35(3):363–380.

(d) Individuals, corporations, and business concerns, and various groups in society must accept responsibility as trustees and guardians of our environment for both present and future generations. We must be accountable environmentally for our individual as well as collective actions which may endanger the environment.
(e) We must acknowledge our responsibility, individually and collectively, of educating our fellow beings about environmental protection and conservation.

These five principles are supplemented by the following tenets which are aimed at securing the future for forthcoming generations:

A. Future generations have a right to an un-manipulated human genetic inheritance that is, a genetic inheritance which is not altered artificially by the present generation of humans.
B. Future generations have a right to the same richness of biogenetic variety in plant and animal world, which is available at present.
C. Future generations have a right to a healthy air, to an intact ozone layer, clean water, fertile soil, and to a vigorous forest cover.
D. Future generations have a right to substantial reserves of nonrenewable energy resources and relevant raw materials.
E. Future generations have a right to a "cultural inheritance," created and bequeathed by the earlier generations, which should not be so altered by the present generation that the future generations cannot enjoy that inheritance.

These basic principles and tenets are the foundation on which the main features of the proposed Code have been formulated. The following ten main features are listed:

(1) A respect for nature and all its constituent parts
(2) The right of all life on earth to perpetuate itself
(3) The duty of each society to act as the environment's keeper
(4) The need for society to encourage restraint and caution in the use of natural resources, and attempt to control human greed and exploitative tendencies
(5) A recognition of the societal obligation to hold natural resources in trust for the appropriate use of not only the present generation but also future generations
(6) A commitment to the moral obligation of all individuals to protect and conserve the environment
(7) The duty to protect and preserve endangered species

(8) The education of each person as to their responsibility for maintaining ecological balance, biological diversity, and environmental sustainability

(9) A determination to secure the right of the public to participate in environmental decision making, to receive information and to be consulted by governmental bodies

(10) A commitment to enhance the flow of information to the public concerning the state of environmental quality, including the possible dangers arising out of industrial and developmental projects.

References

Bosselman, K. (2004). "In Search of Global Law: The Significance of the Earth Charter," *Worldviews*, 8:62–75.

Dwivedi, O.P. (1988). "Man and Nature: A Holistic Approach to a Theory of Ecology," *The Environmental Professional*, 10:8–15.

Dwivedi, O.P. (1992). "An Ethical Approach to Environmental Protection: A Code of Conduct and Guiding Principles," *Canadian Public Administration*, 35(3):363–380.

Dwivedi, O.P. (1997). *India's Environmental Policies, Programmes and Stewardship*, London: Macmillan Press.

Dwivedi, O.P. (2000). "Dharmic Ecology," *Hinduism and Ecology: The Interaction of Earth, Sky and Water*, edited by C.K. Chapple and M.E. Tucker, Cambridge, MA: Harvard University Press, pp. 4–22.

Gorbachev, M.S. (2005). "Foreword," *State of the World* (a Worldwatch Institute Report), Washington, D.C.: Worldwatch Institute, pp. xvii–xviii.

Mackey, B. (2004). "The Earth Charter and Ecological Integrity — Some Policy Implications," *World Views*, 8:76–92.

McChesney, A. and T. Mueller (1997). "The Role of Law in Implementing UNCED Commitments," *Ecodecision*, 24:14–17.

Norton, B. (2000). "Biodiversity and Environmental Values: In Search of a Universal Earth Ethic," *Biodiversity and Conservation*, 9:1029–1044.

Rockefeller, S.C. (1997). "The Earth Charter: A Vision for the Future," *Ecodecision*, 24:70–73.

Shiva, V. (1991). "The Greening of the Global Reach," *Illustrated Weekly of India*, October 12–18.

Singh, Karan (1991). *Brief Sojourn*, Delhi: B.R. Publishing Corporation.

Taylor, P. (1999). "The Earth Charter," *New Zealand Journal of Environmental Law*, 3:193–203.

The Earth Charter (2000). Available online at http://www.earthcharter.org

Timmerman, P. (1992). "Global Environmental Ethics: Towards an Earth Charter," *Global Environmental Change*, 2:154–155.

United Nations Development Program (UNDP), United Nations Environment Program, World Bank, and World Resources Institute (2003). *World Resources*

2002–2004: Decisions for the Earth: Balance, Voice and Power, Washington, D.C.

World Commission on Environment and Development (1987). *Our Common Future*, New York: Oxford University Press.

Chapter 48

Globalization: The Changing Nature of Education and Training for Administration of Government

Paulette Laubsch and Richard Blake

CONTENTS

Introduction

Government, by its very nature, provides an array of benefits and services through executive, judicial, and legislative processes and structures. The extent and quality of these benefits and services, in various jurisdictions and countries, is a correlate of their respective culture, politics, and resources, broadly defined and often embedded for centuries. These jurisdictional boundaries, to some extent and for various reasons, are changing due to globalization of business, immigration, changes in information technology, and other factors (Ball et al., 2002).

The competencies required for employment in government are similarly broad, varied, and changing. As globalization changes how government and the private sector function, it becomes a driving force for how the academy prepares people for managerial and administrative positions in government and the private sector. It simultaneously alters how respective institutions of higher learning function in an era of the globally competitive, and increasingly globally accessible, higher education marketplace. This article discusses change in education and training for public administration that is associated with, if not driven by, globalization.

Public Sector Entry and Advancement: Historical

Those who seek and begin employment in the public sector have innumerable motivations and backgrounds. For some, such as many military personnel, police officers, teachers, and others, public sector employment may represent a career calling since their youth. For others, government employment may represent a career by accident in that they simply completed and fulfilled employment applications and criteria and entered a worksite as generalists to be honed by the respective bureaucracy. Others may have been attracted to what they perceived as stability; others for ideological reasons; others for political reasons and rewards. The list goes on and on; there are as many constellations of reasons as there are people in government. Nevertheless, basic questions derive about the types of knowledge and skill required for entry into government employment and for bureaucratic and career advancement.

Historically, and somewhat typically, the expectation was that novice employees would receive some form of on the job training and then proceed to demonstrate and enhance their competencies with the possibility of promotion to supervisory, managerial, and administrative levels of responsibility. Often, employees were left on their own to seek knowledge, skills, and credentials from the academy, if an institution of higher learning was physically accessible, possibly reimbursed for tuition by the employer.

The Master of Public Administration degree was rarely a requirement for promotion. In many organizations, advanced higher education was *de facto* discouraged as not practical, particularly if the boss lacked such credentials.

Training of public sector administrators and managers is not a new concept, albeit with a contemporary spike in the past two decades in the United States and elsewhere. China's civil examination system for public sector positions dates back over 1400 years. Individuals who were interested in a government position needed to take an examination that required extensive individual study as well as formal education (Kai-Ming et al., 1999). Although this may be the oldest public administrator training process, there are other systems throughout the world that span decades.

In the United States, historically, some bureaucracies, such as the military and police entities, trained and educated their own employees, often as a closed system, which was necessary for technical and security reasons but dysfunctional in terms of potential educational incest. Public schools participated in training and education by serving as sites for the student teaching practicum experience. This carried similar potential for dysfunction with graduates of X College monitoring the progress of their younger counterparts, similarly attending X College and with the profession of teaching lacking national accreditation standards. Some bureaucracies that employed persons who were members of generally accepted professions such as accounting, law, nursing, social work, and others typically relied on the respective person having the requisite credentials and license prior to employment and often left the person on his/her own to satisfy continuing education requirements concomitant with the professional license. Members of these professions were often promoted to supervisory and administrative positions, lacking any formal education and training in this. Other organizations "developed" employees by means of bureaucratic memoranda.

It is only within recent memory that a more open, accessible, diverse, responsive, systematic, and sound protocol for advancement has taken root and begun to institutionalize itself in our public sector organizations. Globalization has been a major contributor to this improvement.

Globalization and Changes in Public Administration Education and Training

Below, we discuss several major, and somewhat recent, changes in the structures and processes of education and training for administration in the public sector. These recognize and incorporate an increasingly global environment in terms of cultural, economic, political, social, and technological dimensions of life. These are not presented with regard to any rank order and we discuss these humbly; the academy, and those of us within it, is struggling.

International Students and International Faculty

The welcome presence of diverse students and faculty in public administration education broadens our worldview. The Fulbright Scholars Program has been a pioneer in these efforts, however, contemporary initiatives transcend the time-bound protocols of programs such as Fulbright, wherein faculty are "loaned" to foreign institutions for a period of time. Obviously, however, this presents challenges in terms of language, both the actual words and the colloquial usage of language. There is much to be learned about how other cultures and nations function, both in terms of us enhancing our own capabilities and by learning how to operate in their homelands and communities. Many entities of government are involved, directly and indirectly, in the operations of businesses that may have local operations but are multinational in nature. Also, law enforcement, monetary policy, financial institutions, and other entities may be domestic in nature, but have obvious implications for how our planet operates.

International Study

At a somewhat elementary level, this would include specific courses that instruct about operations in another country. At Fairleigh Dickinson University (FDU), the Bachelor of Arts in Individualized Study (BAIS) degree requires each student to take such a course. At a more rigorous and sophisticated (and expensive) level, international study could involve an actual learning venture in a foreign country. Colleges and universities have offered these learning opportunities for many years. These are becoming increasingly important and seen less as mere summer school electives. These are typically accomplished with attending faculty from the home college but also are achieved through actual enrollment in a college in a foreign country. These can be arranged by means of formal agreements between the respective colleges (for example, at Seton Hall University a historic reciprocal agreement with the University of Beijing) or students can be left to work this out for themselves using advisors for approvals. At a more extreme level of commitment to globalization and education, a university could merge with a university in another country, for example, Wroxton College in England is part of the FDU structure and is listed as a campus location in university printed materials. Preliminary advisory board meetings with regard to establishment of another doctoral program at FDU have consistently reinforced a requirement for formal education outside the United States.

Change in Philosophy and Methodology of Education

A global worldview, as well as global competency, requires high order cognition and maturity. Our university students already have these qualities; it is time we recognized and respected this and incorporated this into the learning environment. Knowles (1968, 1975, 1980, 1984, 1986) is a seminal thinker regarding attitude, philosophy, and methodology for helping the adult to learn; a process known as *andragogy* (originally spelled *androgogy*).

Another significant change in educational philosophy and methodology relates to competency (Sandwith, 1993); an educational strategy whereby the instructor's job is not to teach, but rather to ensure that the student learns. This learning, as may be applicable to the infinite array of things to be learned, involves knowing, understanding, applying, and integrating. The United States Department of Education has been advocating a competency approach to education for almost 20 years, and this is obvious in examining accreditation standards for universities in general and for professional programs in particular. Competency-based education incorporates what is generally referred to as an educational rubric, in which a course syllabus, or contract, is very specific about what will be learned, when, how, and how learning will be demonstrated. Higher education in a global milieu requires this type of clarity.

Changes in Degrees and Changes in Schools

Higher education, and in this case public administration, is not vocational education nor should it be. But higher education, in many ways, needs to change and is changing. In many ways, we still operate within the framework of our historic intellectual and cultural roots. Public administration, as an academic discipline, has its roots in political science. This has provided a rich, scholarly, theoretically sound educational experience. However, there have been criticisms that content may not be sufficiently "applied" in nature. Innovatively breaking from tradition, some universities are creating new administrative entities with new degrees to address this concern. For example, Central Michigan University (CMU) has the College of Extended Learning that offers, among others, the Master of Science in Administration (MSA) degree and FDU has the New College of General and Continuing

Studies, School of Administrative Science that offers, among others, the Master of Administrative Science (MAS) degree. These degrees do not replace the MPA. Rather, they represent expansion of the continuum of educational offerings. Both the MSA and MAS degree programs have gone through university accreditation protocols, university internal reviews and are supported by many employers in terms of tuition remission and education requirements for continued employment and promotion, and by doctoral education programs. In other words, they are rigorous.

New structures for education for public administration in a global environment also allow for innovations in teaching and learning. The aforementioned degree programs tend to be applied in nature and properly credentialed practitioners are encouraged to apply to teach. Also, these programs are more free to be innovative, a critical dimension regarding globalization. One major innovation is location of the educational experience. Both the aforementioned CMU and FDU masters degree programs in administration have a focus on public sector administration and bring the educational experience to the student. CMU offers courses throughout the United States and in several other countries. FDU offers courses at 50 different employment sites in New Jersey, as well as in other countries. Providing courses to specific employers and offering these courses on site allow opportunity for discounting tuition. Everyone wins.

Less dramatic than offering a new degree in a new academic entity, but nonetheless efficacious insofar as public administration education and globality, is enhanced interdisciplinary, intercollege relationships. For example, at Seton Hall University students have opportunities for studying at The Center for Public Service, historically the MPA degree, and at The School of Diplomacy with its obvious attention to international matters. These types of arrangements in universities, although somewhat tedious insofar as bureaucracy, credit counts, budgeting courses, and the like, are responsive to the needs of students and of our civilization. Again, everyone wins.

The Internet

Education by means of the Internet is an obvious expansion and innovation of the educational enterprise. The University of Phoenix is the most well known and largest provider of Internet education. Internet education certainly allows for anyone to communicate instantly with anyone in the world. In our view, this form of education is in its infancy. Internet education holds significant promise because it is global; most often allows the learner to proceed at his/her own pace; is convenient; and has a host of other attractions. There are potential pitfalls, many of which we may not be aware of yet. This type of education requires, if it is done correctly, a great deal of motivation on the part of the learner. There are questions about the authenticity of the learner; questions about how large a group an instructor can effectively work with; and other issues. Another concern is whether colleges and universities are jumping onto the Internet bandwagon because of loss of student market share. Although this is a legitimate issue, it raises questions about the mission of higher education. One particular concern is that the Internet is faceless and depersonalized, in contrast with many of the requisite functions of a manager in terms of interpersonal skills. Some universities have addressed this by offering what is generally referred to as a blended model, in which a portion of the learning is on the Internet and a portion is in a class setting.

Partnerships

Partnerships, or contracted agreements between organizations, have grown considerably in the past decade. In the past, relationships between institutions of higher learning in public administration and various public and private sector organizations tended to be limited to grant activity, research opportunities, internships, and community service or consultation that faculty would provide. Today, the academy sees itself in partnership and not merely as a recipient or provider.

Although a common type of partnership involves schools at the various levels from community colleges to graduate schools sharing resources and enabling students to move seamlessly through the system, there is the growing partnership between the university and government. We recognize that some public colleges envision themselves and are envisioned by others as entities of government whereas other public institutions of higher education envision themselves and are envisioned by others as almost autonomous. Nevertheless, relationships between universities and government, insofar as the training and education of managers and administrators in the public sector, have been enhanced greatly in recent years. It is through this type of partnership that the various executive MPA programs offered in which senior government officials come together in the university for the MPA. Typically, one has to be nominated, approved, and funded to participate in this.

A more prominent example of partnership is the Certified Public Manager (CPM) program. During the early 1970s, Dr. Kenneth Henning of the University of Georgia envisioned an education and training program for managers in the public sector. His ideas met with the approval of then governor, Jimmy Carter, and the program was spawned. Dr. Henning foresaw a program in which existing supervisors and managers in government, many of whom had little to no formal education in management, would be trained by means of a partnership between training entities in government bureaucracies and respective universities in the various states. His idea was well received, and today the CPM program is peer accredited and awards the CPM credential in 28 states. Persons with the CPM credential can use this as transfer credit for undergraduate or graduate degree programs. This program is rigorous and time-consuming, yet offers a convenient structure and provides an education that is theoretical and applied. Also, the program is contemporary and has educational elements pertinent to diversity, leadership, environment, systems theory, and other dimensions applicable to globalization. Dr. Henning envisioned this as first a national and then an international credential. The program continues to grow.

Certificate Programs

The continuing education needs of our global society is well known to the point of cliché. After a rather slow start, these programs have grown in popularity and significance. Certificate programs meet the needs of many persons for knowledge, skills, and credentials subsequent to, as a prelude to, or in lieu of, a formal degree program. Certificate awarding, continuing education learning experiences, are specialized by nature. We have seen increased interest in certificate programs relating to terrorism, sadly, a dimension of globalization. Public administration programs offer an array of certificate programs as people require more and more competencies and credentials. The potential for certificate programs in virtually any element of globalization is very real in public administration education programs.

Concluding Comment

Globalization is a process involving the breakdown of jurisdictional barriers. It has its proponents and opponents. Nevertheless, this process is ongoing. But like most other processes, it is directed toward some end result. It would seem that the ultimate result of the process of globalization is the end state of globality, however that may be operationalized by our progeny. The academy serves a number of social functions. Yes, it trains and educates and conducts research. But its societal functions and responsibilities are much deeper than that. The academy responds to and shapes our social conscience. Its intellectual freedom protects us from tyranny in word and deed. As civilization engages in globalization, the academy is socially obligated to lead and monitor this process.

References

Ball, D.A., McCulloch, W.H., Frantz, P.L., Geringer, J.M., and Minor, M.S. (2002). *International Business: The Challenge of Global Competition.* Boston: McGraw-Hill Irwin.

Kai-Ming, C., Xinhou, J., and Xiaobo, G. (1999). From training to education: Lifelong learning in China. *Comparative Education, 35,* 119–129.

Knowles, M.S. (1968). Androgogy, not pedagogy! *Adult Leadership, 16,* 350–352, 386.

Knowles, M.S. (1975). *Self-Directed Learning.* New York: Association Press.

Knowles, M.S. (1980). *The Modern Practice of Adult Education.* Chicago: Association Press.

Knowles, M.S. (1984). *The Adult Learner: A Neglected Species.* Houston: Gulf Publishers.

Knowles, M.S. (1986). *Using Learning Contracts.* San Francisco, CA: Jossey-Bass.

Sandwith, P. (1993). A hierarchy of management training requirements: The competency domain model. *Public Personnel Management, 22,* 43–62.

Chapter 49

Global Health and Human Rights: Challenges for Public Health Administrators in an Era of Interdependence and Mobility

Peter H. Koehn

CONTENTS

Introduction

The manifold intersections between globalization and health arise in expanding and occasionally unexpected contexts. Cholera threatens to break out transcontinentally in the wake of a devastating tsunami (Grady, 2005b, p. A10). A strain of polio genetically similar to the one that spread in Nigeria in 2003 appears in Indonesia in 2005 (*Missoulian*, May 4, 2005, p. A12). An epidemic of the deadly Marburg virus might spread across and beyond Angola (LaFraniere, 2005, p. A1). Emerging and reemerging diseases (ERIDs), such as severe acute respiratory syndrome (SARS), avian influenza (Barry, 2004; Heymann, 2005; Lempinen, 2005; Recer, 2005, p. A1; Troedsson & Rychener, 2005), HIV/AIDS (Price-Smith, 2002, p. 164; Fidler, 2003a, p. 97, 130–131; Hunter, 2003, p. 7), and drug-resistant tuberculosis (Porter et al., 2002, p. 185), are rapidly transmitted across permeable borders — infecting skilled public administrators and undermining state capacity and governance along the way (Price-Smith, 2002, pp. 1, 4, 13–14). The number of people at a risk of vector-borne diseases, such as malaria, increases as temperatures rise in far-flung locales (Epstein et al., 1997, p. 68; Martens, 1998, p. 79, 29; Epstein, 2001, pp. 36–39; Price-Smith, 2002, pp. 144–147, 168–169). Rates of obesity are rising in the girth of global advertising. Resource-commanding bioterror-preparedness projects demand the attention of public authorities and non-governmental organizations (NGOs) (Glenn, 2003; Paquette, 2004, pp. 109–110; Lipton, 2005, p. A1, A14). Unrecognized physical- and mental-illness perspectives confound transcultural health promotion efforts (Koehn, 2005b; Sainola-Rodriguez & Koehn, 2005). In inescapable local places, globalization "is generating epidemiological diversity and complexity" (Chen & Berlinguer, 2001, p. 36).

In our era of interdependence and mobility, public health administrators confront daunting transnational challenges to population health. At the same time, globalization provides opportunities for new commitments and breakthrough responses to emerging challenges (Kickbusch & Buse, 2001, p. 729). Health features prominently among the eight millennium development goals. Through the United Nations–founded Global Fund to Fight AIDS, Tuberculosis, and Malaria, about $3 billion has been devoted to projects that address these three illnesses in 120 countries (Lacey, 2004,

p. A3).[1] In the United States, the department of health and human services has created an Office of Global Health Affairs, and the Center for Disease Control (CDC) has prepared a global health strategy (www.ukglobalhealth.org on April 13, 2003). In an educational effort aimed at enhancing the interpersonal medical encounter, three U.S. medical schools are committed to incorporating preparation in transnational competence (TC) into the clinical years of their physician-education curriculums (Swick & Koehn, 2005). In addition, interdisciplinary advanced-degree programs in global or local (rural) health have been introduced at Yale, Oxford (www.ukglobalhealth.org), and the University of Montana. The fundamental right of every human being to realize their full health potential, embraced by the World Health Organization's (WHO) Constitution and other international accords (see Grondin et al., 2003, pp. 85–86), is increasingly recognized for future as well as current generations (Herrell & Mulholland, 1998; Lerer et al., 1998).

The rising commitment to global health has begun to produce results. A promising vaccine for malaria would provide effective protection for most children (McNeil, 2004a, p. A1, A6; also see McNeil, 2005, p. A4). Researchers are developing drugs and vaccines to fight the Ebola and Marburg viruses (Grady, 2005d, p. D9). In August 2003, the World Trade Organization (WTO) agreed to allow poor countries facing public health crises to import inexpensive generic antiretroviral drugs (ARVs) (*Africa Recovery*, October 2003, p. 23). A clinical trial in Cameroon of a simple three-in-one pill made in India confirmed that a generic ARV works as well as brand-name drugs (McNeil, 2004b, p. A5).

Global interdependence, population mobility, epidemiological diversity and complexity, along with emerging technical and political breakthroughs, place fresh demands on frequently overstretched public health administrators. Understanding the nature and intersections of these forces and developments is a prerequisite for advancing public health in the 21st century. This chapter explores the consequences and implications for public health administration arising from interdependence, mobility, and resource challenges.

Interdependence — Arising Challenges

Across the planet, populations and health authorities encounter health threats with roots in an interdependent world. The extralocal origin of factors responsible for noncommunicable illnesses presents special challenges for

[1] The Bush administration prefers its unilateral 5-year, US$9 billion Emergency Plan for AIDS Relief over the Global Fund (Fidler, 2003a, p. 113, 122–123, 135, 142–143). The President's plan proposes to target 15 countries, at least 12 of which are in Africa (*Washington Post*, 23 February 2004).

public administrators whose authority is geographically confined (Fidler, 2001, p. 262; Kickbusch & Buse, 2001, p. 706). These developing challenges are illustrated in this section by reference to the upstream (mainly Northern) forces that impact population health (e.g., advertising and particulate or carbon dioxide (CO_2) emissions), to the midstream impact of social position and social context on health behaviors, and to the downstream impacts of advertising, greenhouse gas (GHG) emissions, and waste disposal.

Upstream Forces

The upstream forces of globalization are associated with numerous contemporary health hazards that possess inescapable reach. The scope and geographical spread of "unhealthy production and consumption patterns" are particularly consequential for population health (Chen & Berlinguer, 2001, p. 37).

The global advertising and marketing of harmful commodities, such as tobacco and high-calorie junk foods, promotes the spread of health-damaging practices (Kickbusch and Buse, 2001, p. 704, 710; Stein, 2004). The impact of such messages is particularly extensive among potential consumers with limited ability to comprehend the health risks associated with practices such as smoking (Kickbusch & Buse, 2001, p. 710).

Increasing outdoor particulate pollution and GHG emissions constitute two escalating transnational environmental health threats that are linked to upstream global production and consumption trends (Cifuentes et al., 2001; Price-Smith, 2002, p. 143). Fine particles that directly affect morbidity and mortality cannot be contained regionally or even intercontinentally (Davis et al., 1997, p. 1341, 1346). For instance, hemispheric winds are transporting vast quantities of transpollutants, including fine particulate matter, within days from the industrialized cities of China to the U.S. west coast (*Missoulian*, February 23, 2004, p. A2). Although the effects will vary, no person or place can escape climatic change. The upstream forces driving anthropogenic climatic change and the generation of a host of air pollutants are extraction, production, and consumption processes that require the combustion of fossil fuels (see Davis et al., 1997, p. 1341; Stern, 1997, pp. 18–19; Cohen, 2001, p. 27; Sprunt, 2001, p. 74; Clapp, 2002, p. 158; Conca, 2002, pp. 143–144; Princen et al., 2002, p. 16).

Midstream Impacts

Many individual risk factors are related to differential exposure associated with social position (levels of education and income) and social context (place of residence, occupation, and work environment) (Davison et al.,

1992, p. 679; Diderichsen et al., 2001, pp. 14, 17–18; Guterman, 2003). Moreover, accumulated health advantages and disadvantages tend to be transferred intergenerationally (Diderichsen et al., 2001, p. 17).

Worldwide, nearly 1 billion people are overweight and over 300 million are obese (Brody, 2005, p. D5). In the United States and seven European countries, more than two thirds of all adults are overweight and roughly one third are obese (Stein, 2004; Payne, 2005). Noncommunicable diseases that are related to diet, physical inactivity, and consequent obesity will soon become the principal cause of death on a global basis (Brody, 2005, p. D5). The spread of unhealthy lifestyles has accompanied urbanization and the geographic expansion of affluence. As the income of populations rises, people's health is increasingly "susceptible to the marketing strategies of global corporations" (Kickbusch & Buse, 2001, p. 710; Brody, 2005, p. D10). Today, the transfer of Northern tastes, fast food and sugar-coated diets, and low physical activity practices is especially pronounced among "the growing middle class of low- and middle-income countries" (Kickbusch & Buse, 2001, p. 710) and among poor people who migrate from rural areas to cities (Brody, 2005, p. D5). In China, for instance, the number of obese people doubled in one decade (from 1992 to 2002) (*New York Times*, October 13, 2004, p. A6; also see Brody, 2005, p. D5, D10). As they become more deeply incorporated in industrial economies and societies, migrants from poor countries (and their children) also tend to adopt unhealthy lifestyles that include less exercise and increased consumption of junk foods (for instance, Williams et al., 1994, p. 35). One recent study found obesity among 8 percent of surveyed immigrants who had resided in the United States for less than 1 year; the presence of obesity rose to 19 percent among immigrants who had lived in the United States for 15 years or more (*New York Times*, December 15, 2004, p. A20).

Downstream Impacts

Worldwide, there are an estimated 1.2 billion smokers and WHO smoking rate surveys indicate that roughly 20 percent of all 13- to 15-year-old children smoke. Public health officials estimate that, by 2030, some 10 million people will die annually from smoking-related illnesses. About 70 percent of these victims will live in poor countries (Yach & Bettcher, 2000, p. 207; *New York Times*, February 28, 2005, p. A8). Tobacco also accounts for one fifth of all deaths in the United States (Leahy, 2005). Although the Framework Convention on Tobacco Control, which came into effect in February 2005, requires ratifying countries (57 on that date, not including China and the United States) to restrict tobacco advertising and sponsorship, the treaty lacks protocols, penalties, and financial support for poor countries (*New York Times*, February 28, 2005, p. A8).

In another downstream impact, global warming resulting from the accumulation of anthropogenic GHGs negatively affects population health directly through system stress and death from heat waves and other extreme weather events and indirectly by promoting wider vector distribution and localized food shortages (Epstein, 1995, p. 228; Patz et al., 1996; McMichael & Haines, 1997; Kickbusch & Buse, 2001, p. 704; Lane & Bierbaum, 2001, p. 201; Price-Smith, 2002, pp. 143–144). Studies published by Pim Martens (1998, p. 79, 29) and others (see Epstein, 2001, pp. 36–39; Price-Smith, 2002, pp. 144–147, 168–169) predict vast increases in the numbers of people at risk of vector-borne diseases — malaria, dengue fever, and schistosomiasis. In addition, the WHO estimates that some 8 million avoidable deaths will occur worldwide by 2020, largely due to suspended particulate matter (Cifuentes et al., 2001, p. 1257). Particulate matter also is associated with increased cardiovascular and respiratory morbidity (Davis et al., 1997, p. 1345). Local people, particularly people living in impoverished environments, increasingly are cognizant of the impact of particulate pollution on community health (Dunlap et al., 1993, p. 14). Based on results from their "Health of the Planet Survey" conducted in 24 nations, Dunlap et al. (1993, p. 15) concluded that "social science analyses of environmentalism . . . have downplayed the role of direct human experience with environmental degradation, which is especially noticeable at the local levels in the poorer nations."

The "distancing" of vast quantities of hazardous, nondegradable, and pharmaceutical wastes constitutes a potent additional downstream consequence of upstream consumption trends (Clapp, 2002). Increasingly, the disposal of such wastes takes place in or offshore of poor countries — out of sight of consumers in affluent lands. The health risks and consequences for poor-country populations are serious. In early 2005, for instance, Somalia began to experience the effects of past hazardous waste dumping off its coast. The Indian Ocean tsunami on December 26, 2004, ruptured dumped containers of hazardous materials. The escaped toxic and radioactive waste that washed onto Somalia's coastline resulted in a wide range of population health problems, including acute respiratory infections, hemorrhaging, and unusual skin disorders (Clayton, 2005, p. A15).

Globally linked initiatives possess considerable potential for addressing interdependent health challenges. In this connection, it is encouraging to note that city-to-city networks have been active in transnational environmental health efforts. The involvement of municipal public health administrators in WHO's Healthy Cities Project offers one avenue for addressing common health threats related to anthropogenic biosphere degradation (Kickbusch & Buse, 2001, pp. 718–719).

Mobility — Arising Challenges

Historically, communicable disease has presented a major challenge to organized communities of human beings. Authorities responsible for population health and safety have focused on transmission mechanisms, and "preventing and controlling disease epidemics" has constituted "the *raison d'être* of public health" (Fidler, 2003a, p. 117). The physical movement of people from one place to another constitutes a particularly potent transmission mechanism. Population mobility is connected to contemporary public health challenges in a number of ways. Mobility-arising challenges for health officials and other public administrators are illustrated in this section by reference to the transmission of communicable diseases across borders, inequities in access to healthcare, discordant health-related perspectives among care seekers and care providers, and the "fatal flow" of professional expertise. Together, these issues signal a growing concern with "migration health" (Grondin et al., 2003, p. 85).

Transmission across Borders

In our mobility era, human interactions across and within porous borders have intensified. More than one million people traverse nation-state borders daily and one million per week move between the global South and the global North (Garrett, 2001, pp. 185–186). Globalization and migration "are mixing people and microorganisms on an unprecedented scale" (Glasgow & Pirages, 2001, p. 196, 203; also Price-Smith, 2002, p. 41, 165) at breakneck speed. Ours is a time of dramatically accelerated transnational human mobility — both proactive and reactive — and of "increasingly rapid exchange of genetic information between microbes" (Glasgow & Pirages, 2001, p. 205). An emerging infectious disease can "traverse entire continents within days or weeks" (Morse, 2001, p. 8). As Julie Gerberding, director of the U.S. CDC, cautions, " 'a problem in a remote corner of the world becomes a world problem overnight. A world problem quickly becomes a local problem, in every corner of the world' " (Lempinen, 2005).

Many of the factors responsible for the emergence of today's particularly threatening new and reemerging infectious diseases are anthropogenic. High-intensity livestock husbandry provides one example. Pandemic influenza viruses involving combinations of gene segments from two influenza strains typically are associated with conditions where humans live in close proximity with integrated pig–duck farming in dense settlements in China and elsewhere in Asia. Researchers have found that "waterfowl, such as ducks, are major reservoirs of influenza and that pigs can serve as mixing vessels for new mammalian influenza strains." Integrated pig–duck farming "puts these two species in contact and provides a natural laboratory for making new influenza recombinants" (Morse, 2001, p. 16). Increased microbial traffic involving novel zoonotic infections that cross from their natural hosts into the human population,[2] and other already present pathogens afforded an opportunity to infect new hosts by changing conditions, are a potent source of emerging pandemic diseases when large numbers of people from diverse places who are uprooted by global economic forces, or by armed conflict, are on the move (Chen & Berlinguer, 2001, p. 38; Garrett, 2001, pp. 186–187; Morse, 2001, p. 11, 17; Price-Smith, 2002, p. 165).

The WHO's International Health Regulations (IHR) aim to prevent the transnational spread of infectious disease with minimum interference in global trade and traffic. Under the IHR, WHO member states are required to report outbreaks of cholera, plague, and yellow fever (see Fidler, 2003b, pp. 1–2). In the past, however, public health administrators and political leaders in headwater states have failed to report and even denied outbreaks — a practice encouraged by the "excessive measures" that other member states have applied "to trade and travelers coming from countries suffering disease outbreaks" (Fidler, 2001, p. 270; also Garrett, 2001, p. 193; Kickbusch & Buse, 2001, p. 707; Smith, 2003, p. B8). The SARS outbreak of 2002/2003 led to changes in prevailing practices. In effect, the WHO expanded its surveillance beyond the three initially identified infectious diseases, although its limited resources are badly stretched (Kickbusch, 2003, p. 4). Heavily infected jurisdictions experienced serious economic losses (see, for instance, Loh and Galbraith, 2003, p. 65),[3] but skilled intervention and reasoned advisories by WHO professionals helped to minimize the damage (BBC, 2004).[4] Another new lesson is that, even in the absence of international legal obligations (Fidler, 2003b, pp. 2–3), global monitoring and media attention (Hu, 2003, p. 62; Zhang, 2003, p. 45) can end the career of top health officials who attempt to cover up the seriousness of an ERID crisis or fail to contain it. SARS demonstrated that transparency and trust are "essential in global health matters" (Kickbusch, 2003, p. 3; Eckholm, 2003, p. A8; Smith, 2003, p. B9). For instance, "precious time was wasted by the initial Chinese refusal to allow the WHO team to visit Guangdong province, where SARS emerged, or visit military hospitals in Beijing where SARS patients were hidden" (Kickbusch,

[2] According to CDC director Gerberding, 12 of the 13 most recent emerging-disease outbreaks have originated in animals (Lempinen, 2005).

[3] Tourism, banking, airlines, restaurants, and higher-education institutions were among those particularly hard hit (Kickbusch, 2003, p. 3).

[4] In Hong Kong, the initiatives undertaken by civic movements helped fill the void in political leadership (Loh & Galbraith, 2003, p. 65).

2003, p. 4; also see Hu, 2003, p. 61; Zhang, 2003, p. 44). Subsequently, "[PRC] Health Minister Zhang Wenkang and the Beijing mayor and deputy party chief Meng Xuenong lost their jobs because of the cover up," false assurances, and inadequate responses (Hu, 2003, p. 63; Zhang, 2003, p. 48). In May 2003, the head of Taiwan's department of health, Twu Siing-Jer, citing personal responsibility for the rapid spread of SARS at two hospitals, stepped down (Grauwels, 2003, p. A5). Finally, in July 2004, Hong Kong's health secretary, Yeoh Eng-kiong, resigned in the wake of a legislative report that held him responsible for the government's slow reaction to the SARS outbreak in that city and for numerous specific response failures (*Missoulian*, July 8, 2004, p. A12).

Given the prominent role played by human mobility in the transmission of infectious diseases, calls for isolation and quarantines typically accompany ERID outbreaks. Isolation involves keeping individuals known to have the focal disease away from the public during the period they are infectious, whereas quarantines involve the separation of persons exposed to it who may or may not be infected (Fidler, 2003b, p. 2; Yee, 2003, p. C3). In the case of the SARS epidemic, public health administrators in a number of countries resorted to isolation and quarantine measures (Yee, 2003, p. C3). Both measures potentially infringe on "civil and political rights recognized in international law, such as freedom of movement and the right to liberty" (Fidler, 2003b, p. 2; also see Smith, 2003, pp. B8–B9). International human rights law allows governments to use isolation and quarantine for public health purposes provided that certain conditions are fulfilled. Specifically, "public health measures that infringe on civil and political rights must (1) be prescribed by law; (2) be applied in a nondiscriminatory manner; (3) relate to a compelling public interest in the form of a significant infectious disease risk to the public's health; and (4) be necessary to achieve the protection of the public, meaning that the measure must be (a) based on scientific and public health information and principles; (b) proportional in its impact on individual rights to the infectious disease threat posed; and (c) the least restrictive measure possible to achieve protection against the infectious disease risk" (Fidler, 2003b, p. 2). The potential advantages of quarantine must also outweigh the potential negative consequences, and it must be feasible both economically and in the sense that exposed persons are willing to cooperate for the duration and can be placed where they can be cared for adequately and safely (Leahy, 2005). In the case of SARS, most of these conditions were satisfied in the principal places that eventually employed isolation and quarantine measures (Fidler, 2003b, p. 3). However, at least Singapore compensated for the shortage of negative-pressure hospital rooms by grouping persons suspected of being infected with SARS in the same ward (Yee, 2003, p. C3).

Access Inequities

Among persons contemplating migration, health issues can trigger or modify the decision to move. In addition, the act of migration can initiate or exacerbate health problems and concerns (Grondin et al., 2003, p. 85). A recent African war-zone study carried out by Physicians for Human Rights concluded that the "first killer is flight" for desperately poor persons driven by conflict from a fragile existence into a hostile environment where health services are nonexistent or not functioning (Lacey, 2005). People on the move can either "introduce new or previously eradicated diseases to the region of destination, or contract diseases unknown to the migrants' region of origin. Moving can also affect mental well-being..." (Grondin et al., 2003, p. 85). As more people in spatial transition compress the distance or time transmission of life-threatening infectious and chronic life-style-linked diseases, the health protection and treatment of migrants assumes increasing consequence for individual patients, receiving societies, and healthcare systems (Koehn, 2006b). Effective public health responses are important because "all members of a community are affected by the poor health status of its least healthy members" (Smedley et al., 2003, p. 37; also see Buse et al., 2002, p. 277).

Policymakers increasingly appreciate that health is a global public good. The distribution of this good remains vastly unequal, however. Individuals and families in transnational spatial transition frequently confront new health risks along with inequities in access and treatment (Smedley et al., 2003, p. 35). Dislocated people are particularly at risk of being bypassed by potentially beneficial interventions (Chen et al., 1999, pp. 284–285, 287, 294).

Disparities in health status reflect, in large measure, lifestyle practices that are mediated by socioeconomic position and ability to access or use healthcare opportunities (Korbin, 2004, p. 10). Given that the transmission of communicable diseases across borders requires population movement, the social determinants of mobility, access, and health status (Whitehead et al., 2001, p. 313) present important context considerations for public health administrators. "Irregular" and undocumented migrations pose special challenges of migration health. At all stages of migration (transportation, transit, and destination), irregular migrants (including persons smuggled and trafficked) "are particularly exposed to contracting or transmitting diseases, to injuries or even death" (Grondin et al., 2003, pp. 90–91). The vulnerability of irregular migrants is exacerbated by poverty, powerlessness, the absence of social and legal protection, and lack of access to reliable healthcare services. This situation often obliges them to seek medical attention through unofficial and unsafe means (Grondin et al., 2003, p. 91).

Although the reasons for disparities in healthcare screening, medical treatments, morbidity, and mortality among persons who lack "voice" in biomedical institutions are multiple and complex (see Roter and Hall, 1992, pp. 46–49), the clinician–patient relationship constitutes an important contributing — and potentially mitigating — factor. For refugees and other migrants at risk of healthcare marginalization, "the medical interview holds the potential to undermine inequalities or to reproduce them" (Fox, 2000, p. 27; also see Kaplan et al., 1995, p. 1177). Based on sensitive and detailed miniethnographic interviews, public health professionals can identify specific resources and support that will empower patients for addressing the external challenges to positive health outcomes they face in the host society. Such support might include facilitating access to traditional healers, medicine, and nutrition; facilitating access to lay (community) health workers; assisting with the development of host-country language proficiency; promoting further education and credential (re-)certification; facilitating employment; promoting the maintenance of children's healthy practices; encouraging legal or policy coalition building and advocacy with host-society institutions and transnational NGOs; and acting as the patient's advocate with government agencies and community associations.

Incongruent Perspectives

Downstream from many of the sources of infectious disease and the onset of chronic illness, migrants and health professionals come together in medical and health promotion encounters. In our mobility-upheaval era, many health outcomes are shaped by transnational interactions among care providers and recipients who meet in settings where nationality or ethnic match is a diminishing option. In such interactions, clinicians, public health administrators, and patients often deal with unfamiliar health risks and threats (Whitehead et al., 2001, p. 313). These transnational encounters are complicated when incongruent perspectives prevail among professionals and service users (Korbin, 2004, p. 11). When migrant perspectives on personal health and illness are withheld from, or incongruent with the perceptions of, host clinicians, their healthcare needs cannot be addressed fully and effectively (Koehn, 2005b, p. 49). Public health professionals are challenged to understand health issues from the migrant's perspective, while health service recipients benefit from understanding provider perspectives (see, for instance, Verwey and Crystal, 2002, pp. 91–92; Koehn, 2005a). Incongruent perspectives regarding the effect of distant premigration and migration contributors on physical and mental health, attitudes toward and use of ethnocultural practices, the role of community and family support networks, proximate factors that confound efforts to deal with mental health problems or to engage in health-promoting activity, and (dis)satisfaction with current healthcare and an unfamiliar healthcare system are especially prone to block the creation of effective transnational health-promoting alliances.

Migrant health is promoted by individual participation in, and community ownership of, partnership strategies (El Ansari et al., 2002, p. 151). The effectiveness of health partnerships depends upon the skills possessed by service users and providers. Interpersonal TC promises to be particularly useful for public health partnerships. TC offers a comprehensive approach for today's diverse and changing multicultural health-promoting encounters. TC analysis treats case-relevant knowledge acquisition, perceptual sensitivity, creative partnering, communicative facility, and effective patient-centered functional behavior as context-specific, interdependent, and ongoing individual skill-based challenges (for details regarding the content of TC's five healthcare-skill domains, see Koehn, 2004). TC on the part of migrant patients and healthcare professionals facilitates the important process of "establishing more common ground than at first is apparent" (Korbin, 2004, p. 11) and promises to mitigate ethnic-based disparities in healthcare (see Koehn, 2005b, pp. 56–69; Koehn, 2006a).

In health-partnership work, "members of the collective action contribute different sets of resources and skills for the task of partnership advancement" (El Ansari et al., 2002, p. 152). In a study conducted in South Africa, El Ansari et al. (2002, p. 152) identified five "domains of stakeholder expertise that are critical to the effectiveness of collaborative projects . . . : (1) educational competencies; (2) partnership fostering expertise; (3) community involvement skills; (4) change agents proficiencies; and (5) strategic and management proficiencies." When asked to rate the skills and abilities of their partners, health professionals considerably underestimated community expertise (El Ansari et al., 2002, p. 152, 155). Other studies have noted that clinicians tend to overlook the resources and resilience of migrants and their families (Muecke, 1992, p. 520; DeSantis, 1997, p. 26; Watters, 2001, p. 1710). Findings from clinical studies also consistently show that, when treated as an interactive, partnership-based process (see Salloway et al., 1997, p. 63), the medical consultation directly and indirectly improves the outcome of healthcare interventions (Jezewski, 1990, p. 511; Street, 1991, pp. 546–547; Roter & Hall, 1992, p. 146; Fox, 2000, p. 27).

A truly comprehensive approach to global and local healthcare appreciates the full "ethnomedical system"; that is, "the total medical resources that are available to, and might be utilized by, a community and society including its biomedical and traditional forms of therapy" (Verwey & Crystal, 2002, p. 83). Incongruent and incomplete perspectives regarding patient, family, and community assets obstruct migrant-health promotion, because the ability to value and express the contributions of both service providers and recipients is a core ingredient in successful collaboration. In community-health initiatives as well as in transnational medical encounters, professional expertise needs to be fused with lay wisdom and experience (El Ansari et al., 2002, p. 156; Koehn & Sainola-Rodriguez, 2005, p. 301). Such fusion enhances the ability of public health personnel "to define public health problems from multiple perspectives and levels of analysis" (Verwey & Crystal, 2002, p. 93).

The "Fatal Flow" of Expertise

Lured by salaries that are unimaginable in their land of origin[5] and by the promise of adequate support facilities, locally trained healthcare workers have been flocking from poor countries to Northern industrialized states.[6] In recent years, for instance, roughly half of the new staff recruited by the British National Health Service held qualifications received abroad. At the start of the new millennium, nearly half of the doctors and one quarter of the nurses in London were foreign-born (Stalker, 2001, p. 32). Medical establishments in Northern countries have been astonishingly successful at skill poaching in the South. More Malawian physicians practice in Manchester (U.K.) today than in Malawi (*Africa Renewal* (January 2005), p. 18). According to Ingida Asfaw, head of the Ethiopian North American Health Professionals Association, more than 400 Ethiopian physicians worked in the United States and Canada in 2004 (Dugger, 2004b, p. A4; also see Koehn et al., 2002).

The "fatal flow" of health professionals, mainly to the United States and Europe, seriously diminishes efforts to prevent and treat infectious and chronic diseases in poor regions (*Africa Renewal* (January 2005), p. 18). According to a 2004 study conducted by the Joint Learning Initiative (a group of more than 100 scholars and health professionals), at least one million additional healthcare professionals need to be trained and retained in Africa over the next decade (Dugger, 2004a, p. A18; *Africa Renewal* (January 2005) p. 18). The migration of healthcare expertise from the global South to the global North also exacerbates prevailing weaknesses in national surveillance systems in low-income countries (see Kickbusch and Buse, 2001, p. 726, 730). In the absence of sufficient personnel trained in

[5] In the early 1990s, "a staff nurse in Manila would get only $146 per month at home, while she or he could earn around... $3,000 in the United States" (Stalker, 2001, p. 32).

[6] Since independence, 550 of the 600 doctors trained in Zambia have emigrated to higher-paying positions (*Africa Renewal* (January 2005), p. 18).

the identification and treatment of ERID outbreaks, diseases are prone to spread both domestically and transnationally (see, for instance, Porter et al., 2002, p. 185). The SARS episode is both disquieting and instructive in this regard. SARS took a disproportionate toll of frontline healthcare providers[7] and forced the closure of well-endowed hospitals in Hong Kong, Taipei, Beijing, and Toronto. A comparable loss of life among an already insufficient and overstretched medical corps could devastate healthcare in most poor countries for decades.[8]

Given the practical and human rights challenges involved in attempting to limit the spread of communicable diseases through border controls, many experts have concluded that improving the medical infrastructure in poor countries, including increased availability of trained public health workers, offers a more promising strategy for reducing ERID outbreaks (Zacher, 1999, p. 275; Grady, 2005e).[9] Expanding the pool of medical workers in Africa, according to recommendations submitted by the Joint Learning Initiative, should include creation of an educational fund that would support the preparation of indigenous paraprofessionals (see Dugger, 2004b, p. A1, A4) and efforts to enhance the emerging reverse flow of health professionals from rich countries — such as the establishment of a volunteer HIV/AIDS corps (Dugger, 2004a, p. A18; also see Grady, 2005e).

Resource — Arising Challenges

Global health and human rights intersect around resource issues. Resource-arising challenges are illustrated in this section by reference to the basic infrastructure and financing of public health administration.

At the end of the 20th century, the World Bank conducted a qualitative study in 60 countries that focused on poor people's economic experiences and perspectives. To the surprise of researchers involved in the interviews and small-group discussions, health emerged as a critical issue. Of particular importance are findings that poor people "overwhelming link disease and ill-health to poverty" and that "good health is not only valued in its own right, but also because it is crucial to economic survival" (WHO and World

---

[7] Of the 193 victims of the Marburg virus outbreak in Angola between October 2004 and April 2005, at least 12 were health workers (Grady, 2005c, p. A4, 2005e, p. A9; also see Hewlett & Hewlett, 2005).

[8] Moreover, as Hu (2003, p. 58) observed, "one of the great mercies in the SARS disaster was that there were no major outbreaks in China's villages.... With far inferior medical facilities and manpower, the hinterlands would have been devastated by a major outbreak."

[9] The CDC's field epidemiological training program provides training courses for health professionals in poor countries (see Zacher, 1999, p. 279).

Bank, 2002, p. 4). WHO's 1998 World Health Report also identified poverty as the principal cause of ill health and premature mortality (see Kickbusch and Buse, 2001, pp. 705–706).

Among the world's poor, the most common social and economic determinants of medical problems are undernourishment, lack of access to safe water, absent or deficient sanitation, and unhygienic housing conditions (Lerer et al., 1998, p. 17; WHO and World Bank, 2002, pp. 4, 6–8). Among the poor, ill health has devastating social and economic consequences. Illness constituted the most frequently cited cause of a downward slide into poverty and despair in the World Bank study:

> Sickness of the family breadwinner is something that poor people particularly fear. It means food and income suddenly stop. Paying for treatment brings more impoverishment — assets may have to be sold and debts incurred.
> (WHO and World Bank, 2002, pp. 15–17; also see Diderichsen et al., 2001, p. 18)

Public health initiatives are dependent upon developments within and beyond the control of nation-states. During the last two decades of the 20th century, the health-sector reforms advanced by the World Bank and the International Monetary Fund (IMF) focused on downsizing the public sector and achieving efficiency objectives (Kickbusch & Buse, 2001, p. 712). The consequences of such policies included the privatization of state health assets, allocation of even smaller budgets to health promotion and care, decreasing public provision and regulation of health and related services, further family impoverishment for treatment that often is inadequate, and expanding health inequities (Chen & Berlinguer, 2001, p. 41; Kickbusch & Buse, 2001, p. 713, 724; Porter et al., 2002, p. 185; Zwi & Yach, 2002, p. 1615, 1617). In China, for instance, "increasing the private provision of public health services has led to serious declines in the quality and equity of such services" (Zwi & Yach, 2002, p. 1619). Moreover, underfunded and overcrowded public health facilities "often become unhygienic centers for the dissemination of disease rather than its control" (Garrett, 2001, p. 188). Thus, some hospitals and clinics in Africa have functioned as "distribution centers" for the Ebola virus (Grady, 2005d, p. D9).

Limited resources and weak initial state capacity make a difference in preventing and treating communicable diseases. Simultaneously, the spread of pathogens further undercuts state capacity (Price-Smith, 2002, pp. 172–175). HIV/AIDS has been especially disruptive with respect to the delivery of health, education, and agricultural services due to high rates of sickness and death among government personnel (Topouzis, 2004, p. 10). Of the 34 African countries reporting adult HIV infection rates above

1 percent, 32 ranked in the lowest 30 percent on the United Nations Development Program's (UNDP) Human Development Index in 2002 (the exceptions are South Africa and Equatorial Guinea). The World Bank has designated 25 of these 34 as "heavily indebted poor countries" (see Fidler, 2003a, pp. 130–131). Public health administrators committed to improving poor people's health need to address the following limitations in prevailing healthcare services identified by participants in the World Bank study: lack of professionally trained staff and required equipments and drugs, abusive treatment by health-center staff, and access obstacles — including the cost of doctor or clinic fees and medicines, bribes for routine services, transportation to care providers, and time lost waiting for treatment (WHO and World Bank, 2002, pp. 17–20, 24–25; also Hsiao & Liu, 2001, p. 262, 269; Whitehead et al., 2001, p. 318; Topouzis, 2004, pp. 9–11).

Although public health remains "a classical 'public good,' meaning that the primary responsibility for protecting and promoting population health falls on the government" (Fidler, 2003a, p. 117), the involvement of independent nonstate actors — for instance, multinational pharmaceutical and insurance corporations (see Kickbusch & Buse, 2001, p. 712), NGOs concerned with women's health, civil-society initiatives such as the People's Health Assembly (Baum, 2001), philanthropic entities such as the Bill and Melinda Gates Foundation (Kickbusch & Buse, 2001, p. 719; Strom, 2005), and public–private partnership ventures such as the Global Fund to Fight AIDS, Tuberculosis, and Malaria (Madamombe, 2005, p. 4) — is increasingly critical in terms of resources, rights, and governance issues (also see Zwi and Yach, 2002, p. 1616, 1618). The mandate of the Global Fund, for instance, involves promoting the "redistribution of financial resources from rich to poor countries for public health purposes" (Fidler, 2003a, pp. 137–138). Under the partnering strategies pursued by the Global Fund, state and nonstate actors combine resources and coordinate project-implementation actions when addressing global disease challenges in poor countries (Fidler, 2003a, pp. 140–141; also see Koehn, 1999; Kickbusch and Buse, 2001, pp. 721–722). However, nonstate actors continue to be fragmented, and given the scale of the public health crisis in poor areas, doubts remain regarding whether partnerization will be sufficiently robust to make a widespread difference. At best, partnerization provides public health administrators with a viable and effective mechanism for global resource redistribution in addressing a single high-visibility health issue (Kickbusch & Buse, 2001, p. 722; also see Topouzis, 2004, p. 11); at worst, it "diverts attention away from the fundamental failure of *governments* to address public health at home and abroad" (Fidler, 2003a, pp. 144–145; Zwi & Yach, 2002, p. 1618; [emphasis added]).

Conclusion

In our era of interdependence and mobility the multiple and complex pathways that link globalization and health merit attention by public health administrators. Although upstream, midstream, and downstream challenges are daunting, globally connected public health administrators have new resources at their disposal and possess enhanced capacity to act. What is called for is attention to "determining the most appropriate mix of policies, directed at both upstream and downstream considerations" (Zwi & Yach, 2002, p. 1619).

Addressing downstream consequences of ERIDs and chronic disease conditions is especially expensive and often ineffectual. Screening at airports and other departure points is costly and not comprehensive. Detection is complicated by incubation periods that "for many incurable contagious diseases may exceed 21 days" (Garrett, 2001, p. 186). Garrett (2001, pp. 185–186) notes that "a person incubating a disease such as Ebola can board a plane, travel 12,000 miles, pass unnoticed through customs and immigration, take a domestic carrier to a remote destination, and still not develop symptoms for several days, infecting many other people before his condition is noticeable" (also see Smith, 2003, p. B8). In addition, no community, even in wealthy countries and global cities, currently possesses or can afford the expense of acquiring specialized facilities, such as negative-pressure (isolation) hospital rooms, in sufficient quantity to contain pandemic infections (Yee, 2003, p. C3). Furthermore, the interorganizational capacity to employ mass quarantines is lacking in most public health systems — including the United States, where the 50 states are primarily responsible for quarantine (and isolation) measures within their borders (Yee, 2003, p. C3).

The SARS experience demonstrated the value of transnational cooperation (and luck) when the public health community is required to act downstream of ERID outbreaks. In recognition that it is not possible to protect the health of U.S. citizens without "addressing infectious disease problems that are occurring elsewhere in the world," for instance, the CDC deployed about 50 public health professionals internationally in response to the SARS crisis (Gerberding, 2003). Instead of abrogating responsibility by stigmatizing migrants, today's public health professional must be skilled in cooperating across borders with state and nonstate counterparts in laboratory work, epidemiological investigations, diagnosis and reporting, exposure management, and specimen handling (Gerberding, 2003). At the same time, support is needed for efforts to strengthen indigenous surveillance and laboratory capacity in the global South and for moves to establish an international system of sanctions and incentives that encourage "global health transparency" (Kickbusch, 2003, p. 4; Barry, 2004, p. B4) rather than denials and cover-ups. Finally, it is critical that public health professionals who decide to resort to isolation and quarantine measures ensure that the advantages outweigh the negative consequences and that the requirements of international law, particularly the obligation not to discriminate on any grounds, be fulfilled before restricting civil or political rights (Fidler, 2003b, p. 2). We know that "quarantines can never be enforced perfectly (imagine the difficulty of shooting to kill when the violator is a kindergartener trying to run home)..." (Smith, 2003, p. B9). Effective quarantines depend upon public support and cooperation. Isolation, which separates dying loved ones from family support networks and cherished cultural practices, is especially difficult to accept (see Grady, 2005a, p. A3). Therefore, "people preparing for careers in public health need to learn that their discipline is as much about politics as medicine, a fact of life that is never clearer than in the imperfect compromises that are often required" (Smith, 2003, p. B9). At the community level, effective policymakers and administrators in public health will possess skills in transnational negotiation, persuasion, and conflict resolution (see Grady, 2005a, p. A3), networking, organizational and institutional analysis, and international law (Kickbusch & Buse, 2001, p. 731).

Upstream health-promotion efforts can reduce transnational health threats, while they benefit needy local populations. At upstream intervention points, local authorities retain a critical role in providing health opportunities for all and in ensuring provider and service quality (Kickbusch & Buse, 2001, p. 705; Zwi & Yach, 2002, p. 1617). One promising approach for public health promotion is to focus on "reducing the excess exposures to health hazards [or avoidable barriers to health] of those occupying lower social positions" — such as dangerous working conditions, unsafe water supplies, nutritional deficiencies, and unhygienic housing and sanitary conditions (Diderichsen et al., 2001, pp. 19–20; Lozano et al., 2001, p. 293; Whitehead et al., 2001, pp. 315–317). Joining forces with the WHO's initiative to combat obesity by supporting restrictions on upstream advertising of junk foods (see Stein, 2004) constitutes an example of another approach that is available to community-health advocates.[10]

Linking behavior to personal or family health is a proven pathway for motivating personal action (Stern, 2000). Linkages to personal or family health concerns have been successful in bringing about dramatic behavior changes in the recent past with regard to smoking cessation, drinking and driving (see Myers, 1997, p. 54), and asbestos removal (Castleman, 2004). Coupling consumption practices with health promotion and psychosocial stress-reduction promises to be a particularly powerful strategy for bringing

[10] Such upstream interventions are particularly important when popular beliefs discount the personal health effects of pathogenic behaviors (Davison et al., 1992, p. 683).

about behavioral change. At the individual and organizational levels, the same actions that reduce GHG emissions over the long term also immediately lower personal stress and dramatically diminish threats to personal and family health (see McQueen et al., 2001, p. 318). Reducing emissions from coal-fire plants and vehicles would provide substantial public health benefits (Cifuentes et al., 2001, pp. 1257–1258). Davis et al. (1997, pp. 1341–1342, 1346–1347) estimate that diminished exposure to the particulate matter that is associated with fossil-fuel combustion processes under a GHG emissions–reduction scenario would avoid 33,000 deaths per year in the United States by 2020 and save far more lives in developing countries. In general, lay publics and political actors are receptive to controlling noticeable emissions that are responsible for pollution and other negative health and economic consequences in one's locality (see, for instance, Frank, 2000; Bickerstaff and Walker, 2001, p. 143; Chandler, et al., 2002, p. 52). Because the detrimental health consequences associated with particulate emissions are proximate and directly and immediately discernable (Bickerstaff & Walker, 2001, pp. 140–143), "air pollution reduction-related health benefits could be a strong motivator for GHG mitigation action" (Cifuentes et al., 2001 p. 1259; Baldassare & Katz, 1992; Hobson, 2003, pp. 107–108).

In addition, to promote health for all in an increasingly borderless world, public administrators responsible for a wide range of health- and nonhealth-specific national and transnational policies, programs, projects, and regulatory instruments need to (re)assess prevailing approaches and new initiatives in terms of "effects on the key social determinants of health: *poverty, economic and ethnic inequalities, violence, war, environmental degradation, and access to healthcare services and technologies*" (Fulbright New Century Scholars, 2002; Lerer et al., 1998, p. 16; Kickbusch & Buse, 2001, p. 703, 711, 722, 729, 732; Price-Smith, 2002, pp. 179–180; Thomas et al., 2002, p. 1058; Zwi & Yach, 2002, p. 1619).[11] Failure to rectify economic, gender, ethnic, and political-power inequities at subnational, national, and global levels perpetuates systematic health disparities between advantaged and marginalized population groups both within and across nation-state borders (Ostlin et al., 2001; Thomas and Web 2004, p. 196). Such inter- and intrastate inequities in health status create "both a human rights and public health travesty" (Baum, 2001, p. 616; Porter et al., 2002, p. 194). The other side of the coin — that investments in improving health "can prevent or offer a route out of poverty" (WHO and World Bank, 2002, p. 23; Kickbusch & Buse, 2001,

[11] For a useful list of global influences on health and their probable impacts, see Kickbusch and Buse (2001, p. 704).

p. 725) — provides further justification for placing public health proponents at the center of coordinated multisectoral development initiatives.

State and nonstate actors concerned with enabling all people to realize their health potential and organizations and individuals struggling to promote human rights can coalesce around a shared vision and action plan that calls for "reductions in discrimination in the distribution of the conditions required for people to have equal opportunity to be healthy" (Zwi & Yach, 2002, p. 1616). Framing public health as a global public good within a human rights and solidarity perspective offers an integrated and ethical foundation for addressing health determinants and generic flaws in policy making by moving beyond issue-specific and country-focused responses (Kickbusch & Buse, 2001, p. 724, 727; Benatar et al., 2003, p. 117). Public health issues are deeply embedded in a political context. Among other changes, the field of public health "must upgrade its capacities in trade and political science so as to effectively participate in such fora as the World Trade Organization" (Zwi & Yach, 2002, p. 1617; Baum, 2001, p. 614; Kickbusch & Buse, 2001, p. 731), where key decisions impacting global health are made in complex contexts of power relations that lack transparency and public accountability (Kickbusch & Buse, 2001, p. 714, 723). Among the lessons of the SARS outbreak are: (1) promoting "transparency is essential in global health matters" (Kickbusch, 2003, p. 3; Zwi & Yach, 2002 p. 1616, 1619) and (2) national and international public health administrators need strengthened mechanisms for cooperation to protect population health in ways that are consistent with a global public goods model (Kickbusch & Buse, 2001, pp. 729–732; Kickbusch, 2003, pp. 3–5). At the local level, public administrators need to implement reforms that will empower the poor with basic health knowledge and enhance the participation of communities as well as marginalized groups and individuals in context-specific health-policy making, implementation, and monitoring (also see Chen & Berlinguer, 2001, p. 43; WHO and World Bank, 2002, p. 22). Public administrators also must be involved in borderless efforts to minimize and compensate for the negative economic impacts on local communities associated with transparency concerning outbreaks of ERIDs (see Garrett, 2001, p. 189). Although global economic forces contribute to the widening gap between haves and have nots that underlies the spread of ERIDs, other aspects of the global communication and transportation revolution, such as the emergence of networks of professional health workers, facilitate the development of effective mitigation and control strategies (Porter et al., 2002, p. 193).[12]

---

[12] In 2004, for instance, ten Southeast Asian countries formed a new veterinary network devoted to generating and sharing expertise related to detection and control of the avian-influenza virus (Altman, 2004, p. A5).

Nonstate actors and networks play an increasingly vital role in addressing global health challenges at a time when states and interstate organizations have not been able to contain the HIV/AIDS pandemic and other ERIDs (Zacher, 1999, p. 278; Price-Smith, 2002, p. 5; Fidler, 2003a, p. 145).[13] In the public health arena, NGOs "act as watchdogs of the pharmaceutical industry, advocate on behalf of primary healthcare and women's health, and ensure that continuing attention is paid to community involvement and human rights in health matters around the globe" (Kickbusch & Buse, 2001, p. 719; also see Whitehead et al., 2001, p. 321). At all levels of action (transnational, national, local, and nongovernmental), training for public health professionals needs to encompass the determinants of population health — particularly those related to mobility, resource distribution, access, governance, power shifts in national and international health systems and in nonstate alliances, and the necessity for building networks and pursuing innovative approaches that address the interface between global and local health (Kickbusch & Buse, 2001, pp. 728–732).

Public administrators need to remain vigilant and critical about interventions employed to address upstream, midstream, and downstream challenges to health. In impact-assessment and monitoring and evaluation processes, cooperation with NGOs and an inclusive array of local residents can promote sustained focus on determinants of health. At the evaluation stage, the crucial considerations should center on whether the chosen interventions not only have improved public health but also have removed barriers to equitable access (see Whitehead et al., 2001, pp. 319–320), enhanced the quality of life of affected populations, and advanced the capabilities of their least-advantaged members (Sen, 2001, p. 72).

---

[13] See, for instance, the principles for action set forth in the People's Charter for Health adopted by public health activists from 93 countries at the 2000 People's Health Assembly in Bangladesh (Baum, 2001, p. 613, 616).

References

Altman, L.K. 2004. "Asian Nations to Cooperate on Avian Flu," *New York Times*, 31 July, p. A5.

Baldassare, M. and C. Katz. 1992. "The Personal Threat of Environmental Problems as Predictor of Environmental Practices," *Environment and Behavior*, 24(5): 602–616.

Barry, J.M. 2004. "Time to Act: Toll from an Influenza Pandemic Would Be Catastrophic," *Missoulian*, 27 October, p. B4.

Baum, F. 2001. "Health, Equity, Justice and Globalisation: Some Lessons from the People's Health Assembly," *Journal of Epidemiology and Community Health*, 55: 613–616.

Benatar, S.R., A.S. Daar, and P.A. Singer, 2003, "Global Health Ethics: The Rationale for Mutual Caring," *International Affairs*, 79(1): 107–138.

Bickerstaff, K. and G. Walker. 2001. "Public Understandings of Air Pollution: The 'Localisation' of Environmental Risk," *Global Environmental Change*, 11: 133–145.

British Broadcasting Corporation (BBC). 2004. *SARS: The True Story*. Princeton, NJ: Films for the Humanities and Social Sciences.

Brody, J.E. 2005. "As America Gets Bigger, the World Does Too," *New York Times*, 19 April, p. D5, D10.

Buse, K., N. Drager, S. Fustukian, and K. Lee. 2002. "Globalisation and Health Policy: Trends and Opportunities," in K. Lee, K. Buse, and S. Fustukian (eds.), *Health Policy in a Globalising World*. Cambridge: Cambridge University Press, pp. 251–280.

Castleman, B. 2004. "The International Struggle over Asbestos," Presidential Lecture, The University of Montana, 5 April.

Chandler, W., R. Schaeffer, Z. Dadi, P.R. Shukla, F. Tudela, O. Davidson, S. Alpan-Atamer. 2002. *Climate Change Mitigation in Developing Countries*. Arlington: Pew Center on Global Climate Change.

Chen, L.C. and G. Berlinguer. 2001. "Health Equity in a Globalizing World," in T. Evans, M. Whitehead, F. Diderichsen, A. Bhuiya, and M. Wirth (eds.), *Challenging Inequities in Health: From Ethics to Action*. Oxford: Oxford University Press, pp. 35–44.

Chen, L.C., T.G. Evans, and R.A. Cash. 1999. "Health as a Global Public Good," in I. Kaul, I. Grunberg, and M.A. Stern (eds.), *Global Public Goods: International Cooperation in the 21st Century*. Oxford: Oxford University Press, pp. 284–304.

Cifuentes, L., V.H. Borja-Aburto, N. Gouveia, G. Thurston, and D.L. Davis. 2001. "Hidden Health Benefits of Greenhouse Gas Mitigation," *Science*, 293 (17 August): 1257–1259.

Clapp, J. 2002. "The Distancing of Waste: Overconsumption in a Global Economy," in T. Princen, M. Maniates, and K. Conca (eds.), *Confronting Consumption*. Cambridge: MIT Press, pp. 155–176.

Clayton, J. 2005. "Tsunami Uncovers Somali Toxic Waste," London Times, 5 March, p. A15.

Cohen, M.J. 2001. "The Emergent Environmental Policy Discourse on Sustainable Consumption," in M.J. Cohen and J. Murphy (eds.), *Exploring Sustainable Consumption: Environmental Policy and the Social Sciences*, Vol. 1. Amsterdam: Pergamon, pp. 21–37.

Conca, K. 2002. "Consumption and Environment in a Global Economy," in T. Princen, M. Maniates, and K. Conca (eds.), *Confronting Consumption*. Cambridge: MIT Press, pp. 133–153.

Davis, D.L., and Working Group on Public Health and Fossil-Fuel Combustion. 1997. "Short-Term Improvements in Public Health from Global-Climate Policies on Fossil-Fuel Combustion: An Interim Report," *Lancet*, 350(8 November): 1341–1349.

Davison, C., S. Frankel, and G.D. Smith. 1992. "The Limits of Lifestyle: Re-assessing 'Fatalism' in the Popular Culture of Illness Prevention," *Social Science and Medicine*, 34(6): 675–685.

DeSantis, L. 1997. "Building Health Communities with Immigrants and Refugees," *Journal of Transcultural Nursing*, 9(1): 20–31.

Diderichsen, F., T. Evans, and M. Whitehead. 2001. "The Social Basis of Disparities in Health," in T. Evans, M. Whitehead, F. Diderichsen, A. Bhuiya, and M. Wirth (eds.), *Challenging Inequities in Health: From Ethics to Action*. Oxford: Oxford University Press, pp. 13–23.

Dugger, C.W. 2004a. "Africa Needs More Health Workers, Report Says," *New York Times*, 26 November, p. A18.

Dugger, C.W. 2004b. "Lacking Doctors, Africa Is Training Substitutes," *New York Times*, 23 November, p. A1.

Dunlap, R.E., G.H. Gallop, and A.M. Gallop. 1993. "Of Global Concern: Results of the Health of the Planet Survey," *Environment*, 35(9): 6–22.

Eckholm, E. 2003. "Hong Kong Bombshell for Beijing," *New York Times*, 10 July, p. A8.

El Ansari, W., C.J. Phillips, and A.B. Zwi. 2002. "Narrowing the Gap between Academic Professional Wisdom and Community Lay Knowledge: Perceptions from Partnerships," *Public Health*, 116: 151–159.

Epstein, P.R. 1995. "Emerging Infections and Global Change: Integrating Health Surveillance and Environmental Monitoring," *Current Issues in Public Health*, 1:224–232.

Epstein, P.R. 1997. "Emerging Infectious Diseases: Symptoms of Global Change," in P.R. Epstein, M. Hoffman, M.J. Kim, J.G. Lipson, J. Mayotte, A.B. McBride, M.L. de Lide Siantz, and R.P. Winter. (eds.), *Global Migration: The Health Care Implications of Immigration and Population Movements*. Washington, D.C.: American Academy of Nursing, pp. 67–77.

Epstein, P.R. 2001. "Climate, Ecology and Human Health," in A.T. Price-Smith (ed.), *Plagues and Politics: Infectious Disease and International Policy*. London: Palgrave, pp. 27–58.

Fidler, D.P. 2001. "Public Health and International Law: The Impact of Infectious Diseases on the Formation of International Legal Regimes, 1800–2000," in A.T. Price-Smith (ed.), *Plagues and Politics: Infectious Disease and International Policy*. London: Palgrave, pp. 262–284.

Fidler, D.P. 2003a. "Racism or *Realpolitik*? U.S. Foreign Policy and the HIV/AIDS Catastrophe in Sub-Saharan Africa," *Journal of Gender, Race, & Justice*, 7(1)(Spring): 97–146.

Fidler, D.P. 2003b. "SARS and International Law," *American Society of International Law Insights* (April): 1–3. www.asil.org/insights/insigh101.htm

Fox, K. 2000. "Provider–Patient Communication in the Context of Inequalities," in E. Silverman (ed.), *Child Health in the Multicultural Environment*. Report of the 31st Ross Roundtable on Critical Approaches to Common Pediatric Problems. Columbus: Ross Products Division, Abbott Laboratories, pp. 27–36.

Frank, A. 2000. "The Environment in U.S.–China Relations: Themes and Ideas from Working Group Discussions," China Environment Series 1, Environmental

Change and Security Project, Woodrow Wilson International Center for Scholars. htttp//ecsp.si.edu/ecsplib.nsf

Fulbright New Century Scholars. 2002. "Scholars' Statement: Challenges to Health in a Borderless World Program," 6 November (Washington, D.C.)

Garrett, L. 2001. "The Return of Infectious Disease," in A.T. Price-Smith (ed.), *Plagues and Politics: Infectious Disease and International Policy*. London: Palgrave, pp. 183–194.

Gerberding, J.L. 2003. "SARS: Assessment, Outlook, and Lessons Learned." Prepared Witness Testimony before the House Committee on Energy and Commerce, 7 May. www.energycommerce.house.gov/108/Hearings/05072003hearing917/Gerberding

Glasgow, S. and Pirages, D. 2001. "Microsecurity," in A.T. Price-Smith (ed.), *Plagues and Politics: Infectious Disease and International Policy*. London: Palgrave, pp. 195–213.

Glenn, D. 2003. "Panic Button," *Chronicle of Higher Education*, 14 March, pp. A14–A15.

Grady, D. 2005a. "Deadly Virus Alters Angola's Traditions," *New York Times*, 19 April, p. A3.

Grady, D. 2005b. "Even Good Health is Overwhelmed by Tsunami," *New York Times*, 9 January, p. A10.

Grady, D. 2005c. "Hospital Errors Jeopardize Angola Virus Battle," *New York Times*, 30 April, p. A4.

Grady, D. 2005d. "Mysterious Viruses as Bad as They Get," *New York Times*, 26 April, p. D1, D9.

Grady, D. 2005e. "Training is First Task in Angola Outbreak," *New York Times*, 13 April, p. A9.

Grauwels, S. 2003. "Health Chief Quits over SARS," *Missoulian*, 17 May, p. A5.

Grondin, D., J. Weekers, M. Haour-Knipe, A. Elton, and J. Stukey. 2003. "Health — An Essential Aspect of Migration Management," in *World Migration 2003: Managing Migration Challenges and Responses for People on the Move*. Geneva: International Organization for Migration, pp. 85–93.

Guterman, L. 2003. "As the Rich Get Richer, Do People Get Sicker?" *Chronicle of Higher Education*, 28 November, pp. A22–A23.

Herrell, I.C. and C.A. Mulholland. 1998. "Reflections on Health in Development and Human Rights," *World Health Statistical Quarterly*, 51: 88–93.

Hewlett, B.L. and B.S. Hewlett. 2005. "Providing Care and Facing Death: Nursing During Ebola Outbreaks in Central Africa," *Journal of Transcultural Nursing* 16(4): 289–297.

Heymann, D. 2005. "Preparing for a New Global Threat — Part I," *Yale Global Online*, 26 January. www.yaleglobal.yale.edu/article.print?id=5174

Hobson, K. 2003. "Thinking Habits into Action: The Role of Knowledge and Process in Questioning Household Consumption Practices," *Local Environment*, 8(1): 95–112.

Hsiao, W.C. and Y. Liu. 2001. "Health Care Financing: Assessing Its Relationship to Health Equity," in T. Evans, M. Whitehead, F. Diderichsen, A. Bhuiya, and

M. Wirth (eds.), *Challenging Inequities in Health: From Ethics to Action.* Oxford: Oxford University Press, pp. 261–275.

Hu J. 2003. "A Tale of Two Crises: SARS vs AIDS," *China Rights Forum*, (3): 56–63.

Hunter, S. 2003. *Black Death: AIDS in Africa.* New York: Palgrave, Macmillan.

Jezewski, M.A. 1990. "Culture Brokering in Migrant Farmworker Health Care," *Western Journal of Nursing Research*, 12(4): 497–513.

Kaplan, S.H., B. Gandek, S. Greenfield, W. Rogers, and J.E. Ware. 1995. "Patient and Visit Characteristics Related to Physicians' Participatory Decision-making Style: Results from the Medical Outcomes Study," *Medical Care*, 33(12): 1176–1187.

Kickbusch, I. 2003. "SARS: Wake-Up Call for a Strong Global Health Policy," *Yale Global Online*, 25 April. yaleglobal.yale.edu/display.article?id = 1476

Kickbusch, I. and K. Buse. 2001. "Global Influences and Global Responses: International Health at the Turn of the Twenty-first Century," in M.H. Merson, R.E. Black, and A.J. Mills (eds.), *International Public Health: Diseases, Programs, Systems, and Policies.* Gaithersburg: Aspen Publishers, pp. 701–732.

Koehn, P.H. 1999. "Operationalizing the Development-Fund Model: Suggestions for Managing Channeled Aid," in P. Koehn and O.J.B. Ojo. (eds.), *Making Aid Work: Innovative Approaches for Africa at the Turn of the Century.* Lanham: University Press of America, pp. 37–64.

Koehn, P.H. 2004. "Global Politics and Multinational Health-Care Encounters: Assessing the Role of Transnational Competence," *EcoHealth*, 1(1)(March): 69–85.

Koehn, P.H. 2005a. "Improving Transnational Health-care Encounters and Outcomes: The Challenge of Enhanced Transnational Competence for Migrants and Health Professionals," in *Proceedings of the Hospitals in a Culturally Diverse Europe Conference on Quality-assured Health Care and Health Promotion for Migrants and Ethnic Minorities, Amsterdam, 9–11 December 2004.* www.mfh-eu.net/conf/results/

Koehn, P.H. 2005b. "Medical Encounters in Finnish Reception Centres: Asylum-seeker and Clinician Perspectives," *Journal of Refugee Studies*, 18(1): 47–75.

Koehn, P.H. 2006a. "Health-care Outcomes in Ethnoculturally Discordant Medical Encounters: The Role of Physician Transnational Competence in Consultations with Asylum Seekers," *Journal of Immigrant Health*, 8(2): 137–147.

Koehn, P.H. 2006b. "Transnational Migration, State Policy, and Local Clinician Treatment of Asylum Seekers and Resettled Migrants: Comparative Perspectives on Reception-centre and Community Health-care Practice in Finland," *Global Social Policy*, 6(1): 21–56.

Koehn, P.H. and K. Sainola-Rodriguez. 2005. "Clinician/Patient Connections in Ethnoculturally Nonconcordant Encounters with Political-Asylum Seekers: A Comparison of Physicians and Nurses," *Journal of Transcultural Nursing*, 16(4): 298–311.

Koehn, N.N., G.E. Fryer, Jr., R.L. Phillips, J.B. Miller, and L.A. Green. 2002. "The Increase in International Medical Graduates in Family Practice Residency Programs," *Family Medicine*, 34(6)(June): 429–435.

Korbin, J.E. 2004. "Cultural Issues in Pediatric Care," in R.E. Behrman, R.M. Kliegman, and H.B. Jensen (eds.), *Nelson Textbook of Pediatrics*, 17th edn. New York: Saunders, pp. 10–12.

Lacey, M. 2004. "U.S. Suggests AIDS Fund Delay Grants," *New York Times*, 17 November, p. A3.

Lacey, M. 2005. "In Africa, Guns Aren't the Only Killers," *New York Times*, 25 April.

LaFraniere, S. 2005. "Health Workers Race to Block Deadly Virus in Angolan Town," *New York Times*, 11 April, p. A1, A9.

Lane, N. F. and R. Bierbaum. 2001. "Recent Advances in the Science of Climate Change," *Natural Resources and Environment*, 15(3)(Winter): 147–151; 199–202.

Leahy, E. 2005. "Public Health and the Public: Negotiating the Intersection," Presentation delivered at the Practical Ethics Center's lecture series, University of Montana 2 May.

Lempinen, E.W. 2005. "CDC Director Gerberding Cites Avian Flu as 'Very Ominous' Threat," *AAAS News*, 21 February. www.aaas.org/news/releases/2005/0221flu.shtml

Lerer, L.B., A.D. Lopez, T. Kjellstrom, and D. Yach. 1998. "Health for All: Analyzing Health Status and Determinants," *World Health Statistical Quarterly*, 51(1): 7–20.

Lipton, E. 2005. "U.S. Lists Possible Terror Attacks and Likely Toll," *New York Times*, 16 March, p. A1, A14.

Loh, C. and V. Galbraith. 2003. "SARS and Civil Society in Hong Kong," *China Rights Forum*, 3: 64–65.

Lozano, R., B. Zurita, F. Franco, T. Ramirez, P. Hernandez, and J.L. Torres. 2001. "Mexico: Marginality, Need, and Resource Allocation at the County Level," in T. Evans, M. Whitehead, F. Diderichsen, A. Bhuiya, and M. Wirth (eds.), *Challenging Inequities in Health: From Ethics to Action*. Oxford: Oxford University Press, pp. 277–295.

Madamombe, I. 2005. "Africans Push to Tame Malaria," *Africa Renewal* (January): 4, 18.

Martens, P. 1998. "Health and Climate Change: Modelling the Impacts of Global Warming and Ozone Depletion." London: Earthscan.

McMichael, A.J. and A. Haines. 1997. "Global Climate Change: The Potential Effects on Health," *British Medical Journal*, 315(7111)(27 September): 805–809.

McNeil, D.G., Jr. 2004a. "Malaria Vaccine Proves Effective," *New York Times*, 15 October, p. A1, A6.

McNeil, D.G., Jr. 2004b. "Study Finds Generic AIDS Drug Effective," *New York Times*, 2 July, p. A5.

McNeil, D.G., Jr. 2005. "New Vaccine Said to Offer Hope against Deadly Bacterium," *New York Times*, 25 March, p. A4.

McQueen, D.V., M.T. McKenna, and D.A. Sleet. 2001. "Chronic Diseases and Injury," in M.H. Merson, R.E. Black, and A.J. Mills (eds.), *International Public Health: Diseases, Programs, Systems, and Policies*. Gaithersburg: Aspen Publishers, pp. 293–330.

Missoulian, 23 February 2004, p. A2

Missoulian, 8 July 2004, p. A12.

Missoulian, 4 May 2005, p. A12

Morse, S.S. 2001. "Factors in the Emergence of Infectious Diseases," in A.T. Price-Smith (ed.), *Plagues and Politics: Infectious Disease and International Policy*. London: Palgrave, pp. 8–26.

Muecke, M.A. 1992. "New Paradigms for Refugee Health Problems," *Social Science and Medicine*, 35(4): 515–523.

Myers, N. 1997. "Consumption: Challenge to Sustainable Development," *Science*, 276(5309): 53–55.

New York Times, 13 October 2004, p. A6.

New York Times, 15 December 2004, p. A20.

New York Times, 28 February 2005, p. A8.

Ostlin, P., A. George, and G. Sen. 2001. "Gender, Health and Equity: The Intersections," in T. Evans, M. Whitehead, F. Diderichsen, A. Bhuiya, and M. Wirth (eds.), *Challenging Inequities in Health: From Ethics to Action*. Oxford: Oxford University Press, pp. 175–189.

Paquette, L. 2004. *Bioterrorism in Medical and Healthcare Administration*. New York: Marcel Dekker.

Patz, J.A., P.R. Epstein, T.A. Burke, and J.M. Balbus. 1996. "Global Climate Change and Emerging Infectious Diseases," *JAMA*, 275(3): 217–223.

Payne, J. 2005. "European Waistlines Gaining on America," *Missoulian*, 16 March, p. A10.

Porter, J., K. Lee, and J. Ogden. 2002. "The Globalisation of DOTS: Tuberculosis as a Global Emergency," in K. Lee, K. Buse, and S. Fustukian (eds.), *Health Policy in a Globalising World*. Cambridge: Cambridge University Press, pp. 181–194.

Price-Smith, A.T. 2002. *The Health of Nations: Infectious Disease, Environmental Change, and their Effects on National Security and Development*. Cambridge: MIT Press.

Princen, T., M. Maniates, and K. Conca. 2002. "Confronting Consumption," in T. Princen, M. Maniates, and K. Conca (eds.), *Confronting Consumption*. Cambridge: MIT Press, pp. 1–20.

Recer, P. 2005. "CDC: World on Precipice of Bird Flu Pandemic," *Missoulian*, 22 February, p. A1, A9.

Roter, D.L. and J.A. Hall. 1992. *Doctors Talking with Patients/Patients Talking with Doctors: Improving Communication in Medical Visits*. Westport: Auburn House.

Sainola-Rodriguez, K. and Koehn, P.H. forthcoming. "The Mental-Health Needs of Political-Asylum Seekers and Resident Foreign Nationals in Finland: Patient Perspectives and Practitioner Recognition," *Journal of Social Medicine* (in Finnish).

Salloway, J.C., F.W. Hafferty, and Y.M. Vissing. 1997. "Professional Roles and Health Behavior," in D.S. Gochman (ed.), *Handbook of Health Behavior Research II: Provider Determinants*. New York: Plenum Press, pp. 63–79.

Sen, A. 2001. "Health Equity: Perspectives, Measurability, and Criteria," in T. Evans, M. Whitehead, F. Diderichsen, A. Bhuiya, and M. Wirth (eds.), *Challenging Inequities in Health: From Ethics to Action*. Oxford: Oxford University Press, pp. 69–75.

Smedley, B.D., A.Y. Stith, and A.R. Nelson (eds.). 2003. *Unequal Treatment: Confronting Racial and Ethnic Disparities in Health Care*. Washington, D.C.: National Academies Press.

Smith, J.S. 2003. "The Personal Predicament of Public Health," *Chronicle of Higher Education*, 49(42)(27 June): B7–B9.

Sprunt, E. 2001. "Emissions Infiltrate Business Issues," *Hart's E&P*, 74(1)(January): 74–76.

Stalker, P. 2001. *The No-Nonsense Guide to International Migration*. London: Verso.

Stein, R. 2004. "White House to Seek Changes to WHO Global Obesity Strategy," *Missoulian*, 20 June.

Stern, P.C. 1997. "Toward a Working Definition of Consumption for Environmental Research and Policy," in P.C. Stern, T. Dietz, V.W. Ruttan, R.H. Socolow, and J.J. Sweeney (eds.), *Environmentally Significant Consumption: Research Directions*. Washington, D.C.: National Academy Press, pp. 12–25.

Stern, P.C. 2000. "Toward a Coherent Theory of Environmentally Significant Behavior," *Journal of Social issues* 56(3): 407–424.

Street, R.L., Jr. 1991. "Information-Giving in Medical Consultations: The Influence of Patients' Communicative Styles and Personal Characteristics," *Social Science and Medicine*, 32(5): 541–548.

Strom, S. 2005. "Gates Charity is Doubling Vaccination Gift," *New York Times*, 25 January, p. A15.

Swick, H. and P.H. Koehn. 2005. "Preparing Transnationally Competent Physicians for Migrant-friendly Health Care: New Directions in U.S. Medical Education," in *Proceedings of the Hospitals in a Culturally Diverse Europe Conference on Quality-assured Health Care and Health Promotion for Migrants and Ethnic Minorities, Amsterdam, 9–11 December 2004*. www.mfh-eu.net/conf/results/

Thomas, C. and M. Weber, 2004. "The Politics of Global Health Governance: Whatever Happened to 'Health for All by the Year 2000'?" *Global Governance*, 10(4): 187–205.

Thomas, J.C., M. Sage, J. Dillenberg, and V.J. Guillory. 2002. "A Code of Ethics for Public Health," *American Journal of Public Health*, 92(7)(July): 1057–1059.

Topouzis, D. 2004. "Moving Therapy to Frontline of AIDS War," *Africa Recovery*, (April): 9–11.

Troedsson, H. and A. Rychener. 2005. "When Influenza Takes Flight," *New York Times*, 5 February, p. A31.

Verwey, S. and A. Crystal. 2002. "Provider-patient Communication in the African Health Context," in A.O. Alali and B.A. Jinadu (eds.), *Health Communication in Africa: Contexts, Constraints and Lessons*. Lanham: University Press of America, pp. 81–108.

Watters, C. 2001. "Emerging Paradigms in the Mental Health Care of Refugees," *Social Science and Medicine*, 52: 1709–1718.

Whitehead, M., G. Dahlgren, and L. Gilson. 2001. "Developing the Policy Response to Inequities in Health: A Global Perspective," in T. Evans, M. Whitehead, F. Diderichsen, A. Bhuiya, and M. Wirth (eds.), *Challenging Inequities in Health: From Ethics to Action*. Oxford: Oxford University Press, pp. 309–323.

Williams, R., R. Bhopal, and K. Hunt. 1994. "Coronary Risk in a British Punjabi Population: Comparative Profile of Non-biochemical Factors," *International Journal of Epidemiology*, 23(1): 28–37.

World Health Organization (WHO) and World Bank. 2002. *Dying for Change: Poor People's Experience of Health and Ill-Health*. Washington, D.C.: WHO and the Bank.

Yach, D. and D. Bettcher, 2000. "Globalization of Tobacco Industry Influence and New Global Responses," *Tobacco Control* 9: 206–216.

Yee, D. 2003. "Officials Size Up SARS Weaknesses," *Missoulian*, 20 May, p. C1, C3.

Zacher, M.W. 1999. "Global Epidemiological Surveillance: International Cooperation to Monitor Infectious Diseases," in I. Kaul, I. Grunberg, and M.A. Stern (eds.), *Global Public Goods: International Cooperation in the 21st Century*. Oxford: Oxford University Press, pp. 266–283.

Zhang, E. 2003. "SARS: Unmasking Censorship in China," *China Rights Forum*, (3): 44–49.

Zwi, A.B. and D. Yach. 2002. "International Health in the 21st Century: Trends and Challenges," *Social Science & Medicine*, 54(11): 1615–1620.

Chapter 50

The Globalization of Public Budgeting in the United States

Patrick Fisher and David C. Nice

CONTENTS

Budgetary decisions affect public bureaucracies in many important ways. If agencies lack adequate funding, they will be less able to accomplish their objectives. The morale of agency employees may suffer if they fail to receive salary increases or if many positions are left unfilled due to hiring freezes. Facilities and equipment that need to be replaced may remain in service because there is no money to replace them; inadequate funding for maintenance may cause premature deterioration of facilities and equipment. If budgetary decisions are subject to repeated revision, agency personnel may fear that a new initiative or an ongoing program may be undercut by the withdrawal of funds that were previously approved. Moreover, the budget's value as an instrument of democratic accountability is reduced if a budget is adopted amid great fanfare but is later revised in ways that are not very visible to the public.

At the risk of some oversimplification, much of the early literature on public budgeting in the United States depicted it as working reasonably well, apart from the lack of revenue available in some jurisdictions and some concerns about pork-barrel spending. Budgetary decisions were made rather smoothly and predictably, and once budgets were decided, they were implemented in a reasonably smooth and predictable fashion. This was in marked contrast to budgeting in some other countries, where prolonged conflict over budgetary decisions sometimes occurred and where budgets were often subject to major revisions after adoption. Although public budgeting was sometimes used to stabilize the U.S. economy, public budgets were not depicted as regularly being used to shape the future development of the economy, in marked contrast to governmental economic planning and economic development policies in some other countries. Moreover, American budgeting was primarily depicted as a domestic process rather than as one that was subject to strong international influences.

In more recent years, scholars and other observers have considerably revised the dominant characterization of public budgeting in the United States. Levels of political conflict have risen considerably in national, state, and local government budgeting, and much of that conflict has followed ideological and partisan lines. The national government and some states have had considerable difficulty in making budgetary decisions according to a regular timetable, and once budgetary decisions are made, they are subject to later revision that may be because of the errors in forecasting revenues or spending or political maneuvering, with people who are unhappy with the original decision trying to modify it. Especially since the September 11, 2001, attacks on the World Trade Center and the Pentagon, a number of observers have also noted the importance of international influences on U.S. budgeting; similar, though less dramatic awareness of international influences surfaced in the aftermath of the 1970s oil shocks and the later discussion of the so-called peace dividend after the end of the Cold War.

We believe that these developments can be usefully characterized as the globalization of American public budgeting. Globalization has a number of different meanings, but for our purposes, two facets of globalization have particular relevance. First, globalization involves a variety of forces and relationships that transcend national boundaries (Fortanier & Maher, 2001; Tarzi, 1999) and may cause different political systems to behave in relatively similar ways, although different systems may respond to those forces in different ways (see Marsh, 1999). Second, globalization may mean that decisions made in one country grow increasingly subject to economic or political forces that primarily arise in other countries — possibly just one other country or region (see Thompson, 1999).

Growing Partisan and Ideological Conflict

One noteworthy development in American public budgeting is the growing partisan and ideological conflict in the budget process. The early literature on American public budgeting often depicted it as having only limited partisan or ideological conflict. Decision makers tried (with varying degrees of success) to minimize the role of overt programmatic issues when working on the budget, and the major parties were too internally diverse to maintain much party unity on budgetary issues. Legislative committees dealing with financial matters tried to achieve bipartisan unity to maximize the committees' influence on floor decisions and sometimes operated behind closed doors, in part to reduce the danger of members playing to external audiences. Old budgetary decisions were rarely re-examined in a thorough fashion, not only because of fears that reopening old questions would produce too much disagreement but also because it risked overloading officials with too many options (see Crecine, 1969; Dye, 1966; Sharkansky, 1968; Wildavsky, 1974). American public budgeting seemed dull in contrast to the livelier ideological and partisan dynamics sometimes found in other countries.

Since the late 1960s, however, the degree of partisan and ideological conflict in American public budgeting has increased significantly. Although members of the Congress have often tried to achieve some degree of bipartisan agreement on budgetary matters (Ellwood, 1984), the process has grown highly partisan in recent years. Votes on congressional budget resolutions during the 1990s reveal the extent of that development (see Table 50.1).

The growing partisan and ideological conflict has been reflected in more than just roll-call voting. Tempers have flared on the floor of the Congress and also in the committee and the subcommittee meetings. Accusations of deception, unreasonableness, bad faith, and failing to deliver on promises have flown back and forth between Republicans and Democrats in Congress and between the White House and opposition party members in the Congress. The most spectacular example of the heightened conflict occurred in the winter of 1995–1996, when a budgetary confrontation between the Clinton administration and congressional Republicans led to several partial government shutdowns.

Table 50.1 Percentage of Members within Each Party Voting in Favor of Congressional Budget Resolutions, 1994–1997

	House		*Senate*	
	Democrats (%)	*Republicans* (%)	*Democrats* (%)	*Republicans* (%)
1994	96	0	96	0
1995	95	0	93	5
1996	3	100	7	100
1997	3	98	0	100

Source: *Congressional Quarterly Almanac* (Washington, D.C.: Congressional Quarterly, various volumes).

These developments reflect, in part, the growing ideological divide between the Democrats and the Republicans, and the related decline in the number of congressional moderates in either party. Those changes are in part an outgrowth of regional shifts in party strength, with the southern wing of the Democratic Party growing smaller and less conservative and the northeastern wing of the Republican Party, a traditional source of moderate Republican strength, declining as well. Democratic and Republican electoral constituencies have become increasingly different from one another on a number of public policy questions, and the political activists in each party have quite different policy views than do their counterparts in the other party (Fisher, 1999).

In a related vein, the social class bases of the two major parties have become more distinctive in recent years, with poorer people leaning in a more Democratic direction and wealthier people leaning in a more Republican direction. Although the party bases continue to overlap to a significant degree, they are more differentiated by social class than was the case in the 1950s and the 1960s (Stonecash, 2000). Not surprisingly, the combination of class differences and differing policy beliefs leads to differing views regarding budgetary priorities. Exit polls from the 2000 presidential election found that people who wanted tax cuts to be a high priority tended to vote for President Bush, while people who were more concerned about prescription drug benefits, education, or social security tended to vote for Vice President Gore (*Gallup Exit Poll*, November 7, 2000).

In addition, the increasing number of interest groups active in national politics has meant growing pressures on members to satisfy or appear to support group positions that sometimes pull the Republicans and the Democrats in different directions. Reforms that have opened up committee deliberations to the press and public have increased opportunities for groups to press their demands on members and have increased incentives for members to play to those divergent groups. The erosion of congressional norms that previously encouraged politeness, specialization, and self-restraint has added to the level of tension. Slow and erratic revenue growth, coupled with the rising cost of entitlement programs, has made accommodating competing demands very difficult (Dodd & Oppenheimer, 2001, Chapters 1, 2, 11, and 12; Maraniss & Weisskopf, 1996; Wildavsky & Caiden, 2001, Chapters 4 and 5).

Similar changes have occurred at the state level as well. State parties have become more polarized in a number of states, and the level and volume of interest group activity has risen significantly. Legislative norms that previously encouraged courtesy and self-restraint have eroded, and the rising cost of some programs, particularly Medicaid, has made finding additional funds difficult for new programs or for expanding old programs. The typical state government is also a major funding source for local government programs; so, many local budget conflicts eventually find their way to the state capitals. State budgetary conflicts, in turn, spillover into local budgeting. These dynamics often produce a high level of partisan and ideological conflict in state budgetary decisions, a trend that is reinforced by budget reforms since the 1950s that have placed greater emphasis on programmatic goals and accomplishments, and, therefore, pressed decision makers to focus more attention on values and priorities (Lee, 1997; Nice, 2002, p. 97; Rosenthal, 1998, Chapters 3, 5, and 6).

International Influences on Budgetary Decisions

Much of the early literature on public budgeting in the United States emphasized internal influences on budgetary decisions. Budgets reflected the beliefs and strategies of elected officials and career administrators, previous budgetary commitments, public expectations, interest group demands, established decision rules, and budgetary procedures. Factors outside the United States were not traditionally seen as major factors in budgetary decision making (for examples, see Campbell & Sachs, 1967; Dye, 1966; Wildavsky, 1974; for some early work that did note the relevance of international factors, see Mosher & Poland, 1964; Sharkansky, 1968, Chapter V).

Events since the late 1960s have helped to produce a greater awareness of the importance of international influences on budgetary decisions in the United States. For the round of inflation that emerged in the 1970s critics blamed the combination of high spending for the Vietnam War and the rising domestic spending. The oil shocks of the 1970s helped to produce rising unemployment and high inflation at the same time, and fluctuations in world oil markets have produced considerable prosperity in oil-producing states and localities in some years and painful economic slumps in other years. Most recently, the attacks on the World Trade Center and the Pentagon, coupled with an already-soft U.S. economy and a slump in the U.S. stock market, have contributed to revenue slumps that are affecting all the levels of government and raising the prospect of painful budgetary decisions, especially in many states and localities ("Aftershocks to Local Budgets," 2001; Broder, 2002; Lester, 2002; Stein, 1994; Wildavsky & Caiden, 2001, pp. 303–304). Pressures to increase funding for various domestic security programs are also being felt by all levels of government, but assessing the long-term impact of those pressures is difficult at this point. Although some of these international dynamics were recognized as early as the 1940s with efforts to bring nations together to discuss worldwide economic issues (Kreinin, 1995; Gilpin, 2000), many observers are placing more emphasis on international budgetary dynamics in the recent years than was the case in the 1950s and the 1960s.

One other development that has received some attention on the national level but has generated considerable interest in a number of states and communities is the prospect of job and investment dynamics that are related to the global economy. The gloomy side of those dynamics is the loss of jobs and investment as companies closedown production facilities in the United States and shift those operations overseas or because foreign companies offer stronger and stronger competition to the U.S. firms. The more positive possibility is the creation of jobs and increased investment because companies based overseas open production facilities in the United States, invest in American firms to help them modernize, or buy products or services from U.S. firms. These dynamics have helped stimulate greater state and local government interest in economic development programs, a point to which we now turn to.

Economic Development Programs

The political culture of the United States has traditionally included a considerable element of skepticism regarding the advisability of governmental involvement in the economy. During the Great Depression, many (but not all) Americans came to accept the premise that government might appropriately work to stabilize the economy, just as many people earlier supported governmental improvements in roads, harbors, and other facilities of great importance to the economy, as well as governmental involvement in education. Even so, many Americans have remained doubtful that government should play a very important role in shaping the future of the economy. Governments in other countries could and did get involved in economic planning or economic development initiatives (Makolo, 1983;

Marsh, 1999), but proposals to have similar programs in the United States traditionally received a barrage of withering criticism.

In recent years, however, many state and local governments have become actively involved in economic development programs. Strictly speaking, some of these programs have existed for a considerable number of years, but the activity has become more public and more accepted, although controversies regarding a number of programs have erupted from time to time. Not all of the economic development programs directly involve government budgeting, but all of them are relevant to budgeting in one or more ways (Bartik, 1996; Iannone, 1994; Saiz & Clarke, 1999).

Some of the oldest economic development programs focus on improving infrastructure in the hope of attracting or retaining businesses. A better harbor, canal, railroad line, highway, or an airport might tip the balance in favor of one community rather than another. Some production processes require large amounts of water or electricity; many firms, especially in the service sector, are interested in the quality of the communications system. Preservation of existing infrastructure may spur public acquisition of a previously private facility; a number of state and local governments have become owners of railroads in precisely this way since the 1950s (Nice, 1997). A major problem for poorer jurisdictions is that major infrastructure improvements are often very costly; in addition, the cost of the improvements may outweigh the value of the business activity attracted or retained.

Another type of economic development program involves a relatively direct subsidy to a business to attract it to the state or locality, keep it from relocating or closing, or encourage expansion. The subsidy may take the form of a tax reduction or postponement, credit assistance, or an outright grant to a firm (the last option is not legal in some jurisdictions). Slightly less direct subsidies include public support for training employees and assistance in assembling and clearing parcels of land, especially in built-up areas. Some of these subsidies have provoked considerable controversy, including some high-profile battles over sports facilities, which critics contend do not produce many benefits for the broader community (Saiz & Clarke, 1999, p. 485). Other critics worry that subsidy programs may degenerate into bidding wars among competing jurisdictions, with large subsidies being granted to large, profitable firms based on their political and economic clout while the smaller firms are overlooked.

Another approach to promoting economic development focuses on regulatory policies. A business may be offered more lenient environmental laws, looser business regulations, or policies that discourage the formation of labor unions. These economic development programs have the advantage of being relatively inexpensive, at least in the short run, but the longer-term consequences may include environmental damage or worker injuries that generate costs for the governments involved.

One of the less controversial approaches to economic development is the adoption of public relations initiatives to promote tourism, sales of important state or local products and services overseas, or attract foreign investment. Many state and local officials have participated in overseas trade missions in recent years, and all of the states and many localities have tourism programs that range from television and magazine advertisements and brochures to the Internet sites that list major attractions and provide links to accommodations, restaurants, and other businesses in the area. Many of these initiatives are comparatively inexpensive, and sometimes businesses that expect to benefit may be willing to pay for some of the costs.

Although interest in state and local economic development programs has remained high, they have a rather mixed record of achievement. Several studies have found that economic development programs have relatively weak or inconsistent effects on economic performance (see Dye, 1990; Saiz & Clarke, 1999). Some of the inconsistencies may reflect the fact that assistance programs are sometimes adopted to attract new businesses but may also be adopted to help existing firms that are in financial difficulty. In some cases, business leaders may select a particular location and then press the state and local governments in the area for assistance that does not actually affect their locational decision. Programs that appear to succeed are often copied, a tendency that will tend to dilute the effects of those programs. The inducements offered by an economic development program may be far outweighed by more fundamental economic considerations. Given that the condition of the economy is a powerful influence on budgeting at all levels of government, but especially at the local level (see Campbell & Sachs, 1967; Dye, 1966), economic development programs are highly likely to retain their appeal, and not just outside the United States.

Budgetary Instability, Rebudgeting, and Uncertainty

In his influential book on budgeting in a variety of countries, Wildavsky (1986, Chapter 5) observed that budgeting in poor countries often includes a high degree of instability. Revenue and spending projections are prone to errors from a host of sources, from deliberate misrepresentation and inadequate record keeping to volatile commodity markets, unanticipated shifts in currency exchange rates, weather changes that affect harvests, and fluctuating interest rates, which are particularly important for poor countries with heavy debt burdens. Poverty also makes those errors more difficult to manage; there is typically little or no economic cushion to soften the impact of errors, in contrast to more prosperous countries, where a modest revenue shortfall may be managed by postponing some expenditures (whether in the public sector or in the private sector) that would be regarded as luxuries in poorer countries (though governments and wealthy individuals in poorer countries may expend funds for luxuries as well).

Adhering to a budget plan for any length of time will often be very difficult in that environment, and the difficulty may be compounded by the political instability within the country or in the neighboring countries. Budgets will be revised and revised again as revenues fall below (or, more happily, rise above) projected levels, as the costs of some programs exceed expectations, or as groups unhappy with earlier decisions press for their revision. Administrators may try to spend or commit money as rapidly as possible because they fear that uncommitted funds may be taken away with little or no advance warning.

In a number of respects, budgeting in the United States displays a significant amount of instability. First, budgets are often revised after adoption. Unexpected needs may lead executives to reprogram funds or to transfer them from one appropriations account to another; the latter method of revision often requires some form of legislative approval. Presidents may impound funds that have been appropriated by Congress, a practice that provoked great controversy during the Nixon administration. Many of the nation's governors have authority to impose spending reductions, often subject to some form of regulation, and a variety of administrative controls may be used to restrain spending. A hiring freeze may leave an agency unable to spend some of its salary funds; denial of approval for equipment purchases or a major agency project may also trim spending. Funding for a particular agency or program may be increased with a supplemental appropriation. People who are unhappy with features of the original budget may press for modifications in it after it has been adopted. In most years, the combined effects of all of these changes will not be very large, relatively to the size of the overall budget, but the effects on individual agencies and programs may be considerable (Nice, 2002, Chapter 7).

Another important aspect of budgetary instability and unpredictability is the recurring tendency for Congress and the President to fail to complete action on budgetary legislation by the beginning of the new fiscal year. The extent of conflict and the complexity of the federal budget combine to make prompt action extremely difficult, and the national government often begins a new fiscal year with one or more spending bills still unfinished (Schick & LoStracco, 2000, pp. 195–201). For several years in a row, some agencies have gone without having a regular appropriations bill adopted for them. These delays provide additional uncertainty for state and local officials as well. The federal government provides more than $200 billion per year in financial aid to state and local governments, and delays in completion of national budgetary legislation can leave state and local officials unsure regarding a significant share of their revenues. Even after the spending bills are adopted, later federal budgetary revisions can leave states and localities with lower revenues than they anticipated. Local reliance on state aid can mean similar difficulties if a state's budget is revised after adoption.

Yet another facet of budgetary instability is the frequent modification of budgetary rules and procedures. This phenomenon has been most studied at the national level; the federal government has adopted a host of budgetary reforms since the early 1970s. Some of these reforms have stemmed from a number of concerns; the Congressional Budget and Impoundment Control Act of 1974 grew out of congressional concerns about presidential impoundment, growing mistrust of the budgetary information provided by the Office of Management and Budget (itself reorganized only a few years earlier), complaints that Congress devoted too little attention to overall budget policy, and the recurring failure of the White House and the Congress to finish work on budgetary legislation by the beginning of the new fiscal year. Recurring federal budget deficits led to a series of reforms, from efforts to produce a balanced budget automatically to the short-lived experiment with giving the President enhanced rescission authority (sometimes called an item veto). The Supreme Court put an end to the experiment when it declared the enhanced rescission authority to be unconstitutional (Nice, 2002, Chapter 6 and 11; Schick & LoStracco, 2000, Chapters 2, 6, and 7; Wildavsky & Caiden, 2001, Chapters 4–6).

Changes in budgetary rules and procedures also have occurred in state and local governments. Some of the most dramatic of these changes have been adopted by the voters, who have sometimes approved new tax policies (often trying to limit various types of taxes, especially property taxes) at the ballot box. State revenue systems have been drastically changed over the last century, with growing emphasis on sales taxes, income taxes, and fees of many kinds. Many states have also adopted lotteries or taxes on gambling in the hope of raising revenues less painfully and, in some cases, raising revenues from nonresidents. Many states and localities, along with the national government, have experimented with different budgetary formats, with a long-term trend toward placing more emphasis on agency activities and the results of agency programs. Those changes have, in turn, produced changes in governmental auditing and accounting, with greater attention devoted to agency performance rather than the more traditional focus on whether spending was in accordance with legislative guidelines (Lee, 1997).

Instability is not necessarily a bad thing. In a changing environment, governments may need to change to adapt to the new conditions. Changing a poor decision may lead to improvement, and complex problems do not always yield to the first remedy applied to them. Large amounts of budgetary instability, however, can mean that agencies have a very difficult time assessing what they will be able to do and how soon they will be able to do it.

Political Difficulties in Taxation

Many recent discussions of the global economy emphasize the belief that capital is increasingly mobile and that wealthy individuals and corporations may migrate from place to place in search of greater opportunities. State and especially local government officials in the United States have long been concerned about the possibility that wealthy people and businesses might leave if they do not believe that their interests are being adequately protected. These concerns are also felt by national officials.

One development that appears consistent with this concern is the decline in personal income tax rates in a number of countries, with declines in the higher tax brackets being particularly noticeable. The declines have not been equally substantial in all countries, and the declines in the United States have been more dramatic than in some other countries, but the pattern is widely distributed (see Table 50.2).

Note that the declines in the top bracket rates have been proportionally much larger than the drops, if any, in the bottom bracket rates. Three countries left the tax rate in the lowest bracket the same, and the three others, including the United States, increased the rate applied to people in the lowest bracket. Comparing rates across countries or over time is a perilous enterprise because definitions of taxable income may vary, but

Table 50.2 Changes in Personal Income Tax Rates, 1975–1989

Country	*Maximum Rate (%)*		*Minimum Rate (%)*	
	1975	*1989*	*1975*	*1989*
Australia	65	49	20	24
Canada	47	29	9	17
France	60	57	5	5
Germany	56	53	22	19
Italy	72	50	10	10
Japan	75	50	10	10
Sweden	56	42	7	5
United Kingdom	83	40	35	25
United States	70	33	14	15

Source: Kay, J.A. 1990. *The Economic Journal*, 100: 18–75.

there appears to be a trend toward shifting tax burdens from the wealthy to the less affluent (Peters, 1991).

In the American case that trend has been reinforced by the gradual shift away from taxing corporate income and a gradual increase in the proportion of revenues coming from social insurance taxes, which tend to be regressive. Bear in mind, however, that the federal revenue system in the United States remains distinctly different from what is found in many other industrial and postindustrial democracies. The United States has no broadly based, national consumption tax, although proposals to adopt one have been discussed on a number of occasions. One important group that opposes a national consumption tax is many state officials, who fear that their ability to generate revenues from sales taxes would be endangered by a federal consumption tax. Proposals for a national consumption tax also strike a sensitive nerve among businesses that sell merchandise to people in other states. Many of those transactions escape state sales taxation, even if the states where the business is located and where the customer is located both have sales taxes in force.

Some Concluding Thoughts

In a number of significant respects, budgetary dynamics that have often been associated with budgeting in other countries in recent years are also found in the budgeting in the United States. Partisan and ideological conflict has grown since the 1950s, and budgets are substantially affected by international forces, including economic fluctuations in other countries, changing prices for various commodities, international capital mobility, civil wars and wars between other countries, and global terrorism. Government budgeting has shown a considerable amount of instability and uncertainty in recent years, although spending levels for many programs show considerable continuity from one year to the next. Many states and localities are substantially involved in economic development programs, although questions regarding the effectiveness of those programs persist.

Globalization has not made American public budgeting identical to budgeting in other Western democracies, however. Military spending in the United States remains proportionally high relative to what is found in a number of other countries, and the United States has yet to adopt a policy to assure that all people have reasonable access to healthcare. Spending on prisons in the United States is relatively high, a reflection of the large prison population in the United States. Globalization does not necessarily produce identical outcomes in all the countries.

References

"Aftershocks to Local Budgets," 2001. *Governing* (November), p. 76.

Bartik, T. 1996. "Strategies for Economic Development," in J.R. Aronson and E. Schwartz, eds., *Management Policies in Local Government Finance*, 4th edn. Washington, D.C.: International City/County Managers Association, pp. 287–312.

Broder, D. "States in Fiscal Crisis," *Washington Post*, May 27–June 2, 2002, p. 4.

Campbell, A., and S. Sachs. 1967. *Metropolitan Area: Fiscal Patterns and Governmental Systems*, New York: Free Press.

Crecine, J. 1969. *Governmental Problem Solving*, Chicago: Rand McNally.

Dodd, L., and B. Oppenheimer, eds. 2001. *Congress Reconsidered*, 7th edn. Washington, D.C.: Congressional Quarterly.

Dye, T. 1966. *Politics, Economics, and the Public*, Chicago: Rand McNally.

Dye, T.R. 1990. *American Federalism: Competition Among Governments*, Lexington, MA: Lexington Books.

Ellwood, J. 1984. "Budget Reforms and Interchamber Relations," in W.T. Wander, F.T. Herbert, and G. Copeland, eds., *Congressional Budgeting*, Baltimore, MD: Johns Hopkins.

Fisher, P. 1999. "The Prominence of Partisanship in the Congressional Budget Process," *Party Politics*, 5: 225–236.

Fortanier, F. and M. Maher. 2001. "Foreign Direct Investment and Sustainable Development," *Financial Market Trends*, 79: 107–130.

Gallup Exit Poll, November 7, 2000.

Iannone, D. 1994. "Economic Development," in J. Banovetz, D. Dolan, and J. Swain, eds., *Managing Small Cities and Counties: A Practical Guide*, Washington, D.C.: International City/County Managers Association, pp. 81–102.

Gilpin, R. 2000. *The Challenge of Global Capitalism*, Princeton, NJ: Princeton University Press.

Kay, J.A. 1990. "Tax Policy: A Survey," *The Economic Journal*, 100: 18–75.

Kreinin, M. 1995. *International Economics*, 7th edn. Fort Worth, TX: Dryden Press.

Lee, R. 1997. "A Quarter Century of State Budgeting Practices," *Public Administration Review*, 57: 133–140.

Lester, W. "State Income Tax Revenues Dropped by 15 Percent," *Moscow-Pullman Daily News*, June 4, 2002, p. 4A.

Makolo, P. 1983. "National Development Through Budgeting," in J. Rabin and T. Lynch, eds., *Handbook on Public Budgeting and Financial Management*, New York: Marcel Dekker, pp. 125–160.

Maraniss, D., and M. Weisskopf. 1996. *Tell Newt to Shut Up!* New York: Touchstone.

Marsh, I. 1999. "The State and the Economy: Opinion Formation and Collaboration As Facets of Economic Management." *Political Studies* XLVII: 837–856.

Mosher, F., and O. Poland. 1964. *The Costs of American Government*. New York: Dodd, Mead.

Nice, D. 1997. "Public Ownership of Railroads in the United States," *Transportation Quarterly* 51: 23–30.

Nice, D.C. 2002. *Public Budgeting*, Stamford, CT: Wadsworth Publishing.

Peters, B.G. 1991. *The Politics of Taxation*, Cambridge, MA: Blackwell.

Rosenthal, A. 1998. *The Decline of Representative Democracy*. Washington, DC: Congressional Quarterly.

Saiz, M. and S. Clarke. 1999. "Economic Development and Infrastructure Policy," in V. Gray, R. Hanson, and J. Herbert, eds., *Politics in the American States*, 7th edn. Washington, D.C.: Congressional Quarterly, pp. 474–505.

Schick, A. and F. LoStracco. 2000. *The Federal Budget*, revised ed. Washington, D.C.: Brookings.

Sharkansky, I. 1968. *Spending in the American States* Chicago: Rand McNally.

Stein, H. 1994. *Presidential Economics*, 3rd edn. Washington, D.C.: American Enterprise Institute.

Stonecash, J. 2000. *Class and Party in American Politics*, Boulder, CO: Westview.

Tarzi, S. 1999. "Financial Globalization and National Macroeconomic Policies: Managerial Challenges to the Nation-State." *The Journal of Social, Political and Economic Studies* 24: 141–161.

Thompson, G. 1999. "Introduction: Situating Globalization." *International Social Science Journal* 51: 139–152.

Wildavsky, A. 1974. *The Politics of the Budgetary Process*, 2nd edn. Boston: Little, Brown.

Wildavsky, A. 1986. *A Comparative Theory of the Budgetary Process*. Piscataway, NJ: Transaction.

Wildavsky, A.B. and N. Caiden. 2001. *The New Politics of the Budgetary Process*, 4th edn. New York: Addison Wesley Longman Publishers.

Chapter 51

Global Climatic Stabilization: Challenges for Public Administration in China and the United States

Peter H. Koehn

CONTENTS

Interdependence Challenges: Climatic Change

In an era of shrinking distances and porous boundaries among nation states (Rosenau, 2003), cross-border transactions profoundly shape local life. Increasingly, public administrators are expected to cope with borderless and interconnected threats to the natural environment. Among these environmental threats, climatic change is particularly problematic.

There is compelling evidence and near-universal scientific agreement that human activities are warming the Earth (see Stevens, 1999, p. D1, D9; Revkin, 2000b, p. A12, 2001d, p. A11; Lane and Bierbaum, 2001, pp. 147–148; Seelye and Revkin, 2001, p. A1, A25). Some forecasters also suggest that unchecked global warming will impact future generations by exacerbating other ecological pressures and social conflicts (Homer-Dixon, 1994, pp. 436–437, 1999, p. 14).[1] Although the predicted consequences for particular regions and countries are not identical in kind, scope, or magnitude, and not uniformly negative (Martens et al., 2000, p. 6), global warming has universal implications. The generation of greenhouse gases (GHGs) "is a problem to which all nations contribute, by which all will be affected, from which no nation can remotely hope to insulate itself, and against which no nation can deploy worthwhile measures on its own" (Myers, 1993b, p. 24). Because global warming is inextricably linked with many natural forces and with deeply entrenched economic interests and social practices, the challenge of climatic stabilization is particularly daunting for policymakers, public administrators, and lay publics (see Newell, 2000, pp. 8–9, 66).

The welfare of local communities in China and the United States increasingly involves linked rather than separate destinies (Koehn, 2001). This interdependence is starkly manifest in the projected ecological and human consequences of anthropogenic global climate change. The following sections of this chapter briefly summarize current expectations regarding the impact of projected global warming on China, the United States, and the global commons.

[1]For critiques of Homer-Dixon's environmental-conflict model, see Peluso and Watts (2001) and Hartmann (2001).

PRC Vulnerabilities

What does global climate change portend for China (PRC). Already, temperature increases since the 1960s have "markedly reduced the rainfall in northern China, resulting in a big rise in the evaporation of surface water and frequent high temperature and drought." At the same time, "southern China is suffering more from rainstorms, floods, and waterlogging. The warm winters have also caused more crop pests" (Hu, 1995, p. 334) and weed growth, and the expanding Pacific Ocean has inundated rich agricultural land along China's east coast (see Ash and Edmonds, 1998, p. 873). China's developed coastal zone accounts for more than half of the country's gross national product (Han et al., 1995, p. 91). Several of China's most dynamic industrial and commercial cities, including Shanghai and Guangzhou, face prospects of significant flooding as a result of the combined effects of rising sea levels and land sinking (Myers, 1993a, p. 755; Han et al., 1995, p. 93; Hu, 1995, p. 334; U.S. Department of Energy, 1999, p. 6). Densely populated coastal areas also are threatened by increased typhoon activity, erosion, and contamination of water supplies by saltwater intrusion (Han et al., 1995, p. 82, 88, 90, 92). Additional croplands would be lost; marine aquaculture would be damaged; and new health and security problems are likely to accompany massive population dislocation (Myers, 1993a, p. 760; Myers & Kent, 1995, pp. 144–145). One "preliminary conclusion" projects that future grain production in China's three main crop sites will diminish by at least 10 percent under a business-as-usual climatic-change scenario (U.S. Department of Energy, 1999, p. 5).

Zhang (2000, p. 749) points out that China is especially vulnerable to global warming because "climate-sensitive sectors such as agriculture" account for a large share of its gross domestic product (GDP). As elsewhere, the effects of anthropogenic global warming on agricultural production in China are likely to be mixed by latitude and even by microclimate, although early official Chinese studies estimate an overall loss of 5 percent in the country's agricultural productivity (NEPA estimates, cited in Economy, 1997, pp. 25–26). In the mountainous areas of western China, an annual temperature rise of a few degrees might be sufficient "to transform formerly non-endemic areas into areas subject to seasonal epidemics" of vector-borne diseases (Martens, 1998, p. 80).

U.S. Vulnerabilities

Projected global warming for the United States over the next century is 5 to 10°F (2.8 to 5.5°C), "slightly higher than the global average because the United States is a continental region at mid-latitudes" (Lane & Bierbaum,

2001, p. 200). Although the effects will be mixed and will differ widely across regions, experts expect increases in total and heavy precipitation and flooding, earlier snowmelt across the Pacific Northwest, uncommon and extreme weather events, coastal erosion, and short-term growth in forest and agricultural productivity followed by long-term decline (Myers, 1993b, p. 174; Adams et al., 1999; Revkin, 2000a, p. A1, A25; Lane & Bierbaum, 2001, p. 200). The impact assessment undertaken by Neumann et al. (2000, p. iii) suggests that the most vulnerable U.S. areas to sea-level rise "are in the mid-Atlantic and south-Atlantic states... and along the Gulf Coast.... The West Coast is generally at lower risk, with the exception of San Francisco Bay and the Puget Sound." However, severe and uncontrolled forest fires are expected to increase dramatically across the west — particularly in western Montana (Devlin, 2003a, p. A1, A10, 2004, p. A1, A5).

Negative indirect effects on U.S. agriculture include "changes in the incidence and distribution of pests and pathogens" and "increased rates of soil erosion and degradation" (Adams et al., 1999, p. 2). A 5°F increase in temperature carries a high risk that malaria and dengue fever will be (re)introduced because "the former breeding sites of several *Anopheles* and *Aedes* species are still available" (Martens, 1998, p. 79; also see Roberts, 2004, p. 121).

Global Threats

From a planetwide view, serious risks are associated with the absence of stringent emission-reduction practices. Temperature change will vary by latitude, with the greatest warming occurring at the poles (Forest et al., 2004, p. 21). Overall precipitation will increase and a higher likelihood of climate-induced natural disasters will exist. Rising sea levels will result in coastal erosion and pose special risks for aquatic and marine ecosystems (Martens et al., 1997, p. 585; Lane & Bierbaum, 2001, p. 149; Forest et al., 2004, p. 22). In addition, "a range of mostly adverse human health impacts is expected, as diseases spread geographically, heat stress increases, and populations become more vulnerable to decreasing food security in developing countries" (Lane & Bierbaum, 2001, p. 201; Patz et al., 1996; McMichael & Haines, 1997; Price-Smith, 2002, pp. 143–144). By activating extreme weather events, global warming indirectly promotes the spread of marine-borne diseases such as cholera (Martens, 1998, pp. 5–7; Price-Smith, 2002, pp. 147–150). Based on impact modeling, Martens (1998, p. 79, 29) predicts vast increases in the numbers of people at risk of vector-borne diseases — malaria, dengue fever, and schistosomiasis (also see Epstein, 2001, pp. 36–39; Price-Smith, 2002, pp. 144–147, 168–169). Climatic change imperils cultural survival as well as human health. Recently, therefore, representatives of poor countries threatened by rising temperatures and seas, such as the Arctic Inuit, have highlighted the ways in which failure to stem GHG emissions constitute an assault on their basic human rights (Revkin, 2004, p. A3).

Culprits and Contributors

Although it supports only 5 percent of the world's population, the United States produces roughly 25 percent of global GHGs (see Revkin, 2000c, p. A13; Zhang, 2000, p. 740). Ultimately, therefore, "no strategy to address global climate change can... succeed without substantial and permanent reductions in U.S. emissions" (Pew Center on Global Climate Change, 2001). Together, China and the United States are responsible for nearly 40 percent of total GHG emissions (Zhang, 2000, p. 739–740). Unchecked, China's future emissions threaten "to wreck the climate for everyone" (Myers, 1993b, p. 173; Claussen & McNeilly, 1998, p. 16; Economy, 1998b, p. 64). Although mainland China is expected to overtake the United States as the number one gross emitter within decades (Logan et al., 1999, p. 2; Zhang, 2000, p. 739; Eckholm, 2001, p. A1) and predicted increases by 2030 will nearly equal those from the entire industrialized world, its per-capita GHG emissions are roughly one eighth of those of the United States (Zhang, 2000, p. 740; Bradsher, 2003, p. A1).

Three of the six GHGs covered by the 1997 Kyoto Protocol (carbon dioxide (CO_2), methane, and nitrous oxide) are produced largely or partly by fossil-fuel production and combustion. The principal focus here is on CO_2 because it is "by far the most plentiful and widely produced greenhouse gas" (Sprunt, 2001, p. 74). On a worldwide basis, "between 75% and 90% of anthropogenic emissions of CO_2 are from combustion of fossil fuels" (Sprunt, 2001, p. 74).[2] If CO_2 emissions from fossil fuels are the principal culprit, then global climatic stability is particularly threatened by prevailing excessive per-capita combustion and consumption patterns within the

[2]Other sources fix CO_2 emissions at about half of post–Industrial Revolution human-induced warming (Monastersky, 2000, p. A16). However, this figure underestimates the current contribution of CO_2 because "Chlorofluorocarbons, responsible for about 20 percent of global warming to date, have been phased out under the regime to deal with ozone depletion" (Paterson, 2000, pp. 258n–259n). Fossil-fuel production and combustion also account for a sizeable proportion of methane and nitrous oxide emissions (Sprunt, 2001, pp. 74–75). Although some scientists argue that aerosol forcing from the combustion of fossil fuels can counteract the warming effects of carbon dioxide forcing by cooling the climate, "carbon-dioxide molecules... survive in the atmosphere for a century or more, on average, spreading around the globe in a relatively even distribution. But aerosols last only a few days or weeks before they drop from the sky, so they concentrate near where they were emitted" (Monastersky, 2000, p. A17).

United States, by U.S. military activity overseas — such as the invasion and occupation of Iraq (Stern, 1997, p. 21), and by population size coupled with consumption and combustion trends in China (see PRC, State Council, 1994, p. 51; Brown, 1995, p. 36; Chai, 1996, p. 272; Banister, 1998, p. 986, 1010, 1014; Tisdell, 1998, pp. 8–9, 20; Porter and Brown, 1999, pp. 112–113; Lew, 2000, p. 271–272; Nordqvist et al., 2002, p. 70, 73, 77–78). In the United States, per-capita energy consumption and automotive-fuel burning continues to rise (Myers, 1993b, p. 175; Myerson, 1998, p. A1; Bradsher, 2001a, p. A1, 2001b, p. A15; Pew Center on Global Climate Change, 2001). GHG emissions are increasing faster in transportation than in any other sector, primarily due to the growing number of cars, sport utility vehicles (SUVs), and trucks in operation (Sperling & Salon, 2002, p. iii). Motor vehicles are directly responsible for roughly one fourth of total U.S. CO_2 emissions and generate other potent GHGs (Walsh, 1989, p. 262). Moreover, as Paterson (2000, pp. 258–259) points out, direct fuel use accounts for "only 60–65 percent of total GHG emissions throughout the life of a car, the rest coming from fuel extraction, processing and transport (15–20 percent), manufacturing (10 percent), and tailpipe emissions other than CO_2."[3] Other emission increases are associated with road construction or repair and deforestation for motorways.

The production and consumption dynamics currently driving the United States and the People's Republic of China (PRC) reflect addiction to a fossil-fuel fueled economy (also see Newell, 2000, p. 9). By itself, reliance on coal has generated huge and recently escalating increases in China's GHG emissions (Lew, 2000, p. 279; Bradsher, 2003, p. A1, A8). From the other direction, by clearing forests for housing, highways, crop production, pastures, and dams, both countries are destroying valuable natural sinks for CO_2 (Sprunt, 2001, p. 74) — although the PRC has implemented large-scale reforestation and afforestation programs in the 1960s and in recent years (see Pan, et al., 2004, p. 211). While China also is developing a growing thirst for petroleum — particularly to fuel the rapid growth in automobiles — the level of U.S. oil consumption is roughly five times greater than estimates for the mainland even though China's population is five times larger than that of the United States (see Lenssen, 1992, pp. 22–23; Brown, 1995, p. 58; Stares and Liu, 1996, pp. 13–16; Shen, 1997, pp. 593–594; Downs, 1999, pp. 5–6; Koehn, 1999, pp. 360–361, 374–375; Manning, 2000, pp. 104–105; Mao and Chen, 2001, pp. 324, 328–329, 331–333).

Transportation accounted for 8 percent of China's total carbon emissions in 1998 — versus 30 percent in the United States (see Sperling and Salon, 2002, p. 14). In 1996, 8 out of every 1000 inhabitants owned a car in the

[3]Lowe (1989, p. 16) notes that "carbon monoxide contributes indirectly to the warming by slowing the removal of methane and ozone, two minor GHGs, from the lower atmosphere."

China mainland — versus 769 per 1000 in the United States (Sperling & Salon, 2002, p. 14, 4). At the turn of this century, China's 20 percent of the world's total population owned 1.5 percent of its automobiles whereas the United States' 5 percent had amassed 25 percent of the world's automotive fleet (Gallagher, 2003, p. 1). If per-capita car ownership and usage in the PRC should reach U.S. levels, China would burn 80 million barrels of petroleum daily — 16 million barrels more than recent worldwide production (*South China Morning Post*, January 12, 1998, p. 15).

Global Warming and Political Cooling

In spite of the growing body of convincing evidence that anthropogenic global warming poses a serious threat to ecological sustainability, the governments of China and the United States have been unwilling to take decisive actions that would reduce GHG emissions. Indeed, both states have been inclined to pursue blocking policies and approaches and to play leadership roles that emphasize confrontation and competition rather than partnership in addressing environmental-protection and resource-consumption issues. For instance, China took the lead in organizing and coordinating the positions of Southern states in the preparation for and during the United Nations Conference on Environment and Development (UNCED) in Rio de Janeiro (Economy, 1997, p. 20, 33–34, 1998a, pp. 272–273). As Ann Kent (2002, p. 359) points out, "identification with the interests of the developing world remains a constituent element of China's own power."[4] From the perspective of many Southern activists and state policymakers, including the government of the PRC, international proposals for reductions in GHG emissions are prone to ignore or insufficiently to account for the disproportionate historical (and per-capita) contributions of developed countries to the problem and have the effect of extending structural inequities embedded in the prevailing international economic order (see Paterson, 1996, pp. 65–66; Bolin, 1997, p. 146; Shi, 1998, pp. 152–153; Hsu, 2000, pp. 70–71; Mwandosya, 2000, pp. 5–6, 74, 139; Kent, 2002, p. 347). Furthermore, developing countries taking part in the 1995 Conference of the Parties of the Climate Convention in Berlin demonstrated an "understandable unwillingness . . . to take on any obligations before developed countries have fulfilled their obligations in accordance

[4]Moreover, guiding the formulation of bases for resisting emission reductions in the South helped "ensure that China, as the developing country with the highest level of CO_2 emissions, would not be singled out and subjected to potentially intense pressures to take immediate action. This was especially important because developing nations such as Bangladesh were expected to be among the most severely harmed by global warming" (Economy, 1997, p. 34).

with the Climate Convention" (Bolin, 1997, p. 147; also see Logan et al., 1999, p. 4; Eckholm, 2001, p. A1, A6; Revkin, 2001b, p. A7).

On its part, the U.S. government, under the administration of the former president George Bush, "blocked secretariat proposals for change in industrialized countries' consumption patterns . . . " at the time of UNCED in Rio and "was prepared to veto any initiatives that could be viewed as redistributing economic power at the global level . . . " (Porter & Brown, 1996, p. 118, 122, 128). Bush's son, George W. Bush, quickly reversed a campaign pledge to treat CO_2 as a pollutant and to regulate the CO_2 emissions of power plants (Jehl & Revkin, 2001, p. A1; Schreurs, 2002, p. 20). It was not surprising, therefore, when the U.S. Environmental Protection Agency ruled in August 2003 that CO_2 cannot be regulated as a pollutant. This action precludes use of the Clean Air Act to reduce CO_2 emissions from automobiles (Borenstein, 2003, p. A3).

In the wake of the second Bush administration's refusal to join agreements reached among 178 countries in Bonn in 2001 (see Revkin, 2001c, p. A1; Schreurs, 2002, pp. 26–27) and later formally adopted in Marrakech, what had been a North–South conflict over GHG emissions became primarily a U.S.–(China-led)South conflict (Johnston, 1998, pp. 572–574; Koehn, 2004, p. 383). The U.S.–China impasse is starkly captured in an argument set forth by President Bush as part of his explanation for opposing the Kyoto Protocol: "The world's second-largest emitter of GHGs is China. Yet, China was entirely exempted from the requirements of the Kyoto Protocol" (Bush, 2001, p. 547; also see Schreurs, 2002, p. 20; Sussman, 2004, p. 363). It also is apparent in the official Chinese response by a ministry of foreign affairs official who reiterated that the United States and other industrialized countries bear a "historical responsibility" for taking the first steps to reduce emissions (cited in Revkin, 2001a, p. A7). Another consequence of this rhetorical contestation is a low level of intergovernmental cooperation on climatic-change projects (Baldinger & Turner, 2002, pp. 26–30, 41–42; Economy, 2004, p. 192, 273).

In both the PRC and the United States, the national political system and the political processes "are loaded against the long run" (Rosenau, 1997b, p. 340). It is not surprising, therefore, that both governments have proven unable to exercise leadership in addressing anthropogenic climatic change. Although China established the interministerial National Climate Change Coordinating Committee in 1990 and signed and ratified the Kyoto Protocol in 2002 (Ross, 1998, pp. 817–820; Chandler et al., 2002, p. 13; Chan, 2004, p. 76), the government has been unwilling to make concrete binding emission commitments (Johnston, 1998, pp. 572–573; Ross, 1998, p. 818; Zhang, 2000, p. 739), views national stability as dependent upon rapid economic growth (Johnston, 1998, p. 566; Ross, 1998, pp. 813–814), and has not allowed other countries to fulfill their Kyoto obligations by undertaking joint implementation activities, such as reforestation, within its territory (Economy, 2004, p. 184). In the United States, voluntary commitments to reduce GHG emissions have not been fully implemented (Barrett, 1999, pp. 196, 203–206) and emphasis has been placed on further research[5] and profitable technology fixes (see, for instance, Logan et al., 1999, p. 11; Schreurs, 2002, p. 27). As justification for the current administration's opposition to the mandatory compliance targets of the Kyoto Protocol, Bush contended on June 11, 2001, that "the Kyoto Protocol was fatally flawed in fundamental ways.... For America, complying with those [Kyoto] mandates would have a negative economic impact" (Bush, 2001, pp. 546–547). The entrenched position of this administration is rooted in the nearly identical outlook of its powerful corporate allies, such as the National Association of Manufacturers (NAM). On April 4, 1998, NAM adopted a resolution stating that "we believe that the Kyoto Protocol to the Convention on Global Climate Change is inherently flawed and, therefore, will damage the U.S. economy without achieving the desired environmental benefits..." (cited in Edwards, 2000, p. 52).[6] Opposition politicians in the United States also show little willingness to call for the sacrifices

---

[5]With the exception of sharing research findings across borders, which the U.S. government has placed under additional restrictions in the name of "national security" (see Skolnikoff, 2002). Boehmer-Christiansen (1996, pp. 191–192) suggests that instead of promoting action-oriented agreements that would produce effective regulation, the international scientific-research establishment has collaborated with governments to "define the global-change problem as a research issue and to suggest solutions, most of which would require further massive research (or subsidisation) efforts" (also see Newell, 2000, pp. 50–51).

[6]In 2000, the influential U.S. Chamber of Commerce also placed priority on "preventing the implementation of the Kyoto Climate Change Treaty" (cited in Edwards, 2000, p. 52). The intransigent U.S. position in international negotiations over global warming can be attributed, in part, to the "exceptional influence of the coal and oil lobbies" along with the Bush family's ties to the oil industry (Paterson, 1996, p. 68; also see Newell, 2000, pp. 97–98). U.S. companies opposing the Kyoto restrictions include Exxon, Southern of Atlanta, and Peabody Energy. According to Frederick D. Palmer, executive vice president for legal and external affairs at Peabody, "'I understand the importance of fossil fuels to the American people. Dick Cheney understands that. The president understands that'" (quoted in Revkin and Banerjee, 2001, p. C6). On the other side are the members of the Social Venture Network (see "Business Leaders Call for U.S. Leadership on Global Warming," full-page open letter addressed to President Bush and Vice President Cheney, *New York Times*, June 21, 2001, p. A23), and the 30-odd firms, including Boeing, Alcoa, DuPont, IBM, and Weyerhaeuser, that belong to the Business Environmental Leadership Council of the Pew Center on Global Climate Change. Collectively, these firms "accept the views of most scientists that enough is known about the science and environmental impact of climate change for us to take actions to address its consequences" and specifically agree that "businesses can and should take concrete steps now in the U.S. and abroad to assess opportunities for emission reductions, establish and meet emission reduction objectives, and invest in new, more efficient products, practices and technologies" (see "Business Environmental Leadership Council" at www.pewclimate.org/belc/index.cfm as of February 2, 2003). Potentially, moreover, the insurance industry's sensitivity to the consequences of global warming could be an important source of supportive action (see Newell, 2000, p. 168).

required to avert serious climatic alterations, especially when they "cannot promise early and satisfying benefits in exchange for the sacrifices" (Rosenau, 1997b, p. 341; Jehl, 2001, p. A14). In both China and the United States, then, the "scale of resistance and inertia that an effective, long-term solution to global warming needs to confront" is exceptionally vast (Newell, 2000, p. 9). Most analysts and international negotiators do not expect either of the national governments to accept binding emission restrictions "any time soon" (Rohter & Revkin, 2004, p. A6).

Concomitantly, the worldwide skill revolution has dramatically enhanced the ability of individuals, acting on their own or through organized groups, to address interdependence challenges (see Rosenau, 1997b, pp. 349–351; Cusimano, 2000, pp. 26–27; Sharp, 2001). In an era of governmental cutbacks, privatization, and loss of confidence and trust in environmental-problem-generating rather than problem-solving political institutions (see Macnaghten and Jacobs, 1997, p. 20), non-governmental organizations (NGOs) and citizen diplomats, operating along and across porous nation-state boundaries through civil-society networks and independent micropolitical processes, have become key players in efforts to resolve issues of collective consequence (see Risse-Kappen, 1995b, p. 280; Rosenau, 1997a, pp. 5–6; Burgess et al., 1998, p. 1447; Koehn, forthcoming). In addition, subnational administrative units in both China and the United States have launched promising initiatives aimed at addressing global warming.

Transnational Networks

If the new century affords a window of opportunity for transition to an ecologically sustainable world, the actions and reactions of residents and professional public administrators in the world's most populous nation and its most gluttonous one will exert an immense influence on the human condition. U.S.–China cooperation on climate-protection measures and approaches is crucial because of the disproportionate impact and dependence of the two societies on the global environment. Both China and the United States are in a position to negate the efforts of the rest of the world community to mitigate global warming and stabilize climate. In a positive vein, the two nations simultaneously offer enormous opportunities for emissions mitigation and possess resources and insights that are vital for addressing contributing factors. Although failure to overcome the fundamental China–U.S. polarization on climate-change issues risks perpetuating the prevailing consumption and emission cycle and smothering potentially powerful incentives to curtail or eliminate unsustainable practices, U.S.–China partnerships that succeed in curbing GHG emissions send a powerful message of progress to the rest of the world.

In terms of administrative responsibility, the challenge of global climatic change can be approached by prevention, mitigation, or emergency responses. This chapter focuses on the current and prospective efforts in China and the United States to promote climatic stabilization through grassroots projects that reduce GHG emissions.[7] Given the entrenched resistance to mandatory reductions that exists at the national government level in both countries, subnational and nonstate opportunities and initiatives receive primary attention. Students of public administration increasingly recognize that administrators must build reliable networks and forge effective "horizontal" partnerships with nonstate actors to deal effectively with complex challenges (Kettl, 2000, p. 494). New actors, new state–nonstate partnerships, and new transnational links and skills are essential if the interdependence challenge of relative climate stability is to be addressed effectively in the 21st century. Given the centrality of the PRC and the United States in the global warming equation, efforts to address the challenges of global climate change must involve partnerships with residents[8] and NGOs in China and the United States (also see Freeman, 1996, p. 8; Oksenberg and Economy, 1998, p. 356). In particular, the involvement of Chinese Americans is likely to be pivotal over the next century.

Chinese Americans: Strategic Positioning

Being Chinese is said to involve early "socialization into the networked society" (Xia, 2000, p. 216; also see Wang, 2001, p. 155). One objective of this chapter is to demonstrate that transnationally competent (TC) Chinese overseas actors are strategically positioned to fill emission-reduction roles. Although they are not the only cross-nationally competent actors at work along the China–U.S. frontier, we are particularly interested here in the capacity of Chinese Americans — both those born in the United States and elsewhere — to span the existing chasms of policy, practice, and values. The prospect that transnational migrants and their descendants can act as a powerful environmental ally in both sending and receiving societies has been overlooked or underestimated by scholars of public administration. With close ties to the world's principal sources of human-induced global

[7] Public administrators in countries where national political leaders who have agreed to reduce GHG emissions face a different set of implementation challenges — including regulation, monitoring and reporting, and oversight of an international trading system (Rohter & Revkin, 2004, p. A6).

[8] As Burgess et al. (1998, p. 1447) note, lay publics "are expert in their own lifeworlds, making rational judgments based on an authority acquired through tacit or local knowledge."

warming, Chinese Americans occupy a privileged vantage point from which to identify and carry out effective strategies of communicating about and exerting influence over interdependence issues in places of origin and residence.

Chinese Americans: Transnational Competence

Particularly important when considering future China–U.S. relations is the evidence that dramatically expanded numbers of people on both sides of the Pacific are moving in the TC direction. Among the most important factors accounting for TC development are permanent and circular migration from East and Southeast Asia to the United States along with the rise of global electronic networks and frequent intercontinental travel by transmigrants who live lives that cross-national borders and participate in local political and bureaucratic processes in both China and the United States.

Transnational competency involves analytic, emotional, creative, communicative, and functional (task) skills.[9] Currently, about three million people of Chinese descent live in the United States. At least 65 percent of these residents are foreign-born (see Yin and Lan, 2003, p. 15). Their awareness of developments in China is sustained at a high level via frequent contact with family members living in the homeland and by physical return to the country of birth. The ability to empathize with Mainland conditions and problems constitutes one important facet of the transnational emotional competence of Chinese Americans — particularly those born in the PRC (see, for instance, Wickberg, 1994, p. 81; Wang, 2002, p. 155). The bilocal or multilocal focus of Chinese transnational families has been constant over time. What is new are the qualitatively and quantitatively enhanced opportunities "for maintaining regular physical contact" among their split components (Ho et al., 2001, p. 25). Today, therefore, bilocality- and multilocality-network-linked immigrant and voluntary transmigrant family members lead a "life that tends to blunt the acute binarism between Asian and American with which earlier generations had to contend strenuously" (Wong, 1995, p. 7). Most Chinese Americans use Mandarin and English and are reasonably fluent in both, interact socially and professionally with mainstream Americans and socially with mainland Chinese nationals, maintain annual contact with at least one individual in the PRC, are self-confident about participating in the two societies,[10] and are able to

---

[9]For a detailed discussion of the five dimensions of transnational competence, see Koehn and Rosenau (2002).

[10]On the importance of a sense of collective efficacy for overcoming obstacles to change, see Bandura (1995, p. 38).

function effectively on both sides of the Pacific (see Wang, 2001, p. 155; Koehn, 2002, p. 238; Lien, 2003, pp. 9–10, 29–30). In short, TC Chinese American professionals increasingly are inclined to perceive their bicultural heritage as an asset rather than a liability in today's world and to become involved in influential transnational and local (within the United States and the PRC) roles (see, for instance, Ying, 1996, p. 12; Cheng, 1999, p. 75; Yin, 1999, pp. 332–336).

The transnational lives and experiences of Chinese overseas provide the basis for critical and independent assessments of culprits and contributors in the global warming scenario. Moreover, Chinese Americans who are TC and "travel" without unwelcome baggage — including certain mainstream U.S. values such as the intense individualism, the arrogance of power, and a missionary complex (Nishi, 1999, p. 183; Wang, 2000, p. 265) — are particularly effective in traversing and shaping trans-Pacific interfaces.

With regard to the specific challenge of climatic stabilization, TC Chinese are differentially positioned to exert influence over critical decisions at various levels of political action. The relevant arenas for participation are international-agreement making by the governments of the PRC and the United States; national policy making and international agreement implementation in China and the United States; civil-society project design and (primarily subnational) administrative implementation in both countries, and individual-to-individual persuasion (see Koehn, 2002, pp. 245–262). This chapter explores bottom-up opportunities to shape climate-change outcomes available to TC Chinese Americans by reference to civil-society projects, partnerships with subnational administrative units, and interpersonal interactions in the PRC and the United States. The exposition involves, first, the identification of potential bases for effective joint action, followed by analysis of specific initiatives and prospects.

Bases for GHG-Reduction Action: Nonstate Partnerships and Subnational Initiatives

In the absence of national political will and the commitment of adequate state financial resources, partnerships among subnational public administrators and nonstate actors become increasingly critical for the foreseeable future (also see Newell, 2000, p. 9, 152). State stalemate over global climate change shifts the focus of attention from failed attempts to reach international agreements to civil-society activity and bottom-up change initiatives (also see Lipschutz, 1997, p. 433; Rabe, 2002, p. 3). Here, we are primarily interested in identifying subnational opportunities for transnational and local project initiatives[11] that possess the potential for reducing GHG emissions when national governments are unwilling to enter into international agreements. These efforts also could become part of any subsequent agreements on climatic stabilization entered into by the governments of the PRC and the United States.

At present, globally linked nongovernmental actors and networks offer "the most exciting arena for innovation in climate change politics" (O'Riordan & Jordan, 1996, p. 358). Among the potentially decisive transnational actors are Chinese American scientists, academics, engineers, investors, charitable donors, and cultural leaders who possess interest and competence in mitigating the detrimental ecological, economic, and health effects of projected anthropogenic climatic changes on China, the United States, and the global commons. The ability of Chinese Americans to contribute to GHG-emission reductions in China and the United States depends, in part, on the strength of their partnerships with government actors. In particular, the curtailment of consumptive behaviors is more problematic in the absence of governmental cooperation through policy and educational initiatives (see O'Riordan and Jordan, 1996, p. 81; SEI, 2002, p. 50).

The project arena allows for a multitude of modest-scale and transnationally partnered (see, for instance, Princen, 1994, p. 34; Porter and Brown, 1996, pp. 51–53) opportunities to address human-induced climate threats. In general terms, such projects encompass research into innovative and sustainable approaches; applications of energy-efficient and renewable-energy technology; exchanges of proven emission-sensitive methods and approaches that possess adaptive potential in the other country; interventions that integrate emission control principles into sustainable development initiatives; and educational efforts that build indigenous capacity for reducing GHG emissions and promote sustainable consumption practices. In terms of promoting the adoption of alternatives to fossil-fuel combustion, for instance, both sides need to cooperate in identifying and adapting approaches, incentives, and technological breakthroughs that will maximize the introduction of solar power, wind power, geothermal power, small-scale hydroelectricity, fuel cells,[12] tidal and wave power, and organic

---

[11]Nonstate actors also perform important roles in generating momentum for policy change and in determining the nature of such changes (see Newell, 2000, p. 7, 9, 26–27, 42–44, 49, 126–129, 139–147, 165). For instance, the China Council for International Cooperation on Environment and Development, a high-level nongovernmental body comprised of specialists and public figures from the PRC and other countries, advises the government on environmental-policy issues (Chan, 2004, p. 75).

[12]Small-scale fuel-cell development holds out the promise of providing an energy bridge from fossil fuels to abundant and clean-burning hydrogen (see McCall, 2001, p. D1).

farming. Wind turbines alone offer the prospect of providing a major share of the total required energy supply in both countries (see Byrne et al., 1996, p. 459; Logan and Zhang, 1998; Johnson, 1999, p. 289; Wald, 1999, p. A25). The range of specific project arenas available for partnerships with Chinese Americans who are adept at working across technical, cultural, political, and administrative divides (Haas, 2004, p. 588) includes:

- Improving energy efficiencies (Zhang, 2000, p. 747; Sprunt, 2001, p. 76)
- Supporting continued progress in the development and adoption of renewable energy sources (Kempton et al., 1995, p. 37; Parson, 2001, p. A23; Short, 2001, p. 14)
- Promoting voluntary reductions in manufacturing emissions (Sprunt, 2001, p. 76)
- Advancing programs that increase the absorption of CO_2 by the terrestrial biosphere (Stevens, 2000, p. D1; Lane & Bierbaum, 2001, p. 201)
- Reorienting the research-focused epistemic community in an action-oriented direction, and building capacity to secure, assess, and utilize scientific evidence (Ross, 1998, p. 832, 835; Botcheva, 2001, p. 221)
- Mobilizing pressure from below (see Edwards, 1999, p. 169), including effective educational efforts (see Kempton et al., 1995, p. 124, 136–137, 219), for resource conservation
- Improving the effectiveness of population control
- Changing emission-exacerbating values and behavior (Kochn, 2006)
- Increasing consumer demands for renewable energy, reusable products, and stringent vehicle-emission standards (Kempton, 1993, pp. 220–221; DeSombre, 2000, p. 251)

Although the effectiveness of these actions in mitigating global warming differs, each of them makes a valuable contribution and, collectively, they would exert a major impact.

In order for Chinese Americans to participate effectively in bottom-up initiatives that address global warming, their actions, investments, and recommendations need to be guided by legitimating and durable principles. The principal basis for trans-Pacific action is available in the idea of common but differentiated responsibility that underlies the Montreal Protocol on the protection of the stratospheric ozone layer and is now widely accepted (Cooper, 1992, p. 305; Paterson, 1996, p. 61, 66; Ross, 1998, p. 819; Barrett, 1999, pp. 210–211; Mwandosya, 2000, p. 147) — even by the Bush administration[13] — although the principle has not yet been applied to public administration partnerships with nonstate actors. Relying, in part, on historical, current, and projected future per-capita emissions, the "common but differentiated responsibility" principle affirms mutual action and cooperation for the sake of collective interests (see Zhang, 2000, p. 749; Mwandosya, 2000, p. 147), and accepts disproportionate contributions or compensation from the North (Newell, 2000, p. 16).[14] The guiding premise behind this principle is that both the rich and the poor will take actions, the magnitude and timing sequence of which are commensurate with relative levels of economic development and respective capacities — with the rich also providing the less advantaged with a larger share of the requisite funding and technology.[15] Adapting this incentive-compatible[16] principle to the partnership context considered here would encourage Chinese American involvement in subnational efforts to address human-induced climate change on both sides of the Pacific. The principle of nonstate common but differentiated responsibility also legitimizes Chinese American participation in transferring resources, technology, and expertise from U.S. sources in support of increasing efforts to reduce CO_2 (and other GHG) emissions within China (also see Birdsall and Lawrence, 1999, pp. 141–143; Zhang, 2000, pp. 749–750).

Although compatibility with prevailing political discourse in both countries underscores its promise as a means of securing U.S.–China cooperation (see Risse, 2002, p. 267), the "common but differentiated responsibility" principle lacks sufficient motivational force on its own. To gain motivational force, it needs to be connected to two other discourse-compatible core principles. The first of these is the linkage with local environmental concerns. In general, lay publics and political actors are receptive to controlling emissions that are responsible for air pollution and other negative health and economic consequences in one's locality (see, for instance, Frank, 2000). The second motivating principle is concern for future generations. Untapped concern for the future of children and descendants offers

[13]In April 2001, the Bush administration agreed to a treaty controlling harmful organic chemicals that "calls for rich and poor countries to move in concert, but... requires industrialized countries to provide the money and technology to help the cleanup in the developing world" (Revkin, 2001b, p. A7).

[14]In the words of Edwards (1999, p. 169), "the North must pay more, the South must demand less, and all of us who care about the future have to make our views known in the political process."

[15]This principle clearly does not absolve China of responsibility for climate-change mitigation. Gielen and Chen (2001, p. 268), for instance, recognize that "given the phenomenal growth of the Chinese economy, and emission levels in Shanghai that are approaching levels in industrialized countries, it seems reasonable that some of the financial burdens are borne by the Chinese side."

[16]Incentive-compatible cooperation "must offer clear net benefits to all participating parties, and all actors must perceive the benefits as fair" (Kaul et al., 1999, p. xxxii).

a powerful common motivator among lay publics and elites in both China and the United States (see Kempton, 1993, p. 237; Kempton et al., 1995, p. 95; Chan, 2004, p. 72).[17] Including the intergenerational principle is especially important in the case of global change because (1) the most damaging impacts of anthropogenic warming are long-term and shared, (2) climate alteration becomes increasingly irreversible for future generations (Claussen & McNeilly, 1998, p. 7), and (3) efforts to control emissions will need to be sustained over time. Therefore, the overall legitimating principle suggested for transnational action in available nonstate arenas by Chinese overseas is "common but differentiated responsibility for present and future generations" (also see Martens et al., 1997, p. 586; Schelling, 1997, p. 8, 14).

Making a Difference: Bottom-Up Applications of Transnational Competency

An extensive and diverse array of civil-society actors — including individuals (see Rosenau, 2003, p. 25), large-scale and small-scale NGOs (both transnational and national), and social movements (transterritorial as well as domestic) — have demonstrated that they can fill key gaps at international, national, and local levels of collective action along interstate frontiers where domestic and foreign issues converge (see Ekins, 1992, pp. 164–165; Princen, 1994, pp. 30–31; Princen and Finger, 1994b, pp. x–xi; Wapner, 1996, p. 149). When it comes to addressing environmental-interdependence issues, nongovernmental change agents possess important capabilities that are not available to national governments (see Princen and Finger, 1994a, pp. 1–11; Wapner, 1995, pp. 336–337; 1996, p. 2; Morphet, 1996, pp. 131–133; Porter and Brown, 1996, p. 51; Keck and Sikkink, 1998, p. 10, 213–214).

This section focuses on bottom-up roles that can be performed by TC Chinese Americans acting individually and as participants in NGOs or government-organized non-governmental organizations (GONGOs) and transnational social movements. Although they are predominantly members of a settled U.S. community (see Yang, 1999, p. 72, 85–86), Chinese Americans actively participate in a rich variety of forums along the U.S.–China frontier. The key to their success lies in the combination of education and professional expertise, transcultural insights and skills, network building, and broad consultation. Transnationally connected and

[17]Concern for future generations must include issues of sustainable development and population control also (see Claussen and McNeilly, 1998, p. 2, 20).

competent Chinese Americans are likely to be trusted on both sides of the Pacific, even by persons holding different views, provided that they "include less powerful actors" in the process of "devising cooperative strategies to deal with global environmental problems" (Botcheva, 2001, pp. 200–201).

As a result of understanding living conditions in both China and the United States and possessing access to local knowledge about successful sustainable-resource-management approaches, a considerable number of Chinese Americans are uniquely positioned to recommend, arrange, and participate in transterritorial and exclusively domestic projects that apply valuable lessons from one country to the other. The particular strategic strengths of the TC Chinese American actor in the United States and the PRC project arenas are likely to include contributions based on local knowledge and practice regarding viable approaches, encouraging participation through persuasion built on trust and cross-cultural knowledge or understanding (see Wang, 2001, pp. 158–159), leveraging resources for initial investments, mobilizing and cooperating with bureaucratically savvy national activists (see Steinberg, 2001, p. 205) and with kinship, native-place, friendship, and religious networks at the local level in China, and identifying qualified and reliable Mainland partners who are committed to initiating demonstration schemes. The latter capability is especially valuable because "many U.S. NGOs that go to China with limited time and support often leave quickly because they can not find . . . suitable partners" (Turner, 2001, p. 11).

Bottom-Up Projects in China

The manifold opportunities for arresting human-induced global warming in the PRC mainly are local and, therefore, tend to be widely dispersed and incremental (Ellerman, 2002, p. 3). The type of environmental protection projects that are most likely to succeed in China will be job-creating initiatives supported by foreign technology and funding (Lieberthal, 1997). Given the broad scope of their networks in the mainland, Chinese overseas are positioned to initiate small-scale, microlevel projects that address the threat of global warming and simultaneously are employment-generating (also see Chen, 1997, p. 90). Coincidentally, Chinese Americans increasingly are being enticed to return permanently by preferential municipal and provincial salary, housing, and job selection policies (Koehn & Yin, 2002, p. xxvii; Zweig, 2002, pp. 178–179, 190–191, 194). In the project arena, the nonstate roles open to Chinese overseas and to returning Chinese include involvement in national and cross-national scientific communities (Committee on Scholarly Communication with the People's Republic of China, 1992; Economy, 1997, pp. 24–30, 38–39; Economy &

Schreurs, 1997, p. 12),[18] professional organizations,[19] ethnic business networks (Peng, 2002, pp. 430–432), environmental NGOs and GONGOs (Wu, 2002, pp. 46–47), multinational corporations (Parson, 2001, p. A23), environmental joint ventures (see Tremayne and de Waal, 1998, p. 1040), philanthropic foundations (Yin & Lan, 2003, pp. 22–25, 29), kinship or ancestral-place networks (see Johnson and Woon, 1997, pp. 45–49, 55; Wang, 2001, p. 155), friendship and sister-city ties (see Shuman and Harvey, 1993, p. 223), and religious organizations.

A growing number of Chinese public administrators are recognizing environmental protection and sustainable development as additional core national policies (see Ross, 1998, p. 813; Baldinger and Turner, 2002, p. 9, 19–21; Chandler et al., 2002, p. 13; Becker, 2004, p. 81; Yardley, 2004, p. A4). However, the bureaucratic apparatus responsible for implementing and enforcing environmental regulations "exhibits fundamental structural weaknesses that undermine the best of intentions" (Economy, 2004, p. 101). These weaknesses include structural fragmentation and interagency competition, the State Environmental Protection Administration's (SEPA) low levels of staffing and funding, and lack of sufficient resources and corruption in the local government regulation process (SEI, 2002, p. 83; Chan, 2004, pp. 73–74; Economy, 2004, pp. 104–111, 127, 259; Koehn, forthcoming). Given the variability that results from the decentralized nature of China's administrative system, however, "when the mayor is environmentally proactive, income levels are high, and the city is tightly integrated into the international community, environmental protection has evidenced substantial progress over the past decade" (Economy, 2004, pp. 117–119, 128, 260).

In such places, Chinese American specialists can propose innovations, assist with renewable-energy-technology transfers (see Johnson, 1999,

---

[18]In 1998, the Chinese Academy of Social Sciences (CASS) and the Social Science Research Council (SSRC) signed an agreement of cooperation that is designed, in part, to respond to CASS' interest in problem-oriented studies (McDonnell, 1999, p. 13). Chinese American scientists are experienced in establishing exchange programs and culturally sensitive joint research projects with PRC scholars (see Wang, 2002, especially 225–227; Committee on Scholarly Communication with the People's Republic of China, 1992, p. 19). Based on its extensive network of contacts in China, the Committee on Scholarly Communicates found (p. 120) that "the Chinese scientific community almost universally considers working on global change topics to be a challenge, an opportunity, and, given China's vulnerability to climatic disasters, a responsibility." Moreover, "China's extensive historical writings contain proxy data for climate change that are a unique contribution to research on past changes" (p. 122).

[19]For instance, a growing number of organizations for Chinese American scientists and engineers, such as the 1500-member society of Chinese bioscientists in America and the 1000-member Chinese American chemical society, are strengthening linkages to China that involve training Mainland scientists in the United States and placing Chinese American experts in positions in Asia as part of an overall effort to "develop more researchers who can contribute scientifically on both sides of the Pacific" (Stone, 1993, p. 350).

p. 277), offer training in new energy-efficient technologies and approaches (Ross, 1998, p. 832; Holt & Haspel, 2001, p. 24), participate in joint ventures with domestically and internationally image-conscious household-appliance firms (Ross, 1998, p. 829), provide advice regarding subnational environmental-policy measures (see, for instance, Ellerman, 2002; Ferris and Zhang, 2002, pp. 452–455, 458), and build diagnostic and monitoring capacity on projects designed to assist (1) China's efforts to improve township, local- and state-enterprise, and household-energy efficiencies (see Smil, 1998, pp. 947–948; Johnson, 1999, p. 289) and (2) moves to adopt renewable-energy alternatives (see Koehn, 1999, p. 368, 386n; Boudri et al., 2002, pp. 418–423; www.efchina.org).[20] In 2002, for instance, Angela Chen of Iowa's department of natural resources led a 2002 China Environment Forum–sponsored workshop session in three mainland cities on the use of municipal bonds to raise capital for energy-efficiency improvements (*China Environment Series* 6, 2003, p. 141).

Another promising project initiative would involve the establishment by Chinese American specialists of independent, but affiliated, mainland-based applied research centers on emissions abatement. These centers might be patterned along the lines of the Beijing University–attached Center for Chinese Economic Research or Battelle Lab's energy-efficiency centers (see Jia and Rubin, 1997, p. A56; Economy, 1998b, p. 67). Most measures that would mitigate China's severe urban air pollution problems, as well as the harmful effects of trans-Pacific pollutants on the western United States (see Baldinger and Turner, 2002, p. 45), would coincidentally reduce GHG emissions[21] and be greeted favorably by local populations and NGOs that are mobilized into action by pressing community concerns (see Lew, 2000, p. 272, 279; Gielen and Chen, 2001, pp. 258, 261–267; Ho, 2001, p. 899; Mao and Chen, 2001, p. 332; Chandler et al., 2002, p. 53). Based on their comparative study of six developing countries, including China, Chandler et al. (2002, p. 52) conclude that the most powerful common drivers for climate change mitigation are "development and poverty alleviation, energy security, and local environmental protection."

---

[20]In the event that both governments agree to the Kyoto Protocol's "clean-development mechanism," emission reductions through sustainable-development projects in China organized and funded by Chinese Americans acting through corporations and NGOs involve the potential to provide credit toward the U.S. national obligation (see Haites and Aslam, 2000, pp. 2–4, 23; Thomas et al., 2001, pp. 172–173; Zhang, 2000, p. 749).

[21]The principal exception is the introduction of SO_2 scrubbers at coal-fired power plants (Gielen & Chen, 2001, p. 258). According to Chandler et al. (2002, p. 63), "desulfurization improves local air quality, but lowers the overall efficiency of power plants, resulting in slightly higher carbon dioxide emissions." The burning of more coal to compensate for decreased energy-extraction efficiency increases CO_2 emissions on a per-unit basis (Dong et al., 1998, p. 122).

In identifying projects that will make a difference, TC Chinese Americans will need to draw upon their insights regarding the PRC political system and their contacts with bureaucrats and party agents. In state-dominated systems, prospects for bringing about policy change are advanced by the activation of influential semigovernmental actors (such as think tanks, research laboratories, and GONGOs) and by gaining access to and generating bridging partnerships with government authorities (see Saich, 2000, p. 139; Risse, 2002, p. 266; Wu, 2002, p. 53, 56; Economy, 2004, p. 135). Once the penetration obstacles are overcome, the policy impact can be profound (Risse-Kappen, 1995a, pp. 25–26). In the absence of permitted institutional channels for public involvement in policy making and for broad consultation in regulatory processes (Tisdell, 1998, pp. 5–6; Lo & Leung, 2000, p. 679, 700–704), moreover, state and nonstate environmental protection advocates find the support and pressure that respected transnational civil-society actors can provide particularly useful for countering entrenched bureaucratic resistance (see Johnston, 1998, p. 585).

A rapidly increasing collection of formal and informal environmental NGOs and GONGOs are active in mainland China (see Ho, 2001, pp. 901–914; Jin, 2001, pp. 5–8; Wu, 2002). Following the downsizing of central government agencies in 1998, many research institutes (e.g., the prestigious Energy Research Institute) have taken on characteristics of semiindependent think tanks that rely on contracted services (SEI, 2002, p. 88) and national and provincial environmental GONGOs have attracted "numerous retired (or nearly retired) high-level officials, environmental scientists, university scholars, respected practitioners, social celebrities, and international experts as leaders and members" (Wu, 2002, p. 48; Liang, 2003, p. 12). A number of China's NGOs and GONGOs are linked to U.S.-based firms, nonprofit organizations, universities, and individuals that are interested in helping to reduce GHG emissions (Turner, 2001, pp. 1–2, 4, Tables 1,3,4, 2002, pp. 163–211). By the turn of the century, some 60 U.S. environmental NGOs, universities, and foundations engaged in five types of mainly small-scale projects in China: "(1) energy efficiency, (2) biodiversity and conservation, (3) pollution control, (4) environmental education, and (5) community capacity-building work" (Baldinger & Turner, 2002, p. 49).

However, many U.S. nonstate actors are finding it difficult to realize project objectives in the PRC due to "language problems and lack of familiarity with China's culture and political system" (Baldinger & Turner, 2002, p. 50). These obstacles show that TC Chinese overseas can play a valuable role by teaming up with the local governments, GONGOs, NGOs, universities, foundations, and firms engaged in, or contemplating involvement in, climate-change-mitigation projects in China. Promising possibilities include the China Sustainable Energy Program supported by grants to NGOs from the Energy Foundation and the David and Lucile

Packard Foundation (www.efchina.org); collaboration with Global Village of Beijing on community-recycling and environmental-education projects (Ho, 2001, pp. 909–910);[22] work with China's Institute for Environment and Development through Leadership for the Environment (an international NGO) on training projects designed to facilitate "the transfer and adoption of green technology by small and medium-size companies" (Ho, 2001, p. 911); participation in Tulane University's joint projects for the 2008 Beijing Green Olympics with the Beijing municipal government (*China Environmental Forum*, 2002, pp. 178–179); cooperation with the International Institute for Sustainable Development on research undertakings that identify sustainable trade opportunities as a World Trade Organization (WTO) member (*China Rights Forum*, No. 1, 2003, pp. 95–96); contributions to the Professional Association of China Environmentalists' online journal of topics related to China's environment (*China Environmental Forum*, 2002, p. 197); and collaboration with the Center for Environmental Education and Communications in raising awareness among mayors and teachers and in the preparation of climatic-stabilization materials for use in schools (SEI, 2002, p. 88).

Although the transportation sector currently is responsible for only about 10 percent of China's total energy-related carbon emissions, the sale of fuel-inefficient automobiles is growing dramatically (see He, 2003, p. 13; Roberts, 2004, p. 159). Domestic automobile production increased by 39.4 percent in 2002 and is expected to grow at an accelerated rate over the next decade (Chandler et al., 2002; Lun, 2003, p. 28, 14; also see Manning, 2000, p. 105). Concomitantly, vehicle imports are escalating as a result of the reduction of import tariffs and quotas following China's accession to the WTO (see Gallagher, 2003, p. 10). Already China is the world's fastest growing automobile market and the prediction of General Motors is that 18 percent of total growth in new vehicle sales through 2012 will occur in the Mainland (Bradsher, 2003, p. A8). Already, as a result of the expansion of automotive sales, "vehicle emissions have replaced coal soot as the major source of air pollution in several major cities" (Baldinger & Turner, 2002, p. 13). Largely due to "rapid increases in long-suppressed car ownership," the Pew Center on Global Climate Change forecasts that transportation GHG emissions in Shanghai will grow between four (low scenario) and seven (high scenario) times the 2000 level by 2020 (see Sperling and Salon, 2002, pp. 31–32).

Transportation-emission-reduction projects are especially likely to be positively received in China because of the "linkage with local environmental

[22]GVB president Sheri Liao also serves as consultant to the Beijing 2008 Olympics Organizing Committee and as a "green ambassador" to other official bodies (Mosher, 2003, p. 82).

concerns" principle. Motor vehicle emissions of hydrocarbons, carbon monoxide, and oxides of nitrogen, combined with lead and particulate emissions, simultaneously are major sources of global warming and negative local health and workforce-productivity effects from ground-level pollution (Walsh, 1989, p. 264; Chan, 2004, p. 80). China's vehicle emissions are associated with "brain damage, respiratory problems and infections, lung cancer, [and] emphysema" among other maladies (Paterson, 2000, p. 259; Sperling & Salon, 2002, p. iv). A recent study also linked China's rise in obesity, diabetes, and abnormal blood lipid levels, in part, to the decline in cycling and walking in favor of car ridership (*New York Times*, October 13, 2004, p. A6).

In preparation for the goal of "blue skies" over Beijing in time for the 2008 Olympics (see Ferris and Zhang, 2002, p. 436), Chinese overseas engineers can assist with the application of state-of-the-art fuel-efficiency technologies in domestic vehicle manufacturing and with leapfrogging to systems that incorporate fuel cells, electric drive, and batteries (see Sperling and Salon, 2002, p. 17, 19; Economy, 2004, p. 261). Prospects for collaboration also exist with the Natural Resources Defense Council's "Initiative for Taipei–Shanghai Cooperation on Fuel Cell Vehicles and Sustainable Transportation." This project is actively promoting the dissemination of fuel-cell-powered motor scooters in the mainland (Turner, 2001, pp. 6–7). Chinese American public health experts can cooperate with the U.S.–China Environmental Fund's "lead-poisoning prevention in China" program (*China Environmental Forum*, 2002, p. 180, 193–194). Local government planners can help transfer "intelligent transportation system" (ITS) technologies (Sperling & Salon, 2002, p. 18). Experts in public policy and public administration can work with mainland municipal governments, such as Shanghai, that are interested in Singapore's successful efforts to restrain vehicle ownership and use (see Willoughby, 2001), in pursuing alternatives to car ownership and usage such as four-stroke motorbikes, and in enhancing the attractiveness of nonmotorized transportation (see Sperling and Salon, 2002, pp. 23–24, 34). A major challenge involved in transferring such emission-reducing technologies and policies is "appropriate application" (Sperling & Salon, 2002, pp. 18–19). In such situations, TC Chinese American professionals are particularly likely to appreciate the indigenous challenges that need to be surmounted, to recognize local possibilities, and to be cognizant of North American "mistakes and detours" (Sperling & Salon, 2002, p. 33).

One particularly ambitious emissions-control project initiative would involve Chinese Americans in the establishment of and transnational funding for a China–U.S. foundation specifically devoted to promoting (1) reciprocal fossil fuel energy conservation and (2) collaborative grassroots projects designed to facilitate transitions to safe, affordable, and renewable alternative energy sources in both countries. Among other projects, the new foundation could help to underwrite the government's interest in "expanding scientific research and exchanges in the study of energy conservation" (PRC State Council, 1994, p. 130; Chen, 1997, p. 87; Gan, 1998, p. 125; Zhang, 1998, p. 135, 2000, p. 749). This initiative also could include a specific program component that facilitates the return of Chinese American experts to the mainland on short-term research, training, and consultancy projects (also see Harding, 1992, p. 353).

Specifically, China's wind resources are "world-class," wind power is one of its "most cost-effective energy supply options," and there are no GHG emissions from wind power (Lew, 2000, pp. 272–275). Although China has been "highly successful in commercial (or near-commercial) dissemination of household-scale renewable energy systems," there is need to adapt advanced (particularly hybrid, and utility-scale) wind turbine technologies from abroad (Lew, 2000, pp. 276–281). For instance, Berger Windpower, a U.S. company, and Xiangtan Electrical Machinery Group Corporation have established a joint venture for the production of 10 kw wind turbines (see Lew, 2000, pp. 277–279). Public administrators in China, particularly at the provincial level, also are challenged to support the nascent wind industry by enforcing existing regulations that mandate or encourage the use of wind power, implementing price-support systems, and coordinating clean development mechanism (CDM) and other renewable energy projects sponsored by the Asian Development Bank and the Global Environmental Facility (Payne, 1998, p. 372; Raufer & Wang, 2003, pp. 44–47; Economy, 2004, p. 189).[23] The development of China's localized wind industry promises to result in considerable employment generation (Raufer & Wang, 2003, p. 46).

Bottom-Up Projects in the United States

Today, ethnic Chinese are "a leading force in U.S. science and technology" (Peng, 2002, p. 432). In the Silicon Valley, "ethnic Chinese account for one fifth of the scientists and technicians" (Peng, 2002, p. 432). TC Chinese American scientists and engineers can connect with a host of respected NGOs for the promotion of mutual learning in the United States. They can do so confident that some 70 percent of the U.S. public believes it is "necessary to take immediate steps to counter global warming" (Andrews, 2001, p. A3). As one example of how this might work, Chinese American

[23]Although entrenched bureaucratic opposition exists to hosting CDM projects, proponents can be found even within China's State Development and Planning Commission (Nordqvist et al., 2002, p. 80).

computer specialists can support the research, education, or advocacy activities of the Silicon Valley Toxics Coalition – a grassroots association devoted to addressing environmental and human-health problems associated with growth of the high-tech electronics industry (*China Rights Forum*, No. 1, 2003, p. 96). Chinese American engineers also can devote their expertise and energies to increasing the fuel efficiency of cars and trucks, to reducing fuel-(including fuel-cell)-manufacturing emissions (Potter, 2001, p. 139), and to finding affordable ways to curb energy use in new and existing dwellings (see Lane and Bierbaum, 2001, p. 201). In a more activist vein, Chinese American lawyers could participate in the efforts to prepare class-action lawsuits on behalf of people or countries that suffer adverse effects of global warming that are aimed at "forcing the United States or corporations to reduce emissions of heat-trapping greenhouse gases" (Seelye, 2001, p. A14). Within Chinese American immigrant communities, existing community-organized workshops on issues such as worker and immigrant rights and domestic violence can be augmented by grassroots conservation-education efforts.[24] The local chapter of the League of Women Voters could join with the Silicon Valley Chinese Engineers' Society or the New York–based Chinese Association of Science and Technology to offer a series of town meetings on the topic of nonrenewable energy consumption trends, the prospective impact of global warming in both countries, and opportunities for increased sales of energy-efficient technologies. Moreover, through participation in U.S. universities, think tanks, churches, professional associations, human rights organizations, labor alliances (see Ngai, 1997, pp. 178–179), and service clubs, Chinese Americans can engage in a "people-to-people dialogue" (Jia & Rubin, 1997, p. A56) over U.S.–China perspectives on and approaches to climatic stabilization. These efforts will be most effective when they occur at the local level (see Burgess et al., 1998, p. 1452) — where members of the Chinese American community are well-known, trusted, and respected. This opportunity dovetails with the propensity for permanent settlement among recent immigrants and the growing tendency of Chinese Americans to become involved politically in "ethnically mixed neighborhoods and communities" (Li, 1999, p. 21; also see Sterngold, 1999, p. A21).

Potter (2001, pp. 139–141) shows that improvements in vehicle technology alone will not reduce CO_2 emissions from automotive transportation to sustainable levels. The most crucial factors in curtailing automobile CO_2 emissions are "the amount and length of journeys" (Potter, 2001, pp. 141–142). According to William Dietz, director of the division of

---

[24]To mention one possibility, environmental education could be included as a UNITE project among the Sunset Park Chinese community in Brooklyn, New York (see Ngai, 1997, pp. 180–181).

nutrition and physical activity at the Centers for Disease Control and Prevention, "a quarter of all trips taken by Americans are under a mile, but 75 percent of those trips are done by car" (cited in Brody, 2000, p. E1). Because "the most energy-intensive activities people engage in are those involving travel" (Schipper et al., 1989, p. 317)[25] and motor vehicles (primarily automobiles) consume roughly two thirds of the petroleum used in the United States "simply in their use,"[26] the provision of cyclist- and pedestrian-friendly routes and the curtailment of short car trips — particularly during peak traffic hours — can bring about a substantial reduction in fossil-fuel emissions (see Schipper et al., 1989, pp. 316–317). Thus, there is much of climatic, health, and resource conservation value that U.S. drivers who value individual mobility could learn from China's designated citywide bike lanes (see Sperling and Salon, 2002, p. 7, 11);[27] free or inexpensive, convenient, and guarded bike-parking areas; extensive system of sidewalk bicycle repair stations; cyclist-commuter subsidies; and bicycle load carrying, delivery, and advertising (see Yang, 1985, pp. 93–104; Lowe, 1989, pp. 20–21, 31–33; Durning, 1992, p. 79; Koehn, 1999, p. 375; Rosenthal, 2000, p. A4). The health benefits of local foot-power projects are considerable. The decline in U.S. bicycle riders (down from 56 million in 1995 to 43.5 million in 1998) parallels the dramatic societal rise in obesity (*UCLA Public Health*, 2004, p. 5). Although 22 percent of U.S. children are obese (according to the Center for Disease Control), less than 1 percent of those aged 7 to 15 currently ride bicycles to school (Kilborn, 1999, p. A1). Although China's urban and rural populations already are experienced with and still prefer the "vehicle of the future" (the bicycle), U.S. bikes are more likely to collect dust in the garage than be used for commuting or shopping (Lowe, 1989, pp. 7–18). As a valuable emissions-reduction step, Chinese Americans can collaborate with U.S. municipal administrators in promoting and facilitating the development of "bicycle-friendly communities," such as those found in Corvallis, Oregon, Palo Alto, California, and Missoula, Montana (Devlin, 2003b, p. B1, B4).

Certain areas of the United States also would benefit by learning from China's successful efforts to produce, disseminate, and maintain small-scale

---

[25]On an individual level, "driving a short distance to a shopping center and burning one gallon of gasoline in the process will produce 22 pounds of CO_2. This would be enough to double the CO_2 content of a half-million cubic feet of air, about the volume of air contained in the entire shopping center" (Kempton et al., 1995, p. 34).
[26]Petroleum is also a major component in asphalt and, hence, in highway construction and repair (Paterson, 2000, p. 260; also see Lowe, 1989, p. 16, 20; Kempton et al., 1995, p. 142).
[27]In Beijing, according to observational studies conducted by Hook in 1996 (p. 4), "bicycle traffic moves at 6–8 kilometres per hour, and the bicycle lanes move 900 more people per lane per hour than the… mixed motor lanes." In China's flat cities, Hook foresees that roller blades "could be the wave of the future."

wind turbines. Chinese public entrepreneurs, particularly at subnational levels, have "instituted some of the most extensive small-scale renewable energy programs in either the developing or industrial world" (Lew, 2000, pp. 272, 283–284). Chinese Americans could fruitfully adapt lessons from China's small-scale wind-turbine and hybrid wind and photovoltaic-systems production and dissemination accomplishments (Lew, 2000, p. 278, 2001) to projects specifically designed for wind-resource-rich places (such as North Dakota and parts of Montana) in the United States.

Many of the most promising venues for Chinese American participation in projects designed to address global warming currently are found at the subnational level. In some U.S. states, concerns about air pollution, waste management, or energy resources have supported efforts to control emissions, adopt renewable energy, protect forests, and reduce automotive transportation (Rabe, 2002). In 2003, Washington state's governor Gary Locke joined the governors of Oregon and California in an agreement to check global warming by promoting renewable energy, developing uniform efficiency standards, and buying fuel-efficient vehicles (Marquez, 2003, p. A2). In 2004, voters approved a ballot initiative (Amendment 37) mandating that 10 percent of Colorado's electricity come from wind and solar power by 2015; the city of Colorado Springs had already introduced an energy program requiring that 15 percent of the energy sold within its limits come from wind sources by 2017 (Johnson, 2004, p. A13).

Collectively, expanding state and local government efforts "constitute a diverse set of policy innovations rich with lessons" for climatic stabilization (Rabe, 2002, p. ii). At the subnational level, the principal "climate-change entrepreneurs" who have contributed to emission reductions have worked for state agencies, legislative staffs, or NGOs. Rabe (2002, p. 10) reports that most of these entrepreneurs are "relatively anonymous figures who are unlikely to seek higher office and are not particularly eager to secure notoriety for their efforts." These are exactly the types of "invisible" roles that TC Chinese Americans prefer to fill (see Koehn and Yin, 2002, p. xxxi). Chinese Americans are also likely to be quite comfortable joining other state-level proponents of climate-change mitigation in emphasizing the accompanying economic development opportunities (Rabe, 2002, pp. 9–10).

Value Change

Energy-efficiency projects and technological breakthroughs in renewable energy will not be sufficient in themselves to prevent increased GHG emissions in China and the United States (see, for instance, Ash and Edmonds, 1998, p. 874). Changes in consumption values also are required. Resource-use values are at once the most important and the most difficult aspects of the global-warming problematic for nonstate actors (or state actors) to change. First, people must recognize a compelling need to transform production processes and to adopt sustainable-consumption lifestyles. Such shifts are facilitated by convincing proof that failure to change will produce proximate danger (see Durning, 1992, p. 25; Rosenau, 1997b, pp. 340–341, 352), by unwillingness to depend on the arrival of technological fixes, by "a feeling of responsibility for one's children and subsequent descendants" or future generations (Kempton et al., 1995, pp. 12–13, 95–96, 101), or by appreciation for the immediate and long-term personal benefits associated with a frugal and simple lifestyle (see De Young, 1990/1991, pp. 215–216, 226; Durning, 1992, pp. 137–139, 149; Kempton et al., 1995, p. 101, 136). Then, public must be assured that any personal sacrifices required by sustainable-consumption behavior will not be negated by the behavior of others — either domestically or globally.

Chinese Americans can play crucial roles in shaping resource-curtailment values — especially with regard to advancing awareness of the intrinsic satisfactions involved in sustainable consumption (higher quality of life, sense of well-being, close interpersonal relationships) as well as framing a shared "anational" identity around the common costs and benefits that are at stake in global climatic change (see Chase and Panagopoulos, 1995, p. 74). The magnitude of this challenge should not be underestimated, however. Decreased per-capita consumption is an ambitious goal. At present, most residents of the United States, who consumed 24 percent of the world's energy usage while constituting only 5 percent of its population in 1990, are not acting to curtail their consumption behavior (see Durning, 1992, pp. 28–29; Kempton et al., 1995, p. 220; Koehn, 1999, p. 368, 386n). In China, the global "priests and prophets of the culture of competition and consumption" have been working assiduously to instill the value of "self-expression through consumption of material goods" (Madsen, 1995, p. 166, 171–172).[28] Many mainland Chinese, at 22 percent of the world's population but using only 8.5 percent of its energy in 1990, aspire to use their newly acquired wealth to increase their access to consumables — including electrical appliances, motorized transport, heating and air conditioning, and status items such as cellular phones (Edmonds, 1994, p. 256; Barber, 1995, pp. 294–295; Brown, 1995, p. 31; Chai, 1996, pp. 256–257, 274, 276; Shen, 1997, p. 595; Banister, 1998, p. 1014; Li, 1998, p. 54–55, 62–63, 131, 156–157, 186; Goldman & MacFarquhar, 1999, pp. 24–25; Davis, 2000, p. 2, 4;

[28]On the Mainland impact of Chinese overseas from the commercialized and consumption-oriented societies of Taiwan and Hong Kong, see Smart and Smart (1998, p. 114); Yang (1997, p. 304). Derived, in part, from the lifestyle of early-20th-century Shanghai, Hong Kong's culture of consumption, with its emphasis on the overt display of material wealth, also has permeated Chinese communities in North American cities (see Mitchell, 1997, pp. 231–232, 236–237).

Landler, 2000, p. C1; Lu, 2000, p. 134; Bradsher, 2003, p. A8). The ostentatious luxury housing and consumption standards set by wealthy and middle-class trendsetters "have created new demands for environmentally damaging products" (Oksenberg & Economy, 1998, p. 354; also see Durning, 1992, p. 52; Goodman, 1999, pp. 259–260).

It is likely that some of the movement of people between the Mainland and the United States has "transformed lower consumers into higher consumers . . . [who] then transfer these values and aspirations back to their places of origin during their periodic returns to home areas" (Skeldon, 1997, p. 211). At the same time, Chinese Americans are presented with an unprecedented opportunity to transform transcontinental migration networks into two-way avenues for transmitting and reinforcing energy conservation and sustainable consumption sensitivities and values. Many more people in the United States — especially young people — embraced attitudes favorable to resource conservation by the end of the 20th century. In the mid-1990s, Willet Kempton, James Boster, and Jennifer Hartley found overwhelming support for protecting the environment even when they explicitly connected this position to a reduced "standard of living today" or to returning to "a less materialistic way of life." The vast majority of their respondents also were convinced that "Americans are going to have to drastically reduce their level of consumption over the next few years" (Kempton et al., 1995, p. 99, 134). Earlier research conducted by Raymond De Young indicated that a substantial proportion of the small-town residents surveyed in the U.S. midwest associated "forms of intrinsic satisfaction with a reduced consumption lifestyle" (De Young, 1990/1991, p. 226; also see Durning, 1992, pp. 38–39, 41–43).

Many mainland Chinese are acutely aware of the seriousness of China's environmental problems (see Lo and Leung, 2000, pp. 683–685, 691–693, 699; Ferris and Zhang, 2002, p. 549) and still derive considerable personal satisfaction from the frugal use of resources in everyday living. The items De Young (1990/1991, p. 222) used to operationalize "frugality" included "keeping things running past normal life," "finding ways to avoid waste," "repairing rather than throwing away," "saving things I might need someday," and "finding ways to use things over and over." These frugal practices are widespread in China (see Madsen, 2000, pp. 316–318; Lu, 2000, p. 141).[29] Given their strong social bonds with mainlanders, Chinese

[29]Lo and Leung (2000, p. 689) report that strong "green values" are widely held at the personal level among residents of Guangzhou — one of China's most industrialized cities. In their 1996 survey, "94.2 percent of respondents agreed or strongly agreed that they ought 'to save water and electricity'; 72.9 percent felt that they ought 'to buy environmentally friendly products'; 68.4 percent advocated 'separating household waste for recycling'; 61.6 percent thought it was right 'to bring one's own shopping bag'; and 55.5 percent felt that 'to spend more on environmentally friendly products is worthwhile.'"

overseas are positioned to build on such indigenous foundations by articulating appealing past and future cultural representations of resourceful living (see Chase and Panagopoulos, 1995, p. 76) that respond to Tu Weiming's (1991, p. 10, 14) call for forms of life that are "not only commensurate with human flourishing but also sustainable in ecological and environmental terms." The mainland-public-interest motives that inspire many Chinese American professionals and family members further enhance prospects that efforts to transmit resource-curtailment values will be viewed as well-intentioned by their counterparts in China.

Openness to the mutually satisfying possibilities inherent in conservation value exchanges will extend further among both populations as analytical and conceptual skills expand (Rosenau, 1997b, pp. 350–351), as lay publics increasingly recognize the unsustainability of fossil-fuel-dependent lifestyles and automotive-centered economies (Durning, 1992, pp. 82–84; Paterson, 2000, pp. 258–260), and as fragmented efforts coalesce in a sustainable-consumption movement (Princen et al., 2002, p. 20). On the promising side of the ledger, public opinion polls indicate that 60 to 80 percent of U.S. electric customers "support renewable energy and would be willing to pay more for it" (Short, 2001, p. 14). A December 2004 poll conducted by the University of Maryland's program on international policy attitudes found 59 percent of Republicans and 74 percent of Democrats in favor of "legislation that limits the United States' emissions of greenhouse gases" (*PA Times*, vol. 28, no. 2, February 2005, pp. 1–2). In China's case, participating in an early and massive transition to renewable energy sources would avoid expensive investments in obsolete fossil-fuel-driven systems (also see Smil, 1993, p. 202; Ryan and Flavin, 1995, p. 129, 115; Hsu, 1999, pp. 29–30). It is encouraging in this connection that China's *Agenda 21* white paper foresees rejection of the industrialized-country development model and acceptance of "appropriate consumption and a low energy-consuming production system" (PRC, State Council, 1994, p. 55). On the other hand, population control and reduction, particularly in rural China, remains to be addressed convincingly (Smil, 1993, pp. 135–137; Yeh, 1996, p. 1522).

Specific recognition of the threats associated with global warming is not highly developed in China at this time.[30] Issues perceived to be personally remote, such as GHG emissions, "receive very little public attention"

[30]Although some enhancement of conceptual tools is occurring and cultural models that would lead to more effective consumer choices exist, Kempton et al. (1995, p. 219, 225) also conclude, on the basis of an extensive anthropological study, that people in the United States "have serious misunderstandings about global environmental issues, which skew public support for policies for irrelevant reasons."

(Vermeer, 1998, p. 953, 960–961; Nordqvist et al., 2002, pp. 79–80). Moreover, "distrust of civil protest or action in any form" hampers "efforts to increase public awareness and political support for environmental actions" (Vermeer, 1998, p. 958). In spite of these constraints, the level of environmental protection activity and public education occurring at the grassroots is expanding rapidly across China today (Bo, 1998; Tremayne & de Waal, 1998, p. 1026; Lo & Leung, 2000, p. 693). In their efforts to advance value and behavioral changes affecting resource use, Chinese Americans likely would find it useful to partner with domestic and international NGOs in China and the United States on educational programs designed to raise awareness regarding the societal and intergenerational virtues and personal benefits associated with (1) local pollution abatement (see Vermeer, 1998, p. 960), (2) recycling, (3) restraining the ownership and use of personal motor vehicles (Sperling & Salon, 2002, pp. 13–14),[31] (4) public and nonmotorized transportation (see Potter, 2001, p. 141; Lowe, 1989), (5) sustainable-consumption practices, (6) "making purchasing decisions based upon [product] source reduction characteristics of durability, repairability and reusability" (De Young, 1990/1991, p. 221), (7) participation in afforestation efforts (Chandler et al., 2002, p. 17; Logan et al., 1999, p. 12), and (8) population control (Chandler et al., 2002, p. 15, 18, 52). Examples of promising opportunities for TC Chinese Americans to join in values-change projects include contributions to the World Wildlife Fund (WWF)–supported graduate program on the human dimensions of climate change at Tsinghua University (China Environmental Forum, 2002, p. 188); support for the Green Ants' "green-life campaign" or the Volunteers Association of Environmental Protection of Yueyang City's efforts to decrease public consumption "by following the reduce, reevaluate, reuse, recycle, and rescue principles" (China Environmental Forum, 2002, p. 202, 209); and participation in the International Awareness Community Theater (IACT)'s "interactive educational program that enables Chinese students to communicate their environmental concerns through role-playing and the performance arts."[32]

[31]Returning Chinese Americans from Los Angeles can speak with authority about "the daily battle with traffic congestion" (see Lowe, 1989, p. 21) and others can share experience with ways of reducing the negative impacts of motorization — such as telecommuting — that are adaptable in the mainland (see Shen, 1997, p. 603; Mao and Chen, 2001, p. 325).

[32]IACT trainers "work with Chinese teachers, drama instructors, and professional actors to organize performances in schools and cultural community centers" (China Environmental Forum, 2002, p. 181).

Conclusion

The continued preoccupation of political leaders in the United States and China with 20th century sensitivities of military-strategic superiority and economic advantage often obscures the need for policy initiatives that address threats to global resources and environmental security. In a milieu characterized by "co-option of the environmental agenda by a traditional security agenda" (Dyer, 1996, p. 24) and national government inaction on GHG emissions, public administrators at subnational levels are responsible for fulfilling key transboundary roles. In both the United States and the PRC, their capacity to address anthropogenic contributors to climatic change is greatly enhanced by linkages with nonstate actors that are committed to emphasizing the importance of maintaining natural resources for future generations in place of pursuing maximum economic growth and consumption. Among the potential nonstate partners, alliances with TC Chinese Americans are particularly important. From a variety of perspectives, all of the contributors to *The Expanding Roles of Chinese Americans* (Koehn & Yin, 2002) highlight the influential, albeit understudied, and typically unreported, roles that Chinese Americans fill in increasingly powerful trans-Pacific civil-society networks — ranging from philanthropy and development to profit-minded business, scientific exchange, and environmental protection.

The transnational competence of Chinese overseas can be employed with important effect to crucial and complex interdependence challenges when state-to-state relations are either unable by themselves to ensure harmonious interactions or likely to exacerbate tensions. As Chinese Americans adopt a shared vision of the double-sided problem of global warming "and see themselves, collectively, as part of the solution, they become [active] stakeholders" (Hardy, 1994, p. 279) along the U.S.–China frontier. By contributing their special insights and skills in project initiation and implementation, TC Chinese overseas fill indispensable roles in addressing global climatic change. The rise of green NGOs and GONGOs that inject new ideas and methods in the China mainland offers fertile ground for cooperation in initiatives aimed at mitigating climate change (Economy, 2004, p. 128, 262). Working with politically connected GONGOs facilitates the approval and successful execution of project opportunities (see Koehn, 2002, pp. 249–251; Ho, 2001, p. 915, 917).

When nonstate actors accept personal responsibility for addressing interdependence issues, they are able to effectuate change through "a myriad [of] small contributions" (Smil, 1993, p. 203). The extent of their impact on direction setting and, ultimately, on reductions in GHG emissions will depend upon the degree to which Chinese Americans are committed to participating in addressing the threats posed by global warming to the PRC, the United States, and the global commons[33]; are able to mobilize their skills, insights, and resources around legitimating and motivating principles; and are successful in employing appropriate grassroots projects and partnering strategies for effectuating change. As the 21st century progresses and global warming increasingly threatens the interests of both populations, climatic stabilization will be of escalating concern to policymakers in China and the United States and non-governmental partnerships with public administrators will expand (Johnston, 1998, p. 585; Economy, 2004, p. 185).

Promoting emissions reductions involves Chinese Americans in an effort to address a mainstream interdependence challenge (see Ungar, 1997, p. 37). At the same time, they are acting on behalf of ethnic community and country-of-origin interests. Although the challenges are formidable, the analysis presented in this chapter indicates that growing numbers of Chinese American scientists, investors (Ong, 1992, p. 129) and corporate executives, engineers (see Kempton, 1993, p. 230), computer technicians, lawyers, forest-resource managers, health professionals (see Martens et al., 1997, p. 586), environmental NGO members, planners, philanthropists, educators, journalists, and other opinion shapers who translate expert discourses (Jamison, 1996, p. 24) are positioned to influence U.S.–China contributions to anthropogenic climatic change in the 21st century as a result of their transterritorial civil-society network building, enhanced activism, transnational competency, and partnerships with farsighted subnational public administrators.

References

Adams, R.M., B.H. Hurd, and J. Reilly. 1999. *Agriculture and Global Climate Change: A Review of Impacts to U.S. Agricultural Resources*. Arlington: Pew Center on Global Climate Change.

Andrews, E.L. 2001. "Frustrated Europeans Set to Battle U.S. on Climate," *New York Times*, 16 July, p. A3.

Ash, R.F. and R.L. Edmonds. 1998. "China's Land Resources, Environment and Agricultural Production," *China Quarterly*, 156(December): 836–879.

Baldinger, P. and J.L. Turner. 2002. *Crouching Suspicions, Hidden Potential: United States Environmental and Energy Cooperation with China*. Washington, D.C.: Woodrow Wilson Center.

Bandura, A. 1995. "Exercise of Personal and Collective Efficacy in Changing Societies," in A. Bandura (ed.), *Self-Efficacy in Changing Societies*. Cambridge: Cambridge University Press, pp. 1–45.

[33]O'Riordan and Jordan (1996, p. 95) maintain that the global commons provides "a force for highly innovative cooperative behavior" because it embodies "a fresh perspective on what truly is self-interest — namely, mutual cooperation in the name of a habitable planet."

Banister, J. 1998. "Population, Public Health, and the Environment in China," *China Quarterly*, 156(December): 986–1015.

Barber, B.R. 1995. *Jihad vs. McWorld*. London: Random House.

Barrett, S. 1999. "Montreal versus Kyoto: International Cooperation and the Global Environment," in I. Kaul, I. Grunberg, and M.A. Stern (eds.), *Global Public Goods: International Cooperation in the 21st Century*. Oxford: Oxford University Press, pp. 192–219.

Becker, J. 2004. "China's Growing Pains: More Money, More Stuff, More Problems. Any Solutions?" *National Geographic* (March): 68–95.

Birdsall, N. and R.Z. Lawrence. 1999. "Deep Integration and Trade Agreements: Good for Developing Countries?" in I. Kaul, I. Grunberg, and M.A. Stern (eds.), *Global Public Goods: International Cooperation in the 21st Century*. Oxford: Oxford University Press, pp. 128–151.

Bo, W. 1998. "Greening the Chinese Media," *China Environment Series 2*, Environmental Change and Security Project, Woodrow Wilson International Center for Scholars. htttp//ecsp.si.edu/ecsplib.nsf

Boehmer-Christiansen, S. 1996. "The International Research Enterprise and Global Environmental Change: Climate-Change Policy as a Research Process," in J. Vogler and M.F. Imber (eds.), *The Environment and International Relations*. London: Routledge, pp. 171–195.

Bolin, B. 1997. "International Scientific Networks," in M. Rolen, H. Sjoberg, and U. Svedin (eds.), *International Governance on Environmental Issues*. Boston: Kluwer Academic, pp. 138–149.

Borenstein, S. 2003. "EPA: Carbon Dioxide Can't Be Regulated," *Missoulian*, 29 August, p. A3.

Botcheva, L. 2001. "Expertise and International Governance: Eastern Europe and the Adoption of European Union Environmental Legislation," *Global Governance*, 7(2): 197–224.

Boudri, J.C., L. Hordijk, C. Kroeze, M. Amann, J. Cofala, I. Bertok, L. Junteny, D. Lin, Z. Shuang, H. Runquing. 2002. "The Potential Contribution of Renewable Energy in Air Pollution Abatement in China and India," *Energy Policy*, 30(5): 409–424.

Bradsher, K. 2001a. "Ethanol Plan Fails to Reduce Use of Gasoline," *New York Times*, 21 June, p. A1, C2.

Bradsher, K. 2001b. "Fuel Economy for New Cars Is at Lowest Level since '80," *New York Times*, 18 May, p. A15.

Bradsher, K. 2003. "China Boom Adds to Global Warming Problem," *New York Times*, 22 October, p. A1, A8.

Brody, J.E. 2000. "Planning Healthier Suburbs, Where Cars Sit Idle and People Get Moving," *New York Times*, 17 October, p. E1.

Brown, L.R. 1995. *Who Will Feed China? Wake-Up Call for a Small Planet*. New York: W.W. Norton.

Burgess, J., C.M. Harrison, and P. Filius. 1998. "Environmental Communication and the Cultural Politics of Environmental Citizenship," *Environment and Planning A*, 30: 1445–1460.

Bush, G.W. 2001. "Global Climate Change: Making Commitments We Can Keep and Keeping Commitments We Can Make," *Vital Speeches of the Day*, 68(18): 546–548.

Byrne, J., B. Shen, and X. Li. 1996. "The Challenge of Sustainability: Balancing China's Energy, Economic and Environmental Goals," *Energy Policy*, 24(5): 455–462.

Chai, J.C.H. 1996. "Consumption and Living Standards in China," in R.F. Ash and Y.Y. Kueh (eds.), *The Chinese Economy under Deng Xiaoping*. Oxford: Clarendon.

Chan, G. 2004. "China's Compliance in Global Environmental Affairs," *Asia Pacific Viewpoint*, 45(1)(April): 69–86.

Chandler, W., R. Schaeffer, Z. Dadi, P.R. Shukla, F. Tudela, O. Davidson, S. Alpan-Atamer 2002. *Climate Change Mitigation in Developing Countries*. Arlington: Pew Center on Global Climate Change.

Chase, J. and I.S. Panagopoulos. 1995. "Environmental Values and Social Psychology: A European Common Market or Commons' Dilemma?" in Y. Guerrier, N. Alexander, J. Chase, and M. O'Brien (eds.), *Values and the Environment: A Social Science Perspective*. Chichester: John Wiley & Sons, pp. 67–79.

Chen, C.-C. 1997. "Beijing's Environmental Protection Strategy," *Issues & Studies*, 33(7)(July): 77–92.

Cheng, L. 1999 "Chinese Americans in the Formation of the Pacific Regional Economy," in E. Hu-De Hart (ed.), *Across the Pacific: Asian Americans and Globalization*. New York: Asia Society, pp. 61–78.

China Environmental Forum. 2000.

China Environmental Series. 6. 2000.

China Rights Forum. 1. 2003.

Claussen, E. and L. McNeilly. 1998. *Equity and Global Climate Change: The Complex Elements of Global Fairness*. Arlington: Pew Center on Global Climate Change.

Committee on Scholarly Communication with the People's Republic of China. 1992. *China and Global Change: Opportunities for Collaboration*. Washington, D.C.: National Academy Press.

Cooper, R.N. 1992. "United States Policy Towards the Global Environment," in A. Hurrell and B. Kingsbury (eds.), *The International Politics of the Environment: Actors, Interests, and Institutions*. Oxford: Clarendon, pp. 290–312.

Cusimano, M.K. 2000. "Beyond Sovereignty: The Rise of Transsovereign Problems," in M. Cusimano (ed.), *Beyond Sovereignty: Issues for a Global Agenda*. Bedford: St. Martin's, pp. 1–40.

Davis, D.S. 2000. "Introduction: A Revolution in Consumption," in D. S. Davis (ed.), *The Consumer Revolution in Urban China*. Berkeley: University of California Press, pp. 1–20.

DeSombre, E.R. 2000. *Domestic Sources of International Environmental Policy: Industry, Environmentalists, and U.S. Power*. Cambridge: MIT Press.

Devlin, S. 2003a. "Changes in Climate Foretell a Hazy Future," *Missoulian*, 23 November, p. A1, A10.

Devlin, V. 2003b. "National Organization Names Missoula a Bicycle-Friendly Community," *Missoulian*, 20 May, p. B1.

Devlin, S. 2004. "Report Details Global Warming, Fire-Threat Links," *Missoulian*, 15 September, p. A1, A5.

De Young, R. 1990/1991. "Some Psychological Aspects of Living Lightly: Desired Lifestyle Patterns and Conservation Behavior," *Journal of Environmental Systems*, 20(3): 215–227.

Dong, F., D. Lew, L. Ping, D.M. Kammen, and R. Wilson. 1998. "Strategic Options for Reducing CO_2 in China: Improving Energy Efficiency and Using Alternatives to Fossil Fuels," in M.B. McElroy, C.P. Nielsen, and P. Lydon (eds.), *Energizing China: Reconciling Environmental Protection and Economic Growth*. Cambridge: Harvard University Press, pp. 119–165.

Downs, E.S. 1999. "China's Thirst for Oil: Energy Security and Interdependence," Paper presented at the 51st Annual Meeting of the Association for Asian Studies, Boston, March.

Durning, A.T. 1992. *How Much Is Enough? The Consumer Society and the Future of the Earth*. New York: W.W. Norton.

Dyer, H.C. 1996. "Environmental Security as a Universal Value," in J. Vogler and M.F. Imber (eds.), *The Environment and International Relations*. London: Routledge, pp. 22–40.

Eckholm, E. 2001. "China Said to Sharply Reduce Emissions of Carbon Dioxide," *New York Times*, 15 June, p. A1, A6.

Economy, E.C. 1997. "Chinese Policy-making and Global Climate Change: Two-front Diplomacy and the International Community," in M.A. Schreurs and E. Economy (eds.), *The Internationalization of Environmental Protection*. Cambridge: Cambridge University Press, pp. 19–41.

Economy, E.C. 1998a. "China's Environmental Diplomacy," in S.S. Kim (ed.), *China and the World: Chinese Foreign Policy Faces the New Millennium*. Boulder, CO: Westview, pp. 264–283.

Economy, E.C. 1998b. "The Environment and Development in the Asia-Pacific Region," in J. Shinn (ed.), *Fires across the Water: Transnational Problems in Asia*. New York: Council on Foreign Relations, pp. 45–71.

Economy, E.C. 2004. *The River Runs Black: The Environmental Challenge to China's Future*. Ithaca, NY: Cornell University Press.

Economy, E.C. and M.A. Schreurs. 1997. "Domestic and International Linkages in Environmental Politics," in M.A. Schreurs and E. Economy (eds.), *The Internationalization of Environmental Protection*. Cambridge: Cambridge University Press, pp. 1–18.

Edmonds, R.L. 1994. *Patterns of China's Lost Harmony: A Survey of the Country's Environmental Degradation and Protection*. London: Routledge.

Edwards, M. 1999. *Future Positive: International Cooperation in the 21st Century*. London: Earthscan.

Edwards, D. 2000. "Getting Back to NAM," *Ecologist*, 30(3)(May): 52.

Ekins, P. 1992. *A New World Order: Grassroots Movements for Global Change*. London: Routledge.

Ellerman, A.D. 2002. "Designing a Tradable Permit System to Control SO_2 Emissions in China: Principles and Practice," *Energy Journal*, 23(2): 1–26.

Epstein, P.R. 2001. "Climate, Ecology and Human Health," in A.T. Price-Smith (ed.), *Plagues and Politics: Infectious Disease and International Policy*. London: Palgrave, pp. 27–58.

Ferris, R.J. and H. Zhang. 2002. "The Challenges of Reforming an Environmental Legal Culture: Assessing the Status Quo and Looking at Post-WTO Admission Challenges for the People's Republic of China," *Georgetown International Environmental Law Review*, 14(3)(Spring): 429–460.

Forest, C., M. Webster, and J. Reilly. 2004. "Narrowing Uncertainty in Global Climate Change," *Industrial Physicist*, 10(4): 20–23.

Frank, A. 2000. "The Environment in U.S.–China Relations: Themes and Ideas from Working Group Discussions," China Environment Series 1, Environmental Change and Security Project, Woodrow Wilson International Center for Scholars. htttp//ecsp.si.edu/ecsplib.nsf

Freeman, C.W., Jr. 1996. "Sino-American Relations: Back to Basics," *Foreign Policy*, 104(Fall): 3–17.

Gallagher, K.S. 2003. "Foreign Technology in China's Automobile Industry: Implications for Energy, Economic Development, and Environment," *China Environment Series*, 6: 1–15.

Gan, L. 1998. "Energy Development and Environmental Constraints in China," *Energy Policy*, 26(2): 9–15.

Gielen, D. and C. Chen. 2001. "The CO_2 Emission Reduction Benefits of Chinese Energy Policies and Environmental Policies: A Case Study for Shanghai, Period 1995–2020," *Ecological Economics*, 39(2): 257–270.

Goldman, M. and R. MacFarquhar. 1999. "Dynamic Economy, Declining Party State," in M. Goldman and R. MacFarquhar (eds.), *The Paradox of China's Post-Mao Reforms*. Cambridge: Harvard University Press, pp. 3–29.

Goodman, D.S. 1999. "The New Middle Class," in M. Goldman and R. MacFarquhar (eds.), *The Paradox of China's Post-Mao Reforms*. Cambridge: Harvard University Press.

Haas, P.M. 2004. "When Does Power Listen to Truth? A Constructivist Approach to the Policy Process," *Journal of European Public Policy*, 11(4): 569–592.

Haites, E. and M.A. Aslam. 2000. *The Kyoto Mechanisms and Global Climate Change: Coordination Issues and Domestic Policies*. Arlington: Pew Center on Global Climate Change.

Han, M., J. Hou, and L. Wu. 1995. "Potential Impacts of Sea-Level Rise on China's Coastal Environment and Cities: A National Assessment," *Journal of Coastal Research*, 14(Winter): 79–95.

Harding, H. 1992. *A Fragile Relationship: The United States and China Since 1972*. Washington, D.C.: Brookings Institution.

Hardy, C. 1994. "Underorganized Interorganizational Domains: The Case of Refugee Systems," *Journal of Applied Behavioral Science*, 30(3)(September).

Hartmann, B. 2001. "Will the Circle Be Unbroken? A Critique of the Project on Environment, Population, and Security," in N.L. Peluso and M. Watts (eds.), *Violent Environments*. Ithaca, NJ: Cornell University Press, pp. 39–62.

He, D. 2003. "Introduction to the China Sustainable Energy Program's Transportation Program," *Sinosphere Journal*, 6(1)(March): 13–17.

Ho, P. 2001. "Greening without Conflict? Environmentalism, NGOs and Civil Society in China," *Development and Change*, 32(5): 893–921.

Ho, E., M. Ip, and R. Bedford. 2001. "Transnational Hong Kong Chinese Families in the 1990s," *New Zealand Journal of Geography*, 111(April): 24–30.

Holt, E.C. and A.E. Haspel. 2001. "The Critical Role of the Private Sector in Addressing Climate Change," *EM* (March): 20–24.

Homer-Dixon, T.F. 1994. "Environmental Changes as Causes of Acute Conflict," in R.K. Betts (ed.), *Conflict After the Cold War: Arguments on Causes of War and Peace*. New York: Macmillan, pp. 425–441.

Homer-Dixon, T.F. 1999. *Environment, Scarcity, and Violence*. Princeton, NJ: Princeton University Press.

Hook, W. 1996. "China Mustn't Copy Western Transport," *China Daily*, 15 October, p. 4.

Hsu, S.-C. 1999. "International Linkage and China's Environmental Policies," Paper presented at the 51st Annual Meeting of the Association of Asian Studies, Boston, March.

Hsu, S.-C. 2000. "International Linkage and China's Environmental Policies" *Issues and Studies*, 36(3): 61–102.

Hu, A. 1995. "China's Environmental Issues," in S. Harris and G. Klintworth (eds.), *China as a Great Power: Myths, Realities and Challenges in the Asia-Pacific Region*. New York: St. Martin's, pp. 328–341.

Jamison, A. 1996. "The Shaping of the Global Environmental Agenda: The Role of Non-Governmental Organizations," in S. Lash, B. Szerszynski, and B. Wynne (eds.), *Risk, Environment and Modernity: Towards a New Ecology*. London: Sage, pp. 224–245.

Jehl, D. 2001. "Members of Congress Begin Effort to Get U.S. to Join in Fighting Global Warming," *New York Times*, 27 July, p. A14.

Jehl, D. and A.C. Revkin. 2001. "Bush, in Reversal, Won't Seek Cut in Emissions of Carbon Dioxide," *New York Times*, 14 March, pp. A1, A16.

Jia, J.J. and K. Rubin. 1997. "A Potential Bridge over Troubled U.S.–China Waters," *Chronicle of Higher Education*, (7 March): A56.

Jin, J. 2001. "The Growing Importance of Public Participation in China's Environmental Movement," in J.L. Turner and F. Wu (eds.), *Green NGO and Environmental Journalist Forum*. Washington, D.C.: Woodrow Wilson Center, pp. 5–8.

Johnson, G.E. and Y.-F. Woon. 1997. "The Response to Rural Reform in an Overseas Chinese Area," *Modern Asian Studies*, 31(1).

Johnson, T.M. 1999. "Foreign Involvement in China's Energy Sector," in E. Economy and M. Oksenberg (eds.), *China Joins the World: Progress and Prospects*. New York: Council on Foreign Relations, pp. 266–295.

Johnson, K. 2004. "Coloradans Vote to Embrace Alternative Sources of Energy," *New York Times*, 14 November, p. A13.

Johnston, A.I. 1998. "China and International Environmental Institutions: A Decision Rule Analysis," in M.B. McElroy, C.P. Nielsen, and P. Lydon (eds.), *Energizing China: Reconciling Environmental Protection and Economic Growth*. Cambridge: Harvard University Press, pp. 555–599.

Kaul, I., I. Grunberg, and M.A. Stern. 1999. "Introduction," in I. Kaul, I. Grunberg, and M.A. Stern (eds.), *Global Public Goods: International Cooperation in the 21st Century*. Oxford: Oxford University Press, pp. xix--xxxviii.

Keck, M.E. and K. Sikkink. 1998. *Activists beyond Borders: Advocacy Networks in International Politics*. Ithaca, NY: Cornell University Press.

Kempton, W. 1993. "Will Public Environmental Concern Lead to Action on Global Warming?" *Annual Review of Energy and the Environment*, 18: 217–245.

Kempton, W., J.S. Boster, and J.A. Hartley. 1995. *Environmental Values in American Culture*. Cambridge: MIT Press.

Kent, A. 2002. "China's International Socialization: The Role of International Organizations," *Global Governance*, 8: 343–364.

Kettl, D.F. 2000. "The Transformation of Governance: Globalization, Devolution, and the Role of Government," *Public Administration Review*, 60(6): 488–497.

Kilborn, P.T. 1999. "No Work for a Bicycle Thief: Children Pedal Around Less," *New York Times*, 7 June, p. A1.

Koehn, P.H. 1999. "Greasing the Grassroots: The Role of Nongovernmental Linkages in the Looming U.S.–China Confrontation over Global Petroleum Reserves," in P.H. Koehn and J.Y.S. Cheng (eds.), *The Outlook for U.S.–China Relations Following the 1997–1998 Summits: Chinese and American Perspectives on Security, Trade, and Cultural Exchange*. Hong Kong: Chinese University Press, pp. 351–390.

Koehn, P.H. 2001. "Cross-National Competence and U.S.–Asia Interdependence: The Explosion of Trans-Pacific Civil-Society Networks," in J. Weiss (ed.), *Tigers' Roar: Asia's Recovery and Its Impact*. Armonk: M.E. Sharpe, pp. 227–235.

Koehn, P.H. 2002. "The Role of Cross-Nationally Competent Chinese+Americans in Environmental-interdependence Challenges: Potential and Prospects," in P.H. Koehn and X.-H. Yin (eds.), *The Expanding Roles of Chinese Americans in U.S.–China Relations: Transnational Networks and Trans-Pacific Interactions*. Armonk: M.E. Sharpe, pp. 235–283.

Koehn, P.H. 2004. "Sustainable-Development Frontiers and Divides: Transnational Actors and U.S./China Greenhouse-Gas Emissions," *International Journal of Sustainable Development and World Ecology*, 11(4): 380–396.

Koehn, P.H. 2006. "Fitting a Vital Linkage Piece into the Multidimensional Emissions-reduction Puzzle: Nongovernmental Pathways to Consumption Changes in the PRC and the USA." *Climatic Change*.

Koehn, P.H. forthcoming. "Globalization, Decentralization, and Public Entrepreneurship: Reorienting Bureaucracy in the People's Republic of China," in A. Farazmand (ed.), *Handbook of Bureaucracy*. New York: Marcel Dekker.

Koehn P.H. and J.N. Rosenau. 2002. "Transnational Competence in an Emergent Epoch," *International Studies Perspectives*, 3(May): 105–127.

Koehn, P.H. and X.-H. Yin. 2002. "Chinese American Transnationalism and U.S.–China Relations: Presence and Promise for the Trans-Pacific Century," in P.H. Koehn and X.-H. Yin (eds.), *The Expanding Roles of Chinese Americans in U.S.–China Relations: Transnational Networks and Trans-Pacific Interactions*. Armonk: M.E. Sharpe, pp. xi–xl.

Landler, M. 2000. "Selling Status, and Cell Phones," *New York Times*, 24 November, p. C1.

Lane, N.F. and R. Bierbaum. 2001. "Recent Advances in the Science of Climate Change," *Natural Resources and Environment*, 15(3)(Winter): 147–151, 199–202.

Lenssen, N. 1992. *Empowering Development: The New Energy Equation*. Worldwatch Paper 111. Washington, D.C.: Worldwatch Institute.

Lew, D.J. 2000. "Alternatives to Coal and Candles: Wind Power in China," *Energy Policy*, 28: 271–286.

Li, C. 1998. *China: The Consumer Revolution*. Singapore: John Wiley & Sons.

Li, W. 1999. "Building Ethnoburbia: The Emergence and Manifestation of the Chinese *Ethnoburb* in Los Angeles' San Gabriel Valley," *Journal of Asian American Studies*, 2(1)(February): 1–28.

Liang, S. 2003. "Walking the Tightrope: Civil Society Organizations in China," *China Rights Forum*, 3: 11–15.

Lieberthal, K. 1997. "China's Governing System and Its Impact on Environmental Policy Implementation," China Environment Series 1, Environmental Change and Security Project, Woodrow Wilson International Center for Scholars. htttp//ecsp.si.edu/ecsplib.nsf

Lien, P.-T. 2003. "What Do Chinese Americans Think and Act Politically? Results from the Multi-Site Asian American Political Survey," Paper Presented at the Second International Conference of Institutes and Libraries for Chinese Overseas Studies, Chinese University of Hong Kong, 13–15 March.

Lipschutz, R.D. 1997. "Networks of Knowledge and Practice: Global Civil Society and Protection of the Global Environment," in L.A. Brooks and S.D. VanDeveer (eds.), *Saving the Seas: Values, Scientists, and International Governance*. College Park: University of Maryland Press, pp. 427–468.

Lo, C.W.H. and S.W. Leung. 2000. "Environmental Agency and Public Opinion in Guangzhou: The Limits of a Popular Approach to Environmental Governance," *China Quarterly*, 163(September): 677–704.

Logan, J.S. and J. Zhang. 1998. "Powering Non-Nuclear Growth in China with Natural Gas and Renewable Energy Technologies," China Environment Series 2, Environmental Change and Security Project. Washington, D.C.: Woodrow Wilson International Center for Scholars. htttp//ecsp.si.edu/ecsplib.nsf

Logan, J. S., A. Frank, J. Feng, and I. John. 1999. *Climate Action in the United States and China*. Washington, D.C.: Woodrow Wilson Center.

Lowe, M.D. 1989. *The Bicycle: Vehicle for a Small Planet*. Worldwatch Paper 90. Washington, D.C.: Worldwatch Institute.

Lu, H. 2000. "To Be Relatively Comfortable in an Egalitarian Society," in D.S. Davis (ed.), *The Consumer Revolution in Urban China*. Berkeley: University of California Press, pp. 124–141.

Lun, J. 2003. "An Update on Efforts to Promote Cleaner Vehicles in China," *Sinosphere Journal*, 6(1)(March): 28–33.

Macnaghten, P. and M. Jacobs. 1997. "Public Identification with Sustainable Development," *Global Environmental Change*, 7(1): 5–24.

Madsen, R. 1995. *China and the American Dream: A Moral Inquiry*. Berkeley: University of California Press.

Madsen, R. 2000. "Epilogue: The Second Liberation," in D.S. Davis (ed.), *The Consumer Revolution in Urban China*. Berkeley: University of California Press, pp. 312–319.

Manning, R.A. 2000. *The Asian Energy Factor: Myths and Dilemmas of Energy, Security and the Pacific Future*. New York: Palgrave.

Mao, B. and H. Chen. 2001. "Sustainability Analysis of Chinese Transport Policy," *International Journal of Sustainable Development and World Ecology*, 8(4): 323–336.

Marquez, J. 2003. "Governors Form Alliance on Global Warming," *Missoulian*, 24 September, p. A2.

Martens, P. 1998. *Health and Climate Change: Modelling the Impacts of Global Warming and Ozone Depletion*. London: Earthscan.

Martens, W.J.M., R. Sloof, and E.K. Jackson. 1997. "Climate Change, Human Health, and Sustainable Development," *Bulletin of the World Health Organization*, 75(6): 583–588.

Martens, P., A.J. McMichael, and J.A. Patz. 2000. "Globalisation, Environmental Change and Health," *Global Change and Human Health*, 1(1): 4–8.

McCall, W. 2001. "Flush with Success: Methane Gas from Decomposing Waste Used to Create Electricity," *Missoulian*, 21 January, p. D1.

McDonnell, M.B. 1999. "Building Bridges with the Chinese Academy of Social Sciences (CASS)," *Items*, 53(1): 12–14.

McMichael, A.J. and A. Haines. 1997. "Global Climate Change: The Potential Effects on Health," *British Medical Journal*, 315(7111): 805–809.

Mitchell, K. 1997 "Transnational Subjects: Constituting the Cultural Citizen in the Era of Pacific Rim Capital," in A. Ong and D.M. Nonini (eds.), *Ungrounded Empires: The Cultural Politics of Modern Chinese Transnationalism*. New York: Routledge, pp. 219–251.

Monastersky, R. 2000. "The Storm at the Center of Climate Science," *Chronicle of Higher Education*, 47(11)(10 November): A16–A18.

Morphet, S. 1996. "NGOs and the Environment," in P. Willetts (ed.), *'The Conscience of the World': The Influence of Non-Governmental Organisations in the UN System*. Washington, D.C.: Brookings Institution.

Mosher, S. 2003. "Resource List," *China Rights Forum*, 3: 81–84.

Mwandosya, M.J. 2000. *Survival Emissions: A Perspective from the South on Global Climate Change Negotiations*. Dar es Salaam: Dar es Salaam University Press.

Myers, N. 1993a. "Environmental Refugees in a Globally Warmed World," *BioScience*, 43(11): 752–762.

Myers, N. 1993b. *Ultimate Security: The Environmental Basis of Political Stability*. New York: W.W. Norton.

Myers, N. and J. Kent. 1995. *Environmental Exodus: An Emergent Crisis in the Global Arena*. Washington, D.C.: Climate Institute.

Myerson, A.R. 1998. "U.S. Splurging on Energy after Falling Off Its Diet," *New York Times*, 22 October, p. A1.

Neumann, J.E., G. Yohe, R. Nicholls. 2000. *Sea-Level Rise and Global Climate Change: A Review of Impacts to U.S. Coasts*. Arlington: Pew Center on Global Climate Change.

Newell, P. 2000. *Climate for Change: Non-state Actors and the Global Politics of the Greenhouse*. Cambridge: Cambridge University Press.

New York Times, 2004. 13 October, p. A6.

Ngai, M.M. 1997. "Who is an American Worker? Asian Immigrants, Race, and the National Boundaries of Class," in F. Steven and J.B. Freeman (eds.), *Audacious Democracy: Labor, Intellectuals, and the Social Reconstruction of America*. Boston: Houghton Mifflin, pp. 173–185.

Nishi, S.M. 1999. "Asian Americans at the Intersection of International and Domestic Tensions: An Analysis of Newspaper Coverage," in E. Hu-De Hart (ed.), *Across the Pacific: Asian Americans and Globalization*. Philadelphia, PA: Temple University Press, pp. 152–190.

Nordqvist, J., C. Boyd, and H. Klee. 2002. "Three Big Cs: Climate, Cement and China," *Greener Management International*, 39(Autumn): 69–82.

Oksenberg, M. and E. Economy. 1998. "China: Implementation under Economic Growth and Market Reform," in E.B. Weiss and H.K. Jacobson (eds.), *Engaging Countries: Strengthening Compliance with International Environmental Accords*. Cambridge: MIT Press, pp. 353–394.

Ong, A. 1992. "Limits to Cultural Accumulation: Chinese Capitalists on the American Pacific Rim," in N.G. Schiller, L. Basch, and C. Blanc-Szanton (eds.), *Towards a Transnational Perspective on Migration: Race, Class, Ethnicity, and Nationalism Reconsidered*. New York: New York Academy of Sciences, pp. 125–143.

O'Riordan, T. and A. Jordan. 1996. "Social Institutions and Climate Change," in T. O'Riordan and J. Jager (eds.), *Politics of Climate Change: A European Perspective*. London: Routledge, pp. 65–105.

Pan, Y., T. Luo, R. Birdsey, J. Hom, and J. Melillo, 2004. "New Estimates of Carbon Storage and Sequestration in China's Forests: Effects of Age-Class and Method on Inventory-Based Carbon Estimation." Climatic Change 67(2–3): 211–236.

Parson, E.A. 2001. "Moving Beyond the Kyoto Impasse," *New York Times*, 31 July, p. A23.

Paterson, M. 1996. "IR Theory: Neorealism, Neoinstitutionalism and the Climate Change Convention," in J. Vogler and M.F. Imber (eds.), *The Environment and International Relations*. London: Routledge, pp. 59–76.

Paterson, M. 2000. "Car Culture and Global Environmental Politics," *Review of International Studies*, 26: 253–270.

PA Times. 2005. 28(2): 1–2.

Patz, J.A., P.R. Epstein, T.A. Burke, and J.M. Balbus. 1996. "Global Climate Change and Emerging Infectious Diseases," *JAMA*, 275(3): 217–223.

Payne, R.A. 1998. "The Limits and Promise of Environmental Conflict Prevention: The Case of the GEF," *Journal of Peace Research*, 35(3): 363–380.

Peluso, N.L. and M. Watts. 2001. "Violent Environments," in N.L. Peluso and M. Watts (eds.), *Violent Environments*. Ithaca, NJ: Cornell University Press, pp. 3–38.

Peng, D. 2002. "Invisible Linkages: A Regional Perspective of East Asian Political Economy," *International Studies Quarterly*, 46(3)(September): 423–447.

People's Republic of China, State Council. 1994. *China's Agenda 21: White Paper on China's Population, Environment, and Development in the 21st Century*. Beijing: State Council.

Pew Center on Global Climate Change. 2001. "Innovative Policy Solutions to Global Climate Change," www.pewclimate.org/policy/program_intro.cfm

Porter, G. and J.W. Brown. 1996. *Global Environmental Politics*, 2nd edn. Boulder, CO: Westview Press.

Potter, S. 2001. "Summing Up the Technology Factor," *Town & Country Planning*, (May): 139–142.

Price-Smith, A.T. 2002. *The Health of Nations: Infectious Disease, Environmental Change, and their Effects on National Security and Development*. Cambridge: MIT Press.

Princen, T. 1994. "NGOs: Creating a Niche in Environmental Diplomacy," in T. Princen and M. Finger (eds.), *Environmental NGOs in World Politics: Linking the Local and the Global* London: Routledge, pp. 29–47.

Princen, T. and M. Finger. 1994a. "Introduction," in T. Princen and M. Finger (eds.), *Environmental NGOs in World Poliitics: Linking the Local and the Global* London: Routledge, pp. 1–25.

Princen, T. and M. Finger. 1994b. "Preface," in T. Princen and M. Finger (eds.), *Environmental NGOs in World Poliitics: Linking the Local and the Global* London: Routledge, pp. ix–xi.

Princen, T., M. Maniates, and K. Conca. 2002. "Confronting Consumption," in T. Princen, M. Maniates, and K. Conca (eds.), *Confronting Consumption*. Cambridge: MIT Press, pp. 1–20.

Rabe, B.G. 2002. *Greenhouse and Statehouse: The Evolving State Government Role in Climate Change*. Arlington: Pew Center on Global Climate Change.

Raufer, R. and S. Wang. 2003. "Navigating the Policy Path for Support of Wind Power in China," *China Environment Series*, 3: 37–49.

Revkin, A.C. 2000a. "Report Forecasts Warming's Effects," *New York Times*, 12 June, pp. A1, A25.

Revkin, A.C. 2000b. "Study Faults Humans for Large Share of Global Warming," *New York Times*, 14 July, p. A12.

Revkin, A.C. 2000c. "U.S. Study Points Out Ways to Cut Emissions," *New York Times*, 16 November, p. A13.

Revkin, A.C. 2001a. "Bush's Shift Could Doom Air Pact, Some Say," *New York Times*, 17 March, p. A7.

Revkin, A.C. 2001b. "Impasse on Gases: Who Moves First?" *New York Times*, 16 June, p. A7.

Revkin, A.C. 2001c. "178 Nations Reach a Climate Accord; U.S. Only Looks On," *New York Times*, 24 July, p. A1, A7.

Revkin, A.C. 2001d. "2 New Studies Tie Rise in Ocean Heat to Greenhouse Gases," *New York Times*, 13 April, p. A11.

Revkin, A.C. 2004. "Eskimos Seek to Recast Global Warming as a Rights Issue," *New York Times*, 15 December, p. A3.

Revkin, A.C. and N. Banerjee. 2001. "Energy Executives Urge Voluntary Greenhouse-Gas Limits," *New York Times*, 1 August, p. C1, C6.

Risse-Kappen, T. 1995a. "Bringing Transnational Relations Back In: Introduction," in T. Risse-Kappen (ed.), *Bringing Transnational Relations Back In: Non-state Actors, Domestic Structures and International Institutions*. Cambridge: Cambridge University Press, pp. 3–33.

Risse-Kappen, T. 1995b. "Structures of Governance and Transnational Relations: What Have We Learned?" in T. Risse-Kappen (ed.), *Bringing Transnational Relations Back in: Non-state Actors, Domestic Structures and International Institutions*. Cambridge: Cambridge University Press, pp. 280–313.

Risse, T. 2002. "Transnational Actors and World Politics," in W. Carlsnaes, T. Risse, and B.A. Simmons (eds.), *Handbook of International Relations*. Thousand Oaks, CA: Sage, pp. 255–274.

Roberts, P. 2004. *The End of Oil: On the Edge of a Perilous New World*. Boston, MA: Houghton Mifflin.

Rohter, L. and A.C. Revkin. 2004. "Cheers, and Concern, for New Climate Pact," *New York Times*, 13 December, p. A6.

Rosenau, J.N. 1997a. *Along the Domestic–Foreign Frontier: Exploring Governance in a Turbulent World*. Cambridge: Cambridge University Press.

Rosenau, J.N. 1997b. "Enlarged Citizen Skills and Enclosed Coastal Seas," in L.A. Brooks and S.D. VanDeveer. (eds.), *Saving the Seas: Values, Scientists, and International Governance*. College Park: University of Maryland Press, pp. 329–355.

Rosenau, J.N. 2003. *Distant Proximities: Dynamics beyond Globalization*. Princeton, NJ: Princeton University Press.

Rosenthal, E. 2000. "Who Needs TV? They Pedal Hard to Peddle Ads," *New York Times*, 3 February, p. A4.

Ross, L. 1998. "China: Environmental Protection, Domestic Policy Trends, Patterns of Participation in Regimes and Compliance with International Norms," *China Quarterly*, 156(December): 809–835.

Ryan, M. and C. Flavin. 1995. "Facing China's Limits," in *State of the World 1995*. New York: W.W. Norton.

Saich, T. 2000. "Negotiating the State: The Development of Social Organizations in China," *China Quarterly*, 161(March): 124–141.

Schelling, T.C. 1997. "The Cost of Combating Global Warming," *Foreign Affairs*, 76(6)(November/December): 8–14.

Schipper, L., S. Bartlett, D. Hawk, and E. Vine. 1989. "Linking Life-Styles and Energy Use: A Matter of Time?" *Annual Review of Energy*, 14: 273–320.

Schreurs, M.A. 2002. "Comparative Perspectives on the Battle over Kyoto: Japan, Germany, and the US Compared," Paper presented at the 43rd Annual International Studies Association Convention, New Orleans, 24 March.

Seelye, K.Q. 2001. "Global Warming May Bring New Variety of Class Action," *New York Times*, 6 October, p. A14.

Seelye, K.Q. and A.C. Revkin. 2001. "Panel Tells Bush Global Warming Is Getting Worse," *New York Times*, 7 June, p. A1, A25.

Sharp, P. 2001. "Making Sense of Citizen Diplomats: The People of Duluth, Minnesota, as International Actors," *International Studies Perspectives*, 2(2): 131–150.

Shen, Q. 1997. "Urban Transportation in Shanghai: Problems and Planning Implications," *International Journal of Urban and Regional Research*, 21(4): 589–606.

Shi, Z.-L. 1998. "Strategies and Policies for Sustainable Development in China," in O. Suliman (ed.), *China's Transition to a Socialist Economy*. Westport: Quorum Books, pp. 145–166.

Short, W. 2001. "Potential of Renewables to Mitigate Global Climate Change," *IEEE Power Engineering Review* (April): 12–14.

Shuman, M.H. and H. Harvey. 1993. *Security without War: A Post-Cold War Foreign Policy*. Boulder, CO: Westview Press.

Skeldon, R. 1997. "Of Migration, Great Cities, and Markets: Global Systems of Development," in W. Gungwu (ed.), *Global History and Migrations*. Boulder, CO: Westview Press, pp. 183–215.

Skolnikoff, E.B. 2002. "Protecting University Research amid National-Security Fears," *Chronicle of Higher Education*, 10 May, pp. B10–B12.

Smart, A. and J. Smart. 1998. "Transnational Social Networks and Negotiated Identities in Interactions between Hong Kong and China," in M.P. Smith and L.E. Guarnizo (eds.), *Transnationalism from Below*. New Brunswick: Transaction Publishers.

Smil, V. 1993. *China's Environmental Crisis: An Inquiry into the Limits of National Development*. Armonk: M.E. Sharpe.

Smil, V. 1998. "China's Energy and Resource Uses: Continuity and Change," *China Quarterly*, 156(December): 935–951.

South China Morning Post, 12 January 1998, p.15.

Sperling, D. and D. Salon. 2002. *Transportation in Developing Countries: An Overview of Greenhouse Gas Reduction Strategies*. Arlington: Pew Center on Global Climate Change.

Sprunt, E. 2001. "Emissions Infiltrate Business Issues," *Hart's E&P*, 74(1)(January): 74–76.

Stares, S. and Z. Liu. 1996. "Motorization in Urban China: Issues and Actions," *China City Planning Review*, 12(1): 13–16.

Steinberg, P.F. 2001. *Environmental Leadership in Developing Countries: Transnational Relations and Biodiversity Policy in Costa Rica and Bolivia*. Cambridge: MIT Press.

Stern, P.C. 1997. "Toward a Working Definition of Consumption for Environmental Research and Policy," in P.C. Stern, T. Dietz, V.W. Ruttan, R.H. Socolow, and J.J. Sweeney (eds.), *Environmentally Significant Consumption: Research Directions*. Washington, D.C.: National Academy Press, pp. 12–25.

Sterngold, J. 1999. "For Asian-Americans, a New Political Resolve," *New York Times*, 22 September, p. A21.

Stevens, W.K. 1999. "Human Imprint on Climate Change Grows Clearer," *New York Times*, 29 June, p. D1, D8.

Stevens, W.K. 2000. "Seas and Soils Emerge as Keys to Climate," *New York Times*, 16 May, p. D1, D4.

Stockholm Environment Institute (SEI). 2002. *China Human Development Report 2002: Making Green Development a Choice*. Oxford: Oxford University Press.

Stone, R. 1993. "The Chinese-American Connection," *Science*, 262(5132)(15 October): 350.

Sussman, G. 2004. "The USA and Global Environmental Policy: Domestic Constraints on Effective Leadership," *International Political Science Review*, 25(4): 349–369.

Thomas, W.L., D. Basurto, and G. Taylor. 2001. "Creating a Favorable Climate for CDM Investment in North America," *Natural Resources and Environment*, 15(3)(Winter): 172–175, 207–209.

Tisdell, C. 1998. *Protecting the Environment in Transitional Situations*. Working Paper No. 29. Brisbane: Department of Economics, University of Queensland.

Tremayne, B. and P. de Wall. 1998. "Business Opportunities for Foreign Firms Related to China's Environment," *China Quarterly*, 156(December): 1016–1041.

Tu, W.-M. 1991. "Cultural China: The Periphery as the Center," *Daedalus*, 120(2)(Spring): 1–32.

Turner, J.L. 2001. "Promoting a Great Green Leap Forward? The Growing Role of U.S. Green NGOs in China," Paper presented at the Annual International Studies Association Meeting in New Orleans, March.

Turner, J.L. (ed). 2002. "Inventory of Environmental and Energy Projects in China," *China Environment Series*, 5: 137–227.

UCLA *Public Health*. 2004.

Ungar, S.J. 1997. "America's New Immigrants: Can 'Fresh Blood' Lead to a Fresh Foreign Policy?" in *Bridges with Asia: Asian Americans in the United States; Summary Report*. New York: Asia Society, pp. 35–37.

United States, Department of Energy, and the State Science & Technology Commission of China. 1999. *China Climate Change Country Study*. Beijing: Tsinghua University Press.

Vermeer, E.B. 1998. "Industrial Pollution in China and Remedial Policies," *China Quarterly*, 156(December): 952–985.

Wald, M.L. 1999. "U.S. Aims to Have 5% of Electricity from Wind by 2020," *New York Times*, 20 June, p. A25.

Walsh, M.P. 1989. "The Global Importance of Motor Vehicles in the Climate Modification Problem," *International Environmental Reporter* (May): 261–267.

Wang, J. 2000. *Limited Adversaries: Post-Cold War Sino-American Mutual Images*. Oxford: Oxford University Press.

Wang, H. 2001. *Weak State, Strong Networks: The Institutional Dynamics of Foreign Direct Investment in China*. Oxford: Oxford University Press.

Wang, Z. 2002. "Chinese American Scientists and U.S.–China Scientific Relations: From Richard Nixon to Wen Ho Lee," in P.H. Koehn and X.-H. Yin (eds.), *The Expanding Roles of Chinese Americans in U.S.–China Relations: Transnational Networks and Trans-Pacific Interactions*. Armonk: M.E. Sharpe, pp. 207–234.

Wapner, P. 1995. "Politics beyond the State: Environmental Activism and World Civic Politics," *World Politics*, 47(April): 311–340.

Wapner, P. 1996. *Environmental Activism and World Civic Politics.* Albany, NY: State University of New York Press.

Wickberg, E. 1994. "Overseas Chinese Adaptive Organizations, Past and Present," in R. Skeldon (ed.), *Reluctant Exiles? Migration from Hong Kong and the New Overseas Chinese.* Hong Kong: Hong Kong University Press.

Willoughby, C. 2001. "Singapore's Motorization Policies 1960–2000," *Transport Policy*, 8: 125–138.

Wong, S-L. 1995. "Denationalization Reconsidered: Asian American Cultural Criticism at a Theoretical Crossroads," *Amerasia Journal*, 21(1–2).

Wu, F. 2002. "New Partners or Old Brothers? GONGOs in Transnational Environmental Advocacy in China," *China Environment Series*, 5: 45–58.

Xia, M. 2000. *The Dual Developmental State: Development Strategy and Institutional Arrangements for China's Transition.* Aldershot: Ashgate.

Yang, J. 1985. "Bicycle Traffic in China," *Transportation Quarterly*, 39(1)(January): 93–104.

Yang, P.Q. 1999. "Sojourners or Settlers: Post-1965 Chinese Immigrants," *Journal of Asian American Studies*, 2(1)(February): 72–86.

Yardley, J. 2004. "Bad Air and Water, and a Bully Pulpit in China," *New York Times*, 25 September, p. A4.

Yeh, K.C. 1996. "Macroeconomic Issues in China in the 1990s," in Y.Y. Kueh (ed.), *The Chinese Economy Under Deng Xiaoping.* Oxford: Clarendon, pp. 11–54.

Yin, X.-H. 1999. "The Growing Influence of Chinese Americans on U.S.–China Relations," in P.H. Koehn and J.Y.S. Cheng (eds.), *The Outlook for U.S.–China Relations Following the 1997–1998 Summits: Chinese and American Perspectives on Security, Trade, and Cultural Exchange.* Hong Kong: Chinese University Press, pp. 331–349.

Yin, X.-H. and Z. Lan. 2003. "Why Do They Give? Change and Continuity in Chinese American Transnational Philanthropy since the 1970s," Paper Presented at the Workshop on Chinese and Indian Diaspora Philanthropy Sponsored by the Asia Center and the John F. Kennedy School of Government, Harvard University, 7–8 May.

Ying, Y.-W. 1996. "Immigration Satisfaction of Chinese Americans: An Empirical Examination," *Journal of Community Psychology*, 24(January): 3–16.

Zhang, Z.X. 1998. *The Economics of Energy Policy in China.* Cheltenham: Edward Elgar.

Zhang, Z.X. 2000. "Decoupling China's Carbon Emissions Increase from Economic Growth: An Economic Analysis and Policy Implications," *World Development*, 28(4): 739–752.

Zweig, D. 2002. *Internationalizing China: Domestic Interests and Global Linkages.* Ithaca, NY: Cornell University Press.

Chapter 52

World Crisis in Public Service and Administration*

Ali Farazmand

CONTENTS

*This is a revised and updated version of the chapter, "Global Crisis in Public Service and Administration," published in another volume, *Handbook of Crisis and Emergency Management* (Marcel Dekker, 2001), edited by the author. Reprinted with permission of the publisher.

Introduction

What is the status of public service and administration in the current age of globalization? Why is public service and administration under attack and in poverty, and what is the fate of public administration as a field of study and practice? These are fundamental and burning questions of our time at the turn of the 21st century. Can public administration be revitalized to perform its noble missions of public service, human development, and world civilization? Elsewhere (Farazmand, forthcoming-a), I have detailed an affirmative answer to this question. However, to understand why a revitalization of the field is needed we must first understand the current global crises that have crippled the field in theory and practice. This is the task of this chapter.

Public service has been one of the longest and most cherished institutions of human history. In fact, civilization, administration, and public service have always developed together, one reinforcing the other. Throughout the history progress has been made toward improving human lot, for which public service and administration have played a key role. Real progress in such a direction was made during the last two centuries when social, economic, and political struggles and innovations led to overall progress in human conditions for citizens worldwide. The rise of the modern nation-states, and the growth of professionalism along with development in education and economic progress also contributed, to some degree, to this human progress around the world.

The rise and expansion of modern capitalism, especially corporate capitalism, produced major organizational and economic progress with advantages over the backward systems of feudalism and slavery. However, it also raised serious concern about the adverse consequences of this historical development. Subsequent struggles by working class peoples and middle class professionals worldwide, as well as the rise of world socialism, resulted in a minimum social safety net, the modern welfare state that absorbed much of the grievances raised by deteriorating human conditions for the mass citizens in the midst of prosperity enjoyed by the few elites.

With the rise and expansion of the welfare state, and the accompanying interventionist state worldwide, public service and administration grew and expanded all over of the capitalist world, resembling a very small degree of the features of socialist countries in place, throughout the 21st century until the big wave of structural changes began to appear in the 1980s. Until then, public service and administration was cherished, as it contributed to civilization, corrected constitutional and political as well economic wrongs, and helped balance against the excesses of market capitalism. However, with the accelerated rate of technological and economic globalization of capital and the rise of the strategic globalization policy of privatization, public service, and administration became the target of the relentless attacks from corporate capitalists, conservative business, and political elites promoting the ideology of market supremacy, and scholars and policy advisors.

With the fall of the USSR, diminution and crisis of public service took a new phase of accelerated pace. Thus, the global system of corporate capitalism declared a death verdict for all that was achieved through public services and administration over decades, in fact over centuries. What was considered "public" and the public sphere were attacked under the banner of efficiency and antipublic sector and through sweeping privatization. The latter has been enforced through supranational organizations such as the World Bank, International Monetary Fund, and World Trade Organization, all of which are heavily influenced by the leading and most powerful governments — the United States and its key Western allies. Public service has therefore been sacrificed for rapid capital accumulation, whereas the character of the state and administration has been changed in favor of strong police security and military systems to promote and protect the corporate interests worldwide. The result has been a global crisis of public service and administration, with three distinct manifest dimensions: institutional, image, and legitimacy crisis.

This chapter outlines this global crisis of public service and administration by addressing the nature of the crisis, its core dimensions, and the factors causing the current crisis in public service worldwide. Consequences and suggestions for policy decisions and administrative action are beyond the limits of this chapter discussions. A major thesis of this chapter is that, whereas there is a need for reform and improvement in public service delivery and administration worldwide, the root causes of the crisis of public service and administration are both political and economic, that much of historical progress toward betterment of human conditions are now expected to be thrown out of windows and people everywhere in the world have become disposable commodities of the new globalization of capital in search of rapid accumulation of capital.

Consequently, public service and administration have been transformed from a public service institution with a long historical tradition to a corporate, coercive state administration enforcing the new rules of corporate welfare state at local, national, and global levels. The global crisis of public service is now connected with other crises impairing human condition: environmental degradation and destruction, child labor, mercenary labor, violations of basic human rights, furtherance of mass poverty, malnutrition, and wage slavery all over the world.

Nature of the Public Service Crisis

Public service is experiencing a crisis globally, nationally, and locally. This global crisis of public service has many dimensions, some of which are discussed in this chapter. Fundamentally speaking, understanding this crisis of public service requires a deeper understanding of the underpinnings that shape the contemporary global trends and changes in socioeconomic and political systems, as well as in the global power structures that have been causing much of the public service crisis experienced all over the globe. It must also be understood in connection with other crises facing the entire planet Earth and the global humanity all together: financial crisis, moral and ethical crisis, environmental crisis, institutional crises, political and cultural crises, and a host of other crises that affect public service and administration worldwide.

This global crisis of public service has not reached its criticality yet. In fact, it has a fairly long way to go before it reaches the criticality that is needed for fundamental social action and qualitative changes. The multitude of contemporary quantitative changes — innovations in technologies, increasing number of nation-states, breakdowns in traditional structures — that have produced some degrees of qualitative changes in human history have had profound effects on the life of billions of global citizens. However, much of these changes have produced fruits that have only benefitted a small number of individuals and governments who have declared the entire globe their realm of kingdom. At the center of this small group of global kingdom are some of the most powerful globalizing barons backed and promoted by the military and political-coercive muscles of the globally hegemonic states, such as the United States and its European allies. Here, both ethnocentrism and superpower arrogance appear to have dominated the psychological as well as political and economic environment of the globe.

The core of this globalization enterprise is a focused onslaught against the realm of public service, public interest, and public sphere all over the world. Behind this global onslaught is the dogmatic, self-proclaimed ideology of global capitalism equated with market-based governance, administration, and democracy. The traditional historical progress of the last four centuries or so against workers' exploitation, human serfdom, child labor, human rights abuse, and other violations of human dignity have all the sudden become matters of nonsense, irrelevant as new concepts of corpocracy and market idolism are invented and propagated. The traditional domains of public service have been claimed and occupied by this new globalizing ideology, and a neocolonization has penetrated deeply into the heart of public service and those areas in which the unprotected had traditionally sought a level of sheltering.

Today, the public service image is totally tarnished by this globalizing ideological corporatism, and its both institutional capacity and philosophical identity have come under serious question. With the governmental elites — elected and nonelected alike — joining as accomplices and, in fact, major partners of this global corporate strategy, public service, and administration have become critically impaired and driven deep into a major crisis that has reached a global scale. In fact, expressions such as "The Quiet Crisis of the Civil Service" (Levine & Kleeman, 1988), "Crisis in the U.S. Civil Service" (Rosen, 1986), "Crisis in the U.S. Administrative State" (Farazmand, 1989), "The Legitimacy Crisis" (Brown, 2000), "Crisis of Morale. . . . " (Ban, 2000), and others are important explanations of and evidence of this global crisis, but they only scratch the surface of the crisis that face public service and administration worldwide.

To understand and explain deeply the core of this global phenomenon, we need to bring into our discussion the macro, big picture and analyze the nature of the current crisis in public service, and the other pervasive crises mentioned earlier, within a broad theoretical framework at the macro level. Here, a global political economy analysis is needed to explain the cause and effect of the crisis, and to outline implications for corrective social action.

Dimensions of the Crisis

Three dimensions comprise the current global crisis of public service and administration: image, institutional, and legitimacy or philosophical.

The Image Crisis

Public service has always been valued as a major part of human civilization. This has been due to many factors, including the nature of humankind as a social creature with concern for both common good and self interest. The state and public sector has always played a leading role in providing this common good and public service throughout the history.

The rise and expansion of the modern state has also contributed significantly to the growth and expansion of the public service. This has been accompanied by the increasing bureaucratization and professionalization of the modern state, as Weber (1946, 1984) predicted. Professionalization has added many values to the administrative and organizational values. Ironically, some of these administrative values have during the last few decades come in conflict with the long cherished human values of citizenship and democratic principles. Professionalization of public service and administrative systems has indeed changed the nature of modern organizations by implanting deeply the instrumental rationality that has dominated societies as well as organizational life around the globe (Farazmand, 1994a, 2002).

This dominance has been more prevalent in the Western societies of the United States and Europe than in developing nations. Rationalism and positivism have become part of the Western culture whereas the normative values are still dominant in the cultures of most developing countries. However, two global observations tend to be the trends: globalization and cultural convergence of this instrumental rationality, especially through the current government reinvention and reengineering, on the one hand, and the concurrent counterpressures from below against this rampant instrumental rationality in developed nations such as the United States and Europe. The result has been a clash of major values underlying the administrative systems and public service around the world, with the invading values of corporate capitalism.

Public service received high values during and after the World War II in both developed and developing nations. In the former countries, professionalization of public service reached the highest stage as bureaucratization of society increased and the role of government and state became more pronounced. This was even more important in underdeveloped and developing countries as these nations freed themselves from the yoke of colonialism and nation-building became a top priority for national development and independence. Nation-building was followed by institution-building, which meant development of infrastructure in society and bureaucratization and administrative capacity building for implementation of national goals. Administrative capacity building also meant expansion of public service and the growth of the administrative state. In both developed and developing nations under capitalism, the administrative welfare state grows significantly in response to the increasing needs and demands of citizens.

The rise of the USSR and expansion of socialism also forced the capitalist nations to adopt mixed economies with a growing welfare state. The Cold War rivalry and competition between capitalism and socialism weakened both the systems from within and made them more vulnerable to external pressures. Eventually, the fall of the USSR and other socialist states resulted in a reconsideration of societal, organizational, and economic arrangement. As the dominant mode of economic system, capitalism appears to have risen to the top as the social and economic system in the world, with the United States and some European nations as the leaders of this global environment. Capitalist ideologies have claimed a supremacy of the marketplace, private enterprise system, and administrative rationality. However, this new global trend has at the same time been accompanied by the pressures from below by mass citizens who seek empowerment, smaller government and less governmental intrusion into their private lives, and democratization of policy, citizenship, and public service. Everywhere, ordinary people resist the empty claims and pressures against public service institutions and demand corrective action through community and global solidarity movements.

The result has been a clash of political citizenship values on the one hand and the professional administrative values on the other. Thus the public service has been badly damaged in terms of institutional capacity, quality, and public image. Corruption has also plagued public service, which has provoked massive resentment and protest against such practices. Resolving this conflict requires a reconciliation of and exercise of administrative ethics with citizenship ethics. It is through this integration that the image of the public service can be revived and enhanced.

Institutional Crisis

Institutional crisis appears when an institution loses credibility and legitimacy, organizational capacity, and ability to function as a viable institution in connection with its environment. An institution may lack organizational capacity, or an organization may exist but has been politically deinstitutionalized, or simply its time and viability have past. In either of these cases, an institutional crisis may be manifest. A market or a government may face institutional crisis when they either lack or lose organizational and legitimacy bases. Without organization and credibility, an institution is shaky and fragile, while an organization without institutionalization is much more fragile and subject to easy breakdown.

The public service values and images have been tarnished severely ever since the rise of the new global corporatism, and its corollary strategic design of privatization, antigovernment and antibureaucracy, anticivil service, and antieverything that is "public" around the world. This is a phenomenon that is totally unprecedented in modern history. Even the ancient civilizations of powerful empires and underdeveloped societies did not experience the current level of hostility toward what is "public" and public service and administration. Why? This is a big question that requires broad, theoretical, and philosophical answers beyond the scope of this limited chapter.

To return to the central point of our discussion, institutional crisis of public service began with the massive onslaught on public service, bureaucracy, and public administration since the 1980s. Led by two major representative speakers of the neocorporate elites of global capitalism, former American president Ronald Reagan and former British prime minister Margaret Thatcher, a global crusade was started with a global political economy agenda that aimed to fundamentally turn around the structural changes and transformations that had taken place for many decades in the 20th century. They were the key speakers of the new global capitalist elites and of globalization that had now demanded: (1) sweeping privatization; (2) questioning the viability and values of public service through governmental organizations and institutional arrangements; (3) reconfiguration of organizational structures of society (public and private sectors); and (4) reduction of the modern state and public administration into a police state for social control, maintenance of order, and promotion of the surplus accumulation of capital, the ultimate objective of capitalism dominated by globalizing financial capital.

As part of this globalization process, the modern states began experiencing a number of strategic of de-institutionalization of the administrative state. This was done by both policy and administrative actions aimed at breaking the institutional capacity of the modern administrative state in the social and economic areas, long established and characterized as the welfare administrative state, and by massive ideological, psychological, and propagating onslaught on the legitimacy of the modern public service, administrative state, and public administration.

Through massive downsizing, reduction in force, destabilization of the civil service structure, businesslike reforms, an all-out propaganda campaign against public service administration, and drastic cutbacks in public personnel and service expenditures, the institutional capacity of administration has been destroyed or seriously diminished to the point of driving it to failure to support the false claims of market supremacy over public sector. The net effect has been an effective strategic implementation of a de-institutionalization of public service and administration and, consequently, a crisis of public service worldwide.

Legitimacy Crisis

The legitimacy crisis has been featured by many aspects of the worldwide assault on public service and administration as inefficient, ineffective, unaccountable, undemocratic, unelected, bureaucratic, and wasteful. Much of these slandering assaults have come from the business sector, especially the business corporate elites, including the corporate media and press, but they also have come from critical organizational and management theorists who aspire to improve organizational life and to improve public service productivity, responsiveness, and accountability to citizens. However, the intellectual suppliers of this worldwide antipublic service and administration have been the neoclassical conservative economic advocates of the rational choice or "public choice theory" (see for example, Buchanan and Tullock, 1962; Niskanen, 1971; Savas, 1987; and others).

The legitimacy crisis has also roots in the philosophical and conceptual grounds of conservative Lockean view of antigovernment, private property and private business, and limited government intervention in economy and society. Further, the legitimacy crisis is rooted in the political culture of the western Anglo-Saxon, Anglo-American, mostly American political culture in which private property and self-interest individualism as well as a culture of possessive consumerism prevail, a phenomenon propagated intensely by corporate business power elites in pursuit of global dominance of market capitalism. The notion of public service, as it has existed and cherished for several millennia, is generally alien to American culture-dominated. Therefore, public service and administration never took deep roots in American political culture.

Sadly, it is this corporate-dominated culture of antipublic service and administration that is now being imposed upon developing countries and less developed nations by various means of coercion — military, security, economic, social, and cultural — and through globalization of economics and politics. Therefore, globalization of corporate capital and of the hegemonic state power of the United States and its European allies is transcending a global crisis of public service in favor of marketization, corporatization, privatization, and self-interested possessive capitalist culture.

Causes and Consequences of the Public Service Crisis

Elsewhere (Farazmand, 1989, 1997), I have discussed in some detail a number of factors that have contributed to the rise, growth, and expansion of the modern administrative state, with which also came an unprecedented degree of professionalization of public bureaucracy and public service. The role of governments in society, economy, and administration grows dramatically. Governments became the engines of national development, of private sector development, of providing public goods, and of solving problems as well as protecting individual rights.

Professionalization of the administrative state and public service has been a common phenomenon of both capitalism and socialism. In the capitalist countries, mixed economies grew and the domain of public–private sector became gradually expanded with blurring boundaries between the two sectors. The competing values of the public–private sectors also merged to an extent, yet the public service values and the commitment and aspirations of those pursuing public service career remained strong. This was also the case in the United States and some other nations, where the rampant political corruption of the 19th and early centuries resulted in a major reform movement, known as the progress movement. It sought to eliminate political and governmental corruption by the application of a modern bureaucratic and administrative rationality based on neutral competence, efficiency, and effectiveness.

These professional administrative values replaced much of the values of the earlier political machine systems prevalent around the nations. Then professionalization of bureaucracy and civil service followed and resulted in the separation of politics and administration (Thayer, 1997). The politics–administration dichotomy was a dominant mode and philosophy in the administrative state and public service (Frederickson, 1994; Van Riper, 1997). However, despite major improvements in public service delivery and in professionalization of public administration, another major dilemma was produced by the mythical dichotomy of politics and administration (Riggs, 1994).

The dichotomy put professional administrators in a major position of vulnerability in that they should not be involved in policy decision making, or be engaged in activities considered in the domain of politics however defined. The democratic values of responsiveness, responsibility, and accountability became major political values claimed to be in conflict and clash with the administrative values of professionalism, efficiency, and effectiveness. Consequently, despite the major earlier strands, the administrative state and the public service and administration came under attacks from an array of crusaders of political values of democracy.

These antipublic service, antibureaucracy, and antigovernment trends have had major ideological, political, social, and economic underpinnings beyond the space limitation of this chapter (see Farazmand, 1989, for a detailed discussion). Consequently, a severe decline of the public service followed both in terms of institutional capacity and of the image in the United States and around the world. The result has been a major crisis of public service and of professionalism in public administration around the world. The contributing critics of public service and administration came from many backgrounds, from left to right, and many factors contributed to this crisis.

Causes of the Public Service Crisis

The causes of the current worldwide crisis in the public service are many. Most of the factors or causes listed here are identified with the terms beginning with the letter C. Some of these factors are macro, national, and even international and they influence shaping the environment in which public service and administration are provided. Others are micro-specific and relate to the profession of public service and public administration, organizationally, individually, and professionally. The ordering of these factors is arbitrary and does not reflect any significance.

Crisis of Legitimacy

This is a political and ideological crisis inflicting regimes and political systems in which the consent of people is not sought and the forms or styles of governance are accompanied by dictatorial rule with consequences of repression, corruption, and other manifestations of abuse of power. Regimes not enjoying legitimacy — the popular consent or perception and aptitudes of citizens toward a government — often have little credibility among citizens, and the public service bureaucracy tends to be also perceived negatively by citizens. Lack of accountability, transparency, and responsiveness compounded by moral and ethical scandals at highest levels of governmental leadership are few reasons why citizens form negative perceptions toward their governments. Simply put, citizens lose confidence and credibility in their governmental and corporate leadership. This has been manifest in the United States for the last 30 years (see Lipset, 1987; Brown, 2000).

Crisis of legitimacy also refers to the crisis or lingering problem of the administrative state in the United States, where its largess and policy-making role have been criticized by many. Legitimacy crisis has roots in the political culture of the America dominated corporate power structure, which favors corporate market capitalism and small government (see Henry, 1995; Rosenbloom, 1995). It also takes roots in the philosophical grounds of the role of government in society, especially of the Lockean view of government. Governments and corporate elites around the world in both industrialized and developing countries suffer a crisis of legitimacy (Lipset, 1987;

Brown, 2000), and this has contributed heavily to the current global crisis of public service and administration.

Corruption

Corruption is a multifaceted and pervasive phenomenon with many forms and degrees. A major impact of corruption is its immediate delegitimation effect on the government, regime, and state bureaucracy. The image of the public service suffers seriously under a corrupt system of governance. Simply put, there is no trust in a government perceived to be corrupt. It also suffers when sectors of the public service are contaminated by corruption. Examples are the Human and Urban Development (HUD) scandals in the United States in the 1980s, bribery and other forms of corruption, the Pahlavi regime under the late Shah of Iran deposed by the popular revolution of 1978–1979, or the Samoza regime in Nicaragua, and Marcos's regime in the Philippines. Other examples are abound.

Corruption may also have a destabilization effect on governments and political regimes. Corruption in public service and administration may benefit a few people, but its negative effect on society's productivity is significant. Corruption also tends to widen the gap between the rich and the poor, therefore having an inequity and injustice effect. All forms of corruption take a big toll on the image of the public service and administration (Gould, 1991). As a universal problem, corruption has been a major contributor to the current crisis of public service around the globe.

Capitalism

Capitalism has also contributed to both corruption and the public service crisis in at least two ways: It has promoted businesslike forms of corruption as a way to increase the bottom line and induced forms of corruption in finalizing contracts with public organizational elites. Bribery and kickbacks are but two examples.

Conflict of interest is another common example. Few Americans know that, for example, the members of the legislature in Florida, and as in most other states, can be and are on the payroll of private corporations. Because most of these legislatures come from the well-to-do class of business/legal elites, their success in election has also been produced by strong support from the corporate power elites, who in turn expect or demand passage of laws favoring those class interests. Conflict of interests is massively reported as private dealing and corporate representation disproportionately affects ordinary and poor citizens. The nature of capitalism promotes business-induced corruption in various forms such as bribery, conflict of interests, special favors, kickbacks, etc.

The second way in which capitalism has caused crisis in public service is the private–corporate sector's antigovernment, antibureaucracy, and probusiness slogans that have eroded the public service institutions' image and legitimacy. This has often been under the banner of business efficiency and free market choice (e.g., the Public Choice theorists arguments; see Farazmand, 1994a,b, 2002). The idea of "money talks" seems to have had an influence on people's perception toward business and government bureaucrats dealing with private corporations, especially the Iron Triangles.

Iron Triangles have special places in capitalist societies. A typical Iron Triangle is found, for example, in the department of defense, between the bureaucratic elites, related legislative members, and corporate business elites producing weapon systems. They are present in every policy area and dictate policy choices in favor of powerful business interests whose protection and promotion are directly linked to the main functions of governmental officials, from the top chief of state, the President or other form of leadership to the lowest possible level of organizational hierarchy.

Capitalism inherently promotes corruption and causes erosion of public service and administration. By nature it is antipublic service, because under capitalism the rich and business elites can afford to buy almost anything, whereas the middle class and working lower classes as well as the poor who are unable to work are in serious need of public goods and services, such as education, health, transportation, and enabling socioeconomic opportunities. The latter group cannot afford to buy them in a marketplace where money is the only purchasing power.

Cutbacks

Massive cutbacks in public-sector expenditures have been a major responsible factor contributing to the current crisis of public service and administration worldwide. Cutbacks in public sector have occurred in at least five major forms: (1) cutbacks in public investments of infrastruture development, or public works; (2) massive cutbacks on social service programs necessary for sustenance of a large number of citizens in need of assistance; (3) cutbacks of organizational capacity such as personnel and operational expenditures; (4) cutbacks in institutional and operational capacities of governmental regulatory functions; and (5) cutbacks in the enabling role of government to provide economic and social opportunities for the vast majority of citizens. Cutbacks have hurt deeply public service and administration systems worldwide.

Communism

Communism provides equitable and massive public services, but equalization and leveling off sometimes are not valued by citizens who take them for granted and are enticed by anticommunism propaganda of the capitalist regimes. The inability of communism to repel effectively the capitalist regime propaganda, its lack of dynamism in producing luxury and appealing goods and services, and its preoccupation with self-defense and protection against the various forms of onslaught of capitalism have made the system vulnerable and therefore contributed to some degree to the current crisis of public service in two ways: Its lack of incentives for individual creativity and opportunity for personal development under some existing socialist systems compounded by the impoverished standard of living as a consequence of slow or lower productivity. Often, public service is viewed by people as being poor in quality as opposed to the privately provided goods and services in mixed economies — regardless of the fact that most public services were provided free of charge.

The fall of the leading socialist states, including especially the USSR, has also fueled the antipublic service and antibureaucracy fervor among peoples and private sector-corporate elites in capitalist nations. The result is a false claim of legitimacy for capitalism and a new world order, which is full of inconsistencies, inequalities, and insecurities for most of world population: in the forms of hunger and poverty, malnutrition, illiteracy, violence, diseases, and other forms of carnage. Worse is the feeling of hopelessness and despair that blanket the entire globe, but mostly the African continent which carries the burden of the problems in the world.

Cost

Cost, especially cost overruns, has been a major cause of public service decline and crisis. Most governments of the world have been operating with significant budget deficit for the last decade or so. National budget deficit has a major negative impact on the image of the public service. Cost overruns in government procurement and other activities — e.g., $700 for toiled seats in Pentagon in the 1980s — tarnished badly the image of the bureaucracy and public service in the eyes of citizens.

Cost also means that monopolistic government bureaucracies are not efficient in delivering services, and that many public services are too costly, especially social services. These latter perceptions have often been fueled mainly by corporate business elite circles to discredit the public-sector organizations, but the shortcomings and excesses or wastefulness of some government bureaucracies cannot be ignored; they must be exposed for transparency and accountability purposes.

Conflict of Interest

Conflict of interest arises when members of the public service engage in contractual or other government transactions with certain private contractors with whom the officials — both political and career — have private interests. Conflict of interest occurs in many forms, and they may contribute to major cost overruns.

Corporatism

Corporatism has been another cause of crisis in public service. It has promoted the corporate ideology of private enterprise against government regulation, and administrative processes. Corporatism has roots in political economy in that its ideological underpinnings dictate corporations as the best and ideal form of organizational arrangement of society.

Corporatism also means corporations as the alternative to formal traditional governance and administration of economy, social services, and legal and professional establishments. Here government intervention may be desirable, under this notion, to help serve the interests of the dominant, corporate power structure, which claims to run the economy and provide goods and services in the marketplace. Corporatism feeds on the rhetorical slogans of freedom, liberty, market, and financial gains. Yet, the fundamental question of corporatism begs explanation of who benefits from these rosy concepts, average citizens or the privileged corporate elites and business class of rich affluent? The latter benefits from the antipublic service and antipublic sector organizational arrangements because it is alien to the social and economic problems the underprivileged or average citizens face on a daily basis.

The corporate ideology attempts to terminate the alternative concepts to the social and economic orders that may be attractive or utilitarian to broad-based populace. There is a global trend of "intolerance" toward any alternative political and economic system, nothing but corporate-defined capitalism, with a global order of market-based political system in service of that order. Simply put, the door is shut to the world outside while classification inside is both constantly tightening and denied opportunities tend to strangle the mass citizenry with "a race to the bottom" (Brecher & Costello, 1994).

Unfortunately, the global war of antiterrorism declared by the United States, accompanied by a host of security-related legislation and laws limiting individual liberty and freedoms in post-September 11, 2001, has also widened the "scope of intolerance," forcing billions of people worldwide into silence, self-censorship, and feardom and insecurity, from both terrorism and political authorities that are fighting them. Sadly, the blind act of terrorism has fed into further injustice and repression with increasing intolerance worldwide. The result is an expected "global bondage" worse than the condition that characterized the inhumane ages of feudalism and slavery.

In such a microscomic world of corporate isomorphism, the broad "public sphere" in which social breathing allows common citizens to think and search for alternative identity is constantly shrinking in favor of "idolism," a notion that subscribes to worshiping of repressive corporate and political idols in control of destiny of masses of citizens. It is this isomorphous "idolic corporatism" that is both stifling and deepening the crises that have already reached a level of criticality worldwide with numerous manifestations in environment, ecosystems, population, governance, and administration.

Only a massive punctuation of glacial magnitude is needed, and will be inevitable, to break down this idolic isomorphism. Heavy price will be paid by the humanity before such as a social breakdown occurs in this idolic corporatism, a phenomenon that social chaos theory attempts to explain. In the meantime, public service crisis will continue to deepen with casualties everywhere around the world.

Colonialism and Neocolonialism

Most developing countries were subjected to colonialism in the last centuries. Colonialism has left major legacies of economic, political, and bureaucratic corruption in newly independent nations, most of which lack a developed free market system, an indigenous administrative and civil service system, and an independent political elite. The result has been a *de facto* colonialism and continuation of the colonial bureaucratic presence in many nations of Africa and Asia. The public sector is often perceived as instruments of former colonial powers.

This phenomenon has also been observed in 20th century countries experiencing neocolonialism and imperialism. Many political, administrative, military, and business elites of these developing countries are under heavy influence of the powerful Western powers such as the United States, Britain, and France. Many regimes in these nations are perceived by their people and intelligentsia as puppets of the foreign powers. Consequently, their state and bureaucratic systems lack popular legitimacy and credibility due to mass corruption and repressive behavior, as well as due to their subservience to foreign neocolonial powers.

Consequently, their public service and administration are heavily affected by the global domination of corporate elites, and the globally dominating governing elites whose primary interests are promotion of financial accumulation of surplus capital and political–military control of the world, creating and promoting the isomorphous ideology of idolic corporatism worldwide.

Cold War

The Cold War also drained the institutional and fiscal capacities of the both capitalist and socialist systems. Indeed, the expansion of the public service and welfare state in capitalist nations with a mixed economy has been perceived and attacked as part of the ideological Cold War strategy. The Cold War took a toll on the public service image — for being viewed socialistic — in capitalist nations. The ideology of idolic corporatism had found the welfare state useful while at the same time it was opposed to its behavioral and structural consequences of public service and administration. This duality and conflicting feature of idolic corporatism has been embodied in American political culture that is shaped by corporate elites.

Culture

Some cultures have an inherent tendency to promote the antipublic service image. This is particularly true in countries like the United States in which corporatism and private enterprise system appear to dominate the American individualistic and political culture. Unlike other nations, public service has never been valued widely in the United States; it is the weakest in the world. Idolic corporatism has planted very deeply a sense of antipublic and proindividualism in American culture, which is now also invading the world far beyond its territory (see, for example, Triandis, 1995; Macpherson, 1987; Bellah, et al., 1985).

Commercialization and Commodification

Commercialization and commodification have similar effect on the public service image and legitimacy in the United States and many other nations. This trend appears to dominate the cultures and societies at a global level, but its origins are the United States and Britain. Commercialization and commodification have intellectual roots in the contemporary neoconservative public choice (misleadingly called public choice while it should be called "elite choice" or "affluent choice") theory and practical roots in Anglo-American idolic corporatism with isomorphic manifestations. Money as an ultimate means of exchange and transaction process has become a gospel of all interactions and social relations, including of human body and soul, of culture and identity, of pride and existence, and everything else (see Parenti, 1995 for the "Land of Idols in America").

Commercialization has degraded and devalued humanity and human dignity as well as all other phenomena and objects in the universe; objectification of all that exists and their valuation by commercial means of exchange, that is the price. Both intellectual and practical roots of commercialization and commodification have contributed to the current crisis of public service and administration, and they are being spread out throughout the world by means of both global capital and global coercion of the hegemonic state power.

Consumerism

Consumerism is another ideological phenomenon dominating the current reforms and reinvention programs of governments and public services around the globe. It is a major by-product of the idolic corporatism, as well as being its major basis of expansion and promotion. Originated in the United States, this conservative neoclassical public choice theory ideology places individual consumers at the center of debate and claims a legitimacy for consumer sovereignty. Its market-oriented consumer ideology is being extended to the public sector, forcing governments and public administrators to view people as consumers, not citizens or owners.

This public choice ideological perspective has in fact degraded citizenship and reduced citizens to consumers of marketplace. The result has been the loss of trust in and appreciation for public service, especially those services and goods that are not quantifiable, measurable, and have no price tags, such as police protection, defense, social services, professor–student and doctor–patient relationships, and the like. As an ideological extension of idolic corporate capitalism, consumerism has advanced to a level of false identity with individual fantasies for perceived ultimate power and control. In such an artificial environment, idolic corporatism thrives and feeds on mass citizenry with short term, partial and "only now" means of subsistence, turning them into consuming animals (like pigs; the more they are fed, the more meat they produce for sale and profit). This would allow the inventories of the idolic corporatism to produce more for further consumption and further surplus accumulation of capital. Consequently, the rich gets richer and the poor poorer.

Once unable to consume, unable to work as wage slave, the modern ordinary citizen is reduced to disposable objects that can be auctioned in the real world of commodity consumerism, where others can offer pennies in exchange for bodies and souls through prostitution, drug dealings, and wage slavery. The utility of mass human beings stops when they are no longer useful to surplus accumulation of capital under idolic corporatism. The public service and administration crisis deepens as consumerism is expanded ideologically and practically worldwide.

Confidence Gap

The erosion and loss of public confidence in governments, democratic as well as authoritarian, and in their governing elites has also contributed to the erosion of the public service image, the institutional and legitimacy crisis worldwide. Although this confidence gap has been experienced in the private-sector leadership (Lipset, 1987), it is the public service that has suffered the most (Farazmand, 1989).

Much of this confidence gap is rooted in the legitimacy crisis in corporate and government leadership in the capitalist world, but it has been masked by events and changes in other global socioeconomic and political systems; thus the spillover of the masked crises to public service and administration has been both expansive and profound. Hard at work, the globalizing idolic corporatism has obstructed continuing historical progress through various systems and has at least temporarily claimed a global hegemony. This confidence gap cannot be filled by injection of more idolic symbolism, as people around the world demand substantive improvement in their lives, communities, and the quality of that environment that must sustain them. The result is continuing crisis of public service, and there is no break in sight.

Careerism

Careerism has also caused public service crisis in that many self-serving and self-conserving bureaucrats engaged in activities or inactivities aimed at preserving and promoting personal career at any cost. This has at times been at the expense of public service, public interests, therefore contributing to the loss of public trust in the civil servants who may be viewed as guardians of public interests. Many senior civil servants refused to speak up or resist the political pressures and intimidation tactics of the Reagan presidency simply to protect their "careers." By refusing to act professionally against immoral, illegal, or unethical political decisions of their bosses, these career civil servants simply violated their basic professional principles and compromised their professional integrity and trusteeship of general public interests.

Similarly, many Danish bureaucrats who cooperated with the Nazi forces during the occupation may be viewed as violating their ethical and moral principles as professional administrators. In the eyes of many citizens, many civil servants are viewed as careerists who are after their personal interests only. Certainly, the public choice theorists as well as corporate elites, including of the media, have strongly perpetuated this idea. Careerism is a major delegitimating problem in public service. Similarly, carelessness on the part of some public servants has contributed to the crisis of public service.

Coercion and Control

By nature, most public organizations are coercive in their relationship with the public. The argument that the public and citizens have become the captives of the administrative state has received considerable attention of experts on modern public administration (Rosenbloom, 1995). As a result, citizens have been learning to become bureaucratic-self to deal effectively with the governmental bureaucrats (Rosenbloom, 1995). The coercive behavior of public organizations emanates from the monopolistic and authoritative nature of government. Citizens have little choice but to pay the required taxes and dues.

The bureaucratic nature of most public organizations makes them highly control oriented. Organizational control performs essential functions of system maintenance and system enhancement in modern governance and administration. However, over control-oriented organizations tend to become dysfunctional and long-run delegitimizers. Examples are the Shah's regime in Iran and Marcos's regime in the Philippines. Simply stated, public bureaucracies become instruments of regime enhancement at the expense of public interests and citizen welfare (Farazmand, 1989, 1997).

Clientelism

Clientelism has also fed to the problem of corruption, conflict of interest, and preferential treatments, leading to organizational injustice and abuse of public trust. Clientelism is a major feature of Iron Triangle operation, which seems to have dominated the political process and the power elite configurations in the United States and most other capitalist nations. Clientelism serves particularistic, private, and strong interest groups at the expense of the broad general public interests. It is discriminatory and unfair, and erodes the public trust in government and its administrators.

Character and Conduct

Character and conduct problems have also been major contributing factors in the public service image crisis. Official conducts and personality characters of public officials — both political and career — are significant symbols of public trust: good character and conduct present a positive image in public service whereas bad character and unethical conduct portray negative images of public service and administration; they have negative impacts on governance and administration, with implications for system legitimacy. It is absolutely inconceivable for citizens to expect high public officials engaged in immoral and unethical behaviors such as sexual scandals in public office, as the U.S. president Bill Clinton did, or others may have done.

These are prime examples of violation of public trust, public confidence, and conduct as well as character. But unethical sexual behaviors are not the only examples of poor character or conduct; diverting public resources to and simply engaging in organization and support of criminal organizations and training criminals to destroy villages, kill innocent people, and destabilize economies and political systems of other nations personally deemed unfriendly is another violation of ethical conduct at the international level. No system can claim to be democratic while at the same time thwarting legitimate democratic governments and violating democratic human rights of citizens outside of its boundaries, no matter what the rationale would be.

Western capitalist democracies have engaged in numerous bloody interventions in developing countries against legitimate and democratically elected public figures whose policies and preferences had favored indigenous national public interests rather than foreign multinational corporate interests. Under various pretexts, the United States and many Western European powers have supported some of the most repressive and fascistic regimes in the world (e.g., Iran in the 1950s, Indonesia in the 1960s, Chile in the 1970s). The U.S. invasion and occupation of Iraq (of course, not with a democratic government) under a false pretext gives another clear example of how the political leadership of a superpower nation (the Bush Administration) lies not only to its people but also to the entire world and stages a war of destruction against innocent people of another country and evades responsibility and accountability to the world.

If such a high level political authority commits violation of international laws and lies to the world, and evades accountability, how can other political leaders and lower level public administrators be held accountable for their unethical and unlawful actions? Therefore, the concepts of good character, ethical conduct, responsibility, and accountability can and should also apply to national governmental behaviors as well as to individual public official's personality and behavior in public service and administration.

Civil Service Crisis

Civil service crisis has also occurred as a result of many forces attacking public bureaucracy and the administrative or welfare state. The largess of the administrative state in the 20th century aroused significant oppositions from left to right who criticized it on different grounds. Politicians, academics, media reporters, press, and the general public all have contributed to the decline and crisis of civil service in many countries around the world including the United States. Their main argument has focused on the ground that career civil servants are nonelected officials who enjoy job security and are not accountable for their actions, and that they are involved in policy making as well as implementation and this is undemocratic.

Such an argument has come from a variety of academic and political circles from the mainstream to the right circles (see, for example, Wilson, 1986; Mosher, 1968; and the public choice theorists such as Buchanan and Tolluck, 1963; Downs, 1967; Niskanen, 1971; Ostrom, 1974; for a detail of this theoretical literature, see Farazmand, 1997, 1989). The crisis in civil service has automatically contributed to the crisis in public service around the world. The more recent challenge to civil service systems has come from the conservative corporate ideological basis of idolic capitalism and market-based values. These values include efficiency at any cost to public interests, temporary and contractual employment, disregard for civil service protection, wage earning jobs, abolition of job security, abolition of employee unions, and disregard for politic responsiveness and political responsibility in serving the public interests.

The whole notion of the civil service system has come under question or abolition. The U.S. 1978 Civil Service Reform Act was a prime example of turning to Right toward conservative, businesslike public personnel system in which civil service system is to be pushed to the back burner in favor of maximizing market values of efficiency and privatization of public services for profit accumulation of capital, again, enhancing the idolic corporate capitalism. This ideological trend is now being pushed worldwide as globalization and global privatization are being implemented.

Privatization

Privatization has been a global strategy of globalization process, which has been transforming the entire world of nations, their governments, and their cultures into a corporate capitalism of grand scale. Armed with forces of antigovernment, antibureaucracy, antipublic service, and in favor of businesslike organizations, market corporatism, and private-sector values, privatization of public services and of public enterprises began to take a global crusade in the early 1980s. Pursued by two conservative right-wing political representatives of the big, globalizing corporate elites, American president Ronald Reagan and British prime minister Margaret Thatcher started the crusade of transforming the public sector into an expanded realm of the corporate sector, claiming a global domain with no restriction.

A number of supranational organizations, such as the International Monetary Fund (IMF), the World Bank (WB), and World Trade Organization (WTO) have been used by the U.S. government as powerful instruments to force developing countries and European nations into this global strategy of capitalist transformation. This global trend of privatization has had devastating consequences for public service and administration worldwide, shrinking the public sector, undermining the institutional capacity of governments to perform their key functions, and causing a severe crisis in legitimacy, performance, and image of the public service and administration (see Farazmand, 1999b, for details on privatization). If privatization has been bad for public service, then globalization has been and will continue to be cutting deep into many aspects of governance, administration, and what has traditionally been considered public service and administration.

Globalization

Globalization has become a worldwide phenomenon with transcending forces of integration, aimed at global restructuring around the ideological corporate capitalism with accompanying global governance and cultural convergence. Different perspectives and meanings of globalization explain the concept, but the most important and common of all is the concept of globalization of capital accumulation by globalizing firms and transnational corporations that do not recognize territorial boundaries and market products through multiple sources of technological means.

Through global factories, global production, global marketing, and global financing, transnational corporations are now able, with the aid of the technological innovations, to make transactions anywhere in the world instantaneously. They are backed and promoted by the globalizing powerful state of the United States and other powerful allies with their military and security might, intimidating developing nations and crushing any government or group on their way for surplus accumulation of capital at rapid rates. Although nothing is new about globalization, for it has been around for many decades, it is the rapid rate of profit maximization by transnational corporations that has made globalization a political and economic phenomenon that never existed before.

A key requirement of globalization is facilitation or way-paving through the global strategies of privatization, deregulation, degovernmentalization, and shrinkage of the public sector to the bone limiting government role to policing and social control, corporatization, marketization, cheap labor forces, cheap natural resources, and structural reforms in favor of corporate business operations without constraints. Global finance backed and promoted by the United States and other big and powerful capitalist governments enter anywhere on the globe deemed profitable and leave whenever they decide, leaving behind destructions in labor structure, environment, economy, and community. Consequently, globalization has caused one of the most severe sources of the global crisis in public service and administration. This is a trend that will likely to continue for many years to come. Degradation of human condition, destruction of the ecological system, deterioration of living conditions of the working people, and reduction of human beings into disposable market commodities have forced millions of global citizens into a "race to the bottom" (see Farazmand, 1999a, forthcoming-b; Korten, 1995; and Costello, 1994 for details on globalization).

Other Trends Deepening the Public Service Crisis

The current global trends that have further deepened the public service crisis may be identified by the following Ds and Rs:

The Ds include deregulation, decentralization and devolution, debureaucratization, degovernmentalization, and democratization. The Rs of public service and governments have included reinvention, reinstitutionalization, realignment and reconfiguration of public–private sector boundaries, reengineering, reparticipation of the public in decision making, reorganization of the bureaucracy, redefinition of the term "public" in society and administration, reform of governmental and administrative systems including the civil service system making it more businesslike, reinstitutionalization, redevelopment, readjustment, and more. These have been the phenomena of governmental reform since the late 1970s, but especially since the 1980s. Central to all these problems and causes of the current public service crisis has been a problem of corruption, calling for an ethical movement in public service and administration around the globe.

Consequences of the Crisis

Consequences of the current global crisis in public service and administration are many, some of which have already been touched upon throughout this chapter. Briefly stated, public-sector infrastructures are in the process of destruction, a trend that will continue as long as the major causes of the crisis are not abated. These public infrastructures have evolved over thousands of years and they have been made possible by sacrifices in human lives as well as in massive investments by various societies; their development has been imperative for sustaining and growth of human civilizations. Without such public infrastructures, no stability and no prosperity could have been achieved. They have up to recently sustained and promoted the viability of private businesses as well as public-sector institutions.

But these public infrastructures are now under severe threat of destruction for profit accumulation purposes. Moreover, humanity and citizenship are in danger as everyone and everything is now put up for grab in the marketplace. Health, education, economic and social opportunities are squeezed and will be lost to the vast majority of citizens and their children who comprise the brain and labor forces of the future civilization. Obviously, not everyone or every nation is affected equally by the destructive crisis underway; citizens of the less developed nations are to suffer most.

The gap between the North and the South will be widened very deep, and the gap between rich and poor among all nations will also enlarge, making it very difficult if not impossible for the average hard working citizens to sustain a decent life. Consequently, more institutions of family and community will break down in the wake of market chaos, causing further crises in societies. The future generations will suffer, but the few, powerful business elites and their children will be enhanced by all opportunities in politics, education, administration, governance, and control of resources. They are the few who rule the many and all (Parenti, 1995). Humanity is heading for a return back to medieval feudalism (Korbin, 1986), a socioeconomic system characterized by few ruling feudal barons, a mass of serves unable to change their destiny, and a village surrounded by other feudal villages, and so on.

Today, the global village is ruled by few corporate elites, and the global governing elites and barons are ruling the world, with little or no opportunity to escape. Until 1990, the two world systems, capitalism led by the United States and socialist systems led by the USSR, checked each other's excesses and their rivalry served global citizens with a degree of calculated, and fragile, security and a minimum extent of public service in the capitalist world. With the fall of that superpower, there is no matching power to stand the abuses of the globalizing corporate barons and to the exploitative, antipublic service wall of the colonizing hegemonic power of the Western capitalism under the U.S. corporate leadership. Sadly, global insecurities emanating from mass hunger and absolute poverty, malnutrition, diseases, health and human crises, and a host of other crises produce more opportunities for crises to come. Unfortunately, the post-September 11, 2001 U.S. global war on terrorism (without a universally defined and agreed definition, and with a vague field of combat that may cover the entire globe) has created a global climate of fear and insecurity for all people as injustices and discriminate acts feed further to the vicious cycle of violence, insecurity, and human suffering around the world.

Despite some positive consequences of this new global world order and corporate hegemony, critics argue, the road to "serfdom and bondage" is widening and shortening, unless something is done locally, nationally, and globally (Korten, 1995; Farazmand, 1999a, forthcoming-b). Unless a global movement of human networks for resistance and reversal of the process takes place, which I believe is inevitable and is already in progress, the road to serfdom for billions of people will be shortened even faster.

Conclusion

There is a global crisis in public service and administration. To some, especially to the neoconservatives and establishment oriented theorists and practitioners, there is no such a thing as a crisis. To them, the new conservative view of public service and administration is summarized in the "new public management," and ideological rhetoric of business managerialism applied to public sector, shrinking it to the bone, stripping it from institutional and financial capacity, and setting it up for failure. This is a global strategy of corporatization, privatization, marketization, and commercialization that is pursued by powerful corporate elites who have captured all realms of life, society, economy, and public service. It is a global strategy to capture all public realms and to turn human citizens consumers of corporate products, for more profits, more surplus accumulation of capital, and in doing so has reduced citizens of the world into "consumer pigs," feeding them with as much as possible to make fatter for more profit return.

The global crisis in public service is felt institutionally, financially, politically, organizationally, and psychologically. The global crisis of public service and administration is accompanied, and accentuated by, other crises facing societies both in the West and East. Crisis in education, family, health, community structure, and other areas are only manifestations of the global crisis caused and perpetuated by the small corporate elites, whose global design of corporate hegemony is set to conquer the entire world and its population, turning them into disposable objects for profit accumulation.

The global crisis of public service and administration can be cured if there is a global break on the greedy and destructive forces of corporate capitalism. This globalizing destructive force of late capitalism has swept away whatever was achieved over decades and even centuries for the general welfare of societies, their average people, and their social systems so that a general harmony could be achieved by the majority of citizens. The welfare administrative state was in part responsible to provide some safety net for the poor and underprivileged so that the upper class elites cold enjoy the benefits of tranquility, peace, and prosperity. With the fall of the USSR as the leader of the socialist world, which had at least served as a deterring force against the excesses of globalizing corporate elites, there are no global checks deterring the new giant power structure of globalizing trans-world corporate elites who have made claim on all corners of the world as their realm of profit seeking crusade.

Public service has been sacrificed for private elite interests, and public means are being used for private corporate ends. In this process, governments are forced by both home-supporting governments of the globalizing states, such as the U.S. Government, and the local subsidiaries — read the business and military elites — to facilitate this globalizing exploitation of public means for private ends, using governmental forces — police, military might, and media propaganda — to promote this global crusade against average, hard working citizens of the globe. The consequences will catch up the entire globe, including the powerful and shameless elites, and everywhere through epidemic education and health crisis, family destruction, increased violence, crimes, and imprisonation of society and people, especially in the United States and Western Europe.

The current trend of global crisis in public service and administration can be turned around by exerting pressures from below, by grassroots people from around the world. Governments need also to revisit their policy options and must play the role of enabling environment for self-organizing organizations and institutions, for citizens to challenge both corporate and government institutions, and to exercise their democratic rights of self-determination. There are many ways to start, and this chapter has mentioned a few.

References

Ban, C. (2000). "The Crisis of Morale and Federal Senior Executives," in Holzer, M., ed. *Public Service: Callings, Commitments, and Contributions*. Boulder, CO: Westview Press.

Bellah, R., R. Madson, W. Sullivan, A. Swiddler, and S. Tipton (1985). *Habits of the Heart: Individualism and Commitment in American Life*. Berkely, CA: University of California Press.

Brecher, J., and T. Costello (1994). *Global Village or Global Pillage?* Boston: South End Press.

Brown, P. (2000). "The Legitimacy Crisis and the New Progressivism," in Holzer, M., ed. *Public Service: Callings, Commitments, and Contributions.* Boulder, CO: Westview Press/ASPA, pp. 105–111.

Buchanan, J., and G. Tullock (1962). *The Calculus of Consent.* Ann Arbor, MI: University of Michigan Press.

Downs, A. (1967). *Inside Bureaucracy.* Boston: Little & Brown.

Farazmand, A. (1989). "Crisis in the U.S. Administrative State," *Administration & Society* 21 (2): 173–199.

Farazmand, A. (1994a). "Organization Theory: An Overview and Appraisal," in Farazmand, A., ed. *Modern Organizations: Administrative Theory in Contemporary Society.* Westport, CT: Praeger, pp. 1–54.

Farazmand, A. (1994b). "The New World Order and Global Public Administration: A Critical Analysis," in Garcia-Zamor, J.-C. and Khator, R., eds. *Public Administration in a Global Village.* Westport, CT: Praeger, pp. 62–81.

Farazmand, A. (1997). "Institutionalization of the New Administrative State/Role: A Political Economy Analysis," Paper Presented at the Annual National Conference of the American Political Science Association (APSA), Washington, D.C., September 1–4.

Farazmand, A. (1999a). "Globalization and Public Administration," *Public Administration Review* 57 (6)/November–December: 209–222.

Farazmand, A. (1999b). "Privatization or Reform? Public Enterprise Management in Transition," *International Review of Administrative Sciences* 65: 551–567.

Farazmand, A. (2002). *Modern Organizations: Theory and Practice*, 2nd edition. Westport, CT: Praeger.

Farazmand, A. (Forthcoming-a). *Revitalizing Public Administration: A Global Strategic Perspective.*

Farazmand, A. (Forthcoming-b). *Globalization, Governance, and Public Administration.*

Frederickson, G. (1994). "Research and Knowledge in Administrative Ethics," in Cooper, T., ed. *Handbook of Administrative Ethics.* New York: Marcel Dekker, pp. 31–46.

Gould, D. (1991). "Administrative Corruption: Incidence, Causes, and Remedial Strategies," in Farazmand, A., ed. *Handbook of Comparative and Development Public Administration.* New York: Marcel Dekker, pp. 467–483.

Korbin, S. (1986)."Back to the Future: Medievalism and the Postmodern Digital Economy," *Journal of International Affairs* 52 (2): 367–409.

Korten, D. (1995). *When Corporations Rule the World.* West Hartford, CT: Kumarian Press.

Levine, C. and R. Kleeman (1988). "The Quiet Crisis of the Civil Service: The Federal Personnel System at the Crossroads," Occasional paper. Washington, D.C.: National Academy of Public Administration.

Lipset, S. (1987). "The Confidence Gap During the Reagan Years: 1981–1987," *Political Science Quarterly* (Spring): 1–23.

Macpherson, C.B. (1987). *The Rise and Fall of Economic Justice*. New York: Oxford University Press.

Mosher, F. (1986). *Democracy and the Public Service*, 2nd edition. New York: Oxford University Press.

Niskanen, W. (1971). *Bureaucracy and Representative Government*. Chicago: Aldein Atherton.

Parenti, (1995). Democracy for the Few. NY: St. Martin's Press.

Ostrom, V. (1974). *Intellectual Crisis in American Public Administration*. Alabama: University of Alabama Press.

Riggs, F. (1994)."Bureaucracy: A Profound Puzzle for Presidentialism." In Ali Farazmand ed. *Handbook of Bureaucracy*. pp. 97 New York: Marcel Dekker

Rosen, B. (1986). "Crisis in the U.S. Civil Service:" *Public Administration Review*. 46(3): 487–501.

Rosenbloom, D. (1995). *Public Administration: Understanding Management, Law, and Politics*. New York: Random House.

Savas, P. (1987). *Privatization: The Key to Better Government*. Chatham, NJ: Chatham House.

Thayer, F. (1997). "The U.S. Civil Service: 1883–1978 (I.R.P.)," in Farazmand, A., ed. *Modern Systems of Government: Exploring the Role of Bureaucrats and Politicians*. Thousand Oaks, CA: Sage Publishers, pp. 95–124.

Triandis, H. (1995). *Individualism and Collectivism*. Boulder, CO: Westview Press.

Van Riper, P. (1997). "The Pendleton Act of 1883 and the Professionalization in the U.S. Public Service," in Farazmand, A., ed. *Modern Systems of Government: Exploring the Role of Bureaucrats and Politicians*. Thousand Oaks, CA: Sage Publications, pp. 196–211.

Waldo, D. (1980/1990). *The Enterprise of Public Administration*. Navota, CA: Chandler & Sharp Publisher.

Weber, M. (1946). *From Max Weber: Essays in Sociology*. Gert, H.H. and Mills Wright, C., (translators and editors). New York: Oxford University Press.

Weber, M. (1984). "Bureaucracy," in Fischer, F. and Cirianni, C., eds. *Critical Studies in Organization and Bureaucracy*, pp. 24–39.

Wilson, J.Q. (1986). "The Bureaucratic State," in Nivolas, P.S. and Rosenbloom, D.H., eds. *Classic Readings in American Politics*. New York: St. Martin's Press.

Index

C

March 10/68.